Goddesses
in World Mythology

Goddesses
in World Mythology

*Martha Ann
Dorothy Meyers Imel*

OXFORD UNIVERSITY PRESS
New York   Oxford

Oxford University Press

Oxford   New York
Athens   Auckland   Bangkok   Bombay
Calcutta   Cape Town   Dar es Salaam   Delhi
Florence   Hong Kong   Istanbul   Karachi
Kuala Lumpur   Madras   Madrid   Melbourne
Mexico City   Nairobi   Paris   Singapore
Taipei   Tokyo   Toronto

and associated companies in
Berlin   Ibadan

Copyright © 1993 by Martha Ann and Dorothy Myers Imel

First published in 1993 by ABC-CLIO Inc.
130 Cremona Drive. P.O. Box 1911
Santa Barbara, California 93116-1911

First issued as an Oxford University Press paperback, 1995

Oxford is a registered trademark of Oxford University Press

Library of Congress Cataloging-in-Publication Data
Ann, Martha.
Goddesses in world mythology /
Martha Ann, Dorothy Myers Imel.
p.   cm.   Originally published: Santa Barbara, Calif.   : ABC-CLIO, c1993.
Includes bibliographical references and indexes.
ISBN 0-19-509199-X
1. Goddesses—Dictionaries.   2. Mythology—Dictionaries.
I. Imel, Dorothy Myers.   II. Title.
[BL473.5.A66   1995]   291.2'114'03—dc20   95-6973

9 8 7 6 5 4 3 2 1

Printed in the United States of America
on acid-free paper

To all the women in the world who were unaware of their heritage.
You are descended from a long line of sacred females
who have been respected and honored for thousands of years.

Remember and make it so.

CONTENTS

Preface, ix

Acknowledgments, xiii

Consultants, xv

Guide to Entry Format, xvii

Introduction, xix

Africa, 1
  (excluding Egypt)

Central America and Mesoamerica, 21

Eastern Europe, 41

Egypt, 75

Far East, 101

Greek and Roman Empires, 141

The Himalaya, 225

Indian Subcontinent, 243

Near East, 315

North America, 355

Northern Europe, 399

Oceania, 423

South America, 473

Southeast Asia, 479

Western Europe, 499

Bibliography, 531

Index of Goddesses by Name, 543

Index of Goddesses by Attribute, 611

PREFACE

Any researcher who embarks upon the study of a subject not usually identified as an area worthy of serious scholarship can expect numerous practical problems in gathering and obtaining data. Information on goddesses from cultures around the world has never before been gathered in a single location. There was no master database of collected sources, no lists of cultures with identified goddesses, and no system for organizing the masses of information about these deities. The serious study of subjects primarily associated with women is a very recent phenomenon.

We have grappled with difficulties ranging from male ethnographers who deemed women's or female deities unworthy of much attention, to the sparseness and obscurity of key sources, which in libraries are scattered among fields as diverse as archaeology, religious studies, and classical literature. Nevertheless, we wanted to obtain as much information as possible on the most important female deities in the world's religious traditions, provide sources for future scholars to begin new research, and to present it all in a manageable volume. We also wanted to offer a taste of the oral traditions from which the stories of these goddesses originate. Never before

has so much information on the topic been collected together.

Even so, we certainly cannot claim that this book covers all goddesses in all cultures throughout time. Such an undertaking would be impossible: a vast amount of information has been lost through the demise of oral traditions, the inaccuracies of history and ethnography, and the natural process of cultural change and transformation.

We consider this work to be only a first step in the serious study of female deities. It is our fondest hope that future scholars will advance the field and go far beyond our tentative efforts. As new and more accurate information comes to light, we hope that it will be gathered, organized, and made accessible to new generations.

Some of our many selection decisions require a note of explanation. In addition to the many clearly identifiable goddesses, we have chosen to include various monsters, evil spirits, and witches as entries because of their supernatural associations. Many of them may have originated as goddesses who were later demonized in an effort to reduce their influence and appeal, or were goddesses whose "dark sides" were emphasized for the same reason. Sometimes, too, fairies or nymphs seem to have been goddesses who were trivialized, perhaps again in an attempt to reduce their attractiveness to worshipers. We have also included some humans who were later deified.

The use of multiple sources presented us with a welter of conflicting spellings and irreconcilable information about the goddesses. It was especially difficult to obtain clarity in names. We generally chose to include rather than exclude the variant names. We have designated both variant names and variant spellings as "Alternate Forms" within the text. The cross-references lead readers to related entries. Occasionally there are goddesses sharing a single name in two or more different regions who may or may not be the same deity. These have been cross-referenced.

We relied on consultants and printed sources for the current usage of diacritics. There are many systems of transliteration, capitalization, and hyphenation; for each major region we chose one system and endeavored, so far as possible, to use it throughout.

Scholarly attempts to package the world within clearly defined boundaries inevitably violate natural cultural boundaries that have ebbed and flowed throughout time. Still, it helps the human mind to have some sort of geophysical boundaries as organizational aids. We therefore have divided the world by continent or subcontinent and placed cultures in one place or the other, but recognize that many cultures have overlapped our geographical divisions.

Various problems were encountered in compiling information on all of the regions: astonishingly large numbers of deities, the deification of virtually every aspect of nature and human culture, a vast linguistic and cultural diversity, and the androgynous characteristics of many deities were among the most difficult problems.

Space limitations prevented us from explaining at greater length the relationships between the goddesses and the whole system of Japanese mythology—the grand system of deities who for the most part symbolize various phases and characteristics of natural phenomena. We hope the reader's interest will be stimulated by the information presented and that he or she will turn to more in-depth sources on Japanese mythology and popular belief for more information. Our intent was not to record every obscure goddess in the region, but rather to identify the most notable female deities, offering a starting point for more research. For Chinese names, we used the standard Pinyin transliteration for the goddess

names. We also listed the original spelling from the citation as an alternate form.

For the Near East, including Arabia and other Muslim countries, we included goddesses who were pre-Islamic amd pre-Christian. We have used the term *Hebrew* to mean the ancient people of the Bible and *Israelite* to refer to the people of the ancient country of Israel. *Canaanite* refers to the people of ancient Canaan. *Semitic* refers to the major peoples of southwestern Asia and northern Africa. We use the term *Jews* to refer to the inhabitants of Judea who are descendants of the ancient Hebrews, as well as to persons whose religion is Judaism.

There is a great body of scholarship on the female deities of the Indian subcontinent and the Greek and Roman empires, and we could not include all of the information. For Greece and Rome, we chose to include only those deities who were clearly worshiped or had cult followings.

Like many cultures, the Aztec conceived of an animistic universe and deified nearly every aspect of nature and human culture, including celestial phenomena, the weather, animals, plants, minerals, and products essential to human survival. Certain symbols and ritual paraphernalia identified specific deities and these elements often took on supernatural qualities as well. Some Aztec deities with distinctly different names and iconography were often apparitions of the same cosmological concept. Many Aztec deities had androgynous characteristics or alternately possessed male and female forms, adding to the difficulty of identifying goddesses. Despite these obstacles, certain patterns exist that suggest that Aztec divinities in general, and goddesses in particular, can be identified and placed within a few overlapping deity complexes. These complexes include creation, maize, water, fertility, fire, death, moon, earth, and mother goddesses. A special effort has beeen made to list and cross-reference the most well-known Aztec goddesses according to their relationships to these complexes and to other deities in the Aztec pantheon. Mayan goddesses include many local variations and alternate titles that overlap deity complexes similar to the Aztecs'. The majority of Mayan goddesses listed here are lunar goddesses related to medicine, childbirth, fertility, water, weaving, and creation.

The collection of ethnic group information is an assignment fraught with controversy. We invite future scholars to add to or delete from our information, and we look forward to further research in this area as it pertains to deities.

The attribute categories sometimes refer to deity complexes. The attribute index is a starting point for finding goddesses with similar characteristics. Often, there are opposing attributes in a single entry; just as humans have opposite sides to their personalities, so do goddesses. We did not include attributes in the *See* entries and used the term *Unknown* for those about whom we found no information. *Demi-animal* is a coined term that we used instead of *zoomorphic*. We think it better describes those goddesses who are part human and part animal or who can transform themselves into animals.

Where appropriate, we have included information about the fathers, sons, or brothers as a point of reference. In each entry, we have tried to eliminate sexism, racism, patriarchalism, and imperialism. Wherever possible, we chose gender-neutral terms, such as *druid* instead of *druidess*.

As researchers, our role has been to compile as much accurate information as possible about goddesses. But we also hope we will contribute to the empowerment of women by increasing the readily available knowledge of female deities and thereby adding to the pool of potential female role models, both fierce and gentle.

ACKNOWLEDGMENTS

We want to offer special thanks to the many friends and family members who assisted us in this project. Dr. Alice Reich's lecture on world goddesses at the Colorado Women's College in Denver was the primary inspiration for the project, and Judy Volc of the Boulder Public Library challenged us to complete it. Mary Headley offered crucial help, including contributing to the organization of the goddesses by attribute. Betty J. Hansch, John Lemp, and Bruce Pollock contributed their knowledge and computer skills. We are most appreciative of the continued support of Suzanne Chance, Acquisitions Editor, and Louis Ruybal, Project Editor, at ABC-CLIO. And most especially, we offer our sincere gratitude to our spouses, who endured and encouraged us through the many years of research and writing.

CONSULTANTS

Jetta Blum
Germanic Languages
University of Colorado at Boulder

John Charlot
Department of Religion
University of Hawaii at Manoa

Frederick Denny
Department of Religious Studies
University of Colorado at Boulder

Lawrence Durdin-Robertson
Dublin, Ireland

Sam Gill
Department of Religious Studies
University of Colorado at Boulder

Joyce Wong Kroll
Oriental Languages and Literatures
University of Colorado at Boulder

Robert Lester
Department of Religious Studies
University of Colorado at Boulder

Lynn Ross-Bryant
Department of Religious Studies
University of Colorado at Boulder

Scott Sessions
Mesoamerican Archives
University of Colorado at Boulder

Reiko Sono
University of Colorado at Boulder

John Thorburn
Classics Department
University of Colorado at Boulder

Peter van der Loo
Northern Arizona University

GUIDE TO ENTRY FORMAT

Entry Name

People

Aataentsic

Region —

Northeast, *Iroquois*

Creator of Life; Destroyer of Life; Immortality; Magic; Sky — Attributes
and Heavens

Translation of Name — "Woman Who Fell from the Sky." Celestial deity who — Description
became First Woman. Mother of Gusts of Wind,
grandmother of Iouskeha and Tawiskaron. She is also
malevolent, causing fatal diseases and then taking charge of
the deceased souls.

Story Icon —

*Aataentsic's father died before she was born, but she was
able to communicate with his spirit. He told her that her
intended mate was Earth-holding Chief. To reach her
husband-to-be, Aataentsic had to face many dangers and*

Story —

*Earth-holding Chief's tests. When she returned to her village and
gave birth to a daughter, her people threw her (or she accidentally
fell) down to the blue lake below. As she was falling, her daughter
Gusts of Wind returned to her mother's womb. The animals and
birds of the blue lake realized that Aataentsic needed some land to
rest on so she could once more give birth to Gusts of Wind and
they quickly set about making land from the lake's mud.*

Synonymy —

Equivalent to *Eagentci.* See also *Awehai, Ketq Skwayne,* — Cross-References
Navajo Woman First, and *Woman Who Fell from the Sky.*

Other Names — Alternate forms: Ataentsic, Ataensic, Atahensic. [Gill 1992; — Bibliographic
or Spellings   Leach 1972; Monaghan 1981; Redfield 1931; Savill 1978; Senior 1985]   Citations

INTRODUCTION

The study of goddesses is just one form of the broad field of women's spirituality. We, like Judith Plaskow and Carol Christ in *Weaving the Visions,* see "the need for a positive past with which feminists can identify, the search for new ways to image and speak about the sacred."

Oral traditions, by their fluid nature, prevent the gathering of consistent information, since storytellers through the generations, and eventually the transcribers, add their own interpretations to the stories. Most of the recent transcribing of myths was completed by male researchers, archaeologists, and linguists, who tended to play down accomplishments by female deities compared to achievements of male deities. The earliest recording was done mostly by church scholars and missionaries, again mostly males, whose bias tended to portray strong male figures and weak female figures.

Religious feminist scholars look at what was not said, what was left out, ignored, changed in translation, and at how female transcribers now are recording indigenous stories with full inclusion of female tales. We search for the ignored stories of goddesses, identify our female religious heritage, and add to our libraries and bookshelves a more gender-balanced view of the world's cultural heritage. The serious study of goddesses and the dissemination of this information is not only an empowerment for women, but for all of humankind. We want women and men to know that the female has been worshiped as sacred for thousands of years, and we believe this contributed to the women in those cultures being accorded respect and honor within their societies.

Female figures have been found by archaeologists in every civilization throughout the world and in every time in human history since the Upper Paleolithic. Among some of the better-known female figures from this era of first human expression are ones found at Laussel, France; Willendorf, Austria; Grimaldi, Italy; and Vagarino, Russia.

Humans existed as hunters and gatherers long before the development of agriculture. Using archaeological information and cross-cultural studies of social life, we might imagine what life was like in those times. Each individual's effort was vital to the success of the group, and so a high degree of gender equality was possible. Women were accorded high status in society because they gathered most of the food needed for the familyf and because they gave birth by what the community thought was magical means.

As the pattern of living changed from nomadic hunting and gathering to settled living, the culture changed. Simple horticulture began without the benefit of plow or draft animals. Women's status probably continued to be high during this period, and female deities continued to be worshiped. Neolithic sites where goddess figures have been found include Hacilar and Çatal Hüyük in Turkey, the Indus Valley of India, Jamor in Iraq, Lepenski Vir in the Danube region, and the Vinåa civilization sites on the Balkan peninsula and the island of Malta.

However, in about the same period, women's status in developing nomadic herding societies began to decline. Men controlled the ownership and management of the herds that produced the majority of the food. With women's loss of control over the major supply of food, and as the male role in procreation was acknowledged, men became more dominant in the social, political, economic, and religious activities of the community. As women's status declined, so did the role of the divine female. The main focus of worship became the male god, but he sometimes had a goddess as mother, wife, or daughter. Finally, when the patriarchal social order had evolved to greater complexity within a culture, a single male god reigned, sometimes even giving birth, and eventually goddesses were eliminated from religious pantheons of many nomadic herding cultures.

Modern women now recognize the loss of their collective female religious heritage. Some remnants of goddesses are discernible in today's modern religions. Some of the "Black Virgins" are the result of Christians subsuming the goddess into their religion by renaming her, changing her role to a saint or other minor character, and taking over an earlier religion's buildings or sacred sites.

So the role of the sacred female deteriorated over time. Long ago people venerated her as the supreme creator. Over time she acquired a son or lover, then became the partner of a god with whom she ruled equally. Her status eroded later to sister, wife, or mother of the supreme god under whom she served. Finally, the male deity ruled as the supreme being, and the goddess was either demonized as a witch or monster; trivialized as an angel, nymph, or fairy; demoted to a subservient and docile saint or "good" wife; or dichotomized as a madonna/whore.

Ultimately, the purpose of this book is to show that goddesses were not just wives, sisters, mothers, or fertility deities, but supreme deities themselves. This is our effort toward returning the feminine sacredness to an honored place in the archives of humanity. ♈

in World Mythology

Goddesses

AFRICA

Ababa
Nigeria
Family and Tribes
   Protector of marriages. [Leach 1992]

Abe
Benin, *Fon (Dahomey)*
Unknown
   She controls the waters. Daughter of **Sogbo.** See also **Abe,** Central America and Mesoamerica. [Bastide 1978; Leach 1992]

Abena Budu
Ghana, *Effutu*
Water; Destroyer of Life
   Sea goddess. She is a white rock in the sea, and passing over her at high tide can be disastrous for a fishing boat. She is sometimes requested by the gods to cause a woman to drown. [Leach 1992]

Abenawa
Ghana, *Effutu*
Water; Fishing and Water Animals
   Water goddess from whom the fishermen seek aid. She draws the fish near to the shore so they can be caught. [Leach 1992]

Aberewa
Ghana, *Akan*
Earth and Nature; Poverty
   "Old Woman Earth." She is found where the earth is unproductive. See also **Asase Yaa.** [Bastide 1978; Monaghan 1981]

Aberewa Awukuwa
Ghana, *Ashanti*
Water
   Goddess of the Aberewa River. Her son is Twe, god of Lake Bosomtwe. [Leach 1992]

Abowie
Ghana, *Effutu*
Health and Healing; Wealth
   Goddess of healing who cures her followers of sterility and makes them prosperous. [Leach 1992]

Abuk
Sudan, *Dinka (Jieng)*
Mother and Guardian; Water; Magic; Agriculture; Family and Tribes
   Mother goddess. Her emblem is a small snake. Associated with streams, she is a guardian of women and what women produce.

 Each day Abuk and her husband were given two grains of corn by the creator. Abuk was able to take the two grains of corn and, by grinding them up, magically make enough meal to feed all the Dinka people. [Leach 1992; Parrinder 1967; Savill 1977; Senior 1985]

Abu-mehsu
Ghana, *Nzema (Akan)*
Water
   River goddess. Her husband is Bobowissi, god of thunder, lightning, and rain. [Leach 1992]

Acek
Sudan, *Padang Dinka*
Creator of Life; Agriculture

Goddess of fertility. She supervises the planting of seeds, pregnancy, and childbirth. Her male counterpart may be Nialic. [Leach 1992]

Afiong Edem
Nigeria, *Efik*
Unknown
In the province of Calabar, Afiong Edem is said to have been a vain young woman whose husband was a skull. [Eliot 1976]

Afrékété
Benin, *Fon (Dahomey)*
Water; Fishing and Water Animals
Sea goddess who protects all that is valuable in the sea. She is also known as a trickster who is fond of gossip. In some areas of Africa, Afrékété is considered a god. [Leach 1972; Leach 1992]

Agada
Western Africa, *Fulbe*
Directions
The goddess *Wagadu* when she faces west. [Bastide 1978]

Aha Njoku
Nigeria, *Ibo (Igbo)*
Agriculture
Goddess of yams. She oversees the behavior of women wherever there are yams—in the home, in the fields, and where the yams are stored. [Leach 1992]

'Aisha Qandisha
Morocco
Demi-animals; Magic; Love and Sexuality
Moroccan "jinniya" (spirit) who is beautiful but has pendulous breasts and goat legs. She is sexually active and a free spirit. [Monaghan 1990]

Aizu
Benin, *Fon (Dahomey)*
Sky and Heavens; Wealth
Sky goddess. Guardian of the people's treasures. She shares this position with her sister, *Akazu.* They are the daughters of *Mawu* and *Lisa.* [Leach 1992]

Aja
Nigeria, *Yoruba*
Earth and Nature; Health and Healing; Education and Knowledge
Benevolent forest goddess who teaches her followers how to use medicinal herbs. See also *Aja,* Near East. [Leach 1992]

Aje
Nigeria, *Idoma*
Earth and Nature
Earth deity. [Leach 1992]

Akazu
Benin, *Fon (Dahomey)*
Sky and Heavens; Wealth
Sky goddess who guards the people's treasures with her sister, *Aizu.* They are the daughters of *Mawu* and *Lisa.* [Leach 1992]

Akpitoko
Ghana, *Gã*
Arts
Kple-dancing goddess. [Leach 1992]

Ala
Nigeria, *Ibo (Igbo)*
Earth and Nature; Mother and Guardian; Justice; Agriculture; Ceremonies
Earth mother. Custodian of her children, she provides all that is life sustaining; establishes laws; guides morality; and, finally, claims them in death. If her children are peaceful, there are bountiful harvests from the earth and the womb. Shrines to Ala are found in Nigerian homes and village squares. There are sculptures of her with children, holding a yam knife, the symbol of fertility of the earth and of death. See also *Ane.* Alternate form: Ale. [Leach 1992; Mbiti 1970; Parrinder 1967; Preston 1982; Senior 1985; Spretnak 1982]

Alajeru
Nigeria, *Yoruba*
Unknown
Revered mother of the people's hero. Heros are important mythical figures. [Savill 1977]

Alasho-Funfun
Nigeria, *Ibadan*
Creator of Life
Fertility goddess. [Leach 1992]

Ale   See *Ala.*

All-bringing-forth
Nigeria
Weather; Water; Demi-animals
Rainbow goddess in Benin who is a deified queen. She is the patron of waters and manifests as a snake. [Johnson 1988]

Alo
Nigeria, *Ibo (Igbo)*
Earth and Nature
Earth mother. She forms a triad with her husband, Eze Chite Okike, the sun, and her son, Igwe, the sky. [Leach 1992]

Ama
Nigeria, *Jukun*
Earth and Nature; Heaven and Hell
Earth mother and underworld goddess. In Kindo (the underworld), she provides a place for those who have died. She is connected with the sky god, Chido. See also *Ama,* Eastern Europe. [Gillon 1984; Leach 1992]

Amakiri
Nigeria, *Okrika*
Earth and Nature
Earth goddess. [Leach 1992]

Amauneit
Kenya; Tanzania
Mother and Guardian; Family and Tribes
Mother goddess who created humans. [Stone 1979]

Amelenwa
Ghana, *Nzema (Akan)*
Water; Justice
River goddess who reigns over the other deities. Because she is merciless and unforgiving, her followers try to avoid offending her. [Leach 1992]

Amirini
Africa
Mother and Guardian
Mother goddess. [Sykes 1968]

Amponyinamoa
Ghana, *Akan*
Earth and Nature; Health and Healing
Earth goddess who grants the blessing of long life.
[Bastide 1978]

Andriamahilala
Madagascar
Creator of Life; Sky and Heavens
"Queen of Heaven." Mother goddess. She gave the first humans their flesh and form, while other deities gave them bones, blood, and breath.

 When the first humans were asked what kind of death they wanted, they were given two choices. Their first choice was to be like the banana tree and send forth shoots that would live on after they died; this meant they would have children but die themselves. The second choice was to have no children, but to be like the moon—to die each month and be born again the next month, thereby living forever. The first humans chose to be like the banana tree. [Cotterell 1979]

Ane
Nigeria, *Ibo (Igbo)*
Earth and Nature
Earth mother of the Ezza people, a subtribe of the Ibo (Igbo). Considered by some to be an alternate name for *Ala*. [Leach 1992; Monaghan 1981]

Ani
Nigeria, *Ibo (Igbo)*
Earth and Nature; Family and Tribes; Agriculture; Justice; Heaven and Hell
Earth goddess of the northern Ibo (Igbo) people of Nigeria. She oversees childbirth, fertility, the farming cycle, morality, and the afterworld. She is associated with Okuke, a fertility god. [Leach 1992]

Annallja Tu Bari
Sudan
Love and Sexuality
Goddess of the Sudan. She began life as an ill-fated lover and was deified. [Eliot 1976]

Anyigba
Togo, *Ewe*
Mother and Guardian; Agriculture; Luck; Hunting and Wild Animals; War; Health and Healing
"Mother of Little Children." Mother goddess who bestows offspring, makes yams grow, and gives good luck in hunting and victory in war. Although she can make people ill, she also heals them. [Leach 1992; Redfield 1931]

Aprija
Nigeria, *Nkum*
Earth and Nature; Agriculture; Mother and Guardian; Ceremonies
Earth goddess who protects crops and is called upon in times of crisis. Women perform springtime rituals in her honor. [Mbiti 1970]

Aquaba
Ghana, *Ashanti*
Family and Tribes
Religious figure whose replica is carried by the women to help them conceive a child.

 Once there was a childless queen of a matriarchal society. She was instructed to carry a wooden figure with her and to treat it as if it were alive. She was soon pregnant and gave birth to a girl child to carry on the family line. [Courlander 1975]

Araua
Kenya; Tanzania, *Ndorobo*
Moon and Night
Moon goddess. Sister or mother of the sun, Asis. [Leach 1992]

Arava
Kenya, *Dorobo (Okiek)*
Moon and Night
Moon goddess. She is the mother of the male deity. [Mbiti 1970]

Asaase Aberewa
Ghana, *Akan*
Heaven and Hell; Demi-animals; Life/Death Cycle; Ceremonies
Goddess of the underworld on the Guinea Coast. She manifests as a scorpion or a snake, symbolizing death and rebirth. Thursday is her sacred day. Also said to be a name for *Nyame*. [Leach 1992]

Asaase Afua   See *Asase Afua.*

Asaase Yaa   See *Asase Yaa.*

Asase Afua
Ghana, *Akan*
Creator of Life; Stars and Planets; Heaven and Hell; Ceremonies
Goddess of fertility and procreation. She is associated with the planet Venus. She is the daughter of Onyame, wife of Nyame, when Nyame is a male deity. She is also a goddess of the underworld and her sacred day is Friday. Alternate form: Asaase Afua. [Courlander 1975; Leach 1992]

Asase Efua   See *Asase Yaa.*

Asase Yaa
Ghana, *Akan*
Heaven and Hell; Earth and Nature; Life/Death Cycle; Ceremonies; Water
"Earth Thursday." Earth goddess. Although she is a very powerful goddess, there is no image or temple in her honor, so she is worshiped in the fields. She gives life, and her followers return to her in death. Thursday is her sacred day. The deities of water and trees are her children. She inhabits the barren places of the earth and the underworld and is associated with the planet Jupiter. See also *Aberewa.* Alternate forms: Asaase Yaa, Asase Efua. [Leach 1992; Mbiti 1970; Monaghan 1981; Redfield 1931; Savill 1977; Sproul 1979]

Ashiakle
Ghana, *Gã*
Water
A secondary sea goddess of the Accra area. [Leach 1992]

Asia
Guinea, *Senegabia, Sengal*; Gambia
Earth and Nature
Earth goddess. [Leach 1992]

Atai
Nigeria, *Efik (Ibibio)*
Creator of Life; Justice; Destroyer of Life; Disorder
Creator goddess who is also said to be responsible for disagreements among children.

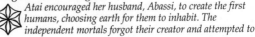 *Atai encouraged her husband, Abassi, to create the first humans, choosing earth for them to inhabit. The independent mortals forgot their creator and attempted to*

become equals of the deities. Atai sent death as a potent reminder that they were only human. [Beier 1966; Cotterell 1979; Leach 1992]

Atete

Ethiopia (Abyssinia), *Galla (Oromo)*

Creator of Life; Water; Earth and Nature

Fertility goddess who controls the fertility of humans and creatures who inhabit rivers. Some people believe she created the world and gave humans the tools necessary for their survival. [Leach 1992]

Atida

Uganda, *Lango*

Hunting and Wild Animals; War; Weather; Fate

Goddess connected with hunting, fighting, and rain. Atida uses the banyan tree, which is sacred to her, as her oracle. She is the female half of Jok, the omnipotent, omnipresent, high god of the Lango. [Leach 1992]

Ato

Nigeria, *Yoruba*

Unknown

Daughter of *Oya's* ninth child, Ogogo Onigbori. Ato was one of a set of triplets and was born with a membrane on her face. She wields *Oya's* sword and is an *egungun* (ancestral spirit of the dead who appears in masquerade form). [Gleason 1987]

Avlekete

Benin, *Fon (Dahomey), Ge*

Water

Sea goddess who is worshiped at the port of Cotonou. [Leach 1992]

Aya

Africa, *Yoruba*

Small Size

Midget jungle goddess who was taken to Cuba and Brazil. In Ghana, the name of a male deity. See also *Aya*, Near East. Alternate form: Aye. [Gonzalez-Wippler 1987]

Ayaba

Benin, *Fon (Dahomey)*

Household Affairs; Agriculture

Household goddess. A daughter of *Mawu* and *Lisa*, she watches over the hearth and food. [Leach 1992]

Aya-eke

Nigeria

Agriculture

Yam goddess. [Leach 1992]

Aye   See *Aya*.

Ayeba

Nigeria, *Tiv*

Creator of Life; Supreme Being

Creator and highest deity worshiped on the Nigerian Delta. [Leach 1992]

Azele Yaba

Ghana, *Nzema*

Earth and Nature; Justice

Earth goddess. Oaths are taken in her name. Blaspheming her or her husband, Nyamenle, will bring punishment unless amends are made immediately. [Leach 1992]

Aziri

Benin, *Fon (Dahomey)*

Water

Freshwater goddess who is the counterpart of the Yoruban *Oxun* and equivalent to *Mistress Ezili,* Mesoamerica. [Bastide 1978]

Babayanmi   See *Bayanni*.

Bayanni

Nigeria, *Yoruba*

Ceremonies

Goddess of the cowrie shell casque of Nigeria and the Americas. A casque is a ceremonial headpiece, a helmet covered with shells. Bayanni is a contraction of *Babayanmi,* which means "Father choose me." Bayanni is Shango's sister.

Bayanni is the weak sister upon whom the feared ineptitude of her younger brother, Shango, is projected, and she is sacrificed for his enablement. Thus, with her own being she crowns him.

Alternate forms: Babayanmi, Dada, Obaneñe. [Gleason 1987]

Bele Alua

Ghana, *Nzema (Akan)*

Earth and Nature

Tree goddess. Her husband is Bobo Arisi. [Leach 1992]

Bitabok

Sudan

Magic

Witches or spirits who have bats as their companions. [Leach 1972]

Bomu Rambi

Zimbabwe

Moon and Night

Moon goddess. [Stone 1979]

Bosumabla

Ghana, *Gã*

Water

Sea goddess in the area of Accra. She is one of their less important deities. [Leach 1992]

Bride of the Barley

Morocco, *Berbers*

Creator of Life; Agriculture; Ceremonies

Fertility goddess. To ensure the fertility of the crops for the next year, the people make images of her out of harvested straw. [Eliade 1987]

Buk

Sudan, *Nuer*

Water

Goddess of rivers and streams. She is the people's source of life. Her son, Deng, is god of thunder, lightning, and rain, and her daughters are *Candit* and *Nyaliep.* [Leach 1992]

Bunzi

Zaire, *Woyo*

Weather; Agriculture; Demi-animals

Rain goddess. She manifests as a rainbow-colored snake and rewards her followers with plentiful rains and harvests. See also *Mboze*.

Bunzi was the daughter of Mboze, the first mother of the Woyo people. When Mboze's husband discovered he was not the father of Bunzi, he killed Mboze. Bunzi then took over the duties of her mother, bringing rain to make the plants grow. [Spretnak 1982; Stone 1979]

Buruku
Ghana, *Akan*
Creator of Life; Supreme Being; Moon and Night
   Creator and highest deity. She is associated with the moon.
In some areas Buruku is considered a male deity. [Leach 1992]

Bushongo Earth Mother
Congo, *Bushongo*
Earth and Nature; Disorder
   Earth Mother and her husband, Heaven, were created by
Bumba, the creator of the Bushongo people.

   *Earth Mother and Heaven lived together as husband and
   wife, closely joined. One day they had a terrible fight and
   Heaven left Earth. They have been apart ever since.*
[Carlyon 1982]

Bwalya Chabala
Zambia, *Bemba (Awemba)*
Family and Tribes; Ceremonies
   Deified founding queen. Her matrilineal clan honors her
by bringing cloth and flour to her burial shrine, where the
offerings are placed in a basket said to have belonged to her.
The flour is used in religious ceremonies. [Eliade 1987]

Candit
Sudan, *Nuer*
Water
   Goddess of streams. Her mother is **Buk.** [Leach 1992]

Ceres Africana
North Africa
Creator of Life; Agriculture
   Fertility goddess who is associated with the harvest. Her
Latin name was given to her by the Roman Tertullian.
Alternate form: Ceres Punica. [Lurker 1984]

Ceres Punica   See *Ceres Africana.*

Chade
Ghana, *Gã*
Agriculture
   Agricultural goddess of the city of Temma. She grants
abundant harvests and supervises the planting of corn.
[Leach 1992]

Chekechani
Malawi, *Anyanja*
Moon and Night
   Wife of the moon. The moon fades because Chekechani
does not feed him. See also **Puikani.** [Leach 1992; Werner
1964]

Chi
Nigeria, *Ibo (Igbo), Ekoi*
Creator of Life; Earth and Nature
   Earth goddess and creator who is a benevolent protector of
the good but punishes the corrupt. Confusion occurs because
Chi is considered one being, male and female—sky god and
earth goddess. Alternate form: Chineke. [Leach 1992]

Chineke   See *Chi.*

Chi-wara   See *Tji-wara.*

Cigoro
Nigeria, *Maguzawa (Hausa)*
Destroyer of Life
   Goddess of disease in Nigeria. Her illnesses affect the eyes.
One of the wives of 'Dan Galadima. See also **Karama.** [Leach
1992]

Coti
Southern Africa, *San (Bushman)*
Creator of Life; Hunting and Wild Animals
   Co-creator, with the god Praying Mantis. She is also the
mother of the antelope. See also **Dasse, Huntu Katt! Katten,**
and **Hyrax.** [Carlyon 1982; Leach 1972; Savill 1977]

Crocodile Woman
Sudan, *Shilluk*
Mother and Guardian; Demi-animals
   Birth goddess who takes the form of a crocodile or
strangely acting animals, presiding over birth and protecting
infants. [Savill 1977]

Dada
Nigeria
Fishing and Water Animals; Water
   Goddess represented by a cowrie shell casque or helmet,
which is also called a *dada.* Also the name of a male deity.
[Gleason 1987; Leach 1992]

Dahomean Moon Woman
Benin; Gambia, *Fon (Dahomey), Serer*
Moon and Night; Mother and Guardian
   Moon goddess.

   *In the beginning Sun was out during the day with his
   children, the stars. Their mother, Moon Woman, saved her
   children from the terrible heat by having them come out
only at night, which made Sun angry. Now he chases Moon
Woman every day, sometimes catching her (an eclipse).*
   There is also a moon goddess of the Serer of Gambia with
this name.

   *Sun and Moon pass a waterfall where their mothers are
   bathing. Sun turns away, but Moon stares. God makes Sun
   bright to remind the people of his modest behavior; Moon is
made dimmer, so the people can stare at her like she stared at her
mother.* [Beier 1966; Carlyon 1982; Courlander 1975]

Damwamwit
Ethiopia, *Gurage*
Ceremonies; Disorder
   Goddess of women. During her festival, the women
can act uncharacteristically by verbally abusing the men.
[Eliade 1987]

Dan
Benin, *Mahi*
Weather; Reptiles; Wealth; Order
   Rainbow serpent goddess. She "symbolizes continuity, the
vital force, and bestows wealth." Also considered a male deity.
[Leach 1992]

Dandalunda   See *Yemanja,* Central America and
Mesoamerica.

Dangira
Nigeria, *Maguzawa (Hausa)*
Destroyer of Life
   Goddess of disease in Nigeria. The people say this goddess
makes them itch. [Leach 1992]

Dariya
Nigeria, *Maguzawa (Hausa)*
Destroyer of Life; Unhappiness
   Goddess of disease. She causes madness by making the
people laugh hysterically. [Leach 1992]

Dasse
Southern Africa, *San (Bushman)*
Unknown

The goddess Dasse is the wife of a god who is a mantis. See also *Coti, Huntu Katt! Katten,* and *Hyrax.* [Jobes 1962]

Data

Nigeria, *Kalabari*

Water

Water deity who is associated with the water god, Agiri, and is the sister of Sabo. [Leach 1992]

Daughter of the Sky   See *Nambi.*

Death Goddess

Ghana, *Ashanti*

Destroyer of Life

Death goddess.

The Death Goddess and the culture hero, Number Eleven, match wits. She tries to obtain as many dead bodies as possible and he tries to keep his friends alive. Because he manages to outwit the Death Goddess, Number Eleven is allowed to become a deity who then becomes the ancestor of the other minor divinities. [Carlyon 1982]

Deung Abok

Sudan, *Shilluk*

Family and Tribes; Domesticated Animals

"Great White Cow." Ancestor goddess. Arising from the Nile River, she became the first ancestor of the kings. [Leach 1992]

Dierra

Western Africa, *Fulbe*

Directions

The goddess *Wagadu* when she faces north. [Courlander 1975]

Dinka First Woman

Sudan, *Dinka*

Destroyer of Life; Agriculture

Deity who brought sickness and death to Earth.

The First Woman was told by the creator to plant just one grain of millet a day. She disobeyed and because the sky was so low, her planting pole kept bumping the sky god. He became angry and withdrew, leaving those on earth to suffer death. [Eliade 1987]

Divine Queen

Transvaal, *Luvedu (Bantu)*

Magic; Earth and Nature

Deified queen. Shielded from evil influences, she is said to have magical powers that she uses to control nature. [Cotterell 1979]

Djaga Woman

Tanzania (Tanganyika Territory), *Djaga*

Destroyer of Life; Life/Death Cycle; Immortality

Goddess in the Lake Tanganyika area. She brought death to earth.

Originally humans did not die. As they grew older, they sloughed off their skin like a snake and became young again. The god Ruwa told them to do this only when no one could see them. Djaga Woman's grandfather sent her out to get some water with a leaky calabash [a container cut from a tree]. He thought this would keep her occupied while he shed his skin, but she quickly patched the holes and returned home. She saw her grandfather half out of his skin and from then on humans died. Djaga Woman was punished by being made the mother of all the monkey family. [Carlyon 1982]

Dogon Earth Mother

Mali, *Dogon*

Creator of Life; Earth and Nature; Love and Sexuality

Earth mother.

It was said that Amma, the Dogon god, created Earth in order to procreate. His first attempt was prevented by a termite hill, Earth Mother's clitoris. After he excised her clitoris, he was able to mate with her. Their children became the elements and the points of the compass.

The Dogon people believe the clitoris represents a woman's masculinity. Even today girls have their clitoris excised. Alternate form: Earth Woman of Dogon. [Carlyon 1982; Eliade 1987]

Dogon Sun Goddess

Mali, *Dogon*

Agriculture

Worshiped by the agricultural people of Mali and the Upper Volta. [Sproul 1979]

Dorina

Nigeria, *Maguzawa (Hausa)*

Hunting and Wild Animals

Hunting deity. Manifested as a hippopotamus, she aids the people during the hunt. [Leach 1992]

Dugbo

Sierra Leone, *Kono*

Earth and Nature

Earth goddess who is responsible for all the plants and trees. Her husband is Yataa, the supreme being. [Leach 1992]

Dziva

Zimbabwe (Rhodesia), *Shona*

Justice; Creator of Life; Goodness; Wealth; Agriculture; Poverty

Shona creator goddess in Zimbabwe (Rhodesia). She is a benevolent deity who provides abundance and fertility but causes pestilence and crop failure as punishment for incest. Said to be the female manifestation of the creator, Mwari. Alternate forms: Mbuya, Zendere. [Leach 1992]

Earth Woman of Dogon   See *Dogon Earth Mother.*

Edinkira

Ghana, *Akan*

Earth and Nature

Tree goddess whose sacred grove is at Nkoranza. She is considered androgynous. [Leach 1992]

Egungun-oya

Nigeria, *Yoruba*

Fate

"Mother of the Dead." An aspect of Yoruban *Oya* when she is practicing divination. [Courlander 1973; Gleason 1987]

Eka Abassi

Nigeria, *Ibibio*

Creator of Life; Primordial Being

"Great First Cause." Creator deity. Her son/husband is Obumo, god of thunder and rain. [Leach 1992; Redfield 1931]

Ekineba

West Africa, *Kalabari*

Arts; Education and Knowledge; Ceremonies

Masquerade goddess in the Niger Delta. She teaches the dancing and drumming that are used at the masquerades. [Leach 1992]

Ekumoke
Nigeria
Creator of Life
    Fertility goddess. [Leach 1992]

Enekpe
Nigeria, *Igala*
Family and Tribes; Mother and Guardian; War
    Guardian of destiny.

 Enekpe saw that her tribe was losing the battle. To save her people, she offered herself as a sacrifice and was buried alive on the battlefield. [Savill 1977]

Esesar
Ghana, *Gbanya*
Earth and Nature
    Earth goddess whose husband is the sky god, Ebore. [Leach 1992]

Eveningstar of Wakaranga
Zimbabwe (Rhodesia), *Wakaranga*
Creator of Life; Hunting and Wild Animals; Insects; Reptiles
    Creator deity who shares her duties with *Morningstar of Wakaranga.* Eveningstar gave birth to domestic animals, antelope, birds, and children, and later, lions, leopards, snakes, and scorpions were born.

 Eveningstar is chased by Moon each night. He is angry with her because she sent Snake to bite him. Moon became ill and drought and famine covered the land. The people thought it was Moon's fault, so they strangled him and threw him into the ocean, from which he continues to arise to chase Eveningstar across the sky. [Beier 1966]

Ewuraba
Ghana, *Effutu*
Water; Fire
    Sea goddess. She is the keeper of the oil lamps that are used when the deities meet. Her home is a "rock in the sea." [Leach 1992]

Ezili
Benin, *Fon (Dahomey)*
Beauty; Love and Sexuality; Water
    Goddess of "sweet" water. Also goddess of beauty and love in Benin. See also *Erzulie*, Central America and Mesoamerica. [Bastide 1978]

Ezili Freda Dahomey   See *Ezili.*

Ezum Mezum
Nigeria
Creator of Life
    Fertility goddess. She is the female half of the dual fertility symbol, the Ibudu. [Leach 1992]

Fa   See *Gbadu* and *Minona.*

Fohsu
Ghana
Agriculture
    White-skinned goddess of salt. Her followers are found among the inhabitants of Cape Coast. [Redfield 1931]

Ganda First Woman
Uganda, *Ganda*
Destroyer of Life
    Deity who brought death. She is the daughter of the sky god and her brother is Death.

 First Woman disobeyed her father, so he sent her brother Death to earth to punish her. Death's first victims were her children. [Eliade 1987]

Ganna
Western Africa, *Fulbe*
Directions
    The goddess *Wagadu* when she faces east. [Bastide 1978]

Gbadu
Benin, *Fon (Dahomey)*
Fate; Order
    "Holy Daughter." Goddess of fate. Gbadu was the first creation of her mother, *Mawu.* She is also considered fate in the abstract and an androgynous deity.

    Gbadu was very sad when she looked down from heaven and saw her mother's creations fighting. She sent her children to earth to remind the people that, when they fight with one another, they are fighting with Mawu, for each of them is a part of Mawu.
    Alternate form: Fa. [Leach 1992; Stone 1979]

Gbenebeka
Nigeria, *Ogoni*
Sky and Heavens; Mother and Guardian
    Sky and mother goddess. [Leach 1992]

Gcagcile
South Africa
Disorder
    "Spirit of Trouble." Her son is the war god, Kibuka, and her husband is Lumukanda. [Leach 1992]

Greedy Woman
Nigeria, *Bini (Edo)*
Agriculture; Evil
    Goddess who is responsible for humans having to work for their living.

    In the beginning people did not work, because the sky was so close to the Earth, they could just reach up and cut off a piece of it to eat. One day, Greedy Woman cut off an enormous chunk of the sky and, even with the help of the whole village, there was no way to finish it so she had to throw the remainder away. The sky was angry about this and rose high above the Earth so the people could no longer take pieces for food. Now people must work for their food. [Beier 1966]

Gyangya'di
Nigeria, *Maguzawa (Hausa)*
Destroyer of Life
    Goddess of disease. She causes sleeping sickness. [Leach 1992]

Haine
Tanzania, *Hadzapi*
Moon and Night
    Moon goddess. Her husband is Ishoye, the sun, and her grandchild is *Shashaya.* Haine is sometimes considered a male deity. [Leach 1992]

Harrakoi Dikko
Nigeria, *Sonrai (Songhai)*
Water; Ceremonies
    "Mother of the Waters." Each year, during the flooding of the Niger River, a cow is sacrificed in her honor. [Gleason 1987]

Hottentot Mother Goddess
Namibia, *Khoikhoin*
Love and Sexuality; Magic

Virgin creator who consumed a magic herb and gave birth to the sorcerer god, Heitsi-Eibib. [Carlyon 1982]

Huntu Katt! Katten
South Africa, *San (Bushman)*
Hunting and Wild Animals; Earth and Nature
   Deity who is worshiped in the form of a rock rabbit and is the wife of the mantis god, Kaggen. See also *Coti, Dasse,* and *Hyrax.* [Leach 1992]

Hyrax
San (Bushman)
Unknown
   Deity who is the wife of I-Kaggen (praying mantis), the creator. See also *Coti, Dasse,* and *Huntu Katt! Katten.* [Aldington and Ames 1968]

Ichar-tsirew
Ghana
Water; Mother and Guardian; Order
   Sea goddess of the people of the Gold Coast. She aids in childbirth and grants tranquility to households. [Leach 1992]

Igbarun
Nigeria
Water
   "Dark River." Deity whose husband is king of the sea, and together they are all the water on earth. [Gleason 1987]

Igoni
Nigeria, *Kalabari*
Water
   Kalabari water goddess in Nigeria. [Leach 1992]

Ii
Nigeria, *Margi*
Earth and Nature; Agriculture
   "The Mother of the Crops." Earth goddess . [Leach 1992]

Ije
Nigeria, *Idoma*
Earth and Nature
   Earth deity. [Leach 1992]

Ikosatana   See *Inkosazana.*

Imo
Nigeria, *Ibo (Igbo)*
Water; Mother and Guardian; Wealth; Ceremonies; Justice
   River goddess who grants children and prosperity. An annual celebration is held for her at her shrine on the Imo River, where her followers come to swear oaths. [Leach 1992]

Inkosazana
South Africa, *Zulu*
Sky and Heavens; Agriculture; Weather; Education and Knowledge
   "Princess of Heaven." Zulu sky goddess and goddess of agriculture in South Africa. She oversees the growth of corn and its harvesting. In the heavens, she manifests as the rainbow, the rain, and the mist. To a chosen few, she appears as a young woman, delivering important revelations that must be kept secret. See also *Nomkubulwana.* Alternate forms: Inkosatana, Inkosazana-ye-zulu. [Bonnerjea 1927; Leach 1992; Mbiti 1970]

Inkosazana-ye-zulu   See *Inkosazana.*

Inkosikasi
South Africa, *Zulu*
Sky and Heavens; Supreme Being
   Omnipotent sky goddess. [Leach 1992]

'Inna
Nigeria, *Maguzawa (Hausa)*
Agriculture; Justice
   Agricultural goddess who provides abundant crops. Her name is used in the swearing of oaths and she protects property and punishes thieves. [Leach 1992]

Isamba
Tanzania, *Issansu*
Moon and Night; Life/Death Cycle
   Moon goddess.
   Isamba, the moon, came down to earth with her husband, the sun. God had given them a pitcher and a basket to help determine who was the wisest. Isamba chose to be guardian of the pitcher and her husband took the basket. God then told them to throw their articles on the ground. Isamba had chosen unwisely because the pitcher broke. When the pitcher "died," death came to humans. [Beier 1966]

Ises
South Africa, *Heikum*
Hunting and Wild Animals
   Goddess of the bow and arrow. [Leach 1992]

Isong
Nigeria, *Ibibio, Ekoi*
Earth and Nature; Creator of Life
   Goddess of the earth and of fertility. See also *Obasi Nsi.* [Leach 1992]

Iya-maase
Nigeria
Ceremonies
   "Essential Woman." She is believed to be the originator of the *egungun* (ancestral spirits of the dead) ritual in Nigeria. [Gleason 1987]

Iyanla
Nigeria; Benin, *Yoruba*
Family and Tribes; Ceremonies
   "Great Mother." She is honored in the Gelede ceremonies used to invoke maternal ancestral power. [Gleason 1987]

Jezanna
Zimbabwe (Rhodesia), *Nashona*
Moon and Night
   Moon goddess. Her sacred lake is the Davisa, where her image dwells at night. She is represented on earth by a high priestess. [Spretnak 1982; Stone 1979]

Juno Coelestis
North Africa, *Berber*
Love and Sexuality
   Goddess of sacred temple sexuality. Associated with debauchery and fertility, she was adopted from the Romans. [Leach 1992]

Kabyle First Woman
North Africa, *Berber*
Creator of Life
   Creator goddess.
   Kabyle First Woman made a ewe from water and flour. She had soot on her hands, so the ewe's head was black. The next day she made a ram out of dough and barley chaff. When the ram tried to butt the sun, the sun seized him. [Eliot 1976]

Kaiala
Congo, *Yoruba*
Unknown
   Equivalent to *Yemanja*, Central America and Mesoamerica.
[Bastide 1978]

Kaikara
Uganda, *Konjo, Banyoro*
Agriculture; Ceremonies
   Harvest deity. Offerings are made to her before the fields
are cut. Her husband is Kalisa, god of the forest and wild
game. [Leach 1992]

Kaiwan
Ethiopia (Abyssinia)
Earth and Nature; Wealth
   Earth goddess of plenty. Corresponds to *Kun*, Indian
Subcontinent. [Jobes 1962]

Kalimulore
Ruanda
Demi-animals
   Shape-changing goddess who appears as a young woman
or a lion. [Savill 1977]

Kamaugarunga
Southwestern Africa, *Herero*
Creator of Life
   First woman in the Herero creation story. [Senior 1985]

Karama
Nigeria, *Maguzawa (Hausa)*
Destroyer of Life
   Goddess of disease who causes diseases of the eye. She
is the youngest wife of 'Dan Galadima. See also *Cigoro*.
[Leach 1992]

Katarwiri
Ghana, *Ashanti, Tshi*
Evil; Water; Ceremonies
   Malevolent river goddess. Human female sacrifices
were made to her. Her husband is the river god, Tando.
[Leach 1992]

Khwora!ma
Namibia, *San (Bushman)*
Insects
   "Mother of the Bees." Deity who can be invoked to help
locate bees' nests. Her husband is Gao!na. [Leach 1992]

Ko
South Africa, *San (Bushman)*
Insects
   Goddess in the Orange Free State. She takes the form of the
mantis. She sometimes tells the hunters where to find
animals. See also *Koki*. [Leach 1992]

Koki
Nigeria; Niger Territory, *Temne, Maguzawa (Hausa)*
Insects
   Goddess who is a praying mantis and is the wife of Spider,
a trickster. See also *Ko*. [Leach 1972]

Koko Mwezi   "Grandmother Moon." See *Mweji*.

Kokobi
Ghana, *Effutu*
Water
   Water goddess who watches over the village's water
supply. [Leach 1992]

Kono
Ivory Coast; Mali, *Senufu*
Ceremonies; Family and Tribes; Wild Birds
   Bird goddess and ancestor deity. She is worshiped in the
form of a large crested crane. Anyone wearing her mask
during rituals "becomes" Kono. [Johnson 1988]

Kono First Woman
Guinea, *Kono*
Family and Tribes
   Ancestor of all the tribes of the world, who are believed to
originate in Guinea. Her husband is god and her father,
Death.
   *First Woman gave birth to three black girls and boys and
   four white girls and boys. When they were born, they spoke
   different languages. From these children came all the
peoples of the world.* [Beier 1966]

Krachi Woman
West Africa, *Krachi*
Earth and Nature
   Earth goddess. [Carlyon 1982]

Kuanja
Angola, *Mbundu*
Hunting and Wild Animals
   Hunting goddess. [Leach 1992]

Kyanwa
Nigeria, *Maguzawa (Hausa)*
Hunting and Wild Animals
   Wildcat spirit who aids in hunting. She is the wife of
Damisa. [Leach 1992]

La-hkima Oqla
Morocco
Evil; Water
   A female "jenn" (spirit) of Morocco. She inhabits the river
Buzemlan and rules over other evil spirits. [Leach 1992]

Lalla Ta Bullat
Morocco
Mother and Guardian
   Goddess of childbirth. She gives aid in difficult deliveries.
To obtain her help, women must visit Lalla Ta Bullat's
gravesite. [Leach 1992]

Leza   See *Lisa*.

Lisa
Benin, *Fon (Dahomey)*
Moon and Night; Ceremonies
   Deity who is the wife or mother of the male Mawu and
forms a trinity with Mawu and Ge. Her daughters are *Aizu,
Akazu,* and *Ayaba.* The Fon (Dahomey) join Lisa with Mawu
into a dual deity, *Mawu-Lisa.* The Fon identify her with the
moon. Sacrifices of white goats and white chickens are made
in her honor. In some areas, Lisa is considered a male deity.
See also *Lissa.* Alternate forms: Leza, Mawu-Lisa. [Carlyon
1982; Leach 1992]

Lissa
Fon (Dahomey)
Sun and Day; Disorder
   Sun spirit. When Lissa and her husband, Gleti, the moon,
have domestic fights, there is an eclipse. Also considered an
alternate form of *Lisa.* [Redfield 1931]

Loa

Tanzania, *Iraqw*
Sun and Day; Destroyer of Life
  Sun goddess. She is the bringer of death. Loa is also a
name for the deities of Vodun (voodoo). See also *Loa*, Central
America and Mesoamerica. [Leach 1992]

Luamerava

South Africa
Love and Sexuality
  Goddess of sexual desire. Associated with Lumukanda.
[Leach 1992]

Ma

South Africa
Creator of Life; Earth and Nature
  "Goddess of Creation." See also *Ma*, Greek and Roman
Empires, and *Ma*, Near East. [Leach 1992]

Mabisalira

Mozambique, *Nyanja*
Magic
  Professional witch-finder. [Bonnerjea 1927]

Macouas First Woman

South-central and Southeastern Africa, *Macouas*
Creator of Life; Agriculture
  First Woman at the Zambesi River.
    *Muluku, the creator, made the earth and dug two holes. Out
    of the holes came a woman and a man. He gave them tools
    and seeds and told them to cultivate the land. Instead, they
ate the seeds and threw the tools away. Afraid of Muluku's anger,
they went to the forest to hide.* [Carlyon 1982]

Mahu

Benin, *Fon (Dahomey)*
Moon and Night
  Moon goddess. Daughter of *Nana Buluku*. See also *Mawu*.
[Baumgartner 1984; Redfield 1931]

Makasa

Nigeria, *Maguzawa (Hausa)*
Destroyer of Life
  Goddess of disease. She lives in the bush with her
husband, Jammarke, and causes diarrhea. [Leach 1992]

Ma-ndəə

Sierra Leone, *Mende*
Earth and Nature
  Earth goddess. [Leach 1992]

Marimba

South Africa
Arts
  Goddess of music, especially singers. Her husband is
Zumangwe, "the Hunter." [Leach 1992]

Maruwa See *Marwe*.

Maryam

Ethiopia, *Amhara-Tigrina*
Earth and Nature
  Name for the *Virgin Mary*, Near East. Maryam live in
sacred natural areas—high mountains, springs, and groves of
sycamore trees. Some worship her in her sacred groves.
[Crim 1981]

Marwe

Kenya
Heaven and Hell; Wealth

Youthful deity of Kenya who was able to go to the
"otherworld" and return with great treasures. Alternate form:
Maruwa. [Senior 1985]

Masai Moon Goddess

Eastern Africa, *Masai*
Mother and Guardian; Disorder; Moon and Night; Health
and Healing
  "New Moon." The people throw a stone at the new moon,
asking for a long life. Pregnant women also request an easy
birth in this manner.
    *Moon and Sun were married. One day they had a terrible
    fight and they were left with many scars. Sun was very
    embarrassed and became a bright light so no one could see
his scars. Moon wants everyone to see her scars so she shines with
less light.* [Courlander 1975]

Mashongavudzi

Zimbabwe (Rhodesia), *Mtawara*
Creator of Life
  Creator-wife of the "great spirit." Today the first wife of
the ruling chief of this tribe takes her name. [Sykes 1968]

Massassi

Zimbabwe (Rhodesia), *Makoni*
Stars and Planets
  "Morning Star." Deity whose children are the grasses,
bushes, and trees. She was the first wife of the moon,
Mwuetsi. See also *Morongo*. [Cotterell 1979; Eliot 1976]

Matu

Zaire
Unknown
  Mother of the hero, an important male in the people's
mythology. Also the name of a male deity. [Leach 1992;
Savill 1977]

Mawa

Benin, *Fon (Dahomey)*
Moon and Night
  Moon goddess. She was sent to Earth by her father to help
the people during a famine. [Jobes 1962]

Mawu

Benin, *Fon (Dahomey)*
Creator of Life; Supreme Being; Moon and Night; Mother and
Guardian; Happiness; Goodness
  Supreme deity. Twin or wife of *Lisa*, the sun. Together they
created all the other deities. Her daughters are *Aizu, Akazu,
Ayaba,* and *Gbadu*. She is identified with the moon, night,
fertility, motherhood, pleasure, relaxation, and forgiveness.
Her mother is *Nana Buluku* or *Minona*. Mawu is known in
different areas as a male deity, a dual deity, or an androgynous
deity and is sometimes called *Mawu-Lisa*. Some of the
confusion about gender is caused by the lack of male and
female pronouns in some African languages. Some researchers
may have assigned a specific sex to androgynous deities.
    *Mawu is a single person with two faces. One face is female
    and her eyes are the moon and is called Mawu. She rules the
    night. The other face is male and is called Lisa and his eyes
are the sun. He rules the day.*
  See also *Mahu* and *Sogbo*. [Bastide 1978; Carlyon 1982;
Cotterell 1979; Leach 1992; Spretnak 1982; Stone 1979]

Mawu Sodza

Togo, *Hoss*
Agriculture; Ceremonies
  Yam goddess. Before digging their fields, the Hoss present
the first two yams of each new crop as an offering to her.
[Mbiti 1970; Redfield 1931]

Mawu-Lisa
Benin, *Fon (Dahomey)*
Creator of Life
    Dual creator deity. Parent of **Naete.** See also **Mawu** and **Lisa.** [Cotterell 1979; Leach 1992]

Mayramu
Nigeria, *Maguzawa (Hausa)*
Destroyer of Life
    Disease goddess. The disease she causes leaves burn-like spots on people's arms. [Leach 1992]

Mbaba Mwana Waresa
South Africa, *Zulu*
Weather; Ceremonies
    Rain goddess. She introduced beer to her people to aid them in their celebrations. Mbaba Mwana Waresa lives in a small house with an ever glowing rainbow on the roof. [Spretnak 1982; Stone 1979]

Mbache
Nigeria, *Yachi*
Earth and Nature
    Earth goddess. Her husband, Ppahia, is a creator deity. [Leach 1992]

Mbale
Uganda
Creator of Life
    Fertility goddess. It is Mbale who brings children. Considered by some to be a male deity. [Leach 1992; Savill 1977]

Mbongwe
Gabon, *Fang*
Creator of Life
    First woman. She was made by Second Man from a tree and together they peopled the earth with their many children. [Aldington and Ames 1968; Beier 1966; Farmer 1978]

Mboze
Zaire, *Woyo*
Mother and Guardian
    Mother goddess. Her daughter is **Bunzi** (see for story). [Spretnak 1982; Stone 1979]

Mbuya   See *Dziva.*

Mebeli
Congo, *Mundang*
Primordial Being; Supreme Being
    Omnipotent primeval mother. [Carlyon 1982; Savill 1977]

Mella
Zimbabwe (Rhodesia), *Buhera Ba Rowzi*
Courage; Health and Healing; Goodness
    Deified Queen.

    Mella's father was dying and there seemed to be no way to save him. Mella solicited the aid of the Moon Goddess, Bomu Rambi. The goddess told her to enlist the aid of the Python Healer. The Python Healer was considered very dangerous, but Mella went to his cave to ask him to help her father. Although very frightened, Mella allowed the Python Healer to wrap himself around her and she carried him to her village. He cured her father and once more wrapped himself around Mella for his return to the cave. Python Healer invited Mella into the cave and again, although she was very frightened, she did what he asked. Deep in the cave were many wonderful riches and the Python Healer told Mella to choose something as a reward for her great courage and love. She asked him to choose for her, and he gave her a necklace

with a pendant of the Ndoro Crescent moon. When she became queen, she had a wooden carving of the Python Healer made and erected it in the center of the village as a reminder of "the one who knew the magic of the Ndoro Crescent moon of Bomu Rambi—and cared for those who lived with courage, honesty and love." [Stone 1979]

Meme
Uganda; Zaire, *Lugbara*
Creator of Life; Health and Healing
    First woman. [Leach 1992]

Mhaya
Tanzania
Love and Sexuality; Unhappiness
    Goddess of "deserted lovers," especially women. [Leach 1992]

Min Jok
Uganda, *Lango*
Weather
    Rain goddess of Uganda. [Leach 1992]

Minona
Benin, *Fon (Dahomey)*
Ceremonies; Agriculture; Education and Knowledge; Goodness; Evil; Fate; Mother and Guardian; Creator of Life; Magic
    Protector of women. She lives in the forest and is the grantor of fertility, for both women and the land. She is variously known as the mother of **Mawu,** the mother or sister of Legba, or the mother of **Fa.** She is a sorceress who teaches both good and evil magic and teaches divination using palm kernels. Every woman has a shrine for Minona in her house at which offerings of fresh fruit are made to guarantee abundant crops. [Leach 1972; Leach 1992; Stone 1979]

Miseke
Tanzania, *Ruanda*
Unknown
    Deity who is the mate of the thunder god.
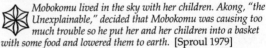
    Miseke's mother was very cold. To get Thunder to come down to Earth and start a fire so she would be warm, she gave him her daughter, Miseke, for his wife. [Savill 1977]

Mobokomu
Zaire, *Ngombe*
Sky and Heavens; Disorder
    Sky goddess. Her children were the parents of the first humans.
    Mobokomu lived in the sky with her children. Akong, "the Unexplainable," decided that Mobokomu was causing too much trouble so he put her and her children into a basket with some food and lowered them to earth. [Sproul 1979]

Moombi
Kenya, *Moombi*
Creator of Life; Family and Tribes
    First woman. She gave birth to nine daughters and nine sons who became the parents of the first nine matrilineal Moombi clans. [Savill 1977]

Morimi
Nigeria, *Yoruba*
Agriculture; Ceremonies
    Agricultural goddess. Her festival takes place when the bush is burned to prepare the fields for planting. [Leach 1992]

Morningstar of Wakaranga
Zimbabwe (Rhodesia), *Wakaranga*
Creator of Life; Earth and Nature; Weather; Agriculture
   Creator deity. She shares her duties with *Eveningstar of Wakaranga.*

It was Morningstar who fed her people. She gave birth to trees and plants. Her trees grew high, touching the sky and bringing the rain. Then there was an abundance of seeds and roots to eat. [Beier 1966]

Morongo
Zimbabwe (Rhodesia), *Makoni*
Mother and Guardian; Stars and Planets; Sky and Heavens; Love and Sexuality; Domesticated Animals; Hunting and Wild Animals
   "Evening Star." Sky goddess. Wife of Mwuetsi, the moon. See also *Massassi.*

Morongo was the second wife of Mwuetsi. When his first wife, Massassi, left Mwuetsi, Morongo became his first wife. It was Morongo who taught humans how to mate. Joining with Mwuetsi, she gave birth to domestic animals and children. When her husband forced himself upon her, making the creator angry, she gave birth to the wild animals. [Cotterell 1979; Eliot 1976; Leach 1992]

Mother of Food
Sudan, *Kariak*
Family and Tribe; Agriculture; Ceremonies; Reptiles
   Deity of the Egyptian Sudan. They honor the spirit of the grandmother or Mother of Food who manifests as a snake. Twice a year they have a meal of beans, wagtail, and snake to celebrate her. [Leach 1972]

Mousso Koroni Koundye
Mali, *Mande*
Primordial Being; Disorder; Weather; Fire; Creator of Life
   Primordial female twin. She and her male twin, Pemba, were part of the "egg of the world." She came down to Earth "on the wind" at Bounan. A tiny, white-headed woman, she is associated with air, wind, and fire but also creates humans, plants, and animals. She is thought to create with haste, disorder, and confusion, and her creations have to be put in order by the god Faro. [Eliade 1987; Long 1963; Sproul 1979]

Muhongo
Angola, *Mbundu*
Family and Tribes
   Ancestor deity.

Muhongo died and her husband sent someone to look for her. Muhongo told the messenger to tell her husband that she could not return from death. [Savill 1977]

Mujaji
South Africa, *Luvedu*
Weather; Ceremonies
   Rain queen of the Transvaal. This is a hereditary position and if she becomes ill she must commit "ritual suicide" so another woman can assume her role. [Savill 1977]

Mukasa
Uganda, *Ganda*
Fishing and Water Animals; Water; Weather; Mother and Guardian; Agriculture
   Water goddess who controls storms, gives safe passage, and provides an abundance of fish and food. She is the mother of *Nagodya.* Sometimes a male or dual god. As a male deity, the husband of *Nalwanga.* [Leach 1992]

Musso Koroni
Nigeria, *Bambara*
Disorder
   Goddess of discord. Her mother is the "Voice of the Void."

Musso Koroni planted a god, Pemba, in the soil and her animals and humans shed their blood on his many thorns in sacrifice to him. Musso Koroni, disliking his thorns, left him and went about the world creating disorder. [Baumgartner 1984; Cotterell 1979]

Mwarega   See *Namboa.*

Mweji
Sudan, *Wapare (Wasu), Kimbi*
Moon and Night; Family and Tribes
   Moon goddess who created human beings. Alternate forms: Koko Mwezi, Mwezi. [Leach 1992]

Mwezi   See *Mweji.*

Nã Afiye
Ghana, *Gã, Osu, Nungwa*
Mother and Guardian
   Goddess of childbirth. [Leach 1992]

Nã Bake
Ghana, *Gã, Osu*
Mother and Guardian; Ceremonies
   Deity of pregnancy rituals. Her husband is Nadu. [Leach 1992]

Na Dede Oyeadu
Ghana, *Gã*
Agriculture
   Agricultural goddess. She oversees the planting of corn. [Leach 1992]

Na Yo
Ghana, *Gã*
Mother and Guardian; Agriculture
   Birth goddess. Originally found in Kpeshi, she became a goddess in Temma when she was given a husband, Sakumo. She also oversees the planting of corn. [Leach 1992]

Nabuzana
Uganda, *Ganda*
Mother and Guardian
   Patron of women who assists in childbirth. [Leach 1992]

Nae   See *Naete.*

Naedona   See *Naete.*

Naete
Benin, *Fon (Dahomey)*
Water
   Sea goddess. She is the mother of *Tokpodun.* She is the twin and wife of Agbe and together they rule the seas. Their children are sea and sky gods, and their parents are *Mawu-Lisa.* Naete also can be found in rivers. Alternate forms: Nae, Naedona. [Bastide 1978; Leach 1972; Leach 1992]

Nagadya
Uganda, *Ganda*
Weather
   Deity who, when there is a drought, is asked to intercede with the other deities to allow the rains to come. See also *Nagawonyi.* [Savill 1977]

Nagawonyi
Uganda, *Ganda*
Weather
    When two of their gods, Gulu and Musoke, are being
difficult, the Ganda people ask Nagawonyi to intercede and
end the drought. See also *Nagadya*. [Leach 1992;
Savill 1977]

Nagodya
Uganda, *Ganda*
Water; Ceremonies
    Lake goddess. Sacrifices are made to her. She is the
daughter of *Mukasa*. [Leach 1992]

Nakiwulo
Uganda, *Basoga*
Justice; Magic
    Goddess of justice. She is invoked to find thieves, lost
property, and missing cattle. [Leach 1992]

Nalongo
Uganda, *Basoga*
Destroyer of Life; Mother and Guardian
    Goddess of disease. She protects her followers from
epidemics. [Leach 1992]

Nalwanga
Uganda, *Ganda*
Creator of Life; Mother and Guardian
    Fertility goddess who can help barren women to conceive.
Her husband is *Mukasa*, a benevolent deity who is
sometimes male and sometimes female. [Leach 1992]

Nambi
Uganda, *Ganda, Masai*
Sky and Heavens; Love and Sexuality; Agriculture
    Sky goddess. She is the daughter of Gulu, the supreme god.
    *Nambi fell in love with the first man on Earth. Her father
    summoned the man, Kintu, to be tested. Gulu wanted to see
    if Kintu was worthy of his daughter. Nambi gave Kintu all
the powers he needed to pass the tests and when they were
completed, Kintu and Nambi went to live on Earth. Nambi's
brother was angry because he was not told about the wedding, so he
brought death to Earth. Since then Nambi has been able to provide
food for her people, but she cannot keep them from dying.*
    The Masai people of the Republic of South Africa tell this
same story about their *Daughter of the Sky*. [Aldington and
Ames 1968; Jobes 1962; Leach 1992]

Namboa
Ghana, *Nankanse*
Moon and Night
    Moon goddess. Namboa and Wuntenga, the sun, are
parents of the stars. Alternate form: Mwarega. [Leach 1992]

Nana   See *Nana Buruku*.

Nana Buluku
Benin, *Fon (Dahomey)*
Primordial Being; Family and Tribes
    Primordial creator of several Fon tribes of Benin. She is the
mother of *Mawu* and *Mahu*. Considered by some to be an
androgynous deity. Alternate form: Nana-buluku. [Leach
1992; Savill 1977; Senior 1985]

Nana Buruku
Nigeria, *Fon (Dahomey), Yoruba*
Earth and Nature; Water; Selflessness
    Earth goddess who is the oldest form of the earth. She is
said to be the parent of the creator. Her son, Omolu

Obaluaiye, is the god of smallpox. She is also considered an
ancient water goddess. See also *Nanen,* South America.
Alternate forms: Nana, Nanan, Nanaburucu. [Bastide 1978;
Gleason 1987; Leach 1972; Leach 1992]

Nana Enna
Ghana
Mother and Guardian
    Protector of women of the people of the Gold Coast. She
protects those whose men are away fighting, and her
husband is the war god, Behnya. [Leach 1992]

Nana Jakpa
Benin, *Fon (Dahomey)*
Fate
    Goddess of prophecy. [Leach 1992]

Nana-buluku   See *Nana Buluku*.

Nanaburucu   See *Nana Buruku*.

Nanan   See *Nana Buruku*.

Nasilele
Zambia, *Barotse, Malozi*
Creator of Life; Life/Death Cycle; Moon and Night;
Ceremonies
    Creator moon goddess. Tribal women are buried facing
west so, in death, they can be closer to her.
    *Nasilele and her husband, Nyambe, created all living
    things, and then stayed on Earth with their creations.
    Nasilele thought that humans should die once and not be
brought back to life. Her husband wanted them to be reborn. When
his dog died, Nasilele would not let him bring the dog back to life.
Then when her mother died, Nasilele asked her husband to bring
her back to life, but he refused.* [Beier 1966; Carlyon 1982; Leach
1992; Mbiti 1970; Savill 1977]

Nawandyo
Uganda, *Basoga*
Health and Healing
    Healing deity who is invoked to cure families of sickness
and adversity. [Leach 1992]

Ndako Gboya
Nigeria, *Nupe*
Magic; Ceremonies
    The Nupe name for *Oya*. Ndako Gboya is actually a
swirling cloth that chases away evil. The Nupe do not have a
pantheon of deities, but they do have "magic medicines" and
rituals. [Gleason 1987]

Ndoi
Sierra Leone, *Mende*
Earth and Nature
    Earth goddess. Her husband is Ngewo, the supreme being
who makes it rain on his wife, the Earth. [Leach 1992]

Ndwanga
Uganda, *Ganda*
Creator of Life; Mother and Guardian; Demi-animals
    Fertility goddess who takes the form of a snake and is
invoked by her devotees to aid barren women in becoming
pregnant. [Savill 1977]

Nebele
Tanzania, *Togo*
Creator of Life
    Creator goddess who created all things except humans.
She was created by her brother, Naka. [Leach 1992]

Neiterogob
Kenya; Tanzania, *Masai*
Earth and Nature
 Earth goddess. [Baumgartner 1984; Leach 1992]

Nejma
Morocco
Health and Healing
 Healing "jenn" (spirit). She is in charge of the other healing spirits inhabiting the grotto of d'El Maqta. [Leach 1992]

Ngame
Ghana, *Akan*
Mother and Guardian
 Mother goddess. [Stone 1979]

Niachero
Zaire, *Alur*
Family and Tribes
 "The Daughter of the Star." Ancestor deity. [Stone 1979]

Nikaiva
Sudan, *Shilluk*
Ceremonies; Reptiles
 Crocodile goddess. Nikaiva's followers sacrifice live sheep to her. [Leach 1992]

Nimba
Guinea, *Baga*
Earth and Nature; Mother and Guardian
 Earth mother. [Savill 1977]

Nimm
Nigeria, *Ekoi*
Water; Demi-animals; Ceremonies
 Water goddess who inhabits the depths of the Kwa River and manifests as a crocodile or snake. There is an oval-shaped stone on the bank of the river that is considered her altar. When her followers want to cross the river safely, they rub a leaf on their forehead and throw then throw the leaf on the altar. [Leach 1992]

Ninavanhu-ma
South Africa
Creator of Life; Mother and Guardian
 Creator and mother goddess. [Leach 1992]

Nkike
Nigeria, *Mbolli*
Earth and Nature
 Earth goddess. [Leach 1992]

Nomkubulwana
South Africa, *Zulu*
Sky and Heavens; Fate
 "Princess of Heaven." Sky goddess.
 As a young maiden, dressed in white, she appears to a chosen believer telling him or her a prophecy that must be kept secret.
 See also *Inkosazana*. [Bonnerjea 1927]

Nomkubulwane
Swaziland, *Swazi*
Sky and Heavens; Ceremonies; Destroyer of Life
 Sky goddess who must be propitiated to avoid illness. [Leach 1992]

Nommo
Mali; Nigeria, *Dogon*
Earth and Nature; Water
 Twin deity, female and male. They were the first perfect pair born to the earth and the god Amma. Nommo is the spirit of the pools. See also *Nummo*. [Carlyon 1982; Leach 1992]

Nsomeka   See *Songi*.

Ntoa
Ghana, *Akan*
Earth and Nature; Stars and Planets; Immortality
 "Fertile Earth." The female aspect of an anthropomorphic deity associated with the planet Venus. She is associated with death and resurrection. [Leach 1992]

Nummo
Mali, *Dogon*
Water; Sun and Day; Creator of Life; Family and Tribes; Demi-animals; Ugliness
 Ancestor deity who has the power of water and light (her embodiment of the creator) and is the animator of all things. The top of her body is human-like and the lower part is serpentine. Covered with glistening, bright green hair, accented by her red eyes and forked tongue, she is a rather frightening goddess. Considered by some to be the fundamental principle of twin-ness in creation, with her twin she is the personification of all the waters, and they are also celestial blacksmiths. See also *Nommo*. [Carlyon 1982; Leach 1992; Savill 1977]

Nyabahasa
Ghana, *Konjo, Kiga*
Creator of Life; Mother and Guardian
 Fertility goddess who aids women in childbirth and barren women in becoming pregnant. [Leach 1992]

Nyabibuya
Uganda, *Konjo, Kiga*
Creator of Life; Mother and Guardian
 Fertility goddess. She aids women in childbirth and barren women in becoming pregnant. Alternate form: Nyabingi. [Leach 1992]

Nyabingi   See *Nyabibuya*.

Nyadeang
Sudan, *Neur*
Moon and Night
 Moon goddess. She is the daughter of Deng, a sky god associated with the weather. [Leach 1992]

Nyakala
Zaire; Uganda, *Amba*
Mother and Guardian; Creator of Life; Supreme Being; Ceremonies
 Fertility goddess. As the most powerful pantheon member, she can be dangerous. Sacrifices are made to her to make barren women fertile. She also protects those trying to escape from warfare. [Leach 1992; Wedeck and Baskin 1971]

Nyakarembe
Tanzania, *Haya*
Agriculture
 Deity of the fields. Her followers pray to her for assistance with their fieldwork. Also worshiped by some males. [Leach 1992]

Nyale

Nigeria, *Bambara*

Creator of Life; Magic; Heaven and Hell

Creator goddess of the upper Niger River valley. Even though the people have become followers of Islam, they continue to worship her. However, to decrease her power, they changed her to a sorceress and sent her to live underground. See also *Odu.* [Gleason 1987]

Nyaliep

Sudan, *Nuer*

Water

Water goddess who is "associated with streams." Her mother is *Buk.* [Leach 1992]

Nyame

Ghana; Ivory Coast, *Ashanti*

Life/Death Cycle; Moon and Night; Earth and Nature; Mother and Guardian

Earth mother who rules over life and death. She created all things on earth—those that are visible and those that are invisible. At death, she provides a place for her children in her "womb," the earth. To some, Nyame (the moon) makes up a trinity with Onyankopon (the sun) and Odomankona (the creative force). These deities are seen as female, male, or androgynous. See also *Asaase Aberewa.* Alternate form: Oyame. [Courlander 1975; Leach 1992; Savill 1977]

Nyamwezi First Woman

Tanzania, *Nyamwezi*

Creator of Life; Life/Death Cycle; Justice

First woman.

God created two women. The first woman was his favorite wife, but she died and was buried in her hut. A plant grew from her grave and the jealous second wife, who was now his first wife, cut the tree down. The god was angry and told her she had killed her co-wife and as a punishment, death would come to all living things. Now all her descendants and all the plants and animals must die. [Beier 1966]

Nyante

Bantu

Primordial Being

Bantu deity. Goddess who personifies the pre-existing universe. Mother of the fertility god, Wamara. [Leach 1992]

Nyinawhira

Uganda, *Banyoro*

Mother and Guardian

Protector of the Banyoro royal family. She shields them from illness and injury. [Leach 1992]

Nyingwan Mebege

Gabon, *Bwiti, Fang*

Moon and Night; Creator of Life; Wealth

Moon goddess and major deity. Representing the female principle, she rules over procreation and prosperity. [Leach 1992]

Nyohwe Ananu

French West Africa, *Fon (Dahomey)*

Creator of Life; Earth and Nature

Creator earth goddess in the town of Abomey. Her husband/twin is Dada Zodji, god of smallpox, with whom she created all the earth deities. [Leach 1992]

Nzambi

Congo, *Bakongo*

Supreme Being; Creator of Life; Mother and Guardian; Justice; Earth and Nature

Bakongo supreme goddess and earth mother in the Congo. She is the "controller of all things." Her husband/father is Nzambi Mpungu.

After Nzambi created the world, she came to earth and appeared to the people as a poor old woman. She went about asking for help. Those who aided her were rewarded and those who refused her were punished.

Also considered a male deity. Alternate form: Nzambi-si. [Baring and Cashford 1991; Carlyon 1982; Courlander 1975; Leach 1992; Redfield 1931]

Nzambi-si   See *Nzambi.*

Nzima Mother

Ghana, *Nzima*

Family and Tribes; Agriculture; Ceremonies

Ancestor goddess who introduced the cultivation of corn and made a sacrifice of her daughter. [Eliade 1987]

Oba

Nigeria, *Yoruba*

Water; Love and Sexuality

Water goddess for whom the Oba River is named. Wife of the storm god, Shango (Chango). In Africa she is protector of prostitutes, but does not perform this function in the Americas.

Oba wanted her husband, Shango, to pay more attention to her. She asked one of his other wives, Oya, how she could accomplish this. Oya, who wanted Oba to lose favor with Shango, told Oba to cut off her own ear and cook it for him. Shango thought the dish was wonderful until he found out it was made with Oba's ear. He was very angry and left Oba. Her unceasing tears formed a river. Now, where the Oba and Oya rivers meet, there is great turbulence—the quarrel between the two goddesses still rages!

Another version says that it is Oshun instead of Oba who goes to Oya for advice. A third version says it is Oshun who gives this advice to Oya. See also *Oba,* Central America and Mesoamerica. [Aldington and Ames 1968; Bastide 1978; Deive 1988; Gleason 1987; Gonzalez-Wippler 1987; Leach 1992]

Obaneñe   See *Bayanni.*

Obasi Nsi

Nigeria; Cameroon, *Ekoi*

Goodness; Earth and Nature; Life/Death Cycle

Benevolent earth goddess. She cares for her followers while they are on earth and makes a home for them under the earth when they die. See also *Isong.* Alternate form: Obassi Nsi. [Leach 1992]

Obassi Nsi   See *Obasi Nsi.*

Obosom

Ghana, *Akan*

Moon and Night; Immortality

Androgynous planetary deity. The female half represents mother and wife. In the Moon Cult, Obosom is considered the visible manifestation of the "kra" (vital force) of the moon. [Leach 1992]

Odame

Ghana, *Nungwa, Gã*

Life/Death Cycle

Goddess who is present when the people are born and when they die. [Leach 1992]

Odu
Nigeria
Fate; Family and Tribes
   "Copious Container." Goddess of the Niger area. She makes wise prophesies and is the ancestor of the "Mothers." Similar to **Nyale.** [Gleason 1987]

Odudua
Nigeria, *Yoruba*
Creator of Life; Earth and Nature; Love and Sexuality
   Earth goddess whose sacred color is black. She brings fertility and love. As the wife of Orishala, who is also known as Obatala, she is a creator of the earth and its people. Sometimes considered a male deity. Alternate forms: Oduduwa, Oduwa. [Aldington and Ames 1968; Leach 1992; Lurker 1984; Preston 1982; Savill 1977; Sykes 1968]

Oduduwa   See *Odudua.*

Oduwa   See *Odudua.*

Ogboinba
Nigeria, *Ijaw*
Magic; Health and Healing; Fate; Intelligence and Creativity; Mother and Guardian; Courage
   Goddess of magic. She is the daughter of **Woyengi.**
   After she was created by Woyengi, Ogboinba asked to be given only magical powers. Woyengi consented, and Ogboinba was able to heal the sick and prophesy the future. She could also communicate with plants and animals. As Ogboinba grew older, she began to wish for children and she decided to return to Woyengi to ask that she be re-created so she could bear a child. To reach Woyengi, Ogboinba passed through seven kingdoms, where everyone warned her that her desires would surely bring death. Ogboinba knew she would need to be very powerful, so at each kingdom she managed to steal the owner's powers to add to her own. By the time she reached Woyengi, she had the powers from Isambi, Egbe, The Sea, Tortoise, Ada, Jasi, and Cock. However, even these powers were not enough and Woyengi was very angry. Ogboinba fled into the eyes of a pregnant woman, where she remains today, looking out on the world. [Beier 1966]

Oia   See *Oya.*

Ol-apa
Kenya, *Masai*
Moon and Night
   Moon goddess. Her husband is Enk-ai. [Leach 1992]

Olokum
Africa, *Edo, Yoruba*
Water; Demi-animals
   Sea goddess who rules the ocean depths. Her husband is Olorun. In some areas, Olokum is the name of a male god. See also **Olokum,** Central America and Mesoamerica. [Leach 1992; Savill 1977]

Olosa
Nigeria, *Yoruba*
Fishing and Water Animals
   Goddess of the fishers. She lives in lagoons. See also *Olosa,* Central America and Mesoamerica. [Gonzalez-Wippler 1987; Leach 1992]

Onile
Benin; Nigeria, *Yoruba, Fon (Dahomey)*
Life/Death Cycle
   "Owner of the Earth." Goddess who expects those to whom she has given life to return to her in death. [Leach 1992; Preston 1982]

Orehu
Guinea, *Irawak*
Water; Magic
   Water goddess. It is from her that her followers receive the charms to ward off Yauhahu, the evil death spirit. [Leach 1992]

Orisha Oko   See *Wife of Orisha Oko.*

Osaka
Ghana, *Effutu*
Destroyer of Life; Justice
   Goddess of stomach disorders.
   Osaka was angry that people were using her sacred grove to bury the dead. To punish them she made them sick to their stomachs. They stopped burying their dead in her grove and were no longer ill. [Leach 1992]

Oshu
Nigeria, *Yoruba*
Moon and Night
   Moon goddess. Alternate forms: Oshupa, Osu. [Leach 1992]

Oshun
Nigeria, *Yoruba*
Water; Health and Healing; Mother and Guardian; Love and Sexuality; Earth and Nature; Wealth
   Goddess of fresh water. Born in the headwaters of the Oshun River, she cures the sick and imparts fertility with her "sweet" water. As Oshun Ana she is the "Goddess of Luxury and Love"; as Oshun Telargo she is the modest one; as Oshun Yeye Moro she is a coquette. She is the wife or mistress of Shango (Chango), god of thunder.
   Oshun wanted to learn how to use shells for divination, but Obatala refused to teach her. One day Obatala was bathing and Elegba (the trickster) stole his "White Cloth." Oshun happened by and agreed to retrieve Obatala's clothes if he would teach her to read the shells. He agreed and once she had learned the skill, Oshun taught divination to all the Orishas [gods].
   See also **Oshun,** Central America and Mesoamerica, and **Oshoun,** South America. [Courlander 1973; Courlander 1975; Gleason 1987; Aldington and Ames 1968; Leach 1972; Leach 1992; Teish 1985]

Oshun Ana   See *Oshun.*

Oshun Telargo   See *Oshun.*

Oshun Yeye Moro   See *Oshun.*

Oshupa   See *Oshu.*

Osu   See *Oshu.*

Ovia
Benin
Water
   River goddess. Her husband is Shango, the storm god. [Leach 1992]

Oxun
Africa, *Yoruba*
Demi-animal
   Mermaid goddess. Second wife of Shango. See also **Oshun** and **Oxun,** Central and Mesoamerica. Alternate forms: Oxun Doco, Oxun Panda. [Bastide 1978]

Oxun Doco   See *Oxun.*

Oxun Panda   See *Oxun*.

Oya
Nigeria, *Yoruba*
Selflessness; Water; Weather; Mother and Guardian; Order
   Goddess of the Niger River. Said to have been the "personified violent rainstorms" that became the river. Seen as a "fierce, bearded goddess," she is the protectress of women who call upon her when they are involved in disputes. She can be destructive or creative and is a wife or sister of Shango, the storm god, to whom she gave "the power of fire and lightning." See also *Oya* and *Egungun-oya*, Central America and Mesoamerica. Alternate forms: Ndako Gboya, Oia, Oya-Ajere. [Bastide 1978; Baumgartner 1984; Courlander 1973; Gleason 1987; Gonzalez-Wippler 1987; Aldington and Ames 1968; Leach 1992; Savill 1977]

Oya-ajere
   "Carrier of the Container of Fire." See *Oya*. [Gleason 1987]

Oyame   See *Nyame*.

Panda
Congo
Creator of Life
   The name for *Yemonja*. See also *Panda*, Greek and Roman Empires. [Bastide 1978]

Pe
Zaire, *Pygmy*
Moon and Night; Creator of Life
   Moon goddess. She makes everything fertile. [Leach 1992]

Pregnant Woman
Nigeria, *Efe*
Destroyer of Life
   God created the people and told them not to eat from the Tahu tree. Pregnant Woman had an irresistible urge to eat the Tahu fruit and asked her husband to pick some for her. The moon goddess saw him pick the fruit and she told the god. He was angry, and to punish them god sent death to the people. [Beier 1966]

Puikani
Malawi, *Anyanja*
Agriculture
   Wife of the moon. Her food makes him grow. See also *Chekechani*. [Leach 1992]

Qandisa
Morocco
Evil; Magic; Water; Charisma; Unhappiness
   Demon who lives in springs and rivers, seducing young men and robbing them of their sanity. She may be a Moroccan form of *Astarte* brought to Morocco from Carthage. [Lurker 1984]

Quabso
Tanzania, *Sandawe*
Weather; Life/Death Cycle; Moon and Night; Creator of Life; Health and Healing
   Moon goddess. The moon is considered female, but not as a being. She is responsible for fertility, growth, health, and rain. She is revered, but no prayers or sacrifices are made to her. [Leach 1992]

Ra
Nigeria, *Maguzawa (Hausa)*
Weather

Goddess of thunder and lightning. Her husband is the rainbow spirit who brings rain. Ra is found in other cultures, especially Egypt, as a male deity. [Leach 1992]

Rakembaranu
Madagascar, *Bara*
Water; Family and Tribes
   Water nymph. Ancestor goddess of the Sihanaki family. [Leach 1992; Lessa 1961]

Randa
Nigeria, *Maguzawa (Hausa)*
Fire; Ceremonies
   Goddess of fire. Randa starts the fires and her husband, Batoyi, gives them animation. Her followers sacrifice chickens in her honor. [Leach 1992]

Ricana
Nigeria, *Maguzawa (Hausa)*
Destroyer of Life; Ceremonies
   Goddess of disease. Followers sacrifice a gray-necked, black chicken to her to cure their eye infections. [Leach 1992]

Sabbath
Ethiopia (Abyssinia), *Falasha, Gallas*
Unknown
   Daughter of a god. See also *Sambata*. [Leach 1992; Monaghan 1981]

Sabulana
Africa, *Machakeni*
Goodness
   Deity who saved her people from starvation. [Monaghan 1981]

Sama Bolowa
Ghana, *Nzema (Akan)*
Heaven and Hell
   Goddess of the underworld. Though powerful, she is considered a lesser deity. [Leach 1992]

Sambata
Ethiopia (Abyssinia), *Gallas*
Unknown
   The sabbath deified as a goddess. See also *Sabbath*. Alternate form: Sambatu. [Leach 1992; Monaghan 1981]

Sambatu   See *Sambata*.

Sarawniya
Nigeria, *Maguzawa (Hausa)*
Destroyer of Life
   Goddess of infertility. She causes women to stop menstruating and men to be impotent. Her husband is Malam 'Alhaji, a Mohammedan deity of illness. [Leach 1992]

Sela
Kenya, *Luyia*
Creator of Life
   First woman.
   She was created so the sun would have a reason to shine. She lived in a house built on sticks to keep the monsters away. Her children were not so fearful and built their houses on the ground. [Cotterell 1979; Savill 1977]

Seta
Kenya, *Sul*
Stars and Planets
   Goddess of the constellation Pleiades. She is the mother of *Topogh* and her husband is Tororut, the sky. [Leach 1992]

Shashaya
Tanzania, *Hadzapi*
Stars and Planets
Goddess of the morning star. She is the granddaughter of the moon, *Haine,* and the sun, Ishoye. [Leach 1992]

Sia Jatta Bari
Sudan
Unhappiness
Deity who loved a serpent. This unnatural union brought her shame and death. [Courlander 1975; Eliot 1976]

Sierra Leone Goddess
Sierra Leone, *Mende*
Life/Death Cycle
Goddess of women and aids in the preparation of young girls for adulthood.

Silla
Western Africa, *Fulbe*
Directions
The goddess *Wagadu* when she faces south. [Bastide 1978]

Sky Woman of Nuer
Sudan, *Nuer*
Life/Death Cycle
Youthful deity who is believed to be responsible for the mortality of humans.

One day Sky Woman came to earth with some of her friends in search of food. She met and fell in love with a mortal and decided to stay on earth. When her friends returned to the sky, they cut the rope they had used to descend to earth, severing the means of immortality. [Eliade 1987]

So
Nigeria, *Pangwe*
Moon and Night
Moon goddess considered by some to be androgynous and chief of the thunder pantheon. See also *Sogbo.* [Bastide 1978; Leach 1992]

Sodza
Togo
Weather
Goddess of thunder. Her loud noise drives away evil spirits. Her husband is the lightning. [Redfield 1931]

Sogbo
Benin, *Fon (Dahomey)*
Weather
Goddess who is the mother of *Abe* and the god of thunder, Agbè.

Agbè cannot produce rain so he sends water from the sea and Sogbo takes it into the sky and causes it to fall as rain.

Her name may be a synonym for *Mawu* and may be an alternate form of *So.* [Bastide 1978; Leach 1972]

Songi
South Africa, *Bantu*
Creator of Life; Wealth
Creator goddess.

There was a young girl who was made wealthy by the goddess Songi. One day Nsomeka met Songi in the forest. Songi filed notches in Nsomeka's teeth. When Nsomeka returned home, all kinds of domestic animals came out of the notches. Nsomeka then taught the other women the special way to file their teeth so they could become wealthy, too. From then on, the men of the village were allowed to live with the women only if they treated the women with great respect.

In some places in Africa, women continue to file their teeth. Alternate form: Nsomeka. [Spretnak 1982; Stone 1979]

Soris   See *!Urisis.*

Tab'a   See *Umm S-subyan.*

Tabhi-yiri
Ghana
Evil; Water; Destroyer of Life
A malevolent sea goddess of the Gold Coast. She is known for drowning people. Her husband is Tahbi, who also participates in the drownings. [Leach 1992]

Tamara
West Africa
Supreme Being
Supreme being of the people who speak the Biloforn dialect on the Niger Delta. "Considered female in the Okita lineage." [Leach 1992]

Tamuno
Nigeria, *Kalabari, Ijaw*
Creator of Life; Fate; Immortality
Creator goddess on the Niger Delta. She created the world and humans. As goddess of fate, at birth she connects each individual with his or her spirit, seeing that the bond is maintained until the individual dies. [Leach 1992]

Tano
Ghana, *Akan*
Moon and Night
Akan moon goddess in Ghana. Also considered a male deity. Alternate form: Twumpuduro. [Leach 1992]

Tega
Ghana, *Kasene*
Earth and Nature
Kasene earth goddess in Ghana. Her husband is the sky god, We. [Leach 1992]

Tenga
Upper Volta; Senegal, *Mossi*
Earth and Nature; Justice
Earth goddess. An omnipotent deity of justice. She punishes immorality and is associated with Wends, the sky deity. [Leach 1992; Wedeck and Baskin 1971]

Ten'gono
Ghana, *Nankanse*
Earth and Nature
Earth goddess. Her husband is Yini, the sky god. [Leach 1992]

Tenye Te'en
Nigeria
Love and Sexuality
Goddess of marital fidelity. [Leach 1992]

Thamuatz
Algeria, *Kabyls*
Mother and Guardian; Hunting and Wild Animals
Mother goddess.

The first living beings on earth were Thamuatz, a buffalo cow, and Itherther, a buffalo. They came from a dark place under the earth called Tlam. When Itherther was separated from Thamuatz, he thought about her and his semen would flow. It was from this semen that the wild animals were created. [Cotterell 1979]

Tingoi, The
Sierra Leone, *Mende*
Goodness; Earth and Nature; Water
  Benevolent "genii" (nature spirits). They appear as beautiful, white-skinned women and live in rivers. [Cotterell 1979; Leach 1992]

Tintai
Ghana, *Isal*
Earth and Nature
  Earth goddess. Her husband is Wea. Alternate form: Tinten. [Leach 1992]

Tinten   See *Tintai.*

Tji-wara
Western Africa, *Bambara*
Agriculture
  Goddess of agriculture in Niger River valley. Pleasing her guarantees an abundant harvest. Alternate form: Chi-Wara. [Spretnak 1982]

Tohar-tsiereur
Ghana
Mother and Guardian
  Protecter of women. She inhabits a rock close to Cape Coast. [Leach 1992]

Tokpodun
Benin, *Fon (Dahomey)*
Water; Sky and Heavens
  Water and sky goddess. Her mother is *Naete* and her father is Agbè.

  Tokpodun lived in the sea with her brothers. Upset by her brothers' brutality, she changed herself into a river and left the sea forever. [Leach 1992]

Topogh
Kenya, *Suk*
Stars and Planets
  Goddess of the evening star. She is the daughter of the sky god, Tororut, and her mother is *Seta.* [Leach 1992]

Totole
Ghana, *Gã, Nugwa*
Water
  Water goddess who inhabits a lagoon. [Leach 1992]

Tsetse
Belgian Congo; Zaire, *Bushongo*
Weather; Fire
  Goddess of lightning.

  Tsetse caused so much trouble on the earth that she was sent back to the sky. She occasionally visits earth to bring fire.
  Alternate form: Tsetse Bumba. [Leach 1956; Leach 1992; Savill 1977; Sproul 1979]

Tsetse Bumba   See *Tsetse.*

Twumpuduro   See *Tano.*

Umm S-subyan
Morocco
Destroyer of Life
  Death goddess who causes infants to die. Alternate form: Tab'a. See also *Am*, Near East, and *Umm S-subyan*, Egypt. [Leach 1992]

Unkulunkulu
South Africa, *Zulu*
Creator of Life; Family and Tribes
  Goddess who emerged from the "primeval cane." She and her husband, who has the same name, are the progenitors of the Zulus and are the creators of everything. [Leach 1992; Lurker 1984]

Untombinde
South Africa, *Zulu*
Justice

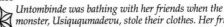
  Untombinde was bathing with her friends when the monster, Usiququmadevu, stole their clothes. Her friends politely asked the monster for their clothes and received them. Untombinde would not demean herself by asking for her clothes and the monster ate her.
  See also *Usiququmadevu.* [Savill 1977]

!Urisis
South Africa, *Khoi-Khoi (Khoikhoin)*
Sun and Day
  Sun goddess of a Hottentot tribe. Her husband is Tsui/goab, a storm god who appears at dawn. Alternate form: Soris. [Leach 1992]

Usiququmadevu
South Africa, *Zulu*
Ugliness; Evil
  Monster deity. Bearded and humpbacked, she devours children. She has a husband by the same name.

  Usiququmadevu found a local chief's children unguarded and promptly swallowed them. When the chief discovered his children were missing, he searched for Usiququmadevu. When he found her, he killed her by stabbing her hump and the children came spewing out of her mouth.
  See also *Untombinde.* [Savill 1977]

Uti
Zaire, *Bambuti*
Family and Tribes
  First ancestor. [Savill 1977]

'Uwardaw
Nigeria, *Maguzawa (Hausa)*
Earth and Nature; Ceremonies; Health and Healing
  "Mother of the Forest Spirits." Nature deity to whom the Maguzawa (Hausa) sacrifice a barren red nanny goat to cure paralysis. [Leach 1992]

Wagadu
Western Africa, *Fulbe*
Physical Prowess; Directions
  Goddess of strength and a legendary city. Her strength comes from the four points of the compass.

  Four different times Wagadu has been lost to the world, "once through vanity, once through false-hood, once through greed, and once through dissension. Should Wagadu ever be found for the fourth time, then she will live so forcefully in the minds of men that she will never be lost again."
  Alternate forms: Agada, Dierra, Ganna, Silla. [Courlander 1975]

Watamaraka
South Africa
Evil
  "Goddess of Evil" who gave birth to all the demons. [Leach 1992]

Wife of Orisha Oko

Nigeria, *Ibadan, Yoruba*
Agriculture

The wife of the god Orisha Oko is the goddess of agriculture who oversees the farm and the harvest. Her name is not known. [Leach 1992]

Woyengi

Nigeria, *Ijaw*
Creator of Life; Mother and Guardian

"Great Mother." Goddess of the Niger River valley.

Woyengi came down from heaven and sat on a chair with her feet on the "Creation Stone." She took earth and formed humans. As she breathed life into them, Woyengi asked them to choose their own sex, their manner of life on earth, and how they wanted to die.

She is the mother of *Ogboinba.* [Beier 1966; Leach 1992]

Yalode

Benin, *Fon (Dahomey)*
Agriculture; Ceremonies; Destroyer of Life

Agricultural goddess. She is worshiped by women, who make offerings to her of cowrie shells and a ram at the Yam Festival. She causes foot infections. [Leach 1992]

Yemanja   See *Yemonja.*

Yemojá

Unknown
Water

Deity of the Ogun River in Africa and in the Americas. See also *Yemonja.* [Courlander 1973; Gleason 1987]

Yemonja

Nigeria, *Yoruba*
Love and Sexuality; Water; Unhappiness; Mother and Guardian

Goddess of saltwater and freshwater. She is the universal mother. She is the sister/wife of Aganju, the soil god.

Aganju had an incestuous relationship with his sister, Yemonja. From this liaison came Orungan, god of the noonday sun. Yemonja cursed her brother, causing his death, and the resulting sorrow caused her death.

Equivalent to *Yemanja,* Central America and Mesoamerica, and *Iamanje,* South America. See also *Yemojá, Ymoja.* Alternate form: Panda. [Baumgartner 1984; Gleason 1987; Leach 1972; Leach 1992; Spretnak 1982]

Ymoja

West Africa, *Yoruba*
Water; Mother and Guardian

River goddess who grants fertility to women. See also *Yemonja.* [Monaghan 1981]

Yukanye

Sudan, *Bari*
Mother and Guardian; Demi-animals

Mother goddess who manifests as a python. [Johnson 1988]

Zat-badar

Ethiopia (Abyssinia)
Sun and Day

Goddess of the sun of the Aksumite religion. She was known as early as the fifth century B.C.E. [Eliade 1987]

Zendere   See *Dziva.*

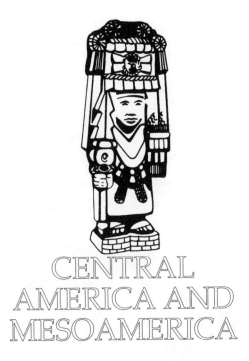

CENTRAL AMERICA AND MESOAMERICA

Abe
Brazil, *Fon*
Water
    Fon sea goddess who rules the waters. Daughter of *Sogbo* (one of the names of *Mawu*). See also *Abe*, Africa. [Bastide 1978; Leach 1992]

Achamommor   See *Olokukurtilisop.*

Acna
Mexico, *Lacandon Maya*
Moon and Night; Mother and Guardian
    "Our Mother." Mother goddess associated with the moon. Patron goddess of childbirth. Alternate form: Akna. [Leach 1992; Perera 1982; Thompson 1970; Wedeck 1971]

Acuecueyotl   See *Acuecueyotlcihuatl.*

Acuecueyotlcihuatl
Mexico, *Aztec*
Mother and Guardian; Water
    "Woman Who Makes the Wave Swell." Goddess of the ocean. Apparition of, or closely associated with, *Chalchiuhtlicue.* Aztec women appeal to her as they go into labor. Alternate form: Acuecueyotl. [Fernandez 1990; Jobes 1962; Teish 1985; Siméon 1988]

Adamisil Wedo
Haiti
Water
    Water goddess at Mirebalais. Identified with *St. Anne.* Alternate form: Si Adaman. [Herskovits 1937; Leach 1992]

Agaman Nibo
Haiti
Ceremonies; Destroyer of Life

Goddess of the dead. Mother of Baron Samedi, father and chief of the gods of the dead and cemeteries. [Leach 1992]

Agwe
Haiti
Magic
    Vodun (voodoo) goddess. A manifestation of *Yemanja.* Agwe is also a male deity. [Savill 1977]

Agweta
Haiti
Water
    Sea goddess. Daughter of Agwe. [Leach 1972]

Ah Uaynih
Guatemala, *Chorti*
Health and Healing
    Goddess of sleep. She causes males to fall asleep. [Leach 1992]

Ah Wink-ir Masa
Guatemala, *Chorti*
Earth and Nature; Hunting and Wild Animals
    Nature deity. Protector of wild animals, especially deer. [Leach 1992]

Ahnt Ahs Pok'
Mexico, *Seri*
Small Size
    "Little Girl." Goddess, two feet tall, who lives with her mother, *Ahnt Kai'* on Tiburon mountain. [Coolidge 1939]

Ahnt Kai'
Mexico, *Seri*
Mother and Guardian; Education and Knowledge; Arts; Ceremonies; Health and Healing

Goddess of women and children. Daughter of First Woman, *Koo-mah'mm hahs-ay' tahm*, mother of *Ahnt Ahs Pok'*. She flies at night and lives above the peak of Tiburon mountain. She is the teacher of singing and dancing, and tells the women and children when to do the Fish Dance. She also heals snake bites. Equivalent to *Athena*, Greek and Roman Empires; *Guanyin*, Far East; and *Estsanatlehi*, North America. [Coolidge 1939; Leach 1992]

Ahuic
Mexico, *Aztec*
Water
"To One Part and To the Other." Her name reflects her role as goddess of the running water in rivers, streams, and waves on the beach. A manifestation of *Chalchiuhtlicue*. [Fernandez 1990; Leach 1992; Siméon 1988]

Aiauh   "Mist" or "Spray." See *Chalchiuhtlicue*.

Aida Ouedo   See *Aida Wedo*.

Aida Wedo
Haiti
Water; Fate; Ceremonies; Family and Tribes; Reptiles
"Rainbow Snake." Goddess of the rainbow and fresh water who determines human destiny. She is said to be fond of red wine. Followers offer sacrifices to her before their marriage. Her husband is Damballa, god of rivers and springs, and they both materialize as snakes. Equivalent to *Mawu*, Africa. Alternate forms: Aida Ouedo, Aido Wedo, Ayida, Ayida Oueddo. [Carlyon 1982; Cotterell 1979; Jobes 1962; Leach 1992; Monaghan 1981; Pelton 1972; Rigaud 1969]

Aido Wedo   See *Aida Wedo*.

Akna   See *Acna*.

Alaghom Naom Tzentel   See *Alaghom Naum*.

Alaghom Naum
Mexico, *Tzental Maya*
Education and Knowledge; Intelligence and Creativity
"Mother of Wisdom." Goddess who created mind and thought, and who is responsible for the immaterial part of nature. Alternate forms: Alaghom Naom Tzentel, Ixtat Ix. [Leach 1972; Leach 1992; Monaghan 1981; Sykes 1968]

Amanjah   See *Emanja*.

Amelia
West Indies
Magic
Vodun (voodoo) *loa* (spirit or deity) of Haiti. Alternate form: Maitresse Amelia. [Savill 1977]

Anne, Saint
West Indies
Fire; Household Affairs; Water; Selflessness
Hearth goddess and deity of fresh water. Identified with *Adamisil Wedo, Emanja, Grande Ezili*, and *Nana Buruku*. [Bastide 1978; Leach 1992]

Apito   See *Atabei*.

Apoconallotl   See *Apozanolotl*.

Apozanolotl
Mexico, *Aztec*
Water; Selflessness

A manifestation of *Chalchiuhtlicue*, represented by foam, suds, or white-capped waves on the water surface, suggesting the virtue of purity. [Fernandez 1990; Siméon 1988]

Atabei
Caribbean, *Taino*
Earth and Nature
"First-in-existence." Earth goddess in Cuba. Alternate forms: Attabeira, Apito, Siella, Suimado, Mamona, Guacarapita, Liella, Guimazoa, Iella. [Jobes 1962; Leach 1992; Sturtet 1979]

Aticpac Calqui Cihuatl
Mexico, *Aztec*
"Woman Who Lives In The Sea." An aspect of *Chalchiuhtlicue*. [Sahagun 1950]

Atlacamani
Mexico, *Aztec*
Water
"Sea Storm." Goddess of ocean storms, an aspect of *Chalchiuhtlicue*. [Siméon 1988]

Atlacoya
Mexico, *Aztec*
Water; Weather
"Sad Waters." A manifestation of *Chalchiuhtlicue*. The name refers to the receding water and drying up of lakes and streambeds during periods of drought. [Fernandez 1990]

Atlatona
Mexico, *Aztec*
Water
"She Who Shines in the Waters." A manifestation of *Chalchiuhtlicue*. She is also associated with *Coatlicue* and the rain god Tlaloc. [Fernandez 1990]

Atlatonin
Mexico, *Aztec*
Mother and Guardian
A name for the Aztec mother goddess. Related to *Toci, Teteoinnan, Tlazolteolt, Cihuacoatl*, and *Xochiquetzal*. [Duran 1971; Sahagun 1950]

Attabeira   See *Atabei*.

Ayauhteotl
Mexico, *Aztec*
Weather; Selfishness; Charisma; Water
Goddess of fog and mist in the early morning or at night. She is associated with fame and vanity. A manifestation of *Chalchiuhtlicue*. [Fernandez 1990]

Ayida   See *Aida Wedo*.

Ayida Oueddo   See *Aida Wedo*.

Ayizan
Haiti
Reptiles; Commerce and Travel
"Mat of the Earth." She was the first "mat" laid on the primeval waters. She is seen as a serpent and represented by a palm leaf. Ayizan protects the market place, public places, roads, doorways, and gates. Alternate form: Ayizan Velequete. [Gleason 1987; Leach 1992; Pelton 1972]

Ayizan Velequete   See *Ayizan*.

Ayopechcatl
Mexico, *Nahua*
Reptiles; Water; Mother and Guardian
"She Who Dwells on the Back of the Tortoise." Protector of newborns and an apparition of *Chalchiuhtlicue*. Alternate form: Ayopechtli. [Stone 1979, Fernandez 1990]

Ayopechtli   See *Ayopechcatl*.

Brigette
Haiti
Immortality
In Haiti, a *loa* (spirit or deity), protector of cemeteries. Also a name for *Oya*, Africa. Alternate forms: Grande Brigette, Maman Brigitte. [Pelton 1972; Teish 1985]

Caha-Paluma   See *Caha Paluna*.

Caha Paluna
Maya
Creator of Life
"Falling Water." First woman mentioned in the *Popol Vuh*, sacred texts of the Mayan. Alternate form: Caha-Paluma. [Eliot 1976; Senior 1985]

Candelaria
West Indies, *Christian*
Fire; Weather; Selflessness
"Our Lady of Candlemas." Catholic counterpart of *Oya*, Africa. She is associated with lightning. Alternate form: Our Lady of Candelaria. [Aldington and Ames 1968; Baumgartner 1984; Gleason 1987; Gonzalez-Whippler 1987]

Caridad
Brazil
Water
"Queen of Sweet Water." Alternate name for the African goddess *Ochun*. [Baumgartner 1984]

Catherine, Saint
West Indies
Selflessness
Identified with *Emanja* and *Oya*, Africa. [Bastide 1978; Baumgartner 1984]

Centeotl
Mexico, *Nahua*
Fishing and Water Animals; Agriculture; Ceremonies
Goddess of maize in the field, she is related to the earth and agricultural fertility. She is depicted in pre-Colombian manuscripts with ears of corn in her headdress, or as a frog. In Tenochtitlan, the Mexican people dedicated at least five temples and three festivals to her. Sometimes Centeotl also refers to a male corn deity. Mother of *Xilonen*. See also *Chicomecoatl*. Alternate forms: Centeotlcihuatl, Iztaccenteol, Tlatlauhquicenteotl, Tzinteotl. [Baring 1991; Leach 1992; Neumann 1972; Nicholson 1971; Redfield 1931; Reville 1884; Siméon 1988; Stone 1979]

Centeotlcihuatl   See *Centeotl*.

Chalchihitlicue   See *Chalchiuhtlicue*.

Chalchiuhcihuatl
Mexico, *Aztec*
Agriculture; Time; Earth and Nature; Wealth
"Precious Woman." Harvest goddess, responsible for the reappearance of plants and flowers in the spring. She is celebrated after an especially abundant harvest. An apparition of *Chicomecoatl*. [Duran 1971; Sahagun 1950]

Chalchiuhcueye   See *Chalchiuhtlicue*.

Chalchiuhtlicue
Mexico, *Aztec*
Water; Fishing and Water Animals; Agriculture; Mother and Guardian; Time
"Jade Skirt." Water goddess of lakes and streams. Patron deity of those who gain their living fishing or selling water. Depicted in the pre-Colombian manuscripts as one of the nine ladies/lords of the night. She represents the period from 12:33 AM to 1:38 AM. Associated with fertility and agriculture, Chalchiuhtlicue is related to Aztec mother goddesses including *Matlalcueye* and *Mayahuel*. Consort of the rain god Tlaloc. Alternate forms: Ahuic, Aiauh, Apozanolotl, Aticpac Calqui Cihuatl, Atlacamani, Atlacoya, Atlatona, Ayauhteotl, Ayopechcatl, Huixtocihuatl, Xixiquipilihui. See also Acuecueyotlcihuatl. [Durdin-Robertson 1982; Jobes 1962; Leach 1972; Leach 1992; Monaghan 1981; Nicholson 1971; Reville 1884; Sahagun 1950; Senior 1985; Siméon 1988; Stone 1979]

Chalchiutlicue   See *Chalchiuhtlicue*.

Chalmecacihuatl
Mexico, *Nahua*
Ceremonies; Heaven and Hell
"Woman of Chalmeca." Goddess of sacrifice who inhabits Mictlan, the lowermost level of the underworld. The terrestrial level of the Aztec universe consisted of quadrants (the four cardinal directions) organized around the center; above the earth existed the celestial levels, and below, the levels of the underworld, each inhabited by several supernatural personalities. Consort of the god Chalmecatl and sister of Yacatecuhtli, the patron deity of Aztec merchants. Alternate form: Chalmecacihutl. [Leach 1992; Nicholson 1971; Duran 1971; Sahagun 1950]

Chalmecacihutl   See *Chalmecacihuatl*.

Chantico
Mexico, *Aztec*
Household Affairs; Fire; Metals and Minerals; War; Fate
"In the House." Goddess of the hearth, related to fire and *Xochiquetzal*. Also patron deity of lapidaries. Warriors made offerings to her before going into battle, and children appealed to her to learn of their destiny. [Carlyon 1982; Fernandez 1990; Leach 1992; Nicholson 1971; Pasztory 1983; Stone 1979]

Charlotte, Mademoiselle
Haiti
Unknown
A non-African *loa* (spirit or deity). She is European but a part of the *loa* pantheon. [Rigaud 1969]

Chebel Yax   See *Ix Chebel Yax*.

Chibilias
Mexico, *Yucatec Maya*
Weather
Rainbow goddess, wife of Iztamna. Daughter of *Ix Chel* and related to *Ix Chebel Yax*. [Brinton 1882; Thompson 1970]

Chich Cohel
Mexico, *Yucatec Maya*
Unknown
"Sacred Woman." Goddess referred to in the *Books of Chilam Balam*. [Kelley 1976]

Chíchipáchu
Panama, *Cuna*
Destroyer of Life; Demi-animals; Domesticated Animals
Demon of sickness. She appears as half-woman, half-dog. An eclipse is said to be this goddess devouring the moon. [Leach 1992]

Chicomecoatl
Mexico, *Aztec*
Agriculture; Weather
"Seven Serpent." Goddess of stored maize and harvested grains. Some say she is responsible for the frosts that kill agricultural plants and cause famines. Related to *Centeotl, Tonalcacihuatl,* and *Xilonen.* Sister of the rain god Tlaloc. Alternate form: Chalchiuhcihuatl. [Brundage 1979; Chicago 1979; Duran 1971; Jobes 1962; Leach 1992; Lurker 1984; Monaghan 1981; Neumann 1972; Nicholson 1971; Sahagun 1950; Stone 1979]

Chimalma
Mexico, *Aztec*
War
"Hand Shield" or "Shield Carrier." War goddess and consort of the hunting god Camaxtle or of the warrior god Mixcoatl, the "Cloud Serpent." Sister or apparition of *Coatlicue.* Alternate form: Chimalman. [Brinton 1882; Brundage 1979; Fernandez 1990; Jobes 1962; Nicholson 1971]

Chimalman See *Chimalma.*

Chimalmat
Guatemala, *Quiché Maya*
Stars and Planets
"Shield Stars." Goddess who represents the Little Dipper constellation. Wife of Seven Macaw, the Big Dipper. See also *Chimalma.* [Tedlock 1985]

Christalline
Haiti
Evil; Water
Evil sea goddess. Equivalent to *Saint Philomena.* [Herskovits 1937; Leach 1992]

Chulavete
Mexico, *Pima*
Stars and Planets
"Morning Star." Stellar deity for the Pima Indians of Mexico and Arizona. [Alexander 1964; Leach 1992]

Chulmetic
Mexico, *Tzeltal*
Earth and Nature
Earth goddess. [Leach 1992; Villa Rojas 1968]

Cihuacoatl
Mexico, *Aztec*
Mother and Guardian; Earth and Nature; reptiles
"Serpent Woman." Mother and earth goddess. Patron deity of Xochimilco. Sometimes called the "eater of men." Related to *The Cihuateteo, Coatlicue, Ilancueitl, Quilaztli, Teteoinnan, Tlaltecuhtli,* and *Toci.* [Clendinnen 1991; Duran 1971; Leach 1992; Nash 1978; Nicholson 1971]

Cihuapipiltin, The
Mexico, *Aztec*
Evil; Immortality
"Women Princesses." Demonic female spirits who haunt people outside of the community. Related to *The Cihuateteo.* [Clendinnen 1991]

Cihuateotl
Mexico, *Aztec*
Mother and Guardian
"Woman Goddess." A manifestation of *Toci, Tonantzin,* and other mother goddesses. [Sahagun 1950]

Cihuateteo, The
Mexico, *Aztec*
Mother and Guardian; Heaven and Hell; Destroyer of Life; Sun and Day
Women who die in childbirth become deified in the level of the underworld called Cihuatlampa—the place of women—and then accompany the sun from its zenith through the underworld at night. Dreaded and propitiated as bringers of childhood sicknesses. Related to *The Cihuapipiltin* and *Cihuacoatl.* See also *La Llorona* and *Chalmecacihuatl.* Alternate form: Ciuateteo. [Fernandez 1990; Jobes 1962; Leach 1972]

Cihuatzin
Mexico, *Aztec*
Mother and Guardian
"Revered Woman." Mother goddess honored in Tenochtitlan during the wars with the Tepaneca. A manifestation of *Toci, Tonantzin,* and other mother goddesses. [Brundage 1979; Siméon 1988]

Cilich Colel
Maya
Unknown
"Holy Lady." Goddess found in the colonial *Books of Chilam Balam,* sacred books of the Mayas. [Kelley 1976]

Cipactónal
Nicaragua, *Nicaro, Nahua*
Creator of Life
Creator goddess. Her husband is Tamagostad. Alternate form: Cipattoval. [Alexander 1920; Bancroft 1886; Leach 1992]

Cipattoval See *Cipactónal.*

Citlalcueyetl See *Citlalicue.*

Citlalicue
Mexico, *Aztec*
Stars and Planets; Heaven and Hell; Mother and Guardian; Sun and Day; Moon and Night
"Star Skirt." Personification of the Milky Way.
Citlalicue birthed a flint knife which in turn begat 1,600 deities. She descended to the underworld, smeared the knife with her own blood and submerged it in a blue bowl of light. Human beings and two deities emerged from the bowl, who set fire to themselves, thereby creating the sun and the moon.
Related to *Omecihuatl* and *Tonalcacihuatl.* Alternate forms: Citlalcueyetl, Citlalinicue. [Brundage 1979; Eliot 1976; Jobes 1962; Leach 1992; Nicholson 1971; Siméon 1988; Sykes 1968]

Citlalinicue See *Citlalicue.*

Ciuateteo See *Cihuateteo.*

Claire, Saint
West Indies
Selflessness; Family and Tribes
May originally have been the mother of the gods of Africa, the *Oddudua.* [Gonzalez-Wippler 1987; Leach 1992]

Clairmé, Mademoiselle

Haiti

Magic; Water

Vodun river loa (spirit or deity). [Herskovits 1937; Leach 1992]

Clairmeziné

Haiti

Water

River goddess. [Herskovits 1937; Leach 1992]

Coatlalopeuh   See Virgin of Guadalupe.

Coatlaxopeuh   See Virgin of Guadalupe.

Coatlicue

Mexico, Aztec

Mother and Guardian; Earth and Nature; Life/Death Cycle; Magic; Ugliness; Reptiles

"Serpent Skirt." The mother goddess of all Aztec deities of Mexico, Coatlicue is a black, disheveled, ugly figure known as an earth goddess, the ruler of life and death, and patron deity of florists. She is depicted as wearing a skirt of swinging serpents, vested in a flayed human skin, and garlanded with hearts and hands. Some say that Coatlicue is one of the Medusa Group, which consists of three bloodthirsty goddesses, Coatlicue, Cihuacoatl, and Itzpapalotl, and some say she has four sisters, with whom she gathers to meditate on Coatepec (Snake Hill).

One day a tuft of feathers descended in front of Coatlicue and she placed it upon her bosom, thereby becoming impregnated. This miraculous conception aroused the fury of her other children, who attempted to kill her to save the family honor. Before they could do so, however, she gave birth to the god Huitzilopochtli ("Hummingbird on the Left"), who was endowed with extraordinary strength and who slew those who attempted to harm his mother. Eventually Coatlicue and Huitzilopochtli ascended to heaven, where she became the Goddess of Flowers.

Related to Atlatona, Chimalma, Cihuacoatl, and Quilaztli. See also Anath, Near East. [Brundage 1979; Chicago 1979; Cotterell 1979; Leach 1992; Monaghan 1981; Neumann 1972; Nicholson 1971; Reville 1884; Sahagun 1950; Stone 1979]

Coatrischie

Caribbean, Taino

Water; Weather; Disorder

"Tempest Raiser." Cuban goddess of water, winds, and storms who causes floods. She is ruled by Guabancex. [Jobes 1962; Leach 1992]

Cochana   See Pitao Huichaana.

Colel Cab

Mexico, Yucatec Maya

Earth and Nature

"Earth Mistress." Earth goddess mentioned in the creation story of the documents called Chilam Balam of Chumayel, a collection of Mayan creation stories. Thought to be another title of Ix Chebel Yax. [Thompson 1970]

Comizahual

Honduras

Magic; Hunting and Wild Animals; Creator of Life; Education and Knowledge

"Flying Tigress." Sorcerer and mother of the first people. She taught them how to live a civilized life. [Jobes 1962]

Coyolxauhqui

Mexico, Aztec

Moon and Night; War; Goodness

"Golden Bells." Moon and warrior goddess. The daughter of Coatlicue, she was slain by her brother Huitzilopochtli ("Hummingbird on the Left"), the Aztec sun god. The struggle between these two deities is seen as representing the opposition of day and night.

When Coatlicue was magically impregnated, her children plotted to kill her. Coyolxauhqui disapproved of her siblings' plans and ran to warn her mother. But the fierce new-born Huitzilopochtli, vowing to protect his mother, rushed out to kill all those approaching his mother and slew Coyolxauhqui. Remorseful after he learned of his sister's goodness, he cut off her head and threw it into the sky to become the moon, where the golden bells in her cheeks could continue to shine. [Carlyon 1982; Cotterell 1979; Jobes 1962; Leach 1992; Monaghan 1981; Nicholson 1971; Sahagun 1950]

Cueravaperi

Mexico, Tarascan, Michoacan

Earth and Nature; Weather; Agriculture; Ceremonies

Mother of the gods and earth. She presides over the rains, germination of seeds, and harvests. She can also bring famine and drought. Human hearts were sacrificed to her at rainmaking ceremonies. Alternate form: Cuerohperi. [Brinton 1882; Jobes 1962; Leach 1992]

Cuerohperi   See Cueravaperi.

Cutzi

Mexico, Tarascan

Moon and Night

Moon goddess. Daughter of Cueravaperi. [Boyd 1969; Leach 1992]

Dabaiaba   See Dabaiba.

Dabaiba

Panama

Water; Weather; Fire

Water goddess. She sent thunder and lightning. See also Dobayba. Alternate form: Dabaiaba. [Leach 1992; Savill 1978]

Damballah

Haiti

Water

Goddess of sweet waters. Equivalent to Maitresse Ezili. [Leach 1992]

Diablesse, The

Haiti

Evil; Justice; Love and Sexuality

Malevolent spirits of dead virgins. They are punished for being virgins by being forced to live in the forest for a long time before the god will allow them to come to heaven. [Savill 1978]

Dobaya   See Dobayba.

Dobayba

Panama, Darien

Water; Mother and Guardian

Water and mother goddess. Alternate form: Dobaya. [Brinton 1876; Jobes 1962; Leach 1992]

Elisabeth, Saint

Haiti

Water; Magic

Vodun (voodoo) *loa* (spirit or deity) of the sea. May be equivalent to *Erzulie*. [Leach 1992]

Emanja
Caribbean, *Trinidad*
Water; Mother and Guardian
River goddess who is a nurse and teacher of children. Identified with *Saint Catherine* or *Saint Anne*. Alternate forms: Emanjah, Amanjah, Omanjah. [Leach 1992]

Emanjah   See *Emanja*.

Erzilie of Damballa   See *Erzulie*.

Erzilie Topicanare   See *Erzulie*.

Erzilie Zandor   See *Erzulie Mapiangueh*.

Erzulie
Haiti, *Dah*
Moon and Night; Love and Sexuality; Health and Healing; Beauty; Luck; Selfishness; Disorder; Reptiles; Magic; Water
"Virgin of the Voodoo." A Caribbean moon goddess and goddess of love associated with health, beauty, and fortune. Mother of *Ursule*. Erzulie can also bring jealousy, discord, and vengeance. She is personified as a water snake whose chief nourishment is bananas. When she is the mistress of the god Agoue T'Arroyo, she is a goddess of salt water and is called *La Sirêne*. As mistress of the god Damballah, she is a goddess of fresh water. Equivalent to *Aziri*, Africa. See also *Grande Ezili*; and *Ezili*, Africa. Alternate forms: Erzilie of Damballa, Erzulie-Freda-Dahomey, Ezili-Freda-Dahomey, Ezili Freda Dahomey, Erzilie Topicanare, Maitresse Erzulie, Grande Erzulie, Maitresse Erzulie Freda, Erzulie Vestery, Mistress Ezili. [Bastide 1978; Carlyon 1982; Leach 1992; Monaghan 1981; Pelton 1972; Rigaud 1969; Savill 1978; Sturtet 1979]

Erzulie-Freda-Dahomey   See *Erzulie*.

Erzulie Mapiangueh
Haiti
Justice; Ugliness
Loa (spirit or deity) of revenge and ugliness. Equivalent to *Erzulie Toho, Erzulie Vestry,* and *Erzulie Zandor*. [Rigaud 1969]

Erzulie Toho   See *Erzulie Mapiangueh*.

Erzulie Vestry   See *Erzulie Mapiangueh*.

Ezili   See *Erzulie*.

Ezili Freda Dahomey   See *Erzulie*.

Ezilie-Freda-Dahomey   See *Erzulie*.

First Mothers
Haiti
Creator of Life; Physical Prowess
Four women who ran swiftly and whose skin was slippery like the skin of eels.
The early inhabitants of Haiti had to live in caves because the sun's rays killed them until they found four women who were not affected by the sun. These women became the mothers of the humans. [Brinton 1876]

Goddess "I"
Mexico, *Yucatec Maya*
Water
Water goddess related to *Ix Chel*. [Kelley 1976; Sykes 1968]

Goddess "O"
Mexico, *Yucatec Maya*
Mother and Guardian; Wild Birds; Household Affairs
An elderly mother goddess depicted with claws in painted manuscripts. Related to weaving and associated with *Ix Chebel Yax, Xkan Le Ox, Xkitza*. [Kelley 1976; Sykes 1968; Thompson 1970]

Grande Brigette   See *Brigette*.

Grande Ezili
West Indies
Magic; Household Affairs; Goodness; Water; Selflessness; Education and Knowledge; Fire
Vodun (voodoo) benevolent goddess of the hearth and fresh water. She represents wisdom and is identified with *Saint Anne*. She is the same as the Dahomean *Aziri*, Africa. See also *Erzulie*. [Bastide 1978; Leach 1992]

Guabancex
Cuba, Haiti, Nicaragua, Puerto Rico, West Indies, Central America, Caribbean; *Taino*
Water; Weather; Disorder
Wind and rain goddess. When she is upset, she brings storms. She rules *Guatauva* and *Coatrischie*. [Aldington and Ames 1968; Alexander 1920; Jobes 1962; Leach 1992]

Guabonito
Haiti, *Taino*
Water; Health and Healing; Ceremonies
Sea goddess. She teaches people about medicines and making shell necklaces for ceremonies. [Jobes 1962; Leach 1992; Savill 1978]

Guacarapita   See *Atabei*.

Guamaonocon
Antilles, *Carib*
Earth and Nature
"Mother Earth." See also *Mama Nono*. [Redfield 1931]

Guatauva
Caribbean, *Taino*
Unknown
Messenger for *Coatrischie*. She is ruled by *Guabancex*. [Jobes 1962]

Guédé l'Oraille
Haiti
Magic; Weather; Disorder; Destroyer of Life
Vodun (voodoo) goddess of violent storms and death. Alternate form: Guede Omsraille. [Leach 1992]

Guede Masaka
Haiti
Evil; Disorder
Evil *loa* (spirit or deity). She has poison leaves that she uses to cause trouble. [Pelton 1972]

Guimazoa   See *Atabei*.

Hamuxa   See *Tatei Hamuxa*.

Haramara   See *Tatei Haramara*.

Hautse Kupúri See *Tāté Hautse Kupúri*.

Hoatziqui
Mexico, *Opata*
Justice; Immortality
  Goddess who cares for the dead.
  Hoatziqui lives on the shore of the lake that the souls of the dead must cross. If the souls have painted faces like the Pima, they are rejected and thrown into the lake. The others she swallows and they have a joyful afterlife in her stomach.
[Leach 1992]

Huechaana
Mexico, *Zapotec*
Fishing and Water Animals; Mother and Guardian; Creator of Life
  Oaxacan fish goddess. She created humans and animals and is the protector of children. [Leach 1992; Whitecotton 1977]

Hueytonantzin "Great Revered Mother." See *Tonantzin*.

Huiçana See *Pitao Huichaana*.

Huichanatao
Mexico, *Zapotec*
Mother and Guardian
  Goddess and protector of children. [Leach 1992; Whitecotton 1977]

Huixtocihuatl
Mexico, *Aztec*
Metals and Minerals; Water; Weather; Ceremonies; Selflessness
  Goddess of salt, worshiped by lake communities as an apparition of *Chalchiuhticue.* Eldest daughter of the rain god Tlaloc. Her festival was celebrated in June by females, young and old, dancing together wearing flowers on their heads. At the end of the ceremony, one of the dancers was sacrificed to Huixtocihuatl at the pyramid of Tlaloc. Alternate form: Uixtocihuatl. [Brundage 1979; Carlyon 1982; Cotterell 1979; Leach 1992; Nicholson 1971; Redfield 1931; Sahagun 1950; Savill 1978;]

Hunahpu-Vuch
Guatemala, *Quiché Maya*
Dawn and Twilight; Hunting and Wild Animals
  Dawn and hunting fox goddess. Also mentioned in the *Popol Vuh*, the sacred books of the Maya. [Leach 1992; Sproul 1979]

Ichpuchtli
Mexico, *Aztec*
Earth and Nature; Love and Sexuality; Household Affairs; Beauty
  "Maiden." Earth goddess associated with flowers, lust, and pleasure. A patron deity of weavers, she represents feminine beauty. Closely related to *Xochiquetzal*. [Nicholson 1971]

Iella See *Atabei*.

Iguanuptigili
Panama, *Cuna*
Evil; Water; Disorder
  Water demon. She brings floods and is a daughter of Olopurguakuayai. See also *Inanupdikile*. [Leach 1992; Nordenskiold 1938]

Iku Oteganaka See *Tāté Ikū Otegañaka*.

Ilamatecihuatl See *Ilamatecuhtli*.

Ilamatecuhtli
Mexico, *Aztec*
Earth and Nature; Moon and Night
  "Woman of the Old Skirt." Mother goddess related to the earth and the moon. A manifestation of *Tonantzin.* Alternate form: Ilamatecuhtli. [Brundage 1979; Jobes 1962; Leach 1992; Sahagun 1950; Siméon 1988; Sykes 1968]

Ilancueitl
Mexico, *Aztec*
Unknown
  "Old Skirt or Old Woman." Incarnation of *Cihuacoatl* as the first wife of Iztacmixcoatl. [Jobes 1962; Sahagun 1950]

Inanupdikile
Panama, *Cuna*
Water; Weather
  One of the rain goddesses and daughter of Olopurguakuayai. See also *Iguanuptigili*. [Jacobsen 1976; Leach 1992]

Isidore, Saint
Haiti
Magic; Selflessness
  Vodun (voodoo) *loa* (spirit or deity) represented by a Catholic saint. [Pelton 1972]

Istsel
Mexico, *Lacandon*
Mother and Guardian
  Childbirth goddess. Her husband is Aquantsob. [Cline 1944; Leach 1992]

Itaba Tahuana
Haiti, *Taino*
Family and Tribes; Weather; Disorder
  Ancestor deity who caused a flood, married the four winds, and bore four sons—the first humans. Alternate form: Itiba Tahuvava. [Brinton 1876; Monaghan 1981]

Itiba Tahuvava See *Itaba Tahuana*.

Itoki
Nicaragua
Insects; Stars and Planets; Immortality; Mother and Guardian
  "Mother Scorpion." Stellar deity who gives souls to newborns and receives the souls again at their death. [Jobes 1962]

Itzcueye
Mexico, *Nahua*
Earth and Nature; Moon and Night
  "Obsidian Skirt." Earth goddess associated with fertility and the moon. Closely related to *Itzpapalotl.* [Brundage 1979; Leach 1992; Nicholson 1971]

Itzpapalotl
Mexico, *Aztec, Chichimec*
Earth and Nature; Mother and Guardian; War; Ceremonies; Wild Birds; Demi-animals
  "Obsidian Butterfly." Earth and mother goddess. Also goddess of sacrifice and war. She is portrayed as winged, with talons for hands and feet. Closely related to *Itzcueye.* Alternate forms: Itpapalotzin, Itzpapalotlcihuatl. [Brundage 1979; Carlyon 1982; Jobes 1962; Leach 1992; Nicholson 1971]

Itzpapalotlcihuatl See *Itzpapalotl*.

Itzpapalotzin   See *Itzpapalotl.*

Ix Ahau
Maya
Moon and Night
"Mistress." Western Highland Maya moon goddess.
Alternate form: Xhau. [Thompson 1970]

Ix Bolon Yol Nicté
Maya
Unknown
"The Nine Heart *Plumiera.*" Goddess found in the
colonial *Books of Chilam Balam,* sacred books of the Mayas.
[Kelley 1976]

Ix Chancab
Maya
Insects
"The Powerful Honey-maker" or "The Female Snake-Bee."
Goddess found in the colonial *Books of Chilam Balam,* sacred
books of the Mayas. [Kelley 1976]

Ix Chebel Yax
Guatemala, Honduras, Mexico, *Maya*
Moon and Night; Mother and Guardian; Household Affairs;
Education and Knowledge
Moon and mother goddess. She taught spinning, dyeing,
weaving, and basketry to the Mayan women. Wife of
Itzamna, creator deity, and daughter of *Ix Chel.* Related to
*Chibilias, Colel Cab, Goddess "O," Xitzam, Xkan Le Ox,
Xkitza.* Alternate forms: Chebel Yax, Ix Hun Tah Dz'ib, Ix
Hun Tah Nok, Ixhunieta, Ixzaluoh. [Leach 1992; Monaghan
1981; Stone 1979; Thompson 1970]

Ix Chel
Mexico, *Putun, Yucatec Maya*
Water; Disorder; Goodness; Wild Birds; Moon and Night;
Household Affairs; Magic; Health and Healing; Mother and
Guardian; Love and Sexuality
"Lady Rainbow." Moon and water goddess. Wife of
the sun and consort of the creator god Itzamna. Mother of
Chibilias and *Ix Chel Yax.* In her benevolent aspect, she is a
goddess of weaving, sorcery, curing, childbirth, and sexual
relations. In her malevolent form, she causes destruction
through water. She is depicted with eagle claws and crowned
with feathers. One of her shrines is on the island of Cozumel.
Related to *Goddess "I," Ix U Sihnal.* Alternate forms: Ixchel,
Ix Ch'up, Ix Hun Zipit Caan. [Baring 1991; Brinton 1882;
Cotterell 1979; Kelley 1976; Leach 1992; Savill 1978; Schele
1986; Stone 1979; Thompson 1970]

Ix Chuah
Maya
Unknown
"She, the Filler." Goddess found in the colonial *Books of
Chilam Balam,* sacred books of the Mayas. [Kelley 1976]

Ix Ch'up
Mexico, *Yucatec Maya*
Moon and Night
Moon goddess of the Toltec period. A manifestation of
Ix Chel. [Savill 1978]

Ix Dziban Yol Nicté
Maya
Unknown
"She, the *Plumiera* of the Painted Heart." Goddess found in
the colonial *Books of Chilam Balam,* sacred books of the Mayas.
[Kelley 1976]

Ix Dzoy
Maya
Unknown
"She the Lazy One." Goddess found in the colonial *Books of
Chilam Balam,* sacred books of the Mayas. [Kelley 1976]

Ix Hun Tah Dz'ib   See *Ix Chebel Yax.*

Ix Hun Tah Nok
Mexico, *Yucatec Maya*
Creator of Life; Household Affairs
Creation goddess who invented weaving. Wife of Kinich
Ahau. A manifestation of *Ix Chebel Yax.* Alternate form: Ix
Zacal Nok. [Thompson 1970]

Ix Hun Zipit Caan   See *Ix Chel.*

Ix Kan Citam Thul
Maya
Demi-animals
"She, the Precious Peccary-Rabbit." Goddess found in the
colonial *Books of Chilam Balam,* sacred books of the Mayas.
[Kelley 1976]

Ix Kan Itzam Thul
Maya
Water; Demi-animals; Magic
"She, the Precious Witch of the Gushing Water" or "The
Precious Lizard-Rabbit." Goddess found in the colonial *Books
of Chilam Balam,* sacred books of the Mayas. [Kelley 1976]

Ix Kanyultá
Maya
Unknown
"Precious Throat." Goddess found in the colonial *Books of
Chilam Balam,* sacred books of the Mayas. [Kelley 1976]

Ix Ku
Mexico, *Yucatec Maya*
Weather; Water
Goddess associated with rain. [Thompson 1970]

Ix Pucyolá
Maya
Water
"She, the Destroyer of the Heart of Water." Goddess found
in the colonial *Books of Chilam Balam,* sacred books of the
Mayas. [Kelley 1976]

Ix Saclactun
Maya
Metals and Minerals
"She Who Is in White Stones." Goddess found in the
colonial *Books of Chilam Balam,* sacred books of the Mayas.
[Kelley 1976]

Ix Tab
Maya
Destroyer of Life
"She of the Noose." Goddess of suicide and the gallows
who is found in the colonial *Books of Chilam Balam,* sacred
books of the Mayas. [Kelley 1976; Leach 1992]

Ix Tan Yol
Maya
Water
"She Who Is in the Heart of the Water." Goddess found in
the colonial *Books of Chilam Balam,* sacred books of the Mayas.
[Kelley 1976]

Ix Tan Yol Ha
Maya
Water
"She Who Is in the Heart of the Showery Water." Goddess found in the colonial *Books of Chilam Balam,* sacred books of the Mayas. [Kelley 1976]

Ix Tol Och
Maya
Demi-animals
"She, the Big-Bellied Opossum." Goddess found in the colonial *Books of Chilam Balam,* sacred books of the Mayas. [Kelley 1976]

Ix Tub Tan
Maya
Reptiles; Metals and Minerals; Weather
Snake goddess who spits out precious stones (rain). Patron of gemstone workers. [Jobes 1962; Leach 1992]

Ix U Sihnal
Mexico, *Yucatec Maya*
Moon and Night; Mother and Guardian; Water; Health and Healing
"Moon Goddess of Birth." Title of a moon goddess who is also associated with water. She is invoked to help with procreation and childbirth and to cure ulcers. Related to *Ix Chel.* [Leach 1992; Thompson 1970]

Ix Ual Cuy
Maya
Demi-animals
"She, the Barn Owl of Extended Wings." Goddess found in the colonial *Books of Chilam Balam,* sacred books of the Mayas. [Kelley 1976]

Ix Ual Icim
Maya
Demi-animals
"She, the Horned Owl of Extended Wings." Goddess found in the colonial *Books of Chilam Balam,* sacred books of the Mayas. [Kelley 1976]

Ix Zacal Nok   See *Ix Hun Tah Nok.*

Ixchel   See *Ix Chel.*

Ixcuina
Mexico, *Aztec*
Moon and Night; Love and Sexuality
Goddess of the moon and of sexuality. Closely related to *Tlazolteotl.* See also *Ixcuiname.* [Brundage 1979; Jobes 1962; Leach 1992; Nicholson 1971; Sahagun 1950]

Ixcuiname, The
Mexico, *Aztec*
Moon and Night; Love and Sexuality
Lunar goddesses representing carnal relations and the different phases of the moon. Sisters of *Tlazolteotl.* See also *Ixcuina.* [Brundage 1979; Fernandez 1990; Leach 1992; Nicholson 1971]

Ixhunieta   See *Ix Chebel Yax.*

Ixma Chucbeni
Maya
Unknown
"She, the Incomplete One." Goddess found in the colonial *Books of Chilam Balam,* sacred books of the Mayas. [Kelley 1976]

Ixquic   See *Xquic.*

Ixtab
Mexico, *Yucatec Maya*
Selflessness; Mother and Guardian; Heaven and Hell; Justice; Moon and Night; Weather; Health and Healing; Household Affairs; Water; Disorder
Goddess of suicide and sacrificial victims, warriors killed in battle, and women who die in childbirth. She brought such people directly to paradise. Also known as a goddess of the moon, rainbow, medicine, weaving, and water as a destructive force. [Cotterell 1979; Jobes 1962; Wedeck 1971]

Ixzaluoh   "Water." See *Ix Chebel Yax.*

Iyalode   See *Oshun.*

Iyerugame   See *Yerugami.*

Iztaccenteol
Mexico, *Aztec*
Agriculture
"White Maize Deity." A variation of *Centeotl.* [Siméon 1988]

Iztaccihuatl
Mexico, *Aztec*
Earth and Nature; Mother and Guardian
"White Woman." Mother goddess worshiped as the mountain on the rim of the Valley of Mexico. [Brundage 1979; Duran 1971; Leach 1992]

Iztat Ix   See *Alaghom Naum.*

Jonaji Belachina
Mexico, *Zapotec*
Mother and Guardian; Luck; Ceremonies
Goddess of women in Coatlan and Oaxaca. They offer her sacrifices for good fortune. See also *Xonaxi Quecuya.* [Leach 1992; Whitecotton 1977]

Karous
Haiti
Magic
Vodun (voodoo) *loa* (spirit or deity). [Savill 1978]

Kaxiwari   See *Tatei Kaxiwari.*

Koo-mah'mm hahs-ay' Tahm
Mexico, *Seri*
Family and Tribes; Beauty
"Painted Woman" or "Beautiful Woman." Mother of the Seri race and *Ahnt Kai'.* [Coolidge 1939]

Kukuru 'Uimari   See *Tatei Kukuru 'Uimari.*

Kwee-kee'kai es-scop'-oh
Mexico, *Seri*
Education and Knowledge
"Flying Around in the Sky." The Wise Old Woman. [Coolidge 1939]

Kwelopunyai
Panama, *Cuna*
Mother and Guardian; Fishing and Water Animals
"Toad." Earth mother's midwife. [Keeler 1960; Leach 1992]

Kyewimoka   See *Tāté Kyewimóka.*

Laloue-diji
Haiti
Magic
> *Vodun* (voodoo) *loa* (spirit or deity). [Savill 1978]

Liella   See *Atabei.*

Llorona, La
Mexico, *Aztec*
Destroyer of Life; Mother and Guardian
"One Who Cries." Spirit who lures people to death by drowning them. Also the Spanish name for *The Cihuateteo,* women who wander the streets looking for their lost children. [Baumgartner 1984; Leach 1972]

Loa
Caribbean
Mother and Guardian; Goodness; Weather; Agriculture; Health and Healing; Luck; Justice; Ceremonies
> *Vodun* (voodoo) deity in Haiti. Benevolent protector of humans. She gives gifts of children, abundant crops, and rain. She also cures disease, but can bring illness and bad luck as punishment to those who break the moral code. She is prayed to but does not require sacrifices. Loa is also a generic term meaning spirit or deity. In Haiti refers to deities belonging to the Haitian pantheon who represent the forces of nature. See also *Loa,* Africa. [Cotterell 1979; Leach 1992]

Madeleine
Haiti
Magic
> *Vodun* (voodoo) *loa* (spirit or deity). Alternate form: Maitresse Madeleine. [Savill 1978]

Mahm-m
Mexico; *Seri*
Mother and Guardian; Luck
> Goddess of women in Sonora. They beseech her for good fortune. Her formal name is *Say-say ai-khai ai'pay.* [Coolidge 1939; Leach 1992]

Maitresse Amelia   See *Amelia.*

Maitresse Erzulie   See *Erzulie.*

Maitresse Erzulie Freda   See *Erzulie.*

Maitresse Karous   See *Karous.*

Maitresse Madeleine   See *Madeleine.*

Maîtresse Philomêne   See *Phillomena, Saint.*

Mama Nono
Antilles, *Carib*
Earth and Nature; Mother and Guardian
> Earth Mother. See also *Guamaonocon.* [Sykes 1968]

Maman Brigitte   See *Brigette.*

Maman Simbi
Haiti
Magic; Water
> *Vodun* (voodoo) goddess of springs. [Leach 1992]

Mamona   See *Atabei.*

Manideakdili
Panama, *Cuna*
Heaven and Hell; Water

Underworld deity. She is the goddess of the underground river Capikundiual. [Leach 1992; Nordenskiold 1938]

Maninupdikili
Panama, *Cuna*
Weather; Disorder; Evil
> Rain demon who causes floods. One of the many daughters of Olopurguakuayai. [Leach 1992; Nordenskiold 1938]

Marie Madeleine, Saint
Haiti
Magic; Selflessness
> *Vodun* (voodoo) *loa* (spirit or deity). [Savill 1978]

Marie-aimée
Martinique
Destroyer of Life; Health and Healing
> Goddess of disease. She can bring disease or take it away. Equivalent of *Mariamma,* Indian Subcontinent. [Horowitz 1963; Leach 1992]

Marinette
Haiti
Earth and Nature; Magic; Wild Birds; Ceremonies
> "Of the Dry Arms." Earth goddess. Wife of Ti-Jean Petro. When she possesses her followers, she makes them wave their arms like wings and curl their hands like claws in imitation of her sreech-owl demon form. Sacrifices of chickens, pigs, and goats are made in her honor. Alternate forms: Marinette Bwa Cheche, Marinette Bois Cheche. [Carlyon 1982; Leach 1992; Monaghan 1981; Savill 1978]

Marinette Bois Cheche   See *Marinette.*

Marinette Bwa Cheche   See *Marinette.*

Mary, Star of the Sea
West Indies
Water
> May originally have been *Yemanja.* [Teish 1985]

Masaya
Nicaragua, *Niquiran*
Fire; Earth and Nature; Disorder; Ceremonies; Fate
> Volcano goddess. She is believed to cause earthquakes, so human sacrifices are made to her after they occur. Her oracles are highly revered. [Aldington and Ames 1968; Carlyon 1982; Leach 1992]

Matinieri, The   See *The Tatei Matinieri.*

Matlalcueye
Mexico, *Aztec*
Water; Weather
> "Blue Skirt." Water and rain goddess who resides on a mountain. Associated with *Chalchiuhtlicue.* [Jobes 1962; Leach 1992; Nicholson 1971]

Mayahuel
Mexico, *Aztec*
Mother and Guardian; Earth and Nature; Moon and Night; Ceremonies
> Agriculture goddess of many breasts. Because of her fruitfulness, she was transformed into the maguey cactus plant, which yields pulque, a milky juice that ferments and can be made into an intoxicating drink. She is associated with fertility, the moon, and ritual drinking. Closely related to *Chalchiuhlicue* and *Tlazolteotl.* [Brundage 1979; Duran 1971; Jobes 1962; Leach 1992; Monaghan 1981; Neumann 1972; Nicholson 1971; Pasztory 1983; Sahagun 1950; Stone 1979]

Me?tik Čič?u
Mexico, *Tzeltal*
Moon and Night
"Our Grandmother the Moon." [Leach 1992; Nash 1970]

Mictanteot
Nicaragua, *Niquiran*
Heaven and Hell; Immortality
Underworld goddess. She cares for some of the souls of the dead. Those souls who go to heaven are considered luckier than those who go to Mictanteot. [Carlyon 1982]

Mictecacihuatl
Mexico, *Aztec*
Destroyer of Life; Heaven and Hell; Time; Moon and Night
Goddess of death who inhabits Mictlan, the lowest level of the underworld, with her consort Mictlantecuhtli. She is the goddess of the fifth hour of the night. See also *Chalmecacihuatl.* [Leach 1992; Nicholson 1971; Sahagun 1950]

Mictlancihuatl
Mexico, *Aztec*
Heaven and Hell; Directions
Goddess associated with the land of the dead and with the north. [Campbell 1974; Neumann 1972; Wedeck 1971]

Mistress Ezili   See *Erzulie.*

Mocihuaquetzque
Mexico, *Aztec*
Mother and Guardian; Immortality
"Valiant Women." Macabre spirits of women who died in childbirth. [Brundage 1979; Nicholson 1971]

Mombu
Haiti
Magic; Weather; Disorder
Vodun (voodoo) *loa* (spirit or deity) who brings severe rain storms. She is said to stammer. [Savill 1978]

Mu
Panama, *Cuna*
Mother and Guardian
San Blas goddess of childbirth. She protects the unborn fetus. [Leach 1992; Nordenskiold 1938]

Mu Alesop
Panama, *Cuna*
Heaven and Hell; Creator of Life
Underworld goddess. With *Mu Aligisai,* she is connected with the creation of humans. [Leach 1992; Nordenskiold 1938]

Mu Aligisai   See *Mu Alesop*

Mu Olokukurtlisop
Panama, *Cuna*
Insects; Creator of Life; Reptiles; Stars and Planets; Earth and Nature; Mother and Guardian; Ceremonies
"Luminescent Giant Butterfly Lady." Creator deity who mated with the sun after she had created it, producing the stars and planets. Her sacred animal is the serpent, with whom she mated to give birth to the plants, animals, and humans. She taught the Cuna young girls' puberty rituals. See also *Olokukurtilisop.* [Johnson 1988; Monaghan 1981; Stone 1979]

Mu Olokundil
Panama, *Cuna*
Heaven and Hell; Creator of Life
One of the underworld goddesses connected with the creation of humans. See also *Mu Olotagisop, Mu Olotakiki,* and *Mu Sobia.* [Leach 1992; Nordenskiold 1938]

Mu Olotagisop
Panama, *Cuna*
Heaven and Hell; Creator of Life
Underworld goddess connected with the creation of humans. See also *Mu Olokundil, Mu Ototakiki,* and *Mu Sobia.* [Leach 1992; Nordenskiold 1938]

Mu Olotakiki
Panama, *Cuna*
Heaven and Hell; Creator of Life
One of the underworld goddesses concerned with the creation of humans. See also *Mu Olokundil, Mu Olotagisop,* and *Mu Sobia.* [Leach 1992; Nordenskiold 1938]

Mu Sobia
Panama, *Cuna*
Heaven and Hell; Creator of Life
Underworld goddess concerned with the creation of humans. See also *Mu Olokundil, Mu Ololtagisop,* and *Mu Olotakiki.* [Leach 1992; Nordenskiold 1938]

Naaliwámi   See *Tāté Naaliwámi.*

Naimetzabok
Mexico, *Lacandon Maya*
Weather
Weather deity. Her husband is Mensabak. [Leach 1992; Perera 1982; Thompson 1970; Tozzer 1937]

Nakawe   See *Takótsi Nakawé.*

Nan Tummat   See *Olokukurtilisop.*

Nana   See *Nana Buruku.*

Nana Buruku
Cuba
Earth and Nature; Water; Selflessness
Earth and water goddess. Identified with *Saint Anne.* See also *Nana Buruku,* Africa; and *Nanen,* South America. Alternate forms: Nana, Nanan, Nanaburucu. [Bastide 1978; Gleason 1987; Leach 1972; Leach 1992]

Nana Olokegepiai
Panama, *Cuna*
Heaven and Hell; Creator of Life
An underworld goddess connected with the formation of humans. [Leach 1992; Nordenskiold 1938]

Nana Olomaguyriai
Panama, *Cuna*
Heaven and Hell; Creator of Life
An underworld goddess connected with the formation of humans. [Leach 1992; Nordenskiold 1938]

Nanaburucu   See *Nana Buruku.*

Nanan   See *Nana Buruku.*

Nanaolonupippisopi
Panama, *Cuna*
Earth and Nature
Earth mother. [Leach 1992]

Nena
Mexico, *Nahua*
Agriculture
  Agriculture deity who protects the harvest. [Jobes 1962]

Netsika   See *The Tatei Netsika.*

Niwetukame   See *Tatei Niwetukame.*

Nohuicana   See *Pitao Huichaana.*

Nohuichana
Mexico, *Zapotec*
Creator of Life; Mother and Guardian; Hunting and
Wild Animals; Fishing and Water Animals; Household
Affairs
  Creation deity at Oaxaca who is the counterpart
of Pitao Cozaana. Also goddess of childbirth, hunting,
fishing, and weaving. See also *Pitao Huichaana.*
[Leach 1992; Whitecotton 1977]

Oba
Puerto Rico
Water; Love and Sexuality; Selflessness; Unhappiness
  Water goddess worshiped in Africa, Brazil, and Puerto
Rico. In Africa, she is a protector of prostitutes, but does
not perform this function in the Americas. See also *Oba,*
Africa. [Aldington and Ames 1968; Bastide 1978; Deive
1988; Gleason 1987; Gonzalez-Wippler 1987; Leach 1992]

Obatala
West Indies
Sky and Heavens
  Sky goddess who became *Our Lady of Mercy.* Also
considered a major male deity. [Teish 1985]

Ochu
West Indies
Moon and Night
  Moon goddess. [Gonzalez-Wippler 1987; Leach 1992]

Ochumare
Puerto Rico
Weather; Happiness
  Rainbow goddess. Also known as *Our Lady of Hope.*
See also *Ochu.* [Gonzalez-Wippler 1987; Leach 1992]

Ochun   See *Oshun.*

Oddudua
Puerto Rico
Mother and Guardian; Selflessness
  Mother of the deities Aganyu and *Yemaya,* and wife
of Obatala. She became known as *Saint Claire.* See also
Odudua, Africa. [Gonzalez-Wippler 1987; Leach 1992]

Olla
Puerto Rico
  Name for the African goddess *Oya.* See also *Oya.*
[Teish 1985]

Olodeakdili
Panama
Water; Heaven and Hell
  Goddess of the river Siakundiual, which runs below
the surface of the earth. [Leach 1992; Nordenskiold 1938]

Olokanigidilisop
Panama, *Cuna*
Heaven and Hell

Guardian of a tree in the underworld. [Leach 1992;
Nordenskiold 1938]

Olokikadiryae
Panama, *Cuna*
Water; Heaven and Hell
  Goddess of the underworld river Kulikundiual in the
fourth layer of the underworld. Olokikadiryae and her
husband Oloueliptol wait by the river for day to come.
[Leach 1992; Nordenskiold 1938]

Olokukurtilisop
Panama, *Cuna*
Earth and Nature; Heaven and Hell
  Earth mother and fertility goddess whose consort/son is
the sun, Olowaipippilele. Her influence extends to humans
on earth and their afterlife. See also *Mu Olokukurtilisop.*
Alternate forms: Achamommor, Nan Tummat. [Leach 1992]

Olokum
West Indies
Water; Love and Sexuality; Demi-animals; Fishing and Water
Animals
  Sea goddess. She rules the ocean depths. Her husband is
Olorun. In some areas, Olokum is the name of a male god. In
Puerto Rico, Olokum is also a hermaphrodite who rules the
mermaids and tritons. See also *Olokum,* Africa. [Aldington
and Ames 1968; Courlander 1973; Leach 1992; Savill 1977]

Olomakriai
Panama, *Cuna*
Earth and Nature; Sun and Day; Stars and Planets
  "Earth Mother." Mother of the sun and stars. [Leach
1992; Keeler 1960]

Olonupdikili   See *Olonuptigile.*

Olonuptigile
Panama, *Cuna*
Weather; Evil; Water; Disorder; Heaven and Hell
  Rain demon and guardian of some of the water in the
underworld. Causes floods. Alternate form: Olonupdikili.
[Leach 1992; Nordenskiold 1938]

Olosa
Puerto Rico, Haiti
Reptiles; Fishing and Water Animals
  Santería goddess who uses crocodiles to carry her
messages and who helps people find fish. She is associated
with the sea god, Olokun. See also African *Olosa.* Santería
is a religion that originated in Cuba and is related to the
worship of saints. [Gleason 1987; Gonzalez-Wippler 1987;
Leach 1992; Monaghan 1981]

Oloueaidili
Panama, *Cuna*
Heaven and Hell
  Goddess who lives with her husband, Uuakua, in the fourth
layer of the underworld. [Leach 1992; Nordenskiold 1938]

Olouiknidilisop
Panama, *Cuna*
Heaven and Hell
  Underworld goddess who is the wife of Masolokuirgikalilel
or Olokuirgikalilel, a rabbit deity. [Leach 1992; Nordenskiold
1938]

Omanjah   See *Amanjah.*

Omecihuatl

Mexico, *Aztec*

Sky and Heavens; Mother and Guardian; Earth and Nature

"Woman of Duality." Celestial goddess who lived in the place of duality and who, as part of the creator couple with Ometecuhtli, gave birth to the Aztec deities. Related to *Citlalicue, Tonalcacihuatl,* and the Aztec earth goddesses. See also *Chalmecacihuatl.* Alternate form: Omeciuatl. [Chicago 1979; Jobes 1962; Leach 1992; Monaghan 1981; Nicholson 1971; Reville 1884; Sahagun 1950]

Omeciuatl   See *Omecihuatl.*

Omeyacigoat

Nicaragua

Supreme Being

Supreme deity. Her husband is Omayateite and she is mother of Quiateot. Alternate form: Omeyatecigoat. [Leach 1992; Lothrop 1926; Krickeberg 1968]

Omeyatecigoat   See *Omeyacigoat.*

Orehu

Guyana, Caribbean, *Arawak*

Water; Health and Healing

"Water Mother." Goddess of healing. [Lovén 1935; Leach 1992]

Oshun

West Indies

Water; Health and Healing; Love and Sexuality; Wealth; Beauty

Originally an African goddess of fresh water and love who cures the sick and imparts fertility. In Puerto Rico, she is associated with money, as indicated by her symbol, the pumpkin. She is also worshiped in Brazil, Cuba, and Haiti where her *orisha* (deity representing the forces of nature in the Yoruban pantheon) form is that of a beautiful woman. When she is the mother of fishes or birds, she is called *Iyaode.* As the mother of sweetness, she is called *Yeye Kari.* She was Christianized as *Our Lady of La Caridad of Cobre.* See also *Oshun,* Africa; and *Oshoun,* South America. Alternate form: Oshoun. [Aldington and Ames 1968; Courlander 1973; Gleason 1987; Leach 1972; Leach 1992; Teish 1985]

Osun   See *Oshun.*

Our Lady of Candelaria   See *Candelarra.*

Our Lady of Hope

West Indies

Selflessness

May have originally been *Ochumare,* a goddess of Africa. [Gonzalez-Wippler 1987; Leach 1992]

Our Lady of La Caridad of Cobre

West Indies

Selflessness

May have originally been *Oshun,* Africa. [Baumgartner 1984; Gonzalez-Wippler 1987]

Our Lady of Mercy

West Indies

Selflessness; Sky and Heavens

May have originally been the African sky goddess, *Obtala.* She was made a saint in Haiti and New Orleans. [Teish 1985]

Our Lady of Regla

Brazil

Selflessness

May have originally been *Yemanja,* Africa. [Baumgartner 1984; Spretnak 1982]

Oxomoco

Mexico, *Aztec*

Moon and Night; Creator of Life; Time; Fate

She and Cipactonal formed the androgynous Aztec creator couple. Oxomoco represents night and Cipactonal represents day. Together they made the first human pair and created the calendar. Oxomoco has divinatory powers. Alternate forms: Oxomuco, Oxomogo. [Brundage 1979; Leach 1992; Nicholson 1971; Sahagun 1950]

Oxomogo   See *Oxomoco.*

Oxomuco   See *Oxomoco.*

Oxum   See *Oshun.*

Oxun

Brazil, *Yoruba*

Demi-animals

Mermaid goddess. Second wife of Shango. See also *Oshun.* Alternate forms: Oxun Panda, Oxun Doco. [Bastide 1978; Leach 1992]

Oxun Doco   See *Oxun.*

Oxun Panda   See *Oxun.*

Oya

West Indies, Brazil, *Yoruba*

Water; Weather

Goddess of violent rainstorms. Wife of Shango. She is identified with *Candelaria* and Saints *Catherine, Philomena,* and *Theresa.* See also *Oya,* Africa. Alternate forms: Brigette, Olla.

Philomena, Saint

West Indies

Magic; Selflessness

Vodun (voodoo) *loa* (spirit or deity). May originally have been *Oya,* Africa. Alternate form: Maîtresse Philomêne. [Baumgartner 1984; Savill 1978]

Picchanto

Mexico, *Zapotec*

Mother and Guardian

Goddess of children. She acts as an intercessor with Pichana Gobeche, a god of healing. [Leach 1992; Whitecotton 1977]

Pitao Huichaana

Mexico, *Zapotec*

Creator of Life; Mother and Guardian

Creator deity. Maker of humans, animals, and fish, and the protector of children. She is called *Cochana* and *Nohuicana* by the Valley Zapotec, and *Nohuichana* by the Southern Zapotec. Equivalent to Aztec *Tonacacihuatl.* [Leach 1992; Whitecotton 1977]

Punauaga Oloeaydili

Panama, *Cuna*

Heaven and Hell; Water

Underworld goddess who guards a river there. [Leach 1992; Nordenskiold 1938]

Punauaga Oloesgidili
Panama, *Cuna*
Heaven and Hell; Water
Underworld goddess of the subterranean river Osikundiual. [Leach 1992; Nordenskiold 1938]

Punauaga Oloibiyalisop
Panama, *Cuna*
Heaven and Hell
Guardian of a tree in the underworld. [Leach 1992; Nordenskiold 1938]

Punauaga Olokurgililiae
Panama, *Cuna*
Insects; Heaven and Hell
Underworld ant goddess. [Leach 1992; Nordenskiold 1938]

Punauaga Oloniskidilisop
Panama, *Cuna*
Heaven and Hell; Water
Underworld deity of the Cacao River. [Leach 1992; Nordenskiold 1938]

Punauaga Olopunalisop
Panama, *Cuna*
Earth and Nature; Disorder
Earthquake goddess. [Leach 1992; Nordenskiold 1938]

Punauaga Olouagaidili
Panama, *Cuna*
Heaven and Hell; Water
Underworld goddess of the Kuilub-kundiual river. [Leach 1992; Nordenskiold 1938]

Punauaga Uisogdili
Panama, *Cuna*
Heaven and Hell; Water
Underworld goddess of the river Kulikundiual in the fourth layer. With her husband Oloueliptol, she waits by the river for the dead. Alternate form: Punauagauisogdilli. [Leach 1992; Nordenskiold 1938]

Punauagauisogdilli   See *Punauaga Uisogdili.*

Puta Santa, La   See *Oshun.*

Quetzaltetlatl
Mexico, *Aztec*
Unknown
"Precious Mat." Sister or wife of the god Quetzalcoatl, the "Feathered Serpent." [Fernandez 1990]

Quetzalmalin
Mexico, *Aztec*
Earth and Nature
Goddess of exuberant plants. Sister of Malinalli. [Fernandez 1990]

Quiamucame
Mexico, *Huichol*
Water
Salt water goddess. [Leach 1992; Peredo 1974]

Quilaztli
Mexico, *Aztec*
Mother and Guardian; War; Magic; Demi-animals; Hunting and Wild Animals; Wild Birds
"Instrument that Generates Plants." Mother goddess associated with war who has the power to transform women and animals, such as jaguars and eagles, into hybrid forms.

An apparition of *Cihuacoatl, Coatlicue, Teteoinnan, Yaocihuatl.* [Brundage 1979; Duran 1971; Fernandez 1990; Leach 1992; Moon 1984; Siméon 1988]

Rapawiyema   See *Tāté Rapawiyama.*

Rosna
Mexico, *Chimalateco*
Earth and Nature
Mountain goddess. She is considered dangerous because she controls the volcano Tajalmulco. [Leach 1992; Wagley 1949]

Rutbe
Costa Rica, *Guaymi*
Family and Tribes; Mother and Guardian
Mother goddess who is the ancestor of all people. [Sykes 1968]

Sahk Kays' Es Yo Sees' Kak Aht
Mexico, *Seri*
Mother and Guardian
"Daughter of the Gods." Daughter of *Koo-mah'mm hahs-ay' Tahm* and the sun. She protects young girls. [Coolidge 1939]

Say-say ai-khai ai'pay   See *Mahm-m.*

Si Adaman   See *Adamisil Wedo.*

Siella   See *Atabei.*

Sirêne, La
Haiti
Magic; Water; Mother and Guardian
Vodun (voodoo) water goddess who presides over both fresh and salt water. Protector of children when they are near or on water. Also said to be an aspect of *Erzulie.* [Carlyon 1982; Leach 1992; Pelton 1972]

Suimado   See *Atabei.*

Sukias, The
Central America
Magic
Witches. [Wedeck 1971]

Sukuyan
Trinidad
Metals and Minerals; Ceremonies; Evil
Vampire.
Sukuyan comes to people's houses in the daytime asking for salt or matches. If you give her salt, there is no way to keep her out of your house. Her power can be overcome by following a ritual that consists of repeating three times, "Thursday, Friday, Saturday, Sunday," marking a cross on each window and door of the house, and hanging a mirror over the door. When Sukuyan sees herself in the mirror, she is frightened and leaves. [Leach 1972]

Tabaminarro
Caribbean, *Achaguas*
Stars and Planets; Dawn and Twilight
"Twilight." Stellar goddess. [Leach 1992; Lovén 1935]

Tāké Vêlika Uimáli
Mexico, *Huichol*
Wild Birds; Mother and Guardian; Stars and Planets
"Our Mother." Maiden eagle who is the mother of Father Sun. Dressed in stars, she grasps the world and guards it. [Seler 1925]

Takótsi Nakawé
Mexico, *Huichol*
Reptiles; Weather; Mother and Guardian; Fire; Earth and Nature
    "Our Grandmother Growth." Mother of all the gods, including the earth goddess, rain serpent, animal goddess, and fire god. Alternate form: Nakawe. [Leach 1992; Seler 1925]

Tãté Haútse Kupúri
Mexico, *Huichol*
Reptiles; Weather; Water; Earth and Nature; Directions; Domesticated Animals
    "Mother North Water." She takes the form of a yellow snake who brings rain and fog from the north to Jalisco, Mexico. The grain plants, flowers, and domestic animals belong to her. Alternate form: Hautse Kupúri. [Leach 1992; Seler 1925]

Tãté Ikū Otegañaka
Mexico, *Huichol*
Agriculture
    Corn and vegetation goddess. Alternate form: Iku Oteganaka. [Leach 1992; Seler 1925]

Tãté Kyewimóka
Mexico, *Huichol*
Weather; Reptiles; Earth and Nature; Directions
    "Mother West Water." She is a white rain serpent who protects the deer, corn, and raven. Alternate form: Kyewimoka. [Leach 1992; Seler 1925]

Tãté Naaliwámi
Mexico, *Huichol*
Weather; Directions; Reptiles; Fire; Domesticated Animals
    "Mother East Water." She is the red snake of Jalisco, Mexico. Goddess of horses, mules, and cattle, who brings the rain and lightning from the east. Alternate form: Naaliwámi. [Leach 1992; Seler 1925]

Tãté Rapawiyama
Mexico, *Huichol*
Directions; Weather; Reptiles; Agriculture
    "Mother South Water." Goddess of seed corn who brings the rain from the south. She manifests as a blue snake. Alternate form: Rapawiyema. [Leach 1992; Seler 1925]

Tãté Tulirkita
Mexico, *Huichol*
Mother and Guardian
    Childbirth goddess who guides conception. Alternate form: Tulirkita. [Leach 1992; Seler 1925]

Tatei Hamuxa
Mexico, *Huichol*
Water; Reptiles
    Serpent water deity. Alternate form: Hamuxa. [Myerhoff 1974]

Tatei Haramara
Mexico, *Huichol*
Water
    Pacific Ocean deity. Alternate form: Haramara. [Myerhoff 1974]

Tatei Kaxiwari
Mexico, *Huichol*
Reptiles; Water
    Serpent goddess of fresh water. Alternate form: Kaxiwari. [Myerhoff 1974]

Tatei Kukuru 'Uimari
Mexico, *Huichol*
Wild Birds; Sun and Day
    "Our Mother Dove Girl." Mother of the sun. See also *The Tatei Netsika.* Alternate form: Kukuru 'Uimari. [Myerhoff 1974]

Tatei Matinieri, The
Mexico, *Huichol*
Water
    "Where Our Mothers Dwell." Water goddesses who live in sacred water holes in the desert. See also *The Tateima.* Alternate form: The Matinieri. [Myerhoff 1974]

Tatei Netsika, The
Mexico, *Huichol*
Agriculture
    The five corn goddesses. They are daughters of *Tatei Kukuru 'Uimari.* Alternate form: Netsika. [Lumholtz 1902; Myerhoff 1974]

Tatei Niwetukame
Mexico, *Huichol*
Mother and Guardian; Immortality
    Birth goddess. She decides if the child will be a girl or boy and then gives it the appropriate soul. Alternate form: Niwetukame. [Myerhoff 1974]

Tatei Utuanaka
Mexico, *Huichol*
Agriculture; Earth and Nature
    "Our Mother Maize." Earth and corn goddess. When the sun and rains have fallen on her, she is ready for corn seeds. Alternate forms: Urinanka, Utuanaka. [Lumholtz 1902; Myerhoff 1974]

Tatei Werika
Mexico, *Huichol*
Wild Birds
    "Our Mother Eagle Girl." The two-headed eagle goddess often associated with the emblem of Mexico and *Virgin of Guadalupe.* Alternate forms: Tatei Werika'Uimari, Werika. [Myerhoff 1974]

Tatei Werika'Uimari   See *Tatei Werika.*

Tatei Xapawiyelkame
Mexico, *Huichol*
Reptiles; Water
    Snake water goddess. Alternate forms: Xapawiyekame, Xapawiyelkame. [Myerhoff 1974]

Tatei Xuturi Iwiekame
Mexico, *Huichol*
Domesticated Animals; Water; Mother and Guardian
    Water goddess and protector of children.
 At first, Tatei Xuturi Iwiekame was called She Dog. She was saved from the flood by Nakawé and changed into a girl named Tatei Xuturi Iwiekame. She mated with Clearer of the Fields and became the mother of the humans who populated the world.
    Alternate form: Xuturi Iwiekame. [Myerhoff 1974]

Tatei Yurienaka
Mexico, *Huichol*
Earth and Nature; Agriculture; Weather
    "Our Mother Earth Softened by Rain." Earth and corn goddess. Alternate form: Yurienaka. [Myerhoff 1974]

Tateima, The
Mexico, *Huichol*
Water
   "Our Mothers." A name for the collective water goddesses. See also *Tatei Matinieri*. [Myerhoff 1974]

Temazcalteci
Mexico, *Aztec*
Health and Healing
   "Grandmother of the Sweat Bath." Goddess of medicinal herbs. A manifestation of *Tlazolteotl*. [Jobes 1962; Leach 1992]

Teresa, Santa
Mexico, *Tzeltal*
Household Affairs; Selflessness
   A remnant of ancient household goddesses. She protects the milpa. [Leach 1992; Nash 1970]

Teteoinnan
Mexico, *Aztec*
Mother and Guardian; Earth and Nature; Health and Healing
   "Mother of Sacred Ones." Mother goddess related to the earth and to maternal fertility. Patron deity of midwives and curers. A manifestation of *Toci*. Closely associated with *Cihuacoatl, Coatlicue, Quilaztli*, and *Tonantzin*. Alternate form: Teteoninnan. [Brundage 1979; Clendinnen 1991; Jobes 1962; Leach 1992; Lurker 1984; Monaghan 1981; Nicholson 1971; Savill 1978; Sahagun 1950; Stone 1979]

Teteoninnan   See *Teteoinnan*.

Tetevinan
Mexico
Moon and Night; Mother and Guardian
   "Mother Moon." Mother of the local god. [Harding 1971]

Tetewan
Mexico, *Cora, Nayarit*
Heaven and Hell; Moon and Night
   Underworld goddess who is in charge of the dark night. [Leach 1992; Pettazoni 1956]

Theresa, Saint   See *Teresa, Santa*.

'Ti Kita
Caribbean
Magic
   Goddess of magic and the dead. One of the Petro, a *Vodun* (voodoo) pantheon. [Herskovits 1937; Leach 1992]

Tlacolteutl
Mexico
Sun and Day; Time
   Fifth Companion of the Day who represents the period from 9:17 A.M. to 10:22 A.M. [Durdin-Robertson 1982]

Tlaltecuhtli
Mexico, *Nahua*
Earth and Nature; Ugliness; Fishing and Water Animals; Life/Death Cycle; Sun and Day; Immortality
   "Earth Monster." Earth deity depicted as a large, toad-like creature that devours blood, human hearts, and the souls of the dead. It is thought that Tlaltecuhtli devours the sun at night and disgorges it before morning. Sometimes also a male deity.

   Two gods brought Tlaltecuhtli down from on high to make the earth. Transforming themselves into two snakes, they grabbed the goddess cross-wise and began pulling. She broke in half, her top half becoming the earth. All the other gods then

came to console her, decreeing that everything required for human life would henceforth issue from her: trees, flowers, and grasses from her hair and skin; rivers, fountains and caves from her mouth and eyes; valleys and mountains from her nose and shoulders.
   Related to *Cihuacoatl*. [Bierhorst 1976; Brundage 1979; Duran 1971; Monaghan 1981; Nicholson 1971; Sahagun 1950]

Tlatlauhquicenteotl   See *Centeotl*.

Tlazolteotl
Mexico, *Aztec*
Love and Sexuality; Mother and Guardian; Health and Healing; Household Affairs; Time; Magic; Immortality
   "Filth Deity." Goddess of carnal pleasures and patron deity of midwives, healers, and weavers. Associated with black magic, she absorbs the sins of those who confess to her, thereby purifying her worshipers. She is depicted in the pre-Colombian manuscripts with spindle whirls in her headdress, as one of the nine ladies/lords of the night. Related to *Ixcuina, Ixcuiname, Mayahuel, Temazcalteci, Xochiquetzal, Yohualticitl*. [Brundage 1979; Carlyon 1982; Clendinnen 1991; Cotterell 1979; Jobes 1962; Leach 1992; Monaghan 1981; Nash 1978; Nicholson 1971; Reville 1884; Sahagun 1950; Savill 1978; Stone 1979]

Toci
Mexico, *Aztec*
Earth and Nature; Mother and Guardian; Ceremonies; Health and Healing
   "Our Grandmother." Earth and mother goddess celebrated during the festival of Ochpaniztli. Believed to be the embodiment of nature's healing powers, she was worshiped under several names, including *Cihuatzin* and *Teteoinnan*. Closely associated with *Cihuacoatl*. [Brundage 1979; Clendinnen 1991; Leach 1992; Monaghan 1981; Sahagun 1950; Savill 1978]

Tonacacíhuatl
Mexico, *Aztec*
Life/Death Cycle
   "Lady of Our Flesh." Creator goddess who, with the creator god Tonacatecuhtli, is the source of life and to whom children go when they die. [Brundage 1979; Jobes 1962; Leach 1992; Savill 1978]

Tonalcacihuatl
Mexico, *Aztec*
Unknown
   "Flesh Woman." Goddess associated with *Chicomecoatl, Citlalicue, Omecihuatl*, and *Xilonen*. [Nicholson 1971; Siméon 1988]

Tonan   See *Tonantzin*.

Tonantsi   See *Tonantzin*.

Tonantzin
Mexico, *Aztec*
Mother and Guardian; Earth and Nature; Agriculture; Ceremonies; Time
   "Revered Mother." Mother goddess of earth and corn celebrated at the time of the winter solstice. Her most sacred shrine was located on Tepeyac Hill. In 1531, she appeared on Tepeyac Hill to an Indian peasant and identified herself as the Virgin (Mary) of Guadalupe. A Catholic church was built in her honor on the site of the apparition. Related to *Teteoinnan*.

See also *Virgin of Guadalupe*. Alternate forms: Cihuatzin, Ilamatecuhtli, Quilaztli, Tonan, Tonantsi, Virgin of Guadalupe. [Brundage 1979; Carrasco 1990; Durdin-Robertson 1982; Jobes 1962; Leach 1992; Monaghan 1981; Nicholson 1971; Preston 1982; Stone 1979]

Tsilah Wedo
Haiti
Magic; Luck; Earth and Nature; Order; Love and Sexuality; Beauty
Vodun (voodoo) goddess of good fortune and beauty. Associated with *Aida Wedo*, with whom she protects the fruits of the earth, peace, and fidelity. [Rigaud 1969]

Tulirkita   See *Tāté Tulirkita*.

Tzapotla Tenan
Mexico
Health and Healing
Healing goddess. She gave *oxitl*, an herb, to the people to cure itches, eruptions, and sore throats. Alternate form: Tzaputaltena. [Bancroft 1886; Leach 1992]

Tzaputaltena   See *Tzapotla Tenan*.

Tzinteotl   "Original Goddess." See *Centeotl*.

Tzitzimime, The
Mexico, *Aztec*
Stars and Planets; Evil; Destroyer of Life; Sun and Day
Stars identified as demonic spirits, both male and female, that haunt the earth and bring about the destruction of humans at the end of the Fifth Age. They are most dangerous during eclipses. Singular form: Tzitzimitl. [Brundage 1979; Monaghan 1981; Nicholson 1971]

Tzitzimitl
Mexico, *Aztec*
Evil
One of the demonic spirits of the *Tzitzimime*. [Nicholson 1971]

Tzultacaj, The
Honduras, *Kekchis*
Agriculture; Water
Agricultural goddesses. A name for the female hot springs. [Leach 1992; Thompson 1930]

U
Honduras
Moon and Night
Moon goddess at San Antonio. [Leach 1992; Thompson 1930]

U Colel Caan
Maya
Sky and Heavens
"Lady of the Skies." Goddess found in the colonial *Books of Chilam Balam*, sacred books of the Mayas. [Kelley 1976]

Uixtocihuatl   See *Huixtocihuatl*.

Urinanka   See *Tatei Utuanaka*.

Ursule
Haiti
Magic; Love and Sexuality
Vodun (voodoo) goddess of love. Daughter of *Erzulie*. [Pelton 1972]

Utuanaka   See *Tatei Utuanaka*.

Vierge Caridad, La
Haiti
Water; Magic
Vodun sea goddess. Equivalent to *Erzulie* and may be the same goddess. [Leach 1992]

Virgin of Guadalupe
Mexico, *Aztec*
Selflessness; Mother and Guardian; Ceremonies
An apparition of *Tonantzin* who appeared in 1531 and proclaimed her love for the Indian natives and desire to protect them. Adopted by the Catholic Church, this brown-skinned goddess became the patron saint of Mexico, the Queen of Mexico, and Empress of the Americas. Her festival on December 9 is the most highly and widely celebrated in Mexico. Alternate forms: Coatlalopeuh, Coatlaxopeuh. [Brundage 1979; Carrasco 1990; Christ and Plaskow 1989; Preston 1982; Teish 1985]

Werika   See *Tatei Werika*.

Werika 'Uimari   See *Tatei Werika 'Uimari*.

White Woman
Honduras
Wild Birds; Magic; Mother and Guardian; Moon and Night
A virgin who gave birth to three sons. Possibly a moon goddess.
White Woman grew old and divided her kingdom among her three sons. She was carried to the highest room in the palace where she changed into a bird and flew from sight in the sky. [Aldington and Ames 1968]

Xapawiyekame   See *Tatei Xapawiyelkame*.

Xapawiyelkame   See *Tatei Xapawiyelkame*.

Xaratanga
Mexico, *Tarascan, Michoacan*
Earth and Nature; Moon and Night; Agriculture; Water; Mother and Guardian
Earth goddess associated with the moon, agriculture, birth, and procreation. She presides over the steam baths where women in labor go for relief from their pain. [Leach 1992]

Xbaquiyalo
Guatemala, *Quiché Maya*
Mother and Guardian; Stars and Planets
Mother goddess associated with the morning star Venus. Wife of One Hunahpu and mother of One Money and One Artisan. [Tedlock 1985]

Xcanil
Guatemala, *Chorti, Quiché Maya*
Agriculture; Ceremonies
Goddess associated with maize and grain. On New Year's Day, Chorti Indian women dedicate the water contained in five sacred coconuts to Xcanil before drinking some of it and then fertilizing the ground with it. Considered a male agrarian deity by the Quiché Indians. [Durdin-Robertson 1982; Leach 1992]

Xcanul
Guatemala, *Quiché Maya*
Fire; Earth and Nature; Disorder
Goddess who represents the volcano Volcán Santa María near Quetzaltenango, Guatemala. [Tedlock 1985]

Xhau   See *Ix Ahau*.

Xilonen
Mexico, *Aztec*
Agriculture; Happiness; Earth and Nature
   Goddess of the tender maize and agricultural fertility.
Daughter of *Centeotl*, she was depicted as a maiden dancing
joyously with outstretched hands holding ears of corn, her
hair flowing like new corn silk. Related to *Chicomecoatl* and
Tonalcacihuatl. [Brundage 1979; Carlyon 1982; Duran 1971;
Leach 1992; Nicholson 1971; Reville 1884; Sahagun 1950]

Xitzam
Mexico, *Yucatec Maya*
Reptiles
   "Woman Lizard." Grandmother of the god Itzam. Probably
an alternate name of *Xkitza* and related to *Ix Chebel Yax*.
[Thompson 1970]

Xixiquipilihui
Mexico, *Aztec*
Water; Weather
   A manifestation of *Chalchiuhtlicue*. Her name refers to the
swelling on lakes created by the wind. [Fernandez 1990;
Jobes 1962; Siméon 1988]

Xkan Le Ox
Mexico, *Lacandon and Yucatec Maya*
Water; Weather; Creator of Life
   "Woman of the Yellow Breadnut Leaf." Rain goddess
related to the rain god Chac. In Lacandon Maya mythology,
she was the creator of women and the wife of the creator god
Hachacyum. Associated with *Goddess "O"* and *Ix Chebel Yax*.
[Thompson 1970]

Xkitza
Mexico, *Yucatec Maya*
Unknown
   Grandmother of the creator god Itzamna. Related to
Goddess "O," Ix Chebel Yax, and *Xitzam*. [Thompson 1970]

Xmucane
Guatemala, *Quiché Maya*
Family and Tribes; Sun and Day; Time; Mother and
Guardian; Fate; Creator of Life; Hunting and Wild Animals
   The androgynous creator couple, Xmucane and Xpiyacoc,
are the divine grandparents of the Mayas. Together, they
represent time and the calendar. Her many titles include
"Grandmother of Day," "Grandmother of Light," "Maker of
the Blue-Green Bowl," "Great White Peccary," "Great White
Tapir," and "Begetter Twice Over." She is a divine midwife
who can foretell the future. [Jobes 1962; Leach 1992; Tedlock
1985; Over 1980]

Xochiquetzal
Mexico, *Aztec*
Love and Sexuality; Beauty; Happiness; Earth and Nature;
Mother and Guardian; Household Affairs
   "Flower Feather." Goddess of love, beauty, sensuality,
pleasure, and flowers. She is associated with childbirth and
weaving. Much loved by women, she was honored with
pottery figurines bearing feathers in their hair. Closely related
to many of the Aztec earth and mother goddesses, including
Chantico, Ichpuchtli, and *Tlazolteotl*. [Brinton 1882;
Brundage 1979; Cooper 1876; Cotterell 1979; Duran 1971;
Jobes 1962; Leach 1992; Monaghan 1981; Neumann 1972;
Nicholson 1971; Reville 1884; Savill 1978]

Xochiquetzalli   See *Xochiquetzal*.

Xonaxi Gualapag   See *Xonaxi Quecuya*.

Xonaxi Peochina Coyo   See *Jonaji Belachina*.

Xonaxi Quecuya
Mexico, *Zapotec*
Heaven and Hell; Destroyer of Life
   Underworld goddess who controls death. To the Sierra
Zapotec she is *Xonaxi Gualapag*, to the southern Zapotec
she is *Xonaxihuilia* or *Jonaji Belachina*. Equivalent to Aztec
Mictecihuatl. [Leach 1992; Whitecotton 1977]

Xonaxihuilia   See *Xonaxi Quecuya*.

Xpuch
Guatemala, *Quiché Maya*
Love and Sexuality; Selflessness
   Xpuch and *Xtah* were two maiden goddesses sent to
seduce the gods, Tohil, Auilix, and Hacauitz, to stop the
abduction and sacrifice of travelers from their village.
[Tedlock 1985]

Xquic
Guatemala, *Quiché Maya*
Creator of Life; Moon and Night; Heaven and Hell; Mother
and Guardian
   "Blood Woman." Creator goddess associated with the
moon, and princess of the underworld. By giving birth to
her children, she established the motions of the universe.
Daughter of one of the Lords of Xibalba, and mother of
Hunahpu and Xbalanque, the Hero Twins. Alternate forms:
Ixquic, Xquiq. [Leach 1992; Schele 1986; Tedlock 1985;]

Xquiq   See *Xquic*.

Xtabai   See *The Xtabay*.

Xtabay, The
Mexico, *Lacandon and Yucatec Maya*
Love and Sexuality; Metals and Minerals
   Seductive goddesses who inhabit the rocks of the forest
and who lure men to their ruin. Alternate form: Xtabai.
[Leach 1992; Perera 1982]

Xtah
Guatemala, *Quiché Maya*
Love and Sexuality
   See *Xpuch* for story. [Tedlock 1985]

Xtoh
Guatemala, *Quiché Maya*
Weather; Water
   Rain goddess. [Leach 1992]

Xuturi Iwiekame   See *Tatei Xuturi Iwiekame*.

Yaocihuatl
Mexico, *Aztec*
War
   "War Woman" or "Mother Warrior." A manifestation of
Quilaztli. [Brundage 1979; Moon 1984]

Yemaja   See *Yemanja*.

Yemanja
Cuba, Haiti, Puerto Rico
Water
   Originally an African ocean goddess whose worship
spread to the West Indies and Brazil. She evolved into *Our
Lady of Regla* in Haa. See also *Yemonja*, Africa. Alternate
forms: Agwe, Yemaja, Yemaya, Yemonja. [Baumgartner 1984;
Gleason 1987; Leach 1972; Leach 1992; Spretnak 1982]

Yemaya
Haiti
Moon and Night; Mother and Guardian
   Moon goddess. Protector of mothers and children. Also alternate name for *Yemanja*. [Leach 1992; Meltzer 1981]

Yemonja   See *Yemanja*.

Yerugami
Mexico, *Terahumara*
Moon and Night; Mother and Guardian
   "Moon Mother." Goddess of women and protector at night. [Leach 1992; Pettazoni 1956]

Yeye Kari   See *Oshun*.

Yohualticitl
Mexico, *Aztec*
Mother and Guardian; Moon and Night

Goddess of the night and guardian of babies. An aspect of *Tlazolteotl*. [Brinton 1876; Brundage 1979; Jobes 1962; Leach 1992]

Yurienaka   See *Tatei Yurienaka*.

Zapotlantenan
Mexico, *Zapotec*
Earth and Nature; Mother and Guardian
   Earth and mother goddess. She gave turpentine to the people. [Leach 1992; Nicholson 1971]

Zipaltonal
Nicaragua, *Niquiran*
Creator of Life
   Creator deity. She made the earth and everything contained there. [Aldington and Ames 1968]

EASTERN EUROPE

Aba-khatun
Slavic; Siberia, *Olkhonian Buriat* or *Baikal*
Water
    Sea goddess. See also *Aba-khatun*, Far East. [Leach 1992]

Äi   See *Ajatar.*

Äijo
Finno-Ugric; Estonia
Evil; Earth and Nature
    "Devil of the Woods." Name for Finnish *Ajatar.* [Leach 1972]

Aino
Finno-Ugric; Finland
Justice, Unhappiness
    Heroine of the *Kalevala*, the Finnish national epic, she is the sister of Sjoukahainaen.

After unwanted overtures by her sister's betrothed, Vainamoinen, Aino drowned herself in the sea. Vainamoinen cried bitterly and tried to catch her on a fishing line. He did catch a fish, but he did not know it was Aino, and she laughed mockingly at his efforts.

    This story reflects the Norse spirit of heroic resignation. "The Norse knew that the gods whom they served could not give them freedom from danger and calamity . . . but only readiness to face the world as it was." Aino gave up her life rather than surrender her freedom. [Crossley-Holland 1980; Guirand 1968; Sykes 1968]

Aisyt   See *Ayisit.*

Aiyjsyt
Slavic; Siberia, *Yakut*
Mother and Guardian
    Placental goddess. See also *Ajysit.* [Eliade 1987]

Ajatar
Finno-Ugric; Finland; Estonia
Destroyer of Life; Demi-animals; Evil
    "Devil of the Woods." Dragon spirit. Ajatar lives in the woods and causes diseases. Her name is used as a curse. In Southern Estonia she is called *Äi, Äijo,* or *Äjätär.* Alternate form: Ajattara. [Leach 1972; Leach 1992]

Äjâtâr   See *Ajatar.*

Ajattara   See *Ajatar.*

Ajy-khoton   See *Ajysit.*

Ajysit
Slavic; Siberia, *Yakut*
Fate; Mother and Guardian; Heaven and Hell; Ceremonies
    "Milk Lake Mother." Birth goddess. She brings the soul to the child, records the child's fate, and lessens the pain of childbirth. In some areas there are two Ajysits who come down to Earth to assist with the birth.

Ajysit lives in heaven on a mountain that is seven stories high. Here she determines everyone's fate, writing it in a golden book as each child is born. She comes to assist at the delivery, and if it is successful, a feast is prepared for her. After eating, she returns to heaven.

    Equivalent to *Khotun.* She is also called *Ajysit-khotun,* "Ajysit-mistress"; *Ajy-khotun,* "Birthgiving mistress"; *Ajysit-ijaksit-khotan,* "Birthgiving, nourishing mother"; *Ajysit-ijäksit,* "Procreating-Nourishing." See also *Ajysit.* Alternate forms: Ajysyt, Ajysyt-ijäksit-khotun, Ijäksit-Khotun. [Cotterell 1979; Jobes 1962; Leach 1992]

Ajysit-ijaksit-khotan   See *Ajysit.*

Ajysit-ijâksit   See *Ajysit.*

Ajysit-khotun   See *Ajysit*.

Ajysyt   See *Ajysit*.

Ajysyt-ijâksit-khotun
Slavic; Siberia, *Yakut*
Mother and Guardian
   "Birthgiving Nourishing Mother." See *Ajysit*.

Akkan, The
Finno-Ugric; Lapland, *Saami*
Creator of Life
   Fertility goddesses. With the exception of *Sarakka*, the first daughter, these deities are worshiped only by women. The others are *Madderakka*, the ur-mother; *Juksakka*, the second daughter; *Ugsakka*, the third daughter. They make animals and women fertile in return for offerings of food, drink, and animals. [Eliade 1987]

Akko   See *Rauni*.

Akkruva
Finno-Ugric; Lapland, *Saami*
Fishing and Water Animals; Demi-animals
   Fish goddess. She is like a mermaid: the top half is human, her head crowned with long hair; the lower part is like a fish. When the catch is excellent, it is because Akkruva has gone to the mouth of rivers taking the fish with her. Similar to *Havfru*, Northern Europe.   [Archaeological Institute 1916–1932; Jobes 1962; Leach 1992; Monaghan 1981]

Albasta
Slavic; Siberia, *Tartar*
Earth and Nature; Evil
   Evil forest spirit. She is a large woman with a big head, breasts to her knees, and long, sharp fingernails. She attacks women who are pregnant, killing them by suffocation. [Archaelogical Institute 1916–1932]

Alencica
Slavic; Slovenia
Heaven and Hell; Courage
   Sister/wife of Kralj Mataz. He rescued Alencica from the Turks or the underworld. [Leach 1972]

Alkonost
Slavic; Russia
Wild Birds; Demi-animals; Justice; Heaven and Hell
   Deity of the land of the dead. Half woman, half bird, she torments the damned with song so that they cannot rest. [Hubbs 1988]

Almoshi
Slavic; Siberia, *Trans-Baikal Buriat*
Domesticated Animals; Health and Healing
   Goddess of animals. Wife of Aikushi. She is invoked to alleviate diseases of cattle. [Leach 1992]

Altan-telgey   See *Teleglen-edzen*.

Alvasta   See *Ovda*.

Ama
Siberia, *Samoyed, Ostyak, Yurak*
Heaven and Hell
   Goddess of darkness and the underworld. See also *Ama*, Northern Europe. [Leach 1992]

Amagandar, The
Slavic; Siberia, *Tungus*
Mother and Guardian
   Protective spirits. Alternate form: Orokannar. [Baumgartner 1984]

Amberella
Slavic; Baltic
Water
   Baltic sea goddess. [Monaghan 1990]

Amins   See *Lusin*.

Ammarik
Finno-Ugric; Finland
Dawn and Twilight
   "Gloaming." In the summer, when the sun in the north never seems to die, it is said she is being kissed by the dawn god, Koit. [Durdin-Robertson 1982]

Amra
Slavic, *Abkhasian*
Sun and Day; Creator of Life
   Caucasus sun goddess. She is invoked for fertility. Associated with Ayt'ar, the god of fertility and procreation. [Leach 1992]

An-alai-chotoun
Slavic; Siberia, *Yakut*
Earth and Nature
   Creator goddess. An Earth mother who presides over vegetation and nature. Associated with the god Urun Ai Toyon. Alternate forms: An-alai-khotun, An-darkhan-khotun. [Archaeological Institute 1916–1932; Leach 1992]

An-alai-khotun   See *An-alai-chotoun*.

An-darkhan-khotun   See *An-alai-chotoun*.

Anakhai, The
Slavic; Siberia, *Buriat*
Evil
   Evil spirits. [Archaeological Institute 1916–1932]

Änâm Jajuci
Slavic; Siberia, *Teleut*
Immortality; Mother and Guardian
   Birth goddess who gives each newborn its soul. [Leach 1992]

Anana-gunda
Slavic, *Abkhasian*
Insects
   Caucasus goddess of the bees. See also *Austheia*. [Leach 1992]

Anapel
Slavic; Siberia, *Koryak*
Mother and Guardian; Immortality; Magic
   "Little Grandmother." She is associated with the birth of children and with reincarnation.
   When a Koryak child is born, the father ties a stone on a string and attaches it to a stick. Holding the stick, he recites the names of all of his and his wife's dead relations. When Anapel makes the stone swing at the mention of a particular name, the parents know that the child has the soul of that ancestor. [Leach 1972]

Anqa-naut
Slavic; Siberia, *Koryak*
Water

Sea goddess. Sometimes called the wife of the supreme being. [Leach 1992]

Anlu-lebie-landet Numakiedeil Emei
Slavic; Siberia, *Yukaghir*
Destroyer of Life
"Out-from-the-Russian-country-here-settled-mother." Goddess of smallpox. [Leach 1992]

Api
Slavic; Scythia
Earth and Nature
Earth goddess who accompanies *Tabiti.* The ancient region of Scythia was located in southern Europe, mainly on the north shore of the Black Sea, on the lower courses of the Don and the Dnieper rivers, and in the Crimea. [Hubbs 1988]

Arapap
Slavic, *Abkhasian*
Evil
Caucasus "mother of the evil spirits." The Caucasus is a mountain system in the former U.S.S.R. between Europe and Asia. [Leach 1992]

As-ava
Slavic; Russia, *Mordvin*
Water
Goddess of fresh water. [Leach 1992]

Aspelenie
Slavic; Lithuania
Household Affairs; Reptiles; Fire
House goddess and goddess of the hearth. She takes the form of a small snake. She is friendly to the family and useful in catching rodents and guarding the holy fire. [Monaghan 1990]

Astrik
Slavic; Armenia
Stars and Planets
Stellar goddess. One of the seven chief deities. She is identified with the planet Venus. [Leach 1992]

Auroras, The
Slavic; Serbia
Sky and Heavens
Sky goddesses, Aurora of the Morning and Aurora of the Evening. These two beautiful virgins lived in a kingdom of light with the sun god. "Seven judges (the planets) and seven messengers who flew across the universe in the guise of stars with tails (comets)" lived with them. Also living in the kingdom of light was the old bald uncle of the sun, the moon god. See also *Zorya.* [Leach 1972]

Ausca
Slavic; Prussia
Dawn and Twilight
Dawn goddess. Equivalent to *Auseklis* and *Ausrine.* [Dexter 1990]

Auseklis
Slavic; Latvia
Dawn and Twilight; Love and Sexuality
Goddess of dawn. She is the morning star, presiding over dawn and love. Equivalent to *Ausca* and *Ausrine.* [Dexter 1990; Leach 1992]

Ausera See *Ausra, Ausrine.*

Aushrine See *Ausrine.*

Ausra
Slavic; Baltic
Dawn and Twilight
Dawn goddess. Alternate form: Ausera. [Wedeck 1971]

Ausrine
Slavic; Lithuania
Dawn and Twilight
"Lady of the Morning Star." Goddess of dawn, she is associated with Venus as the morning star. Daughter of *Saule,* she rules with *Brekstra* and *Zleja.* Each morning she lights the fire for the sun to begin the day. Equivalent to *Ausca* and *Auseklis* and similar to Norse *Aarvak* and Greek *Eos.* Alternate forms: Ausera, Aushrine, Austrine. [Dexter 1990; Jobes 1962; Leach 1992; Monaghan 1981; Savill 1977; Wedeck 1971]

Austheia
Slavic; Lithuania
Insects
Goddess of bees. See also *Anana-gunda.* [Leach 1992]

Austrine See *Ausrine.*

Ava
Finno-Ugric, *Bakshir, Mordvin*
Creator of Life
"Mother." Deity who was created by the male god to populate the Earth. [Farmer 1978; Leach 1972]

Avas, The
Finno-Ugric, *Bakshir, Mordvin*
Mother and Guardian
"Mothers." The names of protective spirits. It is of Turkish-Tartarian origin and is similar to *Awa.* Among the Avas are *Azer-ava, Ban-ava, Cuvto-ava, Hov-ava, Jumon-ava, Jurt-ava, Kaldas-ava, Kov-ava, Kud-ava, Kudo-jurtava, Kugu Shotshen-ava, Mastor-ava, Mor'ava, Nar-azerava, Neškeper-ava, Niski-ava, Norov-ava, Otsuved-azer-ava, P'erna-azor-ava, Sor-ava, Tava-ajk, Tol-ava, Varma-ava, Ved-ava, Ved-mastor-ava, Vel'-ava, Vir-ava, Vir-azerava,* and *Vu-ava.* [Farmer 1978; Leach 1992]

Avezuha
Slavic; Romania
Evil
Demon. This goddess is from an earlier religion absorbed by Christianity. Avezuha was said to have attempted to harm the *Virgin Mary* of Near East before the birth of Jesus. [Jobes 1962]

Avfruvva
Finno-Ugric; Finland, *Saami*
Fishing and Water Animals; Demi-animals
Fish goddess, part human and part fish, like a mermaid. She makes the rivers fruitful by leading the fish to their spawning grounds. Identical to *Akkruva.* Alternate forms: Friis Avfruvva, Havaafru. [Jobes 1962; Leach 1992; Monaghan 1981]

Awa
Slavic; Russia, *Cheremis, Mordvin*
Mother and Guardian
"Mother." It is used in the names of specific deities. Similar to Mordvin *Ava.* [Leach 1972]

Ayisit
Slavic; Siberia, *Tartar, Yakut*
Mother and Guardian; Fate; Immortality

Goddess who presides over fertility and procreation. At childbirth she directs the soul to its appropriate body. She can be invoked to request the birth of sons. See also *Ajysit*. Alternate forms: Aisyt, Ayyysyt. [Leach 1992]

Ayyysyt   See *Ayisit*.

Azelekel   See *Cherlak*.

Azer-ava
Slavic; Russia, *Moksha, Mordvin*
Sky and Heavens; Weather; Agriculture; Justice
   "Mistress." Sky deity and fertility goddess, she belongs to a pantheon of nature divinities. Azer-ava inhabits the upper atmosphere and brings rain and corn. Oaths were taken in her name in local courts of law. The Mordvins have goddesses for natural phenomena as well as one for each place they inhabit. Probably equivalent to *Nishke-ava*. Alternate forms: Ban-ava, Jurt-ava, Nar-azerava, Otsuved-azer-ava, Ved-ava, Vir-ava. [Archaeological Institute 1916–1932; Leach 1992; Monaghan 1981; Redfield 1931]

Bab'e Kasha
Slavic
Family and Tribes; Ceremonies; Agriculture
   "Lady Gruel" of the Kursk province. She arrives the day after *Koliada*, the midwinter birth festival that worships ancestors and casts off the forces of darkness. A special meal is prepared, and the family drinks from a single horned vessel so that the ancestral spirits will bless the harvest. [Hubbs 1988]

Baba-Jaga   See Baba Yaga.

Baba Yaga
Slavic; Russia; Lithuania
Life/Death Cycle; Destroyer of Life; Evil
   Goddess of death and regeneration believed to have come from an Indo-European matrilineal pantheon. She is the totality of the female life cycle—the virgin (she needs no mate), the mother, and the old woman. As the birth-and death-giver, Baba Yaga resembles the Matrioshka doll (a remainder of goddess worship that has lasted into the present), "spilling out" children who are then returned to the goddess. It is Baba Yaga who empowers males. In Russia, she was demoted to a witch who kidnaped and ate her victims, usually children. She survives today in Russian embroideries.
   Baba Yaga lives in a hut, deep in the forest. She can move about on chicken feet. The house is constructed of human body parts, and the fence surrounding it is made of bones and topped by humans skulls with eyes staring from their sockets.
   Similar to *Ragana* and German *Berchta* and *Frau Holle*. Equivalent to Polish *Jedza*. See also *Lamasthu*, Near East. Alternate forms: Baba-Jaga, Yaga-Vasilisa. [Eliade 1987; Hubbs 1988; Jobes 1962; Leach 1972; Leach 1992; Monaghan 1981; Senior 1985]

Baei've   See *Beive-neida*.

Ban-ava
Slavic; Russia, *Mordvin*
Sky and Heavens
   Goddess of the outhouse. Also an alternate form of the sky goddess *Azer-ava*. [Monaghan 1981]

Barbmo-akka
Finno-Ugric; Finland, *Saami*
Wild Birds

"Bird Old Woman." She controls the migratory patterns of birds and calls them back from the warm south. Alternate form: Loddiš-edne. [Archaeological Institute 1916–1932; Jobes 1962; Monaghan 1981]

Beive-neida
Finno-Ugric; Finland, *Saami*
Sun and Day
   "Sun Maiden." Daughter of the sun, *Beiwe*. Alternate form: Baei've, Beiwe-neida. [Leach 1992; Monaghan 1980]

Beiwe
Finno-Ugric; Finland, *Saami*
Sun and Day
   Sun goddess. With her daughter *Beiwe-neida* she returns spring to the world. She brings green plants to feed the the reindeer. Sacrifices are made to her to ensure her return. Alternate form: Paive. [Monaghan 1990]

Beiwe-neida   See *Beive-neida*.

Beregina
Slavic
Unknown
   One of the *Bereginy*. [Hubbs 1988]

Bereginy, The
Slavic
Hunting and Wild Animals; Water; Weather; Demi-animals; Fishing and Water Animals; Earth and Nature; Wild Birds; Ceremonies
   Fertility and hunting goddesses. Nymphs of rivers, lakes, and forests. They provide life-giving moisture from above and below. Portrayed as half woman and half bird or half fish. They are served by a female priesthood. Associated with the early-flowering birch trees. *Beregina* is one of the Bereginy. Alternate forms: Bereguini, Boginki. [Baumgartner 1984; Hubbs 1988]

Bereguini   See *Bereginy*.

Bird and Eye Goddess
Slavic
Hunting and Wild Animals
   Goddess of hunters. Her representation has been found on breast-shaped vessels in the western Ukraine in the Tripol'e (Three Fields) area. She is identified by a double-yolk egg ideogram that is encircled by snakes and deer-antler crescents. [Hubbs 1988]

Bithia
Slavic; Scythia
Magic; Evil
   "Spirit of the Evil Eye." A witch who can cast a spell or kill someone with just a glance. [Jobes 1962]

Boginki   See *The Bereginy*.

Bogoda   See *Dziewanna*.

Boldogasszony
Slavic; Hungary
Mother and Guardian; Family and Tribes
   Virgin goddess whose milk is holy. Protector of mother and child. Christianity transformed her into the *Virgin Mary*, Near East, queen and mother of the Hungarian people. Alternate forms: Kisboldogasszony, Nagyboldogasszony. [Lurker 1984]

Bonto
Finno-Ugric
Evil
"Evil." Wife of Onto. [Jobes 1962]

Bozaloshtsh
Slavic; Germany, *Wend*
Evil; Ugliness; Fate; Destroyer of Life; Directions
Demon of the East. She conveys "the message of death." Bozaloshtsh is a little old woman with long hair. She cries like a child outside the window of a house where someone is about to die. [Bonnerjea 1927; Jobes 1962; Leach 1972; Leach 1992]

Breksta
Slavic; Lithuania
Moon and Night
Goddess of the darkness. She rules with *Ausrine*, the dawn, and *Zleja*, the midday. [Monaghan 1990]

Brieț u-mäte
Slavic; Latvia
Hunting and Wild Animals
"Mother of Elk." One of the seventy sisters of *Zeme*. [Eliade 1987]

Budung-yihe-ibe
Slavic; Siberia, *Buriat*
Goodness; Weather
Benevolent spirit of the mist. [Leach 1992]

Bukura-e Dheut
Slavic; Albania
Goodness; Evil; Heaven and Hell; Magic; Beauty
"Beauty of the Earth." She is powerful and always ready to help, and her castle is guarded by weird and wonderful creatures. If she wishes to communicate with the underworld, she becomes a demon. [Lurker 1984]

Cacce-jienne
Finno-Ugric, *Kola-Lapp*
Water; Physical Prowess; Charisma; Destroyer of Life; Fate; Ceremonies
"Water Mother." A dangerous goddess who has a sirenlike call with which to entice and drown men. To see her foretells disaster, but it can be avoided if one sacrifices bread, a coin, or brandy. Similar to the Slavic *Vodyanoi* and Russian *Rusalka* and *Saive-neida*. [Archaeological Institute 1916–1932]

Cherlak
Finno-Ugric, *Saami*
Water; Ceremonies; Fishing and Water Animals
Volga and Baltic lake goddess. Her sisters *Azelekel* and *Kandralekel* are also lake goddesses.

Cherlak would sometimes go to visit her sisters, taking fish, sea birds, and all her water with her, leaving the lake bed dry. When the people were short of water, they pleaded with her to return and offered her a black bull. She was not pleased with the black bull but accepted their second sacrifice, a black heifer. She then returned with her water, but the water was murky. After her followers sacrificed a black lamb, the water became clear, and the fish and sea birds returned. Sometimes her older sisters came to visit her, causing a flood.

Worshiped in Volga and Baltic areas. [Archaeological Institute 1916–1932]

Chuma
Slavic
Destroyer of Life; Fate
"Fate." Death goddess. Chuma goes from house to house, wrapped in a white veil. She has conversations with those whose death she foretells. Like other death goddesses, she is portrayed clothed in white. Similar to *Kuga* and *Marà*. [Eliade 1987; Leach 1992; Redfield 1931]

Cinderella
Slavic; Finno-Ugric
Goodness; Luck; Magic
Elf of the cinders. She appears in folk literature all over the world. She typifies one whose helpfulness results in good fortune. Her godmother is sometimes considered a goddess. See also *Labismina*, Northern Europe. Alternate form: Ella. [Jobes 1962]

Cinei-new
Slavic; Siberia, *Chukchi*
Water; Fishing and Water Animals
Sea goddess of the maritime people. Her mate is Keretkun (Peruten), god of the sea and sea animals. [Leach 1992]

Colleda
Slavic; Serbia
Time; Fire; Ceremonies; Family and Tribes
Goddess of the winter solstice. She is the keeper of the yule log. In ancient times, fires were lit to celebrate the waxing and waning of the sun. The winter celebration, unlike those in the other seasons, was usually held indoors, part of a smaller family celebration, when the yule log was lit. Some of these festivals are still celebrated by Christians. [Frazer 1959; Monaghan 1981]

Corn Mother
Slavic; Finno-Ugric
Agriculture; Ceremonies
The Corn Mother is made of the last sheaf of corn. The oldest married woman in the village, between fifty to fifty-five years of age, has the honor of shaping the leaves into the figure of a woman. The ears of corn are made into a wreath, entwined with flowers, and carried in a procession by the prettiest girl in the village. The fertilizing power of the Corn Mother is symbolized by having a seven-year-old girl scatter the corn among the new corn on the eve of Easter. The remaining straw is placed in mangers, indicating the Corn Mother's fertilizing influence over the animals. [Durdin-Robertson 1982]

Curche
Slavic; Baltic
Agriculture; Insects; Poverty
A Prussian agricultural deity. She is an insect parasite of grain and is invoked to allay the devastation she brings. [Leach 1992]

Cuvto-ava
Slavic; Russia, *Mordvin*
Earth and Nature
"Tree Mother." Her pardon is sought for any injuries caused to her. [Leach 1992; Monaghan 1981]

Darzamat   See *Dārzu-māte*.

Därzu-mäte
Slavic; Latvia
Earth and Nature
"Mother of the Garden." Goddess of vegetation. One of the seventy sisters of *Zeme*. Alternate form: Darzamat. [Baumgartner 1984; Eliade 1987; Leach 1992]

Debena
Slavic; Czechoslovakia
Hunting and Wild Animals; Earth and Nature
  Goddess of hunting and the forests. [Ergener 1988]

Dekla
Slavic; Baltic
Mother and Guardian; Selflessness; Fate; Unhappiness
  Guardian of newborns. Associated with *Laima* and *Karta*.
Dekla possibly later became the Christian *Saint Thecla*.
When Dekla presides over the birth of a child who is destined
to have an unhappy life, she is very sad. Alternate form:
Delka. [Baumgartner 1984; Leach 1992]

Dekle   See *The Divje Devojke*.

Delka   See *Dekla*.

Derfintos
Slavic; Lithuania
Order
  Goddess of peace. [Leach 1992]

Devana
Slavic; Czechoslovakia
Hunting and Wild Animals
  Goddess of the hunt. Similar to Greek *Diana,* she rides
through the forest with her dogs, searching for game.
Equivalent to Polish *Dziewona* and Serbian *Diiwica*. [Dexter
1990; Savill 1977; Senior 1985; Wedeck 1971]

Dewaite Szwenta
Slavic; Lithuania
Weather
  Weather goddess. She presides over the rain. [Leach 1992]

Dhavata
Slavic; Scythia
Fire
  "The Fire." Sanskrit name for Scythian *Tabiti.* [Cooper 1876]

Didilia
Slavic; Poland
Creator of Life
  Fertility goddess. [Hubbs 1988]

Diiwica
Slavic; Serbia
Hunting and Wild Animals; Earth and Nature
  Goddess of the hunt and forests. Equivalent to Czech
Devana, Polish *Dziewona,* and Slovenian *Divje Devojke*.
Alternate form: Dziwica. [Dexter 1990; Ergener 1988; Savill
1977]

Dive Zeny
Slavic; Bohemia
Disorder; Earth and Nature
  "Wild Woman." Spirit of the woods. As a plural, also said
to be the name for the Polish *Mamony* and equivalent to *The
Divje Devojke*. See also *The Divje Devojke*. [Bonnerjea 1927;
Jobes 1962; Leach 1992]

Divi-te Zeni, The
Slavic; Bulgaria
Earth and Nature
  "Wild Women." Spirits of woods and mountains.
Equivalent to Slovenian *The Divje Devojke* and Bohemian
Divoženky. See also *The Divja Davojka*. Alternate form:
Divi-te Zheny. [Eliade 1987; Jobes 1962; Monaghan 1981]

Divi-te Zheny, The   See *Divi-te Zeni*.

Divja Davojke, The
Slavic; Czechoslovakia
Earth and Nature; Agriculture
  Benevolent spirits who live in forests, mountain caves, or
in homes. They help clean, spin hemp, and reap grain. They
are very good to have around, as they work fast and produce
crops that never diminish. See also *The Divje Devojke*.
[Eliade 1987]

Divje Devojke, The
Slavic; Slovenia
Disorder; Earth and Nature; Weather; Ceremonies
  "Wild Women." Nymphs of woods and mountains.
  *Their wild gatherings cause storms, especially violent ones
  on Midsummer Night, when the frolicking of the Divje
  Devojke is the most intense. They fling their pendulous
breasts over their shoulders so they won't be slowed down while
escaping the storm.*
  Equivalent to *Diiwica, Dive Zeny, Divi-te Zeni,
Divoženky, Dziwožony, Dziwuje Żony, Mamony*. See also
The Divja Davojke. Alternate form: Dekle. [Bonnerjea 1927;
Jobes 1962; Leach 1992; Monaghan 1981]

Divošenky, The
Slavic; Bohemia
Disorder; Earth and Nature
  "Wild Women." Spirits of the forest. Equivalent to Bulgarian
Divi-te Zeni, Slovenian *Divje Devojke,* and Polish *Dziwožony*.
See also *Divja Davojke*. [Eliade 1987; Jobes 1962; Monaghan
1981]

Doda
Slavic; Serbia
Weather
  Goddess of rain. Alternate form: Dodola. [Jobes 1962]

Dodola   See *Doda*.

Dolja   See *Dolya*.

Dolya
Slavic; Russia; Serbia
Fate; Goodness; Evil; Mother and Guardian
  Personal goddess of fate. She can be good or evil, and as
the latter she is sometimes called *Nedolya*. She protects those
she likes. In Serbia she is called *Sreča*. Alternate form: Dolja.
[Dexter 1990; Jobes 1962; Leach 1992; Monaghan 1981]

Drude
Slavic; Bohemia; Moravia
Magic
  Witch. If a female child is born with a tooth, it is considered a
Drude. Wends call them *Murava*. Kasubians call such a child
an *Ohyn,* or vampire; Hungarians, a *Táltos,* or changeling. The
child can be normal and harmless if the tooth is immediately
pulled out. [Leach 1972]

Dsovinar
Slavic; Armenia
Weather
  Storm goddess. Associate of Dsovean, the storm god.
[Leach 1992]

Dugnai
Slavic; Lithuania
Household Affairs
  "That Which Is at the Bottom." Goddess of food. She rules
the kneading of dough. [Monaghan 1990]

Dunna Musun
Slavic; Siberia, *Evenki*
Earth and Nature; Mother and Guardian; Life/Death Cycle
   Earth goddess. She is an old woman who protects the
roads to the realm of the dead. [Leach 1992]

Dzewana   See *Dziewona.*

Dzidzielia
Slavic
Family and Tribes; Creator of Life
   Goddess of fertility who presides over marriage. [Leach
1992]

Dzievona   See *Dziewona.*

Dziewanna
Slavic; Poland
Time; Agriculture; Weather; Ceremonies
   Goddess of spring. As a goddess of agriculture, she was
worshiped by settlers and farmers. Also a goddess of weather.
   ❦ *At the beginning of summer, Dziewanna was carried from
   the woods in the form of a prettily decorated figurine. She
   was followed about the village by a procession of people
collecting gifts and singing.*
   Alternate forms: Bogoda, Zylvie. [Frazer 1959; Leach 1992]

Dziewona
Slavic; Poland
Hunting and Wild Animals; Earth and Nature
   Goddess of forests and hunting. A moon goddess
identified with Greek *Diana.* Equivalent to *Devana* and
Diiwica. Alternate forms: Dzewana, Dzievona. [Ergener
1988; Jobes 1962; Leach 1992; Savill 1977; Wedeck 1971]

Dziparu-māte
Slavic; Baltic
Unknown
   "Mother of Colored Wool." One of the seventy sisters of
Zeme. [Eliade 1987]

Dziwica   See *Diiwica.*

Dziwošony
Slavic; Poland
Disorder; Earth and Nature
   "Wild Women." Spirits of the woods. Possibly the name
of a single goddess. Dziwožony burrow underground in
the forests to find the secrets of nature. Equivalent to *Divje
Dvojke, Divi-te Zeni,* and *Divoženky.* [Eliade 1987; Jobes
1962; Leach 1992; Monaghan 1981]

Dziwuje Zony   See *The Divje Dvojke.*

Dzydzilelya
Slavic; Poland
Love and Sexuality
   Goddess of love. Equivalent to Greek *Aphrodite.* [Jobes
1962; Wedeck 1971]

Edji
Slavic; Siberia
Creator of Life
   "Mother." First woman, who was covered with fur. She
and her husband were placed on a tree with nine branches.
God said "Let nine human beings appear under the nine
branches; from the nine human beings nine races." Similar
to the story of Adam and Eve. [Archaeological Institute
1916–1932]

Egle
Slavic; Lithuania
Reptiles; Family and Tribes; Magic; Water; Unhappiness
   "Queen of the Serpents."
   ❦ *One day Egle was swimming with her sisters. When they
   returned to their clothes, Egle found a serpent coiled in
   hers. The serpent said he would leave if she promised to
marry him, which she did. Several days later, serpent-matchmakers
appeared in her yard, and the marriage was arranged. When Egle
returned with her bridegroom to his palace under the sea, she found
that he was a handsome prince. She lived very happily and had
four children. One of her children asked about his grandparents,
and Egle became homesick. Her husband tried to keep her from
returning home because he did not trust her parents, but he failed.
Once she was back with her family, they elicited her husband's
secret name (which was needed to call him from the water) from
one of the grandchildren and went to the lake and killed him.
Discovering what had happened, Egle ordained that she and the
children be changed into trees: the birch, oak, ash, poplar, and fir.*
[Dexter 1990]

Ehe Tazar
Slavic; Siberia, *Buriat*
Earth and Nature
   "Mother Earth." [Leach 1992]

Ella   See *Cinderella.*

Enakhsys
Slavic; Siberia, *Yakut*
Domesticated Animals
   Cattle goddess. Offerings must be made to her to keep her
from harming the animals. [Leach 1992]

Erce
Slavic; Teutonic
Earth and Nature; Agriculture; Ceremonies; Time
   Earth goddess. She is honored each spring by the pouring
of milk, flour, and water into the newly furrowed earth.
[Leach 1992; Monaghan 1981]

Ether
Finno-Ugric; Finland
Weather
   "Air." Mother of the sea goddess *Ilmater.* [Leach 1972;
Redfield 1931]

Etugen
Siberia, *Mongol*
Earth and Nature
   Earth goddess. She is invoked for good weather, for
abundant crops and animals, and for personal prosperity.
See also *Etugen,* Far East. [Leach 1992]

Ey-vet'ne Kimtaran   See *Tarn.*

Fadza-mama
Slavic; Siberia, *Nanai*
Fire
   Fire deity. She appears as an old woman caring for the fire.
[Leach 1992]

Faraony   See *The Navki.*

Fatit, The
Slavic; Albania
Fate; Insects; Mother and Guardian
   Fate goddesses. They determine each individual's destiny.
Three days after the birth of a child, three Fatit fly into the
baby's room on the backs of butterflies. Approaching the

cradle, they determine the child's fate. See also *Narucnici*. Alternate form: Miren. [Leach 1992; Lurker 1984]

Fevroniia
Slavic; Russia
Earth and Nature

Fertility and tree goddess. Fevroniia was incorporated into Christianity by a monk during the fifteenth century in a story called "Peter and Fevroniia, Wonderworkers of Murom."

Fevroniia cures Peter of an illness and becomes his wife. Because she is a peasant, they are exiled but later return to Murom to rule the city together. When her husband dies, she chooses to join him in death during the feast of Kupala. Her body is buried outside the city because she is a peasant and pagan, but the next morning her grave is discovered next to Peter's in the Cathedral of the Mother of God. [Hubbs 1988]

Fire Mother
Finno-Ugric; Slavic
Mother and Guardian

Goddess of childbirth who is also the guardian of men and women. She is given daily offerings of food and drink at each household's hearth. Her worship is common in Europe and Asia. See also *Tol-ava*. [Eliade 1987]

Firebird, The
Slavic
Wild Birds; Sun and Day; Fire

Deity who is the mother of all birds, the sun, and the hearth fire. She appears in many cultures, including Persian. [Hubbs 1988]

First Woman
Slavic; Russia, *Altai Tartar*
Family and Tribes; Unhappiness; Creator of Life

First Woman was the creation of the god Ulgen.

When Ulgen made First Woman, he could make the body but could not give her life. The devil came and gave her life by blowing his seven-toned flute into her nose and playing his nine-stringed lyre in her ear. She came to life with spirit and mind but with seven bad tempers and nine bad moods. [Farmer 1978]

Friis Avfruvva   See *Akkruva*.

Gabeta   See *Gabija*.

Gabieta   See *Gabija*.

Gabija
Slavic; Lithuania
Fire; Household Affairs; Mother and Guardian; Wild Birds; Ceremonies

Goddess of fire and the hearth. Protector of the "holy fire" and the family. To honor her, salt is thrown on the fire. Gabija was brought to earth by a swallow. The bird was badly burned while performing this duty. Alternate forms: Gabeta, Gabieta. [Leach 1992; Lurker 1984; Savill 1977]

Gabjauja
Slavic; Lithuania
Agriculture; Wealth; Evil

Goddess of corn. Her worship is said to bring prosperity. With the advent of Christianity she became an evil spirit. [Lurker 1984]

Ganis
Finno-Ugric; Finland, *Saami*
Earth and Nature; Love and Sexuality; Hunting and Wild Animals

"Echo." Forest spirit who, seen from the front, is a beautiful maiden. Seen from the back, she has a long tail. To help the people, she brings the reindeer together when they have been in summer pasture and assists in their milking. Sometimes she has sexual intercourse with the men. See also *Metsänneitsyt* and *Tava-ajk*. Alternate forms: Gidne, Kani, Kine. [Archaeological Institute 1916–1932; Jobes 1962]

Gidne   See *Ganis*.

Giltine
Slavic; Lithuania
Destroyer of Life

Goddess of death. Illnesses that cause death by strangulation or suffocation are said to have been the work of Giltine. Like other Slavic deities of death, she appears dressed in white. [Lurker 1984]

Gorska Makva
Slavic; Bulgaria
Ugliness; Demi-animals; Domesticated Animals

Wood hag who is portrayed with the head of an ox. She frightens children at night. Equivalent to *Nocnitsa* and Russian *Kriksy*. [Bonnerjea 1927; Leach 1972]

Gudiri-mumi
Slavic; Russia, *Votyak*
Earth and Nature; Weather

"Mother of Thunder." Nature deity. Alternate form: Gudyri-mumy. [Guirand 1968; Leach 1972]

Gudyri-mumy   See *Gudiri-mumi*.

Haltia
Finno-Ugric, *Baltic Finn*
Directions; Houshold Affairs; Health and Healing; Luck; Domesticated Animals

House goddess. She inhabits the house's structure and brings health and good fortune. If the family destroys the house, they must move some of the wood or ash from the hearth to their new house or risk the anger of Haltia. The female Haltia cares for the cows, sheep, pigs, and poultry. Children are better behaved and become better adults because of the presence of the female Haltia in the house. The Estonians call her *Holdja*. There is also a male deity called Haltia who watches over horses. [Archaeological Institute 1916–1932; Monaghan 1981]

Havaafru   See *Avfruvva*.

Holdja   See *Haltia*.

Hongatar
Finno-Ugric; Finland
Mother and Guardian

Mother goddess. She nursed the bear deity. [Puhvel 1974]

Honoured High Mistress
Slavic; Siberia, *Yakut*
Mother and Guardian; Earth and Nature

Goddess in a creation story. She is the spirit of a tree and is seen as a solemn-eyed, middle-aged woman with flowing locks and a naked bosom.

When White Youth grew tired of living in the tree of life, he asked Honoured High Mistress to let him live as a man should. The tree leaves began to rustle and a warm breeze blew and from under the roots of the tree rose a bare-breasted woman. She gave the youth milk from her breasts and promised him happiness, great power, and protection from all evil.

The Yakut tree of life grows on the yellow navel of the eight-edged Earth. It is a dense, eight-branched tree. The crown of the tree spews forth a heavenly, yellow liquid that refreshes passersby. It is the home of First Man, who is sometimes called White Youth. [Archaeological Institute 1916–1932]

Horsel See *Ursula.*

Hotogov Mailgan
Slavic; Siberia, *Buriat*
Creator of Life; Sky and Heavens
   Goddess of the night heavens. She is also a creator goddess. [Leach 1992]

Hov-ava
Slavic; Russia, *Mordvin*
Moon and Night
   Moon goddess. See also *Avas.* [Leach 1972]

Iarila
Slavic; Russia
Sun and Day; Creator of Life
   "Ardent Sun." She is associated with Iarilo as a fertility deity. [Hubbs 1988]

Idem-huva
Finno-Ugric, *Cheremis*
Agriculture
   "Threshing Barn Woman." She presides over the threshing. Fleeing as the reapers cut down the grain, she takes refuge in the barn. She is placated by being honored at harvest festival ceremonies. The last corn to be threshed is known as Mother Corn. See also *Corn Mother.* Alternate form: Idem-kuva. [Archaeological Institute 1916–1932; Frazer 1959; Monaghan 1981]

Idem-kuva See *Idem-huva.*

Ijâksit-khotun See *Ajysit.*

Ilena
Slavic; Siberia, *Koryak*
Weather
   "Rain Woman" or "Dampness Woman." Sometimes called the wife of the supreme being. Alternate form: Ile-Neut. [Leach 1992]

Ile-neut See *Ilena.*

Illibem Berti
Slavic; Siberia, *Samoyed*
Hunting and Wild Animals; Domesticated Animals
   Goddess of reindeer. She presides over domestic and wild animals. Alternate form: Paduri. [Leach 1992]

Ilma
Finno-Ugric
Weather
   "Atmosphere." Mother of *Luonnotar.* Considered by some to be *Ilmater.* [Jobes 1962; Leach 1992; Monaghan 1981]

Ilmatar See *Ilmater.*

Ilmater
Finno-Ugric; Finland
Creator of Life; Water; Sky and Heavens; Ceremonies
   "Water Mother." Creator deity. Also goddess of water and sky. Daughter of the air, *Ether.*

❁ *Ilmater came down to embrace the sea and remained, tossing on the waves, for seven hundred years. When the celestial duck laid seven eggs, she took them and made the Earth, sun, moon, and the vault of heaven. The wind impregnated her, and she gave birth to three sons, Ilmarinen, Lemminikainen, and Väinämönem (Wainamoinen).*

Her feast day is August 26. See also *Ilma* and *Luonnotar.* Alternate form: Ilmatar. [Durdin-Robertson 1982; Jobes 1962; Leach 1992; Stone 1979]

Ine-shki-ava See *Nishke-ava.*

Irlek-khan
Slavic; Siberia, *Tartar*
Evil
   Evil goddess who came to earth as a black fox. She did much harm to people. Daughter of the king of the dead. [Archaeological Institute 1916–1932]

Isa
Finno-Ugric; Lapland, *Saami*
Intelligence and Creativity
   Goddess of intelligence and perception. Equivalent to Egyptian *Isis.* [Jobes 1962]

Itchita
Slavic; Siberia, *Yakut*
Earth and Nature
   Earth goddess who prevents illness. She lives in birch trees and has spirit servants who aid her with her duties. [Baumgartner 1984; Leach 1992]

Jabme-akka
Finno-Ugric; Lapland, *Saami*
Destroyer of Life; Ceremonies; Heaven and Hell
   Goddess of the dead. An old woman who presides over Jabme-aimo or Jabmeanimo (the region of the dead). She brings illness and death to humans and animals. Sacrifices of black animals, especially cats and cocks, are made to her. She may be an aspect of *Maddarakka.* Alternate form: Jameakka. [Eliade 1987; Leach 1972; Leach 1992]

Jabmeks
Finno-Ugric; Lapland, *Saami*
Heaven and Hell
   Goddess of the underworld and the dead. Alternate forms: Jabmi-akko, Jameakka, and Jami-ajmo-ollmaj. [Leach 1992]

Jaga-baba See *Jezinky.*

Jaja
Slavic, *Abkhasian*
Evil; Agriculture; Wealth
   Caucasus malevolent harvest goddess. She grants abundance only if worshiped properly. [Leach 1992]

Jameakka See *Jabmeks.*

Jami-ajmo-ollmaj See *Jabmeks.*

Ja-neb'a
Slavic; Siberia, *Samoyed*
Earth and Nature; Goodness
   Benevolent earth goddess. [Leach 1992]

Jedza
Slavic; Poland
Evil
   Demon, mother of evil spirits. Equivalent to Russian *Baba Yaga.* [Leach 1992]

Jendzi-baba   See *Jezinky.*

Jendzyna   See *Jezinky.*

Jezenky   See *Jezinky.*

Jezibaba
Slavic; Czechoslovakia
Evil
    Demon, mother of evil spirits. Equivalent to Russian *Baba Yaga.* One of the *Jezinky.* [Leach 1992]

Jezinky, The
Slavic; Czechoslovakia
Evil
    Demons who live in caves. They blind humans and kidnap and devour children. See also *Baba Yaga.* One of the Jezinky is *Jezibaba.* Alternate forms: Jaga-baba, Jendzi-baba, Jendzyna, Jezenky. [Jobes 1962]

Joda-mäte
Slavic; Latvia
Evil
    Mother of the devil. One of the seventy sisters of *Zeme.* [Eliade 1987; Lurker 1984]

Joli-taren
Slavic; Siberia, *Vogul*
Earth and Nature; Creator of Life
    "Giver of Life." Earth goddess, sister of Numi-Tarem, the sky god. She supervised creation. Alternate form: Joli-torem. [Baumgartner 1984; Leach 1992]

Joli-torem   See *Joli-Taren.*

Joukahainen
Finno-Ugric; Lapland, *Saami*
Unknown
    A deity mentioned in the *Kalevala,* the Finish national epic. [Sykes 1968]

Judy, The   See *Vila.*

Juksakka
Finno-Ugric; Lapland, *Saami*
Mother and Guardian; Magic
    "Bow Old Woman." Birth goddess, daughter of *Maddarakka.* She is one of the *Akkah. Maddarakka* gives Juksakka the males, and Juksakka places them in the mother's womb and makes them good hunters. Like her sister *Uksakka,* she can change the sex of an unborn child. She also protects children from accidents. [Jobes 1962; Leach 1992]

Jumala   See *Slatababa.*

Jumon-ava
Slavic; Russia, *Cheremis*
Mother and Guardian; Family and Tribes
    Goddess of childbirth and marriage. Female animals were sacrificed to her in her sacred groves. [Archaeological Institute 1916–1932; Leach 1992]

Juras Mäte
Slavic; Latvia
Water
    "Mother of the Sea." One of the seventy sisters of *Zeme.* May be the same as the Lithuanian mermaid *Jurate.* Alternate form: Jurasmat. [Eliade 1987; Leach 1992; Lurker 1984; Monaghan 1990; Savill 1977]

Jurasmat   See *Juras Māte.*

Jurate
Slavic; Baltic; Lithuania
Water
    Mermaid goddess. May be the same as Latvian *Juras Māte.* [Monaghan 1990]

Jurt-ava
Slavic; Russia, *Mordvin, Moksha*
Household Affairs
    "Dwelling Place Mother." Goddess of the courtyard and outbuildings. A form for the sky goddess *Azer-ava.* See also *Jurt-azerava.* [Archaeological Institute 1916–1932; Leach 1992; Monaghan 1981]

Jurt-azerava
Slavic; Russia, *Moksha*
Household Affairs
    "Dwelling Place Mistress." Goddess of the courtyard and outbuildings. She is a form of *Azer-ava.* See also *Jurt-ava.* [Archaeological Institute 1916–1932; Leach 1992; Monaghan 1981]

Kaldas-ava
Slavic; Russia, *Mordvin*
Domesticated Animals
    Goddess of the cattleyard. [Leach 1992]

Kaldyni-mumas
Slavic; Russia; Siberia, *Votyak*
Mother and Guardian; Family and Tribes
    Goddess of fertility. She is invoked to bring marriage and children. Alternate form: Kildisin. [Leach 1992]

Kalma
Finno-Ugric
Destroyer of Life; Ugliness
    "Corpse-stench." Death goddess who owns a monstrous animal that chases and devours humans. She reigns over graves. [Carlyon 1982; Guirand 1968; Savill 1977]

Kaltas-anki
Finno-Ugric, *Ostyak, Northern, Vogul*
Mother and Guardian; Fate; Immortality
    Goddess of childbirth. Protector of mother and child, it is Kaltas-anki who gives the child its soul. She takes out a golden book at birth and determines the fate and length of life for each child. She may do this when she is in a "gold-embroidered seven-forked tree." See also *Ajysit* and *Kaltes.* [Archaeological Institute 1916–1932; Leach 1992]

Kaltes
Slavic; Siberia, *Ob-Ugric, Vogul, Ostyak*
Earth and Nature; Mother and Guardian; Domesticated Animals
    Earth goddess, goddess of birth. Associated with the sky god Numi-Tarem. The goose and the hare are sacred to her, and she often manifests in their forms. See also *Kaltas-anki.* [Leach 1992; Lurker 1984]

Kamennaia Baba, The
Slavic
Reptiles; Earth and Nature; Domesticated Animals
    "The Stone Mothers." The name given to monolithic stone statues called Menhirs, rounded Matrioshka-like forms found in southern Russia. They are possibly of Scythian origin and are engraved with serpent and animal images, hold a horn, and are flanked by horsemen. The afflicted bring flax, wool,

and sheep to the stones as offerings. Alternate form: Kamennye Baby. [Eliade 1987; Hubbs 1968; Sykes 1968]

Kamennye Baby, The   See *The Kamennaia Baba*.

Kandralekel   See *Cherlak*.

Kani   See *Ganis*.

Kanym
Slavic; Siberia, *Lebed Tartar*
Sky and Heavens
  Wife of one of the seven gods of heaven who serve the "Over god." She and her husband, Ülgön, live in the top story of a seven-storied heaven. [Archaeological Institute 1916–1932]

Kapu Māte
Slavic; Latvia
Destroyer of Life
  "Graveyard Mother." Goddess of the dead. One of the seventy sisters of *Zeme*. [Eliade 1987; Leach 1992; Lurker 1984]

Kardas-ś Arko
Slavic; Russia, *Mordvin*
Household Affairs; Metals and Minerals
  "Yard-śarko." Courtyard deity (female or male) who lives under a stone in the yard. [Archaeological Institute 1916–1932; Leach 1992]

Karta
Slavic; Baltic; Latvia
Fate; Mother and Guardian; Selflessness
  Goddess of destiny. Associated with *Dekla* and *Laima*. She presides over the first few months of a child's life after birth. Her function was assumed by *Saint Thecla*. [Eliade 1987; Leach 1992; Lurker 1984]

Kathshchar-ekva
Slavic; Siberia, *Mansi*
Earth and Nature
  Earth goddess. Sister of the sky god Numi-Torum (Numi-Tarem). [Leach 1992]

Keca Aba
Slavic; Russia, *Cheremis*
Sun and Day
  "Mother Sun." Alternate forms: Ketche Avalon, Os Keca Aba. [Monaghan 1990]

Keren Sotskon Pas   See *Kud-ava*.

Ketche Avalon   See *Keca Aba*.

Ketse-awa
Slavic; Russia, *Cheremis*
Sun and Day
  "Mother of the Sun." [Leach 1972]

Khania Shkwakwa
Slavic, *Abkhasian*
Destroyer of Life
  Caucasus goddess of disease. She causes smallpox and is the wife of the god of smallpox, Akhye Zoshan. [Leach 1992]

Khosadam
Slavic; Siberia, *Ket*, *Yenisei Ostyak*
Evil; Destroyer of Life; Luck

"Eater of Souls." Goddess of evil. Khosadam was banished to Earth by her husband, Ess, because she was unfaithful. She causes illness and misfortune. See also *Khosodam*. Alternate form: Khosedabam. [Baumgartner 1984; Leach 1992]

Khosedabam   See *Khosadam*.

Khosodam
Slavic; Siberia
Evil; Directions; Insects; Destroyer of Life
  Evil demon of the north. Ruler of the dead who created mosquitoes. See also *Khosadam*. [Jobes 1962]

Khotun
Slavic; Siberia, *Yakut*
Mother and Guardian; Wealth; Stars and Planets
  Goddess of birth. Equivalent to *Ajysit*.
 Khotun lives in a lake of milk under the tree of life (see Honoured High Mistress). Her breasts are as large as leather sacks. Her milk is so plentiful that the surplus form the Milky Way.
  See also *Kubai-khotun*. [Jobes 1962]

Kikimora
Slavic; Russia
Household Affairs; Domesticated Animals; Fate
  Slavonic household spirit. She cares for the poultry and sometimes helps with household chores.
  Kikimora created trouble for lazy housekeepers. She would tickle the children of a lazy housekeeper, keeping them and their mother up all night. [Carlyon 1982; Guirand 1968; Jobes 1962; Leach 1992]

Kildisin
Slavic; Russia; Siberia, *Votyak*
Mother and Guardian; Earth and Nature; Agriculture; Ceremonies; Selflessness
  "Procreating Heaven." Birth goddess, earth goddess, and goddess of corn. Wife/mother of Inmar. A white sheep is sacrificed to her at the birth of a child. She makes women and animals fruitful. With the advance of Christianity, she was merged with the *Virgin Mary*, Near East. Like *Ava*, the word for mother, "mumy" or "muni" is used with names of nature deities. Alternate forms: Kaldyni-mumas, Kildisin-mumy, Kugu Shotsen-ava. [Archaeological Institute 1916–1932; Jobes 1962; Leach 1972; Leach 1992]

Kildisin-mumy   See *Kildisin*.

Kine   See *Ganis*.

Kipu-tytto
Finno-Ugric; Finland, *Saami*
Destroyer of Life; Ugliness; Heaven and Hell
  Goddess of illness. The most horrible of the daughters of *Tuonetar* and Tuoni. Her sisters are *Kivutar, Vammatar,* and *Loviatar* who all live together in Tuonela, the Finnish hell. She is said to be very ugly. [Carlyon 1982; Leach 1992; Savill 1977]

Kisboldogasszony   See *Boldogasszony*.

Kivutar
Finno-Ugric; Finland, *Saami*
Unhappiness
  Goddess of pain and suffering. Daughter of *Tuonetar*. Sister of *Kipu-tytto, Loviatar,* and *Vammatar*. [Guirand 1968; Leach 1992; Savill 1977]

Koliada
Slavic; Russia
Time, Sun and Day, Ceremonies
   Goddess of time and personification of the winter solstice. She is symbolized by the sun as it is surrounded by the forces of darkness, needing humanity to drive the darkness away. This task is usually accomplished by women. In Europe, Epiphany is the time of celebration of the winter solstice, a custom that has survived from earlier religions. The festival of *Koliada* takes place at this time to stimulate procreative power. Koliada can also be male, and in this aspect is linked with Saint Nicholas, who assumed the goddess's role as an aide during childbirth and as bearer of fertility. In Bulgaria the festival is called *Kulada*. Alternate form: Koljada. [Hubbs 1988; Leach 1972; Leach 1992]

Koljada   See *Koliada.*

Koš La-kuva
Slavic; Russia, *Cheremis*
Mother and Guardian; Earth and Nature; Domesticatead Animals
   "Old Woman of the Forest." She protects cattle when they are taken to the woods in the spring. She is invoked to help find humans lost in the forest or for protection when people are spending the night there. [Archaeological Institute 1916–1932; Jobes 1962]

Kostroma
Slavic; Russia
Life/Death Cycle; Goodness; Evil
   Benevolent and malevolent fertility goddess. Like Greek *Persephone,* she is the dying and reborn daughter. [Hubbs 1988]

Kostrubonko
Slavic; Russia
Creator of Life
   Fertility goddess. [Monaghan 1981]

Kov-ava
Slavic; Russia, *Mordvin*
Moon and Night
   Moon goddess. See also *The Avas.* [Leach 1992]

Krasnyi
Slavic; Russia
Beauty; Sun and Day
   "Red" or "Beautiful." Epithet that involves a girl and the sun. [Hubbs 1988]

Kriksy
Slavic; Russia
Ugliness; Evil
   Wood hag who torments children at night. Equivalent to Bulgarian *Gorska Makva.* Alternate forms: Nocnitsa, Plaksy. [Bonnerjea 1927; Leach 1972]

Krimba
Slavic; Bohemia
Household Affairs
   Goddess of the house. [Guirand 1968; Leach 1992]

Kuapla   See *Kupalo.*

Kubai-khotun
Slavic; Siberia, *Yakut*
Mother and Guardian; Wealth; Stars and Planets
   "Great Mother." She dwells in the tree of life (see *Honoured High Mistress*) or under its roots and protects and supports both humans and animals. She has "breasts as large as leather sacks" to provide milk, the source of all life. Her milk is the origin of the heavenly Milky Way. See also *Khotun.* [Archaeological Institute 1916–1932]

Kubaiko
Slavic; Siberia, *Tartar*
Courage; Magic
   A woman who braved death to save her brother.
   When her brother's head was cut off by the monster Yebegen, Kubaiko went to the realm of Erlik-Khan to plead for its return. After fulfilling the tasks assigned to her by Erlik-Khan, she was given her brother's head and the water of life. With these she was able to return to the Earth and restore her brother to life. [Archaeological Institute 1916–1932; Eliot 1976; Jobes 1962]

Kubay-khotun-la   See *Nalban-Aiy.*

Kucedre   See *Kulshedra.*

Kud-ava
Slavic; Russia, *Mordvin*
Household Affairs
   "House Mother." Goddess of dwellings. An Erya prayer is "House mother, above is thy lime-bark [the roof is thatched with this material], beneath are thy beams." See also *The Avas.* Alternate forms: Kud-azerava, Kudo-jurtava. [Archaeological Institute 1916–1932; Leach 1972; Leach 1992]

Kud-azerava   See *Kud-ava.*

Kudo-jurtava   See *Kud-ava.*

Kuga
Slavic; Slovenia; Croatia; Serbia
Fate
   "Fate." Life and death goddess. Similar to *Chuma* and *Marà.* [Eliade 1987]

Kugu Shotshen-ava
Slavic; Russia, *Cheremis*
Mother and Guardian
   "Great Birthgiving Mother." Goddess of birth or alternate form for *Kildisin.* A white sheep is sacrificed in her honor at the birth of a child. [Archaeological Institute 1916–1932; Jobes 1962; Leach 1992]

Kukudhi   See *Kukuth.*

Kukuth
Slavic; Albania
Destroyer of Life
   Demon of illness. She causes epidemics. Alternate form: Kukudhi. [Lurker 1984]

Kul
Finno-Ugric, *Siryan*
Water; Fishing and Water Animals
   "Water Dweller." Water spirit with long hair, which she combs with big paws. Her characteristics vary from district to district. She may appear as a woman or small child. As a child, she will be hairy and fishlike, and she may stray into a fisherman's net. See also *Vasa.* [Archaeological Institute 1916–1932]

Kulshedra
Slavic; Albania
Evil; Ugliness; Destroyer of Life; Weather; Ceremonies

Evil hag or dragonlike monster who inhabits the Earth's water. As an enormous hag or a fire-spitting monster, she tries to destroy humankind with storms and floods. She is driven off by Dragoni, the god of thunder and lightning. She is also said to cause droughts and can only be placated with human sacrifices. Alternate form: Kucedre. [Eliade 1987; Leach 1992; Lurker 1984]

Kupal'nitsa
Slavic; Russia
Mother and Guardian; Ceremonies; Fire; Water; Earth and Nature
Mother goddess of the southwest. Her male counterpart is Ivan Kupalo. The festival of Ivan Kupalo celebrates "Mother Moist Earth." The ceremonies involve fire, water, and ritual bathing. See also *Kupalo*. [Hubbs 1988]

Kupalo
Slavic; Russia; Balkans
Time; Ceremonies; Fire; Magic; Mother and Guardian
Midsummer deity associated with water, magic, and herbs. In Russia, Kupalo is represented at her celebration by a woman made of straw. There is a huge bonfire that the young people jump over, dragging the straw woman with them. She then joins them in their bathing ritual the next day and is allowed to float away, carrying any evil away with her. In the Balkans her effigy is made from a birch sapling, which is stripped of all but its topmost branches and dressed in women's clothing. See also *Kupal'nitsa*. Alternate form: Kuapla. [Carlyon 1982; Monaghan 1981; Savill 1977]

Kutug:a
Slavic; Siberia, *Negidal*
Fire
"Mistress of the Fire." [Leach 1992]

Kuutar
Finno-Ugric
Moon and Night; Household Affairs
"Shining." Daughter of the moon. She is associated with the weaving shuttle. [Carlyon 1982; Guirand 1968]

Kybâi-khotun
Slavic; Siberia, *Yakut*
Fate; Mother and Guardian; Family and Tribes
Goddess of birth and fate. Kybäi-Khotun lives in the Zambu tree. She was the mother of the first human. See *Kubai-khotun*. [Archaeological Institute 1916–1932; Jobes 1962]

Lada
Slavic; Lithuania; Poland; Russia
Time; Love and Sexuality; Family and Tribes; Happiness; Ceremonies
Goddess of spring and love. She presides over marriage and happiness. Her worshipers make clay images of larks, smearing them with honey, wrapping the birds' heads in tinsel, and carrying the images through the village singing songs to Lada. Alternate form: Lada-Dida. [Dexter 1990; Hubel 1968; Jobes 1962; Leach 1992; Wedeck and Baskin 1971]

Lada-dida   See *Lada*.

Laima
Slavic; Latvia; Lithuania
Fate; Luck; Demi-animals; Wild Birds; Beauty; Magic
Goddess of fate and good fortune. She is responsible for determining the fate of all living beings.

Laima appeared as a swan, and her feathers were somehow burned, which caused her to be transformed into a beautiful woman. She married a prince and had several

children. *Laima tired of her mortal life and asked the prince to give her some feathers. When he threw them to her, she changed back to her swanlike form and flew away. Laima returned now and then to see her children, but she never regained a mortal form.*

See also *Swan Maidens,* Northern Europe. Alternate forms: Laime, Laima-Dalia. [Dexter 1990; Eliade 1987; Leach 1992; Savill 1977]

Laima-dalia   See *Laima*.

Laimas-mäte
Slavic; Latvia
Luck; Wealth
Mother goddess of fortune. One of the seventy sisters of *Zeme*. [Eliade 1987]

Laime   See *Laima*.

Lamaria
Slavic, *Svan*
Fire; Household Affairs; Mother and Guardian
Caucasus goddess of the hearth and the guardian deity of women. [Lurker 1984]

Laugo-edne
Finno-Ugric; Finland, *Saami*
Household Affairs
Laundry goddess. [Monaghan 1990]

Lauka-mäte
Slavic; Latvia
Agriculture
"Mother of the Plough-land." She is invoked to give abundant crops. One of the seventy sisters of *Zeme*. Alternate forms: Laukumäte, Luakamat. [Baumgartner 1984; Eliade 1987; Leach 1992; Lurker 1984]

Laukosargas
Slavic; Lithuania; Prussia, *Pruthene*
Agriculture
Harvest goddess. She is worshiped in Lithuania as the "guardian of the fields." [Leach 1992]

Laukumäte
"Mother of the Fields." See also *Lauka-mäte*. [Eliade 1987]

Lauma
Slavic; Latvia
Earth and Nature; Household Affairs; Goodness; Evil; Magic
Earth goddess. She also presides over weaving. Benevolent and malevolent, she has come to be known as a fairy or witch. Lauma is also depicted as a plural deity, Laumas. See also *Laumē*.

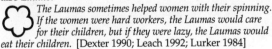 *The Laumas sometimes helped women with their spinning. If the women were hard workers, the Laumas would care for their children, but if they were lazy, the Laumas would eat their children.* [Dexter 1990; Leach 1992; Lurker 1984]

Laumē
Slavic; Lithuania
Magic; Household Affairs; Mother and Guardian; Evil; Fate; Dawn and Twilight
"Earthly Mother." A fairy, she is usually naked and bathes often. She is associated with spinning and weaving. She is also presented in fairy tales as a witch whose sexuality includes large breasts and long blonde hair. She can be demonic. See also *Lauma*. [Dexter 1990; Lurker 1984]

Lazdu-mäte
Slavic; Latvia
Creator of Life
   "Mother of Hazel." Fertility goddess, one of the seventy sisters of *Zeme*. [Eliade 1987]

Lesni Zenka, The
Slavic
Earth and Nature; Love and Sexuality; Goodness
   Wood nymphs. Even though they are benevolent, their love is dangerous to mortals. Also said to be singular and similar to *Meschamaat*. [Jobes 1962; Leach 1992]

Liderc, The
Slavic; Hungary
Evil; Magic; Demi-animals; Fire; Love and Sexuality
   Evil demons who can appear in a variety of forms, among them human, chicken, and fire. They can be helping spirits to humans or witches and demon lovers. The Liderc gather around fires, melting wax to make their lovers' hearts melt with love. [Eliade 1987; Frazer 1959]

Likho
Slavic
Evil
   Goddess of extreme malevolence. She has only one eye. [Jobes 1962; Leach 1992]

Linda
Finno-Ugric; Finland, *Saami*
Wild Birds
   Bird goddess. She manifests as a swan. Wife of Kalev. [Leach 1992]

Linu-mäte
Slavic; Latvia
Creator of Life
   "Mother of Flax." Fertility goddess, one of the seventy sisters of *Zeme*. [Eliade 1987]

Ljubi
Slavic; Albania
Evil; Weather; Ceremonies
   Demon who causes droughts unless proper sacrifices are made to her. [Lurker 1984]

Locid-epie
Slavic; Siberia, *Yukaghir*
Fire
   "Grandmother of the Fire." [Leach 1992]

Loddiŭ-edne
Finno-Ugric; Lapland, *Saami*
Wild Birds
   "Bird Mother." Western protector of birds who presides over their nesting instincts. Alternate form: **Barmo-akka**. [Archaeological Institute 1916–1932; Jobes 1962; Monaghan 1981]

Lopemat
Slavic; Latvia
Domesticated Animals
   "Mother of Cattle." [Baumgartner 1984; Leach 1992]

Louhi
Finno-Ugric; Finland, *Saami*
Magic; Weather; Earth and Nature; Destroyer of Life; Hunting and Wild Animals
   Sorceress. Protector of Pohja (the back country). She is mentioned in the *Kalevala*, the Finnish national epic. As a sorceress, she controls the fog and wind and sends diseases and wild beasts. She sells the wind to becalmed mariners. The wind is tied in three knots: if they untie the first knot, a moderate wind blows; untying the second causes a gale to blow; and if the third knot is untied, a hurricane comes.

 Louhi once stole the sun and the moon and hid them. Vainamoinen captured her and freed them, allowing the light to shine again. [Carlyon 1982; Frazer 1959; Guirand 1968; Leach 1972]

Loviatar
Finno-Ugric
Evil; Ugliness; Destroyer of Life; Unhappiness
   Goddess of disease. Sister of *Kipu-tytto, Kivutar,* and *Vammatar.* Daughter of *Tuonetar.* She is portrayed as an ugly woman with a black face and terribly deformed skin. She is said to have given birth to terrible monsters: Cancer, Colic, Gout, Plague, Pleurisy, Scabies, Tuberculosis, Ulcers, and Envy. [Carlyon 1982; Leach 1992; Savill 1977]

Luakamat See *Lauka-mäte.*

Luojatar
Finno-Ugric
Selflessness
   After the advent of Christianity, a name for the *Virgin Mary,* Near East. See also *Luonnotar.* [Archaeological Institute 1916–1932]

Luonnotar
Finno-Ugric; Lapland, *Saami*
Creator of Life; Water; Earth and Nature; Sky and Heavens; Wild Birds
   "Daughter of Nature." Daughter of *Ilma* and, according to some, mother of Vainamoinen. Her story is similar to that of *Ilmater.*

   A duck flew over the sea where Luonnotar had been floating for seven centuries. The duck built a nest on Luonnotar's knee and laid eggs. When she moved suddenly, the eggs were thrown into the abyss. From the eggs the Earth and the heavens were formed. The yolks became the sun and the whites the moon, and fragments formed the stars and clouds. Luonnotar finished the creation by forming the topography of the land.
   Alternate form: Luojatar. [Archaeological Institute 1916–1932; Guirand 1968]

Luot-chozjik See *Luot-hozjik.*

Luot-hozjik
Slavic; Russia, *Saami*
Hunting and Wild Animals; Demi-animals
   Forest goddess who protects the reindeer as they wander freely in the forests in the summer. She cannot protect them from hunters, and she helps people catch the wild reindeer. She lives on a mountain covered with lichen. She has a human face and feet, but her body is hairy like that of a reindeer. Equivalent to *Pots-hozjik.* Alternate form: Luot-chozjik. [Archaeological Institute 1916–1932; Jobes 1962]

Lusin
Slavic, *Armenia*
Moon and Night
   Moon goddess. Alternate form: Amins. [Leach 1992]

Lymyzn-mam
Slavic; Siberia, *Gilyak*
Household Affairs
   "Mistress of the Threshold." [Leach 1992]

Maa-ema   See *Ma-emma.*

Maa-emae   See *Maan-emo.*

Maan-emo
Finno-Ugric; Finland, *Saami*
Earth and Nature; Mother and Guardian; Agriculture;
Weather
   Earth goddess. Wife of Ukko, god of thunder. She presides
over the fertility of women and the harvest. Also gives aid to
the helpless. See also *Maan-eno.* Alternate forms: Maa-emae,
Maan-emoinen. [Guirand 1968; Jobes 1962; Redfield 1931;
Stone 1979]

Maan-emoinen   See *Maan-emo.*

Maan-eno
Finno-Ugric; Estonia
Earth and Nature; Mother and Guardian
   Fertility goddess of plants and humans. Wife of Ukko, the
supreme being or god of thunder. See also *Maan-emo.*
Alternate form: Rauni. [Guirand 1968; Leach 1992]

Maddar-aka   See *Maddarakka.*

Maddarakka
Finno-Ugric; Sweden; Scandinavia, *Saami*
Earth and Nature; Mother and Guardian; Health and
Healing; Immortality; Magic
   "Old Woman." Earth mother and goddess of childbirth
and healing. Mother of *Juksakka, Sarakka,* and *Uksakka.*

   *She cares for the spirit or soul of a child until it is ready
   for birth. She gives it to Sarakka, who transfers it to the
   woman during labor. Another version of the story says
   that Maddarakka takes the soul from the goddess Serque-edne and
   transfers it to a body. If she entrusts the fetus to her daughter
   Sarakka, it will be female; if Juksaka cares for the fetus, it will
   be male. Uksakka can change the sex before the child is born.*

   See also *Sergue-edne* and *Radien-kiedde.* Alternate form:
Maddar-aka.   [Eliade 1987; Jobes 1962; Leach 1992]

Madder-akku
Finno-Ugric; Finland, *Saami*
Mother and Guardian; Goodness
   Goddess of the blind and deaf. She also protects those who
have lost their way in the wilderness. [Eliade 1987]

Ma-emma
Finno-Ugric; Estonia
Earth and Nature
   Earth goddess. She rules all living beings and provides
their food. Alternate form: Maa-ema. [Monaghan 1981; Stone
1979]

Mahte
Slavic; Lithuania
Creator of Life
   Fertility goddess. Personification of the generative power
of the Earth. Similar to Greek *Demeter.* [Leach 1972]

Majky, The   See *Navki.*

Makosh
Slavic
Water; Agriculture
   Water goddess. She rules over the production of food. See
also *Mokosh.* [Senior 1985]

Mamaldi
Slavic; Siberia, *Amur*
Creator of Life; Magic; Health and Healing
   Creator goddess.

   *Mamaldi created Asia and the island of Sakhalin (an island
   between Russia and Japan). She was killed by her husband
   Khadau but continued to be involved in the creation of
shamans.* [Leach 1992]

Mamony
Slavic; Poland
Disorder; Earth and Nature
   "Wild Woman." Spirit of the woods. Also said to be plural
and equivalent to the *Dive Zeny* and *Divje Devojke.*
[Bonnerjea 1927; Jobes 1962; Leach 1992]

Mampadurei
Slavic; Romania
Earth and Nature
   "Mother of the Forest." [Leach 1992]

Mannu
Finno-Ugric
Earth and Nature
   "Mother Earth." Alternate form: Mother of Mannu.
[Guirand 1968; Savill 1977]

Manzan Gūrmū
Slavic; Siberia, *Buriat*
Mother and Guardian
   "Heavenly Goddess." The overflow of her breast milk
formed the Milky Way. See also *Kubai-khotun* and *Khotun.*
[Archaeological Institute 1916–1932]

Marà
Slavic; Latvia; Russia
Domesticated Animals; Household Affairs; Reptiles
   Goddess of cows in Latvia. She protects and feeds them.
She is also know as *Marsa, Marsava,* and *Maritini.* In Russia
she is a spirit who spins at night, and if not properly invoked,
she will spoil a woman's spinning. She is also a fate goddess
known in her deathly aspect as *Mora* or *Smert.* To the
Slovenes, Marà is a snake goddess, the wife of Kresnik.
[Eliade 1987; Leach 1972; Leach 1992]

Maras, The
Slavic; Germany
Evil; Intelligence and Creativity
   Nightmare spirits in Teutonic and Slavic mythology.
[Leach 1972]

Mardeq Avalon
Slavic; Russia, *Cheremis*
Weather
   Wind goddess. She was worshiped in oak and birch groves.
[Monaghan 1990]

Mardez-awa
Slavic; Russia, *Cheremis*
Weather
   Mother of the wind. [Leach 1972]

Marena
Slavic; Russia
Time; Earth and Nature
   Goddess of winter and the earth. Equivalent to Polish
Marzana. [Monaghan 1981]

Marjatta
Finno-Ugric; Finland
Mother and Guardian; Magic
   Virgin goddess. Her story in the *Kalevala,* the Finnish national epic, shows the overlapping of the earlier religions and Christianity.

   The virgin Marjatta swallows a cranberry and conceives a son. After the birth, Vainamoinen comes to see about this occurrence and suggests that the child is ill-omened and should be put to death. The child is able to speak and tells Vainamoinen his sentence is unjust. Marjatta's son is then baptized as the king of Karelia. Vainamoinen departs, leaving behind his heroic songs and declaring he will come again and be useful to his people. [Leach 1972]

Maruchi
Slavic; Russia
Household Affairs; Small Size
   A tiny old woman. She spins thread while sitting on the stove late at night. [Dexter 1990]

Mary-rusalka
Slavic; Russia
Hunting and Wild Animals; Earth and Nature; Wild Birds
   Tree goddess, mistress of animals and birds. Also a spinner. The Mary-rusalka and the *Virgin Mary* of Near East are closely intertwined (in numerous icons, the Virgin Mary is repesented in association with the tree of life [see also *Honoured High Mistress*]). Mary-rusalka's festival, *Rusalia,* is celebrated in conjunction with Christian Trinity Day. Both Mary-rusalka and the *Virgin Mary* (of the Near East) are associated with the birch tree and water. [Hubbs 1988]

Marzana
Slavic; Poland
Time; Earth and Nature; Destroyer of Life; Ceremonies
   Goddess of winter and the earth. Considered by some to be a goddess of death. Her effigy was carried through the village and thrown away on the outskirts. This was done either to welcome spring or after a death. Equivalent to Russian *Marena.* [Frazer 1959; Monaghan 1981]

Marzyana
Slavic; Poland
Agriculture
   Goddess of grain. She presides over the harvest and is identified with Greek *Demeter.* [Jobes 1962]

Maslenitsa
Slavic; Russia
Agriculture; Ceremonies
   Fertility goddess. Her festival at the winter solstice is also called *Maslenitsa.* In some areas, a doll-like representation of Maslenitsa is carried through the village and taken to the fields, where it is pulled apart and burned or scattered as food for the new growth. [Hubbs 1988]

Mastor-ava
Finno-Ugric, *Erya, Moksha, Mordvin*
Earth and Nature; Health and Healing; Agriculture
   Earth mother. She is invoked for health and a good harvest. Said to be a form of *Azer-ava.* See also *Avas.* [Leach 1972; Leach 1992; Monaghan 1981]

Mat' Syra Zemlya   See *Mati-syra-zemlya.*

Māte
Slavic; Latvia
Mother and Guardian

"Mother." It is used with other words to form the names of goddesses. [Lurker 1984]

Matergabia
Slavic
Household Affairs; Ceremonies
   "Womanfire." Household goddess. She presides over the house and its care. She is offered the first piece of bread after it has been kneaded. Alternate form: Matergabiae. [Guirand 1968; Leach 1992; Monaghan 1990]

Matergabiae   See *Matergabia.*

Mati-syra-zemlya
Slavic; Russia
Earth and Nature; Mother and Guardian; Health and Healing; Luck; Justice; Ceremonies; Agriculture
   "Mother Moist Earth." Earth goddess and protector from misfortune and illness. She also settles disputes and witnesses oaths. In some parts of Russia, breaking the earth before the March 25 is prohibited, to prevent injury to the "pregnant earth." There is still a ritual where farmers pray to Mother Moist Earth. At dawn they offer prayers to each of the four cardinal directions, pouring hemp oil on the fields as they ask her to subdue all evil things, to overcome the power in the boiling earth and burning fires, to calm the south winds that bring whirlwinds and sand, and the north winds that bring the snow and cold. Finally, they break the jar in which they carried the hemp oil by throwing it on the ground. Alternate form: Mat' Syra Zemlya. [Carlyon 1982; Durdin-Robertson 1982; Hubbs 1988; Leach 1972; Leach 1992; Gimbutas 1971; Preston 1982; Savill 1977; Senior 1985]

Matrioshka
Slavic; Russia
Mother and Guardian
   Early mother goddess who has been carried into the present in the form of the Matrioshka doll, considered by some to be a debasement of the deity. She is identified with *Mokosh.* [Hubbs 1988]

Mauthia
Slavic; Albania
Unknown
   Name for *Amalthea,* Greek and Roman Empires. [Eliade 1987]

Mavje, The   See *Navki.*

Mavky, The   See *Navki.*

Medeine
Slavic; Lithuania
Earth and Nature
   Forest goddess. [Savill 1977]

Mejdejn
Slavic; Baltic
Earth and Nature
   Goddess of the woods. [Leach 1992]

Melande-awa
Slavic; Russia, *Cheremis*
Earth and Nature
   "Mother of the Earth." [Leach 1972; Leach 1992]

Mengk, The
Slavic, *Ostyak, Northern, Vogul*
Evil; Earth and Nature

Evil forest spirits. They cause mischief to people disturbing them. [Archaeological Institute 1916–1932]

Mera-māte
Slavic; Latvia
Destroyer of Life
   "Plague Mother." One of the seventy sisters of *Zeme.* [Eliade 1987; Lurker 1984]

Mere-ama
Finno-Ugric; Finland, *Saami*
Fishing and Water Animals
   "Sea Mother." She also manifests in fresh water. She presides over the reproduction of plants and animals, including fish. Alternate forms: Mier-iema, Vete-ema. [Monaghan 1981]

Mereneiu   See *Näkineiu.*

Merenneito   See *Näkki.*

Meschamaat
Slavic; Latvia
Earth and Nature; Love and Sexuality; Destroyer of Life
   Forest goddess. Her love can be fatal to mortals. Similar to *Lesni Zenka.* [Jobes 1962; Leach 1992]

Metsânneitsyt
Finno-Ugric; Finland, *Saami*
Earth and Nature; Beauty; Ugliness
   "Forest Virgin." Equivalent to Swedish *Skogsjungfru.*
   ❀ *When Metsânneitsyt appears to humans, she is a beautiful, well-dressed woman. But if one can catch a glimpse of her from behind, she looks like a stump or bundle of twigs.*
   See also *Ganis* and *Tava-ajk.* Alternate form: Matsanneitsyt. [Jobes 1962; Leach 1972]

Metsarhatija
Finno-Ugric; Finland
Earth and Nature
   Forest goddess. [Monaghan 1990]

Metsola Mother
Finno-Ugric
Earth and Nature; Mother and Guardian
   Forest goddess. [Guirand 1968]

Meža-māte
Slavic; Latvia
Earth and Nature; Mother and Guardian
   "Mother of the Forest." Associated with *Veja Mate.* One of the seventy sisters of *Zeme.* [Eliade 1987; Lurker 1984]

Mielikki
Finno-Ugric; Finland, *Saami*
Earth and Nature; Hunting and Wild Animals; Ceremonies
   "Friendly." Goddess of the forest who is invoked to opprotect and provide game. Wife of Tapio, god of the forest, and mother of *Tuulikki* and Nyyrikki, who are also forest deities. Her feast day is September 23, when the leaves are beginning to turn to gold. Alternate forms: Mielus, Mieulutar, and Mimerkki. [Durdin-Robertson 1982; Guirand 1968; Leach 1972; Stone 1979]

Mielus   See *Mielikki.*

Mier-iema   See *Mere-ama.*

Mieulutar   See *Mielikki.*

Minceskro
Slavic; Transylvania, *Gypsy*
Destroyer of Life
   Demon who causes blood-related diseases. Her children cause smallpox, scarlet fever, and measles. [Leach 1992]

Miren, The   See *The Fatit.*

Mis-khum
Slavic; Siberia
Earth and Nature; Charisma; Luck
   Forest spirit. Her daughters entice young men to live with them. If the men stay in the forest, good fortune comes to their fathers. [Leach 1992]

Mokos   See *Mokosi.*

Mokosh
Slavic; Russia
Water; Earth and Nature; Sky and Heavens; Household Affairs; Fishing and Water Animals; Ceremonies; Metals and Minerals; Weather; Selflessness
   "Moist." She is related to the waters of the sky and the earth, to fertility of the Earth and its inhabitants, to spinning and weaving, and to fishing. Her worship survived into Christian times, and in Christian writings of the sixteenth century, there were complaints that Slavic women still ceremonially honored Mokosh. She is represented by stones, especially those that are breast-shaped, and she is mentioned in the Kievan pantheon. The Czechs prayed to her in time of drought because rain was considered Mokosh's milk. In northern Russia she has survived as a female house deity called *Mokusha* or *Mokysha*, and in the Olonets area, when sheep lose their hair, it is Mokosh who has been out at night spinning. She was later transformed into the East Slavic goddess *Paraskeva* and then *Saint Paraskeva.* She is identified with *Moksha* and *Matrioshka.* See also *Mokosi.* Alternate form: Mokuskha. [Eliade 1987; Gimbutas 1971; Hubbs 1988; Leach 1992; Monaghan 1981]

Mokosi
Slavic; Russia
Mother and Guardian; Domesticated Animals; Selflessness
   "The Moist." Goddess of the official Kievan pantheon. Protector of semen, she presides over childbearing and sheep-breeding. Possibly a name for *Mati-syra-zemlja.* Her functions were transferred to the *Virgin Mary*, Near East, but she is still adored in popular Russian tradition. Closely related to Iranian *Ardvi Sura Anahita.* See also *Mokosh.* Alternate form: Mokos. [Leach 1972; Leach 1992; Lurker 1984]

Moksha
Finno-Ugric; Finland, *Saami*
Mother and Guardian; Ceremonies
   "Giver of Life." She is worshiped in the forests, where there are hollow statues of her. She is portrayed holding a child. Identified with *Mokosh.* [Hubbs 1988]

Mokusa   See *Mokuskha.*

Mokusha   See *Mokuskha.*

Mokuskha
Slavic; Russia
Household Affairs; Ceremonies
   Name for *Mokosh* as a household goddess of spinning.
   ❀ *During Lent, Mokuskha wanders the countryside as a woman. She visits houses, guarding and fleecing sheep herself. Offerings of strands of fleece are laid beside stoves for her.*

Alternate forms: Mokusa, Mokusha. [Durdin-Robertson 1982; Monaghan 1981]

Mora
Slavic
Fate

"Fate." In her death aspect she was a tall white woman who was a shape-changer. When plague was present, she was a slim black woman with long breasts, snake eyes, and cow or horse legs. Similar to *Kuga* and *Chuma*. Alternate forms: Marà, Smert. [Eliade 1987]

Morana
Slavic; Bohemia
Time; Destroyer of Life

Goddess of winter and death. Equivalent to *Hecate*, Greek and Roman Empires. [Bonnerjea 1927; Jobes 1962; Leach 1992]

Mor-ava
Slavic; Russia, *Mordvin*
Water

Sea mother. Equivalent to *Azer-ava*. [Leach 1992; Monaghan 1981]

Moravaya Panna
Slavic
Destroyer of Life

"Black Woman." Goddess of disease. A demon of pestilence who disguises herself as a woman covered in black. [Bonnerjea 1927; Jobes 1962]

Mother Friday   See *Paraskeva*.

Mother of Mannu   See *Mannu*.

Mother of Metsola
Finno-Ugric
Earth and Nature

Goddess of the forest. [Guirand 1968]

Muksort
"Bee Soul." See *Neškeper-ava*.

Mukylcin
Slavic; Russia, *Votyak*
Agriculture

"Earth Wife" of Keremet.

 Once when the Woytaks (Votyaks) of Malmyz were having poor harvests, they decided their god needed a wife. After discussing the matter with the Woytaks of Cura, they went to the sacred grove of Cura and cut a piece of sod to give to their god as a wife. Things went better for Malmyz but got worse for Cura. [Frazer 1959]

Munya
Slavic
Weather; Fire

Goddess of lightning. [Leach 1992]

Murava
Finno-Ugric, *Wend*
Magic

A witch, a child born with a tooth. See also *Drude*. [Leach 1972]

Muzem-mumi   See *Muzem-mumy*.

Muzem-mumy
Slavic; Russia, *Votyak*
Earth and Nature

"Mother of the Earth." Alternate forms: Muzem-mumi, Muzjem-mumi. [Guirand 1968; Leach 1972; Stone 1979]

Muzjem-mumi   See *Muzem-mumy*.

Myesyats
Slavic; Serbia
Moon and Night; Time

Moon goddess.

At the beginning of summer, Myesyats is young and beautiful, and the sun marries her. Their children, the stars, fill the night sky. As the year progresses, her husband moves farther to the south, and Myesyats must wait until spring to enjoy his company once again. [Carlyon 1982; Dexter 1990; Leach 1992; Savill 1977; Senior 1985]

Nagyboldogasszony   See *Boldogasszony*.

Najade
Slavic
Water

Water spirit. [Baumgartner 1984]

Nâkineitsi   See *Näkineiu*.

Nâkineiu
Finno-Ugric; Estonia
Water; Beauty

"Näkki's Maid." Water spirit who is a pretty young girl with long golden yellow or grass-green hair. Sometimes she is naked, other times dressed; sometimes she is fully human and other times she has a fish tail.

Näkineiu sits by the water, running a golden comb through her hair. She sings sweet songs that are wonderful to hear and keeps an eye on her herd of cattle under the water.

See also *Näkki* and *Näkinneito*. Alternate forms: Mereneiu, Näkineitsi, Veeneiu. [Archaeological Institute 1916–1932]

Nâkinneito
Finno-Ugric; Finland, *Saami*
Water; Beauty

Water spirit. Portrayed as a beautiful white-skinned woman with long curly hair. Her breasts are so pendulous and large that she can throw them over her shoulders, a trait of water deities in many cultures. She keeps cattle under the water. See also *Näkineiu* and *Näkki*. [Leach 1972]

Nâkinpiika   "Näkki maid." See *Näkki*.

Nâkki
Finno-Ugric; Estonia
Water; Magic; Beauty; Domesticated Animals; Fishing and Water Animals

"Water Maid." In Österbotten, she is a beautiful woman with a shiny white body and very long curly hair. On the coast and in Nyland, she has large breasts that she throws over her shoulders when busy. She is always busy washing herself, combing her hair, playing in the water, washing her clothes, or watching the cattle near the beach. See also *Näkineiu* and *Näkinneito*. Alternate forms: Merenneito, Näkinpiika, Vedenemäntä, Vedenneito. [Archaeological Institute 1916–1932]

Nalban-aiy

Slavic; Siberia, *Yakut*

Goodness; Creator of Life; Sky and Heavens

Benevolent creator and sky goddess. Alternate form: Kubay-khotun-la. [Leach 1992]

Nalygyr-aissyt-khotun

Slavic; Siberia, *Yakut*

Goodness; Sky and Heavens; Mother and Guardian

Benevolent sky goddess and goddess of childbirth. [Leach 1992]

Nan

Slavic, *Abkhasian*

Creator of Life

Caucasus procreation goddess. [Leach 1992]

Nar-azerava

Slavic; Russia, *Mordvin*

Earth and Nature

Meadow spirit. A form of *Azer-ava*. [Leach 1992; Monaghan 1981]

Narechnitsa

Slavic; Bulgaria

Fate; Mother and Guardian

Fate and birth goddess. Equivalent to Russian *Rozhenitsa*. [Eliade 1987]

Narucnici, The

Slavic; Bulgaria

Fate; Mother and Guardian

Goddesses of fate. Appearing as old women dressed in white, they attend births, announcing the fate of the newborn. Fate goddesses are called *Rodjenice* in Croatia, *Sojenice* in Slovenia, *Sudicky* in Bohemia, *Sudice* in Poland, and *Sudjenice* in Serbia, Slovenia, and Croatia. See also *Fatit*, *Ore*, and *Urme*. Alternate forms: Orisnici, Suzenici, Udelnicy, Uresici, Urisnici. [Jobes 1962; Leach 1992; Monaghan 1981]

Nastasija

Slavic; Russia, *Mordvin*

Health and Healing

Goddess of sleep. [Leach 1992]

Näves-mäte

Slavic; Latvia

Destroyer of Life

"Mother of Death." One of the seventy sisters of *Zeme*. [Eliade 1987]

Navi, The   See *The Navki*.

Navki, The

Slavic

Immortality; Destroyer of Life; Ugliness; Evil

Malevolent spirits of the dead. They are said to be the souls of children who died at birth or of pregnant women who died violent deaths. They confuse people, causing them to drown, or attack women in childbirth. Said by some to be hideous and hairy. Another name for the *Rusalki*. Alternate forms: Faraony, Majky, Mavje, Mavky, Nejky, Navi, Navky, Novjaci, Vodianiani. [Hubbs 1988; Jobes 1962; Monaghan 1981]

Navky   See *The Navki*.

Nay-Ekva

Slavic; Siberia, *Masi*

Fire

Goddess of fire. Sister of Numi-Torum (Numi-Tarem), god of the upperworld. [Leach 1992]

Nedolya

Slavic; Russia; Serbia

Ugliness; Evil; Luck

Malevolent shape-changing spirit represented as an ugly and poor woman. She bestows bad luck. See also *Dolya*. Alternate form: Nesreča. [Eliade 1987]

Nejky, The   See *The Navki*.

Nelaima

Slavic; Latvia

Fate

"Misfortune." Goddess of destiny. The opposite of *Laima*, or her negative aspect. [Leach 1992]

Nemodilky, The

Slavic; Bohemia; Czechoslovakia

Water; Beauty; Charisma

Water spirits.

In Czechoslovakia, the Nemodilky, dressed in red, go out at night searching for young men. When the beautiful maidens with coal-black hair and white skin find them, they entice the men to their underwater world. [Bonnerjea 1927]

Neske-pas

Slavic; Russia, *Mordvin, Erya*

Insects

Goddess (or god) of the beehives. [Leach 1992]

Neŭkeper-ava

Slavic; Russia, *Moksha Mordvin*

Insects

"Bee Garden Mother." Protector of the bees. Alternate form: Muksort. [Archaeological Institute 1916–1932; Jobes 1962; Leach 1992]

Nesreča

Slavic; Russia; Serbia

Fate; Evil; Luck

Slavic malevolent personal fate goddess. If one knows the proper procedure, she can be driven away. Said to be *Sreča* disguised so she can bring bad luck. Alternate form: Nedolya. [Dexter 1990; Eliade 1987; Leach 1992; Monaghan 1981]

Nishke-ava

Slavic; Russia, *Cheremis*

Mother and Guardian; Household Affairs; Selflessness

"Great Birthgiving Mother." Probably equivalent to *Azer-ava* of the Moksha Mordvins. Alternate form: Ine-shki-ava. [Archaeological Institute 1916–1932]

Niski-ava

Slavic; Russia, *Mordvin*

Mother and Guardian; Household Affairs; Selflessness

Goddess of women. Worshiped by women in the privacy of their homes. She has become confused with the *Virgin Mary* of Near East. A form of *Azer-ava*. [Monaghan 1981]

Nocnitsa

Slavic; Russia; Poland; Serbia; Slovakia

Evil; Mother and Guardian; Ceremonies

"Night Hag." Nightmare deity. Mothers place a knife in the cradle or put an axe and a doll under the floor beneath the cradle to keep this creature away. Equivalent to Bulgarian *Gorska Makva*. Alternate forms: Kriksy, Plaksy. [Leach 1972]

Norov-ava
Slavic; Russia, *Mordvin, Erya*
Agriculture
   Goddess (or god) of corn. A form of *Azer-ava*. Alternate form: Norov-Pas. [Leach 1992; Monaghan 1981]

Norov-pas   See *Norov-ava.*

Novjaci, The   See *The Navki.*

Numod-emei
Slavic; Siberia, *Yukaghir*
Household Affairs; Health and Healing
   Deity of the house. She is invoked by the shaman when someone needs healing. [Leach 1992]

Nuset-i-malit, The
Slavic; Albania
Earth and Nature
   Mountain spirits. Equivalent to Greek *Oreadai.* [Eliade 1987]

Obyda
Slavic; Siberia, *Chuvash*
Earth and Nature
   Evil forest spirit. She is naked, with long hair and large nipples. Her feet are turned backward. She makes people lose their way and then tickles or dances them to death. See also *Ovda.* [Archaeological Institute 1916–1932]

Ogu-mäte
Slavic; Latvia
Earth and Nature
   "Berry Mother." One of the seventy sisters of *Zeme.* [Eliade 1987; Lurker 1984]

Ohyn
Finno-Ugric, *Kasubian*
Magic
   Witch or vampire, a child born with a tooth. See also *Drude* and *Mur-ava.* [Leach 1972]

Ojid-emei
Slavic; Siberia, *Yukaghir*
Mother and Guardian; Water
   "Water Mother." She is invoked to guide people safely on the river during the spring thaw. [Leach 1992]

Onmun-emei
Slavic; Siberia, *Yukaghir*
Water
   River goddess. She is both the owner and the mother of the Kolyma river. [Leach 1992]

Ora
Slavic; Albania
Mother and Guardian
   Protective spirit. She accompanies each individual from birth to death. Her visage is white if the person is brave and industrious, black if the person is cowardly and lazy. [Lurker 1984]

Orans
Slavic; Ukraine
Insects
   Paleolithic goddess. A figurine of a bull-horned goddess in the form of a bee was found in Cucuteni (Tripol'e) in the northwestern Ukraine. This image is also found in Russian embroidery today. [Hubbs 1988]

Ore, The
Slavic; Albania
Fate; Mother and Guardian; Goodness
   Benevolent goddesses of fate. They attend all births. [Eliade 1987]

Orisnici, The   See *The Narucnici.*

Orokannar, The   See *The Amagandar.*

Orsel   See *Ursula.*

Os Keca Aba   "White Sun Mother." See *Keca Aba.*

Ot
Slavic; Siberia, *Khakass, Mongol*
Goodness; Fire; Family and Tribes; Ceremonies
   Benevolent goddess of fire. She gives protective warmth and is worshiped at marriage ceremonies. See also *Ot,* Far East. [Leach 1992]

Ot-ânâ
Slavic; Siberia
Fire; Mother and Guardian; Household Affairs
   Goddess of fire in the Altai region. She is a protective spirit with whom the family shares a part of each meal. [Leach 1992]

Otsuved-azer-ava
Slavic; Russia, *Mordvin, Moksha*
Water
   Ruler of the Earth and all its inhabitants. The spirit of moisture, she resides in different forms in all bodies of water. Sacrifices are offered to her by the entire village during agricultural ceremonies. A form of Russian *Azer-ava.* Alternate forms: Ot's'uved-azerava, Ved-ava. [Leach 1992; Monaghan 1981]

Ot's'uved-azerava   See *Otsuved-azer-ava.*

Otygen
Siberia
Earth and Nature
   Mother earth. She is also worshiped in Mongolia. See also *Otygen,* Far East. [Jobes 1962; Leach 1992]

Ovda
Finno-Ugric; Finland, *Chuvash, Volga Finn*
Earth and Nature; Destroyer of Life; Evil
   Evil forest spirit who also lives in rocky outcroppings and in the ruins of old castles.
   She is naked with long hair, her feet are turned backward, and she has such large breasts that she must throw them over her shoulders. Ovda wanders through the woods, sometimes like a whirlwind bending trees to the ground, looking for people to tickle to death. She can be overcome if the victim can find the hole in her left armpit and stick a finger in it.
   See also *Obyda* and *Šurali.* Alternate form: Alvasta. [Archaeological Institute 1916–1932; Monaghan 1981]

Oynyena Maria
Slavic
Fire
   "Fiery Mary." Slavic fire goddess who was eventually subordinated to the thunder god. She became the god's counselor and assistant. [Sykes 1968]

Paduri   See *Illibem Berti.*

Paivatar
Finno-Ugric
Household Affairs
   Goddess of spinning. Daughter of the sun. [Guirand 1968]

Paive   See *Beiwe*.

Paks-av
Slavic; Russia, *Mordvin, Moksha*
Agriculture
   "Mother Field." Goddess of agriculture. [Leach 1992]

Panike
Slavic; Prussia
Fire
   Goddess of fire. [Leach 1992]

Paraskeva
Slavic; Russia
Creator of Life; Time; Selflessness
   "Friday." Fertility goddess associated with spinning, water, health, and marriage. She was officially adopted by the Christian Church as *Saint Paraskeva*. She was a deity of an earlier religion accommodated by the church because of her popularity. Alternate forms: Paraskeva Griaznaia, Paraskeva Piatnitsa. [Eliade 1987; Hubbs 1988]

Paraskeva Griaznaia
   "Muddy." Name for *Paraskeva*.

Paraskeva Piatnitsa   See *Paraskeva*.

Percunatele
Slavic; Poland
Weather
   "Mother of Thunder." [Leach 1992]

Pereplut
Slavic; Balkan
Luck; Agriculture
   Goddess of changing fortune. Also called a goddess of drink. [Baumgartner 1984; Leach 1992]

Perit, The
Slavic; Albania
Earth and Nature; Justice; Health and Healing; Time
   Albanian mountain spirits.

 The Perit, dressed in white, make an appearance if bread is being wasted. They punish the guilty parties by making them hunchbacked.
   See also Egyptian *Perit*. [Durdin-Robertson 1982; Lurker 1984]

Perke
Finno-Ugric
Mother and Guardian
   "Success." Birth deity. [Archaeological Institute 1916–1932]

Perkune Tete
Slavic; Balkan
Weather; Fire; Stars and Planets; Sun and Day
   Goddess of thunder and lightning. Identified with the planet Venus.

 Each night Perkune Tete receives the sun. She returns it to the sky the next morning, bathed and shining. [Archaeological Institute 1916–1932; Jobes 1962; Leach 1992]

P'erna-azor-ava
Slavic; Russia, *Mordvin*
Insects; Ceremonies

Hostess of the keeper of the bees. To honor P'erna-azor-avar she is always given the first taste of honey at the harvest. [Eliade 1987]

Piegulas māte
Slavic; Latvia
Mother and Guardian; Moon and Night
   "Mother of the Night Watch." Protective deity and one of the seventy sisters of *Zeme*. [Eliade 1987]

Pilnitis   See *Piluitus*.

Piluitus
Slavic; Latvia; Lithuania; Prussia
Agriculture; Health and Healing
   Goddess of fertility. She presides over agriculture, harvests, and healing. Sometimes considered a male deity. Alternate forms: Pilnitis, Piluuytis, Pilwittus. [Leach 1992]

Piluuytis   See *Piluitus*.

Pilwittus   See *Piluitus*.

Pirts-māte
Slavic; Latvia; Lithuania
Mother and Guardian; Ceremonies
   "Sauna Mother." She is invoked for an easy childbirth. Offerings of a whisk and clean water are left for her in the sauna. One of the seventy sisters of *Zeme*. [Eliade 1987]

Plaksy   See *Kriksy, Nocnitsa*.

Pogoda
Slavic
Weather; Agriculture; Ceremonies
   "Giver of a Favorable Wind." Weather and agricultural goddess. Those engaged in agriculture make sacrifices of cattle and sheep to her. Also a male deity. [Leach 1992; Redfield 1931]

Pohjan-akka
Finno-Ugric; Lapland, *Saami*
Heaven and Hell
   Goddess of Pohjan (hell). Condemned to live deep in the Arctic Ocean with Pohjan-akka are those who have died violent deaths. [Monaghan 1981]

Poldunica
Slavic; Russia
Agriculture; Evil; Time; Order; Sun and Day
   "Noon." Field spirit. She is also found in other Slavic countries. She is accused of killing children or of causing them to become lost if they are left alone at midday.

 A beautiful girl dressed in white walks about the fields at noon during harvest time. If she finds anyone still working, she stops them by roughly pulling their hair.
   In Serbia she is called *Pszepolnica*. See also *Polednice* and *Zitna-atka*. Alternate forms: Polednica, Poludnitsa, Poludnitza, Prez-poludnica. [Bonnerjea 1927; Carlyon 1982; Durdin-Robertson 1982; Jobes 1962; Lurker 1984; Monaghan 1981; Savill 1977]

Polednica   See *Poldunica*.

Polednice, The
Slavic; Bohemia
Evil; Time; Weather; Sun and Day
   Midday spirits who steal children. Also said to be singular, a whirlwind demon. See also *Poldunica*. [Bonnerjea 1927; Leach 1992]

Polengabia
Slavic; Lithuania
Fire; Household Affairs
"Bright Hearth." Goddess of fire. [Leach 1992]

Polevik See *Polevoi*.

Polevoi
Slavic; Russia
Agriculture
Field spirit. Her hair is as green as grass. Alternate form:
Polevik. [Savill 1977]

Pūlūznitsa
Finno-Ugric, *Siryan*
Agriculture; Justice
Goddess of rye. She punishes those who injure the plant as
it is flowering. Like the Russian *Poludnica*, she does not like
to see children left alone at home at midday. [Hubbs 1988;
Jobes 1962]

Poludnitsa See *Poldunica*.

Poludnitsy, The
Slavic; Ukraine
Moon and Night; Agriculture; Wealth
Moon maidens. They see that the sun's rays cause the
fields to be fertile. May be identified with the *Rusalki*.
[Hubbs 1988]

Poludnitza See *Poldunica*.

Ponyke
Slavic; Lithuania
Fire
Fire goddess. [Leach 1992]

Pūrt-kuva
Slavic; Russia, *Cheremis*
Fate; Household Affairs; Luck; Health and Healing; Mother
and Guardian; Wealth; Ceremonies
"House Woman." A fate goddess who makes herself visible
when illness or disaster is about to strike. If she is angry, she
can bring misfortune to the family, even cause illness. If
properly propitiated, she is happy and protects the home
from robbers, fire, and spirits of sickness, and she can bring
prosperity. In some areas, families leave beer, porridge,
bread, or pancakes under the floor of the house in autumn for
Pört-kuva and Pört-kuguza ("House Man"). When a new
house is occupied, the two are worshiped by the new owners
with bread and pancakes. [Archaeological Institute
1916–1932; Monaghan 1981]

Poshjo-akka
Slavic; Scandinavia, *Saami*
Hunting and Wild Animals
"She Permits Shooting." Goddess of the hunt. Skulls of
the butchered animals are buried at her feet in the storage
hut. If the skulls are not properly buried, the animals do not
reincarnate. [Monaghan 1990]

Possjo-akka
Finno-Ugric; Lapland, *Saami*
Household Affairs
Goddess of the back part of the house called the *kata*.
[Leach 1992]

Pots-hozjik
Slavic; Russia; Finno-Ugric; Lapland
Hunting and Wild Animals

"Reindeer Mistress." Equivalent to *Luot-hozjik*. [Archae-
ological Institute 1916–1932; Jobes 1962]

Poza-mama
Slavic; Siberia, *Amur Ulchi*
Fire
"Mistress of the Fire." [Leach 1992]

Prende
Slavic; Albania
Love and Sexuality; Selflessness; Beauty; Ceremonies; Time
Illyrian goddess of love. Partner of the god of thunder.
Now given the status of saint, Saint Prende is still considered
the "Queen of Beauty." Friday is her sacred day, a day sacred
to many of the early goddesses. Alternate form: Prenne.
[Lurker 1984]

Prenne See *Prende*.

Prez-poludnica See *Poldunica*.

Psezpolnica
Slavic; Serbia
Time; Agriculture; Disorder; Sun and Day
Midday goddess. Equivalent to *Poldunica*. She appears
during harvest time, driving people mad during the hottest
part of the day. [Lurker 1984]

Ptitsy-siriny
Slavic; Russia
Wild Birds
"Bird Maiden." She is associated with vegetation and
animal life. [Hubbs 1988]

Pu'gud-emei
Slavic; Siberia, *Yukaghir*
Sun and Day; Mother and Guardian
"Sun Mother." She provides warmth and protection from
evil. [Leach 1992]

Puges
Slavic, *Ostyak, Vogul*
Mother and Guardian; Fate; Heaven and Hell; Immortality
"Daughter of the Heaven God."

To reach her house in heaven, one must cross seven seas
and climb the mountain of seven stories. She lives in a
golden house with seven cradles hanging from the roof.
When she rocks one of these cradles seven times, a soul is created,
but if the cradle overturns, the soul will not live long.
In the area around Surgut, she is called *Vagneg-imi*.
[Archaeological Institute 1916–1932]

Puirsho
Slavic, *Turco-Tartar*
Creator of Life
"Procreator." Birth deity. [Archaeological Institute
1916–1932]

Pyatnitsa Prascovia
Slavic; Russia
Agriculture; Order; Ceremonies; Time; Justice
Goddess of the harvest. Equivalent to *Seewa*.

Women must not sew, spin, or weave on her ceremonial
day, Friday. If they do, dust may get in their eyes and
bring on the sore-eye curse. [Jobes 1962; Leach 1992]

Queen of the Grain
Slavic; Bulgaria
Agriculture; Ceremonies

Images are made of her out of stalks of grain or straw. [Eliade 1987]

Radegasta
Slavic
War
   War goddess. Similar to Roman *Bellona.* [Wedeck 1971]

Radien-akka
Finno-Ugric, *Saami*
Mother and Guardian
   "Mother." One of the trinity of deities that also includes the child and father. [Monaghan 1990]

Radien-kiedde
Finno-Ugric, *Saami*
Creator of Life
   Creator goddess who gave souls to the mother goddess *Maddarakka* to be made human. [Monaghan 1990]

Ragana
Slavic; Lithuania
Magic; Fishing and Water Animals
   Goddess of clairvoyance. Counterpart of the god Velinas when he is the god of clairvoyance, Ragius. Similar to Russian *Baba Yaga.* Ragana incarnates as a toad. [Eliade 1987; Leach 1992]

Rana Nedia
Finno-Ugric; Lapland, *Saami*
Time; Sky and Heavens; Earth and Nature; Hunting and Wild Animals; Household Affairs
   "Rana Virgin." Goddess of spring. From her heavenly home, she presides over the mountains, making them green and providing moss for the reindeer. Her sacred object is the spinning wheel, and sacrifices are made to her by putting blood on it and leaning it against her altar. Alternate form: Bana-neidda. [Archaeological Institute 1916–1932; Jobes 1962; Leach 1992; Monaghan 1990]

Rana-neidda   See *Rana Nedia.*

Ratainicza
Slavic; Lithuania; Prussia
Domesticated Animals
   Guardian of horses and their stables. Also considered a male deity. Alternate form: Ratainitsa. [Leach 1992]

Ratainitsa   See *Ratainicza.*

Raudna
Finno-Ugric; Lapland, *Saami*
Earth and Nature
   "Rowan," the mountain ash tree. May be related to, or the same as, *Rauni.* [Lurker 1984]

Rauni
Finno-Ugric; Finland, *Saami*
Weather; Earth and Nature; Ceremonies
   "Thunder." Wife of Ukko. She manifests in the rowan tree (mountain ash) and its berries. Reindeer are sacrificed in her honor. She is similar to Norse *Idun* (see Northern Europe). May be related to or the same as *Raudna.*
   Rauni had intercourse with the thunder god, Ukko. From this union came all the plants that grow on the Earth.
   Alternate forms: Akko, Maan-eno, Ravdna, Röönikkä. [Leach 1972; Monaghan 1981; Stone 1979]

Rav-ava
Slavic; Russia, *Mordvin*
Water
   "Mother Volga." River goddess. [Leach 1992]

Ravdna
Finno-Ugric; Finland, *Saami*
Weather; Ceremonies
   "Thunder." In sacred mountain grottoes, reindeer are offered to her. Her favorite tree is the rowan. Alternate forms: Röönikkä, Rauni. [Archaeological Institute 1916–1932; Leach 1992]

Raz-ajk
Slavic; Russia, *Saami*
Earth and Nature
   "Grass Mother" on the Kola Peninsula. [Leach 1992]

Rigiu Boba
Slavic; Lithuania
Agriculture; Ceremonies
   "Old One of the Rye." A representation of her is made from the last sheaf of the harvest. [Leach 1992; Savill 1977]

Risem-edne
Finno-Ugric; Norway, *Saami*
Earth and Nature
   "Twig Mother." [Monaghan 1990]

Rodienitsa   See *Rozhenitsa.*

Rodjenice, The
Slavic; Croatia; Serbia; Slovenia
Fate; Mother and Guardian; Ceremonies
   Fate goddesses. They are said to be deceased mothers. Like the Greek *Fates,* there are three who attend each birth, one spinning, one measuring, and one cutting the thread of life. They are propitiated with the leftovers of the christening feast. Also considered a singular goddess who is one of the three fates along with *Sudnice* and *Sudjenice.* Similar to *Rozanice* and *Rozdenici.* See also *The Narucnici.* Alternate form: Rojenice. [Dexter 1990; Jobes 1962; Leach 1992; Monaghan 1981]

Rodnaia Matushka
Slavic; Russia
Sun and Day; Mother and Guardian
   "Birth Mother." Sun goddess. [Hubbs 1988]

Rojenice, The   See *The Rodjenice.*

Rüünikkâ   See *Rauni.*

Rüugutaja
Finno-Ugric; Estonia
Mother and Guardian
   Birth goddess. [Archaeological Institute 1916–1932]

Rozanice
Slavic; Russia
Fate; Ceremonies
   Fate goddess. She is propitiated with bread, honey, and cheese. Similar to *Rodjenice.* [Leach 1992]

Rozdenici
Slavic; Bulgaria
Fate
   She determines the fate, the time of death, and how each child will die. See *Rodjenice.* [Leach 1992]

Rozenitsa   See *Rozhenitsa*.

Rozhanitsy, The
Slavic
Mother and Guardian; Fate; War
    Guardians of life-giving waters. They are also fate
goddesses and protectors of warriors. Similar to *Rusalka*.
[Hubbs 1988]

Rozhdenitsa   See *Rozhenitsa*.

Rozhenitsa
Slavic; Russia
Mother and Guardian
    "Birth Giver." She determines the fate of newborn children.
Alternate forms: Rodienitsa, Rozenitsa, Rozhdenitsa. [Dexter
1990; Eliade 1987]

Rusalka, The
Slavic; Russia
Water; Life/Death Cycle; Weather; Immortality; Creator of
Life; Ceremonies; Reptiles
    Water spirits. Personification of the regeneration and
rebirth of nature. They rule the sky, the Earth, and all of
their inhabitants. Said to be spirits of unbaptized children
or drowned maidens who remain forever young and free.
They are involved in the fertility of the forests, fields,
And humans. Usually considered beneficent, they can be
dangerous to humans. They must be propitiated with bread
and salt, or evil will befall the community. The Rusalka are
water snakes that are "milked" for rain. Their hair is like that
of *Medusa*—a tangle of serpents. When the Rusalka are angry
with their followers, they are sometimes overzealous in
combing their wet locks and thereby cause floods.
    *Rusalka live a double existence, aquatic and silvan. At the
beginning of summer, they live in water. During Rusalka
Week they emerge from the water and go into the forest.
They choose a weeping willow or birch with long slim branches that
leans over the river and climb up into it. On moonlit nights, they
swing in the branches, call out to each other, then slip down from
the trees to dance in the clearings.*
    They correspond to the Lapp *Cacce-jienne* (see Northern
Europe). They may be identified with the *Poludnitsy* and are
similar to the *Rozhanitsy* and the *Saiva-neida*. See also
Rusalki-siriny. Alternate forms: Navki, Rusalki, Rusalky.
[Bonnerjea 1927; Durdin-Robertson 1982; Hubbs 1988; Jobes
1962; Leach 1992]

Rusalki, The   See *Rusalka*.

Rusalki-siriny, The
Slavic; Russia
Mother and Guardian; Earth and Nature
    Protective spirits who are amuletic. They are nature
mothers. See also *Rusalka*. [Hubbs 1988]

Rusalky, The   See *Rusalka*.

Russian Mother Earth
Slavic; Russia
Earth and Nature; Life/Death Cycle
    Earth deity.
    *Mother Earth complains to god about the pain she feels
from the labor of men. God tells her not to cry because
eventually she will eat them all.*
    Mother Earth (and her Slavic matriarchal followers) may
have been objecting to the introduction of the plow, cattle,
and the patriarchal society of their Indo-European invaders.
[Preston 1982]

Sabaga
Slavic; Siberia, *Yakut*
Fire
    "Mother of Fire." [Jobes 1962; Leach 1992]

Sadsta-akka
Finno-Ugric; Lapland, *Saami*
Magic; Mother and Guardian
    "Cloven Wood." She brings a magic method for assisting
childbirth to make the delivery easier. [Archaeological
Institute 1916–1932]

Saint Paraskeva   See *Paraskeva*.

Saint Prende   See *Prende*.

Saint Thecla   See *Dekla, Karta*.

Saiva-neida, The
Finno-Ugric, *Saami, Western*
Water; Charisma; Love and Sexuality
    "Sea Maids." They love mortals and entice them to their
watery homes. Similar to the Russian *Rusalka* (see Northern
Europe), Lapp *Cacce-jienne* (see Northern Europe), and
Finnish *Savio-neita*. [Archaeological Institute 1916–1932;
Jobes 1962; Leach 1972]

Saivo-neita
Finno-Ugric; Finland, *Lapp*
    Sea maiden. See also *Saiva-neida*. [Leach 1972]

Sakhala
Slavic; Siberia, *Buriat*
Fire
    She rules fire with her husband Sakhadai (Sakhidai-Noin).
Alternate form: Sakhala-khatun. [Leach 1992]

Sakhala-khatun   See *Sakhala*.

Samovila   See *The Vila*.

Samovily   See *The Vila*.

Sangia-mama
Slavic; Siberia, *Udegeis*
Earth and Nature
    "Mistress of the Earth and the World." She is ruler of the
coniferous forests and their inhabitants, including humans.
[Leach 1992]

Santaramet
Slavic; Armenia
Heaven and Hell
    Goddess of the underworld. [Leach 1992]

Sarakka
Finno-Ugric; Lapland, *Saami*
Mother and Guardian; Household Affairs; Hunting and Wild
Animals
    Goddess of childbirth. Daughter of *Maddarakka* and one
of the *Akkah*. She is the protector of the home and of men
and women.
    *When Maddarakka forms the body of a child around its
soul, she gives the female fetuses to Sarakka, who places
them in the mother's womb. Her sister, Juskakka, performs
the same duty for the male fetuses.*
    Also a goddess of spinning and of the birth of reindeer. She
is given daily offerings of food and drink at the hearth.
Sarakka, alone or with *Maddarakka*, was probably worshiped

as the *Virgin Mary* of Near East in later centuries. Alternate form: Sadsta-akka. [Archaeological Institute 1916–1932; Eliade 1987; Jobes 1962; Leach 1992]

Saule

Slavic; Lithuania

Sun and Day; Mother and Guardian; Household Affairs; Arts; Disorder

"Sun." Benevolent deity who presides over childbirth and cares for orphans. She is associated with spinning, weaving, laundering, and music.

> Saule, the sun, and her husband Meness, the moon, did not get along well because they were such opposites. They separated after the birth of their daughter, the Earth. Now Saule watches over her during the day, and Meness watches over her at night.

She is the mother of *Ausrine*. In Latvia she is called *Saules-māte*. See also *Saules Meitas*. [Dexter 1990; Eliade 1987; Leach 1992; Lurker 1984; Savill 1977]

Saules-māte

Slavic; Latvia

Sun and Day

"Mother Sun." Equivalent to *Saules*. One of the seventy sisters of *Zeme*. [Savill 1977]

Saules Meitas

Slavic; Latvia

Sun and Day

"Daughters of the Sun."

> At sunset the Saules Meitas rinse their mother, Saule, the apple-red sun, in the sea. [Eliade 1987; Lurker 1984]

Schastie

Slavic; Russia

Luck; Wealth

Goddess of good fortune. [Dexter 1990]

Schilalyi

Slavic; Transylvania, *Gypsy*

Evil; Destroyer of Life; Hunting and Wild Animals

Demon of disease, wife of the demon Bitoso. She appears as a white mouse and causes colds and fevers. Some consider her a male demon called Schilayi. [Leach 1992]

Seewa

Slavic; Russia

Agriculture; Ceremonies

"Mother Friday." Harvest goddess. Equivalent to *Pyatnitsa Prascovia*. [Jobes 1962]

Selci-syt-emysyt

Slavic; Siberia, *Selkup*

Reptiles

"Mother of Snakes." Goddess of wild animals. [Leach 1992]

Semargla

Slavic

Weather

Weather goddess. She presides over cold and frosty weather. [Leach 1992]

Semik

Slavic; Russia

Ceremonies; Immortality

Chthonic deity who rules the souls of the dead. Her sacred tree is the birch. During the Semik ceremony, a tree is cut down and decorated like a goddess and then drowned in the river in order to provide rain for the crops. [Hubbs 1988]

Semmesmaat

Slavic; Latvia

Immortality

"Keeper of the Grave." [Leach 1992]

Sengi-mama

Slavic; Siberia, *Nanai*

Earth and Nature

She rules the earth, the forests, and the wild animals. [Leach 1992]

Sēnu-māte

Slavic; Latvia

Earth and Nature

"Mother of Mushrooms." One of the seventy sisters of *Zeme*. [Eliade 1987]

Serque-edne

Finno-Ugric; Lapland, *Saami*

Sky and Heavens; Immortality; Mother and Guardian

Sky goddess. She creates souls for the fetus and gives them to *Maddarakka*, who, in turn, gives them to her daughters, *Juksakka* and *Sarakka*, to place in each woman's womb. [Leach 1992]

Shatshektshe, The   See *The Shotshen.*

Shotshen, The

Slavic; Russia, *Cheremis*

Creator of Life

Deities of children, animals, corn, bees, and other living things. These deities are worshiped individually. They are invoked for fruitfulness. See also *Kugu Shothsen-ava.* Alternate form: Shatshektshe. [Archaeological Institute 1916–1932]

Shtrige

Slavic; Albania

Magic; Ugliness; Unhappiness

Witch. There was a widespread belief in witch goddesses who appeared monsterlike, especially to males. The Christian Church denigrated witches, and women took them underground, where their wrathful attributes became accentuated. [Eliade 1987; Hubbs 1988]

Shundimumi

Slavic; Russia, *Votyak*

Sun and Day

"Mother of the Sun." [Guirand 1968]

Si

Slavic; Russia, *Moksha*

Sun and Day; Justice

Sun goddess. Her name is used in swearing oaths, and she punishes perjury. Equivalent to Erya *Tsi*. Alternate form: Si-Bavas. [Leach 1992]

Si-Bavas   See *Si.*

Siriny, The

Slavic

Demi-animals; Fishing and Water Animals

Nature spirits. They assume the form of "fish women," or mermaids. [Hubbs 1988]

Siva
Slavic
Unknown

Slavic goddess of life. Equivalent to Polish **Zywie**. See also **Siva**, Indian Subcontinent. Alternate form: Ziva. [Baumgartner 1984; Jobes 1962; Stutley and Stutley 1984]

Sjantaik
Slavic; Russia
Mother and Guardian; Earth and Nature

"Birth Mother." She presides over humans and animals. [Eliade 1987]

Sjojungfru
Finno-Ugric; Lapland, *Saami*
Water

"Lady of the Sea." [Leach 1992]

Slatababa
Slavic; Russia, *Ugric*
Wealth; Ceremonies

"Golden Woman." Her golden statue was said to have been taken during the sacking of Rome in 410 C.E. She was a representation of Roman **Moneta**. On the way back to Siberia, her name was changed to **Jumala**, and she later became known as Slatababa. The statue was later moved to the junction of the Ob and Irytis rivers. It is believed that the goddess and an immense treasure remain hidden in the marshlands of the Lower Ob. Alternate forms: Jumala, Zlotababa [Sykes 1968]

Smert
Slavic; Russia
Destroyer of Life; Ceremonies

Goddess of death. She is worshiped outdoors under trees, with songs of exorcism or celebration. Similar to Slovene, Croat, and Serb **Kuga**, she is known to the Bulgarians and Russians as **Chuma**. Alternate forms: **Marà, Mora**. [Dexter 1990; Eliade 1987]

Smilšu-māte
Slavic; Latvia
Metals and Minerals

"Mother of Sand." One of the seventy sisters of **Zeme**. [Eliade 1987]

Smrtnice
Slavic; Czechoslovakia
Fate

Death spirit.

Smrtnice walks beneath the windows of the house where someone is dying. She sometimes comes inside, and if she sits at the head of the bed of the sick person, there is no hope. If she sits at the foot of the bed, the invalid may recover. [Bonnerjea 1927]

Sojenice, The
Slavic; Slovenia
Fate

Fate goddesses. See also **Narucnici**. [Jobes 1962; Monaghan 1981]

Solbon
Slavic; Siberia, *Yakut*
Stars and Planets; Weather

Celestial deity. When Solbon, the morning and evening star, and Urgel, the god of the Pleiades, meet, it is a bad omen. There will soon be a violent storm. [Jobes 1962]

Solntse
Slavic
Sun and Day

"Sun." Her husband is the moon, and their children are the stars. [Dexter 1990]

Sor-ava
Slavic; Russia, *Moksha*
Agriculture

"Mother of Corn." [Leach 1992]

Sreča
Slavic; Serbia
Fate; Agriculture; Domesticated Animals

Personal fate goddess. She protects the individual's fields and flocks. Equivalent to Russian **Dolya** (see Northern Europe) and the opposite of **Nesreča**. [Jobes 1962; Leach 1992]

Sudbina
Slavic; Serbia; Croatia
Fate; Mother and Guardian

Birth and fate goddess. Equivalent to Russian **Rozhenitsa**. [Eliade 1987]

Sudice, The
Slavic; Poland
Fate; Mother and Guardian

Fate goddesses. At the birth of an infant, they appear dressed in white and determine the newborn's fate. They are usually considered to be three in number, and information varies as to whether they have the same or different names. See also **Narucnici, Sudicky, Sudjaje,** and **Sudjenice**. [Baumgartner 1984; Jobes 1962; Monaghan 1981]

Sudička
Slavic; Czechoslovakia
Fate; Mother and Guardian

Fate and birth goddess. [Eliade 1987]

Sudicky, The
Slavic; Bohemia
Fate

Fate goddesses. Three women, dressed in white, who decide the fate of each newborn. See also **Narucnici, Sudice,** and **Sudjenice**. [Bonnerjea 1927; Jobes 1962; Monaghan 1981]

Sudjaje, The
Slavic
Fate

Fate goddesses. Equivalent to **Sudice, Sudicky**. [Baumgartner 1984]

Sudjenice, The
Slavic; Serbia; Slovenia; Croatia
Fate

Fate goddesses. See also **Narucnici, Sudice, Sudicky,** and **Sudjaje**. [Eliade 1987; Jobes 1962; Leach 1992]

Sudzenici, The
Slavic

Name for Bulgarian **Narucnici**. [Monaghan 1981]

Sukkamielli
Finno-Ugric; Finland, *Saami*
Love and Sexuality; Disorder

Love deity. Her male counterpart is Lempo. They are thought to be associated with the "frenzy" of love. [Jobes 1962]

Šukšendal

Slavic, *Tartar*

Evil; Household Affairs; Love and Sexuality; Disorder;
Destroyer of Life

Evil household spirit. She appears in the form of a woman
to men and in the form of a man to women. She gives people
nightmares, has sexual intercourse with them in their sleep,
creates disturbances, and can leave changelings in the place
of children who are alone in the house. She can harm people
in the bathhouse and even kill people found there late at
night. [Archaeological Institute 1916–1932]

Sun Virgin

Finno-Ugric; Lapland, *Saami*

Sun and Day

Sun goddess. Her followers make a wooden image of her,
which they smear with the blood of sacrifices—white
reindeer, sheep, or goats. In Norway they smear butter on
their doors when the first rays of the sun appear after the
dark winter. [Archaeological Institute 1916–1932]

Sundi-mumi   See *Sundy-mumy.*

Sundy-mumy

Slavic; Russia, *Votyak*

Sun and Day; Ceremonies

"Mother of the Sun." She is invoked to bring warm
weather and rain. Although not considered a personal being,
she is said to have a soul that requires sacrifices (animal) to
make it stronger. If the nature deities are strengthened, the
Earth is strengthened, and the soil will be more fruitful.
Alternate form: Sundi-mumi. [Leach 1972; Monaghan 1990]

Suonetar

Finno-Ugric; Finland, *Saami*

Immortality; Health and Healing; Magic

Goddess of veins who is able to restore life.

*When Lemminkainen tried to slay the swan of Tuoni, the
god of the underworld, he was torn to pieces. His mother,
Ilmater, took the pieces and fitted them together. With the
help of Suonetar, who reassembled Lemminkainen's veins, Ilmater
was able to restore her son's life.* [Guirand 1968]

Suoyatar

Finno-Ugric; Finland, *Saami*

Evil; Disorder; Reptiles

Serpent goddess. From the abyss, she created all the
trouble possible and put it on Earth. [Redfield 1931]

Šurali

Slavic; Russia, *Votyak, Southern*

Earth and Nature; Charisma; Disorder; Selfishness

Forest spirit who is naked and hairy, with three long
fingers on her hand. She cries out all night in the forest,
causes people to get lost, and entices them to her. Sometimes
she tickles or dances with them until they are totally
exhausted. Sometimes seen as male. See also *Ovda.*
[Archaeological Institute 1916–1932]

Sur-mumy

Slavic; Russia, *Votyak*

Water

"Mother of River." [Leach 1972]

Sweigs-dunka

Slavic; Lithuania

Stars and Planets

"Weaver," or "Bride of the Sky." Star goddess who rules
the morning and evening stars. She weaves the star-blanket
that covers the sky each night. [Leach 1992; Monaghan 1990]

Synnytar   "Birth." See *Luonnotar.*

Syt-kul-amine

Slavic; Siberia, *Buriat*

Mother and Guardian

Birth goddess. [Leach 1992]

Szelanya

Slavic; Hungary

Weather

"Mother of the Winds." [Leach 1992]

Szepasszonyok, The

Slavic; Hungary

Evil; Magic

Evil demons. Speaking their name is taboo. [Eliade 1987]

Tabiti

Slavic; Scythia

Fire; Supreme Being

"Fire." Supreme being. Similar to Greek *Vesta.* She is
assisted by a female deity, Mother Earth, *Api,* and a male
deity, Father Sky. Her Sanskrit name is *Dhavata.* [Cooper
1876; Eliade 1987; Hubbs 1988]

Táltos

Slavic; Hungary

Magic

Witch or changeling, usually a child born with a tooth. See
also *Drude.* [Leach 1972]

Tarn

Slavic; Siberia, *Ostyak*

Fire; Destroyer of Life; War; Weather

"Flames of Fire." Goddess of destruction. She presides
over war, illness, violent storms, and anything that destroys
life. Alternate form: Ey-vet'ne Kimtaran. [Leach 1992]

Tartary and Cathay Earth Goddess

Slavic; Russia

Domesticated Animals; Household Affairs; Ceremonies

Guardian of the flocks and fields. Her husband is Natigai.
Images of the couple and their family are made of felt and
cloth and kept in each house. Offerings are made to them at
each meal. See also *Tartary and Cathay Earth Goddess,* Far
East. [Durdin-Robertson 1976]

Tava-ajk

Slavic; Finno-Ugric; Russia, *Mordvin;* Lapland

Earth and Nature

"Tava Mother." Forest spirit who can be as tall as pine trees
or as small as the underbrush. To the Mordvins she can
appear in human shape but has clumsy feet as big as logs. To
the Finns, she is beautiful from the front but from the back
appears as a rotted stump or bushy tree. She can have a hat of
pine needles, a blue mantle, and if seen as male, a beard of
leaves. See also *Metsänneitsyt, Ganis,* and *Vir-ava.*
[Archaeological Institute 1916–1932]

Tcaridyi

Slavic; Transylvania, *Gypsy*

Evil; Insects; Destroyer of Life

Demon, wife of demon Tculo. Taking the form of a worm,
she invades human bodies, causing fevers, especially
puerperal fever of childbirth. [Leach 1992]

Teleglen-edzen

Slavic; Siberia, *Mongol*

Earth and Nature

Earth goddess. Personification of the Earth's surface. See also *Teleglen-edzen,* Far East. Alternate form: Altan-telgey. [Leach 1992]

Teleze-awa
Slavic; Russia, *Cheremis*
Moon and Night
  "Mother of the Moon." [Leach 1972]

Tenga
Slavic, *Mossi*
Earth and Nature; Justice
  Earth goddess of Senegal and Upper Volta rivers. She presides over justice and morality and avenges wrong. [Leach 1992]

Tōe-ceivune
Slavic; Siberia, *Chukchi*
Dawn and Twilight
  "Dawn-walking-woman." Solar deity. Wife of Tñairgin, god of Morning-Dawn. [Leach 1992]

Togo Musun
Slavic; Siberia, *Evenki*
Fire; Family and Tribes; Immortality
  Fire goddess. She protects the souls of clan members. She is called "mistress of the fire, mother of the clan, head of the tent." [Leach 1992]

Tol-ava
Slavic; Russia, *Mordvin*
Fire; Mother and Guardian; Ceremonies
  The *Fire Mother* of the Eurasians assisted at birth by designating the sex of the child as female. She protected men as well as women, and daily offerings of food and drink were left for her on the hearth. Equivalent to *Tul-awa.* See also *Avas.* [Eliade 1987; Leach 1972; Leach 1992]

Tomam
Slavic; Siberia, *Ket, Yenisei Ostyak*
Directions; Wild Birds
  A goddess of the South and goddess of the migration of birds from south to north. [Leach 1992; Lurker 1984]

Torom Anki
Slavic; Siberia, *Ostyak, Northern*
Mother and Guardian
  Birth goddess. [Leach 1992]

Tshadze-ienne
Finno-Ugric; Lapland, *Saami*
Directions; Water
  "Eastern Water Mother." [Leach 1992]

Tshatse-neida
Finno-Ugric; Lapland, *Saami*
Directions; Water
  "Western Water Mother." [Leach 1992]

Tshuma
Slavic; Russia
Destroyer of Life; Wild Birds
  "Plague." Goddess of disease. She appears as an owl. [Leach 1992]

Tsi
Slavic; Siberia, *Erya*
Sun and Day; Justice

Sun goddess. Her followers swear oaths in her name and invoke her to punish perjury. Equivalent to *Si.* Alternate form: Tsi-pas. [Leach 1992]

Tsi-pas   See *Tsi.*

Tul-awa
Slavic; Russia, *Cheremis*
Fire
  "Mother of Fire." Equivalent to *Tol-ava.* [Leach 1972; Leach 1992]

Tunder Ilona   See *Tundr Ilona.*

Tundr Ilona
Slavic; Hungary, *Ugric*
Creator of Life; Wild Birds
  Creator goddess. Consort of Gander-Chief. As a beautiful swan, she laid an egg, the sun, in the sky. Alternate form: Tunder Ilona. [Leach 1992; Monaghan 1990]

Tuonetar
Finno-Ugric; Finland, *Saami*
Heaven and Hell
  Queen of Tuonela (the underworld or land of the dead, also called Manala). She guides the boat that carries the deceased over the black river of death. It is a land that many enter, but few leave. Her daughters are *Kipu-Tytto, Loviatar,* and *Vammatar.*

  When Vainamoinen came to the isle of Manala, Tuonetar welcomed him by giving him a beer in a pot containing frogs and worms. She told him he would never leave. But Vainamoinen was able to change form and swim beneath the net of iron that had been thrown across the billows of the river of Tuonela and thus escape.

  See also *Tuonetar,* Northern Europe. [Guirand 1968; Jobes 1962; Leach 1972; Leach 1992; Monaghan 1981]

Tñrem Mother
Slavic, *Ostyak, Northern*
Immortality
  The soul-giving deity. [Archaeological Institute 1916–1932]

Turkic Earth Mother
Slavic
Earth and Nature
  Goddess of central Asia. [Eliade 1987]

Tuulikki
Finno-Ugric; Finland, *Saami*
Earth and Nature; Hunting and Wild Animals
  Goddess of the woods. Daughter of *Mielikki* and Tapio, who are also wood deities. She is invoked to assure an abundance of game. [Guirand 1968; Leach 1972; Leach 1992]

Tuurman
Slavic; Siberia, *Gilyak*
Household Affairs; Fire
  Household goddess. An aged woman who presides over the hearth and its fire. [Leach 1992]

Udelnicy, The   See *The Narucnici.*

Udens-mäte
Slavic; Latvia
Water
  "Mother of the Water." One of the seventy sisters of *Zeme.* [Leach 1992]

Uguns-mäte
Slavic; Latvia
Fire
  "Mother of Fire." One of the seventy sisters of *Zeme.* Alternate form: Uggunsmate. [Eliade 1987; Leach 1992; Lurker 1984]

Ugsakka   See *Uksakka.*

Uksakka
Finno-Ugric; Lapland, *Saami*
Household Affairs; Magic; Mother and Guardian
  "Door Woman." Daughter of *Maddarakka* and one of the *Akkah.* She lives in the ground under the door of the tent and protects the family. Uksakka can change the sex of the fetuses that her sisters, *Juksakka* and *Sarakka,* have placed in mothers' wombs. She protects newborns and their first steps. Alternate forms: Ugsakka, Uks-akka. [Archaeological Institute 1916–1932; Eliade 1987; Jobes 1962; Leach 1992]

Uldda
Finno-Ugric; Lapland, *Saami*
Earth and Nature; Evil
  Forest maiden who lives underground and comes to earth with her cattle. To punish people who invade her territory, she harms children who are left alone. Equivalent to Swedish *Huldra* (see Northern Europe). [Archaeological Institute 1916–1932]

Ulgen Ekhe
Slavic; Siberia, *Buriat*
Earth and Nature
  Earth goddess. [Eliade 1987]

Umai
Slavic; Siberia
Mother and Guardian; Fire
  Goddess of human fertility. See also *Umai,* Near East, and *Umai,* Far East. [Baumgartner 1984; Leach 1992]

Unchi-ahchi
Slavic; Siberia, *Ainu*
Fire; Water; Household Affairs
  "Grandmother Hearth." She is the intermediary between the Ainu people and their other deities. Also a goddess of the shore. She is worshiped in Siberia and Japan. See also *Unchi-ahchi,* Far East. [Leach 1992]

Unun-emei
Slavic; Siberia, *Yukaghir*
Water
  "Mother of the Korkodon River." [Leach 1992]

Uresici, The   See *The Narucnici.*

Urisnici, The   See *The Narucnici.*

Urme, The
Slavic; Poland; Russia; Serbia, *Gypsy*
Fate; Mother and Guardian
  Goddesses of fate. Three of them appear at the birth of children. Alternate form: The Ursitory. [Lurker 1984]

Ursel   See *Ursula.*

Ursitory, The   See *The Urme.*

Ut
Slavic; Siberia, *Mongol*
Fire; Household Affairs
  Fire goddess. She presides over the hearth. [Leach 1992]

Vagneg-imi
Slavic, *Ostyak, Vogul*
Mother and Guardian; Fate; Life/Death Cycle
  "Old Woman." Birth goddess and mother of the seven sons of god. She is worshiped in the districts surrounding the town of Surgut. Threads for each person born hang from her wooden staff. When a child is born, she makes a knot in one of the threads denoting the length of the child's life. [Archaeological Institute 1916–1932; Leach 1992]

Vais   See *Vasa.*

Vakarine
Slavic; Lithuania
Stars and Planets
  Goddess of the evening star (the planet Venus). Alternate form: Wakarine. [Leach 1992]

Vakŭ-oza
Slavic; Russia, *Cheremis*
Agriculture; Commerce and Travel; Disorder; Ceremonies
  "Mill Ruler." When appearing as female, she is decorated with silver coins across her breast. She lives under the floor or behind the waterwheel and helps the miller. If she is angry and disrupts the grinding, a dish of porridge is put out for her along with butter and a spoon. [Archaeological Institute 1916–1932]

Va-kul
Slavic; Russia, *Zyrian*
Water; Evil
  Water spirits. They can be male as well as female and are harmful to humans. [Guirand 1968; Leach 1992]

Vammatar
Finno-Ugric; Finland, *Saami*
Destroyer of Life; Unhappiness; Ugliness; Heaven and Hell
  Goddess of illness and pain. Daughter of *Tuonetar* and sister of *Kivutar* and *Luonnotar.* She is portrayed as an ugly hag. [Guirand 1968; Leach 1992; Savill 1977]

Varma-ava
Slavic; Russia, *Mordvin*
Weather
  "Mother Wind." [Leach 1972; Leach 1992]

Vasa
Finno-Ugric, *Siryan, Komi*
Water; Charisma; Beauty; Love and Sexuality
  Water spirit.

> The beautiful Vasa leaves her watery home to entice men to fall in love with her. They follow her into the water and drown, and she takes them to the bottom of the river to be her servants.

  See also *Kul.* Alternate form: Vais. [Archaeological Institute 1916–1932; Leach 1972]

Vasillissa
Slavic
Wild Birds
  Swan maiden. Daughter of the sea king. See also *Swan Maidens,* Northern Europe. [Jobes 1962]

Vechernyaya Zvezda
Slavic
Stars and Planets
"The Morning Star." She and her sister *Zvezda Dennitsa,* the evening star, are companions of the two *Zorya,* two other daughters of Dazhbog, the sun god. [Savill 1977]

Ved-ava
Slavic, *Mordvin, Moksha*
Water; Creator of Life
Mother of water. One of the most important deities, she is a fertility goddess, presiding over the fecundity of humans, animals, and plants. Also considered a form of *Azer-ava.* See also *Avas.* Alternate forms: Otsuved-azer-ava, Ved-azerava, Ved-azer-ava, Ved-mastor-ava. [Leach 1972; Leach 1992; Monaghan 1981]

Ved-azerava See *Ved-ava.*

Ved-azer-ava See *Ved-ava.*

Veden emâ
Finno-Ugric, *Karelian*
Fishing and Water Animals
Fish goddess. Sometimes at the fishers' request, she would drive fish into their nets. [Archaeological Institute 1916–1932]

Vedenemântâ
"Water Mistress." See *Näkki.*

Vedenneito
"Water Maid." See *Näkki.*

Ved'ma
Slavic
Evil; Magic
Witch. She has been changed from a goddess to a flying figure on a broom or rake. She can produce rain and storms. With her magical powers, she can look old and ugly or very beautiful. She can also become invisible. She knows the medicinal uses of plants and is the keeper of the water of life and death. [Eliade 1987]

Ved-mastor-ava
"Water Mother." See *Ved-ava.*

Veela See *The Vila.*

Veele See *The Vila.*

Veeneiu
"Water Maid." See *Näkineiu.*

Vēja-mäte
Slavic; Latvia
Weather; Earth and Nature; Wild Birds
"Wind Mother." Together with *Meza-mäte,* she watches over the forests and the birds. One of the seventy sisters of *Zeme.* Alternate form: Wejamaat. [Eliade 1987; Leach 1992; Lurker 1984]

Vel'-ava
Slavic, *Mordvin*
Family and Tribes
"Village Mother." Protector of the village. Dwelling places as a whole are said to have a special spirit of their own. In addition to the village mother there are others, such as a "bathhouse mother," a "mill mother," and so on. [Archaeological Institute 1916–1932]

Vellamo
Finno-Ugric; Finland
Water
"Rock Oneself." Goddess of the sea and the waters. Wife of Ahit (Ahto), the water god. They both reside in the black slime at the bottom of the sea. Her daughters are the waves. Alternate form: Wellamo. [Guirand 1968; Leach 1972; Leach 1992; Monaghan 1981]

Velu-mäte
Slavic; Latvia, *Letts*
Heaven and Hell
Goddess of the dead and the underworld to the Lettish people of Latvia. One of the seventy sisters of *Zeme.* [Eliade 1987; Leach 1992; Lurker 1984]

Veshianka
Finno-Ugric; Russia
Time
Goddess of spring. [Hubbs 1988]

Veshtitze See *Vyestitsa.*

Vesna
Slavic
Time
Slavic goddess of spring. [Baumgartner 1984; Jobes 1962; Leach 1992]

Vestice, The
Finno-Ugric; Bohemia
Disorder; Magic; Evil
"Wild Women." They can assume the form of every animal. The Vestice steal newborn babies and leave changelings in their places. [Bonnerjea 1927]

Vetca-neut
Slavic; Siberia, *Chukchi*
Stars and Planets
Stellar goddess. Personification of the constellation Leo. Wife of Rultennin, the constellation Orion. [Leach 1992]

Vete-ema See *Mere-ama.*

Vielona
Slavic; Lithuania
Immortality
Goddess of the dead. [Leach 1992; Lurker 1984]

Vila, The
Slavic; Serbia; Slovenia
Earth and Nature; Immortality; Magic; Agriculture; Education and Knowledge; Ceremonies; Health and Healing; Wealth; Justice
Wood spirits. Said to be the souls of unbaptized virgins. They can transform themselves into animals. They empower people by teaching them how to plow, grow abundant crops, and bury the dead. Offerings are made to them in caves and at springs. They give health and wealth to those who have respect but cause harm to those who ignore them. *Veela* is singular for Vila. Alternate forms: Judy, Samovila, Samovily, Vile, Wili, Willi. [Gimbutas 1971; Hubbs 1988; Jobes 1962; Leach 1972; Preston 1982]

Vile See *Vila.*

Viljaneitsi, The
Finno-Ugric
Agriculture
"Maidens of the Cornfield." [Leach 1972]

Viranakka
Finno-Ugric; Lapland, *Saami*
Hunting and Wild Animals
   Goddess of hunting. [Leach 1992]

Vir-ava
Finno-Ugric; Russia, *Mordvin*
Earth and Nature; Goodness; Fire; Hunting and Wild
Animals; Weather
   "Forest Mother" or "Forest Mistress." Benevolent goddess
of the forest. Her male counterpart is Tapio. Assuming a
different shape in each forest, she looks very much like a tree.

   *She has such large breasts that she must throw them over
her shoulders. She has long wild-looking hair and legs as
thick as logs. She can also manifest as a flame burning on
the ground, as a whirlwind, or as any of the forest animals. She is
noted for coming to log fires to warm her long hands.*

   See also *Avas*. A form of *Azer-ava*. Alternate forms: Virava,
Vir-azerava. [Archaeological Institute 1916–1932; Jobes 1962;
Leach 1992; Monaghan 1981]

Vir-azerava   See *Vir-ava*.

Vit'ša-kuva
Slavic; Russia, *Cheremis*
Domesticated Animals; Ceremonies
   "Cattleyard Woman." She appears as an old woman clad
in white. She protects the herd, and if she likes the animals,
she can stimulate their mating. If they displease her, she will
not protect them and is cruel to them at night. A hen is
offered to her as sacrifice to keep her from molesting the
cattle. [Archaeological Institute 1916–1932; Jobes 1962;
Monaghan 1981]

Viz-anya
Finno-Ugric, *Magyar*
Water; Fate; Luck
   "Water Mother." Her appearance foretells misfortune.
[Guirand 1968; Leach 1992]

Vizi-leany
Finno-Ugric, *Magyar*
Water; Fate; Luck
   "Maiden of the Water." Her appearance foretells
misfortune. [Guirand 1968; Leach 1992]

Vodianiani   See *The Navki*.

Vodni Panny, The
Slavic
Water
   Water goddesses. [Monaghan 1981]

Vodyanoi, The
Slavic
Evil; Water; Magic; Immortality
   Malevolent water spirits. They can assume the form of a
log, fish, old man, or beautiful woman. Their favorite habitat
is millponds. Vodyanoi are immortal, but they age and are
then rejuvenated according to the waning and waxing of the
moon. They correspond to *Cacce-jienne*. Alternate form:
Vodyanoy. [Savill 1977]

Vodyanoy   See *The Vodyanoi*.

Vu-ava
Slavic; Russia, *Votyak*
Water; Beauty
   "Water Woman." Naked and beautifully white, she will
come up on the shore to comb her long black hair. Her breasts

are as "big as buckets." She will immediately flee to the water
if she is seen. [Archaeological Institute 1916–1932]

Vüt-kuva
Slavic; Russia, *Cheremis*
Water; Ceremonies; Fishing and Water Animals
   "Water Old Woman." When people swim or fish, they give
this goddess offerings of bread, brandy, a duck, a goose, or a
hen. In the spring, when the first fish is caught, the Eastern
Cheremis boil it and return the bones to the water as an offering.
[Archaeological Institute 1916–1932]

Vyestitsa
Slavic; Serbia
Magic; Evil; Wild Birds; Insects; Destroyer of Life; Moon and
Night
   Sorceress.

   *At night, when Vyestitsa sleeps, a demonic spirit leaves
her body and flies about in the form of a bird or butterfly.
It searches for sleeping humans, especially children, and
tears out and devours their hearts.*

   Alternate form: Veshtitze. [Bonnerjea 1927; Monaghan
1981]

Wakarine   See *Vakarine*.

Walrus Mother
Slavic; Siberia, *Chukchi Inuit*
Water
   Sea goddess. [Wyers 1932]

Wejamaat   See *Vēja-māte*.

Wellamo   See *Vellamo*.

Wesna
Slavic; Bohemia
Time
   Goddess of summer. Equivalent to *Wiosna*. [Leach 1992]

Willi
Slavic
Earth and Nature
   Wood nymphs. See also *Vila*. [Leach 1972]

Wiosna
Slavic
Time
   Goddess of summer. Equivalent to *Wesna*. [Leach 1992]

Wüt-awa
Finno-Ugric, *Cheremis, Mari*
Water
   "Mother of Water." [Leach 1972; Leach 1992]

Wüt-ian uder
Finno-Ugric, *Mordvin*
Water; Time
   Sea goddess. She can have a human husband, but men
fearful of becoming her mate do not fish or bathe at noon,
the hour when water spirits are most active. [Leach 1972]

Xatel-ekwa
Slavic; Siberia, *Vogul*
Sun and Day
   Sun goddess. [Leach 1992]

Xoli-katess
Slavic; Siberia, *Vogul*
Dawn and Twilight

"Dawn Woman." Sister of the sun god Mir-Susne-Khum.
[Leach 1992]

Xotsadam
Slavic; Siberia, *Yenisei Ostyak, Ket*
Supreme Being
    Demon. Former wife of the sky god Ets. [Leach 1992]

Ya'hal-na'ut
Slavic; Siberia, *Koryak*
Weather
    "Cloud Woman." Daughter of the highest being. [Leach 1992]

Yabme-akka
Finno-Ugric; Lapland, *Saami*
Destroyer of Life; Ceremonies; Earth and Nature; Life/Death Cycle
    "Old Woman of the Dead." Underworld deity who is in charge of Tuonela or Manala, the realm under the earth where the dead walk on air. The entrance to this world is the mouth of a river where it flows into the ocean ice. Her hands trembling cause earth tremors. Black cats are sacrificed to her. Encountering old women who are barren (and also priests) is considered an evil omen in northern Europe. Alternate form: Yambe-akka. [Cotterell 1979; Guirand 1968; Leach 1972; Monaghan 1981]

Yaga-vasilisa See *Baba Yaga.*

Yambe-akka See *Yabme-akka.*

Ya-nebya
Slavic; Siberia, *Nentsy*
Earth and Nature; Mother and Guardian; Goodness
    Mother Earth. A benevolent deity who aids women in childbirth. [Leach 1992]

Yaumau-hadaku
Slavic; Siberia, *Yurak Samoyed*
Fishing and Water Animals; Ceremonies; Wealth
    Fish goddess. She inhabits the mouth of the Ob River. A small image of her is placed on the best fish of the first catch of the season. It indicates that the goddess is responsible for bringing the fish into the sea and providing a plentiful catch. Alternate form: Yaumau-haddaku. [Redfield 1931]

Yaumau-haddaku See *Yaumau-hadaku.*

Yegiled-emei
Slavic; Siberia, *Yukaghir*
Fire; Health and Healing
    Fire goddess of the Yassachnaya River area. She is invoked by the shaman to aid in healing. [Leach 1992]

Yine'a-ne'ut
Slavic; Siberia, *Koryak*
Sun and Day
    Solar goddess. Sometimes called the wife of Teikem-Tilaen. [Leach 1992]

Y-lyunda Kotta
Slavic; Siberia, *Selkup*
Supreme Being
    "Mistress of the Universe." [Leach 1992]

Ynakhsyt
Slavic; Siberia, *Yakut*
Domesticated Animals; Ceremonies

Protective goddess of cattle. She is propitiated with the first dairy produce of the spring. [Baumgartner 1984; Leach 1992]

Zallus
Slavic; Lithuania
Disorder
    "Strife." [Leach 1992]

Zarya
Slavic
Health and Healing; Water
    Goddess of healing waters. [Savill 1977; Sykes 1968]

Zarya Utrennyaya See *Zorya Utrennyaya.*

Zarya Vechernyaya See *Zorya Veckernyaya.*

Zeme
Slavic; Latvia
Earth and Nature
    "Mother of the Earth." She is said to have seventy sisters, some of whom have very special functions related to fertility. They include *Briežu-māte, Dziparu-māte, Joda-māte, Kapu-māte, Laimas-māte, Lauka-māte, Lauku-māte, Lazdu-māte, Linu-māte, Mera-māte, Meža-māte, Nāves-māte, Ogu-māte, Piegulas-māte, Pirts-māte, Saules-māte, Sēne-māte, Smilšu-māte, Vēja-māte,* and *Velu-māte.* Alternate form: Zemes-māte. [Leach 1992; Savill 1977]

Zemes-māte See *Zeme.*

Zemyna
Slavic; Lithuania
Earth and Nature
    "Mother Earth." Alternate forms: Zemynele, Ziedkele. [Leach 1992; Lurker 1984]

Zemynele See *Zemyna.*

Zhiva
Slavic
Immortality; Wild Birds; Ceremonies
    Spirit of the dead worshiped by the Elbe River Slavs. She is associated with a female cuckoo that is called on in the spring as a link with the dead. Friday is her sacred day. [Hubbs 1988]

Ziedkele
"She Who Raises Flowers." See *Zemyna.*

Ziedu-māte
Slavic; Baltic
Earth and Nature
    "Mother of the Blossoms." Earth goddess. One of the seventy sisters of *Zeme.* [Eliade 1987]

Zimarzla
Slavic; Russia
Weather
    "The Frozen." Weather goddess. Her breath is icelike, and she is clothed in hoarfrost and snow and crowned with hailstones. [Redfield 1931]

Zitna-atka
Slavic
Time; Agriculture; Destroyer of Life; Intelligence and Creativity

Midday spirit. Equivalent to *Poldunica*. Zitna-atka appears in the cornfields at noon and kills anyone who cannot answer her riddles. [Bonnerjea 1927]

Ziva
Slavic
Health and Healing; Life/Death Cycle

Goddess of life. She is invoked for health and a long life. Alternate forms: Siva, Zywie. [Baumgartner 1984; Jobes 1962; Leach 1992]

Zizilia
Slavic; Poland
Love and Sexuality

Goddess of love. [Hubbs 1988]

Zleja
Slavic; Lithuania
Sun and Day

Goddess of midday. *Ausrine* ruled the dawn, and *Breksta* ruled the darkness. [Monaghan 1990]

Zlotababa
Slavic; Russia
Ceremonies

"Golden Old Woman." In districts around Northern Uras, she is sometimes shown with a child in her arms. Offerings of precious furs were made to her. See also *Slatababa*. [Archaeological Institute 1916–1932; Leach 1972]

Zorya, The
Slavic
Dawn and Twilight; Mother and Guardian

Sky goddesses. The Zorya are *Zorya Utrennyaya*, the "aurora" of dawn, and *Zorya Vechernyaya*, the "aurora" of dusk.

> Each morning Zorya Utrennyaya opens the the palace gates so her father, the sun Dazhbog, can ride out across the sky. When he returns in the evening, Zorya Vechernyaya closes the gates.

Sometimes there are three Zorya, *Zorya Utrennyaya*, *Zorya Vechernyaya*, and their sister, the goddess of midnight, and they are known as the "protectors of the universe."

The three Zorya are the guardians of the world. They watch the god who is chained to Ursa Major to keep him from breaking free. If he is able to escape, the world will end. Alternate form: Zarya. [Guirand 1968; Hubbs 1988; Savill 1977]

Zorya Utrennyaya
Slavic
Sun and Day

"Dawn." Sister of *Zorya Vechernyaya* and daughter of the sun. See also *The Zorya*. Alternate form: Zarya Utrennyaya. [Durdin-Robertson 1982; Savill 1977]

Zorya Vechernyaya
Slavic
Dawn and Twilight

"Dusk." Daughter of the sun. Her sister is *Zorya Utrennyaya*. Alternate form: Zarya Veckernyaya. [Dexter 1990; Graves 1968; Leach 1992; Savill 1977]

Zveyda Dennitsa   See *Zvezda Dennitsa*.

Zvezda Dennitsa
Slavic
Stars and Planets

"The Morning Star." Daughter of the sun god, Dazhbog. Sometimes given as the wife of Myesyats, the moon god.

> She helps her sister, Vechernyaya Zvezda, care for their father's horses, which he uses to cross the sky each day.

See also *Zorya*. Alternate form: Zveyda Dennista. [Durdin-Robertson 1982; Graves 1968; Leach 1992; Savill 1977]

Zvoruna
Slavic; Lithuania
Hunting and Wild Animals

"Bitch." Deity of hunting and game animals. Also considered male. [Leach 1992; Savill 1977]

Zylvie   See *Dziewanna*.

Zywie
Slavic; Poland
Health and Healing

Goddess of life. See *Siva, Ziva*. [Jobes 1962; Leach 1992]

EGYPT

Aahmes-nefertari
Mother and Guardian; Justice
   Deified queen who ruled from 1546 to 1526 B.C.E. As a goddess, she was a protector and punisher of humans.

   ☥ *During her life, Nefertari was called "Amon's wife." She slept in the temple and her children were said to be children of the god.*

   Alternate form: Ahmes-nefertari. [Mackenzie 1913; Savill 1976]

Aakhabit   See *Gate-keeping Goddesses.*

Aa-sheft
Time
   The fourth hour of the night. [Budge 1969; Leach 1992]

Aasith
War; Earth and Nature
   Semitic goddess of war and the desert. Her worship was brought to Egypt from Syria. [Leach 1992]

Aat-aatet
Time
   One of the *Twelve Goddesses of Life and Strength.* [Durdin-Robertson 1982]

Aat-khu
Time
   One of the *Twelve Goddesses of Life and Strength.* [Durdin-Robertson 1982]

Abet-neteru-s
Sky and Heavens
   One of the goddesses who line the path of the sun god, Ra, on his journey across the sky. [Durdin-Robertson 1982]

Ahabit
Time
   "Lady of Hair," "Power," or "Lady of Flame." The sixth hour of the day. [Budge 1969; Durdin-Robertson 1982; Leach 1992; Neumann 1972]

Ahat
Domesticated Animals
   Cow goddess. One of the goddesses who lines the path of the sun god, Ra, on his journey. Wife of Emen. Alternate forms: Emenet, Meh-urt, Net. [Durdin-Robertson 1982; Jobes 1962; Leach 1992]

Ahemait
Heaven and Hell; Demi-animals; Justice; Destroyer of Life
   "Devourer." Underworld deity who is part hippopotamus, part lion, part crocodile. Ahemait eats the souls of the dead who are judged unworthy by *Maât.* See also *Ammit.* [Monaghan 1981]

Ahi
Sun and Day
   Goddess of the day. Daughter of Pa-hra. [Jobes 1962]

Ahmes-nefertari   See *Aahmes-nefertari.*

Ahti
Evil; Demi-animals
   Malevolent goddess. She has the head of an asp and the body of a hippopotamus. [Cooper 1876]

Akarkhentkats
Mother and Guardian; Domesticated Animals
   "Wise One Keeping Her Place." Name of one of the *Hathors.* [Cooper 1876]

Akert-khentet-auset-s
Immortality; Heaven and Hell

One of the *Seven Kine-deities* listed in the Egyptian *Book of the Dead*. They provide the deceased in the underworld with food. The others are *Henemet-em-anh-annuit, Het-kau-nebt-er-tcher, Meh-khebitet-seh-neter, Sekhemet-ren-s-em-abet-s, Shenat-pet-utheset-neter,* and *Ur-mertu-s-teshert-sheni.* They are shown with a solar disk between their horns, much like *Hathor*. Similar to the *Four Uaipu Cow Goddesses* and the *Cow Goddesses,* Near East. [Durdin-Robertson 1975]

Akhet
Time; Water

"Inundations." Goddess of the seasons. She is sometimes called a goddess of the Nile River. [Leach 1992]

Akusaa
Sun and Day

Goddess of the setting sun. Wife of Tum (Atum), god of the setting sun. [Cooper 1876]

Amaunet
Primordial Being; Demi-animals; Heaven and Hell

"Unseen Air." Member of the Hermopolitan Ogdoad (the first living beings who appeared on the flaming isle of the Primeval Beginning). The Ogdoad includes Amon and Amaunet; Huh and *Hauhet*; Kuk and *Kauket*; and Nun and *Naunet* or, according to some, Ka and *Kait*. The goddesses in this group have a serpent's head and instead of feet, the head of a jackal. Originally they lived in the upperworld but later moved to the underworld. See also *Nen*. Alternate form: Amonit. [Durdin-Robertson 1975; Neumann 1972; Sproul 1979]

Amemait   See *Ammit*.

Amemet
Heaven and Hell

Goddess of the underworld. She is named in the *Book of the Dead* as being in the Eleventh Qereret (subdivision), where supplications are made to her. [Durdin-Robertson 1975]

Amenet
Mother and Guardian; Heaven and Hell

Ancient Theban deity thought to be a form of *Neith* of Saïs. Associated with fertility goddesses worshiped in the delta long before gods Amen and Amen-ra. She was replaced by *Mut*. See also *Ament*. [Budge 1989]

Amenit   See *Ament*.

Ament
Heaven and Hell; Directions; Immortality

Goddess of the underworld. She welcomes the shade (spirit) to the west (the place of the dead) with bread and water. She was originally a goddess of Libya, the personification of the west. She is often portrayed with an ostrich feather on her head. Said to be a name for *Isis,* she is associated with *Aukert, Sekhet-hetepet,* and *Unen-em-hetep*. See also *Amenet, Amenit, Amenti,* and *Kerhet*. Alternate forms: Amentet, Amentit. [Carlyon 1982; Durdin-Robertson 1975; Leach 1992; Monaghan 1981]

Amentet   See *Ament*.

Amenti
Heaven and Hell; Creator of Life

Underworld deity who directs the underworld's business. She is also called the "Goddess of Many Names."

Amenti lives in a tree near the World Gates. Here she welcomes the dead, offering them bread and water. If they accept her gifts, they are obligated to the gods and never return from the West, the land of death. Sometimes Nut, Hathor, Neith, or Maât takes Amenti's place by the gates.

See also *Ament*. [Budge 1989; Carlyon 1982; Leach 1992]

Amentit   See *Ament*.

Ament-semu-set
Time

Guardian of the sixth hour of the night in the *Book of Ami Tuat*. This book tells the story of an earthly pharaoh's mystical journey through the Tuat (underworld) in the swamps of the northeastern part of the delta. See also *Fifth Hour Goddess*. [Budge 1989]

Amit
Fire; Heaven and Hell; Immortality

Fire goddess of the underworld. She is associated with the preservation of the body and is mentioned in the *Book of the Dead*. Associated with *Sekhet-bast-ra*. [Durdin-Robertson 1975]

Am-met   See *Ammit*.

Ammit
Justice; Heaven and Hell; Destroyer of Life; Demi-animals

"Devourer of Souls." Goddess of the underworld who is part crocodile, part lion, and part hippopotamus.

It is Ammit who devours those who have died with "hearts heavy with misdeeds" after they have been weighed on the scale with Maât.

See also *Ahemait*. Alternate forms: Amemait, Am-met, Ammut. [Durdin-Robertson 1975; Jobes 1962; Lurker 1984; Monaghan 1981]

Ammut   See *Ammit*.

Amn
Heaven and Hell; Justice

"Invisible." Goddess of the underworld who welcomes those who have led righteous lives. [Stone 1979]

Amonit   See *Amaunet*.

Amunet
Primordial Being

Goddess who inhabited the Isle of Flame in the primeval waters and guided the emerging life from the cosmic egg. Also an alternate name for *Nut*. [Baumgartner 1984; Stone 1979]

Amunta
Sun and Day

Female counterpart of Amen-Ra, the sun. Alternate form: Tamun. [Cooper 1876]

Anatha   See *Anatha Baetyl*.

Anatha Baetyl
Hunting and Wild Animals; Love and Sexuality; War; Sky and Heavens; Earth and Nature

Lion goddess. Associated with *Ashima Baetyl*. She is probably of Syrian origin and is worshiped in the Jewish colony at Elephantine. Called the wife of Jehovah. She is also known as *Anatha* the goddess of love and battle and *Anatha* the Mountain Goddess, Queen of Heaven. [Durdin-Robertson 1975; Graves 1948; Jobes 1962]

Anatis
Moon and Night; Earth and Nature
   Moon and Earth deity. [Harding 1971]

Anenit, The
Heaven and Hell
   "Widows." Goddesses of the underworld. Supplications
are made to them in the Eighth Qereret (subdivision).
[Durdin-Robertson 1975]

Anit
Unknown
   She belongs to the Theban pantheon of 14 deities including
Montu, Atumu, Shu, *Tafnuit*, Sibu, *Nut*, Osiris, *Isis*, Sit,
Nephthys, Horus, *Hathor*, and Tanu. Sometimes the group
includes Mont, *Maut, Mut*, and Khonsu. Said by some to be a
form of *Hathor*. [Cooper 1876; Durdin-Robertson 1975]

Ank   See *Anuket*.

Anka
Creator of Life
   Creator goddess. Wife of Khnum. Equivalent to *Anucis*,
Greek and Roman Empires. See also *Anuket*. [Cooper 1876]

Ankhet
Unknown
   "Lady of Life." She came from the Sudan with *Satet*. See
also *Anuket*. [Stone 1979]

Ankhtith
Demi-animals; Time; Reptiles
   Woman-headed serpent goddess who presides over the
seventh hour of the night. [Durdin-Robertson 1982]

Anouke   See *Anuket*.

Anoukis   See *Anuket*.

Anpet
Time
   The fifth hour of the seventeenth day of the moon. [Leach
1992]

Ānqet   See *Anuket, Isis*.

Anqt   See *Anuket*.

Anquet   See *Anuket*.

Anrn
Unknown
   Goddess about whom nothing is known. [Cooper 1876]

Anta
War; Sky and Heavens
   "Lady of Heaven." Said to be a mother goddess, she can
conceive but cannot bring a child to birth. Thought to form a
triad with *Katesch* and *Reschep*. Possibly an Egyptian name
for *Anat*, Near East, and *Anaitis*, Near East, whose worship
was introduced into Egypt. Alternate form: Anthat. [Budge
1969; Cooper 1876; Jobes 1962]

Antarta
Unknown
   Name for a Khita goddess of the Hittites, Near East.
[Cooper 1876]

Āntat
War

Syrian war goddess introduced into Egypt. She wears the
Crown of the South and holds a spear, shield, and battle-axe.
She had a temple at Thebes during the reign of Thothmes III.
May be similar to *Ānthretju* mentioned in the Hittite Treaty,
Near East. [Budge 1989]

Anthat   See *Anta*.

Anthrathi
Unknown
   Name for the *Anāhita*, Near East; *Anaitis*, Greek and
Roman Empires and Near East; and *Anthat*, Near East.
[Sykes 1968]

Ānthretju
War
   Hittite. May be similar to Syrian war goddess *Āntat*.
[Budge 1989]

Anuke
War
   Deity who presides over battles. [Leach 1992]

Anuket
Water; Mother and Guardian
   "To Embrace." Among her titles are Guardian Goddess
of the Cataracts, The Clasper, The Constrainer, Goddess of
Elephantine, the Goddess of Life, Lady of Life, and Goddess
of Childbirth. Possibly of Nubian origin. She is worshiped in
a temple on the island of Sehel, where she is guardian of the
cataracts of the Nile along with *Satet*. She also had a temple
at Elephantine where she was worshiped as a triad with *Satet*
and Khnum (thought by some to be her husband). She is
sometimes depicted carrying an ankh. According to one scholar,
the word ankh is derived from one of her alternate names.
See also *Anka, Ankhet*. Alternate forms: Ank, Anouke,
Anoukis, Ānqet, Anqt, Anquet, Anukit, Anuqet. [Cooper
1876; Durdin-Robertson 1975; Ions 1982; Jayne 1925; Jobes
1962; Leach 1992; Monaghan 1981; Redfield 1931; Sykes 1968]

Anukit   See *Anuket*.

An-unsser
Domesticated Animals
   One of the *Four Uaipu Cow Goddesses*. [Durdin-
Robertson 1975]

Anuqet   See *Anuket*.

Apet
Hunting and Wild Animals; Mother and Guardian; Justice;
Heaven and Hell
   "The Red Hippopotamus," the "Protectress," and a
goddess of childbirth. She is described as standing upright on
her hind legs and having many teats or a plaited mane. She is
said to be the animal form of *Mut* or her substitute. Also
known as an avenging deity who is depicted with a lion's
head, brandishing a knife in one hand and a cross-like
instrument in the other. In the underworld she nourishes the
dead who are approaching hell. See also *Êpet, Ipet, Reret,
Sheput, Taourt, Ta-urt, Taueret, Thoeris, Thoueris, Tie*.
Alternate forms: Api, Apt, Opet, Rert, Rertu. [Cooper 1876;
Durdin-Robertson 1975; Leach 1992; Monaghan 1981]

Api   See *Apet, Taueret, Ta-urt*.

Apitus
Unknown
   "She Who Is on the Hill." Worshiped in the city of Tuaa.
[Cooper 1876]

Apt
Time

Name for **Uatchet** when she is the goddess of the eleventh month (Eipiphi). Also an alternate name for **Apet**. [Durdin-Robertson 1975; Leach 1992]

Ap-taui   See **Uadjet, Uatchet.**

Apt-hent
Time

Goddess of the eleventh month (Eipiphi). Goddesses of the months can vary. [Leach 1992]

Apt-renpit
Time

Goddess of the twelfth month (Mesore). [Durdin-Robertson 1982; Leach 1992]

Ara-seshap
Sun and Day

Goddess of light. [Durdin-Robertson 1975]

Aritatheth
Sky and Heavens

One of the goddesses who line the path of the sun god, Ra, on his journey across the sky. [Durdin-Robertson 1982]

Arsinoe
Unknown

This is a popular name in history. One was a Greek queen of Egypt and Thrace. Several towns are named after the several queens of this name. One Arsinoe was deified and worshiped as **Venus Zephyritis**, a form of **Venus,** Greek and Roman Empires. Others were Arsinoe Philadelphos and Arsinoe Philopator, who were worshiped in Memphis. [Cooper 1876; Durdin-Robertson 1975; Jobes 1962]

As   See **Isis.**

Aset   See **Isis.**

Ashima Baetyl
Unknown

One of the wives of Jehovah. See also **Anatha Baetyl.** [Graves 1948; Jobes 1962]

Ashtaroth   See **Ashtoreth.**

Ashtarthet   See **Ashtoreth.**

Ashtoreth
Moon and Night; Domesticated Animals; War; Demi-animals

Goddess of the moon, horses, and war. She has the head of a lion. Associated with **Qetesh** and also considered a form of **Hathor.** A Syrian goddess, **Astarte,** Near East, adopted by the Egyptians. The center of her worship was Appollinopolis Magna (Edfû).

☥ *Ashtoreth stands in a chariot drawn by four horses. On the battlefield she drives over any prostrate foes.*
Alternate forms: Ashtaroth, Ashtarthet. [Budge 1969; Budge 1989; Leach 1992; Mackenzie 1913]

Āsit
War

Goddess of the Eastern Desert who is portrayed as riding on a horse while holding a spear and shield. [Budge 1989]

As-neit
Unknown

"Favorite of **Neith.**" Wife of Joseph and mother of Manasseh and Ephrain, who were born in Egypt. [Durdin-Robertson 1975]

Aso
Justice

Deified queen of Ethiopia. She is said to be among the seventy or more who conspired with **Isis** to bring about Osiris's death. [Cooper 1876]

Ast
Time

The third hour of the third day of the moon and the ninth hour of the day. "She watches before Osiris during the fourth and the fifth hours of the night." May be a name for **Isis** meaning "seat" or "throne." See also **Auset.** [Johnson 1988; Leach 1992]

Atem
Time

Egyptian goddess of time who represents the "all-devouring time" involved in the Ritual of the Dead. Alternate form: At-em. [Jobes 1962; Monaghan 1981]

At-em   See **Atem.**

Atet
Sun and Day; Mother and Guardian

Solar goddess or mother goddess. Worshiped at Heracleopolis. The counterpart of the solar god Her-shef. Said to have a cat-like form called **Maau.**

☥ *In the Egyptian* Book of the Dead *there is a hymn to the god Ra which says, "The goddess Nehebka is in the Atet boat, and they both rejoiceth, the two uraei goddesses rise upon thy brow."*

(The uraeus appears on the fore part of the headdress of ancient Egyptian rulers in the form of the sacred asp.) Alternate form: Mersekhnet. [Durdin-Robertson 1975; Jobes 1962; Leach 1992]

Athor   See **Hathor.**

Athtor
Moon and Night

"Mother Night." Darkness covering the primodial abyss. See also **Isthar,** Near East. [Durdin-Robertson 1975]

Athyr   See **Hathor.**

Ator   See **Hathor.**

Au Sept   See **Auset.**

Au Set   See **Auset, Isis.**

Aukert
Heaven and Hell

Goddess of the underworld. Associated with **Ament, Sekhet-hetepet,** and **Unen-em-hetep.** [Durdin-Robertson 1975]

Auset
Family and Tribes; Creator of Life; Stars and Planets

"Exceeding Queen" or "Throne." She is said to be the oldest of the old from whom everything came. Identified with the star Sirius. The Greeks call her **Isis.** See also **Ast.** Alternate forms: Au Sept, Au Set. [Monaghan 1981; Stone 1979]

Auteb   See **Autyeb.**

Autyeb

Happiness

"Joy." Goddess who is the personification of this emotion.
Alternate forms: Auteb, Aut-yeb. [Jobes 1962; Leach 1992]

Aut-yeb   See Autyeb.

Avaris

Unknown

Equivalent to Anat, Near East. [Monaghan 1981]

Bahet

Wealth

"Abundance." Goddess who personifies abundance.
[Jobes 1962]

Bast

Demi-animals; Health and Healing; Earth and Nature; Moon
and Night; Mother and Guardian; Arts; Happiness; Sun and
Day; War

Wife/daughter of Ra. A local deity of the delta. When
depicted with a cat's head, she is a moon goddess presiding
over childbirth and the pleasure given by music and dancing.
In her lion-headed form she is a solar deity presiding over
human healing and the fructification of the earth. She is also
worshiped as a war goddess and protector of cities. She was
worshiped in Babastis. Pi-beseth in the Book of Ezekiel is said
to be the goddess Bast. It is Bast who protects Ra from the
serpent Apep. She is identified with Menhit. See also Pakhit,
Pasht, Ubastet. Alternate forms: Bastet, Bastis, Bubastis,
Ka-harus-apu-saru-ma-hakar-uma, Pacht, Pakht, Uatit, Ubast.
[Budge 1989; Cooper 1876; Cotterell 1979; Durdin-Robertson
1975; Jayne 1925; Leach 1992]

Bastet   See Bast.

Bastis   See Bast.

Bat

Mother and Guardian

Mother goddess. She was later merged with Hathor.
[Jobes 1962]

Behbet

Unknown

Deity of the Nile Delta and patron of the city of Behbet.
[Olson 1983]

Berenice

War; Stars and Planets

"Bringer of Victory." Wife/sister of Ptolemy Euergetes V or
Ptolemy Soter.

☥ Berenice promised the goddess of beauty that she would cut
off her hair if her husband returned home safely from the war.
When he returned, Berenice hung her hair in the temple of
Arsinoe, but it disappeared. The winds carried the hair to heaven,
where it formed the constellation Coma Berenices.

Alternate forms: Berenice Euergetes, Berenike, Berenise,
Bernice. [Cooper 1876; Jobes 1962; Woodcock 1953;
Zimmerman 1964]

Berenice Euergetes   See Berenice.

Berenike   See Berenice.

Berenise   See Berenice.

Bernice   See Berenice.

Beset

Mother and Guardian

Worshiped during the rule of the Ptolemies. Also said to
be an alternate name for Sekhet in her favorable aspect of
protector. She is portrayed holding a sistrum, or a vessel for
libation, and a sacred cat. [Cooper 1876; Lurker 1984]

Bouto   See Buto.

Bubastis   See Bast, Sekhet, Uat.

Buto

Moon and Night; Sky and Heavens; Justice; Mother and
Guardian; Reptiles

Serpent goddess of primal darkness. Goddess of the town
and nome (province) of Buto in lower Egypt. Mother of the
sun and the moon. Sister of Nekhebet. Together Buto and
Nekhebet are called the "Two Mistresses" of Egypt. Buto is
represented wearing the uraeus, or the red crown of lower
Egypt, a symbol of sovereignty. She is also seen carrying a
papyrus stem around which a cobra is coiled or as a cobra
coiled in a basket supported by papyrus plants. It is Buto
who defends the pharaoh. She spits poison on his enemies or
burns them up with her fiery gaze. Equivalent to Eileithyia,
Greek and Roman Empires. See also Uadjet, Uat, Uatchet,
Uto. Alternate forms: Bouto, Edjo, Uajyt, Uazet, Uazit, Udjat,
Uzoit. [Carlyon 1982; Cooper 1876; Ions 1982; Leach 1992;
Monaghan 1981; Savill 1976; Senior 1985; Zimmerman 1964]

Celestial Sow, The

Moon and Night; Domesticated Animals

She evolved as an explanation for eclipses of the moon. It
is said that she swallows the moon, causing its light to go out
suddenly. [Durdin-Robertson 1975]

Celestial Waterer, The

Mother and Guardian; Water

The "Mother of Life pours out the Water of Life." [Durdin-
Robertson 1975]

Chemnis   See Khoemnis.

Chemnu   See Khoemnis.

Chensit

Reptiles

Serpent goddess of the twentieth nome (province) of lower
Egypt. She is depicted with Hathor's crown or Maât's feather,
or both. Associated with the god Sopdu. [Lurker 1984]

Chiun   See Ken.

Clother

Heaven and Hell

Goddess mentioned in the Book of the Dead. One of the
Gate-keeping Goddesses. [Durdin-Robertson 1975; Neumann
1972]

Dikaiosyne

Unknown

Goddess worshiped in Hermopolis (Toth). See also
Nechmetawaj. [Lurker 1984]

Djet

Sky and Heavens

Deity who holds up one of the pillars of the sky on a shrine at
Tutankhamen's tomb. The other pillar is supported by a male
god. [Durdin-Robertson 1975]

Edjo   See Buto.

Ehe
Domesticated Animals
   Portrayed with a cow's head. Possibly a form of *Hathor*.
[Cooper 1876]

Emenet   See *Ahat*.

Enenet-hemset   See *Kerhet*.

Ennit   See *Kerhet*.

Êpet
Mother and Guardian; Hunting and Wild Animals;
Demi-animals
   Protector of children from birth through childhood.
Described as being a hippopotamus with human-like breasts,
carrying a crocodile on her back. Her feet are said to be those
of a lion. In later times she was merged with *Nut*. See also
*Apet, Ipet, Reret, Sheput, Taueret, Ta-urt, Thoeris, Thoueris,
Tie*. Alternate forms: Tueret, Uêret. [Jobes 1962; Leach 1992]

Ermutu
Mother and Guardian
   Goddess of childbirth. Similar to *Meshkent*. [Monaghan
1981]

Ernutet
Agriculture; Reptiles
   "Plentiful Harvests." Portrayed as a woman with the head
of a cobra and wearing a headdress consisting of two plumes,
or a solar disk and a pair of horns. She is often confused with
Renenutet and sometimes merged with *Renenutet*. Alternate
form: Ernutit. [Cooper 1876; Ions 1982; Leach 1992; Sykes
1968]

Ernutit   See *Ernutet*.

Erpuit Goddesses, The
Heaven and Hell
   Goddesses mentioned in the Funeral Text of the Hertu in
the Roman period Egyptian *Books of the Dead*. The two
goddesses may be *Isis* and *Nephthys*. [Durdin-Robertson
1975]

Ese   See *Isis*.

Eset   See *Isis*.

Esi   See *Isis*.

Eus-os   See *Saosis*.

Fifth Hour Goddess
Destroyer of Life; Time
   The goddess who "lived upon the blood of the dead" in
the *Book of Ami Tuat*. See also *Ament-semu-set*. [Budge 1989]

Four Uaipu Cow Goddesses
Domesticated Animals
   Ancient deities mentioned in the Papyrus of Nebseni. Two
of them are *An-unsser* and *Smamet*. They are similar to the
Seven Kine-deities. [Durdin-Robertson 1975]

Gate-keeping Goddesses
Destroyer of Life; Fire; Sun and Day; Physical Prowess;
Courage; Heaven and Hell
   Goddesses of the underworld. Guardians of the Pylons of
the Sekhet-Aanru (Elysian Fields). The deceased must say the
names of the goddesses before they are allowed to pass. Each
pylon has a male and a female deity, but only the females are

characterized in detail. Included are *Aakhabit* and *Clother*.
Of the others, their titles include Mistress of Destruction,
Mistress of the World, Lady of the Altar, Mistress of the Two
Lands, Lady of the Flames, Lady of the Light, Waterflood
which Clotheth, Lady Who Giveth Birth, Lady of Strength,
Lady Who Is To Be Feared, Mistress of Every Pylon, Lady of
Splendor, Lady Whom the Gods Adore, Lady of Might, Lady
of Valor, Lady of Victory, Lady of the Great House, Dispenser
of Light, and Goddess with Face Turned Backwards.
[Durdin-Robertson 1975]

Goddess of Papremis
Unknown
   Mother of the Egyptian counterpart of the Roman god
Mars. She lived in a temple in the city of Papremis.
[Durdin-Robertson 1975]

Goddess-greatly-beloved-with-red-hair
Heaven and Hell
   Goddess of the underworld. She is twentieth on the list in
the *Papyrus of Nu*. [Durdin-Robertson 1975]

Goddess-joined-unto-life-with-flowing-hair
Heaven and Hell
   Goddess of the underworld. Mentioned twenty-first in the
Papyrus of Nu called "Of Making a Man Perfect." [Durdin-
Robertson 1975]

Goose Goddess
Creator of Life; Primordial Being
   "The Great Cackler." Celestial deity who laid the cosmic
egg from which the world came and broke the silence that
had surrounded it.
   ☥ *The egg was laid on the primeval mound and contained
   the bird of light, Ra.* [Durdin-Robertson 1975;
   Ions 1982]

Hagar
Earth and Nature; Moon and Night
   Desert mountain goddess. Named in Hebrew scriptures
as an Egyptian princess. She is worshiped by tribes of the
Southern Desert, and occult tradition links her with the
moon. See also *Hagar*, Near East. [Durdin-Robertson 1975;
Jobes 1962; Monaghan 1981; Senior 1985]

Hak
Heaven and Hell; Immortality; Demi-animals
   Goddess of the underworld. A frog-headed deity
connected with resurrection. Alternate form: Heka. [Redfield
1931]

Hap Cow, The
Domesticated Animals; Ceremonies; Immortality
   Her milk is used in funeral preparations. She is mentioned
in the Papyrus of Nefer-uben-f. [Durdin-Robertson 1975]

Hap-tcheserts
Time
   The twelfth hour of the day. Hours of the day may have
varied names. [Budge 1969; Leach 1992]

Hashepsowe   See *Hatshepsut*.

Hast
Heaven and Hell; Water
   Goddess of the underworld. Mentioned in the Egyptian
Book of the Dead as a pool in the Elysian Fields.
[Durdin-Robertson 1975]

Hatasu   See *Hatshepsut*.

Hathor

Mother and Guardian; Heaven and Hell; Sky and Heavens; Domesticated Animals; Happiness; Sun and Day; Justice; Destroyer of Life

Egyptian mother goddess and goddess of the underworld. Among her many titles are The Celestial Cow, Queen of Heaven, Queen of the Earth, Lady of the Cemetery, Goddess of Joy, and Mother of Light. She is mother of the gods Shu, Khnum, and Ra, and wife/mother of Horus. Like many other goddesses, she is independently creative. Represented with a headdress of a solar disk resting between horns and sometimes with the face of a cow. Her main seat of worship is Dendera, but she is associated with Prosopitis, Atarbechis, Sinai, Mefkait, Serabis, Belbeis, Punt Ethiopia, Somaliland, Libya, Thebes, Luxor Tentyra, Armant, and many other places. The alternate form *Lady of Punt* may suggest an earlier worship by groups living on the Nile in the more southern part of Sudan.

When the sun god, Ra, grew older he became fearful of his enemies and asked Hathor to help him. She took on the job with a vengeance and seemed to enjoy the killing. Ra then worried that she would wipe out the entire human race, so he had red dye mixed in ale and spread about the land. Hathor, thinking it was blood, drank it and became intoxicated. She forgot her assignment and humankind was saved.

Hathor was merged with *Bat, Hetpet, Mht wr.t,* and *Nechmetawaj.* She is idenitified with *Neserit, Noub, Ritho, Saosis, Tefnut,* and *Thenenet.* See also *Akarkhentkats, Anit, Ashtoreth, Ehe, Kerub of Air, Mehet, Meri, Methyer, Naham-ua, Nehemāuit, Nehemcou, Nehimeou, Neith, Qetesh, Sekhmet, Tanen-tu,* and *Isthar,* Near East. Alternate forms: Athor, Athyr, Ator, Hether, Lady of Punt, Meh Urit, Mehet-uret. [Cooper 1876; Durdin-Robertson 1975; Jayne 1925; Leach 1992; Monaghan 1981; Neumann 1972; Olson 1983; Stone 1979]

Hathors, The

Mother and Guardian; Immortality; Ceremonies

Hathor adopted seven forms as a mother goddess. The Seven Hathors nourish the souls of the desceased and the newborns. They include *Akarkhentkats* and *Heb-i.*

Great festivals were celebrated in the temple of Dendera above all on New Year's Day, which was the anniversary of Hathor's birth. Before dawn the priestesses would bring Hathor's image out onto the terrace to expose it to the rays of the rising sun. The rejoicing that followed was a pretext for a veritable carnival . . . the Hathors beat their tabors, the great ladies waved their mystic whips, all those who were gathered together in the town were drunk with wine and crowned with flowers . . . all the children rejoiced in honour of the goddess, from the rising to the setting of the sun. [Durdin-Robertson 1982; Ions 1982]

Hat-mehi

Unknown

Her followers worship her in the city and nome (province) of Chev, in lower Egypt. [Cooper 1876]

Hatmehit

Fishing and Water Animals

Dolphin goddess. Worshiped at Mendes and Punt. She is depicted with a fish on her head. See also *Heru-pa-kaut.* Alternate form: Hat-mehit. [Budge 1969; Johnson 1988; Lurker 1984; Savill 1976]

Hat-mehit   See *Hatmehit.*

Hatshepsut

Justice; Wealth; Order; Family and Tribes; Beauty

Queen of Egypt. Regarded as one of the greatest rulers of Egypt. Her reign was one of peace and prosperity. She restored religious buildings and sent an expedition to Punt to obtain myrrh trees, incense, rare woods, and sacred animals. The tribal chiefs of Syria scorned women rulers, and when she died, her name was erased from all her monuments.

The Hathors attended Hatshepsut's mother, Queen Akmet, during her confinement. At her birth Hathor nursed her. The goddess Uto applauded her divine shapeliness.

Egyptian queens were regarded as goddesses and said to have been more honored and more readily obeyed than kings. Alternate forms: Hashepsowe, Hatasu, Hatshopsiti. [Durdin-Robertson 1975; Mackenzie 1913]

Hatshopsiti   See *Hatshepsut.*

Hauhet

Demi-animals; Primordial Being

Serpent goddess. One of the Hermopolitan Ogdoad. (See *Amaunet* for a description of the Ogdoad.) She represents "the infinity of space." Like the other goddesses in this group she is portrayed "as a woman with a serpent's head and having a jackal's head in place of feet." See also *Heh, Hehet.* Alternate forms: Hauket, Hehut. [Durdin-Robertson 1975; Harding 1971; Leach 1992]

Hauket   See *Hauhet.*

Heb-i

Domesticated Animals

One of the cows of *Hathor.* [Cooper 1876]

Hedetet

Insects

Scorpion goddess. Mentioned in the *Book of the Dead.* She was later merged with *Isis.* [Lurker 1984]

Heh

Primordial Being; Reptiles

Serpent goddess. "One of the initial primeval pairs representing the infinity of space." Also considered half of the primeval pair with *Hauhet* and known as *Huh.* See also *Hehet.* [Cooper 1876; Durdin-Robertson 1975; Leach 1992]

Hehet

Primordial Being

"Infinity." See also *Hauhet, Heh.* [Savill 1976]

Hehut   See *Hauhet.*

Heka   See *Hak.*

Hekenth

Demi-animals; Time

Lion-headed goddess of time. She stands behind Osiris during the seventh hour of the night. [Leach 1992]

Heket

Creator of Life; Demi-animals; Fishing and Water Animals; Mother and Guardian

Frog-headed goddess of childbirth. Her consort fashioned humans' bodies and she gave them life. She is symbolized by germinating grain. See also *Heqet.* [Leach 1992]

Hekt   See *Heqet.*

Hemsut, The

Mother and Guardian; Creator of Life

Protectors of newborns. Also said to be the counterpart of Ka and responsible for the creation of all sustenance. Alternate form: Hemuset. [Long 1963; Lurker 1984]

Hemuset   See *The Hemsut.*

Henemet-em-anh-annuit
Immortality; Heaven and Hell
   One of the *Seven Kine-deities.* They provided food to the deceased in the underworld. See also *Akert-khentet-auset-s.* [Durdin-Robertson 1975]

Hentet-arqiu
Hunting and Wild Animals; Heaven and Hell
   Hippopotamus goddess. Mentioned in the Papyrus of Ani as the keeper of the fifth pylon of the underworld. [Leach 1992]

Hent-nut-s
Time
   One of the *Twelve Goddesses of Life and Strength.* [Durdin-Robertson 1982]

Heptet
Demi-animals; Immortality
   Serpent-headed goddess. She is associated with the resurrection of Osiris. [Leach 1992]

Heqet
Primordial Being; Water; Immortality; Demi-animals; Creator of Life; Mother and Guardian
   Goddess of the Primordial Waters. Wife of Khnemu (Khumn), god of the Nile. Presided over birth of kings and queens and assisted Osiris to rise from the dead in her role over generation, regeneration, and fertility. She is represented as a frog (or toad) or as a woman with a frog's head.

☥ *Heqet is the giver of life. She enlivens the bodies of the rulers of Egypt and the men and women whom Khumn fashions on his potter's wheel.*

   One of the oldest centers of the worship of the frog goddess, Heqet was near the island of Elephantine, where the caverns through which the Nile entered Egypt were situated. She was usurped by *Satet* or *Sati.* See also *Heket.* Alternate forms: Hekt, Heqt, Heqtit, Hequet, Hequit, Hiqit, Hiquit. [Budge 1989; Durdin-Robertson 1975; Ions 1982; Leach 1992; Neumann 1972]

Heqit   See *Nut.* See also *Hecate,* Near East.

Heqt   See *Heqet.*

Heqtit   See *Heqet.*

Hequet   See *Heqet.*

Hequit   See *Heqet.*

Herit
Directions
   Goddess of the North. [Leach 1992]

Her-sha-s
Earth and Nature
   Goddess of the blazing desert. [Leach 1992]

Her-tep-aha-her-neb-s
Time
   The seventh hour of the night. [Durdin-Robertson 1975]

Her-tept
Heaven and Hell; Demi-animals; Immortality
   Serpent-headed goddess of the underworld. She attends the mummified Osiris. [Leach 1992]

Hert-erman
Time
   She stands with the goddess of the North, *Neith,* at the tenth hour. [Durdin-Robertson 1982]

Hert-ketit-s
Time; Demi-animals; Heaven and Hell; Justice
   Underworld goddess of time. This lion-headed deity of the eleventh hour of the night destroys the fiends in the pit of Hatel. [Leach 1992]

Heru-pa-kaut
Fishing and Water Animals; Mother and Guardian
   "Great Mother of Mendes." She is portrayed with a fish on her head. She was displaced by *Isis.* See also *Hatmehit.* [Jobes 1962]

Heru-sekha
Domesticated Animals
   Cow goddess. [Leach 1992]

Hesa
Domesticated Animals; Immortality
   "Divine White Cow." An unguent made of her milk is used to retore the flesh of the deceased. Closely associated with *Isis,* who used a milk unguent to restore Osiris. Alternate form: Hesat. [Durdin-Robertson 1975; Lurker 1984]

Hesamut   See *Reret.*

Hesat   See *Hesa.*

Hesi   See *Isis.*

Hetemitet
Time
   One of the four goddesses of the seventh hour of the night. She is portrayed holding a large knife. [Durdin-Robertson 1982]

Hetepet   See *Hetpet.*

Hetep-sekhus
Heaven and Hell
   Goddess of the underworld. In the Egyptian *Book of the Dead* she is called the "Eye and the Flame." [Durdin-Robertson 1975]

Hether   See *Hathor.*

Het-hert
Time
   Goddess of the third month of the year. [Leach 1992]

Het-kau-nebt-er-tcher
Heaven and Hell
   One of the *Seven Kine-deities.* See also *Akert-khentet-auset-s.* [Durdin-Robertson 1975]

Hetpet
Happiness
   "Happiness." Said to have merged with *Hathor.* Alternate form: Hetepet. [Jobes 1962; Lurker 1984]

Himbuto   See *Uadjet.*

Hiqit   See *Heqet.*

Hiquit   See *Heqet.*

Hoh
Demi-animals
Serpent-headed goddess. [Cooper 1876]

Horit
Sky and Heavens
"Sky." Wife of Horus. [Durdin-Robertson 1975]

Huh See *Heh.*

Huntheth
Sky and Heavens
One of the goddesses who line the path of the sun god, Ra, on his journey across the sky. [Durdin-Robertson 1982]

Ini-herit
Justice; Order
Goddess of politics. She presides over mediators, diplomats, statesmen, and conciliators. It was Ini-herit who convinced Tefnut to return the sun. Alternate form: Onuris. [Baumgartner 1984]

Iou-s-aas
Unknown
"The Great One Who Comes." Daughter of Ra who is worshiped at Heliopolis. [Cooper 1876]

Ipet
Hunting and Wild Animals; Mother and Guardian
Hippopotamus mother goddess who is called the "Queen of Two Lands," upper and lower Egypt. See also *Apet, Êpet, Reret, Sheput, Taourt, Taueret, Ta-urt, Thoeris, Thoueris, Tie.* Alternate form: Ipi. [Lurker 1984]

Ipi See *Ipet.*

Isis
Love and Sexuality; Ceremonies; Health and Healing; Immortality; Time; Stars and Planets; Mother and Guardian; Earth and Nature; Moon and Night
Mother goddess. Daughter of *Nut,* wife of Osiris. Among her many titles are Queen of the Earth, The Moon, Goddess of Life and Healing, Protectress of the Dead, Mother of the Seasons, Queen of the Stars, and the Many-Named Goddess. She is also frequently connected to *Nephthys* with names such as The Divine Merti, The Ur-urti Goddesses, The Two Kites, The Two Divine Hawks, and The Two Exceeding Great Uraei. Also identified with the *Magna Mater,* Greek and Roman Empires. She was worshiped throughout Egypt, the Roman Empire, Chaldaea, Greece, Germany, Gaul, and many other areas. Originally independent, she was united with Osiris, but she remained the more popular deity. She formed a triad with Horus and Osiris, and at Delos she was worshiped as a triad with the gods Anubis and Serapis, invoked for the protection of sailing ships. With the advent of Christianity, many of the chapels of Isis were converted to churches and representations of Isis with the infant Horus became the Virgin Mary holding Jesus. See also *Black Virgins,* Greek and Roman Empires.

☥ *When Osiris was killed by Set, his body was set adrift in the Nile and Isis began her long search for him. The casket washed ashore near the Phoenician city of Byblus, where a tree quickly grew around it. The king of Byblus cut down the tree and used it as a pillar in his house. Isis became a nurse of the monarch's child, who was quite sickly. When Isis cured the boy, the king willingly gave her the pillar. Set, hearing that Isis had found Osiris, stole his body, chopping it into pieces and throwing it into the water again. Isis retrieved her husband and reassembled him. The only part she was unable to find was his penis, so she fashioned a golden phallus for him and they conceived Horus.*

Isis was celebrated at one festival called *The Lychnapsia,* the Festival of Lights, on August 12, to commemorate seeking her spouse in the darkness by torchlight, and her procession resembled those of *Neith* at Sais and of *Bast* at Bubastis. This foreshadowed Candlemas Day of Catholicism. She was merged with *Hedetet, Herupakaut,* and *Sentait.* Equivalent to *Ziza,* Northern Europe. In Sumer and Akkadia she is called *Iahu;* her Nabataean names are *Adb-isi, Amat-isi, Ament, Asdoulos,* and *Isidoulos.* (These goddesses can be found in Near East region.) See also *Amit, Auset, Meri, Methyer, Schent, Sekhet, Selk, Sochet, Watch Merti; Anael,* Near East, and *Isia,* Greek and Roman Empires. Alternate forms: Ānqet, As, Aset, Ast, Au Set, Ese, Eset, Esi, Hesi, Khut, Lady of Life, Mehet-uret, Menhet, Quati, Sara, Schent, Sochet, Stella Maris, Tsont-nofre, Unt. [Cooper 1876; Durdin-Robertson 1975; Durdin-Robertson 1982; Jayne 1925; Jobes 1962; Leach 1992; Olson 1983; Stone 1979; Sykes 1968]

Iusaaset
Sun and Day
Solar goddess. The counterpart of Tem, the rising and setting sun. [Leach 1992]

Iusas See *Iusaset, Juesaes, Saosis.*

Iusaset
Unknown
Goddess of Heliopolis. May be the same as *Iusas.* [Sykes 1968]

Iusasit See *Saosis.*

Juesaes
Unknown
Personification of the "Hand of God." Alternate forms: Iusas, Jusas. [Lurker 1984]

Junit
Unknown
Possibly the personification of a pillar. Worshiped in Tuphium, the modern El Tod. [Lurker 1984]

Jusas See *Juesaes.*

Kadesh See *Qetesh.*

Ka-harus-apu-saru-ma-hakar-uma See *Bast.*

Kahi
Family and Tribes
Possibly the personification of a country. [Cooper 1876]

Kait
Primordial Being
One of the Hermopolitan Ogdoad. (See *Amaunet* for definition of the Ogdoad). Identified with *Kekuit.* See also *Kait,* Near East. [Leach 1992; Wedeck and Baskin 1971]

Kakit See *Kauket.*

Kartek "Spark Holder." See *Thoeris.*

Katesch
Unknown
"Sacred," "Holy." Syrian in origin, she forms a triad with *Anta* and *Reschep.* [Cooper 1876]

Kauket
Moon and Night

"Darkness." One of the goddesses of the Hermopolitan Ogdoad (see *Amaunet* for definition) associated with the phases of light and darkness. See also *Kekuit*. Alternate forms: Kakit, Kekit, Kekiut. [Durdin-Robertson 1975; Leach 1992; Neumann 1972; Sproul 1979]

Kebechet
Immortality; Heaven and Hell; Reptiles; Water
   Snake goddess of the underworld. Personification of the purifying aspect of water. Connected to the revitalization of the dead. [Lurker 1984]

Kebehut
Life/Death Cycle
   "Freshness." Goddess of youth. Daughter of Anubis, jackal god of embalming. She is mentioned in the Pyramid Texts. [Durdin-Robertson 1975; Leach 1992]

Kedesh   See *Qetesh.*

Kefa
Time; Stars and Planets
   "Mother of Time." The goddess of the seven stars (the Great Bear) who gave birth to time in the earliest circle of the year. Alternate forms: Kep, Kepha. [Durdin-Robertson 1975; Durdin-Robertson 1976; Durdin-Robertson 1982]

Kekit   See *Kauket.*

Kekiut   See *Kauket.*

Kek-t
Moon and Night
   Goddess of darkness. [Cooper 1876]

Kekuit
Dawn and Twilight
   "The Period of Night That Immediately Follows the Day." Identified with *Kait*. See also *Kauket*. [Jobes 1962; Leach 1992]

Ken
Love and Sexuality
   Goddess of love. Similar to *Venus*, Greek and Roman Empires. Ken is mentioned in Hebrew scriptures. She is pictured standing on a lion, holding two snakes in one hand and a flower in the other. Alternate forms: Chiun, Kiun. [Durdin-Robertson 1975]

Kenat
Directions; Sun and Day
   Goddess of the South who holds the solar disk as the sun god, Ra, travels on his boat across the sky. [Durdin-Robertson 1982]

Kenemet
Hunting and Wild Animals; Mother and Guardian
   "The Mother." Ape goddess. May be connected to *Mut*. [Durdin-Robertson 1975]

Kenet
Unknown
   Thought to be of Syrian origin. [Sykes 1968]

Kenken-ur   See *Ser-t.*

Kenmut
Stars and Planets
   "Vulture." Name of an Egyptian constellation. [Durdin-Robertson 1975]

Kent
Unknown
   Another name for *Qetesh* or *Qetshu* on the stele in the British Museum. She forms a triad with the gods Reshpu and Min or Amsu. [Budge 1989; Leach 1992]

Kep   See *Kefa.*

Kepha   See *Kefa.*

Kerhet
Moon and Night; Sun and Day
   Goddess of the phases of light and darkness. According to some, one of the members of the Hermopolitan Ogdoad (see *Amaunet* for definition), which includes *Nut, Hauhet,* and *Kauket*. See also *Ament*. Alternate forms: Enenet-hemset, Ennit. [Durdin-Robertson 1975; Jobes 1962]

Kerub of Air
Demi-animals; Wild Birds
   The power of *Hathor* who unites the powers of *Isis* and *Nephthys*. She is personified as a young girl with large and over-shadowing wings. [Durdin-Robertson 1982]

Khaft
Unknown
   "Lady of the Country." Goddess of upper Egypt. [Redfield 1931]

Kha-ra-ta-nek-ha
Unknown
   One of the wives of Horus. [Cooper 1876]

Khebent
Heaven and Hell
   Goddess of the underworld. Daughter of *Sekseket*. [Durdin-Robertson 1975]

Kheftes-hau-hesqet-neha-her
Time
   Guardian of the seventh hour of the night in the *Book of Ami Tuat*. See also *Ament-semu-set*. [Budge 1989]

Khemit
Time; Heaven and Hell
   "Lady of the Boat." Goddess of the fifth hour in the underworld. [Durdin-Robertson 1982]

Khenememtit
Heaven and Hell; Immortality
   Goddess of the underworld. Found in the *Book of Traversing Eternity*. She gives food to the deceased in the "Divine House of the Venerable Goddess." Associated with *Menqet*. [Durdin-Robertson 1975]

Khent
Time
   The sixth hour of the night on the thirteenth or eighteenth day of the moon. [Leach 1992]

Kheperu
Time
   The eighth hour of the day. [Budge 1969; Leach 1992]

Khera
Heaven and Hell
   Goddess of the underworld. She is mentioned in the *Papyrus of Nu*. [Durdin-Robertson 1975]

Khesef-khemt
Time
    The eleventh hour of the night. [Leach 1992]

Khnemet-urt
Immortality
    In the Pyramid Texts, Khnemet-urt plays a part in the re-membering of Osiris after his dismemberment. With the assistance of *Isis*, *Nephthys*, and *Nut*, she breathed life into him and put together his flesh, bones, and heart. [Budge 1989]

Khoemnis
Heaven and Hell; Family and Tribes; Fire; Magic
    Goddess of the underworld. Personification of Egypt. Associated with fire. Her titles include The Mystery Goddess, The Lovely Spectre, Enchantress, and Incuba. The ancient city of Khoemnu or Choemnis is thought to have been named for her. Alternate forms: Chemnis, Chemnu, Khoemnu. [Durdin-Robertson 1975]

Khoemnu See *Khoemnis*.

Khut
Reptiles; Sun and Day
    "The Light-giver." Serpent goddess. Associated with Ra, she encircles the sun. Also a name for *Isis*. [Leach 1992]

Kiun See *Ken*.

Lady of Amenta
Heaven and Hell; Justice; Immortality
    "Heaven." The goddess or goddesses who welcome those who have been judged righteous and are allowed to live in Amenta (heaven).
    ☥ *When the deceased has passed judgment and her/his heart is found to be as light as the feather of Maât, the soul can enter into heaven, where it is greeted by the Lady of Amenta.* [Stone 1979]

Lady of Life See *Isis*.

Lady of Punt See *Hathor*.

Ma
Justice; Heaven and Hell
    "Truth." Daughter of Ra. Also called the "Eternal Mother and Goddess of the Lower World." Also a goddess of Anatolia who was worshiped in Rome and an alternate name for the goddess *Mami*, Near East. Alternate form: Mama. [Cooper 1876; Durdin-Robertson 1975; Monaghan 1981; Neumann 1972; Pike 1951]

Maât
Creator of Life; Heaven and Hell; Justice; Order; Immortality; Primordial Being
    Primeval Egyptian goddess of truth and justice and of law and order. "She does not judge: she is consciousness itself and also the individual consciousness that each person carries in his heart, for she is both the motivating force and the goal of life." She gave the breath of life to the gods. She is sometimes considered two goddesses, *Maati*, goddess of the North and South. Similar to *Tmei*.
    ☥ *Maât is presented to the gods by the pharaoh instead of the ritual meal. In the underworld the figure of Maât or her feather is placed on the opposite side of the scale from the heart of the deceased. If the scale balances, the deceased is allowed to go on to the Elysian Fields. If not, he/she is given to Ammit to devour.*

Alternate forms: Maati, Maet, Mait, Mayet. [Baring and Cashford 1991; Durdin-Robertson 1975; Ions 1982; Leach 1992; Senior 1985; Stone 1979]

Maati See *Maât*.

Maau See *Atet*.

Maet See *Maât*.

Ma'et
Justice
    "Right" or "Truth." [Leach 1992]

Mafdet
Hunting and Wild Animals; Domesticated Animals; Household Affairs
    Lynx goddess or cat goddess. Thought to be of Libyan origin. She keeps the pharaoh's house free from snakes. Alternate form: Maftet. [Durdin-Robertson 1975; Leach 1992; Senior 1985]

Mafiet
War
    Deity of war. [Leach 1992]

Maftet See *Mafdet*.

Mai-hesa
Unknown
    "Fierce-eyed." Worshiped at Bubastis with her consort, the lion. Similar to the *Miysis*, Greek and Roman Empires. [Budge 1989]

Mait See *Maât*.

Mak-nebt-s
Time
    The third hour of the day. [Budge 1969; Leach 1992]

Mama See *Ma*.

Manefertrā
Time; Heaven and Hell
    Pilot goddess of the twelfth hour of the night in the *Book of Ami Tuat*. See also *Ament-semu-set*. [Budge 1989]

Maskhonit See *Meskhent*.

Mauit See *Mut*.

Maut See *Mut*.

Mayet See *Maât*.

Meh Urit See *Hathor*.

Mehen
Reptiles; Heaven and Hell; Water
    Serpent goddess of the underworld. Associated with the "Lake of a Million Years," the Twelfth Qereret (division), and the second division of the Taut (underworld). [Durdin-Robertson 1975; Leach 1992]

Mehenit
Reptiles; Heaven and Hell; Immortality
    Another name for *Sekhmet* as a cobra goddess in the underworld who guarded the head of her father, Rā. Supplications are made to her in the Eleventh Qereret (division). Also said to be a name for *Net* when she clothes the dead in her linens. [Durdin-Robertson 1975; Leach 1992]

Mehet
Directions
   "The Northern One." Also an alternate name for *Sekhmet*.
See also *Hathor, Isis, Mehit, Methyer*. Alternate form:
Mehet-uret. [Lurker 1984]

Mehet-uret   See *Hathor, Isis, Mehet*.

Mehi
Time; Demi-animals
   Goddess of the Eleventh Qereret (division) to whom
supplications are made. Also said to be a lion-headed
goddess, a form of *Pasht* or *Sekhet*. [Cooper 1876;
Durdin-Robertson 1975]

Mehit
Hunting and Wild Animals; Directions
   "The Northern One." Lion goddess. Worshiped in the
nome (county) of Sebennytus. Said by some to be the double
or reincarnation of *Tefnut*. Others say she is associated with
or the same as *Sekhmet*. See also *Mehet*. [Budge 1989;
Durdin-Robertson 1975; Lurker 1984; Savill 1976]

Mehiti
Fishing and Water Animals
   Fish goddess. She fills bodies of freshwater with fish.
[Stone 1979]

Meh-khebitet-seh-neter
Heaven and Hell; Immortality
   One of the *Seven Kine-deities*. See also *Akert-khentet-
auset-s*. [Durdin-Robertson 1975]

Mehueret
Domesticated Animals; Primordial Being; Demi-animals;
Sky and Heavens; Earth and Nature; Heaven and Hell
   Goddess of the Beginning. Among her titles are The
Celestial Cow, The Lady of Heaven, Mistress of Earth,
Goddess of the Watery Abyss, and Underworld Goddess.
She is closely connected to *Methyer, Neith, Hathor*, and *Isis*.
She is represented as a woman with protruding breasts, the
head of a cow, holding a scepter entwined with the stalk of
a lotus flower. Alternate forms: Mehuerit, Mehurt, Meh-urt,
Mihi-uirit. [Durdin-Robertson 1975; Neumann 1972]

Mehuerit   See *Mehueret*.

Mehurt   See *Mehueret*.

Meh-urt   See *Ahat, Mehueret*.

Menat
Hunting and Wild Animals
   Lion goddess. Also worshiped by the Arabians. See also
Menat, Near East. [Leach 1992]

Menhenet
Reptiles
   Serpent goddess. Identified with *Sekhet*. [Leach 1992]

Menhet
Demi-animals
   Lion-headed goddess. Identified with *Bast* in Nubia. Also
the name for *Isis* in Heliopolis. [Leach 1992]

Menhit
Time; War; Hunting and Wild Animals
   The sixth hour of the sixth day of the moon. She is also
identified as a lion goddess and war goddess worshiped in
Latapolis (Esneh). [Leach 1992; Lurker 1984]

Menkheret
Heaven and Hell
   Goddess of the underworld. She assists one of the
barks (boats) that carry the dead on their journey.
[Durdin-Robertson 1975]

Menqet
Heaven and Hell; Immortality
   Goddess of the underworld. She is mentioned in the
Papyrus of Nu. Menqet aids the dead by germinating the
plants they have with them for their afterlife. Associated with
Khenememtit. [Durdin-Robertson 1975]

Meresger   See *Merseger*.

Meret
Water
   Goddess of water. Associated with *Mut*. Also considered
an alternate name for *Mert*. [Leach 1992; Lurker 1984]

Meri
Water
   "Goddess of the Sea." See also *Hathor, Isis*.

Meri-en-sekar   See *Rannu*.

Merit
Creator of Life
   Fertility goddess symbolized by the overflowing of the
rivers. [Stone 1979]

Merseger
Order; Heaven and Hell; Demi-animals; Goodness; Justice;
Magic
   Serpent goddess of the underworld. Goddess of the
Theban Necropolis, companion of the dead who enjoys
silence. She is portrayed as a human-headed snake or as a
snake with three heads, the center a human head with the
head of a snake on one side and a vulture's head on the other.
   ☥ *Merseger was known as a benevolent goddess, but she
      sometimes found it necessary to punish one of her followers.
      Once a man named Neferaboo secretly injured his neighbor,
so Merseger caused him to lose his sight. When Neferaboo publicly
confessed his crime, Merseger returned his vision.*
   Alternate forms: Meresger, Mertseger, Ta-dehnet. [Durdin-
Robertson 1975; Olson 1983; Senior 1985]

Mersekhnet   See *Atet*.

Mert
Time; Heaven and Hell; Wealth
   The eighth hour of the night of the underworld who
manifests as part of the bark that carries the shade (the spirit
of the deceased) through the Borderlands. She is represented
as a woman with a large headdress made from a cluster of
papyrus or lotus, standing on the symbol for gold, and is
sometimes called the "Queen of the Treasury." See also *the
Merti*. Alternate forms: Meret, Merte, Milt. [Budge 1969;
Cooper 1876; Durdin-Robertson 1975; Leach 1992; Lurker
1984]

Merte   See *Mert*.

Merti, The
Time; Reptiles; Heaven and Hell
   Two serpent goddesses who are entwined. See also *Mert,
Watch Merti*. [Durdin-Robertson 1975; Durdin-Robertson
1982]

Mertseger   See *Merseger*.

Mesenet
Mother and Guardian
  Personification of the "birth tile" on which women give birth. See also *Meshkent.* [Lurker 1984]

Meshkent
Mother and Guardian; Fate; Heaven and Hell; Justice
  Goddess of childbirth. Also a goddess of fate who foretells the newborn's future and a goddess of the underworld who accompanies the shade and testifies on his/her behalf at judgment time. Wife of Shai, god of fate. She is sometimes viewed as having four aspects called the Four Meshkents. The four deities are the goddesses of the birth chamber, of the birth stool, and of the two birth bricks on which women squat when the child is delivered. She is depicted with a headdress of two high plumes coiled at the tips. She is also represented as the birth brick with a woman's head. Similar to *Ermutu.* See also *Mesenet.* Alternate forms: Maskhonit, Meshkhenit, Meshkhent, Meshkhoni. [Ions 1982; Leach 1992; Savill 1976]

Meskhenet See *Meshkent.*

Meskhenit See *Meshkent.*

Meskhent
Mother and Guardian; Fate; Heaven and Hell; Justice
  Equivalent to *Meshkent.* Identified with *Shait.* Alternate forms: Maskhonit, Meskhenet. [Durdin-Robertson 1975; Senior 1985]

Meskhoni See *Meshkent.*

Mesta
Unknown
  Spirit or goddess mentioned in the Ritual of the Dead. [Cooper 1876]

Methyer
Primordial Being; Water
  "The Great Flood." Personification of the primordial water. The terrestrial counterpart of the cow of the heavenly ocean. She corresponds to *Isis* and closely parallels *Mehueret.* See also *Hathor, Mehet.* [Durdin-Robertson 1975; Lurker 1984; Neumann 1972; Stone 1979]

Mht wr.t
Primordial Being; Sun and Day
  She arose out of the primeval waters. After giving birth to the sun god, she placed him between her horns. She was replaced by *Hathor.* [Olson 1983]

Mihit
Demi-animals; Hunting and Wild Animals
  Lion goddess. She appears as a lion or as a lion-headed human. Closely associated with *Sekhmet.* [Durdin-Robertson 1975]

Mihi-uirit See *Mehueret.*

Milt See *Mert.*

Mooth See *Mut.*

Mout See *Mut.*

Muit See *Mut.*

Mut
Mother and Guardian; Demi-animals; Creator of Life; Magic; Health and Healing; Immortality
  "Mother." Local vulture goddess who brought forth herself. Her sanctuary was near the lake at Karnak and she was personified as a woman's body with a vulture's head. Later the wife of Amon-Ra and Menes. Among her titles are Our Lady, Queen of Earth, Queen of Heaven, and The Virgin. One of her symbols is the vulture, considered by the Egyptians to be a mother bird who contains the complete power of reproduction. She can assume the cat figure of *Bast* and the lioness head of *Sekhmet.* When in the form of a woman, Mut wears a vulture-shaped headdress and the united crowns of the South and the North. She is considered the "maker of sound bodies."
  ☥ *Mut aided Isis with the reconstitution of the body of Osiris. She replaced his head and heart, and collected the flesh that had been sliced off his body.*
  Identified with *Merit,* and *Hera,* Greek and Roman Empires. See also *Anit.* Alternate forms: Apet, Mauit, Maut, Mooth, Mout, Muit, Muth, Nubit. [Budge 1969; Budge 1989; Cooper 1876; Durdin-Robertson 1975; Guirand 1968; Savill 1976; Senior 1985]

Muth See *Mut.*

Mut-neb-set
Time
  The tenth hour of the night. [Budge 1969; Leach 1992]

Mut-ubastet See *Ubastet.*

Muyt
Creator of Life
  "Seed." Goddess of generation of humans and animals. [Leach 1992]

Nahab
Demi-animals
  Snake-headed goddess. [Monaghan 1981]

Naham-ua
Fishing and Water Animals
  Name for *Hathor* as a fish goddess. [Cooper 1876]

Nahmauit
Goodness
  Like the sound of the sistrum to which her name alludes, she has the power to drive away evil. She forms a triad with her husband, Thoth, and her son, Nofir-horu. She is portrayed with a sistrum on her head. Alternate form: Nemanous. [Durdin-Robertson 1975]

Nakith
Time
  One of the four goddesses of the seventh hour of the night holding a large knife. [Durdin-Robertson 1982]

Naprit
Agriculture
  Goddess of grain. She wears a sheaf of grain on her head. [Durdin-Robertson 1975]

Nau
Time
  Personification of an hour. [Cooper 1876]

Naunet
Mother and Guardian; Water

"Water." Mother goddess. One of the goddesses of the Hermopolitan Ogdoad (see *Amaunet* for definition). Alternate form: Nunut. [Durdin-Robertson 1975; Neumann 1972; Sproul 1979]

Nazit
Demi-animals
   Winged serpent goddess. She is worshiped in the Nile Delta. [Jobes 1962]

Neb-ankhet
Time
   The fifth hour of the night. [Leach 1992]

Neb-anu
Unknown
   Deity about whom nothing is known. She was worshiped during the Ptolemaic period. [Cooper 1876]

Nebetu   See *Nebtuu*.

Nebhat   See *Nephthys*.

Nebheb-ka   See *Nehebka*.

Nebhet Hotep
Metals
   "Lady of the Mine or Quarry" and "Peace of Nebt." Mother of *Tefnut*, wife of Atum, god of the setting sun or darkness. Alternate forms: Nebhet-hotep, Nebthotpit. [Cooper 1876; Durdin-Robertson 1975; Savill 1976]

Nebhet-hotep   See *Nebhet Hotep*.

Neb-oo
Unknown
   Possibly a name for one of the greater goddesses. [Cooper 1876]

Neb-senti
Time
   The ninth hour of the night. [Budge 1969; Leach 1992]

Nebt
Heaven and Hell; Weather
   "Cloud Fiend." Goddess of the underworld who is mentioned in the *Book of the Dead*.
   ☥ *Nebt is often found opposing Ra and Osiris. Once she accompanied Seba and took the form of a cloud, standing in Ra's (the sun's) way at daybreak.*
   Associated with *Seba* and *Seshat*. [Durdin-Robertson 1975]

Nebt-er-tcher
Heaven and Hell
   Goddess of the underworld. She is number sixteen in the *Papyrus of Nu*, "Of Making a Man Perfect." One of the *Seven Kine-deities* is called *Het-kau-nebt-er-tcher*, possibly indicating an association with Nebt-er-tcher. [Durdin-Robertson 1975]

Nebthet   See *Nephthys*.

Nebt-hot   See *Nephthys*.

Nebthotpit   See *Nebhet Hotep*.

Nebti, The
Magic

"Two Mistresses." Name for *Uadjet* and *Nekhebet* as the ruling goddesses of lower and upper Egypt. They are said to be rich in magic. Alternate form: Neb-ti. [Durdin-Robertson 1975; Monaghan 1981]

Neb-ti   See *The Nebti*.

Nebt-mat
Time
   One of the *Twelve Goddesses of Life and Strength*. [Durdin-Robertson 1982]

Nebt-nehi
Unknown
   Deity. [Cooper 1876]

Nebt-setau
Time
   One of the *Twelve Goddesses of Life and Strength*. [Durdin-Robertson 1982]

Nebt-shat
Time
   One of the *Twelve Goddesses of Life and Strength*. [Durdin-Robertson 1982]

Nebt-shefshefet
Time
   One of the *Twelve Goddesses of Life and Strength*. [Durdin-Robertson 1982]

Nebt-thehent
Time
   The first hour of the night. [Budge 1969; Leach 1992]

Nebt-unnut
Heaven and Hell
   "Lady of the Hour." Goddess of the underworld. [Durdin-Robertson 1975]

Nebtusha
Time
   Guardian of the eighth hour of the night in the *Book of Ami Tuat*. See also *Ament-semu-set*. [Budge 1989]

Nebtuu
Earth and Nature
   "Queen of the Fields." Worshiped in Esneh. Alternate form: Nebetu. [Lurker 1984]

Nechbet   See *Nekhebet*.

Nechmetawaj
Justice
   "She Who Takes the Part of the Robbed." Goddess of justice. Worshiped in Hermopolis (Toth) and later merged with *Hathor*. See also *Dikaiosyne*. Alternate form: Nehmet-awai. [Lurker 1984]

Nefertem
Mother and Guardian
   Goddess of childbirth. [Neumann 1972]

Neg   See *Neith*.

Nehebka
Heaven and Hell; Reptiles; Justice; Agriculture
   Serpent goddess of the underworld. Mentioned in the *Book of the Dead*. One of the judges of the dead who supplies them with sustenance and acts as one of the judges for *Maât*. Also

an agricultural goddess associated with plowing. Alternate forms: Nehebkath, Nebheb-ka. [Durdin-Robertson 1975; Jobes 1962; Leach 1992]

Nehebkath   See *Nehebka.*

Nehemāuit
Unknown
   "Sweeper Away of Oppressed." A form of *Hathor* and a counterpart of the male deity Thete. She is depicted as wearing solar and lunar disks on her head, which refers to her solar or lunar origin. [Budge 1989]

Nehemcou
Fishing and Water Animals
   Fish goddess. See also *Hathor.*

Nehimeou
Unknown
   Portrayed wearing a temple headdress. May be a form of *Hathor.* [Cooper 1876]

Nehmet-awai   See *Nechmetawaj.*

Neit   See *Neith.*

Neith
Mother and Guardian; Sky and Heavens; Household Affairs; War; Hunting and Wild Animals; Family and Tribes; Domesticated Animals; Water; Heaven and Hell; Demi-animals
   Ancient goddess whose titles are Mother Goddess, Queen of Heaven, Our Lady of the Starry Vault, Goddess of Weaving, War Goddess, Goddess of Hunting, and Protector of Marriage. The range of her rule is unlimited. One of her names, *Tehenut,* meaning "the Libyan," suggests a Western origin. Neith's early form was that of a heifer, but she later appeared in human form. As a cow goddess she is closely associated with *Mehueret.* Marriage contracts during the time Neith was worshiped required that husbands promise obedience to their wives. She is associated with the Nile Delta and Sais. As a goddess of the underworld, she guards the coffins and canopic jars along with *Selket, Isis,* and *Nephthys.* Neith is represented with wings and either a flat disk signifying the heavens or a weaver's shuttle. She wears the red crown of lower Egypt.
   ♀ *Neith played a part in the tribunal called to decide between the rival claims of Set and Horus. When the gods could not make a decision, they called on Neith, as the oldest of the goddesses, to assist them. She favored Horus and threatened to make the sky collapse if he was not made king, but she also insisted that Set be given just compensation.*
   Identified with *Chaos,* Near East. See also *Hathor* and *Usert.* Alternate forms: Neg, Neit, Neither, Nit, Tehenut. [Cooper 1876; Durdin-Robertson 1975; Jayne 1925; Leach 1992; Monaghan 1981; Neumann 1972; Stone 1979]

Neither   See *Neith.*

Nekhabit   See *Nekhebet.*

Nekhbet   See *Nekhebet.*

Nekhebet
Creator of Life; Mother and Guardian; Demi-animals; Wild Birds
   "Giver of Life and Power." Vulture goddess of Nekhen (Eileithyaspolis) in upper Egypt. Among her titles are Mother Goddess, Creator of the World, Protector of Upper Egypt, Nurse of the Pharaoh, Protector of Childbirth, and sister of

Bruto. Closely associated with *Uadjet,* and they are known together as *the Nebti.* She is represented as a vulture or as a woman with the head of a vulture, and sometimes as a woman wearing the white crown of upper Egypt. She corresponds to *Eileithyia,* Greek and Roman Empires.
   ♀ *Nekhebet spends much time at the palace, where she suckles the royal children, including the pharaoh. When the pharaoh is grown, she accompanies him in battle, hovering over his head in the form of a vulture.*
   Alternate forms: Nechbet, Nekhabit, Nekhbet, Nekhebit. [Durdin-Robertson 1975; Jayne 1925; Leach 1992; Neumann 1972]

Nekhebit   See *Nekhebet.*

Nekhen
Justice
   Goddess of law. [Sykes 1968]

Nekiu
Time
   Seventh hour of the day. [Budge 1969; Leach 1992]

Nemanous   See *Nahmauit.*

Nen
Primordial Being; Water
   Wife of Nau. Variant of the pair of primeval deities representing the watery abyss. See also *Amaunet.* [Leach 1992]

Nephthys
Moon and Night; Heaven and Hell; Immortality; Justice; Water; Weather; Wild Birds
   "Lady of the House." Vulture goddess. Personification of darkness and all that belongs to it. Very early she was a local fetish goddess who became a servant of Osiris. Daughter of *Nut,* sister of *Isis,* and wife of Geb (Seb). Among her titles are Mistress of the West, Protector of the Dead, Goddess of Darkness and Death That Is Not Eternal, One of Word and Power, and Lunar Goddess. She is a member of the Ennead of the Heliopolis and one of those present at the assessment of the souls in the underworld. Earlier, she was considered the personification of the edge of the Nile and the giver of the east wind.
   ♀ *When Nephthys's husband killed Osiris, she went to aid her sister Isis. They governed the country together and when the body of Osiris was found, they reassembled it.*
   Similar to *Anael,* Near East. See also *Anit* and *Ninit.* Alternate forms: Nebhat, Nebthet, Nebt-hot, Nephys, Nepte, Nepthys, Watch Merti. [Budge 1969; Budge 1989; Cooper 1876; Durdin-Robertson 1975; Jayne 1925; Jobes 1962; Leach 1992; Monaghan 1981; Olson 1983; Sykes 1968]

Nephys   See *Nephthys.*

Nepit
Agriculture; Demi-animals
   Goddess of corn. Counterpart of Neper, god of corn. She appears in human form or as a snake. See also *Neprit.* [Lurker 1984]

Neprit
Agriculture
   "Corn." Counterpart of the corn god Nepri. See also *Nepit.* [Leach 1992]

Nepte   See *Nephthys.*

Nepthys   See *Nephthys.*

Nesbet
Time
    Fifth hour of the day. [Budge 1969; Leach 1992]

Neserit
Fire; Magic
    Fire goddess who possesses magical properties. Identified
with *Hathor* and *Sekhet*. Alternate form: Nesert. [Budge 1989;
Leach 1992]

Nesert   See *Neserit*.

Neshtu
Demi-animals
    "The Lioness." Equivalent to *Ishtar,* Near East. [Durdin-
Robertson 1982]

Nesi-khonsu
Heaven and Hell
    Deity of the underworld. [Durdin-Robertson 1975]

Net   See *Ahat, Mehenit, Nut*.

Netert-en-khentet-ra
Time
    One of the *Twelve Goddesses of Life and Strength*.
[Durdin-Robertson 1982]

Netet
Mother and Guardian
    Mother goddess. [Neumann 1972]

Netheth
Directions; Time
    Goddess of the South. She is portrayed supporting a
hatchet at the tenth hour as the sun god, Ra, travels in his
boat. [Durdin-Robertson 1982]

Netpe
Sky and Heavens
    "Goddess of the Firmament." See also *Nut*.

Ninit
Unknown
    Wife of Ninu. Corresponds to *Nephthys*. [Durdin-
Robertson 1975]

Nishem   See *Seben*.

Nit
Hunting and Wild Animals
    Egyptian goddess of hunting at Sais. Also an alternate
name for *Neith* and *Nut*. See also *Niti*, Indian Subcontinent.
[Durdin-Robertson 1975; Durdin-Robertson 1976; Leach 1992]

Noot   See *Nut*.

Noub
Metals
    "Gold." Identified with *Hathor*. Alternate form: Nubt.
[Leach 1992]

Nubait
Unknown
    Deity about whom there is no information. [Cooper 1876]

Nubit   See *Mut*.

Nubt   See *Noub*.

Nuit   See *Nut*.

Nukarā
Unknown
    A Syrian goddess adopted by the Egyptians. May be the
goddess *Ningal,* Near East. [Budge 1989]

Nunet
Primordial Being; Water
    "World Ocean." Nunet, with her counterpart, Nun, formed
the primeval abyss, the Nile of heaven and Earth. Alternate
form: Nunit. [Baumgartner 1984; Budge 1989]

Nunit   See *Nunet*.

Nunut
Time
    The first hour of the day. Also said to be an alternate name
for *Naunet*. [Budge 1969; Durdin-Robertson 1975; Leach 1992]

Nushim
Unknown
    Deity worshiped in the city of Ankaf. [Cooper 1876]

Nut
Sky and Heavens; Mother and Guardian; Demi-animals;
Immortality; Physical Prowess
    Egyptian goddess of the Celestial Vault. Among her other
titles are The Great Deep, The Starry One, Cow Goddess,
Mother of the Gods, Mother of the Sun, Protector of the Dead,
and Mystery of the Heavens. She appears as a woman with a
pear-shaped vessel that resembles the uterus, or she sometimes
manifests as a cow, a sow, or a hippopotamus, and as the
sycamore tree. She represents the four different Egyptian
concepts of sky: a roof, a cow, an ocean, and a woman. She
gave birth to five children: Osiris, Horus, Set, *Isis,* and
Nephthys. One of her shrines was called Het-shenat.
    ✝ *Re asked Nut to raise him into the heavens to remove him
      from the world, which he found distasteful. Carrying him on
      her back, Nut rose upward, but the higher she reached, the
    dizzier she became. She would have crashed to the ground if four
    gods had not steadied her legs and while Shu held up her belly. These
    gods became the four pillars of the sky, and Nut's body became the
    firmament, to which Re attached the stars.*
    She was merged with *Epet*. See also *Anit, Nepte,* and *Ki,*
Near East. Alternate forms: Amunet, Heqit, Net, Nit, Noot,
Nuit, Schent. [Baring and Cashford 1991; Budge 1989;
Cotterell 1989; Durdin-Robertson 1975; Leach 1992; Neumann
1972; Savill 1976; Stone 1979]

Onuris   See *Ini-herit*.

Opet   See *Apet, Taueret, Ta-urt*.

Ouati   See *Sekhet*.

Pacht   See *Bast*.

Pakhet   See *Pakhit*.

Pakhit
Demi-animals
    Cat-headed or lion-headed deity. Worshiped at Speos
Artimedos. Seems to be similar to *Bast* and is associated with
Mut. See also *Pasht*. Alternate forms: Pakhet, Pak-hit, Pekhet,
Pekheth. [Durdin-Robertson 1975; Leach 1992]

Pak-hit   See *Pakhit*.

Pakht   See *Bast*.

Par-neferu-en-neb-set
Time
    Twelfth hour of the night. [Budge 1969; Durdin-Robertson 1982; Leach 1992]

Pasht
Unknown
    Lion-headed goddess worshiped in Benibasin. Also said to be an alternate name for *Bast* and *Sekhet*. See also *Mehi*, *Pakhit*. [Cooper 1876; Durdin-Robertson 1975; Pike 1951]

Pekhet   See *Pakhit*.

Pekheth   See *Pakhit*.

Per Uadjit
    "The Dwelling of Uadjit." See *Uadjet*.

Perit
Time
    One of the *Twelve Goddesses of Life and Strength*. [Durdin-Robertson 1982]

Phut
Unknown
    Deity about whom nothing is known. [Cooper 1876]

Proet
Time; Water
    Goddess of spring. Also said to be a goddess of the Nile. [Leach 1992]

Qadash   See *Qetesh*.

Qadesh   See *Qetesh*.

Qebhsnuf
Heaven and Hell; Immortality
    Goddess of the underworld. She guards the embalmed dead with *Selket*. There is an Egyptian god named Qebhsennuf. [Leach 1992; Monaghan 1981]

Qedeshet   See *Qetesh*.

Qetesh
Love and Sexuality; Moon and Night; Selflessness
    "Holy One." Also a goddess of love and the moon. She was introduced into Egypt from Syria. As *Kent* she forms a triad with Reshpu, the god of war, Min, the storm god and god of reproduction, or Ansu (Amsu), the god of reproduction. She is portrayed as clothed in tights (or naked), riding on the back of a lion, holding lotus flowers in one hand and two serpents in the other. Considered a form of *Hathor*. Identified with *Isis* and three goddesses of the Near East: *Ishtar, Anat*, and *Asherah*. Alternate forms: Kadesh, Kedesh, Qadash, Qadesh, Qedeshet, Qetshu, Qodshu, Quedesh. [Amiet 1977; Budge 1969; Budge 1989; Carlyon 1982; Leach 1992; Mackenzie 1913; Monaghan 1981; Pike 1951; Sykes 1968]

Qetshu   See *Qetesh*.

Qodshu   See *Qetesh*.

Quati   See *Isis*.

Quedesh   See *Qetesh*.

Rait
Disorder; Primordial Being

One of the oldest goddesses of chaos, the beginning, and counterpart of Rā. See also *Rat*. [Budge 1989; Durdin-Robertson 1975]

Ramuit   See *Renenet*.

Ranen   "To Suckle." See *Renenet*.

Raninit   See *Renenet*.

Ranno   See *Renen, Renenet*.

Rannu
Unknown
    Goddess of harvest who is represented by the *uraeus* in the form of the sacred asp. She may be identical to *Renenet* and *Renenutet*. Alternate form: Meri-en-sekar. [Cooper 1876; Leach 1992; Redfield 1931]

Rannut   See *Renenet, Renenutet*.

Ranpu
War
    She carries a sword and a shield and is identified with *Anaitis*, Near East and *Anta*. [Cooper 1876]

Ranuit   See *Renenet*.

Rat
Sun and Day
    Goddess of the sun. Counterpart of Ra, the sun god. Mother of Geb (Seb), *Nut*, Shu, and *Tefnut*. See also *Rait*. [Durdin-Robertson 1975; Leach 1992; Sykes 1968]

Ra-taoui   See *Ritho*.

Ra-to   See *Ritho*.

Ratta
Mother and Guardian
    Goddess who is invoked during the birth of royalty. Wife of Mentu. She wears the solar disk and horns of *Hathor*. Also an alternate name for *Rat-taoui*. See also *Ritho*. [Cooper 1876]

Rat-tanit   See *Tanith*.

Rat-taoui   See *Rat-taui*.

Rat-taui
Sun and Day
    Sun goddess. Wife of Mont (Menthu). Worshiped at Hermonthis and Medamud. She was merged with *Zenenet*. See also *Ratta* and *Ritho*. Alternate form: Rat-taoui. [Durdin-Robertson 1975]

Remute   See *Renenutet*.

Renen
Agriculture
    Goddess of harvest. See also *Renenet*. Alternate form: Ranno. [Cooper 1876]

Renenet
Agriculture; Mother and Guardian; Hunting and Wild Animals; Heaven and Hell
    Lion goddess of the harvest and divine nurse who suckled the pharaohs. She nourishes newborns and sometimes determines their fortune. She also suckles the souls of the dead and is called the earth itself. Renenet is also said to be

a name for *Isis* and identified with *Shait.* See also *Rannu, Renen, Renenutet.* Alternate forms: Ramuit, Ranen, Raninit, Ranno, Rannut, Ranuit, Renenit, Renen-utet, Rennute, Renuntet, Renute, Thermuthis. [Baumgartner 1984; Budge 1989; Cooper 1876; Durdin-Robertson 1975; Leach 1972; Leach 1992; Stone 1979]

Renenit See *Renenet.*

Renenti
Agriculture
    Harvest goddess and goddess of good fortune. [Stone 1979]

Renenutet
Agriculture; Mother and Guardian; Reptiles
    Serpent goddess of the harvest and wine. Daughter of *Saosis.* She wears the horns and solar disk of *Hathor* and is a goddess of nursing. Some say she is also lion-headed. See also *Ernutet, Renenet.* Alternate forms: Rannu, Rannut, Remute, Renen-utet. [Leach 1972; Leach 1992]

Renen-utet See *Renenet, Renenutet.*

Rennute See *Renenet.*

Rennutet
Reptiles; Agriculture; Time; Heaven and Hell
    Snake goddess and goddess of the harvest. She is regent of the eighth month of the year and is associated with the underworld. Alternate form: Renutet. [Durdin-Robertson 1975; Leach 1992]

Renpa
Time
    Goddess of the year who holds a striped palm branch in her hand that represents the calendar. See also *Renpet.* [Cooper 1876]

Renpet
Time; Life/Death Cycle; Immortality
    "Mistress of Eternity." Goddess of time who was connected with the duration of time, the spring tide, and youth. See also *Renpa.* Alternate forms: Renph, Renpit. [Cooper 1876; Durdin-Robertson 1975; Durdin-Robertson 1982; Leach 1992]

Renph See *Renpet.*

Renpit See *Renpet.*

Renuntet See *Renenet.*

Renute See *Renenet.*

Renutet See *Rennutet.*

Repa
Earth and Nature; Heaven and Hell
    Fertility and underworld goddess. Wife of Hapi. [Leach 1992; Redfield 1931]

Reret
Hunting and Wild Animals; Goodness; Stars and Planets
    Hippopotamus goddess identified with *Apet, Ta-urt, Sheput,* and others. The hippopotamus was common in the delta in very early times and appears in the *Book of the Dead* as a friendly goddess. She is a protector from evil, especially that of Set. As a star goddess identified with the constellation Draco, she is called *Hesamut.* May be an alternate name for

Taueret. See also *Apet, Êpet, Ipet, Sheput, Taourt, Taueret, Ta-urt, Thoeris, Thoueris, Tie.* [Leach 1992; Sykes 1968]

Rerit See *Taueret.*

Rert See *Apet, Taueret, Ta-urt.*

Rertu See *Apet, Taueret, Ta-urt.*

Reschep
Unknown
    She is of Syrian origin and forms a triad with *Katesch* and *Anta.* [Cooper 1876]

Ririt See *Taueret.*

Ritho
Mother and Guardian
    Sun goddess. Wife of Menthu, sun god who personifies the destructive heat. She is portrayed with the solar disk and horns of *Hathor* and presides over the birth of royalty. Also an alternate name for *Ratta.* May be the same as *Ra-taui.* Alternate form: Ra-to. [Cooper 1876]

Ronpet
Time
    Goddess of the year. [Leach 1992]

Sa
Heaven and Hell; Immortality
    Goddess of the underworld who protects its inhabitants. Also an alternate name for *Tie.* [Jobes 1962; Leach 1992]

Sachmet
War; Weather
    War goddess who forms the triad of Memphis with her husband, Ptah, and her son, Nefertem. Her breath is the hot winds of the desert. She accompanies the pharaoh, spreading fear and alarm in the battlefield. She has supernatural skills in healing. She is portrayed as a lion or as a woman with a lion's head. See also *Sekhmet.* [Lurker 1984]

Safekh-aabut
Education and Knowledge
    Deity who keeps the records. She is said to have developed the alphabet and to preside over literature and libraries. See also *Seshat.* [Boulding 1976]

Safekh-abui See *Seshat.*

Safkhitabui See *Seshat.*

Sag
Weather; Evil; Demi-animals
    Monster who causes droughts. She has the head of a hawk and the body of a lion with a lotus blossom at the end of her tail. [Jobes 1962]

Sah
Heaven and Hell
    "Great Goddess" of the underworld. She resides with Annu, Ra, Shu, and *Tefnut.* [Durdin-Robertson 1975]

Sakhmet See *Sekhmet.*

Sakhmis
Unknown
    Greek name for *Sekhmet.* [Durdin-Robertson 1975]

Saosis
Earth and Nature

"She Comes, She Grows." Tree goddess. Wife of Atum, mother of *Renenutet*. Associated with the acacia tree and closely connected with *Hathor*. Trees are highly valued in Egypt for their shadows and for the embellishment of the landscape. Other tree goddesses are *Isis* and *Nut*. Alternate forms: Eus-os, Iusas, Iusasit, Uert-hekeu. [Durdin-Robertson 1975; Olson 1983]

Sapt
Unknown

Deity adopted from another country. [Cooper 1876]

Sara   See *Isis*.

Sarset
Time

The second hour of the night. [Budge 1969; Leach 1992]

Satel
Weather; Water

One of the great goddesses in Elephantine with *Ānqet* and the male deity Khnemu.

✝ *The River Nile had been low for seven years and all the supplies had been depleted and people were starving. King Djeser appealed to the governor of Nubia for deities to help. The king journeyed to the south, repaired the deities' temple, and made offerings to them. The triad promised that the Nile would rise annually as before.* [Budge 1989]

Satet
Hunting and Wild Animals; Water; Sun and Day; Heaven and Hell; Immortality

Called The Archer, Goddess of the Sunbeam, and Queen of the Gods and of Egypt. She probably was a local goddess of the chase who became a goddess of inundation. Along with *Anuket*, she guards the cataracts of the Nile. They are worshiped together on the island of Sâhel and very anciently at Elephantine. She probably was of Sûdânî origin. Satet is responsible for the river's current, and its force and speed, sending it on its way like an arrow. She is represented as a woman with the white crown of upper Egypt and a pair of horns, holding arrows and a bow. She also forms a triad with her husband, Khnemu, and *Anuket*.

✝ *Satet stands at the entrance of the underworld. Using water from four vessels, she purifies the pharaoh as he enters the kingdom of the dead.*

See also *Sati, Satis*. Alternate form: Satit. [Budge 1989; Durdin-Robertson 1975; Jobes 1962; Leach 1992; Stone 1979]

Sati
Selflessness

Goddess of the sunbeam. Consort of Khanum (Khnemu). She wears the white crown with lunar horns. Alternate name for *Satet*. Also a goddess of India (Indian Subcontinent), where she represents feminine devotion and piety and is the wife of Siva. [Cooper 1876; Durdin-Robertson 1975; Guirand 1968; Leach 1992]

Sati-abut
Time

Tenth hour of the day. See also *Sati-arut*. [Durdin-Robertson 1982]

Sati-arut
Time

The tenth hour of the day. There is sometimes more than one goddess for the same hour. See also *Sati-abut*. [Budge 1969; Leach 1992]

Satis
Earth and Nature

Fertility goddess of Sehiel (Sâhel), an island near the Nile's first cataract. She purifies the pharaoh with lustrations as he enters the underworld. Wife of Khumn (Khanum or Khnemu) and queen of the gods in the northern kingdom. Alternate name for *Satet*. [Durdin-Robertson 1975; Savill 1976]

Satit   See *Satet*.

Schent
"Lady of Heaven." See *Isis* and *Nut*.

Seba
Heaven and Hell

Goddess of the underworld. She is mentioned in the *Book of the Dead* as the overthrower of enemies. She is called a goddess when helpful to Ra, but a fiend when she opposes him. See also *Nebt*. [Durdin-Robertson 1975]

Seben
Unknown

Worshiped at Syene and Eilethyia. She presides over upper Egypt. Alternate form: Nishem. [Cooper 1876]

Sebit
Time

"Lady of the Boat." Guardian of the eleventh hour of the night in the *Book of Ami Tuat*. See also *Ament-semu-set*. [Budge 1989]

Seb-tet
Unknown

Deity about whom nothing is known. [Cooper 1876]

Sefchet   See *Seshat*.

Sefek-aabui   See *Seshat*.

Sefekh   See *Seshat*.

Sefekh-seshat   See *Seshat*.

Sefkhabu
Heaven and Hell

"Seven-Rayed." Goddess of the underworld. She is mentioned in the Ritual of the Dead. [Cooper 1876]

Sefk-het-abut   See *Seshat*.

Sefkh-tābui   See *Seshat*.

Seher-tut
Time

The third hour of the night. [Budge 1969; Leach 1992]

Sehmet   See *Sekhmet*.

Sekhemet-ren-s-em-abet-s
Heaven and Hell

One of the *Seven Kine-deities*. See also *Akert-khentet-auset-s*. [Durdin-Robertson 1975]

Sekhet
Hunting and Wild Animals; Demi-animals; Destroyer of Life; Heaven and Hell; Justice; Evil; Time

Lion-headed goddess who has the power of destruction, symbolized by the sun's rays. Daughter of Ra, wife of Pthah, mother of I-em-hetop. She wears the lunar horns and solar disk and holds in her hands the *crux ansata* and the papyrus staff, or a shield and a basket. As an underworld deity she directs the torture of the souls of the dead. When she is the goddess of northern Egypt, she is called **Ouati.** As the consort of Shu and his associate in destroying humankind, she is called **Tefnut. Pasht** is her name as the creator of the "yellow race," a race disliked by the Egyptians. In her malevolent aspect she is known as **Beset** or **Bubastis.** She is one of the goddesses who care for the Eye of Horus and is also the goddess of the fourth hour of the fourth day of the moon and of the fourth month of the year. Identified with **Menhenet** and **Neserit.** See also **Isis, Mehi, Sekhment, Sekhmet, Selk.** [Cooper 1876; Leach 1992]

Sekhet-aanru
Weather
   "Lady of the Winds." See also **Sekhet-hetepet.** Alternate form: Sekhet-aaru. [Durdin-Robertson 1975]

Sekhet-aaru   See *Sekhet-aanru.*

Sekhet-bast-ra
Heaven and Hell
   Underworld deity who is associated with **Amit.** [Durdin-Robertson 1975]

Sekhet-hetepet
Heaven and Hell; Agriculture; Weather
   Goddess of the underworld. Among her titles are The Mighty City and The Lady of Winds.
   She is the Elysian Fields, where one can do whatever she or he did on Earth. As Sekhet-aanru she is the Field of Lilies, where reeds, water plants, and grains grow. She has granaries to store the grain used to feed the deceased.
   She is similar to **Ament, Aukert,** and **Unen-em-hetep.** [Durdin-Robertson 1975]

Sekhet-metu
Time
   One of the *Twelve Goddesses of Life and Strength.* [Durdin-Robertson 1982.

Sekhment   See *Sekhet.*

Sekhmet
Fire; Hunting and Wild Animals; War; Justice; Magic; Heaven and Hell; Demi-animals; Courage; Physical Prowess
   "The Powerful." Some of her other titles are Goddess of Fire and Heat, Lion Goddess, Mistress of the Gods, Goddess of War, Goddess of Vengeance, and The Mighty One of Enchantments. She originally came from Sokhem (Letopolis). Wife of Ptah and mother of Nefertum, together with whom she forms a triad. She is similar to **Bast.** In the underworld she presides over the preservation of the body. She is portrayed as a lion or a woman with the head of a lion, often holding an ankh or sistrum.
   She was a pitiless opponent on the battlefield. Sekhmet embodied the strength and bravery of the lion, expressing unbounded delight in the prey that fell to her. . . . In later times, it must have seemed to the Egyptians that Sekhmet hunted with their enemies, for they fell victim in turn to the Assyrians, the Persians, the Greeks and the Romans.
   As many as 600 statues of Sekhmet lined the entrance to the temple of **Mut.** Her Greek name is **Sakhmis** and in Nubia it is **Tekaharesapusaremkakaremet.** Said to also be a name for **Hathor.** See also **Mehenit, Mehit, Mihit, Sachmet, Sekhet, Ubastet.** Alternate forms: Mehet, Pasht, Sakhmet, Sakhmis, Sehmet, Sekmet, Sokhit. [Cotterell 1989; Durdin-Robertson 1975; Eliot 1976; Ions 1982; Jayne 1925; Jobes 1962; Leach 1992; Neumann 1972]

Sekmet   See *Sekhmet.*

Sekseket
Heaven and Hell
   Goddess of the underworld. Mentioned in the *Papyrus of Nu.* Mother of **Khebent.** [Durdin-Robertson 1975]

Selk
Education and Knowledge; Reptiles
   Reptile goddess associated with writing who is identical to **Sekhet.** Possibly a name for **Isis.** According to one author, she has a scorpion on her head and is a protector of the human body with Kabhsenuf in the underworld. See also **Selket.** [Cooper 1876; Durdin-Robertson 1975; Jobes 1962]

Selket
Demi-animals; Immortality; Heaven and Hell; Family and Tribes; Insects
   Scorpion goddess of fertility and the underworld. Wife of Ra. Associated with the male deity Qebhsenuf in guarding the canopic jars containing the intestines and aids **Isis, Nephthys,** and **Neith** in guarding the canopic jars of Osiris. She is also a protector of marriage. She is represented as a woman wearing a scorpion on her head, as a scorpion with a woman's head, and sometimes as a scorpion holding an ankh.
   When Apep participated in an attack against the sun god, Ra, he was defeated and sent to the underworld. Selket was given the duty of guarding him. Because Apep was bound with chains, Selket became known as the goddess who binds the dead with chains.
   See also **Selk.** Alternate forms: Selkhet, Selkit, Selqet, Selquet, Serket, Serkhit, Serq, Serqet. [Durdin-Robertson 1975; Leach 1992; Monaghan 1981; Stone 1979; Sykes 1968]

Selkhet   See *Selket.*

Selkit   See *Selket.*

Selqet   See *Selket.*

Selquet   See *Selket.*

Semt
Time
   Second hour of the day. [Budge 1969; Leach 1992]

Senb-kheperu
Time
   The eleventh hour of the day. [Budge 1969; Leach 1992]

Seneb
Mother and Guardian
   Goddess of childbirth. [Redfield 1931]

Sentait
Heaven and Hell; Domesticated Animals; Immortality
   Cow goddess of the underworld. Protector of the dead. She was merged with **Isis.** [Lurker 1984]

Sept   See *Sothis.*

Septet   See *Sothis.*

Seret
Stars and Planets
   Stellar goddess. The constellation Seret. [Durdin-Robertson 1975]

Serket   See *Selket.*

Serkhit   See *Selket.*

Serq   See *Selket.*

Serqet
Insects; Evil; Stars and Planets
Scorpion goddess originally from Nubia or the Sudan. She was worshiped by the Greeks at a town called Pselchis, near Dakkah. She was evil and associated with Set or Typhon and the stars of the North Pole, the morning star. Also an alternate name for *Selket.* [Budge 1989]

Ser-t
Creator of Life; Hunting and Wild Animals
Goose goddess who laid the cosmic egg but in the *Book of the Dead* is called *Kenken-ur,* the "Great Cackler." [Budge 1989]

Sesat   See *Seshat.*

Sesenet-khu
Demi-animals; Time; Heaven and Hell
Lion-headed goddess of time. The second hour of the night in the underworld. [Leach 1992]

Seshait-safkhitabui   See *Seshat.*

Seshat
Heaven and Hell; Immortality; Arts; Education and Knowledge; Science; Ceremonies
Among her titles are Goddess of Painting and Writing, Mistress of the House of Books, Mistress of the Scribes, Mistress of Architectural Knowledge, Record Keeper of the Gods, and Foundress of Temples. Wife/sister of moon god, Thoth.

☥ *Seshat aids the king of Egypt with the building of temples. It is Seshat, personified in a priestess (Egyptian priesthoods were mainly made up of women in early times), who comes to the spot with a golden mallet and a peg, which is used to mark the position of the axis of the future temple. She is also the king's record keeper and is seen writing the names of the sovereigns on the leaves of the sacred tree at Heliopolis. In the underworld, Seshat provides a house for the shade of the deceased. She is portrayed holding a writing reed and a scribe's palette in her hands as the celestial librarian.*

Associated with *Nebt* and similar to *Nisaba,* Near East, and *Sophia,* Near East. See also *Safekh-aabut, Sheshat, Sheta.* Alternate forms: Safekh-abui, Safkhitabui, Sefchet, Sefek-aabui, Sefekh, Sefekh-seshat, Sefk-het-abut, Sefkh-tābui, Sesat, Seshait-safkhitabui, Sesha't, Seshatu, Sesheta. [Budge 1989; Durdin-Robertson 1975; Leach 1992; Lurker 1984; Monaghan 1981; Stone 1979]

Sesha't   See *Seshat.*

Seshatu   See *Seshat.*

Sesheta   See *Seshat.*

Seshetat
Time
The fourth hour of the day. [Budge 1969; Leach 1992]

Seshetet
Heaven and Hell
Goddess of the underworld mentioned in the *Book of the Dead.* [Durdin-Robertson 1975]

Seven Kine-deities
Heaven and Hell; Immortality

Goddesses of the underworld. They provide the deceased with food. They have a solar disk between their horns like *Hathor.* See *Akert-khentet-auset-s* for a list of the seven names. [Durdin-Robertson 1975]

Shait
Fate
"Human Destiny." She arrives at the moment of birth and stays with each individual throughout her or his life. She speaks at the time of judgment of the soul, for she has observed each person's virtues and crimes. Identified with *Meskhent* and *Renenet.* [Durdin-Robertson 1975; Leach 1992; Monaghan 1981]

Shemat-khu
Time
One of the *Twelve Goddesses of Life and Strength.* [Durdin-Robertson 1982]

Shenat-pet-utheset-neter
Heaven and Hell; Immortality
One of the *Seven Kine-deities.* See also *Akert-khentet-auset-s* for a complete list of the seven. [Durdin-Robertson 1975]

Shenty
Domesticated Animals; Agriculture; Ceremonies; Immortality
Cow goddess associated with agriculture. She is listed in the *Book of Making Perfect the Deceased.*

☥ *Shenty participates in agricultural rituals represented by a cow carved from sycamore and covered with gilt. She watchs as seeds are planted in a "garden" (a vase or pot). Water is poured over Shenty and the "garden" and the grain that grows is a representation of the resurrection of the deity after burial in the earth.* [Durdin-Robertson 1975; Leach 1992; Sykes 1968]

Sheput
Hunting and Wild Animals
One of the forms of the hippopotamus goddess that was very common in the delta in very early times. See also *Apet, Êpet, Ipet, Reret, Taourt, Taueret, Ta-urt, Thoeris, Thoueris, Tie.* Also an alternate name for *Taueret.* [Budge 1989]

Shesat-makey-neb-s
Time
Guardian of the second hour of the night in the *Book of Ami Tuat.* See also *Ament-semu-set.* [Budge 1989]

Shesemtet
Demi-animals; Sky and Heavens
Early lion-headed sky goddess. Associated with the male deity Shesmu. [Jobes 1962]

Sheshat
Unknown
"Mistress of the House of Books." She is said to have invented writing and is the heavenly record keeper. As the heavenly architect, she determines the axis of buildings. After inventing mathematics she became the goddess of fate, responsible for measuring the length of lives. See also *Seshat.* [Monaghan 1981]

Shes-kentet
Unknown
Mentioned in the *Papyrus of the Lady Mut-hetepeth.* [Durdin-Robertson 1975]

Sheta
Heaven and Hell

Goddess of the underworld. One of the deities of the Eighth Qereret (division). May be connected with *Seshat*. [Durdin-Robertson 1975]

Shilluk
Domesticated Animals
    White cow goddess who emerged from the Nile during creation. [Stutley and Stutley 1984]

Smamet
Domesticated Animals
    One of the *Four Uaipu Cow Goddesses.* [Durdin-Robertson 1975]

Sobkit
Unknown
    Wife of Sobku (Sebek), a crocodile-headed god. [Durdin-Robertson 1975]

Sochet
    "Cornfield." See *Isis.* Alternate form: Sochit.

Sochit See *Sochet.*

Sofh
Education and Knowledge
    Goddess of writing worshiped in Memphis. She is portrayed wearing an expanded palm leaf on her head beneath inverted cow horns. [Cooper 1876]

Sokhet
Earth and Nature
    "Country." Goddess of the marsh. [Leach 1992]

Sokhit See *Sekhmet.*

Sopd See *Sothis.*

Sopdet See *Sothis.*

Sopdit See *Sothis.*

Sothis
Sky and Heavens; Time; Heaven and Hell
    Stellar goddess who is said to astronomically be the foundation of the entire religious system. The celestial movements of Sothis (Sirius) determined the Egyptian calendar, and her appearance in the sky in early August heralded the beginning of the new year. Among her titles are The Arrow Star, Sirius, Queen of the Thirty-six Constellations, The Star of Isis, and Star of the Sea. She is also a goddess of the underworld mentioned in the Egyptian *Book of the Dead*. Connected with *Isis.* Alternate names: *Sept, Septet, Sopd, Sopdet, Sopdit.* [Durdin-Robertson 1975; Durdin-Robertson 1982]

Souban
Demi-animals
    Appearing under the form of a vulture, she represents the Southland or Ethiopia. See also *Suvan.* [Cooper 1876]

Sphinx, The
Demi-animals; Water; Intelligence and Creativity
    "Winged One." Daughter of the many-headed monster, Typhon, and the serpent *Echidna*, Greek and Roman Empires. She has the head and breasts of a woman, the body of a dog with lion paws, wings, and a serpent's tail. The Sphinx is a religious symbol of the Egyptians, and it signifies the beginning of the rising of the water in the Nile. She was to guard and protect the pyramids.

⚓ *The Sphinx was sent by the Greek goddess Hera [Greek and Roman Empires] to plague the city of Thebes in Boeotia. She would ask travelers riddles, and if they could not answer they were eaten. One of the travelers to whom she proposed a riddle was Oedipus, when he tried to have the plague lifted by her. When he was able to solve the riddle, she killed herself. [Cotterell 1989; Woodcock 1953]*

Stella Maris See *Isis.*

Suvan
Unknown
    Worshiped at the town of Ten. Probably identical to *Souban.* [Cooper 1876]

Sycamore Tree Goddess
Heaven and Hell; Mother and Guardian
    Goddess of the underworld. She feeds the shade (soul) at night in the cemetery. [Cooper 1876]

Ta-dehnet "Peak." See *Merseger.*

Tafne
Unknown
    Worshiped at Touni or Thinis. Alternate form: Tafnu. [Cooper 1876]

Tafner
Unknown
    Deity whose representation was found at the temple at Kom Ombo. She is portrayed with a headdress of a disk between two horns and carrying an ankh. [Durdin-Robertson 1975]

Tafnu See *Tafne.*

Tafnuit
Unknown
    One of the Theban pantheon that includes 14 deities. See also *Anit.* [Durdin-Robertson 1975]

Tait
Heaven and Hell; Immortality
    Goddess of the underworld. She feeds and clothes the deceased. Mentioned in the *Papyrus of Nu.* [Durdin-Robertson 1975]

Tamun See *Amunta.*

Tanenet See *Taninit.*

Tanenit
Unknown
    Sister of *Anit* and *Meshkent* who wears an object that probably represents the vulva of a cow. [Budge 1989]

Tanen-tu See *Hathor.* Her name when worshiped at the town of Ter near Hermonthis.

Taninit
Heaven and Hell
    Goddess of the underworld mentioned in the *Papyrus Nekhtu-Amen.* Similar to *Isis.* She presides over the region of Tanenet in the underworld. Alternate form: Tanenet. [Durdin-Robertson 1975]

Taourt
Evil; Mother and Guardian; Heaven and Hell; Demi-animals
    Malevolent goddess who presides over the birth of deities and kings. She is also a goddess of the underworld. Taourt is portrayed with the body of an upright hippopotamus with

the skin of a crocodile on her back. See also *Apet, Êpet, Ipet, Reret, Sheput, Taueret, Ta-urt, Thoeris, Thoueris, Tie.* [Redfield 1931]

Ta-repy
Stars and Planets

Name for the constellation Virgo, symbolized by the *Sphinx.* See also the *Zodiacal Virgins*; *Aderenosa,* Near East; and *Kanyā,* Indian Subcontinent. [Durdin-Robertson 1975]

Taueret
Demi-animals; Immortality; Mother and Guardian; Hunting and Wild Animals; Creator of Life; Heaven and Hell; Justice; Stars and Planets

"Great." Hippopotamus goddess of fertility, birth, the underworld, and vengeance. Originally a sky goddess who assisted at the birth of the sun god. Her constellation is the Great Bear (Ursa Major). In childbirth she protects and suckles the newborn. In the underworld she carries the deceased toward a new destiny. She is represented as a hippopotamus standing on her hind legs with pendant breasts. Sometimes her back is that of a crocodile and she has the feet of a lion. As an avenging deity she has the head of a lion and the body of a hippopotamus, brandishes a dagger, and sometimes carries a crocodile on her shoulders. She had temples at Thebes and Deir el-Bahri. See also *Apet, Api, Êpet, Ipet, Opet, Reret, Rerit, Rert, Rertu, Ririt, Sheput, Taourt, Ta-urt, Thoeris, Thoueris, Tie.* Alternate forms: Taur, Taurit, Tie, Toeris, Tueret, Tueris. [Budge 1989; Cooper 1876; Durdin-Robertson 1975; Eliot 1976; Jayne 1925; Jobes 1962; Leach 1992; Monaghan 1981; Stone 1979]

Taur
Unknown

Goddess of Darkness, a region of the underworld. Mentioned in the *Book of the Dead.* Also an alternate name for *Tauret.* Alternate form: Ta-ur. [Cooper 1876; Durdin-Robertson 1975; Monaghan 1981]

Ta-ur See *Taur.*

Tauret See *Taur.*

Taurit See *Taueret.*

Ta-urt
Mother and Guardian; Demi-animals

Ancient hippopotamus mother goddess of childbirth and fertility. See also *Apet, Êpet, Ipet, Reret, Sheput, Taourt, Taueret, Thoeris, Thoueris, Tie.* Alternate forms: Api, Opet, Rert, Rertu. [Jobes 1962; Leach 1992]

Tayt
Heaven and Hell; Immortality

"Clothing." Goddess of the underworld who is involved with the clothing or bandages for mummification. Alternate form: Taytet. [Leach 1992]

Taytet See *Tayt.*

Tcheser-shetat
Time

The sixth hour of the night and also goddess of the ninth hour of the day. [Budge 1969; Durdin-Robertson 1982]

Tchesert
Heaven and Hell; Domesticated Animals

Goddess of the underworld. Personification of the region of Tchesert. She is portrayed as a cow standing on a platform

with a *uraeus,* a symbol of sovereignty, usually on a headdress. [Durdin-Robertson 1975]

Tefenet See *Tefnut.*

Tefent
Unknown

A goddess mentioned in the text of *Unas* with her counterpart, Tefen. [Budge 1989]

Tefnoot See *Tefnut.*

Tefnuit See *Tefnut.*

Tefnut
Sky and Heavens; Order; Justice; Heaven and Hell; Time; Demi-animals; Weather

"The Spitter." Daughter of *Nebhet Hotep,* sister/wife of Shu. Her other titles include Goddess of the Atmosphere, The Lady of Heaven, Goddess of World Order, and The Lady of the Lower Shrine. She helps support the sky and each morning receives the sun in the eastern horizon. Tefnut is one of the "Great Nine" who sit in judgment of the dead. The others are Ra, Shu, Geb, *Nut, Isis, Nephthys, Hathor,* and Horus. Tefnut is also considered the goddess of the second hour of the night of the fourteenth moon. She is portrayed as a lion-headed goddess with a solar disk on her head or as a woman or a lion.

Once Tefnut left Egypt and went to live in the Nubian desert. Ra was lonely and sent the baboon Thoth (and possibly Shu) to ask Tefnut to return to Egypt. She came back as Hathor and there were great celebrations in all the temples. And Ra placed her on his brow as the fierce uraeus serpent.

See also *Mehit, Sekhet.* Alternate forms: Tefenet, Tefnoot, Tefnuit. [Cooper 1876; Durdin-Robertson 1975; Jobes 1962; Leach 1992]

Tehenut See *Neith.*

Tekaharesapusaremkakaremet
Unknown

Nubian name for Egyptian *Sekhmet.* [Durdin-Robertson 1975]

Tekh-heb See *Tekhi.*

Tekhi
Time

Goddess of the first month of the year, Thoth (August 29 to September 27). Alternate form: Tekh-heb. [Durdin-Robertson 1982; Leach 1992]

Temtith
Time

One of the four goddesses of the seventh hour of the night who hold a large knife. [Durdin-Robertson 1982]

Temu
Mother and Guardian

"Mother." [Walker 1986]

Tenemet
Heaven and Hell; Immortality

Goddess of the underworld. She gives ale to the deceased. Similar to *Siduri,* Near East. Alternate forms: Tenemit, Tenenit. [Durdin-Robertson 1975; Jobes 1962; Lurker 1984]

Tenemit See *Tenemet.*

Tenenit See *Tenemet.*

Tenith
Time
One of the four goddess of the seventh hour of the night who hold a large knife. [Durdin-Robertson 1982]

Tent-baiu
Time
Guardian of the third hour of the night in the *Book of Ami Tuat*. See also *Ament-semu-set*. [Budge 1989]

Tentenit-uhert-khakabu
Time
Guardian of the tenth hour of the night in the *Book of Ami Tuat*. See also *Ament-semu-set*. [Budge 1989]

Tentyris
Family and Tribes
Deity of the city of Tentyra. [Cooper 1876]

Tesert
Heaven and Hell; Demi-animals
Goddess of the underworld. She dwells in the Eleventh Qereret (division), where supplications are made to her. She is portrayed as a snake with a woman's head. [Durdin-Robertson 1975]

Tesert-ant
Time
One of the *Twelve Goddesses of Life and Strength*. [Durdin-Robertson 1982]

Thceser-shetat
Time
The sixth hour of the night. [Durdin-Robertson 1982]

Thebean Goddess
Mother and Guardian
Tutelary goddess of the city of Thebes. [Durdin-Robertson 1975]

Themath
Sky and Heavens
One of the goddesses who line the path of the sun god, Ra, on his journey across the sky. [Durdin-Robertson 1982]

Thenenet
Heaven and Hell
Goddess of the underworld and of Hermonthis. Identified with *Hathor* and *Isis*. [Leach 1992]

Thermuthis   See *Renenet*.

Thmei
Justice; Selflessness
Goddess of justice. Also called Mother of All the Virtues and Mirror of Justice. Her headdress is a single ostrich plume, signifying truth. She holds the *crux ansata*. Similar to *Themis*, Greek and Roman Empires, and *Thummim*, Near East. [Cooper 1876; Durdin-Robertson 1976]

Thoeris
Magic; Ceremonies; Mother and Guardian; Hunting and Wild Animals; Reptiles; Justice; Stars and Planets; Ugliness; Heaven and Hell; Health and Healing; Goodness
"Mistress of Talismans." Goddess of conception and childbirth portrayed as a pregnant hippopotamus. She was possibly imported from Africa and has some elements of the crocodile as well as the hippopotamus. She protects children from the moment of birth and has a terrifying aspect that frightens away malevolent spirits. Another of her benevolent aspects is as protector from illness. As an underworld goddess she is portrayed as a hippopotamus standing erect, brandishing a knife. She devours the souls of the wicked dead. She is the constellation Ursa Major. See also *Apet, Êpet, Ipet, Reret, Sheput, Taourt, Taueret, Ta-urt, Thoueris, Tie*. Alternate form: Kartek. [Cooper 1876; Eliot 1976; Jayne 1925]

Thoueris
Mother and Guardian
Goddess of fertility and childbirth. See also *Apet, Êpet, Ipet, Reret, Sheput, Taourt, Taueret, Ta-urt, Thoeris, Tie*. [Leach 1992]

Tie
Education and Knowledge; Magic; Ceremonies; Demi-animals; Intelligence and Creativity
Hippopotamus-headed goddess. Personification of intelligence and wisdom. Talismans of her image are worn for protection. Identified with Ta-urt. See also *Apet, Êpet, Ipet, Reret, Sheput, Taourt, Taueret, Ta-urt, Thoeris, Thoueris*. Alternate form: Sa. [Jobes 1962]

Tiv
Unknown
Deified queen who ruled from 1417 to 1379 B.C.E. She was worshiped in Thebes during the Greek and Roman periods. [Cooper 1876]

Tmei
Heaven and Hell; Goodness; Justice
Goddess of the underworld. Also goddess of mercy and justice. Similar to *Maât*. [Durdin-Robertson 1975]

Toeris   See *Taueret*.

Toses
Unknown
Deity about whom nothing is known. [Cooper 1876]

Tsont-nofre   See *Isis*.

Tuatt-makel-neb-s
Time
Guardian of the ninth hour of the night in the *Book of Ami Tuat*. See also *Ament-semu-set*. [Budge 1989]

Tueret   See *Êpet, Taueret*.

Tueris   See *Taueret*.

Twelve Goddesses of Life and Strength
Time
They protect the ninth hour of the night. They are *Perit, Shemat-khu, Nebt-shat, Nebt-shefshefet, Aat-aatet, Nebt-setau, Hent-nut-s, Nebt-mat, Tesert-ant, Aat-khu, Sekhet-metu*, and *Netert-en-khentet-ra*. [Durdin-Robertson 1982]

Typho
Mother and Guardian
Goddess of childbirth who also presides over gestation. [Jayne 1925]

Ua
Heaven and Hell
Goddess of the underworld who is mentioned in the *Book of the Dead*. [Durdin-Robertson 1975]

Ua Zit   See *Uazit*.

Uadgit See *Uadjet*.

Uadjet
Mother and Guardian; Demi-animals; Ceremonies; Heaven and Hell; Justice; Time

Ancient protector of lower Egypt at Tanis, later Pelusium. Among her titles are The Goddess of Buto, The Lady of Flame, The Uraeus, Queen of the Gods of Egypt, and Goddess of the Placenta. She appears as a cobra, sometimes winged and crowned; as the *uraeus* (symbol of sovereignty); and as a snake with the face of a woman. Her crown is the royal crown of the North. Identified with *Nit* and *Sekhmet* in Hypselis. Uadjet figures importantly in the coronation ceremony and in the underworld, where she endows justice and truth. She is also the goddess of the fifth hour of the fifth day of the moon. She is sister of *Nekhebet*, and together the two goddesses are known as *the Nebti*.

☥ *When Isis was hiding in the swamps, Uadjet came to help her protect her son, Horus, from Set.*
See also *Buto, Per Uadjit, Uatchet, Uazit*. Alternate forms: Ap-taui, Himbuto, Uadgit, Uadjit, Uat, Udjat, Uto, Uzoit, Wadjet, Wazit. [Bonnerjea 1927; Budge 1989; Cooper 1876; Durdin-Robertson 1975; Monaghan 1981; Neumann 1972; Redfield 1931]

Uadjit See *Uadjet*.

Uajyt See *Buto*.

Uat
Water
Goddess of water. Also alternate name for *Buto* or *Bubastis* and for *Uadjet*. [Cooper 1876]

Uatchet
Time; Reptiles; Heaven and Hell; Justice; Fire
Serpent goddess who is sometimes winged. Twin sister of *Nekhebet*. Uatchet is regarded as the goddess of the eleventh month of the Egyptian year, Eipiphi, and the fifth hour of the fifth day of the moon. In the underworld she destroys the enemies of the deceased and with *Nekhebet* accompanied Horus to destroy any remaining rebels with fire. See also *Apt, Buto, Uadjet*. Alternate forms: Ap-taui, Uatchit. [Durdin-Robertson 1975; Durdin-Robertson 1982; Leach 1992]

Uatchit See *Uatchet*.

Uatch-ura
Directions
Goddess of the North. Counterpart of Hep-Meht. See also *Uadjet*. [Leach 1992]

Uati
Mother and Guardian
Guardian deity of lower Egypt. She is portrayed wearing the crown of the North and holding a scepter. [Redfield 1931]

Uatit See *Bast*.

Uazet See *Buto*.

Uazit
Mother and Guardian; Reptiles
Mother goddess called "lady of the night." Cobra goddess worshiped on the Nile Delta. She is "The Eye," or *uraeus*, that is found on the foreheads of other deities and royalty. See also *Buto, Uadjet*. Alternate forms: Ua Zit, Uzoit. [Durdin-Robertson 1975; Leach 1992]

Ubast See *Bast*.

Ubastet
Demi-animals; Hunting and Wild Animals; Health and Healing; Agriculture; Mother and Guardian
"Lady of the West." Goddess of fire. Sister of *Sekhmet*. Ubastet's heat is milder than her sister's and it encourages germination and growth of plants. She is also goddess of healing, of the hunt, and of childbirth and is the protector of children. The cat is sacred to her and she is sometimes called the Cat-Headed Goddess. At Thebes she is called *Mut-ubastet*. See also *Bast*. [Jayne 1925]

Udjat See *Buto, Uadjet*.

Uêret See *Êpet*.

Uert-hekeu See *Saosis*.

Uertheku
Reptiles
Serpent goddess. [Cooper 1876]

Umm s-Subyan
Destroyer of Life
Death goddess who causes infants to die. See also *Umm s-Subyan*, Africa and Near East. [Leach 1992]

Unen-em-hetep
Heaven and Hell; Immortality
"Lady of the Winds" and "Lady of Two Lands." Goddess of the Elysian Fields who is a protector of the dead. Also the name of a lake in the Elysian Fields. Associated with *Ament, Aukert*, and *Sekhet-hetepet*. [Durdin-Robertson 1975]

Unnit
Hunting and Wild Animals; Mother and Guardian
Hare goddess worshiped in the fifteenth nome (county) of upper Egypt, Hermopolis (Toth). Her husband is Unnu/Un, god of the city of Unnu. She later was portrayed as a lion. She was displaced by the god Thot and became a protective deity armed with knives. See also *Unnut*. Alternate form: Unut. [Leach 1992; Lurker 1984]

Unnut
Time
"Lady of Unnu." Also the goddess of Toth (Hermopolis). She is mentioned in the *Book of the Dead*. One writer says she is not the Lady of Unnu, but a "goddess of the hours." See also *Unnit*. [Budge 1989; Durdin-Robertson 1975; Leach 1992]

Unt See *Isis*.

Unut See *Unnit*.

Ur-mertu-s-teshert-sheni
Heaven and Hell
One of the *Seven Kine-deities*. See also *Akert-khentet-auset-s*. [Durdin-Robertson 1975]

Urt-hekau
Magic; Hunting and Wild Animals
"Rich in Magic." Lion goddess (or god) who is the protective power in the Eye of Horus. Also a cobra goddess of magical spells. See also *Urt-hikeu*. Alternate form: Werethekau. [Cooper 1876; Leach 1992; Lurker 1984]

Urt-hikeu
Magic
"Powerful with Magic." Wife of Ra. See also *Urt-hekau*. [Cooper 1876]

Urt-sekhemu
Time
   Guardian of the fourth hour of the night in the *Book of Ami Tuat*. See also *Ament-semu-set*. [Budge 1989]

Usert
Earth and Nature
   Earth goddess. Worshiped in Thebes. Identified with *Isis* and closely resembling *Neith*. [Leach 1992; Mackenzie 1913]

Ushmet-hatu-kheftiu-rā
Time
   Guardian of the first hour of the night in the *Book of Ami Tuat*. See also *Ament-semu-set*. [Budge 1989]

Usit
Unknown
   One of the goddesses who line the path of the sun god, Ra, on his journey across the sky. [Durdin-Robertson 1982]

Uto
Mother and Guardian
   Goddess of protection of the delta and oracles of lower Egypt. Also an alternate name for *Buto* and *Uadjet*. [Durdin-Robertson 1975; Jayne 1925; Leach 1992; Neumann 1972]

Uzoit   See *Buto, Uadjet, Uazit*.

Wadjet   See *Uadjet*.

Watch Merti
Unknown
   Name given to *Isis* and *Nephthys* in the *Book of the Dead*. It may also refer to the *Merti*. [Sykes 1968]

Wazit   See *Uadjet*.

Werethekau
Unknown
   Personifies the magic power in a royal crown. See also *Urt-hekau*. [Lurker 1984]

Whose-name-is-mighty-in-her-works
Heaven and Hell
   Goddess of the underworld. Listed in the *Papyrus of Nu*. [Durdin-Robertson 1975]

Woman-light of the Shadows, The
Moon and Night
   "The Light That Shineth in the Darkness, the Woman-light." Lunar goddess. Mentioned in the *Book of the Dead* as the protector of the moon god, Thot (Thoth). [Durdin-Robertson 1975]

Wosyet
Mother and Guardian; Physical Prowess
   "She Who Is Strong." Protector of Horus and worshiped at Thebes. [Lurker 1984]

Yept
Time
   Goddess of the female apartments. Ruler of the eleventh month of the sothic year (ancient year that has 365-1/4 days), called Eipiphi. Alternate form: Yept Hemet. [Durdin-Robertson 1975; Durdin-Robertson 1982]

Yept Hemet   See *Yept*.

Zenenet
Unknown
   "The Exalted One." Worshiped in the town of Hermonthis. Consort of Month. She was merged with *Rat-taui*. [Lurker 1984]

Zodiacal Virgins, The
Stars and Planets; Love and Sexuality
   Their zodiac sign is between the Lion and the Scales. They are identical to *Ta-repy*; *Aderenosa*, Near East; and *Kanyā*, Indian Subcontinent. [Durdin-Robertson 1975]

FAR EAST

A Hsiang   See *A Xiang.*

A Xiang
China
Weather
   Deity who guides the chariot of the Ministry of Thunder or the Mother of Lightning. Alternate form: A Hsiang. [Werner 1961]

Aba Khatun
China
Water
   Sea goddess. See also *Aba-Khatun,* Eastern Europe. [Klementz 1925; Leach 1992]

Agriculture Goddess, The
Japan
Agriculture
   Deity represented on a frieze of a public building. She is accompanied by the *Goddess of Poetry.* [Durdin-Robertson 1976]

Akaru-hime
Japan
Magic; Mother and Guardian; Metals and Minerals; Love and Sexuality; Unhappiness
   "Bright Princess." Her husband is Ame-no-pi-poko. Born miraculously from a red jewel (or stone).
   When Akaru-hime's mother gave birth to a red jewel, a man who had been watching asked her for it. When the man was arrested, he gave the jewel to Ame-no-pi-poko for his release. The prince took the jewel home and put it in his bed, where it turned into a beautiful woman. He married Akaru-hime, but when he began to mistreat her, she left Korea for her ancestral home in Japan. In her homeland she was enshrined and is worshiped for safety at sea. [Durdin-Robertson 1976]

Aki-bime-no-kami
Japan
Time; Agriculture
   "Autumn Princess." Daughter of *Ō-ge-tsu-hime-no-kami* and Ha-yama-to-no-kami. In popular belief, she is the guardian of grain. A member of the *Izumo Pantheon.* [Durdin-Robertson 1976; Philippi 1968]

Altan-telgey   See *Teleglen-edzen.*

Ama-no-sagu-me
Japan
Intelligence and Creativity; Earth and Nature
   "Heavenly-spying Woman" or "Wise Woman." Earth goddess who is an expert at reading apprehension and dreams. [Durdin-Robertson 1976]

Ama-terasu-oho-hiru-me-no-mikoto   See *Ama-terasu-ō-mi-kami.*

Ama-terasu-ō-mi-kami
Japan
Sun and Day; Mother and Guardian; Family and Tribes; Supreme Being; Education and Knowledge; Unhappiness
   Benevolent Shinto goddess of the sun. Daughter of *Izanami-no-kami* and Izanagi who created the islands of Japan from chaos. She was said to have been the menstrual or birth blood of her mother or to have been the left eye of her father. She is the ancestor of the Imperial Family and taught her people how to cultivate food and to raise silk worms. She is the mother of *Ichiki-shima-hime-no-mikoto* and *Takitsu-hime-no-mikoto.* Sister of *Wakahirume-no-mikoto.* Ama-terasu-ō-mi-kami is the chief deity of the Shinto religion, currently the only religion with a large number of practitioners whose most important divinity is female. She is the ruler of all the other deities and the guardian of the

101

Japanese people. She is the highest manifestation of
Kunitokotachi, the unseen spirit of the universe.

> *Ama-terasu was very unhappy with the rude behavior of
> her brother, Susa-no-wo, the storm god. He neglected his
> duties and caused disturbances on the land which
> Ama-terasu had ruled so carefully. To demonstrate her anger, she
> shut herself in a cave, taking the sunlight with her and leaving the
> world in darkness. The other deities were very upset and wanted the
> sunlight to return, but their pleas to her went unanswered. Finally
> the deities enlisted the aid of Ame-no-uzume who came to the
> entrance of the cave dancing and telling lewd jokes, finally piquing
> Ama-terasu's curiosity. When she looked out of the cave, she saw
> her reflection in a mirror that had been placed there. While she was
> distracted, the deities put the "rope of no return" across the
> entrance, keeping her from going back in. From that time on, the
> sun only disappears at night.*

Equivalent to **Shapash**, Near East; and **Surya**, Indian
Subcontinent. See also **Amitabha, Dainichi-nyorai,** and
Tsukisakaki hime. Alternate forms: Ama-terasu-oho-
hiru-me-no-mikoto, Mikura-tana-no-kami, Ō-hiru-me-no-
muchi, Ten-sho-dai-jin, Tensho, Ten-shkodaijin. See also
Amitabha. [Durdin-Robertson 1976; Philippi 1968; Leach
1992; Monaghan 1981; Ono et al. 1985; Stone 1979]

Ama-tsu-otome, The
Japan
Sky and Heavens
   "Heavenly Girls." Angels. [Durdin-Robertson 1976]

Ama-yorozu-takau-hata chi-hata hime   See
Yorozu-hatatoya-akitsushi-hime-no-mikoto.

Ame-chikaru-mizu-hime
Japan
Sky and Heavens
   Goddess whose husband is O-toshi-no-kami. One of the
Izumo Pantheon. Her name may mean "fresh and youthful of
heaven." [Durdin-Robertson 1976; Philippi 1968]

Ame-no-sade-yori-hime
Japan
Fate; Magic; Health and Healing
   "Heavenly Net-pulling-hither Princess." Princess of the
island of U-Shima between Kyush and Korea. She is an
oracular shaman-medium, an office for which women were
considered to be better qualified than men. [Durdin-Robertson
1976; Philippi 1968]

Ame-no-tanabata-hime-no-mikoto
Japan
Stars and Planets
   Stellar deity. Alternate form: Shokujo. [Herbert 1967; Leach
1992]

Ame-no-toko
Japan
Heaven and Hell
   Heavenly deity. This may be a term for heaven, rather than
an actual goddess. [Jobes 1962]

Ame-no-toko-tachi-no-kami
Japan
Creator of Life
   "Heavenly Eternal Standing Deity." One of the five
Separate Heavenly Deities who existed before gender
division emerged and who represents the female principle.
[Jobes 1962; Ono et al. 1985; Philippi 1968]

Ame-no-tsudoe-chine-no-kami
Japan
Sky and Heavens
   "Heavenly-assembling Deity." Consort of Huka-buchi-
no-mizu-yare-hana-no-kami, mother of Omizu-nu-no-kami.
[Philippi 1968]

Ame-no-uzume
Japan
Family and Tribes; Ugliness; Happiness; Ceremonies; Mother
and Guardian; Life/Death Cycle
   "Magic Ancestor" of the clan of chieftains, the Sarume. The
ugly goddess of mirth and dancing who enticed *Ama-terasu-
ōmi-kami* from a cave. This dance is said to be the one now
performed at Shinto festivals. She is invoked for protection
from evil, longevity, posterity, and honors. She is considered
the archetype of a psychic medium. Alternate forms: Ame-no-
uzume-no-mikoto, Otafuku, Udzume, Uzume. [Durdin-
Robertson 1976; Jobes 1962; Philippi 1968; Leach 1992; Ono
et al. 1985]

Ame-no-uzume-no-mikoto   See *Ame-no-uzume.*

Ami Goddess, The
Formosa
Reptiles; Magic
   Deity.

> *The Ami Goddess escaped the great flood with her brother
> and they were later married. She gave birth to a snake
> and a frog.* [Durdin-Robertson 1976]

Ami-tanne-mat
Japan, *Ainu*
Fishing and Water Animals; Mother and Guardian; Magic
   "Long-fingered Woman." She appears as a crab whose
magic iron hook can pull a baby from the birthing mother's
womb to save the woman's life. [Meltzer 1981]

Amida   See *Amitabha.*

Amitabha
Japan
Education and Knowledge
   "Buddha of Infinite Light and Life." May be a
manifestation of *Ama-terasu-ō-mi-kami.* Also worshiped in
Southeast Asia. Alternate forms: Amida, Kanro-o, Muryoju,
Muryoka. [Jobes 1962]

Ao-numa-nu-oshi-hime
Japan
Water
   Possibly "Blue Pond" or "Swamp Horse." One of the
"Feminine Deities of the Seventeen Generations" mentioned
in the *Kojiki.* Daughter of Shiki-yama-nushi-no-kami, consort
of Miro-nami-no-kami, and mother of Nuno-oshi-tomi-tori-
narumi-no-kami. [Durdin-Robertson 1976; Philippi 1968]

Ape-huchi
   "Fire Grandmother." See *Apemeru-ko-yan-mat
Unameru-ko-yan-mat.*

Apemeru-ko-yan-mat Unameru-ko-yan-mat
Japan, *Ainu*
Fire; Household Affairs; Ceremonies; Family and Tribes
   "Fire-sparks-rise-woman," or "Cinder-sparks-rise-woman."
She lives in the fireplace of every home and is central to the
Ainu religious life. Prayers offered to any deity are addressed
through her. Ancestor of all Ainu women. Alternate forms:
Ape-huchi, Kamui Huchi. [Philippi 1982]

Asa-ma   See *Konohana-sakuya-hime.*

Ashi-nadaka-no-kami
Japan
Unknown
   Possibly "Evermore Flourishing Reed." One of the
"Feminine Deities of Seventeen Generations" mentioned
in the *Kojiki.* Wife of Kuni-osi-tomi-nokami, mother of
Paya-mika-no-take-sapayadi-numi-no-kami. Alternate form:
Yagawa-e-hime. [Durdin-Robertson 1976]

Ashke-tanne-mat
Japan, *Ainu*
Insects; Mother and Guardian; Magic
   "Long-fingered-woman." Spider goddess worshiped by
women. She assists at childbirth by pulling the baby out of
the womb. She can overcome male marauders by using her
superior shamanistic powers.
   *Poro-nitne-kamui, Big Demon, came to marry Ashke-
   tanne-mat. Not interested in this stupid and boorish
   intruder, she quickly turned him away and went back to
her needlework as if nothing had happened.* [Leach 1992; Meltzer
1981; Philippi 1982]

Ata
Japan
War
   Warrior goddess. Also the name of a location. [Jobes 1962]

Aunt Piety
China
Magic; Education and Knowledge
   Vixen deity noted for her magical qualities. Mother of
Eterna. She frequently appears in human form. Corresponds
to Japanese **Inari.** Aunt Piety is also worshiped in India,
Tibet, and Japan.
   *Aunt Piety was assigned several tasks by Wu, the Queen
   of Heaven. Her first task was to be detained by Yang,
   which means "aspen." Aunt Piety discovered that there
was a government official in a nearby city by the name of Yang.
Seeking a way to get the official to require her skills, she went to his
house. Here she discovered that he had in his possession a Sanskrit
scripture which he was unable to read. She told Yang's gate keeper
that she could read Sanskrit and if Yang needed her help, all he had
to do was face southeast and call her name. Deciding Aunt Piety
was a holy woman, Yang called her name and she appeared
immediately. Wanting to make the most of her abilities, Yang
offered Aunt Piety permanent housing on his estate. And this is
how Wu's first assignment for Aunt Piety was carried out.*
[Durdin-Robertson 1976]

Avalokita
China
Primordial Being
   A Buddhist male god who, in China, became identified
with the personification of the cosmic female energy, evolving
into *Guanyin.* [Leach 1972]

Awa-nami-no-kami
Japan
Water; Order
   "Foam Female Deity." Daughter or granddaughter of
Izanami-no-kami and Izanagi. Counterpart of Awa-nagi-
no-kami. Some believe this name indicates the surface of
calm water. See also *Deities of the Third Earthly Generation.*
[Durdin-Robertson 1976; Leach 1992; Philippi 1968]

Aya-kashiko-ne-no-kami
Japan
Creator of Life

"Ah-how-awesome-deity." A term of endearment for one
of a pair of the Seven Generations of the Age of the Gods who
represent the gradual progress of creation. Sister/wife of
Omo-daru-no-kami. [Ono et al. 1985; Philippi 1968]

Ba
China
Weather; War
   Drought goddess. Sometimes called the daughter of
Huang Di, the Yellow Emperor or August Monarch.
   *Ba came to earth to assist her father in a war against
   Chiyu who used the spirits of rain and fog as weapons.
   Ba drove the spirits away and caused a great drought.*
Her prolonged presence threatened to destroy the earth so her father
exiled her to the north, beyond the Red Water. She occasionally
returns for visits, once again causing a drought.
   Alternate form: Pa [Durdin-Robertson 1976; Senior 1985]

Baäbai
Taiwan, *Tosou*
Agriculture
   Grandmother of rice. [Er-Wei 1959; Leach 1992]

Bai Mundan
China
Wealth; Love and Sexuality; Beauty; Charisma
   "White Peony." The peony symbolizes wealth, honor,
love, and feminine loveliness. She is given the job of
distracting those who practice asceticism, a job also given
to the *Apsarases,* Indian Subcontinent. Equivalent to
Pramlocha, Indian Subcontinent. Alternate form: Pai Mu-Tan.
[Durdin-Robertson 1976]

Baiji
China
Domesticated Animals; Unhappiness; Magic; Health and
Healing
   "The White Hen."
   *A ten-year-old girl was given the name Baiji when she
   committed suicide after her father killed himself when the
   conquering Mings entered their city. The people of the
city built a temple in her honor. Another story says an old white
hen changed into a girl and cured people during an epidemic with
magic medicine. Then one bright day she flew away.*
   Alternate form: Pai Chi. [Werner 1961]

Banzhen
China
Destroyer of Life
   Disease deity who causes scarlet fever. Alternate name
Pan-chen. [Day 1940; Leach 1992]

Baowa   See *Nüwa.*

Bear Woman
China
Family and Tribes
   Ancestor deity of the Wang Clan. There are indications that
in early times Chinese society may have been matriarchal, and
when a man married he went to his wife's village to live.
   *A young man named Wang was caught in a terrible
   storm and his boat was tossed by the waves onto a
   mountain where Bear Woman was waiting. She took
Wang for her husband and when she went to look for food she
would shut him in a cave. Several years passed and Bear Woman
allowed Wang to leave the cave when he wanted to and soon they
had two children. One day Wang took the children and left Bear
Woman. Catching a passing ship, he returned to China.* [Durdin-
Robertson 1976; Leach 1972]

Benten

Japan

Luck; Happiness; Wealth; Arts; Water; Reptiles; Mother and Guardian; Ceremonies

One of the Seven Deities of Luck or Happiness and the only female. She is a goddess of luck, wealth, music, love and the sea. Originally a Hindu goddess called *Sarasvati*, she became the Buddhist deity Benten.

Benten took the form of a dragon woman and swam under the islands of Japan, mating with the white snakes that lived there. She did this to prevent earthquakes that could injure her followers. Also as one of the Seven Deities of Luck, on New Year's Eve she accompanies the Takara-bune ("Treasure Ship") as it sails into port. It contains treasures for the people, the hat of invisibility, the lucky rain-coat, the sacred key, the inexhaustible purse, the precious jewel, the clove, the weight, and a flat object apparently representing a coin. All who buy a picture of the Takara-bune and put it under their pillow will have a lucky dream.

Alternate forms: Benzaiten, Benzai-tennyo, Ichiki-shima-hime-no-mikoto. [Cottrell 1979; Durdin-Robertson 1976; Durdin-Robertson 1982; Jobes 1962; Leach 1992; Monaghan 1981; Philippi 1968]

Benzaiten See *Benten.*

Benzai-tennyo See *Benten.*

Bilig-un cinadu-kijaghar-a kuruksen

Mongolia

Education and Knowledge

Goddess of wisdom. Equivalent to *Prajmaparamita,* Indian Subcontinent. [Leach 1992]

Bixia Yuangun See *Bixia Yuanjin.*

Bixia Yuanjin

China

Dawn and Twilight; Mother and Guardian; Luck; Health and Healing;

Weather Princess of the Purple and Azure Clouds. Taoist goddess of dawn and childbirth. She attends each birth accompanied by six divine helpers, protecting the mother and bringing good health and fortune to the child. There are two primary goddesses with this name, one worshiped in Fukien and one in Tai Shan (Tian Xian or T'ien Hsien). Bixia Yuanjin Tai Shan is a wind diety, the daughter of the sacred mountain of the east, Tai Shan. See also *Fecundity Lady* and *Yu nü.* Alternate forms: Bixia Yuangun, Bixia Yuanjun, Chen Furen, Chu-shêng Niangniang, Niangniang Songzi, Pi-hia-yü-kün, Pi-Hsia Yuan-Chin, Pi-hsia Yuan-Chun, Pi Hia Yuan Kiun, Shengmu, Shen Mu, Tianxian Songzi, Tia Shan, Tia Shan Niang-niang, T'ien-hsien Sung-tzu, Zheseng Niang-niang. [Jobes 1962; Leach 1972; Leach 1992; Werner 1961]

Bixia Yuanjun See *Bixia Yuanjin.*

Bixiao

China

Household Affairs

One of the *Keng San Giuniang,* a goddess of the latrine. See also *Guodeng* and *Maozi Shenju.* Alternate form: Pi-hsiao. [Leach 1992; Werner 1961]

Blue Lotus

China

Immortality; Heaven and Hell

Deity. Wife of Liu Ch'uan and mother of two daughters.

Blue Lotus and her husband's souls were taken by messengers to the underworld. Then a strong, dark wind blew through the open gates of death and carried Blue

Lotus and Liu back to the city of Ch'angan where she was installed in the inner gardens and he in the Imperial storehouse.

The color blue represents the water and the moon-like principle in the occult. [Durdin-Robertson 1976]

Can Nü

China

Insects; Stars and Planets; Magic; Heaven and Hell

Goddess of silkworms and of the star Tiansi (T'ien Ssŭ).

One day Can Nü was out walking and passed by a horse that her father had killed. The skin of this magic horse was spread on the ground, but as Can Nü passed by the skin rose up, covered her and carried her towards heaven. Ten days later the skin was found beneath a mulberry tree and Can Nü had been changed into a silkworm and was in the tree, eating mulberry leaves and spinning silk.

Alternate form: Ts'an Nü. [Leach 1992; Werner 1961]

Chang E

China

Moon and Night; Reptiles; Immortality; Primordial Being

Moon goddess. Wife of the Divine Archer, Shen I.

When Chang E lived on earth, she drank some stolen liquid, the elixir of life. Her husband was angered by her behavior so she fled to the moon. There she was changed into a toad, some say a three-legged one.

As *Heng E* she is the cold, dark female principle, *Yin. Heng E* lives in the Palace of Great Cold. Her husband built the palace of cinnamon wood and he visits her there once a month when the moon is dark. She is called the "Celestial Toad," a toad with three legs—the legs representing the three ten-day phases of the moon. Alternate forms: Chang O, Heng E, Heng O, Chang Ngo. [Durdin-Robertson 1976; Durdin-Robertson 1982; Eliot 1976; Jobes 1962; Leach 1992; Lurker 1984; Monaghan 1981]

Ch'ang Yung See *Chang Yong.*

Chang Hsi See *Zhang Xi.*

Chang Xi

China

Moon and Night

Mother of ten moons. She bathed them regularly in a pool at the foot of a tree. [Senior 1985]

Chang Yong

China

Primordial Being; Immortality; Justice

Deity who is the personification of the male principle in nature. She was said to have been a princess of the Shang dynasty who became immortal and inhabited the mountains. She is forever young and casts no shadow. Alternate form: Ch'ang Yung. [Werner 1961]

Chang Ngo See *Chang E.*

Chang O See *Chang E.*

Chao San Niang See *Zhao Sanniang.*

Chedi Furen

China

Stars and Planets; War

Goddess of the star Yüeh-k'uei. The wife of the general Tou Jung. She was deified after being killed at Yu-hun Kuan. Alternate form: Ch'e-Ti Fu-jen. [Leach 1992; Werner 1961]

Chen
China
Mother and Guardian
   Goddess of childbirth. She once appeared to a great lady during labor and has subsequently been worshiped by women during childbirth. [Werner 1961]

Chen Furen   See *Bixia Yuanjin.*

Chên, Queen   See *Mi Fei.*

Chen-te P'u-sa   See *Zhende Pusa.*

Ch'e-Ti Fu-jen   See *Chedi Furen.*

Ch'i Ku-tzu   See *The Qi Guzi.*

Chia Shih   See *Jia Shi.*

Chiang, The Empress
China
Moon and Night
   Goddess of the star Taiyin (T'ai-yin), the moon. [Leach 1992; Werner 1961]

Chieh   See *Jie.*

Chih Nu   See *Zhinü.*

Chih-nii   See *Zhinnü.*

Ch'i-hsien-niangniang   See *Qixian Niangniang.*

Chikisani-kamui
Japan, *Ainu*
Family and Tribes; Earth and Nature
   Elm goddess and ancestor of Ainu people. Mother of Aeoina-kamui, the father of whom was either the Pestilence god, Pa-kor-kamui or a sky god. The elm tree was used to strike a fire and believed by the Ainu to be the first tree in the human world. Alternate form: Chikisanti. [Jobes 1962; Leach 1992; Philippi 1982]

Chikisanti   See *Chikisani-kamui.*

Chin Ku   See *Jin Gu.*

Chin Mu   See *Jin Mu.*

Chin Nü   See *Zhinü.*

Chin-hua Niang-niang   See *Jinhua Niangniang.*

Chiu T'ien Hou Mu   See *Jiutian Houmu.*

Chiu T'ien Hsuan-nu   See *Jiutinan Xuannu.*

Ch'iung Hsiao   See *Qiongxiao.*

Chiu-rang-guru, The
Japan, *Ainu*
Water; Disorder
   "Senders Down of the Currents." River deities who inhabit rough waters, rapids, and waterfalls. [Batchelor ca. 1927; Leach 1992; Munro 1963]

Chi-shiki-no-ō-kami   See *Izanami-no-kami.*

Chiwashekot-mat
Japan, *Ainu*
Water; Fishing and Water Animals
   "She Who Governs the Place Where the Fresh and Salt Waters Mingle." Water deity who presides over the mouths of rivers where salt and fresh water meet. She protects the fish that live in these waters and the ones who come to spawn. [Batchelor ca. 1927; Leach 1992]

Chiwash-kor-kamui
Japan, *Ainu*
Water; Disorder; Mother and Guardian; Education and Knowledge; Ceremonies
   Goddess of the river rapids. Along with *Pet-ru-ush-mat (Wakka-ush-kamui)*, she saves humankind from famines by teaching them the proper rituals to use when hunting and fishing. [Leach 1992; Philippi 1982]

Chang-bu
Taiwan
Mother and Guardian
   Guardian of young children. [Diamond 1969; Leach 1992]

Chuan Hou
China
Water
   Goddess of streams. Equivalent to *Tian Hou.* [Jobes 1962]

Chuang Mu
China
Household Affairs; Order; Mother and Guardian
   Goddess of the bedchamber. She is invoked to keep harmony in the marital bed so progeny can be created. She is associated with wine. Alternate form: Ch'uang Mu (Po). [Jobes 1962; Leach 1992]

Ch'uang Mu   See *Chuang Mu.*

Chuh Kamuy
Japan, *Ainu*
Sun and Day; Moon and Night; Ceremonies
   Sun and moon deity who mediates for her followers with the other deities. She is the daytime sun and the dark moon and is the most important of the sky deities. See also *Goddess of the Sun and Moon.* [Leach 1992]

Chui-shen Niangniang   See *Juishen Niangniang.*

Chun T'i   See *Jun Ti.*

Chu-shêng Niangniang   See *Bixia Yuanjin.*

Corner Goddess
China
Fate
   Fortune deity. Young ladies seek out this goddess to have their fortunes told. [Werner 1961]

Corpse Goddesses
China
Immortality; Heaven and Hell; Justice; Ceremonies
   Death deities. Three nuns who are ghosts and reside in the dead body. To keep them from leaving the body to go to heaven and informing the gods of the person's sins, a night watch is held by friends and relatives of the deceased. The three are *Pang Che, Pang Jiao,* and *Pang Zhu.* [Werner 1961]

Cui Sheng
China
Mother and Guardian
Deity of midwifery who presides over childbirth to make it easier. [Leach 1992; Werner 1961]

Cuisheng Sheng Mu
China
Mother and Guardian; Health and Healing
"The Saintly Mother Who Hastens Childbirth." She is the deified Danai Furen, a specialist of the celestial Ministry of Medicine who safely and painlessly delivered the Empress of an heir. See also *Peitai Niangniang.* Alternate forms: Ta-nai Fu-jen, Ts'ui Shêng Shêng-mu. [Leach 1992; Werner 1961]

Cunda
Japan
Deity of the Buddhist pantheon. See also *Cunda,* Indian Subcontinent. [Getty 1962]

Da Ma Niangniang   See *Deo Ma Niangniang.*

Da'an Nü
China
Insects
Silkworm deity. Alternate form: Ts'an Nü. [Leach 1992; Werner 1961]

Dabiancai Tiannü
China
Arts
Goddess of music and poetry. Equivalent to Indian *Sarasvati.* See also *Miao Yin Fomu.* Alternate form: Ta-pien-ts'ai-t'ien-nü. [Getty 1962; Leach 1992]

Daiboth, The Female
Japan
Large Size
A clay idol of enormous size who has many hands. May be a representation of *Quanyin.* [Durdin-Robertson 1976; Redfield 1931]

Dainichi-nyorai
Japan
Goodness; Sun and Day
"Great Illuminator." Benevolent sun deity who belongs to the great Buddhist trinity. Considered either a male or female deity. May be an incarnation of *Ama-terasu-ō-mi-kami* and said to be associated with Fudo, the god of wisdom. [Jobes 1962; Sykes 1968]

Daiyou Taiping Xiang Yuxian Niangniang   See *Yu Nü.*

Daji
China
Justice
Deity who invented a punishment called "roasting." Wife of Chou Hsin. Daji's punishment consisted of walking over heated copper. If the victim slipped, he or she fell into a pit of hot coals. Alternate form: Tachi. [Jobes 1962]

Danai Furen   "The Greatly Honored Dame." See *Cuisheng Sheng Mu.*

Dao
China
Earth and Nature
"The Way" or "The Path." Not generally considered a goddess but it is accepted that Daoists follow the ways of Mother Nature and important values are usually referred to as feminine and maternal. See also *Dao,* Southeast Asia; and *Estsanatlehi,* North America. Alternate form: Tao. [Stone 1979]

Dao Mu   See *Dou Mou.*

Dara Eke
Mongolia
Goodness
Mother of mercy and compassion. Equivalent to Chinese *T'o-lo.* [Leach 1992]

Dark Maid, The
China
Weather
Weather deity who sends down frost and snow. [Durdin-Robertson 1976]

Dashizhi
China
Education and Knowledge
Bodhisatva (one whose essence is perfect knowledge and is believed to be a future Buddha). In India she is the male Mahāsthamparata, "he who has attained to great power." Alternate form: Da-shi-zhi. [Lurker 1984]

Da-shi-zhi   See *Dashizhi.*

Daxian Furen
China
Evil
"Great (Fox) Fairy Dame." Malevolent deity who must be appeased. Alternate form: Ta Hsien Fu Jên. [Leach 1992]

Deities of the Third Earthly Generation
Japan
Unknown
Grandchildren of *Izanami-no-kami* and Izanagi. They include *Awa-nami-no-kami, Kaya-no-hime-no-kami, Kuni-no-kuhiza-mochi-no-kami, Kuni-no-mi-kumari-no-kami, Kuni-no-kura-do-no-kami, Kuni-no-sa-giri-no-kami, Kuni-no-sa-zuchi-no-kami, Ō-to-mato-hime-no-kami, Toyo-uke-bime-no-kami,* and *Tsura-nami-no-kami.* [Durdin-Robertson 1976]

Deo Ma Niangniang
China
Health and Healing
Goddess of health who cures measles and smallpox worshiped in Sichuan. Deo is not a Chinese word so this goddess' name may be *Da Ma Niangniang* or *Ma Niangniang.* [Graham 1928; Leach 1992]

Di Mu
China
Earth and Nature; Agriculture; Ceremonies; Family and Tribes
Ancestor of the world. Daoist earth mother and agricultural growth deity. The Emperor is considered a husbandman and at the vernal equinox, he goes to the fields richly attired and, using his own plow, turns the first earth. Offerings to Di Mu are placed in the earth, not burned. In south China, she is represented by a clod of earth in front of which an offering of burning incense is given to thank her for an abundant harvest. Alternate forms: Di Ya, Ti Mu. [Leach 1992; Lurker 1984; Werner 1961]

Di Ya
China
Earth and Nature

Earth mother. Also said to be name of a servant of the god of literature. Alternate form: Di Mu. [Lurker 1984; Senior 1985]

dKar-mo
China
Earth and Nature
Mountain deity of southwest China. Alternate form: Seng-ge Ga-mu. [Leach 1992]

Dong Mu
China
Mother and Guardian
Mother of ancient China worshiped during the Shang and Zhou (Chou) periods. Alternate form: Tung Mu. [Chang 1976]

Dou Mou
China
Stars and Planets; Family and Tribes; Justice; Health and Healing; Mother and Guardian; War; Commerce and Travel; Education and Knowledge; Fate
Goddess of the North Star. The constellation is also called the Star-Bushel and the Southern Bushel, and Dou Mou is sometimes called the bushel goddess. She has nine children, the Renhuang (Jen Huang), who were the first human rulers on earth. Worshiped by the Buddhists and the Daoists, she is invoked for protection from disease, from war, and while traveling. She is the record keeper of births and deaths and is the patron of fortune tellers. She upholds the sun and the moon and passes easily between them. She may have been *Marichi*, Indian Subcontinent, adopted in China. In the Daoist religion, she is similar to the Buddhist *Guanyin*. Equivalent to *Maritchi*, Indian Subcontinent. Alternate forms: Dao Mu, Dou Mu, Tian Mu, T'ien Mu, Tou Mu. [Jobes 1962; Leach 1992; Monaghan 1981; Sykes 1968; Werner 1961]

Dou Mu   See *Dou Mou.*

Douizhen   See *Doushen Niangniang.*

Doushen Niangniang
China
Destroyer of Life; Justice
Daoist goddess of smallpox. Mother of four sons who represent four kinds of smallpox. She is a specialist attached to the celestial Ministry of Medicine and is also responsible for punishing those committing infanticide. She is sometimes portrayed wearing a shawl which is protecting her smallpox infected skin from the cold. Alternate forms: Douizhen, Tou-shen Niang-niang. [Leach 1992; Werner 1961]

Dragon Mother, The
China
Mother and Guardian; Magic; Education and Knowledge
Mother goddess.
 Monkey visited the Dragon King looking for a suitable weapon. The Dragon King offered him several different ones, but Monkey was not satisfied. The Dragon King said he had no more weapons, then Dragon Mother appeared and suggested the magic iron with which the Milky Way had been pounded flat. She said it had been glowing with a strange light for several days and perhaps it was an omen indicating the iron should be given to Monkey. The magic iron satisfied Monkey and he took it away. [Durdin-Robertson 1976]

Earth Cow, The
China
Agriculture; Domesticated Animals; Ceremonies
Earth deity. A representation of her is carried during an agricultural celebration. It is made of baked earth, decorated with gilt ears and ornaments. Inside of the cow are many earthen calves. At the end of the ceremony the cow is broken open and the pieces of the figure and the calves are distributed among the people. In one village there is a stone cow who is invoked during droughts. [Durdin-Robertson 1976]

Earth Goddess   See *Tartary and Cathay Earth Goddess.*

Eastern Mother
China
Magic; Health and Healing
Deity associated with Shamanism. [Durdin-Robertson 1976]

Edji
China; Mongolia
Creator of Life
"Mother." First woman. [Jobes 1962]

Embroidery Goddess
China
Household Affairs
Needlework deity. Companion of Hsüan Yüan. Because of her skill with the needle and embroidery, she was appointed its goddess. Young girls learning to do needlework worship her. [Werner 1961]

Eterna
China
Magic; Family and Tribes; Heaven and Hell
Sorcerer. Daughter of *Aunt Piety.*
Eterna disappeared in a black wind while her mother was off visiting Wu. Aunt Piety discovered that Eterna had been reborn into a family of a rich shopkeeper named Hu. Aunt Piety visited her daughter in secret and taught her the skills of sorcery. When Hu's house and business burned down, Eterna started practicing her magic. She provided coins and great quantities of rice. When Hu found out that Eterna was using a book of magic, he burned it. As food and money became scarce, Hu decided that Eterna should be allowed to use her magic after all. Hu became rich once again. Eterna married, but when her husband was accidentally killed, the authorities became curious about her activities and Eterna decided to leave. Aunt Piety helped Eterna to escape to a beautiful place under the earth, where mother and daughter now live together. [Durdin-Robertson 1976]

Etogon
China
Earth and Nature
Earth goddess of Kansu. [Leach 1992; Schram 1957]

Etugen
Mongolia, *Mongol*
Earth and Nature; Weather; Agriculture; Wealth
Mongolian earth goddess. She is invoked for good weather, abundant crops and animals, and for personal prosperity. See also *Etugen*, Eastern Europe. [Czaplicka 1969; Leach 1992]

Ezo Goddess
Japan, *Ainu*
Earth and Nature
Creator of Ezo (Hokkaido). She spends a lot of time talking with other goddesses. [Durdin-Robertson 1976]

Fecundity Lady
China
Unknown
Attendant of Lady of Tai Shan, *Bixia Yuanjin.* [Leach 1972]

Fei, Lady
China
Unknown
   Companion to the gods. [Eliot 1976]

Feng Po
China
Weather; Hunting and Wild Animals; Order
   "Mistress Wind." Feng Po controls the winds while riding
on a tiger. When the winds are calm, she has the winds stuffed
away in a bag she carries over her shoulder. Alternate form:
Feng Popo. [Carlyon 1982; Durdin-Robertson 1976;
Monaghan 1981; Senior 1985]

Feng Popo   See *Feng Po.*

Flower Goddesses
China
Earth and Nature; Time
   There are twelve of these deities, including male as well
as female, one for each month. They are worshiped on the
twelfth day of the second moon by florists. [Werner 1961]

Frost Goddess
China
Weather; Time; War
   Called the Green Maiden, she determines that there will be
frost on the third day of the ninth moon and is worshiped by
the military. [Werner 1961]

Fuchi   See *Fuji.*

Fuji
Japan, *Ainu*
Fire; Earth and Nature; Disorder; Household Affairs
   Fire goddess who presides over volcanic fires as well as
hearth fires. Mount Fujiyama on Honshu island bears her
name. See also *Apemeru-ko-yan-mat, Aetna,* Greek and
Roman Empires, *Pele,* Oceania, and *Chuginadak,* North
America. Alternate forms: Fuchi, Huchi-fuchi, Huzi. [Leach
1992; Monaghan 1981; Stone 1979]

Funadama-sama
Japan
Fishing and Water Animals
   "Ship Spirits." Goddess of the seafarers and their boats.
[Herbert 1967; Leach 1992; Norbeck 1954]

Fupao
China
Magic; Mother and Guardian; Sky and Heavens
   Mother of the Yellow Emperor, Huang-Ti.

   *One spring evening, Fupao was sitting outside watching
   a light show in the sky. She was miraculously impregnated
   and remained pregnant for two years.* [Jobes 1962;
Monaghan 1981]

Fute-mimi-no-kami
Japan
Unknown
   Possibly "Fat Ear." Daughter of Hu-no-zu-no-no-kami,
wife of O-mi-zu-nu-no-kami, mother of Ame-no-puya-
kinu-no-kami. [Durdin-Robertson 1976; Philippi 1968]

Fuzhou Princess
China, *Zhong (Jung)*
Family and Tribes
   Ancestor deity in Fuzhou (Fuchow). [Durdin-Robertson
1976]

Gao Lanying
China
Stars and Planets
   Stellar deity, the star T'ao-hua. Alternate form: Kao
Lan-ying. [Leach 1992; Werner 1961]

Gaomei   See *Nüwa.*

Ge Gu
China
Mother and Guardian; Health and Healing; Ceremonies
   "Wise Lady Ge." Childbirth specialist attached to the
celestial Ministry of Medicine. She has a temple in Liiu-kuo
Hsiang Village. A tablet inscribed with her title is taken into
the room where a woman is having a difficult delivery so it
can be prayed to for aid. Alternate form: Ko Ku. [Werner
1961]

Gogome   See *Yomo-tsu-shiko-me*

Good Sight Lady
China
Mother and Guardian; Health and Healing
   Protector of children's eyes. [Durdin-Robertson 1976]

Guanyin
China
Goodness; Mother and Guardian; Health and Healing;
Physical Prowess; Education and Knowledge
   Goddess of Mercy. She protects women and children,
giving them health and making them fertile. Sister of *Miao
Yin.* Also associated with sound and called "The Melodious
Voice." Guanyin may have originally been the older deity
Nügua. She is equivalent to the Avalokitesvara, who was
a male deity, and *Vac* and *Vach,* Indian Subcontinent. In
Buddhism she is a *bodhisatva,* one whose essence is perfect
knowledge and is believed to be a future Buddha.

   *Guanyin was so concerned for humanity, that when she
   became enlightened, she chose to keep her human form
   and remain on earth until all living creatures attained
enlightenment.*
   Guanyin has taken many different forms, an unusual
happening for a Buddhist deity, being depicted in at least
thirty-three different ways, both female and male. In Japan
she is called *Kwannon.* See also *Avalokita, Daitboth, Songzi,
Songzi Guanyin; Ahnt Kai',* Central and Mesoamerica;
Tho-og, the Himalaya. Equivalent to *Chuin,* Near East,
and *Kun,* Indian Subcontinent. Alternate forms: Kuan Yin,
Kwanyin, Miao Shan. [Durdin-Robertson 1976; Getty 1962;
Leach 1972; Leach 1992; Monaghan 1981; Werner 1961]

Guiling Shenamu
China
Reptiles
   "Saintly Mother Turtle." Alternate form: Kuei-ling Sheng-mu.
[Werner 1961]

Gum Lin
China
Mother and Guardian
   "Self-esteem." Cantonese goddess who was committed to
protecting the people of her village. See also *Yi Long.* [Stone
1979]

Guodeng
China
Household Affairs
   Goddess of Latrine. See also *Bixiao, Keng San Guniang,
Maozi Shenju,* and *Qiongxiao.* Alternate form: Kuo-teng.
[Werner 1961]

Hachi-kazuki-hime
Japan
Beauty; Metals and Minerals; Ceremonies
"Princess with a Helmet."

 Hachi-kazuki-hime was a beautiful woman who always hid her charms with a wooden helmet. When she married, the helmet would not come off her head until the end of the ceremony when it split into many pieces. Each piece fell to the floor and turned into a precious jewel.
Alternate form: Hatschihime. [Durdin-Robertson 1976]

Hana-yama-hime   See *Hani-yasu-bime-no-kami*

Hani-yasu-bime-no-kami
Japan
Earth and Nature; Household Affairs; Commerce and Travel
"Hani-yasu Princess Deity"or "Clay-tempering Princess Deity." Goddess of clay and patron of potters. In popular belief, she was the goddess of industry. Daughter of *Izanami-no-kami,* wife of Haniyasu-hiko-no-Kami. Alternate forms: Hana-yama-hime, Haniyasu-hime. [Durdin-Robertson 1976; Leach 1992; Ono et al. 1985; Philippi 1968; Sproul 1979]

Haniyasu-hime   See *Hani-yasu-bime-no-kami.*

Haritei-mo   See *Helidi.*

Hashinau-kor-kamui
Japan; *Ainu*
Goodness; Hunting and Wild Animals
Benevolent goddess of the hunt. [Leach 1992; Philippi 1982]

Hashinau-uk-kamui   See *Hash-inau-uk-kamui.*

Hash-inau-uk-kamui
Japan, *Ainu*
Hunting and Wild Animals; Mother and Guardian
Goddess of the hunt. Protector and guide of the hunters. Alternate form: Hashinau-uk-kamui. [Leach 1992; Philippi 1982]

Hatschihime   See *Hachi-kazuki-hime.*

Haya-aki-tsu-hime-no-kami
Japan
Time; Water
"Rapid Autumn Princess Deity." Goddess of harbors, river mouths, estuaries, and rivers. Daughter of *Izanami-no-kami* and Izanagi, a deity of the *Second Earthly Generation.* Mother of the water, mountain, tree, wind and meadow deities and grandmother of the bird, fertility, fire, and land deities. [Durdin-Robertson 1976; Jobes 1962; Leach 1992; Philippi 1968]

He   See *Xi Wang mu.*

He Ku
China
Family and Tribes; Magic; Water; Fishing and Water Animals; Immortality
"Immortal of the Waters."

He Ku was gathering flowers along the bank of a river when three youths appeared and told her that the Duke of the Eastern Seas had chosen her for his wife. The youths laid a carpet on the water and He Ku walked across the water toward the Eastern Seas. Before she left, she sent a message to her parents telling them that she had become the "Immortal of the Waters" and that she would send fish on the fourth month of each year. The fish would bring her family news of He Ku from her
new home. A temple was built in her honor on the spot where she first received the message.
Alternate forms: Ho Ku, Nü Chün. [Werner 1961]

He Xiangu
China
Immortality; Mother and Guardian; Sky and Heavens
One of the "Eight Immortals," the only female. Daoist patron deity of women and housewives. She is portrayed holding a lotus blossom and a peach or ladle.

He Xiangu obtained immortality by eating a supernatural peach, powdered mother-of-pearl, and moonbeams. She lives in the heavens with Xi Wangmu and was once seen floating on a cloud and once in Canton.
Alternate forms: Ho Sian Gu, Ho Hsien-ku. [Bonnerjea 1927; Carlyon 1982; Leach 1992; Lurker 1984; Monaghan 1981]

Helidi
China
Evil; Mother and Guardian; Life/Death Cycle
Demon. She became a protector of children and aided couples in conceiving, after the intervention of the Buddha. Equivalent to *Hariti,* Indian Subcontinent. Alternate forms: Hariti, Haritei-mo, Kishimojin. [Lurker 1984]

Heng E   See *Chang E.*

Heng O   See *Chang E.*

Hettsui-no-kami
Japan
Household Affairs; Fire; Ceremonies
"Kitchen Deity." Shinto goddess of the kitchen stove. She is associated with the other household deities. Her feast, the Feast of the Bellows, *Fuigo Matsuri,* takes place on November 8. [Durdin-Robertson 1976; Durdin-Robertson 1982]

Hi-haya-bi-no-kami   See *Hi-no-haya-hi-no-mikoto.*

Hi-kawa-hime
Japan
Sun and Day; Water; Ceremonies
"Sun River Princess." Daughter of O-kami-no-kami. Her husband Huha-no-mojikunusu-nu-no-kami (Pupa-no-mondi-kunusunu-no-kami) was a descendant of *Kushi-nada-hime.* Her shrine was located in the province of Musashi, probably where the famous Hikawa Shrine, now in Omiya-shi, Saitama-ken, is located. [Durdin-Robertson 1976; Philippi 1968]

Hime-jima
Japan
Earth and Nature
"Maiden Island." The name of a number of small islands born of the union of *Izanami-no-kami* and her brother, Izanagi-no-mikoto. Alternate form: Hime-shima. [Durdin-Robertson 1976]

Hime-shima   See *Hime-jima.*

Hime-tatara-isuke-yori-hime   See *Hoto-tatara-isusuki-hime-no-mikoto.*

Hime-tatara-isuzu-himen-no-mikoto   See *Hoto-tatara-isusuki-hime-no-mikoto.*

Hi-naga-hime
Japan
Reptiles; Demi-animals

"Long Princess of Pi." Snake princess who has the body of a snake and a human face. Married to the prince Homutsu-wake (Homuchiwake).

> When Hi-naga-hime's husband saw her on their wedding night, he was very frightened and ran away. He set out to the sea in a boat, but Hi-naga-hime pursued him in another boat. The prince fled to land and carried his boat up into the mountains.

See also *Kiyo-hime*. [Durdin-Robertson 1976; Philippi 1968]

Hi-narashi-bime
Japan
Unknown

One of the *Seventeen Generations Deities*. Daughter of O-kami-no-kami, wife of Mika-nushi-hiko-no-kami, mother of Tahirikishimarumi-no-kami. [Durdin-Robertson 1976; Philippi 1968]

Hina-teri-nukata-bichi-o-ikochini-no-kami
Japan
Unknown

Possibly "rustic regions to shine." Wife of Tori-narumi-no-kami, mother of Kuni-oshi-tomi-no-kami. One of *Seventeen Generations Deities*. [Durdin-Robertson 1976; Philippi 1968]

Hi-no-haya-hi-no-mikoto
Japan
Fire

"Fire-vigorous-force-deity." She is manifest in the fire. Alternate form: Hi-haya-bi-no-kami. [Herbert 1967; Leach 1992]

Hinomahe-no-kami
Japan
Unknown

Goddess of the Province of Kii. [Durdin-Robertson 1976]

Hirose-no-kawaai-no-kami See *Waka-uka-no-me-no-mikoto*.

Hisa-me, The
Japan
Heaven and Hell; Ugliness

Eight underworld deities who are bogies and frighten children. They also aided *Izanami-no-kami* (see for story) in her pursuit of Izanagi. One of the Hisa-me is named *Yomo-tsu-hikmo-me*. [Durdin-Robertson 1976; Jobes 1962]

Hiyoi Kwan-non
Japan
Unknown

Equivalent to *Parnasavari*, Indian Subcontinent. Alternate form: Jgyo-kongo. [Getty 1962]

Ho Hsien-ku See *He Xiangu*.

Ho Ku
China
Water

River goddess of the river Han. Alternate form: He-ku. [Leach 1992; Werner 1961]

Ho Sian Gu See *He Xiangu*.

Hongluan Xingjun
China
Stars and Planets; Family and Tribes

Stellar deity who presides over engagements and weddings. Alternate form: Hung Luan Hsing Chün. [Day 1940; Leach 1992]

Horkeu-kamui
Japan, *Ainu*
Hunting and Wild Animals

Wolf goddess who wears white robes.

> She was living in the land of humans when she was attacked by a monster bear. Her cubs called to their father in the upper heavens and he came to rescue them.

[Philippi 1982]

Horokariyep
Japan; *Ainu*
Water; Disorder

"The Spirit Who Turns Back." Spirit of the eddy. A very short-tempered deity who attacks people if she is jealous. [Batchelor ca. 1927; Leach 1992]

Hoto-tatara-isusuki-hime-no-mikoto
Japan
Beauty

"Genitals Bellows Panicky Princess Lady." A woman of remarkable beauty, second or "great wife" of Emperor Jimmu. Daughter of *Seya-tatara-hime* (see for story) and Ō-mono-hushi. Alternate forms: Hime-tatara-isuke-yori-hime, Hime-tatara-isuzu-hime-no-mikoto, Isuke-yori-hime. [Durdin-Robertson 1976; Ono et al. 1985; Philippi 1968]

Hou T'u Kuo Huang See *Houtu Guohuang*.

Hou Tu See *Hou Tu Nainai* and *Hu Tu*.

Hou Tu Nainai
China
Earth and Nature

Earth goddess. Originally a male deity (Hou Tu) who became a female deity. Alternate forms: Hou-t'u nai nai, Moutu, Hou Tu. [Jobes 1962]

Houtu Guohuang
China
Earth and Nature

Earth goddess. Alternate form: Hou Tú Kou Huang. [Day 1940; Leach 1992]

How Kung See *Hoy Kong*.

Hoy Kong
China
Stars and Planets

"The Empress." Stellar goddess in the Ursa Minor Constellation. Alternate form: How Kung. [Durdin-Robertson 1976]

Hsi Ho See *Xi Hou*.

Hsi Shih See *Xi Shi*.

Hsi Wang Mu See *Xi Wangmu*.

Hsi-ling Shih See *Xiling Shi*.

Hsiang, Lady See *Xiang, Lady*.

Hsieh, Lady See *Xie, Lady*.

Hsieh Jên Hsing Chün See *Xieren Xingjun*.

Hsiu-chi See *Xiu Zhi*.

Hsü T'ien-chu See *Xu Tianju*.

Hsueh Hu Niang Niang   See *Xuehu Niangniang.*

Hsuk'ung Tsang   See *Xu Kongcang.*

Hu Tu
China
Creator of Life
   "Empress Earth." Fertility goddess whose altar is in the
Forbidden City in Beijing. [Monaghan 1981]

Hua Hsien   See *Hua Xian.*

Hua Xian
China
Earth and Nature
   Flower goddess. [Jobes 1962]

Huang
China
Stars and Planets
   "The Phoenix." Dihou (Ti-hou) star goddess. Also a symbol of
the Empress. [Durdin-Robertson 1976; Leach 1992]

Huang Daopo
China
Earth and Nature
   Goddess of cotton in Jiangnan (Kiangnan). Alternate form:
Huang Tao-P'o. [Werner 1961]

Huang Tao-p'o   See *Huang Daopo.*

Huchi-fuchi
Japan, *Ainu*
Fire; Household Affairs; Mother and Guardian; Health and
Healing
   Goddess of the hearth fire. She cooks food, warms people,
and purifies diseased bodies. Mother of *Shu-koyan-mat.* Also
an alternate name for *Fuji.* [Durdin-Robertson 1976; Leach
1992]

Huchu Xing   See *Yuefu Taiyin.*

Hung Luan Hsing Chün   See *Hongluan Xingjun.*

Huoling Shengmu
China
Stars and Planets; War
   Stellar deity, the star Huofu. She was slain while defending
the ancient capital of the Yin dynasty. Alternate form: Hou-
ling Sheng-mu. [Leach 1992; Werner 1961]

Hushan Dashi   See *Zhende Pusa.*

Hu-shan Ta-shih   See *Zhende Pusa.*

Huzi   See *Fuji.*

Ichiki-shima-hime-no-mikoto
Japan
Fishing and Water Animals; Wealth; Luck
   "Ichiki-shima Princess Goddess." A deity of seafarers,
goddess of luck and wealth, and one of the three *Munakata
Goddesses,* daughter of *Ama-terasu-ō-mi-kami.* Ichiki-shima-
hime-no-mikoto was an ancient name of *Benten,* and the
island Itsukushima, where she is enshrined, later became a
center of goddess worship. See also *Munakata Goddesses.*
Alternate forms: Sayori-bime-no-mikoto, Itiki-sima, Itiki-
sima-pime-no-mikoto. [Durdin-Robertson 1976; Jobes 1962;
Leach 1992; Ono et al. 1985]

Idumo Pantheon Deities   See *Izumo Pantheon Deities.*

Idunome-no-kami   See *Izu-no-me-no-kami.*

Idzu-no-me-no-kami   See *Izu-no-mo-no-kami.*

Iha-naga-hime   See *Iwa-naga-hime.*

Ihatsutsu-nome   See *Iwa-tsutsu-no-me-no-mikoto.*

Ikuguhi   See *Iku-gui-no-kami.*

Iku-gui-no-kami
Japan
Unknown
   "Life-integrating Deity." Sister/wife of the Germ-
Integrating Deity, Tsuno-gui-no-kami. One of the Seven
Generations of the Age of the Gods, deities born without
parents. Alternate forms: Ikuguhi, Iku-kuhi-no-mikoto.
[Durdin-Robertson 1976; Jobes 1962; Philippi 1968]

Iku-kuhi-no-mikotu   See *Iku-gui-no-kami.*

Iku-tama-saki-tama-hime-no-kami
Japan
Luck
   "Living-spirit, Lucky-spirit-princess." One of the deities
of the Seventeen Generations. Daughter of Hihiragi-no-sono-
hana-mazumi-no-kami, consort of Tahirikishimarumi-no-kami,
mother of Miro-nami-no-kami. See also *Iku-tama-yori-bime.*
[Durdin-Robertson 1976; Philippi 1968]

Iku-tama-yori-bime
Japan
Family and Tribes; Luck; Love and Sexuality
   "Life-spirit, Lucky-spirit Princess." Ancestor of the
Dukes of Miwa and Kamo.
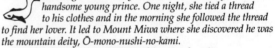   *Each night Iku-tama-yori-bime was visited by a
   handsome young prince. One night, she tied a thread
   to his clothes and in the morning she followed the thread
to find her lover. It led to Mount Miwa where she discovered he was
the mountain deity, Ō-mono-nushi-no-kami.*
   See also *Iku-tama-saki-tama-hime-no-kami.*
[Durdin-Robertson 1976; Jobes 1962; Ono et al. 1985;
Philippi 1968]

In
Japan
Creator of Life; Directions
   Female principle who is passive and rules the north, while
the male principle is considered active and rules the south.
Equivalent to *Yin,* Far East, *Yoni,* Indian Subcontinent, and
Yum, the Himalaya. See also *Kami-musubi-no-kami.* [Jobes
1962]

Inada-hime
Japan
Love and Sexuality
   "Rice-land-lady." May be an alternate form of *Kushi-nada-
hime.* Said to be a Shinto goddess of love. [Bonnerjea 1927;
Jobes 1962]

Inagami-hime   See *Kushi-nada-hime.*

Inari
Japan
Commerce and Travel; Wealth; Life/Death Cycle; Love and
Sexuality; Hunting and Wild Animals
   Shinto vixen goddess associated with rice and smithcraft.
She is invoked for prosperity, long life, and a successful

love relationship. She corresponds to *Aunt Piety*. *Tama-no-maye* may be a form of Inari. Alternate forms: Inari-m'yojim, Uka-no-kami. [Durdin-Robertson 1976; Jobes 1962; Monaghan 1981]

Inari-m'yojim   See *Inari*.

Ino-hime
Japan
Unknown
  "Princess of Ino." A goddess of the *Izumo Pantheon*. Consort of O-toshi-no-kami. [Durdin-Robertson 1976]

Inoshishi
Japan
Hunting and Wild Animals; Reptiles; Mother and Guardian
  "Boar." Said to be a goddess who drives away poisonous snakes. [Jobes 1962]

Iresu-huchi
Japan, *Ainu*
Fire
  Fire goddess. [Eliade 1987]

Isa
Mongolia
Directions
  Goddess of the Northeast. [Leach 1992; Percheron 1953]

Ishi-kori-dome-no-mikoto
Japan
Commerce and Travel
  "Stone-cutting Old Woman." She assists the celestial blacksmith, Amatsu-mara. Ishi-kori-dome-no-mikoto made the mirror that the deities used in luring *Amaterasu-ō-kami* (see for story) out of the cave. [Durdin-Robertson 1976; Jobes 1962; Leach 1992; Ono et al. 1985; Philippi 1968]

Isuke-yori-hime   See *Hoto-tatara-isusuki-hime-no-mikoto*.

Itiki-sima-pime-no-mikoto   See *Ichiki-shima-hime-no-mikoto*.

Iwa-naga-hime
Japan
Life/Death Cycle; Unhappiness
  "Rock-long Princess." Goddess of longevity. Consort of Ninigi, sister of *Konohana-sakuya-hime*.
  Iwa-naga-hime was rejected by Ninigi, who found her younger sister more attractive. Iwa-naga-hime cursed her sister's children with short lives, lives that lasted only as long as a blossom's. Iwa-naga-hime blessed her own children with long lives, lives as long as that of a rock.
  Alternate form: Iha-naga-hime. [Bonnerjea 1927; Durdin-Robertson 1976; Monaghan 1981; Philippi 1968]

Iwa-su-hime-no-kami
Japan
Metals and Minerals
  "Rock-nest-princess Deity." Daughter of *Izanami-no-kami* and Izanagi. Also called the goddess of sand. Alternate forms: Iwasubime-no-kami [Durdin-Robertson 1976; Leach 1992; Philippi 1968]

Iwa-tsutsu-no-me-no-mikoto
Japan
Magic; Fire

"Stone-spark-woman Deity." One of the feminine deities of the *Second Earthly Generation*. She was born from the blood of the fire god when Izanagi killed him. Counterpart of Iwa-tsutsu-no-o-no-mikoto. Alternate forms: Iwatsutsu-nome,Iha-tsutsu-nome. [Durdin-Robertson 1976; Ono et al. 1985]

Iwasubime-no-kami   See *Iwa-su-hime-no-kami*.

Iwatsutsu-nome   See *Iwa-tsutsu-no-me-no-mikoto*.

Izanami-no-kami
Japan
Creator of Life; Earth and Nature; Heaven and Hell; Ugliness
  "Female-who-invites." Creator, earth goddess, and underworld deity. Mother or grandmother of *Awa-nami-no-kami, Haya-aki-tsu-hime-no-kami, Hime-jima, Kaya-no-hime-no-kami*, and *Deities of the Third Earthly Generation*. *Mitsu-ha-no-me-no-kami* was born from *Izanami-no-kami's* urine.
  Izanami-no-kami and her brother/consort, Izanagi-no-mikoto, descended from heaven on the Celestial Bridge, the Milky Way. They stirred the watery chaos and when it solidified they alighted. After stepping onto the island, Izanami-no-kami spoke first which angered Izanagi and he arranged to change the event so he could speak first. Then they had intercourse and began to have numerous progeny: the sea, other islands, rivers, mountains, vegetation and many deities, the first being Amaterasu-ō-mi-kami. The deities of the earth came from her feces, other deities came from her urine, and still others from her vomit. When Izanami-no-kami had birthed all of the deities, she went to the underworld and built a castle. Izanagi was sad to have lost her companionship and went in search of her. When he found her, she agreed to accompany him to the upper world. But first she said she needed to be alone for awhile, so telling Izanagi not to disturb her, she shut herself in a room in her castle. Izanami-no-kami became impatient and went into the room where he discovered that Izanami-no-kami was now in a more primitive body. Attending her were the eight thunder demons. Frightened by Izanami's appearance and her anger, Izanagi fled. He was pursued by the Shikomes, the eight thunder demons, fifteen hundred assistant devils, and Izanami-no-kami. When they reached the Even Pass between the upper and lower worlds, Izanami-no-kami and Izanagi stopped and discussed the situation. Izanami-no-kami returned to the underworld and Izanagi went to the upperworld.
  Izanami-no-kami is worshiped by offerings of flowers, drums, flutes, flags, singing, and dancing. Alternate forms: Izanami-no-mikoto, Yomo-tsu-ō-kami, Chi-shiki-no-ō-kami. [Durdin-Robertson 1976; Durdin-Robertson 1982; Jobes 1962; Leach 1992; Monaghan 1981; Philippi 1968; Sproul 1979; Stone 1979]

Izanami-no-mikoto   See *Izanami-no-kami*.

Izu-no-me-no-kami
Japan
Health and Healing
  "Consecrated-woman Deity." Goddess of purification. She was born when Izanagi bathed. One of the deities of the *Second Earthly Generation*. Alternate forms: Idunome-no-kami, Idzu-no-me-no-kami. [Durdin-Robertson 1976; Leach 1992; Philippi 1968]

Izumo Pantheon Deities
Japan
Agriculture; Household Affairs
  Land-protecting, agricultural, and household goddesses. Descendants of O-toshi-no-kami. Worshiped in a variety of localities, they are not necessarily related. They are *Aki-bime-no-kami, Ami-chikaru-mizu-hime, Ino-hime, Kagayo-hime,*

Natsu-taka-tsu-hi-no-kami, Nunakawa-hime, Oki-tsu-hime, Ō-tsuchi-no kami, Uke-mochi-no-kami, Waka-sana-me-no-kami. Alternate form: Idumo Pantheon Deities. [Durdin-Robertson 1976; Philippi 1968]

Izushio-tome   See *Izushi-otome-no-kami*.

Izushi-otome-no-kami
Japan
Time; Love and Sexuality
   "Izushi-maiden Deity."
   *Izushi-otome-no-kami was desired by two brothers. The older brother had been unable to attract her attention.
   The younger brother enlisted the aid of his mother who made him clothes and a bow and arrow out of wisteria vines. When the younger brother approached Izushi-otome-no-kami in this odd outfit, she was very curious and took him inside her house. Having conjugal relations, they became husband and wife. The brothers are Autumn and Spring and when Izushi-otome-no-kami married Spring, Autumn did not give them a wedding gift. Their mother, Nature, was angry and she cursed him, causing him to wither.*
   Alternate form: Izushio-tome. [Durdin-Robertson 1976; Jobes 1962]

Japanese Mother Goddess
Japan
Mother and Guardian
   Progenitor of the Seven Generations of the Age of the Gods. She is compared to the mother goddess of Gnostic tradition, *Aeons*, Near East, who bore the seven material spirits. She may be *Kami-musubi-no-kami*. [Durdin-Robertson 1976]

Jen, Queen   See *Mi Fei*.

Jende Pusa   See *Zhende Pusa*.

Jgyo-kongo   See *Hiyoi Kwan-non* and *Parnasavari*, Indian Subcontinent.

Jia Shi
China
Stars and Planets
   Stellar deity, the star Maoduan (Mao Tuan). Alternate form: Chia Shih. [Leach 1992; Werner 1961]

Jian Lao
China
Earth and Nature
   Buddhist earth goddess. She represents permanence. [Lurker 1984]

Jiang Yuan
China
Agriculture
   Grain deity. Mother of Hou Tsi, Prince Millet, who taught the people how to grow grain. Alternate form: Kiang Yuan. [Durdin-Robertson 1976]

Jie
China
Household Affairs; Fire
   Hearth deity. Can be female or male or a couple. If the hearth and fire are considered separately, the hearth is female and the fire is male. Alternate form: Chieh. [Leach 1992; Schram 1957]

Jin Gu
China
Magic

Song (Sung) dynasty goddess who is a form of *Bixia Yuanjin*. Jin Gu performed numerous miracles. Alternate form: Chin Ku. [Werner 1961]

Jin Mu
China
Earth and Nature; Immortality
   Mountain Goddess who dispenses the pill of immortality. Alternate forms: Chin Mu, Xi Wangmu. [Eliot 1976; Leach 1992]

Jin Nü   See *Zhinü*.

Jinhua Niangniang
China
Arts
   Drum and violin goddess. Alternate form: Chin-hua Niang-niang. [Leach 1992; Werner 1961]

Jiutian Houmu
China
Unknown
   "Empress Mother of Heaven." Alternate form: Chiu T'ien Hou Mu. [Day 1940; Leach 1992]

Jiutinan Xuannu
China
Heaven and Hell; Magic; Love and Sexuality; Ceremonies
   "Dark Maiden." She lived in the Ninth Heaven. During the Han period, heaven was thought to have nine ascending partitions.
   Jiutinan Xuannu came down to earth to live with a mortal. A man bought a picture of a beautiful girl. He took it home and hung it on the wall, worshiping it each day. About six months went by and strange things began to happen. The man would come home and find food on his table and the household chores done. He hid himself and watched. He saw a young woman cooking and he noticed that the picture was just a white piece of paper. The next day, he left as usual, but returned early and burst into the cottage. He rolled up the blank paper and hid it. The woman said that since he had found her they should become husband and wife. They lived happily together and had a daughter. Finally, Jiutinan Xuannu told her husband she was the "Dark Maiden" and had come from the Ninth Heaven to live on earth for a few years. One day she asked him to give her the roll of paper. When he unrolled it, his wife disappeared and the woman reappeared on the paper. He hung the picture back on the wall and worshiped it as he had before.
   Alternate form: Chiu T'ien Hsuan-nu. [Durdin-Robertson 1976]

Jokwa
Japan
Justice; War; Order
   "Royal Lady of the West." Japanese mythical empress who aided humans by waging war against the demons and giants and setting the world in order. Equivalent to Chinese *Nügua*. [Jobes 1962]

Juishen Niangniang
China
Mother and Guardian
   Childbirth goddess. Alternate forms: Chin-hua Niang-niang, Chui-shen Niangniang. [Graham 1961; Leach 1992]

Jun-tei Kwan-non
Japan
Unknown
   Goddess who may have come from India, a form of *Durga* or *Hariti*, Indian Subcontinent. She is said to be a form of

Kwannon. As the mother of Buddhas, she is called *Cunda,* or *Sapta-koti-buddha-matri-cunti-devi,* Indian Subcontinent. Alternate form: Koti-sri. [Getty 1962]

Jun Ti
China
Dawn and Twilight; War

Dawn goddess who is light personified. She is portrayed with eight arms, one holding the sun and another the moon. Jun Ti is worshiped by the Hindus, Daoists, and Japanese Buddhists. She is said to be the same as *T'ien Hou* or *Tou Mu.* When she is represented with three heads, one is that of a sow. The Daoists say she is one of the Immortals and has warlike attributes. In Tantra Buddhism, she is also warlike and is portrayed with sixteen or eighteen arms. She holds a sword, hatchet, bow, arrow, thunderbolt, rosary, lotus, and vase. Equivalent to *Cunda,* Indian Subcontinent. Alternate forms: Chun T'i, Tian Hou. [Werner 1961]

Jūni-sama
Japan
Time; Creator of Life

"Mrs. Twelve." Mountain goddess. Once a year she bears twelve children symbolizing the months of the year. [Hori 1968]

Kagayo-hime
Japan
Unknown

"Shining Princess." Goddess of the *Izumo Pantheon.* [Durdin-Robertson 1976; Philippi 1968]

Kaguya-hime-no-mikoto
Japan
Beauty; Moon and Night; Immortality; Small Size; Luck

"Radiance and Beauty." Moon princess. She came to earth from the great city in the moon. The moon is thought to be a cinnamon tree.

A wood-cutter was in the forest cutting bamboo. A young, slender cane he had cut shone with a radiance and a song came from its roots. Looking more closely, the wood-cutter saw a tiny young woman. She was dressed like a princess and she gave off a wonderful flowery scent. The wood-cutter took her home and he and his wife adopted her. Their fortunes increased and news of their beautiful daughter reached the surrounding countryside, attracting even the Emperor to their home. Kaguya refused all suitors or gave them impossible tasks to perform. When Kaguya announced that she must return to her own people, the Emperor sent an army to prevent her leaving. On the night of her departure, a palanquin accompanied by many beautiful beings, dressed in kimonos of every color, came to carry her back to the moon. Before she left, she gave the Emperor a poem and a pitcher containing a potion for eternal youth.

Alternate form: Konohana-sakuya-hime. [Durdin-Robertson 1976]

Kalapiat
Taiwan, *Ami*
Weather; Fire; Disorder

Goddess of lightning. Her quarrels with the god of thunder, Kakring, produce storms. [Campbell 1925; Leach 1992]

Kami-ata-ka-shi-tsu-hime   See *Konohana-sakuya-hime.*

Kami-mima-subi   See *Kami-musubi-no-kami.*

Kami-musubi-no-kami
Japan
Creator of Life

"Divine-generative-force Parent Deity." The third primeval creative deity who originally had no gender, but with her counterpart Taka-mi-musubi-no-kami, is the the parent of Sukuna-hiko-ha-no-kami. She is also said to be the female principle *In.* She may be the same as the *Japanese Mother Goddess.* Alternate forms: Kami-mima-subi, Kamu-mimusubi. [Durdin-Robertson 1976; Jobes 1962; Leach 1992; Philippi 1968]

Kaminari
Japan
Weather

"Thunder woman." [Jobes 1962]

Kami-naru   See *Naru-kami.*

Kamu-ata-kashi-tsu-hime   See *Konohana-sakuya-hime.*

Kamu-ata-tsu-hime   See *Konohana-sakuya-hime.*

Kamu-hata-hime
Japan
Household Affairs

Deity of weaving. [Herbert 1967; Leach 1992]

Kamu-mimusubi   See *Kami-musubi-no-kami.*

Kamu-ō-ichi-hime
Japan
Unknown

"Divine Ōiti Princess." A goddess enshrined in Ōiti. Daughter of O-yama-tsu-mi-no-kami, consort of Susa-no-wo, and mother of Ō-toshi-no-kami and Uku-no-ami-tama-no-kami. See also *Ō-ichi-hime.* [Durdin-Robertson 1976; Philippi 1968]

Kamui-fuchi
Japan, *Ainu*
Household Affairs; Fire; Family and Tribes; Ceremonies; Mother and Guardian

"Supreme Ancestress." Hearth deity. Prayers to other deities must be addressed first to Kamui-fuchi. She protects her followers, especially pregnant women, from evil spirits, but will punish those who do wrong.

Kamui-fuchi watches over the hearth in each Ainu home. The hearth is where the meals are prepared and is used for warmth, but it is also the entrance to the world of the dead. Kamui-fuchi rests at night when the hearth fire is banked with ashes. The fire is never extinguished, so this is her only chance to sleep.

Alternate forms: Kamui-fuji, Kamuy-fuchi. [Abingdon 1981; Leach 1992; Meltzer 1981]

Kamui-fuji   See *Kamui-fuchi.*

Kamui-huchi
"God Grandmother." See also *Apemeru-ko-yan-mat Unameru-ko-yan-mat.*

Kamui-matne-po
Japan, *Ainu*
Water

"Divine Daughters." Water deities who are daughters of the goddess of the headwaters. [Batchelor ca. 1927; Leach 1992]

Kamui-menoko
Japan, *Ainu*
Hunting and Wild Animals

"She-bear" or "Goddess." [Philippi 1982]

Kamuy-fuchi See *Kamui-fuchi.*

Kamu-ya-tate-hime-no-mikoto
Japan
Unknown
   "Divine-eight-shields-princess Goddess" or "Divine house-erection-princess Goddess." Consort of O-kuni-hushi-no-kami, mother of Koto-shiro-hushi-no-kami. [Durdin-Robertson 1976; Philippi 1968]

Kana-yama-bime-no-kami
Japan
Metals and Minerals; Magic
   "Metal-mountain-princess Deity." Goddess born from the vomit of her mother *Izanami-no-kami,* along with her male counterpart Kana-yama-biko-no-kami. Alternate form: Kanayama-hime. [Durdin-Robertson 1976; Philippi 1968]

Kana-yama-hiko
Japan
Metals and Minerals
   Deity of metals. Also the name of a male deity. [Herbert 1967; Leach 1992]

Kanayama-hime See *Kana-yama-bime-no-kami.*

Kanro-o See *Amitabha.*

Kao Lan-ying See *Gao Lanying.*

Kao Mei See *Nüwa.*

Kararat
Japan, *Ainu*
Wild Birds; Ceremonies
   Carrion crow goddess.
   When Kararat hears the gods are eating and drinking, she begins her dance of "glittering treasures," dropping acorns and chestnuts. The gods reward her by including her in the festivities. [Leach 1992; Philippi 1982]

Karitei-mo See *Kichi-jō-ten*

Karu-no-ō-iratsume
Japan
Arts; Beauty
   "Great Lady of Karu." Muse of poetry. Sister/lover of Prince Kinashi Karu. She is identified with or may be the same as *So-tohoshi-no-iratsume* who is said to be so lovely that her beauty radiates through her clothing. Karu-no-ō-iratsume and *So-tohoshi-no-iratsume* are both also known as *Oto-hime.* See also *Oto.* [Durdin-Robertson 1976]

Kasenko
Japan
Physical Prowess
   Goddess. Kasenko eats mother-of-pearl which allows her to move as swiftly as a bird. Equivalent of Chinese *He Xiangu.* [Jobes 1962]

Kaya-no-hime-no-kami
Japan
Earth and Nature
   "Grassy-plains-princess Deity." Daughter of *Izanami-no-kami* and Izanagi, one of the four daughters of the *Deities of the Third Earthly Generation* and possibly the wife of Oyamatsumi-no-kami. Mother of *Kuni-no-kura-do-no-kamie, Kuni-no-sa-giri-no-kami, Kuni-no-sa-zuchi-no-*

kami, and *Ō-to-matohi-me-no-kami.* She presides over all herbaceous plants. Alternate form: No-zuchi-no-kami. [Bonnerjea 1927; Durdin-Robertson 1976; Leach 1992; Ono et al. 1985; Philippi 1968]

Kayanohime
Japan
Earth and Nature
   "Mistress of Grass" or "Spirit of Grass." [Kato 1971]

Kele-yin ükin tegri
Mongolia
Education and Knowledge
   Goddess of the intellect including speech and knowledge. Equivalent to *Sarasvati,* Indian Subcontinent. [Getty 1962; Leach 1992; Percheron 1953]

Keng San Gu
China
Household Affairs
   Three ladies of the latrine. See also *Keng San Guniang.* Alternate forms: K'eng San-ku, Tzu-ku-Shën, Zigu Shen. [Leach 1992; Werner 1961]

Keng San Guniang
China
Household Affairs
   Three goddesses of the latrine. They are *Bixiao, Qiongxiao,* and *Yunxiao.* A small round tub, colored red, is usually used in a pit for a toilet. They are frequently given as wedding presents and are used to receive a baby during delivery. The tub is also called the "Golden bushel of troubled origins." See also *Guodeng* and *Maozi Shenju.* Alternate forms: Keng San Gu, K'eng San Hu-niang. [Werner 1961]

K'eng San Hu-niang See *Keng San Guniang.*

K'eng San-ku See *Keng San Gu.*

Kenru-katkimat
Japan, *Ainu*
Household Affairs
   Household deity. [Leach 1992; Munro 1963]

Kerep-nove
Japan, *Ainu*
Hunting and Wild Animals
   "Scratch and Stagger." Her husband is Kerep-Turuse, "Scrape and Infect." They are deities of poisons used for hunting. [Batchelor ca. 1927; Leach 1992]

Kesou Niangniang
China
Health and Healing
   Goddess of healing. She cures coughs. [Chavannes 1910; Leach 1992]

Kiang Yuan See *Jiang Yuan.*

Kichi-jō-ten
Japan
Luck; Beauty
   Goddess of good fortune and beauty. She is the equivalent of *Lakshimi* or *Sri,* Indian Subcontinent. Alternate forms: Karitei-mo, Kishijo-ten, and Kisshō-ten. [Durdin-Robertson 1976; Leach 1992]

Kisagai-hime
Japan
Fishing and Water Animals; Sky and Heavens; Immortality

"The Ark-shell Princess." A shell-fish goddess who lives in the heavens and has the power to revive the dead.

Kisagai-hime and Umugi-hime restored O-kuni-hushi-no-kami to life after he was fatally injured by some mischievous deities. Kisagai-hime covered him with pulverized shells and Umugi-hime brought water to rub on him. He changed into a young man and walked away. [Durdin-Robertson 1976; Philippi 1968]

Kishijo-ten See *Kichi-jō-ten.*

Kishijoten
Japan
Mother and Guardian
   Protector of children. Said to be Kishimojin's daughter. A goddess who came from India, by way of China, to Japan. Originally a mother of demons, she became a more peaceful deity through the influence of Buddha. Newborn infants are brought to ceremonies in her honor, to seek her lifetime protection from danger. Equivalent of **Hariti** and **Churalin,** Indian Subcontinent, and **Lilith,** Near East. [Cotterell 1979; Durdin-Robertson 1976; Leach 1992; Lurker 1984; Monaghan 1981]

Kishimojin See *Helidi, Lamasthu,* Near East.

Kisshō-ten See *Kichi-jō-ten.*

Kissiang
China
Water
   River goddess. [Leach 1992]

Kitchen Range Goddess
Japan
Household Affairs
   Shinto household deity. Food-giving and food-transforming deities are usually considered feminine. [Durdin-Robertson 1976]

Kiyo-hime
Japan
Evil; Justice; Reptiles; Magic
   An Oni or demon. Equivalent of **Kundalini,** Indian Subcontinent.

The young widow, Kiyo-hime, was attracted to a man named Anchin who stopped near her home while on a pilgrimage. Anchin told her he would return, but he did not keep his promise. Kiyo-hime followed him to a temple that was on the other side of the river. Turning herself into a snake, she crossed the river. Finding Anchin hiding inside the temple bell, she coiled around it and the heat of her anger killed him.

   See also *Hi-naga-hime.* Alternate form: Kyohime. [Durdin-Robertson 1976; Jobes 1962]

Ko Ku See *Ge Gu.*

Kokuzo
Japan
Primordial Being
   Name for the primordial being. See also *Akasagarabha,* Indian Subcontinent. [Leach 1992]

Kongde
China
Goodness; Justice
   Benevolent goddess of rewards. Alternate form: Kung-te. [Leach 1992; Puini 1880]

Konohana-chiru-hime
Japan
Earth and Nature
   "Blossoms-of-the-trees-falling Princess." Daughter of O-yama-tsu-mi-no-kami, consort of Ya-shima-jinumi-no-kami, and mother of Pupa-no-modi-kunusunu-no-kami. [Durdin-Robertson 1976; Philippi 1968]

Konohana-no-sakuya-bime See *Konohana-sakuya-hime.*

Konohana-sakuya-hime
Japan
Earth and Nature; Unhappiness; Fire; Courage; Ceremonies
   "Blossoms-of-the-trees-blooming Princess." Daughter of Opo-yama-tu-mi-no-kami, a mountain deity, wife of Ninigi, mother of Po-deri-no-mikoto (Fire-Shine), Po-suseri-no-mikoto (Fire-Full), and Po-wori-no-mikoto (Fire-Fade).

After Konohana-sakuya-hime married Ninigi, he began to ridicule her because she was pregnant sooner than he expected. This made her sad, and she hid herself away. She set fire to her hiding place and when the flames became bright, her first son was born; her next son was born during the height of the fire; and her third son was born as she escaped the fire. Neither Konohana-sakuya-hime nor her sons were harmed by the fire and her husband apologized and said she possessed a wonderful and extraordinary dignity.

   Konohana-sakuya-hime probably is responsible for a festival involving sake called Nihi-nahe. It is celebrated November 23 and includes an offering to the gods of the newly harvested rice. See also **Banana-Maiden,** Southeast Asia. Equivalent to **Sita,** Indian Subcontinent. See also **Kaguya-hime-no-mikoto** and **Sengen-sama.** Alternate forms: Asa-ma, Kamu-ata-tsu-hime, Kami-ata-kashi-tsu-hime, Konohana-no-sakuya-bime, Konshana-sakuya-hime, Sakuya-bime, Sengen-sama. [Durdin-Robertson 1976; Leach 1992; Monaghan 1981]

Konshana-sakuya-hime See *Konohana-no-sakuya-hime.*

Koti-sri See *Jun-tei Kwan-non.*

Koyasu Kwan-non
Japan
Mother and Guardian
   Buddhist goddess who makes childbirth easy and protects children. See also **Hariti,** Indian Subcontinent. [Getty 1962; Hori 1968; Leach 1992]

Kuan Yin See *Guanyin.*

Ku-doku-niyo
Japan
Goodness
   Deity of good works. [Leach 1992; Puini 1880]

Kuei-ling Sheng-mu See *Guiling Shenamu.*

Kuguri-gami
Japan
Mother and Guardian; Water
   Guardian of the professional diving women. [Herbert 1967; Leach 1992]

Kujaku-myō-ō
Japan
Wild Birds; Mother and Guardian; Weather
   "Great Peacock Goddess." Buddhist protector. She prevents harm and brings rain during droughts. Equivalent to **Mahamayuri,** Indian Subcontinent. [Eliseev 1963; Guirand 1968; Leach 1992]

Kukuri-hime-no-kami
Japan
Order
Mediation Deity. She negotiates between the deities.
 *Kukuri-hime-no-kami was the mediator during the discussion between Izanami-no-kami and Izanagi at Even Pass.* [Durdin-Robertson 1976]

Kun
China
Earth and Nature
Earth goddess. The feminine spirit, *yin*. [Durdin-Robertson 1976]

Kun-syo-ming-wang
China
Wild Birds; Mother and Guardian
Great Peacock Goddess. She protects humans from harm. See also *Mahamayuri*, Indian Subcontinent. [Getty 1962; Leach 1992]

Kung-te See *Kongde*.

Kuni-no-kuhiza-mochi-no-kami
Japan
Water
"Earthly-dipper-holder Deity." Goddess of watering. Daughter of Haya-aki-tsu-hiko and *Haya-aki-tsu-hime-no-kami*. Her counterpart is Ame-no-kuhiza-mochi-no-kami. See also *Deities of the Third Earthly Generation*. [Leach 1992; Philippi 1968]

Kuni-no-mi-hashira
Japan
Earth and Nature
"Sacred Pillar of the Land" or "Sacred Deity of the Land." [Jobes 1962]

Kuni-no-mi-kumari-no-kami
Japan
Water
"Earthly-water-partings Deity." Probably a goddess of irrigation. Daughter of Haya-aki-tsu-hiko and Haya-aki-tsu-hime. She is one of the *Deities of the Third Earthly Generation*. Her counterpart is Ame-no-mi-kumaui-no-kami. [Durdin-Robertson 1976; Leach 1992; Philippi 1968]

Kuni-no-kura-do-no-kami
Japan
Unknown
"Earthly-dark-door Deity." Daughter of Ō-yama-tsu-mi-no-kami and *Kaya-no-hime-no-kami*. One of the *Deities of the Third Earthly Generation*. Her counterpart is Ame-no-kura-do-no-kami. [Durdin-Robertson 1976; Philippi 1968]

Kuni-no-sa-giri-no-kami
Japan
Weather
"Earthly Mist Deity." Daughter of Ō-yama-tsu-mi-no-kami and *Kaya-no-hime-no-kami*. One of the *Deities of the Third Earthly Generation*. Her counterpart is Ame-no-sagiri-no-kami. [Durdin-Robertson 1976; Philippi 1968]

Kuni-no-sa-zuchi-no-kami
Japan
Unknown
One of the *Deities of the Third Earthly Generation*. Her parents are Ō-yama-tsu-mi-no-kami and Kaya-no-hime-no-kami. Her counterpart is Ame-no-sa-zuchi-no-kami. [Durdin-Robertson 1976; Philippi 1968]

Kuo-teng See *Guodeng*.

Kura-mitsu-ha-no-kami
Japan
Magic
"Valley-water-greens Deity." Born from the blood of the fire god when Izanagi killed him. One of the deities of the *Second Earthly Generation* who may be genderless. See also *Mitsu-ha-no-me-no-kami*. [Durdin-Robertson 1976; Philippi 1968]

Kushi-nada-hime
Japan
Agriculture; Reptiles
"Wondrous Inada Princess." Rice goddess. Daughter of A-shi-na-zuchi and *Te-na-zuchi-no-kami*. Mother of a number of generations of deities with Susa-no-o.
 Kushi-nada-hime was threatened by a great serpent. Susa-no-o helped her to escape and built a grand palace where they lived together.
Alternate form: Inagami-hime. [Durdin-Robertson 1976; Ienaga et al. 1967; Jobes 1962; Leach 1992; Philippi 1968]

Kuzo-no-ha
Japan
Hunting and Wild Animals
A fox. She married a human warrior. [Jobes 1962]

Kwannon
Japan
Goodness; Water; Fishing and Water Animals
Buddhist deity of compassion. Japanese form of Chinese *Quanyin*. She has a temple in the Asakusa district of Edo (Tokyo). Associated with the sea, she is portrayed riding a dolphin or fish. In Japan, the masculine form of this deity is more prominent. See also *Jun-tei Kwan-non* and *Kwanseieun*. Alternate form: Kwannung. [Cottrell 1979; ; Getty 1962; Leach 1992; Monaghan 1981; Senior 1985; Stone 1979]

Kwannung See *Kwannon*.

Kwanseieun
Korea
Goodness
Goddess of mercy. See also *Kwannon*. [Clark 1932; Leach 1992]

Kwanyin See *Guanyin*.

Kyohime See *Kiyo-hime*.

Lan Caihe
China
Earth and Nature; Arts
Daoist protector of horticulture. She is the "Red Footed Genius," a street musician who was said to appear dressed in women's clothes, but to have the voice of a man. Also patron of florists. Alternate form: Lan Ts ai-ho. [Eliot 1976; Leach 1992; Monaghan 1981]

Lan Ts ai-ho See *Lan Caihe*.

Lei-tsu See *Lei-zi*.

Lei-zi
China
Insects; Household Affairs; Weather
Deity who originated silk-worm breeding. Wife of the Yellow Emperor. She is worshiped by weavers and is also a goddess

of thunder. See also *Liu Zu*. Alternate form: Lei-tsu. [Leach 1992; Wu Che-lin 1942]

Lengdin
China, *Ahom*
Earth and Nature
　Earth goddess. [Gurdon 1925; Leach 1992]

Li
China
Fire; Time
　Goddess of fire. Fire is thought to have no form but clings to what is burning, thus being bright. She is associated with summer. [Durdin-Robertson 1976]

Lincui Hu
Taiwan
Health and Healing; Mother and Guardian
　Healing deity who protects children. Alternate form: Lin-cui-hu-zin. [Diamond 1969; Leach 1992]

Lin-cui-hu-zin See *Lincui Hu*.

Liu Tsu See *Liu Zu*.

Liu Zu
China
Household Affairs
　Goddess of silk-making. See also *Lei-zi*. Alternate form: Liu Tsu. [Durdin-Robertson 1976]

Lo Shen
China
Water
　Lo River goddess. [Ferguson 1937; Leach 1992]

Longji Kongju
China
Stars and Planets
　Stellar deity, the star Hongluan (Hung-luan). Alternate forms: Lung-chi Kung-chu, Longzhi Kongju.

Longzhi Kongju See *Longji Kongju*.

Longzhi Kongju See *Longji Kongju*.

Loy Yi Lung See *Yi Long*.

Lung-chi Kung-chu See *Longji Kongju*.

Ma Gu
China
Immortality; Magic; Agriculture; Goodness; Ceremonies; Heaven and Hell; Health and Healing
　Name of three women who became Immortals. The first one lived during the Han dynasty. An image of her is given to married couples on their silver and golden wedding anniversaries. She was a sorcerer who used her magic to reclaim land from the sea for mulberry orchards. The second Ma Gu lived during the Hou-chao dynasty. This Ma Gu became a hermit and then ascended to heaven after her cruel father became angry with her. She was a forgiving person and restored her father's vision after he lost it weeping for her, but then she returned once more to heaven. The third Ma Gu lived during the Sung dynasty. Alternate form: Ma Ku. [Werner 1961]

Ma Ku See *Ma Gu*.

Ma Ming Shêng Mu See *Maming Shengmu*.

Ma Niangniang See *Deo Ma Niangniang*.

Ma Shi
China
Stars and Planets
　Stellar deity, the star Saozhou (Sao-chou). Alternate form: Ma Shih. [Leach 1992; Werner 1961]

Ma Shih See *Ma Shi*.

Ma Tsu See *Ma Zu*.

Ma Tsu P'o See *Ma Zupo*.

Ma Zu
China
Mother and Guardian; Fishing and Water Animals
　Protector of sailors. Alternate form: Ma Tsu. [Leach 1992; MacLagen 1925]

Ma Zupo
China
Weather; Mother and Guardian; Fishing and Water Animals
　Southern Sea goddess who controls the weather and protects sailors. Alternate form: Ma Tsu P'o [De Groot 1925; Leach 1992; Williams 1976]

Ma-cha Shên See *Mazha Shen*.

Maing Jini
China
Mother and Guardian; Small Size
　Childbirth goddess who is only three inches tall. She protects the womb. Alternate form: Mang Ching'i. [Leach 1992; Werner 1961]

Mamaldi
China, *Amur*
Earth and Nature
　Creator of earth.
 Mamaldi's husband became jealous when she created Asia, so he killed her. [Baumgartner 1984]

Maming Shengmu
China
Insects
　Silkworm goddess. Alternate form: Ma Ming Shêng Mu. [Day 1940; Leach 1992]

Mang Ching'i See *Maing Jini*.

Manzan Gormo
Mongolia
Mother and Guardian; Stars and Planets
　Mother goddess. Her abundant milk overflowed and formed the Milky Way. [Jobes 1962]

Mao Tzu Shên Chüu See *Maozi Shenju*.

Maozi Shenju
China
Household Affairs; Fate
　Latrine goddess. She predicts the future. See also *Bixiao, Guodeng,* and *Keng San Guniang*. [Day 1940; Leach 1992]

Marishi-ten
Japan
Sun and Day; War

Buddhist goddess of light. She is the embodiment of the first ray of light that appears before sunrise and invisibly precedes the sun throughout the day. Humans cannot possess her, but anyone who knows her name can gain her powers. She is the goddess *Marichi*, Indian Subcontinent, who was brought to Japan. She became the protector of the warrior class, who placed an image of her on their helmets. She is portrayed sitting or standing on charging boars, holding weapons in each of her two, six, or eight arms. [Durdin-Robertson 1976]

Marōdo
Japan
Time
Shinto goddess of the eleventh day. She guards the imperial court. [Kato 1971]

Matnau
Japan, *Ainu*
Directions; Weather; Disorder
North Wind goddess. When she dances on top of the mountains, there are storms at sea.

> Okikurmi and Samai-un-kur were caught in a storm in their boat. Samai-un-kur was killed and Okikurmi, blaming Matnau, killed her.

The Gilyak people of Sakhalin also have a wind goddess. When she is at home working, the weather is calm. When she goes outside to dance, the wind begins to blow. If she dances too long, strong winds begin to blow. [Leach 1992; Philippi 1982]

Matou Niang
China
Demi-animals; Domesticated Animals; Insects
"Horse-headed Dame." She is part human and part horse. Goddess of silkworms. [Leach 1992; Werner 1961]

Matsu   See *Mazu.*

Mazha Shen
China
Insects; Agriculture
Goddess of Locusts. Wife of Chiang Tai Kong (T'ai-King). Worshiped in the north, where she is asked not to bring her plague to the fields. There is a proverb that says: "O Locust Goddess, Locust Goddess! eat all our neighbor's crops, but don't touch ours!" Alternate form: Ma-cha Shên. [Leach 1992; Werner 1961]

Mazu
China
Water; Heaven and Hell
Sea deity worshiped on the southeast coast of China. Also the name of the goddess of heaven in Taiwan. Alternate forms: Matsu, Mhatzuu. [Jordan 1972; Leach 1992; Lurker 1984]

Meng Chiang Nü   See *Meng Jiangnii.*

Meng Jiangnü
China
Family and Tribes; Order; Magic; Agriculture
"Pumpkin Girl."

> The Meng and the Jiangnü families lived on opposite sides of a wall. They both planted pumpkins and the vines climbed the wall and met on the top. A wonderful pumpkin formed. Unable to decide which family the pumpkin belonged to, they split it in half. When they did this, they found a beautiful little girl inside. She was named Meng Jiangnü for both the families and they raised her together.

Alternate form: Meng Chiang Nü. [Durdin-Robertson 1976]

Meng Po Niangniang
China
Heaven and Hell; Justice; Immortality
"Lady Meng." She waits at the exit door of hell where she gives the souls of those about to be reincarnated the broth of oblivion. The drink wipes out the soul's memory of everything except pain. Alternate form: Peng Po. [Carlyon 1982; Leach 1992; Monaghan 1981; Werner 1961]

Menluzipu
China
Mother and Guardian; Magic
Protector from demons who is invoked by sorcerers. Alternate form: Mun-lu-dzi-pu. [Leach 1992; Rock 1959]

Mhatzuu   See *Mazu.*

Mi Fei
China
War
Lo river goddess. Alternate forms: Queen Jen, Queen Chên. [Leach 1992; Werner 1961]

Mi-bou-do
China
Earth and Nature
Mother earth. [Frazer 1926; Leach 1992]

Miao Qing
China
Unknown
Older sister of *Guanyin.* Alternate form: Miao Yu. [Werner 1961]

Miao Shan
China
Family and Tribes; Selflessness; Heaven and Hell; Immortality; Magic
Alternate form of *Guanyin.*

> Miao Shan was the daughter of King Miao Tohoang. Having only daughters, the king found them suitable husbands so that they might produce an heir to the throne. Miao-shan refused to marry, preferring to dedicate herself to becoming a Buddha. Her father tried persuasion, and then cruelty, to change her mind. When she still refused, he ordered her decapitation. Her body was carried off by a deity who appeared in the form of a tiger. She visited hell, where she set free some of the damned. On her return, Buddha gave her a divine peach that would provide her with food and drink and give her eternal life. After nine years she attained the rank of Buddha. Once, for saving the life of a son of the Dragon King, Miao Shan was given a pearl that lit up the dark, allowing her to read sacred books at night. She became the "Saviour of Men" and refused to enter paradise until all humans could also enter.

See also *Miao Yin.* [Getty 1962; Werner 1961]

Miao Yin
China
Unknown
Second sister of *Guanyin.* See also *Miao Shan.* [Werner 1961]

Miao Yin Fomu
China
Arts
Goddess of music and poetry. Equivalent of *Sarasvati,* Indian Subcontinent. See also *Dabiancai Tiannii.* [Getty 1962; Leach 1992]

Miao Yu   See *Miao Qing.*

Midwives, Goddess of
China

Mother and Guardian; Ceremonies
    Deities who aid childbirth. Prayers and offerings are
made to them both before and after a delivery. Red eggs are
used in their worship and the eggs are sometimes stolen by
infertile women to aid them in becoming pregnant. [Werner
1961]

Midzuha-no-me-no-kami   See *Mitsu-ha-no-me-no-kami.*

Mifuto-hime
Japan

Fate; War
    Goddess of Muraya. One of three deities who aided the
Emperor Temmu in his campaigns.
    *Using a priest as her oracle, Mifuto-hime predicted that
    an army would attack the Emperor, coming down the
    middle road to her shrine. Several days later soldiers
appeared on the road, but the Emperor was prepared and defeated
the invading army.* [Durdin-Robertson 1976]

Mihotsu-hime
Japan

Unknown
    "Heavenly Deity." Daughter/wife of Omo-mono-nushi.
[Durdin-Robertson 1976]

Miketsu-kami
Japan

Mother and Guardian
    Shinto goddess of food. [Herbert 1967; Kato 1971; Leach
1992]

Miko
Japan

Ceremonies
    Shinto priest who is said to be the bride of the gods. [Jobes
1962]

Mikura-tana-no-kami
Japan

Agriculture
    "Deity of the August Storehouse Shelf." The name of the
necklace bestowed on *Ama-terasu-ō-mikami* by her father
Izanagi and an aspect of the goddess herself. The necklace, a
symbol of delegated power and provider of fertility, was so
precious it was kept by *Ama-terasu-ō-mikami* on a shelf in
her storehouse. [Jobes 1962]

Milun
China

Earth and Nature; Directions
    Mother of the gods of mountains and the directions.
[Werner 1961]

Ming, Lady
China

Heaven and Hell; Mother and Guardian
    Underworld deity. She takes away the memory of newborns
during rebirth. [Jobes 1962]

Mintuchi-kamui
Japan, *Ainu*

Water; Health and Healing
    Water nymph. She is invoked to exorcize Pauchi Kamui,
god of disease. [Leach 1992; Munro 1963]

Mirume
Japan

Justice; Education and Knowledge
    "Knower of All Secrets." Buddhist double-faced deity
whose eyes see all secret sins. [Jobes 1962]

Mishima-no-mizo-kui-hime
Japan

Water
    Water deity who presides over "water-channel-piles." See
also *Mizo-kuhi-hime.* Alternate forms: Tama-kushi-hime,
Seya-tatara-hime. [Ienaga et al. 1967; Philippi 1968]

Mitsu-ha-no-me-no-kami
Japan

Water; Magic
    "Water-greens-woman Deity." Water goddess born from
the urine of *Izanami-no-kami* after she bore the fire god. See
also *Kura-mitsu-ha-no-kami.* Alternate forms: Midzuha-no-
me-no-kami, Mizuha-no-me.

Miyazu-hime
Japan

Family and Tribes; Mother and Guardian
    Japanese princess and ancestor of the Kuni-no-miyatuko of
Owari (Wopari). Consort of Yamato-takem-no-mikoto.
    *When Miyazu-hime met her husband to be, Yamato-
    takem-no-mikoto, he noticed menstrual blood on the
    hem of her cloak. He sang a song to her, referring to the
blood as the moon having risen.*
    It has been suggested that menstrual blood might be a sign
of ritual holiness or that it may be identified with the holy fire
kindled in religious worship. [Durdin-Robertson 1976;
Kramer 1961b]

Mizo-kuhi-hime
Japan

Water
    "Water-pole Princess." She had intercourse with an
eight-fathom bear/sea monster, which is one form of the
god Koto-shiro-hushi-no-kami. She is similar to *Seya-tatara-
hime* and is associated with the "water-channel-pile." See
also *Mishima-no-mizo-kui-hime.* Alternate form: Mizohuhi
hime, Tama-kushi-hime. [Durdin-Robertson 1976; Ienaga
et al. 1967]

Mizohuhi hime   See *Mizo-kuhi-hime.*

Mizu-tsu-hime
Japan

Water
    Water deity. [Herbert 1967; Leach 1992]

Mizuha-no-me   See *Mitsu-ha-no-me-no-kami.*

Mizunoe   See *Oto.*

Mo   See *Nok.*

Mo Bo
China

Mother and Guardian
    "Maternal Goodness." Mother of Meng.
    *Mo Bo was widowed soon after the birth of her son. She
    did such an excellent job of raising him that outstanding
    mothers are complimented by being referred to as
"Mother of Meng."* [Durdin-Robertson 1976]

Mo Ye
China
Metals and Minerals; Commerce and Travel; Magic; Mother and Guardian; Justice
Maker of swords.

 Mo Ye, with her husband Kan Chiang, was commissioned by the king of Wu to make some swords. Mo Ye and Kan Chiang gathered suitable ore from the mountains and then began to make the swords. To make the iron malleable, Mo Ye threw clippings from her hair and nails into the furnace (or she went into the furnace herself). Kan Chiang gave the king only one sword and kept one for himself. This made the king angry and he killed Kan Chiang. Mo Ye became pregnant by walking along a river bank and being encircled by a rainbow. Her son Fohe (Fo-Hi) was born twelve years later and when he grew up, he revenged the death of Kan Chiang.

Alternate forms: Moye, Mo Yeh. [Durdin-Robertson 1976; Jobes 1962; Redfield 1931]

Mo Yeh   See Mo Ye.

Moire-mat
Japan, *Ainu*
Insects; Household Affairs
Spider goddess. Household deity who is invoked during house-warming ceremonies. [Leach 1992; Munro 1963]

Moshir-huchi
Japan, *Ainu*
Poverty; Water
"Earth Crone." She seems to be a famine deity who lives on the ocean floor.

 Moshir huchi is attacked by Aeoina-kamui. She uses her tangled hair to catch his spear and sword, but cannot keep him from destroying her wickerwork fish trap. The fish are freed and the humans are saved from famine.

See also *Sedna*, North America. [Philippi 1982]

Mother of Ten Thousand Things
China
Creator of Life
"The Void" or "The Way." Daoist feminine principle who was the mother of the world. [Durdin-Robertson 1976]

Mt. Unebi Goddess
Japan
Earth and Nature
Spirit of the Yamato Mountains.

Unebi is loved by the spirits of Mount Kagu and Miminashi who compete for her attention. [Durdin-Robertson 1976]

Mou-t'u   See Moutu.

Moutu   See Hou Tu Nainai. Alternate form: Mou-t'u.

Moye   See Mo Ye.

Mu   See Nok.

Mu Je   See Mu Re.

Mu Re
China
Sky and Heavens; Family and Tribes
Sky goddess. She came to the earth to marry the first man, have children, and then return to her heavenly home.
Alternate form: Mu Je. [Graham 1958; Leach 1992]

Mun-lu-dzi-pu   See Menluzipu.

Munakata Goddesses
Japan
Unknown
"Province-ruler Possessors." Three goddesses born from the breath of *Ama-terasu-ō-mi-kami* who made them to test the sincerity of Susa-no-wo's motives. They descended from heaven to live on the Central Land Reed-plain. They are *Ichiki-shima-hime-no-mikoto*, *Takiri-bime-no-mikoto*, and *Takitsu-hime-no-mikoto*. [Durdin-Robertson 1976]

Muryoju   See Amitabha.

Muryoka   See Amitabha.

Mysterious Female
China
Creator of Life
"Root of Heaven and Earth." From her womb was born the universe. [Durdin-Robertson 1976]

Na-naki-me   See Nakime.

Nai Mu
China
Mother and Guardian
Goddess of wet nurses who protects children. [Day 1940; Leach 1992]

Nai-orun-kamui
Japan, *Ainu*
Water
Fresh water deity who presides over the springs and pools of the valleys. [Leach 1992; Munro 1963]

Nakime
Japan
Unhappiness; Wild Birds
"Weeping Woman."

Ame-no-waka-hiko was sent to subdue and pacify the earth deities. When he failed to return, the deities sent the pheasant, Nakime, to inquire why. Angered by her inquiry, Ame-no-waka-hiko shot an arrow at her. The arrow missed its mark and sailed to the heavens, where it was caught and returned to his breast, killing him. Nakime wept at his funeral.

Alternate forms: Nanaki, Na-naki-me. [Durdin-Robertson 1976; Ienaga et al. 1967; Leach 1992; Philippi 1968]

Naki-saha-me-no-kami   See Naki-sawa-me-no-kami.

Naki-saha-no-me-no-mikoto   See Naki-sawa-me-no-kami.

Naki-sawa-me-no-kami
Japan
Unhappiness; Magic
"Weeping-marsh-woman Deity." Daughter of Isanagi-no-kami, formed from his tears over the death of *Izanami-no-kami*. She lives at the base of the trees in the foothills of Mt. Kagu. Alternate forms: Naki-saha-me-no-kami, Naki-saha-no-me-no-mikoto, Naki-sawame-no-mikoto. [Durdin-Robertson 1976; Ienaga et al. 1967; Jobes 1962; Leach 1992; Philippi 1968]

Naki-sawame-no-mikoto   See Naki-sawa-me-no-kami.

Nanaki   See Nakime.

Napuri-kor-kamui-kor-matnepo
Japan, *Ainu*
Evil; Hunting and Wild Animals; Immortality; Destroyer of
Life
    Malevolent Bear Maiden.
        *Napuri-kor-kamui-kor-matnepo had an evil disposition.
        Wanting to kill a human, she slipped away from her
        benevolent family and killed a woman. The Fire Goddess*
demanded that Napuri-kor-kamui-kor-matnepo restore the woman's
life, which she did. Repenting her evil deed she said to the other
deities, "I bid you, o she-bears, do not, on any account, do such
deeds as these!" [Philippi 1982]

Naru-kami
Japan
Weather; Earth and Nature; Arts
    Thunder goddess. She protects trees and artisans. Alternate
form: Kami-naru. [Monaghan 1981]

Natsu-no-me-no-kami   See *Natsu-taka-tsu-hi-no-kami.*

Natsu-taka-tsu-hi-no-kami
Japan
Agriculture
    "Summer-high-sun Deity." In popular belief, she is a
guardian goddess of grain. Daughter of Hayama-to-no-kami
and *O-get-su-hime-no-kami.* See also *Izumo Pantheon.*
Alternate forms: Natsutakatsuhi-no-Kami, Natsu-no-me-
no-kami. [Durdin-Robertson 1976; Leach 1992; Philippi 1968]

Nda-la-a-ssaw-mi
China, *Na-khi*
Weather
    Wind deity. [Leach 1992; Rock 1947]

Niangniang
China
Earth and Nature; Weather; Mother and Guardian
    Tai Shan mountain goddess. Also weather deity who
protects against hail. See also *Bixia Yuanjin.* [Jobes 1962;
Leach 1992]

Niangniang Songzi
China, *Na-khi*
Mother and Guardian
    Goddess who brings children. She is worshiped in the
Yunnan Province. Alternate forms: Bixia Yunajun, Niang-
niang Sung-tzu. [Leach 1992; Werner 1961]

Niang-niang Sung-tzu   See *Niangniang Songzi.*

Nibu-tsu-hime
Japan
Unknown
    Deity of Mt. Koya. Goddess of the hunters in northeast
Honshu. [Hori 1968; Leach 1992]

Ningyo, The
Japan
Fishing and Water Animals; Demi-animals; Immortality
    Mermaids. Ethereal in nature, they sometimes manifest so
they can be seen by humans. They are said to cry pearl tears
and any woman, by eating their flesh, acquires eternal youth
and beauty. [Durdin-Robertson 1976; Jobes 1962; Monaghan
1981]

Nish-kan-ru-mat
Japan, *Ainu*
Stars and Planets
    Stellar deity. [Leach 1992; Munro 1963]

Nitat-unarabe
Japan, *Ainu*
Evil; Water
    Malevolent deity of marshy areas who gave birth to many
demons. [Batchelor 1925; Leach 1992]

Niu   See *Nok.*

Niu She
China
Stars and Planets; Education and Knowledge
    "Literary Woman." Goddess of the Constellation Draco.
She is also called "The Palace Governess." [Durdin-Robertson
1976]

Nochiu-e-rant-mat
Japan, *Ainu*
Stars and Planets
    Air and stellar deity. With her husband, Nochiu-e-ran-
guru, she cares for the stars. [Batchelor 1925; Leach 1992]

Nok
China
Stars and Planets
    Stellar deity, the constellation Aquarius. Alternate forms:
Mo, Mu, Niu, Woo Neu. [Durdin-Robertson 1976]

No-zuchi-no-kami   See *Kaya-no-hime-no-kami.*

Nts'ai Hwa
China
Sky and Heavens; Health and Healing
    "Girl Cloud." Sky goddess who is called on to exorcise
demons of sickness and death. [Graham 1937; Jobes 1962]

Nü
China
Family and Tribes
    Goddess of marriage. Later identified with *Zhinu.* Also an
alternate name for *Nok.* [Jobes 1962]

Nü Chün   See *He Ku.*

Nu Hsi   See *Nüwa.*

Nu Kwa   See *Nügua.*

Nümei   See *Nügua.*

Nü She
China
Destroyer of Life
    "Female Snake Charm." Disease deity. [Day 1940; Leach 1992]

Nü Kua   See *Nügua.*

Nu-chiao   See *Nüjiao.*

Nügua
China
Creator of Life; Order; Demi-animals; Reptiles; Weather;
Education and Knowledge; Family and Tribes; Agriculture;
Directions; Sky and Heavens; Water; Mother and Guardian
Creator
    "Restorer of Cosmic Equilibrium." Like Egypt, early China
had a matriarchal hierarchy and worshiped a Great Mother
Goddess. Nügua was an early Mother Goddess. She has a
human head and a dragon body, although she is, at times,
portrayed as a rainbow dragon or as a woman. It is Nügua

who civilized life, instituted marriage, tamed wild animals, and presided over irrigation.

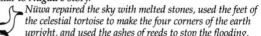 *Nügua lived on earth by herself. She was lonely so she formed a tiny creature out of yellow clay, the first human. This being gave her so much joy, she quickly made many more. They danced about her and she was no longer lonely. Then Nügua discovered that the four cardinal directions were misplaced, the sky did not cover all the earth, the waters flowed all over, and the wild animals and birds were devouring her creations, the people. Nügua took the stones of five colors to repair the sky, the feet of a tortoise to fix the directions, and the ashes of reeds to stop the waters. Then the earth was peaceful.*

Equivalent to *Atargatis, Nina,* and *Mami,* Near East. See also *Nüwa;* and *Estsanatlehi,* North America. Alternate forms: Nü Kua, Nu Kwa. [Durdin-Robertson 1976; Eliot 1976; Leach 1992; Lurker 1984; Monaghan 1981; Senior 1985; Stone 1979]

Nüjiao
China
Metals and Minerals; Magic; Mother and Guardian
"Mother Stone." Wife of Yu, mother of Chhi (Split).

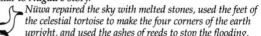 *Nüjiao took the form of a boulder. The boulder split open and a son came forth.*
Alternate form: Nu-Chiao. [Durdin-Robertson 1976]

Nümei   See *Nüwa.*

Nunakawa-hime
Japan
Family and Tribes
"Princess of Nunakawa" was wooed by Ya-chi-hoko-no-kami. Some suggest that her marriage was a diplomatic one—an attempt by Izumo leaders to gain control of Kosi by marrying its woman leader. [Durdin-Robertson 1976; Philippi 1968]

Nunurao
Taiwan, *Yami*
Creator of Life
Creator of the universe. [Del Re 1951; Leach 1992]

Nupka-ush-ma
Japan, *Ainu*
Unknown
"Chestnut-tree Grandmother." A heavenly deity who came to live on earth for awhile. [Leach 1992; Philippi 1982]

Nupki-ot-mat
Japan, *Ainu*
Water; Evil
"Female of Muddy Places." Water demon. She lives near the edge of the river with her river demon husband. They make the water muddy and erode the banks. [Batchelor ca. 1927; Leach 1992]

Nusa-kor-huchi
Japan, *Ainu*
Reptiles
Goddess of the Spirit Fence, the place where the deities gather to talk. She manifests as a snake. [Leach 1992; Philippi 1982]

Nüwa
China
Family and Tribes; Demi-animals; Reptiles; Sky and Heavens; Order
"Snail Maid." Goddess of marriage arrangers, the go-betweens. She is portrayed with a long head and two

horns or with a human head and snake's body. Her story is similar to *Nügua's* story.

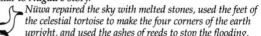 *Nüwa repaired the sky with melted stones, used the feet of the celestial tortoise to make the four corners of the earth upright, and used the ashes of reeds to stop the flooding.*

See also *Nügua.* Alternate forms: Baowa, Kao Mei, Nuwo, Nü mei, Nu Hsi, Nüxi, Gaomei. [Durdin-Robertson 1976; Werner 1961]

Nuwa   See *Nügua.*

Nüxi   See *Nüwa.*

Ō-to-ma-hime-no-mikoto   See *Ō-to-no-be-no-kami.*

O-be-hime-no-kami   "Great-hearth-princess Deity."
See *Okitsu-hime-no-mikoto.*

O-getsu-hime   See *Uke-mochi-no-kami.*

O-ge-tsu-hime-no-kami   "Great-food-princess Deity."
See *Uke-mochi-no-kami.*

Ogtarghui-in jiruken
Mongolia
Unknown
Mongolian name for *Akasagarabha,* Indian Subcontinent. [Getty 1962; Leach 1992]

Ō-hiru-me-no muchi   See *Ama-terasu-ō-mi-kami.*

Ō-hiru-no muchi   See *Ama-terasu-ō-mi-kami.*

Oho-to-no-be-no-kami   See *Ō-to-no-be-no-mikoto.*

Ohoyatsu-hime   See *Ō-yatsu hime.*

Ō-ichi-hime
Japan
Love and Sexuality; Creator of Life
"Divine Ō-ichi Princess." Goddess of sexual attraction and the fertility of plants and humans. See also *Kamu-ō-ichi-hime.* Alternate form: Oichi-hime. [Leach 1992]

Oichi-hime   See *Ō-ichi-hime.*

Oimi-no-kami   See *Waka-uka-no-me-no-mikoto.*

Okame
Japan
Luck; Ugliness; Goodness
Good luck deity. With her puffy face, Okame is unattractive, but she is known for her goodness. A mask of her face is used as a good luck charm. [Jobes 1962]

Okikurmi kot tureshi
Japan, *Ainu*
Unknown
"Younger Sister." Goddess greatly loved by the Ainu. [Leach 1992]

Oki-tsu-hime
Japan
Household Affairs
"Embers-princess Deity." Goddess of the *Izumo Pantheon.* Daughter of Ō-toshi-no-kami and *Ame-chikaru-mizu-hime.* Household deity of the kitchen range and furnace with her husband Okitsuhiko. She presides over the pots and pans. Alternate form: Okitsu-hime-no-mikoto. [Durdin-Robertson 1976; Leach 1992; Philippi 1968]

Okitsu-hime-no-mikoto   See *Oki-tsu-hima.*

Oki-tsu-shima-hime-no-mikoto
"Offshore-Island-Princess Deity." See *Takiri-bime-no-mikoto.*

Omiya-hime
Japan
Fate; Magic; Life/Death Cycle; Mother and Guardian
   "Goddess of the Jingikwan, the Department of Religion."
Sorcerer and prophet invoked for longevity, posterity,
protection from evil, and honors. [Leach 1992]

Onne-chip-kamui
Japan, *Ainu*
Commerce and Travel
   "Old Boat Goddess."
   *Onne-chip-kamui inhabited a tree that grew at the top of
   a waterfall. For many years she resisted the pleas of other
   deities that she be cut down. Finally, deciding she would
   like to travel, she allowed a boat maker to carve her into a boat and
   she set out upon the sea as a trader.* [Leach 1992; Philippi 1982]

Ō-no-de-hime
Japan
Earth and Nature
   "Great-plain-hand Princess." She is identified with the
natural phenomena and physical features of the island of
Azuki-shima. Daughter of *Izanami-no-kami* and Izanagi-no-
kami. [Durdin-Robertson 1976; Philippi 1968]

Ori-hime   See *Shokujo.*

O-ryu
Japan
Earth and Nature
   Spirit of an old willow tree. O-ryu was married to a
warrior. They were parted when the tree she inhabited was
cut down. See also *Fangge,* Northern Europe. [Jobes 1962]

Ot
Mongolia, *Mongols*
Goodness; Fire; Family and Tribes
   Benevolent fire deity and goddess of marriage. See also *Ot,*
Eastern Europe. [Baumgartner 1984; Leach 1992]

Otafuku   See *Ame-no-uzume.*

Oto
Japan
Heaven and Hell; Water; Life/Death Cycle; Magic
   "Dragon Princess." Ruler of paradise, which is in the
depths of the sea. Her palace is large and beautiful and, for
those who live there, time seems to stand still.
   *One day a young man named Urashima rescued a turtle
   who was being tormented by some children. He put the
   turtle gently back into the sea and returned home. Several
   days later, when Urashima was fishing, the turtle called to him and
   offered to take him to the Dragon Princess. Urashima climbed onto
   the turtle's back and was carried to the bottom of the sea. He was
   welcomed at the palace with food and entertainment. After a time,
   Urashima asked to return to his old home and the Princess reluctantly
   granted his request. As he was leaving she gave him a beautiful box
   and told him that she hoped he would return quickly. When he
   arrived at his village, Urashima discovered it had been three hundred
   years since he had left. Wanting to return to the Dragon Princess,
   he opened the box she had given him and he was enveloped in a mist
   that quickly aged him. Soon he was ready to die and return to his
   wonderful home under the sea.*
   See also *Karu-no-ō-iratsume; Sotohoshi-no-iratsome.*
Alternate form: Mizunoe. [Durdin-Robertson 1976]

Oto-hime   See *Karu-no-ō-iratsume* and *So-tohoshi-
no-iratsume.*

Ō-to-ma-hime-no-mikoto   See *Ō-to-no-be-no-kami.*

Ō-to-matohi-me-no-kami
Japan
Earth and Nature
   "Great-door-mislead-woman Deity." Goddess of the slopes
and gentle mountain folds. Daughter of Ō-yama-tsu-mi-no-
kami and *No-zuchi-no-kami (Kaya-no-hime-no-kami).*
Her husband is Oto-madoiko-no-kami. Alternate forms:
Oto-matoiko, Otomatoime. See also *Deities of the Third
Earthly Generation.* [Leach 1992; Philippi 1968]

Ō-to-mato-hime-no-kami
Japan
Unknown
   Princess of the *Deities of the Third Earthly Generation.*
Her counterpart is Ō-to-mano-hiko-no-kami. [Durdin-
Robertson 1976]

Oto-matoiko   See *Ō-to-matohi-me-no-kami.*

Otomatoime   See *Ō-to-matohi-me-no-kami.*

Ō-to-no-be-no-kami
Japan
Mother and Guardian; Earth and Nature
   "Great-female-genital Deity." One of the seven generations
of the Age of the Gods. Primal deity born without a progenitor.
She symbolizes the female genitalia and personifies the
incipient earth. Her counterpart is Ō-to-no-ji-no-kami.
Alternate forms: Oho-to-no-be-no-kami, Ō-to-ma-hime-
no-mikoto. [Ienaga et al. 1967; Jobes 1962; Philippi 1968]

Oto-tachibana-hime-no-mikoto
Japan
Order; Courage
   "Younger-sister-orange Princess." She often accompanied
her husband Yamato-takeru-no-mikoto on his travels.
   *Oto-tachibana-hime-no-mikoto calmed the angry sea by
   sitting on its surface. Another story says she saved her
   husband's life and her country by jumping into the sea to
   appease the sea god, thereby calming the water and averting a
   disaster.*
   Alternate form: Tachibana. [Durdin-Robertson 1976; Jobes
1962]

Ō-tsuchi-no-kami
Japan
Earth and Nature
   "Great-soil Deity." One of the *Izumo Pantheon.* Alternate
form: Tsuchi-no-mi-oya-no-kami. [Durdin-Robertson 1976]

Otygen
Mongolia, *Mongols*
Earth and Nature
   Earth mother. See also *Otygen,* Eastern Europe. [Jobes
1962; Leach 1992]

Ō-ya-tsu-hime-no-mikoto
Japan
Earth and Nature
   "Great-mansion-princess Deity." She plants trees. Daughter of
Susano-wo, older sister of *Tsuma-tsu-hime-no-mikoto.*
Alternate form: Ohoyatsu-hime. [Durdin-Robertson 1976;
Herbert 1967; Leach 1992; Philippi 1968]

Pa   See *Ba.*

Pai Chi   See *Baiji*.

Pai Mu-tan   See *Bai Mundan*.

Pan-chen   See *Banzhen*.

P'an Chin-lien   See *Pan Jinlian*.

Pan Jinlian
China
Love and Sexuality; Beauty; Justice
   Goddess of Brothels.
   *Pan Jinlian, who had been recently widowed, lived with
   her brother-in-law. A passer-by was struck by her great
   beauty and managed an introduction. They soon became
   intimate, and when her brother-in-law found them together, he
   cut off Pan Jinlian's head. Since then, she has been honored by
   prostitutes as they enter their place of business.*
   Alternate form: P'an Chin-lien, P'an Kin-lien. [Carlyon
1982; Durdin-Robertson 1976; Leach 1972; Leach 1992;
Werner 1961]

P'an Kin-lien   See *Pan Jinlian*.

Pan Niang
China
Health and Healing
   Vaccination goddess. Alternate form: P'an Niang. [Leach
1992; Werner 1961]

Pang Che
China
Heaven and Hell; Justice; Ceremonies
   One of the corpse goddesses. The others are *Pang Jiao* and
Pang Zhu. The deceased's family and friends must keep a
night watch over the dead body or these three goddesses will
inform the gods about the sins of the deceased. [Leach 1992;
Werner 1961]

P'ang Chiao   See *Pang Jiao*.

P'ang Chu   See *Pang Zhu*.

Pang Jiao
China
Heaven and Hell; Justice; Ceremonies
   One of the *Corpse Goddesses*. See also *Pang Che* and *Pang
Zhu*. Alternate form: P'ang Chiao. [Leach 1992; Werner 1961]

Pang Zhu
China
Heaven and Hell; Ceremonies; Justice
   One of the *Corpse Goddesses*. See also *Pang Che* and *Pang
Zhu*. Alternate form: P'ang Chu. [Leach 1992; Werner 1961]

Patrinia
Japan
Time; Goodness
   Goddess who symbolizes autumn and eternal devotion.
[Jobes 1962]

P'ei-t'ai Niang-niang   See *Peitai Niangniang*.

Peitai Niangniang
China
Creator of Life; Mother and Guardian
   Conception deity. She is worshiped along with the childbirth
goddess, *Cuisheng Sheng Mu*. Alternate form: P'ei-t'ai
Niang-niang. [Leach 1992; Werner 1961]

P'ei-yang   See *Peiyang*.

Peiyang
China
Mother and Guardian
   Guardian of children who provides their food. Alternate
form: P'ei-Yang. [Day 1940; Leach 1992]

Peng Po   See *Meng Po Niangniang*.

Pe-poso-koshimpuk
Japan, *Ainu*
   "Demons which pass through the water." Mermaids and
mermen. [Batchelor ca. 1927]

Perasia
China
Ceremonies; Magic; Fire
   An Asiatic deity worshiped in Hieropolis-Castabala in
eastern Cilicia. She is honored by priests who walk over fire
in their bare feet. [Monaghan 1981; Redfield 1931]

P'er Ndzi Ssaw Ma
China, *Na-khi*
Health and Healing; Education and Knowledge
   Healing goddess. She gave the people information about
healing divination, the Tso-la Books. [Leach 1992]

Pet-etok-mat
Japan, *Ainu*
Water
   "Head-water-female." Water deity. She presides over the
source of rivers and maintains their flow. [Batchelor ca. 1927;
Leach 1992]

Petorush-mat   See *Pet-ru-ush-mat*.

Pet-ru-ush-mat
Japan, *Ainu*
Education and Knowledge; Ceremonies; Fishing and Water
Animals; Hunting and Wild Animals
   "Women-dwelling-in-the-watering Place." Deities who
protect whole rivers from their source to the sea. Offerings
are made to them either at the river's edge or at the spirit
fence (outside of the individual's house) for good fishing and
protection from the rapids. Pet-ru-ush-mat taught the people
proper hunting and fishing rituals so they would not starve
to death. There seems to be confusion as to whether this is a
single goddess or group of goddesses. See also *Chiwash-
kor-kamui*. Alternate forms Petorush-mat, Wakka-ush-kamui.
[Batchelor ca. 1927; Leach 1992; Philippi 1982]

Pi hia yuan kiun   See *Bixia Yuanjin*.

Pi-hia-yü-kün   See *Bixia Yuanjin*.

Pi-hsia Yuan-chin   See *Bixia Yuanjin*.

Pi-hsia Yuan-chun   See *Bixia Yunajin*.

Pi-hsiao   See *Bixiao*.

Poetry Goddess
Japan
Arts
   Represented on a frieze of a public building. See also
Agriculture Goddess. [Durdin-Robertson 1976]

Poi-soya-un-mat
Japan, *Ainu*
Commerce and Travel; Hunting and Wild Animals
"The Woman of Poi-Soya." A woman who "exalted herself above the gods." She committed indignities by dressing like a man and hunting or sailing around as a trader. [Philippi 1982]

Qi Guzi, The
China
Earth and Nature; Mother and Guardian; Weather; Health and Healing
"The Seven Young Ladies." Mountain or earth goddesses. They are sought for protection against drought, floods and disease. Alternate form: Ch'i Ku-tzu. [Werner 1961]

Qiongxiao
China
Household Affairs
Latrine goddess. One of the *Keng San Guniang*. See also *Bixiao, Guodeng,* and *Maozi Shenju*. Alternate form: Ch'iung Hsiao. [Werner 1961]

Qixian Niangniang
China
Household Affairs
Goddess of weavers. Alternate form: Ch'i-hsien-niangniang. [Graham 1961; Leach 1992]

Quan Hou
China
Water
Fresh water goddess. Also said to be another name for *Tian Hou*. Alternate form: Chuan Hou. [Ferguson 1937; Leach 1992]

Rafu-sen
Japan
Earth and Nature; Moon and Night
"Buoyant Subtlety." Goddess of plum blossoms. She appears on moonlit nights, the perfume of the blossoms floating like a veil around her. Alternate form: Rafusne. [Jobes 1962; Monaghan 1981]

Rafusne   See *Rafu-sen*.

Randeng
China
Education and Knowledge
"Burning Lamp."
Randeng was a beggar-woman who spent her money on a lamp to light Buddha's altar. As a well-known Daoist teacher, she introduced Buddha to the teaching that leads to perfection. As her reward, she later became a Buddha. [Lurker 1984]

Ro-tara-ni-bi
Japan
Goodness; Creator of Life
Goddess of mercy. Buddhist Bodhisatva who represents the feminine principle. Consort of Avalokitesvara. Alternate form: Tara Bosatsu. [Leach 1992]

Ru-be-sei
China
Earth and Nature; Weather; Agriculture
Earth goddess. She brings rain and good crops for the people in Sichuan. [Graham 1958; Leach 1992]

Saho-yama-hime
Japan
Time
Goddess of spring. [Jobes 1962; Leach 1992]

Saki-tama-hime
Japan
Luck
"Lucky Spirit Princess." One of the deities of the *Seventeen Generations*. Daughter of Ame-no-milea-nushi-no-kami. [Durdin-Robertson 1976; Philippi 1968]

Sakuya-bime   See *Konohana-no-sakuya-bime*.

San Fu Jên   See *The San Furen*.

San Furen, The
China
Mother and Guardian
"Three Matrons." Protectors of women. Alternate form: San Fu Jên. [Day 1940; Leach 1992]

San Gufuren
China
Insects; Earth and Nature
Silkworm goddess who protects the mulberry trees. She is important to the farmers and villagers, so is invoked and appeased often. Alternate form: San Ku Fu Jen. [Day 1940; Leach 1972; Leach 1992]

San Ku   See *San Gu*.

San Ku Fu Jen   See *San Gufuren*.

Sao Ch'ing Niang   See *Saoqing Niang*.

Saoqing Niang
China
Weather; Stars and Planets; Ceremonies
"Broom Lady." Weather deity who provides good weather by sweeping away the clouds and rain. She lives on the Broom Star, Sao Chou. A human figure representation of her is cut from paper and hung near the gate of the compound to stop heavy rains or to bring rain when there is a drought. Alternate forms: Sao-ts'ing Niang, Sao Ch'ing Niang. [Leach 1972; Leach 1992; Monaghan 1981]

Sao-ts'ing Niang   See *Saoqing Niang*.

Sapta-koti-buddha-matri-cunti-devi   See *Jun-tei Kwan-non*.

Sarak-kamui
Japan, *Ainu*
Evil; Water
Malevolent river deity. She is the cause of river disasters. [Batchelor 1894; Czaplicka 1969; Leach 1992]

Sayo-hime
Japan
Metals and Minerals
"Wife Rock."
Sayo-hime was married to a man who spent a great deal of time at sea. She stood on a rock by the shore watching for him for so long that she turned into a rock. [Monaghan 1981]

Sayori-bime-no-mikoto   See *Ichiki-shima-hime-no-mikoto*.

Se-o-nyo

Korea

Magic; Commerce and Travel

"Fire-raven Woman." Wife of Yon-o-nang.

One day, Yon-o-nang went to gather seaweed. When he stood on a rock by the shore he was carried across the water to Japan, where the people made him king. When Se-o-nyo, looking for her husband, stood on the same rock, it took her to Japan where she was reunited with Yon-o-nang. Soon the sun and moon became less brilliant over their homeland. A messenger was sent to Japan to summon them home. They said they could not leave, but Se-o-nyo sent back a fine cloth she had woven for use in ceremonies in their former land. Soon after, radiance returned to the sun and moon. [Durdin-Robertson 1976]

Second Earthly Generation Deities

Japan

Earth and Nature

Deities born to *Izanami-no-kami* and Izanagi-no-kami. They inhabit the Japanese islands and represent various natural phenomena and physical features of the land. Some seem to be genderless. The female deities she birthed include *Ama-terasu-o-me-kami, Haya-aki-tsu-hime-no-kami, Iwa-tsutsu-no-me-no-mikoto, Iwasu-hime-no-kami, Izunome-no-kami, Kana-ama-bime-no-kami, Kaya-no-hime-no-kami, Mitsu-ha-no-me-kami, Naki-sawa-no-me-no-kami, Wakahirume-no-mikoto.* [Durdin-Robertson 1976]

Sei-o-bo

Japan

Directions

Goddess of the West. Equivalent to Chinese *Xi Wang Mu*. [Jobes 1962; Leach 1992]

Seng-ge Ga-mu

China

Earth and Nature

Mountain goddess worshiped in the southwest. Equivalent to *dKar-mo*. [Leach 1992; Rock 1947]

Seng-ge Karmo

China

Earth and Nature

"White Lioness." Mountain deity who takes possession of lamas at the Yongning (Yung-ning) Lamasery. [Leach 1992; Rock 1959]

Sengen-sama

Japan

Earth and Nature

Blossom goddess of Fujiyama. See also *Konohana-sakuya-hime*. [Jobes 1962; Leach 1992; Redfield 1931]

Senjo, The   See *The Senyo*.

Senyo, The

Japan

Magic; Small Size

Japanese female genii and fairies of Chinese origin. Alternate form: Senjo. [Durdin-Robertson 1976]

Seoritsu-hime

Japan

Water; Immortality

Water deity who lives in the rapids of a stream. She carries the stream to the sea and purges sins. [Jobes 1962]

Seven Sisters of Industry

China

Stars and Planets

The Pleiades. Equivalent to the *Krittika,* Indian Subcontinent and *Seven Sisters,* North America. [Durdin-Robertson 1976]

Seventeen Generations Deities

Japan

Unknown

Deities who are descendants of Sasa-no-wo, the brother of *Ama-terasu-ō-mi-kami.* They are listed in the *Kojiki.* Female deities include *Ao-numa-nu-oshi-hime, Ashi-nadaka-no-kami, Hi-narashi-bime, Hinateri-nukata-bichi-o-ikuchini-ne-no-kami, Ikutama-sakutama-hime-no-kami, Saki-tama-hime, Toho-tsu-machi-no-kami,* and *Wakahirume-no-mikoto.* [Durdin-Robertson 1976]

Seya-tatara-hime

Japan

Family and Tribes

Goddess who became the wife of Ō-mono-hushi-no-kami. Mother of *Hoto-tatara-isusuki-hime-no-mikoto.*

The god Ō-mono-hushi-no-kami greatly admired Seya-tatara-hime. He transformed himself into a red painted arrow and floated down a ditch in which she was defecating. When the arrow touched her intimate parts, she fled in alarm. She took the arrow with her and placed it in her bed, where the arrow returned to the form of Ō-mono-hushi-no-kami. The couple was quickly married.

Similar to *Mizo-kuhi-hime.* See also *Mishima-no-mizo-kui-hime.* [Durdin-Robertson 1976; Philippi 1968]

Shan-tien P'o-tzu   See *Shandian Pozi*.

Shandian Pozi

China

Fire; Weather; Justice; Heaven and Hell; Reptiles

Goddess of lightning.

Dressed in a beautiful gown of blue, green, red, and white, Shandian Pozi stands holding a mirror in each hand, directing her "golden snakes" of lightning into the hearts of humans. Whatever is in their hearts is revealed to the god of thunder to be used in deciding just punishments. No one escapes her light.

Alternate form: Shan-tien P'o-tzu. [Werner 1961]

She Mu

China

Reptiles; Evil; Destroyer of Life; Time; Ceremonies

Mother of Serpents. Evil goddess eats people unless she is given children as sacrifices each year on the ninth day of the ninth moon. [Werner 1961]

She Sang Neu   See *Shesang Nü*.

Shen Deity

China

Earth and Nature; Primordial Being

Earth goddess. Wife of Phan-ku. She is responsible for managing the earth and is the basis for the Yin principle. [Durdin-Robertson 1976]

Shen Mu   See *Bixia Yuanjin*.

Shenggu

China

Magic; Water; Immortality; Weather; Disorder

Magician. She could walk on water.

Shenggu was killed by her husband. Her corpse stayed fresh and natural looking for seven hundred years. If people were disrespectful to her, their boats would be delayed or overturned by violent winds.

Alternate form: Sheng-ku. [Werner 1961]

Sheng-ku. See *Shenggu*.

Shêng Mu   See *Shengmu*.

Shengmu
China
Magic
　　Goddess of sorcery associated with *Bixia Yuanjin* or an alternate name for *Bixia Yuanjin*. Alternate form: Shêng Mu. [Jobes 1962; Leach 1992; Werner 1961]

Shepe
China
Mother and Guardian
　　Goddess of females. Alternate form: She-p'er. [Graham 1958; Leach 1992]

She-p'er   See *Shepe*.

Shesang Nü
China
Stars and Planets
　　Stellar deity. She is the contellation Virgo. Equivalent to *Kanya*, Indian Subcontinent. Alternate form: She Sang Neu. [Durdin-Robertson 1976]

Shi
China
Agriculture; Household Affairs
　　Protector of grain in storage who is worshiped in Sichuan. Wife of Ts'u-ga-shi. [Graham 1958; Leach 1992]

Shi-nish-e-ran-mat
Japan, *Ainu*
Weather
　　Japanese goddess of air. She lives in the clouds with her husband, Shi-nish-e-ran-guru. [Batchelor 1925; Leach 1992]

Shi-nun-manuri
Taiwan, *Yami*
Fate; Mother and Guardian; Sky and Heavens
　　Chief deity of the fourth plane of the heavens. She controls and supervises all the goddesses on that plane. They in turn are responsible for equalizing the births of both sexes and for determining the length of each infant's life. [Del Re 1951; Leach 1992]

Shih Hu Shih   See *Shihu Shi*.

Shih-chi Niang-niang   See *Shiji Niangniang*.

Shihu Shi
China
Reptiles
　　Dragon Mother. Alternate form: Shih Hu Shih. [Werner 1961]

Shiji Niangniang
China
Stars and Planets
　　Stellar deity, the star Yueh-yu. She was slain by a magic mirror. Alternate form: Shih-chi Niang-niang. [Werner 1961]

Shiko-me   "Ugly Woman." See *Yomo-tsu-shiko-me*.

Shinatsuhime
Japan
Weather
　　Japanese wind goddess. Her counterpart is the wind god, Shinatsuhiko. [Holtom 1965; Kato 1971; Leach 1992]

Shing Moo   See *Xing Mu*.

Shio-mi-ma
Taiwan, *Yami*
Sky and Heavens
　　Goddess of the second plane of the heavens. [Del Re 1951; Leach 1992]

Shir-kor-kamui
Japan, *Ainu*
Earth and Nature
　　Ruler of the earth. [Leach 1992; Philippi 1982]

Shitateru-hime-no-mikoto   "Lower-Radiant Princess" or "Red Shining Princess." See *Takahime-no-mikoto*.

Shiu-mu Niang-niang   See *Xiumu Niangniang*.

Shokujo
Japan
Stars and Planets; Ceremonies
　　"Heavenly Weaver-girl." Stellar deity, the star Vega near the Milky Way. Wife of Kengyu, the herdsman. At the Festival of Tanabata on the seventh day of the seventh month, Shokujo and Kengyu are worshiped. Poems are written on strips of paper and stuck to bamboo grass in various places. They are of Chinese origin. See also Chinese *Zhinü*. Alternate forms: Ame-no-tanabata-hime-no-mikoto, Ori-hime, Tanabata hime, Tanabata tsume. [Durdin-Robertson 1976; Leach 1992]

Shozu-ga-no-baba
Japan
Commerce and Travel; Immortality
　　Guardian of the crossroads. It is at the crossroads that the three ways of the transmigration of the soul begins. [Jobes 1962; Leach 1992]

Shuhiji-no-kami   See *Su-hiji-ni-no-kami*.

Shui-i Shih   See *Shuiyi Shi*.

Shui-mu Niang-niang   See *Shuimu Niangniang*.

Shuimu Niangniang
China
Water; Weather
　　Water goddess who may cause floods. Alternate form: Shui-mu Niang-niang. [Leach 1992; Schram 1957; Werner 1961]

Shuiyi Shi
China
Earth and Nature; Directions
　　Goddess of the sacred mountain of the east, Tai Shan (T'ai Shan). Wife of Chin Hung, mother of five sons. Alternate form: Shui-i Shih. [Werner 1961]

Shu-koyan-mat
Japan, *Ainu*
Household Affairs
　　Household deity. Goddess of the cooking pot. Daughter of *Huchi-fuchi*. [Batchelor ca. 1927; Leach 1992]

Shun I Fu-jen   See *Shunyi Furen*.

Shunyi Furen
China
Weather; Poverty
　　Deity of drought (or famine) and flood. Alternate form: Shun I Fu-jen. [Leach 1992; Werner 1961]

Si Ling She   See *Siling Shen.*

Si Wang Mu   See *Xi Wangmu.*

Sien-tsan   See *Xiancan.*

Sieou Wen-yin   See *Xiu Wenyin.*

Siling Shen
China
Justice; Insects
   Goddess of silkworms who was a deified empress.
Alternate form: Si Ling She. [Leach 1992; MacLagen 1925]

Silla Mountain Goddess
Korea
Mother and Guardian
   Mother goddess. Wife of Che-syang.
   *When Che-syang went to Wa country (Japan) and was
   killed, Silla Mountain Goddess took her three daughters
   and went to the top of the mountain where she could see
Wa country. She was made Goddess mother and a shrine honoring
her was built on the spot.* [Durdin-Robertson 1976]

So Wang-mo
Korea
Small Size; Immortality
   Daoist Queen Mother of the West. She is ruler of the fairies
(the Immortals). The Fairy Peach grows in her orchard in the
K'un Lun Mountains and the phoenix is her messenger. See
also Chinese *Xi Wangmu.* [Leach 1992; Moes 1983]

Somber Maiden
China
Sun and Day; Moon and Night
   Sun goddess. Her story tells of the struggle between light
and dark at the beginning of history. [Werner 1961]

Song Tseu Niang Naing   See *Songzi Niangniang.*

Song Tsi Kuan Yin   See *Songzi Guanyin.*

Songzi
China
Mother and Guardian
   Goddess of children. Alternate form: Sung Tzǔ. [Day 1940;
Leach 1992]

Songzi Guanyin
China
Mother and Guardian
   "Dispenser of Fecundity." Fertility deity who gives
children, especially sons. A form of the androgynous deity,
Avalokitesvara. See also *Guanyin.* Alternate forms: Song
Tsi Kuan Yin, Sung Tzǔ Kuan-yin [Day 1940; Getty 1962;
Leach 1992]

Songzi Niangniang
China
Mother and Guardian; Health and Healing
   Goddess who gives children. She brings female infants, but
is invoked for sons. She is also a healer. Alternate forms: Song
Tseu Niang Niang, Sung Tzi Liang Liang, Sung-tzi
niang-niang, Sun-tzu Niang Niang, Tseu Souen Nai Nai,
Zisong Nai Nai. [Durdin-Robertson 1976; Leach 1992]

Sotohori-irat-sume   See *So-tohoshi-no-iratsume.*

So-tohoshi-no-iratsume
Japan
Beauty
   "Clothing-penetrating-through Lady." Her skin was so
beautiful, her body's radiance came through her garments.
There are apparently two deities with this name; one is the
sister of the Empress Osaka no Oho-nakatsu and the other
is her daughter. See also *Oto.* Alternate forms: Oto-hime,
Karu-no-ō-iratsume, Sotohori-irat-sume. [Durdin-Robertson
1976]

Sse
China, *Na-khi*
Creator of Life
   Female principle. Deity of creation worshiped in the
Yunnan Province. [Leach 1992]

Sti-per-sei
China, *Ch'iang*
Mother and Guardian
   Childbirth goddess. [Graham 1958; Leach 1992]

Su-hiji-ni-no-kami
Japan
Earth and Nature
   "Mud-earth Lady." The personification of sand or earth.
One of the seven generations of the Age of the Gods. Her
counterpart is U-hiji-ni-no-kami. In ancient times, newborn
females were said to be laid on the earthen floor for three days.
This is thought to have been a way of connecting the woman
to the earth. Alternate form: Shuhiji-no-kami. [Durdin-
Robertson 1976; Jobes 1962; Ono et al. 1985; Philippi 1968]

Sun and Moon, Goddess of the
Japan, *Ainu*
Sun and Day; Moon and Night
   Sometimes a single deity, but in some regions the sun
and moon are separate deities. See also *Chuh Kamuy.*
[Eliade 1987]

Sun Goddess
Japan, *Ainu*
Sun and Day
   Her story is similar to *Ama-terasu-ō-mikami.* [Durdin-
Robertson 1976]

Sun Goddess, Formosan
Formosa (Taiwan), *Ami*
Sun and Day
   Solar deity. [Durdin-Robertson 1976]

Sun-tzu Niang Niang   See *Songzi Niangniang.*

Sung Tzi Liang Liang   See *Songzi Niangniang.*

Sung Tzǔ   See *Songzi.*

Sung Tzǔ Kuan-yin   See *Songzi Guanyin.*

Sung-tsi Niang-niang   See *Songzi Niangniang.*

Sung-tzu Niang Niang   See *Songzi Niangniang.*

Suseri-bime-no-mikoto
Japan
Heaven and Hell; Physical Prowess; Magic; Mother and
Guardian; Love and Sexuality
   "Forward Princess." A forceful, vigorous and energetic
underworld deity. Daughter of Sasa-no-wo and consort of
Opo-kuni-hushi (Okuninushi).

Suseri-bime-no-mikoto meets her husband in the underworld. After they are married, her father Sasa-no-wo begins to persecute Opo-kuni-hushi. His father-in-law sends him to sleep in a snake house, a centipede house, and a wasp house. Each time Suseri-bime-no-mikoto provides her husband with a protective scarf so he will not be harmed. The couple tries to escape the underworld, pursued by Sasa-no-wo. At the Even Pass the three reach an agreement and the couple is allowed to leave and they settle in Izumo.

The couple are enshrined in several areas, embracing as husband and wife. [Durdin-Robertson 1976; Philippi 1968]

Suserihime
Japan
Unknown
A daughter of the storm god Susano-o-no-Kami. [Kato 1926]

Ta Hsien Fu Jên   See *Daxian Furen.*

Tachi   See *Daji.*

Tachibana   See *Oto-tachibana-hime-no-mikoto.*

Tagi-tsu-hime   See *Takitsu-hime-no-mikoto.*

Tagorihime   See *Takiri-bime-no-mikoto.*

T'ai Chün Hsien Niang   See *Taijun Xianniang.*

Tai Shan Niangniang   See *Bixia Yuanjin.*

Tai Yuan
China
Selflessness; Magic; Mother and Guardian; Heaven and Hell
Deity who lives in the clouds on the highest mountains.

Tai Yuan led a celibate life, but was impregnated by a beam of light when she was eighty years old. Her child became the ruler of the underworld.

Alternate forms: Taiyuan, T'ai Yuan. [Monaghan 1981]

Taijun Xianniang
China
Mother and Guardian
Childbirth goddess who gives aid to make the delivery easier. Alternate form: T'ai Chün Hsien Niang. [Day 1940; Leach 1992]

Taiyin
China
Moon and Night
Moon deity. [Day 1940; Leach 1992; Werner 1961]

Tai-yo T'ai-p'ing-hsiang Yu-hsien Niangniang
See **Yu Nü.**

Taiyuan
China
Magic; Mother and Guardian
Creator.

Every day Taiyuan climbed to the top of the mountain where she was nourished by the sun, moon, and clouds. A spark from the male creator impregnated her and she gave birth to a holy man.

Alternate form: T'ai Yuan. [Eliot 1976]

Ta'nai Fu-jen   See *Ta-nai Fu-jen.*

Takahime-no-mikoto
Japan
Ceremonies; Unhappiness; Wild Birds
"High-princess Lady." Daughter of Ō-kuni-nushi and *Takiri-bime-no-mikoto,* sister of Aji-shiki-taka-hikone-no-kami, consort of Ame-no-waka-piko.

Ame-no-waka-piko came from heaven to the Central Land Reed-Plain. Here he married Takahimi-no-mikoto. When her husband died, Takahimi-no-mikoto built a funeral house. She then assigned a wild goose to be the bearer of funeral offerings; the kingfisher became the bearer of food offerings, the heron a broom-bearer, a sparrow the grinding woman, and the pheasant a weeping-woman. The birds then celebrated the funeral by singing and dancing for eight days. When her brother Adi-siki-taka-pikone came he was mistaken for the corpse because they looked so much alike. This made Takahime-no-mikoto's brother angry and he flew away in a rage, knocking down the funeral house as he left. Takahime-no-mikoto tried to make amends by singing a song telling that her brother was also a god.

Alternate form: Shitateru-hime-no-mikoto. [Durdin-Robertson 1976]

Takiri-bime-no-mikoto
Japan
Weather; Fishing and Water Animals
"Mist-princess Goddess." A goddess of seafarers who was one of the three *Munakata Goddesses,* daughter of *Ama-terasu-ō-mi-kami.* Consort of Ō-kuni-nushi and the mother of Aji-shiki-taka-hikone-no-kami (Kamo-no-ō-kami) and *Takahime-no-mikoto.* Alternate form: Oki-tsu-shima-hime-no-mikoto, Tagorihime. [Durdin-Robertson 1976; Leach 1992; Philippi 1968]

Takitsu-hime-no-mikoto
Japan
Water; Disorder; Fishing and Water Animals
"Seething-waters Princess." River goddess and deity of seafarers. One of the three *Munakata Goddesses,* daughter of *Ama-terasu-ō-mi-kami.* See also *Ichiki-shima-hime-no-mikoto* and *Takiri-bime-no-mikoto.* Alternate forms: Tagi-tsu-hime, Takitu-pime-no-mikoto. [Durdin-Robertson 1976; Leach 1992]

Takitu-pime-no-mikoto   See *Takitsu-hime-no-mikoto.*

Tama-kushi-hime   See *Mishima-no-mizo-kui-hime* and *Mizo-kuhi-hime.*

Tamamo-no-maye
Japan
Magic; Demi-animals; Hunting and Wild Animals
Shape changer. Possibly an incarnation of *Inari.*

Tamamo-no-maye could become a flying fox at will. When confronted with a mirror, she lost her power of transformation. [Monaghan 1981]

Tama-yori-bime-no-mikoto
Japan
Water; Magic; Health and Healing; Mother and Guardian
"Spirit-medium Princess." Sea goddess with shamanistic powers. She is also a goddess of childbirth. Daughter of Wata-tsu-mi-no-kami, sister of Toyo-tama-bime. Tama-yori-bime-no-mikoto nursed her brother's son, Ama-tsu-hiko-hiko-nagisa-take-u-gaya-huki-aezu-no-mikoto (Ugaya-fuki-aezu) and later married this nephew. Alternate form: Tamayorihime. [Durdin-Robertson 1976; Ienaga et al. 1967; Leach 1992; Philippi 1968]

Tamayorihime   See *Tama-yori-bime-no-mikoto.*

Tanabata hime   See *Shokujo.*

Tanabata tsume   See *Shokujo.*

Ta-nai Fu-jen   "The Greatly Honored Dame." See *Cuisheng Sheng Mu.*

T'ang   See *Tang.*

Tang
China
Justice
   Empress. Heavenly goddess who lives in the palace of the Golden Bells. Alternate form: T'ang. [Durdin-Robertson 1976]

Ta-pien-ts'ai-t'ien-nü   See *Dabiancai Tiannü.*

Tao   See *Dao.*

Tao Mu   See *Dao Mu.*

Tara Bosatsu   See *Ro-tara-ni-bi.*

Tartary and Cathay Earth Goddess
Mongolia
Domesticated Animals; Household Affairs; Ceremonies
   Guardian of the flocks and fields. Her husband is Natigai. Images of the couple and their family are made of felt and cloth and kept in each house. Offerings are made to them at each meal. See also *Cathay Earth Goddess,* Eastern Europe. [Durdin-Robertson 1976]

Tathagata mahavai-rokana   See *Dainichi-nyorai.*

Tatsu-ta-hime
Japan
Weather; Agriculture; Time; Mother and Guardian
   Wind goddess. Along with the god Tatsuta-hiko, she is prayed to for abundant harvests. Each autumn she weaves a tapestry of multicolored leaves and then blows them away. Her devotees, especially fishermen and sailors, wear her amulet for protection from storms. Alternate form: Tatsuta-hime. [Durdin-Robertson 1976; Guirand 1968; Leach 1992; Monaghan 1981]

Tatsuta-hime   See *Tatsu-ta-hime.*

Taxankpada Agodales
Taiwan
Directions; Weather
   Goddess of the east. Her husband is Tamagisanbach. Thunder occurs when she is upset with him for not sending rain. See *Tekarpada.* [Coleman 1832; Leach 1992]

Tekarpada
Taiwan
Directions
   Goddess of the east. See also *Taxankpada Agodales.* [Campbell 1925; Leach 1992]

Teleglen-edzen
Mongolia, *Mongols*
Earth and Nature
   Earth goddess. Personification of the earth's surface. See also *Teleglen-edzen,* Eastern Europe. Alternate form: Altan-telgey. [Klementz 1925; Leach 1992]

Te-na-zuchi-no-kami
Japan
Mother and Guardian

"Hand-stroking Elder." Consort of Asi-na-duti, mother of eight daughters. Her youngest daughter is *Kushi-nada-hime.* Te-na-zuchi-no-kami's name refers to her caressing her daughter when she was threatened by the great serpent. [Durdin-Robertson 1976; Ienaga et al. 1967; Philippi 1968]

Tennin, The
Japan
Immortality; Wild Birds; Demi-animals; Arts
   Buddhist ethereal beings, angels. Possibly of Chinese origin. They are portrayed as winged and wearing feathered robes, playing instruments and singing. They are perpetually youthful. Equivalent to the *Gandharvis,* Indian Subcontinent. [Durdin-Robertson 1976]

Tensho   See *Ama-terasu-ō-mi-kami.*

Ten-sho-dai-jin   See *Ama-terasu-ō-mi-kami.*

Tenth Aunt
China
Mother and Guardian; Agriculture
   Village deity who protects crops and humans. [Durdin-Robertson 1976]

Third Lady
China
Magic
   Witch. Equivalent of *Circe,* Greek and Roman Empires. [Durdin-Robertson 1976]

Ti Mu   See *Di Mu.*

Tia Shan Niang-niang   See *Bixia Yuanjin.*

Tian Fei
China
Commerce and Travel; Mother and Guardian
   Goddess of navigation and sailors. She is invoked for safe passage and also for children. Alternate form: T'ien Fei, Tian Hou. [Durdin-Robertson 1976; Leach 1992; Monaghan 1981; Stone 1979; Werner 1961]

Tian Hou
China
Dawn and Twilight; Commerce and Travel; Mother and Guardian; Fishing and Water Animals
   "Queen of Heaven." Goddess of dawn and protector of sailors and navigators. She also protects fishermen and their catches. May be identical to *Quan Hou* and is equivalent to *Chuan Hou.* Alternate forms: Jun Ti, Mazu, Tian Fei, Tian Hou niangniang, T'ien Hou. [Durdin-Robertson 1976; Leach 1992; Monaghan 1981; Stone 1979; Werner 1961]

Tian Hou niangniang   See *Tian Hou.*

Tian Mu   See *Dou Mou.*

Tian Mu Niangniang
China
Weather; Fire
   Goddess of lightning. The mirrors she holds in her hands cause the bolts to bounce about the sky and sometimes to strike the earth, starting fires. She works in conjunction with Yu-tzu, the "Master of Rain." Alternate form: Tien Mu Niang Niang. [Guirand 1968; Leach 1992]

Tian Nü, The
China
Stars and Planets

Stellar attendants. Equivalent to *Apsarases,* Indian
Subcontinent. [Werner 1961]

Tiangong Dimu
China
Creator of Life
   Fertility deity. Alternate form: T'ien Kung Ti Mu. [Day 1940;
Leach 1992]

Tianxian Songzi   See *Bixia Yuanjin.*

T'ien Fei   See *Tian Fei.*

T'ien Hou   See *Jun Ti* and *Tian Hou.*

Tien Hou   See *Tian Hou.*

T'ien Kung Ti Mu   See *Tiangong Dimu.*

T'ien Mu   See *Dou Mou.*

Tien Mu Niang Niang   See *Tian Mu Niangniang.*

Tien Nu   See *The Tian Nü.*

T'ien-hsien Sung-tzu   See *Bixia Yuanjin.*

Tilan Xian   See *Bixia Yuanjin.*

Toho-tsu-machi-ne-no-kami
Japan
Unknown
   "Distant cove." One of the *Seventeen Generations Deities.*
Daughter of Ame-no-sa-giri-no-kami, wife of Ame-no-hi-bara-
ō-shina-do-mi-no-kami, mother of Toho-tsu-yama-saki-
tarashi-no-kami. Alternate form: *Totsu-machine-no-kami.*
[Durdin-Robertson 1976; Philippi 1968]

Toi-kura-puni-mat
Japan, *Ainu*
Earth and Nature
   Vegetation deity. [Batchelor 1925; Leach 1992]

Toikunrari-mat
Japan, *Ainu*
Evil; Hunting and Wild Animals; Mother and Guardian
   Land demon. She is friendly to hunters and they invoke
her when in danger. [Batchelor 1925; Leach 1992]

T'o-lo
China
Goodness
   Mother of mercy and compassion. Equivalent to *Dara Eke,*
Mongolia. [Leach 1992]

Tori-mimi-no-kami
Japan
Unknown
   "Bird-ear" or "To Take Ear." Daughter of Ya-shima-mu-ji-
no-kami, wife of Ō-kuni-nushi, mother of Tori-naru-mi-no-
kami. [Durdin-Robertson 1976; Philippi 1968]

Tortoise Goddess
China
Magic
   Goddess of magic. She carries nine cauldrons on her back.
The cauldron is an instrument of women's magic, the vessel
of fertility. [Durdin-Robertson 1976]

Totsu-machine-no-kami   See *Toho-tsu-machi-ne-
no-kami.*

Tou Mou   See *Dou Mou* and *Jun Ti.*

Tou-shen Niang-niang   See *Doushen Niangniang.*

Toyotama   See *Toyo-tama-bime-no-mikoto.*

Toyo-tama-bime-no-mikoto
Japan
Water; Mother and Guardian; Reptiles
   "Abundant Jewel Princess" or "Abundant Spirit Princess."
Sea goddess who married Ho-wori-no-mikoto, a mortal who
was a descendant of the sun goddess.
   *Toyo-tama-bime-no-mikoto made her husband promise
not to watch her while she gave birth. Unable to restrain
his curiosity, Ho-wori-no-mikoto looked into the room
and discovered that his wife had become a sea crocodile. Toyo-tama-
bime-no-mikoto left her baby in the care of her younger sister and
returned to the ocean depths. She sang a song to him as she left,
telling of her eternal love. He sang to her in return, a song he
continued to sing each night to the sea until he died.*
   Alternate forms: Toyotama. [Durdin-Robertson 1976]

Toyo-uke-bime-no-kami
Japan
Mother and Guardian
   "Abundant Food-princess Deity." Daughter of Waku-musubi-
no-kami. She was enshrined at Watarai (Watarapi). Alternate
forms: Toyo-uke-hime-no-kami, Toyu-uke-no-kami. See also
Deities of the Third Earthly Generation. [Durdin-Robertson
1976; Ienaga et al. 1967; Leach 1992; Philippi 1968]

Toyo-uke-hime-no-kami   See *Toyo-uke-bime-no-kami.*

Toyonkenime-no-kami   See *Uke-mochi-no-kami.*

Toyouke-Daijin
Japan
Mother and Guardian
   Shinto food deity. [Kato 1971; Leach 1992]

Toyoukehime-no-Kami
Japan
Agriculture
   Shinto cereal goddess or the "Spirit of the rice plant."
[Kato 1971]

Toyu-uke-no-kami   See *Toyo-uke-bime-no-kami.*

Travel Goddess
China
Justice
   Deified empress. [Werner 1961]

Triple Pussa
China
Unknown
   Buddhist triple goddess. [Durdin-Robertson 1976]

Ts'an Nü   See *Da'an Nü* and *Can Nü.*

Tse-Sun   See *Zesun.*

Tseu Souen Nai Nai   See *Songzi Niangniang* and *Zesun
Nainai.*

Ts'i Ma Niang Tsai

China, *Ch'uan Miao*

Sky and Heavens; Mother and Guardian; Goodness

Benevolent sky goddess who protects ill-fated children. [Graham 1937; Leach 1992]

Ts'i Kuan Niang

China

Fate; Family and Tribes

Goddess of visions. She allows young maidens to view their future husbands. [Jobes 1962]

Tsua Sen Niang Niang

China

Mother and Guardian

Childbirth goddess who makes the delivery easier. [Graham 1928; Leach 1992]

Ts'uai-shen Niang Niang

China

Mother and Guardian; Health and Healing

"The Matron Who Hastens Childbirth." Deity who gives sons. She is attached to the celestial Ministry of Medicine and accompanies *Bixia Yuanjin*. She is portrayed carrying a child and a stick of cinnamon. Alternate form: Ts'ui-sheng Niang-niang. [Leach 1992; Werner 1961]

Tsubura-hime

Japan

Water

Sea goddess. She lives at the entrance of Oka Bay and decides which ships may pass. [Durdin-Robertson 1976; Leach 1992]

Tsuchi-no-mi-oya-no-kami   "Earth Mother Deity." See *Ō-tsuchi-no-kami.*

Ts'ui sheng Niang-niang   See *Ts'uai-shen-niang-niang.*

Ts'ui Shêng Shêng-mu   See *Cuisheng Sheng Mu.*

Tsukisakaki hime

Korea

Earth and Nature

Awful spirit of the Cleyera Japonica tree, the holy tree of Shinto. She dwells in the split-bell Isuzu at Ise. She may be *Ama-terasu-ō-mi-kami* representing herself as a Korean deity. [Durdin-Robertson 1976]

Tsuma-tsu-hime   See *Tsuma-tsu-hime-no-mikoto.*

Tsuma-tsu-hime-no-mikoto

Japan

Earth and Nature

A planter of tree seeds. Daughter of Susano-wo, younger sister of *O-ya-tsu-hime-no-mikoto.* Alternate form: Tsuma-tsu-hime. [Ienaga et al. 1967; Leach 1992]

Tsura-nami-no-kami

Japan

Order; Water

"Calm-water-surface Deity." One of the *Deities of the Third Earthly Generation.* Her counterpart is Tsura-nagi-no-kami. [Durdin-Robertson 1976; Philippi 1968]

Tudi Furen

China

Earth and Nature; Agriculture

Guardian of the earth, especially the grain crop. Wife of Tudi Laoye (T'u Ti Lao Yeh). Alternate form: T'u Ti Fu Jên. [Day 1940; Leach 1992]

Tudi Nainai

China

Earth and Nature

Earth goddess who protects the soil. Alternate form: T'u Ti Nai-nai. [Ferguson 1937; Leach 1992]

Tui

China

Water; Happiness

"Goddess of Joy." She is symbolized by the "smiling lake" and its ability to refresh living things. She is associated with autumn. [Durdin-Robertson 1976]

Tung Mu   See *Dong Mu.*

Turesh

Japan, *Ainu*

Water; Ugliness; Fishing and Water Animals; Justice; Goodness

Heavenly deity who appeared as a sea monster.

 Turesh carried fish caught by Okikurumi in the celestial sea down to the Ainu. They lived happily, always having enough to eat, until one day one of the people grabbed her hand and pulled her inside. This broke a law which forbade asking for a benefactor's name or seeing the benefactor, and from that day on the Ainu had to struggle for their food. [Monaghan 1981]

Turesh machi

Japan, *Ainu*

Education and Knowledge; Household Affairs

Seamstress deity. She taught her followers how to sew. [Chamberlain 1887; Leach 1992]

Tushan, Lady

China

Family and Tribes; Metals and Minerals; Magic; Mother and Guardian

Ancestor of the Xia (Hsia) dynasty.

When Lady Tushan's husband changed into a rock, she changed into a stone. She was pregnant and gave birth by splitting open.

Lady Yu is also said to be the ancestor of the Xia (Hsia) dynasty. [Chang 1983]

T'u Ti Fu Jên   See *Tudi Furen.*

T'u Ti Nai-nai   See *Tudi Nainai.*

Tzŭ Kou   See *Zi Gou.*

Tzu Sun Niang Niang   See *Zisun Niangniang.*

Tzu-ku Shën   See *Zigu Shen* and *Keng San Gu.*

Uba-gami

Japan

Health and Healing

Nurse goddess enshrined in the icho tree. [Holtom 1931; Leach 1992]

Udzume   See *Ame-no-uzume.*

Ugadama

Japan

Commerce and Travel; Agriculture

Deity of carpenters and contractors worshiped at the Fushimi-Inari Shrine. She is also said to be a food goddess connected with Dosojin, an agricultural fertility god who protects the rice fields. [Leach 1992]

Ugly Females of Yomi
Japan
Ugliness; Evil
Eight demons who aided *Izanami-no-kami* (see for story) in her pursuit of Izanagi. [Sproul 1979]

Uka-no-kami   See *Inari.*

Uka-no-mitama   See *O-ge-tsu-hime-no-kami.*

Uka-no-mitama-no-kami   "Food Spirit Deity." See *Ugadama.*

Uke-mochi-no-kami
Japan
Agriculture; Mother and Guardian; Domesticated Animals
Food goddess, mother of *Waka-sana-ma-no-kami.*
Uke-mochi-no-kami had an unusual way of providing food: she would vomit it from her mouth. If she faced the land, rice ready to eat would come out; if facing the sea, fish and seaweed would spew forth; when she turned toward the mountains she produced wild game. One day Susa-no-o saw her doing this and he became so disgusted he killed Uke-mochi-no-kami. Out of her body grew millet, rice, barley, beans, grass, and the mulberry tree with the silkworm, while her head grew into a horse and cow.
See also *Corn Woman,* North America. Alternate forms: O-ge-tsu-hime-no-kami, Toyonkenime-no-kami. [Durdin-Robertson 1976; Leach 1992; Monaghan 1981; Stone 1979]

Uke-no-kami   See *Inari.*

Um
Korea
Unknown
Goddess. Partner of Yang. [Jobes 1962]

Umai
Mongolia, *Altai*
Goodness; Mother and Guardian
Benevolent deity who protects children. See also *Umai,* Eastern Europe and Near East. [Baumgartner 1984; Leach 1992]

Uminai-gami
Okinawa; Ryukyu Islands
Creator of Life
Creator deity worshiped in the Ryukyu Islands. She created the land and humans with her brother, Umikii-gami. Alternate form: Winagu-gami. [Leach 1992; Lebra 1966]

Umugai-hime   See *Umugi-hime.*

Umugi-hime
Japan
Fishing and Water Animals; Immortality
"Clam Princess." A heavenly deity who has the power to restore life. See also *Kisagai-hime.* Alternate form: Umugai-hime. [Durdin-Robertson 1976; Leach 1992; Philippi 1968]

Unchi-ahchi
Japan, *Ainu*
Fire; Household Affairs

"Grandmother Hearth." Fire goddess who is the intermediary between humans and other deities. See also *Unchi achi,* Eastern Europe. [Leach 1992]

Urara-e-ran-mat
Japan, *Ainu*
Weather
Air goddess. She and the god Urara-e-ran-guru preside over low clouds and fog. [Batchelor 1925; Leach 1992]

Uzume   See *Ame-no-uzume.*

Vatiaz
Mongolia, *Buriat*
Physical Prowess
Woman of great strength.
Vatiaz went to heaven seeking help after her brother was murdered. She pretended to be a man and competed for the three daughters of the chief god. She won all of the contests, and even though the god had been told that Vatiaz was a woman, he allowed her to take his three daughters back to earth to help in returning her brother to life. [Monaghan 1981]

Virgin Jasper
China
Magic; Mother and Guardian
The mother of the supreme spirit, Dao (Tao). This miraculous birth allowed him to have contact with humans. [Jobes 1962]

Wakahirume   See *Wakahirume-no-mikoto.*

Wakahirume-no-mikoto
Japan
Dawn and Twilight; Household Affairs
"Young-sun-female." One of the *Seventeen Generations Deities.* Daughter of *Izanami-no-kami,* sister of *Ama-terasu-ō-mi-kami.* She is one of the heavenly weavers appearing at dawn to harmonize the day and to weave garments for the other deities. Alternate form: Wakahirume, Ori-hime. [Durdin-Robertson 1976; Jobes 1962; Leach 1992; Philippi 1968]

Waka-sana-me-no-kami
Japan
Agriculture
"Young-rice-planting-maiden Deity." Daughter of *Uke-mochi-no-kami* and Hayamato-no-kami. She presides over the transplanting of rice plants. One of the *Izumo Pantheon Deities.* [Durdin-Robertson 1976; Leach 1992; Philippi 1968]

Waka-uka-hime waka-uke-nome
Japan
Mother and Guardian
"The Young-food Lady." Food goddess. [Durdin-Robertson 1976]

Waka-uka-no-me-no-mikoto
Japan
Weather; Agriculture
Young food goddess who is associated with rain. Alternate forms: Hirose-no-kawaai-no-kami, Oimi-no-kami. [Herbert 1967; Leach 1992]

Wakka-ush-kamui   See *Pet-ru-ush-mat.*

Wang   See *Xi Wangmu.*

Wangmu Niangniang
China
Wild Birds; Beauty

Queen Mother. Identified with *Xi Wangmu*. She is sometimes portrayed as a beautiful young woman attended by peacocks. [Durdin-Robertson 1976; Monaghan 1981]

Weiwobo   See *Xi Wangmu*.

Wen Ch'iao   See *Wen Qiao*.

Wen Cheng
China
Unknown
Princess who was deified and called *Sitatara* by the Buddhists. She married the Tibetan emperor, Song-tsen-gam-po, to prevent a war. See also *Sitatara*, Indian Subcontinent. [Jobes 1962]

Wen Qiao
China
Unknown
Wife of Ch'en O, mother of Hsuan Tsang. Alternate form: Wen Ch'iao. [Durdin-Robertson 1976]

Wenchen
China
Goodness
"White Dolma" or "White Tara." Compassionate deity who helps all who suffer. She brought Buddhism into Tibet. See *Konjo*, The Himalaya. [Durdin-Robertson 1976]

Western Mother
China
Ceremonies; Magic; Health and Healing
"Western Royal Mother." Shaman of Mt. Kunlun. She handles religious ceremonies and leads the troops of genii. [Durdin-Robertson 1976; Bonnerjea 1927]

White Wave
China
Magic; Small Size; Insects; Goodness
Fairy who appears as a Snail Maiden

Hsieh Tuan, returning home late at night, found a snail on the edge of the path. He picked it up and took it home. He put the snail in an earthenware jar and gave it some leaves to eat. When he returned from work the next day, his supper was on the table and his house was clean. This continued every day for a week, but Hsieh Tuan could not discover who was doing this wonderful thing for him. He hid outside of the house and he saw a lovely young woman emerge from the earthenware jar. He ran inside and confronted her and she told him her name was White Wave. She said she was doing these things because he had no family to help him, but that she must return to her own land. She left him the shell which magically filled with food when he was hungry. White Wave flew off during a storm and Hsieh Tuan built a shrine in honor her. [Durdin-Robertson 1976]

Winagu-gami   See *Uminai-gami*.

Woo Neu   See *Nok*.

Xi Hou
China
Sun and Day; Mother and Guardian
"Mother of Ten Suns."

Xi Hou is responsible for the proper functioning of her ten children. Early in the morning Xi Hou bathes the suns in the lake at the eastern edge of the world. They climb into a tree by the shore and the sun who is to shine that day climbs to the top of the tree and Xi Hou places the "duty" sun in a chariot driven by dragons for a ride across the sky.

Alternate form: Hsi Ho. [Durdin-Robertson 1976; Durdin-Robertson 1982; Leach 1992; Stone 1979]

Xi Shi
China
Commerce and Travel
Patron of cosmetic sellers, especially those who sell perfume and face cream. She smells very sweet. Alternate form: Hsi Shih. [Leach 1972; Leach 1992]

Xi Wangmu
China
Hunting and Wild Animals; Directions; Creator of Life; Destroyer of Life; Immortality; Demi-animals
Royal mother of the western air from which she was formed. Mother of *Yunhua Furen*. She is the female principle, *yin*. With Mu Kung, *yang*, she created heaven and earth and all the living beings of the universe. She is also the goddess of plague and pestilence. As guardian of the herb (or peach) of immortality, she can also bestow immortality. Xi Wangmu lives on Mt. Kunlun (Kwen-lun) and commands the troops of genii. She is portrayed as a composite deity, human but with the tail of a leopard (or panther), the teeth of a tiger (or dog), and disheveled hair. Equivalent to *Sei-o-bo*. See also Korean *So Wang-mo*. Alternate forms: He, Hsi Wang Mu, Jin Mu, Wangmu Niangniang, Weiwobo, Si Wang Mu, Yang, Wang. [Bonnerjea 1927; Durdin-Robertson 1976; Jobes 1962; Leach 1992; Monaghan 1981; Senior 1985; Werner 1961]

Xiancan
China
Insects; Education and Knowledge; Household Affairs
Silk goddess. She introduced silkworm breeding to the people. Alternate form: Sien-tsan. [Leach 1992; Redfield 1931]

Xiang, Lady
China
Goodness
"Pottery Seller." She was deified because of her good works. Alternate form: Lady Hsiang. [Durdin-Robertson 1976]

Xie, Lady
China
Family and Tribes; Magic; Mother and Guardian; Wild Birds
Ancestor of the Shang dynasty.

Lady Xie ate an egg that was dropped by a dark bird. After eating the egg, she became pregnant and the mother of the Shang dynasty.

The story of ancestral birth from a bird's egg is widespread among the peoples in the eastern coastal areas of China and Northeast Asia. Alternate form: Lady Hsieh. [Chang 1983]

Xieren Xingjun
China
Stars and Planets; Mother and Guardian
Stellar deity who protects women in childbirth. Alternate form: Hsieh Jên Hsing Chün. [Day 1940; Leach 1992]

Xiling Shi
China
Justice; Insects; Education and Knowledge
Empress. Wife of the Yellow Emperor, Huang-ti. She invented silk and introduced silkworm culture. Alternate form: Hsi-ling Shih [Jobes 1962; Monaghan 1981]

Xing Mu
China
Intelligence and Creativity
"Holy Mother." She personifies perfect intelligence. Alternate form: Shing Moo. [Harding 1971]

Xiu Wenyin
China
Fire; Weather
   Goddess of lightning and thunder in China. Alternate form: Sieou Wen-yin. [Chavannes 1910; Leach 1992]

Xiu Zhi
China
Stars and Planets; Magic; Mother and Guardian
   Stellar deity. Mother of the Yellow Emperor, Yu.
      Xiu Zhi was a falling star. She became pregnant when she swallowed a pearl.
         Alternate form: Hsiu-chi. [Jobes 1962]

Xiumu Niangniang
China
Water; Weather
   "Water Mother."
      When Xiumu Niangniang went to the well for water, she would strike the pail once and it would fill. If she struck it twice water flowed out of it endlessly, devastating the country with floods. The Lord of the Skies, Yü Huang, sent troops to capture her, but they were unsuccessful and the floods continued. After several other attempts, Quanyin Pusa was enlisted and she captured Xiumu Niangniang and put her in the bottom of a well where she has stayed forever.
   Alternate form: Shiu-mu Niang-niang. [Durdin-Robertson 1976; Werner 1961]

Xu Kongcang
China
Unknown
   Primordial being identical to *Akasagarabha,* Indian Subcontinent. Alternate form: Hsuk'ung Tsang. [Leach 1992]

Xu Tianju
China
Household Affairs
   Goddess of the latrine. Alternate form: Hsü T'ien-chu. [Werner 1961]

Xuehu Niangniang
China
Heaven and Hell
   Underworld goddess associated with the "Pool of Blood." Alternate form: Hsueh Hu Niang Niang. [Day 1940; Leach 1992]

Ya Hsek Khi
China
Earth and Nature; Creator of Life
   Earth goddess who was shaped like a tadpole. Wife of Ta Hsek Khi (Yatawan).
      Ya Hsek Khi, the earth, and her husband, Ta-hsek-khi, the water, ate three gourds from heaven. When they spit out the seeds, all the animals and the sixty races of humans grew from them. The people were root, rice, corn, or flesh eaters.
   Alternate form: Yatai. [Durdin-Robertson 1976]

Yachimata-hime
Japan
Agriculture; Commerce and Travel
   Goddess of agriculture, travel, and the crossroads. [Kato 1971; Leach 1992; MacCulloch 1925]

Ya-gami-hime
Japan
Family and Tribes

"Princess of Ya-gami." She chose Ō-kuni-nushi as her husband over his eighty brothers who had come to seek her hand in marriage. Mother of Ki-no-mata-no-kami. [Durdin-Robertson 1976; Philippi 1968]

Yagawa-e-hime   See *Ashi-nadaka-no-kami.*

Yakami
Japan
Courage; Selflessness
   Buddhist heroine who offered herself as a sacrifice and killed the sea serpent. [Kramer 1961; Stone 1979]

Yal-un eke
Mongolia
Fire
   Fire mother. [Lurker 1984]

Yama-hime
Japan
Earth and Nature
   "Mountain Maiden." Mountain goddess. [Hori 1968]

Yama-no-Shinbo
Japan
Wealth; Luck
   "Divine Mother of the Mountain." She brings success and happiness. [Hori 1968]

Yama-omba
Japan
Evil; Destroyer of Life
   "Mountain-old Woman." A demon who devours humans. Alternate form: Yama-uba. [Jobes 1962]

Yama-uba   See *Yama-omba.*

Yamato-hime
Japan
Magic; Ceremonies
   Sorceress and priest. Aunt of Yamato-take. She gave him a magic fire-striker to protect him in battle. [Jobes 1962]

Yamato-hime-no-mikoto
Japan
Ceremonies
   "Yamato Princess Deity." Chief priest of *Ama-terasu-ō-mi-kami* at the Temple of Ise. Daughter of the Emperor Suinin. She performed her duties for several hundred years. [Durdin-Robertson 1976; Ienaga et al. 1967; Philippi 1968]

Yametsu-hime
Japan
Earth and Nature
   Shinto mountain deity who lives in the mountains in the district of Yame. [Durdin-Robertson 1976; Leach 1992]

Yamni-huchi
Japan, *Ainu*
Immortality
   "Chestnut-tree Grandmother." She restored the life of a young maiden who had been killed by her sister. [Philippi 1982]

Yang   See *Xi Wangmu.*

Yang Chen
China
Education and Knowledge

Buddhist goddess of learning and teaching. Protector of books. Equivalent to *Sarasvati*, Indian Subcontinent, and *Tibetan Sarasvati*, the Himalaya. [Durdin-Robertson 1976]

Yang Shih
China
Stars and Planets
Stellar deity, the star Hungyan (Hung-yen). [Werner 1961]

Yang T'ai Chün   See *Yang Taijun*.

Yang Taijun
China
Mother and Guardian
Childbirth goddess. Alternate form: Yang T'ai Chün. [Day 1940; Leach 1992]

Yanguang Nainai   See *Yanjing Niangniang*.

Yanguang Pusa
China
Health and Healing
"Goddess of the Light of the Eye." A specialist connected to the celestial Ministry of Medicine. She is represented in all the medicine gods' temples and worshiped to help cure illnesses of the eyes or to ward them off. Also said to be a male deity, god of tailors. Alternate form: Yen-kuang P'u-sa. [Leach 1992; Werner 1961]

Yanjing Niangniang
China
Health and Healing
Eye deity who protects the people from eye disease. Alternate forms: Yen Tsing Niang Niang, Yanguang Nainai. [Chavannes 1910; Leach 1992]

Yao Chi   See *Yao Ji*.

Yao Ji
China
Water; Weather
"Turquoise Courtesan." Water deity who presides over rain and fertility. The rainbow is her symbol and her essence. Her home is on Wu shan in the area of the Yangtze River. Alternate form: Yao Chi. [Leach 1992; Schafer 1973]

Yaoshkep-kamui
Japan, *Ainu*
Insects; Mother and Guardian
Spider goddess who is a childbirth deity. [Leach 1992; Philippi 1982]

Yasak-no-iri-bime-no-mikoto
Japan
Unknown
Deity of Suta. Consort of the Emperor Keikō. [Durdin-Robertson 1976]

Yatai   See *Ya Hsek Khi*.

Yaye-zakura
Japan
Earth and Nature
Cherry-tree goddess. [Monaghan 1981]

Yen Tsing Niang Niang   See *Yanjing Niangniang*.

Yen-kuang P'u-sa   See *Yanguang Pusa*.

Yi Long
China
Mother and Guardian
The third daughter of the Dragon Mother and the Dragon King.

 Yi Long helped Gum Lin release the water in a lake for the benefit of the village of P'o-lo, which was suffering from a long drought. Yi Long's father banished his daughter, who was also called Third Dragon Princess, for acting independently, so she went to live with Gum Lin.

See also *Gum Lin*. Alternate form: Loy Yi Lung. [Durdin-Robertson 1976; Stone 1979]

Yin
China
Creator of Life
"Female Principle." See also *Chang E*. Equivalent to *In*; *Yoni*, Indian Subcontinent; and *Yum*, the Himalaya. [Jobes 1962]

Ying Hsi-niang   See *Yingxi Niang*.

Yingxi Niang
China, *Monguors*
Happiness
Goddess of joy worshiped in Kansu. Alternate form: Ying hsi-niang. [Leach 1992; Schram 1957]

Yin-meng Niang-niang   See *Yimeng Niangniang*.

Yimeng Niangniang
China
Mother and Guardian
"Saintly Mother." Childbirth deity. Alternate form: Yin-meng Niang-niang. [Werner 1961]

Yomo-tsu-hisame   See *Yomo-tsu-shiko-me*.

Yomo-tsu-ō-kami   Goddess of the underworld. See *Izanami-no-kami*.

Yomo-tsu-ō-kami   See *Izanami-no-kami*.

Yomo-tsu-shiko-me
Japan
Heaven and Hell; Ugliness
Underworld bogey. She aided *Izanami-no-kami* (see for story) in her pursuit of Izanagi. Alternate forms: Gogome, Hisame, Shiko-me, Yomo-tsu-hisame. [Durdin-Robertson 1976]

Yorozu-hatatoya-akitsushi-hime-no-mikoto
Japan
Unknown
Goddess who aided in the preparations for the descent of the god Ninigi into the Central of the Reed Plains. Alternate form: Ama-yorozu-takau-hata-chi-hata-himi. [Durdin-Robertson 1976]

Yu Mu Sei
China, *Ch'iang*
Mother and Guardian
Childbirth deity who protects the unborn child and guards the newborn. She is also invoked to give sons. [Graham 1958; Leach 1992]

Yu Neu   See *Yu Nü*.

Yu Nü
China
Stars and Planets; Selflessness
   "Honorable Lady," "Jade Lady." Daoist stellar deity, the constellation Leo or a small red star in the constellation. She is also called "The Immortal Jade Mother of the Sacred Mountain Taishan [T'ai-shan]." It was on the mountain that she lived her life of asceticism. Because she washed her hands in the lake, it is called Jade Maiden's Lake. See also *Bixia Yuanjin.* Alternate forms: Bixia Yuanjin, Yu Nü Daxian, Daiyou Taiping Xiang Yuxian Niangniang, Taishan Niangniang, Tai-yo T'ai-p'ing-hsiang Yu-hsien Niangniang, Yu Neu. [Durdin-Robertson 1976; Monaghan 1981; Werner 1961]

Yu Nü Daxian   See *Yu Nü* and *Tai Shan Niangniang.*
Alternate form: Yu-nu Ta-hsien.

Yu, Lady
China
Family and Tribes; Agriculture; Mother and Guardian; Magic
   Ancestor of the Xia (Hsia) dynasty.
      Lady Yu gave birth to the first human after eating some grains of Job's tears, the oldest domesticated crop in eastern Asia.
   See also *Lady Tushan.* [Chang 1983]

Yuan, Lady
China
Family and Tribes; Mother and Guardian; Magic
   Ancestor of the Zhou (Chou) dynasty.
      Lady Yuan became pregnant when she stepped on the big toe of a footprint made by the supreme god. [Chang 1983]

Yu-nu Ta-hsien   See *Yu Nü Daxian.*

Yuede Xingjun   See *Yuefu Taiyin.*

Yuefu Taiyin
China
Moon and Night; Agriculture; Time
   Moon goddess. She presides over the harvest, months, and tides and is a symbol of *Yin.* Alternate forms: Yueh Fu T'ai Yin, Yuede Xingjun, Huchu Xing. [Day 1940; Leach 1992]

Yueh Fu T'ai Yin   See *Yuefu Taiyin.*

Yuki-onne
Japan
Weather; Life/Death Cycle
   "Snow Maiden." Death spirit of freezing. She appears to the dying as a calm, pale woman, helping them to die quietly and painlessly. [Monaghan 1981]

Yun Hwa Fu-jen   See *Yunhua Furen.*

Yun Hsiao   See *Yunxiao.*

Yunhua Furen
China
Earth and Nature
   Daughter of *Xi Wangmu.* She inhabits the peaks of Wu shan. Alternate form: Yun Hwa Fu-jen. [Bonnerjea 1927]

Yunxiao
China
Household Affairs
   One of the *Keng San Guniang.* Alternate form: Yun Hsiao. [Leach 1992; Werner 1961]

Zesun
China
Mother and Guardian; Education and Knowledge
   Guardian of children and posterity. Alternate form: Tse-Sun. [Day 1940; Leach 1992]

Zesun Nainai   See *Songzi Niangniang.*

Zhang Xi
China
Moon and Night
   Creator goddess of the Shang and Zhou dynasties who gave birth to twelve moons. Alternate form: Chang Hsi. [Chang 1976]

Zhao Sanniang
China
Goodness; Commerce and Travel
   Deified woman who is the patron of wig makers.
      Zhao Sanniang's in-laws died and there was not enough money for coffins. She sold her hair to get the money, but then was ashamed to face her husband with a shaved head. She searched until she had enough hair to make a wig.
   Alternate form: Chao San Niang. [Jobes 1962; Leach 1972; Leach 1992]

Zhende Pusa
China
Mother and Guardian
   Mother of Buddha. She is portrayed with thirty-four arms and eighteen heads. Alternate forms: Chen-te P'u-sa, Hu-shan Ta-shih, Jende Pusa. [Werner 1961]

Zhinnü   See *Zhinü.*

Zhinü
China
Stars and Planets; Family and Tribes; Order; Sky and Heavens; Time; Wild Birds; Household Affairs
   "Weaving Woman of Heaven" or "Heavenly Weaver Girl." Stellar deity, the star Alpha in the constellation Lyre (Lyra) or the star Vega. Patron of weavers. She harmonizes night and day, is the goddess of marriage, and weaves the clothing for the Heavenly Emperor's family. Identified with *Nü.*
      Zhinü and six other nymphs were bathing in a stream on earth. A herdsman stole one of their dresses from the bank while they were in the water. When they came out of the water her six friends were able to return to heaven, but Zhinü had to follow the herdsman to try and get her dress back. For three years she lived with the man as his wife. When she finally found where he had hidden her dress, she put it on and returned to heaven. Zhinü now lives on one side of the Milky Way and the herdsman, who followed her to heaven, lives on the other. On the seventh day of the seventh month, all the magpies fly from earth to form a bridge over the Milky Way so Zhinü and her husband can meet.
   There are many versions of this story in China, Korea, and Japan. See also *Swan Maidens,* Northern Europe and Japanese *Shokujo.* Alternate forms: Chih Nu, Chin Nü, Jin Nü, Zhinnü. [Durdin-Robertson 1976; Jobes 1962; Leach 1972; Leach 1992; Monaghan 1981]

Zhuseng Niang-niang   See *Bixia Yuanjin.*

Zi Gou
China
Commerce and Travel
   Manure deity. Worshiped by the manure traders.

      A companion of Mr. Li, Zi Gou was killed by his head wife. The Ancient Original appointed her the goddess of manure.
      Alternate form: Tzǔ Kou. [Leach 1972]

Zigu Shen
China
Household Affairs
"The Violet Lady Spirit." Goddess of latrines. She is one of the **Keng San Guniang.**

When Zigu Shen was murdered out of jealousy in a latrine, she was made the Spirit of the Latrines by the Supreme Being.

Alternate form: Tzu-ku Shën. [Leach 1992; Monaghan 1981; Werner 1961]

Zisong Nai Nai See *Songzi Niangniang.*

Zisun Niangniang
China
Ceremonies
Goddess of weddings. Alternate form: Tzu Sun Niang Niang. [Leach 1972]

GREEK AND ROMAN EMPIRES

Abarbarea
Grecian
Water
   One of the *Naiades,* daughter of Oceanus and *Tethys.* Wife of Bucolion and mother of several sons, but only two are known—Asespus and Pedasus. [Bell 1991; Leach 1992]

Abeona
Roman
Mother and Guardian; Commerce and Travel
   Goddess of departing. She is guardian of children as they begin to explore the world. Also guardian of travelers. Similar to *Adiona.* [Jobes 1962; Meltzer 1981; Redfield 1931]

Abundantia
Roman
Wealth
   Goddess of abundance. Alternate form: Abundita. [Monaghan 1981; Redfield 1931]

Abundita   See *Abundantia.*

Acacalis
Grecian
Earth and Nature
   Daughter of *Pasiphae* and Minos, granddaughter of the sun, Helios. Her sisters are *Ariadne* and *Phaedra.* Alternate forms: Acacallis, Acalle, Deione. Also a nymph, mother of Phylacides and Philandros. See also Nymphs. [Bell 1991; Guirand 1968]

Acacallis   See *Acacalis.*

Acalanthis
Grecian
Hunting and Wild Animals
   One of the nine *Pierides.* Daughter of Pierus of Emathia in Macedonia. [Bell 1991]

Acalle   See *Acacalis.*

Acantha
Grecian
Earth and Nature; Water
   Nymph. She was so loved by Apollo, the sun god, that when she died, he changed her into the Acanthus flower. See also *Nymphs.* [Monaghan 1981; Zimmerman 1964]

Acasta   See *Acaste.*

Acaste
Grecian
Water
   One of the *Oceanides.* Daughter of *Tethys* and Oceanus. Alternate forms: Acasta, Akaste. [Bell 1991; Leach 1992]

Acaviser
Roman; Etruscan
Fate
   One of the *Lasas.* She is associated with *Turan.* Alternate form: Achvistr. [Lurker 1984]

Acca
Roman
Unknown
   Goddess associated with Hercules. [Graves 1948]

Acca Larentia
Roman; Etruscan
Earth and Nature; Hunting and Wild Animals; Mother and Guardian; Ceremonies

Earth goddess. Foster mother, she-wolf that nursed Romulus and Remus, the founders of Rome. She is identified with *Lupa* and may be identified with *Tacita.* There may have been two goddesses with this name. She is honored on the last day of April and on December 23 with the festival *Laurentia.* See also *Lara.* Alternate forms: Acca Laurentia, Larentia, Laurentia. [Bell 1991; Durdin-Robertson 1992; Jobes 1962; Wedeck and Baskin 1971]

Acca Laurentia   See *Acca Larentia.*

Acco
Grecian
Evil
   It was said she swallowed newborns. [Graves 1948]

Achaea
Roman, Grecian
Earth and Nature; Fate
   1) Earth goddess and a name for *Demeter* in Athens. She is identified with *Ceres.*
   ╫ *By drinking the blood of a bull, she is able to predict the future. Achaea likes to do her prophesying in a cave, a place sacred to the Greeks.*
   2) Roman name for *Minerva* at Luceria in Apulia. Alternate form: Achaia. [Bell 1991; Jobes 1962; Street 1804]

Achaia   See *Achaea.*

Achaiva   "Spinner." See *Demeter.*

Acheloides, The
Grecian
Water
   Water nymphs. Their name denotes their father, Achelous, the river god. Their mother is *Sterope.* See also *Nymphs.* Alternate forms: Potameides, Sirens. [Bell 1991; Zimmerman 1964]

Achelois
Grecian
Arts; Sciences; Intelligence and Creativity; Evil
   One of the *Muses.* Daughter of Pierus. [Bell 1991]

Achiroe
Grecian
Unknown
   Daughter of Nilus, the Nile river god. There may have been two women by this name, one Egyptian and one Macedonian, which would account for a confusing history that lists several husbands, children, and locations. Alternate form: Archiroe. [Bell 1991]

Achlys
Grecian
Moon and Night; Unhappiness; Primordial Being
   "Eternal Night." Said to exist before Chaos. Some say she is the personification of misery and sadness. She is depicted on the shield of Heracles as pale and emaciated, with a bloody face and dust on her shoulders. [Bell 1991]

Acholoe
Grecian
Weather; Justice; Ugliness; Demi-animals; Heaven and Hell; Wild Birds
   One of the *Harpies.* [Bell 1991]

Achvistr   See *Acaviser.*

Acidalia
Grecian; Roman
Disorder
   "Restlessness." Name for Greek *Aphrodite* and Roman *Venus.* The name is taken from a fountain in Boeotia where Aphrodite bathes with the *Graces.* [Bell 1991; Zimmerman 1964]

Acidusa
Roman
Unknown
   "Mother of the Maidens". The maidens were minor Greek divinities. There is a Boeotian spring named for her. Her husband was Scamander. [Bell 1991]

Acleme   See *Alcmena.*

Acme
Grecian
Time; Order
   One of the *Horae.* [Bell 1991]

Acmenes, The
Grecian
Earth and Nature
   Nymphs who were worshiped at Elis. See also *Nymphs.* [Bell 1991; Lewis 1956]

Acraea
Grecian
1) Water; 2) Mother and Guardian; 3) Mother and Guardian
   "Topmost." 1) Water nymph. Daughter of the river god Asterion. With her sisters *Euboea* and *Prosymna,* she served as a nurse to *Hera.* There is a hill near Mycenae (Acrea) named for her. 2) Name for *Athena,* "protectress of towns, fortresses, and harbors." 3) Name referring to *Aphrodite, Artemis* and *Hera.* See also *Nymphs.* Alternate forms: Acrea, Acria, Rhea. [Bell 1991; Jobes 1962; Redfield 1931; Street 1804]

Acrea   See *Acraea.*

Acria   See *Acraea.*

Actaea
Grecian
Water; Fate; Beauty
   One of the *Nereides.* Goddess of the shores. [Bell 1991; Leach 1992]

Adamanteia   See *Adamanthea.*

Adamanthea
Grecian
Mother and Guardian
   Nymph and nurse of Zeus. She hid Zeus and his cradle in a tree, to protect him from his malicious father, Cronus. See also *Nymphs.* Alternate form: Adamantei. [Bell 1991; Monaghan 1981; Zimmerman 1964]

Addephagia   See *Adephagia*

Adeona
Roman
Mother and Guardian
   Goddess who guards schoolchildren on their way to and from school and in their early explorations. Similar to *Abeona.* Alternate form: Adiona. [Meltzer 1981; Monaghan 1990]

Adephagia
Grecian
Disorder
    "Gluttony." She is portrayed joyfully eating and drinking. She had a temple in Sicily that also contained a statue of *Ceres.* Alternate form: Addephagia. [Jobes 1962; Leach 1992; Redfield 1931; Wedeck and Baskin 1971]

Adicia
Grecian
Justice; Ugliness
    "Injustice." She is depicted as an ugly woman being dragged and beaten by *Dice,* the personification of justice. [Bell 1991]

Adiona   See *Adeona.*

Admeta
Roman
Ceremonies
    Priestess of *Juno.* Equivalent to Greek *Admete.* [Guirand 1968; Zimmerman 1964]

Admete
Grecian
Earth and Nature
    "Untamable." Nymph daughter of *Tethys* and Oceanus whose task was to help young boys achieve manhood. See also *Nymphs* and *Admeta.* [Bell 1991; Guirand 1968; Leach 1992; Zimmerman 1964]

Adraste
Grecian
Weather; Stars and Planets
    One of the *Hyades.* Sister of *Eidothea* and *Althaea.* [Bell 1991]

Adrastea
Grecian
1) Fate; 2) Earth and Nature; Mother and Guardian
    "Unyielding." 1) A name for *Nemesis,* "she whom none can escape." 2) A Greek nymph and nurse of the child Zeus.
    By request of Zeus's mother, Rhea, the nymph Adrastea protected the young Zeus from his malicious father, Cronus. Adrastea cared for Zeus in a cave on Mount Dicte. Here he slept in a golden cradle and was amused by the golden ball given to him by Adrastea.
    See also *Nymphs, Rhea.* Alternate form: Adrasteia. [Bell 1991; Jobes 1962; Leach 1992]

Adrasteia   See *Adrastea.*

Adryades, The   See *The Dryades.*

Aea
Grecian
Hunting and Wild Animals; Magic
    A hunter. She was metamorphosed into an island to escape the advances of Pasis, the river god. [Bell 1991]

Aeaea
Grecian
Magic
    A name for *Calypso, Circe,* and *Medea.* [Bell 1991; Zimmerman 1964]

Aeaga   See *Aega.*

Aeantis
Grecian
Unknown
    "Ajacian." Name for *Athena.* [Avery 1962]

Aedos
Grecian
Selflessness
    "Shame" or "Modesty." A companion of *Nemesis.* Her Roman name is *Pudicitia.* [Bell 1991]

Aeetias
Grecian
Unknown
    Name for *Medea* used by Roman poets. Alternate forms: Aeetine, Aeetis. [Bell 1991]

Aeetine   See *Aeetias.*

Aeetis   See *Aeetias.*

Aega
Grecian
1) Sun and Day; 2) Domesticated Animals
    "She Who Shines for All" or "Goat." 1) Sun goddess, daughter of *Gaea* and Helios, sister of *Circe* and *Pasiphae.* Others say she is the daughter of Oleus and sister of *Helice.* This goddess may supercede a pre-Hellenic deity consisting of three sisters who together ruled the sun. 2) Aega is also the human personification of the goat goddess *Amalthea.* Alternate forms: Aeaga, Aegia. [Bell 1991; Leach 1992; Redfield 1931]

Aegea   See *Aega.*

Aegeria
Roman
Fate; Mother and Guardian
    "Giver of Life." Roman prophetic deity, one of the *Camenae.* Identified with *Diana.* She is invoked by pregnant women. There is a grove sacred to her in the valley of Aricia. See also *Nemorensis.* Alternate form: Egeria. [Bell 1991; Monaghan 1981]

Aegia   See *Aega.*

Aegiale
Grecian
Unhappiness; Magic; Earth and Nature
    1) One of the *Heliades.* 2) Daughter of Apollo, sister of *Aigle* and Phaeton. 3) A daughter of Asclepius. Alternate form: Aegialeia. [Bell 1991; Zimmerman 1964]

Aegialeia   See *Aegiale.*

Aegilae   See *Aigle.*

Aegina
Grecian
Unknown
    Daughter of the river god Asopus. Mother of Aeacus by Zeus, who abducted her to the island Oenone, or Oenopia, which later bore her name. Alternate form: Aigina. [Bell 1991; Redfield 1931; Zimmerman 1964]

Aeginaea
Grecian
Domesticated Animals
    "Goat Goddess." Name for *Artemis* at her sacred site at Taenarus. [Avery 1962]

Aegle   See *Aigle.*

Aegophaga
Grecian
Domesticated Animals
   A name for *Aphrodite* when a goat is sacrificed to her.
[Wedeck and Baskin 1971]

Aegophagos
Grecian
Domesticated Animals
   "Goat Eater." Name for *Hera* at Sparta. [Bell 1991]

Aello
Grecian
1) Weather; Demi-animals; Beauty; Directions; Destroyer of
Life; 2) Weather; Physical Prowess
   "Tempest." 1) One of the *Harpies.* Daughter of *Electra* and
Thaumas, sister of *Celaeno* and *Ocypete.* A swift-winged
maiden who personified a whirlwind. She is represented as
clawed, beak-faced, and a demon of the south wind that
brings death and destruction. 2) A name for *Iris.* Alternate
forms: Aellopos. [Bell 1991; Jobes 1962; Leach 1992; Redfield
1931]

Aellopos
Grecian
Physical Prowess
   "Swifted-footed Like a Storm Wind." A name for *Iris.* See
also *Aello.* [Bell 1991]

Aeolis   See *Alcyone.*

Aer
Grecian
Sky and Heavens
   Represents the lowest region of the sky. She was loved by
Orion. [Bell 1991; Guirand 1968; Jobes 1962]

Aero   See *Merope.*

Aesa
Grecian
Fate
   "Destiny." Sometimes thought to be one of the *Moirae* or
an Argive deity. Identified with *Ate.* [Bell 1991]

Aestas
Roman
Time
   Goddess of summer. Of the deities who collected around
the sun, Aestas is portrayed as naked and adorned with
garlands made from ears of corn. [Durdin-Robertson
1982]

Aesyle
Grecian
Weather; Stars and Planets
   One of the *Hyades.* [Bell 1991]

Aetae, The   See *The Litae.*

Aeterna   See *Vesta.*

Aether
Grecian
Sky and Heavens
   The highest level of the sky. She is in one of the dawn
myths explaining the daily birth of the sun. Daughter of *Nyx*

and Erebus. Alternate forms: Aethre, Aither, Ether. [Guirand
1968; Jobes 1962]

Aetheria
Grecian
Unhappiness; Magic
   One of the *Heliadae.* Daughter of Helios and *Clymene.*
[Bell 1991; Zimmerman 1964]

Aethra
Grecian
Water
   One of the *Oceanides.* Mother of the *Hyades.* [Bell 1991;
Leach 1992; Zimmerman 1964]

Aethre   See *Aether.*

Aethyia
Grecian
Science; Water
   Name for *Athena* at Megaris. Possibly refers to her as
goddess of the art of shipbuilding or navigation. [Bell 1991]

Aetna
Roman
Fire
   Goddess of Mount Etna. See also *Fuji,* Far East; *Pele,*
Oceania; *Chuqinadak,* North America. [Monaghan 1981;
Zimmerman 1964]

Aetole
Grecian
Unknown
   Name for *Artemis* at Naupactus. [Bell 1991]

Agamede
Grecian
Health and Healing
   "Healer." Along with her husband, Augeus the
herbologist, she was proficient in using herbs to heal the sick.
Agamede in Lesbos may be named for her. [Bell 1991; Jayne
1925; Zimmerman 1964]

Aganippe
Grecian
Intelligence and Creativity; Earth and Nature; Water
   A nymph whose spring is at the foot of Mount Helicon in
Boeotia. The spring is sacred to the *Muses* and inspires those
who drink from it. See also *Nymphs.* [Bell 1991]

Aganippides, The
Grecian
Water
   Name for the *Muses.* Their fountain was located at
Aganippe at the foot of Mt. Helicon. [Bell 1991; Woodcock
1953; Zimmerman 1964]

Agathe Tyche
Grecian
Luck
   "Good Fortune." Her consort is listed as Agathos Daemon
or Zeus Philius. [Leach 1992]

Agave
Grecian
Water; Fate; Beauty
   1) Daughter of *Harmonia* and Cadmus, sister of *Autonoe,*
Ino, and *Semele.*

⚕ *Men were not allowed to participate in the religious rituals of Dionysus. Pentheus, king of Thebes, hid in a tree to watch the rites. Some say Agave mistook him for a wild beast and killed him; others say he was killed because he intruded on women's ceremonies.*

2) A *Nereid*. 3) A *Danaid*. [Bell 1991; Jobes 1962; Leach 1992; Zimmerman 1964]

Agdistis
Grecian
Unknown
   1) Name for *Rhea* at Pessinus. 2) A name for *Cybele*. [Bell 1991]

Agdos
Grecian
Earth and Nature
   Name for *Cybele* when she takes the form of a rock. [Monaghan 1981]

Ageleia
Grecian
Unknown
   "The Forager." Name for *Athena*. Alternate form: Ageleis. [Bell 1991]

Ageleis   See *Ageleia*.

Aglaia
Grecian
Charisma
   "Brightness" or "Splendor." The youngest of the *Charites* who presides at banquets, dances, and social occasions, daughter of Zeus and *Eurynome* and youngest sister of *Thaleia* and *Euphrosyne*. [Bell 1991; Jobes 1962; Leach 1992; Zimmerman 1964]

Aglaope
Grecian
Beauty; Charisma; Demi-animals; Fate; Destroyer of Life; Wild Birds
   "Glorious Face." One of the *Sirens*. [Bell 1991; Monaghan 1981]

Aglaopheme
Grecian
Beauty; Charisma; Demi-animals; Fate; Destroyer of Life; Wild Birds
   One of the *Sirens*. Sister of *Thelxiepeia* and *Peisinoe*. [Jobes 1962]

Agno
Grecian
Earth and Nature; Mother and Guardian
   A nymph and nurse of Zeus. See also *Nymphs*. [Zimmerman 1964]

Agoraea
Grecian
Justice
   "Protector of the People." Name for *Athena* and *Artemis* at Sparta. Alternate form: Agoraia. [Bell 1991; Leach 1972]

Agoraia   See *Agoraea*.

Agraea   See *Agrotera*.

Agraulids, The   See *The Augralids*.

Agraulos
Grecian
Creator of Life; Agriculture; Weather; Unhappiness; Magic
   1) Goddess of the "dew." She is responsible for agricultural fertility. Sister of *Herse, Pandrosos*, and Erysichthon. One of the *Augralids* of Attica. Daughter of Cecrops and the son of *Gaea* who was half serpent, half man.

⚕ *Agraulos had a sister named Herse. The god Hermes came to visit Herse. Agraulos, jealous of her sister, tried to interfere with his visit by refusing to move out of his way. Hermes was very angry and turned Agraulos into stone.*

   2) Also the name of a daughter of the first king of Athens, Actaeus, who was the mother of *Herse, Pandrosos*, Erysichthon, and the above Agraulos. [Bell 1991; Leach 1992; Zimmerman 1964]

Agrotera
Grecian
Hunting and Wild Animals; Mother and Guardian; Health and Healing
   Name for *Artemis* as the hunter. Protector of the young and of good health. A temple to her at Agrae contains a statue of her carrying a bow. Alternate forms: Agraea, Agrotora. [Bell 1991; Jobes 1962; Leach 1992]

Agrotora   See *Agrotera*.

Aidos
Grecian
Unhappiness
   "Shame." A companion of *Nemesis*. [Leach 1992]

Aigina   See *Aegina*.

Aigle
Grecian
1) Unknown; 2) Mother and Guardian; Earth and Nature; 3) Unhappiness; Magic; 4) Health and Healing; 5) Beauty and Charisma
   1) Daughter of *Panope*. *Aegle* is the Latinized spelling of her name. Equivalent to *Phoebe*. 2) One of the three *Hesperides* who guarded the Golden Apples. 3) One of the *Heliadae*. 4) The youngest daughter of Asclepius, god of medicine, and sister of *Hygeia, Iaso*, and *Panacea*. 5) One of the three *Charites*. Alternate forms: Aegle, Aegilae.

⚕ *Aigle changed herself into a willow tree after hearing the pitiable prayers of Orpheus.* [Bell 1991; Jobes 1962; Leach 1992; Redfield 1931; Zimmerman 1964]

Aither   See *Aether*.

Aithuia
Grecian
Wild Birds
   "Diver" or "Water-hen." Name for *Athena* and possibly the name of an earlier goddess who was later merged with Athena. [Jobes 1962]

Akaste   See *Acaste*.

Akeso
Grecian
Health and Healing
   "Healer." Daughter of Asclepius, she is associated with her sisters *Panacea* and *Iaso* [Leach 1992]

Akhuvitr
Roman; Etruscan
Unknown
   Deity. Alternate form: Akhvizer. [Cooper 1876]

Akhvizer   See *Akhuvitr.*

Akraia
Grecian
Earth and Nature
   "Goddess of Hilltops." Name for *Hera.* [Leach 1992]

Alala
Grecian
War
   "Battle Cry." Goddess of war. [Leach 1992]

Alalcomenia   See *Alalkomenia.*

Alalcomene
Grecian
Justice
   "War Cry" and "Long Hair." Name for *Athena* possibly
derived from the Boeotian village of Alalcomenae where she
was born. Also a name for *Hera.* [Bell 1991; Zimmerman
1964]

Alalkomenia
Boeotia
Earth and Nature
   Earth goddess. One of the *Praxidicae.* Sister of *Thelxinoea*
and *Aulis.* Alternate form: Alalcomenia. [Bell 1991; Leach
1992; Zimmerman 1964]

Albina
Grecian; Roman; Etruscan
1) Domesticated Animals; 2) Sun and Day; Dawn and
Twilight; Love and Sexuality
   "White Goddess." 1) A white sow goddess similiar to the
Celtic *Cerridwen.* See also *Alphito.* 2) An Etruscan light and
dawn goddess. Protector of ill-fated lovers. [Jobes 1962;
Leach 1992]

Albuna
Roman
Fate
   A prophetic nymph or priestess. See also *Nymphs.*
Alternate form: Albunea. [Wedeck and Baskin 1971;
Zimmerman 1964]

Albunea   See *Albuna.*

Alceste   See *Alcestis.*

Alcestis
Grecian
Selflessness; Immortality; Courage
   One of the *Pleiades,* daughter of *Anaxibia* and Pelias,
sister of *Amphinome, Asteropeia, Euadne, Hippothoe,*
Medusa, Peisidic, Pelopeia, and Acastus.
   ♀♀ *Alcestis took poison and died to keep her husband, Admetus,*
   ♀♀ *alive. The Fates granted him immortality as long as he could*
      find a family member to die in his place. Alcestis was
returned from Hades by Persephone or Heracles.
   Alternate form: Alceste. [Bell 1991; Jobes 1962; Senior 1985;
Woodcock 1953; Zimmerman 1964]

Alcimache
Grecian
1) War; 2) Earth and Nature
   "Defender in Battle." 1) Name for *Athena.* 2) Name of one
of the *Maenades.* [Bell 1991]

Alcippe
Grecian
Domesticated Animals; Justice; Love and Sexuality
   "Mighty Mare." Daughter of *Agraulos,* mother of
Daedalus.
   ♀♀ *Alcippe was raped by a son of Poseidon. Her father, Ares, killed*
   ♀♀ *Halirrhotius and was brought before the court of the gods and*
      acquitted. [Bell 1991; Evans 1904; Zimmerman 1964]

Alcis
Macedonia
Physical Prowess
   "The Strong." Name for *Athena* in Macedonia.. [Bell 1991]

Alcmena
Grecian
Family and Tribes; Immortality; Ceremonies
   Ancestor of the Heraclid dynasty. Daughter of *Anaxo* and
mother of Hercules by Zeus. She was mortal when
impregnated by Zeus but was later worshiped as a goddess.
   ♀♀ *When Alcmena died, Zeus had her body removed from the*
   ♀♀ *coffin, leaving a stone in its place. She was taken to the Isles*
      of the Blessed, where she was brought back to life. The stone
that had been left in her place was set in a sacred grove at Thebes
that became a place of worship.
   Alternate forms: Acleme, Alkmene, Electryone, Mideatis.
[Bell 1991; Savill 1977; Zimmerman 1964]

Alcyone
Grecian
Unhappiness; Love and Sexuality; Magic; Water; Wild Birds
   One of the *Pleiades,* daughter of *Pleione* and Atlas. Also
the name of a daughter of *Enarete* or *Aegiale* and Aeolus who
is a member of the family from which the Greek royal houses
Magnesia, Corinthia, Boeotia, Elis, Messenia, and Phocis
sprang. See also *Seven Sisters,* North America. Alternate
forms: Aeolis, Cleopatra, Halcyon, Halcyone.
[Bell 1991; Redfield 1931; Wedeck and Baskin 1971;
Woodcock 1953; Zimmerman 1964]

Alea
Arcadia
Unknown
   Name for *Athena.* She was worshiped in Alea, Mantineia,
and Tegea. [Bell 1991; Leach 1972]

Alecto
Grecian
Justice; Ugliness
   "Vengeance," "Never-ending." One of the three *Erinyes.*
Along with *Megaera* and *Tisiphone,* she pursues lawbreakers
until their punishment is deemed satisfactory. If the punishment
has not been adequate in life, she follows them into death.
With snakes coiled in her hair and carrying a torch and whip.
She plays a prominent role in the Aeneid, where she terrifies
Turnus in a dream and causes him to make war against the
Aeneidae. Alternate form: Allekto. [Bell 1991; Cotterell 1979;
Leach 1992; Savill 1977; Woodcock 1953; Zimmerman 1964]

Alectrona
Grecian
Unknown
   Daughter of the sun. [Monaghan 1981]

Aletheia   See *Alethia.*

Alethia
Grecian
Justice

"Truth." Daughter of Zeus. Known as *Veritas* in Rome. Alternate form: Aletheia. [Leach 1992; Zimmerman 1964]

Aletis   See *Erigone.*

Alexida
Grecian
Health and Healing
   "Healer." Daughter of Amphiaraos. She protects her followers from epilepsy. The *Elasii* were her descendents. [Bell 1991; Leach 1992]

Alexirrhoe
Grecian
Earth and Nature
   Nymph and daughter of the Granicus river god. See also *Nymphs.* [Bell 1991]

Algea
Grecian
Unhappiness
   "Pain and Sorrow." Daughter of *Eris.* One of the *Androktiasi.* Alternate form: Algia. [Bell 1991; Jobes 1962; Leach 1992]

Algia   See *Algea.*

Alimede
Grecian
Water; Fate; Beauty
   One of the *Nereides.* Daughter of Nereus and *Doris.* [Bell 1991; Leach 1992]

Alkmene   See *Alcmena.*

Allekto   See *Alecto.*

Alma
Roman
Unknown
   Later name for *Venus.* [Bell 1991]

Alma Mammosa   See *Ceres.*

Alpan
Roman; Etruscan
Unknown
   One of the *Lasas.* She is attendant to *Turan,* similar to the *Charites.* [Cooper 1876]

Alpanu
Roman; Etruscan
Unknown
   Associated with *Akhuvitr* and *Thanr.* Her attendant is *Sipna.* Alternate form: Alpnu. [Cooper 1876]

Alpnu   See *Alpanu.*

Alphaea
Grecian
Unknown
   Name for *Artemis* derived from Alpheius, the river god. Alpheius was captivated by *Artemis* and pursued her relentlessly. [Bell 1991]

Alpheias
Sicily
Water
   Nymph who inhabits the Sicilian fountain of *Arethusa.* See also *Nymphs.* [Bell 1991]

Alphito
Grecian
Agriculture
   "White Goddess." Goddess of barley. She lives on a cliff top in never-ending snow in Argos. See also *Albina.* Alternate form: Cerdo. [Graves 1948; Jobes 1962]

Alseides, The
Grecian
Earth and Nature
   Nymphs of forests, groves, and glens. See also *Nymphs.* [Bell 1991]

Altria
Roman; Etruscan
Unknown
   Goddess. [Cooper 1876]

Amalthea
Grecian
Magic; Stars and Planets; Water
   A Greek nymph of springs, associated with Apollo. *Aega* is Amalthea's human personification. See also *Nymphs.* Alternate form: Amaltheia. [Bell 1991; Chicago 1979; Leach 1972; Leach 1992; Redfield 1931; Wedeck and Baskin 1971]

Amaltheia   See *Amalthea.*

Amathaon   See *Amathaounta.*

Amathaounta
Grecian
Water; Family and Tribes
   Sea goddess of the Aegean who was imported from the Near East. In Samaria, she was worshiped as *Ashmia* (see Near East). She founded tribes in both Syria and Palestine. Alternate form: Amathaon. [Jobes 1962; Sykes 1968; Wedeck and Baskin 1971]

Amatheia
Grecian
Unknown
   One of the *Nereides.* [Bell 1991]

Amathuntia   See *Amathusia.*

Amathusia
Grecian
Unknown
   Name for *Aphrodite* when worshiped at Amathus on Cyprus. Alternate name: *Amathuntia.* [Bell 1991]

Ambologera
Grecian
Immortality
   "Delaying Old Age." Name for *Aphrodite* at Sparta. [Bell 1991]

Ambrosia
Grecian
Stars and Planets
   Star goddess. One of the *Hyades,* who bring storms. Daughter of *Aethra* and Atlas. [Bell 1991; Leach 1992]

Ambulia
Grecian
Immortality
   "Goddess Who Delays Death." Name for *Artemis* at Sparta and a name for *Athena.* [Bell 1991]

Amica
Roman
Unknown
   Name for *Venus*. [Woodcock 1953]

Amnisiades, The
Grecian
Water; Hunting and Wild Animals
   Nymphs of the Amnisus River. Attendants of *Artemis,* they care for her sacred deer. See also *Nymphs.* [Bell 1991]

Amphictyonis
Grecian
Justice; Ceremonies
   Name for *Demeter* at Anthela. Offerings were made to her at the opening of the meetings of the amphictyons of Thermopylae. [Bell 1991]

Amphilogea
Grecian
Unknown
   One of the *Androktiasi,* daughter of *Eris.* [Jobes 1962; Leach 1992]

Amphinome
Grecian
1)Water; Fate; Beauty; 2) Stars and Planets; Magic; 3) Water
   1) One of the *Nereides.* 2)Name of one of the *Pleiades.* 3) One of the *Oceanides.* [Bell 1991; Leach 1992]

Amphiro
Grecian
Water
   "Flowing Water." An *Oceanid.* Daughter of *Tethys* and Oceanus. [Leach 1992]

Amphissa   See *Metope.*

Amphithoe
Grecian
Water; Fate; Beauty
   One of the *Nereides.* Alternate form: Ampithoe. [Bell 1991; Leach 1992]

Amphitrite
Grecian
Water; Weather; Fishing and Water Animals; Fate; Beauty
   "The Mediterranean Sea." As daughter of Nereus and *Doris,* she is one of the *Nereides.* She is the wife of Poseidon, mother of Triton and *Rhode.* She is often depicted with crab claws on her forehead and a fishing net covering her hair. She is responsible for the foaming waves and for sea monsters. She can calm the winds and the sea. Equivalent to the Roman *Salacia.* Alternate form: Halsodyne. [Bell 1991; Jobes 1962; Leach 1992; Neumann 1972; Woodcock 1953; Zimmerman 1964]

Ampithoe   See *Amphithoe.*

Amymone
Grecian
Earth and Nature
   An early Earth goddess. [Bell 1991; Jobes 1962; Zimmerman 1964]

Anadyomene
Grecian
Water
   Name for *Aphrodite* as she rose from the ocean. [Bell 1991; Jobes 1962]

Anagke   See *Ananke.*

Anaea   See *Anaitis.*

Anagtia
Roman; Oscan
Health and Healing
   Goddess of healing. Member of the Roman pantheon. Alternate forms: Anagtia Diiva, Angitia. [Avery 1962; Jayne 1925]

Anagtia Diiva   See *Anagtia.*

Anaitis
Grecian
Creator of Life
   Asiatic goddess worshiped in Greece. She represents the creative powers of nature. She is identified by Greek writers with *Aphrodite* and *Artemis.* See also *Anthrathi,* Egypt. Alternate forms: Anaea, Aneitis, Nanaea, Tanais. [Bell 1991]

Ananke
Grecian
Fate
   "Necessity" or "Fate." Daughter of *Nyx* and Erebus. She controls the destiny of the world and its occupants. Some say she was the mother of the *Moirae.* Her Roman counterpart is *Fatum,* although some scholars say Ananke is the name for *Necessitas.* Euripides called her "the most powerful of all the deities." Alternate form: Anagke. [Bell 1991; Graves 1948; Leach 1992; Redfield 1931]

Anatole
Grecian
Time; Order
   One of the *Horae.* [Bell 1991]

Anaxarete
Grecian
Magic; Love and Sexuality; Unhappiness; Justice
   Greek princess/goddess.
   Anaxarete was loved by Iphis but felt only scorn for him. He was devastated by her rejection and committed suicide. Venus punished her by turning her to stone.
   The same story is told about *Arsinoe* and Arceophon. [Bell 1991; Jobes 1962; Zimmerman 1964]

Anaxibia
Grecian
Unknown
   Mother of the *Peliades* by Pelias. [Bell 1991]

Anaxiroe
Grecian
Unknown
   Mother of *Hermione.* [Bell 1991]

Anaxo
Grecian
Unknown
   Mother of *Alcmena.* [Bell 1991; Zimmerman 1964]

Anceta
Roman; Paelignian
Health and Healing
   Goddess of healing. Member of the Roman pantheon. She is identified with Angitia. [Jayne 1925]

Anchiale
Grecian
Earth and Nature
1) Nymph. Mother of the Idean *Dactyls*. Anchiale threw dust into a cave in Crete where Zeus was reared, creating the *Dactyls*. 2) Phrygian nymph. Mount Ida is named for her. 3) A nymph who cared for Zeus. See also *Nymphs*. Alternate form: Ida. [Bell 1991]

Anchinoe See *Achiroe*.

Anchiroe
Grecian
Water
Daughter of the river god Eranisus. [Bell 1991]

Androctasia
Grecian
Unknown
"Slaughter." Her name also appears in the plural, *Androktiasi*. Daughter (or daughters) of *Eris*. [Jobes 1962; Leach 1992]

Androktiasi, The
Grecian
Unknown
Daughters of *Eris*. They are *Algea, Amphilogea, Androctasia, Dysnomia,* and *Phonos.* They may also include *Ate.* [Jobes 1962; Leach 1992]

Andromeda
Grecian
Family and Tribes; Beauty; Unhappiness; Magic; Water; Stars and Planets
"Chained Lady" of astronomy. Ancestor of important royal lines. Daughter of *Cassiopeia* and Cepheus. Wife of Perseus. *Cassiopeia bragged that Andromeda was more beautiful than the Nereides. This angered Poseidon, and he caused the land to be flooded and sent a sea monster to destroy ships. To stop these catastrophes, Andromeda was chained to a rock as an offering to the sea monster. Perseus saved her by turning the monster to stone. She was later placed in the heavens as a constellation.* [Bell 1991; Evans 1904; Woodcock 1953; Zimmerman 1964]

Aneitis See *Anaitis*.

Anemotis
Grecian
Weather
"Subduer of Winds." Name for *Athena* at Methone, Messenia. [Bell 1991]

Anesidora
Grecian
Goodness
"Sender of Gifts." Name for *Demeter, Gaea,* and *Pandora.* [Bell 1991; Monaghan 1981]

Angelos
Grecian
Unknown
Name for *Artemis* at Sparta and, according to some scholars, the original name of *Hecate.* [Bell 1991]

Angerona
Roman
Unhappiness; Time; Ceremonies; Order; Mother and Guardian
"Silence." Goddess of fear and anguish, which she can produce or relieve. Her early form was probably as goddess of the winter solstice. Later statues show her with her mouth bound or a finger to her lips; the interpretation is that she is guarding a secret, probably the secret name of Rome. Her sacred day, *Angeronalia,* is December 12. Alternate forms: Angeronia, Volupia. [Bell 1991; Carlyon 1982; Evans 1904; Jayne 1925; Jobes 1962; Leach 1992; Woodcock 1953]

Angeronia See *Angerona*.

Angina
Roman
Health and Healing
Goddess of health. Invoked to cure sore throats. [Jayne 1925]

Angitia
Roman
Health and Healing; Magic
Goddess of healing. She is skilled in the use of medicinal plants and antidotes for poison. She can cure people of venomous snake bites and can kill serpents with incantations. The forest of Angitia near Lake Fucinus is named for her. She may be of Greek origin. She is identified with *Anceta* and is equivalent to *Bona Dea*. Alternate forms: Anagtia, Anguitia, Diiva. [Bell 1991; Jayne 1925; Wedeck and Baskin 1971]

Anguitia See *Angitia*.

Anieros
Grecian
Unknown
Goddess of autumn. Mother of *Axiokersa*. Anieros is a name given in Greece during Roman times to a goddess who resembles *Demeter*. Hers was an ancient religion in Asia Minor. [Durdin-Robertson 1982; Monaghan 1981]

Anigriades, The See *Anigrides*.

Anigrides, The
Grecian
Health and Healing; Water
"Healers." These nymphs inhabit warm sulfur springs in a grotto near the mouth of the Anigrus River in Elis. They cure skin diseases. See also *Nymphs*. Alternate form: Anigriades. [Bell 1991; Jayne 1925]

Anima Mundi
Roman
Immortality
"Soul of the World." Name for a Roman Gnostic being. [Monaghan 1981]

Anippe
Grecian
Water
Daughter of the Nile river god. [Bell 1991]

Anna Perenna
Roman
Health and Healing; Wealth; Happiness; Ceremonies; Moon and Night; Fate
"Giver of Life, Health, and Abundance." Also a moon and fate goddess. As Anna, she is a feminine personification of the year (New Year) and as Perenna (Old Year), she is a personification of the endless procession of the years. Some scholars suggest she was an earlier Etruscan goddess. Her festival on March 15 welcomes spring with joyfulness and merriment. Identified with Greek *Themis* and *Anu*, Western Europe. [Bell 1991; Durdin-Robertson 1982; Graves 1948; Jayne 1925; Wedeck and Baskin 1971]

Antaea
Grecian
Unknown
Name for *Cybele, Demeter,* and *Rhea.* May signify "a goddess whom people may approach in prayers." [Avery 1962; Bell 1991]

Anteia
Grecian
Dawn and Twilight
"Light." She is the dusk that follows the setting sun. This phenomenon is often explained in mythology as attempts to destroy the sun. Her daughters by Proetus are *Iphinoe, Iphianassa, Lysippe,* and *Maera.* Some scholars consider *Calaene, Elege, Hipponoe* to be daughters as well. See also *Anticleia.* Alternate forms: Antia, Stheneboea. [Bell 1991; Jobes 1962; Zimmerman 1964]

Antevorta
Roman
Mother and Guardian; Fate; Moon and Night
Goddess of childbirth. One of the *Camenae.* She has the ability to see into the past and reminds people of what happened before. She is said to represent the waning moon. She was possibly an attribute of *Carmentis,* who subsequently became known as a separate deity. See also *Postvorta.* [Bell 1991; Leach 1992]

Anthea   See *Antheia.*

Anthedon
Boeotia
Earth and Nature
Nymph. She gave the Boeotian town of Anthedon her name. See also *Nymphs.* [Bell 1991]

Antheia
Grecian
Earth and Nature
"Flowering One." Name for *Hera* at Argos. Also a name for *Aphrodite* at Cnossus (Knossos, Crete). Alternate form: Anthea. [Avery 1962; Bell 1991; Monaghan 1981]

Anthracia
Grecian
Earth and Nature
An Arcadian nymph. Possibly a nurse of Zeus. See also *Nymphs.* [Bell 1991]

Anticleia
Grecian
Dawn and Twilight
"Dusk." The personification of the light that "flushes" the sun from the sky. Like many women of Greek religion, this name appears in a variety of stories and a variety of times and probably refers to several different women. See also *Anteia.* [Bell 1991; Jobes 1962]

Antigone
Grecian
Dawn and Twilight; Love and Sexuality; Unhappiness
Goddess of light at dusk who follows the sun to his death. [Bell 1991; Chicago 1979; Jobes 1962; Senior 1985; Woodcock 1953; Zimmerman 1964]

Antinoe
Grecian
Fate; Family and Tribes
1) One of the *Peliades.* 2) A daughter of Cepheus and sister of *Sterope.* [Bell 1991]

Antioche
Grecian
Unknown
Mother of *Iole* by Eurytus. Alternate form: Antiope. [Bell 1991]

Antiope
Grecian
1) Dawn and Twilight; 2) Dawn and Twilight; Earth and Nature
"Dawn." 1) Daughter of Aeolus. Mother of Boeotus, Aeolus, and Hellen by Poseidon. 2) Nymph who was the mother of nine daughters by Pierus.

Pierus encouraged his daughters to enter a contest with the Muses. His daughters lost and were metamorphosed into different kinds of birds.

See also *Nymphs.* Alternate forms: Antioche, Menstro. [Bell 1991; Chicago 1979; Evans 1904; Jobes 1962; Senior 1985; Zimmerman 1964]

Anucis   See Egyptian *Anka.*

Aoede
Grecian
Arts
One of the original *Muses.* Her name signifies one of the strings on a three-stringed lyre. [Bell 1991; Woodcock 1953]

Aonides, The
Grecian
Arts; Sciences; Intelligence and Creativity; Evil
Name for the *Muses* in Aonia. [Woodcock 1953]

Apanchomene
Grecian
Unknown
"The Strangled Goddess." Name of *Artemis* at Caphyae. [Bell 1991]

Apaturia
Grecian
Evil
"The Deceitful." Name for *Athena* and a name for *Aphrodite* at Phanagoreia. [Leach 1972]

Aphaia   See *Aphaea.*

Aphaea
Grecian
Water; Demi-animals; Moon and Night
"Lady of the Beasts." Associated with fish pools, she appears as a mermaid on the islands of Crete and Aegina. Possibly a moon goddess, this is the name of *Britomartis* on Aegina. Alternate form: Aphaia. [Bell 1991; Jobes 1962; Leach 1992; Neumann 1972]

Aphacitis   See *Aphrodite.*

Aphrodite
Grecian
Mother and Guardian; Fate; War; Sky and Heavens; Beauty; Love and
   Sexuality
"Foam." One of the twelve Olympian divinities. Mother of *Beroe.* Originally an ancient mother goddess of the Eastern Mediterranean islands, she was revered as a multifaceted deity with special powers of prophesy and battle. Known as the *Queen of Heaven* by the Phoenicians (see Near East), she was introduced to Greece during the Greek colonization of Canaan. In their attempt to assimilate this complex goddess,

the Greeks converted her into the personification of physical beauty. Plato gave her two names, thereby splitting her persona: *Urania,* who represented spiritual love, and Aphrodite Pandemos, who represented sexual love.

⑂ *Aphrodite's overwhelming passion was for Adonis. However, she had to share this dying-and-rising god with Persephone, the queen of the dead. To settle their dispute, Zeus ruled that for one third of the year, Adonis was to dwell by himself, for another third with Persephone, and for the remaining third with Alphrodite.*

She is equivalent to Roman *Venus; Aslik,* Near East; *Biducht,* Near East; and is identified with *Genetyllis,* Roman *Marica,* Sabine *Nerine,* and Etruscan *Turan.* See also *Isthar,* Near East; *Branwen,* Western Europe. Alternate forms: Acidalia, Acraea, Aegophaga, Amathuntia, Amathusia, Ambologera, Anadyomene, Anaitis, Androphonos, Antheia, Apaturia, Aphacitis, Apostrophia, Aracynthias, Areia, Argennis, Callipygos, Cnidia, Colias, Ctesylla, Cypria, Cypris, Cyprigeneia, Cyprogenes, Cythera, Delia, Despoena, Dionaea, Epistrophia, Epitragia, Epitymbia, Erycina, Euploia, Hecaerge, Hippodameia, Idalia, Kypris, Kythereia, Limenia, Machanitis, Melaenis, Melinaea, Migonitis, Morpho, Nymphaea, Pandemos, Paphia, Pasiphae, Peitho, Pelagia, Philia, Pontia, Scotia, Urania, Zephyritis, Zerynthia. [Bell 1991; Bolen 1984; Carlyon 1982; Cotterell 1989; Harding 1971; Johnson 1988; Leach 1992; Monaghan 1981; Stone 1979; Zimmerman 1964]

Apollonis
Grecian
Arts; Sciences; Intelligence and Creativity; Evil
One of the three *Muses* at Delphi, sister of *Borysthenis* and *Cephisso.* [Bell 1991]

Apostrophia
Grecian
Selflessness; Magic
"The Expeller" or "The Rejecter." Name for *Aphrodite* at Thebes. She expels lust and carnal memories from men's minds. Alternate form: Apotrophia. [Bell 1991]

Apotrophia   See *Apostrophia.*

Appiades, The
Roman
Water
Nymphs of the Appian Spring in Rome. Also said to refer to the five deities *Concordia, Minerva, Pax, Venus,* and *Vesta.* See also *Nymphs.* [Bell 1991; Zimmerman 1964]

Appias
Roman
Water
Nymph who inhabits the fountain in the Forum of Rome. Name for *Minerva.* See also *Nymphs.* [Leach 1992]

Apseudes
Grecian
Water; Fate; Beauty
One of the *Nereides.* [Bell 1991; Leach 1992]

Apteros
Grecian
Unknown
"The Wingless." Name for *Nice* at Athens. [Bell 1991]

Ara   See *Arai.*

Aracynthias   See *Aphrodite.*

Arae   See *Arai.*

Arai
Grecian
Destroyer of Life; Justice
Deities of destruction and revenge. They perform the same function as the *Erinyes,* but are distinct from them. They have been confused with the *Erinyes* and the *Eumenides.* The Latin spelling is *Arae* and the singular is *Ara.* [Bell 1991; Jobes 1962]

Arantides, The   See *Erinyes.*

Arcadian
Grecian
Earth and Nature; Hunting and Wild Animals
"Chaste Hunter and Goddess of Nymphs." Name for *Artemis.* [Jobes 1962]

Arce
Grecian
Unknown
Sister of *Iris* and the *Harpies,* daughter of *Electra* and Thaumas. [Avery 1962]

Arche
Grecian
Arts; Sciences; Creativity and Intelligence; Evil
"Beginning." One of the four *Muses.* [Bell 1991]

Archiroe   See *Achiroe.*

Ardalides, The
Grecian
Arts; Sciences; Creativity and Intelligence; Evil
Name for the *Muses* at Troezen. Alternate form: Ardaliotides. [Bell 1991]

Ardaliotides   See *The Ardalides.*

Area   See *Areia.*

Areia
Grecian
War
"The Warlike." Name for *Athena, Aphrodite,* and *Artemis.* Alternate form: Area. [Avery 1962; Bell 1991; Leach 1972]

Areta   See *Arete.*

Arete
Grecian
Justice
"Virtuous Rule." Goddess of Justice. Wife of Alcinous, king of the Phaeacians.

⑂ *The Colchians landed on Scheria demanding Medea. Alcinous said he would give her to them if she and Jason were not married. Arete warned the lovers, and they were quickly married, preventing the Colchians from taking Medea.*

Alternate form: Areta. [Bell 1991; Jobes 1962; Zimmerman 1964]

Arethusa
Grecian
1) Water; Fate; Beauty; 2) Mother and Guardian; Earth and Nature
1) A *Nereid.* She is said to inspire pastoral poetry and is an attendant to *Artemis.*

⑂ *The river god, Alpheius, fell in love with Arethusa. She was not interested in him, but he pursued her continuously. She asked Artemis to help her, and Artemis changed her into a spring. When Alpheius returned to his river form and attempted to mingle his water with Arethusa's spring, Artemis intervened again and carried Arethusa through an underground passage all the way to Ortygia, an island off the coast of Sicily.*

2) One of the *Hesperides,* a daughter of Abas, for whom the springs at Chalcis and Euboea were probably named. [Bell 1991; Jobes 1962; Leach 1992; Woodcock 1953; Zimmerman 1964]

Arge
Grecian

1) Hunting and Wild Animals; 2) Earth and Nature

1) A hunter who was changed into a deer by Apollo. 2) A nymph, daughter of *Hera.* See also *Nymphs.* [Bell 1991; Zimmerman 1964]

Argeia
Grecian

1) Unknown; 2) Water

1) Name for *Hera* at Argos. 2) Name of one of the *Oceanides.* [Bell 1991]

Argennis   See *Aphrodite.*

Argimpasa
Grecian

Love and Sexuality; Family and Tribes; Order

Scythian goddess of love, marriage, and harmony. Similar to *Aphrodite* as Aphrodite Urania. [Leach 1992]

Argiope
Grecian

1) Earth and Nature; 2) Water

1) A Parnassian nymph. 2) Name of a daughter of the Nile river god. See also *Nymphs.* [Bell 1991; Leach 1992; Zimmerman 1964]

Argyra
Grecian

Water

Water nymph. She inhabits the spring at Achaja (Achaia). See also *Nymphs.* [Bell 1991; Leach 1992]

Aria   See *Furies.*

Ariadne
Grecian

Love and Sexuality; Creator of Life; Mother and Guardian

Goddess of love and fertility on the island of Crete. Daughter of the second Minos, king of Crete, sister of *Acacalis* and *Phaedra.* According to some, the wife of Dionysus. She also spent a lot of time with Theseus, by whom she had several children.

♁ *Ariadne gave Theseus a ball of string to unwind when he went into the labyrinth to kill the Minotaur. After he had successfully destroyed the Minotaur, he followed the unwound string back to the entrance. He and Ariadne then fled from Crete, taking with them the seven boys and seven girls who had been sent as victims to appease the Minotaur.*

Originally a strong Minoan goddess, her power was later greatly diminished when she became considered human, not divine. Alternate forms: Aridela, Minoid. [Bell 1991; Hultkrantz 1983; Leach 1992; Lurker 1984; Senior 1985; Woodcock 1953; Zimmerman 1964]

Aricina
Grecian

Unknown

Name for *Artemis.* It is derived from the town of Aricia in Latium, Italy. [Bell 1991]

Aridela   See *Ariadne.*

Ariste
Grecian

Unknown

"The Best." Name for *Artemis* at Athens. [Bell 1991]

Aristobule
Grecian

Education and Knowledge

"The Best Adviser." Name for *Artemis* at Athens. [Bell 1991]

Armata
Roman

Unknown

Name for *Venus* in Sparta. [Woodcock 1953]

Arne
Grecian

Unknown

Daughter of Aeolus, king of winds.

♁ *Aeolus banished Arne from his kingdom, and she became a lover of Poseidon. She was the mother of twins, Boeotus and Aeolus, by Poseidon.* [Bell 1991]

Arrhippe
Grecian

Hunting and Wild Animals

Hunter and attendant of *Artemis* on Mount Carmanor in Lydia. [Bell 1991]

Arsinoe
Grecian

1) Unhappiness; 2) Mother and Guardian

1) Daughter of Phegeus, king of Psophis in Arcadia.

♁ *Her husband was Alcmaeon, who deserted her and was killed by her brothers. One source says she in turn was killed (another says that she was sold by her brothers as a slave) because she was angry about the murder of her unfaithful husband.*

See also *Anaxarete.* 2) Name of a nurse of Orestes. She was able to prevent his murder by sneaking him out of the palace. [Bell 1991; Jobes 1962; Zimmerman 1964]

Artemis
Grecian

Moon and Night; Earth and Nature; Hunting and Wild Animals; Mother and Guardian; War

Virgin moon goddess, nature goddess, goddess of the hunt and of childbirth. She is also the warrior goddess of the Amazons. She is the daughter of *Leto* and Zeus. She is a tree, a bear, the moon, a nymph, and the "Lady of Beasts." The most complex of the twelve Olympian deities, Artemis has come to represent the variable energies of the feminine psyche. She evolved from earlier Mediterranean and Eastern deities, including *Atargatis,* Near East, and is equivalent to *Artio,* Western Europe, and *Diana. Saint Artemidos,* Near East, is the Christianized Artemis. She is identified with *Bendis, Britomartis, Eileithyia, Genetyllis,* and *Tauropolis.* See also *Nymphs.* Alternate forms: Acraea, Aeginaea, Aetole, Agoraea, Agrotera, Alphaea, Ambulia, Anaitis, Angelos, Apanchomene, Arcadian, Areia, Aricina, Ariste, Aristobule, Astrateia, Brauronia, Calliste, Caryatis, Cedreatis, Chitone, Cnagia, Colaenis, Condyleates, Cordaca, Coryphaea, Corythallia, Curotrophos, Cynthia, Daphnaea, Delia, Delphinia, Derrhiatis, Diana, Dictynna, Elaphios, Ephesia, Eucleia, Eurynome, Gaeeochos, Hecaerge, Hegemone, Hemeresia, Heurippe, Hymnia, Iphigeneia, Issoria, Kaukasis, Laphria, Letogeneia, Leucophryne, Limenia, Limnaea, Limnatis, Locheia, Loxo, Lyceia, Lycoatis, Lygodesma,

Lysizona, Meleagrian, Melissa, Munychia, Mysia, Oenoatis, Opis, Orthia, Ortygia, Paedotrophus, Partheria, Peitho, Pheraea, Phoebe, Phosphoros, Pitanatis, Polymastus, Potamia, Pyronia, Saronia, Sarpedonia, Savior, Soteira, Stymphalia, Tauro, Tauropolis, Thermaia, Thoantea, Triclaria, Upis. [Avery 1962; Bell 1992; Chicago 1979; Jobes 1962; Leach 1992; Stone 1979]

Artimpasa
Grecian
Unknown
  "Noble Lady." Scythian goddess similiar to Roman *Venus*. [Cooper 1876]

Ashima   See *Amathaounta*.

Asia
Grecian
1) Unknown; 2) Water; 3) Water; Fate; Beauty
  1) Name for *Athena* in Colchis. 2) Name of one of the *Oceanides*, a daughter of *Tethys* and Oceanus. Considered by some to be the mother of Atlas, Prometheus, Epimetheus, and Menoitios. Asia may have been named for her. 3) One of the *Nereides*, daughter of *Doris* and Nereus. [Bell 1991; Leach 1992]

Asine
Grecian
Unknown
  Daughter of *Sparta* and Lacedaemon. Sister of *Eurydice* and Amyclas. Three towns in the Peloponnesus bore her name. [Bell 1991]

Asopo
Grecian
Arts; Science; Intelligence and Creativity; Evil
  One of the seven *Muses*. [Bell 1991; Leach 1992]

Assaros
Grecian
Mother and Guardian; Family and Tribes
  Mother goddess. Ancestor of the first triad of Greco-Babylonian male deities. [Cooper 1876]

Asseneth
  Equivalent to *As-neit*, Egypt. [Durdin-Robertson 1975]

Assesia
Grecian
Unknown
  Name for *Athena* at Assesus in Ionia. [Bell 1991]

Asteria
Grecian
1) Love and Sexuality; 2) Stars and Planets; Magic
  1) Titan goddess. Inhabitant of Olympus. Daughter of *Phoebe* and Coeus, sister of *Leto*, mother of *Hecate*.
  ♉ *Asteria was pursued by Zeus even though she was married to Perses. To escape from Zeus, she changed into a quail. When this attempt was unsuccessful, she dove into the sea, where she became the island of Asteria (Delos).*
  2) One of the *Pleiades*. See also *Asterodeia*. [Bell 1991; Zimmerman 1964]

Asterodeia
Grecian
1) Moon and Night; 2) Earth and Nature
  1) Possibly a moon goddess. 2) A nymph. See also *Nymphs*. Alternate forms: Asteria, Asterodia. [Bell 1991; Jobes 1962]

Asterodia   See *Asterodeia*.

Asterope
Grecian
1) Stars and Planets; Magic; 2) Water; 3) Water
  1) One of the *Pleiades*. 2) One of the *Oceanides*.
3) Asterope, who is sometimes called *Hesperia*, is the daughter of Cebren, a river god. [Bell 1991; Zimmerman 1964]

Asteropeia
Grecian
Stars and Planets; Magic
  One of the *Peliades*. Sister of *Amphinome, Euadne, Hippothoe, Medusa, Peisidice, Pelopeia*, and Acastus. [Bell 1991]

Astraea
Grecian
Selflessness; Justice; Stars and Planets
  "Innocence, Perfection, and Justice." Daughter of *Themis* and Zeus.
  ♉ *Seeing humans become more corrupt, Astraea retreated to the heavens, where she lives in the constellation Virgo.*
  Alternate form: Astrea. [Bell 1991; Leach 1992; Redfield 1931]

Astrea   See *Astraea*.

Astrateia
Grecian
War
  "Invasion Stopper." Name for *Artemis* in Laconia. [Bell 1991]

Astyageia
Grecian
Unknown
  Daughter of *Creusa* and Hypseus. Sister of *Alcaea, Cyrene*, and *Themisto*. [Bell 1991]

Atae   See *Ate*.

Atalanta
Grecian
Hunting and Wild Animals; Water
  Huntress. Mentioned as Arcadian and Boeotian, it is not clear whether there are one or two Atalantas. She may have been one of the Argonauts. A spring near the ruins of Cyphanta in Laconia was thought to have gushed forth when Atalanta struck a rock with her spear. Alternate form: Atalante. [Bell 1991; Chicago 1979; Redfield 1931; Woodcock 1953; Zimmerman 1964]

Atalante   See *Atalanta*.

Ate
Grecian
Disorder; Justice
  "Discord." Banned from Olympus because of the trouble she caused, Ate fell to Earth on the spot where Troy was built. She is blamed for the Trojan War. She was later seen as an avenger of evil, rather than its creator. She may be one of the *Androktiasi*. Equivalent to Roman *Discordia* and Etruscan *Nathum*. See also *Aesa* and *Ate*, Near East. Alternate form: Atae. [Bell 1991; Leach 1992; Redfield 1931; Wedeck and Baskin 1971]

Athana Lindia
Grecian
Agriculture
  Harvest goddess in Lindos. [Monaghan 1981]

Athena
Grecian
War; Order; Goodness; Arts; Household Affairs

Protector during war. Benevolent during peace, she is responsible for rational activity, the arts, literature, and the practical arts. She is considered the protector of Athens as well as other parts of Greece and is identified with Sabine *Nerine;* Roman *Minerva; Anat* and *Anaitis,* Near East. See also *Ahnt Kai',* Central America and Mesoamerica; *Enyo* and *Blodeuwedd,* Western Europe. Alternate forms: Acraea, Aeantis, Aethyia, Ageleia, Agoraea, Aithuia, Alacomene, Alcimache, Alcis, Aleia, Ambulia, Anemotis, Apaturia, Areia, Asia, Assesia, Athenaia, Athene, Atthis, Axiopoenos, Boarmia, Boulaia, Budeia, Bulia, Chalcioecus, Chalinitis, Chryse, Cleidouchos, Colocasia, Coryphasia, Curotrophos, Cydonia, Damasippus, Ergane, Glaucopis, Gorgopa, Hellotia, Hippia, Hippolaitis, Hygeia, Iasonia, Itonia, Laosoos, Laphria, Larissaea, Lindia, Longatis, Machanitis, Magarsia, Meter, Munychia, Narcaea, Nedusia, Nice, Nike, Onca, Ophthalmitis, Optiletis, Oxydercis, Paeonia, Pallas, Pallenis, Panachaea, Panatis, Pareia, Parthenia, Parthenos, Phratria, Polias, Poliatas, Poliuchos, Polyboulos, Promachorma, Promachus, Pronaea, Pronoia, Pylaitis, Saitis, Salpinx, Sciras, Soteira, Sthenias, Telchinia, Tritogeneia, Xenia, Zosteria. [Avery 1962; Bell 1991; Bolen 1984; Cotterell 1979; Leach 1992; Stone 1979; Zimmerman 1964]

Athena of Ilium See *Anāhita,* Near East.

Athenaia See *Athena.*

Athene See *Athena.*

Athene Boarmia
Grecian
Domestic Animals

"The Ox-yoker." Name for *Athena* as worshiped in Boeotia. [Leach 1972]

Athra See *Aethra.*

Atlantia
Grecian
Earth and Nature

One of the *Hamadryades,* mother of one of the *Danaides, Iphimedusa.* [Bell 1991]

Atlantides, The
Grecian
1) Mother and Guardian; Earth and Nature; 2) Stars and Planets; Magic

1) Name for the *Hesperides.* Daughters of Atlas and *Hesperis.* 2) Name for the *Pleiades,* celestial nymphs, daughters of Atlas and *Pleione.* See also *Nymphs.* [Bell 1991; Jobes 1962; Zimmerman 1964]

Atlantis See *Maia.*

Atropos
Grecian
Fate; Moon and Night

"Inexorable" or "Inflexible." Fate. One of the three sisters called the *Moirae* (their Latin name is the *Fates*). She is the one who cuts the thread of life, ending each person's existence. Atropos is the old moon who rules over the past. Her Roman name is *Morta.* See also *Heimarmene.* [Graves 1948; Leach 1992; Redfield 1931; Zimmerman 1964]

Atthis
Grecian
Dawn and Twilight

"Dawn Goddess." See *Athena.* [Jobes 1962]

Auge
Grecian
Time; Order

Name of one of the *Horae.* [Bell 1992; Jobes 1962; Zimmerman 1964]

Augralids, The
Grecian
Mother and Guardian

Name for a triad of goddesses including *Agraulos, Herse,* and *Pandrosos.* Alternate form: Agraulids. [Jobes 1962; Monaghan 1981; Redfield 1931]

Aulis
Grecian
One of the *Praxidicae.* Sister of *Alalkomenia* and *Thelxinoea.*

[Bell 1991]

Auloniades, The
Grecian
Earth and Nature

Nymphs of forests, groves, and glens. See also *Nymphs.* [Bell 1991]

Aura
Grecian
1) Weather; 2) Earth and Nature

1) "Goddess of the Morning Wind" or a nymph who personifies a gentle breeze. 2) One of the *Maenades.* See also *Nymphs.* Alternate form: Aurae. [Bell 1991; Jobes 1962; Leach 1992; Zimmerman 1964]

Aurae See *Aura.*

Aurita
Roman
Health and Healing

Name for *Bona Dea* as healer of the ears. [Jayne 1925; Redfield 1931]

Aurora
Grecian
Dawn and Twilight

"Dawn." The eqivalent of *Eos.* Her mother was *Thea* or *Gaea.* Similar to Etruscan *Tesana.* See also *Aarvak,* Northern Europe, and *Albina,* Western Europe. Equivalent to *Aya,* Near East. Alternate forms: Heos, Rhododactylos. [Bell 1991; Cooper 1876; Leach 1992; Woodcock 1953; Zimmerman 1964]

Automatia
Grecian
Luck

"Chance." Name for Roman *Tyche* or *Fortuna.* Her luck can be good or bad. [Bell 1991; Leach 1992]

Autonoe
Grecian
Intelligence and Creativity

"Giver of Inspirations." One of the *Nereides,* daughter of Nereus and *Doris.* Mother of *Macris.* Sister of *Agave, Ino,* and *Semele.* [Bell 1991; Leach 1992; Zimmerman 1964]

Auxesia
Grecian
Agriculture
"Increase." Earth goddess of agriculture—the fertility of its crops and its drudgery. She came from Crete with *Damia* to Troezen. Some say Auxesia and *Damia* were later merged with *Demeter*. Also a name for *Persephone*. [Bell 1991; Jayne 1925; Leach 1992; Wedeck and Baskin 1971]

Auxo
Grecian
1) Time; Order; 2) Beauty; Charisma
1) Name of one of the *Horae*. 2) One of the *Charites* who is associated with *Hegemone*. [Bell 1991; Jobes 1962]

Aventina
Roman
Unknown
Name for *Diana* in her many-breasted aspect when she was worshiped on the Aventine Hill in Rome. [Monaghan 1990]

Avernales
Roman
Water; Heaven and Hell; Intelligence and Creativity; Fate
Nymphs of the rivers of the underworld. Their Grecian name is *Nymphae Infernae Paludis*. [Bell 1991]

Averruncus
Roman
Mother and Guardian
Deity of childbirth. Guardian of the delivery. [Jayne 1925]

Aversa
Etruscan
Unknown
Etruscan goddess with an ax. See also *Asera*, Near East. [Lurker 1984]

Axieros
Grecian
Earth and Nature
One of the *Cabeiriae*. Identified with *Demeter*. [Bell 1991]

Axiocersa   See *Axiokersa*

Axiokersa
Samothrace, Phrygia
Earth and Nature
"Daugher of Cabiro." Her mother was *Anieros* and she is the sister of the *Cabeiriae*. To the Phrygians of the island, she was the sister/daughter (spring) of the mother goddess (autumn) in a seasonal story. Axiokersa is the sun at the equinox who initiates summer or brings winter—gently giving or taking away life. She corresponds to *Demeter* and *Persephone*. Similar to *Anael*, Near East. Alternate form: Axiocersa. [Durdin-Robertson 1982; Monaghan 1981]

Axioche
Grecian
Earth and Nature
Nymph. See also *Nymphs*. Alternate form: Danais. [Bell 1991]

Axiopoenos
Grecian
Justice
"The Avenger." See *Athena*. [Bell 1991]

Azesia
Grecian
Agriculture
"Harvest." Name for *Demeter* and *Persephone* at Troezen. [Bell 1991]

Bacchae, The   See *The Maenades*.

Bacchantes, The   See *The Maenades*.

Bacche
Grecian
Weather; Stars and Planets
One of the *Hyades*. [Bell 1991]

Bakchetis   See *Begoe*.

Balneorum
Roman
Unknown
Name for *Fortuna*. [Jayne 1925; Jobes 1962; Monaghan 1981]

Barbata
Roman
Unknown
"The Bearded." Name for Roman *Venus*. Bearded representation of Venus may relate to earlier time period when Atticans cross-dressed for a festival honoring the mixed-gender goddess *Selene* (later Barbata). [Bell 1991]

Bassarae, The
Grecian
Earth and Nature
Maenades whose name may derive from the fact that their long robes were made of fox skins. Alternate form: Bassarides. [Bell 1991]

Bassarides, The   See *The Bassarae*.

Bateia
Grecian
Water; Health and healing; Intelligence and Creativity; Fate
One of the *Naiades*. [Bell 1991; Leach 1992]

Befana
Sicily
Magic; Goodness; Ceremonies; Selflessness
Either a good fairy or hag (a goddess who has become a wise old woman) who can expel evil spirits with noise. She is said to appear on January 5, possibly to witness winter's darkness passing. She later evolved into Saint Befana, an old woman who leaves presents in stockings of Italian children on the eve of Epiphany, or Twelfth Night. Alternate forms: La Strega, La Vecchia. [Durdin-Robertson 1982; Leach 1972; Monaghan 1981]

Begoe
Roman; Etruscan
Weather; Water; Justice
Goddess of lightning and thunder. Said by some to have been the deity responsible for giving the sacred laws to the people. Alternate forms: Bakchetis, Bergoia, Bigoe, Bigone, Vegoia. [Jobes 1962; Leach 1992; Monaghan 1981]

Bellona
Roman; Sabine
War
Goddess of war. Identified with Sabine *Vacuna* and the Sabine war goddess *Nerio*. Equivalent to *Enyo*. Her temple

was in the Campus Martius, and human sacrifices were made in her honor. Companion of *Discordia,* the *Furies,* and Mars. She assimilated *Mah-Bellona.* [Bell 1991; Leach 1972; Monaghan 1981; Neumann 1972; Woodcock 1953; Zimmerman 1964]

Bendis
Grecian
Moon and Night; Earth and Nature
"Moon." She had great power over heaven and Earth and is identified with the Brauronian *Artemis, Hecate, Rhea,* and *Persephone.* Her worship was introduced into Attica by the Thracians and was so favored that she was celebrated in a ceremonial at Athens called *Bendideia.* During this festival, there were races and processions of Athenians and Thracians at the Piraeus. Popular in Asia Minor with the Phrygians and Thracians. Alternate form: Mendis. [Bell 1991; Carlyon 1982; Durdin-Robertson 1982; Jobes 19962; Leach 1992; Neumann 1972)

Berecynthia
Grecian
Unknown
Name for *Cybele* when worshiped on Mount Berecynthis in Phrygia. [Bell 1991]

Bergoia   See *Begoe.*

Beroe
Grecian
1) Water; Fate; Beauty; 2) Water; 3) Unknown
1) One of the *Nereides.* 2) One of the *Oceanides.* 3) A daughter of *Aphrodite* and Adonis who was loved by Poseidon. [Bell 1991; Leach 1992]

Bia
Grecian
Physical Prowess
"Force." Daughter of the Titan Pallas and *Styx.* She was upset when the Titan Prometheus was discovered stealing heavenly fire for humans. Bia bound him to a rock where he was condemned to perpetual torment. [Bell 1991; Monaghan 1981]

Biblis   See *Byblis.*

Bigoe   See *Begoe.*

Bigone   See *Begoe.*

Black Virgin
Europe
Selflessness
In Roman times the worship of *Isis* was widespread throughout Europe. With the advent of Christianity, many of the chapels of Isis became Christian churches and the representations of *Isis* holding Horus began to be called the *Virgin Mary* (see Near East) carrying Jesus. Because Isis was dark skinned, these representations became known as Black Virgins. Scholars characterize them by the community of people who worship them, by color, and by the miracles some have performed. They have been discovered on most continents: Europe (France, Germany, Italy, Poland, Spain, and Switzerland), the Americas (Mexico, Central America, and South America), Africa, Asia, and the Pacific. See also *Amari De,* Indian Subcontinent. [Begg 1985; Preston 1982]

Boarmia
Grecian
Intelligence and Creativity; Agriculture

"Inventor of the Plow." Name for *Athena* when in Boeotia. [Leach 1992]

Boeotia
Grecian
Unknown
Name sometimes given for the mother of the *Hyades.* [Bell 1991]

Bolbe
Grecian
Water
Goddess of Lake Bolbe on the Bay of Strymon. [Bell 1991; Leach 1992]

Bona
Roman
Unknown
Goddess of female characteristics. Alternate form: Bona Fortuna. [Jobes 1962]

Bona Dea
Roman
Health and Healing
"Good Goddess." Goddess of healing. Only women are allowed to participate in her worship, but either sex can be a recipient of her healing powers. The serpent is her symbol in her reign as Earth mother. The anniversary of the foundation of her temple was held on the first of May when prayers were offered to her for the averting of earthquakes. She is equivalent to *Angitia* and identified with Roman *Ops, Ceres, Fauna, Maia,* and *Tellus* and the Greek goddesses *Damia, Hecate, Medea, Persephone, Rhea,* and *Semele.* Alternate forms: Aurita, Bona Oma, Cybele, Fatua, Fauna, Magna Mater, Oculata Lucifera. [Bell 1991; Chicago 1979; Durdin-Robertson 1982; Evans 1904; Jayne 1925; Redfield 1931; Zimmerman 1964]

Bona Oma
Roman
Unknown
Name for *Bona Dea.* [Bell 1991; Wedeck and Baskin 1971]

Bormonia
Roman
Health and Healing
Goddess of healing. She presides over the fountain at Bourbon-Lancy in Gaul. [Jayne 1925; Leach 1992]

Borysthenis
Grecian
Arts; Sciences; Intelligence and Creativity; Evil
One of the three *Muses* at Delphi. Sister of *Cephisso* and *Apollonis.* [Bell 1991]

Boulaia
Grecian
Justice
"Upholding the Authority of the Law." Name for *Athena.* [Bell 1991]

Brauronia
Grecian
Hunting and Wild Animals
Name for *Artemis* when associated with the bear. The name is also considered by some to have come from the deme (a political division) of Brauron. [Bell 1991; Jobes 1962; Leach 1992]

Brimo
Grecian
Destroyer of Life

"The Terrifying One." Goddess of death. Also a name for *Cybele, Demeter, Hecate,* and *Persephone.* [Bell 1991; Jobes 1962; Leach 1992; Neumann 1972]

Brisa
Grecian
Mother and Guardian; Earth and Nature

Nymph, nurse of Dionysus. One of his names, Brisaeus, is derived from her. See also *Nymphs.* [Bell 1991]

Briseis
Grecian
Moon and Night

"Moon." Moon goddess over whom the two aspects of the sun quarreled. Related to the Vedic *Brisaya,* Indian Subcontinent. [Bell 1991; Jobes 1962; Zimmerman 1964]

Britomartis
Grecian
Moon and Night; Fishing and Water Animals; Hunting and Wild

Mammals; Earth and Nature; Immortality; Demi-animals; Love and Sexuality; Unhappiness

Originally a Cretan moon goddess. Associated with Mt. Dicte (Dictynnaeus). Daughter of *Carme.* Protector of fishermen, sailors, and hunters. She is also a nature goddess connected to the earth, wild animals, and trees. As a chthonic goddess, she guards the dead. Closely identified with *Artemis,* who may have been her lover. She is portrayed as a mermaid.

⚸ *Britomartis was chased by Minos, the god of law, from early spring until harvest time. To escape Minos, she threw herself into the sea, where she became entangled in a fishing net. Artemis rescued her and made her a goddess.*

Alternate forms: Aphaea, Dictynna, Laphria. [Bell 1991; Chicago 1979; Jobes 1962; Leach 1992; Zimmerman 1964]

Brizo
Grecian
Moon and Night; Fishing and Water Animals; Fate; Mother and Guardian; Intelligence and Creativity

Aegean moon goddess on Delos. Guardian of sailors and ships. She prohibits the sacrifice of fish and is a prophetic goddess who interprets dreams. [Bell 1991; Jobes 1962; Leach 1992; Wedeck and Baskin 1971]

Brome
Grecian
Mother and Guardian; Earth and Nature

One of the *Nyscides* who was nurse of Dionysus. One of his names, Bromius, is said by some to have been taken from her name. See also *Nymphs.* [Bell 1991]

Bubastos
Grecian
Unknown

The deified *Parthenos,* daughter of Staphylus. Sister of *Molpadia* and *Rhoeo.* [Bell 1991]

Bubona
Roman
Domesticated Animals

Protector of oxen and cows. Small figurines representing her are placed in buildings where cattle are kept. [Bell 1991]

Budeia
Grecian
Education and Knowledge; Agriculture

Name for *Athena.* Refers to her teaching people how to use oxen to plow the earth. Also the name of the wife of Clymenus, mother of *Eurydice.* The Boeotian town of Budeion is named for her. Alternate form: Byzyge. [Bell 1991]

Bulia
Grecian
Justice

"Goddess of the Council." Name for *Athena.* [Leach 1972]

Byblis
Roman
Water; Unhappiness; Love and Sexuality

Water nymph who suffered from unrequited love and was changed into a spring, fountain, or well. One of the *Hamadryades.* The city of Byblos in Phoenicia is said to have been named for her. See also *Nymphs.* [Bell 1991; Jobes 1962; Woodcock 1953; Zimmerman 1964]

Byzyge
Grecian
Unknown

Probably a nickname for *Budeia.* [Bell 1991]

Cabeiri   See *Cabeiriae.*

Cabeiriae
Grecian
Earth and Nature

Greek nymphs *Axieros* and *Axiokersa,* who are found in Samothrace and Boeotia. They were worshiped in secrecy, so very little is known about them. See also *Nymphs.* Alternate forms: Cabeiri, Kabeiroi. [Bell 1991; Jayne 1925]

Cabeiria
Grecian
Unknown

Name for *Demeter* when at Thebes. [Bell 1991]

Cabeiro
Grecian
Water

Sea nymph. Daughter of *Anchinoe* and Proteus. See also *Nymphs.* [Bell 1991]

Caca
Roman
Fire; Evil

Goddess of fire or vice. Her sanctuary contains a perpetual flame. She was later supplanted by *Vesta.* See also *Tanaquil.* Alternate forms: Cacia, Kakia. [Bell 1991; Jobes 1962; Lurker 1984; Zimmerman 1964]

Cacia   See *Caca.*

Caecilia   See *Tanaquil.*

Caelestis   See *Dea Caelestis.*

Caeneus   See *Caenis.*

Caenis
Grecian
Magic; Love and Sexuality; War

Daughter of Atrax or *Hippe* and Elatus. Sister of *Hippodameia.*

♌︎ *At her request, she was changed by Poseidon into a man and was then called Caeneus. He waged war, became a king, married, and had a son. Invulnerable to weapons, he was eventually smothered. His soul left in the form of a bird, and his body returned to its female state.*

Alternate form: Caeneus. [Bell 1991; Leach 1972; Zimmerman 1964]

Calaene
Grecian
Unhappiness; Selfishness; Health and Healing
One of the *Proetides.* [Bell 1991]

Calaeno See *Celaeno.*

Cale
Grecian
1) Beauty and Charisma; 2) Water; Fate; Beauty
1) One of the *Charites.* The other two are *Euphrosyne* and *Pasithea.* 2) Name of one of the *Nereides.* [Bell 1991]

Caliadne
Grecian
1) Water; Health and Healing; Intelligence and Creativity; Fate; 2) Water
1) One of the *Naiades.* 2) One of the *Oceanides.* [Bell 1991; Leach 1992]

Caligo
Grecian
Moon and Night; Primordial
"Darkness." Mother of primordial goddess *Chaos.* [Bell 1991; Leach 1992]

Callianassa
Grecian
Water; Fate; Beauty
One of the *Nereides.* [Bell 1991]

Callianeira
Grecian
Water; Fate; Beauty
One of the *Nereides.* [Bell 1991]

Calligeneia
Grecian
Mother and Guardian; Ceremonies
Name for *Demeter* as mother of *Persephone.* [Bell 1991]

Calliope
Grecian
Arts
"Epic Poetry." One of the nine *Muses* at Athens. She is the mother of the poets and musicians Hymen, Ialemus, Linus, Orpheus. The *Sirens* were also her children. [Bell 1991; Leach 1992; Redfield 1931; Senior 1985; Zimmerman 1964]

Callipygos
Grecian
Beauty
"Beautiful Buttocks." Aspect or surname of *Aphrodite.* [Bell 1991]

Callirhoe See *Callirrhoe.*

Callirrhoe
Grecian
Water
"Beautiful Stream." 1) One of the *Oceanides.* Daughter of *Tethys* and Oceanus. She was the mother of *Echidna* by

Chrysaor and of *Chione* by the Nile River. 2) Name given to water nymphs who are daughters of the rivers Achelous, Scamander, and Maeander. See also *Nymphs.* Alternate forms: Callirhoe, Kallirhoe. [Bell 1991; Jobes 1962; Zimmerman 1964]

Calliste
Grecian
Unknown
Name of *Artemis.* Not to be confused with *Callisto,* the companion of Artemis. [Bell 1991]

Callisto
Grecian
Hunting and Wild Animals; Magic; Love and Sexuality; Stars and Planets
Arcadian nymph. Companion of *Artemis.* Not the same as *Calliste.*

♌︎ *Callisto was raped by Zeus and became pregnant. Zeus changed her into a bear to protect her from Hera. Hera discovered the trick and sent Artemis to have Callisto killed during a hunt. After her death, Zeus turned her into the constellation Ursa Major. Her son became Ursa Minor.*

See also *Cynosura* and *Nymphs.* Alternate forms: Kalliste, Kallisto, Megisto, Phace. [Bell 1991; Evans 1904; Jobes 1962; Leach 1992; Woodcock 1953]

Calva
Roman
Unknown
"The Bald." Name for Roman *Venus* possibly derived from a recounting of Roman women sacrificing their hair to be made into bow strings during a seige by the Gauls and the subsequent temple to Calva raised in honor of the women. [Bell 1991]

Calybe
Roman
Water
A nymph. [Bell 1991]

Calypso
Grecian
Water; Immortality; Charisma
One of the *Oceanides* and one of the *Nereides.* It is not clear whether there were two nymphs by this name or whether they are one and the same. Sometimes confused with *Circe.*

♌︎ *Calypso inhabited the island of Ogygia where Odysseus was shipwrecked. She promised him eternal youth if he would stay with her on the island. At the insistence of the gods, Odysseus did finally leave.*

Alternate forms: Aeaea, Kalypso. [Bell 1991; Jobes 1962; Leach 1992; Zimmerman 1964]

Camenae, The
Roman
Water; Fire
Prophetic nymphs of fountains and springs. They are especially identified with the springs in a grove at the Porta Capena of Rome, from which the Vestal Virgins drew water. Among those included in this classification are *Aegeria, Antevorta, Carmentis* (said to be the leader), *Porrima, Prorsa, Proversa, Postvorta, Tiburtis,* and *Timandra.* See also *Nymphs.* Alternate form: Casmenae. [Bell 1991; Jobes 1962; Leach 1992; Redfield 1931]

Camise
Roman
Water

Roman water nymph associated with a spring. Mother of Tibernius by Janus. See also *Nymphs*. [Leach 1992]

Campe
Grecian
Heaven and Hell
   Jailor of Tartarus (the underworld). She kept the giant Cyclopes and Hecatoncheires imprisoned. [Bell 1991; Monaghan 1981]

Candelifera
Roman
Mother and Guardian
   Deity of childbirth. She lights and carries candles during the confinement and delivery. [Jayne 1925; Leach 1992]

Canente
Roman
Water; Unhappiness; Love and Sexuality
   Roman ocean nymph who grieved so much over the loss of her husband that she disappeared. Some say she dissolved in tears. See also *Nymphs*. [Jobes 1962; Zimmerman 1964]

Canidia
Grecian
Magic; Moon and Night
   Sorceress who can make the moon descend from the sky. [Jobes 1962; Wedeck and Baskin 1971]

Capheira
Grecian
Mother and Guardian
   One of the *Oceanides*. *Rhea* gave Capheira and the nymphs of Techiniae Poseidon to raise. [Bell 1991]

Capita   See *Capta*.

Capta
Roman
Unknown
   Name for *Minerva*. She had a chapel at the foot of the Caelian Hill, one of the Seven Hills of Rome. Alternate form: Capita. [Bell 1991]

Cardea
Roman
Household Affairs; Mother and Guardian
   Goddess of door hinges, that is, domestic life and humans. She guards against evil spirits, sharing duties with Janus, god of the thresholds. She is invoked to protect children from the night spirits who kidnap them and suck their blood. Her emblem is a white thorn, which she uses to banish evil. Her festival is on June 1. See also *Carna*. [Bell 1991; Durdin-Robertson 1982; Jobes 1962; Redfield 1931]

Carme
Grecian
Earth and Nature
   A nymph. Mother of *Britomartis* and attendant of *Artemis*. See also *Nymphs*. Alternate forms: Charme, Charmel. [Bell 1991; Zimmerman 1964]

Carmenta   See *Carmentis*

Carmentis
Roman
Health and Healing; Fate; Mother and Guardian; Education and Knowledge
   Chief of the Camenae. Goddess of healing with prophetic powers, singing the future and the past, who attends the birth of children. Some believe she is an earlier Arcadian goddess named *Nicostrata* or *Nicostrate*. Carmentis is sometimes represented as two goddesses, the Carmentes, called *Postverta* and *Prorsa*. She had a sanctuary at the foot of the Capitoline Hill and altars near the Porta Carmentalis in Rome. She is said to have invented fifteen characters of the Roman alphabet using the Greek alphabet. Her festival, the *Carmentalia*, was celebrated on January 11 and 15, when protection of children was sought. One date was for celebrating the birth of girls, the other for boys. Alternate forms: Carmenta, Tiburtus. [Bell 1991; Carlyon 1982; Jayne 1925; Leach 1972; Leach 1992; Redfield 1931; Zimmerman 1964]

Carna
Roman
Health and Healing
   Goddess of physical well-being who presides over the internal organs: heart, lungs, and liver. The festival of *Calendae Fabrariae* on June 1 is celebrated in her honor. She had a sanctuary on the Caelian Hill, one of the Seven Hills of Rome. Also a goddess of the hinge: "By her divine power she opens what is closed and closes what is open." In other words, she is guardian of family life among the Romans. See also *Cardea*. [Bell 1991; Durdin-Robertson 1982; Graves 1948; Leach 1972; Wedeck and Baskin 1971]

Carpo
Grecian
Time
   "Autumn." One of the *Horae*. She was worshiped at Athens, Argos, Corinth, and Olympia. [Bell 1991; Jobes 1962; Leach 1992; Zimmerman 1964]

Carpophori
Grecian
Agriculture
   "Fruit-bearers." Name for *Demeter, Kore,* and *Persephone* at Tegea. Demeter was also worshiped by this name at Paros. [Bell 1991]

Caryatid   See *Caryatis*.

Caryatis
Grecian
Earth and Nature; Intelligence and Creativity; Health and Healing
   "She of the Walnut Tree." Name for *Artemis* referring to her inspiration and healing. Her statue stood in the open air at Caryae in Laconia.
   When Carya was turned into a walnut tree, Artemis carried the news, hence her name Caryatis. The worship of Carya was soon replaced by that of Artemis.
   Alternate form: Caryotis. [Bell 1991; Jobes 1962]

Caryotis   See *Caryatis*.

Casmenae, The   See *The Camenae*.

Cassiopeia
Grecian
Moon and Night; Beauty
   Night deity. Mother of *Andromeda* and wife of Cepheus. Also considered the mother of Phoenix, *Libya, Lysianassa,* and Atymnius.
   Cassiopeia boasted that her beauty and that of her daughter Andromeda were greater than the beauty of the Nereides. The Nereides told Poseidon of the insult, and he sent a sea monster to attack the coast. Poseidon declared the only salvation for the country would be the sacrifice of Andromeda to the monster. Andromeda was strapped to a rock awaiting the inevitable but was

saved by Perseus when he turned the monster to stone by showing it the head of Medusa.

A constellation in the northern sky is named for her. Alternate form: Iope. [Bell 1991; Jobes 1962; Leach 1972; Senior 1985; Woodcock 1953; Zimmerman 1964]

Cassotis
Grecian
Water; Fate

Nymph. A spring at Delphi is named for her. Water from the spring imparts the power of prophecy. See also *Nymphs*. [Bell 1991; Leach 1992]

Castalia
Grecian
Water; Unhappiness

Nymph. Daughter of the Achelous river god. Pursued by Apollo, she drowned herself in a spring on Mount Parnassus, near Delphi, which now bears her name. See also *Nymphs*. [Bell 1991; Zimmerman 1964]

Castalides, The
Grecian
Water

The Muses believe the spring at Castalia is sacred. See also *Nymphs*. [Bell 1991; Woodcock 1953; Zimmerman 1964]

Castitas
Roman
Earth and Nature

"Protectress of Olive Trees." Name for *Minerva*. [Leach 1992]

Cataclothes, The
Grecian
Fate

"Fate." Similar to the *Harpies* and *Keres*. [Jobes 1962]

Cedreatis See *Artemis*.

Celaeno
Grecian
1) Stars and Planets; Magic; 2) Weather; Justice; Ugliness; Demi-animals; Heaven and Hell; Wild Birds

1) One of the *Pleiades*. 2) One of the *Harpies* (the one who causes cloudiness). See also *Aello* and *Ocypete*, and the *Harpies*. Alternate forms: Calaeno, Celeno, Clonia. [Bell 1991; Leach 1992; Redfield 1931; Zimmerman 1964]

Celedones, The
Grecian
Happiness; Magic; Arts

"Singers." The soothing goddesses. [Bell 1991]

Celeno See *Celaeno*.

Cephisso
Grecian
Arts; Sciences; Intelligence and Creativity; Evil

One of the three *Muses* recognized at Delphi. Sister of *Apollonis* and *Borysthenis*. [Bell 1991]

Cer
Grecian
Destroyer of Life; Fate; Justice

"Violent Death" (or personification of the inevitability of death). Daughter of *Nyx* and sister of the *Moirae*. Alternate form: Ker. [Bell 1991; Zimmerman 1964]

Cerceïs
Grecian
Water

One of the *Oceanides*. Alternate name: *Kerkeis*. [Bell 1991; Leach 1992]

Cercyra
Grecian
Unknown

A nymph daughter of *Metope* and the river god Asopus. The island Corcyra (Corfu) is named for her. See also *Nymphs*. Alternate form: Corcyra. [Bell 1991; Zimmerman 1964]

Cerdo See *Alphito*, *Peitho*, and *Teledice*.

Ceres
Roman; Grecian
Agriculture; Destroyer of Life; Fate; Justice

Earth mother, goddess of corn and harvests. Equivalent to Greek *Demeter*, who was brought to Italy via Sicily. She was worshiped in conjunction with her children, *Libera* and Liber, divinities of viticulture. Her festival, *Cerealia*, was held in the spring in Rome to honor the founding of her temple, and another festival to Ceres was held in August. Her worship was one of the oldest plebeian cults of Rome. The early Catholic Church instituted the Feast of Lights on February 2, telling the people to replace the honoring of Ceres with the honoring of the Virgin. Another of her festivals is the *Ambarvalia*, held May 29 to celebrate the plowed fields and bless them. Similar to *Aneal*, Near East. She is identified with *Achaea, Bona Dea, Dea Dia, Demeter, Hera, Tellus*, and *Vacuna*. See also *Kerres*. Alternate forms: Alma Mammosa, Magna Dea, Thesmorphonis. [Bell 1991; Durdin-Robertson 1982; Durdin-Robertson 1990; Harding 1971; Jobes 1962; Leach 1972; Neumann 1972; Woodcock 1953; Zimmerman 1964]

Ceto
Grecian
Water; Luck

"Perils of the Sea." 1) One of the *Nereides*. 2) Daughter of *Gaea* and Pontus. Sister of Phorcys, with whom she bore the *Graeae* and *Gorgons*. [Bell 1991; Jobes 1962; Zimmerman 1964]

Chalcioecos
Grecian
Unknown

"Goddess of the Bronze House." Name for *Athena* when at Sparta. The Latin spelling is Chalcioecus. [Bell 1991; Leach 1972]

Chalcioecus See *Chalcioecos*.

Chalinitis
Grecian
Domesticated Animals

"Horse Bridler." Name for *Athena*. There was a temple dedicated to Athena Chalinitis at Corinth. [Bell 1991; Leach 1972]

Chamyne
Grecian
Earth and Nature

Name for *Demeter* that refers to her relationship to the Earth when she is at Olympia. [Bell 1991]

Chaos
Grecian
Primordial Being
The vacant abyss before the creation of the Earth. Daughter of *Caligo.* Some say Chaos is male. [Bell 1991]

Chariboea
Grecian
Water; Ugliness
Sea monster. Sometimes called *Curissia.* [Bell 1991]

Chariclo
Grecian
Water
Water nymph. Daughter of Oceanus, Apollo, or Perses. See also *Nymphs.* [Leach 1992]

Charis
Grecian
Beauty; Charisma
One of the *Charites,* she personifies grace and beauty. Her husband is Hephaestus (Hephaistos). [Bell 1991; Jobes 1962; Leach 1992; Zimmerman 1964]

Charites, The
Grecian
Beauty, Charisma
"Grace and Beauty." They are responsible for those things believed to enhance life, the social graces. They are sometimes said to be the daughters of *Coronis,* sometimes the daughters of *Eunomia* or *Eurynome,* and are variously named *Aigle, Aglaia, Auxo, Cale, Charis, Cleta, Euphrosyne, Hegemone, Pasithea, Peitho, Phaenna,* and *Thaleia.* See also *Kathirat, The,* Near East. Alternate forms: Graces, Gratiae. [Bell 1991; Jobes 1962; Zimmerman 1964]

Charme   See *Carme.*

Charmel   See *Carme.*

Charybdis
Grecian
Water; Destroyer of Life
Personification of the whirlpool in the strait between Italy and Sicily. Daughter of *Gaea* and Poseidon.

   ☩ *Charybdis inhabits a rock in the sea opposite the one inhabited by the monster Scylla. Passing boats must go between the rocks, trying to avoid the whirlpool that is formed when Charybdis vomits seawater. Sailors must choose to fight either the whirlpool or Scylla, who snatches them from their boats and devours them.* [Bell 1991; Jobes 1962; Zimmerman 1964]

Chelone
Grecian
Earth and Nature; Justice; Magic; Fishing and Water Animals
A nymph.

   ☩ *For refusing to attend the wedding of Hera and Zeus, Chelone was punished by Hermes (the purveyor of the invitation). She was dumped into the river that ran through her house, and she was changed into a tortoise. Her house became her shell.*
See also *Nymphs.* [Bell 1991; Jobes 1962; Zimmerman 1964]

Chera
Grecian
Unknown
"The Widowed." A name for *Hera.* [Bell 1991; Redfield 1931]

Chimaira   See *Chimaera.*

Chimaera
Grecian
Demi-animals; Ugliness; Love and Sexuality
1) Monster who is part lion, part goat, part dragon, with a head for each animal represented. The dragon head breathes fire. Said to have been the mother of the Neaeman lion and Egyptian *Sphinx.* 2) Seducer of Daphnis. See also *Nomia.* Alternate forms: Chimera, Chimaira. [Bell 1991; Jobes 1962]

Chimera   See *Chimaera.*

Chione
Grecian
1) Weather; 2) Unknown
"Snow Cloud." 1) A daughter of *Callirrhoe* and the Nile river god. 2) Daughter of *Oreithyia* and the god of the north wind, Boreas. Alternate form: Deiope. [Bell 1991; Jobes 1962; Zimmerman 1964]

Chitone
Grecian
Hunting and Wild Animals
Name for *Artemis.* This name may refer to a *chiton,* a loose garment sometimes worn while hunting, or to the town of Chitone in Attica where she was worshiped. [Bell 1991]

Chlidanope
Grecian
Water; Health and Healing; Intelligence and Creativity; Fate
One of the *Naiades.* Mother of *Alcaea, Astyageia, Cyrene,* and *Themisto.* [Bell 1991]

Chloe
Grecian
Earth and Nature; Life/Death Cycle
"The Blooming." Name for *Demeter* when associated with sprouting young plants. [Bell 1991; Jobes 1962; Leach 1992]

Chloris
Grecian
1) Goodness; 2) Unknown; 3) Earth and Nature
1) Goddess "who hears the prayers of supplicants." Daughter of *Niobe* and Amphion.

   ☩ *Niobe was punished for bragging that she had so many children while Leto had only two. Ten of her children were killed, but Meliboea and her brother were spared. The trauma caused Meliboea to turn white, and from then on she was called Chloris.*
2) Daughter of Amphion who has *Persephone* for a mother and is also named Chloris. Her husband is Neleus, with whom she had twelve sons and one daughter, *Pero.* 3) Goddess of buds and flowers. Her husband is Zephyrus, the west wind, and she is identified with Roman *Flora.* See also *Nymphs.* [Bell 1991; Jobes 1962; Leach 1992; Redfield 1931; Zimmerman 1964]

Choro
Grecian
Water; Fate; Beauty
One of the *Nereides.* [Leach 1992]

Chryse
Grecian
1) Unknown; 2) Earth and Nature
1) Name for *Athena* on the island of Chryse. 2) Nymph on the island of Chryse. [Bell 1991]

Chryseis
Grecian
Water
One of the *Oceanides.* [Bell 1991; Jobes 1962; Leach 1992; Senior 1985; Zimmerman 1964]

Chrysopeleia
Grecian
Earth and Nature
One of the *Hamadryades.* [Bell 1991]

Chthonia
Grecian
Earth and Nature
"The Subterranean Goddess of the Earth." Name for *Hecate, Nyx, Melinoe,* and especially *Demeter.* [Bell 1991]

Chthoniae, The
Grecian
Earth and Nature; Family and Tribes
Nymphs connected with a locality or race. See also *Nymphs.* [Bell 1991]

Cidaria
Grecian
Unknown
Name for *Demeter* at Pheneus in Arcadia. *Cidaris* refers to a dance and to the royal headdress. [Bell 1991]

Cilla
Grecian
Unknown
Daughter of *Strymo* and Laomedon. Sister of *Hesione* and *Astyoche.* Alternate form: Cylla. [Bell 1991]

Cinxia
Roman
Family and Tribes
Name for Roman *Juno* that relates to the marriage ceremony. [Bell 1991; Jayne 1925; Monaghan 1981]

Circe
Grecian
Magic; Hunting and Wild Animals; Education and Knowledge
Sorceress. Daughter of *Perse* and Helios and sister of *Aega.* Sometimes confused with *Calypso.* She lives on the enchanted island of Aeaea, probably off the coast of Italy. She is identified with Roman *Marica.*

On the island of Aeaea were many subdued wild animals. When men landed on the island, Circe gave them drugged food, and upon awakening they were wild boars. Once Odysseus came to the island, but he had an antidote for Circe's herbs and was not harmed. He stayed on the island and fathered several children, but he eventually left Circe, who gave him advice on how to return home safely.

Equivalent to *Third Lady,* Far East. Alternate forms: Aeaea, Kirke. [Bell 1991; Chicago 1979; Jayne 1925; Johnson 1988; Leach 1992; Senior 1985; Woodcock 1953; Zimmerman 1964]

Cirrha
Grecian
Earth and Nature
Nymph. The town of Cirrha in Phocis is believed to be named for her. See also *Nymphs.* [Bell 1991]

Cisseis
Grecian
Earth and Nature; Stars and Planets; Mother and Guardian
One of the *Nyseides.* [Bell 1991]

Citherides, The
Grecian
Earth and Nature
Nymphs of Mt. Citheron. See also *Nymphs.* Alternate form: Cithaeronides. [Bell 1981; Woodcock 1953]

Cleeia   See *Cleia.*

Cleia
Grecian
Weather; Stars and Planets
One of the *Hyades.* Alternate form: Cleeia. [Bell 1991]

Cleidouchos   "Warlike." See *Athena.*

Cleio   See *Clio.*

Cleis
Grecian
Weather; Stars and Planets
One of the *Hyades* in Naxos. With her sisters *Coronis* and *Philia,* she raised Dionysus. [Bell 1991]

Cleochareia
Grecian
1) Water; 2) Water; Health and Healing; Intelligence and Creativity; Fate
1) An *Oceanid.* 2) One of the *Naiades.* See also *Nymphs.* [Bell 1991; Leach 1992]

Cleone
Grecian
Water
Water goddess. Daughter of the Asopus river god. The Greek city of Cleone is named for her. [Bell 1991; Monaghan 1981]

Cleta
Grecian
Mother and Guardian
"Sound." One of the *Charites.* With her sister, *Phaenna,* she was worshiped at Sparta. [Bell 1991; Jobes 1962; Leach 1992]

Clio
Grecian
Education and Knowledge
"History." One of the *Muses* at Athens. She is depicted with a laurel wreath on her head and an open book in her hands. Alternate forms: Cleio, Kleio [Bell 1991; Jobes 1962; Leach 1992; Senior 1985; Zimmerman 1964]

Cloacina
Roman
Love and Sexuality; Family and Tribes
Name for *Venus* as protector of sexual intercourse in marriage. She also presided over the sewers of Rome to ward off disease and filth. [Bell 1991; Jayne 1925; Redfield 1931; Woodcock 1953]

Clonia
Grecian
Earth and Nature
Name of a nymph who was sometimes called *Celaeno.* See also *Nymphs.* [Bell 1991]

Clotho
Grecian
Fate

One of the *Moirae*. Present at births, she spins the thread of life. See also *Decuma* and *Heimarmene*. Alternate form: Klotho. [Bell 1991; Jobes 1962; Leach 1992; Neumann 1972]

Cluacina
Roman; Sabine
Unknown
Name for *Venus* given to her when the Sabines and the Romans signed a pact of reconciliation near one of her statues. [Woodcock 1953]

Clymene
Grecian
1) Water; Fate; Beauty; 2) Water
1) One of the *Nereides*. 2) One of the *Oceanides*. See also *Nymphs*. Alternate form: Klymene. [Bell 1991; Jobes 1962; Redfield 1931; Zimmerman 1964]

Clytia
Grecian
1) Water; 2) Earth and Nature
1) One of the *Oceanides*. 2) Nymph who loved Helios, who changed her into a sunflower. Alternate forms: Clytie, Klytia. [Bell 1991; Jobes 1962; Leach 1992; Zimmerman 1964]

Clytie   See *Clytia*.

Cnagia
Grecian
Unknown
Name for *Artemis* at Sparta. [Bell 1991]

Cnidia
Grecian
Unknown
Name for *Aphrodite* from the town of Cnidus in Caria. [Bell 1991]

Cnossia
Grecian
Earth and Nature
Nymph. See also *Nymphs*. [Bell 1991]

Coccymo
Grecian
Stars and Planets; Magic
One of the *Pleiades*. [Bell 1991]

Cocythiae, The
Grecian
Earth and Nature
Nymphs of Elis. See also *Nymphs*. [Bell 1991]

Coinquenda
Roman
Earth and Nature
Goddess of trees. She oversees their care and removal, especially on sacred ground. [Leach 1992]

Colaenis
Grecian
Unknown
Name for *Artemis* in the Attic deme of Myrrhinus. [Bell 1991]

Colias
Grecian
Mother and Guardian

Name for *Aphrodite* as goddess of maternal care and birthing in Colias. Alternate form: Kolias. [Bell 1991; Jayne 1925]

Collatina
Roman
Earth and Nature
Goddess of the hills. [Leach 1992]

Colocasia
Grecian
Unknown
Name for *Athena* when at Sicyon. [Bell 1991]

Comitia
Roman
Mother and Guardian
Goddess of childbirth. May be the same as *Carmentis*. [Jayne 1925; Leach 1992]

Conciliatrix
Roman
Order; Family and Tribes
Name for *Juno* at Rome as restorer of marital harmony. [Bell 1991]

Concordia
Roman
Order; Ceremonies
Goddess of peace, harmony, and domestic concord. Maybe one of the *Appiades*. She was invoked with *Venus* and *Fortuna* by married women at the festival of *Veneralia* on April 1. Another of her festivals, the *Charistia*, is on February 22. The Roman Senate met in one of her temples. She is also honored on January 30 along with *Pax, Salus,* and Janus. [Bell 1991; Durdin-Robertson 1982; Durdin-Robertson 1990; Zimmerman 1964]

Condyleates
Grecian
Unknown
Name for *Artemis* when at Caphyae. [Bell 1991]

Conservatrix   See *Fortuna*.

Copia
Roman
Wealth
Goddess of plenty. [Monaghan 1981; Zimmerman 1964]

Cora   See *Core*.

Corcyra   See *Cercyra*.

Cordaca
Grecian
Ceremonies
Name for *Artemis* at Pisa in Elis. It is the name of a dance that is performed in her honor at victory celebrations. [Bell 1991]

Core
Grecian
Unknown
"Maiden." Name for *Persephone* when she lived on earth with her mother *Demeter*. Alternate forms: Cora, Corinna, Corinne, Kore. [Bell 1991; Jobes 1962; Zimmerman 1964]

Corinna   See *Core*.

Corinne See *Core.*

Coronides, The
Grecian
Unknown
   Daughters of Orion: *Menippe* and *Metioche.* [Bell 1991]

Coronis
Grecian
1) Weather; Stars and Planets; 2) Earth and Nature;
3) Unknown
   1) One of the *Hyades.* Daughter of *Aethra* and Atlas.
2) Naxian nymph who with her sisters, *Philia* and *Cleis,*
raised Dionysus. 3) The Coronis who is sometimes said to be
the mother of the *Charites.* [Bell 1991; Jobes 1962; Leach
1992; Zimmerman 1964]

Corycia
Grecian
Earth and Nature
   Nymph. One of the *Coryciae.* The Corycian cave on Mount
Parnassus was named for her. See also *Nymphs.* [Bell 1991]

Coryciae, The
Grecian
Earth and Nature
   Mountain nymphs. Daughters of the Pleistus who inhabits
the Corycian cave. See also *Corycia.* [Bell 1991]

Coryphaea
Grecian
Earth and Nature
   "Goddess of the Summits." Name for *Artemis* on Mount
Coryphum. [Bell 1991]

Coryphasia
Grecian
Earth and Nature
   "Head," "Summit." Name for *Athena.* She had a temple on
the point of Coryphasium in Messenia. [Bell 1991; Leach
1972]

Corythallia
Grecian
Unknown
   Name for *Artemis* when at Sparta. [Bell 1991]

Cotys
Grecian
Ceremonies; Creator of Life
   Thracian fertility goddess. She is celebrated with orgiastic
rites. Her followers are called *baptai.* See also *Cotys,* Near
East. Alternate forms: Cotytto, Kottuto, Kotus, Kotyto. [Bell
1991; Wedeck and Baskin 1971]

Cotytto See *Cotys.*

Cranto
Grecian
Water; Fate; Beauty
   One of the *Nereides.* [Bell 1991]

Crataeis
Grecian
Unknown
   Name of *Hecate.* Mother of *Scylla,* the sea monster, whose
genealogy is disputed. Alternate form: Crateis. [Bell 1991;
Zimmerman 1964]

Creneis
Grecian
Unknown
   One of the *Nereides.* [Bell 1991]

Cretan Snake Goddess
Grecian
Heaven and Hell
   "Nether Regions Lady." Very popular chthonic fertility
deity in Neolithic Crete. [Burkert 1985]

Creta See *Crete.*

Crete
Grecian
Unknown
   There are several deities by this name. One may be the
mother of *Pasiphae.* Another gave her name to the island of
Crete. Alternate form: Creta. [Bell 1991; Zimmerman 1964]

Creusa
Grecian
Water; Family and Tribes
   Water nymph. Daughter of Oceanus and *Gaea* or *Tethys.*
Sometimes considered the mother of *Daphne.* The river
Peneius in Thessaly is her husband or half-brother, by whom
she gave birth to the royal line of Thessaly. See also *Nymphs.*
[Bell 1991; Jobes 1962; Leach 1992]

Crinaiae, The
Grecian
Water
   Freshwater nymphs. They inhabit fountains, brooks, rivers,
and lakes and are more commonly called *Naiades.* See also
Nymphs. [Bell 1991]

Cteis
Grecian
Earth and Nature
   "Earth." Greek name for the Sanscrit *Yoni,* Indian
Subcontinent. Alternate form: Kteis. [Jobes 1962]

Ctesylla
Grecian
Unknown
   Name for *Aphrodite* when at Ceos. [Bell 1991]

Cuba
Roman
Mother and Guardian
   Goddess of infants. She induces slumber and *Edulica*
blesses their food and *Portina* blesses their drinking. Sister of
Cunina and *Rumina.* [Bell 1991; Jobes 1962; Wedeck and
Baskin 1971]

Culsa
Roman
Heaven and Hell
   Goddess of the underworld. One of the *Vanths.* Alternate
form: Culsu. [Lurker 1984; Monaghan 1981]

Culsu See *Culsa.*

Cunina
Roman
Mother and Guardian
   Goddess of infants. Sister of *Cuba* and *Rumina.* [Bell 1991;
Dames 1979; Meltzer 1981]

Cupra
Roman
1) Life/Death Cycle; Goodness; Sun and Day; 2) Unknown
   1) Benevolent Roman Earth and death goddess. Thought to be the personification of light or day. Worshiped in Umbria and Picenum, with shrines at Veii, Falerii, and Persuia. Associated with the Greek *Ilythyia-Leucothea.* 2) Name for *Juno* in Etruria. [Bell 1991; Leach 1992; Redfield 1931]

Curiatia
Roman
Justice
   Name for *Juno* when involved in affairs of state. [Bell 1991]

Curissia
Grecian
Ugliness; Water
   The name of a sea monster more commonly called *Chariboea* or *Periboea.* [Bell 1991]

Curitis
Roman
Mother and Guardian; Health and Healing
   "Of the Spear." Name for Roman *Juno.* Protector of married women who promises healthy children. [Jayne 1925]

Curotrophos
Grecian
Mother and Guardian; Hunting and Wild Animals
   "Nurse of Youth." Name for *Gaea* at Athens. Also a name for *Artemis* as hunter and protector of youth and for *Athena* as nurturer of children. See also *Kourotrophos.* [Bell 1991; Leach 1972]

Cyane
Sicily
1) Earth and Nature; Water; 2) Water
   1) Nymph. Companion of *Proserpina.* Cyane was so grief-stricken over the loss of her friend *Proserpina* that she was changed into a well. 2) Daughter of the Maeander River. See also *Nymphs.* [Bell 1991]

Cybele
Roman
Mother and Guardian; Ceremonies
   "The Great Mother."
   Her festival, the *Megalensia,* or *Megalesia,* was celebrated on April 4 and was the first festival of the year because Cybele came first. It was she who gave birth to the gods. See also *Cybele,* Near East. She is identified with Roman *Fauna* and *Ops* and merged with *Magna Mater.* See also *Misa.* Alternate forms: Agdistis, Agdos, Antaea, Berecynthia, Bona Dea, Brimo, Genetrix, Idaea, Mater Turrita, Pessinuntia, Phrygia. [Durdin-Robertson 1982]

Cycladic Goddesses, The
Grecian
Unknown
   Neolithic marble figures, believed representative of goddesses, found in funerary sites. Voluptuous nude female fertility figurines. [Eliade 1987]

Cydippe
Grecian
Water; Fate; Beauty
   Name of one of the *Nereides.* Alternate form: Lycippe. [Bell 1991; Jobes 1962]

Cydonia
Grecian
Unknown
   Name for *Athena* when in Elis. [Bell 1991]

Cylla   See *Cilla.*

Cyllene
Grecian
Earth and Nature
   A nymph, mother of Lycaon by Pelasgus. See also *Nymphs.* [Bell 1991]

Cymatolege
Grecian
Water; Fate; Beauty
   One of the *Nereides.* [Bell 1991]

Cymo
Grecian
Water
   "Waves." One of the *Nereides.* Alternate form: Kymo. [Bell 1991; Leach 1992]

Cymodoce
Grecian
Water; Order
   "Wave-receiving." One of the *Nereides,* she calms the seas. Alternate form: Kymodoce. [Bell 1991; Jobes 1962; Leach 1992]

Cymothoe
Grecian
Water
   "Swift Wave." One of the *Nereides.* Alternate form: Kymothoe. [Bell 1991; Leach 1992]

Cynosura
Grecian
Earth and Nature; Mother and Guardian; Stars and Planets
   Nymph. One of the nurses of Zeus. One story says she was changed by Zeus into the constellation Ursa Major to escape Cronus. A place in Crete is named for her. See also *Nymphs.* [Bell 1991; Jobes 1962]

Cynthia
Grecian
Unknown
   Name for *Artemis* derived from Mt. Cynthus on Delos. [Bell 1991]

Cypete   See *Ocypete.*

Cypria
Grecian
Water
   Name for *Aphrodite* on Cyprus. Cyprus is close to where she is said to have risen from the sea, and there are many of her temples on the island. Also a name for *Venus* when worshiped on Cyprus. Alternate forms: Cypris, Cyprigeneia, Cyprogenes. [Bell 1991; Woodcock 1953; Zimmerman 1964]

Cypridos
Grecian
Time; Order
   One of the *Horae.* [Bell 1991]

Cyprigeneia   See *Cypria.*

Cypris   See *Cypria.*

Cyprogenes   See *Cypria.*

Cyrene
Grecian
Justice
   Queen of Lybia. Daughter of *Chlidanope* and Hypseus. Her sisters are *Alcaea, Themisto,* and *Astyageia.* The city of Cyrene is named for her. [Bell 1991; Jobes 1962]

Cythera
Grecian
Water
   Name for *Aphrodite.* She is said to have landed on an island by this name when she rose from the sea. Alternate forms: Cytherea, Cythereia, Cytherias. [Bell 1991; Jobes 1962; Woodcock 1953; Zimmerman 1964]

Cytherea   See *Cythera.*

Cythereia   See *Cythera.*

Cytherias   See *Cythera.*

Da
Grecian
Earth and Nature
   Possibly an early name for the Earth mother. [Monaghan 1981]

Dactyls, The
Grecian
Arts; Magic; Household Affairs
   Attendants of *Cybele* who introduced ironworking into Greece. Said to be skilled in music and magic. Scholars disagree on who their mother is—*Anchiale* or *Ida.* Alternate form: Dactyli. [Bell 1991; Redfield 1931; Monaghan 1981]

Dactyli   See *Dactyls.*

Daeira
Grecian
Education and Knowledge
   "The Knowing." One of the *Oceanides,* daughter of *Tethys* and Oceanus. Sometimes called sister of *Styx.* [Bell 1991; Jobes 1962; Leach 1992]

Dais
Grecian
Agriculture; Weather
   Goddess who is the personification of a plentiful meal. [Leach 1992]

Damasippus
Grecian
Domesticated Animals; Order
   "Horse-taming." Name for *Athena.* [Leach 1972]

Damatres, The
Sicily
Unknown
   "The Mothers." Name for *Demeter* and *Persephone.* [Monaghan 1990]

Damia
Grecian
Mother and Guardian; Agriculture
   Responsible for the fertility of corn and humans. Closely identified with *Auxesia* and Roman *Bona Dea.* Alternate forms: Damoia, Lochia. [Bell 1991; Jayne 1925; Jobes 1962; Leach 1992; Redfield 1931]

Damoia   See *Damia.*

Danais   See *Axioche.*

Danu
Grecian
Mother and Guardian
   Aegean mother goddess. Alternate form: Danuna. [Graves 1948]

Danuna   See *Danu.*

Daphnaea
Grecian
Earth and Nature
   Name for *Artemis* at Hypsi in Laconia. The name comes from a type of laurel called daphne. [Bell 1991]

Daphne
Grecian
1) Water; 2) Unknown; 3) Water 4) Unknown
   1) Daughter of *Creusa* and the Peneius river god in Thessaly.

☿ *Pursued by Apollo, Daphne asked Gaea to protect her. Mother Earth opened, taking Daphne within and transforming her into a laurel tree.*

   2) Name for *Manto.* 3) Daughter of the Ladon river god in Elis. 4) Name for *Pasiphae.* [Bell 1991; Chicago 1979; Jobes 1962; Senior 1985; Woodcock 1953]

Daulis
Grecian
Earth and Nature
   Nymph. The city of Daulis is named for her. See also *Nymphs.* [Zimmerman 1964]

Dea Caelestis
Roman; Carthage
Unknown
   Roman name for the Carthaginian goddess *Tanit.* Identified with *Magna Mater.* See also *Caelestis,* Near East. Alternate forms: Caelestis, Nutrix. [Jobes 1962; Redfield 1931]

Dea Dia
Roman
Agriculture
   Ancient corn and agricultural goddess. Later identified with *Acca Larentia,* goddess of the cornfields, and *Ceres.* Twelve priests, the Arval Brothers, were selected as lifetime members from distinguished senatorial families (the reigning emperor was always a member). They performed her complicated worship with a festival on three days in May. The first and third days were celebrated in her temple in Rome; the second day was celebrated in her sacred grove. [Durdin-Robertson 1982; Eliade 1987; Leach 1972; Wedeck and Baskin 1971]

Dea Febris   See *Febris.*

Dea Marica
Roman
Earth and Nature; Water
   "Goddess of the Marshes." Roman nature goddess. [Avery 1962]

Dea Matuta   See *Mater Matuta.*

Dea Quartana   See *Febris.*

Dea Syria
Roman
Unknown
  Roman name for the Syrian goddess *Atargatis*, Near East. [Harding 1971; Monaghan 1981; Redfield 1931]

Dea Tertiana See *Febris.*

Deae Matres, The
Roman
Mother and Guardian
  Mother goddesses of Celtic or Teutonic origin who were absorbed into the Roman pantheon. [Monaghan 1981; Wedeck and Baskin 1971]

Decima See *Decuma.*

Decuma
Roman
Fate
  One of the *Parcae.* Said to be the same as Greek *Clotho* or *Lachesis.* Alternate form: Decima. [Bonnerjea 1927; Redfield 1931]

Deianeira
Grecian
Unknown
  One of the *Nereides.* Daughter of *Doris* and Nereus. Alternate form: Dejanira. [Bell 1991; Jobes 1962; Leach 1992; Zimmerman 1964]

Deima
Grecian
Courage
  "Fear." [Bell 1991]

Deino
Grecian
Water
  "The Terrifier." One of the *Graeae,* personifications of the white foam of the sea. [Bell 1991; Leach 1992; Redfield 1931; Zimmerman 1964]

Deiois See *Deione.*

Deione
Grecian
Unknown
  "Daughter of *Demeter.*" A name for *Persephone.* Alternate forms: Acacalis, Deiois, Deoine. [Bell 1991]

Deiope See *Chione.*

Deiopea
Grecian
1) Water; Fate; Beauty; 2) Earth and Nature
  1) One of the *Nereides.* 2) A Lydian nymph. See also *Nymphs.* [Bell 1991; Leach 1992]

Deipara
Grecian
Unknown
  1) "Mother of God." Latin name for *Theotokos.* 2) At one time, it referred to the Virgin Mary. [Jobes 1962]

Deiphobe
Grecian
Fate
  Prophetess. Daughter of Glaucus. An alternate form for the *Cumaean Sibyl.* [Bell 1991; Zimmerman 1964]

Dejanira See *Deianeira.*

Delia
Grecian
Unknown
  Name for *Artemis* referring to her birthplace at Delos. [Jobes 1962; Zimmerman 1964]

Deliades, The
Grecian
Earth and Nature
  Nymphs of Delos and other deities worshiped in Delos. See also *Nymphs.* [Bell 1991]

Delight
Grecian
Unknown
  Daughter of *Psyche.* [Zimmerman 1964]

Delphinia
Grecian
Unknown
  Name for *Artemis* when at Athens. [Bell 1991]

Demeter
Grecian
Mother and Guardian; Agriculture; Justice; Life/Death Cycle; Unhappiness; Time
  Mother goddess. One of the twelve great Greek Olympian deities. She has power over the productivity of the Earth and the social order of humans. She forms a triad with her daughter, *Persephone,* and *Hecate.*

  ⚸ *Demeter's daughter, Persephone, was kidnapped and taken to the underworld by Hades to be his mate. Demeter searched for her for nine months. During this time, no plants would grow on Earth. Demeter was able to obtain Persephone's release from the underworld, but Persephone was forced to return for three months (winter) each year because she had eaten a few pomegranate seeds while there.*

  This mother-and-daughter relationship is said to symbolize the cycle of life, death, and regeneration. The *Thesmophoria* was the festival of Demeter. In Athens the festival took three days. On the first day, worshipers went down into caves to celebrate the founding of agriculture and the rite of marriage. Her Roman name is *Ga Mater.* See also *Anieros, Axiokersa, Ceres, Enyo; Chaabou* and *Deo,* Near East. Alternate forms: Achaea, Achaia, Achaiva, Amphictyonis, Anesidora, Antaea, Auxesia, Axieros, Azesia, Brimo, Cabeiria, Calligeneia, Carpophori, Carpophoros, Chamyne, Chloe, Chthonia, Cidaria, Damatres, Demo, Deo, Despoena, Eleusinia, Epipole, Erinys, Europa, Gemeter, Hercyna, Himalis, Karpophoros, Kidaria, Lernaea, Malophorus, Meilichia, Mycalessia, Mysia, Panachaea, Panteleia, Pelagia, Pelasga, Prosymna, Rharias, Sito, Stiria, Thesmia, Thesmophoros. [Bell 1991; Bolen 1984; Chicago 1979; Jobes 1962; Leach 1992; Neumann 1972; Stone 1979; Stutley 1984]

Demo See *Demeter.*

Dendritus
Grecian
Earth and Nature
  "Goddess of the Tree." [Bell 1991; Monaghan 1981]

Deo
Grecian
Unknown
  Name for *Demeter.* [Bell 1991]

Deoine See *Deione.*

Dero
Grecian
Water; Fate; Beauty
    One of the *Nereides*. [Bell 1991; Leach 1992]

Derrhiatis   See *Artemis*.

Despoena
Grecian
Ceremonies
    1) Goddess worshiped in Arcadia. Daughter of *Demeter* and Poseidon Hippius.

⚡ *When Demeter was wandering the world searching for Persephone, she was persued by Poseidon. She changed into a mare, but Poseidon, not to be denied, changed into a stallion and impregnated her. She gave birth to twins, Despoena and Areion.*
    Despoena is her cult name, her real name is known only to those who worshiped her in secret rites. 2) "The Mistress." Name for *Aphrodite, Demeter,* and *Persephone*. Alternate form: Despoina. [Bell 1991; Bonnerjea 1927; Jobes 1962]

Despoina   See *Despoena*.

Deverra
Roman
Mother and Guardian; Household Affairs
    One of three goddesses who protect young mothers. She sweeps the threshold to prevent the god Silvanus from entering the house. The other two goddesses are *Intercidona* and *Pilumnus*. [Jayne 1925]

Dexamene
Grecian
Water; Fate; Beauty
    One of the *Nereides*. [Bell 1991; Leach 1992]

Dia
Grecian
Unknown
    Name for *Hebe* or *Ganymeda* at Phlius and Sicyon. There are several other deities with this name. [Bell 1991]

Diana
Roman; Sabine
Moon and Night; Mother and Guardian; Water; Hunting and Wild Animals; Earth and Nature
    Goddess who was probably an earlier Latin or Sabine deity. She is a goddess of the moon, women, procreation and birth, springs, woods, and hunting. Diana (growth) is a member of the trinity of goddesses that also includes *Lucina* (birth), and *Hecate,* (death). Her chief festival was called the Festival of Candles or Torches and was celebrated on August 15th when her groves shone with a multitude of torches. This day is still celebrated as a Festival of Candles, but the torches are lit for the *Virgin Mary,* Near East. It is the day of Mary's Assumption. Diana is the Roman equivalent of *Artemis*. Identified with *Aegeria*. Alternate forms: Aventina, Dictynna, Diviana, Jana, Lucifera, Lucina, Luna, Nemorensis, Noctiluca, Opifera, Proserpina, Sospita, Tergemina, Thermia, Titania, Trivia. [Bell 1991; Durdin-Robertson 1982; Harding 1971; Jayne 1925; Jobes 1962; Leach 1992; Neumann 1972; Woodcock 1953]

Diana of Ephesians
Grecian
Unknown
    "Great Goddess." Resembling the characteristics of the Egyptian goddess *Ashtoreth,* she represents nature. Her many breasts offer nurture and comfort. Her first temple in Turkey was built in 580 B.C.E. and burned by Erostratus in 356 B.C.E. The second temple was built during the time of

Alexander the Great in Ephesus, the capital of Asia. Her worship was restored and flourished. See also *Artemis;* and *Artemis Ephesus,* Near East. [Jobes 1962; Lockyer 1967]

Dice
Grecian
Justice; Order
    "Justice." One of the *Horae*. She represents order in nature and human beings. Associated with *Poena* and *Adicia*. Alternate form: Dike. [Bell 1991; Evans 1904; Jobes 1962; Zimmerman 1964]

Dicte
Grecian
Earth and Nature
    Nymph. She gave her name to Mount Dicte in Crete. See also *Nymphs*. [Bell 1991]

Dictynna
Grecian, Roman
Fishing and Water Animals
    "Fish goddess." Name for *Artemis, Britomartis,* and Roman *Diana*. Alternate form: Diktynna. [Bell 1991; Bonnerjea 1927; Jobes 1962; Neumann 1972; Woodcock 1953; Zimmerman 1964]

Dike   See *Dice*.

Diktynna   See *Dictynna*.

Dindymene
Grecian
Unknown
    A name for *Cybele*. The name may be related to Mt. Dindymus in Phrygia, where she had a temple, or from her mother, Dindyme. [Bell 1991; Jobes 1962; Leach 1992; Woodcock 1953; Zimmerman 1964]

Dionaea
Grecian
Unknown
    Name for *Aphrodite* derived from her mother *Dione*. Dionaea is sometimes applied to objects that are sacred to *Aphrodite,* such as the dove. Alternate form: Dionea. [Bell 1991; Bonnerjea 1927]

Dione
Grecian
1) Water; Fate; Beauty; 2) Weather; Stars and Planets; 3) Water; 4) Unknown
    1) One of the *Nereides*. 2) One of the *Hyades*. 3) A Titan daughter of Uranus and *Gaea* said to be the mother of *Aphrodite* (see also *Dionaea*). Some say the latter Dione is one of the *Oceanides*. 4) A daughter of Atlas, mother of *Niobe* by Tantalus. See also *Dione,* Near East. [Bell 1991; Jobes 1962; Leach 1992; Senior 1985; Woodcock 1953; Zimmerman 1964]

Dionea   See *Dionaea*.

Dios
Grecian
Unknown
    The counterpart of Zeus. See also *Diwya*. [Harding 1971]

Dioxippe
Grecian
Unhappiness; Magic
    One of the *Heliades*. [Bell 1991]

Dirae, The
Roman
Unknown
Name for the Greek *Erinyes*. Also called the *Furies*. [Bell 1991; Woodcock 1953; Zimmerman 1964]

Dirce
Grecian
Water
Wife of Lycus. The cruel aunt of *Antionpe*. She was changed into a spring by Dionysus. [Bell 1991; Jobes 1962; Zimmerman 1964]

Disciplina
Roman
Justice
Goddess of discipline. [Monaghan 1990]

Discord   See *Discordia*.

Discordia
Roman
Disorder; War
Goddess of discord and war. Companion to *Bellona*. Similar to Greek *Eris*. Alternate form: Discord. [Bell 1991; Redfield 1931; Zimmerman 1964]

Diuturna   See *Juturna*.

Diviana
Roman
Unknown
Italian name for *Diana*. [Harding 1971]

Diwja   See *Diwya*.

Diwya
Grecian
Sky and Heavens
Mycenaean sky goddess. May be a female counterpart of Zeus at Pylos. See also *Dios*. Alternate form: Diwja. [Leach 1992]

Dodone
Grecian
Water
One of the *Oceanides*. Daughter of *Tethys* and Oceanus. The oracle of Dodona is believed to have taken her name. [Bell 1991; Leach 1992]

Dodonides, The
Grecian
1) Earth and Nature; Mother and Guardian; 2) Weather; Stars and Planets
1) Nymphs who raised Zeus. 2) Name for the *Hyades*, daughters of *Aethra*. [Bell 1991; Redfield 1931; Zimmerman 1964]

Domiduca
Roman
Family and Tribes
"Leading Home." Name for Roman *Juno* pertaining to her role as matrimonial goddess. [Bell 1991]

Dorides, The
Grecian
Water; Fate; Beauty
A name for the *Nereides* taken from their mother's name, *Doris*. [Zimmerman 1964]

Doris
Grecian
1) Water; 2) Water; Fate; Beauty
1) One of the *Oceanides*, daughter of *Tethys* and Oceanus. With her husband, Nereus, she had fifty daughters called the *Nereides*. The sea is sometimes called Doris. 2) Also the name of one of her daughters. [Bell 1991; Leach 1992; Redfield 1931]

Doto
Grecian
Fishing and Water Animals; Wealth; Water; Fate; Beauty
One of the *Nereides* associated with the abundance of the sea. [Bell 1991; Leach 1992; Woodcock 1953]

Dove Goddess
Grecian
Unknown
Goddess worshiped in Minoan-Mycenaean times. [Wedeck and Baskin 1971]

Drimo
Grecian
Water; Fate; Beauty
One of the *Nereides*. Alternate form: Drimo. [Bell 1991; Leach 1992]

Dryades, The
Grecian
Earth and Nature
Tree nymphs. Probably Arcadian in origin. The life of each is connected to an individual tree; when the tree dies, the Dryad dies. Nymphs inhabiting fruit trees were known as *Meliades* or *Hamaelides*. See also *Nymphs*; and *Fange*, Northern Europe. Alternate forms: Adryades, Dryads, Hamadryades. [Bell 1991; Leach 1992; Redfield 1931; Woodcock 1953; Zimmerman 1964]

Dryads, The   See *The Dryades*.

Drymo   See *Drimo*.

Dryope
Grecian
Earth and Nature
Daughter of Eurytus or Dryops who became one of the *Hamadryades*. [Bell 1991; Jobes 1962; Zimmerman 1964]

Dynamene
Grecian
"Capable." One of the *Nereides*, daughter of *Doris* and Nereus. [Bell 1991; Leach 1992]

Dysis
Grecian
Sun and Day
"Sunset." One of the *Horae*. [Leach 1992]

Dysnomia
Grecian
Disorder
"Lawlessness." Daughter of *Eris*. One of the *Androktiasi*. [Leach 1992]

Echenais
Grecian
Love and Sexuality; Water; Health and Healing; Fate; Intelligence and Creativity
One of the *Naiades*, she fell in love with Daphnis, a Sicilian shepherd. [Bell 1991; Monaghan 1981]

Echidna
Grecian
Ugliness; Demi-animals; Love and Sexuality
Monster. Primarily considered the daughter of *Gaea* and Tartarus. She may have been the daughter of *Callirrhoe* and Chrysaor, *Styx* and Peiras, or Keto and Phorcys. Half woman and half serpent, Echidna mated with her brother Typhon and produced many monster children, including *Hydra*. [Bell 1991; Jobes 1962; Leach 1992; Redfield 1931; Zimmerman 1964]

Echo
Grecian
Earth and Nature; Physical Prowess
Mountain nymph and one of the *Oreades.*

Echo was quite a conversationalist, talking almost continuously. She often had conversations with Hera, distracting her when Zeus was having sexual relations with other nymphs. Hera, learning of the deception, punished her. Echo can no longer initiate conversation, she can only repeat the last words that she hears. [Bell 1991; Jobes 1962; Leach 1992; Woodcock 1953; Zimmerman 1964]

Edulica
Roman
Mother and Guardian
Protector of children, blesses their food. Similar to *Cuba,* who blesses their sleep, and *Potina,* who blesses their drinking. [Bell 1991]

Edusa
Roman
Mother and Guardian
She helps mothers wean their children. [Monaghan 1990]

Egeria   See *Aegeria.*

Eidothea
Grecian
1) Water; Mother and Guardian; 2) Weather; Stars and Planets
1) An *Oceanide.* 2) One of the *Hyades* and a nurse to Zeus. Sister of *Adraste* and *Athala.* Alternate forms: Eurynome, Idothea. [Bell 1991; Zimmerman 1964]

Eidyia   See *Idyia.*

Eileithyea   See *Eileithyia.*

Eileithyia
Grecian
Mother and Guardian
"Childbirth." Daughter of *Hera* and Zeus. It is suggested that two goddesses with this name, one responsible for easy births and one for difficult deliveries, were merged.

At the request of Hera, it was Eileithyia who delayed the birth of Heracles so that Eurystheus would be born first.

There were many temples to Eileithyia with carved representations of her. She is sometimes identifed with the Greek *Artemis, Elionia,* and *Hera*; the Roman *Juno* and *Nascio*; and the Egyptian *Bubastis* and *Nekhebet.* She is equivalent to the Etruscan *Ethausva.* Alternate forms: Eilethyia, Eileithyea, Eleithyia, Eleutho, Ilithyia, Lucina, Lysizona. [Bell 1991; Jayne 1925; Leach 1992; Meltzer 1981; Neumann 1972]

Eilethyia   See *Eileithyia.*

Eione
Grecian
Water

"Goddess of the Shore." One of the *Nereides.* [Bell 1991; Leach 1992]

Eirene
Grecian
Order
"Peace." Daughter of *Themis* and Zeus. One of the *Horae.* Her counterpart is Roman *Pax.* There is also an Eirene who is the daughter of *Melanthea* and Poseidon. See also *Opora.* Alternate form: Irene. [Bell 1991; Leach 1992; Zimmerman 1964]

Elais
Grecian
Magic
One of the *Oenotropae.* She could change berries into olives. [Bell 1991]

Elasii, The
Grecian
Health and Healing
"Healers." Daughters of *Alexida.* They prevented epileptic seizures. [Bell 1991]

Elate
Grecian
Large Size; Unhappiness
Giant. Elate wept unceasingly when her brothers Otus and Ephialtes were killed. She was changed into a spruce tree. [Bell 1991]

Electra
Grecian
1) Water; 2) Stars and Planets; Magic
1) One of the *Oceanides,* who was the mother of *Arce,* the *Harpies,* and *Iris.* 2) One of the *Pleiades.* Alternate form: Elektra. [Bell 1991; Evans 1904; Senior 1985; Zimmerman 1964]

Electryone
Grecian
1) Moon and Night; 2) Unknown; 3) Unhappiness; Magic
1) Moon goddess. 2) Name for *Alcmena.* 3) One of the *Heliades,* daughter of *Rhodos* and Helios. [Bell 1991]

Eleionomae
Grecian
Water; Health and Healing; Intelligence and Creativity; Fate
Name for *Naiades* of the marshes. [Bell 1991]

Eleithyia   See *Eileithyia.*

Elektra   See *Electra.*

Eleos
Grecian
Goodness
"Pity" or "Mercy." She was worshiped only in Athens. [Bell 1991]

Eleusina
Grecian
Unknown
Name for *Demeter* and *Persephone* when in Eleusis, Attica. [Bell 1991]

Eleusina   See *Eleusinia.*

Eleuthera
Grecian
Family and Tribes
   "Mother of Greece." [Neumann 1972]

Eleutho   See *Eileithyia.*

Elionia
Grecian
Mother and Guardian
   "Childbirth." She was worshiped at Argos and may be the
same as *Eileithyia.* [Bell 1991]

Elpis
Grecian
Happiness
   "Hope." Her Roman equivalent is *Spes.* [Bell 1991]

Empanada
Roman
Mother and Guardian; Goodness
   Goddess of asylum. Her temple was always open, providing
food and shelter to those in need. May be a name for *Juno.*
Alternate form: Panda. [Bell 1991; Redfield 1931]

Empusa
Grecian
Evil; Ugliness; Demi-animal
   Monster. Empusa has "one leg of brass and one of an ass."
She was said to have been an over-protective mother who
died young and who now appears as a vampire, snatching
away children. See also *Empusae.* [Bell 1991; Evans 1904;
Jobes 1962; Neumann 1972]

Empusae
Grecian
Evil; Ugliness; Commerce and Travel
   Monsters who suck blood from their male victims and
frighten travelers. Similar to *The Qlippoth,* Near East. See
also *Empusa,* the *Lamiae,* and *Mormo.* [Bell 1991; Evans
1904; Jobes 1962; Neumann 1972]

Enarete
Grecian
Family and Tribes
   Mother of important royal lines in mythological dynastic
history. Daughter of Deimachus, wife of Aeolus, mother of
Canace, Alcyone, Peisidice, Calyce, and *Perimede.* [Bell 1991]

Endeis
Grecian
Earth and Nature
   Nymph, daughter of *Chariclo* and Sciron. See also *Nymphs.*
[Bell 1991; Redfield 1931]

Enhydria
Grecian
Water
   "Abundance of Water." Nymph who inhabits a spring.
See also *Nymphs.* [Leach 1992]

Enkrateia
Grecian
Selflessness
   "Abstinence." [Leach 1992]

Enodia
Grecian
Commerce and Travel
   Goddess of "crossroads and gates." [Leach 1992]

Enyo
Grecian
1) War; 2) Water; Ugliness; Mother and Guardian
   "The Shaker." 1) Goddess of war, daughter of Ares. She is
celebrated along with *Demeter, Athena,* and Zeus at the
festival of *Homoloia.* She is equivalent to *Bellona.* 2) One of
the *Graeae.* [Bell 1991; Leach 1992; Neumann 1972; Woodcock
1953; Zimmerman 1964]

Eos
Grecian
Dawn and Twilight; Weather; Stars and Planets; Love and
Sexuality; Immortality; Life/Death Cycle; Unhappiness
   "Dawn." Daughter of *Theia* and Hyperion. Mother of stars
and winds.
   *As the result of a curse by Aphrodite, Eos was constantly in
need of young male lovers. Her greatest love was for Tithonus,
for whom she obtained immortality. However, she forgot to
ask Zeus for eternal youth for Tithonus, so he grew old and dried
up, metamorphosing into a cricket. When her son, Memnon, was
killed, she persuaded Zeus to give him immortality in the afterworld.
Eos, still saddened that Memnon was no longer on Earth, wept
profusely, and her tears became the morning dew.*
   Equivalent to *Aurora; Aarvak,* Northern Europe; and *Aya,*
Near East. Alternate forms: Heos, Phosphoros, Tito. [Bell
1991; Cooper 1876; Leach 1992; Redfield 1931; Zimmerman
1964]

Epaine
Grecian
Unknown
   "The Awesome." Name for *Persephone.* [Bell 1991]

Epeione   See *Epione.*

Ephesia
Grecian
Earth and Nature
   "The Nourishing Powers of Nature." A name of *Artemis.*
Ephesia was an earlier Asian deity, possibly the Persian
goddess *Metra,* Near East, over whom Artemis was
superimposed. She is represented crowned and with
multiple breasts (identified by some as a necklace of bull
testicles); the lower part of her body tapers to a point. Her
symbol is the bee. Her temple at Ephesus was one of the
seven wonders of the ancient world. [Bell 1991; Jobes 1962]

Epimelides   See *Meliades.*

Epione
Grecian
Health and Healing
   "Soothing." A Healer. Wife of Asclepius and mother of
Aegle, Iaso, and *Panaceia.* Alternate form: Epeione. [Bell
1991; Leach 1992]

Epipole
Grecian
War; Justice
   Name for *Demeter* at Lacedaemon. [Bell 1991]

Epipyrgidia
Grecian
Unknown
   "On the Tower." Name for *Hecate* on the Acropolis at
Athens. [Bell 1991]

Epistrophia
Grecian
Unknown

Name of *Aprodite*. Her Roman name is *Verticordia*. [Woodcock 1953]

Epitragia   See *Aphrodite*.

Epitymbia
Grecian
Unknown
"Of the Tombs." Name for *Aphrodite* as goddess of "death-in-life." Alternate form: Epitymbria. [Avery 1962]

Epitymbria   See *Epitymbia*.

Epona
Roman
Domesticated Animals
"Protector of Horses." See also *Epona*, Western Europe. [Bell 1991]

Equestris
Roman
Domesticated Animals
Name for *Venus*. [Bell 1991]

Erato
Grecian
1) Earth and Nature; 2) Arts; Sciences; Intelligence and Creativity; Evil; 3) Weather; Stars and Planets; 4) Magic; Wild Birds; Unhappiness; 5) Earth and Nature; Mother and Guardian; Stars and Planets
1) A prophetic Arcadian nymph. 2) One of the nine *Muses* at Athens who presides over erotic poetry. 3) One of the *Nereides*. 4) One of the *Hyades*. 5) One of the *Nyseides*. [Bell 1991; Bonnerjea 1927; Leach 1992; Redfield 1931; Senior 1985; Zimmerman 1964]

Ergane
Grecian
Commerce and Travel
"The Worker." Name for *Athena*. Alternate form: Ergatis. [Leach 1972; Leach 1992]

Ergatis
Roman
Household Affairs
"Work Woman." Name for *Minerva* as inventor of spinning and weaving. As a name for *Athena*, see *Ergane*. [Woodcock 1953]

Eriboea
Grecian
Unknown
Wife of Aloeus and stepmother of the Aloeidae, twin giants, sons of Poseidon. [Bell 1991; Zimmerman 1964]

Erigone
Grecian
1) Justice; Unhappiness; Stars and Planets; 2) Justice
"Righteousness." 1) A faithful daughter who hung herself after discovering the body of her murdered father, Icarius. She was placed among the stars by Dionysus. Alternate form: Aletis. 2) Daughter of Themis. She was the personification of righteousness. [Bell 1991; Jobes 1962; Zimmerman 1964]

Erinnys, The   See *Erinyes*.

Erinyes, The
Grecian
Justice; Heaven and Hell; Ugliness; Family and Tribes

"Vengeance." Daughters of *Gaea* (Earth) and Uranus (heaven), although several other deities are also given as their parents, including Cronus and *Euonyme*, *Nyx* (night), Scotus (darkness) and *Gaea*, or *Persephone* and Hades.
Older than the Olympian deities, their early appearance was similiar to the *Gorgons*—clad in black, with serpents in their hair and bloody eyes. Later they were portrayed in a less frightening form. They are guardians of Tartarus (the underworld) and attendants of *Nemesis*, pursuing those who have committed crimes against social or natural laws, particularly crimes against their families. Sisters of the *Moirae*. Originally they were probably more in number, but the Erinyes came to be known as only four, *Alecto, Magaira, Megaera*, and *Tisiphone. Telphusia* is also called one of the Erinyes. See also *Semnai Theai*. Alternate forms: Arantides, Dirae, Erinnys, Eumenides, the Roman Furies, Maniae, Melanaegis, Mixoparthenos. [Bell 1991; Cotterell 1979; Jobes 1962; Leach 1992; Woodcock 1953; Zimmerman 1964]

Erinys
Grecian
Disorder
"Fury." Name for *Demeter*. She became very angry when she was unsuccessful in hiding from her brother, Poseidon. [Bell 1991]

Eripha
Grecian
Earth and Nature; Mother and Guardian; Stars and Planets
One of the *Nyseides*. [Bell 1991]

Eriphyle
Grecian
Evil
Deity who was willing to sacrifice her family members for personal gain. Daughter of *Lysimache* and Talaus. [Bell 1991; Jobes 1962]

Eris
Grecian
Disorder; War
"Discord." Daughter of *Hera* and Zeus, although some say she is the daughter of *Nyx*. Eris calls forth war; her brother, Ares, carries out the destruction. Her children, apparently virgin births, are *Algea* (sorrow), *Amphilogea* (dispute), *Androctasia* (slaughter), *Dysnomia* (lawlessness), Limos (famine), Neicea (quarrel), and Phonos (murder), who are collectively called the *Androktiasi*. Also listed are *Ate* (error) and Harcus (the oath). Her Roman counterpart is *Discordia*. [Bell 1991; Guirand 1968; Jobes 1962; Leach 1992; Redfield 1931; Senior 1985; Zimmerman 1964]

Ersa
Grecian
Weather
"Dew." Daughter of *Selene* and Zeus. Sister of *Nemea* and *Pandeia*. See also *Herse*. Alternate form: Erse. [Bell 1991; Leach 1992]

Erse   See *Ersa*.

Erycina
Sicily
Earth and Nature
1) Name for Roman *Venus* when associated with Mt. Eryx. 2) Roman name for *Aphrodite*. [Bell 1991; Jobes 1962; Woodcock 1953; Zimmerman 1964]

Erythea

Grecian

Mother and guardian; Earth and Nature

One of the *Hesperides*. Guardian of the golden apples in the garden of the Hesperides. Alternate forms: Erytheia, Erytheis. [Bell 1991; Redfield 1931; Zimmerman 1964]

Erytheia   See *Erythea.*

Erytheis   See *Erythea.*

Esenchebis

Grecian

Unknown

Isis when worshiped on the Island of Chembis. [Lurker 1984]

Ethausva

Roman; Etruscan

Mother and Guardian

Goddess of childbirth. Equivalent to Greek *Eileithyia*. [Bell 1991]

Ether   See *Aether.*

Etna

Grecian

Water

One of the *Oceanides*. The mother of the Palici, twins, whose father was Hephaestus. [Guirand 1968; Leach 1992; Zimmerman 1964]

Euadne

Grecian

1) Stars and Planets; Magic; 2) Unknown; 3) Water; 4) Unknown

1) One of the *Pleiades*. 2) Daughter of *Pitane* and Poseidon. She was the ancestor of a great family of prophets. 3) Daughter of *Neaera* and the river god Styron. 4) Daughter of Iphis, wife of Copaneus. [Bell 1991]

Euagora   See *Evagora.*

Euarne   See *Evarne.*

Euboea

Grecian

1) Mother and Guardian; 2) Unknown

1) With her sisters, *Acraea* and *Prosymna*, nurse to *Hera*. Daughter of Asterion. 2) Daughter of the river god Asopus, mother of Tychius, for whom the island of Euboea was probably named. [Bell 1991; Redfield 1931]

Eucharis

Grecian

Earth and Nature

A nymph. An attendant of *Calypso*. See also *Nymphs*. [Bonnerjea 1927]

Eucleia

Grecian

War ·

1) Name for *Artemis* at Athens. 2) A goddess, the personification of "glory in battle," who may have been connected with Artemis. [Bell 1991]

Eucrante

Grecian

Water; Luck

"Successful Venture." One of the *Nereides* of the waves. Daughter of *Doris* and Nereus. Alternate forms: Eukrante, Eukrate. [Bell 1991; Leach 1992]

Eudane   See *Evadne.*

Eudaimonia

Grecian

Ceremonies

"Benediction." Associated with *Aphrodite*. [Leach 1992]

Eudia

Grecian

Water; Fate; Beauty

One of the *Nereides*. [Leach 1992]

Eudora

Grecian

1) Goodness; Water; Fate; Beauty; 2) Water; Goodness; 3) Sky and Heavens; Goodness; 4) Weather; Stars and Planets; Goodness

"Gifts," "Good Giver." 1) One of the *Nereides*. 2) One of the *Oceanides*. 3) One of the *Atlantides*. Daughter of Atlas and *Hesperis*. 4) One of the *Hyades*. [Bell 1991; Leach 1992; Zimmerman 1964]

Eugora

Grecian

Justice; Water; Fate; Beauty

"Good Assembler." One of the *Nereides* associated with organization and political leadership. [Leach 1992]

Eukrante   See *Eucrante.*

Eukrate   See *Eucrante.*

Eulimene

Grecian

Travel and Commerce; Goodness

"Good Haven." One of the *Nereides,* she is associated with sailing. [Bell 1991; Leach 1992]

Eumenides, The   See *The Erinyes.*

Eumolpe

Grecian

Water; Fate; Beauty

One of the *Nereides*. [Bell 1991; Leach 1992]

Euneike   See *Eunike.*

Eunice   See *Eunike.*

Eunike

Grecian

Water; Luck

"Successful Venture." One of the *Nereides* who inhabits a spring or fountain. Alternate forms: Eunice, Euneike. [Leach 1992]

Eunoe

Grecian

Unknown

Mother of *Hecuba* according to some authors. [Bell 1991]

Eunomia

Grecian

1) Order; Justice; 2) Unknown

"Lawfulness," "Legality," "Legislation." 1) One of the *Horae.* 2) Name sometimes used for the mother of the *Charites.* Alternate form: Soteira. [Bell 1991; Jobes 1962; Leach 1992; Redfield 1931; Zimmerman 1964]

Eunoste
Grecian
Earth and Nature
    Nymph of Boeotia. See also *Nymphs.* [Bell 1991]

Eunostos
Grecian
Agriculture
    Goddess of flour mills. [Bell 1991]

Euonyme
Grecian
Unknown
    Goddess about whom little is known. Euonyme may be another name for *Gaea.* [Bell 1991]

Eupheme
Grecian
Mother and Guardian
    Nurse of the *Muses.* [Bell 1991]

Euphrosyne
Grecian
Happiness
    "Mirth and Hospitality." One of the *Charites.* [Bell 1991; Leach 1992; Redfield 1931; Zimmerman 1964]

Euploia
Grecian
Travel and Commerce; Goodness
    "She Who Confers a Good Voyage." Name for *Aphrodite* in coastal areas. [Lurker 1984]

Eupompe
Grecian
Travel and Commerce; Goodness
    "Good Voyage." One of the *Nereides,* she is associated with sailing. [Bell 1991; Leach 1992]

Euporia
Grecian
Time; Order
    One of the *Horae.* [Bell 1991]

Europa
Grecian
1) Family and Tribes; 2) Unknown; 3) Unknown; 4) Water
    1) Eponymous goddess of southern Greece. Daughter of *Parthenope,* sister of *Thrace.* 2) Name for *Demeter* at Lebadeia. 3) Name for *Merope.* 4) One of the *Oceanides.* Alternate form: Hellotia. [Bell 1991; Chicago 1979; Evans 1904; Johnson 1988; Leach 1992; Neumann 1972; Zimmerman 1964]

Euryale
Grecian
Evil; Ugliness
    One of the *Gorgons.* [Bell 1991; Jobes 1962; Zimmerman 1964]

Eurybia
Grecian
Water

"Restless Might." Sea goddess, daughter of *Gaea* and Pontus. Mother of Astraeus, Pallas, and Perses. [Bell 1991; Jobes 1962; Leach 1992; Zimmerman 1964]

Eurydice
Grecian
1) Love and Sexuality; Unhappiness; Earth and Nature; 2) Water; Fate; Beauty
    1) A nymph.

Eurydice and Orpheus were very happy together. One day, while attempting to escape the advances of Aristaeus, Eurydice stepped on a poisonous snake. She died from its bite and was transported to Hades. Orpheus went in search of her. The deities told him they would allow her to return, walking behind him, to Earth, as long as he did not look back. Unable to quell his doubts, he turned to see whether she was there, and Eurydice vanished. Orpheus was forever deprived of his love, and some say he hung himself.

    2) One of the *Nereides.* See also *Nymphs.* [Bell 1991; Davis 1971; Guirand 1968; Senior 1985; Zimmerman 1964]

Eurynome
Grecian
1) Water; 2) Unknown; 3) Unknown
    1) One of the *Oceanides,* daughter of *Tethys* and Oceanus. 2) Mother of the *Charites* by Zeus. 3) Name for *Artemis* at Phigalia in Arcadia. Alternate form: Eidothea. [Bell 1991; Evans 1904; Leach 1992; Zimmerman 1964]

Euryphaessa
Grecian
Dawn and Twilight
    "Far-shining," an aspect of the dawn. A Titan, daughter of *Gaea* and mother of Helios, the sun god. [Jobes 1962]

Euryphassa   See *Euryphaessa.*

Eurysternos
Grecian
Unknown
    "Goddess with the Broad Chest." Name for *Gaea.* [Bell 1991]

Euryte
Grecian
Earth and Nature
    Nymph. See also *Nymphs.* [Bell 1991]

Euterpe
Grecian
Arts
    "Lyric Poetry." One of the nine *Muses* at Athens, she is shown holding a flute. [Bell 1991; Cooper 1876; Leach 1992; Redfield 1931; Woodcock 1953; Zimmerman 1964]

Eutychia
Grecian
Happiness
    "Happiness." She is equivalent to the Roman *Felicitas.* [Bell 1991]

Evadne
Grecian
Unknown
    Daughter of Poseidon and *Pitane.* Mother of Iamus by Apollo. Alternate form: Eudane. [Bell 1991; Jobes 1962; Guirand 1968; Leach 1992; Zimmerman 1964]

Evagora
Grecian
Water; Fate; Beauty
   One of the *Nereides*. Daughter of *Doris* and Nereus, wife of Sangarius, mother of *Hecuba*. Alternate form: Euagora. [Leach 1992]

Evan
Roman; Etruscan
Fate
   "Personal Immortality." One of the *Lasas*. [Lurker 1984]

Evarne
Grecian
Water; Fate; Beauty
   One of the *Nereides*. Alternate form; *Euarne*. [Leach 1992]

Fama
Roman
Commerce and Travel
   Goddess of rumor. She is said to have many eyes and mouths. She travels about the world, first whispering her information to only a few, then becoming louder and louder, until even heaven hears her news. Equivalent to Greek *Ossa*, she is also identified with Greek *Pheme*. [Bell 1991; Redfield 1931; Zimmerman 1964]

Fata
Roman
Magic; Evil
   Spirit or supernatural being who is in the service of other evil spirits. See also *Fata Alcina* and *Fata Morgana*. [Jobes 1991]

Fata Alcina
Roman
Magic; Evil
   Supernatural being. Sister of *Fata Morgana*.
   Fata Alcina took her lover, Astolpho, to her island, carrying him there on the back of a whale. When she tired of him, she changed him into a myrtle tree. [Jobes 1962]

Fata Morgana
Roman
Magic; Evil
   1) Supernatural being who serves evil spirits. sister of *Fata Alcina*. 2) Name for Celtic *Morgan Le Fay*, Western Europe. [Jobes 1962; Monaghan 1981; Stone 1979]

Fates, The   See *Parcae*

Fatua   See *Bona Dea, Fauna.*

Fatuella   See *Fauna.*

Fatum
Roman
Fate
   "Unalterable Necessity." Equivalent to Greek *Ananke*. [Redfield 1931]

Faula   See *Fauna.*

Fauna
Roman
Earth and Nature
   Goddess who personified the Earth and its fertility. She is the wife or daughter of Fanus. Associated with *Bona Dea, Bona Mater, Cybele, Mater Matuta, Ops,* and *Tellus.*

Alternate forms: Fatua, Fatuella, Faula. [Bell 1991; Harding 1971; Jayne 1925; Leach 1992; Redfield 1931]

Febris
Roman
Health and Healing
   Goddess of fevers. Addressed as *Dea Febris, Dea Quartana,* and *Dea Tertiana.* When the fevers are caused by a specific illness, she is asked to heal by destroying the disease. Alternate forms: Quartana, Tertiana. [Jayne 1925; Redfield 1931; Woodcock 1953]

Februa
Roman
Mother and Guardian; Health and Healing
   Goddess of purification. She presides over the delivery of the afterbirth and over purgation. [Jayne 1925; Leach 1992]

Februlis
Roman
Health and Healing; Mother and Guardian
   Goddess of purification. She aids in impregnation by driving away evil spirits. [Jayne 1925]

Fecunditas
Roman
Mother and Guardian
   Goddess of fertility. She is appealed to for aid in becoming pregnant. [Jayne 1925]

Felicitas
Roman
Happiness
   "Happiness." She is equivalent to the Greek *Eutychia*. [Bell 1991]

Ferentina
Roman
Mother and Guardian; Water
   Goddess of protection for the Latin League and the town of Ferentium. She is a spring and fountain nymph. See also *Nymphs*. [Leach 1992; Wedeck and Baskin 1971]

Feronia
Roman
Earth and Nature; Justice
   Ancient Earth goddess presiding over orchards, groves, and woods. She was introduced to the Romans by the Sabines and Faliscans, although Greek writers describe her as Greek in origin. She is also considered a goddess of liberty because slaves were given freedom in her temple in the Campus Martius on November 13. She is identified with *Juno*. [Bell 1991; Durdin-Robertson 1982; Jayne 1925; Jobes 1962; Redfield 1931; Woodcock 1953; Zimmerman 1964]

Fides
Roman
Goodness; Selflessness
   Personification of honesty and faithfulness.
   As Fides Publica, or Honour of the People, this goddess had a temple on the Capitol . . . to which the flamines of Jupiter, Mars and Quirinus rode in a covered chariot on the 1st of October. At the offering they had their right hands wrapped up to the fingers with white bands. The meaning of the covered chariot was that honor could not be too carefully protected; of the covered right hand, that the right hand, the seat of honor, should be kept pure and holy. The goddess was represented with outstretched right hand and a white veil. Her attributes were ears of corn and fruits, joined hands, and a turtle-dove. [Bell 1991; Durdin-Robertson 1982; Redfield 1931; Zimmerman 1964]

Flora
Roman; Sabine
Earth and Nature; Time; Ceremonies; Magic

Goddess of flowers and spring. Also a goddess of the flower of youth and its pleasures. See also *Chloris*. April is her sacred month, and the *Floralia* is her festival, which began in 238 B.C.E. as a festival of unrestrained pleasure. From 173 B.C.E., the festival was annual and lasted for six days, from April 28, the anniversary of the founding of her temple, to May 3. The origin of the maypole and collecting May baskets of flowers came from her festival.

⁂ *Flora provided Juno with a special flower that allowed her to become pregnant without male assistance and to give birth to Mars.* [Bell 1991; Durdin-Robertson 1990; Jobes 1962; Redfield 1931; Zimmerman 1964]

Fluona   See *Fluonia*.

Fluonia
Roman
Magic

Name for *Juno* as the goddess who stops the menstrual flow. Alternate forms: Fluona, Fluvinoa. [Bell 1991; Jayne 1925]

Fluvinoa   See *Fluonia*.

Fons
Roman
Water

Goddess of fountains. [Monaghan 1990]

Fornax
Roman
Agriculture; Ceremonies

Goddess of bread. She presides over the entire process, from the growing of the grain to baking. She is celebrated at the *Fornacalia*, the Festival of Ovens. Identified with *Vesta*. [Bell 1991; Durdin-Robertson 1982; Jobes 1962; Redfield 1931; Zimmerman 1964]

Fors
Roman
Unknown

"She Who Brings." Name for *Fortuna*. [Jobes 1962; Monaghan 1981]

Fortuna
Roman
Luck

"Fortune." Identified with *Tyche* and *Nortia*. Her ancient temple in the Forum Boarium at Rome had the same dedication day as that of *Mater Matuta*, June 11. She presides over the fertility of the earth and its inhabitants. She has many epithets, including *Balneorum, Conservatrix, Fors, Mala, Muliebris, Navirilis, Nortia, Praenestina, Primigenia, Privata, Publica, Redux, Salutaris, Virginalis, Virginensis, Virilis*, and *Virgo*. Identical to *Tyche* and to *Ardokhsho*, Near East. See also *Mah*, Near East. Alternate form: Fors. [Bell 1991; Durdin-Robertson 1982; Jayne 1925; Jobes 1962; Woodcock 1953; Zimmerman 1964]

Fraud
Roman
Evil; Demi-animals

Goddess of betrayal. She is portrayed with a human face and a serpentlike body, with a scorpion stinger at the end of her tail. Alternate form: Fraus. [Jobes 1962; Woodcock 1953; Zimmerman 1964]

Fraus   See *Fraud*.

Fulgora
Roman
Weather

Goddess of lightning. Invoked for protection from thunderstorms. [Zimmerman 1964]

Furies, The
Roman
Justice

Avenging goddesses. They include *Alecto* and sometimes *Furina*. They are companions of *Bellona*. There are also said to be Etruscan Furies, one of whom is *Nathum*. Roman equivalent of Greek *Erinyes*. Alternate forms: Aria, Dirae, Furiae, Megaera, Mixoparthenos, Poenae, Semnae, Waelcyrge. [Bell 1991; Cooper 1876; Cotterell 1979; Davidson 1964; Neumann 1972; Senior 1985; Woodcock 1953; Zimmerman 1964]

Furiae   See *The Furies*.

Furina
Roman; Etruscan
Moon and Night; Earth and Nature

Ancient deity of a spring or springs. She had a grove and an annual festival, the *Furrinalia*, which was a state holiday that required annual offerings and a special priest. Said to be a goddess of darkness, of robbers, or of the Earth. Considered by some to be one of the *Furies*. Alternate form: Furrina. [Bell 1991; Durdin-Robertson 1982; Jobes 1962; Leach 1992; Zimmerman 1964]

Furrina   See *Furina*.

Gaea
Grecian
Primordial Being; Creator of Life; Supreme Being; Family and Tribes

"Earth." She is believed to have emerged from Chaos. A supreme power, she created everything—the universe, deities, and humans; an "all-producing and all-nourishing" goddess. She may have been an earlier Phoenician goddess whom the Greeks took as their own. She had many children, including *Agdistis, Ceto*, and *Charybdis*, some by herself and some with male impregnation. She was the mother of the first race, the Titans. She was also the mother of the *Moirae*, the *Erinyes*, and the *Muses* with Uranus or Aether. In later times she was assimilated by other goddesses, just as she had assimilated *Titaea*. Her Roman name is *Tellus*. Similar to *Mulaprakriti*, Indian Subcontinent. Equivalent to *Apia* and *Ghe*, Near East. Alternate forms: Anesidora, Curotrophos, Euonyme, Eurysternos, Gaia, Ge, Ma, Pandora. [Bell 1991; Eliot 1976; Leach 1992; Monaghan 1981; Neumann 1972; Stone 1979; Zimmerman 1964]

Gaeeochos
Grecian
Earth and Nature ⁊

"Holder of the Earth." Name for *Artemis* when at Thebes.

Gaia   See *Gaea*.

Galatea
Grecian
Magic; Love and Sexuality

One of the *Nereides*. Daughter of *Doris*, beloved by the Cyclops Polyphemus. When her lover, Acis, was killed, she changed the blood that flowed from his body into a river, the river Acis, which runs at the foot of Mount Aetna. Alternate forms: Galateia, Gallathaea. [Bell 1991; Jobes 1962; Leach 1992; Redfield 1931; Woodcock 1953; Zimmerman 1964]

Galateia See *Galatea.*

Galaxaura
Grecian
Order; Water
"Calm Sea." One of the *Nereides,* daughter of *Doris* and Oceanus. Also the name of one of the *Oceanides.* Alternate form: Galaxaure. [Bell 1991; Leach 1992]

Galaxaure See *Galaxaura.*

Galene
Grecian
Water
"Mirrorlike." One of the *Nereides,* she is associated with the sea. [Bell 1991; Leach 1992]

Gallathaea See *Galateia.*

Gamelia
Roman
Family and Tribes
1) A name for *Juno* when presiding over marriages. The *Gamelia* was a festival that celebrated marriage, a birthday, or the anniversary of the death of someone. It was usually held on January 1. 2) Also a name for *Hera.* [Bell 1991; Durdin-Robertson 1982; Durdin-Robertson 1990]

Ganymeda See *Hebe.*

Ganymede See *Hebe.* Alternate form: Ganymeda.

Ge See *Gaea.*

Gello
Grecian
Magic; Evil
Female demon. [Jobes 1962]

Gemeter See *Demeter.*

Genetrix
Grecian
Unknown
1) Latin name for *Cybele.* 2) Latin name for Roman *Venus.* [Bell 1991]

Genetyllides, The
Grecian
Mother and Guardian
Goddesses of birth and generation. See also *Genetyllis.* Alternate form: Gennaides. [Bell 1991]

Genetyllis
Grecian
Mother and Guardian
"Protector of Births." One of the *Genetyllides.* She was later identified with *Aphrodite, Artemis,* and *Hecate.* [Bell 1991; Jayne 1925; Leach 1992]

Genita Mana
Roman
Life/Death Cycle; Mother and Guardian
Goddess with power over life and death. She presides over childbirth. [Jayne 1925; Leach 1992]

Gennaides See *The Genetyllides.*

Giane
Sardinia
Earth and Nature; Household Affairs
Wood spirit. She presides over spinning. [Monaghan 1981]

Gigantia
Roman
Unknown
Goddess of the Island of Gozo near Malta. [Monaghan 1990]

Glauce
Grecian
1) Water; Fate; Beauty; 2) Earth and Nature
1) One of the *Nereides.* 2) An Arcadian nymph; mother of *Diana.* See also *Nymphs.* [Bell 1991; Jobes 1962; Zimmerman 1964]

Glaucia
Grecian
Water
Daughter of the Scamander river god. A stream in Boeotia is named for her. [Bell 1991]

Glauconome
Grecian
Water; Fate; Beauty
One of the *Nereides.* [Bell 1991]

Glaucopis
Grecian
Unknown
"Gleaming Eyes." Name for *Athena* as an owl. [Leach 1972]

Glauke
Grecian
Water; Fate; Beauty
"Mirror of the Sea Full of Splendor and Light." One of the *Nereides.* [Leach 1992]

Glaukonome
Grecian
Water; Fate; Beauty
"The Dweller in the Green Sea." One of the *Nereides.* [Leach 1992]

Glaukopis
Roman
Unknown
"Blue Eyes." Name for Roman *Minerva.* [Woodcock 1953]

Gorgons, The
Grecian
Evil; Ugliness
Monsters. Said originally to have been only one, they are now three—*Euryale, Stheno,* and *Medusa.* Their parents were either *Ceto* and Phorcys or *Echidna* and Typhon. Frightening in appearance, with snakes in their hair, tusks, hands of metal, and wings, anyone looking into their eyes would turn to stone. They were guarded by their sisters, the *Graeae.* Alternate form: Phorcides. [Bell 1991; Jobes 1962; Neumann 1972; Senior 1985; Zimmerman 1964]

Gorgopa
Grecian
Destroyer of Life

"Death." Also a name for *Athena*. Alternate form: Grogopa.
[Jobes 1962]

Graces, The   See *The Charites*.

Graeae, The
Grecian
Water; Ugliness
"Old Women." Daughters of *Ceto* and Phorcys. Sisters of
the *Gorgons*. They may personify the white sea foam. Their
names are *Deino*, *Enyo*, *Pemphredo*, and *Perso*. They had
only one eye and one tooth among them, which they shared.
They used the eye for guarding the *Gorgons*, warning them
of danger. Alternate forms: Graiai, Phorcides. [Bell 1991;
Neumann 1972; Senior 1985; Zimmerman 1964]

Graiai   See *The Graeae*.

Gratiae, The
Roman
Beauty; Charisma
Name for Greek *Charites*. [Bell 1991; Zimmerman 1964]

Grogopa   See *Gorgopa*.

Gymnasia
Grecian
Time; Order
One of the *Horae*. [Bell 1991; Stone 1979]

Haero   See *Merope*.

Hagno
Grecian
Earth and Nature; Mother and Guardian
An Arcadian nymph. Nurse of Zeus with *Neda* and
Theisoa. See also *Nymphs*. [Bell 1991; Leach 1992]

Halcyon   See *Alcyone*.

Halcyone   See *Alcyone*.

Halia
Grecian
Water
"The Saltiness of the Sea." 1) One of the *Nereides*. 2) Sister
of the Telchines and mother of *Rhodos* in Rhodes She became
the personification of the sea. Alternate form: Leucothea.
[Bell 1991; Leach 1992]

Haliae, The
Grecian
Water
Marine nymphs. See also *Nymphs*. [Bell 1991]

Halimede
Grecian
Water; Education and Knowledge
"Sea Goddess of Good Counsel." One of the *Nereides*, she
is associated with the salty sea. [Bell 1991; Leach 1992]

Halsodyne
Grecian
1) Water; 2) Unknown; 3) Water; Fate; Beauty
"Sea-fed" or "Sea-born." 1) Sea goddess. 2) Name for
Amphitrite and *Thetis*. 3) One of the *Nereides*. [Bell 1991;
Leach 1992]

Hamadryades, The
Grecian
Earth and Nature
Tree nymphs, daughters of *Hamadryas*. They appear as
human females above the waist and as trees below. Their
mother was *Hamadryas*. *Atlantia*, *Byblis*, *Chrysopeleia*,
Dryope, and *Sagaritis* were Hamadryades. They belong to
the larger classification *Dryades*. See also *Nymphs*. Alternate
form: Hamadryads. [Bell 1991; Jobes 1962; Zimmerman 1964]

Hamadryads   See *Hamadryades*.

Hamadryas
Grecian
Unknown
Mother of the *Hamadryades*. [Bell 1991]

Hamaelides, The
Grecian
Earth and Nature
Nymphs of fruit trees. They belong to the larger classification
Dryades. See also *Nymphs*. [Bell 1991]

Harmonia
Grecian
1) Unknown; 2) Water; Health and Healing; Fate; Intelligence
and Creativity
1) Daughter of *Aphrodite* and Ares. By her husband
Cadmus, the mother of *Agave*, *Autonoe*, *Ino*, Polydorus, and
Semele. 2) One of the *Naiades*, said by some to be the mother
of the *Amazons*. Alternate form: Hermiona. [Bell 1991; Jobes
1962; Redfield 1931; Senior 1985; Zimmerman 1964]

Harpies, The
Grecian
Weather; Justice; Ugliness; Demi-animals; Heaven and Hell;
Wild Birds
Orginally goddesses of the storm winds. Included
are *Aello*, *Celaeno*, *Kelaino*, *Lelaino*, *Nicothoe*, *Ocypete*,
Podarge. They later became "the Snatchers." They are said
to number from one to as many as eight, and there is no
agreement as to their parentage. They are sisters of *Arce*
and *Iris*. In their later form, they are portrayed as monsters
with female heads and vulturelike bodies and appendages.
They are said to "carry away the souls of the dead, serve
as ministers of divine vengeance, and punish criminals."
Similar to the *Cataclothes*. [Bell 1991; Bonnerjea 1927; Leach
1992; Lurker 1984; Redfield 1931; Zimmerman 1964]

Hebe
Grecian
Ceremonies; Life/Death Cycle
"Youth." Daughter of *Hera* and Zeus. One of her tasks was
cupbearer to the deities. This responsibility was assumed by a
young man, Ganymede, and Hebe is sometimes known by
his name, both in its masculine and feminine forms (Ganymede
and *Ganymeda*). As wife of Heracles she had two sons,
Alexiares and Anicetus. Equivalent to the Roman *Juventas*.
Alternate form: Dia. [Bell 1991; Leach 1992; Redfield 1931;
Senior 1985; Zimmerman 1964]

Hecaerge
Grecian
Physical Prowess
"Hitting at a Distance." 1) Name for *Artemis* and *Aphrodite*
in reference to marksmanship. 2) Name of a daughter of Boreas
who was a Hyperborean maiden. [Bell 1991]

Hecate
Grecian
Moon and Night; Magic; Wealth; Education and Knowledge;
Goodness; Ceremonies
Originally a Thracian moon goddess, she was absorbed
as a Titan by the Greeks. Her parents are listed variously as
Asteria and Perses, *Pheraea* and Zeus, or *Nyx* and Tartarus.
Her powers extend to all regions. She has the power of magic
and sorcery and bestows wealth and wisdom. Hecate forms a
trinity with *Diana* and *Lucina.* On August 13 a great festival
was held for Hecate, the moon goddess, and *Diana,* her Roman
successor. Her aid was invoked to avert storms which might
harm the coming harvest. It has been suggested that August
15, the Assumption of the Blessed Virgin when prayers are
offered to the Virgin to turn aside storms until the fields are
reaped, was derived from Hecate's festival. Small replicas of
Hecate are placed at the entrances of houses and at crossroads to
protect those who pass from evil. Hecate forms a triad with
Demeter and *Persephone.* Identified with *Bendis, Bona Dea,*
and *Genetyllis.* See also *Hecate,* Near East. Alternate forms:
Angelos, Brimo, Chthonia, Cratais, Epipyrgidia, Munychia,
Perseis, Phosphoros. [Bell 1991; Durdin-Robertson 1982;
Harding 1971; Leach 1992; Monaghan 1981; Neumann 1972;
Senior 1985; Stone 1979; Woodcock 1953; Zimmerman 1964]

Hegemone
Grecian
Justice; Agriculture
"Leader" or "Ruler." 1) Name for *Artemis.* 2) Name of one
of the *Charites,* who was invoked in the swearing of oaths.
Said by some to be a goddess of plants, responsible for their
fruition. Associated with *Auxo.* [Bell 1992; Jobes 1962; Leach
1992]

Hegetoria
Grecian
Earth and Nature
Nymph in Rhodes. See also *Nymphs.* [Bell 1991]

Heimarmene
Grecian
Fate
"Fate." She is more abstract than the *Fates,* and they are
probably included collectively in this name. The Phoenicians
said she became one of the wives of Cronus. See also *Atropos,*
Clotho, and *Nemesis.* [Bell 1991; Durdin-Robertson 1982]

Helen
Grecian
1) Beauty; War; 2) Unknown
1) Beautiful daughter of *Leda* and Zeus, known as Helen of
Sparta. It is said that her journey (it may have been voluntary,
or she may have been kidnapped) with Paris to Troy
precipitated the Trojan War. 2) A daughter of Epidamnius
who was a goddess and an attendant of *Aphrodite*; a daughter
of Fasustulus. Alternate forms: Helena, Dendritus. [Bell 1991;
Chicago 1979; Jobes 1962; Redfield 1931; Senior 1985]

Helena
Grecian
Moon and Night; Health and Healing
Moon goddess in Sparta who possessed the ability to heal.
Said by some to have incarnated as *Helen.* [Durdin-
Robertson 1975; Jayne 1925; Leach 1992]

Helia
Grecian
Sun and Day
Sun Goddess. Daughter of Helios and sister of Phaethon.
[Leach 1992]

Heliadae, The
Grecian
Unhappiness; Magic
Female descendents of Helios, the sun god. Their mothers
were *Rhodos* and *Clymene.* The male descendents were
called Heliades. The children of Rhodos were Actis,
Candalus, Cercaphus, *Electryone,* Macareus, Ochimus,
Tenages, and Triopas. The children of *Clymene* were *Aegiale,*
Aigle, Aetheria, Dioxippe, Merope, and Phaethon.
Lampethusa, Phaethusa, and *Phatusa* are also Heliadae.

⚕ *When Phaethon drove the chariot of the sun across the sky,*
his sisters yoked the horses for him. Losing control of the
horses, Phaethon swung too close to the Earth, setting it on
fire. Zeus sent a lightning bolt to knock him from the chariot. Helios
managed to gain control of the chariot and save the world, but
Phaethon was drowned. His sisters, believing they were responsible,
wept unceasingly and were changed into poplar trees; their tears
became pieces of amber.
Alternate form: Phaethonides. [Bell 1991; Monaghan 1981;
Zimmerman 1964]

Helice
Grecian
1) Water; Fate; Beauty; 2) Water; 3) Stars and Planets
1) One of the *Nereides.* 2) An *Oceanid,* daughter of *Tethys*
and Oceanus. Nurse of Zeus. 3) Daughter of Lycaon who
aided *Demeter* in her search for *Persephone* and was changed
into the constellation Ursa Major. See also *Aega, Callisto,* and
Cynosura. [Bell 1991; Leach 1992; Monaghan 1981]

Heliconides, The
Grecian
Unknown
Name for the *Muses* on Mt. Helicon. [Woodcock 1953;
Zimmerman 1964]

Helike
Grecian
Earth and Nature
"Willow." A nymph. See also *Nymphs.* [Leach 1992]

Helle
Grecian
Water
Daughter of *Nephele* and Athamas.
⚕ *The ram with the Golden Fleece was sent by Nephele to*
rescue Helle and her brother, Phrixus. While riding on the
ram, Helle fell off. The sea into which she fell was named the
Hellespont after her. She was rescued by Poseidon and became a sea
deity. [Bell 1991; Jobes 1962; Leach 1972; Redfield 1931;
Zimmerman 1964]

Hellotia
Grecian
Ceremonies
1) Name for *Europa* in Crete, where she had a festival by
this name. 2) Name for *Athena* at Corinth. [Bell 1991]

Hemera
Grecian
1) Sun and Day; 2) Earth and Nature
"Day." 1) Daughter of *Nyx* and Erebus (brother of Aether)
and mother of *Thalassa.* 2) A nymph. See also *Nymphs.*
Alternate form: Himera. [Bell 1991; Leach 1992; Redfield
1931; Zimmerman 1964]

Hemeresia
Grecian
Water

"The Soothing Goddess." Name for *Artemis* when she was worshiped at the spring Lusi in Arcadia. [Bell 1991]

Hemithea
Grecian
Unknown
Name for *Molpadia*, the daughter of Staphylus. [Bell 1991]

Henioche
Grecian
Unknown
"Charioteer." Name for *Hera* in Lebadeia. [Bell 1991]

Heos   See *Aurora, Eos.*

Heptapora
Grecian
Arts and Sciences; Intelligence and Creativity; Evil
One of the *Muses.* [Bell 1991]

Hera
Grecian
Supreme Being; Family and Tribes; Mother and Guardian; Fate; Weather
Supreme goddess. Goddess of marriage and childbirth. One of the twelve Olympian deities. Daughter of *Rhea* and Cronus, her husband was Zeus, and she was mother of Ares, *Hebe,* and Hephaestus. She is also the mother of the nymph *Arge.* She can bestow the gift of prophecy. As deity of the atmosphere, her bad moods are displayed in violent storms. Known as *Juno* in Rome. She is identified with *Ceres, Eileithyia.* Alternate forms: Acraea, Aegophagos, Akraia, Ammonia, Antheia, Argeia, Chera, Gamelia, Henioche, Hercyna, Hippia, Hypercheiria, Imbrasia, Kourotrophos, Lucina, Nympheuomene, Pais, Parthenia, Pelasga, Pharygaea, Prodromia, Telchinia, Teleia, Theria, Syzygia, Zygia. [Bell 1991; Bolen 1984; Leach 1992; Stone 1979; Zimmerman 1964]

Hercyna
Grecian
1) Unknown; 2) Water
1) Name for *Hera* and for *Demeter* at Lebadeia. 2) Daughter of Trophonios. There is a spring named for her. Alternate form: Herkyna. [Bell 1991; Leach 1992]

Herkyna   See *Hercyna.*

Hermiona   See *Harmonia.*

Hermione
Grecian
Unknown
Name for *Persephone* at Syracuse. Alternate forms: Hyrmine, Iphiboe, Ledaea. [Bell 1991; Woodcock 1953; Zimmerman 1964]

Herse
Grecian
Agriculture; Weather
Goddess of agriculture and the dew. Sister of *Agraulos, Pandrosos,* and Erysichthon. The three sisters served *Athena,* blessing the fruitfulness of the fields. [Bell 1991; Durdin-Robertson 1982; Leach 1992; Redfield 1931]

Hespera
Grecian
Mother and Guardian; Earth and Nature
One of the *Hesperides.* Alternate forms: Hesperie, Hesperia. [Bell 1991; Redfield 1931; Zimmerman 1964]

Hesperia   See *Asterope, Hespera.*

Hesperides, The
Grecian
Mother and Guardian; Earth and Nature
Guardians of the golden apples given to *Hera* at her wedding by *Gaea.* The names, numbers, and parents of these nymphs vary. One set of parents is given as Atlas and *Hesperis;* another source gives *Themis* as their mother. The Hesperides include *Aigle, Arethusa, Erythea, Hestia,* and *Hespera.* They were aided in their duties by the dragon Ladon. See also *Nymphs.* Alternate form: Atlantides. [Bell 1991; Jobes 1962; Neumann 1972; Woodcock 1953; Zimmerman 1964]

Hesperie   See *Hespera.*

Hesperis
Grecian
Unknown
Mother of the *Hesperides.* Daughter of Hesperus and wife of Atlas. [Bell 1991; Redfield 1931; Zimmerman 1964]

Hestia
Grecian
1) Fire; Household Affairs; Family and Tribes; 2) Mother and Guardian; Earth and Nature
1) Virgin goddess of the hearth flame. Guardian of the family and the community. She was worshiped at the hearth, both at home and in public. Her perpetual flame embraces the centricity of the universe. *Vesta* is her Roman counterpart. 2) One of the *Hesperides.* [Bell 1991; Bolen 1984; Leach 1992]

Heurippe
Grecian
Domesticated Animals
"Finder of Horses." Name for *Artemis* when at Pheneus. [Bell 1991]

Hilaeira
Grecian
Moon and Night
"The Shining." Name for *Selene.* Alternate forms: Hilaira, Hilara, Ilaeira, Talaira. [Bell 1991; Zimmerman 1964]

Hilaira   See *Hilaeira.*

Hilara   See *Hilaeira.*

Himalia
Grecian
Agriculture
Benediction Goddess who blessed the harvest. Mother of Cronius, Spartaeus, and Cytus by Zeus. [Bell 1991; Leach 1992]

Himalis
Grecian
Agriculture
"Goddess of Grain." Name for *Demeter* when in Syracuse. [Leach 1992]

Himera   See *Hemera.*

Himeropa
Grecian
Charisma
"Arousing Face." A *Siren.* [Monaghan 1981]

Hippe
Grecian
1) Earth and Nature; Mother and Guardian; 2) Unknown;
3) Unknown
   1) A nymph, nurse of Dionysus. 2) A daughter of the
Centaur Cheiron. 3) A wife of Elatus and mother of Caeneus
who became *Caenis.* This Hippe was also called *Hippeia.* See
also *Nymphs.* [Bell 1991]

Hippeia   See *Hippe.*

Hippia
Grecian
Domesticated Animals
   "Horse Goddess." Name for *Hera* at Olympia. Also the
name of *Athena* at Athens, Tegea, and Olympia. A name for
Minerva because she taught humans how to use horses.
Alternate form: Hippias. [Bell 1991; Leach 1972; Monaghan
1981; Woodcock 1953]

Hippias   See *Hippia.*

Hippo
Grecian
Demi-animals; Water
   One of the *Oceanides,* associated with horses and swift
currents. [Bell 1991; Leach 1992; Monaghan 1981]

Hippocrenides, The
Grecian
Arts; Sciences; Intelligence and Creativity; Evil
   Name for the *Muses* that derives from the fountain at
Hippocrene. [Woodcock 1953]

Hippodameia
Grecian
Domesticated Animals
   Name for *Aphrodite* when connected with horses. [Bell
1992; Jobes 1962; Senior 1985; Zimmerman 1964]

Hippolaitis
Grecian
Unknown
   Name for *Athena* when at Hippola in Laconia. [Bell 1991]

Hippona
Roman
Domesticated Animals
   Roman goddess who presides over horses. [Jobes 1962;
Redfield 1931; Woodcock 1953]

Hipponoe
Grecian
Water; Fate; Beauty; Disorder
   "Unruly As a Mare." One of the *Nereides.* [Bell 1991;
Leach 1992]

Hippothoe
Grecian
1) Water; Fate; Beauty; Physical Prowess; 2) Stars and
Planets; Magic
   "Swift As a Mare." 1) One of the *Nereides.* 2) One of the
Pleiades, and a daughter of Mestor and *Lysidice.* [Bell 1991;
Leach 1992]

Hora
Roman
Earth and Nature
   Roman goddess who presides over time and space or
beauty. [Bell 1991; Zimmerman 1964]

Horae, The
Grecian
Time; Order
   Goddesses of the seasons, they are concerned with order in
nature and in the lives of humans. Sisters of the *Moirae.* Like
other deities, their names and ancestry vary. Some consider
their mother to be *Themis.* They include *Acme, Auxo,
Anatole, Carpo, Dice, Dysis, Eirene, Eunomia, Euporia,
Gymnasia, Mesembria, Musike, Nymphes, Orthosia,
Pherusa, Sponde, Telete, Thallo,* and *Titanis.* Alternate form:
Horai. [Bell 1991; Leach 1992; Redfield 1931; Zimmerman
1964]

Horai   See *The Horae.*

Horme
Grecian
Physical Prowess
   "Energetic Activity." Worshiped in Athens. [Bell 1991]

Horta
Roman; Etruscan
Earth and Nature
   Goddess of gardens. [Redfield 1931]

Hosia
Grecian
Ceremonies
   Goddess of holy rituals. [Leach 1992]

Hostilina
Roman
Agriculture
   Roman goddess of growing corn. [Wedeck and Baskin
1971; Woodcock 1953]

Hyades, The
Grecian
Weather; Stars and Planets
   "Rainy." The nymphs whose appearance foretells rain
when the constellation of the Pleiades is in conjunction
with the sun. Daughters of *Aethra* or, by some accounts,
Boeotia. Their father is Atlas. The Hyades were placed in
the sky as a constellation by Zeus. They include *Adraste,
Aesyle, Ambrosia, Bacche, Boeotia, Cleia, Cleis, Coronis,
Dione, Eidothea, Erato, Eudora, Nysa, Pedile, Phaeo, Phyto,
Polyxo, Thyene.* See also *Nymphs.* Alternate form: Dodonides.
[Bell 1991; Leach 1992; Redfield 1931; Zimmerman 1964]

Hyale
Grecian
Earth and Nature
   The name of a nymph of Roman *Diana.* See also *Nymphs.*
[Bell 1991]

Hybla
Sicily
Earth and Nature
   Earth goddess. [Monaghan 1981]

Hydra
Grecian
Immortality
   Guardian of the underworld for *Hera.* Daughter (some say
son) of *Echidna.* [Monaghan 1981]

Hydria
Grecian
Water
   Water nymph. See also *Nymphs.* [Jobes 1962]

Hygea   See *Hygeia*

Hygeia
Grecian
Health and Healing
   1) "Health." Daughter of Asclepius and *Epione*. Sister of *Aegle, Iaso,* and *Panacea*. 2) A name for *Athena* as the guardian of mental health. Identified with Roman *Salus*. Equivalent to Roman *Valetudo*. Alternate forms: Hygea, Hygieia. [Bell 1991; Jayne 1925; Leach 1972; Leach 1992; Zimmerman 1964]

Hygieia   See *Hygeia*.

Hymnia
Grecian
Unknown
   Name for *Artemis* when worshiped in Arcadia. [Bell 1991]

Hypate
Grecian
Arts; Sciences; Intelligence and Creativity; Evil
   One of the *Muses*. Worshiped at Delphi with her sisters *Mese* and *Nete*. [Bell 1991]

Hypercheiria
Grecian
Mother and Guardian
   "Goddess with the Protecting Hands." Name for *Hera* in Sparta. [Bell 1991]

Hypereia
Grecian
Water
   A nymph who had a spring named for her. See also *Nymphs*. [Leach 1992]

Hypermestra   See *Mestra*.

Hyrmine   See *Hermione*.

Iaera
Grecian
Earth and Nature
   One of the *Nereides*, daughter of *Doris* and Nereus. Also the name of a wood nymph whose children were Pandarus and Bitias and whose husband was Alcanor. See also *Nymphs*. Alternate form: Iaira. [Bell 1991; Leach 1992]

Iaira   See *Iaera*.

Iambe
Grecian
Happiness; Arts
   Servant in the house of Celeus and *Metaneira*. Daughter of *Echo* and Pan. It was Iambe who, by joking and dancing, was able to cheer *Demeter* during her search for *Persephone*. It is believed that the term *iambic* (a type of poetry) derives from her name. [Bell 1991; Jobes 1962; Leach 1972]

Ianassa
Grecian
Water; Fate; Beauty
   One of the *Nereides*. [Bell 1991; Leach 1992]

Ianeira
Grecian
1) Water; 2) Water; Fate; Beauty

1) One of the *Oceanides,* daughter of *Tethys* and Oceanus.
2) One of the *Nereides,* daughter of *Doris* and Nereus. Alternate form: Ianira. [Bell 1991; Leach 1992)

Ianira   See *Ianeira*.

Ianthe
Grecian
Water
   One of the *Oceanides,* daughter of *Tethys* and Oceanus. She was a friend of *Persephone*. [Bell 1991; Leach 1992]

Iasis
Grecian
Health and Healing; Water
   One of the *Ionides*, a nymph at a healing spring in Elis. See also *Nymphs*. [Jayne 1925; Leach 1992]

Iaso
Grecian
Health and Healing
   "Recovery." Goddess of medicine, daughter of Asclepius and *Epione* and sister of *Aegle, Hygeia,* and *Panacea*. [Wedeck and Baskin 1971; Zimmerman 1964]

Iasonia
Grecian
Unknown
   Name for *Athena* at Cyzicus. [Bell 1991]

Ichnaea   See *Themis*.

Ida
Grecian
1) Mother and Guardian; 2) Earth and Nature; 3) Earth and Nature
   Name of several nymphs. 1) Daughter of Melisseus who was one of the nurses of Zeus. 2) An Idaean nymph who was the mother of the *Dactyls*. See also *Anchiale*. 4) A nymph who was loved by Hyrtacus. See also *Nymphs*. [Bell 1991; Monaghan 1981]

Idaea
Grecian
1) Earth and Nature; 2) Unknown
   1) A nymph who inhabited Mount Ida. Daughter of Dardanus and *Bateia*. 2) Sometimes given as a name for *Cybele*. [Bell 1991; Jobes 1962]

Idalia
Grecian
Unknown
   Name for *Aphrodite* where she is worshiped at Idalion in Cyprus. [Bell 1991; Jobes 1962]

Idothea   See *Eidothea*.

Idya   See *Idyia*.

Idyia
Grecian
Water
   One of the *Oceanides,* daughter of *Tethys* and Oceanus. Wife of Aeetes and mother of *Medea* and *Chalciope*. Alternate forms: Eidyia, Idya. [Bell 1991; Leach 1992; Zimmerman 1964]

Ignea   See *Vesta*.

Ilaeira   See *Hilaeira*.

Ilia
Roman
Unknown
    Name for *Rhea Silvia*. [Bell 1991; Monaghan 1981; Zimmerman 1964]

Ilissiades, The
Grecian
Arts; Sciences; Intelligence and Creativity; Evil
    Name for the *Muses* in Attica. [Bell 1991]

Ilithyia   See *Eileithyia*.

Ilythyia-Leucothea
Grecian
Unknown
    Greek goddess associated with the Roman *Cupra*. [Sykes 1968]

Imbrasia
Grecian
Water
    Name for *Hera* on the banks of the Imbrasus River in Samos. [Bell 1991]

Inferna
Roman
Heaven and Hell
    "Underworld." Name for *Proserpina* and *Juno*. [Bell 1991; Woodcock 1953]

Ino
Grecian
Water
    Daughter of *Harmonia* and Cadmus, sister of *Agave*, *Autonoe*, Polydorus, and *Semele*. She was transformed into a sea goddess called *Leucothea*. She is identified with *Mater Matuta*. [Bell 1991; Jobes 1962; Leach 1972; Redfield 1931; Zimmerman 1964]

Intercidona
Roman
Mother and Guardian; Household Affairs
    Roman protectress of children. Also known as the goddess of the axe and firewood. Using her axe, Intercidona guards new mothers from evil spirits, especially Silvanus, by pounding on door thresholds. Companion of *Deverra* and *Pilumnus*. [Bell 1991; Jayne 1925; Leach 1992; Wedeck and Baskin 1971]

Interduca
Roman
Family and Tribes
    Name for Roman *Juno* related to the marriage ceremony. [Bell 1991]

Invidia
Grecian
Unhappiness
    "Envy." Daughter of Pallas and *Styx*. [Bell 1991]

Inyx
Grecian
Earth and Nature; Magic; Wild Birds
    Woodland nymph. Daughter of Pan and either *Echo* or *Peitho*. She was changed into a bird, the wryneck, by *Hera*, who was angry about the attention Zeus gave to Inyx. See also *Nymphs*. [Bell 1991]

Iodama
Grecian
1) Health and Healing; 2) Earth and Nature
    "Healer." 1) Daughter of *Melanippe*. 2) Mother of *Thebe*, a nymph and priestess of *Athena*. See also *Nymphs*. [Bell 1991; Jobes 1962]

Iole
Grecian
Dawn and Twilight
    Dawn. Daughter of *Antioche* and Eurytus. [Bell 1991; Jobes 1962]

Ione
Grecian
Water; Fate; Beauty
    One of the *Nereides*. Daughter of *Tethys* and Oceanus. [Bell 1991; Leach 1992]

Ioniades, The   See *The Ionides*.

Ionides, The
Grecian
Health and Healing; Water
    Nymphs of healing. They were associated with a mineral spring in Ellis. They include *Iasis* and *Kalliphaeia*. See also *Nymphs*. Alternate forms: Ioniades, Pegaeae, Synallaxis. [Bell 1991; Jayne 1925]

Iope   See *Cassiopeia*.

Iophossa   See *Chalciope*.

Ioulo, The
Grecian
Unknown
    Goddesses who are invoked by howling. [Stutley and Stutley 1984]

Iphianassa
Grecian
Water; Fate; Beauty
    One of the *Nereides*. [Bell 1991; Leach 1992]

Iphiboe   See *Hermione*.

Iphigeneia
Grecian
Unknown
    A name for *Artemis* at Hermione. Alternate forms: Iphianassa, Oreilochia, Orsiloche. [Bell 1991; Jobes 1962; Redfield 1931; Woodcock 1953; Zimmerman 1964]

Iphimedeia
Grecian
Courage
    Mother of the giant twins Otus and Ephialtes. Daughter of *Atlantia*.

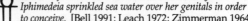 *Poseidon fathered them, but in an unusual way. Iphimedeia sprinkled sea water over her genitals in order to conceive.* [Bell 1991; Leach 1972; Zimmerman 1964]

Iphthime
Grecian
1) Water; Fate; Beauty; 2) Unknown
    1) One of the *Nereides*. Mother of the Satyrs. 2) Daughter of Icarius and sister of *Penelope*. Athena is said to have assumed Iphthime's shape when she needed to visit Penelope. [Bell 1991]

Irene   See *Eirene*.

Iris
Grecian
Weather
"Messenger of Light." Goddess of the rainbow. Daughter of *Electra* and Thaumas, sister of *Arce* and the *Harpies.* Alternate form: Aellopos. [Leach 1992; Redfield 1931]

Isia
Grecian
Intelligence and Creativity
Name for Egyptian *Isis.* Goddess of intelligence and perception. [Harding 1971; Jobes 1962]

Issoria
Grecian
Unknown
Name for *Artemis* in Sparta. [Bell 1991]

Ithome
Grecian
Earth and Nature; Mother and Guardian
Nymph and nurse of Zeus. She gave her name to the Messenian hill of Ithome. See also *Neda, Nymphs.* [Bell 1991]

Itonia
Grecian
Unknown
Name for *Athena* at Iton, Thessaly, and Corona. Alternate forms: Itonias, Itonis. [Bell 1991; Jobes 1962; Leach 1972]

Itonias   See *Itonia.*

Itonis   See *Itonia.*

Iuno   See *Juno.*

Iustitia   See *Justitia.*

Iuturna   See *Juturna.*

Iuventas   See *Juventas.*

Jana
Roman
Moon and Night
Roman moon goddess. Wife of Janus. Alternate form: Diana. [Bell 1991; Zimmerman 1964]

Juga
Roman
Family and Tribes
Name for Roman *Juno* as goddess of marriage. Alternate form: Jugalis. [Bell 1991]

Jugalis   See *Juga.*

Juno
Roman
Mother and Guardian; Family and Tribes; Justice; Commerce and Travel
Supreme goddess. Wife of Jupiter. She forms a trinity with *Minerva* and Jupiter. Protecting everything connected with women, she is especially involved in marriage and children. She is also involved in public affairs, money, and politics. Unlike *Hera,* she is little concerned about the activities of her husband. She may have evolved from Etruscan *Uni.* She is identified with Roman *Feronia, Mater Matuta,* and *Proserpina;* Greek *Eileithyia, Hera; Astroarche,* Near East; and *Nicnevin,* Western Europe. On March 7 her festival, the *Junonalia* is held.

⩲ *In the solemnity . . . two images of Juno, made of cypress, were borne in procession. Then marched 27 girls, habited in long robes, singing a hymn to the goddess; then came the decemviri, crowned with laurel, investments edged with purple. This pompous company, going through the Vicus Jugarius, had a dance in the great field of Rome; from thence they proceeded through the Forum Boarium to the temple of Juno.*

Some goddesses that were absorbed into her worship are *Empanada, Matuta,* and *Mephistis.* Alternate forms: Cinxia, Concilciatrix, Cupra, Curiatia, Curitis, Domiduca, Inferna, Iuno, Interduca, Juga, Jugalis, Lacinia, Luceria, Lucetia, Lucina, Megale, Moneta, Natalis, Ossipaga, Parthenos, Pertunda, Populonia, Prema, Pronubia, Quiritis, Regina, Sororia, Sospita, Thana, Unxia, Virginalis, Viriplaca. [Avery 1962; Bell 1991; Durdin-Robertson 1975; Durdin-Robertson 1982; Leach 1992; Neumann 1972; Redfield 1931; Woodcock 1953]

Justitia
Roman
Justice
"Justice." She is portrayed blindfolded, holding two evenly balanced scales and a sword. Alternate form: Iustitia. [Durdin-Robertson 1982; Jobes 1962]

Juturna
Roman
Water; Ceremonies
Goddess of fountains and waters, she is a nymph at the spring in Latium. Some say she is the wife of Janus, mother of Fons. She had a sanctuary in the Campus Martius, and her sacred celebration, the *Juturnalia,* was celebrated on January 11, the date on which her temple was erected. See also *Nymphs.* Alternate forms: Diuturna, Iuturna. [Bell 1991; Durdin-Robertson 1982; Leach 1972; Leach 1992; Redfield 1931; Zimmerman 1964]

Juventas
Roman
Life/Death Cycle
Goddess of youth. Her sanctuary predated Jupiter's. Equivalent to Greek *Hebe.* Alternate forms: Iuventas, Juventus. [Bell 1992; Leach 1992; Lurker 1984; Redfield 1931]

Juventus   See *Juventas.*

Kabeiroi, The   See *Cabeiriae.*

Kakia
Grecian
Evil
"Vice." A name for *Caca.* [Monaghan 1981; Zimmerman 1964]

Kallianassa
Grecian
Water; Fate; Beauty
One of the *Nereides.* [Leach 1992]

Kallianeira
Grecian
Water; Fate; Beauty
One of the *Nereides.* [Leach 1992]

Kalliphaeira
Grecian
Earth and Nature
One of the *Ionides.* She is found at Elis. [Leach 1992]

Kallirhoe   See *Callirrhoe.*

Kalliste   See *Callisto.*

Kallisto   See *Callisto.*

Kalypso   See *Calypso.*

Karpophoros
Grecian
1) Earth and Nature; 2) Agriculture
   "She Who Bears Fruits." 1) Goddess of wild things.
2) Name for *Demeter.* [Jobes 1962; Stutley and Stutley 1984]

Kaukasis
Grecian
Unknown
   Name for *Artemis* in the village of Caucasia on the island
of Chios. Inhabited by the Pelasgians, this village was the
center of worship of *Artemis.* [Ergener 1988]

Kelaino
Grecian
Weather; Justice; Ugliness; Demi-animals; Heaven and Hell;
Wild Birds
   One of the *Harpies.* [Lurker 1984]

Ker   See *Cer.*

Keraunia
Grecian
Unknown
   Name for *Semele* when killed by Zeus by lightning.
[Bonnerjea 1927; Jobes 1962]

Keres, The
Grecian
Goodness
   Malevolent death spirits.
   *When the Moirai had arranged a mortal's time of death, the
   malevolent Keres appeared. These female spirits, with pointed
   claws and bloodstained cloaks, delivered the fatal blow and
took their victims to the land of shadows.*
   See also *Cataclothes.* [Cotterell 1989]

Kerkeis   See *Cerceïs.*

Kerres
Roman
Mother and Guardian
   Mother goddess. Probably an early form of *Ceres.* [Jobes
1962]

Kidaria
Grecian
Unknown
   "Mask." Name for *Demeter.* [Monaghan 1981]

Kirke   See *Circe.*

Kleio   See *Clio.*

Klothes
Grecian
Household Affairs
   Goddess of spinning. [Neumann 1972]

Klotho   See *Clotho.*

Klymene   See *Clymene.*

Klytia   See *Clytia.*

Kolias
Grecian
Earth and Nature
   Goddess of the foothills. See also *Colias.* [Leach 1992]

Komodia
Grecian
Arts; Happiness
   Goddess of music and amusement. [Leach 1992]

Kore
Grecian
Unknown
   "Maiden." She may have been equivalent to or entirely
separate from *Persephone.* She is identified with Roman
Libera. In a Christianized version of her worship on the "Eve
of the Epiphany of Kore," the Koreion on January 5, was
celebrated by Clement of Alexandria:
   *The people spent the night in the temple, singing to the
   accompaniment of flutes. A troop of torchbearers entered and
   went down into the underground cult chamber whence they
brought up a statue: A wooden idol and its seals, but otherwise
naked, were placed in a litter and carried seven times round the
inner temple.*
   Alternate forms: Carpophori, Core. [Chicago 1979; Leach
1992; Neumann 1972; Stone 1979; Zimmerman 1964]

Kore-Arethusa
Grecian
Unknown
   Name for *Persephone* when she assumed *Arethusa's* role.
[Lurker 1984]

Koros
Grecian
Happiness
   Goddess of exuberance. [Leach 1992]

Kottutto   See *Cotys.*

Kotus   See *Cotys.*

Kotyto   See *Cotys.*

Kourotrophos
Grecian
1) Mother and Guardian; 2) Unknown
   "Nourisher of Children." 1) Samian goddess who protects
infants. 2) Name for *Hera.* See also *Curotrophos.* [Jobes 1962;
Leach 1992; Redfield 1931]

Kranto
Grecian
Water; Fate; Beauty
   One of the *Nereides.* Daughter of *Doris* and Nereus.
[Leach 1992]

Kratesis
Grecian
Justice; War
   "Ruling." Goddess of victory. [Leach 1992]

Kteis   See *Cteis.*

Kulmu   See *Kulsu.*

Kulsu
Roman; Etruscan
Heaven and Hell
   Chthonic goddess. Alternate form: Kulmu. [Cooper 1876]

Kuttuto   See *Cotys.*

Kymathea
Grecian
Unknown
   One of the *Nereides.* Daughter of *Doris* and Nereus.
[Leach 1992]

Kymatolege
Grecian
Water; Order; Fate; Beauty
   "Wave-stiller." One of the *Nereides.* [Leach 1992]

Kymo   See *Cymo.*

Kymodoce   See *Cymodoce.*

Kymothoe   See *Cymothoe.*

Kypris
Grecian
Unknown
   Name for *Aphrodite* at her shrines on Cyprus and Kythera.
[Lurker 1984]

La Strega
Roman
Unknown
   Name for *Befana.* [Leach 1972]

La Vecchia
Roman
Unknown
   Name for *Befana.* [Bell 1991]

Lachesis
Grecian
Fate
   One of the *Moirae.* She measures the length of the thread
of life. See also *Decuma.* [Bell 1991; Leach 1992; Redfield
1931; Zimmerman 1964]

Lacinia
Roman
Unknown
   Name for *Juno.* [Woodcock 1953]

Lactura
Grecian
Agriculture
   Corn goddess. [Woodcock 1953]

Lala   See *Losna.*

Lalal
Roman; Etruscan
Moon and Night
   Moon goddess. See also *Losna* and *Lucna.* [Monaghan
1990]

Lamia
Grecian
Ugliness; Unhappiness; Evil
   One of the *Lamiae.*

   *Driven insane when Hera kidnapped her children,
   Lamia became an ugly, frightening monster who devoured
   children.*
   See also *La Masthu,* Near East. [Bell 1991; Redfield 1931;
Zimmerman 1964]

Lamiae, The
Grecian
Evil; Magic; Ugliness
   Monsters related to *Lamia.* They are child snatchers and
vampirelike murderers of young men. They can change their
appearance at will. Similar to *Empusae* and *Mormo.* See also
The Qlippoth, Near East. [Bell 1991; Redfield 1931]

Lampado
Grecian
Unknown
   One of the *Pleiades.* [Bell 1991]

Lampatho
Grecian
Stars and Planets; Magic
   One of the *Pleiades.* [Bell 1991]

Lampethusa
Grecian
Unknown
   One of the *Heliades,* daughter of Helios. [Monaghan 1981;
Zimmerman 1964]

Lampetia
Grecian
Domesticated Animals
   Guardian of the herds of Helios. Daughter of *Neaera* and
Helios. Half-sister of the *Heliades.* [Bell 1991]

Laodice
Grecian
Earth and Nature
   A nymph, mother of *Niobe.* See also *Nymphs.* [Bell 1991;
Leach 1992; Zimmerman 1964]

Laomedeia
Grecian
Justice; Water; Fate; Beauty
   "Leader of the People." One of the *Nereides.* [Bell 1991;
Leach 1992]

Laonome
Grecian
Earth and Nature
   Nymph. See also *Nymphs.* [Bell 1991]

Laosoos
Grecian
Charisma
   "Rouser of Nations." Name for *Athena* and *Eris.* [Bell
1991]

Laphria
Grecian
Unknown
   Name for *Artemis* when worshiped in Calydon. Also a
name given to *Athena* and *Britomartis.* [Bell 1991]

Lara
Roman
Heaven and Hell; Immortality
   "Mother of the Dead." Goddess of the underworld. She
may be the same as *Acca Larentia.* She is identified with
Larunda, Muta, and *Tacita.* Alternate forms: Larentia, Mater
Larum. [Monaghan 1981]

Larentia   See *Acca Larentia* and *Lara.*

Lares, The
Roman, Spain
Family and Tribes; Ceremonies
Household goddesses celebrated by the Romans on January 12 and March 6 in the crossroads at the festival of *Compitalia*. See also *Lares*, Western Europe. [Durdin-Robertson 1982; Eliade 1987]

Larissaea
Grecian
Unknown
Name for *Athena* at her sanctuary on the Larissus River between Elis and Achaia. [Bell 1991]

Larunda
Roman; Sabine
Family and Tribes
House goddess. Generally supposed to be chthonian. Her celebration was held on December 23. Identified with *Lara*, *Muta*, and *Tacita*. [Durdin-Robertson 1982; Monaghan 1981; Wedeck and Baskin 1971]

Larymna
Grecian
Unknown
This goddess gave her name to two towns in Boeotia. [Bell 1991]

Lasa
Roman; Etruscan
Fate
Goddess of fate. One of the *Lasas*. She is represented with wings or with a hammer and nail. [Lurker 1984; Redfield 1931]

Lasa-Rakuneta
Roman; Etruscan
Demi-animals
Etruscan winged goddess. [Cooper 1876]

Lasas, The
Roman; Etruscan
Fate
Etruscan goddesses of fate. They are *Acaviser, Alpan, Evan, Lasa,* and *Mean*. [Lurker 1984; Redfield 1931]

Lato   See *Leto*.

Latona
Roman
Unknown
"Woman." Roman name for the Greek goddess *Leto*. [Bell 1991; Ergener 1988; Redfield 1931; Zimmerman 1964]

Laurentia   See *Acca Larentia*.

Laverna
Roman
Evil
Roman patron goddess of thieves. The Porta Lavernalis was named for her, and she had an altar near there. She also had a sacred grove on the Via Salaria in Rome. [Bell 1991; Redfield 1931; Zimmerman 1964]

Lavinia
Roman
Earth and Nature
Roman goddess of the Earth's fertility. The city of Lavinium was named for her. [Bell 1991; Jobes 1962; Leach 1972]

Leagore
Grecian
Justice; Charisma
"Assembler of the People." One of the *Nereides*, her name relates to leadership. [Bell 1991; Leach 1992]

Leda
Grecian
Love and Sexuality; Mother and Guardian; Magic
Daughter of *Eurythemis* and Thestius.

⚮ *Leda was raped and impregnated by Zeus, who appeared as a swan. She was also impregnated by Tyndareus the same night. She produced two eggs. Out of one came Helen and Polydeuces, out of the other, Clytemnestra and Castor.* [Monaghan 1981; Woodcock 1953]

Ledaea   See *Hermione*.

Leiagora
Grecian
Water; Fate; Beauty
One of the *Nereides*. Alternate form: Leiagore. [Leach 1992]

Leiagore   See *Leiagora*.

Leirioessa   See *Leiriope*.

Leiriope
Grecian
Unknown
Mother of Narcissus by the river god Cephissus. Alternate forms: Liriope, Leirioessa. [Bell 1991; Zimmerman 1964]

Lelaino
Grecian
Weather; Justice; Ugliness; Demi-animals; Heaven and Hell; Wild Birds
One of the *Harpies*. [Lurker 1984]

Leprea
Grecian
Selflessness
Goddess of lepers. [Jobes 1962]

Lernaea
Grecian
Unknown
Name for *Demeter* when at Lerna. [Bell 1991]

Letham
Roman; Etruscan
Unknown
Etruscan deity who was merged with *Minerva*. [Cooper 1876]

Lethe
Grecian
Health and Healing; Heaven and Hell; Immortality
"Oblivion."

⚮ *The river Lethe flows in the underworld. Here the dead drink its water to forget about their earthly life. If they should return to Earth, they must drink from Lethe to erase their memory of Hades.*

There is also a spring named Lethe at the oracle of Trophonius at Lebadeia. [Bell 1991]

Leto
Grecian
Health and Healing; Mother and Guardian

Goddess of healing and childbirth. She is also the protector of children. Mother of *Phoebe*. Mother of *Artemis* and Apollo by Zeus, she became an object of the jealous wrath of *Hera*. Alternate forms: Lato, Latona, Phytia. [Bell 1991; Leach 1992; Neumann 1972; Senior 1985]

Letogeneia
Grecian
Unknown
Name for *Artemis* that comes from her mother, *Leto*. [Bell 1991]

Leuce
Grecian
Water
An *Oceanid*. She was kidnapped by Hades, and when she died, she was changed into a white poplar tree. See also *Nymphs*. [Bell 1991]

Leucippe
Grecian
1) Water; 2) Earth and Nature
1) One of the *Oceanides* who accompanied *Persephone* when she was kidnapped by Hades. 2) One of the *Maenades*. [Bell 1991; Leach 1992]

Leucophryne
Grecian
1) Unknown; 2) Earth and Nature
1) Name for *Artemis* when worshiped in Phrygia. 2) Nymph associated with her. See also *Nymphs*. [Bell 1991]

Leucosia
Grecian
Beauty; Charisma; Demi-animals; Fate; Destroyer of Life; Wild Birds
"White Goddess." One of the *Sirens*. [Bell 1991; Monaghan 1981; Zimmerman 1964]

Leucothea
Grecian
Water
"Goddess of the Spray of the Sea." Sea goddess who protects her followers from being shipwrecked. Alternate form: Halia. [Bell 1991; Jobes 1962; Leach 1992]

Leucothoe
Grecian
Water; Fate; Beauty
One of the *Nereides*. [Bell 1991; Jobes 1962]

Levana
Roman
Mother and Guardian
"To Lift Up." Goddess associated with lifting a child from the Earth after birth. Equivalent to *Selene*. [Bell 1991; Meltzer 1981; Wedeck and Baskin 1971]

Libentina
Roman
Love and Sexuality
Name for Roman *Venus* as goddess of sexual pleasure. Alternate forms: Lubentia, Lubentina. [Bell 1991]

Libera
Roman
Agriculture; Ceremonies
Goddess of viticulture. Daughter of *Ceres*. With her brother Liber, she presides over viticulture. She is identified with the

Greek *Kore*. March 16 is the date of her festival, the *Liberalia*, which celebrates the return of vegetation after the winter. During the festival, elderly women wearing crowns of ivy sold cakes that were burned by her followers as offerings to the gods. [Bell 1991; Leach 1972]

Liberalitas
Roman
Unknown
"Generosity." [Monaghan 1990]

Libertas
Roman
Justice
Goddess of liberty. She had three temples in Rome, and her statue was in the Forum. Her temple, the Atrium Libertatis, later became the first public library. She is depicted with a laurel wreath and sometimes a tight cap that seems to represent liberty. [Bell 1991; Lurker 1984]

Libethrides, The   See *The Muses*.

Libitina
Roman
Destroyer of Life; Ceremonies
Goddess of death. She presides over funerals. Believed to have been an earlier Italian Earth goddess. Identified with *Proserpina*. [Bell 1991; Jobes 1962; Redfield 1931; Woodcock 1953; Zimmerman 1964]

Libya
Grecian
1) Mother and Guardian; 2) Water
1) Mother goddess. 2) An *Oceanid*, daughter of Oceanus. [Bell 1991; Jobes 1962]

Ligankdikei   See *Lignaco Dex*.

Ligea   See *Ligeia*.

Ligeia
Grecian
1) Water; Beauty; Charisma; Demi-animals; Fate; Destroyer of Life; Wild Birds; 2) Earth and Nature; 3) Water; Fate; Beauty
1) "Shrill Sounding." One of the *Sirens*. 2) Name of a Roman nymph. See also *Nymphs*. 3) One of the *Nereides*. Alternate form: Ligea. [Bell 1991; Zimmerman 1964]

Lignaco Dex
Roman
Earth and Nature
Forest goddess. Alternate form: Ligankdikei. [Monaghan 1981]

Lilaea
Grecian
1) Water; Fate; Beauty; 2) Water; Health and Healing; Intelligence and Creativity; Fate
1) One of the *Nereides*. 2) One of the *Naiades*. Alternate form: Lilaia. [Bell 1991; Leach 1992]

Lilaia   See *Lilaea*.

Limenia
Grecian
Water
"Protector of the Harbor." Name for *Artemis* and *Aphrodite*. [Bell 1991]

Limnades, The
Grecian
Water; Destroyer of Life; Commerce and Travel
   Nymphs who inhabit bodies of fresh water. Said by some to be dangerous, luring travelers to their deaths. See also *Nymphs*. Alternate form: Lymniades. [Bell 1991; Leach 1992; Monaghan 1981; Woodcock 1953; Zimmerman 1964]

Limnaea
Grecian
Water
   "Lake-born or Lake-dwelling." Name of *Artemis*. [Bell 1991; Leach 1992]

Limnatides, The
Grecian
Water; Health and Healing; Intelligence and Creativity; Fate
   Name for the *Naiades* who inhabit lakes. [Bell 1991]

Limnatis
Grecian
Unknown
   "Marshes." A name for *Artemis* in Sparta at Limnaion. [Ergener 1988]

Limnoreia
Grecian
Water; Fate; Beauty
   One of the *Nereides*. [Bell 1991; Leach 1992]

Limoniades, The
Grecian
Earth and Nature
   Nymphs of plants and flowers. See also *Nymphs*. [Zimmerman 1964]

Lina
Grecian
Household Affairs
   Goddess of flax weaving. [Redfield 1931; Woodcock 1953]

Lindia
Grecian
Unknown
   Name for *Athena* when worshiped at Lindus on the island of Rhodes. [Bell 1991]

Linos
Grecian
Earth and Nature
   Nymph, mother of Pelops. See also *Nymphs*. [Bell 1991]

Lips
Grecian
Weather; Directions
   Wind goddess of the southeast. [Leach 1992]

Liriope   See *Leiriope*.

Litae, The
Grecian
Goodness; Justice
   "Prayers." Benevolent goddesses. They make amends for those who have committed criminal acts or who are unforgiving. Daughters of Zeus. Alternate forms: Aetae, Litai. [Bell 1991; Monaghan 1981; Redfield 1931; Zimmerman 1964]

Litai, The   See *The Litae*.

Locheia
Grecian
Mother and Guardian
   "Childbirth." 1) An early Spartan goddess who was merged with Artemis. 2) Name for *Artemis* and *Damia*. Alternate form: Lochia. [Bell 1991; Jobes 1962]

Lochia   See *Locheia*.

Longatis
Grecian
Unknown
   Name for *Athena*. [Bell 1991]

Losna
Roman; Etruscan
Moon and Night
   Etruscan moon goddess. See also *Lalal* and *Lucna*. [Cooper 1876; Leach 1992]

Lotis
Grecian
Earth and Nature; Magic
   Nymph. While being pursued by the ugly god Priapus, Lotis appealed for help from the gods and was metamorphosed into the lotis tree. See also *Nymphs*. [Bell 1991; Redfield 1931; Zimmerman 1964]

Loxo
Grecian
Unknown
   Name for *Artemis*. [Bell 1991]

Lua
Roman
War; Destroyer of Life
   Italian goddess to whom captured weapons were dedicated. She was also invoked to cause plagues among enemies. She is also called *Lua Mater* or *Lua Saturni* and is identified with *Ops*. [Bell 1991; Jobes 1962]

Lua Mater   See *Lua*.

Lua Saturni   See *Lua*.

Lubentia   See *Libentina*.

Lubentina   See *Libentina*.

Lucania
Roman
Justice
   Mother of *Roma*, she was involved with the founding of Rome. [Bell 1991]

Luceria
Roman
Mother and Guardian
   "Giver of Light." Name for *Juno* as goddess of childbirth, representing the bringing of the newborn into the light. See also *Lucina*. Alternate form: Lucetia. [Bell 1991; Leach 1992]

Lucetia   See *Luceria*.

Lucifera
Roman
Moon and Night
   Name for *Diana* as moon goddess. [Jayne 1925]

Lucina
Roman, Grecian
Mother and Guardian
   1) Name for Roman *Juno* and *Diana.* "She who brings the light." Related to bringing newborns into the light. Lucina (birth) is part of a trifold goddess with *Diana* (growth) and *Hecate* (death). The festival, the *Matronalia,* celebrates the founding of the temple of Juno Lucina on the Esquiline Hill of Rome. In the temple, women prayed to her, brought gifts, and celebrated her goodness bestowed on them. She was portrayed as a veiled figure with a flower in her right hand, holding an infant. See also *Opigena.* Alternate form: Luceria. [Bell 1991; Jobes 1962]
   2) Name for Greek *Hera* and *Eileithyia* as goddesses of childbirth. [Durdin-Robertson 1990; Jobes 1962; Redfield 1931; Zimmerman 1964]

Lucna
Roman, Etruscan
Moon and Night
   Moon goddess. See also *Lalal* and *Losna.* [Monaghan 1990]

Luna
Roman
Moon and Night; Time
   "The Moon That Rules the Months." Moon goddess who regulates the seasons and the months and is associated with the first day of the waning moon. She had an ancient sanctuary on the Aventine Hill in Rome and was worshiped on the last day of March (the first month of the old Roman year). In heaven, *Diana*'s name was Luna. Equivalent to *Selene* and *Levanah,* Near East. [Dames 1979; Durdin-Robertson 1990; Leach 1992; Woodcock 1953; Zimmerman 1964]

Lupa
Roman
Demi-animals; Mother and Guardian; Ceremonies
   Goddess who appears as a she-wolf. She suckled Romulus and Remus, the founders of Rome. Identified with *Acca Larentia.* A festival called *Lupercalia* is celebrated on February 15. Alternate form: Luperca. [Bell 1991; Johnson 1988]

Luperca See *Lupa.*

Lybica
Roman
Fate
   One of the *Sibyls.* [Jobes 1962]

Lyce
Grecian
Earth and Nature
   Nymph. Some say she loved Daphnis, but most say that that nymph was *Nomia.* See also *Nymphs.* [Bell 1991]

Lyceia
Grecian
Hunting and Wild Animals
   "Wolfish." Name for *Artemis* at Troezen. [Bell 1991]

Lycippe
Grecian
Unknown
   Some say this is the name of a wife of Thestius. May be another spelling of *Leucippe.* Alternate form: Cydippe. [Bell 1991]

Lyco
Grecian
Fate
   Prophetess, daughter of *Iphitea* and Prognaus, sister of *Carya* and *Orphe.* Lyco and Orphe were metamorphosed into rocks, Carya into a walnut tree. [Bell 1991]

Lycoatis
Grecian
Unknown
   Name of *Artemis* when worshiped at Lycoa in Arcadia. [Bell 1991]

Lycorias
Grecian
Water; Fate; Beauty
   One of the *Nereides.* [Bell 1991]

Lygodesma
Grecian
Unknown
   Name for *Artemis* at Sparta. [Bell 1991]

Lykorias
Grecian
Water; Fate; Beauty
   One of the *Nereides.* [Leach 1992]

Lymniades, The See *The Limnades.*

Lympha
Roman
Health and Healing
   Roman goddess of healing. She typifies the healing properties of water. Alternate form: Lymphae. [Jobes 1962]

Lymphae See *Lympha.*

Lysianassa
Grecian
Justice; Water; Fate; Beauty
   "Royal Deliverer." One of the *Nereides,* she is associated with politics. [Bell 1991; Leach 1992]

Lysidice
Grecian
Unknown
   Name of a daughter of Phelops. [Bell 1991]

Lysimache
Grecian
Unknown
   Wife of Talaus; mother of *Eriphyle.* [Bell 1991]

Lysizona
Grecian
Mother and Guardian
   "Girdle Loosener." Name for *Artemis* and *Eileithyia* at Athens as associated with childbirth. [Bell 1991]

Lyssa
Grecian
Heaven and Hell
   Goddess of the underworld. [Monaghan 1981]

Ma
Grecian
1) Unknown; 2) Unknown

"Mother." 1) Lydian name for *Rhea.* 1) A name for *Gaea.* She was merged with *Magna Mater.* See also *Ma,* Africa. [Bell 1991]

Machanitis
Grecian
Love and Sexuality; Intelligence and Creativity
"Deviser," or "Contriver." Name for *Aphrodite* at Megalopolis. The name refers to physical items or forms of speech used to enhance love. Also a name for *Athena* referring to her general inventiveness. See also *Mechanitis.* [Bell 1991]

Macris
Grecian
Mother and Guardian; Goodness
Nurse of Dionysus. Daughter of *Autonoe* and Aristaeus of Euboea. She took Dionysus to a cave on the island of Scheria. It was here that she became known for helping people. [Bell 1991; Zimmerman 1964]

Maenades, The
Grecian
Earth and Nature
Nymphs, companions of Dionysus. They include *Alcimache, Aura,* and *Leucippe.* Also called *Thyiades.* See also *Nymphs.* Alternate forms: Bacchae, Bacchantes, Bassarae, Bassarides, Maenads, Mimallones. [Bell 1991; Redfield 1931; Monaghan 1981; Zimmerman 1964]

Maenads, The   See *Maenades.*

Maeonides, The
Grecian
Arts; Sciences; Intelligence and Creativity; Evil
A name for the evil *Muses* as related to Maeonia. [Zimmerman 1964]

Maera
Grecian
1) Water; Fate; Beauty; Unhappiness; Selfishness; Health and Healing; 2) Demi-animal
1) One of the *Nereides.* 2) Name of *Hecuba* when she was changed into a dog after jumping from a Trojan ship. [Bell 1991]

Maerope   See *Merope.*

Magarsia
Grecian
Unknown
Name for *Athena* at Magarsos. [Bell 1991]

Magna Dea   See *Ceres.*

Magna Mater
Roman
Mother and Guardian; Demi-animals
"She Who Shines for All." The great Asiatic mother goddess who was brought to Rome and later merged with *Cybele, Ma, Dea Caelestis, Ops,* and *Rhea.* She incarnates as a dove, and doves are her messengers. Her worshipers were prominent opponents of Christianity until they were overcome by the new religon. Her festival, the *Megalesia,* the "Festival of the Great Mother," was celebrated on April 4 with games and processions. She is identified with *Bona Dea, Mah-Bellona, Mater Matuta, Tanit; Atargatis,* Near East; and *Isis,* Egypt. See also *Megale.* Alternate forms: Anāhita, Mater Magna. [Durdin-Robertson 1990; Harding 1971; Leach 1992; Monaghan 1981; Neumann 1972; Woodcock 1953; Zimmerman 1964]

Mah-Bellona
Roman
War
Cappadocian (Near East) goddess *Mah,* an earth deity, was assimilated by Roman goddess *Bellona* who represents territorial sovereignty and armed conflict and became known as Mah-Bellona. She is identified with *Magna Mater* and *Enyo.* See also *Mah,* Near East. [Leach 1992; Monaghan 1981]

Maia
Grecian, Roman
1) Stars and Planets; 2) Earth and Nature; Love and Sexuality
1) One of the *Pleiades.* Daughter of *Pleione* and Atlas. Mother of Hermes. Alternate form: Atlantis,. 2) Roman goddess of spring growth who rules the warmth, including sexual heat. Wife of Vulcan. The month of May is taken from her name and on May 1 offerings are made to her. The Greek aia is the mother of Hermes and the two are sometimes confused. Maia is identified with *Bona Dea, Fauna,* and *Ops.* Alternate form: Majesta. [Bell 1991; Bonnerjea 1927; Durdin-Robertson 1980; Harding 1971; Leach 1992; Lurker 1984; Senior 1985; Zimmerman 1964]

Maira
Grecian
Water; Fate; Beauty
One of the *Nereides.* [Leach 1992]

Majesta   See *Maia.*

Malaviskh
Roman; Etruscan
Unknown
Etruscan goddess. [Cooper 1876]

Maliades   See *Meliades.*

Malophorus
Grecian
Earth and Nature; Domestic Animals
"Apple-bearer" or "Sheep-bearer." Name for *Demeter.* [Avery 1962]

Mana
Roman
Mother and Guardian; Immortality
Goddess presiding over generation conception and infants who die at birth. Alternate form: Mana Geneta. [Bell 1991]

Mana Geneta   See *Mana.*

Mania
Roman
Heaven and Hell; Magic; Immortality
"Mother of the Manes." "Mother of Ghosts" or "Grandmother of Ghosts." Her image, in the form of woolen effigies of women and men, or loaves of bread, are hung in household doorways to spare the living for another year and to ward off evil. They were also used in the festival of the *Compitalia* in Rome. Equivalent to *Ida,* Indian Subcontinent. [Bell 1991; Zimmerman 1964]

Maniae   See *The Erinyes.*

Manto
Grecian
Fate; Earth and Nature
1) A prophet also known as *Daphne,* who is the mother of *Tisiphone;* 2) A nymph whose lover was the Tiber river god. See also *Nymphs.* [Bell 1991; Monaghan 1981]

Marica
Roman
Water
   Nymph worshiped at Minturnae. Identified with Greek *Aphrodite* and *Circe.* See also *Nymphs.* [Bell 1991]

Marpessa
Grecian
Love and Sexuality
   Deity who chose a mortal, Idas, over Apollo for her husband. Mother of *Alcyone.* [Bell 1991; Zimmerman 1964]

Mater Larum   See *Lara.*

Mater Magna   See *Magna Mater.*

Mater Matuta
Roman
Dawn and Twilight; Mother and Guardian; Water; Commerce and Travel; Ceremonies
   "Morning Mother." Similar to *Aurora* and identified with *Magna Mater* and *Fauna.* When identified with *Ino* and *Leucothea,* she is a protector of seafarers, the sea, and harbors. She was worshiped throughout central Italy and into Africa. Her festival of *Matralia,* the festival of mothers, is celebrated to honor the women of Rome on June 11 at her temple in the Forum Boarium. During this festival women pray for the protection of their nieces and nephews first and then for their own children. They make flower offerings to the goddess. As *Dea Matuta,* she is the "light-bringing" mother. Alternate form: Matuta. She was assimilated by and is considered a name for *Juno.* [Bell 1991; Dexter 1990; Durdin-Robertson 1982; Jayne 1925; Jobes 1962; Leach 1992; Lurker 1984; Zimmerman 1964]

Mater Turrita
Roman
Unknown
   Name for Roman *Cybele.* [Zimmerman 1964]

Matres   See *Matres Britanne.*

Matres Britanne
Roman
Earth and Nature
   Name for the Celtic Earth mothers. They are triune goddesses of birth, growth, and death, self-creating and self-sustaining. See also *Matres,* Western Europe. Alternate form: Matres. [Jobes 1962]

Matrona
Roman
Mother and Guardian
   Name for *Juno* as protector of women from birth to death. [Bell 1991]

Matuta   See *Mater Matuta.*

Mean
Roman
Fate
   One of the *Lasas.* [Cooper 1876]

Mechanitis
Grecian
Intelligence and Sexuality
   "Discoverer of Devices." Name of *Athena.* [Leach 1972; Zimmerman 1964]

Medea
Grecian
Magic; Love and Sexuality
   Purveyor of magic. Medea fell in love with Jason and aided him in stealing the Golden Fleece from her father, Aeetes. Her mother was *Idyia,* and she had a sister, *Chalciope.* Identified with *Bona Dea.* Alternate forms: Aeaea, Aeetias. [Bell 1991; Zimmerman 1964]

Meditrina
Roman
Health and Healing; Magic; Ceremonies
   Goddess of healing. She uses wine, herbs, and magic formulas for healing. She was celebrated at the festival of *Meditrinalia* on October 3 with the statement, "Wine new and old I drink, of illness new and old I'm cured." [Baskin 1971; Bell 1992; Durdin-Robertson 1982; Jayne 1925; Wedeck and Baskin 1971; Zimmerman 1964]

Medusa
Grecian
1) Magic; Love and Sexuality; Ugliness; 2) Stars and Planets; Magic
   One of the *Gorgons.*
   ♁ *After her head was cut off by Perseus, Athena placed it on her shield and used vials of her blood for good and harmful purposes. According to some, this was to punish Medusa for sleeping with Poseidon in one of Athena's temples.*
   One of the *Pleiades.* [Bell 1991; Neumann 1972; Woodcock 1953; Zimmerman 1964]

Mefitis   See *Mephitis.*

Megaera
Grecian
1) Justice; Heaven and Hell; Ugliness; Family and Tribes; 2) Justice
   1) One of the Greek *Erinyes.* 2) One of the Roman *Furies.* See also *Megaira.* [Bell 1991]

Megaira
Grecian
Unhappiness
   One of the *Erinyes.* Goddess of "envious anger." See also *Megaera.* Alternate form: Megatra. [Leach 1992; Zimmerman 1964]

Megale
Grecian
Unknown
   Greek name of *Magna Mater* in Rome. [Woodcock 1953]

Megatra   See *Megaira.*

Megisto
Grecian
Unknown
   Name for *Callisto.* [Bell 1991]

Meiboia
Grecian
Sky and Heavens; Insects
   Bee goddess of heaven of ancient Greece. [Jobes 1962]

Meilichia
Grecian, Roman
Heaven and Hell
   Underworld goddess. May have been a name for *Demeter.* [Monaghan 1981]

Meilinoe See *Melinoe.*

Melaenis
Grecian
Moon and Night
   "The Dark." Name for *Aphrodite* at Corinth. [Bell 1991]

Melanaegis, The
Grecian
Unknown
   "Black-Shielded." Name for the *Erinyes.* [Bell 1991]

Melanippe
Grecian
Earth and Nature
   A nymph who was the mother of Boeotus, *Chromia* and *Iodama.* See also *Nymphs.* Alternate form: Menanippe. [Bell 1991; Monaghan 1981; Zimmerman 1964]

Meleagrian
Grecian
Destroyer of Life
   Name for *Artemis* as hunter of members (parts of the body) ravaged by disease. [Jobes 1962]

Melete
Grecian
Arts; Sciences; Intelligence and Creativity; Evil
   One of the *Muses* worshiped on Mt. Helicon. [Bell 1991; Leach 1992]

Melia
Grecian
1) Water; 2)Earth and Nature
   1) One of the *Oceanides.* Mother of the Argive nation with her brother Inachus, god of the Inachus River. 2) An ash tree nymph, mother of Amycus by Poseidon. See also *Nymphs.* [Bell 1991; Leach 1992]

Meliades
Grecian
1) Domesticated Animals; Agriculture; 2) Earth and Nature
   1) Nymphs, protectors of flocks and fruit trees. They belong to the larger classification of *Dryades.* 2) Name of the nymphs near Trachis on the Spercheius River. See also *Nymphs.* Alternate forms: Epimelides, Malides. [Bell 1991; Jobes 1962]

Meliae, The
Grecian
1) Earth and Nature; Magic; 2) Earth and Nature; Mother and Guardian
   1) Nymphs.
   When drops of blood from the severed genitals of Uranus fell on Mother Earth Gaea, they were given life and became the Meliae.
   2) Name of the nymphs who nursed Zeus who take their name from *Melissa.* [Bell 1991; Monaghan 1981]

Meliboea
Grecian
1) Unknown; 2) Water
   "Sweet-Voiced." 1) Name for *Persephone.* 2) One of the *Oceanides,* a daughter of Oceanus and *Tethys.* [Bell 1991]

Melides See *Meliades.*

Melinaea
Grecian
Unknown
   Name for *Aphrodite* when worshiped at Meline. [Bell 1991]

Melinoe
Grecian
Heaven and Hell; Disorder
   Goddess of the underworld sometimes called *Chthonia.* Daughter of *Persephone* and Zeus. She visits the Earth nightly, causing fear and confusion. Alternate form: Meilinoe. [Bell 1991]

Melissa
Grecian
1) Mother and Guardian; 2) Unknown
   1) Nurse of Zeus who fed him honey. The bees, *melissae,* are probably named for her. 2) A name for *Artemis.* See also *Meliae.* [Bell 1991; Jobes 1962; Zimmerman 1964]

Melissae, The
Grecian
Earth and Nature; Ceremonies
   Nymphs. Later the name was was used to refer to priestesses in general. See also *Nymphs.* [Bell 1991]

Melite
Grecian
1) Health and Healing; Water; Intelligence and Creativity; Fate; 2) Water; Fate; Beauty; 3) Water
   1) One of the *Naiades.* 2) One of the *Nereides.* 3) One of the *Oceanides.* [Bell 1991; Leach 1992]

Melitodes
Grecian
Goodness
   "Sweet as Honey." Name for *Persephone.* [Bell 1991]

Mellona
Roman
Agriculture
   Protector of honey. Alternate form: Mellonia. [Bell 1991; Monaghan 1980; Wedeck and Baskin 1971]

Mellonia See *Mellona.*

Melobosis
Grecian
Goodness; Water
   One of the *Oceanides,* goddess of beneficence. Alternate form: Melobote. [Bell 1991; Leach 1992]

Melobote See *Melobosis.*

Melpomene
Grecian
Unhappiness; Arts
   "The Singing." One of the *Muses* at Athens. The *Muse* of tragedies and elegies. [Bell 1991; Leach 1992; Redfield 1931; Zimmerman 1964]

Memphis
Grecian
Water
   1) A daughter of the Nile river god. 2) Mother of *Lysianassa,* one of the *Nereides.* [Bell 1991]

Menanippe See *Melanippe.*

Mendeis
Grecian
Earth and Nature
  Macedonian nymph. See also *Nymphs.* [Bell 1991]

Mendis See *Bendis.*

Mene
Grecian
Moon and Night; Time
  Goddess of the moon. She presides over the months.
Similar to *Selene.* [Bell 1991; Leach 1992]

Meneruva
Roman; Etruscan
Unknown
  Etruscan name for *Minerva.* Alternate form: Menerva.
[Cooper 1876]

Menerva See *Meneruva.*

Menestho
Grecian
Order
  "Steadfastness." One of the *Oceanides,* daughter of *Tethys*
and Oceanus. [Bell 1991; Leach 1992]

Menippe
Grecian
1) Courage; Water; Fate; Beauty; 2) Courage; 3) Water;
Courage
  "Courageous Mare" 1) One of the *Nereides.* 2) One of the
Coronides. 3) Daughter of the Peneius river god. [Bell 1991;
Leach 1992]

Menrfa
Roman; Etruscan
Unknown
  Name for *Minerva.* Alternate form: Menrva. [Jobes 1962]

Menrva See *Menrfa.*

Mens
Roman
Mother and Guardian
  "Right Moment." The word *menstruation* comes from her
name. Her name is also said to mean "mind." The Roman
Senate prayed to her during war. See also *Shakti,* Indian
Subcontinent; *Adamu* and the *Holy Spirit,* Near East.
[Durdin-Robertson 1982; Monaghan 1981]

Menstro See *Antiope.*

Mentha See *Menthe.*

Menthe
Grecian
Heaven and Hell; Earth and Nature
  Underworld nymph who was also called *Nais.* The spirit
of the mint plant. See also *Nymphs.* Alternate forms: Mentha,
Mintha, Minthe, Nais. [Bell 1991; Leach 1992; Zimmerman
1964]

Mephitis
Roman
Health and Healing
  Goddess of noxious vapors. She protects her followers
from inhaling poisonous gasses and cures those who are
exposed to them. She had a temple surrounded by a grove on

the Esquiline Hill in Rome. Alternate form: Mefitis. [Jayne
1925; Redfield 1931]

Meroe
Grecian
Magic
  Witch in Thessaly. [Monaghan 1981]

Merope
Grecian
1) Stars and Planets; Magic; 2) Water; 3) Unhappiness; Magic;
4) Sky and Heavens
  1) One of the *Pleiades.* She is the seventh and least visible
star in the constellation. Some say she is hiding because of the
embarrassment of having a mortal, Sisyphus, for a husband.
2) One of the *Oceanides.* 3) One of the *Heliades.* 4) One of
the *Atlantides.* Alternate forms: Aero, Europa, Haero, and
Maerope. [Bell 1991; Leach 1992; Redfield 1931; Zimmerman
1964]

Mese
Grecian
Arts
  One of the *Muses* worshiped at Delphi. Her name signifies
one of the strings of a three-stringed lyre. [Bell 1991]

Mesembria
Grecian
Time
  One of the *Horae,* she represents the noon hour. [Bell 1991;
Leach 1992]

Mesma
Grecian
Water
  Nymph who inhabits a mineral spring. See also *Nymphs.*
[Leach 1992]

Messeis
Grecian
Water
  Nymph who inhabits a mineral spring in Thessaly. See also
Nymphs. [Leach 1992]

Messene
Grecian
Unknown
  Daughter of *Euboea* by Phorbas. Wife of Polycaon with
whom she settled Messenia. They were worshiped as deities.
[Bell 1991]

Messia
Roman
Agriculture
  Roman goddess of agriculture. Identified with *Tutilina.*
[Bell 1991]

Mestra
Grecian
Magic
  A shape-changing deity. Daughter of Erysichthon. She
tried unsuccessfully to save her father from death. [Bell 1991]

Meter
Grecian
Mother and Guardian
  "Mother." Name for *Athena* at Elis. [Bell 1991; Monaghan
1981]

Meteres
Grecian
Mother and Guardian
   Goddess of maternity and fecundity on Crete. [Sykes 1968]

Methe
Grecian
Disorder
   Personification of alcoholic intoxication. [Bell 1991]

Metioche
Grecian
Unknown
   One of the *Coronides*. [Bell 1991]

Metis
Grecian
Order; Water
   "Prudence." One of the *Oceanides*, daughter of *Tethys* and Oceanus. [Bell 1991; Leach 1992; Redfield 1931; Zimmerman 1964]

Metope
Grecian
Water
   Water nymph. Daughter of the river god, Ladon, wife of Asopus. She is sometimes called *Parnassa*. See also *Nymphs*. Alternate form: Amphissa. [Bell 1991; Leach 1992]

Mida
Grecian
Justice
   Goddess of oaths. [Leach 1992]

Mideatis
Grecian
Unknown
   Name for *Alcmena* at Midea in Argolis. [Bell 1991]

Mideia
Grecian
Earth and Nature
   Nymph, lover of Poseidon. See also *Nymphs*. [Bell 1991]

Migonitis
Grecian
Unknown
   Name for *Aphrodite*. [Bell 1991]

Militaris
Roman
Unknown
   Name for *Venus*. [Bell 1991]

Mimallones, The
Grecian
Disorder
   "Wild Women." Name for the *Maenades* in Macedonia. Followers of Dionysus. [Bell 1991; Woodcock 1953]

Minerva
Roman; Etruscan
Intelligence and Creativity; War; Household Affairs
   Personification of "thinking, calculating, and invention." She forms a trinity with *Juno* and Jupiter. One of the *Appiades*. Identified with the Greek *Athena, Mnemosyne, Nerine*. Patron goddess of domestic skills and military abilities. She had temples in Rome on the Aventine Hill, the Caelian Hill, and the Capitoline Hill, where the oldest one was erected. Her festival, the *Quinquatria*, celebrated her birthday five days after the Ides of March. Another festival for Minerva was the *Panathenaea*, which may have been the same as the *Quinquatria*. She is named as one of the mothers of the *Muses*, and is identified with *Pallas*.

⚕ *Outside the city, a ship was built that carried Minerva's garment as a sail. The garment was transported to the temple of Ceres Eleusinia and then to the citadel, where it was placed on Minerva's statue. A procession followed, with people carrying olive branches, soldiers carrying spears and shields, foreigners, young men crowned with millet singing hymns to the goddess, and selected virgins of the noblest families carrying baskets of offerings.*

   See also *Letham* (this section) and *Belisama*, Western Europe. Alternate forms: Achaea, Aglauros, Appias, Capta, Castitas, Ergatis, Glaukopis, Hippias, Meneruva, Menerva, Menrfa, Menrva, Parthenos, Promachus, Pylotis, Sais, Tritonia. [Bell 1991; Cooper 1876; Durdin-Robertson 1976; Durdin-Robertson 1982; Lurker 1984; Woodcock 1953]

Mintha   See *Menthe*.

Minthe   See *Mentha*.

Misa
Grecian
Intelligence and Creativity
   A mystic being who may be the same as *Cybele* or who may be an attribute of *Cybele*. [Bell 1991]

Miseria
Roman, Grecian
Poverty; Unhappiness
   "Poverty," "Lament." Roman/Grecian goddess. Daughter of Roman *Nox*/Greek *Nyx* and Erebus. [Leach 1992]

Mixoparthenos, The
Grecian; Roman
Justice; Heaven and Hell; Ugliness; Family and Tribes
   "Half-maiden." Name for the Greek *Erinyes* and the *Furies* in Rome. [Bell 1991]

Miysis
Grecian
Unknown
   Similar to Egyptian *Mai-hesa*. [Budge 1989]

Mlakukh
Roman; Etruscan
Love and Sexuality
   Etruscan love goddess. [Cooper 1876]

Mnasa
Grecian
Unknown
   "Memory." Mycenaean goddess. Related to *Mnemosyne*. [Monaghan 1981]

Mneiae, The
Grecian
Arts; Sciences; Intelligence and Creativity; Evil
   "Remembrances." Name for the nine *Muses*. [Bell 1991]

Mneme
Grecian
Arts; Sciences; Intelligence and Creativity; Evil
   "Memory." One of the three *Muses* worshiped on Mt. Helicon. [Bell 1991; Leach 1992]

Mnemonides, The
Grecian
Arts; Sciences; Intelligence and Creativity; Evil
   Name for the *Muses*. [Bell 1991]

Mnemosyne
Grecian
Intelligence and Creativity
   "Memory." Daughter of *Gaea* and Uranus, and as such,
one of the *Titanides*. Mother of the nine Athenian *Muses*,
who are *Calliope* (epic song), *Clio* (history), *Euterpe* (lyric
song), *Thalia* (comedy), *Melpomene* (tragedy), *Terpsichore*
(dancing), *Erato* (erotic poetry), *Polymnia* (sacred songs),
and *Urania* (astronomy). She is worshiped in Athens and
Lebadeia, where her sacred fountain is located. Her festival is
called the Nativity of the Muses and is held on June 13.
Identified with the Roman *Minerva*. Related to *Mnasa*.
Alternate form: Moneta. [Bell 1991; Durdin-Robertson 1982;
Leach 1992; Monaghan 1981; Redfield 1931]

Moera, The   See *The Moirae*.

Moerae, The   See *The Moirae*.

Moirae, The
Grecian
Fate; Life/Death Cycle
   "Allotters." Goddesses of fate. Variously considered
daughters of *Nyx, Gaea,* or *Ananke,* with or without a mate.
Their names are *Clotho, Atropos,* and *Lachesis*. Depending
on who their parent or parents were, they are sisters to the
Horae and *Erinyes* and to the Roman goddess *Ceres*. Some
consider the Moirae to be daughters of *Themis*. *Aesa* is
sometimes considered one of the Moirae. As triune goddesses,
they are responsible for the beginning, the middle, and the
end of each life. Equivalent to *Gulses,* Near East.
   *The Moirae appear as three old women, spinning out human
destinies like strands of thread. Clotho draws the thread from
the spindle, Lachesis measures their length, and Atropos cuts
the thread when life is to end. The malevolent Keres then appear,
delivering the final blow and taking their victims to the land of
shadows.*
   See also *Parcae*. Alternate forms: Moera, Moerae, Moirai.
[Bell 1991; Cotterell 1979; Cotterell 1989; Leach 1992;
Neumann 1972]

Moirai, The   See *The Moirae*.

Molae, The
Roman
Household Affairs
   Goddesses who preside over mills. [Bell 1991]

Molpadia
Grecian
Mother and Guardian
   A goddess of childbirth. Daughter of Staphylus and
Chrysothemis, she is also called *Hemithea*. Her sisters are
Parthenos and *Rhoeo*. She comforts women in labor. [Bell
1991; Jayne 1925]

Molpe
Grecian
Beauty; Charisma; Demi-animals; Fate; Destroyer of Life;
Wild Birds
   One of the *Sirens*. [Bell 1991]

Moneta
Roman
Wealth; Fate; Family and Tribes

Name for *Juno* as guardian of finances. Mother of the *Muses*.
She had a temple on the Capitoline Hill. Also said to be a name
for *Mnemosyne*. [Bell 1991; Leach 1972; Monaghan 1981]

Morae, The   See *The Moirae*.

Mormo
Grecian
Immortality; Evil
   Specter used to frighten children. Similar to *Empusea* and
Lamiae. See also *The Qlippoth,* Near East. [Bell 1991; Leach
1972]

Morpho
Grecian
Unknown
   "The Fair-shaped." Name for *Aphrodite* at Sparta. [Bell
1991]

Mors
Grecian
Destroyer of Life
   "Death." Daughter of *Nyx*. [Woodcock 1953]

Morta
Roman
Destroyer of Life
   Name for Greek *Atropos*. The goddess who cuts the thread
of life. One of the *Parcae*. [Bonnerjea 1927; Redfield 1931]

Muliebris
Roman
Selflessness; Mother and Guardian
   Name for *Fortuna* relating to chastity and womanhood.
See also *Pudicitia*. [Jobes 1962]

Munthkh   See *Munthukh*.

Munthukh
Roman; Etruscan
Health and Healing
   Etruscan goddess of health. Alternate form: Munthkh.
[Cooper 1876]

Munychia
Grecian
Moon and Night
   "Moon Goddess." Name for *Artemis* at the harbor of
Athens. Also a name for *Athena* and *Hecate*. [Bell 1991;
Leach 1992]

Murcia
Roman
Unknown
   Name for *Venus* at Rome, where she had a chapel in the
Circus. Alternate forms: Murtea, Murtia. [Bell 1991]

Murtea   See *Murcia*.

Murtia   See *Murcia*.

Musae, The   See *The Muses*.

Muses, The
Grecian
Arts; Sciences; Intelligence and Creativity; Evil
   Goddesses of the arts and sciences and inspiration. They
vary in number, name, and parentage. There are three Muses
on Mount Helicon in Boeotia, *Aoede, Melete,* and *Mneme*.
At Sicyon there are three, but only one name survives,

Polymatheia. At Delphi, they are called *Hypate, Mese,* and *Nete,* or *Apollonis, Borysthenis,* and *Cephisso.* At one time they were four in number and were called *Aoede, Arche, Melete,* and *Thelxinoe.* There were also the seven Muses, *Achelois, Asopo, Heptapora, Neilo, Rhodia, Tipoplo,* and *Tritone.* At Athens there are nine, *Calliope, Clio, Erato, Euterpe, Melpomene, Polymnia, Terpsichore, Thaleia,* and *Urania. Myrtis of Anthedon* and *Nete* are also considered Muses. Their parents are listed variously as *Mnemosyne* and Zeus, *Gaea* and Uranus, *Antiope* and Pierus, Apollo, *Moneta* and Zeus, *Minerva* and Zeus, or *Gaea* and Aether. Their nurse was *Eupheme.* They confer their talents on humans and also use their talents to perform a variety of functions. They can also be malevolent if someone offends them. They are called *Heliconides* (their place of worship being Mt. Helicon) or *Parnassides* (named for their place of birth, the foot of Mt. Parnassus). Similar to *Namaqiri,* Indian Subcontinent. Alternate forms: Aganippides, Aonides, Ardalides, Castalides, Hippocrenides, Ilissiades, Libethrides, Maeonides, Mneiae, Mnemonides, Musae, Olympiades, Pegasides, Pimpleides. [Bell 1991; Bonnerjea 1927; Leach 1992; Neumann 1972; Woodcock 1953; Zimmerman 1964]

Musike
Grecian
Time; Order
   One of the *Horae.* [Leach 1992]

Muta
Roman
Order
   Goddess of silence. Identified with *Lara, Larunda,* and *Tacita.* [Monaghan 1981; Zimmerman 1964]

Mycalessia
Grecian
Unknown
   Name for *Demeter* at Mycalesus in Boeotia. [Bell 1991]

Mycalessides, The
Grecian
Earth and Nature
   Mountain nymphs on the promontory of Mycale. See also *Nymphs.* [Bell 1991]

Myrtis of Anthedon
Grecian
Arts; Sciences; Intelligence and Creativity; Evil
   One of the *Muses.* She was a teacher of Pindar the Poet. [Chicago 1979]

Myrtoessa
Grecian
Water
   Nymph in Arcadia. A spring is named for her. See also *Nymphs.* [Bell 1991]

Mysia
Grecian
Unknown
   Name for *Demeter.* [Bell 1991]

Mystis
Grecian
Mother and Guardian; Education and Knowledge
   Nurse of Dionysus who instructed him in the Mysteries. [Bell 1991]

Naenia
Roman
Unhappiness; Ceremonies
   Goddess of funerals. Personification of lamentation for the newly dead. Her sanctuary was outside the walls of Rome, near the Viminal Gate. All chapels for this Roman goddess of death were placed outside the city walls. Alternate form: Nenia. [Bell 1991; Redfield 1931; Zimmerman 1964]

Naiades, The
Grecian
Water; Health and Healing; Intelligence and Creativity; Fate
   Nymphs of fresh water. They inhabit springs, brooks, rivers, and lakes. Their powers vary. Some heal the sick, and others confer inspirational powers or prophetic powers. Their lives are connected to the water, and if their source dries up, they die. They are classified according to the body of water they inhabit: *Crinaea* (fountains), *Eleionomae* (marshes), *Limnatides* (lakes), *Pegaeae* (springs), and *Potameides* (rivers). Those who inhabit the rivers of the underworld are the *Nymphae Infernae Paludis.* Naiades include *Abarbarea, Aigle, Bateia, Caliadne, Chlidanope, Cleochareia, Echenais, Eleionomae, Harmonia, Lilaea, Melite, Oenoie, Polyxo, Pronoë.* See also *Nymphs.* Alternate form: Naiads. [Bell 1991; Woodcock 1953; Zimmerman 1964]

Naiads   See *The Naiades.*

Nais   See *Menthe.*

Nanaea   See *Anaitis.*

Napaea, The
Grecian
Earth and Nature
   Forest nymphs. Followers of *Artemis* in dells, glens, and woods. Alternate form: Napaeae. [Bell 1991; Jobes 1962]

Napaeae, The   See *The Napaea.*

Narcaea
Grecian
Unknown
   Name for *Athena* at Olympia. [Bell 1991]

Nascio
Roman
Mother and Guardian
   Goddess of childbirth. Protector of infants and assistant to *Lucina.* Identified with Greek *Eileithyia.* Her sanctuary was in the neighborhood of Ardea, an ancient town of southeast Lavinium. [Bell 1991; Jayne 1925; Woodcock 1953]

Natalis
Roman
Unknown
   Name for *Juno.* [Bell 1991]

Nathum
Roman; Etruscan
Unknown
   One of the Etruscan *Furies.* Equivalent to Greek *Ate.* [Cooper 1876]

Nausithoe
Grecian
Water; Fate; Beauty
   One of the *Nereides.* [Bell 1991]

Navirilis
Roman
Luck
   Name for *Fortuna* relating to manhood. [Jayne 1925; Jobes 1962; Monaghan 1981]

Neaera
Grecian
1) Earth and Nature; 2) Water; 3) Earth and Nature
   1) A nymph loved by Helios, the mother of *Lampetia* and *Phaethusa*. 2) The wife of the Strymon river god and mother of *Euadne*. 3) A nymph who was the mother of *Aigle* by Zeus. See also *Nymphs*. [Bell 1991; Zimmerman 1964]

Necessitas
Roman
Fate
   Roman goddess of destiny. Her symbol is the nail, which holds fast the decrees of fate. She is called *Anake* by the Greeks. [Redfield 1931; Zimmerman 1964]

Neda
Grecian
Water; Mother and Guardian
   Arcadian nymph who, along with *Hagno* and *Theisoa*, was a nurse of Zeus. The Messenians say she and *Ithome* bathed Zeus in the fountain of Clepsydra. A river in Messenia is named for her. See also *Nymphs*. [Bell 1991; Monaghan 1981]

Nedusia
Grecian
Unknown
   Name for *Athena* when worshiped in Messenia and Ceos. [Bell 1991]

Neilo
Grecian
Arts; Sciences; Intelligence and Creativity; Evil
   One of the seven *Muses*. [Bell 1991]

Neis
Grecian
1) Water; 2) Unknown
   1) Name of a water nymph, or possibly a generic name for water nymphs. 2) Name of a daughter of *Niobe* by Amphion. It is believed that the Neitian gate at Thebes was named for her. See also *Nymphs*. [Bell 1991; Leach 1992]

Nemea
Grecian
Unknown
   Goddess of Nemean games, daughter of *Selene* and Zeus. Sister of *Pandeia* and *Ersa*. The games were held in the valley of Nemea near Cleonae. They were one of the four great national festivals. The other three were the Olympian, Pythian, and Isthmian games. [Avery 1962; Bell 1991; Leach 1992]

Nemertes
Grecian
Justice
   "Truthful, Unerring." One of the *Nereides*. [Bell 1991; Leach 1992]

Nemesis
Grecian
Justice; Unhappiness
   Goddess of righteous anger. She is a primordial deity who emerged from Chaos. The Greeks celebrated a festival called *Nemesia* in memory of their dead. Nemesis defended the belongings and memory of the dead from all insult. Also seen as an avenger because she takes away happiness if she thinks her sister *Tyche* has given too much. Daughter of *Nyx* and Erebus or Oceanus. Associated with *Aedos, Aidos,* and *Poena*. Alternate forms: Adrastea, Heimarmene, Rhamnusia. [Bell 1991; Durdin-Robertson 1982; Leach 1992; Neumann 1972; Redfield 1931; Woodcock 1953; Zimmerman 1964]

Nemorensis
Roman
Mother and Guardian
   Name for *Diana* when assisting in obstetric activities. She usually assists *Aegeria* in these functions. She had a very famous and wealthy temple at Aricia in Italy. [Avery 1962; Jayne 1925]

Nenia   See *Naenia*.

Neomeris
Grecian
Water; Fate; Beauty
   One of the *Nereides*. [Bell 1991]

Nephele
Grecian
Weather; Mother and Guardian
   "Mist of the Morning Tide." Her husband was Athamas. Nephele sent the ram of the Golden Fleece to rescue her children *Helle* and Phrixus. [Bell 1991; Jobes 1962; Redfield 1931]

Neptunine
Grecian
Unknown
   Name for *Thetis* as the granddaughter of Neptune. [Bell 1991]

Nereides, The
Grecian
Water; Fate; Beauty
   Saltwater nymphs. They are also oracular. Daughters of *Doris* and Nereus. Generally thought to be fifty in number, their names and numbers vary from writer to writer. They are beautiful naked women who live on the sea bottom with Nereus, and they watch over sailors. They occasionally surface and mate with humans. They variously include *Actaea, Agave, Alimede, Amatheia, Amphinome, Amphithoe, Amphitrite, Apseudes, Arethusa, Asia, Autonoe, Beroe, Cale, Callianassa, Callianeira, Callidice, Calypso, Ceto, Choro, Clymene, Cranto, Creneis, Cydippe, Cymatolege, Cymo, Cymodoce, Cymothoe, Deianeria, Deiopea, Dero, Dexamene, Dione, Doto, Drimo, Dynamene, Eione, Erato, Euarne, Eucrante, Eudia, Eudora, Eugora, Eulimene, Eumolpe, Eunike, Eupompe, Evagora, Evarne, Galatea, Galaxaura, Galene, Glauce, Glauconome, Glauke, Glaukonome, Halia, Halimede, Halsodyne, Helice, Hipponoe, Hippothoe, Iaera, Ianassa, Ianeira, Ione, Iphianassa, Iphthime, Kallianassa, Kallianeira, Kranto, Kymathea, Kymatolege, Laomedeia, Leagore, Leiagora, Leucothoe, Ligeia, Lilaea, Limnoreia, Lycorias, Lykorias, Lysianassa, Maera, Melite, Memphis, Menippe, Nausithoe, Nemertes, Neomeris, Nesaea, Neso, Opis, Oreithyia, Panope, Pasithea, Pherusa, Phyllodoce, Plexaura, Ploto, Polynoe, Polynome, Pontomedusa, Pontopereia, Pronoë, Protho, Proto, Protogeneia, Protomedeia, Psamathe, Sao, Speio, Thaleia, Themisto, Thetis, Thoeë,* and *Xantho*. Alternate forms: Dorides, Nereids. [Bell 1991; Leach 1992; Redfield 1931; Woodcock 1953; Zimmerman 1964]

Nereis
Grecian
Water; Fate; Beauty
A patronymic form of Nereus given to individual *Nereides*. Alternate form: Nerine. [Bell 1991]

Nerine
Roman
Unknown
Sabine name identified with Greek *Athena* and Roman *Minerva* or Greek *Aphrodite* and Roman *Venus*. Her festival is on March 23 in celebration of her marriage to the god Mars. Alternate forms: Nereis, Neiro. [Bell 1991; Durdin-Robertson 1982; Durdin-Robertson 1990]

Nerio
Roman
War
"Valor." See *Nerine*.

Nesaea
Grecian
Water; Fate; Beauty
"The Dweller on Islands." One of the *Nereides*. Alternate form: Nesaia. [Bell 1991; Leach 1992]

Nesaia   See *Nesaea*.

Neso
Grecian
Water; Fate; Beauty
One of the *Nereides*. [Bell 1991]

Nete
Grecian
Arts; Sciences; Intelligence and Creativity; Fate
A *Muse* worshiped at Delphi. Her name signifies one of the strings on a three-stringed lyre. [Bell 1991]

Nice
Grecian
War
1) Alternate form for *Nike*, goddess of victory. 2) A name for *Athena* in Athens and Megara. 3) Name for *Apteros*. [Bell 1991]

Nicephorus
Grecian
War
"Bringing Victory." A name for *Aphrodite*. [Bell 1991]

Nichta   See *Nikta*.

Nicostrata
Roman
Unknown
The original name for *Carmentis* or an earlier goddess who was assimilated by *Carmentis*. Alternate form: Nicostrate. [Bell 1991; Leach 1972]

Nicostrate   See *Nicostrata*.

Nicothoe
Grecian
Weather, Justice; Ugliness; Demi-animals; Heaven and Hell; Wild Birds
One of the *Harpies*. [Bell 1991]

Nike
Grecian
War
Goddess of victory. Daughter of *Styx* and Pallas. Equivalent to Roman *Victoria*. She is also known in Palestine. Also a name for *Athena*. See also *Mah*, Near East. Alternate form: Nice. [Avery 1962; Bell 1992; Leach 1972; Leach 1992; Zimmerman 1964]

Nikta
Grecian
Moon and Night
Goddess of the night. Alternate form: Nichta. [Stone 1979]

Nissa
Grecian
Earth and Nature
A nymph, mother of the sun. See also *Nymphs*. [Jobes 1962]

Nixi, The
Roman
Mother and Guardian
Roman deities who assist women during childbirth, relieving the pain. Alternate form: Nixi Dii. [Bell 1991]

Nixi Dii, The   See *The Nixi*.

Noctiluca
Roman
Moon and Night
"Shines During the Night Season." Latin name for *Diana*. She had a sanctuary on the Palatine Hill in Rome. [Redfield 1931]

Nomia
Grecian
Earth and Nature; Domesticated Animals; Love and Sexuality; Justice
An Arcadian nymph whose name was given to a mountain in the area. See also *Nymphs*. Alternate form: Echenais. [Bell 1991]

Nona
Roman
Mother and Guardian
Goddess of fetal formation. One of the *Parcae*. [Monaghan 1990]

Nortia
Roman; Etruscan; Volsci
1) Luck; Ceremonies; Magic; 2) Health and Healing
"Fortune." 1) Worshiped mainly at Vulsinni as a special deity of Volsci tribes. Each year a nail is driven into the wall of her temple. Some say it is to mark the passing of time, and others suggest that it is symbolic of nailing down evil. 2) A Tuscan goddess of healing identified with *Fortuna*. Alternate forms: Nursia, Nurtia. [Bell 1991; Carlyon 1982; Jayne 1925; Jobes 1962; Redfield 1931]

Nox
Roman
Moon and Night
Goddess of night. Equivalent to Greek *Nyx*. [Bell 1991; Bonnerjea 1927; Redfield 1931; Woodcock 1953; Zimmerman 1964]

Numeria
Roman
Mother and Guardian

Women in childbirth invoke her, perhaps to speed up the birth. [Bell 1991; Jayne 1925]

Numina, The
Roman

Mother and Guardian; Agriculture; Household Affairs

Roman protective spirits of individuals, households, gardens, and fields. *Pales* and *Pomona* are Numina. [Zimmerman 1964]

Nundina
Roman

Mother and Guardian; Ceremonies

Goddess who presides over a child's naming day, the ninth day after birth. [Wedeck and Baskin 1971; Woodcock 1953]

Nursia   See *Nortia.*

Nurtia   See *Nortia.*

Nutrix
Roman

Mother and Guardian

"She Who Gives Nourishment." Roman name for *Dea Caelestis* and *Tanit.* Also refers foster motherhood. [Lurker 1984]

Nycheia
Grecian

Earth and Nature

One of the *Oceanides,* daughter of *Tethys* and Oceanus. [Leach 1992]

Nymphae, The   See *The Nymphs.*

Nymphae Infernae Paludis
Grecian

Water; Heaven and Hell; Intelligence and Creativity; Fate

Nymphs of the rivers of the underworld. In Rome they are called *Avernales.* [Bell 1991]

Nymphaea
Grecian

Unknown

"Bridal." Name for *Aphrodite.* [Avery 1962]

Nymphes
Grecian

1) Earth and Nature; 2) Order; Time

1) Another name for the *Nymphs.* 2) One of the *Horae.* [Bell 1991]

Nympheuomene
Grecian

Unknown

Name for *Hera* as a mature woman. [Monaghan 1981]

Nymphs, The
Grecian

Earth and Nature; Water

Deities who are classified according to the areas of nature they represent. Water nymphs are *Haliae, Limnades, Nereides, Naiades, Oceanides,* and *Pagaeae.* Nymphs of mountains and grottoes are *Oreades* or *Sphragitides.* Nymphs of trees are *Dryades* and *Hamadryades.* Nymphs of plants and flowers are *Limoniades.* (See their entries for further subdivisions.) Their worship is widespread; among the more notable places it is found are Athens, Cyrtone, Megara, Olympia, and Sicyon. They are offered sacrifices of

goats, lambs, milk, and oil. Alternate forms: Nymphae, Nymphes. [Bell 1991; Lurker 1984; Redfield 1931; Woodcock 1953; Zimmerman 1964]

Nysa
Grecian

1) Earth and Nature; Mother and Guardian; Stars and Planets; 2) Weather; Stars and Planets

1) One of the *Nyseides* or 2) *Hyades.* [Bell 1991]

Nyseides, The
Grecian

Earth and Nature; Mother and Guardian; Stars and Planets

Nymphs who nursed Dionysus on Mt. Nysa. They include *Brome, Cisseis, Erato, Eripha, Nysa, Polyhymno.* See also *Nymphs.* [Bell 1991; Woodcock 1953; Zimmerman 1964]

Nyx
Grecian

Moon and Night; Order; Heaven and Hell

"Night." She came from Chaos. She is the subduer of all and lives in Hades. Sister/wife of Erebus, mother of *Aether, Ananke, Hemera.* Without the help of a mate she became the mother of *Ceres, Eros, Mors, Nemesis, Oizys, Pugna,* and *Senecta.* She is considered by some to be the mother of the *Moirae.* Same as Roman *Nox.* Alternate form: Chthonia. [Bell 1991; Leach 1992; Redfield 1931; Zimmerman 1964]

Obsequens
Roman

Unknown

Later name for Roman *Venus.* [Bell 1991]

Oceanides, The
Grecian

Water

Water nymphs, daughters of *Tethys* and Oceanus. Although they were called nymphs of the ocean, they were not always confined to water, and some seem to have been connected to fresh, rather than salt, water. Their numbers vary greatly. They seem to have had no altars or special form of worship. Along with Apollo and their brothers the Rivers, they aid in the rites that bring young boys to manhood. They variously include *Acaste, Aethra, Amphinome, Amphiro, Argeia, Asia, Asterope, Beroe, Caliadne, Callirrhoe, Calypso, Capheira, Cerceïs, Chryseis, Cleochareia, Clymene, Clytia, Daeira, Dione, Dodone, Doris, Eidothea, Electra, Etna, Eudora, Europa, Eurynome, Galaxaura, Hippo, Ianeira, Idyia, Leuce, Leucippe, Melia, Meliboea, Melite, Melobosis, Menestho, Merope, Metis, Nycheia, Pasiphae, Pasithoe, Peitho, Perse, Perseis, Petraea, Phaeno, Pleione, Plexaura, Plouto, Polydora, Polyxo, Prymno, Rhodope, Stilbo, Styx, Telesto, Theia, Thoë, Torone, Tyche, Urania, Zeuxippe,* and *Zeuxo.* See also *Nymphs.* Alternate forms: Oceanids, Okeaninai. [Bell 1991; Leach 1992; Redfield 1931; Woodcock 1953]

Oceanids, The   See *The Oceanides.*

Oculata Lucifera
Roman

Health and Healing

"Healer of Eyes." Name for *Bona Dea.* [Jayne 1925]

Ocypete
Grecian

Weather

Goddess of storm winds. One of the *Harpies.* Sister of *Aello* and *Celaeno.* Alternate forms: Cypete, Ocypode,

Ocythoe, Okypete. [Bell 1991; Leach 1992; Redfield 1931; Woodcock 1953; Zimmerman 1964]

Ocypode   See *Ocypete.*

Ocyrhoë   See *Ocyrrhoë.*

Ocyrrhoë
Grecian
1) Water; 2) Fate; 3) Earth and Nature
   1) One of the *Oceanides,* mother of Phasis by Helios, associated with the mobility of water. 2) The prophetic daughter of *Chariclo* and the Centaur Cheiron. 3) A nymph of Mysia, mother of Caicus by Hermes. See also *Nymphs.* Alternate forms: Ocyrhoe, Okyrhoe, Okyrrhoë. [Bell 1991; Leach 1992; Woodcock 1953; Zimmerman 1964]

Ocythoe   See *Ocypete.*

Odyne
Grecian
Unhappiness
   "Pain." She is the personification of pain. [Leach 1992]

Oeno
Grecian
Magic
   One of the *Oenotropae.* She can change water into wine. [Bell 1991]

Oenoatis
Grecian
Unknown
   Name for *Artemis* at Oenoe in Argolis. [Bell 1991]

Oenoe
Grecian
Mother and Guardian; Earth and Nature
   An Arcadian nymph who was a nurse of Zeus. See also *Nymphs.* [Bell 1991]

Oenoie
Grecian
Health and Healing; Fate; Intelligence and Creativity
   One of the *Naiades.* [Bell 1991]

Oenotropae, The
Grecian
Magic
   "Changers into Wine." Although it was *Oeno* who made wine, all three are known by this name. Three daughters of Anius, king of Delos. They are a later version of the cornucopia. Their names are *Elais, Oeno,* and *Spermo.* [Bell 1991]

Oeroe
Grecian
Water
   Goddess of the river Oeroe. Daughter of Asopos. [Leach 1992]

Oizys
Grecian
Unhappiness
   "Woe." Daughter of *Nyx.* [Bell 1991; Leach 1992]

Okeaninai, The   See *The Oceanides.*

Okypete   See *Ocypete.*

Okyrhoe   See *Ocyrrhoë.*

Okyrrhoë   See *Ocyrrhoë.*

Olympiades, The
Grecian
Sky and Heavens
   Name for the *Muses.* Refers to their being heavenly rather than earthly. [Bell 1991]

Onca
Grecian
Unknown
   Name for *Athena* when worshiped at Onca (just outside Thebes) in Boeotia. Alternate form: Onga. [Bell 1991]

Oncaea
Grecian
Earth and Nature
   Nymph on the island of Lesbos. Mother of Arion by Poseidon. See also *Nymphs.* [Bell 1991]

Onga   See *Onca.*

Ophthalmitis
Grecian
Health and Healing
   "Patron Goddess of Eyesight." Name for *Athena.* [Bell 1991; Leach 1972]

Opifera   See *Ops* and *Diana.*

Opigena
Roman
Mother and Guardian
   Goddess of childbirth. Assistant to *Lucina.* [Jayne 1925]

Opis
Grecian
Unknown
   One of the *Nereides.* Also a name for *Artemis.* Alternate form: Upis. [Bell 1991]

Opora
Grecian
Time
   "Autumn." An attendant of *Eirene.* [Leach 1992]

Ops
Roman
Agriculture; Mother and Guardian; Ceremonies
   Earth goddess. Protector of everything associated with agriculture. A nurturing goddess to newborns and adults. As Ops Consiva, "The Lady Bountiful, the Planter," her festival, the *Opeconsivia,* was celebrated on August 25. She had a sanctuary on the Capitoline Hill in Rome and a shrine in the Regia that was so small that only the Vestal Virgins and the state priest could enter. As Opifera she helps newborn humans. Ops was assimilated by *Magna Mater.* Identified with *Bona Dea, Cybele, Eire* (Western Europe) *Fauna, Lua, Maia, Pomona, Proserpina, Rhea, Tellus,* and *Tutilina.* Alternate forms: Patella, Runcina, Thya. [Bell 1991; Cooper 1876; Durdin-Robertson 1982; Jayne 1925; Redfield 1931; Woodcock 1953; Zimmerman 1964]

Optiletis
Grecian
Physical Prowess
   "Keen Sight." Name for *Athena.* [Leach 1972]

Orbona
Roman
Mother and Guardian; Health and Healing
Goddess of children. Some say she protects orphans; others say she protects siblings of children who have died or children with life-threatening diseases. [Bell 1991; Wedeck and Baskin 1971; Woodcock 1953]

Oreadai, The   See *The Oreades*.

Oreades, The
Grecian
Earth and Nature
Mountain nymphs. They also inhabit caves. They include *Echo*. See also *Nymphs*. Alternate forms: Oreadai, Orodemniades. [Bell 1991; Eliade 1987; Wedeck and Baskin 1971; Zimmerman 1964]

Oreilochia
Grecian
Unknown
Name for *Iphigeneia* on the island of Leuce. [Bell 1991]

Oreithyia
Grecian
Water; Fate; Beauty
One of the *Nereides*. Alternate form: Orithyia. [Bell 1991; Leach 1992; Monaghan 1981; Zimmerman 1964]

Orithyia   See *Oreithyia*.

Orodemniades, The   See *The Oreades*.

Orseis
Grecian
Earth and Nature; Family and Tribes
Nymph, wife of Hellen, the ancestor of the Hellenes (Greeks) and mother of Aeolus (the founder of the Aeolian branch of the Hellenes), Dorus (the ancestor of the Dorians), and Xuthus (the founder of the Achaians and Ionians). See also *Nymphs*. [Bell 1991]

Orthia
Grecian
Unknown
"Upright Position." A name of *Artemis*. A form of the goddess brought to Sparta from Tauris. Alternate form: Orthosia. [Bell 1991; Leach 1992]

Orthosia
Grecian
1) Order; Time; 2) Unknown
1) One of the ten *Horae*. 2) A name for *Artemis* (see *Orthia*). [Bell 1991; Leach 1992]

Ortygia
Grecian
Earth and Nature
Name for *Artemis* refering to her birth island, Ortygia. [Bell 1991]

Ossa
Grecian
1) Selfishness; 2) Earth and Nature
"Rumor." 1) She is equivalent to Roman *Fama*. 2) Also the personification of Mt. Ossa. [Bell 1991; Leach 1992]

Ossilago   See *Ossipaga*.

Ossipaga
Roman
Mother and Guardian; Health and Healing
She strengthens and hardens the bones of fetuses and infants. Also considered a name for *Juno*. Alternate forms: Ossilago, Ossipagina, Ossipago, Ossipanga. [Bell 1991; Meltzer 1981; Monaghan 1981]

Ossipagina   See *Ossipaga*.

Ossipago   See *Ossipaga*.

Ossipanga   See *Ossipaga*.

Ourania   See *Urania*.

Oxyderces   See *Oxydercis*.

Oxydercis
Grecian
Intelligence and Creativity; Physical Prowess
Name for *Athena*. Refers to her keen sight or strong intellect. Alternate form: Oxyderces. [Bell 1991; Leach 1972]

Paedotrophus
Grecian
Mother and Guardian
"Nurse of Children." Name for *Artemis*. [Avery 1962]

Paeonia
Grecian
Health and Healing; Immortality; Reptiles
"The Healer." Name for *Athena* at Athens and Oropus. Her sacred symbol is the serpent, the representation of perpetual renewal. [Bell 1991]

Pais
Grecian
Unknown
"Maiden." Name for *Hera*. [Bell 1991; Monaghan 1981]

Palato
Roman
Weather; Directions
Daughter of the north wind and wife of the Roman god of agriculture. [Jobes 1962]

Pales
Roman
Domesticated Animals
Goddess of flocks and shepherds. One of the *Numina*. Her festival, the *Palilia*, was celebrated on April 21 during the celebration of the founding of Rome. Pales was sought by the people to bless their animals, to keep away diseases, and to avert drought and famine as the shepherds' benefactor. She was sometimes described as a male or androgynous deity. Associated with the Greek god Pan. [Bell 1991; Durdin-Robertson 1976; Redfield 1931; Zimmerman 1964]

Pallas
Grecian
Unhappiness
Name for *Athena*. Early on, it appeared as Pallas Athena. There are several possible origins for this name.
Athena killed the giant Pallas and used his skin as her aegis (shield). Or she accidentally killed her childhood friend, Pallas. Athena made a wooden image of Pallas and left it with Zeus. It became the famous Palladium.
She is identified with Roman *Minerva*. [Bell 1991; Woodcock 1953; Zimmerman 1964]

Pallenis
Grecian
Unknown
Name for *Athena*. She had a temple between Athens and the plain of Marathon in Attica. [Bell 1991]

Pallor
Roman
Courage
"Fear." Similar to *Pavor*. [Monaghan 1981]

Pamphile
Grecian
Magic; Moon and Night
Sorceress who could control the moon. [Monaghan 1981]

Panacea
Grecian
Health and Healing
Goddess of healing. Daughter of *Epione* and Asclepius and sister of *Aigle, Hygeia,* and *Iaso.* Alternate forms: Panaceia, Panakeia. [Bell 1991; Redfield 1931; Zimmerman 1964]

Panaceia See *Panacea.*

Panachaea
Grecian
Unknown
"Goddess of the Achaians." Name for *Demeter* at Aegae in Macedonia. Name for *Athena* in the precinct of Laphria in the city of Patrae. [Bell 1991]

Panakeia See *Panacea.*

Panatis
Grecian
Household Affairs
Name of *Athena* as goddess of weaving. [Leach 1992]

Pandeia
Grecian
Unknown
Daughter of *Selene* and Zeus. See also *Pandia.* [Bell 1991]

Pandemos
Grecian
Ceremonies
"Common to All the People." Name for *Aphrodite.* She is worshiped with this name at Megalopolis and Thebes with a festival and the sacrifice of white goats. [Bell 1991; Monaghan 1981]

Pandia
Grecian
Moon and Night
Moon goddess. Daughter of *Selene* or *Luna.* See also *Pandeia.* [Durdin-Robertson 1982; Monaghan 1990]

Pandora
Grecian
Earth and Nature; Intelligence and Creativity; Evil; Selflessness
"The Giver of All." Name for *Gaea,* Earth. Mother of *Pyrhha.* Pandora later became equivalent to the Old Testament Eve, the original cause of evil on Earth. [Baring and Cashford 1991; Bell 1991; Redfield 1931; Walker 1983; Woodcock 1953; Zimmerman 1964]

Pandrosos
Grecian
Agriculture; Household Affairs
"All-bedewing." Goddess of agriculture. One of the *Augralids.* Pandrosos is credited with the introduction of spinning. [Bell 1991; Leach 1992; Redfield 1931; Zimmerman 1964]

Panope
Grecian
Water; Fate; Beauty
Name of one of the *Nereides.* Mother of *Aigle.* Alternate forms: Panopea, Panopeia. [Bell 1991; Leach 1992; Zimmerman 1964]

Panopea See *Panope.*

Panopeia See *Panope.*

Panteleia
Grecian
Supreme Being
"Perfection." May be a name for *Demeter.* [Leach 1992]

Paphia
Grecian
Unknown
Name for *Aphrodite* as worshiped in the temple at Paphos on Cyprus. [Bell 1991; Neumann 1972; Woodcock 1953; Zimmerman 1964]

Paraca See *Parca.*

Parca
Roman
Mother and Guardian
"Childbirth." Alternate forms: Paraca, Partula. [Jayne 1925; Wedeck and Baskin 1971]

Parcae, The
Roman
Fate
Name for the *Fates* or the Greek *Moirae.* Their names are *Decuma, Morta,* and *Nona.* See also *Wyrdes,* Western Europe. [Bell 1991; Bonnerjea 1927; Leach 1992]

Paregoros
Grecian
Charisma; Goodness
Goddess of persuasion and consolation. Daughter of *Tethys* and Oceanus but not a water deity. [Leach 1992]

Pareia
Grecian
Earth and Nature
Name for *Athena* at Laconia. She had a statue made of Parian marble there. Also the name of a nymph on Crete. See also *Nymphs.* [Bell 1991]

Parnassa See *Metope.*

Parnassides, The
Grecian
Arts; Sciences; Intelligence and Creativity; Evil
Name for the *Muses* from Mt. Parnassus. [Woodcock 1953]

Partenope See *Parthenope.*

Parthenia
Grecian
1) Unknown; 2) Earth and Nature; 3) Stars and Planets; Magic
1) Name for *Athena, Hera,* and *Artemis.* 2) A nymph on the island of Samos, which was Parthenia in earlier times. 3) One of the *Pleiades.* [Bell 1991; Zimmerman 1964]

Parthenope
Roman
1) Beauty; Charisma; Demi-animals; Fate; Destroyer of Life; Wild Birds; 2) Unknown
1) One of the Roman *Sirens.* 2) The mother of *Europa* and *Thrace.* Alternate form: Parthenos. [Bell 1991; Zimmerman 1964]

Parthenos
Grecian
Unknown
"Virgin" (the original meaning of the word *virgin* meant "not belonging to a man"). Name for *Athena* at Athens, associated with the Parthenon. Also a name for Roman *Minerva* and *Juno.* Alternate form: Parthenope. [Bell 1991; Redfield 1931; Woodcock 1953]

Partula
Roman
Mother and Guardian
Goddess of childbirth. She determines the time of gestation. Alternate form: Parca. [Meltzer 1981; Redfield 1931]

Pasiphae
Grecian
1) Moon and Night; 2) Unknown; 3) Water; 4) Unknown
"Shining on All." 1) Moon goddess. Daughter of *Perseis* and Helios. Some say she may be the daughter of *Crete.* Wife of the second Minos, king of Crete, and mother of *Ariadne* and *Phaedra.* She mated with a white bull and produced the Minotaur. 2) Name of an oracular goddess at Thalamae in Laconia. 3) One of the *Oceanides.* 4) Name for *Aphrodite.* Alternate form: Daphne. [Bell 1991; Harding 1971; Leach 1992]

Pasithea
Grecian
1) Water; Fate; Beauty; 2) Beauty; Charisma
"Brilliance." 1) One of the *Nereides.* 2) One of the *Charites.* [Bell 1991; Jobes 1962; Leach 1992; Zimmerman 1964]

Pasithoe
Grecian
Water
One of the *Oceanides.* [Bell 1991]

Patelina   See *Patella.*

Patella
Roman
1) Agriculture; 2) Unknown
1) Agricultural goddess. She presides over the grain, "opening the stem on a stalk of wheat so that the ears might come forth and develop." 2) Also thought to have been a name for *Ops.* Alternate form: Patelina. [Bell 1991; Wedeck and Baskin 1971]

Pavor
Roman
Courage
"Fear." Similar to *Pallor.* [Monaghan 1990]

Pax
Roman
Order; Ceremonies
"Peace." One of the *Appiades.* Equivalent to the Greek *Eirene.* On January 30, a festival is celebrated honoring Pax, *Salus, Concordia* and Janus. Alternate form: Pax Augusta. [Bell 1991; Baumgartner 1984; Durdin-Robertson 1982; Redfield 1931; Zimmerman 1964]

Pax Augusta   See *Pax.*

Pecunia
Roman
Wealth
Goddess who presides over money. [Graves 1985; Wedeck and Baskin 1971]

Pedile
Grecian
Weather; Stars and Planets
One of the *Hyades.* Daughter of *Aethra* and Atlas. [Bell 1991; Leach 1992]

Pegaeae, The
Grecian
Health and Healing; Water
Healing nymphs of springs. Sometimes called *Ionides.* See also *Nymphs* and *Naiades.* Alternate form: Pegaia. [Bell 1991; Jayne 1925]

Pegaia, The   See *The Pegaeae.*

Pegasides, The
Grecian
1) Arts; Sciences; Intelligence and Creativity; Evil; 2) Water
1) Name for the *Muses.* 2) Name for nymphs of springs and brooks. See also *Nymphs.* [Bell 1991]

Peirene
Grecian
Water; Unhappiness
Daughter either of the river god Achelous or the Asopus river god. Mother of Leches and Cenchrias by Poseidon. When Cenchrias was accidentally killed by *Artemis,* the spring of Peirene at Corinth was formed of Peirene's tears. See also *Pyrene.* [Bell 1991; Zimmerman 1964]

Peisdice
Grecian
1) Stars and Planets; Magic; 2) Unknown
1) One of the *Peliades.* 2) A daughter of *Enarete* and Aeolus. [Bell 1991]

Peisinoe
Grecian
Charisma; Love and Sexuality
"Seductress." One of the *Sirens.* Sister of *Aglaopheme* and *Thelxiepeia.* [Bell 1991; Monaghan 1981]

Peitho
Grecian
1) Justice; Charisma; 2) Justice; Beauty; Charisma; 3) Justice; Water; 4) Justice
"Persuasion." Associated with leadership. 1) Daughter of *Aphrodite* and Hermes. In Rome she is called *Suada.* 2) One of the *Charites.* 3) One of the *Oceanides.* 4) A name for *Aphrodite* and *Artemis.* Alternate forms: Cerdo, Pitho. [Jobes 1962; Leach 1992]

Pelagia
Grecian
Unknown
Name for *Aphrodite*. [Zimmerman 1964]

Pelasgian Goddess   See *Pelasga*.

Pelasga
Grecian
Unknown
Name for *Hera* at Iolcus in Thessaly. A name for *Demeter* at Argos. Alternate forms: Pelasgis, Pelasgian Goddess. [Bell 1991]

Pelasgis   See *Pelasga*.

Peliades, The
Grecian
Immortality; Justice
Daughters of Pelias and *Anaxibia*. They include *Amphinome, Euadne, Peisdice,* and *Pelopeia.*

⚷ *They were deceived by Medea into dismembering their father and putting him into a cauldron, thinking that this would make him young again. Medea thereby exacted her revenge against Pelias and escaped.* [Bell 1991; Zimmerman 1964]

Pelonia
Roman
Magic; Mother and Guardian
Goddess who is invoked to ward off enemies. [Bell 1991; Wedeck and Baskin 1971]

Pelopeia
Grecian
Immortality and Justice
One of the *Peliades*. [Bell 1991]

Pemphredo
Grecian
Water
"White Foam." One of the *Graeae*. Daughter of *Phorcys* and Ceto. Alternate form: Pephredo. [Bell 1991; Leach 1992; Zimmerman 1964]

Penia
Grecian
Poverty
Goddess who is the personification of poverty. She was the consort of Porus, the personification of expediency. [Bell 1991; Leach 1992]

Penteteris
Grecian
Time
The personification of a four-year cycle. [Leach 1992]

Pephredo   See *Pemphredo*.

Pepromene
Grecian
Fate
"Predestination." [Bell 1991]

Periboea   See *Curissa*.

Pero
Grecian
Unknown
1) Mother of the river god Asopus by Poseidon. 2) Name of a daughter of *Chloris*. [Bell 1991; Monaghan 1981]

Perse
Grecian
Water; Magic
One of the *Oceanides*. Wife of Helios, mother of Aeetes, *Aega, Circe, Pasiphae,* and Perses (and some sources also include Aloeus in this list), who are collectively known as the *Perseides*. All of her children are endowed with magical powers. Alternate forms: Persea, Perseis. [Bell 1991; Leach 1992; Zimmerman 1964]

Persea   See *Perse*.

Perseides, The   See *Perse*.

Perseis
Grecian
1) Unknown; 2) Water; Magic
1) Name for *Hecate*. 2) A name for one of the *Oceanides*, sometimes called *Perse*. [Bell 1991]

Persephatta   See *Persephone*.

Persephone
Grecian
Mother and Guardian; Heaven and Hell; Life/Death Cycle; Health and
Healing
Goddess of death and the underworld. Daughter of *Demeter* and Zeus. Some say she is the daughter of *Styx*. The story of her descent to the underworld and her eternally recurring return to the Earth has been a central religious theme from early times. As *Kore* she is goddess of seed corn and was kidnapped by Hades. She is also the goddess of healing and childbirth.

⚷ *Demeter came from Crete to Sicily, where, near the springs of Kayane, she discovered a cave. There she hid her daughter Persephone and set two serpents as guardians over her. At other times the serpents were harnassed to her chariot. In the cave the maiden worked in wool—the customary occupation for maidens. . . . Persephone began weaving a great web, a robe for her father or her mother, which was a picture of the whole world.*

Similar to *Aneal*, Near East; *Cordelia* and *Kernaby*, Western Europe. She is equivalent to Roman *Proserpina*. Although Persephone is sometimes called *Despoena*, Despoena was actually a separate goddess who was merged with Persephone. Identified with *Aiokersa, Bendis, Bona Dea* (this region), and *Kunhild*, Northern Europe. Alternate forms: Auxesia, Azesia, Brimo, Carpophori, Cora, Core, Deione, Despoena, Eleusinia, Epaine, Hermione, Kore, Kore-Arethusa, Meliboea, Melitodes, Persephassa, Persephatta, Persephoneia, Phersephassa, Soteira. See also Damatres and Demeter. [Bell 1991; Bolen 1984; Jobes 1962; Leach 1992; Leeming 1981; Lurker 1984; Zimmerman 1964]

Persephoneia   See *Persephone*.

Persian Artemis
Grecian
Unknown
Name for Persian *Anāhita*, Near East. [Leach 1972]

Perso
Grecian
Water; Ugliness; Mother and Guardian
One of the *Graeae*. [Bell 1991]

Persphassa   See *Persephone*.

Pertunda
Roman
Love and Sexuality
Name for *Juno* related to newlyweds' first sexual intercourse. [Bell 1991]

Pessinuntia
Grecian
Unknown
Name for *Cybele*. [Bell 1991]

Petraea
Grecian
Water
"Rocky." 1) One of the *Oceanides*. 2) Also a name for *Scylla*. Alternate form: Petraia. [Bell 1991; Leach 1992]

Petraia   See *Petraea*.

Phace
Grecian
Unknown
Name for *Callisto*. [Bell 1991]

Phaea
Grecian
Ugliness; Evil; Domesticated Animals
Monstrous wild sow of Crommyon. Possibly a daughter of *Echidna* and Typhon. [Bell 1991]

Phaedra
Grecian
Unknown
1) Daughter of *Pasiphae* and the second Minos, king of Crete. Sister of *Ariadne* and *Acacalis*. Wife of Theseus before or after the death of *Antiope*. 2) Some say Phaedra is a literary creation based on an earlier Cretan goddess. [Bell 1991; Bonnerjea 1927; Monaghan 1981; Zimmerman 1964]

Phaenna
Grecian
Sun and Day
"Brilliant" or "Light." One of the *Charites*. She was with *Cleta* at Sparta. [Bell 1991; Jobes 1962; Leach 1992]

Phaeno
Grecian
Water
One of the *Oceanides*. [Bell 1991]

Phaeo
Grecian
Weather; Stars and Planets
One of the *Hyades*. [Bell 1991]

Phaethonides, The
Grecian
Unhappiness; Magic
Name for the *Heliadae*. Daughters of Helios and sisters of Phaethon. Alternate forms: Phaethontiades, Phaethontides. [Bell 1991]

Phaethontiades, The   See *The Phaethonides*.

Phaethontides, The   See *The Phaethonides*.

Phaethusa
Grecian
Weather; Unhappiness; Magic

One of the *Heliades*. Daughter of *Neaera*. She, with *Lampetia*, "fed the clouds" to make it rain. [Bell 1991; Jobes 1962; Zimmerman 1964]

Pharmaceia
Grecian
Water; Magic
Nymph. Her spring has poisonous powers and is near the Ilissus River in Athens. See also *Nymphs*. [Bell 1991]

Pharmacides, The
Grecian
Magic; Health and Healing
Minor deities or witches. They have knowledge of drugs and aided *Hera* and *Eileithyia* in delaying the birth of Heracles. [Bell 1991]

Pharygaea
Grecian
Unknown
Name for *Hera* at Pharygia in Locris, where she had a temple. [Bell 1991]

Phatusa
Grecian
Unhappiness; Magic
One of the *Heliadae*. [Monaghan 1981; Zimmerman 1964]

Pheme
Grecian
Charisma
"Fame." *Fama* is her Roman counterpart. [Zimmerman 1964]

Phemonoe
Grecian
Arts
Goddess of poetry. Inventor of hexameter verse. Daughter of Apollo. [Bell 1991]

Pheraea
Grecian
Order; Hunting and Wild Animals
Name for *Artemis* and *Hecate*. Some say she is a Cretan goddess, "Lady of Beasts Who Tames the Masculine and Bestial." Alternate form: Pheraia. [Bell 1991; Leach 1992; Monaghan 1981; Neumann 1972]

Pheraia   See *Pheraea*.

Pherousa   See *Pherusa*.

Pherusa
Grecian
1) Water; Fate; Beauty; 2) Order; Time
1) One of the *Nereides*. 2) One of the *Horae*. Alternate form: Pherousa. [Bell 1991; Leach 1992]

Phigalia
Grecian
Earth and Nature
One of the *Dryades*. The town of Phigalia in Arcadia is believed to have been named for her. [Bell 1991]

Philia
Grecian
Love and Sexuality; Mother and Guardian; Earth and Nature
"Friendship." 1) The name of a nymph of Naxos who, with her sisters *Cleis* and *Coronis*, cared for the infant Dionysus. 2) Name for *Aphrodite*. [Bell 1991; Leach 1992]

Philotes
Grecian
Love and Sexuality
"Friendship." Daughter of *Nyx,* sister of Apate, Geras, and *Eris.* [Leach 1992]

Philyra
Grecian
Mother and Guardian
An *Oceanid.* Mother of Cherion by Cronus. Cherion has the upper body of a human and lower body of a horse. [Bell 1991; Redfield 1931]

Phobos
Grecian
Courage
Goddess of fear. [Lurker 1984]

Phoebe
Grecian
1) Moon and Night; 2) Earth and Nature; 3) Supreme Being; 4) Moon and Night
1) Name for *Artemis* as goddess of the moon. 2) One of the *Hamadryades*; a daughter of *Leda* and Tyndareus. 3) A Titan, daughter of *Gaea* and Uranus (and thus one of the *Titanides*), mother of *Asteria* and *Leto,* who is said to have been in possesion of the Delphic oracle before Apollo. 4) Some say Phoebe is a moon goddess, daughter of Helios and *Neaera* and the same as *Aigle.* [Bell 1991; Bonnerjea 1927; Leach 1992]

Phonos
Grecian
Unknown
One of the *Androktiasi.* [Jobes 1962; Leach 1992]

Phorcides, The
Grecian
Evil; Ugliness; Water
Name for the *Gorgons* and the *Graeae.* Daughters of Phorcys and *Ceto.* Alternate forms: Phorcydes, Phorcynides. [Bell 1991]

Phorcydes, The   See *Phorcides.*

Phorcynides, The   See *The Phorcides.*

Phosphoros
Grecian
1) Dawn and Twilight; Mother and Guardian; 2) Dawn and Twilight; 3) Fire
"Bringing Light." 1) Name for *Artemis,* probably related to childbirth. 2) A name of *Eos* as the bringer of dawn. 3) A name for *Hecate* when bearing a torch. [Bell 1991]

Phratria
Grecian
Family and Tribes
Name for *Athena* as head of the Athenian family. [Leach 1972]

Phrygia
Grecian
Unknown
Name for *Cybele.* [Bell 1991]

Phyllodoce
Grecian
Water; Fate; Beauty

One of the *Nereides.* Alternate form: Phyllodoke. [Bell 1991; Leach 1992]

Phyllodoke   See *Phyllodoce.*

Physis
Grecian
Earth and Nature
Goddess of nature. [Leach 1992]

Phytalus
Grecian
Unknown
A demigoddess, a human raised to the status of deity, who greeted *Demeter* at Eleusis. [Wedeck and Baskin 1971]

Phytia
Grecian
Magic; Mother and Guardian; Ceremonies
"Creator." Name for *Leto* at Phaestus in Crete. She changed a female child to a male child to prevent the father from killing the baby. The festival of *Ecdysia* commemorates *Leto* for this act. [Bell 1991]

Phyto
Grecian
Weather; Stars and Planets
One of the *Hyades.* Daughter of *Aethra* and Atlas. [Bell 1991; Leach 1992]

Pieria
Grecian
Earth and Nature
A nymph, wife of Oxylus. See also *Nymphs.* [Bell 1991]

Pietas
Roman
Justice
"Duty to One's Gods, State, and Family." [Bell 1991; Zimmerman 1964]

Pilumnus
Roman
Mother and Guardian; Household Affairs
She protects young mothers from the god Silvanus by striking the threshold with a pestle. Two other goddesses assist her in this task, *Deverra* and *Intercidona.* [Jayne 1925]

Pimpleia   See *Pipleia.*

Pimpleides, The
Grecian
Arts; Sciences; Intelligence and Creativity; Evil
Name for the *Muses.* Pimpleia in Pieria is sacred to them. [Bell 1991]

Pipleia
Grecian
Earth and Nature
Nymph loved by Daphnis. See also *Nymphs.* Alternate form: Pimpleia. [Bell 1991]

Pirene   See *Pyrene.*

Pistis
Grecian
Goodness
"Loyalty and Faith." [Leach 1992]

Pitanatis
Grecian
Unknown
Name for *Artemis* at Pitane in Laconia where she had a temple. [Bell 1991]

Pitane
Grecian
Unknown
Daughter of the Eurotas river god in Laconia. Mother of *Euadne* by Poseidon. The town of Pitane is named for her. [Bell 1991]

Pitho   See *Peitho*.

Pithys   See *Pitys*.

Pitys
Grecian
Earth and Nature; Magic; Weather; Unhappiness
Nymph.
Pitys was loved by Pan, but in fleeing from him she fell onto a rock and was killed. She was changed into a pine tree.
Others say she was loved by Pan and Boreas, the north wind. She chose Pan, and Boreas blew her off a cliff. Gaea changed her into a pine tree, which weeps when the north wind blows.
Alternate form: Pithys [Bell 1991; Jobes 1962; Zimmerman 1964]

Placida
Roman
Unknown
Later name for *Venus*. [Bell 1991]

Pleiades, The
Grecian
Stars and Planets; Magic
Daughters of *Pleione* and Atlas. Half-sisters of the *Hyades*. Their names vary among writers, but those named include *Alcyone, Antinoe, Asteria, Asterope, Celaeno, Coccymo, Electra, Euadne, Hippothoe, Lampado, Lampatho, Maia, Medusa, Merope, Parthenia, Protis, Sterope, Stonychia,* and *Taygete*. They were transformed together into a constellation. Equivalent to *The Vergiliae, Krittika,* Indian Subcontinent, and *Kimah,* Near East. Their Roman name is the *Vergiliae*. Alternate form: Atlantides. [Bell 1991; Leach 1992; Redfield 1931; Zimmerman 1964]

Pleias   See *Maia*.

Pleione
Grecian
Water
One of the *Oceanides*. Wife of Atlas and mother of the *Pleiades*. [Bell 1991; Redfield 1931; Zimmerman 1964]

Plexaura   See *Plexaure*.

Plexaure
Grecian
1) Water; Fate; Beauty; 2) Water
"Like a Dashing Brook." One of the *Nereides,* daughter of *Tethys* and Oceanus. Also said to be the name of one of the *Oceanides*. Alternate form: Plexaura. [Bell 1991; Leach 1992]

Ploto
Grecian
Water; Fate; Beauty
"The Swimmer." One of the *Nereides,* she is associated with sailing. [Bell 1991; Leach 1992]

Plouto
Grecian
Water; Wealth
"Gifts and Wealth." One of the *Oceanides,* daughter of *Tethys* and Oceanus. [Leach 1992]

Pluto
Grecian
Water
One of the *Oceanides*. [Bell 1991]

Podarge
Grecian
Weather; Justice; Ugliness; Demi-animals; Heaven and Hell; Wild Birds
One of the *Harpies*. She is sometimes called *Celaeno*. [Bell 1991; Jobes 1962; Leach 1992; Zimmerman 1964]

Poena
Grecian, Roman
1) Unknown; 2) Justice
1) An attendant of *Nemesis*. 2) Roman Goddess of punishment. See also *Poene*. [Boulding 1976; Leach 1992; Zimmerman 1964]

Poenae, The   See *The Furies*.

Poene
Grecian
Unknown
The personification of retaliation. See also *Poena*. [Bell 1991]

Polias
Grecian
Unknown
"Protector of Cities." Name for *Athena*. [Bell 1991; Leach 1972; Redfield 1931]

Poliatas
Grecian
Unknown
"Keeper of the City." Name for *Athena*. [Avery 1962]

Polimastos   See *Polymastus*.

Poliuchos
Grecian
Unknown
"Protecting the City." Name for *Athena* at Sparta in her aspect Chalcioecos. [Bell 1991]

Polyboulos
Grecian
Education and Knowledge
"Exceedingly Wise." Name for *Athena*. [Bell 1991]

Polydora
Grecian
Luck
"Good Fortune." One of the *Oceanides*. Daughter of *Tethys* and Oceanus. [Bell 1991; Leach 1992]

Polyhymnia   See *Polymnia*.

Polyhymno
Grecian
Earth and Nature; Mother and Guardian; Earth and Planets
One of the *Nyseides*. [Bell 1991]

Polymastus

Grecian

Earth and Nature

"Many-breasted." Name for *Artemis*. Her likeness as a fertility goddess was in a great temple in Ephesus. Originally an Asiatic deity adopted by the Greeks and assimilated into their *Artemis*. Alternate form: Polimastos. [Avery 1962; Ergener 1988]

Polymatheia

Grecian

Arts; Sciences; Intelligence and Creativity; Evil

One of the three *Muses* in Sicyon. [Bell 1991]

Polymnia

Grecian

Arts; Sciences; Intelligence and Creativity; Evil

One of the nine *Muses* at Athens. She presides over lyric poetry and is said to have invented the lyre. Alternate form: Polyhymnia. [Bell 1991; Redfield 1931; Zimmerman 1964]

Polynoe

Grecian

Intelligence and Creativity; Water; Fate; Beauty

"Richness of Mind and Reason." One of the *Nereides*. [Bell 1991; Leach 1992]

Polynome

Grecian

Water; Fate; Beauty

One of the *Nereides*. [Bell 1991]

Polyxo

Grecian

1) Water; 2) Weather; Stars and Planets; 3) Water; Health and Healing; Fate; Intelligence and Creativity

1) One of the *Oceanides*. 2) One of the *Hyades*. 3) One of the *Naiades*. [Bell 1991; Leach 1992; Zimmerman 1964]

Pomona

Roman

Agriculture

Goddess of fruit trees. She represents autumn. One of the *Numina*. Her sacred grove, Pomonal, was on the road from Rome to Ostia. Identified with *Ops*. [Bell 1991; Jobes 1962; Redfield 1931; Zimmerman 1964]

Pontia

Grecian

Water

"Of the Deep Sea." Name for *Aphrodite*. [Avery 1962]

Pontomedusa

Grecian

Water; Fate; Beauty

One of the *Nereides*. [Bell 1991; Leach 1992]

Pontopereia

Grecian

Water

"The Seafarer." One of the *Nereides*. [Bell 1991; Leach 1992]

Populonia

Roman

Justice; Creator of Life

Name for *Juno* when involved in affairs of state. Others say it relates to her involvement with conception. [Bell 1991; Monaghan 1981]

Porrima

Roman

Fate

One of the *Camenae*. [Bell 1991; Jayne 1925]

Posidaeia

Grecian

Unknown

Goddess of the Pylians of Mycenae. Female counterpart of Poseidon. [Leach 1992]

Postvorta

Roman

Mother and Guardian

1) One of the *Camenae*. Prophetic goddess of the waning moon. She is associated with the breech presentation in childbirth. Guardian of women. See also *Prorsa* and *Antevorta*. 2) A name for *Venus*. [Leach 1992; Monaghan 1981; Zimmerman 1964]

Potameides, The

Grecian

Water

River nymphs. They are further classified by specific rivers. See also *Naiades*. Alternate form: Acheloides. [Bell 1991; Jobes 1962; Zimmerman 1964]

Potamia

Grecian

Water

Name for *Artemis* as a river goddess. [Leach 1992]

Potina

Roman

Mother and Guardian

Goddess of children. She blesses their drinks. Her companions are *Edulica* and *Cuba*. [Bell 1991; Zimmerman 1964]

Potnia

Grecian

Earth and Nature

Earth goddess of Pylos, Mycenae, and Greece, associated with smiths. She is similar to *Cuba* and *Eudlica*. [Leach 1992]

Potnia Theron

Grecian, Crete

Earth and Nature

"Mistress of Animals, Lady of Wild Things." Possibly of Asian origin. [Eliade 1987]

Praenestina

Roman

Unknown

Name for *Fortuna* when worshiped at Praeneste. [Bell 1991]

Praxidice

Grecian

Justice

Goddess of oaths. See also *Praxidicae*. Alternate form: Praxidike. [Bell 1991]

Praxidicae, The

Grecian

Justice

Demi-goddesses. They see to the delivery of justice, expecially if an oath is sworn. As a single goddess, her name is *Praxidice*. The sisters in this group include *Aulis*,

Alalkomenia, and *Thelxinoea.* Alternate form: Praxidikae. [Bell 1991; Jobes 1962]

Praxidikae, The   See *The Praxidicae.*

Praxidike   See *Praxidice.*

Praxithea
Grecian
Water
   Water nymph, probably the daughter of the Cephissus river god in Attica. Also the name of a daughter of *Diogeneia* and Phrasimus who had fifteen or more children, including *Chthonia, Creusa, Merope, Oreithyia, Otionia, Pandora, Procris, Protogeneia,* and one of the *Leontides.* See also *Nymphs.* [Bell 1991]

Prema
Roman
Love and Sexuality; Mother and Guardian
   Name for *Juno.* Relates to newlyweds' first sexual intercourse. Later she is invoked to grant an easy labor during childbirth. [Bell 1991]

Primigenia
Roman
Luck
   Name for Roman *Fortuna* as the first daughter of Jupiter. [Jayne 1925; Jobes 1962; Monaghan 1981]

Prisca
Roman
Unknown
   Name for *Vesta.* [Woodcock 1953]

Privata
Roman
Unknown
   Name for *Fortuna.* [Bell 1991]

Prodromia
Grecian
War
   "Advance Guard." Name for *Hera* when worshiped in Sicyon. [Bell 1991]

Promachorma
Grecian
Water
   "Protector of the Bay." Name for *Athena* when worshiped in her sanctuary on Mount Buporthmus near Hermione. [Bell 1991]

Promachus
Grecian
War
   "Front of Battle." A name for *Athena* and Roman *Minerva.* [Cooper 1876; Leach 1972]

Pronaea
Grecian
Unknown
   "Fore-temple." Name for *Athena* at Delphi. Alternate form: Pronoea. [Leach 1972]

Pronoë
Grecian
1) Water; Fate; Beauty; Justice; 2) Water; Health and Healing; Fate; Intelligence and Creativity

"The Provident" or "Forethought." 1) One of the *Nereides,* she is associated with leadership. 2) Name of one of the *Naiades* in Lycia. [Bell 1991; Leach 1992]

Pronoea   See *Pronaea.*

Pronoia
Grecian
Unknown
   "Forethought." Name for *Athena.* [Avery 1962]

Pronubia
Roman
Family and Tribes
   Name for *Juno* related to the marriage ceremony. [Bell 1991]

Prorsa
Roman
Mother and Guardian; Fate
   Name for *Carmentis.* Related to a headfirst birth presentation. One of the *Camenae.* See also *Postvorta.* [Bell 1991; Jayne 1925; Leach 1992; Monaghan 1981]

Proserpina
Roman
Agriculture; Heaven and Hell
   Originally a Roman goddess presiding over the germination of seeds. Her festival was the *Lupercalia,* which was absorbed by the Christian church as "Holy Virgin Mary" day, or Candlemas (because many candles were lighted), on February 2. Proserpina used candles to search for her mother, *Ceres.*
   She later became the Roman equivalent of the Greek *Persephone,* goddess of the underworld. Prosperina is considered a name for *Diana* in the infernal regions. She is identified with *Juno, Libitina,* and *Ops.* See also *Virgin Mary,* Near East, and *Inferna* (this section). Alternate forms: Inferna and Proserpine. [Bell 1991; Durdin-Robertson 1982; Eliot 1976; Jayne 1925; Jobes 1962; Redfield 1931; Woodcock 1953; Zimmerman 1964]

Proserpine   See *Proserpina.*

Prosymna
Grecian
1) Mother and Guardian; Moon and Night; 2) Earth and Nature; Heaven and Hell
   "Lofty." 1) The new moon. Nurse of *Hera,* sister of *Acraea* and *Euboea,* and daughter of Asterion, the river god. The town of Prosymna, near the Heraion, the temple of Hera, is named for her. 2) Name for *Demeter* as the Earth mother in her underworld aspect at Lerna. [Bell 1991; Durdin-Robertson 1982; Redfield 1931]

Protageneia   See *Protogenia.*

Protho
Grecian
Water; Fate; Beauty
   One of the *Nereides.* [Leach 1992]

Protis
Grecian
Stars and Planets; Magic
   One of the *Pleiades.* [Bell 1991]

Proto
Grecian
Luck; Water; Fate; Beauty

"Successful Venture." One of the *Nereides.* [Bell 1991; Leach 1992]

Protogenia
Grecian
1) Luck; Selflessness; 2) Water; Fate; Beauty
   1) Earth goddess associated with successful venture.
2) One of the *Nereides.* Alternate form: Protageneia. [Bell 1991; Leach 1992; Monaghan 1981; Zimmerman 1964]

Protomedea   See *Protomedeia.*

Protomedeia
Grecian
Justice
   "First in Leadership." One of the *Nereides.* Alternate form: Protomedea. [Bell 1991; Leach 1992]

Proversa
Roman
Water; Fate
   One of the *Camenae.* [Bell 1991]

Providentia
Roman
Unknown
   "Forethought." [Monaghan 1990]

Prymno
Grecian
Water
   "Ship's Stern" or "Like a Cascade." One of the *Oceanides,* daughter of *Tethys* and Oceanus. [Bell 1991; Leach 1992]

Psamathe
Grecian
1) Magic; Hunting and Wild Animals; 2) Unknown
   "Sand Goddess." 1) One of the *Nereides.* She could become a seal at will. Mother of Phokos (Phocus) by Aiakos (Aeacus). 2) The name of the wife of Proteus. [Bell 1991; Jobes 1962; Leach 1992]

Psyche
Grecian
Immortality
   "Soul." She represents the emergence of the soul after death. Mother of *Volupta* (Pleasure). Her symbol is a butterfly, the only one mentioned in Greek and Roman literature. *Venus* had Psyche put to death because of her fervent love for Cupid, but Jupiter granted Psyche immortality. Equivalent to *Leilah,* Near East. [Bell 1991; Monaghan 1981; Redfield 1931; Woodcock 1953; Zimmerman 1964]

Publica
Roman
Unknown
   Name for *Fortuna.* [Bell 1991]

Pudicitia
Roman
Unknown
   "Modesty." Her sanctuaries were Pudicitia Patricia and Pudicitia Plebeia. In Greece she is called *Aedos,* and she is equivalent to *Fortuna* in her aspect *Muliebris.* [Bell 1991; Redfield 1931]

Pugna
Grecian
Disorder

"Combat and Conflict." Daughter of *Nyx* and Erebus. [Leach 1992]

Purikh
Roman; Etruscan
Unknown
   Etruscan deity. [Cooper 1876]

Puta
Roman
Earth and Nature
   Goddess of pruning of trees. [Monaghan 1990]

Pylaitis
Grecian
Commerce and Travel
   "Gate-keeper." Name for *Athena* as protectress of towns. [Bell 1991]

Pylotis
Roman
Unknown
   Name for *Minerva.* [Woodcock 1953]

Pyrene
Grecian
1) Evil; Magic; Love and Sexuality; Reptiles; 2) Unknown
   1) A daughter of Bebryx, king of the Gauls.
   Pyrene was raped by Heracles and gave birth to a snake. Frightened, she ran into the mountains and was killed by wild animals. The mountian range, the Pyrenees, was named for her.
   2) The mother of Cycnus. Alternate forms: Peirene, Pirene. [Bell 1991; Zimmerman 1964]

Pyronia
Grecian
Fire
   "Fire Goddess." Name for *Artemis.* [Avery 1962]

Pyrrha
Grecian
Earth and Nature; Weather; Magic; Life/Death Cycle
   Goddess of the fiery red earth. Daughter of *Pandora* and Epimetheus.
   Pyrrha and her husband Deucalion were survivors of a storm, a nine-day deluge sent by Zeus, that flooded the Earth. Having built a boat, they were able to float to safety on Mount Parnassus. The couple asked Zeus to repopulate the world. They were told to throw the bones (stones) of their mother, Gaea (Pandora), behind them. When they did this, men and women sprang from the stones. [Bell 1991; Jobes 1962; Monaghan 1981]

Quies
Roman
Unknown
   "Rest." Her temple was just outside the Colline gate of Rome. [Woodcock 1953]

Quiritis
Roman; Sabine
1) Unknown; 2) Mother and Guardian
   "Of the Spear." 1) Another name for *Juno.* 2) A goddess of motherhood. [Avery 1962; Lurker 1984]

Redux
Roman
Luck

"Fortune Leads Back." Name for *Fortuna,* a goddess of happy journeys and prosperous returns. [Bell 1991; Durdin-Robertson 1982]

Regina
Roman
Sky and Heavens

"Queen of Heaven." Name for Roman *Juno.* Her festival is June 2. She had a temple on the Aventine Hill in Rome. Name for Welsh *Rhiannon,* Western Europe. [Bell 1991; Durdin-Robertson 1982; Stone 1979]

Rhamnusia
Grecian
Unknown

1) Name for *Nemesis.* At the famous temple at Rhamnus in Attica, there is a statue of her carved from a piece of stone ten cubits high. 2) Name for Roman *Venus.* [Bell 1991; Woodcock 1953]

Rharias
Grecian
Unknown

Name for *Demeter* when worshiped on the Rharian Plain near Eleusis. [Bell 1991]

Rhea
Grecian
Mother and Guardian; Earth and Nature

Mother of the gods; she is also called Mother Earth. Daughter of *Gaea* and Uranus, she is one of the *Titanides.* Wife of Cronus. Sister of *Astarte* and *Dione,* Near East. She is identified with Thracian and Asiatic goddesses. She was assimilated by *Magna Mater.*

Cronus had been told that he would be overthrown by one of his children, so he swallowed them as soon as they were born. When Zeus was about to be born, Rhea, his mother, went to Crete. After the birth, Rhea left Zeus in the care of the Curetes, Dactyls, and several nymphs, including Adrastea and Ida. She returned to Cronus with a stone wrapped like an infant, which he swallowed. When Zeus grew up, he induced his father to vomit up all of the children, including the rock, and they joined in declaring war on Cronus.

Rhea was worshiped in an ancient temple at Knossos and at Thebes, Chaeroneia, Plataea, Arcadia, the islands of Lemnos and Samothrace, in Phrygia, and at Pessinus in Galatia, where her name is *Agdistis.* From there, her worship was carried to Rome. Identified with *Bendis, Bona Dea,* and *Ops.* See also *Deo* and *Mater Kubile,* Near East. Alternate forms: Acraea, Antaea, Ma, Titan Rhea. [Bell 1991; Harding 1971; Jobes 1962; Leach 1992; Neumann 1972; Zimmerman 1964]

Rhea Silvia
Roman
Selflessness

A Vestal Virgin whom the god of the Anio River caused to become a goddess. Mother of Remus and Romulus by Mars. Alternate forms: Ilia, Rhea Sylvia, Silvia. [Bell 1991; Zimmerman 1964]

Rhea Sylvia   See *Rhea Silvia.*

Rhene
Grecian
Earth and Nature

Nymph. See also *Nymphs.* [Bell 1991]

Rhode
Grecian
Unknown

Name of a daughter of Poseidon by Amphitrite. Rhode and *Rhodos* are sometimes confused. [Bell 1991]

Rhodea   See *Rhodeia.*

Rhodeia
Grecian
Water

One of the *Oceanides,* daughter of *Tethys* and Oceanus and companion to *Persephone.* Alternate form: Rhodea. [Bell 1991; Leach 1992]

Rhodia
Grecian
Arts; Sciences; Intelligence and Creativity; Evil

One of the *Muses.* [Bell 1991]

Rhododactylos
Grecian
Unknown

Name for *Aurora.* [Cooper 1876]

Rhodope
Grecian
1) Earth and Nature; Justice; Magic; 2) Water

1) Daughter of the Strymon river god. A companion of *Persephone.*

Rhodope and Haemus had a following in Thrace and called themselves Hera and Zeus. This angered Zeus and Hera, and they turned the imposters into mountains, which later bore their names.

2) One of the *Oceanides.* [Bell 1991; Jobes 1962; Leach 1992; Zimmerman 1964]

Rhodos
Grecian
Earth and Nature

Nymph, daughter of *Halia* and Poseidon. Wife of Helios and mother of the *Heliades* (also the name of the children by Helios and *Clymene*). The island of Rhodes is named for her. She is sometimes confused with *Rhode.* [Bell 1991]

Rhoeo
Grecian
Water

Daughter of the Scamander River. [Bell 1991]

Robigo
Roman
Agriculture

Goddess of grain, especially corn. Her festival, called *Robigalia,* was celebrated on April 25, when she was called upon to preserve the corn from disease. [Durdin-Robertson 1982; Zimmerman 1964]

Roma
Roman
Family and Tribes

"Strength" or "Might." Personification of Rome who was later worshiped as a goddess by some cities of Asia Minor in the second century B.C.E. Her mother was *Lucania.* The festival of the *Parilia* was held in her honor on April 21, the traditional day of the founding of Rome. Some portrayals show her wearing a crown or winged helmet with all the attributes of prosperity and power. Alternate form: Tyche. [Bell 1991; Durdin-Robertson 1982; Zimmerman 1964]

Rumia Dea
Roman
Mother and Guardian
Protector of infants. [Woodcock 1953]

Rumina
Roman
Mother and Guardian
"Mother's Breast." She was one of three deities who protects sleeping infants. The other two are her sisters, *Cuba* and *Cunina*. [Bell 1991; Redfield 1931; Woodcock 1953; Zimmerman 1964]

Rumor
Grecian
Physical Prowess; Disorder; Selfishness; Demi-animals; Wild Birds
Feathered and swift-footed deity who runs about with messages— truthful or untruthful. Sometimes perverse and mischievous. [Monaghan 1981; Zimmerman 1964]

Runcina
Roman
Agriculture
Goddess of agriculture. She presides over weeding. Alternate form for *Ops* as the promoter of the harvest. [Bell 1991; Wedeck and Baskin 1971]

Rusina
Roman
Agriculture; Earth and Nature
Goddess of fields and open country. [Leach 1992]

Sacra   See *Vesta.*

Sagaris
Grecian
Earth and Nature
Nymph. See also *Nymphs*. [Jobes 1962]

Sagaritis
Grecian
Earth and Nature
One of the *Hamadryades*. [Bell 1991]

Sais
Roman, Egypt
Unknown
A name for *Minerva* when worshiped at Sais, Egypt. See also *Saitis*. [Woodcock 1953]

Saitis
Grecian
Unknown
Name for *Athena* when worshiped at her sanctuary on Mount Potinus near Lerna in Argolis. It is related to her worship in Egypt as *Sais*. [Bell 1991]

Salacia
Roman
Water
"Salt." Sea goddess. Equivalent to the Greek *Amphitrite* and similar to *Venilia*. Equivalent to Greek *Tethys*. Also possibly a name for *Venus*, related to her rising from the sea. Equivalent to *Mara*, Near East. Alternate form: Salatia. [Bell 1991; Jobes 1962; Leach 1992; Redfield 1931; Woodcock 1953; Zimmerman 1964]

Salatia   See *Salacia.*

Salmacis
Grecian
Earth and Nature; Love and Sexuality
Nymph.
⚠ *Hermaphroditus was sitting next to the spring where Salmacis lived. She fell in love with him and asked to be united with him in a single body. They became a bisexual being, a hermaphrodite.*
See also *Nymphs*. [Bell 1991; Leach 1992; Lurker 1984; Monaghan 1981]

Salmaone
Grecian
Mother and Guardian; Directions
"Lady of the East." Mother goddess. [Jobes 1962]

Salpinx
Grecian
Unknown
"Trumpet." Name for *Athena* at Argos. [Bell 1991]

Salus
Roman
Health and Healing; Agriculture; Goodness; Wealth
Goddess of health. Said to be an earlier Sabine agricultural goddess who was incorporated into the Roman pantheon and identified as a goddess of well-being responsible for the general welfare of the city and state. She became goddess of health after her identification with Greek *Hygeia*. Corresponds to Sabine *Strenia*. She is celebrated along with *Concordia*, Janus, and *Pax*. Also called *Salus Hygeia* and *Salus Publica*. [Bell 1991; Jayne 1925; Leach 1972; Redfield 1931; Zimmerman 1964]

Salus Hygeia   See *Salus.*

Salus Publica   See *Salus.*

Salutaris
Roman
Unknown
Name for *Fortuna*. [Bell 1991; Jayne 1925; Monaghan 1981]

Sao
Grecian
Mother and Guardian; Water
"The Rescuer" or "Safety." One of the *Nereides* associated with sailing. [Bell 1991; Leach 1992]

Sapientia
Roman
Unknown
"Wisdom." Counterpart of the Hebrew-Greek *Sophia*, Near East. In medieval times, she was known as *Sapientia-Sophia*. [Durdin-Robertson 1982]

Sapientia-Sophia   See *Sapientia.*

Saronia
Grecian
Ceremonies
Name for *Artemis* at Troezen. The festival of *Saronia* is held in her honor. Alternate form: Saronis. [Bell 1991]

Saronis   See *Saronia.*

Sarpedonia
Grecian
Unknown
Name for *Artemis*. [Bell 1991]

Savior
Grecian
Unknown
   Name for *Artemis* in her aspect of saving the people. Many sanctuaries were raised in her honor. [Avery 1962]

Scabies
Roman
Health and Healing
   "Skin Diseases." She was invoked for their cure. [Jayne 1925]

Sciras
Grecian
Unknown
   Name for *Athena* at her temple in Phaleron in Attica and on the island of Salamis. [Bell 1991]

Scotia
Grecian, Cyprus
Water
   "Dark One." Sea goddess. Name for *Aphrodite*. [Avery 1962; Jobes 1962]

Scylla
Grecian
Magic; Evil; Water; Beauty; Ugliness; Destroyer of Life
   "Witch of the Shoals."
   Having been changed from a beautiful woman into a monster by either Circe or Amphitrite, Scylla inhabited the rocks in the strait between Italy and Sicily. Ships sailing too close lost some of their crew members, who were snatched and devoured by a monster that barked like a dog and had "twelve feet, six long necks, and mouths with rows of sharp teeth."
   Alternate form: Petraea. [Bell 1991; Jobes 1962; Neumann 1972; Woodcock 1953; Zimmerman 1964]

Secia
Roman
Agriculture
   Goddess of seeds. May be the same as *Seia*. See also *Tutilina*. [Bell 1991]

Segetia
Roman
Agriculture
   Goddess who presides over the planted seeds. She controls their sprouting. Member of a triad; the other two goddesses are *Seia* and *Tutilina*. May be the same as *Seja*. [Bell 1991; Monaghan 1990]

Seia
Roman
Agriculture
   One of three goddesses who control the sprouting of seeds. Seia protects the seeds beneath the ground. The others are *Segetia* and *Tutilina*. May be the same as *Secia*. [Monaghan 1990]

Seirenes   See *Sirens*.

Seitho   See *Pitho*.

Seja
Roman
Agriculture
   Goddess of seeds. May be the same as *Segetia*. [Bell 1991]

Selena   See *Selene*.

Selene
Grecian, Norman
Moon and Night; Stars and Planets; Selfishness; Love and Sexuality
   Goddess of the moon and "Mistress of the Stars." Similar to *Mene*. Daughter of *Theia* and Hyperion, although other parents are sometimes mentioned. She is associated with the first day of the waning moon. Mother of *Ersa, Herse, Nemea,* and *Pandeia.*
   She drives her chariot across the heavens, drawn by two white steeds. Selene fell in love with Endymion, whom she put into a narcoleptic state and visited nightly. They had fifty daughters.
   Equivalent to *Luna* and *Levanah,* Near East. Alternate forms: Hilaeira, Selena. [Bell 1991; Dames 1979; Durdin-Robertson 1982; Leach 1992; Neumann 1972; Zimmerman 1964]

Semele
Grecian
Love and Sexuality
   Daughter of *Harmonia* and Cadmus. Sister of *Agave, Autonoe, Ino*, and Polydorus. Mother of Dionysus.
   Semele became a lover of Zeus, but he always appeared to her in disguise. When she asked him to appear in his godly state, he appeared as the great thunderer and wielder of lightning and Semele was burned to death.
   Sometimes identified with *Bona Dea* at Rome. Alternate forms: Keraunia, Stimula, Thyone. [Bell 1991; Jobes 1962; Monaghan 1981; Redfield 1931; Wedeck and Baskin 1971; Zimmerman 1964]

Semnai Theai, The
Grecian
Earth and Nature
   Earth goddesses of fertility. Worshiped in a cave on an island. Later identified with the *Erinyes*. Alternate form: Furies. [Lurker 1984]

Senecta
Grecian
Life/Death Cycle
   "Old Age." Daughter of *Nyx* and Erebus. Alternate form: Senectus. [Leach 1992]

Senectus   See *Senecta*.

Sepeo   See *Speio*.

Silvia   See *Rhea Silvia*.

Simaethis
Grecian
Water
   Water nymph. See also *Nymphs*. [Redfield 1931]

Sinoe
Grecian
Earth and Nature
   Arcadian nymph. She helped raise Pan. See also *Nymphs*. [Bell 1991]

Sipna
Roman; Etruscan
Unknown
   Divinity who is the attendant of *Alpanu*. [Cooper 1876]

Sirens, The
Grecian, Roman
Beauty; Charisma; Demi-animals; Fate; Destroyer of Life;
Wild Birds
  Temptingly beautiful, half-woman, half-birdlike creatures
who sing seductively. Some suggest that they were early
Greek prophets of both sexes. They are the daughters of
Calliope or, some say, *Sterope*. Their names and numbers
vary from writer to writer. They variously include *Aglaope,*
Aglaopheme, Himeropa, Ligeia, Molpe, Peisinoe, Teles,
Thelchtereia, Thelxiepeia. Roman sirens are said to include
Leucosia and *Parthenope.* They are said to lure sailors from
ships to their deaths. There was a temple to them near
Surrentum (Sorrento). See also *Mermaids,* Western Europe;
and *Yara,* South America. Alternate forms: Acheloides,
Seirenes. [Bell 1991; Redfield 1931; Monaghan 1981;
Zimmerman 1964]

Sito
Grecian
Agriculture
  "Giver of Food or Grain." Name for *Demeter.* [Bell 1991]

Sleparis
Roman; Etruscan
Unknown
  Divinity who is represented on a mirror at the Vatican.
[Cooper 1876]

Smyrna
Grecian
Unknown
  Daughter of *Oreithyia* and Theias. She gave her name to
the city of Smyrna. [Bell 1991]

Snake Goddess of Knossos
Crete; Minoan
Heaven and Hell; Immortality
  Chthonic goddess with a reviviscent (reviving the dead)
function. [Boulding 1976; Eliade 1987]

Sophrosyne
Grecian
Order
  "Safe Mind." Personification of "soundness, temperance,
wise moderation." [Jobes 1962]

Sororia
Roman
Unknown
  Name for *Juno.* [Bell 1991]

Sospita
Roman
Mother and Guardian
  "Savior." Name for *Juno* and *Diana* as goddesses of
childbirth related to labor. *Juno* had temples at Lanuvium
and Rome under this name. On February 1 new shrines were
constructed for her. She is said to have communicated on a
psychic level with her followers. [Bell 1991; Jobes 1962;
Lurker 1984; Monaghan 1981; Woodcock 1953]

Soteira
Grecian
Mother and Guardian
  "Saving Goddess." Personification of safety or recovery.
Name for *Artemis, Athena, Eunomia,* and *Persephone.* [Bell
1991; Zimmerman 1964]

Sparta
Grecian
Unknown
  Daughter of *Cleta* and Eurotas. Mother of *Asine, Eurydice,*
and Amyclas by Lacedaemon. The city of Sparta was named
for her. [Bell 1991; Monaghan 1981]

Speio
Grecian
Earth and Nature; Water; Fate; Beauty
  Goddess of caves. One of the *Nereides.* Alternate forms:
Speo, Sepeo. [Bell 1991; Leach 1992]

Speo See *Speio.*

Spermo
Grecian
Magic; Agriculture
  One of the *Oenotropae.* She can change grass into wheat.
[Bell 1991]

Spes
Roman
Happiness
  "Hope." Equivalent to the Greek *Elpis.* [Bell 1991;
Monaghan 1981]

Sphragitides, The
Grecian
Earth and Nature
  Mountain nymphs. They have a grotto on Mount
Cithaeron in Boeotia. See also *Nymphs.* [Bell 1991]

Sponde
Grecian
Order; Time
  One of the *Horae.* [Bell 1991]

Stata Mater
Roman
Unknown
  Her statue stood in the Forum at Rome, where fires were
kept burning during the night. May be a name for Greek
Vesta. Alternate form: Statua Mater. [Bell 1991; Wedeck and
Baskin 1971]

Statua Mater See *Stata Mater.*

Sterope
Grecian
1) Stars and Planets; Magic; 2) Unknown; 3) Unknown
  1) One of the *Pleiades.* Daughter of *Pleione* and Atlas. 2) A
daughter of *Euryte* and Porthaon, said by some to be the
mother of the *Sirens.* 3) Daughter of Helios. [Bell 1991;
Redfield 1931; Zimmerman 1964]

Sthenele
Grecian
Unknown
  Daughter of *Astydameia* and Acastus, sister of *Sterope.*
[Bell 1991]

Sthenias
Grecian
Physical Prowess
  "Strong." Name for *Athena* in Troezen. [Avery 1962]

Sthenno See *Stheno.*

Stheno
Grecian
Physical Prowess
"Strength." One of the *Gorgons.* Alternate form: Sthenno. [Monaghan 1981; Zimmerman 1964]

Sthenoboea See *Antea.*

Stilbe
Grecian
1) Water; 2) Unknown
1) Daughter of *Creusa* and the Peneius river god. Sister of *Daphne.* 2) Daughter of Eosphorus, who, according to some, is the mother of Autolycus by Hermes. [Bell 1991]

Stilbo
Grecian
Water
One of the *Oceanides.* [Bell 1991]

Stimula
Roman
Unknown
Name for *Semele* given to her by the Romans. [Bell 1991]

Stiria
Grecian
Unknown
Name for *Demeter* at Stiris in Phocis. Alternate form: Stiritis. [Avery 1962]

Stiritis See *Stiria.*

Stonychia
Grecian
Stars and Planets; Magic
One of the *Pleiades.* [Bell 1991; Leach 1992]

Strenia
Roman; Sabine
Health and Healing; Mother and Guardian
Goddess of health and protector of youth. A celebration connected with Strenia took place on January 1 in Rome. People exchanged *strenae,* gifts of bay and palm branches, and sweetmeats made of honey and dates or figs. These gifts were accompanied with wishes for happiness in the new year. She corresponds to the Roman *Salus.* [Durdin-Robertson 1982; Durdin-Robertson 1990; Jayne 1925; Leach 1992; Redfield 1931]

Strenua
Roman
Physical Prowess
Goddess of vigor. She gives energy to the weak. [Zimmerman 1964]

Strymo
Grecian
Water
Daughter of the Scamander River. Mother of *Cilla, Hesione,* and *Astyoche* by Laomedon. [Bell 1991]

Stymphalia
Grecian
Unknown
Name for *Artemis* when worshiped at her temple at Stymphalus in Arcadia. [Bell 1991]

Styx
Grecian
Water; Heaven and Hell; Justice

River nymph. One of the *Oceanides.* Daughter of *Tethys* and Oceanus. She inhabits the River Styx in the underworld. It is her name that is used when oaths are sworn. Her children are *Bia,* Cratus, *Nike,* and Zelus. Some say that *Persephone* and *Echidna* are her daughters, and the Romans add *Invidia.* See also *Nymphs.* [Bell 1991; Leach 1992; Redfield 1931; Zimmerman 1964]

Suada
Roman
Intelligence and Creativity; Charisma
"Persuasion." Equivalent to Greek *Peitho.* Alternate form: Suadela. [Bell 1991; Zimmerman 1964]

Suadela See *Suada.*

Syllis
Grecian
Earth and Nature
Nymph. Wife or lover of Zeuxippus. See also *Nymphs.* [Bell 1991]

Synallaxis, The See *The Ionides.*

Syrinx
Grecian
Earth and Nature; Magic; Arts
Arcadian nymph. Pursued relentlessly by Pan, she was metamorphosed into a clump of reeds by the Ladon River god (probably her father) to escape Pan's attentions. From these reeds, Pan fashioned a musical instrument, known as the Pipes of Pan. See also *Nymphs.* [Bell 1991; Redfield 1931; Zimmerman 1964]

Syzygia
Grecian
Family and Tribes
Name of *Hera* as goddess of the union of marriage. [Leach 1992]

Tabliope
Grecian
Luck
Goddess of gambling. [Leach 1992]

Tacita
Roman
Order
"The Silent." One of the Roman *Camenae.* Identified with *Lara, Larunda, Muta,* and possibly *Acca Larentia.* Her festival is February 18 through 21. [Monaghan 1981; Wedeck and Baskin 1971]

Talaira See *Hilaeira.*

Tamfana
Roman; Marsi
Agriculture
"Provider of Harvests." Italian Marsi Earth goddess. [Jobes 1962]

Tanais See *Anaitis.*

Tanaquil
Roman
Household Affairs
A queen of Rome who was deified. Her worship centered around the hearth and domestic life. Alternate forms: Caecilia, Caia. [Bell 1991; Jayne 1925]

Tanit
Roman, Carthage
Moon and Night
Goddess of the moon at Carthage. Her symbol is the crescent moon or the full moon. In her temple was a veil, which was regarded as the city's palladium, the object upon which the safety of the city depended. She is identified with *Astarte*, Near East, *Dea Caelestis*, and *Magna Mater*. Also called *Tanit Pele Baal*. Alternate forms: Nutrix, Tanith, Tinnit. [Jobes 1962; Leach 1992]

Tanit Pele Baal   See *Tanit*.

Tanith   See *Tanit*.

Taurian Artemis   See *Tauropolis* and *Trivia*.

Taurione   See *Tauropolis*.

Tauro
Grecian
Unknown
"Bull." A name for *Artemis*. See *Tauropolis*. [Ergener 1988]

Tauropolis
Grecian
Ceremonies
Worshiped at Tauris on the Black Sea. Identified with *Artemis*. Her rites are said to be "bloody and savage." See also *Trivia*. Alternate forms: Taurian Artemis, Taurione, Tauro, Tauropolos, Tauropos, Thoantea. [Bell 1991; Leach 1972]

Tauropolos   See *Tauropolis*.

Tauropos   See *Tauropolis*.

Taygete
Grecian
Stars and Planets; Magic
One of the *Pleiades*. A mountain in Laconia is named for her. [Bell 1991; Redfield 1931; Zimmerman 1964]

Techne
Grecian
Arts
Goddess of art. [Leach 1992]

Teisiphone   See *Tisiphone*.

Telchinia
Grecian
Unknown
1) Name for *Athena* at her temples at Teumessus in Boeotia and at Cameirus on Rhodes. 2) Name for *Hera* at Ialysus on Rhodes. [Bell 1991]

Telecleia
Grecian
Unknown
Wife of Cisseus who is said by some authors to be the mother of *Hecuba* and *Theano*. [Bell 1991]

Teledice
Grecian
Earth and Nature
Nymph. Alternate form: Cerdo. See also *Nymphs*. [Bell 1991]

Teleia
Grecian
Life/Death Cycle
"Complete One." Name for *Hera* as a mature female. [Bell 1991; Jobes 1962; Redfield 1931]

Telephassa
Grecian
Sun and Day
"Wide-shiner." Early goddess of light, probably from Phoenicia. Later called the mother of *Europa*. She participated in the search for her daughter when her daughter was kidnapped by Zeus, who took the form of a bull. [Bell 1991; Bonnerjea 1927; Monaghan 1981]

Teles
Grecian
Unknown
One of the *Sirens*. [Bell 1991]

Telesto
Grecian
Ceremonies
"Goddess of Initiations." One of the *Oceanides*, daughter of *Tethys* and Oceanus. [Leach 1992]

Telete
Roman, Grecian
1) Selflessness; 2) Order; Time
1) Spirit of mystery religions. She is the personification of consecration. 2) One of the *Horae*. [Bell 1991; Monaghan 1990]

Tellus
Roman
Earth and Nature; Immortality; Justice; Ceremonies
Goddess of the earth and its fertility. She is also associated with the fertility of humans. Corresponds to Greek *Gaea* and *Hertha*, Northern Europe. Tellus has a closer association with the world of the dead, receiving them into her bosom. Oaths are sworn by her by facing the palm downwards. Her festival is the *Fordicidia* or *Hordicalia* on April 15, which also honors *Ceres*. Tellus is identified with *Bona Dea, Ceres,* and *Ops*. Alternate names: *Tellus Mater, Terra, Terra Mater*. [Cooper 1876; Durdin-Robertson 1990; Harding 1971; Leach 1992; Monaghan 1982; Woodcock 1953; Zimmerman 1964]

Tellus Mater   See *Tellus*.

Telphusa
Grecian
Water
Nymph. Her fountain at the foot of Mount Tilphossium was said to have such cold water that anyone drinking it would die. Telphusa was also the name of a daughter of the Ladon river god from whom the city of Telphusa in Arcadia is named. Alternate form: Thelpusa. [Bell 1991; Monaghan 1981; Zimmerman 1964]

Telphusia
Grecian
Justice; Heaven and Hell; Ugliness; Family and Tribes
One of the *Erinyes*. [Bell 1991]

Tempestates
Roman
Weather
Roman goddess of storms and storm winds. [Zimmerman 1964]

Tergemina
Roman
Life/Death Cycle
Name for *Diana* relating to her as a trinity, goddess of heaven (*Lucina* or *Luna*), Earth (*Diana*), and the underworld (*Hecate*). Alternate form: Trivia. [Jobes 1962; Woodcock 1953]

Terpsichore
Grecian
Arts
One of the nine *Muses* at Athens. She presides over lyric poetry, choral singing, and dancing. Said to be the mother of the *Sirens*. [Bell 1991; Leach 1992; Redfield 1931; Zimmerman 1964]

Terra See *Tellus*.

Terra Mater See *Tellus*.

Tesana
Roman; Etruscan
Dawn and Twilight
"Dawn." The spirit of the dawn, similar to *Aurora*. She is good and comes with the first hint of red color in the sky to softly awaken the sleeping. Alternate form: Thesan. [Durdin-Robertson 1982; Leach 1992]

Tethys
Grecian
Water
Sea goddess. Daughter of *Gaea* and Uranus, and as such, one of the *Titanides*. Wife of Oceanus and mother of thousands of sea deities, including the *Oceanides*, the *Naiades*, and the river gods. Roman goddess *Salacia* is her equivalent. [Bell 1991; Bonnerjea 1927; Leach 1992; Redfield 1931]

Thalaeia See *Thaleia*.

Thalana
Roman; Etruscan
Unknown
Attendant of *Thanr*. [Cooper 1876]

Thalassa
Grecian
Water
"Vast and Lonely Primitive Sea" (the Red Sea or the Mediterranean). Daughter of Aether, the upper sky, and *Hemera*, the day. See also *Thalassa*, Near East. Alternate form: Thalassa Erythra. [Bell 1991; Leach 1992]

Thalassa Erythra See *Thalassa*.

Thaleia
Grecian
1) Arts; Sciences; Intelligence and Creativity; Evil; 2) Water; Fate; Beauty; 3) Beauty; Charisma
1) One of the nine *Muses* at Athens. She rules comedy. 2) One of the *Nereides*. 3) One of the *Charites*. Alternate forms: Thalaeia, Thalia. [Bell 1991; Bonnerjea 1927; Leach 1992; Redfield 1931; Zimmerman 1964]

Thalia See *Thaleia*.

Thallo
Grecian
Time; Earth and Nature
Goddess of spring blossoming. One of the *Horae*. [Bell 1991; Jobes 1962; Leach 1992]

Thalna
Roman; Etruscan
Beauty; Time
"Beauty," "Spring." [Cooper 1876]

Thana
Roman; Etruscan
Unknown
Name for *Juno*. [Cooper 1876]

Thanr
Roman; Etruscan
Mother and Guardian
Goddess who aids in childbirth. Attendant of *Akhuvitr*. [Cooper 1876]

Thea See *Theia*.

Theia
Grecian
Sun and Day
Goddess from whom light emanates. May be pre-Hellenic. One of the *Titanides*, daughter of *Gaea* and Uranus. She is the mother of Helios (the sun), *Eos* (the dawn), and *Selene* (the moon). Theia is also the name of one of the *Oceanides*. Alternate forms: Thea, Thei, Titan Theia. [Bell 1991; Monaghan 1981; Zimmerman 1964]

Thebe
Grecian
1) Earth and Nature; 2) Unknown
1) Nymph. Daughter of Prometheus and *Iodane*. The Boeotian city of Thebes was named for her. Also the name of a daughter of *Metope* and Asopus. See also *Nymphs*. [Bell 1991; Jobes 1962; Zimmerman 1964]

Thei See *Theia*.

Theisoa
Grecian
Earth and Nature; Mother and Guardian
Nymph. Along with *Hagno* and *Neda*, she helped raise Zeus. Worshiped at Theisoa in Arcadia. See also *Nymphs*. [Bell 1991]

Thelchtereia
Grecian
Charisma
"Enchantress." One of the *Sirens*. [Monaghan 1981]

Thelpusa See *Telphusa*.

Thelxiepeia
Grecian
Beauty; Charisma; Demi-animals; Fate; Destroyer of Life; Wild Birds
One of the *Sirens*. Sister of *Aglaopheme* and *Peisinoe*. [Bell 1991; Jobes 1962]

Thelxinoe
Grecian
Arts; Sciences; Intelligence and Creativity; Evil
One of the earliest *Muses*. [Bell 1991]

Thelxinoea
Grecian
Justice
One of the *Praxidicae*. Sister of *Alalkomenia* and *Aulis*. [Bell 1991]

Themis
Grecian
1) Order; Justice; Education and Knowledge 2) Earth and Nature
   1) "Of the order of things established by law, custom, and ethics." Mother of the *Horae*, the *Moirae*, the *Hesperides*, and *Astraea* by Zeus. Daughter of *Gaea* and Uranus, she is one of the *Titanides* and is worshiped at Athens, Olympia, Tanagra, Thebes, and Troezen. Identified with Roman *Anna Perenna*. Similar to Egyptian *Thmei*. See also *Thummin*, Near East. Alternate form: Ichnaea. 2) Themis is also the name of an Arcadian nymph. [Bell 1991; Bonnerjea 1927; Jayne 1925; Leach 1992; Redfield 1931; Stone 1979; Woodcock 1953; Zimmerman 1964]

Themisto
Grecian
Justice; Order
   "Law" or "Representing the Law-enforcing Tendencies of the Universe." One of the *Nereides*. Daughter of *Doris* and Nereus. According to some, the mother of *Callisto*. [Bell 1991; Leach 1992]

Theotokos
Grecian
Mother and Guardian
   "Mother of God" or "Bringing Forth a God." Her name is applied to the *Virgin Mary*, Near East. Alternate form: Deipara. [Jobes 1962]

Theria
Grecian
Life/Death Cycle
   "Crone." Name for *Hera* as an old woman. [Monaghan 1981]

Therma
Grecian
Water
   Nymph of the springs of Apameia. See also *Nymphs*. [Leach 1992]

Thermaia
Grecian
Health and Healing
   Name of *Artemis* as goddess of health. [Leach 1992]

Thermia
Roman
Health and Healing; Water
   Name for *Diana* when presiding over healing springs and fountains. [Jayne 1925]

Thermuthis
Grecian
Unknown
   Name for Egyptian *Maut* [Cooper 1876]

Thesan
Roman; Etruscan
Unknown
   "Dawn." Name for *Tesana*. [Cooper 1876]

Thesmia   See *Thesmophoros*.

Thesmophoros
Grecian
Justice; Ceremonies
   "Lawgiver." Name for *Demeter*. A celebration, the *Thesmophoria*, is held in her honor in Athens. Alternate form: Thesmia. [Bell 1991; Monaghan 1981]

Thesmorphonius
Roman
Unknown
   Name for *Ceres*. [Woodcock 1953]

Thespeia
Grecian
Earth and Nature
   Nymph. Daughter of the Asopus river god. The town of Thespiae in Boeotia is named for her. See also *Nymphs*. [Bell 1991]

Thetis
Grecian
Water
   Sea goddess. One of the *Nereides*, daughter of Doris and Nereus. Mother of Achilles by the mortal Peleus. She had a temple called the *Thetideion* near Pharsalus in Thessaly. She was also worshiped in Sparta and Messenia. Alternate forms: Halsodyne, Leda, Neptunine. [Bell 1991; Bonnerjea 1927; Leach 1992; Redfield 1931; Zimmerman 1964]

Thisbe
Grecian
Earth and Nature
   Boeotian nymph. The town of Thisbe (to the south of Mount Helicon) is named for her. See also *Nymphs*. [Bell 1991]

Thoantea   See *Tauropolis*.

Thoë
Grecian
1) Water; Physical Prowess; 2) Water; Fate; Beauty; Physical Prowess
   "Quick" or "Nimble." 1) One of the *Oceanides*, daughter of *Tethys* and Oceanus. 2) One of the *Nereides*, daughter of *Doris* and Nereus, who is associated with sailing. [Bell 1991; Leach 1992]

Thriae
Grecian
Fate; Earth and Nature
   Prophetic nymphs. They taught Hermes the art of prophecy. See also *Nymphs*. Alternate form: Thriai. [Bell 1991; Jobes 1962]

Thriai   See *Thriae*.

Thya
Roman
Unknown
   Name for *Ops*. [Woodcock 1953]

Thyades   See *The Thyiades*.

Thyene
Grecian
Weather; Stars and Planets
   One of the *Hyades*. [Bell 1991]

Thyia
Grecian
Unknown
   Nymph, a companion of Dionysus. Daughter of Castalius or the Cephissus river god. One of the *Thyiades*. See also *Nymphs*. [Bell 1991]

Thyiades, The
Grecian
Unknown
Nymphs who are companions of Dionysus. Also called *Maenades*. See also *Thyia* and *Nymphs*. Alternate form: Thyades. [Bell 1991; Zimmerman 1964]

Thyone   See *Semele*.

Tiburtis
Roman
Water; Fate
One of the *Camenae*. [Bell 1991]

Timandra
Roman
Water; Fate
One of the *Camenae*. [Bell 1991]

Tinnit   See *Tanit*.

Tipanu
Roman; Etruscan
Unknown
Attendant of *Alpanu*. [Cooper 1876]

Tiphanati
Roman; Etruscan
Unknown
Name for *Turan*. [Cooper 1876]

Tipoplo
Grecian
Arts; Sciences; Intelligence and Creativity; Evil
One of the seven *Muses*. [Bell 1991]

Tisiphone
Grecian
1) Justice; 2) Unknown
1) One of the *Erinyes*. Goddess of retaliation, especially for murder. 2) Name of a daughter of *Manto* and Alcmaeon. Alternate form: Teisiphone. [Bell 1991; Bonnerjea 1927; Cotterell 1979; Leach 1992; Neumann 1972; Zimmerman 1964]

Titaea
Grecian
Earth and Nature
Early Earth goddess who was later assimilated by *Gaea*. Alternate form: Titaia. [Jobes 1962; Leach 1992; Zimmerman 1964]

Titaia   See *Titaea*.

Titan Rhea   See *Rhea*.

Titan Theia   See *Theia*.

Titania
Roman
Unknown
Name for *Diana*. [Jobes 1962; Woodcock 1953]

Titanides, The
Grecian
Supreme Being
Daughters of *Gaea* and Uranus. They are *Mnemosyne, Phoebe, Rhea, Tethys, Theia,* and *Themis*. Sometimes their children are included in this classification. See also *Titanides, Near East*. Alternate form: Titanids. [Bell 1991; Zimmerman 1964]

Titanids, The   See *The Titanides*.

Titanis
Grecian
Order; Time
One of the *Horae*. [Bell 1991]

Tithorea
Grecian
Earth and Nature
Nymph of Mount Parnassus. The town of Tithorea may be named for her. See also *Nymphs*. [Bell 1991]

Tito   See *Eos*.

Torone
Grecian
Water
One of the *Oceanides,* daughter of *Tethys* and Oceanus. Wife of Proteus. [Bell 1991; Leach 1992]

Tragasia
Grecian
Unknown
Daughter of Celaeneus, wife of Miletus, mother of *Byblis*. [Bell 1991]

Triclaria
Grecian
Unknown
Name for *Artemis* in Achaia. [Bell 1991]

Trito   See *Tritogeneia*.

Tritogeneia
Grecian
Unknown
Name for *Athena*. This name may come either from Lake Tritonis in Libya, near where she is said to have been born; from the stream called Triton near Alalcomenae in Boeotia, where she might have been born; or from the Aeolian word for "head"; or it may mean "thrice-born." Alternate forms: Trito, Tritogenis, Tritonia, Tritonis. [Bell 1991; Leach 1972; Woodcock 1953; Zimmerman 1964]

Tritogenis   See *Tritogeneia*.

Tritone
Grecian
Arts; Sciences; Intelligence and Creativity; Evil
One of the *Muses*. [Bell 1991]

Tritonia
Roman, Grecian
Unknown
Name for Roman *Minerva*. Also an alternate form for Greek *Tritogeneia*. [Woodcock 1953]

Tritonis   See *Tritogeneia*.

Tritopatores
Grecian
Weather
Goddess of the winds. Alternate form: Tritopatreis. [Leach 1992]

Tritopatreis   See *Tritopatores*.

Trivia
Roman
Commerce and Travel
   Name for *Diana*. It may indicate that she has three heads
or that she is the guardian of the crossroads where three
roads meet. It may also refer to her in her aspect as triune
goddess. Latin name for *Taurian Artemis*. Alternate form:
Tergemina. [Jobes 1962; Redfield 1931; Woodcock 1953;
Zimmerman 1964]

Tuchulcha
Roman; Etruscan
Heaven and Hell; Destroyer of Life; Ugliness; Demi-animals
   "Underworld." A death demon that is frightening in
appearance: part human, part bird, and part animal, with
serpents in her hair and around her arm. [Chicago 1979;
Cooper 1876; Monaghan 1981]

Turan
Roman; Etruscan
Love and Sexuality
   Goddess of love. Identified with *Venus* and Greek
Aphrodite and associated with *Acaviser*. Alternate form:
Tiphanati. [Cooper 1876; Monaghan 1981]

Tursa
Roman
Evil
   Goddess of terror. [Jobes 1962]

Tutela   See *Vesta*.

Tutelina   See *Tutilina*.

Tutilina
Roman
Agriculture
   Roman agricultural goddess. She protects the crops at
harvest time and in the granaries. She incorporates the
worship of several other agricultural deities: *Messia, Secia,
Segetia, Seia,* and *Seja*. She is identified with *Messia* and *Ops*
and may be an attribute of *Ops*. Alternate forms: Tutelina,
Tutulina. [Bell 1991; Monaghan 1990; Wedeck and Baskin
1971; Woodcock 1953]

Tutulina   See *Tutilina*.

Tyche
Grecian
1) Luck; 2) Earth and Nature; 3) Water
   "Luck or chance." 1) Daughter of Zeus Eleuthereus, sister
of *Nemesis*. Identical to *Fortuna;* and *Ardokhsho*, Near East.
2) Name of a nymph associated with *Persephone*. 3) One of
the *Oceanides*. Alternate forms: Automatia, Roma. See also
Band Goddesses, Western Europe.   [Bell 1991; Jobes 1962;
Monaghan 1981; Redfield 1931]

Uni
Roman; Etruscan
Mother and Guardian
   Protector of cities and their women. May have evolved into
Juno. She had a sanctuary at the port of Pyrgi in the town of
Caere. [Durdin-Robertson 1982; Monaghan 1981]

Unxia
Roman
Family and Tribes
   Name for *Juno*. Protector of the newly married. [Woodcock
1953]

Upis
Grecian
1) Mother and Guardian; Luck; 2) Unknown
   1) Goddess of childbirth and fortune. 2) A name for
Artemis at Ephesus, where she had a temple. Alternate form:
Opis. [Bell 1991; Redfield 1931]

Urania
Grecian
1) Sciences; Stars and Planets; 2) Arts; Sciences; Intelligence
and Creativity; Evil; 3) Water
   1) Goddess of astronomy. 2) One of the nine *Muses* at
Athens. A name for *Aphrodite,* said to be the "heavenly one."
3) Name of one of the *Oceanides* associated with *Persephone*.
Alternate form: Ourania. [Bell 1991; Graves 1948; Leach 1992;
Redfield 1931; Stone 1979; Zimmerman 1964]

Vacuna
Roman; Sabine
War
   Sabine goddess of victory as associated with freedom from
duties. Among the Romans, she evolved into a war goddess.
There was an ancient sanctuary for her on the Tiber River
near the villa of Horace and also one at Rome. She is equivalent
to *Victoria* and identified with *Bellona, Ceres,* and *Venus*.
[Bell 1991; Jayne 1925; Redfield 1931; Zimmerman 1964]

Vagitanus
Roman
Mother and Guardian
   Newborns were encouraged to cry by this goddess.
[Monaghan 1990]

Valetudo
Roman
Unknown
   Roman name for Greek *Hygeia*. [Leach 1972]

Vanth
Roman; Etruscan
Destroyer of Life; Demi-animals
   Goddess of death. She is portrayed with wings, a cap on
her head, and a key in her hand, which she uses to open the
tomb. One of the *Vanths*. [Cooper 1876]

Vanths, The
Roman; Etruscan
Destroyer of Life
   Death spirits. One is named *Vanth*. [Monaghan 1981]

Vegoia   See *Begoe*.

Venilia
Roman
Weather; Water
   Roman goddess of the wind and the sea. Sister of *Amata*
and wife of Daunus. Mother of *Juturna* and Turnus. Similar
to *Salacia*. [Bell 1991]

Venus
Roman
Life/Death Cycle; Order; Love and Sexuality; Family and
Tribes; Beauty
   Goddess of growth and the beauty of orderly nature. The
Romans call her the goddess of love, especially sensual love.
She may be one of the *Appiades*. She is identified with Sabine
Vacuna, Etruscan *Turan,* and the Greek *Aphrodite* and *Nerine*,
and she is considered the mother of the Roman people. She
had been transferred from Eryx in Sicily to Rome at the direction
of one of the Sibyls because Venus chose to be worshiped in

the city of her people. The largest temple in Rome belonged to Venus and stood on the Circus Maximus. Her festival, the *Vinalia* was celebrated on April 23, honoring *Venus* as the protector of gardens and vineyards. Similar to *Rembha,* Indian Subcontinent.

Equivalent to *Anunit* and *Arusyak,* (Near East). See also *Concordia;* and *Isthar,* Near East. Alternate forms: Acidalia, Alma, Amica, Armata, Barbata, Calva, Cloacina, Cluacina, Cypria, Equestris, Erycina, Genetrix, Libentina, Militaris, Murcia, Obsequens, Placida, Postvorta, Rhamnusia, Salacia, Verticordia, Victrix, Zephyritis. [Bell 1991; Durdin-Robertson 1975; Durdin-Robertson 1976; Durdin-Robertson 1982; Leach 1972; Leach 1992]

Vergiliae, The
Roman
Stars and Planets
Goddesses representing the constellation Pleiades. Equivalent to Greek *Pleiades; Krittika,* Indian Subcontinent; and *Kimah,* Near East. [Durdin-Robertson 1976; Zimmerman 1964]

Veritas
Roman
Justice
"Truth." Identical to Greek *Alethia.* [Durdin-Robertson 1975; Zimmerman 1964]

Verticordia
Roman
Love and Sexuality
Name for *Venus* relating to the power of love to change the inflexible. Equivalent to Greek *Epistrophia.* [Woodcock 1953]

Vesta
Roman
Household Affairs; Ceremonies; Fire; Mother and Guardian
Virgin goddess of the hearth. One of the *Appiades.* She is similar to the married *Vesuna Erinia.* Equivalent to the Greek *Hestia,* she is identified with *Fornax* and may be a name for *Stata Mater.* She absorbed *Caca.* She was worshiped daily at mealtimes in each home. Her temple contained the eternal fire and was cared for by the Vestal Virgins. On March 1, her sacred fire and the laurel tree above her hearth were renewed. The festival of *Vestalia* was celebrated at Rome on the 9th of June. Banquets were then prepared before the houses, and meat was sent to the Vestals to be offered to the gods, millstones were decked with garlands, and the asses that turned them were led round the city covered with garlands. Only women were allowed in the temples for this festival. Alternate forms: Aeterna, Felix, Prisca, Ignea, Sacra, and Tutela. [Bell 1991; Durdin-Robertson 1982; Harding 1971; Leach 1992; Woodcock 1953; Zimmerman 1964]

Vesuna Erinia
Roman
Household Affairs; Fire
Married hearth goddess. Similar to unmarried *Vesta.* [Monaghan 1990]

Victoria
Roman
War
"Victory." Equivalent to Greek *Nike* and Sabine *Vacuna.* She had four sanctuaries in Rome—one was on the Palatine Hill. [Bell 1991; Redfield 1931; Zimmerman 1964]

Victrix
Roman
War
"The Victorious." Name for *Venus.* [Bell 1991]

Virginalis
Roman
Unknown
Name for *Fortuna* and *Juno.* [Jayne 1925; Jobes 1962; Monaghan 1981]

Virginensis
Roman
Love and Sexuality
Name for *Fortuna* relating to married women and virginity. [Baring and Cashford 1991; Jayne 1925; Monaghan 1981]

Virginia
Roman
Justice
Roman goddess of politics. [Monaghan 1981]

Virgo
Roman
Luck; Selflessness
Name for *Fortuna* relating to virginity. [Jayne 1925; Jobes 1962; Monaghan 1981]

Virilis
Roman
Love and Sexuality
Name for Roman *Fortuna* relating to sexual attractiveness. Women worship her with this name, asking to continue to be exciting to their husbands. Also a name for *Tyche.* [Bell 1991; Jayne 1925; Jobes 1962; Monaghan 1981]

Viriplaca
Roman
Family and Tribes
Name for *Juno* when she restores marital peace. She had a sanctuary on the Palatine where women could go to seek redress from their husbands. [Bell 1991]

Virtus
Roman
Courage
The personification of valor in war. [Bell 1991]

Voleta
Roman
Intelligence and Creativity
Goddess of "will or wishing." [Meltzer 1981]

Voltumna
Roman; Etruscan
Justice
Tutelary goddess of the Etruscan Federation. Her shrine. [Redfield 1931]

Volumna
Roman
Mother and Guardian; Health and Healing
Roman goddess of the nursery. She presided over the health and welfare of infants. [Lurker 1984]

Volupia   See *Angerona.*

Volupta
Grecian
Unknown
"Pleasure." Daughter of *Psyche* and Cupid. [Bell 1991]

Voluptas
Roman
Love and Sexuality
  Roman goddess of sensual pleasure. [Zimmerman 1964]

Waelcyrge   See *The Furies*.

Xantho
Grecian
Water; Fate; Beauty
  One of the *Nereides*. [Bell 1991]

Xenia
Grecian
1) Justice; 2) Earth and Nature
  "Presiding Over the Laws of Hospitality and Protecting
Strangers." 1) Name for *Athena*. 2) A nymph in love with
Daphnis. See also *Nymphs*. [Bell 1991]

Zana
Roman
Beauty; Courage
  Pre-Roman goddess in the Balkans. She lived in the
Albanian mountains, where she was revered for beauty and
courage. May have been absorbed by *Diana*. [Lurker 1984]

Zephyritis
Grecian, Roman
1) Earth and Nature; 2) Unknown
  1) Name for *Aphrodite*, derived from the Egptian
promontory of Zephyrium. 2) Name for Roman *Venus*. [Bell
1991]

Zerynthis
Grecian
Unknown
  Name for *Aphrodite*. She was worshiped in a temple in the
town of Zerynthus in Thrace. [Bell 1991]

Zeuxippe
Grecian
Water
  1) An *Oceanid*, daughter of *Tethys* and Oceanus. 2) Daughter
of the Eridanus river god. [Bell 1991; Leach 1992]

Zeuxo
Grecian
Water
  One of the *Oceanides*, daughter of *Tethys* and Oceanus.
[Bell 1991; Leach 1992]

Zirna
Roman; Etruscan
Moon and Night
  Companion of *Turan*. Moon goddess represented by a
half-moon. [Monaghan 1981]

Zosteria
Grecian
War
  "Girded" (for battle). Name for *Athena* when worshiped
by the Epicnemidian Locrians. [Bell 1991]

Zygia
Grecian
Family and Tribes
  "Joiner or Yoker." Name for *Hera* as related to marriage.
[Bell 1991]

THE HIMALAYA

aBru-gu-ma

Tibet

Earth and Nature

Wife of the weather god Kesar. She performs the activities for the earth goddess *sKyabs-mdun.* [Francke 1923; Leach 1992; von Furer-Haimendorf 1964]

âkâsha-dahatû-ishvarî

Tibet

Sky and Heavens

"Sovereign Lady of the Space of Heaven." See *Nam-kha-ing-kya-wang-chug-ma.* [Durdin-Robertson 1976]

âloka See *sNang-gsal-ma.*

âloke See *sNang-gsal-ma.*

Altan-telgey

Mongolia; Siberia

Earth and Nature

"Golden Surface." Earth goddess. Alternate form: Teleglen-Edzen. [Leach 1992; Monaghan 1981]

Ankushâ "She Holding the Goad." See *Chags-kyu-ma.*

A-phyi-gung-rgyal

Tibet

Sky and Heavens

"Heavenly Space." Bon deity. Daughter of Chu Icam Icam and Shang po, consort of gNam gyi Ihaa rgod thog pa, the god of heaven. When she resides at Ti se, Mount Kailasa, she is called *Srid-pa'i-sman.* Bon (Pon) is a pre-Buddhist religion practiced by the aboriginal inhabitants of Tibet, who some believe were of Mongolian origin. The Black Bon (Pon) practiced sorcery. The White Bon (Pon) faith is very similar to Buddhism. Alternate form: gNam-phyi-gung-rgyal. [Durdin-Robertson 1976; Jobes 1962; Leach 1992; Tucci 1980]

Atugan

Mongolia

Earth and Nature

Earth goddess who is the source of all living things. [Baumgartner 1984; Leach 1992; Queval 1968]

Bardo Goddesses

Tibet

Heaven and Hell; Immortality; Intelligence and Creativity

Goddesses associated with Bardo. They include faith-guarding and door-keeping deities, the *Htamenmas,* the *Kerimas,* and the *Wang-Chugmas.* Bardo is the after-death state of transition before rebirth. One can enter Bardo by dying or during deep meditation, dreams, or a trance. Those who are intuitive or psychically sensitive can also experience Bardo. When in Bardo the body is a duplicate of the human body and has all of its senses and the ability to move about unimpeded. The astral light in Bardo is like Earth's twilight. The inhabitants of Bardo live on the ethereal essences that they extract from food given as offerings from Earth or from nature's storehouse. From Bardo one can be reborn or enter another realm. Those who fall over one of the three precipices, the White, Red, or Black Deep, fall into the womb. Those who find shelter in the hollows of trees or in the cavities or crevices of the earth become ghosts or enter the animal world. Equivalent to the *Sheol,* Near East; *Amenet* and *Tauret,* Egypt; *Yoni,* Indian Subcontinent; and the Greek god Hades. Among the Bardo goddesses are *bDug-spös-ma, Buddha Krotishaurima, Cha-dog-ma, Chags-kyu-ma, Clear-light Mother, gLu-ma Ghirdhima, Gokarmo, Hphreng-ba-ma, Karma Dakinis, Karma-krotishaurima, Khahdoma, Kuntu-bzang-mo, Mâmakî, Me-tog-ma, Nam-kha-ing-kya-wang-chug-ma, Padma Dakinis, Padma*

225

Krotishaurima, Pândurâ, Pukkase, Ratna Krotishaurima,
Sangs-rgyas-spyan-ma, sGrol-mas, Shal-za-ma, Smasha,
sNang-gsal-ma, Til-bu-ma, Tsandhali, Tseurima, Vajra
Krotishaurima, Zhag-pa-ma, and *Zhal-zas-ma.* [Durdin-
Robertson 1976; Evans-Wentz 1960; Jobes 1962; Leach 1992;
Waddell 1925]

bDud-mo-gshin-rej-mgo-dgu-ma
Tibet
Water; Mother and Guardian; Weather
    Lake deity who offers protection from hail and lightning.
[de Nebesky-Wojkowitz 1952; Leach 1992]

bDud-mo-gshin-rje-lag-brgya-ma
Tibet
Water; Mother and Guardian; Weather
    Lake deity who offers protection from hail and lightning.
[Leach 1992]

bDud-mo-gsod-mo-gsod-byed-ma
Tibet
Water; Mother and Guardian; Weather
    Lake deity who offers protection from lightning and hail.
[de Nebesky-Wojkowitz 1952; Leach 1992]

bDud-mo-phung-khrol-ma
Tibet
Water; Mother and Guardian; Weather
    Lake deity who offers protection from lightning and hail.
[de Nebesky-Wojkowitz 1952; Leach 1992]

bDud-mo-rno-myur
Tibet
Earth and Nature
    Mountain deity. [de Nebesky-Wojkowitz 1952; Leach 1992]

bDug-spös-ma
Tibet
Heaven and Hell; Time
    Buddhist afterworld deity who appears on the third day in
Bardo (see *Bardo Goddesses*). Her color is yellow like the
earth. Her Tibetan Sanskrit name is *Dhupema.* Equivalent to
Dhupa, Indian Subcontinent. Associated with *Sangs-rgyas-*
spyan-ma. Alternate form: Dug-po-ma. [Durdin-Robertson
1976; Evans-Wentz 1960; Leach 1992]

Bhavani
Nepal
Creator of Life
    "Giver of Existence." Wife of Siva and equivalent to
Vajravarahi, Indian Subcontinent. [Cooper 1876; Durdin-
Robertson 1976; Jobes 1962; Stutley and Stutley 1984]

bKur-dman-rgyalmo
Tibet
Sky and Heavens
    Co-ruler of heaven. Wife of gLing-chö. Mentioned in the
Kesar Saga, a story that seems to indicate a religion somewhat
different from Bon (see *A-phyi-gung-rgyal*), perhaps of an
even earlier origin.
    The white-colored heaven is ruled by bKur-dman-rgyalmo
    and her husband. They have three sons, Donyod, Donaldan,
    and Dongrub. Here is a world tree with six branches, each
with a bird, nest, and egg. Below heaven is Bar-btsan, the red middle
place. It is the Earth, the land of humans where Dongrub was sent.
Yog-klu is the blue-colored underworld. Sometimes a fourth realm is
included, the black or violet-colored land of the devil, bDud.
[Leach 1972]

Black Crow-headed One
Tibet
Heaven and Hell; Wild Birds
    One of the *Htamenmas.* [Durdin-Robertson 1976; Jobes
1962]

Black Cuckoo-headed Mystic Goddess
Tibet
Heaven and Hell; Wild Birds; Intelligence and Creativity;
Directions; Demi-animals
    One of the *Wang-Chugmas* and Door-Keeping *Yogini.* She
holds an iron hook and comes from the eastern quarter.
[Durdin-Robertson 1976; Jobes 1962]

Black Petali
Tibet
Heaven and Hell; Directions
    One of the *Kerimas* who is colored black. She comes from
the north to Bardo (see *Bardo Goddesses*) on the thirteenth
day holding a *dorje* (thunderbolt symbol) and a blood-filled
bowl. Alternate form: Petali. [Durdin-Robertson 1976; Leach
1992]

Black Sow-headed Sow Goddess
Tibet
Heaven and Hell; Domesticated Animals; Directions;
Demi-animals
    One of the *Wang-Chugmas.* She holds a noose made of
fangs and comes from the northern quarter. [Durdin-
Robertson 1976; Jobes 1962]

Black Vixen-headed One
Tibet
Heaven and Hell; Hunting and Wild Animals
    One of the *Htamenmas.* [Durdin-Robertson 1976; Jobes
1962]

Blue Monkey-headed Goddess of Inquisitiveness
Tibet
Heaven and Hell; Intelligence and Creativity; Directions;
Demi-animals
    One of the *Wang-Chugmas.* She holds a wheel and comes
from the eastern quarter. [Durdin-Robertson 1976; Jobes 1962]

Blue Serpent-headed Water Goddess
Tibet
Heaven and Hell; Reptiles; Directions; Demi-animals
    One of the *Wang-Chugmas.* She holds a noose made of
serpents and comes from the northern quarter. [Durdin-
Robertson 1976; Jobes 1962]

Blue Wolf-headed Wind Goddess
Tibet
Heaven and Hell; Hunting and Wild Animals; Weather;
Directions; Demi-animals
    One of the *Wang-Chugmas.* She waves a pennant and
comes from the northern quarter. [Durdin-Robertson 1976;
Jobes 1962]

brDa'i 'phrad
Tibet
Water; Evil; Unhappiness
    Malevolent lake deity who causes madness. [de Nebesky-
Wojkowitz 1952; Leach 1992]

Bribsun
Tibet, *Nepal*
Mother and Guardian
    The *Green Tara* or *Green Dolma.* Bribsun is a mother
goddess and a *Shakti.* She is said to have been embodied in a

Nepalese princess who married a Tibetan king and was responsible for the establishment of Buddhism in Tibet. In Nepal she is called *Khadiravani Tara*. Alternate form: Dol Jyang. [Durdin-Robertson 1976]

'Brog-bza'-lha-icam-ma
Tibet
Fate
Prophetic deity. She uses an arrow and a mirror for divination. [de Nebesky-Wojkowitz 1952; Leach 1992]

brTan-ma
Tibet
Earth and Nature
Earth goddess. May be identical to *sKyabs-mdun*. [Francke 1923; Leach 1992; von Furer-Haimendorf 1964]

brTar-byed-ma   See *sKyabs-mdun*.

'Brug-gi-sgra-sgrog-ma
Tibet
Weather; Sky and Heavens
Sky goddess who presides over the weather. [de Nebesky-Wojkowitz 1952; Leach 1992]

bStan-ma   See *Tan-ma*.

bTsan-Idan-blo-sgron-ma
Tibet
Fate
Prophetic Bon (see *A-phyi-gung-rgyal*) deity. She is invoked to aid in divination. [de Nebesky-Wojkowitz 1952; Leach 1992]

Buddha Dakinis
Tibet
Magic; Education and Knowledge; Intelligence and Creativity; Justice
"Chief of the *Khahdoma*." Air deity who bestows supernatural powers on her followers. She is the Dakini who grants completeness through understanding. Her color is white and her emblems are the wheel, the skull cup, and the ritual wand. Her color is also given as dark blue; her characteristic is knowledge of truth, and she comes from the center (the four cardinal directions are represented by the other four gods). There are five orders of Tibetan Dakinis including *Karma Dakinis, Padma Dakinis, Ratna Dakinis,* and *Vajra Dakinis*. See also *Buddha Dakini*, Indian Subcontinent. [Durdin-Robertson 1976; Jobes 1962]

Buddha Krotishaurima
Tibet
Heaven and Hell; Justice; Time
Mighty, wrathful mother. She appears in the Bardo (see *Bardo Goddesses*) on the eighth day, embracing Buddha Heruka and giving him blood to drink from a red shell. Alternate form: Bud-dha Kro-ti-shva-ri-ma. [Durdin-Robertson 1976]

Bud-dha Kro-ti-shva-ri-ma   See *Buddha Krotishaurima*.

Cha-dog-ma
Tibet
Heaven and Hell; Directions; Demi-animals; Hunting and Wild Animals; Love and Sexuality; Time
"She Holding the Chain." Door-keeper and guardian of the west door of Bardo (see *Bardo Goddesses*) who comes on the sixth day. She has the head of a lion and is associated with love. She is also the *Shakti* of the god Hayagriva. Her Sanskrit name is *Vajra-Shringkhala*. See also *Chags-kyu-ma*,

Kuntu-bzang-mo, Til-bu-ma, and *Zhag-pa-ma*. Alternate form: Lghags-sgrog-ma. [Durdin-Robertson 1976; Leach 1992]

Chags-kyu-ma
Tibet
Heaven and Hell; Directions; Demi-animals; Hunting and Wild Animals; Goodness; Order; Time
Door-keeper and *Shakti* of the god Vijaya and guardian of the east door of Bardo (see *Bardo Goddesses*) who comes on the sixth day. She has the head of a tiger and is associated with compassion and the four peaceful methods of instruction. Her Sanskrit name is *Ankushā*. See also *Cha-dog-ma, Kuntu-bzang-ma, Til-bu-ma,* and *Zhag-pa-ma*. Alternate form: Chak-yu-ma. [Evans-Wentz 1960; Leach 1992]

Chak-yu-ma   See *Chags-kyu-ma*.

Chi-chi-gyal-mo
Tibet
Time
Buddhist goddess of spring. Equivalent to *Vasanta*, Indian Subcontinent. Alternate form: dPyid-kyi-rgyal-mo. [Jobes 1962]

Chit   See *Chit*, Indian Subcontinent.

Chu-lcam-rgyal-mo
Tibet
Water
Freshwater deity of the Bon religion. Mother of bsKal med 'bum na, who was born from the black egg and of the 18 srid pa'i ming sring. Her consort is Ye smon rgyal po. [de Nebesky-Wojkowitz 1952; Leach 1992]

Chu'i lha mo
Tibet
Water
Freshwater deity who is invoked to aid in removing pollution. [de Nebesky-Wojkowitz 1952; Leach 1992]

Chu'i lha mo Mamaki
Tibet
Water
Freshwater deity who is invoked to aid in removing pollution. [de Nebesky-Wojkowitz 1952; Leach 1992]

Chu'phrul can
Tibet
Evil; Water; Destroyer of Life
Malevolent freshwater deity who causes jaundice. [de Nebesky-Wojkowitz 1952; Leach 1992]

Clear-light Mother
Tibet
Heaven and Hell; Intelligence and Creativity
Goddess of primal light. She appears when one is falling deeply asleep and also on the twelfth day in Bardo (see *Bardo Goddesses*). She has a son named Offspring Clear-light. [Durdin-Robertson 1976]

Dakini Guru
Tibet
Education and Knowledge; Magic
Teacher of the Buddha Padma.
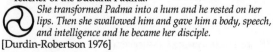 *She transformed Padma into a hum and he rested on her lips. Then she swallowed him and gave him a body, speech, and intelligence and he became her disciple.*
[Durdin-Robertson 1976]

Dakini Queen   See *Khadoma Queen*.

Dakinis   See *Dakinis*, Indian Subcontinent. See also
*Buddha Dakinis, Karma Dakinis, Padma Dakinis, Ratna
Dakinis, Vajra Dakinis,* and *Ye-she-tsho-gyal,* both in this
section and in Indian Subcontinent.

Dam-tshig-mkha'-'gro-ma
Tibet
Weather
    Weather deity who presides over the rainfall. [de Nebesky-
Wojkowitz 1952; Leach 1992]

Dark-blue Owl-headed One
Tibet
Heaven and Hell; Wild Birds
    One of the *Htamenmas.* [Durdin-Robertson 1976; Jobes
1962]

Dark-blue Smasha
Tibet
Heaven and Hell; Directions
    One of the *Kerimas.* She comes from the northeast to Bardo
(see *Bardo Goddesses*) on the thirteenth day.
[Durdin-Robertson 1976]

Dark-blue Wolf-headed One
Tibet
Heaven and Hell; Hunting and Wild Animals
    One of the *Htamenmas.* [Durdin-Robertson 1976; Jobes
1962]

Dark-brown Lion-headed One
Tibet
Heaven and Hell; Hunting and Wild Animals
    One of the *Htamenmas.* [Durdin-Robertson 1976; Jobes
1962]

Dark-brown Yak-headed Rakshasa Goddess
Tibet
Heaven and Hell; Hunting and Wild Animals; Directions;
Demi-animals
    One of the *Wang-Chugmas.* She holds a *dorje* (thunderbolt
symbol) and comes from the eastern quarter. [Durdin-
Robertson 1976; Jobes 1962]

Dark-green Fox-headed Baton Goddess
Tibet
Heaven and Hell; Hunting and Wild Animals; Directions;
Demi-animals
    One of the *Wang-Chugmas.* She holds a club and comes
from the southern quarter. [Durdin-Robertson 1976; Jobes
1962]

Dark-green Ghasmari
Tibet
Heaven and Hell; Directions; Time
    One of the *Kerimas.* She comes to Bardo (see *Bardo
Goddesses*) on the thirteenth day from the southwestern
quarter. She carries a bowl filled with blood in her left hand
and stirs it with the *dorje* (thunderbolt symbol) in her right
hand. Alternate form: Ghasmari. [Durdin-Robertson 1976]

dBang-bsdud-ma
Tibet
Evil; Water; Destroyer of Life
    Malevolent lake deity who causes blood diseases.
[de Nebesky-Wojkowitz 1952; Leach 1992]

dBang-sdud-kyi-mkha'-'gro-ma
Tibet
Weather

Weather deity invoked for control of the weather. [Leach
1992]

dByangs-can-ma
Tibet
Arts
    Goddess of music and poetry. Identical to *Sarasvati,*
Indian Subcontinent. Alternate form: dByans-can-ma.
[de Nebesky-Wojkowitz 1952; Leach 1992; gt]

dByans-can-ma   See *dByangs-can-ma.*

dByar-gyi-rgyal-mo
Tibet
Time
    Goddess of spring. Equivalent to *Grismadevi,* Indian
Subcontinent. [Jobes 1962]

Demon Protector of the Grand Lama
Tibet
Mother and Guardian; Magic
    Goddess worshiped in Lhasa by the lamas for the
protection of the Grand Lama. She is said to manifest in an
old woman in the city and when the woman is in a trance, the
goddess speaks through her. [Durdin-Robertson 1976]

dGra-lha-ma-lha-bu-rdzi
Tibet
Mother and Guardian
    Maternity deity who presides over childbirth. [de Nebesky-
Wojkowitz 1952; Leach 1992]

dGra-lha-thab-lha-g·yu-mo
Tibet
Fire; Household Affairs
    Fire deity who presides over the hearth. [de Nebesky-
Wojkowitz 1952; Leach 1992]

Dharti Mata   See *Dharti Mata,* Indian Subcontinent.

Dhupema   See *bDug-spös-ma.*

Didun
Tibet; Apa Tanis
Sky and Heavens
    Himalayan sky goddess. [Wedeck and Baskin 1971]

Dinsangma
Tibet
Unknown
    Buddhist deity. One of the *Long-life Sisters.* Her emblems
are a mongoose and a vase and her *vahana* (mount or throne)
is an antelope. [Jobes 1962]

dMag-zor-ma
Tibet
Fate
    Prophetic deity who is asked about the future. [Leach
1992; Tucci 1980]

Dol Jyang   See *Bribsun.*

Dolma
Tibet
Love and Sexuality; Goodness
    Generic name for all the *Taras.* Dolma holds an important
place in the Buddhist pantheon. Her different colors reflect
her different natures: white, green, and yellow indicate
gentleness and love; red and blue are threatening. The Green
Dolma is particularly worshiped in Tibet, whereas the White

Dolma is more recognized in China and Mongolia. See also *Tara,* Indian Subcontinent. Alternate forms: Dol-ma, Song-tsen-gam-po. [Durdin-Robertson 1976; Jobes 1962]

Dom-gdon-can
Tibet
Magic; Demi-animals; Hunting and Wild Animals
Buddhist bear-headed witch. She confers supernatural powers on her followers and is yellow in color. Equivalent to *Rksavaktradakini,* Indian Subcontinent. [Jobes 1962]

Dorje Naljorma
Tibet
Mother and Guardian; Education and Knowledge; Happiness
"The Divine Lady." She symbolizes the truth and her spiritual energy is inexhaustible bliss. See also *rDo-rje-rnal-hbyor-ma* and *Toma.* Alternate form: Vajrayogini. [Durdin-Robertson 1976]

Dorje Phagmo
Tibet
Magic; Demi-animals; Domesticated Animals
"Thunderbolt Sow." She is incarnate in one Tibetan female at a time and is highly venerated and accorded great privileges.

Once the monastery was being attacked and Dorje Phagmo changed all the monks, nuns, and herself into pigs. The invaders thought the place deserted and would not loot it because there were only swine guarding it. Then Dorje Phagmo changed everyone back into their human form and the terrified invaders bowed in awe and presented gifts.

Her Sanskrit name is *Vajra-Vārāhī.* Her story is similar to that of *Vajravaraki.* [Durdin-Robertson 1976]

Dorje-pa-mo
Tibet
Mother and Guardian
Buddhist guardian deity. She is one of four tutelary deities of the Kargyupta sect. One of her incarnations is *Senga-dong-ma.* She is portrayed brandishing a copper hook knife and holding a bowl in her left hand. [Durdin-Robertson 1976]

Dosangma
Tibet
Unknown
Buddhist deity. One of the *Long-life Sisters,* whose symbols are a spike of rain and a serpent. Her *vahana* (mount or throne) is a dragon. [Jobes 1962]

dPal-gyi-pho-nya-las-mkhan-mo
Tibet
Weather; Fire
Weather deity who sends hail and lightning as messages. [de Nebesky-Wojkowitz 1952; Leach 1992]

dPal-ldan Lha-mo
Tibet
Justice; Ugliness
Terrifying revenge goddess of Lamaism. Wife of Shin-je, Prince of Hell. Identical to *Sridevi* and *Lha-mo.* [Leach 1992; Lurker 1984; Ribbach 1940]

dPyid-kyi-rgyal-mo   See *Chi-chi-gyal-mo.*

Drag-ppo'i-klog-khyung-ma
Tibet
Weather
Weather deity. [de Nebesky-Wojkowitz 1952; Leach 1992]

Dri-chab-ma   See *Dri-chha-ma.*

Dri-chha-ma
Tibet
Education and Knowledge
"She Spraying Perfume." She is associated with the light of wisdom, indicated by her green color. Said to be one of the eight *Matris,* Indian Subcontinent, of the Hindu pantheon. Her Sanskrit name is *Gandhema.* Alternate form: Dri-chab-ma. [Durdin-Robertson 1976; Jobes 1962]

Dril-bu-ma   See *Til-bu-ma.*

Dröl-ma
Tibet, Nepal
Goodness
"Deliverer." Deity of compassion. Identical to *Tara.* [Bell 1931; Leach 1992]

Dug-po-ma   See *bDug-spös-ma.*

Dur-khrod-kyi-bdag-mo-khros-ma-nag-mo
Tibet
Destroyer of Life
Cemetery deity who governs the gods of lightning and hail. [de Nebesky-Wojkowitz 1952; Leach 1992]

Dur-khrod-lha-mo
Tibet
Destroyer of Life
Cemetery deity. Identified with *Ekajata,* Indian Subcontinent. [Leach 1992; Snellgrove 1957]

Dvang-phyng-ma   See *Wang-Chugmas.*

Earth Goddess
Tibet
Unknown
Deity who brought a yellow robe for Padma during his ordination ceremony. [Durdin-Robertson 1976]

Ekadzati
Tibet
Intelligence and Creativity; Education and Knowledge
One-eyed guardian deity of mystic cults who is associated with wisdom. [Durdin-Robertson 1976]

Gandhema   See *Dri-chha-ma.*

Gangkar Shame
Tibet
Earth and Nature
Mountain deity portrayed with clothing of glacial ice and carrying a blood-spattered banner. [de Nebesky-Wojkowitz 1952; Leach 1992]

Gangs-dkar-sha-med
Tibet
Ugliness
Terrifying white snow goddess. She has no flesh. [Leach 1992; Tucci 1980]

Gar-ma
Tibet
Order; Mother and Guardian
Mother of Buddhism. A peaceful deity portrayed as green in color and with two or four arms. Equivalent to *Nrtya,* Indian Subcontinent. [Jobes 1962]

Ghasmari   See *Dark-Green Ghasmari.*

Ghirdhima   See *gLu-ma Ghirdhima.*

Gita   See *gLu-ma Ghirdhima.*

Glog-bdag-mo
Tibet
Weather; Fire
   Weather deity who presides over lightning. [de Nebesky-Wojkowitz 1952; Leach 1992]

gLu-ma Ghirdhima
Tibet
Arts; Fire; Order; Heaven and Hell; Time
   Goddess of music and song. One of the Eight Mothers of Buddhism who is peaceful in aspect. Related to fire, her color is red. She is portrayed holding a lyre and she is usually dancing. A Bodhisatva (one whose essence is perfect knowledge and who is believed to be a future Buddha) who appears in Bardo (see *Bardo Goddesses*) with Amitabha on the fourth day. Her Sanskrit name is *Gita.* Alternate forms: Ghirdhima, Gita, Lu-ma. [Evans-Wentz 1960; Leach 1992; Waddell 1925]

gNam-Iha dkar-mo
Tibet
Sky and Heavens
   "White Goddess of Heaven." She is found in the vicinity of Mount Everest. [Hoffman 1956; Leach 1992]

gNam-Iha-byang-sman-mthing-gi-go-zu-can
Tibet
Sky and Heavens; Weather; Disorder
   Sky goddess of the Bon religion (see *A-phyi-gung-rgyal).* She causes weather disturbances. [de Nebesky-Wojkowitz 1952; Leach 1992]

gNam-lcags-thog-'bebs-ma
Tibet
Weather
   Weather deity. [de Nebesky-Wojkowitz 1952; Leach 1992]

gNam-phyi-gung-rgyal   See *A-phyi-gung-rgyal.*

Gokarmo
Tibet
Mother and Guardian; Heaven and Hell; Time; Immortality
   "She-in-white-raiment." Mother goddess who on the fourth day of Bardo (see *Bardo Goddesses*) is invoked to be the rear-guard of the deceased. Shakti of Amitabha, wife of Nang-ya-tha-yay. Alternate forms: Gos-dhar-mo, Gös-dkar-mo. [Durdin-Robertson 1976]

Gos-dhar-mo   See *Gokarmo.*

Gös-dkar-mo   See *Gokarmo.*

Gos-ster-ma-dkar-mo
Tibet
Wealth
   Goddess belonging to the group of wealth deities. [de Nebesky-Wojkowitz 1952; Leach 1992]

Grahamatrka
Nepal
Stars and Planets
   Stellar deity portrayed with three faces or three heads and many arms. Alternate form: Mahavidya. [Leach 1992; Pal and Phattacharyya 1969]

Green Deer-headed Wealth-guardian Goddess
Tibet
Heaven and Hell; Mother and Guardian; Wealth; Directions; Demi-animals
   One of the *Wang-Chugmas.* She holds an urn and comes from the western quarter. [Baring and Cashford 1991; Durdin-Robertson 1976]

Green Dolma   See *Bribsun.*

Green Tara   See *Bribsun* and *Khadiravani Tara.*

Greenish-black Elephant-headed Big-nosed Goddess
Tibet
Heaven and Hell; Hunting and Wild Animals; Directions; Demi-animals
   One of the *Wang-Chugmas.* She holds a noose made of serpents and comes from the northern quarter. [Durdin-Robertson 1976; Jobes 1962]

Greenish-black Leopard-headed Great Goddess
Tibet
Heaven and Hell; Hunting and Wild Animals; Directions; Demi-animals
   One of the *Wang-Chugmas.* She holds a trident and comes from the eastern quarter. [Durdin-Robertson 1976; Jobes 1962]

Greenish-black Serpent-headed Mystic Goddess
Tibet
Heaven and Hell; Reptiles; Intelligence and Creativity; Directions; Demi-animals
   One of the *Wang-Chugmas* and a Door-Keeping *Yogini* who comes from the northern quarter. [Durdin-Robertson 1976; Jobes 1962]

Greenish-black Vulture-headed Eater Goddess
Tibet
Heaven and Hell; Wild Birds; Directions; Demi-animals
   One of the *Wang-Chugmas.* She holds a baton and comes from the western quarter. [Durdin-Robertson 1976; Jobes 1962]

gshin-rje-mo
Tibet
Destroyer of Life
   Death demons. Their ruler is *Srog-bdag-mo.* [de Nebesky-Wojkowitz 1952; Leach 1992]

gSum-brag-ma
Tibet
Evil; Destroyer of Life
   Malevolent disease goddess of dysentery. [de Nebesky-Wojkowitz 1952; Leach 1992]

Gu-lang   See *Pashupati.*

'Gying-dkar-ma
Tibet
Evil; Water
   Malevolent lake deity who causes dropsy. [de Nebesky-Wojkowitz 1952; Leach 1992]

Hlamos, The
Tibet
Beauty; Love and Sexuality
   Eight divine mothers. They are so beautiful that they often appear in disguise so their followers are not overwhelmed with sensual desire. See also *Matris,* Indian Subcontinent. Alternate form: Matrikas. [Durdin-Robertson 1976]

Hod-zer-can-ma
Tibet
Dawn and Twilight
   Dawn goddess. Equivalent to *Marichi*, Indian Subcontinent. Alternate form: Od-zer-'c'an-ma. [Durdin-Robertson 1976; Getty 1962; Leach 1992]

Hphreng-ba-ma
Tibet
Heaven and Hell; Time; Education and Knowledge
   Bodhisatva (one whose essence is perfect knowledge and who is believed to be a future Buddha) who appears on the third day in Bardo (see *Bardo Goddesses*) with the god Ratna-Sambhava. Her Sanskrit name is *Mâlâ* and her Tibetan Sanskrit name is *Mahlaima*. Associated with *Sangs-rgyas-spyan-ma*. Alternate form: Phreng-ta-ma. [Durdin-Robertson 1976; Evans-Wentz 1960; Leach 1992]

Htamenmas
Tibet
Heaven and Hell; Demi-animals; Hunting and Wild Animals; Wild Birds
   The wrathful animal-headed Bon deities (see *A-phyi-gung-rgyal*). They inhabit Bardo (see *Bardo Goddesses*), holding corpses and skeletons. They are called **Black Crow-headed One, Black Vixen-headed One, Dark-blue Owl-headed One, Dark-blue Wolf-headed One, Dark-brown Lion-headed One, Red Tiger-headed One,** and **Yellowish Bird-headed One.** See also *Karma-Krotishaurima.* Alternate form: Pharmen-ma. [Durdin-Robertson 1976; Jobes 1962]

Jejamo-karpo
Tibet
Unknown
   Buddhist princess of the Yaksas. Alternate form: Pho-zem-na-po. [Jobes 1962]

Jewel Goddesses
Tibet
Unknown
   Twelve Buddhist goddesses who are companions of *Sridevi*. They ride on a variety of animals or sit on clouds. See also *Lha-mo.* [Jobes 1962]

'Jig-rten-mkha'-'gro-ma
Tibet
Weather
   Weather deity invoked for rainfall. [de Nebesky-Wojkowitz 1952; Leach 1992]

'Jigs-pa'i-zer-mo-mig-gcig
Tibet
Evil; Ugliness; Destroyer of Life; Weather; Unhappiness
   Malevolent, misshapen deity who causes illness and bad weather and is responsible for unpleasant feelings. [de Nebesky-Wojkowitz 1952; Leach 1992]

Jo-mo-lha-ri
Tibet
Earth and Nature
   Mountain deity who is worshiped close to the Bhutanese border. [de Nebesky-Wojkowitz 1952; Leach 1992]

Kadomas   See *Khahdoma.*

Kando-ye-shes-chogyel
Nepal; Sherpa
Education and Knowledge

"Goddess Ocean of Wisdom." Her husband is Guru Rimpoche. [Francke 1923; Leach 1992; von Furer-Haimendorf 1964]

Karma Dakinis
Tibet
Mother and Guardian; Heaven and Hell; Directions; Time
   Stern mother goddesses who are green in color. One of the five orders of *Dakinis*. They are associated with the astral plane and Bardo (see *Bardo Goddesses*). Arriving in Bardo from the north on the seventh day, they carry the "Spear of Great Impartiality." See also *Dakinis*, Indian Subcontinent. [Durdin-Robertson 1976]

Karma Kro-ti-shvr-ri-ma   See *Karma-krotishaurima.*

Karma-krotishaurima
Tibet
Heaven and Hell; Directions; Time
   Guardian deity of Bardo (see *Bardo Goddesses*) who arrives from the northern quarter on the twelfth day. She is accompanied by the *Kerimas, Htamenmas, Wang-Chugmas,* and Karma-Heruka. Alternate form: Karma Kro-ti-shvr-ri-ma. [Durdin-Robertson 1976]

Kerimas
Tibet
Destroyer of Life; Unhappiness
   Eight wrathful goddesses who haunt cemeteries and cremation grounds. They include **Black Petali, Dark-blue Smasha, Dark-green Ghasmari, Red Pramoha, Red Pukhase, White Kerima, Yellow Tseurima,** and **Yellowish-white Tsandhali,** who are the Eight Kerimas of the Abodes (or eight directions). Their Sanskrit name is *Keyûrî*. See also *Karma-krotishaurima.* [Durdin-Robertson 1976]

Keyûrî   See *Kerimas.*

Khadhomas   See *Khahdoma.*

Khadiravani Tara
Nepal
Goodness; Earth and Nature; Education and Knowledge
   "Acacia Forest." Benevolent deity known as the *Green Tara*. The color green is associated with the occult. She is portrayed as a green-skinned woman, dressed like a Bodhisatva (one whose essence is perfect knowledge and who is believed to be a future Buddha), sitting on a throne with her left foot resting on a lotus. See also *Bribsun.* [Durdin-Robertson 1976]

Khados   See *Khahdoma.*

Khahdoma
Tibet
Magic; Heaven and Hell; Sky and Heavens; Ceremonies; Education and Knowledge; Evil
   Tantric fairy-like deities who possess occult powers that they can impart to their followers. They inhabit the astral plane and Bardo (see *Bardo Goddesses*). Their ruler is said to be *Sangye-khado.* They preside over the heart, throat, and brain and, if asked, give assistance to those who are about to perform difficult rituals. Also considered malevolent demons. According to one author there are two kinds of Khahdoma. One kind belongs to another world and is called "Wisdom Khahdomas" and the second belongs to our world and sometimes incarnates as a woman. They are equivalent to the *Dakinis*, Indian Subcontinent. See also *Khadoma Queen* and *Yeshe-Khaholome.* Alternate forms: Kadomas,

Khadhomas, Khados, Khandros, Mkhah-hgro-ma. [Durdin-Robertson 1976]

Khadoma Queen
Tibet
Education and Knowledge; Beauty; Magic; Metals and Minerals
Goddess of knowledge.

The Khadoma Queen, disguised as a beggar, appears briefly to Tilopa, a holy man, as he is reading a philosophic treatise. She questions his knowledge, utters a word he cannot understand, and departs. Tilopa, disturbed by this strange woman, sets out in search of her. After much roving about the countryside, he finds her seated alone in a wooded area (or perhaps a cemetery), her eyes gleaming in the darkness. She tells him to go to the land of the Dakinis in order to meet their queen. After an arduous journey, including roaring torrents, ferocious animals, ghastly apparitions, and tempting maidens who try to distract him from his trip, Tilopa arrives at the enchanted castle. Here he finds a beautiful fairy, the Khadoma Queen, welcoming him from her jewel-adorned throne. This may be the beginning or the ending of his search for knowledge.

See also *Sangye-khado.* Alternate form: Dakini Queen. [Durdin-Robertson 1976]

Kha-la-me-'bar-ma
Tibet
Destroyer of Life
Disease goddess. [de Nebesky-Wojkowitz 1952; Leach 1992]

Khandros   See *Khahdoma.*

Khôn-ma
Tibet
Evil
"Old Mother" of the earth-demons. She is portrayed riding a ram, dressed in yellow robes, and holding a golden noose in her hand. She is propitiated to keep the other demons from causing injury to household members. [Durdin-Robertson 1976; Leach 1992; Monaghan 1981]

Khrag-gi-ser-'bebs-ma
Tibet
Weather; Water
Weather deity who inhabits the ocean. [de Nebesky-Wojkowitz 1952; Leach 1992]

Khro-gner-can-ma   See *Bhrkuti,* Indian Subcontinent.

Kinkini-dharî   See *Til-bu-ma.*

Kiru
Tibet; Apa Tanis
Mother and Guardian; Ceremonies
Guardian deity who oversees the general welfare of her followers. Female counterpart of Kilo. The annual festival, Mloko, is held in Kiru's and Kilo's honor. [Wedeck and Baskin 1971]

Klu-mo-dung-skyong-ma
Tibet
Sky and Heavens
Sky goddess. Consort of the god of the thunderbolt, lHa rgod thog 'bebs. [de Nebesky-Wojkowitz 1952; Leach 1992]

Kongtsun Demo
Tibet
Earth and Nature; Magic

Mountain goddess. She is portrayed riding a turquoise-maned horse and carrying a magic dart for protection. [de Nebesky-Wojkowitz 1952; Leach 1992]

Krodhesvari
Tibet
Unhappiness
Wrathful goddess. Partner of the god Heruka. [Leach 1992; Snellgrove 1957]

Kule
Tibet
Directions
Deity associated with the southeast. [de Nebesky-Wojkowitz 1952; Leach 1992]

Kun-bzang-ma
Tibet
Earth and Nature
Mountain goddess. [de Nebesky-Wojkowitz 1952; Leach 1992]

Kuntu-bzang-mo
Tibet
Mother and Guardian; Heaven and Hell; Time
Mother goddess who arrives in Bardo (see *Bardo Goddesses*) on the sixth day. She accompanies the Door-Keepers, *Cha-dog-ma, Chags-kyu-ma, Til-bu-ma,* and *Zhag-pa-ma.* Her Sanskrit name is *Samanta-Bhadra.* [Durdin-Robertson 1976]

Kurukulle
Tibet
Directions; Wealth; Fate; Love and Sexuality
Goddess of the southeast, wealth, and divination. She is also called *Red Tara* and worshiped by disappointed lovers. See also *Kurukulla,* Indian Subcontinent. [de Nebesky-Wojkowitz 1952; Jobes 1962; Leach 1992]

Lasema   See *Sgeg-mo-ma.*

Las-kyi-mkha'-'gro-ma
Tibet
Weather
Weather deity invoked for rain. [de Nebesky-Wojkowitz 1952; Leach 1992]

Las-kyi-mkhah-hgro
Tibet
Magic
Equivalent to *Karmadakini,* Indian Subcontinent. [Jobes 1962]

Lâsyâ   "Belle." See *Sgeg-mo-ma.*

Lghags-sgrog-ma   See *Cha-dog-ma.*

Lha-ma-yin
Tibet
Evil; Health and Healing; Heaven and Hell
Buddhist name for *Asuri,* Indian Subcontinent. [Jobes 1962]

Lha-mo
Tibet
Destroyer of Life; Time
Tibetan name for the Hindu goddess *Devi,* Indian Subcontinent. She sends disease and destroys nonbelievers. Her assistants are the *Long-life Sisters* and the *Jewel Goddesses.* When she manifests as time, the four seasons

emerge from her hair. One author says she has no mild aspects whereas another says she is called *Ma-cig-dpal-lho-mo* in her mild aspect. Her Sanskrit name is *Shri-devi.* Identical to *dPal-ldan Lha-mo.* Alternate form: Lha-mo-kar-po. [Getty 1962; Jobes 1962; Leach 1972; Leach 1992; Waddell 1925]

Lha-mo-gos-dkar-ma
Tibet
Fate
   Goddess associated with divination. [de Nebesky-Wojkowitz 1952; Leach 1992]

Lha-mo-kar-po   See *Lha-mo.*

Living Goddess
Tibet
Ceremonies
   A goddess said to be incarnate in a young Brahmin girl who is enshrined so that the Newari Hindus and Tibetans can worship her. At a certain festival she is brought to the door of the temple, where she showers her followers with flower petals and *rakshi* (a sweet fruit wine). After the ceremony, she is replaced by another young girl, and the retired Living Goddess can return to her normal life. This is said to still occur in Katmandu. [Durdin-Robertson 1976]

Lobsangma
Tibet
Metals and Minerals; Hunting and Wild Animals
   Buddist deity. One of the *Long-life Sisters.* Her emblems are a bowl of jewels and a mongoose. Her *vahana* (throne or mount) is a tiger. [Jobes 1962]

Locana
Tibet
Order
   A peaceful goddess. Partner of Vajrasattva, the Buddha of Consciousness, and *Shakti* of the god Akshobhya. She belongs to Akshobhya's *vajra*-family (*vajra* represents magical powers). Her color is blue. [Leach 1992; Snellgrove 1957]

Long-life Sisters
Tibet
Unknown
   Buddhist goddesses who accompany *Sridevi.* They are *Dinsangma, Dosangma, Lobsangma, Tashitsheringma,* and *Thinggishalsangma.* Their ruler is *Machi-pal Lha-mo.* See also *Lha-mo.* [Jobes 1962]

Lu
Tibet
Water; Reptiles; Demi-animals
   Water deities and nymphs. They appear as snakes or with half-snake, half-human bodies and live in the earth, the air, and freshwater. [Leach 1992; Ribbach 1940]

Lu-ma   See *gLu-ma Ghirdhima.*

Machi-pal Lha-mo
Tibet
Unknown
   Buddist deity. Chief of the *Long-life Sisters.* Alternate form: Mac-ig-dpal. [Jobes 1962]

Mac-ig-dpal   See *Machi-pal Lha-mo.*

Ma-cig-dpal-lho-mo   See *Lha-mo.*

Ma-gcig-dpal-lha-mo
Tibet
Mother and Guardian; Ceremonies
   Protective deity. In her presence, Lhasa women are able to perform certain religious rituals. [Leach 1992; Tucci 1980]

Mahavidya   See *Grahamatrka; Mahavidya,* Indian Subcontinent.

Mahlaima   See *Hphreng-ba-ma.*

Mâlâ   "She Who Holds or Bears the Rosary." See *Hphreng-ba-ma.*

Mâmakî
Tibet
Heaven and Hell; Directions
   One of the four *Devis,* Indian Subcontinent. The *Devis* include *Pândurâ, Rochanî,* and *Tara.* Wife of Vajra-Sattva. Also a deity of Bardo (see *Bardo Goddesses*) who comes from the east and is asked by those who are entering to be "our rearguard." Associated with *Me-tog-ma.* [Durdin-Robertson 1976]

Ma-mo
Tibet
Evil; Destroyer of Life
   Indigenous deity. A she-devil who causes disease. [Jobes 1962]

Ma-mo-sgam-pa-ma
Tibet
Destroyer of Life
   Goddess of illness. [de Nebesky-Wojkowitz 1952; Leach 1992]

Mangu-srî   See *Manjusris.*

Manjusris
Tibet
Education and Knowledge; Heaven and Hell
   Human Bodhisatvas (one whose essence is perfect knowledge and who is believed to be a future Buddha) of the Northern Buddhists. Their Sanskrit name is *Mangu-srî.* [Durdin-Robertson 1976]

Matrikas   See *Hlamos.*

Maya   See *Maya,* Indian Subcontinent.

Me'-ilha-mo Gos-dkar-mo
Tibet
Fire
   Goddess of fire. She is invoked to eliminate pollution. [de Nebesky-Wojkowitz 1952; Leach 1992]

Me-tog-ma
Tibet
Heaven and Hell; Time; Love and Sexuality; Earth and Nature
   "She Who Offers Blossoms." She appears in Bardo (see *Bardo Goddesses*) on the second day accompanied by *Mâmakî.* The meaning of her name is said to include flowers as menses, sentimental speeches, and pledges of love. Her Sanskrit name is *Pushpâ* and her Tibetan Sanskrit name is *Pushpema.* Identical to *Puspa,* Indian Subcontinent. [Durdin-Robertson 1976; Jobes 1962]

Mkhah-hgro-ma   See *Khahdoma.*

Mokum
Tibet; Apa Tanis
Earth and Nature
    Earth goddess. [Wedeck and Baskin 1971]

Mo-lha-mo
Tibet
Mother and Guardian; Household Affairs; Family and Tribes
    Protector of women. She lives in the area of their activities
and presides over the interior of the house, the female line,
and the left armpit. [de Nebesky-Wojkowitz 1952; Leach
1992; Tucci 1980]

Mother Khahdoma
Tibet
Justice; Mother and Guardian
    "Mother Fairy." She admonished that no one had the
authority to destroy another's life if they could not
reconstruct the being or establish that person in a better place.
See also *Khahdoma*. [Durdin-Robertson 1976]

mThing-gi-zhal-bzang-ma
Tibet
Earth and Nature; Fate
    Mountain deity who also presides over divination.
[de Nebesky-Wojkowitz 1952; Leach 1992]

mTsho-sman-g·yu-thang-cho-longs-ma
Tibet
Water
    Lake deity. [de Nebesky-Wojkowitz 1952; Leach 1992]

mTsho-sman-gzi-ldan-ral-gcig-ma
Tibet
Water
    Lake deity. [de Nebesky-Wojkowitz 1952; Leach 1992]

mTsho-sman-klu-yi-rgyal-mo
Tibet
Water
    Lake deity. She inhabits the mTsho sngon khri shor.
[de Nebesky-Wojkowitz 1952; Leach 1992]

mTsho-sman-mthing-gi-lha-mo
Tibet
Water
    Lake deity. [de Nebesky-Wojkowitz 1952; Leach 1992]

mTsho-sman-nyi-ma'i-byan-goig-ma
Tibet
Water
    Lake deity. [de Nebesky-Wojkowitz 1952; Leach 1992]

mTsho-sman-rgyal-mo-mkhro'i-gtso
Tibet
Water; Justice
    Queen or ruler of the *mtsho sman* (lake goddesses).
[de Nebesky-Wojkowitz 1952; Leach 1992]

mTsho-sman-ru-phyug-rgyal-mo
Tibet
Water; Justice
    Queen or leader of the *mtsho sman* (lake goddesses). She
may be the sister or *Shakti* of the god Khyung Inding nag po.
[de Nebesky-Wojkowitz 1952; Leach 1992]

Naivedya "She Holding Sweetmeats." See *Zhal-zas-ma*.

Nam-kha-ing-kya-wang-chug-ma
Tibet
Heaven and Hell
    "Sovereign Lady of the Space of Heaven." Wife of
Vairochana and a *Shakti*. She comes to Bardo (see *Bardo
Goddesses*) from the Central Realm on the first day. She
is invoked to be a "rearguard." Her Sanskrit name is
âkâsha-dahatû-ishvarî. Alternate form: Nam-mkh-ah-
dvyings-kyi-dvang-phyug-ma. [Durdin-Robertson 1976]

Nam-mk'ahi-snin-po
Tibet
Primordial Being
    "Void Space." Buddhist deity whose essence is ether.
Equivalent to *Akasagarabha*, Indian Subcontinent. [Getty
1962; Leach 1992]

Nam-mkha'g·yu-mdog-snang-srid-mdzod
Tibet
Weather; Disorder
    Bon (see *A-phyi-gung-rgyal*) deity who causes weather
disturbances. [de Nebesky-Wojkowitz 1952; Leach 1992]

Nam-mkh-ah-dvyings-kyi-dvang-phyug-ma
See *Nam-kha-ing-kya-wang-chug-ma*.

Nam-mkha'i-lha-mo-gsal-byed-ma
Tibet
Sky and Heavens
    Sky deity. [de Nebesky-Wojkowitz 1952; Leach 1992]

Nam-mkha'i-lha-mo-Kun-tu-bzang-mo
Tibet
Sky and Heavens; Ceremonies
    Sky deity who presides at ceremonies to eliminate
pollution. [de Nebesky-Wojkowitz 1952; Leach 1992]

Nam-mkha'i-lha-mo-snyoms-byed-ma
Tibet
Sky and Heavens; Directions
    Sky deity who inhabits the northwest. [de Nebesky-
Wojkowitz 1952; Leach 1992]

Nam-mkha'i-lha-mo-sprin-tshogs-ma
Tibet
Sky and Heavens; Directions
    Sky and weather deity who inhabits the northeast.
[de Nebesky-Wojkowitz 1952; Leach 1992]

Nam-mkha'i-lha-mo-tsha-gsang-snyoms
Tibet
Sky and Heavens; Directions
    Sky and weather deity who inhabits the southwest.
[de Nebesky-Wojkowitz 1952; Leach 1992]

Nam-mkha'i-lha-mo-tshod-'dzin-ma
Tibet
Sky and Heavens; Directions
    Sky and weather deity who inhabits the southeast.
[de Nebesky-Wojkowitz 1952; Leach 1992]

Nang-sal-ma   See *sNang-gsal-ma*.

Naro-kha-choma
Tibet
Magic; Weather
    Name for *Sarvabuddhadakini*, Indian Subcontinent.
Alternate form: Naro-mk-a-spyod-ma. [Jobes 1962]

Naro-mk-a-spyod-ma See *Naro-kha-choma*.

Nguntre
Tibet; Apa Tanis
Creator of Life
   One of three creator goddesses. The other two are
Ni-ngurre and *Ui Tango*. [Wedeck and Baskin 1971]

Nidhema   See *Zhal-zas-ma*.

Ni-ngurre
Himalayas
Creator of Life
   One of three creator goddesses. The other two are *Nguntre*
and *Ui Tango*. [Wedeck and Baskin 1971]

Nor-rgyun-ma
Tibet
Fate
   Divination deity. [de Nebesky-Wojkowitz 1952; Leach 1992]

Nor-ster-ma-sngon-mo
Tibet
Wealth
   Deity associated with the gods of wealth. [de Nebesky-
Wojkowitz 1952; Leach 1992]

Nye-pha'i-btsun-mo
Tibet
Domesticated Animals
   Grandmother of the cattle deities. Wife of Zia ba'i phyugs
po, grandfather of the cattle deities. [de Nebesky-Wojkowitz
1952; Leach 1992]

Od-zer-'c'an-ma   See *Hod-zer-can-ma*.

'Og-gis-bdag
Tibet; Nadir
Earth and Nature
   Earth goddess. Identical to Ananta, Hindu serpent god.
[Leach 1992; Waddell 1925]

Ogress of Lust
Tibet
Love and Sexuality; Sky and Heavens; Ceremonies; Directions
   An elemental spiritual being who inhabits the astral plane.
She appears in the Yogic Dance of the Five Directions (the
four cardinal directions and the center). Worshiped by the
Ningmapa sect of the Primitive Unreformed Church, which
probably originated from the Bon faith (see *A-phyi-gung-
rgyal*. [Durdin-Robertson 1976]

Padma Dakinis
Tibet
Love and Sexuality; Heaven and Hell; Directions
   "Lotus." They come from the west and carry the Spear of
Great Affection. They inhabit the astral plane and Bardo (see
Bardo Goddesses). Their color is red and their characteristic is
fascination. See also *Buddha Dakinis* and *Dakinis*, Indian
Subcontinent. [Durdin-Robertson 1976]

Padma Krotishaurima
Tibet
Mother and Guardian; Heaven and Hell; Directions; Time
   Mother goddess and *Shakti*, Indian Subcontinent. Wife of
Padma-Heruka. She comes from the western quarter to Bardo
(see *Bardo Goddesses*, on the eleventh day. Alternate form:
Padma Kro-ti-shvr-ri-ma. [Durdin-Robertson 1976]

Padma Kro-ti-shvr-ri-ma   See *Padma Krotishaurima*.

Padma mkha' 'gro ma
Tibet
Weather
   Weather deity invoked for rain. [de Nebesky-Wojkowitz
1952; Leach 1992]

Padma-mkhah-Ngro   See *Padmadakini*, Indian
Subcontinent.

Pags-ma-gdugs-dkar
Tibet
Mother and Guardian
   White parasol goddess who protects her followers from
harm. See also *Sitatapatra Aparajita*, Indian Subcontinent.
Alternate form: Phe-ma-du-kar. [Getty 1962; Jobes 1962;
Leach 1992]

Pândurâ
Tibet
Heaven and Hell
   One of four *Devis*, Indian Subcontinent, who inhabit Bardo
(see *Bardo Goddesses*). The others are *Mâmakî*, *Rochanî*, and
Tara. [Durdin-Robertson 1976]

Pâshadharî   "The Noose Bearer." See *Zhag-pa-ma*.

Pashupatî
Tibet; Nepal
Earth and Nature
   "Lady of Beasts." Sanskrit name of a goddess primarily
of the Nepalese and a deity of the Brahmins who is
propitiated by mothers. She may correspond to *Devi*,
Indian Subcontinent. Alternate form: Gu-lang. [Durdin-
Robertson 1976]

Pelden Lhamo
Tibet
Mother and Guardian; Fate
   Protective Buddhist deity. She can see into the future and
can determine one's fate. [de Nebesky-Wojkowitz 1952;
Leach 1992]

Petali   See *Black Petali*.

Pharmen-ma   See *Htamenmas*.

Phe-ma-du-kar   See *Pags-ma-gdugs-dkar*.

Pho-zem-na-po   See *Jejamo-karpo*.

Phreng-ta-ma   See *Hphreng-ba-ma*.

'Phrog-'chang-ma
Tibet
Directions
   Deity of direction associated with the northeast.
[de Nebesky-Wojkowitz 1952; Leach 1992]

'Phur-'debs-ma
Tibet
Directions
   Guardian deity associated with the northwest direction.
[de Nebesky-Wojkowitz 1952; Leach 1992]

Phyugs-bdag-btsun-mo
Tibet
Domesticated Animals
   Mother of the cattle deities whose husband is their father,
Phyugs rje btsan po. [de Nebesky-Wojkowitz 1952; Leach
1992]

Prajnaparamita
Tibet
Education and Knowledge; Mother and Guardian
  Goddess of transcendental wisdom. *Shakti,* Indian Subcontinent, of Vajradhara. She is considered the personification of the perfected wisdom of Yoga. She is the Mother of the Bodhisatvas (one whose essence is perfect knowledge and who is believed to be a future Buddha), bringing them to birth and suckling them to Buddhahood. Prajnaparamita is also the title of one of the most important Buddhist scriptures. Identical to *Yum-chen-mo.* See also *Dolma, Tara,* and *Prajnaparamita,* Indian Subcontinent. Alternate form: Ses-rab-kyi-pha-rol-ta-phyin-pa. [Durdin-Robertson 1976; Hoffman 1956; Hooykaas 1964; Leach 1992; Marchall 1963; Zimmer 1955]

Pukkase
Tibet
Unhappiness; Directions; Time; Heaven and Hell
  Wrathful deity who comes to Bardo (see *Bardo Goddesses*) from the southeast on the thirteenth day. See also *Red Pukhase.* [Evans-Wentz 1960; Leach 1992]

Pushpâ See *Me-tog-ma.*

Pushpema See *Me-tog-ma.*

Rab-brtan-ma
Tibet
Earth and Nature
  Earth diety. [de Nebesky-Wojkowitz 1952; Leach 1992]

Ral-gcig-ma
Tibet
Fate; Justice
  Goddess of great power who has only one eye, ear, tooth, breast, arm, foot, etc. Ruler of the *Tan-ma* furies. She can see into the past, present, and future and destroys all of her enemies. Equivalent to *Ekajata,* Indian Subcontinent. [de Nebesky-Wojkowitz 1952; Eliade 1964; Evans-Wentz 1960; Getty 1962; Jobes 1962; Leach 1992]

Ratna Dakinis
Tibet
Goodness
  "Precious." One of the five orders of Tibetan Dakinis. Their color is yellow and their characteristic is compassion. See also *Dakinis.* [Durdin-Robertson 1976; Jobes 1962]

Ratna Krotishaurima
Tibet
Mother and Guardian; Heaven and Hell; Time; Directions; Wealth
  "Rich in Treasures." Guardian deity who is a mother goddess and *Shakti.* She appears in Bardo (see *Bardo Goddesses*) from the southern quarter on the tenth day. Alternate form: Ratna Kro-ti-shavr-ri-ma. [Durdin-Robertson 1976]

Ratna Kro-ti-shavr-ri-ma See *Ratna Krotishaurima.*

rDerje-mkhah-hgro See *Vajradakini,* Indian Subcontinent.

rDo-rje-dpal-gyi yum
Tibet
Evil; Earth and Nature
  Malevolent mountain goddess whose name appears in Tibetan liturgy. Alternate form: Rong gi Jo-mo-kha-rag. [Leach 1992; Tucci 1980]

rDo-rje-drag-mo-rgyal
Tibet
Mother and Guardian; Earth and Nature
  Guardian of Buddhist doctrine who is also a mountain deity and protective goddess. [de Nebesky-Wojkowitz 1952; Leach 1992]

rDo-rje-mkha'-'gro-ma
Tibet
Weather
  Weather deity who is invoked to bring rain. [de Nebesky-Wojkowitz 1952; Leach 1992]

rDo-rje-ne-ne-gnam-sman-sgron
Tibet
Sky and Heavens
  Sky deity. [de Nebesky-Wojkowitz 1952; Leach 1992]

rDo-rje-rnal-hbyor-ma
Tibet
Education and Knowledge; Weather
  Deity of truth, spiritual energy, and knowledge that dispels ignorance. rDo-rje is the Tibetan symbol for the thunderbolt. She is also the chief guardian of the esoteric practices of Tibetan Tantric Yoga. Her color is red and she is portrayed with one face, two hands, three eyes, and a halo of the flames of wisdom. She is worshiped in Tibet and Afghanistan and is associated with the *Yogini* and *Shakti,* and *Kundalini,* Indian Subcontinent; Shakti Yoga, and the Yoga of the Psychic-heat. See also *Dorje Naljorma.* Alternate form: Vajrayogini. [Durdin-Robertson 1976; Leach 1992; Sierksma 1966; Snellgrove 1957]

Red Crow-headed Thunderbolt Goddess
Tibet
Heaven and Hell; Wild Birds; Directions; Demi-animals
  One of the *Wang-Chugmas.* She comes from the northern quarter. [Durdin-Robertson 1976; Jobes 1962]

Red Hoopoe-headed Desire Goddess
Tibet
Heaven and Hell; Wild Birds; Directions; Demi-animals
  One of the *Wang-Chugmas.* She holds a bow and arrow that is ready to shoot and comes from the western quarter. [Durdin-Robertson 1976; Jobes 1962]

Red Horse-headed Delight Goddess
Tibet
Heaven and Hell; Happiness; Domesticated Animals; Directions; Demi-animals
  One of the *Wang-Chugmas.* She holds a club in her hand and comes from the western quarter. [Durdin-Robertson 1976; Jobes 1962]

Red Ibex-headed Woman Goddess
Tibet
Heaven and Hell; Hunting and Wild Animals; Directions; Demi-animals
  One of the *Wang-Chugmas.* She comes from the northern quarter. [Durdin-Robertson 1976; Jobes 1962]

Red Lion-headed Mystic Goddess
Tibet
Heaven and Hell; Hunting and Wild Animals; Intelligence and Creativity; Directions; Demi-animals
  One of the *Wang-Chugmas* and a Door-Keeping *Yogini.* She holds an iron chain and comes from the western quarter. [Durdin-Robertson 1976; Jobes 1962]

Red Makara-headed Peaceful Goddess
Tibet
Heaven and Hell; Order; Directions; Demi-animals
   One of the *Wang-Chugmas*. She holds an urn and comes from the southern quarter. [Durdin-Robertson 1976; Jobes 1962]

Red Pramoha
Tibet
Heaven and Hell; Time; Directions
   One of the *Kerimas*. She comes to Bardo (see *Bardo Goddesses*) on the thirteenth day from the western quarter holding a makara-banner. (The makara is a bird.) [Durdin-Robertson 1976]

Red Pukhase
Tibet
Heaven and Hell; Directions; Time
   One of the *Kerimas*. She comes to Bardo (see *Bardo Goddesses*) from the southeast quarter on the thirteenth day. See also *Pukkase*. [Durdin-Robertson 1976]

Red Scorpion-headed Amrita Goddess
Tibet
Heaven and Hell; Insects; Directions; Demi-animals
   One of the *Wang-Chugmas*. She holds a lotus and comes from the southern quarter. [Durdin-Robertson 1976; Jobes 1962]

Red Snow-bear-headed Virgin Goddess
Tibet
Heaven and Hell; Hunting and Wild Animals; Directions; Demi-animals
   One of the *Wang-Chugmas*. She holds a short spear and comes from the eastern quarter. [Durdin-Robertson 1976; Jobes 1962]

Red Tara   See *Kurukulle*.

Red Tiger-headed One
Tibet
Heaven and Hell; Hunting and Wild Animals
   One of the *Htamenmas*. [Durdin-Robertson 1976; Jobes 1962]

Reddish-yellow Serpent-headed Brahma Goddess
Tibet
Heaven and Hell; Reptiles; Directions; Demi-animals
   One of the *Wang-Chugmas*. She holds a lotus and comes from the eastern quarter. [Durdin-Robertson 1976; Jobes 1962]

Remati
Tibet
Mother and Guardian
   Guardian deity considered a form of *Kali*, Indian Subcontinent. She is important to the Gelugpa and Ningmapa sects of Tibetan Buddhism. [Durdin-Robertson 1976]

Ri-bu-mo
Tibet
Evil
   "Maiden of Caste." Demon. Alternate form: Rigs-bu-mo. [Jobes 1962]

Rigs-bu-mo   See *Ri-bu-mo*.

Rin-chen-mkha'-'gro-ma
Tibet
Weather

Weather deity invoked to bring rain. [de Nebesky-Wojkowitz 1952; Leach 1992]

Rin-chen-mkhah-ngro
Tibet
Weather; Magic
   Equivalent to *Ratnadakini*, Indian Subcontinent. [Jobes 1962]

Rlung-gi-lha-mo-dam-tshig-sgrol-ma
Tibet
Weather
   Wind goddess who helps to eliminate pollution. [de Nebesky-Wojkowitz 1952; Leach 1992]

rMa-bya-c'en-mo
Tibet
Wild Birds; Magic; Mother and Guardian
   "The Great Peacock Goddess." She casts magic spells to ward off harm. Equivalent to *Mahamayuri*, Indian Subcontinent. [Getty 1962; Leach 1992]

Rochanî
Tibet
Beauty
   One of the *Devis*, Indian Subcontinent. The others are *Mâmakî, Pândurâ*, and *Tara*. Rochanî is bright and lovely and stimulates the appetite. [Durdin-Robertson 1976]

Ro-kha-ma
Tibet
Ceremonies
   Cemetery deity. [de Nebesky-Wojkowitz 1952; Leach 1992]

Rong gi Jo-mo-kha-rag   See *rDo-rje-dpal-gyi yum*.

Sa'i-lha-mo Sangs-rgyas-spyan-ma
Tibet
Earth and Nature
   Earth deity invoked to eliminate pollution. [de Nebesky-Wojkowitz 1952; Leach 1992]

Samanta-Bhadra   See *Kuntu-bzang-mo*.

Sangs-rgyas-mkha'-'gro-ma
Tibet
Weather
   Rain goddess. [de Nebesky-Wojkowitz 1952; Jobes 1962; Leach 1992]

Sangs-rgyas-spyan-ma
Tibet
Heaven and Hell; Directions; Time
   Shakti of Ratna-Sambhava, Indian Subcontinent. She appears in Bardo (see *Bardo Goddesses*) from the southern realm on the third day accompanied by *Hphreng-ba-ma* and *bDug-spös-ma*. Alternate form: Sangyay Chanma. [Durdin-Robertson 1976; Evans-Wentz 1960; Leach 1992]

Sangyay Chanma   "She of the Buddha Eye [or Eyes]." See *Sangs-rgyas-spyan-ma*.

Sangye-khado
Tibet
Magic; Heaven and Hell; Sky and Heavens; Ceremonies; Education and Knowledge
   Chief of the *Khahdoma*. See also *Buddha Dakinis* and *Khahdoma Queen*. Alternate form: Sans-rgyas-mkhah-hgro. [Durdin-Robertson 1976; Jobes 1962]

Sans-rgyas-mkhah-hgro See *Sangye-khado.*

Sa-rgyal-dong-gi-dbal-mo
Tibet
Earth and Nature
  Bon (see *A-phyi-gung-rgyal*) earth deity. Consort of the earth god Sa bla dog rum. [Leach 1992; Tucci 1980]

Sa-yi-lha-mo-bstan-ma
Tibet
Mother and Guardian; Magic; Ceremonies
  Protective deity invoked during magic ceremonies. She is portrayed holding a "vessel in front of her heart." [de Nebesky-Wojkowitz 1952; Leach 1992]

Senga-dong-ma
Tibet
Demi-animals; Hunting and Wild Animals
  Lion-faced demon. See *Dorje-pa-mo* and *Seng-ge Dolma.* [Durdin-Robertson 1976]

Sengdroma
Tibet; Sherpa
Hunting and Wild Animals; Demi-animals; Mother and Guardian; Domesticated Animals; Ceremonies
  Lion-faced deity. The female manifestation of Guru Rimpoche, she is invoked during the rite of summer to protect the herds in Nepal. [Francke 1923; Leach 1992; von Furer-Haimendorf 1964]

Seng-ge Dolma
Tibet
Immortality
  Savior. Corresponds to *Senga-dong-ma.* [Durdin-Robertson 1976]

Seng-ge'i-gdong-can
Tibet
Magic; Demi-animals; Hunting and Wild Animals
  Goddess of magic. She is portrayed with a lion face. [Leach 1992; Waddell 1925]

Ses-rab-kyi-pha-rol-ta-phyin-pa See *Prajnaparamita.*

Sgeg-mo-ma
Tibet
Beauty
  Goddess of beauty. Her Sanskrit name is *Lâsyâ* and she is portrayed holding a mirror in a coquettish manner. Her Tibetan Sanskrit name is *Lasema.* [Durdin-Robertson 1976]

sGrol-dkar-po See *Sitatara,* Indian Subcontinent.

sGrol-ma See *sGrol-mas.*

sGrol-mas
Tibet
Mother and Guardian; Heaven and Hell; Time; Health and Healing
  As *Tara* she protects humans from lions, elephants, snakes, fire, thieves, enemies, water, and epidemics. She is also the *Shakti* of Amogha-Siddhi. Together they appear in Bardo (see *Bardo Goddesses*) on the fifth day. See also *Tara,* Indian Subcontinent. Alternate form: sGrol-ma. [Evans-Wentz 1960; Jobes 1962; Leach 1992; Waddell 1925]

Shakti
Tibet
Creator of Life; Primordial Being

Creative power and energy. Their energy activates and empowers the male deities. Tibetan Shaktis are *Bribsun, Cha-dog-ma, Chags-kyu-ma, Gokarmo, Locana, mTsho-sman-ru-phyug-rgyal-mo, Nam-khu-ing-kya-wang-chug-ma, Padma Krotishaurima, Prajnaparamita, Ratna Krotishaurima, rDo-rje-rnal-hbyor-ma, Sangs-rgyas-spyan-ma, sGrol-mas, Thog-gi-bu-yug,* and *Zhag-pa-ma.* See also *Shakti,* Indian Subcontinent.

Shal-za-ma See *Zhal-zas-ma.*

Shri-devi "Glorious Goddess." See *Lha-mo.*

Singhinî
Nepal
Evil
  Guardian demon. She is one of the guards of the Devi Bhawani Temple at Bhatgaon. [Durdin-Robertson 1976]

Sipe Gyalmo
Tibet
Justice
  "Queen of the World." A Bon (see *A-phyi-gung-rgyal*) deity who has one head, three eyes, and six arms. Her arms hold a banner of victory, a sword, a royal sunshade, a swastika, a skull-bowl, and a trident. Her *vahana* (throne or mount) is a red mule. [Lurker 1984]

sKyabs-mdun
Tibet
Earth and Nature
  "Helpful Spouse." The highest earth deity, her active role is transferred to *aBru-gu-ma,* the wife of the weather god Kesar. She may be identical to the earth deities *brTan-ma* or *brTar-byed-ma.* [Francke 1923; Leach 1992; von Furer-Haimendorf 1964]

Skyes-bu-ber
Tibet
Magic; Education and Knowledge; Ceremonies
  Goddess of magic who teaches her followers exorcism and propitiation. [Beier 1966; Leach 1992]

Smasha
Tibet
Unhappiness; Heaven and Hell; Directions; Time
  Wrathful deity whose color is dark blue. She comes to Bardo (see *Bardo Goddesses*) from the northeast on the thirteenth day. Alternate form: Smashali. [Evans-Wentz 1960; Leach 1992]

Smashali See *Smasha.*

sNa tshogs nkha' 'gro ma
Tibet
Weather
  Weather deity invoked for rain. [de Nebesky-Wojkowitz 1952; Leach 1992]

sNang-gsal-ma
Tibet
Heaven and Hell; Directions; Time; Fire
  Goddess of light. She arrives in Bardo (see *Bardo Goddesses*) on the fourth day from the western realm. Related to fire, her color is red. Her Sanskrit name is *âloka* and her Tibetan Sanskrit name is *âloke.* Alternate form: Nang-sal-ma. [Durdin-Robertson 1976; Evans-Wentz 1960; Leach 1992]

sNa-tshogs-rdorje-mkha-hgro See *Visvadakini*, Indian Subcontinent.

Sobha
Nepal
Moon and Night
   Wife of the moon god Candra. [Leach 1992; Pal and Phattacharyya 1969]

Song-tsen-gam-po See *Dolma*.

Sridevi
Tibet
Justice
   She serves as a guardian of the Dalai Lama. As a chthonic deity she plays a part in the judgment of the dead, keeping a record of human sins. Identical to *dPal-ldan Lha-mo*. See also *Jewel Goddesses* and *Long-life Sisters*. [Leach 1992; Lurker 1984; Ribbach 1940]

Srid-pa'i-sman See *A-phyi-gung-rgyal*.

Srimati
Tibet
Fate
   Goddess of prophecy who presides over good omens. [Hackin et al. 1963; Hoffman 1956; Leach 1992]

Sring-mo-no-chung-gzi-byin-ma
Tibet
Commerce and Travel
   Guardian of travelers. A Bon (see *A-phyi-gung-rgyal*) deity. [de Nebesky-Wojkowitz 1952; Leach 1992]

Srinmo
Tibet
Evil; Destroyer of Life; Life/Death Cycle
   Demon of death. Srinmo holds the Great Round, the Tibetan cosmic wheel, upon which the ascending and descending cycle of human life is represented. [Durdin-Robertson 1976; Leach 1992; Monaghan 1981]

Srog-bdag-mo
Tibet
Destroyer of Life; Evil
   Demon of death. Ruler of the *gshin-rje-mo*. [de Nebesky-Wojkowitz 1952; Leach 1992]

Stag-gdon-can See *Vyaghravaktradakini*, Indian Subcontinent.

Ston-gyi-rgyal-mo
Tibet
Time
   Equivalent to *Saraddevi*, Indian Subcontinent. [Jobes 1962]

Tan-ma
Tibet
Hunting and Wild Animals; Evil; Health and Healing
   Buddhist "she-furies" who are ruled by *Ral-gcig-ma*. There are 12 and they are divided into three classes—four ferocious great she-devils, four ferocious great injuries, and two moderate medicine females. They are mounted on dragons, lions, tigers, or other wild animals. They were originally Bon (see *A-phyi-gung-rgyal*) deities. Alternate form: bStan-ma. [Jobes 1962]

Tara
Tibet
Unknown

One of the four *Devis*, Indian Subcontinent. The others are *Mâmakî*, *Pândurâ*, and *Rochanî*. See also *Tara*, Indian Subcontinent. [Durdin-Robertson 1976]

Tashitsheringma
Tibet
Unknown
   One of the *Long-life Sisters*. [Jobes 1962]

Teleglen-Edzen See *Altan-telgey*.

Thab-lha-g•ui-mo
Tibet
Fire; Household Affairs
   Hearth deity. [de Nebesky-Wojkowitz 1952; Leach 1992]

Thab-lha-g•yu-mo
Tibet
Fire; Household Affairs
   Hearth deity. [de Nebesky-Wojkowitz 1952; Leach 1992]

Thinggishalsangma
Tibet
Unknown
   One of the *Long-life Sisters*. [Jobes 1962]

Tho-ag See *Tho-og*.

Thog-ag See *Tho-og*.

Thog-gi-bu-yug
Tibet
Sky and Heavens
   Sky deity and *Shakti* of Yar lha sham po, a mountain god. [de Nebesky-Wojkowitz 1952; Leach 1992]

Tho-og
Tibet
Primordial Being
   The Eternal Mother who is self-formed. She is the preexisting space. Similar to *Aditi*, Indian Subcontinent, and *Guanyin*, Far East. Equivalent to *Mother Space*, Indian Subcontinent. Alternate forms: Tho-ag, Thog-ag. [Durdin-Robertson 1976]

Tibetan Sarasvati
Tibet
Education and Knowledge
   Goddess of teaching and learning. Wife of Manjushri Jampal. *Ye-she-tsho-gyal* is said to be her incarnation. She is similar to *Yang-Chen*, Far East. See also *Sarasvati*, Indian Subcontinent. [Durdin-Robertson 1976]

Til-bu-ma
Tibet
Reptiles; Demi-animals; Heaven and Hell; Directions
   Faith-guarding deity. She has the head of a serpent and is the guardian of the north door of Bardo (see *Bardo Goddesses*) with her husband, Amrita-Dhari. Like the other female door-keepers, she is portrayed as naked with long flowing hair, in dancing position, and with her genitals exposed. Her Sanskrit name is *Kinkini-dharî*. See also *Cha-dog-ma*, *Chags-kyu-ma*, *Kuntu-bzang-mo*, and *Zhag-pa-ma*. Alternate form: Dril-bu-ma. [Durdin-Robertson 1976]

Toma
Tibet
Unhappiness; Intelligence and Creativity
   "The Wrathful She." As an aspect of *Dorje Naljorma*, she seems to be associated with the intellect. She is red in

color and has two eyes plus the third eye of wisdom. She is portrayed nude, decorated with symbolic ornaments, and dancing. [Durdin-Robertson 1976]

Tonagma
Tibet
Evil; Unhappiness; Ceremonies
"Wrathful Black-one." Tantric deity who is the malevolent aspect of *Vajra Dakinis.* She is called black because of her wrathful appearance, but is actually red in color. She appears at the Tibetan Red Feast Ritual. [Durdin-Robertson 1976]

Tsandhali
Tibet
Unhappiness; Heaven and Hell; Directions; Time
Wrathful goddess. She is yellowish-white and comes from the northwest to Bardo (see *Bardo Goddesses*) on the thirteenth day. [Evans-Wentz 1960; Leach 1992]

Tse-ring Chhe-nga
Tibet
Earth and Nature
The Tibet Earth and Nature Mountain spirits. They are the five sisters of Mount Everest. They are portrayed in flowing robes, holding emblems of fertility: jewels, a spear, a sun, and a golden staff. [Jobes 1962]

Tseurima
Tibet
Unhappiness; Heaven and Hell; Directions; Time
Wrathful goddess. She is yellow and comes to Bardo (see *Bardo Goddesses*) from the south on the thirteenth day. [Evans-Wentz 1960; Leach 1992]

Tsha-ba'i-brtan-ma-chen-mo
Tibet
Earth and Nature
Mountain deity. Ruler of the Tshab sgang ridge in Tibet. [de Nebesky-Wojkowitz 1952; Leach 1992]

Tsho-gyalma
Tibet
Education and Knowledge; Happiness
"She Who Conquers the Lake." She confers the blissfulness of understanding with her knowledge about the space of truth. [Durdin-Robertson 1976]

Ugtsho Yamasil
Tibet
Earth and Nature
Mountain deity. Her color is red and her *vahana* (throne or mount) is a nine-headed tortoise. [de Nebesky-Wojkowitz 1952; Leach 1992]

Ui Tango
Tibet; Apa Tanis
Creator of Life
Creator deity. She is one of three. The others are *Nguntre* and *Ni-ngurre.* [Wedeck and Baskin 1971]

Ushnishavijaya
Tibet
Intelligence and Creativity
"Intelligence." See also *Ushnishavijaya,* Indian Subcontinent. [Getty 1962; Leach 1992]

Vajra Dakinis
Tibet
Ceremonies; Intelligence and Creativity

One of the five orders of Tibetan *Dakinis.* They appear in the Rite of the Living and the Rite for the Dead. Their followers are asked to visualize a Dakini with an arrow-like reed extending through the center of the body, the median nerve, which is white on the outside and red inside. It ends about four inches below the navel and the upper part opens from the crown of her head. See also *Buddhadakini,* Indian Subcontinent, and *Dakinis* and *Tonagma,* this region. [Durdin-Robertson 1976]

Vajra Krotishaurima
Tibet
Heaven and Hell; Directions; Time
Guardian deity who comes to Bardo (see *Bardo Goddesses*) from the eastern quarter on the ninth day. She accompanies her husband, Vajra-Heruka. Alternate form: Vajra Kro-ti-shrv-ri-ma. [Durdin-Robertson 1976]

Vajra Kro-ti-shrv-ri-ma   See *Vajra Krotishaurima.*

Vajra-Shringkhala   See *Cha-dog-ma.*

Vajra-Vārāhī
Tibet
Hunting and Wild Animals
Boar deity. Partner of Vajradāka, one of the fearful gods. Also Sanskrit name for *Dorje Phagmo.* See also *Vajravarahi,* Indian Subcontinent. [Durdin-Robertson 1976; Leach 1992; Snellgrove 1957]

Vajravaraki
Tibet
Magic; Mother and Guardian; Domesticated Animals
"Wanderer of the Air." A goddess who incarnates as a Buddhist abbess who never sleeps. Her story is similar to that of *Dorje Phagmo.*

 To protect the nuns in her care, she used her magical powers to make the abbey disappear. The Mongol chieftain who was attacking the abbey found only a herd of pigs with a wild sow as their leader. The nuns were returned to human form when the danger passed. [Monaghan 1981]

Vajrayâna Devatas
Tibet
Education and Knowledge
An order of devatas who are collectively personified as *Dorje Naljorma.* One of their order instructed Padma Buddha in the secret Tantric method. [Durdin-Robertson 1976]

Vajrayogini   "Insight and Knowledge." See *Dorje Naljorma* and *rDo-rje-rnal-hbyor-ma.*

Vasudhara   See *Vasudhara,* Indian Subcontinent.

Vinasa
Tibet
Education and Knowledge; Health and Healing; Magic; Mother and Guardian
Wine-seller and guru.

 A king of the Urgyan country was bitten by a snake. When the physicians were unable to cure him, they sent Vinasa to the deepest part of the ocean to get some water. When the water cured him, the king made Vinasa his spiritual adviser. Vinasa tired of her service to the king and wanted to leave. Since he wanted her to stay, she magically presented him with a child to take her place as guru. The child later became the sage, La-wa-pa. [Durdin-Robertson 1976]

Vīras
Tibet
Courage; Ceremonies

Heroines belonging to an order of elementary spiritual beings. They participate in the Yogic Dance of the Five Directions (the four cardinal directions and the center). In the east they dance in a crescent-shaped area, in the south it is a triangular area, in the west it is circular, and in the north it is square. When they dance in the center, the area is blessed by their presence. [Durdin-Robertson 1976]

Vyaghrini
Tibet
Evil

Guardian demon of Nepal. Associated with *Singhini*. [Durdin-Robertson 1976]

Wang-Chugmas
Tibet
Heaven and Hell; Time

Mighty goddesses of Bardo (see *Bardo Goddesses*) who arrive on the fourteenth day. There are 28 including *Black Cuckoo-headed Mystic Goddess, Black Sow-headed Sow Goddess, Blue Monkey-headed Goddess of Inquisitiveness, Blue Serpent-headed Water Goddess, Blue Wolf-headed Wind Goddess, Dark-brown Yak-headed Rakshasa Goddess, Dark-green Fox-headed Baton Goddess, Green Deer-headed Wealth-guardian Goddess, Greenish-black Elephant-headed Big-nosed Goddess, Greenish-black Leopard-headed Great Goddess, Greenish-black Serpent-headed Mystic Goddess, Red Crow-headed Thunderbolt Goddess, Red Hoopoe-headed Desire Goddess, Red Horse-headed Delight Goddess, Red Ibex-headed Woman Goddess, Red Lion-headed Mystic Goddess, Red Makara-headed Peaceful Goddess, Red Scorpion-headed Amrita Goddess, Red Snow-bear-headed Goddess, Reddish-yellow Serpent-headed Brahma Goddess, White Bear-headed Indra Goddess, White Eagle-headed Mighty Goddess, White Kite-headed Moon Goddess, Yellow Bat-headed Delight Goddess, Yellow Dog-headed Rakshasi, Yellow Goat-headed Mystic Goddess,* and *Yellowish-black Tiger-headed Rakshasi.* See also *Karma-krotishaurima.* Alternate form: Dvang-phyng-ma. [Durdin-Robertson 1976; Jobes 1962]

White Bear-headed Indra Goddess
Tibet
Heaven and Hell; Hunting and Wild Animals; Directions; Demi-animals

One of the *Wang-Chugmas.* She holds a noose made of intestine and comes from the eastern quarter. [Durdin-Robertson 1976; Jobes 1962]

White Eagle-headed Mighty Goddess
Tibet
Heaven and Hell; Wild Birds; Directions; Demi-animals

One of the *Wang-Chugmas.* She holds a club and comes from the western quarter. [Durdin-Robertson 1976; Jobes 1962]

White Kerima
Tibet
Heaven and Hell; Time; Directions

One of the *Kerimas.* She comes to Bardo (see *Bardo Goddesses*) on the thirteenth day from the eastern quarter. She holds a club in her right hand and a bowl filled with blood in her left. [Durdin-Robertson 1976; Leach 1992]

White Kite-headed Moon Goddess
Tibet
Heaven and Hell; Moon and Night; Directions; Demi-animals

One of the *Wang-Chugmas.* She holds a *dorje* (thunderbolt symbol) and comes from the southern quarter. [Durdin-Robertson 1976; Jobes 1962]

Yami
Tibet
Water

River goddess. See also *Yami,* Indian Subcontinent. [Durdin-Robertson 1976; Jobes 1962; Leach 1992; Monaghan 1981]

Yellow Bat-headed Delight Goddess
Tibet
Heaven and Hell; Happiness; Directions; Demi-animals

One of the *Wang-Chugmas.* She holds a shaving knife and comes from the southern quarter. [Durdin-Robertson 1976; Jobes 1962]

Yellow Dog-headed Rakshasi
Tibet
Heaven and Hell; Domesticated Animals; Directions; Demi-animals

One of the *Wang-Chugmas.* She holds a *dorje* (thunderbolt symbol) and a shaving knife and comes from the western quarter. [Durdin-Robertson 1976; Jobes 1962]

Yellow Goat-headed Mystic Goddess
Tibet
Heaven and Hell; Domesticated Animals; Intelligence and Creativity; Directions; Demi-animals

One of the *Wang-Chugmas* and a Door-Keeping *Yogini.* She holds a noose and comes from the southern quarter. [Durdin-Robertson 1976; Jobes 1962]

Yellow Tseurima
Tibet
Heaven and Hell; Time; Directions

One of the *Kerimas.* She comes to Bardo (see *Bardo Goddesses*) on the thirteenth day from the southern quarter holding a bow and arrow in shooting position. [Durdin-Robertson 1976; Leach 1992]

Yellowish Bird-headed One
Tibet
Heaven and Hell; Wild Birds

One of the *Htamenmas.* [Durdin-Robertson 1976; Jobes 1962]

Yellowish-black Tiger-headed Rakshasi
Tibet
Heaven and Hell; Hunting and Wild Animals; Directions; Demi-animals

One of the *Wang-Chugmas.* She holds a blood-filled bowl and comes from the southern quarter. [Durdin-Robertson 1976; Jobes 1962]

Yellowish-white Tsandhali
Tibet
Heaven and Hell; Directions; Time

One of the *Kerimas.* She comes to Bardo (see *Bardo Goddesses*) on the thirteenth day from the northwest quarter. [Durdin-Robertson 1976]

Yeshe-khahdoma
Tibet
Education and Knowledge

"The All-fulfilling Wisdom." One of her identifying symbols is a tiara. She gives divine assistance to those who appeal to her before the performance of a difficult ritual, especially in yoga. She is one of the *Khahdomas*. [Durdin-Robertson 1976]

Ye-shes-mkha'-'gro-ma
Tibet
Weather
　　Rain goddess. Her consort is mGon po dkar po. [de Nebesky-Wojkowitz 1952; Leach 1992]

Ye-she-tsho-gyal
Tibet
Education and Knowledge
　　"Victorious One of the Ocean of Wisdom." Her memory is so great that she remembers forever whatever she has heard. She is a *Dakini*. See also *Tibetan Sarasvati*. [Durdin-Robertson 1976]

Yid-'prog-ma
Tibet
Evil; Life/Death Cycle; Goodness; Health and Healing; Wealth; Mother and Guardian
　　Name for Buddhist *Hariti*, Indian Subcontinent. [Getty 1962; Leach 1992]

Yogini
Tibet
Evil; Magic; Mother and Guardian
　　Demon or witch. See also *Yogini*, Indian Subcontinent. [Danielou 1964; Stutley and Stutley 1984]

Yum
Tibet
Creator of Life
　　Female principle. Corresponds to *Yoni*, Indian Subcontinent, and to *Yin* and *In*, both Far East. Yum is coupled with Yab, the male principle. [Durdin-Robertson 1976; Jobes 1962]

Yum-chen-mo
Tibet
Education and Knowledge
　　Deity of wisdom. Identical to *Prajnaparamita*. [Leach 1992; Snellgrove 1957]

Zas-ster-ma-dmar-mo
Tibet
Wealth
　　Deity who belongs to a group of gods and goddesses of wealth. [de Nebesky-Wojkowitz 1952; Leach 1992]

Zhag-pa-ma
Tibet
Heaven and Hell; Time; Love and Sexuality; Demi-animals; Domesticated Animals
　　Door-keeper of the south in Bardo (see *Bardo Goddesses*) who appears on the sixth day. *Shakti* of Yamantaka, she is associated with fondness. She has the head of a sow and bears a noose that represents the *Yoni*, Indian Subcontinent, and the umbilical cord, the latter of which restricts and nourishes. See also *Cha-dog-ma, Chags-kyu-ma, Kuntu-bzang-mo,* and *Til-bu-ma*. Alternate forms: Pâshadharî and Zhags-pa-ma. [Durdin-Robertson 1976; Leach 1992]

Zhags-pa-ma　　See *Zhag-pa-ma*.

Zhal-zas-ma
Tibet
Education and Knowledge; Directions; Time
　　Bodhisatva (one whose essence is perfect knowledge and who is believed to be a future Buddha) who comes from the north to Bardo (see *Bardo Goddesses*) on the fifth day with Amogha-Siddhi, the Buddha of Infallible Magic. Her Tibetan Sanskrit name is *Nidhema* and her Sanskrit name is *Naivedya*. Alternate form: Shal-za-ma. [Durdin-Robertson 1976; Evans-Wentz 1960; Leach 1992]

INDIAN SUBCONTINENT

A Nyit A Jom
India, *Lepcha*
Agriculture
Sikkim goddess of agricultural fertility. [Leach 1992]

Abhraganga   See *Ganga.*

Abhramu
India
Weather; Magic; Hunting and Wild Animals
"Cloud Knitter." A shape-changer who could take the shape of her children, the clouds. Hindu deity who was originally a female elephant and the mate of the elephant form of Indra. [Monaghan 1981; Stutley and Stutley 1984]

Abrayanti
India
Stars and Planets; Mother and Guardian
One of the *Krittikas.* [Durdin-Robertson 1976]

Acheri, The
India
Destroyer of Life; Mother and Guardian; Immortality
Disease-bringing ghosts of young girls.
At night the Acheri come down from the mountain tops, bringing illness. Mothers place a scarlet thread around their children's necks because the Acheri do not bother anyone wearing red. [Bonnerjea 1927; Leach 1972]

Adanari
India
Earth and Nature; Justice; Magic; Hunting and Wild Animals
Hindu deity of nature, religion, and truth. She is portrayed with long hair and four arms inside a hexagram. Each hand holds a different emblem: a circle or coin, a cup, a magician's rod, and a sword. Beneath her are the heads of a lion, an ox,

and a leopard. Identified with *Isis,* Egypt. Alternate form: Adda-nari. [Durdin-Robertson 1976; Jobes 1962]

Adda   See *Ida.*

Adda-nari   See *Adanari.*

Addittee   See *Aditi.*

Adhararani
India
Fire
"Tinder Wood." A fire deity who is the lower piece of *Arani.* Used in kindling holy fires. See also *Uttararani.* [Durdin-Robertson 1976]

Adhidevatas, The
India
Mother and Guardian
Tutelary deities. One of the classifications of the *Devatas.* [Durdin-Robertson 1976]

Adimata   "Primal Mother." See *Manasa.*

Adishakti   "Primeval Power or Energy." See *Shakti.*

Adit   See *Aditi.*

Aditi
India
Creator of Life; Primordial Being; Sky and Heavens; Supreme Being
"Mother of the Gods," "Cow of Light," "Freedom." Supreme creator of all that has been created. A pre-existent Hindu first goddess of the primordial vastness. Originally considered the mother of Iranian deities, she became known

later as the mother of all the deities. She is also the mother of all the heavenly bodies, including the sun and planets. See also *Mother Space, Mulaprakriti, Prithivi, Revati, Vac.* Opposite of *Diti.* Equivalent to *Shekinah,* Near East, and *Tho-og,* the Himalaya. Alternate forms: Adit, Addittee, Aditya, Kadru. [Danielou 1964; Durdin-Robertson 1976; Leach 1992; Monaghan 1981; Senior 1985; Stutley and Stutley 1984; Sykes 1968]

Aditya, The

India

Wealth; Order; Mother and Guardian; Goodness; Health and Healing; Weather

In Vedic belief, one of the *Vasus,* divine attendants of *Aditi.* [Stutley and Stutley 1984]

Adkaya   See *Prithivi.*

Adrija   "Mountain Born." See *Parvati.*

Adrika

India

Magic; Fishing and Water Animals; Mother and Guardian; Sky and Heavens; Goodness; Immortality; Water; Magic; Weather

One of the *Apsarases.*

↑ *Adrika was changed into a fish. When she magically gave birth to a son and daughter, the spell ended and she rose to the heavens.* [Stutley and Stutley 1984]

Aginvati

India

Small Size; Magic

"She with the Purse." One of the *Khekaris.* [Durdin-Robertson 1976]

Agnayi

India

Fire

One of the *Gnas.* A fire deity in the Vedic pantheon. [Durdin-Robertson 1976; Stutley and Stutley 1984]

Agni   See *Varsus.*

Agwani

India

Fire; Destroyer of Life

Hindu fire goddess. She is a deity of pustular diseases who causes fever. One of the six sisters of *Sitala.* [Leach 1972; Leach 1992]

Ahalya

India

Beauty; Love and Sexuality; Justice

A Hindu deity of great beauty.

↑ *Indra saw Ahalya and fell in love with her. When her husband, Gautama, was away, Indra tried to seduce Ahalya, but Gautama's return ended the scheme. Indra then conspired with the moon god, Soma. Indra took the form of a cock and crowed at midnight, which lured Gautama out of the house to perform his morning exercises. Indra then assumed Gautama's form and went to Ahalya. As punishment for having sex with her, Indra's skin was covered with marks looking like yoni (female reproductive organs) or eyes.*

Alternate form: Maitreyi. [Durdin-Robertson 1976; Stutley and Stutley 1984]

Ahana

India

Dawn and Twilight

Vedic dawn deity. [Leach 1992]

Aie Lacha

India

Poverty

Lohar caste famine deity. [Leach 1992]

Aindri   See *Saci.*

Aingini   See *Ganesani.*

Aitan

India, *Khasi*

Water

Assam stream goddess. [Leach 1992]

Aiyulaniza   See *Niseginyu.*

Akasa

India

Mother and Guardian

"Mother," "Pure Essence." Ether. Identified with *Nari.* [Durdin-Robertson 1976]

Akasaganga   See *Ganga.*

Akasagarabha

India

Primordial Being

Void space whose essence is ether. A Buddhist Dhyani-Bodhisatva. She is called *Nam-mk'ahi snin-po,* the Himalaya, *Ogtarghui-in jiruken, Xu Kongcang* or *Kokuzo,* Far East. [Leach 1992]

Aksara

India

Ceremonies

"Syllable of Sound." Speech expressing praise or prayer. She is invoked to remember her worshipers. [Stutley and Stutley 1984]

Aksaya   "Undecaying." See *Prithivi.*

Akuti

India

Intelligence and Creativity

"Will," "Intention." Daughter of Syayambhuva Manu, mother of *Dakshina* and Yajna, who became the parents of the gods called Yamas. [Bonnerjea 1927; Stutley and Stutley 1984]

Al Shua

India

Stars and Planets

Stellar goddess. Personification of the constellation Ursa Major. Corresponds to *Arundhati.* [Durdin-Robertson 1976]

Alakhani

India

Goodness; Earth and Nature; Selfishness

Assam benevolent vegetation spirit.

↑ *Alakhani mischievously waits in a mushroom-shaped plant in a bamboo grove. She possesses anyone who passes, but never harms them.* [Monaghan 1990]

Alakshmi

India

Luck; Poverty

"Misfortune" or "Non-prosperity." Hindu deity, sister and opposite of *Lakshmi*. Alakshmi is also called *Jyestha*, elder sister. Alternate form: Nirriti. [Leach 1992; Stutley and Stutley 1984]

Alambusha

India

Sky and Heavens; Goodness; Immortality; Wealth; Water; Magic; Fishing and Water Animals

One of the *Apsarases*. [Durdin-Robertson 1976]

Alopurbi

India, *Baiga*

Hunting and Wild Animals

Hunting deity. [Leach 1992]

Alwantin

India

Destroyer of Life; Immortality; Mother and Guardian

Death deity. The spirit of a woman who died in childbirth. Worshiped in the Deccan region, a plateau triangular in shape that covers most of peninsular India. [Bonnerjea 1927]

Amari De

India, *Gypsy*

Mother and Guardian; Earth and Nature

"Great Mother." Gypsy personification of nature. It is suggested that the gypsies originated in India or Hindustan (India and Pakistan). Amari De appears today as *Sara-Kali*, a *Black Virgin*, Greek and Roman Empires, or *Sara*, in statue form among modern Gypsy families. Alternate form: De Develski. [Durdin-Robertson 1976]

Amavasya

India

Mother and Guardian; Ceremonies

"New Moon." Hindu deity. Daughter of Sraddha.

The first day of the first quarter when the moon is invisible is when Amavasya and the sun live together. [Leach 1992; Stutley and Stutley 1984]

Amba

India

Mother and Guardian; Ceremonies; Justice; Stars and Planets

"Mother." Possibly a pre-Aryan deity. One of the *Krittikas*. Either an alternate name for *Durga* or a goddess who was absorbed by her. She is also said to have been absorbed by *Parvati* and *Uma*. Worshiped into modern times near Jaipur as Amba, she is honored with a sacrifice of black goats. Another goddess by this name is the eldest daughter of the King of Kasi who committed suttee in order to be able to incarnate as Sikhandin to seek revenge for wrongs done to her by Bhisma. Alternate form: Amber. [Durdin-Robertson 1976; Monaghan 1981; Stutley and Stutley 1984]

Amba Bai

India

Mother and Guardian

"Mother." Tutelary deity. Worshiped in Kilhapur (Kolsapur, Kolhapaur). On April fifteenth, her statue is carried about the town in a triumphal vehicle. [Durdin-Robertson 1976]

Ambabachi   See *Bhudevi*.

Amber   See *Amba*.

Ambika

India

Mother and Guardian; Agriculture

"Mother." A merciful Hindu nature deity of Kilhapur. She is worshiped during harvest season and before the digging of water holes. The Shaktas consider *Jyestha, Raudri*, and *Vama* as aspects of this goddess.

Ambika coalesced the energies of all the deities and destroyed the buffalo-demon who was attacking them. She was successful, but later lost to the demons Shumbha and Nishumbha. When Ambika rejected Shumbha, he sent an army against her. Kali saved her and Ambika gave Kali the name Camunda.

See also *Shakti* and *Amikas*. Alternate forms: Durga, Parvati. [Danielou 1964; Lurker 1984; Stutley and Stutley 1984]

Amma

India

Mother and Guardian

"Mother." Dravidian earth goddess. As protector of all beings and as creator of life, she is the symbol of fertility. She manifests as a cow. Sometimes used in the plural form, *Ammas*. See also *Uma*. [Durdin-Robertson 1976; Stutley and Stutley 1984]

Ammal   "Earth Mother." See *Parvati*.

Ammas   See *Amma*.

Ammavaru

India

Primordial Being; Mother and Guardian; Hunting and Wild Animals

Telugu mother goddess of a Dravidian people in east central India. She existed before the creation of the world and rides on a jackal.

Ammavaru laid an egg in the Sea of Milk. From the egg rose Brahma, Vishnu, and Shiva. [Lurker 1984]

Amrit

India, *Kol*

Immortality; Love and Sexuality; Water; Magic

Hindu deity of immortality. She appeared at the Churning of the Milk Ocean. Associated with love potions, soma and nectar (vehicles of transformation), and water-life forms. Sometimes considered a male deity.

Amrit's belly contained the "water of immortality." Anyone who drank the water became immortal. One day Amrit's belly was punctured by the horn of a cow and all the water seeped out. Death came to the world. The cow, as punishment, works behind a plow.

Alternate form: Amrita. [Durdin-Robertson 1976; Leach 1992]

Amritika   See *Amrita*.

Ana

India

Mother and Guardian

"Mother" in Sanskrit. See also *Ana*, Near East, and *Ana*, Western Europe. Alternate form: Anu. [Jobes 1962]

Anakulam-Bhagavathi

India, *Kadar*

Mother and Guardian; Hunting and Wild Animals

"Goddess of the Elephant Tank." Deity who protects against attacks by elephants. [Leach 1992]

Anala

India

Agriculture; Goodness; Health and Healing; Weather; Wealth; Order; Mother and Guardian

Hindu deity of food. One of the *Vasus*. Daughter of *Surabhi*. She is the mother of seven kinds of trees that yield pulpy fruit: coconut, date, nut, palm, milk, and tali. [Jobes 1962; Leach 1992; Stutley and Stutley 1984; Sykes 1968]

Anapurna   See *Annapurna*.

Anasuya

India

Education and Knowledge; Justice; Love and Sexuality

"Free from Envy." Hindu goddess of wisdom. Daughter of Daksha, wife of Atri, and mother of Soma, Durvasas, and Dattatreya.

⚲ One day Anasuya was sitting on the bank of the Ganges with Atri when the three gods, Shiva, Vishnu, and Brahma, appeared. They all were possessed by passion for her. They tried to take her body by force, but she rose against them. She told them if they expected to be worthy as holy beings they must know her as their mother only. [Stone 1979; Stutley and Stutley 1984]

Angana

India

Magic; Hunting and Wild Animals; Sky and Heavens; Goodness; Immortality; Water; Wealth; Fishing and Water Animals

Queen of the monkeys. One of the *Apsarases*. Wife of Kesari and mother of Hanuman, a monkey god. Angana manifests as a monkey. Alternate form: Anjana. [Durdin-Robertson 1976]

Angarmati Bhawani

India

Fire; Sun and Day; Destroyer of Life

"Blazing Charcoal."

⚲ On hot days, Angarmati Bhawani rides through the sky in her chariot causing those on earth to suffer sunstroke. [Leach 1992]

Anila

India

Wealth; Order; Mother and Guardian; Goodness; Health and Healing; Weather

One of the *Vasus*. [Sykes 1968]

Anjana   See *Angana*.

Ankamma

India

Destroyer of Life; Household Affairs

Goddess of disease worshiped in the Nellore (Ellore) district, Andhra Pradesh. She is frequently chosen as the household deity. [Leach 1992]

Anna Kuari

India, *Oraon*

Agriculture; Luck; Ceremonies

Fertility goddess worshiped during the threshing of grain on the Chota Nagpar Plateau of Bihar. She gives good fortune and crops for which she is said to require human sacrifices. Alternate form: Anna Kurari. [Durdin-Robertson 1976; Leach 1992]

Anna Kurari   See *Anna Kuari*.

Annal   See *Parvati*.

Annapatni

India

Agriculture

Hindu deity who presides over food. [Stutley and Stutley 1984]

Annapurna

India

Goodness; Agriculture; Household Affairs; Wealth

Benevolent household deity who provides food for the people of Benares (Varanasi). Considered a form of *Parvati* in Tanjore, Bengal, or a form of *Durga*, she is said to live on the top of Annapurna Mountain. Worshiping her guarantees food for all the world. She is a corn goddess in Bania. Similar to Greco-Roman *Anna Perenna*. See also *Apnapurna*. [Durdin-Robertson 1976; Leach 1992; Monaghan 1981; Stutley and Stutley 1984]

Anoi Diggan Juje

India, *Dhammai*

Creator of Life; Fishing and Water Animals

First woman.

⚲ Anoi Diggan Juje and her brother were human children of frogs, but were born covered with hair. They became the parents of three sons, Lubukhanlung, Sangso-Dungso, and Kimbu Sangtung. [Sproul 1979]

Anrita

India

Unknown

Deity. Wife of Adhrama and mother of *Maya*. [Durdin-Robertson 1976]

Antai

India

Health and Healing

Deity who causes and protects against whooping cough. Worshiped in Gujarat. [Leach 1992]

Antariksha

India

Sky and Heavens; Wealth; Order; Mother and Guardian; Goodness; Health and Healing; Weather

"Sky." One of the *Vasus*. [Sykes 1968]

Anu   See *Ana*.

Anumati

India

Luck; Magic; Moon and Night; Wealth; Intelligence and Creativity; Mother and Guardian; Life/Death Cycle

"Divine Favor." A Vedic moon deity, she is said to preside over the full moon with *Raka*. With *Sinivali*, Anumati is invoked to form a male child. She also gives her worshipers "wealth, inspiration, insight, offspring, and longevity." [Durdin-Robertson 1976; Jobes 1962; Leach 1992; Stutley and Stutley 1984]

Anushakti

India

Creator of Life; Primordial Being

One of the *Shaktis*. [Durdin-Robertson 1976]

Anushayini

India

Sun and Day

Sun goddess. Her blue eyes are so radiant, they can light up a room. When she descended to earth, she was called *Shri*. [Jobes 1962]

Ap, The
India

Water; Creator of Life; Health and Healing; Luck; Immortality

"The Waters." Hindu personifications of celestial and terrestrial waters, they are mentioned in the Vedas. Original creator deities used water, liquid or solidified, as the basis for everything. As the representatives for all deities, they cure, purify, grant favors, and give immortality. Also the name of one of the *Vasus*. See also *Apo*, Near East. Alternate forms: Apa, Apah, Apas. [Durdin-Robertson 1976; Leach 1992; Stutley and Stutley 1984]

Apa   See *Ap*.

Apah   See *Ap*.

Apala
India

Earth and Nature; Health and Healing; Magic

Creator of animals.

Apala was afflicted with a severe skin disease. Indra cleansed her. Three times he pulled her through holes, one in a chariot, one in a wagon, and one in a yoke. Each time she lost some skin and the skin changed into a hedgehog, an alligator, and a chameleon. [Stutley and Stutley 1984]

Aparajita
India

Unknown

"The Unconquered One." Buddhist deity portrayed as yellow and covered with jewels. See also *Durga*. [Lurker 1984]

Aparna
India

Selflessness

"Without a Leaf." Originally a non-Aryan deity, she became known as *Uma*. Eldest daughter of Himavat and *Mena*, sister of *Ekaparna* and *Ekapatala*.

Aparna and her sisters practiced austerities and abstinences. Her sisters existed on one leaf each while Aparna existed on none at all. [Stutley and Stutley 1984]

Apas   See *Ap*.

Apnapurna
India

Wealth

"To Nourish by Water," "To Produce." Hindu goddess of plenty. She is bent over by the weight of her full breasts. Similar to Roman *Anna Perenna*. See also *Annapurna*. [Jobes 1962]

Apsarases, The
India

Sky and Heavens; Goodness; Immortality; Water; Magic; Weather; Fishing and Water Animals

Hindu celestial nymphs who provide solace to the deities and the souls of dead warriors, similar in this aspect to the *Valkyries*, Northern Europe. The essence of waters, they may symbolize clouds or mists. They are able to change shapes, often appearing as water birds. Their numbers vary, but there may be thirty-five million or more. Their parentage is also unclear. Possibly they sprang from the Churning of the Ocean, or from *Bhasi* or *Vac*. Among the Apsarases are *Adrika, Alambusha, Angana, Aukshagandhii, Caksusi, Ghrtaci, Guggulu, Harini, Jamadagni, Keshini, Lavangi, Madhava, Malini, Manasi, Marisha, Masrakesi, Mena, Naladi, Pramandani, Pramlocha, Pururavas, Purvachitti,* *Rambha, Rati, Sahaganya, Sanumati, Sasilekha, Saudamani, Sukanthi, Surabhidatta, Surapamsula, Tilottama, Uravari, Urvasi, Vadaba,* and *Vasistha*. Equivalent to *Bai Mundan*, Far East. See also *Kshiti-apsarases*. [Cooper 1876; Durdin-Robertson 1976; Stutley and Stutley 1984]

Apu
India

Health and Healing; Weather; Wealth; Order; Mother and Guardian; Goodness

One of the *Vasus*. [Sykes 1968]

Apvā
India

Courage; War; Health and Healing

Goddess of fear, according to Sāyana (a fourteenth-century author). Apvā is also possibly the personification of intestinal problems that affect warriors in the field. [Stutley and Stutley 1984]

Aramati
India

Selflessness; Earth and Nature; Mother and Guardian

"Piety." Personificaton of devotion and, according to some, of the earth. Similar to *Armaiti*, Near East, and *Pietas*, Greek and Roman Empires. She protects those who worship the gods. [Durdin-Robertson 1976; Leach 1992; Stutley and Stutley 1984]

Arani
India

Family and Tribes; Earth and Nature; Fire; Ceremonies; Love and Sexuality

"Mistress of the Race." Arani is a piece of wood of the Shami tree, which is used for kindling holy fires. The lower piece is called *Adhararani* and the upper piece is *Uttararani*. Fire and the making of fire, sometimes interpreted as a sexual act, are considered feminine. Cults of Arani are associated with rites of lesbian intercourse. [Durdin-Robertson 1976]

Aranya
India

Mother and Guardian; Health and Healing

Bengal deity who is invoked to make children healthy and to cure infertility. Alternate form: Jamai Sashthi. [Leach 1992]

Aranyani
India

Earth and Nature; Mother and Guardian; Health and Healing

"Mother of Beasts." Hindu deity of the jungle, Vedic deity of the forest. She provides curative unguents and food. [Jobes 1962; Leach 1992; Redfield 1931; Stutley and Stutley 1984]

Arayi, The
India

Evil; Ugliness; Destroyer of Life

"Mean." Hindu demons. Hags who have one eye and limp about destroying human embryos. [Stutley and Stutley 1984]

Ardhanari
India

Earth and Nature

"Capable." She is mentioned in the ancient catechism of Madras referred to in *The Secret Doctrine*. She is portrayed on a lotus leaf floating on the water. She may be connected to *Lakshmi*. Also said to be the androgynous form of Shiva in which the left side of the body is female. [Durdin-Robertson 1976; Stutley and Stutley 1984]

Aruna

India

Love and Sexuality

"Illicit Love." One of the *Nayikas.* [Stutley and Stutley 1984]

Arundhati

India

Love and Sexuality; Creator of Life; Stars and Planets; Family and Tribes

"Fidelity." Daughter of Daksha, wife of Dharma or Vasishtha. She gave birth to the divisions of the earth. Also the name of a stellar deity who is the personification of the star Alkor in the constellation Ursa Major. Arundhati is invoked in marriage ceremonies. She is portrayed standing on a lotus leaf floating on the water. Corresponds to *Al Shua.* [Durdin-Robertson 1976; Stutley and Stutley 1984]

Arwut

India

Unknown

Hindu deity who lives in the city of Soonbhedra on the banks of the Nerbudda. She is the mother of a male dwarf, Bamun Owtar, who lived a thousand years. He was an Avatar (incarnation) of Vishnu. [Durdin-Robertson 1976]

Arya "Noble One." See *Sarasvati.*

Aryajangulitara See *Sitatara.*

Asa Poorna

India, *Chohan*

Happiness; Mother and Guardian; Creator of Life; Primordial Being

"Hope Fulfilled." Tutelary deity and *Shakti.* [Durdin-Robertson 1976]

Asapishachikis, The

India

Evil

Demons of false hope. A form of *Pisachis.* [Durdin-Robertson 1976]

Asapura

India

Mother and Guardian; Health and Healing

Deity of reproduction. She is invoked to help the women of Gujarat become pregnant. [Leach 1992]

Asapurna

India, *Charan, Hinglaj, Rajput*

Earth and Nature; Happiness; Ceremonies

"She Who Fulfills Desire." Hindu earth mother who represents hope. She is worshiped by the Rajputs as an incarnation of *Gauri.* At Madh in Cutch, she is worshiped in the form of a red painted rock and honored with sacrifices of seven male buffaloes. [Leach 1972; Leach 1992]

Ashi

India

Justice; Education and Knowledge; Health and Healing; Wealth

"Reward." Daughter of *Armati.* She is the messenger who brings wisdom from heaven to earth. She uses plants and waters for healing. Said to give riches, abundance, and prosperity, but according to some, she brings them only after death. See also *Ashi,* Near East. [Jayne 1925; Jobes 1962; Leach 1992]

Ashis

India

Happiness

"Hope" is personified as the daughter of the Hindu god, Bhaga. [Stutley and Stutley 1984]

Ashva

India

Dawn and Twilight; Domesticated Animals

"Horse" or "Mare." Vedic deity of dawn. Similar to the *Usas.* [Durdin-Robertson 1976; Stutley and Stutley 1984]

Asikni See *Virini.*

Aso See *Niseginyu*

Asokakanta

India

Domesticated Animals

She is portrayed as golden yellow, is covered with jewels, and rides a pig. See also *Marici.* [Lurker 1984]

Asra

India

Water

Water deity who lives near rivers. [Leach 1992]

Asrapas The "Blood Sippers." See *Dakinis.*

Asri

India

Luck

"Bad Luck." Deity of misfortune. [Durdin-Robertson 1976; Stutley and Stutley 1984]

Assam Mother Earth

India, *Khasi*

Earth and Nature; Water; Fire; Sun and Day; Moon and Night; Unhappiness; Life/Death Cycle; Immortality

Earth deity who is the mother of waters, *Ka Um;* of fire, *Ka Ding;* of the sun, *Ka Sngi;* and the moon, U Bnai.

When Mother Earth grew old and died, her daughters were grieved. They sought to perform funeral rites to free their mother's soul from her body. Ka Sngi sent down waves of heat but her mother's body retained its shape. Ka Um made a flood, but she was also unsuccessful. Then Ka Ding sent her fire and her mother's body burst into flame. Her body was changed and her soul set free. [Stone 1979]

Assuras See *The Asuris.*

Astabhuja Kurukulla See *Kurukulla.*

Asu Mainao

India, *Kachari*

Agriculture

Agricultural deity who presides over the asu crop. [Leach 1992]

Asuniti

India

Ceremonies; Immortality

"Spirit Life." Vedic deity who is invoked to prolong life by giving strength and nourishment. Also thought to preside over funerals. Asuniti may be an alternate form for Yama, the ruler of the dead. [Stutley and Stutley 1984]

Asura See *The Asuris.*

Asuri See *The Asuris.*

Asuris, The
India
Evil; Health and Healing; Heaven and Hell
Originally Iranian deities who were demoted to demons and driven to the nether regions where they became enemies of the Hindu gods. They were adopted by the Buddhists. In the singular, a demon who created a remedy for leprosy. She is called *Lha-Ma-Yin*, The Himalaya. See also *Mohini.* Alternate forms: Asura, Assuras. [Durdin-Robertson 1976; Jobes 1962; Stutley and Stutley 1984]

Asvini
India
Domesticated Animals
"Mare." One of the *Gnas.* Wife of the Asvins, two sky gods who appear before dawn, she was later called their mother. [Stutley and Stutley 1984]

Ati-canda
India
Love and Sexuality
One of the *Nayikas.* A form of *Durga.* [Stutley and Stutley 1984]

Auksagandhi
India
Earth and Nature; Sky and Heavens; Goodness; Immortality; Water; Weather; Magic; Fishing and Water Animals
"Having an Ox Smell." One of the *Apsarases.* See also *Guggulu.* [Stutley and Stutley 1984]

Ausinari
India, *Usinari*
Fire; Justice
Fire deity. Wife of Pururavas and queen of Madhyadesa. She was responsible for a vessel containing the celestial fire. [Durdin-Robertson 1976]

Avantimatrikas   See *The Avantimatris.*

Avantimatris, The
India, *Avanti*
Family and Tribes
"Divine Mothers" of the Avanti people. Alternate form: Avantimatrikas. [Durdin-Robertson 1976]

Avany
Sri Lanka
Mother and Guardian; Magic
Virgin mother of the Buddha Sakyamuni. [Durdin-Robertson 1976]

Awejsirdenee
India
Unknown
Wife of Bishenjun. Mother of Kalki, the tenth Avatar (incarnation) of Vishnu. [Durdin-Robertson 1976]

Ayepi
India, *Naga*
Household Affairs; Wealth
Household deity who gives prosperity. Worshiped by the Angami branch of the Naga in Assam and Nagaland. [Leach 1992]

Badi Mata
India
Destroyer of Life
Smallpox goddess who mainly infects children. Worshiped in the state of West Bengal. [Leach 1992]

Bagala
India
Evil; Demi-animals
"Deceitful." A crane-headed goddess said to revel in cruelty and suffering. Originally a village deity, a *Gramadevata*, she is now identified with *Durga.* Also a *Mahavidya.* [Leach 1992; Stutley and Stutley 1984]

Bagula
India
Household Affairs
Household deity. [Leach 1992]

Bahu
India
Mother and Guardian; Stars and Planets
"Creating Mother." Personification of the star Denebola in the constellation Leo. See also Mesopotamian and Accadian *Bahu* in Near East. [Cooper 1876; Durdin-Robertson 1975; Durdin-Robertson 1976; Monaghan 1981]

Bahucharaji
India
Ceremonies; Health and Healing
Dravidian deity called the "Looking Glass Goddess." Her worshipers look at their own image in a mirror while praying to her. In Gujarat, she is invoked by "the lame, the blind, the impotent, and the children." [Leach 1992; Redfield 1931]

Bai Haldahin
India, *Baiga*
Destroyer of Life
Deity of disease who "causes a yellow vomit." Alternate form: Hardahin. [Leach 1992]

Baihi
India, *Baiga*
Destroyer of Life; Unhappiness
Deity of illness who causes madness. [Leach 1992]

Bala
India, *Punjab*
Household Affairs
Household deity worshiped in Mandi, a city and/or district in both Himachal Pradesh and Madhya Pradesh. A manifestation of *Shakti.* [Leach 1992]

Balambika
India
Unknown
"Girl Mother." Deity worshiped by the southern Indian Tantrists of Cape Comorin. Equivalent to *Kanyā Kurmārī.* [Stutley and Stutley 1984]

Balini
India
Love and Sexuality
"Illicit Love." One of the *Nayikas.* [Stutley and Stutley 1984]

Baluchistan Goddesses
India
Unknown
Female figurines that are thought to represent goddesses found at Baluchistan, c. 3000 B.C.E. They are about one inch long, full-breasted, with their knees bent, wearing necklaces, with strands of hair reaching the top of their breasts. [Fairservis 1971]

Banasankari
India, *Lambadi*
Earth and Nature
   Forest deity of the south. Alternate form: Banasamkari.
[Leach 1992]

Banasamkari   See *Banasankari.*

Banjari
India, *Banjara*
Mother and Guardian
   Tutelary deity. She is invoked for protection when a person
is in the forest. [Leach 1992]

Banka Mundi
India, *Khond*
Hunting and Wild Animals; Courage
   Hunting deity. Saying her name out loud makes one
fearless of the wild animals of the jungle. [Monaghan 1990]

Bansapti
India, *Musahar*
Earth and Nature
   Nature deity. She presides over the woods. She increases
the productivity of all the plants used by humans, including
fruit trees and bulbs. [Leach 1992]

Bardaichila
India
Weather; Disorder; Ceremonies
   Assam storm goddess who creates gales when traveling
from her home to earth. During the festival of Bohag Bihu she
creates a storm just before the festival begins and just after it
ends. [Monaghan 1990]

Barhishmati
India
Ceremonies
   Deity who provides the grass used in rituals, especially
those of Vedi. Sister of *Samgna.* [Durdin-Robertson 1976]

Basanti
India
Destroyer of Life
   Deity of smallpox. Called the "yellow goddess" because
the color of the skin of those infected appears yellow. She
arrives in the spring when the disease is rampant. One of the
sisters of *Sitala.* [Leach 1972; Leach 1992]

Basany
India
Unknown
   Vedic deity. Wife of Bais. [Durdin-Robertson 1976]

Baski Mata
India, *Bhuiya*
Earth and Nature; Life/Death Cycle
   Earth deity.
   *Baski Mata supports the earth on her feet. She stands on
   her head on a lotus flower at the bottom of the sea, and
   when she tires and changes position, there is an
earthquake.* [Leach 1992]

Basuli
India
Earth and Nature
   Ancient deity who inhabits the Kandagiri caves. She is
portrayed nude, standing in a lotus bush, and holding a lotus
stalk in each hand. [Durdin-Robertson 1976]

Basumati
India, *Juang*
Agriculture
   Fertility goddess worshiped in West Bengal. Offerings are
made to her during planting and harvest time. Also a name
for *Bhudevi.* [Leach 1992]

Basundhara   See *Bhudevi.*

Bauri Bai
India, *Baiga*
Destroyer of Life; Unhappiness
   Deity of illness who causes madness. [Leach 1992]

Bela Pinnu
India, *Khond*
Earth and Nature
   Earth goddess worshiped in the Central Provinces and in
the state of Orissa. Also the name of a male deity. [Leach
1992]

Bentakumari
India
Water
   Assam water deity. Her followers give her the first catch of
the season. [Monaghan 1990]

Bera Pennu   See *Tari Pennu.*

Bettada Chicama
India, *Kurumba*
Domesticated Animals; Household Affairs; Travel and
Commerce; Intelligence and Creativity; Immortality;
Destroyer of Life
   "Mother of the Hill" to a caste of shepherds, weavers, and
stone masons in the south.
   *When the dead appear in the dreams of the living and
   direct that offerings be made to Bettada Chicama,
   dreamers had better obey or she will cause illness.*
[Leach 1992]

Bhadrā
India
Luck; Justice; Domesticated Animals
   "Auspicious," "Fortunate." Deity of fertility cycles. The
name of several deities including: an alternate name for
Durga; a daughter of Soma and wife of Utathya; one of
Krishna's queens; a daughter of Rohini and mother of goats
and sheep; and the wife of the Garuda, a bird god.
   *Bhadrā, the daughter of Soma, was kidnapped by Varuna.
   Her husband, Utathya, demanded her return. When
   Utathya dried up the rivers and made the earth a desert,
Varuna returned her.*
   Alternate form: Carvi and Durga. [Jobes 1962; Stutley and
Stutley 1984]

Bhadrakali
India, *Kadar, Izhava*
Destroyer of Life; Earth and Nature; Health and Healing; War
   Hindu death goddess or nature deity who later became a
form of *Durga/Kali.* As a manifestation of *Kali* to the Kadar
people, she protects humans and cattle from disease. Also a
manifestation of *Shakti* and an alternate form of *Uma.*
Among the Izhava, she is a war goddess who aids in military
undertakings. [Durdin-Robertson 1976; Leach 1992; Stutley
and Stutley 1984]

Bhagadevi
India, *Jalari, Vada*
Health and Healing
Deity who protects against cholera. [Leach 1992]

Bhagavathi
India, *Kshatriya*
Family and Tribes; Ceremonies
Vedic marriage deity who is worshiped on the fourth day of the marriage ceremonies. [Leach 1992]

Bhagavati
India, *Coorg*
Supreme Being; Creator of Life
"Supreme Goddess." The joint powers of Brahma, Vishnu, and Shiva combined in Bhagavati. Also said to be a Hindu creator goddess of the Coorg (Kodagu) people. Alternate forms: Devi and Khermai. [Leach 1992; Stutley and Stutley 1984]

Bhageseri
India
Destroyer of Life
Deity of pustular disease. One of the sisters of *Sitala.* Worshiped by the Dom caste (musicians, weavers, traders, and moneylenders). [Leach 1992]

Bhagirathamma
India, *Jalari, Vada*
Health and Healing; Fishing and Water Animals
Protector of night fishermen. She keeps them from becoming ill. [Leach 1992]

Bhagirathi
India
Water; Health and Healing
See also *Ganga.* She was given the name Bhagirathi when Shiva allowed her to flow to the sea and the nether regions, purifying Sagara's sons. [Stutley and Stutley 1984]

Bhagvati   See *Mindhal.*

Bhairava, The
India
Evil; Sky and Heavens; Goodness; Immortality; Water; Magic; Weather; Fishing and Water Animals
"Fearful Ones." A class of *Apsarases.* Alternate form: Nirriti. [Danielou 1964; Stutley and Stutley 1984]

Bhairavi
India
Evil; Life/Death Cycle
"Terror" or "The Power To Cause Terror." Hindu death goddess. A form of *Devi.* She carries out the perpetual process of decay that occurs throughout life. Often regarded as a demon. Alternate forms: Nirriti Parvati, Mahavidya. [Stutley and Stutley 1984]

Bhandarin
India, *Gadba*
Agriculture
Deity worshiped in the Central Provinces. [Leach 1992]

Bharadi
India
Education and Knowledge
Deity of history. Alternate form: Suraswati. [Leach 1992]

Bharati
India, *Bharat*
Charisma; Ceremonies; Mother and Guardian
"Eloquence." Deity of speech and one of the *Gnas.* Along with *Sarasvati* and *Ila,* she represents a form of worship. She became the tutelary deity of the Bharat people who lived in the Sarasvati River valley. Some say that Bharati is another name for Sarasvati. [Danielou 1964; Stutley and Stutley 1984]

Bhasa   See *Bhasi.*

Bhasi
India
Wild Birds; Weather
Deity of flight. Daughter of *Tamra* and Kashyapa. She is said to be the mother of kites or birds. Alternate form: Bhasa. [Stutley and Stutley 1984]

Bhattarika   "Noble Lady." See *Durga.*

Bhaumi   "Produced from the Earth." See *Sita.*

Bhavani(s)
India, *Todas*
Creator of Life; Ceremonies
"Giver of Existence." Hindu Great Mother of the Trimurti—Brahma, Vishnu, and Shiva. In Nepal, she is the wife of Siva and equivalent to *Vajravarahi.* When plural, "a class of women who are dedicated to the service of the temple." Alternate forms: Bhawani, Bhowani, Kali, Parasu-pani, Mother Earth. [Cooper 1876; Durdin-Robertson 1976; Jobes 1962; Stutley and Stutley 1984]

Bhawani   See *Bhavani.*

Bherunda   See *Kali* and *Yakshi.*

Bhgavati
India, *Kol*
Destroyer of Life
Smallpox goddess worshiped in central India. One of the *Matris.* [Leach 1992]

Bhgavatiamman
India
Destroyer of Life; Evil
Malevolent smallpox goddess worshiped in the Trichinopoly (Tiruchirapalli) district. [Leach 1992]

Bhima
India
Evil
A form of *Durga.* Also the name of one of the *Apasarases* meaning "fearful" or "terrible." [Durdin-Robertson 1976; Stutley and Stutley 1984]

Bhisana
India
Evil
Hindu goddess of terror. [Stutley and Stutley 1984]

Bhogavati
India
Reptiles; Earth and Nature
Serpent-nymph and the name of one of the attendants of the god Skanda, who are called *Matris* (mothers). This is also the name used for the capital of the Nagas (serpents) and a sacred river of serpent-demons. [Stutley and Stutley 1984]

Bhowani   See *Bhavani.*

Bhrkuti
India
Unhappiness
"She Who Frowns." Buddhist yellow *Tara*. Her Tibetan name is *Khro-gner-can-ma*, the Himalaya. [Jobes 1962]

Bhudevi
India, *Bangladesh*
Mother and Guardian
Benevolent aspect of *Dharti Mata* worshiped in the state of Bengal. Alternate forms: Ambabachi, Basumati, Basundhara, Bhumi, Prithivi, Thakurani Mai. [Leach 1972; Leach 1992; Stutley and Stutley 1984]

Bhukhi Mata
India
Poverty
Deity of famine. [Leach 1992]

Bhulli Buri   See *Mainao*.

Bhumi
India
Earth and Nature
"Existing." Personification of the earth as one of three spheres of existence: celestial, atmospheric, and terrestrial. She is closely identified with *Mother Earth* or may be the same as *Prithivi* or *Bhudevi* and corresponds to *Sukara-preyasi*. Alternate form: Bhumidevi. [Durdin-Robertson 1976; Jobes 1962; Stutley and Stutley 1984]

Bhumidevi   See *Bhumi*.

Bhumiya Rani
India, *Dangis*
Earth and Nature; Family and Tribes; Agriculture; Evil; Destroyer of Life; Reptiles
Earth deity of the north worshiped during marriage, childbirth, and harvest in northern India. The male god by this name sometimes changes sex and becomes malevolent, causing illness to those who show disrespect. The Dangis of the United Provinces worship her as a snake. [Leach 1972; Leach 1992]

Bhumme Nari
India, *Naga*
Earth and Nature
Earth goddess worshiped in Assam. [Leach 1992]

Bhutamatri
India
Immortality; Ceremonies; Agriculture
"Mother of Spirits." Her festival is celebrated during the ripening of the crops, from May to June. See also *Krodha*. [Stutley and Stutley 1984]

Bhuti   "Well-being," "Prosperity," "Good Fortune." See *Lakshmi*.

Bhuvanesvari
India
Supreme Being
"Mistress of the World." An epitaph of many goddesses. See also *Rajarajvari*, and *Mahavidya*. [Leach 1992; Stutley and Stutley 1984]

Bhuyian
India, *Dom*
Earth and Nature
Earth goddess who is an aspect of *Devi*. [Leach 1992]

Bibi Miriam
India
Mother and Guardian; Goodness
Indian name for *Virgin Mary*, Near East. [Durdin-Robertson 1976]

Bija-garaba   "Womb of the Elements of Speech." See *Sarasvati*.

Bijaldeo Kanya
India, *Khond*
Weather
Weather deity presiding over lightning. Daughter of Megh Raja and Megh Rani who is worshiped in the Central Provinces. [Leach 1992]

Bijloki
India, *Rajnengi Pardhan*
Weather
Lightning deity. One of the wives of Lakshman. [Leach 1992]

Biliku
India
Creator of Life; Goodness; Insects; Directions; Weather; Fire; Arts; Wild Birds
Andaman Island creator of the earth who sometimes manifests as a spider. She is benevolent and malevolent and, being connected with the northeast monsoon, sends all the winds except the south wind.

When the world was plunged into darkness by the monsoon, Biliku taught the people how to bring the light back with fire, song, and dance. When the kingfisher stole fire from her, Biliku left the earth forever.

See also *Biliku*, Southeast Asia, and *Spider Woman*, North America. Alternate forms: Mimi Biliku, Puluga. [Johnson 1988; Leach 1992; Monaghan 1981; Savill 1978]

Bisal Mariamna
India
Sun and Day; Ceremonies; Creator of Life; Primordial Being
Solar deity. The *Shakti* of sunlight in Mysore. One of seven sister goddesses, she is worshiped in an open-roofed shrine where the sun can shine unhampered. In the shrine is a brass pot filled with water and called Kunna-Kannadi ("eye-mirror"). On top of the water float pepper leaves and coconut flowers, and a small mirror is leaned against it. [Monaghan 1990]

Bisam Thakurani
India, *Santal*
Health and Healing
Deity who protects her followers from disease. [Leach 1992]

Bisari
India, *Kachhi*
Destroyer of Life
Disease goddess who causes ophthalmia. [Leach 1992]

Bomong   See *Bong*.

Bong
India, *Minyong*
Sky and Heavens
Sister deities of a people who are neither Hindu nor Buddhist. They are daughters of the earth and sky who began glowing the moment they were born.

Bong and Bomong grew brighter and brighter in the care of their nurse. When their nurse died suddenly, the sisters died, too. The world became dark, and the people, thinking the nurse had stolen the light, dug up her body. All that remained were her eyes which held the reflections of Bong and Bomong. A carpenter cut the images from the eyes and the girls were once again alive and there was light in the world.

Alternate form: Bomong. [Monaghan 1990]

Bonga

India, *Santal*

Evil; Earth and Nature; Love and Sexuality; Immortality

Evil spirit, usually female, who lives in hills, trees, or rivers. They are said to marry or have intercourse with humans. People who die become *bongas,* except uninitiated children who become *bhuts,* and women who die in childbirth and are not cremated become *Churels. Bhut* or *bhuta* is also a general term in Hindu belief for a malignant spirit of a person whose death was accidental, suicide, or a result of capital punishment. [Leach 1972]

Boodh   See *Buddhi.*

Boorbi Pennu

India, Bangladesh, *Khond*

Agriculture

Fertility goddess who presides over new growth and first fruits. [Leach 1992]

Brahmani

India

Creator of Life; Mother and Guardian

Non-Vedic, serpent-headed deity. Said to be one of the seven divine mothers (*Matrikas*) and a form of *Durga.* One of the *Saptamatrakas.* A *Shakti* of Brahma. Alternate forms: Sarasvati, Satarupa, Savitri. [Danielou 1964; Stutley and Stutley 1984]

Brahmi   "The Power of the Immense Being." See *Sarasvati* and *Savitri.*

Brisaya

India

Moon and Night

Vedic moon goddess who presides over darkness. Similar to *Briseis,* Greek and Roman Empires.

Brisaya is sought by the solar hero, Aharyu. He must capture her before he can recover the morning dew stolen by the Panis. [Jobes 1962]

Buddha Dahinis   See *Buddha Dakinis.*

Buddhadakini

India

Weather; Magic; Ceremonies

Buddhist air deity who bestows supernatural powers. Her emblems are the wheel, skull cup, and ritual wand. In Tibet she represents understanding and justice, and her color is dark blue. See also *Dakinis* and *Buddha Dakins,* the Himalaya.. Alternate form: Buddha Dahinis. [Durdin-Robertson 1976; Jobes 1962]

Buddhi

India

Intelligence and Creativity; Earth and Nature

"Intellect." One of the seven principles of the Great Mother, Buddhi is the breath. Also called one of the seven planes of nature, the intuitional plane, called by some the Buddhic plane. Alternate form: Boodh. [Durdin-Robertson 1976; Stutley and Stutley 1984]

Buddhi Nagin

India, *Kulu*

Reptiles; Weather

Serpent deity associated with the rainbow and worshiped in northern India. [Johnson 1988]

Buddhi Pallien

India

Earth and Nature; Hunting and Wild Animals

Assam forest deity. She manifests as a tiger in the jungle. [Monaghan 1990]

Bugarik

Assam, *Garo*

Water; Physical Prowess; Destroyer of Life

Sea goddess.

Bugarik has the upper body of a woman, but no legs. She floats on the current, killing any humans she can catch. [Bonnerjea 1927]

Burhi Mata

India, *Gadba, Bondo*

Destroyer of Life; Ceremonies

Goddess of disease. She causes smallpox in humans and rinderpest in cattle. She is propitiated with flowers and incense, but her followers abuse her if the epidemic doesn't subside. Alternate form: Thakurani Mata. [Leach 1992]

Burhi Thakurani

India, Bangladesh

Water

Tista River deity in eastern Bangladesh and West Bengal, India. [Leach 1992]

Bursung

India, *Bondo*

Creator of Life; Evil; Goodness; Mother and Guardian

Earth deity who is benevolent and malevolent and presides over fecundity. She feeds or starves the life she created and receives the dead. As the wife of Maoli, she protects cattle from disease and danger. Alternate form: Hundi. [Leach 1992]

Caksusi

India

Sky and Heavens; Goodness; Immortality; Water; Magic; Weather; Fishing and Water Animals

One of the *Apsarases.* [Durdin-Robertson 1976]

Camdhen   See *Kamadhenu.*

Camunda

India

Mother and Guardian; Goodness; Ugliness; Creator of Life; Love and Sexuality

"Destroyer of Demons." A deity of non-Aryan origin, she is one of the forms of *Durga* (a *Nayika*), one of the *Saptamatrakas* and a form of *Kali.* Also called *Pretasana.*

Kali sprang from the forehead of Ambika to destroy the asuras Candala and Munda. After destroying them, Kali was given the name Camunda. As Camunda she reveals herself as Kumari, a scrawny, frightening old woman, with a robe of elephant's hide and a necklace of corpses.

One of the *Saptamatrakas.* See also *Ambika, Narasimhi,* and *Navadurgas.* Alternate forms: Camundi, Candi, Kaumari, Kumari. [Danielou 1964; Stutley and Stutley 1984]

Camundi   See *Camunda* and *Candi.*

Cana Aulola
India
Fishing and Water Animals
"Mother Fresh-water Shrimp." Wife of Puluga. She had many daughters but only one son, Pijcor. Andaman Islands. Alternate form: Cana Palak. [Leach 1992]

Cana Palak
India
Fishing and Water Animals
"Mother Eel." Andaman Islands. Alternate form: Cana Aulola [Leach 1992]

Cancala   "The Fickle One." See *Lakshmi* and *Lola*.

Canda
India
Love and Sexuality; Evil
"Wrathful." One of the *Nayikas*. See also *Candi* and *Durga*. [Monaghan 1981; Stutley and Stutley 1984]

Candasya Naptyas, The
India
Household Affairs
"The Wrathful." Class of household demons. Daughters of *Candi*. [Stutley and Stutley 1984]

Candanayika
India
Love and Sexuality
One of the *Nayikas*. See also *Durga*. [Stutley and Stutley 1984]

Candavati
India
Love and Sexuality
One of the *Nayikas*. [Stutley and Stutley 1984]

Candi
India
Unhappiness; Moon and Night; Mother and Guardian; Love and Sexuality
"Wrathful." A fierce form of *Durga* in which she destroyed the asura Mahisa. One of the *Nayikas* and mother of the *Candasya Naptyas*. Said to also be a moon goddess. In Mysore she is called *Camundi* and is a tutelary deity. Equivalent to *Kali* and the non-Aryan autochthonous goddesses. Alternate forms: Canda, Candika, Chandi, Parvati. [Monaghan 1981; Stutley and Stutley 1984]

Candika   See *Candi*.

Candogra
India
Love and Sexuality
One of the *Nayikas*. See also *Durga*. [Stutley and Stutley 1984]

Caraki
India
Evil
Hindu demon who is propitiated with meat and ghee. [Stutley and Stutley 1984]

Carvi   "Splendor." See *Bhadrā*.

Chakrisvari
India
Weather; Earth and Nature; Evil; Goodness

One of the *Yakshini*. At Palitana she guards the entrance to a Jain temple with her sixteen arms. [Durdin-Robertson 1976]

Chala
India
Luck
"To Move, Sway, Tremble, or Quiver." Goddess of fortune. [Durdin-Robertson 1976]

Challalamma
India
Agriculture
Masulipatam village goddess worshiped in Telugu who watches over the buttermilk. [Leach 1992]

Chamariya
India
Destroyer of Life
Smallpox goddess, oldest and most malignant sister of *Sitala*. [Leach 1992]

Chamconda Mata
India, *Bheel*
Agriculture
Agricultural deity who presides over the harvest. [Leach 1992]

Chamunda   See *Durga*.

Chamundi
India
Mother and Guardian
Hindu deity of protection. [Jobes 1962]

Chandi
India
Hunting and Wild Animals; War
Deity appearing in different forms who presides over hunting and war. Bachelors are the only ones allowed to make offerings to her. Alternate forms: Candi and Devi. [Leach 1992; Monaghan 1981]

Chandi Mata
India
Moon and Night; Family and Tribes
Moon deity. Her tattooing symbol can only be worn after marriage when the hair is parted. If the husband dies, hair parting must end. [Leach 1992]

Chandika   See *Devi*.

Chandra
India
Wealth; Order; Mother and Guardian; Goodness; Health and Healing; Weather
One of the *Vasus*. [Sykes 1968]

Chandragupta
India
Mother and Guardian
Hindu mother.
⚥ *Chandragupta protected her son from his father's murderer by hiding him in a vase. She left him at the gate of a cattle pen, where a bull named Chando guarded him.* [Jobes 1962]

Chapala
India
Luck
A fickle deity of fortune. [Durdin-Robertson 1976]

Charani Devi
India
Arts
  Deity of the bards worshiped in Rajasthtan. [Leach 1992]

Chaurashi Devi
India
Fishing and Water Animals
  Fishing deity of the Kewat caste, who keeps boats from sinking, worshiped in the Central Provinces. [Leach 1992]

Chausath Joginis   See *Chausathi Yoginis.*

Chausathi
India
Unknown
  Goddess for whom a stepped passageway, leading to the Ganges at Benares (Varanasi), is named. She also has a temple nearby. [Durdin-Robertson 1976]

Chausathi Yoginis, The
India, *Jahoti*
Evil
  Sixty-four demons who are adept at yoga. There are at least two existing ancient temples dedicated to them in Khajuraho and one each in Ranipur Jharial, south of Sambhalpus, and in Bheraghat. See also *Yogini.* Alternate form: Chausath Joginis. [Durdin-Robertson 1976]

Chauturopayini
India
Creator of Life
  Fertility deity. She is portrayed with four arms, with her lower right hand in a giving gesture and her lower left hand holding a vessel. [Durdin-Robertson 1976]

Chaya
India
Family and Tribes
  "Shadow." The dark form of *Saranyu.* See also *Chhaya* and *Samgna.*
  ⛎ *Saranyu created Chaya as her identical form when she left Vivasvant. Chaya became the mother of Mamu, the ancestor of all people.*
  Alternate form: Khaya. [Jobes 1962; Leach 1992; Stutley and Stutley 1984]

Chhatmata
India, *Oraon*
Sun and Day
  "Shade." Sun deity. The counterpart and consort of the male sun god. [Leach 1992]

Chhaya
India
Sun and Day
  "Shadow." Her body is composed of etheric substance from which a "double" is formed. Said to be the mother of Saturn and Visti. Similar to *Lilith,* Near East, and *Nephele,* Greek and Roman Empires. See also *Chaya.*
  ⛎ *Chhaya was a sister and handmaid of Sanja and took her place when Sanja left the sun god, Surya.*
         Alternate form: Khaya. [Durdin-Robertson 1976; Leach 1992]

Chhotimai
India
Destroyer of Life

Goddess of disease who causes "small poxes" while *Mahamai* causes "large poxes." Sisters of *Sitala.* [Preston 1982]

Chigrinad
India, *Oraon, Kurukh*
Household Affairs; Ceremonies; Health and Healing; Luck
  Household deity. Daughter of the household god, Barnda. Sacrifices are made to Chigrinad to prevent illness and misfortune. [Leach 1992]

Chilkin Piri
India, *Baiga*
Destroyer of Life
  Disease deity who causes stomach pains. [Leach 1992]

Chingan Mata
India, *Baiga*
Destroyer of Life
  Disease goddess who causes rheumatism. [Leach 1992]

Chinnamasta
India
Ceremonies; Destroyer of Life
  "Beheaded." A Buddhist deity of ritual sacrifice who is also worshiped by the Hindus. The fifth *Mahavidya* who represents the end of life at the beheading of a sacrificial victim. She is portrayed headless, holding the head in her hand, the mouth open to receive the blood spurting from her neck. Similar to Tantric *Vajrayogini.* Alternate forms: Chinnamastaka, Durga, Tara, Viaratri, Vidya. [Leach 1992; Lurker 1984; Stutley and Stutley 1984]

Chinnamastaka   See *Chinnamasta*

Chinnintamma
India
Household Affairs
  Household deity. [Monaghan 1990]

Chit
India
Justice; Intelligence and Creativity
  Deity of intellect, the "Voice of Conscience." In Tibet (the Himalaya) she "appears to be one of the agents leading to earthly incarnation." See also *Chitti.* Alternate form: Chiti. [Durdin-Robertson 1976]

Chitarhai Devi
India
Wealth
  "The Goddess of Rags" worshiped in the Central Provinces. She is offered bits of old rags in hopes that she will replace them with new cloth. [Redfield 1931]

Chiti   See *Chit.*

Chitkuar Devi
India, *Khond*
Agriculture; Ceremonies
  Grain goddess who presides over the threshing floor. Chicken and pigs are sacrificed to her. [Leach 1992]

Chitti
India
Unknown
  "A Voice with Mystic Life." Identified with *Guanyin,* China-Mongolia. See also *Chit.* [Durdin-Robertson 1976]

Chola Pacho
India, *Oraon*
Earth and Nature; Weather
  Deity of the sacred grove. Worshiped in the Central Provinces, she provides the rain to produce good crops. [Leach 1992]

Choorail
India
Immortality; Mother and Guardian
  Moslem ghost of a pregnant woman. See also *Churalin, Churel,* and *Cudel.* [Bonnerjea 1927]

Chowa
India, *Pulaya*
Health and Healing
  Health goddess. She is invoked by conjurers to help drive out the evil spirits that cause illness. [Leach 1992]

Chunda
India
Happiness
  Buddhist deity of happiness. [Leach 1992]

Chupunika
India
Stars and Planets; Mother and Guardian
  One of the *Krittikas.* [Durdin-Robertson 1976]

Churalin
India
Destroyer of Life; Evil; Immortality; Mother and Guardian
  Hindu monster. See also *Choorail, Churel,* and *Cudel.* Equivalent to *Kishijolen,* Far East, and *Lilith,* Near East.
  Churalin is the repository for the souls of all those who die in childbirth. She wanders around looking for and killing infants. [Monaghan 1981]

Churel
India, *Oraon*
Evil; Beauty; Immortality; Mother and Guardian
  Hindu demon of Bengal. The Oraon say she is beautiful, dresses in white, and hovers around gravestones. In Deccan, she is the ghost of a woman who died in childbirth and was not cremated. In either case, her feet are inverted with the heels in front and toes behind. See also *Choorail, Churalin,* and *Cudel.* [Bonnerjea 1927; Leach 1972; Redfield 1931]

Churelin Mata
India, *Baiga*
Destroyer of Life
  Disease deity who causes impotency in young men. [Leach 1992]

Cosmic Waters, The
India
Sun and Day; Weather
  "Mothers of the Sun." They are said to low like cattle and let down the rain. [Durdin-Robertson 1976]

Cotton Mother
India
Agriculture
  Agricultural deity. Worshiped in Punjab, where her followers make a representation of her out of the most beautiful cotton plant. [Eliade 1987]

Cudel
India
Evil; Mother and Guardian

Hindu demon. A woman who dies in childbirth and is purified by cremation. See also *Churel, Churalin,* and *Choorail.* [Stutley and Stutley 1984]

Cunda
India
Unknown
  Deity of the Buddhist pantheon, a Bodhisatva. Sometimes called the mother of Buddha, she has a pleasant appearance, which contrasts with some of her emblems which are threatening. Her emblems are the amrta vase, sword, rosary, lotus, alms bowl, and book. She is portrayed with four or sixteen arms and her color is red. Similar to *Kakini, Kurukulla.* Equivalent to *Jun Tei Kwan-non,* Far East. See also *Cunda,* Southeast Asia. Alternate forms: Cunti, Kunda. [Durdin-Robertson 1976; Getty 1962; Jobes 1962]

Cunti See *Cunda.*

Dadju
India
Hunting and Wild Animals
  Goddess of good hunting worshiped in the Central Provinces by the Beria, a caste of gypsies and thieves. [Leach 1992]

Daginis, The See *The Dakinis.*

Daini
Bangladesh
Magic
  A Bengal witch who is similar or equivalent to a *Dakini.* [Bonnerjea 1927]

Daintary
India
Large Size
  A giant. Daughter of the race of giants and wife of the first Brahman. [Durdin-Robertson 1976]

Daityas, The
India
Large Size; Water
  Giants or titans. Daughters of *Diti* who live in Pātāla and are generally opposed to the gods. Pātāla is the name for seven nether regions collectively, each being under the ocean (some suggest that it includes South America) and 10,000 leagues in depth and ruled by a separate regent. Each region has soil of a different color, and Pātāla, as a separate region, has gold soil and is said to be a place of splendor. The Daityas wear jewels the size of boulders. There are also male Daityas. See also *Danavis.* [Durdin-Robertson 1976; Stutley and Stutley 1984]

Daiviprakriti
India
Primordial Being
  "Primordial Light." Associated with the *Shaktis* and similar to Hebrew *Shekinah.* [Durdin-Robertson 1976]

Dakini
India
Evil
  A demon. One of six divinities who govern the bodily substances. The others are *Hakini, Kakini, Lakini, Rakini,* and *Shakini.* They correspond to the *Krittika(s).* In one of her incarnations, Dakini is called *Mandarava.* [Durdin-Robertson 1976; Stutley and Stutley 1984]

Dakinis, The
India
Destroyer of Life; Evil; Magic; Mother and Guardian; Unhappiness

Hindu fiends. Attendants of *Kali* who delight in blood and eating flesh. In Tibet, the Himalaya, they are regarded as mother goddesses who preside over occult powers and grant insights to their followers. Buddhist Dakinis wander in the air, conferring supernatural powers on those they favor. They are also prone to anger. One of the more important Buddhist Dakinis is *Vajravarahi*. Others who are considered Dakinis are *Dakini, Makaravaktra, Mandarava,* and *Sarvabuddhadakini*. See also *Buddhadakini, Padmadakini,* and *Shakinis*. Alternate forms: Asrapas, Daginis, Daini, Khahdomas, Makaravaktra. [Danielou 1964; Durdin-Robertson 1976; Jobes 1962; Monaghan 1981; Stutley and Stutley 1984]

Dakshina
India
Mother and Guardian; Creator of Life; Domesticated Animals

"The Cow." Personification of the "gift" given as a sacrifice. She is invoked for protection from harm. Identified with the Cosmic Cow as the giver of all life. [Durdin-Robertson 1976; Stutley and Stutley 1984]

Daksinakalika   See *Durga*.

Damayanti
India, *Rajput*
Justice; Love and Sexuality; Ceremonies

Queen of Nishada. Daughter of *Vaidarbhiganani*, wife of Nala, mother of Indrasena and Indrasena, a son and a daughter.

☿ *Damayanti and Nala lived a week's journey apart, but each had heard many reports of praise about the other. A magical swan appeared to Nala and said he would fly to Damayanti and praise him to her. The swan did as he promised and Damayanti sent the swan on an identical return mission. In this way Damayanti and Nala fell in love.*

Among the Rajput (a matriarchal tribe), women choose their own husbands at a ceremony called the Svayamvara.

☿ *Nala was on his way to Damayanti's Svayamvara when three gods stopped him and demanded that he inform Damayanti that she was to choose one of them for her husband. Nala did as he was told and on the day of the Svayamvara there appeared four men all looking exactly like Nala. Damayanti was not fooled, as she saw that only one cast a shadow and moved his eyes. She placed the garland around the real Nala's neck and they were married.* [Durdin-Robertson 1976; Jobes 1962; Stutley and Stutley 1984]

Danavis, The
India
Evil; Large Size; Metals and Minerals; Water

Giant demons. Daughters of *Danu* and sisters of the Danavas. Like the *Daityas*, they are said to wear jewels the size of boulders and to live in the depths of the ocean. See also *Kalaka*. [Durdin-Robertson 1976]

Dantesvari   "The Goddess with Teeth." See *Mata*.

Danu
India
Order

"Restraint." Daughter of *Diti* and mother of demons, the *Danavis* (female) and the Danavas (male). [Durdin-Robertson 1976; Stutley and Stutley 1984]

Danus, The
India
Evil
Demons. [Durdin-Robertson 1976]

Daridra   "Poor," "Deprived." See *Dhumavati*. See also *The Mahavidyas*.

Darmit
India, *Lepcha*
Justice
Goddess of morality who rewards and punishes her followers in Sikkim. [Leach 1992]

Dasabhuja   Destroyer of Sumbha's army. See *Durga*.

Dasara
India
Water
Ganges River deity. [Leach 1992]

Davata
India
Fire
Goddess of fire. [Monaghan 1981]

Daya
India
Goodness
"Sympathy and Compassion." Daughter of Daksha. [Stutley and Stutley 1984]

Dayan
India, *Oraon*
Magic; Evil; Creator of Life; Destroyer of Life

A witch who knows the spell for destroying and creating life. She frequents burial grounds or cremation sites, drinking blood and giving children the evil eye.

☿ *If a woman of the tribe desires the power of a Dayan she can go into a cave dressed in a girdle made of twigs taken from a broken broom. Here she studies the spells for a year and when she conducts a seance, she drops a stone in a hole. If the hole is completely filled at the end of the year, she can destroy and create life; if not, she can only destroy life.* [Leach 1972]

De Develski   See *Amari De*.

Debee   See *Devi*.

Delight Goddess, The
India
Charisma; Magic

One of the deities of temptation who is skilled in the magical arts of desire. See also *Lust Goddess, Thirst Goddess*.

☿ *The three sisters of temptation visited a Gautama reproaching him for forsaking his duty to his wife, family, and home.* [Durdin-Robertson 1976]

Desahai Devi
India
Directions

Dravidian deity of directions. She presides over the "four quarters of the hamlet." [Leach 1992]

Deshtri
India
Education and Knowledge
"The Instructress." [Durdin-Robertson 1976]

Desini   See *Durga*.

Deva Kanyakas   "Celestial Maidens." See also *Devis.* Alternate form: Deva-Kanyas.

Deva Kanyas   See *Deva Kanyakas.*

Devabhuti   "Flowing from Heaven." See *Ganga.*

Devaki
India
Education and Knowledge; Mother and Guardian
   "Mother of Wisdom." Daughter of Devaka, wife of Vasudeva, mother of Krishna. Alternate forms: Deywuckee, Dhriti, Niti, Samnati.

⚨ Kansa, the king of Mathura, had been told that he would one day be killed by one of Devaki's sons. He killed her first six sons, but her seventh son was transferred to the womb of Rohini before his birth, keeping him from being killed. The eighth son, Krishna, arranged that when he was born he would be replaced by a newly born girl. The prediction was fulfilled by Krishna who restored King Kansa's father to the throne. [Durdin-Robertson 1976; Stutley and Stutley 1984]

Devala
India
Arts
   "Music." Hindu deity. [Bonnerjea 1927]

Devananda
India
Happiness
   "She of Divine Joy." Wife of Rishabhadatta, mother of Vardhamana (Mahavira). See also *Trisala.* [Durdin-Robertson 1976]

Devanganas, The   "Celestial Women." See *Devis.*

Devasena
India
Unknown
   "Divine Array." According to some, one of the *Matris.* Devasena is also another name for *Sena, Kaumari* and *Jayanti.* [Jobes 1962; Stutley and Stutley 1984]

Devasuni   "The Wind." See *Sarama.*

Devatas, The
India
Household Affairs; Earth and Nature
   Household and sylvan (genii of fountains and trees) deities associated with the earth. Among the classes of Devatas are *Adhidevatas, Digdevatas, Ghihadevatas, Mangadevatas, Mantradevatas, Purvadevatas, Rajyadidevatas, Rakshodhidevatas, Sakunadevatas, Shastradevatas, Sthalidevatas, Ushodevatas, Vanadevatas,* and *Vrikdevatas.* There are also male Devatas. [Durdin-Robertson 1976; Jobes 1962; Stutley and Stutley 1984]

Devayani
India
Immortality; Heaven and Hell
   Chthonic deity who knows how to raise the dead. [Monaghan 1990]

Devayoshas, The   "Divine Women." See *Devis.*

Devee   See *Devi.*

Devi
India, *Bhmata, Rajput*
Supreme Being; Mother and Guardian; War; Goodness; Evil; Life/Death Cycle; Creator of Life; Primordial Being
   Post-Vedic goddess, *Shakti* of Shiva, who has a mild and a fierce form. In her mild form, she is *Ambika, Bhagavati, Gauri, Haimavati, Kanya, Parvati, Sati, Uma.* In her fierce form, she is *Bhairavi, Chandi, Chandika, Durga, Kali, Kamaksi,* and *Syama.* She is also called *Bhuyian, Haimavati, Ida,* and *Malini.* She is the absolute power of the universe—creating, maintaining, and destroying. Also the tutelary goddess of the Bhmata and the war goddess of the Rajput who protects the virtue of women. Originally *devi* was a general term for a goddess. See also *Bhumidevi, Devis, Khermata, Mahadevi, Manasa* (this region), *Agusan Devi,* Southeast Asia, and *Lha-mo,* the Himalaya. Alternate forms: Devee, Debee. [Durdin-Robertson 1976; Jobes 1962; Leach 1992; Monaghan 1981; Senior 1985; Stone 1979; Stutley and Stutley 1984]

Devikas, The   See *Devis.*

Devis, The
India
Sky and Heavens; Immortality
   Celestial females or angelic beings. Similar to the *Apsarases.* Frequently referred to as wives of the gods or as parts of religious worship personified as goddesses, such as *Bharati, Hotra,* and *Ida. Amritika, Malini,* and *Mandaramala* are also called Devis. They are also referred to as nature spirits, often manifested in trees. See also *Devi.* Alternate forms: Devikas, Deva-Kanyakas, Devanganas, Devatas, Devayoshas, and the Vidyadevis. [Durdin-Robertson 1976; Stutley and Stutley 1984]

Dewel
Sri Lanka
Evil
   Demon. She is portrayed as a heavyset woman wearing a red jacket and an Elizabethan frill around her neck. [Durdin-Robertson 1976]

Deywuckee   See *Devaki.*

Dhahu Dhukan
India, *Baiga*
Destroyer of Life
   Disease goddess who "causes sudden pains in the chest." [Leach 1992]

Dhanada
India
Weather
   Deity of wealth. Associated with Kubera. Alternate form: Dhanesvari. [Pal 1981]

Dhanesvari   "Divinity of Wealth." See *Sarasvati.*

Dhara
India
Wealth; Order; Mother and Guardian; Goodness; Health and Healing; Weather
   One of the *Vasus.* [Sykes 1968]

Dharani
India
Earth and Nature; Wealth
   Earth deity associated with fertility, prosperity, and abundance. See also *Lakshmi.* [Danielou 1964; Stutley and Stutley 1984]

Dharni Deota
India, *Khond*
Unknown
   Formerly a goddess who was called *Tari Pennu.* Now the
name of a male deity. [Leach 1992]

Dharni Pinnu
India, *Khond, Gadba*
Earth and Nature; Health and Healing; Mother and Guardian
   Earth mother of the Khond and goddess of health for the
Gadba of the Central Provinces. [Leach 1992]

Dharti   See *Dharti Mata.*

Dharti Mai   See *Dharti Mata* and *Bhudevi.*

Dharti Mata
India
Mother and Guardian; Agriculture; Ceremonies
   "Mother Who Supports." Hindu earth goddess who
presides over human, animal, and vegetable life. She is
worshiped throughout the agricultural season with the
sacrifice of goats, pigs, and fowl. As a village goddess, her
altar is a pile of stones or a pot. Alternate forms: Bhudevi,
Dharti, Dharti Mai. [Jobes 1962; Leach 1972; Leach 1992]

Dhisana
India
Wealth; Fire; Sun and Day; Moon and Night; Stars and
Planets; Sciences; Mother and Guardian
   Vedic goddess of abundance. One of the *Gnas.* Closely
associated with the ritual drink, soma. In the plural, Dhisanas
are divine guardians associated with the sacred fire, days and
nights, stars, and the sciences. They are invoked to prevent
harm and to give their followers strength. Identified with *Vac.*
[Jobes 1962; Leach 1992; Stutley and Stutley 1984]

Dhriti
India
Order
   "Steadfast," "Resolute." Deity of fortitude. Daughter of
Daksha and one of the wives of Dharma. One of the *Matris.*
Associated with Krishna. May also be an alternate form for
Devaki. Alternate form: Dhrti. [Durdin-Robertson 1976;
Leach 1992; Stutley and Stutley 1984]

Dhrtarastri
India
Wild Birds
   Hindu deity of ducks. Daughter of *Tamra.* [Stutley and
Stutley 1984]

Dhrti   See *Dhriti.*

Dhruva
India
Wealth; Order; Mother and Guardian; Goodness; Health and
Healing; Weather
   One of the *Vasus.* [Sykes 1968]

Dhumavati
India
Fire; Ugliness; Weather; Destroyer of Life
   "The Smoky One." One of the wives of Yama, ruler of the
dead. Dhumavati, the seventh *Mahavidya,* is the personification
of the final stage of destruction of the universe by fire, when
only the smoke remains. She is invoked to injure enemies.
Portrayed as an ugly crone carrying a winnowing basket, she
is associated with the rainy season. Alternate form: Daridra,
Vidhava. [Leach 1992; Stutley and Stutley 1984]

Dhumorna
India
Ceremonies
   "Shroud of Smoke." Personification of the smoke of the
funeral pyre. One of the wives of Yama, the ruler of the dead.
[Stutley and Stutley 1984]

Dhupa
India
Mother and Guardian
   "Bearer of the Incense." Buddhist mother goddess. She
appears on the third day of the Bardo, Buddhist region of
after-death, for transition before rebirth. Her color is the same
as the earth, yellow. Her Tibetan name is *bDug-spös-
ma,* the Himalaya. Alternate form: Dhupema. [Durdin-
Robertson 1976; Jobes 1962; Leach 1992]

Dhupema   See *Dhupa.*

Diarrhoea
India, *Gypsy*
Destroyer of Life
   Deity of illness. [Leach 1992]

Digdevatas
India
Household Affairs; Earth and Nature
   A class of *Devatas.* Similar to the *Dik-kanya.* [Durdin-
Robertson 1976]

Dik-kanya
India
Sky and Heavens
   Personification of the feminine quarter of the sky. Similar
to the *Digdevatas.* [Durdin-Robertson 1976]

Dikkumari, The
India
Directions
   Deities of direction. There are fifty-six who assist in
important functions. [Jobes 1962]

Dilli Polasi
India
Household Affairs
   Household deity and village goddess worshiped in the
Nellore district in Andhra Pradesh. [Leach 1992]

Dishai Devi
India, *Gadaria*
Domesticated Animals
   She presides over the sheep pen and may be personified as
a sheep. Worshiped in the Central Provinces. [Leach 1992]

Dispirir Mata
India, *Baiga*
Destroyer of Life
   Syphilis deity worshiped in central India. [Leach 1992]

Diti
India
Earth and Nature; Family and Tribes; Selflessness
   "Limited" or "Bounded." Opposite of *Aditi.* Vedic goddess
of earthly phenomena, a shadowy figure who is not
worshiped. Wife of Kashyapa. Said to be the mother of two
races of humanity—the giant *Daityas* who live in Patala (the
nether regions) on the bottom of the ocean and who are often
hostile toward the gods, and the Maruts (male storm spirits).
She may also be the mother of the *Asuris.* Also mother of
Danu.

Diti wanted Indra killed and asked her husband to give her a son who could carry out her wish. Kashyapa agreed to do so if Diti remained physically and mentally chaste and carried the fetus for one hundred years. One night, just before the baby was to be born, Diti retired without performing the necessary ablution of washing her feet. Indra took this opportunity to attack Diti and divided the fetus into seven parts. When the child cried, he divided the seven parts into seven again, and from these divisions came the Maruts, a class of the Hindu deities. [Danielou 1964; Durdin-Robertson 1976; Monaghan 1981; Stutley and Stutley 1984]

Divo Duhita
India
Unknown
"Daughter of Heaven." Vedic deity. [Eliade 1987]

Diwali
India, *Bhil*
Happiness; Ceremonies
Goddess of merriment who presides over singing and festivals. Wife of Nandervo and sister of *Holi.* She is worshiped in Madhya Pradesh. [Leach 1992]

Doini
India, *Adi*
Sun and Day
Sun goddess. Daughter of *Sitking Kedding* and Peddo Dodum, sister of Polo, the moon. As a dual deity, Doini Polo, they are the guardians of truth and law. [Leach 1992]

Doljang
India
Unknown
Hindu goddess. She is said to have stigmata on her hands and feet like those of Jesus and Francis of Assisi. [Jobes 1962]

Dolma   See *Tara.*

Dongar Dai
India
Earth and Nature
Nature deity who presides over the forests and hills of Orissa. [Leach 1992]

Donyi
India, *Kadeng, Dafla, Gallong*
Sun and Day
Sun goddess worshiped in Assam. Said to be the second most powerful deity of these tribes. Among the Gallongs, she forms a dual deity with her brother the moon, Doini Polo, and their names are used in the taking of sacred oaths. [Leach 1992]

Doorga   See *Parvati* and *Durga.*

Draupadi
India
Ceremonies; Courage
Deity said to have been born from the sacrificial fire and considered an incarnation of *Sri.* She is one of the main heroes of the *Mahabharta,* an Indian epic. Alternate form: Krisna. [Durdin-Robertson 1976; Monaghan 1981; Stutley and Stutley 1984]

Druh
India
Weather
"Hostile." A drought demon, female or male, opposed to Indra. [Stutley and Stutley 1984]

Duhkharni Mai
India, *Dom*
Destroyer of Life
Deity of illness, of "eruptive diseases." A sister of *Sitala.* [Leach 1992]

Dula
India
Stars and Planets; Mother and Guardian
One of the *Krittikas.* [Leach 1992]

Dundubhi   "The Drum." See *Manthara.*

Durga
India
Justice; Evil; Earth and Nature; Fire; Life/Death Cycle; War; Intelligence and Creativity; Love and Sexuality
"Avenger," "Unapproachable." A composite goddess, Durga embodies a number of local Hindu divinities and demons associated with mountains, vegetation, and fire, as well as being a manifestation of *Devi.* Durga represents the end of all things. Known primarily as a bloodthirsty warrior, she symbolizes both the power of the struggle against evil and that of the intellectual sphere. Those seeking to understand her are believed to be engaging in the most powerful intellectual exploration possible. Durga is said to have many forms, each of which is given a different name. Alternate forms: Amba, Ambika, Annapurna, Aparajita, Bhadra, Bhadrakali, Bhattarika, Bhima, Brahmani, Chamunda, Daksinakalika, Dasabhuja, Desini, Doorga, Durja, Ekanamsa, Gautami, Hindi, Hindira, Iravati, Isana, Jagaddhatri, Jagadgaur, Jaganmatr, Jatavedasi, Kali, Kali Mata, Kalika, Kalilika, Kamakhya, Kamaksi, Kapalini, Karali, Karttiki, Kesini, Kirati, Kokamukha, Kottavei, Ksama, Laksmi, Lakshmi Mahisasuramardin, Madira, Mahadevi, Mahamaya, Mahasveta, Mahesvari, Mahisasuramardini, Mari, Muktakesi, Navadurgas, Nayikas, Parvati, Puramdhi, Raktadantika, Revati, Rudrani, Sasti, Shakinis, Shaktis, Simhavahini, Sokarahita, Sri, Syama, Tara, Tripurasundari, Uma, Vijaya, Vindhyavasini, Yoganidra, Yogini. Equivalent to *Jun-tei Kwan-non,* Far East. See also *Chalonarang,* Southeast Asia. [Cooper 1876; Jobes 1962; Monaghan 1981; Neumann 1972; Stutley and Stutley 1984]

Durga Mata
India, *Kamar*
Destroyer of Life
Smallpox goddess worshiped in the Central Provinces. See also *Durga.* [Leach 1992]

Durgamma
India
Reptiles; Mother and Guardian
Bengal snake goddess worshiped on the Telangana Plateau of Andhra Pradesh. Her shrine is built over a snake-stone close to a nim tree. When worshiped in homes, she is represented by a silver cobra's head. Mothers put out offerings of milk to encourage her to protect their children. In Bengal she is called *Manasa.* [Leach 1992; Stutley and Stutley 1984]

Durgapunja   See *Kali.*

Durja   See *Parvati* and *Durga.*

Durpatta Mata
India, *Baiga*
Destroyer of Life
Goddess of disease. She prevents delivery, causing the death of the fetus and mother. [Leach 1992]

Dyaush-pitir
India
Sun and Day
   Early sun goddess who later became an Aryan sky father.
[Sykes 1968]

Dyava-matar   "Earth Mother." See *Prithivi.*

Dyava-Prthivi
India
Earth and Nature; Sky and Heavens; Creator of Life
   "Earth and Sky." A combined Hindu deity who is said to
be the primeval parent(s). See also *Prithvi.* [Leach 1992;
Stutley and Stutley 1984]

Dyu
India
Sky and Heavens; Wealth; Order; Mother and Guardian;
Goodness; Health and Healing; Weather
   "Heaven." One of the *Vasus.* [Sykes 1968]

Dzurawu
India, *Angami Nagas*
Hunting and Wild Animals
   Deity of wild animals worshiped in Assam. Wife of
Tsukho, god of wild animals and hunting. [Leach 1992]

Earth Goddess
India, *Khond*
Creator of Life
   Fertility deity of one of the most ancient Indian tribes.
[Durdin-Robertson 1976]

Earth Mother of Hrusso
India
Earth and Nature; Sky and Heavens; Creator of Life
   Goddess of the earth.
   In the beginning there were two great eggs. The eggs
   collided and broke open, discharging Earth and Sky. Earth
   was too big for Sky to hold, so he asked her to make herself
smaller. She became pliable and started shrinking, forming the
mountains and valleys. Then Sky was able to make love to her and
as a result, all the plants and living creatures were created.
[Farmer 1978]

Egattala
India
Mother and Guardian
   Tutelary deity of Madras, Tamil Nadu. Probably non-Aryan.
[Stutley and Stutley 1984]

Ekajata
India
Happiness; Supreme Being; Luck
   Buddhist Blue *Tara* of the Mahayana pantheon. A fierce
deity, the most powerful of all of the goddesses. Just listening
to her mantra being spoken removes all obstacles, bringing
good fortune and religious pleasure. She is portrayed with
one head, three eyes, and an angry face. Her emblems are the
staff, skull cup, conch shell, and ornaments. In Tibet she is
called *Ral-gcig-ma* and identified with *Dur-khrod-lha-mo,*
the Himalaya. Alternate forms: Ugratara, Vidyujjvalakarali,
Ekajati. [Getty 1962; Jobes 1962; Lurker 1984]

Ekajati   See *Ekajata.*

Ekanamsa   "The Single Portionless One," "The New
Moon." See *Durga.*

Ekaparna
India
Unknown
   One of the two sisters of *Aparna* (see for story). [Stutley
and Stutley 1984]

Ekapatala
India
Unknown
   One of the two sisters of *Aparna* (see for story). [Stutley
and Stutley 1984]

Ekash-Taka
India
Mother and Guardian
   Mother goddess whose son is the moon god. [Monaghan
1990]

Ekastaka
India
Time; Mother and Guardian; Health and Healing
   "The Eighth Day after the Full Moon." Invoked to give
healthy children. See also *Shakti.* [Stutley and Stutley 1984]

Elamadichi
India
Health and Healing; Mother and Guardian
   Village goddess of health worshiped in the Trichinopoly
(Tiruchirapalli) district, Madras, Tamil Nadu. She ends
sickness and relieves suffering. She also grants children.
[Leach 1992]

Ellamma
India, *Donga Dasari, Tamil*
Health and Healing; Luck; Ceremonies
   Southern goddess of good health and fortune. Sacrifices
are made to her by the Donga Dasari before their thieving
expeditions. To the Tamil and Delugu Paraiyan people, she is
the goddess of the boundary. As a village deity of the
Talagana and of Vizagapatam, Ellamma is invoked to prevent
illness, and to cure boils and eye problems. [Leach 1992]

Empusae   See *Ghuls.*

Eternal Mother
India
Primordial Being
   She "who gives birth to the form that combines all forms."
Her bosom sends out a "kind of cosmic electricity." [Durdin-
Robertson 1976]

Gajalakshmi   See *Lakshmi.*

Galadevi
India, *Baiga*
Destroyer of Life
   Disease goddess who causes mumps. [Leach 1992]

Gan Gaur
India
Life/Death Cycle
   Goddess of life who is worshiped in the village of
Nimkhera, Madhya Pradesh. She is invoked by wives to
grant their husbands long lives. [Leach 1992]

Ganapatihrdaya
India
Demi-animals; Ceremonies; Creator of Life; Primordial Being

Buddhist Tantric goddess. She is the personification of a mantra. She has the head of an elephant and is probably the **Shakti** of Ganesha. [Stutley and Stutley 1984]

Gandha   "She Spraying Perfume." See **Dri-chha-ma,** The Himalaya.

Gandhari
India
Justice; Magic; Destroyer of Life; Mother and Guardian
Queen of Kuru. Daughter of Saubala and wife of the blind Dhrtarastra. She is also said to be a Hindu goddess of smallpox. Alternate form: Gundhary.

Gandhari was rewarded by the seer Dvaipayana for her hospitality. He said he would grant her wish for one hundred sons. She became pregnant, but after two years she still had not delivered. When she struck her womb violently, a hard lump of flesh appeared. Dvaipayana sprinkled it with water and it divided into one hundred small pieces. These were placed in a hundred jars of ghee. When the lids were removed two years later, one hundred sons appeared. Gandhari also wished for a daughter, so an excess piece of flesh was put into another jar of ghee and Duhsala was born. [Durdin-Robertson 1976; Jobes 1962; Stutley and Stutley 1984]

Gandharvadatta
India
Domesticated Animals; Charisma; Water
"Giving." One of the **Gandharvis.** [Durdin-Robertson 1976]

Gandharvi
India
Domesticated Animals; Charisma; Water
One of the **Gandharvis.** Daughter of **Surabhi.** Ancestor of all horses, she is a seductive water nymph who inhabits the banks of rivers. [Leach 1992; Stutley and Stutley 1984]

Gandharvis
India
Demi-animals; Arts; Earth and Nature; Sky and Heavens
Celestial deities who are half-human, half-bird. They are skilled musicians—"angels of song"—who haunt the forests and mountains at twilight. They are often found in the heaven of Indra with the **Apsarases,** singing and playing their instruments. Equivalent to the **Tennin,** Far East. See also **Gandharvadatta, Gandharvi, Manthara.** [Durdin-Robertson 1976; Stutley and Stutley 1984]

Gandini
India
Domesticated Animals; Ceremonies
"Cow Daily." Hindu deity.

Gandini had been in her mother's womb for twelve years when she told her father to offer a cow each day to the Brahmas. After three more years, the time foretold by Gandini, she was born. She continued the daily presentation of a cow until she died. [Bonnerjea 1927; Stutley and Stutley 1984]

Ganesani
India
Creator of Life; Primordial Being
Shakti of Ganea. Also called **Aingini** and **Vinayika.** [Stutley and Stutley 1984]

Ganga
India
Water; Earth and Nature; Sky and Heavens; Heaven and Hell; Health and Healing; Happiness; Wealth; Creator of Life; Demi-animals

"The Swift Goer." Personification of the Ganges River. Daughter of **Mena** and Himavat, sister of **Uma** or **Parvati,** wife of all the celestial gods and the mortal Santanu. Ganga waters three worlds: the celestial realms from which she came, earth, and Patala (the nether regions, see **Daityas**). Ganga may have originally been a river spirit with whom other local river goddesses became identified. She has become the chief river deity of a vast area and is endowed with amazing traits. She bestows health, happiness, fertility, and material wealth. In southern India she is portrayed as a mermaid, and in Bengal she is depicted as a woman, colored white, who cleanses and purifies. Alternate forms: Abhraganga, Akasaganga, Bhagirathi, Devabhuti, Gung, Gunga, Kirati, Mandakini, Visnupadi.

Bhagiratha, a descendant of Sagara, propitiated Ganga to descend from heaven to purify the ashes of Sagara's sixty thousand sons so they could attain paradise. Ganga came down in great torrents and would have flooded the earth had not Shiva caught the waters in his matted hair. Ganga flowed to the sea and finally to Patala where she purified Sagara's sons. [Durdin-Robertson 1976; Leach 1992; Monaghan 1981; Stutley and Stutley 1984]

Ganga Devi
India, *Badaba*
Health and Healing; Domesticated Animals; Ceremonies
Goddess of life and good health for humans and cattle worshiped in southern India. Pigs, goats, and pigeons are sacrificed in her honor. Alternate form: Takurani. [Leach 1992]

Gangaji
Bangladesh, India
Water; Ceremonies
River deity to whom Patni boatmen make sacrifices in the state of Bengal. [Leach 1992]

Gangamma
India, *Telugu*
Health and Healing
Southern water deity who protects against smallpox. [Leach 1992]

Gangammal
India, *Paraiyan*
Destroyer of Life
Disease goddess of the south who presides over cholera. [Leach 1992]

Gaon Mataa   "Village Mother." See **Ujali.**

Gara Satamai
India, *Hos*
Evil; Ceremonies; Reptiles; Fishing and Water Animals
Malevolent deity worshiped on the Chhotanagpur Plateau in the state of Bihar. She must be propitiated when one dreams of "a snake, a crocodile, or a fish." [Leach 1992]

Garita
India
Wild Birds
Goddess of birds. Similar to **Simorgh,** Near East. [Durdin-Robertson 1976]

Gasain Era
India, *Santal*
Mother and Guardian; Earth and Nature
Guardian deity who is worshiped at the foot of the mowah tree. [Leach 1992]

Gau
India
Earth and Nature
   Name of an ancient earth goddess prior to *Prithivi*. [Leach 1992]

Gauri
India
Ceremonies; Water; Creator of Life; Weather; Wealth; Domesticated Animals; Family and Tribes
   "Yellow," "Brilliant," "Golden One." The fertilizing rain flows from her. She symbolizes the waters before creation and is considered the source of the world, the Cosmic Cow. A Hindu deity of abundance, she is worshiped with Ganesha at wedding ceremonies in the Central Provinces and is the patron deity with Eklinga in fertility ceremonies in Rajputana. The *Gauris* are a class of goddesses that includes *Ambika, Asapurna, Parvati, Rambha, Totala, Tripura,* and *Uma.* Their mother is *Sirsootee.* See also *Matris, Sri, Varunani.* Alternate forms: Devi, Gouri. [Jobes 1962; Leach 1992; Monaghan 1981; Stutley and Stutley 1984]

Gauris   See *Gauri.*

Gauri Sankara
India
Earth and Nature
   Goddess of Mt. Everest. [Monaghan 1981]

Gautami   See *Durga, Kripi,* and *Rakshasi.*

Gavariamma
India
Health and Healing; Large Size; Evil; Charisma; Beauty; Destroyer of Life
   Village deity worshiped to prevent illness by the people in the Vizagapatam district of Madras, Tamil Nadu. One of the *Rakshasis.* [Leach 1992]

Gayatri
India
Ceremonies; Wild Birds; Magic; Sky and Heavens
   "Morning Prayer."
   Gayatri was a Hindu eagle who stole the Soma (sacred drink) from heaven and brought it to earth. She was shot by the archer guarding the Soma and the nail of her left foot was cut off. It became a porcupine and the fat that dripped from the wound became a goat.
   Alternate form: Vac. [Danielou 1964; Durdin-Robertson 1976; Jobes 1962; Stutley and Stutley 1984]

Ghar Jenti
India
Luck; Household Affairs
   "Light of the House." Assam good fortune deity said to be manifest in the ticking noises that a house makes at night. The occupants also feel her passing in their dreams. [Monaghan 1990]

Ghatchindan
India, *Baiga*
Destroyer of Life
   Disease goddess of animals. [Leach 1992]

Ghihadevatas   See *Devatas.*

Ghoshinis   See *Ghosinis.*

Ghosinis
India
Evil; Disorder
   "Noisy Ones." Female attendants of Rudra. Said to be demons. Alternate form: Ghoshinis. [Durdin-Robertson 1976; Stutley and Stutley 1984]

Ghritachi   See *Ghrtaci.*

Ghrtaci
India
Family and Tribes; Love and Sexuality; Sky and Heavens; Goodness; Immortality; Water; Magic; Weather; Fishing and Water Animals
   "Abounding in Ghee." One of the Hindu *Apsarases* who is the mother of more than one hundred daughters including *Shrutavati.* She had love affairs with many and the offspring from her alliance with Vishvakarman were said to be the origin of the mixed castes. Alternate form: Ghritachi. [Bonnerjea 1927; Stutley and Stutley 1984]

Ghuls
India
Evil; Ugliness
   Monsters who assume many forms and have shrill cries. Alternate form: Empusae. [Durdin-Robertson 1976]

Ginoo moong
India, *Lepcha*
Unhappiness; Destroyer of Life
   Goddess of envy worshiped in the state of Sikkim. She kills the prosperous and those who are dissatisfied with their material wealth. [Leach 1992]

Girija   "Mountain-born." See *Parvati.*

Girl Twin of Mithuna
India
Stars and Planets
   Stellar deity. She is the female half of the constellation Mithuna (Gemini). [Durdin-Robertson 1976]

Gnas, The
India
Creator of Life; Love and Sexuality
   Possibly non-Aryan fertility deities. They are creative forces of enormous potency. Considered by some to be the consorts of gods. Among those considered to be Gnas are *Agnayi, Asvini, Bharati, Dhisana, Indrani, Rodasi, Sarasvati,* and *Varunani.* [Stutley and Stutley 1984]

Godavari
India
Water
   River deity. [Leach 1992]

Gomaj
India, *Gorku*
Moon and Night
   Moon goddess worshiped in the Berar region of Madhya Pradesh on the Deccan Plateau. Gomaj is also the male god of the sun and used as a general term for god. [Leach 1992]

Gonti
India
Weather
   Rain goddess of the Dravidians. Alternate form: Gontiyalamma. [Leach 1992]

Gontiyalamma   See *Gonti.*

Gopis, The
India
Domesticated Animals; Ceremonies; Creator of Life
  Herdswomen among whom Krishna lived as a youth.
They dance a circular dance, each holding Krishna's hand (he
multiplied himself so there was one of him between two of
the Gopi), probably to promote fertility. [Stutley and Stutley
1984]

Gopya
India
Earth and Nature
  Nymphs. [Woodcock 1953]

Gosae-era
India, *Santal*
Arts
  Goddess of music. [Leach 1992]

Gouri See *Gauri* and *Isani.*

Grahis, The
India
Evil; Destroyer of Life
  "Seizers." Malevolent spirits who cause death. They are
said to come from the "rajasa" essence of the goddesses
Ganga, Krittika, and *Uma.* [Danielou 1964; Stutley and
Stutley 1984]

Gramadevatas, The
India
Mother and Guardian; Ceremonies; Creator of Life; Fishing
and Water Animals
  Tutelary deities of villages. According to some authorities
they were worshiped in pre-Dravidian, archaic times. They
are associated with the water jar or pot (symbol of the
womb), indicating a connection with a fertility cult. In
southern India their shrines in small rural communities are
usually located near trees. Their icons are images of yoni (the
womb). Sacrifices of sheep, goats, and buffaloes are made in
their honor. They are also worshiped by fishermen and those
who make their living from lakes and rivers. See also *Bagala,
Kumbhamata,* and *Pidari.* [Stutley and Stutley 1984]

Grhadevi
India
Household Affairs; Magic
  Household deity. She can assume any form and is highly
venerated. Alternate form: Jara. [Stutley and Stutley 1984]

Grhalaksmi
India
Mother and Guardian; Household Affairs; Wealth;
Happiness; Health and Healing; Life/Death Cycle
  Guardian deity of new houses. She is invoked to give
happiness, wealth, children, health, and a long life. [Stutley
and Stutley 1984]

Grihadeva
India
Household Affairs
  Hindu household goddess. [Leach 1992]

Grilya Burhin
India, *Dhoba*
Earth and Nature; Life/Death Cycle
  Earth goddess.
  *Grilya Burhin "supports the middle of the world on her
  head. When her husband insists on lying with her, there is
  an earthquake."* [Leach 1992]

Grismadevi
India
Time; Demi-animals
  "Summer." Buddhist seasonal deity. The others are
Vasanta, Saraddevi, and *Hemantadevi.* Grismadevi's color is
red, her vahana (mount or throne) is a blue yak, and her
emblems are an axe and skull cup. She is usually portrayed
with the head of an animal. In Tibet she is called
dByar-gyi-rgyal-mo, the Himalaya. [Jobes 1962]

Guggulu
India
Magic; Earth and Nature; Sky and Heavens; Goodness;
Immortality; Water; Weather; Fishing and Water Animals
  "Bedellium." One of the *Apsarases.* Her name represents
the odor of the bedellium plant. A spell is used to drive the
odor away, to make her go back to the source of the odor. The
spell includes the recognition of the supernatural being,
which causes her to lose some of her power. The others with
unpleasant odors are *Aukshagandhii, Naladi,* and
Pramandani. [Stutley and Stutley 1984]

Gulsalia Mata
Bangladesh, India
Destroyer of Life
  Bengal and Bangladesh smallpox goddess. [Leach 1992]

Gundhary See *Gandhari.*

Gung See *Ganga.*

Gunga See *Ganga.*

Gungu
India
Moon and Night; Mother and Guardian
  Moon goddess who presides over procreation and
childbirth. [Durdin-Robertson 1976; Leach 1992; Stutley and
Stutley 1984]

Hada Bai
India
Wealth; Luck
  Assam goddess of wealth. She can be invoked to cause
one's enemies to lose their wealth as well as for one's own
gain. [Monaghan 1990]

Hadakai
India
Domesticated Animals; Health and Healing
  Animal deity worshiped in Gujarat. She controls rabid
dogs and prevents hydrophobia. [Leach 1992]

Hadphoran Marhi
India, *Baiga*
Destroyer of Life
  Goddess of smallpox. [Leach 1992]

Haimavati "Daughter of the Himalaya Mountains."
See *Devi.*

Hakini
India
Health and Healing
  One of the six deities governing the six bodily substances.
See *Dakini* for the others. [Durdin-Robertson 1976]

Hamsadhirudha "Mounted on a Goose." See *Sarasvati.*

Hamsika
India
Directions; Sky and Heavens
   Hindu goddess who supports the southern corner of the sky. Daughter of *Surabhi*, sister of *Surupa, Subhadra,* and Sarvakamdugha, who support the other corners. [Jobes 1962; Leach 1992]

Harahvaiti
India
Water
   Avesta (Zoroastrian) river goddess. Equivalent to Vedic *Sarasvati* and *Helmund,* Near East. [Jobes 1962]

Harbadevi
India, *Son Kolis*
Fishing and Water Animals
   Deity of fishermen. [Leach 1992]

Harappan Goddesses
India
Mother and Guardian
   Clay deities, c. 3000 B.C.E., found in the Indus Valley area in the Mohendaro and Harappan civilizations. Modeled of clay, they are voluptuous figures, decorated with shell, bone, iron, agate, turquoise, carnelian, lapis lazuli, steatitea beads, and gold jewelry. [Fairservis 1971]

Hardahin   See *Bai Haldahin.*

Hari
India
Hunting and Wild Animals; Happiness
   Hindu animal deity. One of the nine angry daughters of *Krodha.* She is the mother of the "cow-tailed" animals, i.e., monkeys, horses, etc. As "remover of sorrow," another name for *Lakshmi.* [Danielou 1964; Stutley and Stutley 1984]

Harini
India
Sky and Heavens; Goodness; Immortality; Water; Magic; Weather; Fishing and Water Animals
   One of the *Apsarases.* [Durdin-Robertson 1976]

Hariti
India
Evil; Life/Death Cycle; Goodness; Health and Healing; Wealth; Mother and Guardian
   Mother of five hundred demons. She originally combined the three archetypal activities of a mother goddess: creation, preservation, and destruction. Her conversion from Hinduism to Buddhism changed her from a demon into a benevolent deity of health and abundance who gives and protects children. She is also worshiped in Chinese Turkestan. Equivalent to *Koyasu Kwan-non, Jun-tei Kwan-non, Karitei-Mo,* and *Kishijoten,* Far East. [Cotterell 1979; Durdin-Robertson 1976; Getty 1962; Jobes 1962; Leach 1992; Lurker 1984]

Harits, The
India
Dawn and Twilight; Domesticated Animals
   Hindu sisters who are the winged steeds of Indra. They are the shining lights of dawn who bring the bright morning. [Jobes 1962]

Hariyali
India
Hunting and Wild Animals; Time
Deity who "guards the crops for hunters." She is worshiped during the month of Sawan. [Leach 1992]

Hariyari Mata
India, *Majhwar*
Agriculture; Ceremonies
   Agricultural deity who guards the crops. Sacrifices are made to her during mowing and harvesting. [Leach 1992]

Harsiddh Mata
India
Water
   Terrestrial deity, goddess of the seashore. The people in the state of Rajasthan believe she swallows boats. [Leach 1992]

Hastakamala   "Lotus in Hand." See *Lakshmi.*

Hastimukha   See *Jyestha.*

Hathay
India
Family and Tribes; Unhappiness
   "Grandmother." As a young girl this deity refused to marry the man her father had chosen. After drowning herself in a pool, she appeared in peoples' dreams telling them she had been an incarnation of *Parvati.* [Monaghan 1990]

Havirbhu
India
Ceremonies
   "Oblation-born." Personification of the place of sacrifice. Daughter of Dardama, wife of Pulastya. [Stutley and Stutley 1984]

He-li Di   See *Hariti.*

Hemambika
India
Ceremonies; Love and Sexuality; Mother and Guardian
   "Golden Mother." Tantric *Shakti* worshiped in Palghat, southern Malabar. At her shrine she is represented by a pair of hands protruding from a small well. This representation is said to have resulted because of the "lewd attentions" of a priest who ritually bathed her. [Stutley and Stutley 1984]

Hemantadevi
India
Time
   "Winter." Buddhist seasonal deity. See also *Grimsmadevi, Saraddevi,* and *Vasanta.* [Jobes 1962]

Hemaprabha
India
Small Size; Magic
   "Golden Splendor." One of the *Khekaris.* [Durdin-Robertson 1976]

Hidimba
India
Fate; Magic; Love and Sexuality; Large Size; Evil; Destroyer of Life; Charisma; Beauty
   One of the *Rakshasis.*
   Hidimba's brother used her as a decoy against the Pandavas because she could fly, change shape, and possessed the knowledge of the past and future. Instead of protecting her brother, she fell in love with one of the Pandavas, Bhima, who killed her brother. Hidimba then lived with Bhima during the day, returning him to the Pandavas at night.
   Alternate form: Hidimva. [Durdin-Robertson 1976; Jobes 1962; Stutley and Stutley 1984]

Hidimva   See *Hidimba*.

Hima
India
Sky and Heavens; Weather
   "Snow." A celestial deity who inhabits the mountains.
[Stutley and Stutley 1984]

Himsa
India
Evil
   "Injury," "Harm," "Violence." She is personified as the
wife of Adhrama, god of injustice. [Stutley and Stutley 1984]

Hindi   "Pomegranate-carrying Death Queen." See *Durga*.

Hindira   See *Durga*.

Hinglajin
India, *Pardham*
Creator of Life; Agriculture
   Fertility goddess worshiped in the state of Madhya
Pradesh. She presides over the crops. [Leach 1992]

Hira   "Jewel." See *Lakshmi*.

Hiranyavaksas   "Golden-breasted." See *Vasudhara*.

Holi
India, *Bhil*
Happiness
   Deity of merriment who presides over singing and
dancing. Wife of Mashru Dev, sister of *Diwali*. Alternate
form: Jogan Mata. [Leach 1992]

Holika
India
Fire; Ceremonies
   Fire deity associated with a famous fire festival.
[Monaghan 1981]

Hotra
India
Ceremonies
   "Call." Personification of the invocation to priestly office.
Wife of Agni. [Durdin-Robertson 1976; Stutley and Stutley
1984]

Howanmata
India, *Bhil*
Health and Healing
   Deity of protection during epidemics in Madhya Pradesh.
She is invoked by women. [Leach 1992]

Hri
India
Unhappiness
   "Shame." [Leach 1992]

Huliamma
India
Hunting and Wild Animals
   Tiger goddess worshiped in the state of Karnataka
(Mysore). [Leach 1992]

Huligama
India
Creator of Life
   Goddess of males who presides over virility. [Leach 1992]

Huligavva
India, *Donga Dasari*
Health and Healing; Ceremonies; Mother and Guardian
   Southern goddess who is invoked to help heal sick
children. She is also sacrificed to before her followers leave on
their thieving missions. [Leach 1992]

Hulka Devi
Bangladesh
Destroyer of Life
   Bengal deity of cholera and vomiting. [Leach 1992]

Hulki Mai
India, *Chamar, Nat*
Destroyer of Life
   Deity of cholera and smallpox. [Leach 1992]

Hundi   See *Bursung*.

Hunwarmata
India, *Bhil*
Health and Healing
   Goddess of health invoked by women during illness.
[Leach 1992]

Hyrania
India
Unknown
   "Womb of Gold." Associated with *Nari*. [Durdin-
Robertson 1976]

Ichchhashakti
India
Intelligence and Creativity; Creator of Life; Primordial Being
   "Power of the Will." One of the six primary forces in
nature. A classification of *Shaktis*. See also *Mantrikashakti*.
[Durdin-Robertson 1976]

Ida
India
Earth and Nature; Agriculture; Wealth; Domesticated
Animals; Ceremonies
   Hindu earth goddess. Personification of the sacrificial
food: clarified butter or ghee, sour milk, whey, and curds.
Also said to be personified as a cow symbolizing abundance.
One of the *Nadis*, she is associated with the left nostril which
is influenced by the moon. Considered by some to be an aspect
of *Kundalini*. Equivalent to *Vac, Devi*, and Greco-Roman
Mania. Alternate forms: Adda, Ila. [Durdin-Robertson 1976;
Leach 1992; Stutley and Stutley 1984; Zimmerman 1964]

Idavida
India
Mother and Guardian; Wealth
   Birth goddess. Mother of the god of wealth, Kubera.
Alternate form: Ilavija, Ilavila. [Stutley and Stutley 1984]

Ideal Nature
India
Creator of Life; Primordial Being
   Procreating power. The space from which everything in the
universe is generated. [Durdin-Robertson 1976]

Ilavija   See *Idavida*.

Ila
India
Earth and Nature; Domesticated Animals; Justice; Magic
   Ancient earth goddess who may be the same as *Ida*. She is
the mother of cattle, i.e., the food intended for sacrifice. She is

also called the goddess of revelation. There are a variety of stories about Ila where she is changed from male to female, or the reverse. Sometimes her sex changes several times, which makes it unclear as to whether she is a female or male deity. Alternate form: Bharati. [Cooper 1876; Durdin-Robertson 1976; Leach 1992; Stutley and Stutley 1984]

Ilavila   See *Idavida.*

i-lha-mo
India
Earth and Nature
   Earth goddess worshiped in the state of Sikkim. [Leach 1992]

Ilura
India
Moon and Night
   Moon goddess. Sister of Parama Shiva. Identified with *Parvati.* [Leach 1992]

Inde
India
Family and Tribes
   Mother goddess of the nations. Worshiped in Ireland and India. Associated with *Cessair,* Western Europe. [Durdin-Robertson 1976]

Indira   "Powerful One." See *Lakshmi.*

Indrani
India
Love and Sexuality; Immortality; Mother and Guardian; Creator of Life
   Goddess of sensual pleasure. One of the *Gnas.* Wife of Indra. Also called the goddess of arrows. Indrani owns the parijata, the celestial wishing tree. The sight of her tree reinvigorates the old. She is similar to *Lakshmi* and *Venus,* Greek and Roman Empires, *Mahendri,* and one of the *Saptamatrakas.* Alternate form: Paulomi, Shaci. [Danielou 1964; Durdin-Robertson 1976; Stutley and Stutley 1984]

Ira
India
Earth and Nature; Creator of Life; Agriculture; Sky and Heavens; Goodness; Immortality; Water; Magic; Weather; Fishing and Water Animals
   One of the *Apsarases.* Daughter of Daksha, wife of Kashyapa, and mother of three vegetal goddess-daughters, *Lata, Valli,* and *Virudha.* Closely allied with *Ida.* [Stutley and Stutley 1984]

Iravati
India
Hunting and Wild Animals
   The name of a daughter of Krodhavasha, wife of Pulaha. Mother of four divine elephants. A name for *Durga.* [Stutley and Stutley 1984]

Isana   See *Durga.*

Isani
India
Wealth; Ceremonies; Agriculture
   Hindu goddess of abundance. There is a festival in her honor at Oodeypoor in Rajputana. An earthen image of Isani and her husband Ishwara is made and placed by a trench where barley is sown. When the grain sprouts, the women of the village dance around it, invoking a blessing from Isani on

their husbands. Alternate form: Gouri. [Durdin-Robertson 1976; Leach 1992]

Isi
India
Stars and Planets
   Hindu stellar deity associated with the constellation Argo Navis.
   ⚥ *The Argo Navis is the ark that carried Isi and her husband Iswara over the Deluge.* [Durdin-Robertson 1976]

It Mu
India, *Lepcha*
Creator of Life; Domesticated Animals
   Creator goddess worshiped in Sikkim. She created all the other deities including Tak Bo Thing and *Na Zong Nyo,* who were assigned to create humans. She gave her people their domestic animals. [Leach 1992]

Jagad-dhatri   "Sustainer of the World." See *Parvati, Sarasvati,* and *Durga.*

Jagadgauri
India
Mother and Guardian
   "Yellow Woman" or "Fairest in the World." Name for *Durga* when she is praised by gods and men for delivering them from demons. Also a name for *Parvati.* [Stutley and Stutley 1984]

Jagad-yoni
India
Creator of Life
   "Womb of the World." Personification of female reproduction. Some of her symbols are an inverted triangle, an egg, a lotus flower, and a discus. Her colors are red and black. [Durdin-Robertson 1976]

Jaganmatr   "World Mother." See *Durga* and *Lakshmi.*

Jaher Era
India, *Santal*
Arts
   Goddess of music who is worshiped in Bihar. [Leach 1992]

Jahira Buru
India, *Hos*
Goodness; Earth and Nature
   Benevolent tree deity who presides over the sacred grove. Wife of Dessauli. [Leach 1992]

Jakhamata   See *Jakhmata.*

Jakhmata
India
Household Affairs
   Household deity worshiped in the Poona district, an ancient region in the state of Maharashtra. Alternate form: Jakhamata. [Leach 1992]

Jaladhija   "Ocean-born." See *Lakshmi.*

Jalia
India, *Savara*
Evil; Destroyer of Life
   Southern malevolent goddess of death and disease who can be appeased if propitiated properly. In some areas, a male deity. [Leach 1992]

Jalkamni

India

Water

Water goddess worshiped in the state of Orissa. Sometimes a male deity. [Leach 1992]

Jalpa Mai

India, *Basor*

Destroyer of Life

Goddess of death and disease, especially the plague, worshiped in Jabalpur (Jubbulpore), a district in Madhya Pradesh. Equivalent to *Mari Mai.* [Leach 1992]

Jamadagni

India

Sun and Day; Time; Sky and Heavens; Goodness; Immortality; Water; Magic; Weather; Fishing and Water Animals

One of the *Apsarases* who accompanies the sun on its journey during January-February. [Stutley and Stutley 1984]

Jamai Sashthi   See *Aranya.*

Jamants

India, *Holeya*

Ceremonies; Commerce and Travel

Deity worshiped once a month by Holeya caste of field laborers and village servants. She also has a yearly festival. Associated with *Kali.* [Durdin-Robertson 1976]

Jami

India

Mother and Guardian

Hindu deity of maternity or femininity. [Stutley and Stutley 1984]

Janguli

India

Health and Healing; Reptiles

"The Poisonous One." Buddhist deity who is invoked to cure snakebites. Janguli is identified with the Mansasa cult found in some Bengali Moslem communities. She is portrayed with one head, four arms, holding a musical instrument and a white snake. At other times she is shown with three faces and six arms, and colored yellow. May be an alternate form for Mahavidya and also said to be a form of Tara. [Leach 1992; Lurker 1984; Stutley and Stutley 1984]

Jappi Mata

India, *Baiga*

Destroyer of Life

Goddess of illness who causes sleeping sickness. [Leach 1992]

Jara

India

Household Affairs; Evil; Magic; Immortality; Large Size; Destroyer of Life; Charisma; Beauty

"Decrepitude." Household deity, a *Rakshasi,* who devours flesh and changes her shape at will. Alternate form: Grhadevi.

Jara found two stillborns at the crossroads who had only one eye, ear, arm, and leg, and she joined them together. They became a single healthy child whom she gave to the childless king of Magadha. He named the child Jarāsandha, meaning "Joined by Jara." [Leach 1992; Stutley and Stutley 1984]

Jassuju

India, *Dhammai*

Fishing and Water Animals; Creator of Life

Frog deity.

Jassuju was the daughter of the Earth and the Sky. She had a twin brother, Lujjuphu, who was also a frog. The two frogs mated and produced the first humans, Anoi-Diggan-Juje and Abugupham-Bumo. [Leach 1992; Sproul 1979]

Jatavedasi

India

Creator of Life

Feminine form of name for the god Agni. See also *Durga.* [Stutley and Stutley 1984]

Jatila

India

Education and Knowledge; Selflessness

Dedicated student of Vedic knowledge who incinerated herself so she could be reunited with her teachers in the other world. Alternate form: Shabari. [Stutley and Stutley 1984]

Jaya

India

War

Goddess of victory in the *Manavagrihyasutra* text. See also *Matris.* [Leach 1992]

Jayani   See *Jayanti.*

Jayanti

India

Unknown

Hindu goddess. Daughter of Indra. Alternate forms: Devasena, Jayani, Tavisi. [Stutley and Stutley 1984]

Jayini

India

Love and Sexuality

"Illicit Love." One of the *Nayikas.* [Stutley and Stutley 1984]

Jesodha   See *Yashoda.*

Jhulan Devi

India, *Khond*

Mother and Guardian

Cradle goddess worshiped in the Central Provinces. To support and protect her child, a mother has a tatoo of Jhulan put on her body where her child's head rests. [Leach 1992]

Jibbi-Jang-Sangne

India, *Dhammai*

Earth and Nature

Mountain deity. Earth's daughter. [Leach 1992; Long 1963; Sproul 1979]

Jnanashakti

India

Intelligence and Creativity

"Power of Intellect." A class of *Shaktis.* See also *Mantrikashakti.* [Durdin-Robertson 1976]

Jogan Mata   See *Holi.*

Jumna   See *Yami.*

Jumna Ji
India
Water
Benevolent river deity. [Leach 1992]

Jyaya See *Jyestha.*

Jyestha
India
Destroyer of Life
"Elder Sister." Sister of *Lakshmi* or another name for *Alakshmi.* Jyestha is also said to be one of three aspects of *Ambika.* She was a local goddess of smallpox in southern India who is now called *Sitala.* Alternate forms: Hastimukha, Jyaya, Kaladi, Kapila-patini, Kumbhi, Mudevi, Mugadi, Nirriti, Tauvai, and Vighaparsada. See also Matris. [Danielou 1964; Stutley and Stutley 1984]

Jyestha Alakshmi
India
Destroyer of Life; Life/Death Cycle
Goddess of smallpox. Counterpart of *Sitala.* Portrayed as old and decrepit, symbolizing decay. [Leach 1992]

Jyotsna
India
Moon and Night; Dawn and Twilight
"Moonlight," "Twilight." Wife of the moon, Candra, and beloved of the moon, Soma. Alternate form: Kaumudi. [Durdin-Robertson 1976; Stutley and Stutley 1984]

Ka Blai Synshar
India, *Khasi*
Justice; Wealth; Happiness
Assam deity who embodies the "Divine Law." She can grant or withhold material prosperity and spiritual happiness, and she empowers or punishes the evil spirits who harass humans. [Leach 1992]

Ka Blei Sam Um
India, *Khasi*
Water; Fishing and Water Animals; Ceremonies
Assam river goddess. Fishermen make offerings to her before they begin fishing. Offerings are also made to her after the loss of the umbilical cord. [Leach 1992]

Ka Di
Pakistan
Reptiles; Mother and Guardian
"Lady of Life." Serpent mother goddess worshiped at Dir. [Leach 1992]

Ka Ding
India, *Khasi*
Fire
Assam fire goddess. One of the four children of *Assam Mother Earth* (see for story). The others are *Ka Um, Ka Sngi,* and U Bnai, the moon. [Stone 1979]

Ka Duba
India, *Khasi, Synteng*
Destroyer of Life
Assam fever goddess. [Leach 1992]

Ka Khlam
India, *Khasi, Synteng*
Destroyer of Life
Assam cholera goddess. [Leach 1992]

Ka Ksaw Ka Jirngam
India, *Khasi*
Luck; Household Affairs; Hunting and Wild Animals
Assam household deity of good fortune, especially in hunting. [Leach 1992]

Ka 'Lei Aitan
India, *Khasi*
Water
Assam river deity. She is apparently associated with the same river as the goddess *Aitan.* [Leach 1992]

Ka 'Lei Iing
India, *Khasi*
Household Affairs
Assam household deity. [Leach 1992]

Ka 'Lei Synshar
India, *Khasi*
Ceremonies
Assam deity to whom her followers sacrifice a pig. [Leach 1992]

Ka Niangriang
India, *Khasi*
Evil; Destroyer of Life
Assam malevolent deity of disease. She makes children sick by causing an infection in the navel. [Leach 1992]

Ka Ram-ew
India, *Khasi*
Earth and Nature
Assam earth goddess. [Leach 1992]

Ka Rasong
India, *Synteng*
Household Affairs; Commerce and Travel; Mother and Guardian
Assam household deity who presides over her followers' work and trading. She also supervises the young unmarried. [Leach 1992]

Ka Rih
India, *Khasi, Synteng*
Evil; Destroyer of Life
Assam malevolent deity who causes malaria. [Leach 1992]

Ka Ron
India, *Khasi, Synteng*
Evil
Assam evil deity. [Leach 1992]

Ka Shwar
India, *Khasi*
Destroyer of Life
Assam disease goddess who causes convulsive cramps. [Leach 1992]

Ka Singi
India, *Khasi*
Sun and Day
Assam sun goddess. Her brother, the moon, had incestuous intentions toward her. See also *Ka Sngi.* [Leach 1992]

Ka Smer
India; *Khasi*
Destroyer of Life
Assam death goddess who causes people to die violently. [Leach 1992]

Ka Sngi
India, *Khasi*

Sun and Day; Love and Sexuality; Justice; Moon and Night

Assam sun goddess. One of the four children of *Assam Mother Earth* (see for story). The others are *Ka Ding, Ka Um,* and U Bnai, the moon. See also *Ka Singi.*

Ka Sngi's younger brother at first shone as brightly as his sister the sun. As they grew older, U Bnai became enamoured of Ka Sngi. She tried to explain to him that his desires were inappropriate, but one day he assaulted her. Angry, Ka Sngi threw some of the ashes from her fire on him. They dimmed the light of U Bnai and scarred his face and the vain young man seldom appeared in the light of day after that. [Stone 1979]

Ka Syrtieh
India, *Khasi*

Unhappiness

Assam goddess of pain. She causes cuts and scratches from tools. [Leach 1992]

Ka Taben
India, *Synteng*

Household Affairs

Assam mother of all the household deities. [Leach 1992]

Ka Taro   See *Ka Taroh.*

Ka Taroh
India, *Khasi, Synteng*

Evil; Destroyer of Life; Wealth

Assam malevolent disease goddess who causes delirium. Among the Synteng, she is also the demon of wealth. Alternate form: Ka Taro. [Leach 1992]

Ka Um
India, *Khasi*

Water

Assam goddess of the waters. One of the four children of *Assam Mother Earth.* See also *Earth.* [Stone 1979]

Kadru
India

Reptiles

Mother of the *Nagis.* One of the thirteen daughters of Daksha, wife of Kashyapa. The *Nagis* were created to inhabit Patala (the nether regions, see *Daityas*). She is a one-eyed goddess who lost her eye when she cheated on a bet with her sister, *Vinata.*

Kadru wanted to be the mother of a thousand snakes and laid a thousand eggs. Vinata wanted two children and laid only two eggs. After five hundred years, Kadru's eggs hatched. Vinata broke open one of her eggs to find a partially formed son. Vinata was cursed to wait another five hundred years before the second egg hatched.

Kadru is sometimes called *Aditi.* [Durdin-Robertson 1976; Monaghan 1990]

Kahasumma
India, *Kotas (Kotah)*

Creator of Life

Creator goddess worshiped in the Neelgerry Hills. [Durdin-Robertson 1976]

Kaika
Cruel stepmother of Rama. See also *Kaikeyi.* [Jobes 1962]

Kaikeyi
India

Family and Tribes

Hindu deity. One of the three principal wives of Dasharatha, and mother of Bharata.

Dasharatha promised two boons to Kaikeyi when he married her. She had never collected them, so when his eldest son Rama was to become heir-apparent, Kaikeyi demanded that her son, Bharata, be proclaimed heir and Dasharatha had to honor his promise. It was Manthara who told her to make such a demand.

See also *Kaika.* [Stutley and Stutley 1984]

Kairadeshahi
India, *Baiga*

Destroyer of Life; Mother and Guardian

Goddess of disease and death who causes stillbirths. [Leach 1992]

Kaki
India

Wild Birds

Mother of the crows. Daughter of *Tamra* and Kashyapa. [Stutley and Stutley 1984]

Kakini
India

Health and Healing

One of the *Shakti.* She is one of the six deities governing the six bodily substances. The others are *Dakini, Hakini, Lakini, Rakini, Shakini.* They correspond to the *Krittika.* Kakini is portrayed seated on a red lotus and having four arms (symbolizing four powers or functions). She is similar to Buddhist *Kurukulla* and *Cunda.* [Durdin-Robertson 1976]

Kakubh
India

Sky and Heavens

"Peak," "Summit." A later definition is "region" or "quarter of heaven." A sky deity personified as the daughter of Daksha and wife of Dharma. [Stutley and Stutley 1984]

Kala Pidari   See *Pidari.*

Kaladi   See *Jyestha.*

Kalaka
India

Unknown

"Dark Blue," "Black." Mother of the Danavas with her sister *Puloma.* See also *Danavis.* [Durdin-Robertson 1976]

Kalamahichandi
India, *Santal*

Destroyer of Life; Life/Death Cycle

Disease goddess of men and cattle. She can be propitiated to prevent illness. [Leach 1992]

Kalaratri
India

Time; Life/Death Cycle

"Time." Hindu deity. She presides over the darkness that follows the end of the world that is said to occur at the end of each age. She is usually depicted carrying a noose, which she uses to catch her victims. Alternate forms: Kali, Kutumbini, Mahalakshmi, Mahakali, Mahamaya, and Yoganidra. [Stutley and Stutley 1984]

Kali
India

Ceremonies; Health and Healing; Mother and Guardian; Time; Life/Death Cycle; Courage; Luck; Education and Knowledge; War; Creator of Life; Primordial Being

Hindu goddess, the symbol of eternal time, who gives life and also destroys it. An aspect of *Devi*. The *Shakti* of Shiva. Sister of *Devi, Sirsootee, Sri,* and Brahma. She appears naked, clothed only in space. She is black, "the color in which all distinctions dissolve." Her hands show the fear-removing and boon-granting *mudras* (symbolic poses)—she allays the fears of those who invoke her and grants the "supreme realization of truth." *Durga* was called Kali when she fought the army of a giant. The Eravallar ask her for protection when they are in the forest; the Naya make sacrifices to her during cholera and smallpox epidemics; the Badhaks, a tribe of criminals, believe that if things go wrong they have somehow displeased Kali; and in southern India, offerings are made to her during plowing, sowing, and reaping. She is sometimes portrayed with the head of jackal. Frequently seen as only a frightening, human-devouring demon, her gift-giving and fear-allaying aspects, and the naturalness of death following life, are overlooked. Kali is one of the *Mahavidyas*. Like *Durga,* Kali has many forms, each having a different name. Included in these are *Amari De, Ambika, Bhadrakali, Bhavani, Bherunda, Bhradrakali, Camunda, Candi, Durga, Durgapunja, Kalaratri, Kalika, Kalimata, Kamakhya, Kottavei, Mahadevi, Mahakali, Mari-Mai, Parvati, Sara Kali, Sati, Shakti, Tara, Uma, Vindhyavasini.* See also *Rernati,* the Himalaya. [Leach 1992; Monaghan 1981; Neumann 1972; Stone 1979; Stutley and Stutley 1984; bg]

Kaliamma

India

Travel and Commerce

Village deity who is a boundary goddess worshiped in the Tanjore District, Tamil Nadu. [Leach 1992]

Kalika

India

Mother and Guardian; Earth and Nature; Time; Ceremonies

One of the nine forms of *Durga* in vegetal form, a *Navadurga*. She inhabits a plant, Arum colocasia, which is invoked for protection. The nine forms are celebrated at an autumn ceremony in Bengal. It is also her name as the mother of the gods who, at the dissolution of the world, will return and disappear within her. The Tharus people worship her as a goddess of childbirth who will end sterility. Alternate name for *Kali*. Alternate form: Kalilika. [Leach 1992; Monaghan 1981; Stutley and Stutley 1984]

Kalilika   See *Kalika*.

Kalimata

"Goddess of the Cow Shed." See *Kali*.

Kaliyani

India, *Kadar*

Earth and Nature

Goddess of the mountains. [Leach 1992]

Kalumaiamman

India

Health and Healing; Domesticated Animals

Protection goddess who keeps cattle and humans from becoming ill. She is worshiped in the Trichinopoly (Tiruchirapalli) district of Madras. [Leach 1992]

Kaluvaliamma

India

Destroyer of Life; Commerce and Travel

Epidemic goddess and goddess of travelers who propitiate her when they return from a trip. [Leach 1992]

Kamadhenu

India

Domesticated Animals; Luck; Family and Tribes; Mother and Guardian

Cow of plenty who grants all wishes and who emerged from the Churning of the Ocean. She represents motherhood and reproduction. She created the people outside of the four Hindu castes, who are called Milleetch (Mlechchhas).

A powerful king called at the home of a brahmin, whose wife offered the king hospitality. While visiting he saw the cow Kamadhenu and decided he must have the miraculous animal. The woman tried to convince him not to take Kamadhenu, but the king left, driving the cow ahead of him. When the woman's son came home and heard what happened, he pursued the king and killed him, bringing Kamadhenu back home.

Alternate forms: Camdhen, Kamdhen, Sarasvati, Savala, Surabhi. [Danielou 1964; Durdin-Robertson 1976; Jobes 1962; Leach 1992; Stutley and Stutley 1984; Sykes 1968]

Kamakhya

India

Love and Sexuality; Ceremonies

Goddess of sexual desire, a form of *Kali* or "wanton-eyed," a form of *Durga*, to whom human sacrifices, said to be voluntary, were made. Worshiped by the Dom caste (scavengers, musicians, weavers, traders, and moneylenders). Alternate form: Kamaksi. [Leach 1992; Stutley and Stutley 1984]

Kamaksi

India

Goodness; Ceremonies; Creator of Life; Primordial Being

"She Who Ogles." Benign goddess worshiped in the south. She is the highest *Shakti* and is portrayed with four arms, seated on a lotus. Her chief temple is in Assam, where cruel rites were performed. Also said to be a form of *Devi* and *Durga*. Alternate form: Kamakhya. [Lurker 1984; Stutley and Stutley 1984]

Kamala

India

Earth and Nature

"Lotus." See *Lakshmi*. Also the name of several other Indian deities including the tenth *Mahavidya*, the lotus girl, who is said to be the "enjoyer and enjoyed." [Leach 1992; Monaghan 1981; Stutley and Stutley 1984]

Kamashi

India

Love and Sexuality

"Wanton-eyed." May be an early fertility goddess who was merged with *Parvati*. Kamashi is considered an aspect of *Paravati* in Vedic theology. [Sykes 1968]

Kamasshi   See *Parvati*.

Kamdhen   See *Kamadhenu*.

Kamesvari

India

Love and Sexuality

"Illicit Love." One of the *Nayikas*. [Danielou 1964; Leach 1992]

Kami   See *Rati*.

Kamthi Mata

India

Destroyer of Life

Plague goddess. [Leach 1992]

Kanaka Durgamma
India
Domesticated Animals; Health and Healing
Cattle goddess who is invoked to protect them from disease. [Leach 1992]

Kangra Goddess, The
India, *Kutoch Rajput*
Creator of Life
Creator deity.

⚧ *The tribe began with the first Rajah of Kangra. He came to life full grown, created from the perspiration from the brow of the Kangra Goddess.* [Durdin-Robertson 1976]

Kankali
India, *Bondo*
Luck
Deity of disaster. Identified with *Thakurani Bakorani*. [Leach 1992]

Kankar Mata
India
Destroyer of Life
"The Most Dreaded." Smallpox goddess of Bengal. [Leach 1992]

Kannae
"Virgin of Light." See *Kanyā*.

Kannagi
India, *Tamil*
Selflessness; Justice; Family and Tribes
Goddess of chastity. She also represents spirituality and conceptualizes the Tamil heritage of justice, and their linguistic and cultural purity. Tamilnad is a linguistic region in the extreme southeast. [Preston 1982]

Kanni Amma
India
Water
Sea goddess who is propitiated during the launching of sailing vessels when setting sail. She is sometimes worshiped collectively with Hanniammar. [Leach 1992]

Kanni, The
India
Family and Tribes; Magic; Ceremonies
Terrestrial spirits who are the virgin ancestors of the Indians. They are propitiated with offerings of cakes and fruit. [Durdin-Robertson 1976]

Kanniha Paramesvare
India
Commerce and Travel
Deity of southern traders. [Leach 1992]

Kannimar, The
India, *Eravallar*
Family and Tribes
Guardian deities for specific families who watch over their well-being. [Leach 1992]

Kanti
India
Destroyer of Life
Smallpox deity who causes swelling in the neck. One of the wives of the moon god, Chandra. [Leach 1992; Preston 1982]

Kanyā
India
Stars and Planets

"The Virgin." Deity of the constellation Kandra (Virgo), and the most ancient divinity of the Indian pantheon. Either a name for, or closely associated with, *Devi*. Equivalent to *Aderenosa* and *Adra Nedefa*, Near East. See also *Ta-Repy* and *Zodiacal Virgins*, Egypt, and *Shesang Nü*, Far East. Alternate forms: Kannae, Kanyabara, Kauni, Kunnyan, Uma-Kanya. [Durdin-Robertson 1976; Stutley and Stutley 1984]

Kanyā Kumārī
India
Unknown
"Girl Mother." Goddess of Cape Comorin in the Kanniyakumari district of Tamil Nadu. Equivalent to *Balambika*. [Stutley and Stutley 1984]

Kanyabara
See *Kanyā*.

Kapalini
India
Unknown
Name for *Durga* as wife of Shiva-Kapalin. [Stutley and Stutley 1984]

Kapenopfu
India, *Naga*
Goodness; Supreme Being; Creator of Life; Hunting and Wild Animals
Benevolent supreme being who created humans and the large cats. She is worshiped by the Angami group in the states of Assam and Nagaland. [Leach 1992]

Kapila-patni
See *Jyestha*.

Kapisha
India
Mother and Guardian
Mother of the *Pisachis*. Wife of Pulaha. [Stutley and Stutley 1984]

Kapni Piri
India, *Baiga*
Destroyer of Life
Disease goddess who causes fever and chills. [Leach 1992]

Karaikkal Asmmaiyar
India
Selflessness; Arts
Vaishnava Hindu saint and poet. Those needing to overcome their bodily appetites honor her. [Monaghan 1990]

Karala
See *Parvati*.

Karali
India
Evil
"The Terrific." See also *Durga*. Alternate form: Karili. [Jobes 1962]

Karicag
India, *Baiga*
Earth and Nature
Earth deity.

⚧ *Karicag was a daughter of god. She made the earth by putting it in a pot made of leaves and stirring it for eight days and nine nights. She then took it to god and he rolled earth out like a chapati and spread it on top of the water. It grew until it covered all the waters.* [Farmer 1978]

Karili
See *Karali*.

Karisini   "Abounding in Dung." See *Lakshmi*.

Karitei-mo   See *Hariti*.

Karmadakini
India
Magic
   Buddhist deity of the air who confers supernatural powers. Her emblems are a skull cup, sword, and ritual wand, and her color is green. See also *Las-kyi-mkhah-hgro*, the Himalaya. [Jobes 1962]

Karttiki
India
Agriculture
   "Barley." One of the *Navadurgas*. [Stutley and Stutley 1984]

Kastha
India
Domesticated Animals
   Hindu mother of cloven-footed animals. One of the wives of Kashyapa. [Stutley and Stutley 1984]

Kataputanas, The
India
Evil
   Demons. [Durdin-Robertson 1976]

Kateri
India
Destroyer of Life; Mother and Guardian
   Cholera deity of the forest who is propitiated by pregnant women. [Leach 1992]

Kati Ankamma
India
Destroyer of Life; Evil
   Deity who presides over cremation and cemeteries. She devours corpses and kills children and cattle. She also sets fire to houses. [Leach 1992]

Katukilal
India, *Tamil*
Earth and Nature
   "The Lady of the Jungle." Deity of the woods worshiped in the southeast. Alternate form: Korrawi. [Lurker 1984]

Kaulesi
India
Love and Sexuality
   "Illicit Love." One of the *Nayikas*. [Stutley and Stutley 1984]

Kaumari
India
Mother and Guardian; Creator of Life
   "Power of Youth." One of the *Saptamatricas* as "power of youth." Alternate forms: Camunda, Devasena, and Sena. [Danielou 1964; Durdin-Robertson 1976; Stutley and Stutley 1984]

Kaumudi   "Moonlight." See *Jyotsna*.

Kauni   "Virgin of Light." See *Kanya*.

Kausalya
India
Justice; Selflessness

Queen of Kosala. First wife of Dasaratha, mother of Rama, the seventh avatar (incarnation) of Vishnu. She is "blessed with virtue." Alternate form: Kooshelya. [Durdin-Robertson 1976]

Kausiki
India
Water
   Hindu deity who "issued from *Parvati's* body." Also the name of a river identified with *Satyavati*. [Stutley and Stutley 1984]

Kaveri
India, *Coorg*, *Kaveri*
Water; Ceremonies
   River deity, mother goddess of the Kaveri River. Said to be a manifestation of *Parvati* who is given offerings of fruit and money. [Durdin-Robertson 1976; Leach 1992]

Kawalkamata
India, *Bhil*
Health and Healing
   Deity of health who is invoked to "cure lameness and pain." [Leach 1992]

Kelikila   "Wanton." See *Rati*.

Kelu Devaru
India, *Kuraba*
Household Affairs; Ceremonies
   Household deity who presides over the pot. She is worshiped during the Dasara festival and weddings. Alternate form: Hennu Devaru. [Leach 1992]

Keshini
India
Family and Tribes; Justice; Sky and Heavens; Goodness; Water; Immortality; Magic; Weather; Fishing and Water Animals
   "Queen of Solar Race." Name of several Hindu deities including: one of the *Apsarases*; the mother of Ravanaa and Kumbhakarna; and queen of the solar race. Alternate form: Durga. [Durdin-Robertson 1976; Leach 1992]

Kesora
India
Unknown
   Hindu deity. There is an idol of her in a temple at Puri which has a head and body of sandalwood, diamond eyes, and a robe of gold. Associated with Krishna. [Durdin-Robertson 1976]

Keyum
India, *Miris*
Creator of Life
   Great Mother, worshiped in the northeast, who existed at the beginning and "out of whom came *Sedi-Melo*." See also *Sadi*. [Leach 1992]

Keyuri
India
Destroyer of Life
   Goddess of cemeteries. [Durdin-Robertson 1976]

Khahdomas   See *Dakinis*.

Khala Kumari
Bangladesh
Fishing and Water Animals; Ceremonies

Water deity to whom fishermen sacrifice the best of their first catch. [Leach 1992]

Khasias Celestial Woman
India, *Khasi*
Moon and Night; Unhappiness; Love and Sexuality
Celestial deity who is the mother of the wife of the moon god.

Every month the moon god falls in love with his mother-in-law. Annoyed by this, she throws ashes at him. [Durdin-Robertson 1976]

Khaya   See *Chaya* and *Chhaya*.

Khekaris, The
India
Small Size; Magic
Fairies who move through the air by flying. They include *Aginvati, Hemaprabha, Kutamangari, Lalitalochana, Mandaradevi, Maruttaruni, Mgigalekha, Ratnamangari, Shaktiyasas, Svarnarekha, Vegavati.* See also *Siddhis.* [Durdin-Robertson 1976]

Khermai   See *Bhagavati*.

Khermata
India
Earth and Nature
Dravidian earth deity identified with *Devi*. [Leach 1992]

Khir Bhawani
India
Water
"Milk Goddess" worshiped in Kashmir. Springs are sacred to her. [Leach 1992]

Khulungma
Bangladesh, *Tipara*
Household Affairs
Bengal deity of cotton. [Leach 1992]

Kimnaris, The
India
Sky and Heavens; Demi-animals
Sky deities who inhabit the astral plane and are half-human, half-animal. One is *Raktadhara*. Alternate form: Kinnaris. [Durdin-Robertson 1976]

Kine Nane
India, *Adi*
Creator of Life; Heaven and Hell; Earth and Nature; Wealth
Chthonic earth goddess of the northeast who presides over abundance and fertility. She is said to represent "universal motherhood." [Leach 1992]

Kinkin
India, *Baiga*
Evil
Malevolent deity who is invoked to cause evil. [Leach 1992]

Kinnaris   See *Kimnaris*.

Kirati   See *Durga* and *Ganga*.

Kirteka, The   See *Krittikas*.

Kirti
India
Charisma
Deity of fame who is associated with Krishna. [Leach 1992]

Kitro Bai
Bangladesh, *Oraon*
Household Affairs
Bengal household deity. Daughter of Barnda. [Leach 1992]

Kodamata
India, *Bhil*
Health and Healing
Goddess of health in Madhya Pradesh who is invoked by women who are ill. [Leach 1992]

Kokamukha   "Wolf-face." See *Durga*.

Kokkalamma
India
Destroyer of Life
Goddess of disease who causes coughs at Bangalore in Mysore. [Leach 1992]

Kol First Woman
India, *Kol*
Family and Tribes
Ancestor of the first people.

God made a girl and boy and put them in a cave. When they didn't come out, he taught them to make rice beer. Soon they came out and had twelve daughters and twelve sons. [Farmer 1978]

Kolapuriamma
India
Fate
Deity of fortune tellers who use rice and winnowing fans for divination. [Leach 1992]

Kolin Sutti Bhavani
India, *Baiga*
Hunting and Wild Animals
Hunting goddess. [Leach 1992]

Kooshelya   See *Kausalya*.

Korraval
India, *Tamil*
War
Goddess of victory worshiped in the extreme southeast. [Sykes 1968]

Korrawi
India, *Tamil*
War
Goddess of battle and victory whose temples are found in forests, guarded by dead spirits. Alternate form: Katukilal. [Lurker 1984]

Kotari   See *Kottavei*.

Kotavi   See *Kottavei*.

Kotma Ma
India, *Baiga*
Creator of Life
Creator deity. Mother of the Pandwa brothers.

Kotma took the grain of earth that was stolen from the lower world and churned it with water. It increased so much that she could cover the middle world and make it fertile. [Leach 1992]

Kottavei
India, *Tamil*
War; Evil; Mother and Guardian

　　War goddess and powerful demon who was later identified with *Durga*. Mother of Bana. Said to correspond to *Kali* as a naked woman and mystical deity and one who feeds on the carnage of war. She is the tutelary goddess of the *Daityas*. Alternate forms: Kotavi, Kotari, Kotavi. [Bonnerjea 1927; Delaney 1980; Durdin-Robertson 1976; Guirand 1968; Leach 1992; Stutley and Stutley 1984]

Kraunca
India
Wild Birds

　　Hindu bird goddess. Mother of the curlews. [Stutley and Stutley 1984]

Kripi
India
Goodness

　　"Compassion." There is some confusion about her name and parentage. She is possibly the daughter of Saradvata, also called Gautama, so Kripi is also called *Gautami*. Or she may have been born with her brother Kripa in a bed of grass and rescued by a king who adopted them out of compassion. [Stutley and Stutley 1984]

Krisna　See *Draupadi.*

Krittika, The
India
Stars and Planets; Mother and Guardian

　　Stellar deities. Personification of the constellation Pleiades whose energy animates all matter. Their names and numbers vary. In *The Secret Doctrine,* they are *Abrayanti, Amba, Chupunika, Dula, Maghayanti, Nitatui,* and *Varshayanti.* Equivalent to *The Pleiades* and *The Vergiliae* Greek and Roman Empires, and *Kimah,* Near East. Alternate forms: Dakinis, Kirteka, Sakis.

　　♇　The Krittika became the foster-mothers of Karttikeya after
　　　　　he was born to Ganga. All six wanted to suckle the baby,
　　　　　so he developed six heads so they could each have the honor.

　　See also *Seven Sisters,* North America, and *Seven Sisters of Industry,* Far East. [Durdin-Robertson 1976]

Kritya
India
Magic

　　"Spell." Personification of witchcraft. Sacrifices are made to her to obtain magical powers or for the destruction of one's enemies. She is blue and red as she clings to her victim. [Stutley and Stutley 1984]

Krityakas, The
India
Magic

　　Witches and fairies. [Durdin-Robertson 1976]

Kriya
India
Unknown

　　"Activity." Abstract deity mentioned in the *Vayupurana,* a Sanskrit book of ancient and medieval Indian theology. [Leach 1992]

Kriyashakti
India
Intelligence and Creativity

　　A class of *Shaktis.* They preside over one of the seven great potencies, the power of creative thought or divine activity. Their thoughts produce external, perceptible results. See also *Mantrikashakti.* [Durdin-Robertson 1976; Leach 1992]

Krodha
India, *Baiga*
Evil; Unhappiness

　　"Anger." Mother goddess of malignant spirits called Bhutas. Daughter of Daksha and wife of Kashyapa. See also *Bhutamatri.* [Leach 1992; Stutley and Stutley 1984]

Ksama
India
Selflessness; Earth and Nature

　　Goddess of patience. Daughter of Daksha. Also the name for the personified earth and *Durga.* [Stutley and Stutley 1984]

Ksetrasya Patni
India
Mother and Guardian; Earth and Nature

　　"Queen of the Soil." Hindu tutelary deity. [Stutley and Stutley 1984]

Kshama
India
Goodness

　　Deity of forgiveness who is associated with Krishna. [Leach 1992]

Kshanti
India
Goodness

　　Deity of forgiveness who is named in the *Vayupurana.* [Leach 1992]

Kshiti-apsarases, The
India
Earth and Nature; Goodness; Immortality; Water; Magic; Weather; Fishing and Water Animals

　　Terrestrial *Apsarases.* [Durdin-Robertson 1976]

Ksirabdhitanaya　"Daughter of the Ocean of Milk." See *Lakshmi.*

Ksudha　See *Mahakali* and *Mahalakshmki.*

Kubjika
India
Household Affairs

　　Tutelary deity of potters. [Stutley and Stutley 1984]

Kuhu
India
Moon and Night; Wealth; Charisma

　　"New Moon." Either the personification of the first day of the waxing moon (when the moon is not visible) or the first day of the moon's disappearance (when it is waning). She is invoked to provide a great hero with material wealth or to give her followers the fame and glory of their ancestors. See also *Sinivali.* [Leach 1992; Stutley and Stutley 1984]

Kujaku-myō-ō　See *Mahamayuri.*

Kujum-Chantu
India
Earth and Nature; Selflessness; Sky and Heavens

　　Earth goddess.

⚧ *Kujum-Chantu looked like a human being, with a head, arms and legs, and a very large stomach. The first humans lived on her stomach. When she realized that everyone would fall off and be killed if she stood up, she died of her own accord. Her eyes became the sun and the moon.* [Leach 1992; Long 1963]

Kukar Mari
India
Domesticated Animals

Guardian of dogs. The professional dog-slayers, who are members of the Dom caste (scavengers, musicians, weavers, traders, and moneylenders) in the United Provinces propitiate her. [Stutley and Stutley 1984]

Kul Devi
India
Household Affairs

Household deity of the Central Provinces who must be worshiped when the family is alone. She is also worshiped at weddings. [Leach 1992]

Kul Gosain
India, *Pahari, Mal*
Agriculture

Agricultural deity who presides over the sowing of crops. [Leach 1992]

Kulagollamma
India
Agriculture

Dravidian agricultural deity who makes farmers prosperous by making the grain crop abundant. [Leach 1992]

Kulanthalamman
India
Commerce and Travel

Deity of the boundary stone, who is also the collector of debts and is worshiped in the Trichinopoly (Tiruchirapalli) district of Madras, Tamil Nadu. [Leach 1992]

Kuleswari
India, *Magahiya*
Destroyer of Life

Goddess of eruptive diseases. Sister of *Sitala* worshiped in the Gaya district in the state of Bihar. [Leach 1992]

Kumari
India, *Tamil*
Life/Death Cycle; Ceremonies

"The Damsel." Among her officiants in the south are young girls who "run races on the beaches . . . in her honor." In Vedic religion she is one of the aspects of *Parvati*, but was probably an earlier deity who was absorbed by her. See also *Camunda*. [Durdin-Robertson 1976; Sykes 1968]

Kumbhamata
India
Household Affairs; Ceremonies; Creator of Life

Pot goddess, a *Gramadevata*. At the marriage ritual, a pile of pots is made that is said to be where the fertility deities reside, and a pot becomes an object of worship. The pot is a symbol of fertility. [Stutley and Stutley 1984]

Kumbhi   See *Jyestha*.

Kumbhinasa
India
Household Affairs; Evil; Large Size; Destroyer of Life; Charisma; Beauty

Pot deity. One of the *Rakshasis*. [Durdin-Robertson 1976]

Kun
India
Wealth

Hindu goddess of abundance. Corresponds to *Guanyin*, Far East, *Kaiwan*, Africa, and *Chiun*, Near East [Jobes 1962]

Kunda   See *Cunda*.

Kundalini
India
Primordial Being

Hindu mother goddess. Personification of latent energy which has the character of a coiled serpent of fire. She is the great force underlying all organic and inorganic power. Equivalent to *Kiyo-himo*, Far East. See also *Do-rje-mal-hbyor-ma*, the Himalaya, and *Sushumna*. [Danielou 1964; Durdin-Robertson 1976; Leach 1992; Stutley and Stutley 1984]

Kundalini Shakti
India
Primordial Being

A class of *Shaktis* whose power moves in a curved path and is the universal life-principle. See also *Mantrikashakti*. [Durdin-Robertson 1976]

Kunnyan   "Virgin of Light." See *Kanya*.

Kunti
India
Mother and Guardian

"Mother." Mother goddess who was replaced by other deities. Wife of Pandu, mother of Karna, Yudishthira, Bhima, and Arguna; the latter three are Pandavas. She figures in the Hindu epic, the *Mahabharata*.

⚧ *Pritha was the daughter of Shula, a Yadava king. He gave his first-born daughter, Pritha to his childless cousin, Kuntibhoja, and her name became Kunti.*
Alternate form: Pritha. [Durdin-Robertson 1976; Monaghan 1981]

Kupli
India, *Khasi*
Water; Ceremonies

Water deity. She is invoked during a June fertility ritual in Assam. [Leach 1992]

Kurmar Devis, The
India
Domesticated Animals

Goddesses of the Kurumbar shepherds from Keljhar. [Durdin-Robertson 1976]

Kurukule   See *Kurukulla*.

Kurukulla
India, Tibet
Love and Sexuality; Wealth; Unhappiness; Magic

Buddhist Red *Tara*. Goddess of love and wealth. Said by some to be terrifying. Depending on the character of the person seeing her, she is bearing arms or symbols of divine charity. She is worshiped by unhappy lovers. It is said that repeating her mantra ten thousand times will lead to the granting of all wishes. See also *Kuru Kulle*, the Himalaya.

Alternate forms: Astabhuja Kurukulla, Cunda, Kurukule, Tara. [Durdin-Robertson 1976; Getty 1962; Leach 1992; Lurker 1984]

Kurumbai
India
Commerce and Travel
   Deity of boundaries worshiped in Irungalur in the south. [Leach 1992]

Kusumamodini
India
Earth and Nature
   Himalayan mountain deity. [Monaghan 1990]

Kutamangari
India
Earth and Nature; Small Size; Magic
   "Mango Blossoms." One of the *Khekaris*. [Durdin-Robertson 1976]

Kutumbini
India
Ugliness
   Black, half-clad, blood-spattered woman. See also *Kalaratri*. [Stutley and Stutley 1984]

Kwuyuniza   See *Niseginyu*.

Lairmena
India, *Meitheis*
Fate; Intelligence and Creativity
   Goddess of divination who comes to her followers in dreams. Worshiped in Assam. [Leach 1992]

Lajja
India
Selflessness; Unhappiness
   "Modesty." Daughter of Daksha, wife of Dharma, and mother of Vinaya. Also said to be the goddess of shame in the *Vayupurana*. [Leach 1992; Stutley and Stutley 1984]

Lakini
India
Health and Healing; Creator of Life; Primordial Being
   One of six deities governing the six bodily substances. A *Shakti*. See also *Kakini*. [Durdin-Robertson 1976]

Lakshmi
India
Health and Healing; Heaven and Hell; Wealth; Beauty; Creator of Life; Luck; Ceremonies; Earth and Nature; Creator of Life; Primordial
   Goddess of prosperity and beauty. *Shakti* of Vishnu, wife of Dharma and consort of Indra and Vishnu, mother of Kama. Her sister, *Alakshimi*, or *Jyestha*, is said to be her opposite. She may have been a pre-Aryan earth deity who was later incorporated into Vedic theology. She is said to have risen from the Churning of the Ocean at the beginning of time and she is then called *Ksirabdhitanaya* or *Jaladhija*. When she is seen standing on or holding a lotus, she is called *Padma* or *Kamala*. *Sri* refers to her as beauty. As *Sita* and *Dharani*, she is associated with fertility, abundance, and prosperity. She can be represented by a basket full of unhusked rice or seedlings growing in a winnowing basket. Her image appears on coins, which suggests she is a deity of good fortune. Holly basil is sacred to her and is grown in pots near Hindu dwellings and temples. It is used to protect the body, to ensure children, and to open the gates of heaven. Some of her reincarnations are as *Kamala, Radha,* and

Varahini. Equivalent to *Kichi-jo-ten,* Far East. See also *Phra Naret,* Southeast Asia. Alternate forms: Alaksimi, Bhuti, Cancala, Durga, Gajalakshmi, Hari, Hastakamala, Hiri, Indira, Jaganmatr, Jaladhija, Karisini, Ksirabdhitanaya, Laxmi, Loka-mata, Lola, Lutchmeen, Mahalakshmi, Navadurga, Rama, Rukimi, Rukmini, Sambhu, Shri, Sita, Sri Lakshmi, Sree. [Durdin-Robertson 1976; Leach 1972; Leach 1992; Monaghan 1981; Pal 1981; Senior 1985; Stutley and Stutley 1984]

Laksmana
India
Unknown
   Hindu goddess. Wife of Krishna. [Stutley and Stutley 1984]

Lakshmi mahisasuramardini   See *Durga*.

Lalbai Phulbai
India
Metals and Minerals; Health and Healing
   "Dear Flower Lady." Personified as a stone, she is worshiped during cholera epidemics. [Leach 1992]

Lalita
India
Happiness; Love and Sexuality
   "The Amorous." Hindu deity who is the personification of playfulness. A playful young girl for whom the world is a toy and whose form is the universe. She enjoys both childish things and womanly delights. Alternate forms: Lolita, Mahadevi, Mahavidyas, Nitya. [Danielou 1964; Durdin-Robertson 1976; Leach 1992; Stutley and Stutley 1984]

Lalita Tripurasundari
India
Primordial Being; Creator of Life
   Tantric goddess of cosmic energy. *Shakti* of Shiva. From their union of energies comes the "transitory world of deception." [Lurker 1984]

Lalitalochana
India
Small Size; Magic
   One of the *Khekaris*. [Durdin-Robertson 1976]

Lambodari
India
Unknown
   Hindu pot-bellied goddess. Wife of Ganesha. [Stutley and Stutley 1984]

Lamkariya
India
Destroyer of Life
   Goddess of pustular disease. Sister of *Sitala*. [Leach 1972; Leach 1992]

Lankini
India
Mother and Guardian
   Tutelary deity of Lankala.
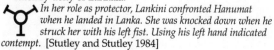   *In her role as protector, Lankini confronted Hanumat when he landed in Lanka. She was knocked down when he struck her with his left fist. Using his left hand indicated contempt.* [Stutley and Stutley 1984]

Lata
India
Earth and Nature

"Creeper." Daughter of *Ira* and Kashyapa. She is the mother of trees. [Stutley and Stutley 1984]

Lavangi
India
Earth and Nature; Goodness; Immortality; Water; Magic; Weather; Fishing and Water Animals
"She of the Clove Tree." One of the *Apsarases*. [Durdin-Robertson 1976]

Laxmi   See *Lakshmi*.

Lenju
India, *Khasi*
Water
Water deity who presides over a stream and is worshiped in the state of Assam. [Leach 1992]

Lesini   See *Durga*.

Limnate
India
Water
Water deity who inhabits salt marshes. Daughter of *Ganga*, mother of Athis who was born "beneath these crystal caves" of salt. Alternate form: Limniace. [Durdin-Robertson 1976]

Limniace   See *Limnate*.

Lohasur
India, *Agar, Baiga*
Metals and Minerals; Commerce and Travel; Household Affairs
Deity of iron and the furnace to the Agar people. Worshiped by smelters and forgers. To the Baiga, a household deity found in the axe. Also considered a male deity. [Leach 1992]

Loka-mata   "Mother of the World." See *Lakshmi*.

Lola
India
Luck; Weather
Goddess of fortune and fickleness. Also said to be a deity of lightning. Alternate forms: Cancala, Lakshmi. [Durdin-Robertson 1976; Stutley and Stutley 1984]

Lolita   See *Lalita*.

Lopamudra
India
Magic; Love and Sexuality; Selfishness
Hindu deity. Personification of finger gestures (mudras) that are important in magic and Hindu religion. Wife of Agastya (Dattoli).
Agastya made Lopamudra from the most beautiful parts of several different animals. Then he took her to the king of Vidarbha who adopted her. When she was old enough, she married Agastya and became the embodiment of wifely devotion. [Durdin-Robertson 1976; Stutley and Stutley 1984]

Lust Goddess
India
Love and Sexuality
Goddess of desire, who with her sisters, *Thirst* and *Delight* (see for story), displayed their charms to Gautama. [Durdin-Robertson 1976]

Lutchmeen   See *Lakshmi*.

Ma Dharti
India, *Bhil*
Earth and Nature; Household Affairs; Ceremonies; Agriculture
Earth deity who is worshiped during the building of a house, during sacrifices to the deceased, and at harvest time. [Leach 1992]

Ma Nu
India
Primordial Being
"Primal Ocean." Primal mother. [Walker 1986]

Ma Paudi
India
Order
Goddess of the state of Bihar who symbolizes unity. [Leach 1992]

Machandri
India
Earth and Nature; Agriculture
Earth goddess who is invoked to encourage fertility after the seeds have been planted. She is worshiped on the Hoshanabad plain, Madhya Pradesh. [Leach 1992]

Madhava
India
Love and Sexuality; Sky and Heavens; Goodness; Immortality; Water; Magic; Weather; Fishing and Water Animals
One of the *Apsarases*.
Indra sent Madhava to distract Vishnu, keeping him from concentrating and interrupting his flow of cosmic force.
This story probably points to the period when the Vedic deities were beginning to be replaced by Vishnu and Shiva. [Stutley and Stutley 1984]

Madhavi Devi
India
Earth and Nature; Love and Sexuality
Earth goddess.
When Sita's chastity was questioned, she called upon Madhavi Devi for help. She asked Madhavi Devi to let her return to the earth, if Sita had in fact been true to her husband. Madhavi Devi appeared and placed Sita on a throne and the earth swallowed her. [Stutley and Stutley 1984]

Madhukasa
India
Wealth; Weather
"Honey Whip." Goddess of abundance. The significance of her name is not clear. Honey is considered a potent fertilizing fluid, and she may have been involved in mixing it with soma, the sacred drink. She is also said to represent lightning, which is considered to be a whip and brings the rains. [Stutley and Stutley 1984]

Madhusri
India
Time
Goddess of spring. [Durdin-Robertson 1976]

Madira
India
Agriculture
Hindu goddess of wine. Alternate forms: Durga, Varuni. [Leach 1992; Stutley and Stutley 1984]

Madri
India
Justice
   Goddess and princess of Madra. Wife of Krishna or King Pandu. [Durdin-Robertson 1976; Stutley and Stutley 1984]

Madu-Ammal
India, *Kadar*
Domesticated Animals
   Animal deity who protects cattle. [Leach 1992]

Maghayanti
India
Stars and Planets; Mother and Guardian
   One of the *Krittikas*. [Durdin-Robertson 1976]

Mahadevi
India
Creator of Life; Supreme Being; Fishing and Water Animals; Primordial Being
   "Great Goddess." *Shakti* of Shiva, representing all aspects of his cosmic energy. Along with *Lalita*, all of these goddesses are sometimes called Mahadevi. When Mahadevi is worshiped by fishermen, as a goddess born from the sea, she is called *Mahagramadevata*. See also *Devi*.
   Mahadevi was asked by the other gods to create the Shaktis of the Hindu triad from her three colors. White became Sarasvati, the Shakti of Brahama; red became Lakshmi, the Shakti of Vishnu; and black became Parvati, the Shakti of Shiva.
   Alternate forms: Durga, Kali, Nitya, Uma. [Stutley and Stutley 1984]

Mahagramadevata
India
Fishing and Water Animals
   Goddess of water who is worshiped by fishermen and anyone whose livelihood is connected with lakes and rivers. See also *Mahadevi*. [Stutley and Stutley 1984]

Mahakali
India, *Banjara*
Destroyer of Life; Fate; Health and Healing
   Destructive goddess, a form of *Kali* as the personification of cholera. An emanation of *Mahalakshmi*. Sister of *Sitala*. She is also called *Kalaratri* and *Ksudha* when she is involved with the dissolution of the world. When worshiped by the Banjaras, she is said to inspire oracles through the medicine shaman. Alternate forms: Kali, Mahamari, Nidra, Trsna, Uma. [Leach 1992; Redfield 1931; Stutley and Stutley 1984]

Mahalakshmi
India
Supreme Being; Creator of Life; Primordial Being
   "Great *Lakshmi*." *Shakti* of Narayana (Vishnu). She is a primary deity, worshiped in the state of Orissa, from whom other goddesses emanate, including *Kalaratri, Ksudha, Mahakali, Mahamaya, Mahamari, Mahasarasvati, Mahavidya, Vac, Vedagarbha,* and *Yoganidra*. She is also identified with *Kali, Ksudha, Nidra, Parvati, Sarasvati,* and *Trsna*. [Danielou 1964; Leach 1992; Stutley and Stutley 1984]

Mahalaya
India
Primordial Being
   "The Source of the Universe." [Leach 1992]

Mahamai
India
Destroyer of Life

Hindu deity of pustular disease. She causes large poxes while *Chhotimai* causes small poxes. Sister of *Sitala*. [Leach 1972; Preston 1982]

Mahamantranusarini
India
Mother and Guardian; Magic; Goodness; Life/Death Cycle
   One of the *Pancaraksa*. Her spell protects against disease. [Jobes 1962]

Mahamari   See *Mahakali, Mahalakshmi,* and *Mahamaya*.

Mahamaya
India
Justice; Intelligence and Creativity
   Goddess of illusion. Said to be a queen of the Sakyas people whose capital is Kapila-vastu. An emanation of *Mahalakshmi*. Identified with *Durga; Maya;* and *Maia,* Greek and Roman Empires. Alternate forms: Kalaratri, Mahamari, Mayadevi, Tripura Bhairavi. [Durdin-Robertson 1976; Stutley and Stutley 1984]

Mahamayuri
India
Wild Birds; Magic; Reptiles; Goodness; Life/Death Cycle; Mother and Guardian
   Golden peacock goddess and queen of magic who protects against snakebites. One of the *Pancaraksa*. She is called *rMa-bya-c'en-mo,* The Himalaya; *Kun-syo-ming-wang,* Far East; and *Kujaku-myō-ō,* Far East. Alternate form: Maya Mayuri. [Getty 1962; Jobes 1962; Leach 1992; Lurker 1984]

Mahapratisara
India
Magic; Mother and Guardian; Goodness; Life/Death Cycle
   Buddhist spell goddess, one of the *Pancaraksa*. Her spell guards against physical dangers and sin. [Jobes 1962; Lurker 1984]

Mahanidra   See *Uma*.

Mahari
India, *Irula, Neilgherries*
Destroyer of Life
   Goddess of smallpox. Alternate form: Mariatha. [Leach 1992]

Mahasahasrapramardani
India
Magic; Mother and Guardian; Weather; Evil; Goodness; Life/Death Cycle
   "The Great Lady of the Void." Buddhist spell goddess. One of the *Pancaraksa*. She is invoked for protection from earthquakes, evil spirits, and storms. [Jobes 1962; Leach 1992; Lurker 1984]

Mahasarasvati
India
Supreme Being
   Supreme goddess who emanates from *Mahalakshmi*. One of the *Pancaraksa*. Alternate form: Vedagarbha. [Stutley and Stutley 1984]

Mahasitaviti
India
Magic; Mother and Guardian; Hunting and Wild Animals; Insects; Earth and Nature; Goodness; Life/Death Cycle
   Buddhist spell goddess, "the Great Lady of the Cool Grove." She is invoked for protection from ferocious beasts, poisonous insects, and plants. [Jobes 1962; Lurker 1984]

Mahasveta
India
Earth and Nature
"Dazzling White." Earth goddess. Consort of Surya, the sun god. Also a name for *Durga* and *Sarasvati*. [Durdin-Robertson 1976; Stutley and Stutley 1984]

Mahavani   "Transcendent Word." See *Sarasvati*.

Mahavidya
India
Education and Knowledge; Stars and Planets
"Transcendent Knowledge." Her concern is not with knowledge for its own sake, but with knowledge that will lead to the attainment of ultimate liberation. A post-Vedic deity who probably evolved from a prehistoric mother goddess. An emanation of *Mahalakshmi*. She is closely connected to *Vac*. In Nepal, the Himalaya, she is worshiped as a stellar deity who is portrayed as many-armed, with three faces or heads. See also the *Mahavidyas* and *Sarasvati*. [Danielou 1964; Leach 1992; Stutley and Stutley 1984]

Mahavidyas, The
India
Education and Knowledge
Ten Hindu goddesses of transcendent knowledge and magical powers. Seven of them belong to the creative manifestation stages of the universe, and three to the withdrawal stages. *Kali* (or her manifestation *Lalita*) and *Tara* (or her manifestation *Janguli*) are the two principal deities. The others are *Sodasi, Bhuvanesvari, Bhairavi, Chinnamasta* (or her manifestation *Viraratri*), *Dhumavati* (or her manifestations *Daridra* or *Vidhava*), *Bagala, Matangi,* and *Kamala*. See also *Mahavidya*. [Stutley and Stutley 1984]

Mahavyahriti, The
India
Unknown
Names of the first three of the seven worlds who are personified as the daughters of Savitr and *Prishni*. [Stutley and Stutley 1984]

Mahendri
India
Creator of Life; Primordial Being; Mother and Guardian; Earth and Nature; Water
One of the *Matris*. *Shakti* of Indra. Corresponds to *Indrani*. [Durdin-Robertson 1976]

Mahesvari
India
Supreme Being; Creator of Life; Mother and Guardian
"Power of Universal Dominion." Hindu supreme goddess. *Shakti* of Shiva. One of the *Saptamatrakas*. Also a name for *Durga* and *Parvati*. [Danielou 1964; Stutley and Stutley 1984]

Mahi
Earth and Nature; Stars and Planets; Ceremonies; Wealth; Domesticated Animals
"Great." Earth goddess who is said to be the mother of the planet Mars. With *Ila* and *Sarasvati*, she attends the sacrifice. Also called the *Soma Cow* from whom all prosperity and abundance flow. [Durdin-Robertson 1976; Stutley and Stutley 1984]

Mahisasuramardini
India
War
The form of *Durga* when slaying the buffalo form of Shumbha. [Stutley and Stutley 1984]

Mai Dharitri
India, *Baiga*
Earth and Nature
Earth goddess. [Durdin-Robertson 1976]

Maia   See *Maya*.

Maimungma
Bangladesh, *Tiparas*
Agriculture
Bengal and Bangladesh agricultural deity who presides over the paddy fields. Wife of the agricultural god, Thunai. [Leach 1992]

Mainao
India, *Kachari*
Household Affairs; Agriculture
Household deity and guardian of the rice fields worshiped in the state of Assam. Alternate form: Bhulli Buri. [Leach 1992]

Maisamma
India
Agriculture; Mother and Guardian
Protective village deity who presides over agricultural prosperity. Worshiped on the Telangana Plateau in the state of Andhra Pradesh. [Leach 1992]

Maitreyi   See *Ahalya*.

Maitri
India
Goodness; Love and Sexuality
"Goodwill," "Friendship." [Durdin-Robertson 1976]

Maiya Andhiyari
India, *Dhanwar*
Moon and Night
Goddess of the night worshiped in the Central Provinces. She represents "the dark fortnight of the month." Alternate forms: Rat Devi, Rat Mai. [Leach 1992]

Makara
India
Ceremonies
Buddhist Tantric deity who was adopted by the Hindu Tantrists. She may be the personification of the "five Ms" of the "left-handed" Tantric ritual. They are *mada* (wine), *matsya* (fish), *mamsa* (meat), *mudra* (parched grain or kidney beans, which are considered aphrodisiacs), and *maithuna* (ritualistic copulation). [Stutley and Stutley 1984]

Makaravaktra
India
Magic
Buddhist *Dakini* who is able to confer supernatural powers on those who invoke her. [Jobes 1962]

Makaris, The
India
Fishing and Water Animals; Evil; Ugliness
Sea monsters. They are portrayed as amphibious animals, possibly a crocodile or a monster fish with the head of a deer and legs of an antelope. Similar to Chaldean *Tiamat*. [Durdin-Robertson 1976]

Malin Budhi
India, *Santal*
Creator of Life
Creator goddess.

☿ *Malin Budhi was commanded by the god, Thakur Kiu (Jiu), to make human beings. Her first attempt failed when she gave humans the lives of birds and they flew away. She tried several more times before successfully hatching two eggs into human beings.* [Leach 1992]

Malini
India
Sky and Heavens; Goodness; Immortality; Water; Magic; Weather; Fishing and Water Animals
"She with the Garland." Wife of Ruci, mother of Manu Raucya. One of the *Apsarases*. Also referred to as a "celestial female *Devi*" who is similar to the *Apsarases*. [Durdin-Robertson 1976; Stutley and Stutley 1984]

Mallana Devi
India, *Khond*
Domesticated Animals; Ceremonies; Health and Healing
Goddess of shepherds worshiped in Keljhar. She is represented by a stone that is kept in a dolmen (shrine or temple). Offerings of wooden figures are made to her by those who are ill in hopes of averting their death. [Durdin-Robertson 1976]

Mallinatha
India
Magic
A Jain rishi (a holy person or sage) who possesses supernatural powers, equal to or superior to the gods. [Durdin-Robertson 1976; Leach 1972]

Mamata
India
Mother and Guardian; Love and Sexuality; Unhappiness
Hindu deity.
☿ *Mamata was assaulted by her brother-in-law, Brihaspati, when she was pregnant, but the fetus prevented him from actually having intercourse with her. He cursed the unborn child and, afraid that her husband would be angry, Mamata tried to abandon the baby. The gods commanded her to raise the child "born of two fathers."* [Stutley and Stutley 1984]

Mamili
India, *Koyi*
Agriculture; Ceremonies
Agricultural deity worshiped in southern India. She is said to be propitiated with sacrifices, preferably human, to prevent crop failure. [Leach 1992]

Manasa
India, *Mal*
Intelligence and Creativity; Reptiles; Earth and Nature; Heaven and Hell; Creator of Life; Ceremonies; Health and Healing
"Mind, Thought." Snake goddess worshiped in the state of Bengal and in parts of Bihar, Orissa, and Assam. She is connected with the earth, the nether world, and as a fertility goddess she is involved in marriage ceremonies. She protects her followers against the bites of poisonous snakes. When she removes poison, she is called *Visahari*; when she controls poison, she is called *Visadhari*. See also *Devi*. Alternate forms: Adimata, Durgamma, Padma, Padmavati, Shaivi. [Durdin-Robertson 1976; Johnson 1988; Leach 1972; Leach 1992; Monaghan 1981; Stutley and Stutley 1984]

Manasi
India
Intelligence and Creativity; Immortality; Sky and Heavens; Goodness; Immortality; Water; Magic; Weather; Fishing and Water Animals

"The Intelligent One." One of the *Apsarases* who welcome the souls after death. [Durdin-Robertson 1976]

Mandakini   "Milky Way." See *Ganga*.

Mandaradevi
India
Small Size; Magic
One of the *Khekaris* who is the goddess of the paradise tree. [Durdin-Robertson 1976]

Mandaramala
India
Earth and Nature
"Wreath of Mandara Flowers." One of the *Devis*. [Durdin-Robertson 1976]

Mandarava
India
Magic
Buddhist deity. Incarnation of *Dakini*. She is a shape-changer and accompanies Padmasambhava. [Jobes 1962]

Mandodari
India
Justice; Unhappiness
"Narrow-waisted." Daughter of *Maya*, wife of Ravana, mother of Indrajit. Queen of Lanka.
☿ *After mourning her husband who was killed in battle, she married his brother, Bibhishan, who then became king of Lanka.* [Durdin-Robertson 1976; Stutley and Stutley 1984]

Mandwa Rani
India, *Kawar*
Earth and Nature; Mother and Guardian
Protective nature deity worshiped in the Central Provinces. She inhabits Mandwa Hill and helps those who are lost in the forest. [Leach 1992]

Mane Hennu Devaru   See *Kelu Devaru*.

Mane Manchamma   See *Mane Manchi*.

Mane Manchi
India
Reptiles
Serpent deity worshiped in Karnataka (Mysore). Alternate form: Mane Manchamma. [Leach 1992]

Mangadevatas
India
Mother and Guardian
A class of *Devatas*. Protective deities. [Durdin-Robertson 1976]

Mangalamai
India
Destroyer of Life; Commerce and Travel
Goddess of pustular disease worshiped by the Dom caste (scavengers, musicians, weavers, traders, and moneylenders) in the state of Bihar. One of the sisters of *Sitala*. [Leach 1992]

Manota
India
Unknown
Deity to whom an offering is made during the manota hymn. She is mentioned in the *Rig Veda* (sacred Hindu

literature whose hymns are addressed to personifications of the powers of nature). [Durdin-Robertson 1976; Leach 1972]

Manthara
India
Evil; Destroyer of Life
Name for *Dundubhi,* a *Gandharvi,* when she was reincarnated as a provoker of hate. She was killed by Indra when she tried to destroy the world. Also the name of a deformed slave who was the servant of Queen *Kaikeyi.* [Stutley and Stutley 1984]

Mantradevatas
India
Household Affairs; Earth and Nature
A class of *Devatas* who are invoked in a scripture text. [Durdin-Robertson 1976]

Mantrikashakti
India
Education and Knowledge; Arts
"Power of Letters, Speech, and Music." A class of *Shaktis.* One of the six forces who, in their unity, represent the Astral Light. The others are *Ichchhashakti, Jnanashakti, Kriya-shakti, Kundalini Shakti,* and *Parashakti.* [Durdin-Robertson 1976]

Manusha-Rakshasis, The
India
Evil
Devils who appear in human form. [Durdin-Robertson 1976]

Marahi Devi   See *Marai Mata.*

Marai Mata
India
Destroyer of Life
Cholera goddess who is worshiped by the Kohil caste. Similar to *Sitala.* Alternate form: Marahi Devi. [Monaghan 1981; Pike 1951]

Maraki
India
Destroyer of Life
Disease deity who causes cholera and is worshiped in Gujarat. [Leach 1992]

Maramma
India
Destroyer of Life
Goddess of cholera in Karnataka (Mysore). See also *Mariamma.* [Leach 1992]

Margavati
India
Commerce and Travel; Mother and Guardian
Protector of travelers who guards the paths and roads. [Stutley and Stutley 1984]

Marhai Devi   See *Marai Mata.*

Marhai Mata
India, *Kunbi, Kurmi*
Destroyer of Life
Disease goddess who causes smallpox and cholera in the Central Provinces. [Leach 1992]

Mari
India
Destroyer of Life; Weather
Hindu deity. Personification of pestilence and death who is identified with *Durga.* Also a Dravidian village mother goddess who causes smallpox or makes it rain. See also Celtic *Mari,* Western Europe. [Durdin-Robertson 1976; Eliade 1987; Leach 1992; Stutley and Stutley 1984]

Mari Bhavani
India
Destroyer of Life
Brahman disease goddess of pestilence in Mirzapur, Uttar Pradesh. Similar to Oba. [Leach 1992]

Mari Mai
India
Destroyer of Life; Commerce and Travel; Agriculture
Cholera goddess of the Dom caste (scavengers, musicians, weavers, traders, and moneylenders) who is called "Mother of Death." Also worshiped for abundant crops. Alternate forms: Jalpa Mai, Kali. [Leach 1992]

Mari Mata
India, *Banjara*
Destroyer of Life
Cholera goddess in Madhya Pradesh. See also *Mariamma.* [Leach 1972; Leach 1992]

Mariai   See *Mariamma* and *Mari.*

Mariama   See *Mariamma.*

Mariamma
India, Sri Lanka
Destroyer of Life; Mother and Guardian; Ceremonies
Village deity or mother goddess who brings smallpox, cholera, and other fatal diseases. Disease goddesses are feared more than loved so they are propitiated with sacrifices. In southern India and Ceylon, Mariamma is also a protector of seafarers. See also *Maramma, Mari Mati.* Alternate forms: Mariai, Mariama. [Leach 1972; Leach 1992]

Mariamman
India
Weather; Destroyer of Life
"Mother of Death or Rain." Sister of *Sitala.* [Preston 1982]

Mariatha   See *Mahari.*

Marichi
India
Dawn and Twilight; Ugliness
"Queen of Heaven." Buddhist dawn goddess. The frightening counterpart of *Ushas.* Marichi has three faces, ten menacing arms, and an eye in her forehead. May be equivalent to *Dou Mou,* Far East, and *Hod-zer-can-ma,* the Himalaya. See also *Asokakanta,* this section, and *Marishi-ten,* Far East. Alternate form: Marishi. [Durdin-Robertson 1976]

Marici
India
Dawn and Twilight; Domesticated Animals
"Diamond Sow." Buddhist dawn goddess. Alternate form: Asokakanta. [Leach 1992]

Maridama
India
Evil; Destroyer of Life

Malevolent disease deity who brings cholera. Alternate form: Maridiamma. [Leach 1992]

Maridiamma   See *Maridama*.

Marisha
India
Sky and Heavens; Goodness; Immortality; Water; Magic; Weather; Fishing and Water Animals
Celestial deity. One of the *Apsarases*. Daughter of *Pramlocha*, wife of Prachetases, mother of Daksha. Alternate form: Marsha. [Durdin-Robertson 1976]

Marishi   "Queen of Heaven." See *Marichi*.

Maritchi
India
Unknown
Vedic goddess. Equivalent to *Dou Mou*, Far East. [Sykes 1968]

Mariyammai
India
Destroyer of Life
"Mother Death" to the Tamil-speaking people of southeastern India. Alternate form: Sitala. [Stutley and Stutley 1984]

Mariyamman
India
Family of Life
Village deity of the Tamil-speaking people of southeastern India. [Olson 1983]

Mariyayi
India, *Malayali*
Destroyer of Life
Disease goddess who brings cholera. [Leach 1992]

Marsha   See *Marisha*.

Maru Devi
India
Unknown
Hindu deity. Wife of Nabhi, mother of Rishabha, who is considered the founder of Jainism (a form of Hindu religion that resembles Buddhism, founded in 500 B.C.E.). [Durdin-Robertson 1976]

Marulupolamma
India, *Vada*
Water
Southern goddess of the sea. [Leach 1992]

Maruttaruni
India
Small Size; Weather
"Wind Maiden." One of the *Khekaris*. [Durdin-Robertson 1976]

Maryatale
India
Unknown
Headless Hindu goddess worshiped by the Pariah caste. [Cooper 1876]

Masan
India
Destroyer of Life; Commerce and Travel

Deity of the cremation grounds. Sometimes considered male. Worshiped by the Dom caste (scavengers, musicians, weavers, traders, and moneylenders). [Leach 1992]

Masani
India
Destroyer of Life
Hindu goddess of pustular disease. Sister of *Sitala*. [Leach 1972]

Masanyatha
India, *Kadar*
Justice
Goddess of justice. She presides over the trials of lawbreakers so she can detect the wrongdoers. [Leach 1992]

Maswasi
India, *Baiga, Dhanwar*
Hunting and Wild Animals
Goddess of hunting to the Dhanwar. Maswasi is a god of the chase to the Baiga. [Leach 1992]

Mata
India, *Khond, Bhil, Hos, Bhunjia, Korku*
Mother and Guardian; Moon and Night; Time; Fate; Destroyer of Life
"Mother or Moon." As the moon, she is the measurer of time and as a mother, her womb determines (measures) the potential of each human being. Also said to be a goddess of smallpox and cholera. Alternate forms: Dantesvari, Mata Devi. [Leach 1992; Redfield 1931; Stutley and Stutley 1984]

Mata Devi   See *Mata*.

Mata Januvi
India, *Rajput*
Mother and Guardian
Goddess of childbirth. [Leach 1992]

Matabai
India
Mother and Guardian; Ceremonies
Mother goddess worshiped in the village of Nimkhera, state of Madhya Pradesh. She is invoked for children, particularly "at the Havan, a nine-day sacred-fire ceremony in December." [Leach 1992]

Matamgi   See *Matangi Shakti*.

Matangi
India
Hunting and Wild Animals; Moon and Night; Intelligence and Creativity; Order; Wealth; Magic
"The Night of Delusion." Night deity. Also mother of elephants. She reveals a day of peace and prosperity which is really a dream or mirage that appears at night. As one of the ten sources of preternatural power, a *Mahavidya*, she is the personification of domination. Also a manifestation of *Shakti*. [Leach 1992; Stutley and Stutley 1984]

Matangi Shakti
India
Destroyer of Life
Disease deity associated with smallpox. She can take the form of *Sitala* or other similar goddesses. Alternate form: Matamgi. [Leach 1992]

Mataras, The
India
Mother and Guardian

"Little Mothers." Seven to nine goddesses whose functions are not clearly defined. They may be *Shaktis*. Alternate form: Ambikas. [Lurker 1984]

Mathyalamma See *Mutyalamma*.

Matrikas, The See *Matris*.

Matri-Padma
India
Water; Primordial Being; Creator of Life
  "Universal Mother." Personification of the waters of space. Associated with the opening lotus, a symbol of the vulva. [Leach 1992]

Matris
India
Mother and Guardian; Earth and Nature; Water; Travel and Commerce; Magic; Destroyer of Life
  In the singular, "Divine Mother." The plural is *Matrikas.* Both names refer to a class of goddesses identified with Vedic *Gnas,* ancient mother goddesses, and attendants of *Skanda.* They are connected with water and earth and are sometimes called the "seven mother streams." They are equated with the *Shaktis.* Similar to Gallic *Matres,* Western Europe, and *Hlamos,* the Himalaya. Their numbers vary according to the source but included are *Bhogavati, Devasena, Dhriti, Gauri, Jaya, Mahendri, Medha, Padma, Pushti, Savitri, Svadha, Svaha, Tushti,* and *Ambika* and her three aspects *Jyestha, Raudri,* and *Vama.* Also said to be spirits who practice witchcraft and dwell in cemeteries, at crossroads and on mountains, and are disease demons.
  The Seven Mothers assisted Candika in her struggle against Sumbha and his followers. The Seven Mothers, personifiying the energy of their respective deva, quickly stopped the enemies of the gods, and then broke into a victory dance.
  Alternate form: Matrikas. [Jobes 1962; Stutley and Stutley 1984]

Matrix of the Universe
India
Creator of Life
  Hindu teaching compares the Matrix to the female uterus. This womb contains mighty oceans, the continents, seas, mountains, stars, planets, the gods, demons, and humankind. [Durdin-Robertson 1976]

Maura Mata
India, *Baiga*
Destroyer of Life
  Disease goddess who causes seizures in children. [Leach 1992]

Mawshai
India, *Khasi*
Commerce and Travel
  Market deity worshiped in the state of Assam. [Leach 1992]

Maya
India
Intelligence and Creativity; Creator of Life; Sun and Day; Water; Magic
  "Illusion" personified as a Hindu and Buddhist goddess. Also worshiped in Nepal, Tibet, eastern Asia, and the Himalaya. She gives life and the desire for life. Also called "The Mother of Creation" and the "Material Universe." Connected to light, to the sea, with witchcraft and magic, she seems to have endless manifestations. See also *Mulaprakriti.* Corresponds to *Prakriti.* Alternate forms: Mahamaya, Maia,

Maya, Mayadevi, Mayavati. [Durdin-Robertson 1976; Monaghan 1981; Stutley and Stutley 1984]

Maya Mayuri See *Mahamayuri*.

Mayadevi "Illusion." See *Maya* and *Mahamaya*.

Mayarani
India
Water
  Fresh water deity. [Leach 1992]

Mayavati "Deceiver." See *Rati* and *Maya*.

Mayavva
India
Health and Healing
  Disease goddess in Sivapur propitiated to cure chicken pox and other contagious diseases in children. [Leach 1992]

Meana See *Mena*.

Medha
India
Intelligence and Creativity; Education and Knowledge
  "Intelligence or Wisdom." Personified as the daughter of Daksha and wife of Dhrama. Also a form of *Sarasvati.* See also *Matris.* [Durdin-Robertson 1976; Stutley and Stutley 1984]

Medini
India
Earth and Nature; Stars and Planets; Love and Sexuality
  "Illicit Love." Earth goddess, mother of the planet Mars, and one of the *Nayikas.* [Durdin-Robertson 1976; Stutley and Stutley 1984]

Mena
India
Mother and Guardian; Goodness; Love and Sexuality; Magic; Health and Healing; Sky and Heavens; Immortality; Water; Weather; Fishing and Water Animals
  "Mind-born" daughter of Svadha and wife of Himavat, mother of *Ganga, Parvati,* and Mainaka. Also the name of an *Apsarases.* Alternate forms: Meana, Menaka, Merna. [Danielou 1964; Durdin-Robertson 1976; Stutley and Stutley 1984]

Menaka See *Mena*.

Merna See *Mena*.

Mesabai
India
Water
  Fresh water deity. Alternate form: Mesako. [Leach 1992]

Mesako See *Mesabai*.

Mgigalekha
India
Moon and Night; Small Size; Magic
  "Moon-streak." Princess of the *Khekaris.* [Durdin-Robertson 1976]

Mimi Biliku See *Biliku*.

Mina
India
Fishing and Water Animals

Hindu deity. Mother of fish and makaras, metaphysical aquatic animals. [Stutley and Stutley 1984]

Minachiamman
India
Evil; Justice; Beauty

Village deity of Madura. Her demon form is called *Thurgai*.

☥ *When a king closed her temples, Minachiamman incarnated as a young child to take revenge. She appeared wearing a bracelet that was an exact replica of one belonging to the queen. The king was going to adopt the child, but he was advised not to, so she was thrown into a river. Saved by a passing merchant, she became a beautiful young woman who caught the eye of Shiva, who had incarnated as a poor man. When he tried to sell his wife's bracelet because they needed money, he was accused of stealing the queen's jewels and was killed.*

Minachiamman became Thurgai and killed the king. [Monaghan 1990]

Minaksi
India
Charisma; Love and Sexuality; Ceremonies

"Fish-eyed." An ancient southern goddess, an incarnation of *Parvati*. As a daughter of Kubera, she is a *Yakshi*. Wife of Sundara who is worshiped in Madurai. Her lustrous eyes subdue all who see her.

☥ *Minaksi had three breasts, but when she met Shiva her third breast disappeared. Their wedding took place in the riverbed of the Vaigai. Minaksi's brother was given the wrong time for the wedding and arrived late. He left in anger and sulked in a tent on the far side of the river. Every year since, he arrives late and retires to sulk. Thousands of people gather each year in the same riverbed to celebrate Minaksi's wedding and her brother's disappointment.*

See also *Tadatagei*. [Durdin-Robertson 1976; Leach 1992; Stutley and Stutley 1984]

Mindhal
India
Metals and Minerals

Goddess worshiped in Himachal Pradesh.

☥ *Mindhal rose out of the earth in the form of a large black stone. When the stone began to emerge, the woman, in whose yard it was happening, tried to push her back into the ground. When she began to worship the stone her friends made fun of her so she changed her seven sons and herself into stones and surrounded Mindhal.*

Alternate forms: Bhagvati, Mindhal Devi. [Monaghan 1990]

Mindhai Devi See *Mindal*.

Mirgi Devi
India, *Baiga*
Destroyer of Life

Disease goddess who causes epilepsy. [Leach 1992]

Mirzapore Forest Goddess
India
Earth and Nature

Titular forest deity worshiped in the Mirzapore (Mirzapur), a city/district in the state of Uttar Pradesh. [Durdin-Robertson 1976]

Misrakesi
India
Sky and Heavens; Goodness; Immortality; Water; Magic; Weather; Fishing and Water Animals

One of the *Apsarases*. [Durdin-Robertson 1976]

Mngilamma
India, *Paraiyan*
Earth and Nature

Southern bamboo goddess. [Leach 1992]

Mohani
India
Evil

"The Beguiler." Demon of deception who causes human fetuses to be born as snakes, frogs, etc. [Stutley and Stutley 1984]

Mohenjo-Daro Goddesses
India
Creator of Life

Many figures, thought to be goddesses and dated around the third millenium B.C.E., were found at Mohenjo-Daro in the Indus Valley. For example, there is a figure that is naked, wide-hipped, and lifting her breasts with her hands, similar to earth mother figures of other regions. To the soil-tillers this figure has remained the goddess of fertility, "the Possessor of Dung." For others, as male deities gained ascendancy in the more complicated pantheon, this figure became a consort, sublimated to a male deity. [Fairservis 1971; Leach 1972]

Mohini
India
Beauty; Magic

"Beautiful Enchanter." Female form assumed by Vishnu to bewitch the *Asuri*, depriving them of their share of the ambrosia that arose during the Churning of the Ocean. [Stutley and Stutley 1984]

Monkey Goddess of Hampi
India
Mother and Guardian

"Queen Mother." There is a stone carving of her from Hampi. [Durdin-Robertson 1976]

Moothevi
India, *Korava*
Evil; Health and Healing

Goddess of sleep worshiped in the south. She helps criminals by keeping them awake and making their victims sleepy. [Leach 1992]

Mother Earth
India
Earth and Nature; Water; Mother and Guardian

The earth described as the body of a woman, the water is her blood. At first, she existed under the water, but then she rose above the water and broke apart, forming the "Eternal Land" and many islands. She corresponds to *Bhavani, Bhumi, Prishni, Prithivi,* and Chaldean *Tiamat.* [Durdin-Robertson 1976]

Mother Fish
India
Creator of Life; Fishing and Water Animals

"Mother," "Fiery Fish of Life." Creator goddess who "spawned" the whole cosmos. [Durdin-Robertson 1976]

Mother Globes
India
Mother and Guardian; Health and Healing; Intelligence and Creativity; Immortality

"The Mother Being of This Planet." She personifies seven principles: the gross body, fluidic double, life principle, creative impulse, physical intelligence, Buddhi, and spiritualized akasa. [Durdin-Robertson 1976]

Mother Space
India
Sky and Heavens
  "The Womb of Space." Creator of the sun and planets. Corresponds with *Aditi*, this section, and *Tho-og*, The Himalaya. [Durdin-Robertson 1976]

Mother Water
India
Creator of Life; Water
  "Mystic Mother." Creator goddess who created from her womb or from her breast, the water of the "Great Sea" from which everything evolved. Water is the symbol of the female element. [Durdin-Robertson 1976]

Motho
India
Earth and Nature; Agriculture
  Deity of the grains, vetch and pulse. Sister of *Mungo*. [Leach 1972]

Moti Mata
India
Metals and Minerals; Destroyer of Life
  "Pearl Mother." She is manifested in a stone that is worshiped during cholera epidemics. [Leach 1992]

Mrtyu
India
Destroyer of Life; Goodness; Unhappiness
  Goddess of death.
  Mrtyu was a compassionate being and did not like to kill people. Because she cried about her duty, Brahma turned her tears into fatal diseases.
  Also considered by some to be a male deity. See also *Prithivi*. [Leach 1992]

Mudevi
India
Unknown
  "The Crow-bannered, the Ass Rider," whose weapon is a sweeping broom. A form of *Jyestha*. [Stutley and Stutley 1984]

Mugadi   See *Jyestha*.

Muhurta
India
Time
  Goddess of moments of time. Daughter of Dalsa, wife of Dharma or Manu. [Stutley and Stutley 1984]

Mukhambika
India
Mother and Guardian
  "Mouth Mother." She has a shrine in northern Cannanore on the Malabar coast in the state of Kerala. [Stutley and Stutley 1984]

Mukta Devi
India, Bangladesh
Creator of Life
  Fertility deity worshiped in the state of Bengal. Wife of Dharma Thakur, a fertility, prosperity, and healing god. [Leach 1992]

Muktakesi
India
War

Durga's
name as destroyer of the giant's troops. [Stutley and Stutley 1984]

Mulaprakriti
India
Primordial Being
  Primordial goddess. Personification of the primal substance and its derivatives, the most basic element of nature from which all forms are derived. Her three aspects are *Shakti, Prakriti,* and *Maya.* She corresponds to *Aditi.* Similar to the Hebrew goddesses *Nepesh,* Near East, *Shekinah,* Near East, and to *Gaea,* Greek and Roman Empires. [Durdin-Robertson 1976]

Mungo
India
Earth and Nature; Agriculture
  Deity of the grains pulse and vetch. Sister of *Motho*. [Leach 1972]

Murala
India
Earth and Nature; Love and Sexuality; Unhappiness
  Mother of bamboo.
  Murala was a Brahman girl who unknowingly married a man of the Sudra caste. When the deception was discovered, she decided to end her life by throwing herself on a funeral pyre. Her ashes grew into bamboo. [Leach 1972]

Mutyalamma
India, *Telangana, Koyi, Konda Dora, Koya*
Health and Healing; Destroyer of Life
  Disease goddess who causes smallpox and cholera and is invoked to avert these illnesses. Also said to be a goddess in eastern India. Alternate form: Mathyalamma. [Leach 1992; Monaghan 1990]

Muzamuza
India, *Sema Naga*
Evil; Earth and Nature; Unhappiness
  Malevolent wood spirit worshiped in the state of Assam. She causes men to disappear or go mad. [Leach 1992]

Na Rip Nom
India
Family and Tribes
  Marriage deity. She originated marriage with Tarbong-bo and Komsithing, and is worshiped in the state of Sikkim. [Leach 1992]

Na Zong Nyo   See *It Mu*.

Nadi
India
Water
  A river personified as a goddess. In the Hindu tantras (a division or chapter of sacred works in Sanskrit), Nadi is "the channel through which energies flow through the human subtle body." See also *Ida*. [Durdin-Robertson 1976; Stutley and Stutley 1984]

Nage-bonga
India, *Hos*
Goodness; Water; Destroyer of Life
  Benevolent river goddess. If offended she can cause diseases of the eyes and ears. [Leach 1992]

Nage-Era
India, *Munda*
Destroyer of Life

Disease goddess.

🜬 *Nage-Era's brother was destroying humans. She rescued two of them and would not return them to Singbonga until he promised to stop his destructive behavior. Her share of humankind was those with leprosy. It is said she infects people with the disease to increase the size of her share.* [Leach 1992]

Naginis, The See the *Nagis*.

Nagis, The
India
Evil; Demi-animals; Heaven and Hell
Serpent demons whose upper body is human and whose lower body is snake-like; but rather than creep, they walk and run. Alternate forms: Naginis, Nagnis.

🜬 *Kadru and her husband Kashyapa gave birth to one thousand Nagis, with whom they peopled Patala, the seven infernal regions below the surface of the earth.*
[Durdin-Robertson 1976; Stutley and Stutley 1984]

Nagnis See *Nagis*.

Naikin Bai
India, *Baiga*
Destroyer of Life; Domesticated Animals
Goddess of disease in cattle. [Leach 1992]

Naina Devi
India
Domesticated Animals; Wealth
Goddess of eyes. She was transported to earth by a divine cow. The cow stayed at Naina Devi's sacred spot, producing great amounts of milk. [Monaghan 1990]

Nakshatras, The
India
Moon and Night; Goodness; Health and Healing; Weather; Wealth; Order; Mother and Guardian
Hindu moon goddesses. Wives of the moon. Also said to be the name of one of the *Vasus*. [Redfield 1931; Sykes 1968]

Naktamcharis, The
India
Evil; Ugliness; Moon and Night
Night goblins. [Durdin-Robertson 1976]

Nakti Devi
India, *Baiga*
Agriculture
Agricultural deity who presides over the fields. Sometimes said to be the wife of Thakur Deo, god of cultivation. [Leach 1992]

Naladi
India
Earth and Nature; Fishing and Water Animals; Immortality; Water; Magic; Weather; Sky and Heavens; Goodness
"Nard." One of the *Apsarases*. She has the unpleasant odor of the nard plant. See also *Guggulu*. [Stutley and Stutley 1984]

Namagiri
India
Intelligence and Creativity
Inspiration goddess who inspires knowledge. Similar to the *Muses*, Greek and Roman Empires.

🜬 *About ninety years ago a brahmin of Madras prayed for a grandchild in the temple of Namagiri and his prayer was answered. Shortly before the birth, Namagiri appeared to the man's daughter and predicted that her son would be very gifted. When, as an adult, the son Ranamujan was invited to Cambridge,*

his mother refused to let him go. Namagiri once again appeared, this time convincing the mother that her son would not endanger his soul by going to England. [Durdin-Robertson 1976]

Namamdamma
India, *Kannadiyan*
Destroyer of Life; Directions; Ceremonies
Village disease goddess of the south who is propitiated with the sacrifice of a goat to ward off cholera and cattle disease. [Leach 1992]

Nanda Devi
India
Earth and Nature
"Blessed Goddess" of the Himalaya Mountains. [Leach 1992]

Nandi
India
Happiness
Hindu goddess of joy. [Woodcock 1953]

Nandini
India
Domesticated Animals; Wealth; Immortality
"Cow of Abundance." Daughter of *Surabhi*. Worshiped in northern India, which is denoted as the land of plenty by her name. Her milk rejuvenates humankind. [Stutley and Stutley 1984]

Nanga Baigin
India, *Baiga, Agar*
Earth and Nature
Earth deity. Wife of Nanga Baiga, god of earth and animals. [Leach 1992]

Narasimhi
India
Demi-animals
One of the Hindu *Saptamatrakas* who is sometimes substituted for *Camunda* as one of the seven. She has the head of a lion. [Leach 1992; Stutley and Stutley 1984]

Narayani Mai
India, *Magahiya*
Destroyer of Life; Commerce and Travel
Goddess of pustular disease. Sister of *Sitala*. Worshiped in the Gaya district in the state of Bihar. Also worshiped by the Dom caste (scavengers, musicians, weavers, traders, and moneylenders). [Leach 1992]

Nari
India
Creator of Life
Elemental mother who becomes *Tanmatra*, the mother of air, water, fire, earth, and ether. Similar to *Mari* and *Mariamma*. See also *Akasa* and *Hyrania*. Associated with *Trigana*. [Durdin-Robertson 1976; Jobes 1962]

Narmada
India
Water; Health and Healing; Reptiles; Ceremonies; Goodness
A river and the goddess personifying it. The river rises from Mt. Mekala in the Vindhya Mountains, Madhya Pradesh. The Nagas gave Narmada the ability to annul the effects of snake venom, and the sight of the river absolves one from all sin. It is considered a meritorious act for her followers to walk on the banks of the river from the sea to her source and back, a two-year pilgrimage. Alternate form: Reva. [Durdin-Robertson 1976; Stutley and Stutley 1984]

Navadurgas, The
India
Agriculture

Nine plant forms of *Durga* including *Brahmani* (plantain), *Camunda* (rice), *Durga* (turmeric), *Kalika* (Arun colocasia), *Karttiki* (barley), *Lakshmi* (rice), *Raktadantika* (pomegranate), *Siva* (wood apple), and *Sokarahita* (Saraca indica). They are invoked to protect their followers. See also *Sri*. Alternate form: Navapatrikas. [Stutley and Stutley 1984]

Navapatrikas, The See *Navadurgas*.

Nayikas, The
India
Love and Sexuality

Eight minor forms of *Durga* including *Ati-Canda*, *Camunda, Canda, Candanayika, Candavati, Candogra*, *Pracanda*, and *Ugracanda*. Also the name of a class of deities who are the personifications of illicit love including *Aruna*, *Balini, Candi, Jayini, Kamesvari, Kaulesi, Medini*, *Sarveshvari*, and *Vimala*. [Stutley and Stutley 1984]

Nidra
India
Health and Healing; Creator of Life

Deity personifying sleep. She emerged from the Churning of the Ocean.

At the end of each age, when the world is dissolved, Nidra enters the body of Vishnu. He goes to sleep on the causal waters until Nidra, instructed by Brahma, departs. Vishnu then awakens and re-creates the world.

Alternate form: Mahakali. [Stutley and Stutley 1984]

Nikumbhila
India
Mother and Guardian; Magic; Ceremonies

Guardian deity of Lanka (Raksasas). She has the power to make humans invisible. Groves are dedicated to her where there is dancing, drinking of wine, and human sacrifice in her honor. [Stutley and Stutley 1984]

Ninda Kando (Chando)
India, *Santal*
Moon and Night

Moon deity. Wife of the sun, Sing Chando, mother of the stars. [Leach 1992]

Ning-Bonga
India, *Binjhia*
Moon and Night

"Mother of the Stars." Dravidian moon goddess worshiped in the north. [Redfield 1931]

Nirantali
India, *Kind*
Creator of Life

Creator deity. [Leach 1992]

Nirriti
India
Destroyer of Life; Unhappiness; Evil; Wild Birds; Hunting and Wild Animals; Justice; Poverty; Heaven and Hell; Large Size; Beauty; Charisma

"Corruption, Evil, and Decay." Goddess of death and misery. Wife/daughter of Adharma and *Himsa*, mother of the *Rakshasis* and Rakshasas. The much feared owl, pigeon, and hare are sacred to her. Worshiped by Hindus and Buddhists. Black in color, she finds those who do not honor her properly. She is asked to avoid the paths of the good and follow those of thieves and robbers. Those who are

born into poverty and crime, but are virtuous, are protected by Nirriti. She is the guardian of the southwestern quarter of the compass, the underworld. Alternate forms: Alakshmi, Bhairava, Bhairavi, Jyestha, Nirrti. [Danielou 1964; Durdin-Robertson 1976; Leach 1992; Stutley and Stutley 1984]

Nirrti See *Nirriti*.

Nisacharis, The
India
Evil; Ugliness; Moon and Night

Goblins and courtesans. [Durdin-Robertson 1976]

Niseginyu
India, *Rengma Naga*
Agriculture

Agricultural deity, "a Spirit of the Crops." Alternate forms: Aiyulaniza, Aso, Kwuyuniza. [Leach 1992]

Nishtigri
India
Earth and Nature

Hindu earth goddess. Wife of Dyaus. [Jobes 1962]

Nit See *Niti*. See also *Nit*, Egypt.

Nitatui
India
Stars and Planets; Mother and Guardian

One of the *Krittikas*. [Durdin-Robertson 1976]

Niti
India
Justice; Education and Knowledge

Deity of "Royal Policy" associated with guidance, wisdom, morality, and ethics. See also *Nit*, Egypt. Alternate form: Devaki. [Durdin-Robertson 1976]

Nitya
India
Supreme Being; Magic

Great goddess, *Mahadevi*, who embraces all women and entrances the world. The highest female in the supreme mandala of Tantric female deities. Associated with Krishna. Alternate form: Lalita. [Stutley and Stutley 1984]

Niyati
India
Fate

Fate goddess. [Durdin-Robertson 1976]

Nona Chamari
India
Health and Healing; Reptiles; Commerce and Travel

Goddess of health who is invoked in times of illness and to avert death from poisonous snakebites. Worshiped by the Chamar caste (shoemakers, skinners, tanners, and leather workers) in the state of Uttar Pradesh. [Leach 1992]

Nostu Nopantu
India, *Garo*
Creator of Life; Insects

Creator deity worshiped in the state of Assam.

Nostu Nopantu was sent by Tatara Rabuga, the creator god, to create the earth. She had a beetle bring up clay from under the primordial water and she fashioned the earth. [Leach 1992]

Nrtya
India
Mother and Guardian

Buddhist mother goddess, one of the eight mothers of Buddhism. Her aspect is peaceful, her color is green, and she is portrayed with two or four arms, dancing. See *Gar-ma*, The Himalaya. [Jobes 1962]

Nukalamma
India
Health and Healing; Destroyer of Life

Disease goddess who is worshiped in the south to avert illness, especially smallpox. [Leach 1992]

Nukulamma
India
Evil; Luck; Health and Healing; Destroyer of Life

Malevolent deity who causes misfortune and harm. She is worshiped to avert illness. [Leach 1992]

Nustoo
India
Creator of Life

Dravidian creator deity worshiped in the north.

☿ *Nustoo came into being from a self-evolved egg. She inhabited the petals of a water lily that floated on the primal ocean until she formed and molded the earth.* [Redfield 1931]

Ola Bibi
India, Bangladesh
Destroyer of Life

Disease deity who causes cholera in the state of Bengal. As the Muslim goddess *Ola Chandi*, she is said to be the goddess of cholera. Alternate form: Olabibib. [Leach 1992; Preston 1982]

Ola Chandi   See *Ola Bibi*.

Olabibib   See *Ola Bibi*.

Oraon Earth Goddess
India, Bangladesh, *Oraon*
Creator of Life; Ceremonies

Fertility goddess worshiped in the state of Bengal. A festival intended to encourage this goddess to make the earth fruitful is held when the sal tree is in blossom. [Durdin-Robertson 1976]

Orusandiamma
India
Water; Fishing and Water Animals

Sea goddess. She is worshiped by fishermen on the eastern coast. Sister of Ramasondi, a water god. [Leach 1992]

Pa Janjali   See *Pae Devi*.

Padma   "Lotus." See *Lakshmi, Manasa, Matris*, and *Sri*.

Padmadakini
India
Magic; Weather

Buddhist atmospheric deity who can confer supernatural powers. Her color is red and her emblems are the skull cup, ritual wand, and lotus. See also *Dakinis* and *Padma-mkhah-Ngro*, the Himalaya. [Jobes 1962]

Padmavati
India
Justice; Mother and Guardian

"Messenger." Nagi Queen. Wife of Parshvanatha.

☿ *With Dharanendra, Padmavati saved her husband from death during a flood by protecting him with her cloak.*

Alternate form: Manasa. [Durdin-Robertson 1976; Stutley and Stutley 1984]

Pae Devi
India, *Bhil*
Water; Fishing and Water Animals

Water deity. Wife of Sunagi Moru. She presides over salt water and fresh water, and all the animal life in the water. She is worshiped in the state of Madhya Pradesh. Alternate form: Pa Janjali. [Leach 1992]

Paharon
India
Destroyer of Life

"She of the Hills." Disease goddess who causes smallpox. [Preston 1982]

Pan Dong Cyu
India, *Lepcha*
Earth and Nature; Weather; Health and Healing; Time

Mountain deity who is invoked at the beginning of the rains and winter to avert illness and death. Wife of the mountain god, Pan Dong. They are worshiped in the state of Sikkim. [Leach 1992]

Pancaraksa, The
India
Mother and Guardian; Magic; Goodness; Life/Death Cycle

Buddhist five-spell goddesses. They are invoked for longevity and protection. Benevolent deities who are the personifications of five magical formulas first uttered by Gautama Buddha. The five are *Mahamantranusarini, Mahamayuri, Mahapratisara, Mahasahasrapramardani*, and *Mahasarasvati*. [Jobes 1962; Lurker 1984]

Pandara
India
Fire

"White One." Buddhist fire goddess. [Lurker 1984]

Paniharin
India, *Baiga*
Household Affairs; Mother and Guardian

Household deity. Protector of women who bring the water into the house, she lives beside the water pots. [Leach 1992]

Pansahi Mata
India, Bangladesh
Destroyer of Life

Disease deity who causes smallpox in young children. She is worshiped in the state of Bengal. [Leach 1992]

Panthoibi
India, *Neitheris*
Life/Death Cycle; Sun and Day

Deity of life and death. Associated with the sun. Wife of Khaba, she is worshiped in Manipur and Assam. [Leach 1992]

Parashakti, The
India
Fire; Sun and Day

"Great Force" including the powers of heat and light. A class of *Shaktis*. See also *Mantrikashakti*. [Durdin-Robertson 1976]

Parasu-pani   "Mother of India." See *Bhavani*.

Para-vac
India
Primordial Being
Vedic mother of the "Supreme Logos." Alternate form: Vac. [Stutley and Stutley 1984]

Parbutta
India
War
Hindu goddess of war. Sometimes called the consort of Shiva. [Redfield 1931]

Parendi
India, Iran
Wealth
Goddess of material wealth. In Iran she is one of the wives of Ahura Mazda. Equivalent to *Purandhi*. [Leach 1992]

Parnasavari
India
Health and Healing; Mother and Guardian
"Savari of the Leaves." Ancient goddess of protection who later became a Buddhist deity. She has two forms, one yellow and one green, and wears a loincloth of leaves. She conquers all epidemics. In Japan she is called *Hiyoi Kwan-non* or *Jgyo-kongo,* Far East. Alternate form: Sarvasavaaranaambhagavati. [Getty 1962; Lurker 1984]

Parooa
India
Commerce and Travel; Physical Prowess; Charisma; Disorder; Weather
Female spirit of the crossroads in Assam.
☿ *Parooa plays a flute-like instrument to lure travelers from the road. She then envelopes them in a thick fog from which they cannot escape.*
Similar to Celtic *Dames Vertes,* Western Europe. [Monaghan 1990]

Parrapotamma
India, *Paraiyan*
Health and Healing; Domesticated Animals
Deity who cures cattle disease. [Leach 1992]

Parvati
India
Earth and Nature; Love and Sexuality; Intelligence and Creativity; Ceremonies; Time; Creator of Life; Primordial Being
One of the aspects of *Devi.* Her energy represents passionate attachment to sexuality. Personification of the Himalaya Mountains and the conscious substance of the universe. Daughter of ether and intellect, she is the ruler of the elves and spirits of the earth. In her fierce aspect as *Kali,* the "Power of Time," she is fierce-looking and fond of intoxicants, lust, and bloody sacrifices. Sister of *Ganga,* wife and *Shakti* of Shiva, mother of Skanda (Karttikeya, Kumara) and Ganesha. Some of Parvati's aspects may come from regional goddesses whom she absorbed or from *Devi.* She is one of the *Gauris* with *Rambha, Totala, Tripura,* and *Uma.* She is identified with Jagadmata.
☿ *One day Parvati was sitting nude on the lap of Shiva when some holy men walked in unannounced. Her embarrassment was so great that Shiva promised that any man who intruded in the future would be instantly transformed into a female.*
Alternate forms: Adrija, Ambika, Ammal, Annal, Annapurna, Bhairavi, Candi, Doorga, Durga, Durja, Gauri, Girija, Ilura, Jagad-Dhatri, Kali, Kamashi, Kamasshi, Karala,

Kaveri, Kumari, Mahalakshmi, Mahesvari, Minaksi, Radha, Syama. [Cooper 1876, Danielou 1964; Durdin-Robertson 1976; Lurker 1984; Monaghan 1981; Neumann 1972; Olson 1983; Stutley and Stutley 1984]

Pasupati
India
Mother and Guardian
Pre-Aryan mother goddess. [Johnson 1988]

Pathya
India
Wealth; Commerce and Travel; Directions; Sky and Heavens
"Auspicious Path." Goddess of prosperity and protector of travelers. Wife of Pusan, protector deity of paths and travelers. Said to be associated with the eastern quarter of the heavens. [Stutley and Stutley 1984]

Pathyarevati
India
Wealth
"Genius of Plenty." [Durdin-Robertson 1976]

Pathya Svasti
India
Luck; Wealth
"Prosperous Way or Path." Goddess of success and well-being. Equivalent to *Sevasti-devi.* [Stutley and Stutley 1984]

Paulomi   See *Indrani.*

Pauri Pat
India, *Santal*
Commerce and Travel; Luck
Hill deity invoked for successful journeys. [Leach 1992]

Paurnamasi
India
Moon and Night
Celestial deity who presides over the full moon. The night of the full moon is especially sacred to the Hindus. [Leach 1992; Stutley and Stutley 1984]

Pavanarekha
India
Justice
Queen of the Yadavas, a peace-loving, agricultural people who lived during the Second Age of the world. [Durdin-Robertson 1976]

Petni
India, Bangladesh
Evil; Earth and Nature
Malevolent tree spirit worshiped in the state of Bengal. See also *Sankini.* [Bonnerjea 1927]

Pharka Undharan Mata
India, *Baiga*
Destroyer of Life
Disease deity. [Leach 1992]

Phoki Mata
India, *Baiga*
Destroyer of Life; Domesticated Animals
Disease deity who causes dysentery in cattle. [Leach 1992]

Phorcis
India
Mother and Guardian; Domesticated Animals

Sow goddess worshiped as a mother goddess in the north. She is portrayed with large breasts, sitting on a lotus throne, with a child on her lap. She was masculinized into Phorcys. [Johnson 1988]

Phulmata
India, Bangladesh
Destroyer of Life
   Disease goddess who causes smallpox in young children in the state of Bengal. [Leach 1992]

Phulmati
India
Destroyer of Life
   Goddess of a mild form of pustular disease. Younger sister of *Sitala*. [Leach 1992]

Pidari
India
Unhappiness; Immortality; Mother and Guardian; Reptiles
   Snake deity and village goddess, a *Gramadevata*, who presides over suicides and violent death. By controlling the spirits of those who died in this manner, she prevents them from becoming malevolent demons. She guards the villages by frightening evil spirits away with her noose and drum. Alternate forms: Kala-Pidari, Pitali. [Monaghan 1990; Stutley and Stutley 1984]

Pingala
India
Sun and Day
   "Red-eyed." Sun goddess. Alternate forms: Pingela, Pingeela, Soorenjnaree. [Durdin-Robertson 1976]

Pingeela   See *Pingala*.

Pingela   See *Pingala*.

Pisaca   See *Pishacha*.

Pisacas   See *Pishacha* and *Pisachis*.

Pisachis, The
India
Immortality; Moon and Night; Large Size; Evil; Destroyer of Life; Beauty; Charisma
   "Flesh-eater." Hindu bloodthirsty demons who inhabit the north. Similar to the *Rakshasis*. They are said to be very pious and are the souls of those who have met violent or untimely deaths, created from drops of water by Brahma. Other authors say they are the daughters of *Pishacha*, they emerged from the god Pulaha, or they were produced by Darkness. Another form of the Pisachis are the *Asapishachikis*. Alternate forms: Pisacas, Pishachis, Pishachakis. [Durdin-Robertson 1976; Leach 1972; Stutley and Stutley 1984]

Pishacha
India
Evil
   Mother of demon daughters, the *Pisachis* and demon sons, the Pisachas. Alternate form: Pisacas. [Durdin-Robertson 1976; Stutley and Stutley 1984]

Pishachakis   See *Pisachis*.

Pishachis   See *Pisachis*.

Pitali   See *Pidari*.

Piteri
India, *Khond*
Creator of Life
   Creator deity. Worshiped in the city/district of Madras in the state of Tamil Nadu with her husband, Bura Penu. [Leach 1992]

Pochamma
India
Destroyer of Life
   Disease deity who causes smallpox in the Telangana area in the state of Andhra Pradesh. [Leach 1992]

Podamata
India, *Bhil*
Health and Healing
   Health goddess invoked by sick women in the state of Madhya Pradesh. [Leach 1992]

Polamde
India
Destroyer of Life
   Goddess of pustular disease. Sister of *Sitala*. [Leach 1972]

Poleramma
India
Commerce and Travel; Destroyer of Life
   A boundary goddess in Ellore (Eluru) district in the state of Andhra Pradesh. In the Telugu region in the same state, she is a smallpox goddess. [Leach 1992]

Pollamma
India
Destroyer of Life
   Disease goddess who causes smallpox. [Olson 1983]

Ponniyayi
India
Health and Healing; Mother and Guardian
   Village goddess of health. She presides over the relief of suffering and the granting of children in the Trichinopoly (Tiruchirapalli) district of Madras in the state of Tamil Nadu. [Leach 1992]

Poramai
India, *Nadiya*
Earth and Nature
   Jungle goddess. Alternate form: Poru Mai. [Leach 1992]

Poru Mai   See *Poramai*.

Pos Bai
India, *Oraon*
Household Affairs
   Household deity. Daughter of Barnda, guardian of the household. [Leach 1992]

Prabha
India, *Kanjar*
Dawn and Twilight; Health and Healing; Domesticated Animals
   "Radiance." Dawn goddess who presides over the health of humans and cattle. Daughter of Svarbhanu. Also the name of Sagara's wife who is the mother of sixty thousand sons. Alternate form: Prabhata. [Leach 1992; Stutley and Stutley 1984]

Prabhasa
India
Health and Healing; Weather; Wealth; Order; Mother and Guardian; Goodness
One of the *Vasus*. [Sykes 1968]

Prabhata   See *Prabha*.

Pracanda
India
Love and Sexuality
One of the *Nayikas*. Alternate form: Durga. [Stutley and Stutley 1984]

Pracriti
India
Earth and Nature
Nature deity. [Woodcock 1953]

Pragna   "Goddess of Knowledge." See *Prajna*.

Prajna
India
Education and Knowledge; Intelligence and Creativity; Creator of Life; Primordial Being
Buddhist goddess. Personification of the female principle of knowledge and the basis of cognition. For those who practice Zen Buddhism, the activation of Prajna is the ultimate goal. She corresponds to Hindu *Shakti;* Hebrew *Chokmah,* Western Europe; and Gnostic *Sophia,* Near East. Alternate form: Pragna. [Durdin-Robertson 1976; Stutley and Stutley 1984]

Prajnaparamita
India
Education and Knowledge; Heaven and Hell; Ceremonies
Tantric Buddhist bodhisatva of transcendent wisdom, "wisdom that has gone to the other shore." "Mother of all the Buddhas." Offerings of flowers and perfumes are made to her. See also *Prajnaparamita* and *Ses-rab-kyi-pha-rol-ta-phyin-pa,* the Himalaya; and *Bilig-un-cinadu-kijaghar-a-kuruksen,* Far East. [Getty 1962; Jobes 1962; Leach 1972; Stutley and Stutley 1984]

Prajnapti
India
Magic
Goddess of information, a magic art. [Durdin-Robertson 1976]

Prakriti
India
Life/Death Cycle; Earth and Nature
Hindu goddess. Personification of "the active female principle through which the inactive male principle of the cosmos is manifested." With the male principle, she constitutes Nature, its generation and destruction. During evolution she was responsible for every Deva being associated with a *Shakti*. She corresponds to *Aditi* and *Maya*. See also *Mulaprakiti* and the *Seven Females*. Alternate form: Prakrti. [Durdin-Robertson 1976; Jobes 1962; Stutley and Stutley 1984]

Prakrti   See *Prakriti*.

Pramandani
India
Earth and Nature; Sky and Heavens; Goodness; Immortality; Water; Magic; Weather; Fishing and Water Animals

"A Pungent-smelling Plant." One of the *Apsarases.* See also *Guggulu.* [Stutley and Stutley 1984]

Pramlocha
India
Evil; Sky and Heavens; Love and Sexuality; Goodness; Immortality; Unhappiness; Magic; Water; Weather; Fishing and Water Animals
Celestial demon. One of the *Apsarases.*

⚥ *Pramlocha was sent by the gods to distract Kandu from his penances. She gave him so much pleasure that he was distracted for nine hundred and seven years, six months, and three days. When he realized that he had been distracted for so long (it had seemed like only a day), he angrily sent Pramlocha away. She was so troubled about leaving that she began to sweat profusely. As she flew away the moisture dripped on the trees below. Collected by the winds and matured by the rays of the moon, her perspiration grew into a beautiful girl called Marisa.*
Equivalent to *Bai Mundan,* Far East. [Durdin-Robertson 1976; Stutley and Stutley 1984]

Pratyusha
India
Wealth; Order; Mother and Guardian; Goodness; Health and Healing; Weather
One of the *Vasus*. [Sykes 1968]

Pretasana   See *Camunda*.

Prishni
India
Earth and Nature; Domesticated Animals; Weather
"Variegated" or "Ray of Light." Earth goddess manifested as a many-colored cow or perhaps as a spotted storm cloud. Wife of Rudra or Savitr, mother of the Maruts (male storm spirits). See also *Mother Earth*. Alternate form: Prsni. [Durdin-Robertson 1976; Leach 1992; Stutley and Stutley 1984]

Pritha   See *Kunti* and *Prithivi*.

Prithivi
India, Bali
Domesticated Animals; Earth and Nature; Life/Death Cycle; Wealth; Order; Mother and Guardian; Goodness; Weather; Health and Healing
"Broad One." The earth manifested as a cosmic cow who feeds everyone with her milk. Sometimes jointly personified with the sky as *Dyava-Prthivi*. When she is the earth, her children are all the forms of life found there. She is closely connected to animal husbandry, the occupation of the great majority of people who worship her. One of the *Vasus*.

⚥ *During an early population explosion, Prithivi is said to have been unable to endure all the people and appealed to Brahma to reduce their numbers. He did so by creating death, Mrtyu.*
Identified with *Aditi,* she also closely corresponds to *Bhudevi*. Also worshiped in Bali. See also *Bhumi, Dyava-mata, Gai, Mother Earth, Mrtyu,* and *Sukarapreyasi.* Alternate forms: Adkaya, Aksaya, Pritha, Ritha. *[Danielou 1964; Durdin-Robertson 1976; Leach 1992; Monaghan 1981; Stutley and Stutley 1984; Sykes 1968]*

Priti
India
Happiness
Goddess of joy. [Durdin-Robertson 1976]

Priyadarsana
India
Beauty

"Good Looking." Daughter of **Yashoda** and Mahavira. [Durdin-Robertson 1976]

Priyakarini
India
Education and Knowledge
Goddess of knowledge. One of the **Vidyadevis.** See also **Trisala.**

Prsni   See **Prishni.**

Puloma
India
Evil
Demon. Wife of Bhrigu but loved by Puloman. With her sister **Kalaka,** she is the mother of thirty million Danavas (giant demons). She is said to have lived with her family in a golden city that floats in air. [Durdin-Robertson 1976]

Puluga   See **Biliku.**

Puramdhi
India
Creator of Life
Ancient fertility goddess. Corresponds to **Durga.** [Stutley and Stutley 1984]

Purandhi
India
Wealth
Hindu goddess of material abundance. Associated with Bhaga and equivalent to **Parendi.** [Jobes 1962; Leach 1992]

Puranjani
India
Intelligence and Creativity
Goddess of intellect. Wife of King Puranjana.
Puranjani lived happily with her husband for one hundred years, disapproving only of his great desire to hunt. [Stutley and Stutley 1984]

Pururavas
India
Sky and Heavens; Goodness; Immortality; Water; Magic; Weather; Fishing and Water Animals
One of the **Apsarases.** She and **Urvasi,** under certain conditions, agree to become the lovers or wives of some notable person. [Stutley and Stutley 1984]

Purvachitti
India
Fate; Sky and Heavens; Goodness; Immortality; Water; Magic; Weather; Fishing and Water Animals
"Presentiment." One of the **Apsarases.** [Durdin-Robertson 1976]

Purvadevatas
India
Primordial Being
"Primeval Deity." A class of **Devatas.** [Durdin-Robertson 1976]

Pushti
India
Physical Prowess
Deity of strength. See also **Matris.** [Leach 1992]

Puspa
India
Mother and Guardian

One of the eight mothers of Buddhism. She is peaceful in aspect and her color is white. Holding a flower and having two or four arms, she is usually depicted dancing. Identical to **Me-tog-ma,** the Himalaya. [Jobes 1962]

Putana
India
Evil; Destroyer of Life; Mother and Guardian; Fate
Giant vampire-like demon. One of the **Rakshasis,** she is a child killer.
 When Krishna was born, Putana suckled him with her poison milk. Instead of killing him, she was killed, fulfilling the prophecy that Krishna would become a slayer of demons. [Durdin-Robertson 1976; Stutley and Stutley 1984]

Radha
India
Luck; Love and Sexuality; Mother and Guardian
"Success, Achievement" or "Beloved One." There are several women in the Hindu religion with this name. One is said to be the lover or wife of Krishna. In Tantrism her infinite love is the essence of Krishna and she presides over life and its energies. The Radha who is the wife of Adhiratha became the foster mother of Karna when he was rescued from the Ganges River. A form of **Lakshmi** and an alternate form of Parvati. [Danielou 1964; Durdin-Robertson 1976; Olson 1983; Stutley and Stutley 1984]

Ragalata   "Vine of Love." See **Rati.**

Rahabasin Mata
India, *Baiga*
Destroyer of Life; Courage
Disease deity who brings sickness caused by fear. [Leach 1992]

Rajamma
India, *Jalari, Oriya Kumbaro, Vada*
Mother and Guardian; Health and Healing; Luck; Fishing and Water Animals
Goddess of childbirth worshiped in the south. She makes barren women fertile and determines the size of the fishermen's catch. [Leach 1992]

Rajarajeshvari
India
Justice; Education and Knowledge
"Queen of Queens." The embodiment of all transcendent knowledge. Alternate form: Bhuvanesvari. [Stutley and Stutley 1984]

Rajyadidevatas, The
India
Justice; Mother and Guardian
Guardian deities of royalty. A class of **Devatas.** [Durdin-Robertson 1976]

Rajyasri
India
Justice
"Royal Dignity." Queen Victoria was worshiped by a sect in the state of Orissa. [Durdin-Robertson 1976]

Raka
India
Moon and Night; Agriculture; Wealth; Courage; Mother and Guardian; Ceremonies
Moon goddess associated with the full moon. Daughter of Angiras and Sraddha. She may have been an earlier

fertility goddess involved in agriculture. Associated with childbirth, she is invoked for children, to endow heroism in sons, and to make her followers prosperous. See also *Sinivali*. [Durdin-Robertson 1976; Stutley and Stutley 1984]

Rakini
India
Unknown
One of the *Shaktis* who governs bodily substances. See also *Dakini* and *Kakini*. [Durdin-Robertson 1976]

Raksasis   See *Rakshasis*.

Rakshasis, The
India
Large Size; Evil; Charisma; Beauty; Destroyer of Life
Giant demons who allure with their beauty. Their offspring are adult at the moment of conception. Sisters of the male Rakshasas. They are said to be carnivorous and capable of destroying entire cities. Some of them are *Gautami, Gavariamma, Hidimba, Jara, Kumbhinasa, Nirriti, Pisachi, Putana, Surpanakha, Tadaka, Taraka,* and *Trigata.* Alternate form: Raksasis. [Bonnerjea 1927; Durdin-Robertson 1976; Stutley and Stutley 1984]

Rakshodhidevatas, The
India
Evil; Justice
Leaders of the demons. A class of *Devatas.* [Durdin-Robertson 1976]

Raksin Mata
India, *Baiga*
Destroyer of Life
Disease goddess who causes large sores that itch. [Leach 1992]

Raktadantika
India
Earth and Nature
A *Navadurga.* A plant form of *Durga,* the pomegranate. [Stutley and Stutley 1984]

Raktadhara
India
Sky and Heavens
Cosmic deity. One of the *Kimnaras.* [Durdin-Robertson 1976]

Raktipurbi
India, *Baiga*
Hunting and Wild Animals
Hunting goddess. [Leach 1992]

Rama
India
Charisma
"Charming." See *Lakshmi.* Also the name of male deities. [Stutley and Stutley 1984]

Ramaladevi
India
Moon and Night; Beauty; Charisma
"Dark-colored," "Pleasing," "Darkness." Night goddess who is charming and lovely. Mother of Gayadeva. [Durdin-Robertson 1976]

Rambha
India
Beauty; Sky and Heavens; Goodness; Immortality; Water; Magic; Weather; Fishing and Water Animals
One of the *Apsarases.* Whatever her guise, she is always described as beautiful. Said to be one of the Fourteen Treasures connected with the Churning of the Ocean and one of the six variants of the goddess *Gauri.* [Durdin-Robertson 1976; Stutley and Stutley 1984]

Ramchandi
India, *Kol*
Earth and Nature
Worshiped in the Central Provinces as Mother Earth. [Leach 1992]

Ranaghanti
India
War; Metals and Minerals; Mother and Guardian
War goddess worshiped in Assam in the form of a large red stone. She is invoked to give protection and victory in battle. [Monaghan 1990]

Rangda
India, Bali
Creator of Life; Magic; Ugliness; Fire; Life/Death Cycle; Ceremonies; Agriculture
Goddess of fertility and a witch. With tusks and striped breasts, she goes about spewing fire from her tongue. In Bali she is associated with the paddy fields and offerings are made to her. She is also said to be a "widow" who is associated with death and menopause, the end of the fertility of life. See also *Rangda,* Southeast Asia. [Durdin-Robertson 1976; Neumann 1972; Preston 1982]

Ranu Bai
India, *Nimadi*
Mother and Guardian; Water; Creator of Life
Fertility deity. She is invoked by barren women.
Ranu Bai carried a golden pitcher on a silver cord. To fill the rivers of India, she poured water from her wondrous pitcher. [Monaghan 1990]

Rat Devi   See *Maiya Andhiyari.*

Rat Mai   See *Maiya Andhiyari.*

Rati
India
Love and Sexuality; Creator of Life; Mother and Guardian; Sky and Heavens; Goodness; Immortality; Water; Magic; Weather; Fishing and Water Animals
"Desire, Passion, Love." An *Apsarases.* One of the wives of Kama, the god of desire. The Balinese version of this Hindu fertility goddess is a very pregnant woman with distended breasts.
Rati reincarnated as Mayavati and was the wife of Shambhara when Kama was reborn as Pradyumna. Shambhara, heeding a warning that he had received, threw Pradyumna into the sea where he was swallowed by a fish. The fish was caught and arrived in the kitchen of Shambhara, where it was cut open by Mayavati and the still living child was recovered. Because Pradyumna (Kama) was able to become invisible, Mayavati was able to raise him to adulthood. Then he killed Shambhara in single combat. Mayavati and Pradyumna eventually resumed their forms of Rati and Kama.
Alternate forms: Kami, Kelikila, Ragalata, Reva, Subhangi. [Cotterell 1979; Durdin-Robertson 1976; Leach 1992; Pike 1951; Stutley and Stutley 1984]

Ratnadakini

India
Weather; Magic
Buddhist air deity who confers supernatural powers on those who invoke her. See also *Rin-chen-mkhah-ngro*, The Himalaya. [Jobes 1962]

Ratnamangari

India
Earth and Nature; Small Size; Magic
"Abundance of Blossoms." One of the *Khekaris*. [Durdin-Robertson 1976]

RatriIndia

Moon and Night; Mother and Guardian; Health and Healing
Goddess of the night. With her sister *Usas*, the mother of celestial order. They follow similar paths but they never cross paths. Ratri provides her followers with rest, protecting them from wolves and thieves. [Leach 1992; Stutley and Stutley 1984]

Raudri See *Ambika* and *Matris*.

Rddhi

India
Wealth
Deity of prosperity. Wife of Kuvera (Kubera), god of wealth. Alternate form: Riddhi. [Leach 1992]

Rembha

India
Happiness
Goddess of pleasure. Associated with Indra. Similar to *Venus*, Greek and Roman Empires. [Street 1804]

Renuka

India
Love and Sexuality; Selflessness
Hindu deity. Daughter of King Rasenajit, wife of Jamadagni, mother of Parasurama (sixth incarnation of Vishnu).

Renuka's husband was an ascetic who became a hermit, deserting his wife. She was visiting him after having seen a couple involved in erotic behavior and the resulting stimulation was transferred from her mind to Jamadagni. Unable to drive Renuka from his mind, he gave up being a hermit and lived with his wife.

Alternate form: Runeeka. [Durdin-Robertson 1976; Stutley and Stutley 1984]

Reva

India
Water; Love; Sexuality
Water goddess and embodiment of wifely love. Personification of running water. Alternate forms: Rati, Narmada. [Durdin-Robertson 1976; Leach 1992; Stutley and Stutley 1984]

Revali

India
Health and Healing
Healing goddess who gives relief to those afflicted with blindness and paralysis. [Leach 1992]

Revati

India
Wealth
A *Yogini*. Identified with *Aditi* and *Durga*. Also the name of a daughter of King Raivata who is the wife of Balarama

and associated with abundance. [Durdin-Robertson 1976; Stutley and Stutley 1984]

Riddhi See *Rddhi*.

Ritha See *Prithivi*.

Rksavaktradakini

India
Weather; Magic; Demi-animals
Buddhist air goddess portrayed as a yellow, bear-headed witch. She confers superhuman powers on her followers. See also *Dom gdon-can*, The Himalaya. [Baring and Cashford 1991]

Rodasi

India
Weather; Wealth
Vedic goddess of lightning who bestows wealth. Wife of Ruda, mother or wife of the Maruts (male storm spirits). One of the *Gnas*. [Durdin-Robertson 1976; Stutley and Stutley 1984]

Rohina See *Rohini*.

Rohini

India
Domesticated Animals; Stars and Planets; Health and Healing; Love and Sexuality; Unhappiness
"Red One." A cow goddess and a constellation. Counterpart to the personified rising sun, Rohita. In post-Vedic writing, she is the daughter of *Surabhi*, mother of *Kamadhenu*. Her red color is said to signify health.

Rohini was loved by the moon god and her father became angry that they were spending so much time together. He cursed the moon with consumption. Rohini's sisters intervened and convinced their father to make the disease chronic rather than fatal. This explains why the moon comes and goes.

See also *Devaki*. Alternate form: Rohina. [Durdin-Robertson 1976; Jobes 1962; Leach 1992; Monaghan 1981; Stutley and Stutley 1984]

Rokime

India, *Garo*
Agriculture
Agricultural deity. Worshiped in the state of Assam and invoked for a good rice crop. [Leach 1992]

Ronkini

India, *Santal*
Earth and Nature; Ceremonies
Hill goddess. In earlier times she required human sacrifices. [Leach 1992]

Rtuharika

India
Evil; Destroyer of Life
Hindu demon who makes women infertile by obstructing the menses. [Stutley and Stutley 1984]

Rudrani

India
Ceremonies; Evil; Destroyer of Life; Unhappiness
"Goddess of Tears." Malevolent storm goddess who causes sickness and death to emerge from the forests. She is mentioned in the Brahaman (priestly compositions) as requiring blood sacrifices. In post-Vedic writings she is identified with *Durga*. Alternate form: Uma. [Jobes 1962; Leach 1992; Stutley and Stutley 1984]

Rukmini
India
Dawn and Twilight; Family and Tribes; War
"Gloaming." Hindu deity. Wife of Krishna, sister of Rukmin, mother of Pradyumna. She is also considered an incarnation of **Lakshmi.**

⚥ *Rukmini's brother, Rukma, had arranged her betrothal to Sisupala, a cousin of Krishna's. Before the marriage took place, Rukmini sent a letter to Krishna asking him to prevent the wedding. Krishna rescued her on her wedding day and a battle ensued. Rukma supported Sisupala, but his life was spared when his sister interceded.* [Danielou 1964; Durdin-Robertson 1976; Jobes 1962; Stutley and Stutley 1984]

Runeeka   See *Renuka.*

Saci
India
Physical Prowess; Earth and Nature; Primordial Being
"Divine Power." Hindu strength goddess. Wife of Indra. Vedic name for **Indrani,** she is also called **Aindri.** She is the owner of the divine *parijata* tree.

⚥ *Saci's tree came from the Churning of the Ocean and was planted in Indra's heaven. The coral tree yielded all the objects anyone could wish for and was desired by Satyabhama who had Krishna steal it for her.*
See also **Satyabhama.** [Stutley and Stutley 1984]

Sacontala   See *Sakuntala.*

Sacti   See *Shakti.*

Sadanvas, The
India
Evil; Household Affairs; Ceremonies
Hindu demons who inhabit the foundations on which houses are built. Rudra and Indra are invoked to remove them and a pearl shell amulet is worn for protection against them. Because so little is known about them, they are greatly feared. [Stutley and Stutley 1984]

Sadbhavasri
India
Life/Death Cycle
"Becoming." A goddess. [Durdin-Robertson 1976]

Sahaganya
India
Family and Tribes; Sky and Heavens; Goodness; Immortality; Water; Magic; Weather; Fishing and Water Animals
"Bridesmaid." An **Apsarases.** [Durdin-Robertson 1976]

Sakambhari
India
Agriculture; Wealth
Agricultural deity worshiped in Pandharpu in the Solapur district in the state of Maharashtra. She presides over vegetation and prosperity. [Leach 1992]

Saki
India
Physical Prowess; Charisma
"Competence, Power, Might, Grace, and Skill." Wife of Indra. May correspond to **Indrani.** [Durdin-Robertson 1976]

Sakis   See *Krittika.*

Sakunadevatas
India
Luck

A class of **Devatas.** They preside over good omens. [Durdin-Robertson 1976]

Sakunadhisthatri
India
Luck
Hindu goddess of omens, usually good. Alternate form: Sakunadhishthatri. [Durdin-Robertson 1976; Stutley and Stutley 1984]

Sakuni
India
Destroyer of Life
Disease demon of children. Sometimes associated with **Durga.** [Stutley and Stutley 1984]

Sakuntala
India
Sky and Heavens; Family and Tribes
Celestial nymph. Daughter of **Menaka** who married a mortal. Wife of Dushyanta, mother of Bharata. Ancestor of the human race of Bharat. Alternate forms: Sacontala, Shakuntala. [Durdin-Robertson 1976; Stutley and Stutley 1984]

Sali Minao
India, *Kachari*
Agriculture
Agricultural deity who presides over the *sali* crop. [Leach 1992]

Samaiya
India
Mother and Guardian; Health and Healing; Commerce and Travel
Goddess of childbirth worshiped by the Dom caste (scavengers, musicians, weavers, traders, and moneylenders.) Wife of Gandak, god of thieves. She offers protection during childbirth, teething, and illness. [Leach 1992]

Samalamma
India, *Jalari, Vada*
Health and Healing; Fishing and Water Animals
Fishing deity of the south who protects fishermen from fevers. [Leach 1992]

Sambhu
India
Mother and Guardian; Order
"O Giver of Peace," a birth goddess. See also **Lakshmi.** Alternate form: Sambhuti. [Danielou 1964; Durdin-Robertson 1976]

Sambhuti   See *Sambhu.*

Samdhya   See *Sandhya.*

Samgna
India
Intelligence and Creativity; Unhappiness; Magic; Domesticated Animals; Love and Sexuality; Order
Goddess of understanding and harmony. Daughter of Visvakarma(n). Wife of Surya, mother of **Yami,** Manu, Yama, the twin Asvins, and Revanta.

⚥ *Samgna was bothered by the brightness of her husband Surya, the sun. Samgna changed her handmaid Chaya (Chhaya) into her own likeness and left Surya. She went to the forest and became a mare. When Surya discovered the ruse, he looked for his wife and then changed into a stallion. They lived in the forest for a time. When Surya agreed to have some of his brightness reduced, Samgna returned with him to the celestial sphere where Vishvakarma(n) reduced Surya's size by seven-eighths. Samgna then stayed with her husband.*

See also *Chaya* and *Saranyu*. Alternate forms: Samjna, Sanjna, Tvastri. [Durdin-Robertson 1976; Jobes 1962; Stutley and Stutley 1984]

Samjna   See *Samgna*.

Samjuna
India
Education and Knowledge
Goddess of knowledge. Her story is the same as *Samgna*'s. Alternate form: Saranya. [Monaghan 1981]

Samnati
India
Unknown
Hindu deity. Wife of Dharma. Associated with *Devaki*. Alternate form: Sannati. [Durdin-Robertson 1976]

Samriddhi
India
Wealth
Goddess of prosperity. [Leach 1992]

Samundra
India
Water
River goddess. [Monaghan 1990]

Sandhya
India
Dawn and Twilight; Earth and Nature; Goodness; Evil; Magic
"Juncture." Buddhist goddess of twilight. Daughter of Bhrama, wife of Shiva. She can cause good or evil and may have originally been a nature deity. Alternate form: Samdhya. [Durdin-Robertson 1976; Stutley and Stutley 1984]

Sandi
India
Mother and Guardian; Goodness
Buddhist guardian of the world. At one time violent, she is now a benign deity. [Preston 1982]

Sandili
India
Ceremonies
Brahman who was considered divine. Probably mother of Agni. [Durdin-Robertson 1976]

Sangvo Nimu
India, *Lepcha*
Agriculture
Sikkim earth spirit associated with grains. Wife of Alau Yook and Addo Yook. [Leach 1992]

Sanjna   See *Samgna*.

Sankata
India, *Migahiya*
Destroyer of Life
Goddess of pustular disease worshiped in the Gaya district in the state of Bihar. Sister of *Sitala*. [Leach 1992]

Sankchinni
India
Evil; Moon and Night

Demons who have white complexions. They are seen standing by tree trunks in the middle of the night, looking like white sheets. [Bonnerjea 1927]

Sankini
India
Unknown
Bengal spirit closely related to *Petni* and *Dakini*. [Bonnerjea 1927]

Sannati   See *Samnati*.

Sansari Mai
India
Earth and Nature; Commerce and Travel; Evil; Destroyer of Life
Earth mother who is a goddess of the Dom caste (scavengers, musicians, weavers, traders, and moneylenders). Identified with Jagadamba as goddess of smallpox, she is invoked before thieves wage a raid. [Leach 1992]

Santa
India
Order
Goddess of tranquility. [Durdin-Robertson 1976; Jobes 1962]

Sanumati
India
Earth and Nature; Sky and Heavens; Goodness; Immortality; Water; Magic; Weather; Fishing and Water Animals
One of the *Apsarases*. She is a mountain with a plateau or ridge. [Durdin-Robertson 1976]

Sapta-koti-buddha-matri-cunti-devi
India
Mother and Guardian
Mother of the Buddhas. In Japan her name is *Jun-tei Kwan-non* (Far East). [Getty 1962]

Saptamatrakas
India
Mother and Guardian; Creator of Life
"The Seven Mothers." They were worshiped in pre-Vedic India. Their names vary and were not assigned until the post-Vedic era. They are usually considered to be: *Brahmani, Camunda, Indrani, Kaumari, Mahesvari, Vaisnavi*, and *Varahi*. Occasionally *Narasimhi* is substituted for *Camunda*, and Virabhadra and Ganesa act as guardians, occasionally along with Skanda. The arrangement of these goddesses on icons varies according to the desired outcome, i.e., if the destruction of enemies is desired, *Brahmani* is placed at the center; to increase the population of a village, *Camunda* is in the center. Seven is a sacred number and is used to express an indeterminate number. [Danielou 1964; Stutley and Stutley 1984]

Sara   See *Amari De*.

Sarada   See *Sarasvati*.

Saraddevi
India
Time
Buddhist season goddess—autumn. The other Buddhist season goddesses are *Vasantadevi, Grismadevi*, and *Hemantadevi*. Saraddevi's Tibetan name is *Ston-gyi-rgyal-mo*, The Himalaya. See also *Saradavadhu*. [Jobes 1962]

Saradvadhu

India

Time

Goddess of autumn. See also *Saraddevi.* [Durdin-Robertson 1976]

Sara-kali   See *Amari De.*

Sarama

India

Domesticated Animals; Immortality; Mother and Guardian; Dawn and Twilight; Stars and Planets

"Swift One." Goddess who is the mother of dogs and especially the two dogs that guard the path the deceased must follow to the underworld. She is also said to help those who are lost in dark places and to be a dawn goddess and one of the twin watchdogs of the Milky Way. Alternate form: Devasuni. [Durdin-Robertson 1976; Jobes 1962; Stutley and Stutley 1984]

Saranjus

India

Sky and Heavens; Weather

Sky goddess. Possibly the personification of a thunder-cloud. [Leach 1992]

Saranya   See *Sumjuna.*

Saranyu

India

Weather; Domesticated Animals; Love and Sexuality; Magic

Cloud goddess. Daughter of Tvashtri, wife of Vivasvat, god of the rising sun. She is the mother of the Asvins, twin gods of dawn and morning. Her dark form is *Chaya.*

⚧ *Saranyu left her twin children in the care of her double, Chaya, whom she created. Vivasvat was unaware of the substitution and impregnated the double with Manu. When he discovered Saranyu had left and taken the form of a mare, Vivasvat became a stallion and went in search of her. He became so excited when he found her that his semen spilled on the ground. Just sniffing the semen impregnated her with the twin Asvins, Nāsatya and Dasara.*

See also *Samgna, Savarna,* and *Vrishakapayi.* [Durdin-Robertson 1976; Jobes 1962; Leach 1992; Stutley and Stutley 1984]

Sarassouadi

India

Order; Sciences

Goddess of harmony and the sciences. [Street 1804]

Sarasvati

India

Education and Knowledge; Water; Creator of Life; Wealth; Arts; Ceremonies

"The Flowing One." Goddess of knowledge, personification of the Sarasvati River (an ancient river in northwestern India). As a river goddess, she is associated with fertility and prosperity. She was later recognized as the originator of speech and, eventually, of all the arts. The guardian deity of writers and poets, she is worshiped in libraries with offerings of fruit, flowers, and incense. She is one of the trinity which includes *Devi* and *Lakshmi* and is portrayed as a graceful woman with white skin, sitting on a lotus or peacock, her brow adorned with a crescent moon. One of the *Gnas,* Sarasvati is revered by the Buddhists and Hindus. Similar to *Vac.* Equivalent to *dByengs-can-ma* and *Tibetan Sarasvati,* the Himalaya; *Benten* and *Kele-yin-ukin-tegri,* Far East. See also *Dabiancai Tiannu, Miao Yin Fomu; Yang Chen,* Far East; and *Helmund,* Near East. Alternate

forms: Arya, Bharati, Bija-garabha, Brahmi, Dhanesvari, Hamsadhirudha, Harahvaiti, Jagad-dhatri, Kamadhenu, Mahalakshmi, Mahasveta, Maha-vani, Mahavidya, Medha, Sarada, Saraswati, Satarupa, Savitri, Vagisvara, Vac, Vijagarbha. [Bonnerjea 1927; Danielou 1964; Durdin-Robertson 1976; Getty 1962; Leach 1992; Monaghan 1981; Stutley and Stutley 1984]

Saraswati   See *Sarasvati.*

Sarduli

India

Hunting and Wild Animals

Hindu mother of animals of prey. [Stutley and Stutley 1984]

Sarmishtha   See *Sarmistha.*

Sarmistha

India

Family and Tribes

Goddess of delight. Daughter of Vrsaparvan, mother of three sons by Yayati of whom only the youngest's name is given, Puru.

⚧ *Sarmistha quarreled with Devayani and was thrown into a well. She would have died, but Yayati discovered and rescued her. Thwarted, Devayani then insisted that Sarmistha be made her servant. This accomplished, Devayani married Yayati by pratiloma (a marriage arranged by a woman who has had three monthly periods to a "blameless man"). Devayani's father agreed to this even though Yayati was of a different caste. Sarmistha then came to Yayati and, even though he had promised his father-in-law, Sukra, that he would be faithful, Yayati and Sarmistha had three sons together. Sukra then cursed Yayati, saying he should immediately become old. Yayati begged that the curse be mitigated and Sukra said it could be if one of his sons would accept the curse. Puru agreed to accept his father's punishment.*

Alternate form: Sarmishtha. [Durdin-Robertson 1976; Stutley and Stutley 1984]

Sarna Burhia

India

Agriculture; Ceremonies; Earth and Nature

Agricultural deity to whom the winnowing basket is sacred. She is given offerings of the first picking of her followers' crops. In Bengal she is a tree goddess. [Leach 1992; Monaghan 1981]

Sarparajni

India

Reptiles; Earth and Nature; Primordial Being; Life/Death Cycle; Heaven and Hell; Sky and Heavens; Weather

Serpent goddess who is the earth. According to one writer she was originally a long trail of cosmic dust that writhed like a serpent. She is also said to shed her skin during geological changes. She is associated with the lower realms, the air, and the heavens. [Durdin-Robertson 1976]

Sarpis, The

India

Reptiles; Earth; Heaven and Hell; Sky and Heavens; Demi-animals; Weather

Snake goddesses. Associated with the earth and its lower realm, air, and the heavens. Like the *Nagis,* they are half-human and half-serpent, but while the *Nagis* walk upright, the Sarpis move about in a snake-like manner. They are similar to Egyptian *Buto* and the Egyptian *Uraeus.* [Durdin-Robertson 1976]

Sarvabuddhadakini
India
Magic; Weather
Buddhist air goddess. She confers superhuman powers on her followers. One of the *Dakinis*. In Tibet she is called *Naro-kha-choma* or *Naro-mk-a-spyhod-ma*, The Himalaya. [Jobes 1962]

Sarvakamadugha
India
Domesticated Animals; Directions; Sky and Heavens; Magic; Immortality; Physical Prowess
Hindu cow goddess who holds up the northern corner of heaven while her sisters *Hamsika, Subhadra,* and *Surupa* support the other three corners. Daughter of *Surabhi.* Her milk is so potent that any young human who drinks it will be "strong for a thousand years." Alternate form: Sarvakamdugha. [Jobes 1962; Leach 1992]

Sarvari
India
Water
Water deity. [Monaghan 1990]

Sarvasavaaranaam-bhagavati   See *Parnasavari.*

Sarvayoni
India
Creation of Life; Mother and Guardian
Goddess of female anatomy, the *yoni.* She is the source of all. [Durdin-Robertson 1976]

Sarveshvari
India
Love and Sexuality
"Illicit Love." One of the *Nayikas.* [Stutley and Stutley 1984]

Sasana-devi
India
Heaven and Hell; Ceremonies
Jain goddess who is raised above all earthly things, but is accessible via prayer. [Lurker 1984]

Sasilekha
India
Moon and Night; Sky and Heavens; Goodness; Immortality; Water; Magic; Weather; Fishing and Water Animals
"Lunar Crescent." One of the *Apsarases.* [Durdin-Robertson 1976]

Sasthi
India
Domesticated Animals; Wealth; Mother and Guardian; Health and Healing
"Sixth." Hindu deity. Personification of the sixth day after childbirth, she protects children. She is also worshiped by women desiring children, and for protection from smallpox. The cat is sacred to her. She may have been merged with *Sri* and therefore may also represent prosperity. Alternate form: Skandamata. [Jobes 1962; Leach 1992; Stutley and Stutley 1984]

Sasti
India
Mother and Guardian
"Goddess of the Sixth." Birth deity who is a form of *Durga.* [Monaghan 1990]

Sat Matra
India
Metals and Minerals; Health and Healing
Dravidian stone deity worshiped in the north. She is invoked to protect against cholera. [Leach 1992]

Satarupa
India
Family and Tribes; Time; Arts; Destroyer of Life
"Having a Hundred Forms." Primary Hindu ancestor. Wife or daughter of Bhrama.

> *Satarupa with Bhrama became the creator of innumerable children, including time, the arts, and death.*

Alternate forms: Brahmi, Brahmani, Sarasvati, Savitri. [Stutley and Stutley 1984]

Sati
India
Mother and Guardian; Dawn and Twilight; Time; Ceremonies
Hindu mother goddess. Personification of the dawn that disappears in the fire of the sun, or spring disappearing in summer's heat. Daughter of Daksha, wife of Visvamitra or Shiva. The burning of a widow on her husband's funeral pyre is a commemoration of her and is called *sati* or *suttee.* See also *Devi; Kali;* and *Sati*, Egypt. [Durdin-Robertson 1976; Jobes 1962; Monaghan 1981]

Satvai
India, *Mahar*
Destroyer of Life
Smallpox goddess. [Leach 1992]

Satyabhama
India
Heaven and Hell
"Having True Luster." Wife of Krishna. It was Satyabhama who went to heaven with Krishna and convinced him to steal *Saci's* divine *parijata* tree. [Stutley and Stutley 1984]

Satyavati
India
Justice
Goddess of truth. Daughter of *Adrika.* Mother of Krishna-Dvaipayana, a legendary compiler of texts. His father was Parasara. Satyavati later became the wife of King Santanu. Also the name of a daughter of the king of Kanyakubja, Gadhi. [Durdin-Robertson 1976; Stutley and Stutley 1984]

Saudamani
India
1) Weather; Fire; 2) Sky and Heavens; Goodness; Immortality; Water; Magic; Fishing and Water Animals; 3) Weather; Earth and Nature; Evil; Goodness
1) Goddess of lightning from a rain cloud. 2) One of the *Apsarases.* 3) One of the *Yakshi.* [Durdin-Robertson 1976]

Savadamma
India
Household Affairs
Deity worshiped by the weaver caste in the Coimbatore district in the state of Tamil Nadu. [Leach 1992]

Savala   See *Kamadhenu.*

Savari
India
Stars and Planets; Weather

"Star-spangled Night." Associated with the Maruts (male storm gods). [Durdin-Robertson 1976]

Savarna
India
Unknown

"Having the Same Appearance."

⚥ *Savarna was left by Saranyu as her substitute. She lived as Surya's wife until he discovered the ruse.*

See also *Chaya* and *Saranyu*. [Durdin-Robertson 1976]

Savitri
India
Mother and Guardian; Goodness; Immortality

Name given to many goddesses and humans by the Hindus. One of the eight divine mothers. She is mentioned in connection with *Vac* as the "Hymn to the Sun."

⚥ *Savitri compelled the god of death, Yama, to restore her husband, Satyavana, to life again. Because of this, she is considered the model of a devoted wife.*

See also *Matris*. Alternate forms: Brahmani, Brahmi, Sarasvati, Satarupa, Surya. [Bonnerjea 1927; Danielou 1964; Durdin-Robertson 1976; Stutley and Stutley 1984]

Sedhu
India
Ceremonies

Attendant to *Sitala*. Their shrines are located to the northwest of the village where she is given offerings of vegetarian foods, pigs, and hens. [Preston 1982]

Sedi
India, *Minyong*
Family and Tribes; Earth and Nature; Unhappiness; Mother and Guardian

Earth goddess worshiped in the state of Assam. She forms a dual deity with her brother/husband Melo, the sky, and together they are parents of the human race. Her daughters are the sun goddesses, *Sedi-Irkong-Bomong* and *Sedi-Irkong-Bong*. Equivalent to *Sichi*.

⚥ *Sedi and Melo were married and when they came together the humans and animals feared they would be crushed between them. One of the men, Sedi-Diyor, caught the sky and beat him and Melo fled to the heavens. When Sedi, the earth, gave birth to two daughters, she was so sad over the loss of her husband that she could not take care of them. Sedi-Diyor found a woman to be their nurse. When Sedi-Irkong-Bomong and Sedi-Irkong-Bong began to walk, they also began to radiate light, each day becoming brighter and brighter. When their nurse died, they were very sad and died, their light dying with them. They people tried various things to bring them back to life. Eventually they were successful and daylight returned.*

Equivalent to *Sichi*. See also *Keyum*. Alternate form: Shedi. [Leach 1992; Long 1963; Sproul 1979]

Sedi-Irkong-Bomong
India, *Minyong*
Sun and Day

Sun goddess. Daughter of *Sedi*. [Long 1963; Sproul 1979]

Sedi-Irkong-Bong
India
Sun and Day

Sun goddess. Daughter of *Sedi*. [Long 1963; Sproul 1979]

Sena
India
War; Family and Tribes

"An Armed Force." Wife of Skanda. Also the name of a wife of Indra.

⚥ *Sena met Indra one day in the forest and asked him to help her find a husband. Because of her name, Indra thought she should have a military husband, because with her help, the husband could lead the gods. Indra chose Skanda and Sena married him.*

Alternate forms: Devasena, Kaumari. [Durdin-Robertson 1976; Stutley and Stutley 1984]

Senamuki
India
War

"Van of the Army." [Durdin-Robertson 1976]

Sevasti-devi
India
Household Affairs; Wealth; Mother and Guardian

Household deity who confers prosperity on and protects its members. Her male counterpart is possibly Pusan, the protector of roads and travelers. May be equivalent to *Pathya Svasti*. [Stutley and Stutley 1984]

Seven Females, The
India
Earth and Nature; Physical Prowess

Inhabitants of the holy forest. Closely associated with the senses and *Prakriti* and sometimes called the Seven Prakritis. They are Ahamkara, Mahat, and the five *Tanmatras*. [Durdin-Robertson 1976]

Shabari   See *Jatila*.

Shaivi   See *Manasa*.

Shakini
India
Evil

A demon. [Durdin-Robertson 1976]

Shakinis, The
India
Evil

"Able Ones" or "Helpful." Demons. Attendants of *Durga* and Shiva. Similar to the *Dakinis*. [Danielou 1964; Durdin-Robertson 1976; Stutley and Stutley 1984]

Shakti
India
Primordial Being; Love and Sexuality; Destroyer of Life

"Divine Power or Energy." Her power is dynamic as opposed to the passive power of the male deities. Each male god has a Shakti as his energizer and creative force, energy being the ultimate source of everything. She is known as the goddess of lust and destruction and wife and energy of Shiva. Among the Kaniyan people in the south, she is worshiped in her many manifestations: *Ambika, Bala, Bhadrakali, Durga,* and *Matangi*, in the belief that this will give more accuracy to their astrological predictions. See also *Mulaprakriti, Rakini* (this region); *Adishakti, Ekastaka, Mens*, Greek and Roman Empires; and *Holy Spirit*, Near East. [Bonnerjea 1927; Danielou 1964; Durdin-Robertson 1976; Leach 1992; Stutley and Stutley 1984]

Shaktis, The
India
Creator of Life; Primordial Being

Creative power and energy. Their energy activates and empowers the male deities. Among the Shaktis are *Anushakti, Asa Poorna, Bisal Mariamma, Devi,*

Ganapatihrdaya, Ganesani, Hemambika, Kali, Kamaksi, Lakini, Lakshmi, Lalita Tripurasundari, Mahadevi, Mahalakshmi, Parvati, Prajna, Sitala, Tripura Bhairavi, Uma, and *Yashodhara.* Associated with *Daiviprakriti* and *Matras.* See also *Adishakti* and *Ekastaka.* Alternate forms: Ichchhashakti, Jnanashakti, Kriyashakti, Kundalini Shakti, Mantrikashakti, Parashakti, Sacti, Sushakti. Mataras may be an alternate name for the Shaktis. [Bonnerjea 1927; Danielou 1964; Durdin-Robertson 1976; Leach 1992; Stutley and Stutley 1984]

Shaktiyasas
India
Small Size; Magic
   One of the *Khekaris.* [Durdin-Robertson 1976]

Shakuntala   See *Sakuntala.*

Shamidevi
India
Earth and Nature; Fire; Immortality; Order; Commerce and Travel
   Tree goddess. Personification of a hardwood tree believed to contain fire. She brings peace to the dead and her tree is planted to define boundaries. Closely associated with Agni, god of fire. [Stutley and Stutley 1984]

Shanti
India
Order
   "Tranquility." Daughter of Sraddha. She is the absence of passion. [Stutley and Stutley 1984]

Shashthi   See *Shasti.*

Shasthi
India
Mother and Guardian
   Hindu goddess of childbirth who protects women and children. [Leach 1992]

Shasti
India
Domesticated Animals; Mother and Guardian; Earth and Nature
   Feline goddess and deity of childbirth who is the guardian of children. First worshiped in the state of Bengal where she is depicted riding a cat. Closely connected with *Manasa.* In Ksirahar there is a representation of her holding a child in her lap and in one of her hands is a leafy branch, indicating a relationship to plants and water. Alternate forms: Shashthi, Sitala. [Durdin-Robertson 1976; Johnson 1988]

Shastradevatas
India
War
   Goddesses of war. A class of *Devatas.* [Durdin-Robertson 1976]

Shatarupa   See *Vac.*

Shaterany
India
War
   Vedic goddess. Wife of the warrior Raettris. [Durdin-Robertson 1976]

Shavasi
India
Mother and Guardian
   "Mighty." Mother of Indra. [Stutley and Stutley 1984]

Shedi   See *Sedi.*

Shidkin-kede
India, *Minyong Abor*
Earth and Nature
   Earth goddess worshiped in the state of Assam. [Leach 1992]

Shing-rum
India, *Lepcha*
Hunting and Wild Animals
   Wild animal goddess worshiped only by male hunters in the state of Sikkim. [Leach 1992]

Shitala   See *Sitala.*

Shitla   See *Sitala.*

Shraddha
India
Intelligence and Creativity
   "Faith." Wife of Sharma or Angiras, mother of Kama. She is asked to give her worshipers invincible faith and certainty. [Durdin-Robertson 1976; Leach 1992; Stutley and Stutley 1984]

Shri
India
Unknown
   "Luster" or "Sacred Lotus." Wife of Vishnu. Before descending from the sun she was known as *Anushayini.* Alternate form: Lakshmi. [Jobes 1962; Monaghan 1981]

Shrutavati
India
Selflessness
   Practitioner of extreme austerities. Daughter of *Ghrtaci* and Bharadavja, wife of Indra. [Stutley and Stutley 1984]

Shuci
India
Wild Birds
   Hindu bird goddess, mother of parrots. Daughter of *Tamra* and Kashyapa. See also *Shuki.* Alternate form: Suki.

Shuki
India
Wild Birds
   Hindu bird goddess, mother of parrots. Daughter of *Surabhi.* See also *Shuci.* [Jobes 1962; Leach 1992]

Shurpanakha
India
Large Size
   "Having Fingernails Like Winnowing Fans." Giant demon, one of the *Rakshasi.*

Shushtee
India
Earth and Nature
   Hindu goddess of fertility of plants and animals. [Leach 1992]

Shuska-Revati
India
Justice

Goddess created by Vishnu to aid Shiva in destroying Andhaka when he and his followers were trying to take the divine *parijata* tree. She drank their blood and Shiva was able to kill them. [Stutley and Stutley 1984]

Shyavi
India
Moon and Night
"Dark Brown." Night deity. [Durdin-Robertson 1976]

Shyeni
India
Wild Birds
Hindu bird deity. Mother of birds of prey including eagles and hawks. Daughter of *Tamra* and Kashyapa. [Stutley and Stutley 1984]

Sichi
India, *Gallong*
Creator of Life; Mother and Guardian
Creator and mother goddess. Equivalent to *Sedi*. [Leach 1992]

Siddhanganas
India
Magic; Heaven and Hell
Sorcerer. Possessors of occult power who inhabit the middle regions (the land of the blessed) between heaven and earth. [Durdin-Robertson 1976]

Siddha-Yoginis, The
India
Magic; Education and Knowledge
Sorcerers, fairies, and witches who are adept at yoga. See also *Yogini*. [Durdin-Robertson 1976]

Siddhikari
India
Magic
Sorcerer. [Durdin-Robertson 1976]

Siddhis
India
Magic; Wealth; Education and Knowledge
"Successful Achievement." Wife of Ganesha, the overcomer of obstacles. Also said to be the deity of realization as wife of Bhaga, and deity of success as wife of Ganapati. Siddhis are generally associated with fortune, personal perfection, and fulfillment, as well as having specific powers, including changing in size and weight and the power to move objects from one place to another. Among the Siddhis are Khekarisiddhi, who has the magical power to fly; Layasiddhi, the subtle, who has the knowledge of creation; Mahasiddhi, the possessor of great magical power; Manorathasiddhi, the realization of a wish; Sadhyasiddhi, successful achievement; and Sarvasiddhi, accomplishment of all goals. [Durdin-Robertson 1976; Leach 1992; Stutley and Stutley 1984]

Sila
India
Goodness
"Good Behavior." [Monaghan 1990]

Simhavahini   "She Rides a Lion." See *Durga*.

Simhavaktra
India
Weather; Magic

Buddhist air deity who confers supernatural powers on her followers. [Jobes 1962]

Simhika
India
Sky and Heavens; Hunting and Wild Animals
"Lioness." Celestial deity. Mother of Rahu. [Durdin-Robertson 1976]

Sinavali
India
Creator of Life; Mother and Guardian; Moon and Night
Fertility goddess. She aids in pregnancy and delivery. Daughter of Angiras. Representative of the first day of the new moon. See also *Sinivali*. [Leach 1992]

Sindhu
India
Water
River goddess. She flows quickly and unrestrained across the plains, and flowers grow along her banks. [Durdin-Robertson 1976]

Singarmati Devi
India
Insects
Silkworm goddess worshiped in the Mirzapur district in the state of Uttar Pradesh. She cares for the silkworms as if they were human. [Durdin-Robertson 1976]

Singhbahani
India
Commerce and Travel
Goddess worshiped in the Central Provinces by the Tamera, a caste of coppersmiths. [Leach 1992]

Singhbahini
India, *Pahari*
Hunting and Wild Animals; Reptiles; Insects
Goddess of noisome animals including tigers, snakes, and scorpions. [Leach 1992]

Siniboi
India, *Bondo*
Household Affairs
Household guardian. [Leach 1992]

Sinivali
India
Moon and Night; Mother and Guardian; Ceremonies; Domesticated Animals
"New Moon." She is invoked to form a male embryo in the womb. She presides over procreation with *Anumati, Kuhu,* and *Raka*. Wife of Vishnu. Offerings of heifers are given to her and she appears in the shape of a crescent moon on Shiva's headdress. [Durdin-Robertson 1976; Leach 1992; Stutley and Stutley 1984]

Sirsootee
India
Water
River goddess. Daughter of *Mahalakshimi;* sister of *Devi, Mahakali, Sri,* and Brahma; mother of the *Gauris* and Vishnu. She may be equated with another deity of the early Indian pantheon. [Durdin-Robertson 1976]

Sita
India
Agriculture; Ceremonies; Earth and Nature; Goodness

"Furrow." Agricultural goddess, possibly a corn mother. Wife of Rama. The earth is ritually ploughed by the king or chieftain at the beginning of the planting season (a ritual that also occurs in China and Ceylon). The furrows are considered the earth's reproductive organs.

Sita is falsely accused by her husband of unfaithfulness. At the edge of a lake, she asks Mother Earth to carry her to the other side if she has been a faithful wife, and she is borne to the other shore.

Equivalent to *Banana Maiden,* Southeast Asia; *Konohana-sakuya-hime,* Far East; and *Kornmutter,* Northern Europe. Alternate forms: Bhaumi, Lakshmi. [Bonnerjea 1927; Danielou 1964; Leach 1972; Leach 1992; Stutley and Stutley 1984]

Sitala
India
Destroyer of Life; Mother and Guardian; Health and Healing; Ceremonies; Domesticated Animals; Creator of Life; Primordial Being

Disease goddess. Sister of *Agwani, Basanti, Lamkariya, Mahamai, Masani,* and *Polamde.* Her sisters are also given as *Bhagavati, Bhageseri, Bhandra Kali, Chamariya, Chhotimai, Duhkharnimai, Durga Kali, Kuleswari, Mahakali, Mangalamai, Mariamman, Mariyammai, Narayanimai, Phulmati, Sankata, Sitala Mata,* and *Sitlamata.* Together they preside over pustular diseases. Sitala is probably the most worshiped goddess in India and is called mother (Mata) of each village where her shrine sits to the northeast. She causes or prevents smallpox.

Sitala was born later than the other goddesses and humans did not pay attention to her. She invented smallpox to force humans to invent rituals for her. She roams the countryside on an ass, looking for victims.

See also *Matangi-Shakti* and *Ujali Mata.* Alternate forms: Jyestha, Shakti, Shasti, Shitala, Shitla, Sitla, Sitala-Devi. [Durdin-Robertson 1976; Leach 1972; Leach 1992; Monaghan 1981; Stutley and Stutley 1984]

Sitala Devi   See *Sitala.*

Sitala Mata   See *Sitala.*

Sitalamma
India
Water
Water deity worshiped in the south. [Leach 1992]

Sitatapatra Aparajita
India
Mother and Guardian; Physical Prowess
Buddhist invincible goddess of the white parasol. With her eight arms, she keeps all harm away. Her Tibetan name is *Pags-ma-gdugs-dkar* or *Phe-ma-du-kar,* The Himalaya. Alternate form: Sitataptra. [Getty 1962; Jobes 1962; Leach 1992]

Sitatara
India
Education and Knowledge; Happiness; Immortality
Buddhist White *Tara* whose knowledge can lead to everlasting bliss. A staunch defender of the faith, she is portrayed with seven eyes. Her emblems are the serpent and the lute. She is an incarnation of the Chinese *Wen Chheng,* Far East. Her Tibetan name is *sGrol-dkar-po,* The Himalaya. Alternate form: Aryajangulitara. [Getty 1962; Jobes 1962]

Sitking-Kedding
India, *Bori (Adi)*
Earth and Nature

Earth goddess worshiped in the northeast. Wife of the sky, Peddo Dodum, mother of *Doini* (the sun) and Pollo (the moon). [Leach 1992]

Sitla   See *Sitala.*

Sitlamata
India, *Bhil*
Health and Healing; Mother and Guardian
Goddess of health. Invoked for protection from smallpox and to make sterile women fertile. See also *Sitala.* [Leach 1992]

Siva
India
Earth and Nature
A *Navadurga.* One of the nine plant forms of *Durga,* the wood apple. [Stutley and Stutley 1984]

Sixty-four Yoginis, The   See *Chausathi Yoginis.*

Skandamata   See *Sasthi.*

Smriti
India
Education and Knowledge
Deity of memory and tradition. Wife of Angiras, the teacher of transcendent knowledge. Associated with Krishna. [Leach 1992]

Sodasi
India
Creator of Life; Order; Heaven and Hell
"Maiden of Sixteen." Goddess of perfection and the divine night. In Hindu religion, the number sixteen signifies totality (perfection). She is Shiva's activating power and gives life to all mortals and immortals. She rules over all that is perfect, complete, and beautiful and is worshiped after dawn. One of the *Mahavidyas.* Identified with *Tripurasundari.* [Durdin-Robertson 1976; Stutley and Stutley 1984]

Sokarahita
India
Earth and Nature
A *Navadurga.* One of the nine plant forms of *Durga,* the Saraca indica. [Stutley and Stutley 1984]

Soma   See *Vasus.*

Soma Cow   See *Mahi.*

Somlai
India
Intelligence and Creativity
Goddess of inspiration in the city/district of Sambalpur in the state of Orissa, Central Provinces. When she inspires her followers, they shake and their heads roll. [Frazer 1959]

Sonnolipenu
India, *Khond*
Agriculture
Agricultural deity invoked for good crops. [Leach 1992]

Sookhmurna   See *Sushumna.*

Soora   See *Sura.*

Soorenjnaree   See *Pingala.*

Sree   See *Lakshmi.*

Sri
India

Wealth; Goodness; Earth and Nature

"Prosperity." A Hindu deity who has been adopted by the Buddhists. She embodies all that is good and is desired by gods and men. She is identified with *Lakshmi*. Also considered one of the six variants of *Gauri,* or as Gauri, and as one of the *Navapatrikas* (one of the nine plant forms of *Durga*). The coconut is her sacred fruit, although her plant form is rice. In Indonesia and Bali, Sri is called *Giriputri,* Southeast Asia. Equivalent to *Kichi-jo-ten,* Far East. See also *Navadurgas.* Alternate forms: Draupadi, Padma. [Danielou 1964; Leach 1992; Redfield 1931; Stutley and Stutley 1984]

Sri Lakshmi   See *Lakshmi.*

Sringatpadini
India

Magic; Demi-animals; Weather; Earth and Nature; Evil; Goodness

A *Yukshi.* She can create horns and change humans into animals. [Durdin-Robertson 1976]

Sruta-Kriti
India

Beauty; Goodness

"Lovely Princess." Wife of Satrughna. She is honored for her "acts of goodly grace." [Durdin-Robertson 1976]

Sthalidevatas
India

Unknown

A class of *Devatas,* a local deity. [Durdin-Robertson 1976]

Suaha
India

Love and Sexuality; Magic

"So Be It." Her name is uttered at the end of many mantras. Wife of Agni or Rudra.

When the god Agni was in the forest trying to quell his desires for the Krittikas, Suaha saw him and made amorous overtures toward him. When she saw, through her magic, that he was occupied with thoughts of the Krittikas, she disguised herself as each of the Krittikas to attract his attention. Six times she overcame Agni's hesitations and had relations with him.

Alternate forms: Svaha, Swaha. [Durdin-Robertson 1976]

Subbu Khai Thung
India, *Dhammai*

Earth and Nature; Mother and Guardian; Insects

Earth goddess. Daughter of *Zumiang Nui* and Shuzanghu.

When Subbu Khai Thung, the earth, and her brother Jongsuli Young Jongbu, the sky, were born they fell from the sky and were swallowed by a worm, Phangnalomang. When their mother was pregnant again, she asked her husband to protect the new child. He set traps and when Phangnalomang came to get the next child he was caught. When Shuzanghu cut the monster open, the children were still inside and they returned to their places as the earth and the sky. [Leach 1992; Long 1963; Sproul 1979]

Subhadra
India

Mother and Guardian; Sky and Heavens; Ceremonies; Directions; Physical Prowess

Goddess of the female principle. An *Asuri* who, with her sisters *Hamsika, Sarvakamadugha,* and *Surupa,* supports the four directional corners of the heavens. Wife of Arjuna, sister of Krishna and Balarama. The three siblings are honored at great festivals at Puri where the members of all four castes are allowed together to eat and celebrate, perhaps suggesting an earlier time when there were no castes and everyone was considered equal. [Durdin-Robertson 1976; Leach]

Subhangi   See *Rati.*

Substance Mother
India

Mother and Guardian; Primordial Being

"The Mother." She is the nucleus of all living and existing forces in the universe. [Durdin-Robertson 1976]

Sudakshina
India

Justice

"Having a Good Right Hand." Goddess and queen, wife of the king of Ayodhya. [Durdin-Robertson 1976]

Sudesna   See *Tara.*

Sugrivi
India

Domesticated Animals

Hindu animal goddess. Mother of beasts of burden, camels, horses, and asses. Daughter of *Tamra* and Kashyapa. Sugrivi is a part of the "secondary" creation. [Stutley and Stutley 1984]

Sukanthi
India

Physical Prowess; Sky and Heavens; Goodness; Immortality; Water; Magic; Weather; Fishing and Water Animals

"Sweet Voiced." An *Apsarases.* [Durdin-Robertson 1976]

Sukanya
India

Immortality; Magic

"Well-known Maiden." Wife of the sage, Cyavana.

The Asvins visited Sukanya and her husband on several occasions. They suggested she should come and enjoy herself with them, as her husband was so old and decrepit. At her husband's suggestion, Sukanya told the Asvins that they were incomplete and if they would make her husband young, she would tell them how they could become complete and be included in the god's celebrations. They told her to take Cyavana to a nearby body of water and to have him submerged in it. He emerged from the water a young man and Sukanya and Cyavana then gave the Asvins the promised information. [Durdin-Robertson 1976; Stutley and Stutley 1984]

Sukarapreyasi
India

Earth and Nature; Hunting and Wild Animals

"Beloved of the Boar." Earth goddess. Vishnu, in the form of a boar, brought the earth, Sukarapreyasi, up from the depths of the ocean. She corresponds to *Bhumi* and *Prithivi.* [Durdin-Robertson 1976]

Sukhajamma
India

Destroyer of Life

Disease goddess who causes measles and smallpox. There is a shrine to her in the city of Bangalore in the state of Karnataka (Mysore). [Leach 1992]

Suki
India

Domesticated Animals; Sun and Day

Cow goddess. Wife of the sun. [Monaghan 1981; Stutley and Stutley 1984]

Sulochana
India
Beauty; Weather; Earth and Nature; Evil; Goodness
 "Lovely-eyed." One of the *Yakshi*. [Durdin-Robertson 1976]

Sumati
India
Mother and Guardian
 Creator goddess. Daughter of *Vinata*, wife of Sagara. Sumati gave birth to a gourd, out of which came sixty thousand sons. [Durdin-Robertson 1976]

Sumaya
India
Unknown
 "Having Noble Counsels." Daughter of *Maya*. [Durdin-Robertson 1976]

Sumitra
India
Justice; Goodness
 "Kind Friend." Queen. Wife of Dasaratha, mother of Satrughna and Laksmana. Also the name of one of the *Yakshi*. [Durdin-Robertson 1976]

Sumu Mung
India, *Lepcha*
Evil; Love and Sexuality
 Demon. In the state of Sikkim she seduces young men and attacks those who venture into the forest at night by themselves. [Leach 1992]

Sundari
India
Beauty; Earth and Nature
 Goddess who takes the form of a beautiful woman or a tree. [Durdin-Robertson 1976]

Sunkalamma
India
Destroyer of Life
 Disease goddess who causes measles and smallpox. She is worshiped by the pariahs in the Cuddapah and Kurnool districts in the state of Andhra Pradesh and in the Bellary district in the state of Karnataka. [Leach 1992; Monaghan 1981]

Sunrta
India
Wealth
 "Gladness." Hindu goddess of wealth. [Stutley and Stutley 1984]

Sura
India
Health and Healing; Ceremonies
 "Intoxicating Liquor" or "Wine." Hindu goddess of wine used in religious rituals as an anesthetic or stimulant. She may be connected to *Varunani*. Alternate forms: Suradevi, Soora. [Bonnerjea 1927; Durdin-Robertson 1976; Leach 1992; Stutley and Stutley 1984]

Surabhi See *Kamadhenu*.

Surabhidatta
India
Sky and Heavens; Goodness; Immortality; Water; Magic; Weather; Fishing and Water Animals
 "Giving." One of the *Apsarases*. [Durdin-Robertson 1976]

Suradevi See *Sura*.

Surapamsula
India
Sky and Heavens; Goodness; Immortality; Water; Magic; Weather; Fishing and Water Animals
 "Divine Courtesan." One of the *Apsarases*. [Durdin-Robertson 1976]

Surasa
India
Water; Reptiles
 "Abounding in Water." Creator of serpents and dragons. Wife of Kashyapa. [Durdin-Robertson 1976]

Suraswati See *Bharadi*.

Suratamangari
India
Magic; Small Size; Love and Sexuality
 Connected to fairies and associated with sexual enjoyment. [Durdin-Robertson 1976]

Suris, The
India
Unknown
 Great goddesses. Daughters of *Aditi*. Correspond to Greek and Roman Olympian deities. [Durdin-Robertson 1976]

Surupa
India
Sky and Heavens; Directions; Physical Prowess
 Sky goddess. Daughter of *Surabhi*, who, with her sisters *Hamsika*, *Sarvakamadugha*, and *Subhadra*, supports the four corners of the heavens. [Leach 1992]

Surya
India
Sun and Day; Wild Birds; Demi-animals
 Vedic solar deity. Daughter/wife of Surya, the sun god. Also said to be the wife of the Asvins who won her away from Soma. Sister of Pusan. She is also called a swan-maiden. Equivalent to *Shapash*, Near East, and *Ama-terasu-o-mi-kami*, Far East. See also *Swan Maidens*, Northern Europe. Alternate forms: Savitri, Surya-Bai. [Durdin-Robertson 1976; Eliade 1987; Leach 1992; Stutley and Stutley 1984]

Surya-Bai See *Surya*.

Suryasya Duhita
India
Unknown
 "Daughter of the Sun." Vedic deity. [Eliade 1987]

Susana
India
Mother and Guardian
 Hindu birth goddess. She is responsible for the "loosening" of the uterus, making the birth easier. [Stutley and Stutley 1984]

Sushakti
India
Primordial Being; Love and Sexuality; Destroyer of Life
 "Easy Matter." A class of *Shakti*. [Durdin-Robertson 1976]

Sushumna
India
Moon and Night; Health and Healing

Vital air and moon deity. She is the energy that travels through the middle of the spinal cord and her power is revered by the yogis. An aspect of **Kundalini.** She aids the moon's light in permeating humans and animals. Her color is blue. Alternate forms: Susumna, Sookhmurna. [Durdin-Robertson 1976]

Susime
India, *Garo*
Moon and Night; Health and Healing; Wealth; Ceremonies
Daughter of Asima-Dingsima. Associated with the moon, she causes or cures lameness and blindness. Also said to give wealth. She is worshiped in the state of Assam where offerings of pigs, fowl, and intoxicating drink are made to her. [Leach 1992]

Susumna   See *Sushumna.*

Sutrooka
India
Family and Tribes; Creator of Life
Progenitor of the human race. Wife of Munnoo. [Durdin-Robertson 1976]

Suttibhavani
India, *Baiga*
Hunting and Wild Animals
Hunting deity. [Leach 1992]

Sutudri
India
Water
River goddess. [Durdin-Robertson 1976; Leach 1992]

Svadha
India
Family and Tribes
"Offering." Daughter of Daksha or Agni and Prasuti. Wife of one class of *pitrs* (fathers or ancestors of families) and mother of the others. See also **Matris.** [Stutley and Stutley 1984]

Svaha
India
Ceremonies
"Invocation at an Offering." Wife of Agni or possibly Rudra. Identified with **Uma.** See also **Matris.** Alternate forms: Suaha, Svahariti, Swaha. [Danielou 1964; Durdin-Robertson 1976; Stutley and Stutley 1984]

Svahariti
India
Ceremonies
Deity of the *Apri* hymns. See also **Svaha.** [Durdin-Robertson 1976]

Svarnarekha
India
Small Size; Magic
"Gold Streak." One of the **Khekaris.** [Durdin-Robertson 1976]

Svayamvaraprabha
India
Unknown
"Self-choosing Splendor." Deity. [Durdin-Robertson 1976]

Swadha
India
Ceremonies

Deity who presides over funeral rituals. See also **Suaha** and **Uma.** [Leach 1992]

Swaha   See *Svaha* and *Suaha.*

Syama
India
Unknown
"Black." A Tantric form of **Durga.** Alternate forms: Devi, Parvati, Uma. [Stutley and Stutley 1984]

Syamatara   See *Tara.*

Tadaka
India
Earth and Nature; Evil
Hindu vegetal **Yakshi** who was changed into a malevolent **Rakshasi** and killed by Rama for disturbing the devotions of a seer. [Stutley and Stutley 1984]

Tadatagei
India
War; Physical Prowess
War goddess and princess of Tamil (Tamilnad, a linguistic region in the extreme southeast). Extremely strong and very knowledgeable in military tactics. She was born with three breasts. See also **Minaksi.** [Durdin-Robertson 1976]

Takurani   See *Ganga Devi.*

Talyeu Nimu
India, *Lepcha*
Earth and Nature; Agriculture
Earth spirit worshiped in the state of Sikkim who participates in the rice harvest. One of the wives of Adoo Yook and Alau Yook. [Leach 1992]

Tamil Mountain Fairies, The
India
Earth and Nature
Dravidian spirits in Tamil (Tamilnad, a linguistic region in the extreme southeast) who inhabit the mountains. [Durdin-Robertson 1976]

Tamra
India
Wild Birds
"Copper-colored." Hindu ancestor of birds. Daughter of Daksha, wife of Kashyapa, mother of **Bhasi, Dhrtarastri, Kaki, Sugrivi, Suki,** and **Shyeni.** Her grandson, Garuda, was a king of the feathered peoples. [Durdin-Robertson 1976; Stutley and Stutley 1984]

Tanmatra
India
Unknown
Mother of the five elements, a form of **Nari.** [Durdin-Robertson 1976]

Tanmatras   See *Seven Females.*

Tanum
India, *Minyong Abor*
Hunting and Wild Animals; Wild Birds
Goddess of wild animals. She forms a dual deity with Shikom and together they preside over all the wild animals. Worshiped in the state of Assam. [Leach 1992]

Tapati

India

Water; Sky and Heavens; Beauty; Family and Tribes

River goddess and celestial nymph. She presides over the Tapti River in the Surat district in the state of Gujarat. Daughter of *Samjna*.

The god Surya arranged for King Samvarana to see and fall in love with Tapati, but as soon as he saw her, Tapati disappeared. The king searched everywhere for her, and finally, she came to him in a vision and told him to go to Surya to obtain permission for their marriage. After twelve days Surya agreed to the wedding and had a sage escort Tapati down to earth for the marriage. Tapati and the king lived happily in the mountain forests for twelve years until they had to return to the capital, where there was great unrest. They were able to restore peace and prosperity to the capital and remained there with their subjects. [Durdin-Robertson 1976; Stutley and Stutley 1984]

Tara

India

Stars and Planets; Mother and Guardian; Immortality; Physical Prowess

"Star." Wife of Brhaspati who was kidnapped by Soma. She bore Soma's son, Buddha. Also the name of a Tantric goddess, one of the *Mahavidyas*, and considered a savior, protecting humans from dangers and redeeming them. She presides over the senses and elements. She figures in Hindu, Jain, and Buddhist Tantric religion and represents the ancient mother goddess religion of aboriginal India. Tara has five main forms: *Sitatara*, white Tara; *Syamatara*, green Tara, *Ekajata*, blue Tara; *Bhrkuti*, yellow Tara; and *Kurukulla*, red Tara. In Nepal the green Tara is called *Khadiravani Tara*, The Himalaya. In Tibet she is called *sGrol-mas*, The Himalaya. See also *Dolma* and *Tara*, the Himalaya. Alternate forms: Chinnamasta, Dolma, Durga, Janguli, Kali, Maya, Sudesna, Taraka, Ugratara. [Durdin-Robertson 1976; Jobes 1962; Neumann 1972; Stutley and Stutley 1984]

Tara Bai

India

Stars and Planets; Magic; Physical Prowess

Hindu star goddess who bewitches humans with her songs. [Jobes 1962]

Tarai

India

Weather

Andaman Island weather deity associated with monsoons. Wife/sister of Biliku, a weather god. [Leach 1972]

Taraka

India

Evil; Disorder

Demon. Daughter of Sunda or Suketu. She was changed into a *Rakshasi* by Agastya and she ravaged the countryside until killed by Rama. Alternate form: Tara. [Stutley and Stutley 1984]

Tari Pennu

India, *Khond*

Earth and Nature; Evil; Destroyer of Life; Luck; Ceremonies; Agriculture; Sun and Day

Dravidian earth goddess worshiped in Bengal. Said to be malevolent, causing disease, misfortune, and death. Human sacrifices are made to her for abundant crops, especially for turmeric, which requires blood to give it color.

Tari Pennu was desired by the sun god, but she rejected his advances. He then created human women, but they began worshiping Tari Pennu instead, and so the struggle between Tari Pennu and the sun still goes on.

Alternate forms: Bera Pennu, Dharni Deota. [Durdin-Robertson 1976; Leach 1992; Monaghan 1981]

Tauvai   See *Jyestha*.

Tavisi   See *Jayanti*.

Teeree

India

Creator of Life; Metals and Minerals

Creator. She formed an egg or was the egg that divided into two parts. One half became celestial beings and the other half became all other living creatures, plants, and minerals. [Durdin-Robertson 1976]

Teikirzi

India, *Todas*

Justice; Ceremonies; Immortality

Goddess who presides over laws and rituals. She is worshiped in the Nilgiri Hills in the state of Orissa. Teikirzi was able to bring humans back to life, but when she saw their mixed reactions, she decided not to interfere. [Leach 1992]

Thadha Pennu

India, *Goomsur*

Agriculture; Wild Birds

Earth goddess who takes the form of a peacock and who is invoked for abundant crops. [Leach 1992]

Thakurani Bakorani

India, *Gadba, Bondo*

Destroyer of Life; Domesticated Animals; Ceremonies; Health and Healing

Goddess of pustular diseases among humans and cattle. She is given offerings of flowers and incense to help cure the illness, but she is abused if it does not subside. Identified with *Kankali*. Alternate form: Thakurani Mata. [Leach 1992]

Thakurani Mai

India

Earth and Nature

Earth deity worshiped in the Central Provinces. Thakurani is an alternate form for Bhudevi in Bengal. [Leach 1992]

Thakurani Mata   See *Thakurani Bakorani* and *Burhi Mata*.

Thirst Goddess

India

Magic; Love and Sexuality

One of three sisters skilled in the magic arts including desire and voluptuousness. The others are *Lust* and *Delight*. They visited Gautama and censured him for not properly performing his duties to his wife, family, and home. [Durdin-Robertson 1976]

Thurgai   See *Minachiamman*.

Tilottama

India

Time; Weather; Metals and Minerals; Beauty; Sky and Heavens; Goodness; Immortality; Water; Magic; Fishing and Water Animals

One of the *Apsarases* who escort the sun as guardians during January-February. They preside over the temperature and rainfall.

Bhrama created Tilottama from precious stones. She was so beautiful, Shiva became four-faced so he would never lose sight of her. [Durdin-Robertson 1976; Jobes 1962; Stutley and Stutley 1984]

Tola   See *Tula.*

Totala
India
Family and Tribes; Weather; Wealth; Domesticated Animals;
Ceremonies; Water; Creator of Life
   One of the *Gauris.* Alternate form: Parvati. [Stutley and
Stutley 1984]

Trigana
India
Wealth; Love and Sexuality; Goodness
   "Of the Three Elements." She presides over richness, love,
and mercy. Closely connected to *Nari,* this section, and *Isis,*
Egypt. [Durdin-Robertson 1976]

Trigata
India
Destroyer of Life; Large Size; Evil; Charisma; Beauty
   "Wearing Three Braids." One of the *Rakshasis.* [Durdin-
Robertson 1976]

Trijata
India
Destroyer of Life; Large Size; Evil; Charisma; Beauty
   One of the *Rakshasis.* She aided Sita when she was
kidnapped by Ravana. [Stutley and Stutley 1984]

Tripura   See *Gauri* and *Parvati.*

Tripura Bhairavi
India
Metals and Minerals; Destroyer of Life; Earth and Nature;
Sky and Heavens; Heaven and Hell; Creator of Life;
Primordial Being
   Goddess of the triple city, Tipura, the fabulous city of the
Asuras that is constructed of gold, silver, and iron, or of their
three fortresses—earth, atmosphere, and heaven. She is the
Shakti of Shiva when he is the ruler of death and she carries
out his work. See also *Tripurasundari.* Alternate form:
Mahamaya. [Stutley and Stutley 1984]

Tripurasundari
India
Beauty
   Tantric goddess of the city of Tripura (see *Tripura
Bhairavi*). She is also a form of *Durga* as the most beautiful
being in the three realms: earth, air, and heaven. Identified
with *Sodasi.* [Stutley and Stutley 1984]

Trisala
India
Goodness; Fate; Mother and Guardian; Magic
   "Showing Everyone a Kindness." She believed in resisting
the "urge to kill," which was later a principal of the Jain
philosophy. She also had prophetic dreams.
   ☿ *Trisala had a son who, just before birth, was transferred
      from the womb of Devananda to hers. This child,
      Mahavira, became a great proponent of Jainism, just
as Trisala's dreams had foretold.*
   See also *Devananda.* Alternate form: Priyakarini. [Durdin-
Robertson 1976]

Trsa   See *Trsna.*

Trsna
India
Love and Sexuality

Thirst goddess as related to desire. Daughter of *Rati* and
Kama. Alternate forms: Mahakali, Trsa. [Stutley and Stutley
1984]

Tseurima
India
Destroyer of Life
   Cemetery goddess. [Durdin-Robertson 1976]

Tsun Kyanske
India
Destroyer of Life; Heaven and Hell
   Death goddess of Khymer who is the ruler of the afterlife.
[Monaghan 1990]

Tuima
India
Water
   River goddess of the Tiparas River in eastern Bengal (now
Bangladesh). She has become identified with the Ganga River.
[Leach 1992; Stutley and Stutley 1984]

Tula
India
Stars and Planets
   Stellar deity. The constellation Libra. Alternate forms:
Tulam, Tola. [Durdin-Robertson 1976]

Tulsi
India
Earth and Nature
   Agricultural deity who presides over the basil plant.
[Monaghan 1990]

Tushti
India
Order
   Goddess of satisfaction. See also *Matris.* [Leach 1992]

Tvastri   See *Samgna.*

Ugracanda
India
Ceremonies; Sun and Day; Love and Sexuality
   One of the *Nayikas.* [Stutley and Stutley 1984]

Ugratara
India
Destroyer of Life
   The terrifying form of *Tara.* She appears and becomes
all-consuming when offerings are not made to the sun.
Ugratara is also the name of a Mahayana Buddhist Tantric
deity adopted by the Hindus. Alternate form: Ekajata.
[Stutley and Stutley 1984]

Ujali
India
Destroyer of Life
   "White Lady." Smallpox goddess. Her shrine sits to the
southeast of the village and she is given only vegetarian
offerings. Alternate form: Gaon Mataa. [Preston 1982]

Ujali Mata
India
Destroyer of Life; Ceremonies
   Disease goddess worshiped in the Muzaffarnagar district
in the state of Uttar Pradesh. Equivalent to *Sitala.* [Leach
1992]

Ukepenopfu
India, *Angami Nagas*
Family and Tribes
Ancestor deity. [Monaghan 1990]

Ulupi
India, *Naga*
Heaven and Hell; Reptiles
Underworld serpent goddess. Wife of Arjuna, who descended to Patala (the nether regions, see *Dayitas*) to marry her. [Durdin-Robertson 1976]

Uma
India
Selflessness; Intelligence and Creativity; Immortality; Earth and Nature; Primordial Being; Creator of Life
"Light," "The Peace of Night," or "Desist." Non-Vedic goddess with whom local goddesses were gradually identified. Uma Haimavati, daughter of Himavat, may have been her original name and she may have been a mountain ghost haunting the Himalayas. Or her name may have been derived from the Dravidian *Amma*. As the *Shakti* of Shiva, she is the power of light that makes perception possible. Uma is also said to be a name for *Aparna*. Identified with *Svaha* and *Swadha*.

Aparna carried her self-denial to such an extreme—no nourishment of any kind—that her mother cried out to her, "Uma!" (desist). She was then called Uma.
Alternate forms: Ambika, Bhadrakali, Devi, Durga, Gauri, Kali, Mahadevi, Mahakali, Mahanidra, Parvati, Rudrani, Sakambhari, Syama. [Danielou 1964; Stutley and Stutley 1984]

Uma Kanya   See *Kanyā*.

Umariya Mata
India, *Chamar*
Destroyer of Life
Goddess of cholera worshiped in the state of Uttar Pradesh. [Leach 1992]

Uradamma
India
Luck
Goddess of fortunes. She presides over the well-being of the people of the Telangana Plateau in the state of Andhra Pradesh. [Leach 1992]

Uravari
India
Earth and Nature; Sky and Heavens; Goodness; Immortality; Water; Magic; Weather; Fishing and Water Animals
"Fertile Soil." One of the *Apsarases*. [Stutley and Stutley 1984]

Urja   See *Urjani*.

Urjani
India
Physical Prowess; Stars and Planets
Hindu goddess of strength. Associated with the Asvins (twin stars that appear before dawn). May be the same as post-Vedic *Urja*, daughter of Daksha. [Stutley and Stutley 1984]

Urmila
India
Beauty
Goddess of beauty. Sister of *Sita*, wife of Lakshimana. [Durdin-Robertson 1976]

Urmya
India
Moon and Night; Mother and Guardian
Vedic night goddess. She protects her followers from thieves and wolves. [Stutley and Stutley 1984]

Uruasi   See *Urvasi*.

Uruki   See *Urvasi*.

Urvashi   See *Urvasi*.

Urvasi
India
Water; Dawn and Twilight; Beauty; Fire; Ceremonies; Love and Sexuality; Sky and Heavens; Goodness; Immortality; Magic; Weather; Fishing and Water Animals
"Widespreading." Considered a Hindu spring or dawn deity. One of the *Apsarases* whose beauty attracted the Vedic gods and humans. Her name is sometimes used for *Usas*. She is connected with the fire-generating ritual, one of the sticks being called Urvasi and the other stick Pururavas, and the resulting fire is called their child. She is invoked by lovers for success with their love.

Urvasi incurred the wrath of some of the gods, so she decided to live on earth for a while. When Pururavas saw her, he desired her for his wife. She agreed to live with him on three conditions: if she could keep her pet rams by the bed; that he would not appear naked before her; and that she would be given clarified butter to eat. When they had lived together for sixty one thousand years (or four autumns), the gods wanted Urvasi to return to the heavens. They sent someone to steal the rams. When Pururavas went after the robbers, the gods made it lightning so Urvasi would see him naked and she disappeared. After much searching, Pururavas found her again and they met once a year for five years and had five sons. When the gods offered Pururavas one wish, he asked to live with Urvasi forever. His wish was granted.
See also *Pururavas*. Alternate forms: Uruasi, Uruki, Urvashi, Usas. [Durdin-Robertson 1976; Jobes 1962; Stutley and Stutley 1984]

Usas
India
Dawn and Twilight; Wealth; Life/Death Cycle; Immortality
Dawn goddess. She gives life and abundance, but is also said to drain life away from men. She remains eternally young, while men grow old. The Asvins (two stars that appear before dawn) precede her across the sky and she may be their mother. Sister of *Ratri*, Agni, Bhaga, Varuna, and possibly Indra, mother of Rudra. She rides across the sky in a chariot drawn by reddish cows, a woman dressed in rose-red garments, veiled in gold. See also *Ashva* and *Vrishakapayi*. Alternate forms: Ushas, Urvasi. [Durdin-Robertson 1976; Stutley and Stutley 1984]

Ushas   See *Usas*.

Ushnishavijaya
India
Intelligence and Creativity; Goodness
Buddhist goddess of intelligence. She represents charity and reassurance. Worshiped also in Tibet and Mongolia. [Getty 1962; Leach 1992]

Ushodevatas
India
Dawn and Twilight
Goddesses of dawn. A class of *Devatas*. [Durdin-Robertson 1976]

Usnisavijaya
India
Selflessness
   Buddhist goddess of virtue. She is white in color with a white mandal. [Lurker 1984]

Uttararani
India
Fire
   Fire deity. The upper fire stick, a piece of *Arani* used in kindling holy fires. See also *Adhararani*. [Durdin-Robertson 1976]

Vac
India
Education and Knowledge; Intelligence and Creativity; Magic; Mother and Guardian; Domesticated Animals
   "Feminine Voice." Goddess of speech. She communicates occult wisdom and knowledge to humans. Wife of Indra. She is considered the mother of the Vedas, the supreme sacred knowledge; the power of the mantras; and the inspirer of the seers. She is believed to be invested with magical powers. Vac also takes the form of a cow who gives nourishment and vigor. An emanation of *Mahalakshmi*. Equivalent to *Guanyin*, Far East. Similar to *Sarasvati* and *Aditi*. She corresponds to the Chinese *Guanyin*, Far East; and to the Hebrew *Chokmah, Sophia,* and *Shekinah*, Near East. Closely connected to *Mahavidya*. Alternate forms: Dhisana, Gayatri, Ida, Para-vac, Shatarupa, Vach, Vacha. [Danielou 1964; Durdin-Robertson 1976; Stutley and Stutley 1984]

Vach   See *Vac*.

Vacha   See *Vac*.

Vadaba
India
Domesticated Animals; Sky and Heavens; Goodness; Immortality; Water; Magic; Weather; Fishing and Water Animals
   "Mare." One of the *Apsarases*. Mother of the Asvins (the two stars that precede dawn). Alternate forms: Badava, Vadava. [Durdin-Robertson 1976; Stutley and Stutley 1984]

Vadava   See *Vadaba*.

Vadra-Kali
India
Unknown
   Hindu goddess who aided her father in overcoming the giant Darida. [Cooper 1876]

Vagisvara   See *Sarasvati*.

Vaidarbhiganani
India
Unknown
   Princess of Vidarbha. Wife of Bhima, mother of *Damayanti*, Dama, Danta, and Damana. [Durdin-Robertson 1976]

Vaisnavi
India
Mother and Guardian; Creator of Life
   "Power of Pervasion." One of the *Saptamatrakas*. [Stutley and Stutley 1984]

Vajar Mata
India, *Bhil*
Mother and Guardian

Goddess of procreation worshiped in the west-central part of the state of Madhya Pradesh and invoked to give children. Wife of Shiva. [Leach 1992]

Vajradakini
India
Magic; Weather
   Buddhist air deity who confers supernatural powers on her followers. Her color is blue. In Tibet she is called *rDerje-mkhah-hgro*, The Himalaya. [Jobes 1962]

Vajravarahi
India
Magic; Charisma; Ceremonies
   Goddess of enchantment, she bewitches men and women. The most important of the *Dakinis*, she is said to be incarnate in the priestess who heads the Tibetan monastery bSam-ldin. Also worshiped in Tibet and Nepal as *Vajra-Vārāhī*, the Himalaya. Equivalent to *Bhavani*. [Jobes 1962; Stutley and Stutley 1984]

Vajrayogini
India
Unknown
   Headless Buddhist Tantric goddess. Similar to *Chinnamasta*. She has been absorbed by the Hindus into their pantheon. [Stutley and Stutley 1984]

Valli
India
Earth and Nature
   "Creeping Plant." One of the daughters of *Ira* who, with her sisters *Lata* and *Virudha*, became the mother of trees, plants, and shrubs. [Stutley and Stutley 1984]

Vama
India
Mother and Guardian
   "Lovely Woman." Jain goddess. One of the aspects of *Ambika*. See also *Matris*. [Durdin-Robertson 1976; Stutley and Stutley 1984].

Vana
India
Earth and Nature; Fire
   "Fire Stick." Forest deity. Similar to *Arani*. [Durdin-Robertson 1976]

Vanadevatas
India
Earth and Nature
   Sylvan deities. A class of *Devatas*. [Durdin-Robertson 1976]

Vanaspati Mai
India
Earth and Nature
   Forest deity worshiped in the Northwest Provinces. [Leach 1992]

Vandya
India
Beauty; Weather; Earth and Nature; Evil; Goodness
   "Adorableness." One of the *Yakshi*. [Durdin-Robertson 1976]

Varahi
India
Hunting and Wild Animals; Mother and Guardian; Creator of Life

"Power of the Boar." Wife of Varaha, the boar form of Vishnu. One of the *Saptamatrikas*. [Danielou 1964; Durdin-Robertson 1976]

Varshayanti
India
Weather; Stars and Planets; Mother and Guardian
"Rainy Season." One of the *Krittikas*. [Durdin-Robertson 1976]

Varu-dasa-rabbi
India
Earth and Nature
Hindu earth goddess. [Cooper 1876]

Varunani
India
Agriculture; Creator of Life
Goddess of intoxicating liquid. Wife of Varuna. One of the *Gnas*, she is said to have appeared at the Churning of the Milk Ocean. She may have originally been a fertility goddess of a non-Aryan cult. See also *Gauri, Madira, Sura*. Alternate forms: Mada, Varuni. [Durdin-Robertson 1976; Leach 1992; Monaghan 1981; Stutley and Stutley 1984]

Varuni See *Varunani*.

Varutri(s)
India
Mother and Guardian; Magic
"Protector." Hindu guardian deity with great powers to help her followers. Also the name of protective genii. [Stutley and Stutley 1984; Durdin-Robertson 1976]

Vasanta
India
Time
Goddess of spring. Sister of *Grismadevi, Hemantadevi,* and *Saraddevi*. Her color is blue. In Tibet she is called *Chi-chi-gyal-mo* or *dPyid-kyi-rgyal-mo*, The Himalaya. Alternate forms: Vasantadevi, Vassanti, Visanti. [Durdin-Robertson 1976; Jobes 1962; Leach 1992]

Vasantadevi See *Vasanta*.

Vasistha
India
Sky and Heavens; Goodness; Immortality; Water; Magic; Weather; Fishing and Water Animals
One of the *Apsarases*. Also the name of a male deity. [Jobes 1962; Stutley and Stutley 1984]

Vassanti See *Vasanta*.

Vasudhara
India
Wealth; Domesticated Animals; Earth and Nature
"Golden-breasted." Hindu earth goddess of abundance who sometimes takes the form of a cow. Wife of Jambhala, the god of wealth, mother of *Sita* and Naraka. Also the name of a Mahayana Buddhist goddess associated with the Dhyani Buddhas. Also worshiped in Tibet and Nepal. Alternate form: Hiranyavaksas. [Durdin-Robertson 1976; Leach 1992; Stutley and Stutley 1984]

Vasus, The
India
Wealth; Order; Mother and Guardian; Goodness; Health and Healing; Weather

"Good." Eight divine attendants of Indra who are considered atmospheric powers and are invoked for material wealth, to defeat enemies, to end discord, and to cure convulsions. They are: *Aditya, Antariksha, Agni, Chandra, Dyu, Nakshatras, Prithivi,* and *Vayu*. Another list says they are *Anala, Anila, Ap, Apu* (Apa), *Dhara, Dhruva, Prabhasa, Pratyusha* and *Soma*. [Stutley and Stutley 1984; Sykes 1968]

Vatsasur
India
Evil; Domesticated Animals
Cow demon. One of those who attacked Krishna. [Durdin-Robertson 1976]

Vayu See *Vasus*.

Vedagarbha See *Mahalakshmi* and *Mahasarasvati*.

Vegavati
India
Disorder
"Impetuous." One of the *Khekaris*. [Durdin-Robertson 1976]

Verdatchamma
India
Water
Fresh water deity associated with the Cumbum irrigation holding tank. [Leach 1992]

Veyyi Kannula Ammavaru
India
Fishing and Water Animals
Goddess of fishermen. Worshiped in the south, she is said to have one thousand eyes. [Leach 1992]

Viaratri See *Chinnamasta*.

Vibudhastris, The
India
Education and Knowledge; Sky and Heavens
Wise women who live in the celestial realms. [Durdin-Robertson 1976]

Vidhava See *Dhumavati* and *Mahavidyas*.

Vidya See *Chinnamasta*.

Vidyadevis, The
India
Education and Knowledge; Arts
Jain goddesses of knowledge. They include Gandhara, Handharva, and *Priyakarini*. The third tone in the Hindu scale of tones is known as Vidya-devi. See also *Devis* and *Vidyadharis*. [Durdin-Robertson 1976]

Vidyadharis, The
India
Education and Knowledge; Magic; Wild Birds; Demi-animals
"Bearers of Wisdom." Aerial genii of the Himalayas who have a knowledge of spells. They can be half-human and half-bird or all human in form. They possess a weapon, but are not warlike. See also *Vidyadevis*. [Durdin-Robertson 1976; Stutley and Stutley 1984]

Vidyavadhus, The
India
Arts
Muses. [Durdin-Robertson 1976]

Vidyujjvalakarali
India
Ugliness; Fire; Weather
   Buddhist goddess of terror. A form of *Ekajata* when she is
the fire of lightning and when she has twelve heads and
twenty-four arms. [Lurker 1984]

Vigayavati
India
Reptiles
   Snake demon. [Durdin-Robertson 1976]

Vighaparsada   See *Jyestha.*

Vijagarbha   See *Sarasvati.*

Vijaya   See *Durga* and *Vijayasri.*

Vijaya Sakti
India
Directions; Sun and Day
   Buddhist keeper of the door to the east, from which she
releases rays of light. [Jobes 1962]

Vijayasri
India
War
   Goddess of victory. May be an alternate form for Vijaya.
[Durdin-Robertson 1976; Sykes 1968]

Vikesi
India
Earth and Nature; Love and Sexuality
   Earth goddess. [Leach 1992]

Vimala
India
Love and Sexuality
   "Illicit Love." One of the *Nayikas.* [Stutley and Stutley
1984]

Vinata
India
Heaven and Hell; Wild Birds; Evil; Destroyer of Life
   Underworld goddess. Wife of Pasyapa, mother of *Sumati*
and possibly Garuda, the bird king. Vinata is said to have laid
an egg from which Garuda hatched after a thousand years.
Also the name of a demon who causes diseases. Indian
mother of eagles, sister of *Kadru* (see for story). [Durdin-
Robertson 1976; Stutley and Stutley 1984; Sykes 1968]

Vinayika   See *Ganesani.*

Vindhya
India
Earth and Nature
   Goddess of the Vindhyan Mountain Range, which crosses
the states of Madhya Pradesh and Uttar Pradesh. See also
Vindhyavasini. Alternate form: Vindhyesvari. [Leach 1992]

Vindhyacalavasini   See *Vindhyavasini.*

Vindhyavasini
India
Ceremonies
   "Dweller on the Vindhya." Tribal goddess who was offered
human sacrifices. See also *Vindhya.* Alternate forms: Durga,
Kali, Vindhyacalavasini. [Stutley and Stutley 1984; Sykes
1968]

Vindhyesvari   See *Vindhya.*

Vipas
India
Water
   "Unfettered." River goddess of the Punjab. [Durdin-
Robertson 1976; Leach 1992]

Viraj
India
Primordial Being; Water
   Primordial deity, the cosmic waters, who is sometimes
male. [Leach 1992]

Virani   See *Virini.*

Virini
India
Family and Tribes
   Mother of five thousand sons by Daksha. He hoped they
would people the world. Alternate forms: Asikni, Virani.
[Stutley and Stutley 1984]

Virudha
India
Earth and Nature
   "A Plant That Grows Again after Being Cut." Daughter of
Ira. With her sisters *Lata* and *Valli,* mother of trees, plants,
and shrubs. [Stutley and Stutley 1984]

Visadhari   "Controller of Poison." See *Manasa.*

Visahari   "Poison Remover." See *Manasa.*

Visanti   See *Vasanta.*

Vishnupadi
India
Stars and Planets
   "Flowing from Vishnu's Left Foot." A reference to the
Milky Way. Name for *Ganga.* [Stutley and Stutley 1984]

Vishpala
India
War
   Warrior deity. She lost her leg in a battle, but the Asvins
(the two stars that precede the dawn) gave her an artificial leg
so she could continue to participate in battles. [Stutley and
Stutley 1984]

Visvadakini
India
Magic; Weather
   Buddhist air spirit who confers supernatural powers on
her followers. In Tibet she is called
sNa-tshogs-rdorje-mkha-hgro, The Himalaya. [Jobes 1962]

Vrikdevatsas, The
India
Earth and Nature
   Tree deity. A class of *Devatas.* [Durdin-Robertson 1976]

Vrishakapayi
India
Unknown
   She is listed in the *Rig Veda.* Wife of Vrishakapi, the great
ape. Associated with *Usas, Saranyu,* and *Surya.* [Durdin-
Robertson 1976]

Vumdhati
India
Stars and Planets
    Stellar deity. The constellation Vumdhati (Vas). [Durdin-Robertson 1976]

Vyaghravaktradakini
India
Magic; Weather
    Buddhist air goddess who confers supernatural powers on her followers. In Tibet she is called *Stag-gdon-can,* The Himalaya. [Jobes 1962]

Waghai Devi
India
Hunting and Wild Animals
    Tiger goddess worshiped in Berar in the state of Madhya Pradesh on the Deccan Plateau. [Leach 1992]

Woman in a Ship
India
Stars and Planets
    Stellar deity. The constellation Virgo worshiped in Cingalese. [Durdin-Robertson 1976]

Woman with Cord
India
Stars and Planets
    Buddhist stellar deity. The constellation Gemini. [Durdin-Robertson 1976]

Yagas, The
India
Magic
    Genii. [Durdin-Robertson 1976]

Yakshi, The
India
Weather; Earth and Nature; Evil; Goodness
    Atmosphere and tree deities. The plural form is *Yakshini.* Their male counterparts are the Yaksas. They generally inhabit each village's sacred tree. They are often depicted as the ideal of feminine beauty, their tall, rounded figures clad in transparent garments. A Yakshi is sometimes seen gently kicking a tree to make it blossom. Benevolent or malevolent, they are sometimes called ogres because they supposedly devour children. Among the *Yakshini* are *Bherunda, Chakrisvari, Minaksi, Saudamani, Sringatpadini, Sulochana, Sumitra, Tadaka,* and *Vandya.* Alternate form: Yakshini. [Durdin-Robertson 1976; Stutley and Stutley 1984]

Yakshini   See the *Yakshi.*

Yami
India
Creator of Life; Water
    River goddess. Sister of Yama, the ruler of the dead. Yami is the river *Yamuna (Jumna)* and is called the mother of the human race because it was created at her entreaty. Also worshiped in Tibet. [Durdin-Robertson 1976; Jobes 1962; Leach 1992; Monaghan 1981]

Yamuna   See *Yami.*

Yanta
India
Justice; Heaven and Hell
    "Vengeance." Hindu deity who is the "torments of hell." Daughter of Bhaya (fear) and *Mrtyu* (death). [Stutley and Stutley 1984]

Yaparamma
India
Commerce and Travel
    Deity who presides over business in eastern India. [Monaghan 1990]

Yasasvati
India
Mother and Guardian
    "Magnificent." Wife of Rishabha, mother of *Brahmi* and one hundred sons, sister of Sunanda. [Durdin-Robertson 1976]

Yashoda
India
Mother and Guardian
    Foster mother of Krishna and mother of *Priyadarsana.* Alternate forms: Yasodha, Ysodha, Jesodha. [Cooper 1876, Durdin-Robertson 1976; Monaghan 1981; Stutley and Stutley 1984]

Yasodha   See *Yashoda.*

Yashodhara
India
Charisma; Magic; Primordial Being; Creator of Life
    "Preserver of Fame." Goddess of occult power and *Shakti* of Siddhartha. Also the name of the mother of Trishiras and Vishvarupa. [Stutley and Stutley 1984; Durdin-Robertson 1976]

Yatudhanis, The
India
Sun and Day; Evil
    Sun demons. [Durdin-Robertson 1976]

Yauni
India
Water
    River goddess. [Monaghan 1981]

Yechu
India, *Daphla*
Wealth; Goodness
    Benevolent goddess of wealth worshiped in the states of West Bengal and Assam. [Leach 1992]

Yerenamma
India, *Jalari*
Fishing and Water Animals; Mother and Guardian
    Fishing goddess. She protects her followers from drowning or being caught by a large fish. [Leach 1992]

Yerra Gadipati Ganga
India
Domesticated Animals
    Dravidian deity of shepherds. [Leach 1992]

Yoganidra
India
Life/Death Cycle
    "Meditation-sleep." A form of *Durga* and a name for *Kalaratri* and *Mahalakshmi.* She is the interval between cosmic periods. [Stutley and Stutley 1984]

Yoginis, The
India
Evil; Magic; Mother and Guardian
    Demon or witch. There are eight, sixty, sixty-four, or sixty-five. They were created by *Durga* who is also called Yogini. Also the name of a protective deity associated with *Shakti* worship. One of the Yogini is *Revata.* Equivalent to

dDorrjernal-hbyor-ma, the Himalaya. See also *Siddha-Yoginis* and *Chausathi Yoginis.* [Danielou 1964; Stutley and Stutley 1984]

Yoni
India
Mother and Guardian
   Female principle of reproductive organs. Equivalent to *In* and *Yin,* both Far East. [Jobes 1962; Stutley and Stutley 1984]

Ysodha   See *Yashoda.*

Zumiang Nui
India, *Chammai/Dhammai*
Creator of Life
   Creator goddess. Mother of the earth, *Subbu-Khai-Thung* and the sky, Jongsuli Yong Jongbu. Wife of Shuzanghu. [Leach 1992; Long 1963; Sproul 1979]

NEAR EAST

A
Mesopotamia; Sumer; Chaldea
Moon and Night; Water
   A moon goddess. Her disk has eight rays, a number associated with goddesses of light in many cultures. Alternate forms: Aya, Ai, Sirdu, Sirrida. [Durdin-Robertson 1975; Jobes 1962; Monaghan 1981]

Ai   See *A*.

Absusu   See *Ishtar*.

Abtagigi   "She Who Sends Messages of Desire." See *Ishtar*.

Abyss Lady
Mesopotamia; Babylonia
Supreme Being; Education and Knowledge
   "Unfathomable Wisdom" and "Voice of the Abyss." Supreme deity. [Jobes 1962]

Abyzu
Israelite
Evil; Magic
   A demon.
   She made mothers' milk cold and frightened children in their sleep. Saint Michael took away her power by forcing her to reveal her forty names.
   See also *Lilith*. [Jobes 1962]

Achamoth   See *Sophia-achamoth*.

Ada
Persia
Mother and Guardian
   A guardian who gives strength to those who seek her. [Gray 1930; Leach 1992]

Adamah
Israelite
Earth and Nature
   "Earth." As the earth, Adamah "opened her mouth" to receive Abel when he died. Similar to *Aretz*. [Durdin-Robertson 1975]

Adamina
Israelite
Earth and Nature
   "Earth Woman." She is Adam's counterpart; her symbol is the red earth. [Jobes 1962]

Adamu
Mesopotamia; Chaldea
Mother and Guardian
   "The Red One." She makes souls from her blood, which represents the blood of childbearing and menstruation. See also *Mens*, Greek and Roman Empires. [Durdin-Robertson 1975; Monaghan 1981]

Adb-isi
Arabia; *Nabataean*
Unknown
   Name for *Isis* of Egypt.   [Negev 1986]

Aderenosa
Mesopotamia; Babylonia
Stars and Planets
   "Celestial Virgin." Ruler of the constellation Virgo. In Babylonia, she can be seen seated on an embroidered throne, nursing an infant. Equivalent to *Adra Nedefa, Kanya,* Indian Subcontinent; and *Ta-repy* and *Zodiacal Virgins*, Egypt. [Durdin-Robertson 1975]

Adnigkishar
Mesopotamia; Sumer, *Bedu*
Family and Tribes
     Patron of the Sumerian city-state of Kazallu. Consort of the
god Martu by which union she consolidated the power of
Kazallu with that of the nomadic Semitic-speaking people
who lived to the west and southwest of Sumer. [Durdin-
Robertson 1975]

Adra Nedefa
Mesopotamia; Babylonia
Stars and Planets
     Associated with the constellation Virgo. She is portrayed
holding an ear of corn in each hand and a baby on her arm.
Equivalent to *Aderenosa,* this section, and *Kanya,* Indian
Subcontinent. [Durdin-Robertson 1975]

Aeons, The
Near East
Creators of Life
     Gnostic angels of "Great Manifested Thought," they
created all things. They number anywhere from eight to
thirty and are the daughters of *Barbelo.* Among the Aeons are
Aletheia, Charity, Ecclesia, Ennoia, Enthumesis, Epinoia,
Mother of Life, Sige, Sophia, Sophia-achamoth, Sophia
Prunikos, and *Zoe.* Equivalent to *Japane Mother Goddess,*
Far East. [Durdin-Robertson 1975]

Afka
Mesopotamia; Babylonia
Water
     She is present in a sacred spring. Another name for
Mylitta. [Monaghan 1981]

Agasaya
Israelite
War
     "The Shrieker." A war goddess who was assimilated into
Ishtar. [Monaghan 1981]

Aggareth   See the *Qlippoth.*

Agrat Bat Mahalat
Israelite
Evil
     Leader of 180,000 demons. According to the Talmud, she
will attack anything that moves on Wednesday and Friday
nights; the rest of the week, she is kept under control by the
rabbis. Alternate form: Igirit. [Monaghan 1981]

Agusaya
Mesopotamia; Babylonia
War
     "The Loud-crying One." A war goddess who subdued
Saltu ("Discord") at *Ishtar's* command. Also an aspect of
Ishtar. [Jobes 1962; Leach 1992]

Aharišvang
Persia
Wealth; Justice
     A goddess of wealth. She represents righteous sovereignty
and truth. [Gray 1930; Leach 1992]

Ahera   See *Asherah.*

Ahurani
Persia
Health and Healing; Wealth; Ceremonies; Water

"She Who Belongs to Ahura." A water deity who was
propitiated for healing and prosperity. Offerings to her could
be made only during the day. [Jayne 1925; Leach 1992;
Lurker 1984]

Ailo   See *Lilith.*

Aima   "Great Mother." See *Aima,* Western Europe.

Aisera   See *Asera.*

Aja
Mesopotamia; Babylonia
Dawn and Twilight; War; Earth and Nature
     "The Unborn." A war goddess identified with *Ishtar* and
the consort of the sun god, she represents unmanifested
nature; her qualities are light, enjoyment, and secretiveness.
See also *Aya,* this section, and *Aja,* Africa. [Danielou 1964;
Leach 1992; Monaghan 1981]

Aka
Anatolia
Mother and Guardian
     Her name means "Mother" in some dialects. See also *Akka*
and *Maddarakka,* Eastern Europe. Alternate forms: Akka,
Ekki Maan-eno Mader-akka. [Monaghan 1981]

Akka   See *Aka.*

Āl
Armenia
Reptiles; Fire
     Demon of childbirth who blinds unborn children and
causes miscarriages and stillbirths. She has fiery eyes,
snake-like hair, brass fingernails, and iron teeth. Originally Āl
was an androgynous demon who hid in damp places. Āl was
also a goddess in Afghanistan. [Archaeological Institute vol. 5
1916–1932; Leach 1972]

Alat   See *Asherah.*

Alath
Persia, *Nabataean*
Unknown
     A goddess who was the female counterpart of Elga.
[Cooper 1876]

Aletheia
Near East
Justice
     "Truth." The principal *Aeon.* She is one angle of the square
upon which Gnosis rests and is called the "Truth of the
Mysteries." Alternate forms: Alitia, Veritas. [Durdin-
Robertson 1975]

Alitia   See *Aletheia.*

Allat
Chaldea; Arabia
Hell; Planets
     Ruler of Aralu, the land of the dead. In Chaldea she is
portrayed as having a woman's body upon the head of a lion
and claws like those of a bird of prey. Similar to *Ereshkigal*
and *Irkalla.*
          Allat rides through her empire standing on the back of a
          horse, greeting the "ekimmu," or spirits of those who have
          just died. Her domain is so large that she sometimes sails
down her river to meet the endless number of deceased. Her boat
resembles a bird and moves without oars or sails.
     See also *Asherah* and *Allatu.* [Durdin-Robertson 1975]

Allatu
Mesopotamia; Akkad; Assyria; Babylonia; Carthage
Heaven and Hell; Justice
   She is the queen of the underworld where she judges the
dead with her consort, Nergal. See also *Allat* and *Ashtart*.
Alternate forms: Alukah, Ereshkigal. [Leach 1992; Monaghan
1981; Stone 1979]

Allatum   See *Arsai, Arsay,* and *Ereshkigal*.

Alukah   See *Allatu*.

Am
Sumer
Intelligence and Creativity; Creator of Life; Mother and
Guardian
   "Muse" in Aryan and "Mother" in Semitic languages, she
is the mother of humankind and the creator of all things.
Alternate forms: Ama, Mama, Mami, Umm. [Jobes 1962;
Monaghan 1981]

Ama   See *Am* and *Mama*.

Ama Usum Gal Ana   "Great Mother Serpent of Heaven."
See *Inanna*.

Amadubad   "All Mother." See *Mami*.

Amanoro
Armenia
Water
   A goddess of springs. [Jobes 1962]

Amat-isi
Arabia; *Nabataean*
Unknown
   Name for *Isis* of Egypt. [Negev 1986]

Amatudda   See *Mami*.

Ament
Arabia; *Nabataean*
Unknown
   Name for *Isis* of Egypt. [Negev 1986]

Ameretāt
Persia
Immortality; Earth and Nature
   "Immortality" or "Long Life." She rules the physical and
spiritual aspects of never-ending life and protects all growing
things. One of the *Amesha Spentas* with *Spentā Ārmaiti* and
Haurvatāt. See also *Ardokhsho*. Alternate form: Amerodat.
[Eliade 1987; Leach 1972; Leach 1992; Monaghan 1981]

Amerodat   See *Ameretāt*.

Amesha Spentas, The
Persia
Immortality; Earth and Nature; Water
   "Immortal Holy Ones." Archangels, attendants of Ahura
Mazda, and guardians of the elements. *Spentā Ārmaiti*
guards the earth; *Haurvatāt*, water; and *Ameretāt*,
vegetation. Animals, fire, and metals are cared for by male
Amesha Spentas. Originally there were only six, but over
time others have been added. [Eliade 1987; Leach 1972]

Amma Attar   See *Asherat*.

Amona   See *Amona*, Western Europe.

Amurdat   See *Zam*.

Ana
Babylonia
Heaven and Hell
   "Spirit of Heaven." See also *Ana*, Indian Subcontinent; and
Ana, Western Europe. Alternate forms: Anan, Anat, Anu.
[Durdin-Robertson 1975; Jobes 1962]

Anael
Near East
Immortality; Stars and Planets
   "Angel." Ruler of the Astral Light (a supernatural
substance). Similar to *Axiokersa, Ceres,* and *Persephone,*
Greek and Roman Empires; and to *Isis* and *Nephthys,* Egypt.
Probably of Babylonian origin. See also *Celestial Virgin* and
Sophia-achamoth. [Durdin-Robertson 1975]

Anahid
Armenia
War
   Equivalent to Assyrian *Anaitis*. See also *Anāhita*. [Cooper
1876]

Anāhit   See *Anāhita* and *Anatu*.

Anāhita
Persia
Moon and Night; Water; Love and Sexuality; Creator of Life;
War; Selflessness; Mother and Guardian
   "Without Blemish" or "Immaculate One." Zoroastrian
moon and fertility goddess, the most popular of seven major
deities. She rules water, the fertilizing force of the earth. As
the patron of love and childbirth, she purifies the sperm and
the womb. She is associated with orgiastic religion and sacred
sexuality. In the Avesta, the sacred book containing the
teachings of Zoroaster, she is a goddess of war who drives a
chariot pulled by four white horses (wind, rain, cloud, and
hail). Possibly equivalent to *Anath*, she is known in
Babylonia as a goddess of love and war and in Egypt as the
"Lady of Heaven." In Armenia she is called *Anāhit*. The
Greeks called her *Anaitis*. They sometimes confused her with
Aphrodite, Greek and Roman Empires, and, because the bull
was sacred to her, she was also confused with *Artemis*, Greek
and Roman Empires. She was worshiped as *Magna Mater* in
the Latin world. Alternate forms: Anahid, Anahit, Anta,
Anthat, Ardvi Anahita, Aredvi Sura Anahita, Ardvī Surā
Anāhita, Mater Artemis, Nahunta. [Cooper 1876; Dexter
1990; Harding 1971; Jobes 1962; Leach 1972; Leach 1992;
Malandra 1983; Monaghan 1981; Senior 1985; Stone 1979]

Anaitis
Persia
War
   Greek name for *Anāhita* or *Anat*. Egyptian name for
Anthrathi. Assyrian war goddess introduced into Egypt in
the fifteenth century B.C.E. See also *Anahid*. She was
identified with *Athena*, Greek and Roman Empires, and said
to resemble *Mylitta* and *Anat*. Alternate forms: Anait, Anta.
[Cooper 1876; Harding 1971; Jobes 1962; Monaghan 1981;
Stone 1979]

Anan   See *Ana*.

Anat
Mesopotamia; Ugarit; Canaan, *Hurrian*
War; Disorder; Love and Sexuality
   "Lady of Death and Life." A warrior goddess associated
with great violence and intense sexuality. *Shakti* (see Indian
Subcontinent) of Assyrian deity Oannes and wife of Anu.

Regarded in Canaan as the sister/wife of Baal. In Egypt she was called *Anaitis* and was either the feminine form or the wife of Reseph and the daughter of Ra. She is identified with the war goddesses *Anthyt* and *Antaeus* and also with *Athena*, Greek and Roman Empires. See also *Anaitis, Anath* and *Anat*, Southeast Asia, and *Anta,* Egypt. Equivalent to *Avaris,* Egypt. Alternate forms: Ana, Anata, Anna-nin, Anatu, Anit, Antu, Antum, Ba'alatu Darkati, Ba'alatu Mulki, Ba'alatu Samen Ramen, and Hanata. [Amiet 1977; Carlyon 1982; Cooper 1876; Durdin-Robertson 1975; Eliade 1987; Leach 1972; Leach 1992; Monaghan 1981; Stone 1979]

Anata   See *Anat.*

Anat-bethel
Canaan
Stars and Planets; War; Love and Sexuality
    An early androgynous deity, represented by the morning and evening stars. In the morning she is a god of war, in the evening, a goddess of love and sacred sexuality. Alternate form: Anat-yaw. [Jobes 1962]

Anath
Mesopotamia; Ugarit; Canaan; Phoenicia; Syria, *Israelite*
Creator of Life; War; Hunting and Wild Animals; Destroyer of Life
    A goddess of fertility and war associated with Baal. She is sometimes identified with *Astarte* and *Asherah* and was said to be the wife of Jehovah. Anath is portrayed as a lion deity.
    Anath followed Baal one day when he went hunting, and when he turned around and saw her he was overcome by desire. They made love as a bull and a cow, and from that bovine union there issued a wild ox. Later, Anath killed many people during a battle and waded through their blood with severed heads slung over her shoulder and the hands of corpses tied around her waist.
    See also *Coatlicue,* Mesoamerica, and *Anat* and *Anāhita,* this section. May be similar to *Anthretjo.* Alternate form: Anatha. [Baring and Cashford 1991; Durdin-Robertson 1975; Jobes 1962; Leach 1972; Leach 1992; Olson 1983; Patai 1967; Savill 1976]

Anatha   See *Anath.*

Anatu
Mesopotamia; Sumer; Armenia; Anatolia; Urartu
Earth and Nature; Sky and Heavens
    "Ruler of the Earth and Queen of the Sky." *Ishtar's* mother, who was later assimilated into *Ishtar.* A primeval goddess. Granddaughter of *Tiamat.* Alternate forms: Anat and Anahit. [Archaeological Institute vol. 7 1916–1932; Monaghan 1981]

Anat-yaw   See *Anat-bethel.*

Anaxšti
Persia
Disorder; Evil
    "Dissension." A demon. [Gray 1930; Leach 1992]

Anghairya
Persia
Mother and Guardian
    A goddess of childbirth. [Gray 1930; Leach 1992]

Ani   See *Mami.*

Anit
Mesopotamia; Ugarit
Sun and Day

A solar goddess, she is the mother of Heru-shu-p-khart. Alternate form: Anat. [Leach 1992; Monaghan 1981]

Anna-nin   See *Anat.*

Anta   See *Anāhita, Anthat, Anaitis.*

Antaeus
Phoenicia
War
    War goddess who is associated with *Anat* and *Anthat.* [Leach 1972]

Anthat
Phoenicia; Assyria
Mother and Guardian; War
    A mother goddess and a goddess of battle. See also *Antaeus* and *Anthyt* and *Anthrathi,* Egypt. Alternate forms: Anāhita, Anta. [Jobes 1962; Leach 1992]

Ānthretju
Hittite
War
    A war goddess mentioned in a treaty between the Hittites and the Egyptians. May be similar to Assyrian *Anath.* [Budge 1989]

Anthyt
Phoenicia
War
    A war goddess associated with *Anat* and *Anthat.* [Leach 1972]

Antu   See *Anat.*

Antum   See *Anat.*

Anu   See *Ana.*

Anuna
Mesopotamia; Akkad
War
    War goddess. [Jacobsen 1970; Leach 1992]

Anunit
Mesopotamia; Babylonia; Assyria; Chaldea
War; Stars and Planets
    "Heavenly One" or "Morning Star." Patron of the city of Nineveh. A war goddess who was eventually assimilated into *Ishtar.* Equivalent to *Venus,* Greek and Roman Empires. [Cooper 1876; Durdin-Robertson 1975; Durdin-Robertson 1990; Leach 1992; Olson 1983]

Anush
Armenia
Reptiles
    A dragon deity who lives in a ravine that is high up on a mountain. [Archaeological Institute vol. 5 1916–1932; Jobes 1962; Wedeck and Baskin 1971]

An.zu
Mesopotamia
Life/Death Cycle; Ugliness; Primordial Being; Water and Earth; Nature
    She is a sea monster, the primal water, and the generator of life, which she also destroys so that it can be renewed again. Equivalent to *Ishtar.* [Johnson 1988]

Aphek   See *Mylitta.*

Apia
Scythia
Earth and Nature
    An earth goddess, equivalent to *Ge* and *Gaea*, both Greek and Roman Empires, and *Armaiti*, this section. [Gray 1930; Leach 1992]

Apo, The
Persia
Water; Ceremonies
    Goddesses of water, equivalent to the *Apas*, Indian Subcontinent. Offerings were made to them only during the day, and it was a sin to make offerings at any other time. [Leach 1992]

Ararat
Anatolia
Creator of Life
    Creator of the world. A mountain is named for her in modern Armenia. [Monaghan 1981]

Ardat Lili   "Belonging to the Night." See *Lilith* and *Lilithu*.

Ardokhsho
Persia
Justice
    "Augmenting Righteousness." Equivalent to *Tyche* and *Fortuna*, both Greek and Roman Empires. May be equivalent to *Ameretāt*. [Jobes 1962]

Arduisur
Persia
Water; Directions
    A goddess symbolized by a fountain out of which four rivers flow in the four cardinal directions. [Brinton 1876]

Ardvi Anahita   See *Anāhita*.

Ardvī Surā Anāhita   "The Watery, Strong, and Immaculate One." See *Anāhita*.

Ardvi Vaxsha
Persia
Water
    A water goddess associated with *Anāhita*. [Hinnells 1973; Leach 1992]

Aredvi Sura Anahita   "Lady Who Is Lofty, Mighty, and Spotless." See *Anāhita*.

Aretia
Armenia
Earth and Nature; Creator of Life
    "Earth." The mother of all living things. Equivalent to *Rhea* and *Vesta*, both Greek and Roman Empires, and to the Hebrew *Aretz*. Alternate forms: Titae Aretia, Titaea Magna, Horchia. [Durdin-Robertson 1975; Lurker 1984]

Aretz
Israelite
Earth and Nature; Justice; Heaven and Hell; Physical Prowess
    "The Earth." In Hebrew scriptures, Aretz is sometimes the earth and sometimes a fertile mother personifying the earth. Her mouth is the entrance to the underworld, and when she opens it she can swallow people whole along with their houses and all their possessions. She also witnesses oaths. Equivalent to *Aretia* and similar to *Adamah*. Alternate form: Eretz. [Durdin-Robertson 1975]

Ariel
Near East, *Israelite*
Family and Tribes; Evil; War
    The personification of Jerusalem. In the Hebrew scriptures, Ariel is mentioned in connection with the terrible strangers and munitions within her (within the city). [Durdin-Robertson 1975]

Ariniddu   See *Arinna*.

Arinitti   See *Arinna*.

Arinna
Mesopotamia, *Hittite*
Sunshine and Daytime
    "Queen of the Hatti." A sun goddess, her consort was the weather god, U or Im, to whom she was considered superior, indicating that a matriarchal society might have existed during her time. Also identified with *Kubaba* and *Hepat*. Alternate forms: Ariniddu, Arinitti, Wurusemu. [Leach 1992; Lehmann 1975; Lurker 1984; Monaghan 1981]

Arisya
Mesopotamia; Ugarit
Earth and Nature
    "Earthy." An earth goddess and a consort of Baal. [Savill 1976]

Armaita   See *Armaiti*.

Armaiti
Persia
Creator of Life; Agriculture; Earth and Nature
    Zoroastrian goddess who presides over fertility, she is a daughter of Ahura Mazda.
    Armaiti wandered over the face of the earth, converting deserts and wilderness into food-bearing fields and gardens.
    See also *Spentā Ārmaiti*. Equivalent to *Apia*, this section, and *Aramati*, Indian Subcontinent. Alternate form: Armaita. [Leach 1992; Monaghan 1981; Redfield 1931]

Armat
Armenia
Earth and Nature
    An earth goddess. Alternate forms: Erkir, Perkunas. [Archaeological Institute vol. 5 1916–1932; Jobes 1962; Leach 1992]

Arsa   See *Rusa*.

Arsai
Mesopotamia; Syria; Canaan
Earth and Nature; Heaven and Hell
    "Girl of the Earth." A nature deity and goddess of the underworld, she was the daughter of Baal and the sister of *Pidrai* and *Tallai*. Alternate forms: Allatum, Arsay, Arsy. [Durdin-Robertson 1975; Eliade 1987; Leach 1992]

Arsay
Canaan; Ugarit
Heaven and Hell
    A goddess of the underworld and a daughter of Baal. Alternate forms: Allatum, Arsai. [Eliade 1987; Leach 1992]

Arsiya
Anatolia
Earth and Nature
    Companion of *Asherah* and a consort of Baal. [Olson 1983]

Arstât
Persia
Justice
   "Truthfulness." She was known for her honesty, and her words made all living things grow and prosper. Alternate form: Aršti. [Durdin-Robertson 1982; Leach 1992]

Aršti   See *Arstât.*

Arsy   See *Arsai.*

Artemides   See the *Titanides.*

Artemidos, Saint
Near East
Selflessness
   A Christian version of the goddess *Artemis*, Greek and Roman Empires, as she appears in the Eastern Orthodox religion. [Jobes 1962]

Artemis Ephesus
Anatolia
Justice; Immortality; Education and Knowledge; Creator of Life; Mother and Guardian
   "Great, Invincible, and Magnificent Founder and Savior, Commander and Guide, Legislator and Queen." A creator goddess and mother goddess. A statue at Ephesia, Anatolia, portrays her with many breasts, to represent her fecundity. She was so popular that a huge temple was built in her honor at Ephesia, and it is known today as the second wonder of the world. Her renown throughout the world was unparalleled. See also *Diana of Ephesians*, Greek and Roman Empires. [Durdin-Robertson 1982; Ergener 1988; Monaghan 1981]

Arubani
Armenia; Urartu
Creator of Life; Primordial Being
   Creator goddess, consort of Haldi. [Der Nersessian 1969; Senior 1985]

Aruru
Mesopotamia; Sumer
Earth and Nature; Creator of Life
   "The Potter." She fashioned humans out of a clay that was mixed with the blood and flesh of a slain deity. In the Epic of Gilgamesh, she creates Enkidu out of this clay to be a companion for Gilgamesh. Some believe that she was originally *Sarpanitu*, one of Marduk's wives. Alternate forms: Mami, Ninhursag, Nintu, Sarpanitum, Zarpandit. [Chicago 1979; Durdin-Robertson 1975; Leach 1972; Leach 1992; Monaghan 1981; Savill 1976]

Aruru-ishtar   See *Ishtar.*

Arusyak
Armenia
Love and Sexuality
   "Little Bride." A goddess of love. She was known earlier as *Astghik*, and Arusyak may have also been a title of *Ishtar*. Arusyak was one of seven important Armenian deities. Equivalent to *Venus*, Greek and Roman Empires. [Jobes 1962; Jones 1932]

Asakhira   See *Ishara.*

Asdoulos
Arabia; *Nabataean*
Unknown
   Name for *Isis* of Egypt. [Negev 1986]

Asenath   See *As-neit*, Egypt.

Asera
Mesopotamia; Syria; Palestine, *Semite*
Mother and Guardian; Water
   Goddess of the Semitic Amorites. "Mother of the Gods and Queen of the Sea." Similar to *Astarte*. Alternate forms: Aserat, Aisera, Aserat. [Lurker 1984]

Aserat   See *Asera.*

Asfandarmad   See *Spentā Ārmaiti.*

Ashdar
Ethiopia
Mother and Guardian
   An Abyssinian mother goddess, equivalent to *Asherah, Ashtoreth,* and *Ishtar.* [Jobes 1962; Monaghan 1981]

Asherah
Mesopotamia; Anatolia; Assyria; Ugarit; Ebla; Phoenicia; Canaan, *Hittite*
Mother and Guardian; Justice; Earth and Nature; Goodness
   "The Great Mother Goddess." Asherah was worshiped in many areas and was said to have been the mother of seventy deities. She was both mother and consort to Baal and a consort of El. She is mentioned frequently in the Hebrew scriptures and in the ancient Ras Shamra tablets. Her symbol is a living tree; in her temples, her presence was represented by an unshaped piece of wood, called an *asherah.* See also *Allat, Ashdar.* Alternate forms: Ahera, Alat, Asherat, Asherat-of-the-sea, Asherath, Asrath, Asheratian, Ashertu, Asirat, Asratu, Astarte, Astratu, Asirtu, Atherat, Athirat, Elat, Elath, Lat, Qadash. [Carlyon 1982; Dexter 1990; Durdin-Robertson 1975; Durdin-Robertson 1982; Leach 1992; Lockyer 1967; Monaghan 1981; Stone 1979]

Asherat   See *Asherah.*

Asherath   See *Asherah.*

Asheratian   See *Asherah.*

Asherat-of-the-sea   See *Asherah.*

Ashertu   See *Asherah.*

Ashi
Persia
Creator of Life; Health and Healing; Wealth; Justice
   A goddess of fertility, abundance, and healing, she blesses the dead as well as the living. See also *Ashi*, Indian Subcontinent. [Jayne 1962; Leach 1992; Littleton 1965]

Ashi Vanguhi   See *Ashish Vanuhi.*

Ashi Yast   "Piety." See *Ashish Vanuhi.*

Ashima
Samaria
Moon and Night; Justice
   "Moon." She was introduced into Samaria from Syria, possibly by the men of Hamath, who worshiped her and brought images of her with them. Her name is used in oath-taking. She may be connected with *Ashima Baetyl* and is identified with *Seimia* and *Shimti.* [Durdin-Robertson 1975; Graves 1948; Jobes 1962; Leach 1992]

Ashima Baetyl

Samaria

Mother and Guardian

A mother goddess worshiped by the Aramaic-speaking Jews at Elephantine in ancient Egypt. She was one of Jehovah's wives. She may have originally been connected with the people of Hamath. See also *Ashima*. Alternate form: Symbetylos. [Durdin-Robertson 1975; Graves 1948; Jobes 1962]

Ashimbabbar

Mesopotamia; Babylonia; Sumer; Akkad

The Moon

"New Light." A form of *Nanna*, Ashimbabbar is the new moon. [Jacobsen 1970; Leach 1992]

Ashi-oxsho

Persia

Fate

Goddess of fate. A daughter of Ahura Mazda. [Hinnells 1973; Leach 1992]

Ashirat

Mesopotamia; Akkad; Ugarit

Sun and Day; Stars and Planets

A sun goddess worshiped by the people of Ugarit. She was Venus, the evening star, to the Akkadians. Alternate form: Ashirtu. [Dexter 1990; Sykes 1968]

Ashirtu   "Sanctuary." See *Ashirat*.

Ashish Vanuhi

Persia

Wealth; Justice

"The Good Truth." A goddess of wealth and fortune, and a sister of the *Amesha Spentas*. She responds to anyone who calls on her for help, and was often invoked along with *Pârendi*. Equivalent to *Lakshimi*, Indian Subcontinent. Alternate forms: Ashishang, Ashi Yast, Ahsi Vanguhi. [Durdin-Robertson 1982]

Ashishang   See *Ashish Vanuhi*.

Ashmunikal

Anatolia, *Hittite*

Justice

A goddess queen of the early Hittites. Mentioned in one version of the Poem of Telepinus. [Durdin-Robertson 1975; Kramer 1961a]

Ashnan

Mesopotamia; Sumer

Agriculture

A goddess of grain and harvests, she presided over the cultivated fields and their produce. Sister of *Lahar*.

Ashnan provided clothes and food for the other gods. One day, after overindulging in her wine, some of them forgot to attend to their duties, so humans were created to do their work for them.

Alternate forms: Asnan and Emmer. [Durdin-Robertson 1975; Leach 1992; Lurker 1984; Savill 1976]

Ashtarchemosh

Moabite

War

Probably the female counterpart of the god Chemosh. [Cooper 1876]

Ashtar-kemosh

Mesopotamia, *Moabite*

Love and Sexuality; War; Creator of Life

A goddess who was equivalent to *Ishtar* or *Astarte*. [Eliade 1987]

Ashtaroth, The

Israelite

War

Goddesses. See also *Ashtart* and *Ashtoreth*. Alternate form: the Ashthraroth. [Crossley-Holland 1980; Leach 1992; Lockyer 1967]

Ashtart

Canaan; Assyria

Sky and Heavens; Creator of Life; Love and Sexuality; War

"Goddess of Heaven." She presides over fertility, love, and sacred sexuality, and as "Venus of the Morning" she is a war goddess. Identified with *Zam*. She is mentioned in Jewish Scripture in Samuel, 1 Kings, Judges, and Jeremiah. Alternate forms: Urania (with the Greek occupation of the Near East). In Arabia she is called *Amma Attar, Malkatu Ashar Amaim,* or Allatu, and in Byblos, Phoenicia, she is called Ra'alat Ashtart. See also *Ashtaroth*. Alternate form: Ashtoreth. [Leach 1992; Stone 1979]

Ashtartu

Mesopotamia; Ebla; Persia

Unknown

One of two great goddesses of the empire of Ebla. The other was *Asherah*. [Matthiae 1981]

Ashtharoth, The   See *Ashtoreth* and *The Ashtaroth*.

Ashtoreth

Canaan, *Zidonian*

Creator of Life; Domesticated Animals

Worshiped in Palestine, she presided over fertility and horses, and is mentioned in Jewish Scripture in 1 Kings. The plural of her name is the *Ashtharoth*. See also *Ashdar* and *Ashtoreth*, Egypt. Alternate forms: Astarte, Ashtart. [Deen 1955; Leach 1972; Leach 1992; Lurker 1984; Monaghan 1981; Zimmerman 1964]

Ashuritu   See *Belit*.

Asi

Palestine

Sky and Heavens

A goddess of the heavens. Alternate form: Asiti. [Cook 1930; Leach 1992]

Aši

Persia

Health and Healing; Wealth; Education and Knowledge

"Just Recompense." She brings healing, wealth, and wisdom. Daughter of *Armaiti* and Ahura Mazda. [Gray 1930; Jayne 1962; Leach 1992; Littleton 1965]

Asiah   See *Asiah*, Western Europe.

Asirat   See *Asherah*.

Asirtu   See *Asherah*.

Asiti   See *Asi*.

Aslik

Armenia

Stars and Planets; Love and Sexuality; Small Size

A goddess of stars and love, equivalent to *Ishtar,* this section, and to *Aphrodite,* Greek and Roman Empires. She has been reduced by later patriarchal religions to being the mother of fairies and nymphs. [Lurker 1984]

Asmodaeus   See *Asmodeus.*

Asmodeus
Near East
Love and Sexuality; Evil
    A Hebrew demon of lust who causes men to be unfaithful; sister of Tubal-Cain. Can also be male. Alternate form: Asmodaeus. [Jobes 1962]

Asmun Nikal
Anatolia
Sun and Day
    A sun goddess. [Stone 1979]

Asnan
Mesopotamia; Sumer
Agriculture
    A goddess of grain. She was called *Emmer* in Sumer. Alternate form: Ashnan. [Lurker 1984]

Asrath   See *Asherah.*

Asratu   See *Asherah.*

Asrušti
Persia
Disorder; Evil
    "Disobedience." A demon. [Gray 1930; Leach 1992]

Astar   See *Ishtar.*

Astart   See *Astarte.*

Astarte
Phoenicia, *Assyrian*
Creator of Life; Love and Sexuality; Heaven and Hell; Moon and Night; Mother and Guardian; Water; Justice
    "Queen of Heaven." The mother of many Assyrian deities, she was their goddess of fertility, love, and sacred sexuality, also a guardian of ships and sailors and a patron of the law. According to some, she is equivalent to *Ashtoreth* in Jewish Scripture. She may also be equivalent to *Anat, Anath, Asherah, Atargatis,* and *Ishtar.* She is identified with *Tanit,* Greek and Roman Empires, and *Qandisa,* Africa. Alternate forms: Ashtoreth, Astart, Astert, Athtarath, Kaukabhta. [Amiet 1977; Baring and Cashford 1991; Durdin-Robertson 1975; Jones 1932; Leach 1992; Monaghan 1981; Patai 1967; Savill 1976]

Astert   See *Astarte.*

Astghik
Armenia
Stars and Planets
    "Little Star." Identical to *Astarte.* A summer festival honoring Astghik and *Anāhita* was called Vardavar ("the bearing of roses"). See also *Arusyak.* [Der Nersessian 1969; Eliade 1987]

Astratu   See *Asherah.*

Astroarche   See *Juno Caelestis,* Greek and Roman Empires.

Astronoe
Phoenicia
Mother and Guardian
    A mother goddess, equivalent to *Cybele.* [Jobes 1962; Monaghan 1981]

Atar   See *Atargatis.*

Atarate   See *Atargatis.*

Atargata   See *Atargatis.*

Atargatis
Syria
Creator of Life; Demi-animals; Fishing and Water Animals; Ceremonies
    A fertility goddess who created the universe. One legend says that she herself was born of an egg that had descended from heaven into the Euphrates while another says she was formed out of the body of a woman who had thrown herself into a lake. She is frequently represented as a mermaid, with the head and body of a woman and the tail of a fish; out of respect for her, her worshipers abstained from eating fish. Her main temples were at the cities of Hierapolis (Mabig) and Askalon on the coast of ancient Palestine. Atargatis eventually came to be revered in Asia Minor and Greece, as well as in Egypt. In Greece and Egypt she is pictured with snakes, and in Rome a monument shows her seated on a throne between lions. Her name is a compound of *Astarte* and *Anat,* whose functions she took over. The Armenians called her *Tharatha.* Equivalent to *Nügua,* Far East. See also *Ate,* this section, and *Artemis* and *Dea Syria,* both Greek and Roman Empires. Alternate forms: Atar, Atarate, Atargata, Atergata, Atergatis, Atharate, Athi, Derketo. [Cooper 1876; Durdin-Robertson 1975; Durdin-Robertson 1982; Leach 1992; Monaghan 1981]

Ate
Anatolia
Mother and Guardian; Hunting; Wild Animals; Birds
    An Aramaic and Cilician mother goddess worshiped at Tarsus. Identified with *Atargatis.* She rides a lion and is accompanied by a sacred dove; her effigy appears on coins found at Tarsus. See also *Ate,* Greek and Roman Empires. Alternate form: Atheh. [Jobes 1962; Leach 1992; Redfield 1931; Woodcock 1953; Zimmerman 1964]

Atergatis   See *Atargatis.*

Atharate   See *Atargatis.*

Atheh   See *Ate.*

Atherat   See *Asherah.*

Athi   See *Atargatis.*

Athirat
Canaan
Water; Mother and Guardian
    "Lady Who Treads upon the Sea." She is the mother of the Canaanite gods, and frequently intervenes on behalf of her children. Alternate forms: Asherah and Ilat. [Eliade 1987]

Athtarath   See *Astarte.*

Atum
Canaan
Heaven and Hell

A goddess of the underworld and female counterpart of Resheph. [Albright 1968; Leach 1992]

Aūṭak See *Vatak.*

Axšti
Persia
Order
"Victorious Peace." [Gray 1930; Leach 1992]

Aya
Mesopotamia; Babylonia
Dawn and Twilight
"Bride." A dawn goddess, she is identified with the eastern mountains and the sunrise. She is the wife of the sun god, Shamash. See also *Aya,* Africa. Equivalent to *Eos* and *Aurora,* both Greek and Roman Empires. She became *A, Aja,* and finally was assimilated into *Ishtar.* [Durdin-Robertson 1975; Monaghan 1981; Senior 1985]

Ayish
Israelite
Stars and Planets
"Great Bear." A stellar deity, probably worshiped in Judah. [Durdin-Robertson 1975]

Az
Persia
Evil; Selfishness
A demon who encourages greed and lust. [Durdin-Robertson 1975; Leach 1992]

A-zi-mu-a
Mesopotamia; Sumer
Heaven and Hell
A chthonic goddess. Daughter of *Ninhursag,* wife of Ningishzida. [Jacobsen 1970; Leach 1992]

Azuiti
Persia
Large Size
A goddess of obesity and a wife of Ahura Mazda. [Gray 1930; Leach 1992]

Ba'alat See *Beltis.*

Ba'alat Ashtart
Canaan
Reptiles; Stars and Planets; Metals; Ceremonies
A serpent lady worshiped in Serabit El Khadim and at Byblos (a port on the Levantine coast) in Canaan. She is said to have fallen from the sky as a fiery star and landed in the waters of the holy Lake Aphaca where her sacred stone was kept in a temple. [Stone 1979]

Baalath
Israelite
Earth and Nature; Primordial Being
A goddess associated with earth energy. The female counterpart of Baal, or another fertility deity who was replaced by Baal. See also *Ba'alath Gebal.* Equivalent to *Baalti* and *Beltis.* Alternate form: Belet. [Jobes 1962; Sykes 1968]

Ba'alath Gebal
Syria, *Assyrian*
Earth and Nature; Primordial Being
Female counterpart of Baal. See also *Baalath.* [Redfield 1931]

Ba'alatu Darkati See *Anat.*

Ba'alatu Mulki See *Anat.*

Ba'alatu Samen Ramen See *Anat.*

Baalith
Mesopotamia
Love and Sexuality; Heaven and Hell; Moon and Night
"Great Goddess." A goddess of love, the underworld, and the moon, she preceded *Ishtar.* [Carlyon 1982]

Baalti
Phoenicia
Mother and Guardian
"My Lady." Mother goddess of the city of Byblos. This name is also used in connection with *Astarte* and *Ishtar.* Equivalent to *Baalath* and *Beltis.* Alternate forms: Belti, Zerbanit. [Jobes 1962; Savill 1976]

Baaltis See *Beltis.*

Baau See *Bau.*

Baba
Mesopotamia; Sumer
Health and Healing
A goddess of healing, identified with *Gula.* Daughter of Anu, consort of Ningirsu and/or Zababa. Her emblem is the goose. See also *Gula.* Alternate form: Bawu. [Amiet 1977; Leach 1992; Moscati 1962; Roberts 1972]

Babaia
Mesopotamia
Mother and Guardian
In Damascus, she was a protector of children. Alternate form: Babia. [Leach 1992]

Babelah
Mesopotamia; Babylonia
Love and Sexuality
In Babylon, a goddess of love. She is mentioned in Hebrew and Greek writings. Associated with *Tiamat.* Babelah is said to have been worshiped around the ancient world. [Durdin-Robertson 1975]

Babia See *Babaia.*

Babu See *Bau.*

Baev See *Bau.*

Bagbarti
Anatolia, *Hurrian*
Unknown
A goddess. [Eliade 1987]

Bagmashtu
Persia, *Urartu*
Primordial Being
She was brought to the city of Musasir, in Persia, by the people of Urartu where she superseded *Arubani* as the consort of Haldi. See also *Bagmasti.* [Der Nersessian 1969; Senior 1985]

Bagmasti
Armenia
Creator of Life
A creator goddess and consort of Haldi. Worshiped at Muzazin in Ararat. See also *Bagmashtu.* [Cooper 1876]

Bagvarti
Urartu
Unknown
    A goddess worshiped by the people of Urartu. [Lurker 1984]

Bahu
Mesopotamia; Akkad
Unknown
    Alternate form of Mesopotamian *Bau*. Also an Akkadian name for Assyrian *Gula*. See also *Bahu*, Indian Subcontinent. [Cooper 1876; Durdin-Robertson 1975; Monaghan 1981]

Balthi
Phoenicia; Cyprus
Justice
    "Queen." Worshiped first in Cyprus and later in Phoenicia. Associated with Tamuz. Also said to be a name for *Belit Ilani*. Alternate form: Belit Ile. [Jobes 1962; Teixidor 1977]

Bamya
Persia
Dawn and Twilight
    "Dawn." She guides the vehicle of the Zoroastrian sun god, Mithra. [Gray 1930; Leach 1992]

Ban
Mesopotamia; Babylonia
Creator of Life
    Prominent goddess and consort of Ningirsu. [Bonnerjea 1967]

Banit
Mesopotamia; Babylonia
Unknown
    A goddess. [Eliade 1987]

Barbelo
Near East
Creator of Life
    Gnostic personification of the "Spirit Father's" thought. Sometimes considered androgynous. Also called *Sophia*, she is similar to *Ennoia*. She is mother of the Archon Ialdabaoth, Sabaoth, or Jehovah, and also mother of the *Aeons*. A special Gnostic sect was devoted to Barbelo and she is closely connected to *Sophia-achamoth*. [Carlyon 1982; Durdin-Robertson 1982]

Bar-juchne
Babylonia
Wild Birds; Sun and Day
    An enormous bird deity: When she extends her wings, they eclipse the sun. She may be connected to the Babylonian zoomorphic deities. [Durdin-Robertson 1975]

Baruth   See *Beruth*.

Basmu Usum   "Holy Cobra." See *Nidaba*.

Bathkol
Israelite
Fate
    "Daughter of a Voice." A symbol of female puberty and gestation. Oracles from this goddess were received through a young girl during her first menstrual period. [Durdin-Robertson 1982; Durdin-Robertson 1990; Redfield 1931]

Bau
Mesopotamia; Babylonia; Sumer
Creator of Life; Mother and Guardian; Health and Healing; Goodness; Ceremonies
    "Great Mother." The chief deity at Lagash where she protected the health of her people. Her husband is Ningirsu. In the role of creator she is identified with *Gula, Mah,* and *Nintu*. She may be a beneficent aspect of *Tiamat*; she was later assimilated into *Ishtar*. The Festival of Bau opened the new year in Lagash. In Phoenicia she was called *Baau*. Alternate forms: Baba, Babu, Baev, Bahu, Gur, Ishtar, Niritu. [Cooper 1876; Durdin-Robertson 1975; Durdin-Robertson 1976; Durdin-Robertson 1982; Leach 1972; Leach 1992; Monaghan 1981; Saggs 1962; Savill 1976]

Baubo
Asia Minor
Earth and Nature
    "Lady of Beasts." [Leach 1992; Neumann 1972]

Bawu   See *Baba*.

Belatsunat
Mesopotamia
Justice
    A goddess. She may be a deified queen. [Durdin-Robertson 1975]

Belet   See *Baalath*.

Beletekallim
Mesopotamia; Mari
Mother and Guardian
    Worshiped by women during the third milllenium B.C.E. [Achtemeier 1985]

Beletersetim   See *Belit Seri*.

Beletseri   See *Belit Seri*.

Beli Sheri   See *Belit Seri*.

Belili
Mesopotamia; Babylonia; Phoenicia; Sumer
Moon and Night; Love and Sexuality; Water; Heaven and Hell
    "Wise Old Lady." A Sumerian moon and love goddess; a water deity who presides over springs, wells, and the willow tree; and a goddess of the underworld. She is the consort of Alala and the sister of Tamamuz. Equivalent to *Ishtar*. She is called *Beltis* in Phoenicia. [Jobes 1962; Leach 1992; Monaghan 1981; Savill 1976]

Belisheri   See *Belit Seri*.

Belit
Mesopotamia; Assyria; Babylonia
Mother and Guardian
    "Lady." A mother goddess and patron of the Assyrian city of Nippur. She is the consort of Bel, Enlil, Marduk, or Ashur. See also *Bilit*. Equivalent to *Astarte, Belili, Ishtar,* and *Ninlil*. Alternate forms: Ashuritu, Beltis, Beltu, Nin-gelal. [Jobes 1962; Leach 1972; Leach 1992; Saggs 1962]

Belit Ilani
Mesopotamia; Babylonia
Mother and Guardian
    "Star of Desire." A mistress of the gods and patron of childbirth and procreation. Equivalent to *Nintu*. Alternate forms: Belit-ilani, Belit Ile, Balthi, Makh, Mah, Belit-illi, Nin-edin. [Carlyon 1982; Jobes 1962; Monaghan 1981]

Belit Ile   See *Balthi* and *Belit Ilani.*

Belit Seri
Mesopotamia; Babylonia; Akkad
Heaven and Hell; Justice
    "Lady of the Underworld." She records all human events.
Alternate forms: Gestinanna, Beli Sheri, Nin-edin, Beletseri,
Belisheri, Beletersetim. See also Makh. [Carlyon 1982;
Durdin-Robertson 1975; Monaghan 1981; Stone 1979]

Belit-itani   See *Makh.*

Belit-matate   See *Ninlil.*

Belti   See *Baalti, Beltis.*

Beltia   See *Beltis* and *Zarpanitu.*

Beltis
Phoenicia; Chaldea; Babylonia
Mother and Guardian; Love and Sexuality; Ceremonies
    "Our Lady" or "Virgo." A mother goddess who shares
power equally with her consort, Bel. Orgiastic rituals were
performed in her honor. She is portrayed as a naked woman,
with an ample body and large breasts. Some say she is
identical to *Cybele* or *Ishtar.* Others identify her with *Astarte,
Baalath, Baalti, Belit, Nana, Ninhursag,* or *Zarpandit.*
Alternate forms: Ba'alat, Baaltis, Belti, Beltia, Beltu. [Cooper
1876; Durdin-Robertson 1982; Jobes 1962; Monaghan 1981]

Beltiya   See *Zarpandit.*

Beltu   See *Beltis* and *Belit.*

Berecynthia   See *Cybele.*

Berit   See *Beruth.*

Berith   See *Beruth.*

Beroth   See *Beruth.*

Beruth
Phoenicia
Family and Tribes
    "Mother." Progenitor of the human race. She gave her
name to the city of Beruth, which is present-day Beirut. Her
consort was either Eliun or Hypsistus. Alternate forms: Baruth,
Berit, Berith, Beroth. [Cooper 1876; Durdin-Robertson 1975;
Jobes 1962; Monaghan 1981]

Biducht
Persia
Love and Sexuality
    A goddess of love, equivalent to *Aphrodite,* Greek and
Roman Empires, and similar to the Celtic *Bidhgoe,* Western
Europe. [Jobes 1962]

Bilit
Assyria
Mother and Guardian
    "Mother of the Gods." Consort of Bel. Associated with
Mylitta, Greek and Roman Empires. See also *Belit.* Alternate
form: Bilit Taauth. [Cooper 1876]

Bilit Taauth   See *Bilit.*

Binah   See *Binah,* Western Europe.

Bithiah
Near East, *Israelite*
Unknown
    "Daughter of Jehovah." An Egyptian who married the
Israelite chief Meted. [Cooper 1876; Deen 1955]

Black Virgins, The   See *Black Virgins,* Greek and Roman
Empires.

Briah
Spain, *Cabalist*
Primordial Being; Earth and Nature
    "The Throne." Her world is called the Briatic. She is
associated with *Neshamah.* See *Briah,* Western Europe.
[Durdin-Robertson 1975]

Broxa
Near East
Wild Birds; Evil
    "Nightjar." A bird who steals milk from goats during the
night. Another name for the Jewish *Lilith.* [Monaghan 1981]

Bubrostis
Anatolia
Unknown
    In Smyrna, a goddess of ravenous hunger. [Leach 1992;
Roscher 1965]

Bushyasta
Persia
Evil
    A demon of sloth and drunken stupors. [Malandra 1983]

C
Near East
Night and Moon
    "Crescent Moon." Gnostic great sea mother. [Jobes 1962]

Cabira
Phoenicia
Mother and Guardian
    "The Cabirian Mother." The Cabirian deities were
probably of Phoenician origin and are found in many
pantheons. [Durdin-Robertson 1975]

Caelestis
Carthage
Moon and Night; Mother and Guardian
    A moon goddess and tutelary deity of Carthage. See also
Dea Caelestis, Greek and Roman Empires. [Jobes 1962; Leach
1992]

Cajiah   See *Chaiah.*

Çatal Hüyük Goddesses, The
Anatolia
Mothers and Guardians
    Mother goddesses depicted sitting or squatting among
wild animals. Their breasts are large and sagging, their hips
large and round. The height of the civilization was around
7000 B.C.E., and it lasted about 1,500 years. Many female
figures have been found but only one carved figure of a male
in this major religious center; it is thought the males were
represented by bulls' heads. [Ergener 1988]

Celestial Virgin
Mesopotamia
Mother and Guardian; Evil and Goodness; Stars and Planets

"Mother of Gods and Devils." She is benevolent and loving; according to some, she is the Astral Light. See also *Anael* and *Sophia-achamoth*. [Durdin-Robertson 1975]

Chaabou
Israelite, Nabataean
Earth and Nature; Mother and Guardian
   "Earth Mother." A virgin goddess and mother of the sun god, Dusura. Her cult is said to parallel that of *Demeter* and *Persephone*, both in Greek and Roman Empires. Alternate form: Chaabu. [Jobes 1962; Leach 1992; Monaghan 1981]

Chaabu   See *Chaabou*.

Chaiah
Near East
Intelligence and Creativity; Primordial Being
   Giver of intuition and understanding. The Gnostic Chaiah is a realm of nature with a density halfway between that of the heavier *Neshamah* and the lighter *Yechidah*, and all humans must pass through Chaiah. Alternate form: Cajiah. [Durdin-Robertson 1975]

Chaos
Mesopotamia; Babylonia
Mother and Guardian
   Mother of the gods. Identified with *Neith*, Egypt, and with *Tiamat*. [Jobes 1962]

Charity   See the *Aeons*.

Chasbei
Moabite
Unknown
   Worshiped by the Semitic-speaking people and the people of Moab, an ancient kingdom in Syria. Alternate forms: Cosbi, Kozbi. [Durdin-Robertson 1975]

Chavah
Near East
Mother and Guardian
   "Mother of All That Lives." In Hebrew tradition she is a form of *Eve*. Alternate form: Chavva. [Jobes 1962]

Chavva   See *Chavah*.

Cherubim, The
Near East
Demi-animals; Wild Birds; Immortality
   Winged female creatures, usually shown squatting and facing each other. Considered by some to be demigods, halfway between humans and gods. One statue shows a male and a female Cherub engrossed in unending intercourse, symbolizing a unifying and transfiguring spiritual force. Some believe that the Cherubim are like the clouds upon which higher gods ride across the sky. They appear in Israelite temples and tabernacles, especially in connection with the Ark. [Monaghan 1981; Patai 1967]

Chiun
Israelite
Wealth; Stars and Planets
   "Plenty." Possibly associated with the planet Saturn. Equivalent to *Kaiwan* or *Guanyin*, both Far East. Alternate forms: Kiun, Remphan. [Jobes 1962]

Chokmah   See *Chokmah*, Western Europe.

Cista
Persia
Physical Prowess; Stars and Planets
   "Morning Star." She gives physical prowess and good eyesight. She is also the goddess of those who pursue spiritual paths. Alternate form: Razishta Cista. [Leach 1992; Malandra 1983]

Cosbi   See *Chasbei*.

Cotys
Anatolia, *Phrygian*
Earth and Nature; Love and Sexuality; Ceremonies
   An earth goddess and a patron of debauchery. Identified with *Cybele*. She was introduced to Athens and Corinth, where private orgies were held in her honor. Her followers were called *baptai*. Perhaps they performed a ritual of dipping their clothes or their hair in water before their orgies. See also *Cotys*, Greek and Roman Empires. Alternate form: Cotytto. [Jobes 1962; Leach 1992; Redfield 1931; Woodcock 1953; Zimmerman 1964]

Cotytto   See *Cotys*.

Cow Goddesses, The
Syria
Domesticated Animals
   Goddesses mentioned in the Assyrian epic *The Building of Baal's House* in which the goddesses are present at a great feast commemorating the event. Also known as the *Ewe Goddesses*, the *Jar Goddesses*, and the *Throne Goddesses*. Similar to the *Seven Kine-deities*, Egypt. [Durdin-Robertson 1975]

Cybele
Anatolia, *Phrygian*
Mother and Guardian; Earth and Nature; Creator of Life; Hunting and Wild Animals; War; Family and Tribes
   "Great Mother." A goddess of forests, mountains, and the fertility of all living things. Her worship was introduced into Greece and Italy. She is often represented as a lion wearing a turreted crown, indicating that she was a war goddess and a founder of cities. Cybele is said to have originally been the goddess *Kubaba*. A statue of her is carved out of rock on the face of Mt. Sipylos, and her image is also said to be seen on some meteorites. See also *Cybele*, Greek and Roman Empires, *Berecynthia*, Western Europe. Equivalent to *Astrone*. Alternate forms: Kybele, Berecynthia, Kubele. [Harding 1971; Jobes 1962; Leach 1992; Monaghan 1981; Neumann 1972; Redfield 1931; Stone 1979; Zimmerman 1964]

Daath   See *Daath*, Western Europe.

Dadmish
Canaan
War
   Possibly a warrior goddess. [Eliade 1987]

Daena
Persia
Mother and Guardian; Time; Justice; Heaven and Hell; Immortality; Domesticated Animals
   "That Which Has Been Revealed." A guardian of women, she presides over the twenty-fourth day of the lunar month. Daughter of *Armaiti* and Ahura Mazda.
   Daena meets the souls of the dead on the fourth day, and then leads them either to heaven or hell. She is aided in her decision by a dog who can distinguish between good and evil.

She is often invoked along with *Kista.* [Durdin-Robertson 1982; Leach 1992; Lurker 1984]

Dagon
Phoenicia, Syria, *Philistine*
Demi-animals; Fishing and Water Animals
   Deity who is part fish, part human. (Can also be a male god.) [Bulfinch 1898; Langdon 1931; Leach 1992]

Damake   See *Damkina.*

Damgalnunna
Mesopotamia; Sumer
Justice
   "Great Wife of the Prince." She became the mother goddess, *Ninhursag.* See also *Damkina.* [Lurker 1984; Savill 1976]

Dam-ki   See *Damkina.*

Damkina
Mesopotamia; Babylonia; Akkad
Sky and Heavens; Mother and Guardian
   "Mistress of the Earth." A Babylonian sky goddess and protector of childbirth, she is the spouse of Ea and the mother of Marduk. Associated with *Damgalnunna, Ninhursag,* and the Sumerian *Ki.* Alternate forms: Damake, Dam-ki, Dauke, Daukina, Dauthe, Davkina, Dawkina, Gashan-ki, Ninella, Ninki, Nin-ki. [Carlyon 1982; Durdin-Robertson 1975; Monaghan 1981; Saggs 1962]

Da-mu-gal   See *Gula.*

Daukina   See *Damkina.*

Dauthe   See *Damkina.*

Davcina
Mesopotamia; Babylonia; Chaldea
Earth and Nature
   An earth goddess. Wife of Aos, mother of Bel. Alternate form: Davke. [Cooper 1876]

Davke   See *Davcina.*

Davkina   See *Damkina.*

Dawi
Persia
Evil
   "Deceit." A demon. [Gray 1930; Leach 1992]

Dawkina   See *Damkina.*

Dazimus
Mesopotamia; Sumer
Health and Healing
   A goddess of healing, her story is told in the epic *Paradise of Dilmun.* [Savill 1976]

Ddrvaspa
Persia
Domesticated Animals
   A protector of animals, she presides over the health of cattle and horses. [Gray 1930; Jayne 1962; Leach 1992]

Deo
Akkad
Agriculture; Demi-animals; Domesticated Animals
   A barley-planting goddess. She is portrayed with a mare's head and holds a porpoise and a black dove. She was later

assimilated into *Demeter,* Greek and Roman Empires, and is identified with *Rhea,* Greek and Roman Empires. [Jobes 1962; Wedeck and Baskin 1971]

Dercetis   See *Derketo.*

Derceto   See *Derketo.*

Derketo
Mesopotamia; Babylonia; Chaldea
Demi-animals; Water Animals and Fishing; Mother and Guardian; Moon and Night
   A mermaid goddess whose early worship started in Chaldea and spread extensively throughout Syria and the land of the Philistines where she was known as a mother goddess. She was the mother of *Semiramis* and was closely connected with *Atargatis* and *Astarte.* Also a moon goddess associated with fertility. Alternate forms: Derceto, Dercetis. [Durdin-Robertson 1975; Harding 1971; Jobes 1962; Leach 1992; Monaghan 1981]

Dewy
Canaan
Weather
   A goddess of rain, she is the female counterpart of Baal. [Gray 1957; Leach 1992]

Dianoia
Near East
Intelligence and Creativity
   "Thought." A Gnostic deity. [Durdin-Robertson 1975]

Dido
Phoenicia
Dawn and Twilight
   "The Fugitive." She is the gloaming, which dies when the fire of the sun departs. A title used by *Elissa,* deified queen of Tyre, and by succeeding generations of queens. Dido's city was Cartha-Elissa, which was later called Carthage. In the center of the city was the sacred grove of *Elissa,* which was destroyed by the Romans. Alternate forms: Dido Anna, Didon, Didone. [Chicago 1979; Cooper 1876; Jobes 1962; Monaghan 1981; Senior 1985; Woodcock 1953; Zimmerman 1964]

Dido Anna   See *Dido.*

Didon   See *Dido.*

Didone   See *Dido.*

Dilbah
Mesopotamia
Unknown
   A name for *Ishtar* when she rises and sets as the morning and evening stars, and when she is warlike and lustful. [Monaghan 1981]

Dilbali   See *Ishtar.*

Dimme
Mesopotamia; Sumer
Destroyer of Life
   A goddess of disease who causes puerperal fever and other illnesses in newborns. Daughter of An. Equivalent to *Lamashtu.* [Leach 1992]

Dimtabba
Mesopotamia; Sumer
Unknown
   A goddess who was worshiped in the city of Ur (2112–2015
B.C.E.). [Savill 1976]

Dingirmah   "Exalted Deity." See *Hannahannas.*

Dione
Phoenicia
Unknown
   Daughter of *Ghe*, consort of Ouranos. Sister of *Astarte*
(this region) and *Rhea* and *Dione*, Greek and Roman Empires.
[Durdin-Robertson 1975]

Dizane
Afghanistan, *Kaffir*
Agriculture; Ceremonies
   A goddess who protects the growing grain. A goat was
sacrificed to her when a male child was born. [Leach 1992;
Robertson 1925]

Dodah
Israelite
Unknown
   Deity who was honored in Israel. [Durdin-Robertson 1975]

Druj
Persia
Evil
   An embodiment of deceit and treachery, she accompanied
the devil, Angra Mainyu. Equivalent to *Drude*, Northern
Europe, and *Nasu*, this section. [Jobes 1962; Leach 1972;
Lurker 1984]

Druxsans, The
Persia
Evil; Magic
   Demons connected with enchantment. [Durdin-Robinson
1976]

Drvaspa
Persia
Health and Healing; Immortality
   "Possessing Sound Horses." A goddess who is prayed to in
order to avert illness and aging, she heals animals as well as
humans. [Jayne 1925; Leach 1992]

Dsovinar
Armenia
Water; Disorder
   Born from the sea, she is an angry goddess who brings
destructive storms. [Jobes 1962; Jones 1932]

Dudu Hepa
Anatolia
Sun and Day
   A sun goddess. [Stone 1979]

Dughda
Persia
Mother and Guardian; Goodness and Evil
   Mother of Zoroaster.
   *During the sixth month of her pregnancy, Dughda dreamed
   that good and evil spirits were fighting for control of her
   child. A monster tried to tear the future Zoroaster from
Dughda's womb, but a light-bearing deity came to the rescue and
put the embryo back.*
   Alternate form: Dughdhova. [Jobes 1962; Leeming 1981]

Dughdhova   See *Dughda.*

Dumuziabzu
Sumer; Babylonia
Creator of Life; Earth and Nature; Water; Mother and
Guardian
   A fertility goddess who protects the marshlands. In
Babylonia she was the tutelary goddess of Kinirsa. Alternate
form: Dumuzid-abzuk. [Jacobsen 1970; Leach 1992; Lurker
1984]

Duttur
Mesopotamia; Sumer
Domesticated Animals
   Goddess of the ewes. The mother of the shepherd god
Dumuzi. [Jacobsen 1970; Leach 1992]

Dynamis
Mesopotamia; Sumer
Immortality; Family and Tribes
   A Gnostic deity. With *Phronesis* and *Sophia*, she created
principalities and angels. Also an eagle goddess associated
with *Ishtar* and *Ana*. [Durdin-Robertson 1975]

Ecclesia
Near East
Education and Knowledge; Family and Tribes
   One of the *Aeons*. Represented as "Israel" or the "Bride,"
her heart sends forth streams of spirit-nourishing wisdom.
Similar to *Malkuth*, Western Europe, and *Tiphereth*, Western
Europe. [Durdin-Robertson 1975]

Edem
Near East
Evil
   A Gnostic deity who causes evil but is not necessarily evil
herself. [Carlyon 1982]

Eden
Near East
Demi-animals; Earth and Nature; Mother and Guardian;
Reptiles
   "Earth." A Gnostic deity, half woman and half serpent, said
to have a "double mind" and a "double body." As the mate of
Elohim, Eden gave birth to twenty-four angels, twelve of
whom were archons, or demons. [Buckley 1986]

Egitummal
Mesopotamia; Sumer
Agriculture
   A grain goddess and the tutelary deity of the city of
Tummal. [Jacobsen 1970; Leach 1992]

Eimaramene
Phoenicia
Fate
   A goddess of fate. With *Hore*, she waged war against
Cronus; they were defeated when Cronus won them over
with his charms. Alternate form: Heimarmene. [Durdin-
Robertson 1975]

Ekki   See *Aka.*

Elat   See *Asherah.*

Elath   See *Asherah.*

Elissa
Phoenicia; Carthage
Unknown

Goddess identified with *Dido.* Also the name of an Arabian goddess associated with Mitra, the sun god. [Jobes 1962; Wedeck and Baskin 1971]

Emmer
Mesopotamia; Sumer
Agriculture
Sumerian name for *Asnan,* an ancient goddess of wheat. [Lurker 1984]

Ennoe   See *Ennoia.*

Ennoia
Near East
Disorder; Magic; Education and Knowledge
"Designing Thought." One of the *Aeons,* she created the angels of the lower worlds; it was said that her demonic progeny brought her down from heaven to earth where she inhabits the bodies of women and causes strife by inflaming their passions. She was supposed to have taught magic to the sorcerer Simon Magus. Alternate form: Ennoe. [Carlyon 1982; Durdin-Robertson 1975; Durdin-Robertson 1982]

Ensum   "Half Moon." See *Nanna.*

Enthumesis
Near East
Goodness
"Consideration" or "Esteem." Daughter of *Sophia* and one of the *Aeons.* Very similar to *Epinoia.* Alternate form: Enthymese. [Durdin-Robertson 1975]

Enthymese   See *Enthumesis.*

Epinoia
Near East
Intelligence and Creativity; Earth and Nature
"Power of Thought." One of the *Aeons.* Connected with the earth. She is similar to *Aletheia.* [Durdin-Robertson 1975]

Eres Ki Gala   See *Ereshkigal.*

Ereshkigal
Mesopotamia; Sumer
Destroyer of Life; Moon and Night; Goodness; Heaven and Hell
A goddess of death and darkness and the elder sister of *Inanna.* She was the sole ruler of Irkalla, the Land of the Dead, until she stopped Nergal from killing by making him her co-ruler. Her beneficent aspect becomes apparent when she allows the wealth (gold, oil, etc.) of the underworld to surface on earth. Alternate forms: Allatu, Allatum, Ganzir, Irkalla, Ninkigal, Eriskegal, Eres Ki Gala. [Chicago 1979; Cotterell 1979; Durdin-Robertson 1975; Jobes 1962; Leach 1992; Monaghan 1981; Stone 1979]

Eretz   See *Aretz.*

Eriskegal   See *Ereshkigal.*

Erkir   See *Armat.*

Erua
Mesopotamia; Babylonia
Water
A goddess of the waters, possibly the daughter of Eal. She was assimilated into *Sarpanitu.* Also an alternate name for *Mami.* [Leach 1992; Lurker 1984; Monaghan 1981]

Esharra
Mesopotamia
Wealth
A goddess of productive fields, she protected the private ownership of land. [Durdin-Robertson 1975; Monaghan 1981]

Eshtar
Ebla; Syria
Mother and Guardian; Stars and Planets
Mother goddess and stellar deity of Semitic-speaking people who was worshiped in Ebla. Said to be the old Akkadian form of *Ishtar.* Equivalent to *Inanna* and *Ishtar.* [Leach 1992; Matthiae 1981; Stone 1979]

Eve
Mesopotamia; Phoenicia; Sumer
Heaven and Hell; Mother and Guardian
Phoenician goddess of the underworld who is invoked in inscriptions. Possibly identified with *Ishtar.* Also the first or second mate of Adam and mother of all humans. See also *Chavah, Lilith,* and *Meshiane.* [Baring and Cashford 1991; Deen 1955; Eliade 1925; Leach 1993; Monaghan 1981; Neumann 1972; Senior 1972]

Ewe Goddesses, The   See *The Cow Goddesses.*

Ezinu
Mesopotamia; Sumer
Agriculture
A grain goddess.   [Jacobsen 1970; Leach 1992]

Feminine Powers, The
Persia
Creators of Life
In the Manichean system, five goddesses who created the first couple, Adam and *Eve.* [Durdin-Robertson 1975]

Ferašti
Persia
Education and Knowledge
"Teachability." Goddess who was a wife of Ahura Mazda. [Gray 1930; Leach 1992]

Filia Vocis   See *Filia Vocis,* Western Europe.

First Woman, The
Persia
Creator of Life; Love and Sexuality
First Woman is said to have begun life inside a reed.
Long ago, before the beginning of time, there was nothing but a tall reed, and inside this reed there lay a man and a woman, so deeply entwined with each other that they seemed to be inseparable, until a god came along and separated them, and kept them apart for fifty long years. After they were reunited they had a son and daughter, but their love for their children was so great that they devoured them, so once again, the god intervened. This time, he reduced the couple's love for their offspring, and they had fourteen more children, seven boys and seven girls, who were able to grow to maturity.
See also *Mashyoi.* [Farmer 1978]

Frasasti
Persia
Charisma
"Fame." A wife of Ahura Mazda. [Leach 1992]

Fravakain
Persia
Family and Tribes

One of two primeval children. Daughter of *Nashak* and Siyakmak, sister of Fravak, mother of *Tazhak*, Taxh, *Guzhak*, and Haoshyangha. *Tazhak* became the mother of the Arabs, and *Guzhak* the mother of the Persians. [Jobes 1962]

Fravashis, The
Persia
Immortality; Creators of Life; Earth and Nature; Heaven and Hell
"The Chosen Ones." Everlasting and deified souls. They helped create the world, especially things that grow, and are defenders of heaven.   [Durdin-Robertson 1982; Lurker 1984]

Fšeratu
Persia
Primordial Being
Divine goddess. [Gray 1930; Leach 1992]

Ganzir   See *Ereshkigal.*

Gashan-ki   See *Damkina.*

Gasmu
Mesopotamia
Water; Education and Knowledge
"Lady of the Ocean" or "The Wise One." An ancient sea goddess who was later associated with *Zarpanitu.* [Durdin-Robertson 1975]

Gatamdug
Mesopotamia
Fate; Water
Goddess of the Tigris and a goddess of fate, later assimilated into *Gula.* See also *Ninmuk.* [Monaghan 1981]

Ga-tum-dug
Mesopotamia; Babylonia
Earth and Nature
Earth goddess and mother goddess worshiped in Lagash, a city in Sumer, South Babylonia. Other goddesses worshiped there were *Inanna* and *Ninhursag.* [Guirand 1968; Leach 1992]

Ge   See *Ghe.*

Gea
Phoenicia
Earth and Nature
Mother earth in the creation legend of Philo Byblos. Also said to have risen from the primeval egg. Alternate form: Keb. [Sykes 1968]

Geburah   See *Geburah*, Western Europe.

Gedulah   See *Gedulah*, Western Europe.

Gelou   See *Lilith.*

Genea
Phoenicia
Creator of Life
"First Mother of Humanity." [Durdin-Robertson 1975; Monaghan 1981]

Gephen
Near East
Earth and Nature; Family and Tribes
"The Vine." A Gnostic feminine symbol representing the wife or mother of Israel. She corresponds to *Sophia,* who is also like a vine. See also *Geshtin.* [Durdin-Robertson 1975]

Geshtin
Mesopotamia; Sumer; Babylonia
Earth and Nature
A goddess of the vine. See also *Gephen.* Alternate form: Geshtinanna. [Guirand 1968; Leach 1992; Mole 1966]

Geshtinanna   See *Geshtin* and *Gestinanna.*

Gestinanna
Mesopotamia; Babylonia; Sumer
Justice; Heaven and Hell; Intelligence and Creativity; Water
"She Who Keeps Records in the Underworld" and "Lady of the Vine." An underworld goddess who lives on earth for half of the year, a divine poet and dream interpreter, and the sister of Dumuzi. According to some she is the "queen of water," a fish goddess whose earlier name was *Nina.* Alternate forms: Belit Seri, Geshtinanna, Nin-edin. [Durdin-Robertson 1975; Leach 1992; Mercer 1925b; Monaghan 1981; Savill 1976]

Geush Urvan
Persia
Domesticated Animals; Earth and Nature; Health and Healing
"Soul of the First Ox." An androgynous deity who contained the seeds of all species of animals, grains, and medicinal plants. [Jobes 1962]

Gevurah   See *Gevurah*, Western Europe.

Ghe
Phoenicia
Earth and Nature
Earth goddess. The earth was named after her. She was worshiped at Bylbos, which became the cities of Beruth and Eliun. Equivalent to *Gaea*, Greek and Roman Empires. Alternate form: Ge. [Durdin-Robertson 1975]

Gilou   See *Lilith.*

Gubarra
Mesopotamia; Babylonia
Earth and Nature
"Lady of the Mountain." Her husband is Mâtu. [Leach 1992; Sayce 1898]

Gula
Mesopotamia; Babylonia; Akkad
Health and Healing; Destroyer of Life; Evil; Mother and Guardian
Mother goddess and great physician. An amalgamation of *Bau, Gatamdug,* and *Mama.* She lives in a beautiful garden at the center of the world. She gives life and also brings misfortune and can either cause or cure disease. See also *Baba* and *Hala.* Alternate forms: Da-mu-gal, Gula Bau, Ninkarrak, Ninudzalli. [Durdin-Robertson 1975; Jayne 1925; Johnson 1988; Leach 1992; Monaghan 1981; Saggs 1962]

Gula Bau   See *Gula.*

Gulses, The
Anatolia, *Hittite*
Fate
"The Scribes of Fate." Mentioned in the Poem of Telpinus. They mete out good and evil, life and death. Equivalent to *Moirae*, Greek and Roman Empires. Their Hurrian name is *Hutena.* [Durdin-Robertson 1975; Lurker 1984]

Gumshea
Mesopotamia
Earth and Nature

A plant goddess, later assimilated into *Ishtar*. [Monaghan 1981]

Gur   See *Bau*.

Guzhak
Persia
Family and Tribes
    Mother of the Persians, daughter of *Fravakain* and Fravak, and wife of Haoshyangha. [Jobes 1962]

Hacilar Goddess
Anatolia
Creator of Life
    A mother goddess worshiped by the ancient community of Hacilar that existed from 7000 to 5450 B.C.E.

Hagar   See *Hagar*, Egypt.

Hala
Mesopotamia; Kassite
Health and Healing
    A goddess of healing, equivalent to *Gula*. [Lurker 1984]

Halmssuitta
Mesopotamia, *Hittite*
Supreme Being
    Halmssuitta protects the king.
 Once a king promised Halmssuitta wonderful gifts if she would guard a mountain that was far away from him, hoping to keep her from meddling in his affairs.
    See also *Hanwasuit*. [Lehmann 1975; Wedeck and Baskin 1971]

Hambarus, The
Armenia
Household Affairs
    "House Spirits." Spirits who have human bodies and sometimes live in ruins; they were probably feminine. [Archaeological Institute vol. 5 1916–1932]

Ham-vareti
Persia
Mother and Guardian; Weather; War
    "Morning Mist." She hides warriors from their enemies. [Gray 1930; Leach 1992]

Hanata
Near East
War
    "Warrior." See *Ishtar* and *Anat*.

Hannahannas
Anatolia, *Hittite*
Mother and Guardian; Insects
    "Mother of the Gods." She is associated with the bee. Alternate forms: Dingirmah, Nintu. [Durdin-Robertson 1975; Ergener 1988; Kramer 1961; Lurker 1984; Stone 1979]

Hanwasuit
Anatolia, *Hittite*
Supreme Being
    A throne goddess of the city of Zalpa on the Black Sea. See also *Halmssuitta* and *Hatti Throne Goddess*. [Lurker 1984]

Hapantili
Mesopotamia, *Hittite*
Moon and Night
    Sky goddess.

The moon fell out of the sky into a city, and Hapantili took the moon's place in the heavens. [Lehmann 1975]

Hashat
Mesopotamia; Ugarit
Unknown
    A goddess associated with *Anath*. [Savill 1976]

Hatepinu
Anatolia, *Hittite*
Unknown
    The mother of Telepinu and consort of Taru. [Wedeck and Baskin 1971]

Hatti Throne Goddess
Anatolia, *Hittite*
Supreme Being
    A throne goddess who protects the king. See also *Hanwasuit*. [Durdin-Robertson 1975; Kramer 1961b]

Haurvatāt
Persia
Water; Health and Healing
    "Integrity" or "Health." One of the *Amesha Spentas* with *Ameretāt* and *Spentā Ārmaiti*. She guards the spiritual and physical aspects of water. [Eliade 1987; Monaghan 1981]

Hea
Mesopotamia; Ugarit
Earth and Nature; Education and Knowledge
    An earth goddess and a goddess of wisdom. [Leach 1992; Seligmann 1948]

Heba   See *Hebat*.

Hebat
Anatolia, *Hurrian, Hittite*
Sun and Day; Hunting and Wild Animals
    A sun goddess who was later assimilated into *Wurusemu*. Her constort is the weather god, Tsehub, and she is the mother of Sharruma. She is portrayed as a matronly woman astride a lion. Alternate forms: Hepatu, Hebatu, Hepit, Heba, Hepat. [Eliade 1925; Leach 1992; Monaghan 1981]

Hebatu   See *Hebat*.

Hecate
Anatolia
Unknown
    An ancient goddess who lives both in the water and on dry land. Worship of her began on the coast of western Anatolia; in Egypt she is called *Heqit*. See also *Hecate*, Greek and Roman Empires. [Stone 1979]

Heimarmene   See *Eimaramene*.

Helmund
Afghanistan
Water
    A river goddess, equivalent to *Harahvaiti* and *Sarasvati*, both Indian Subcontinent. [Jobes 1962]

Henti
Anatolia
Sun and Day
    A sun goddess. [Stone 1979]

Hepat
Anatolia, *Hurrian*
Justice
A goddess who presides over the Hurrian pantheon. The lion was sacred to her, and she was often portrayed standing on one. She is identified with *Wurusemu* and *Arinna.* Alternate forms: Hepit, Kubebe Kupapa. [Amiet 1977; Durdin-Robertson 1975; Stone 1979]

Hepatu   See *Hebat.*

Hepit   See *Hebat* and *Hepat.*

Hidaba
Mesopotamia; Sumer
Education and Knowledge
A goddess of writing. [Johnson 1988]

Hir Nineveh
Mesopotamia
Magic
"Well-favored Harlot." A tutelary goddess of Nineveh who presides over witchcraft and is mentioned in Hebrew Scriptures. [Durdin-Robertson 1975]

Hod   See *Hod,* Western Europe.

Holy Ghost, The   See the *Holy Spirit.*

Holy Spirit, The
Israelite
Primordial Being; Creator of Life
"The Life-giving Principle." Among those who considered the Holy Spirit to be feminine were the Gnostics, the Nazarenes, and the Essene Ebionites. In the "Life of Jesus," attributed to the Jews, Jesus refers to "My Mother, the Holy Spirit (Pneuma)." Associated with *Sophia,* this section; *Mens,* Greek and Roman Empires; and *Shakti,* Indian Subcontinent. Alternate form: the Holy Ghost. [Durdin-Robertson 1975]

Horchia   See *Aretia.*

Hore
Phoenicia
War
Accompanied *Eimaramene* in a campaign to defeat Cronus. [Durdin-Robertson 1975]

Houri, The
Persia
Earth and Nature; Justice; Heaven and Hell
Moslem nymphs who accompany the faithful in paradise. [Jobes 1962]

Hubar   See *Hubur.*

Hubur
Mesopotamia; Babylonia
Primordial Being; Evil
A primordial mother goddess. She gave birth to monsters who went to war with *Tiamat.* Alternate form: Hubar. [Durdin-Robertson 1975; Gray 1930; Leach 1992]

Hulla
Anatolia, *Hittite*
Unknown
A goddess who was the daughter of *Wurusemu.* [Durdin-Robertson 1975]

Huriya
Syria
Mother and Guardian
A goddess whose special son was nursed by *Asherah* and *Anath.* She was the mother of six other sons and a daughter, *Thitmanat,* and was the consort of Keret, the king of Huber. She was mentioned in the Ras Shamra Tablets of Syria. Alternate form: Hurriya. [Durdin-Robertson 1975; Savill 1976]

Hur-ki
Mesopotamia; Akkad; Babylonia
Moon and Night
A moon goddess. [Goldziher 1877; Leach 1992]

Hurriya   See *Huriya.*

Husbishag
Akkad, *Israelite*
Heaven and Hell; Fate
A goddess of the underworld. In her secret book, the *Land of the Dead,* kept at Arallu, is written the hour of death for every living creature. Possibly an aspect of *Ereshkigal.* Alternate form: Hushbishag. [Monaghan 1981]

Hushbishag   See *Husbishag.*

Hushiti
Persia
Household Affairs; Mother and Guardian
A goddess of the home who protects its occupants. [Gray 1930; Leach 1992]

Hutena   See the *Gulses.*

Huwassanas
Anatolia, *Hittite*
Weather; Disorder
A goddess who is the consort of the weather god. Alternate forms: Sahassaras, Tasimis. [Durdin-Robertson 1975; Savill 1976]

Huyairya
Persia
Time
"Good Year." A pre-Zoroastrian goddess, one of the *Pairikas.* [Durdin-Robertson 1982]

Iahu
Mesopotamia; Akkad, *Sumerian*
Unknown
Name for *Isis* of Egypt. [Durdin-Robertson 1975]

Iahu Anat
Israelite
Unknown
Believed by some to have been an ancient Hebrew goddess who was later assimilated into the god Yahweh, or Jehovah. [Monaghan 1981]

Id
Mesopotamia; Babylonia
Water
"Pure Waters." The mother of the god Ea. [Leach 1992; Thompson 1903]

Igirit   See *Agrat Bat Mahalat.*

Igrath Bath Mahalath
Israelite
Unknown
    An early Hebrew deity. [Leach 1992; Patai 1967]

Ilat   See *Athirat*.

Inanna
Mesopotamia; Sumer
Heaven and Hell; Earth and Nature; Creator of Life and
Death; Unhappiness
    "Queen of Heaven." A Sumerian goddess, ruler of the sky,
the earth, and fertility. She presides over the growth of plants
and animals and the fertility of humans. She has the power of
death and rebirth.
    *One day, Inanna decided to visit her sister, Ereshkigal, in
the underworld and to attend the funeral of Ereshkigal's
husband. As she passed through each of the Seven Gates
of the Underworld she had to leave behind one article of clothing,
so that when she reached her destination she would be completely
stripped of worldly power. When Ereshkigal saw her sister coming,
she set upon her and killed her, then she hung her corpse on a
meathook, and left it there to rot in the sun. . . . Before she left her
palace, Inanna had instructed Ninhursag to get help if she didn't
return within three days; so after three days had gone by, Ninhursag
went to the god of wisdom, Enki, for aid, and the two of them went
to the underworld to help Inanna escape. Before she left, Inanna
was told that she would have to find someone to take her place in
the underworld. She decided to send her husband, Dumuzi, because
he had not mourned for her while she was gone, but when he was
missed by his sister, Gestinanna, and his mother, Ninsu, Dumuzi
and his sister arranged to trade places with each other every six
months, so that each would only have to spend half of the year
in the underworld.*
    See also *Ininni* and *Ishtar*. Alternate forms: Innin, Nini,
Ninni, Ama Usum Gal Ana. [Carlyon 1982; Cotterell 1979;
Durdin-Robertson 1975; Durdin-Robertson 1982; Leach 1992;
Stone 1979; Tyler 1964]

Inaras
Mesopotamia; *Hittite*
Intelligence and Creativity; Reptiles
    "The Lady of Tarukka."
    *After the weather god, possibly Teshub, had been defeated by
Illuyankas, the dragon, he asked the other gods for help and
Inaras came to his aid. She enticed the dragon out of his lair
with wine, and when he got drunk they tied him up and killed him.*
    Alternate form: Inara. [Cotterell 1979; Durdin-Robertson
1975; Kramer 1961b; Lehmann 1975; Monaghan 1981]

Inin
Mesopotamia; Akkad
War
    A war goddess. [Jacobsen 1970; Leach 1992; Roberts 1972]

Ininni
Mesopotamia; Babylonia; Sumer
War; Earth and Nature; Mother and Guardian; Water; Reptiles
    "Venus." A mother goddess who shines in the light of
Venus and is also very present here on earth, where she is
identified with water and snakes. She was associated with
Ishtar as a goddess of war. Another name for *Inanna*.
Alternate form: Innin. [Jobes 1962; Leach 1992; Monaghan
1981; Saggs 1962]

Innin   See *Inanna* and *Innini*.

Irkalla
Mesopotamia; Sumer
Heaven and Hell

An underworld goddess, the twin of *Ishtar*. Equivalent to
Allat. Also another name for *Ereshkigal*. [Chicago 1979;
Leach 1992; Monaghan 1981]

Irnina
Mesopotamia; Akkad
War
    A goddess of victory. [Leach 1992]

Irnini
Lebanon
Earth and Nature
    A goddess of the cedar-tree mountains. Later assimilated
into *Ishtar*. [Leach 1992; Monaghan 1981; Savill 1976]

Irsirra
Anatolia, *Hurrian*
Fate
    A goddess of fate. [Baumgartner 1984]

Iš
Persia
Unknown
    "Wish." A wife of Ahura Mazda. [Gray 1930; Leach 1992]

Isdustaya   See *Istustaya*.

Ishara
Babylonia, *Israelite*
Insects; Love and Sexuality; Fishing and Water Animals
    "The Scorpion." Deity of sacred sexuality of the Semitic-
speaking people who was later assimilated into *Ishtar*.
Also a Babylonian deity of aquatic animals and conquest.
Wife of Nin-dar-a. Identified with *Nina*. Alternate form:
Asakhira. [Durdin-Robertson 1982; Leach 1992; Monaghan
1981]

Ishhara   See *Ushharay*.

Ish-khanna
Mesopotamia; Babylonia
Insects
    A scorpion deity. [Hommel 1925; Leach 1992]

Ishkhara
Anatolia, *Hittite*
Mother and Guardian
    "The Mother." Mentioned in the Epic of Kumarbi.
[Durdin-Robertson 1975]

Ishtar
Mesopotamia; Babylonia; Assyria
Love and Sexuality; War; Creator; Mother and Guardian;
Health and Healing; Justice; Heaven and Hell
    A prominent and very popular goddess in the Assyro-
Babylonian pantheon. Of Semitic origin, she was worshiped
throughout Mesopotamia as a goddess of love, fertility,
childbirth, and healing. She could also cause disease and
inflict punishments. Ishtar was the tutelary deity of many
cities, and many other goddesses were assimilated into her,
including *Anatu, Anunit, Gumshea, Irnini, Ishara, Mashti,
Ninlil,* and *Sherua*. She is known by many names, including
Anunit, Bau, Belit, Inanna, Mylitta and *Nana*. Equivalent to
Aslik, and *Nishtu*, Egypt.
    *In a story very much like the story of Inanna, Ishtar
descended to the underworld to rescue her husband,
Tammuz. Here the ruler was Allat. She passed through the
seven gates and was gone for a long time. The other deities became
concerned because nothing grew on earth while Ishtar was gone.
With the help of the other deities, Tammuz was allowed to leave the*

*underworld, and as part of the bargain Ishtar had to return to the
underworld once a year to repeat the ritual of Tammuz's death and
rebirth.*

Ishtar is closely associated with *Ashdar, Astarte, Eshtar,
Kubaba,* and *Siduri.* See also *Arusyak* and *Shaushka.*
Alternate forms: Absusu, Abtagigi, An.zu, Aruru-ishtar,
Astar, Dilbali, Hanata, Istara, Istaru, Isthar, Kilili, Nahunta,
Ninharrissi, Nin Si Anna, Nin-si-anna, Sharrat Shame, Sharis,
Tiskhu, Tsikhu, Ulsiga, Zanaru, Zib. [Cotterell 1979; Durdin-
Robertson 1975; Leach 1992; Lurker 1984; Monaghan 1981;
Saggs 1962; Stone 1979]

Isidoulos
Arabia; *Nabataean*
Unknown
   Name for *Isis* of Egypt. [Negev 1986]

Island Paradise Lady
Mesopotamia
Unknown
   A goddess mentioned in the Epic of Gilgamesh. [Durdin-
Robertson 1975]

Istara   See *Ishtar.*

Istehar
Israelite
Love and Sexuality; Magic; Heaven and Hell; Stars and
Planets; Intelligence and Creativity
   *Istehar was once a Jewish maiden who was desired by the
   angel Shemhazai. When he tried to force himself upon her,
   she agreed to sleep with him if he would tell her Jehovah's
secret name. Shemhazai kept his part of the bargain, but Istehar
didn't keep hers. Instead, she used the secret name to transport her
to heaven, where she became the constellation Pleiades.*
[Monaghan 1981]

Isthar
Mesopotamia
Stars and Planets
   "Queen of the Stars." Another name for *Ishtar.* She was
Ashtoreth in the Book of Kings and the original *Aphrodite* of
Greece and *Venus* of Rome. Perhaps equivalent to *Athyr,
Athor,* or *Hathor,* all Egypt, and to *Astarte,* this section.
[Durdin-Robertson 1982]

Istustaya
Anatolia, *Hatti*
Heaven and Hell; Fate
   Primeval goddess of the netherworld; with *Papaya,* a
goddess of fate. While spinning the thread of life, she also
uses her spindle, along with a mirror, for divination.
Alternate form: Isdustaya. [Durdin-Robertson 1975; Kramer
1961b; Lurker 1984; Stone 1979]

Iza
Persia
Justice
   "Zeal." A wife of Ahura Mazda. [Gray 1930; Leach 1992]

Jahi
Persia
Evil; Love and Sexuality; Destroyer of Life
   A demon harlot who leads men to commit evil deeds.
Alternate forms: Jaki, Jeh. [Bonnerjea 1927; Jobes 1962; Leach
1972; Monaghan 1981; Stone 1979]

Jaki   See *Jahi.*

Jar Goddesses, The   See *Cow Goddesses.*

Jauthe
Mesopotamia; Babylonia
Mother and Guardian
   Primordial mother of the gods and consort of Apason.
[Cooper 1876]

Jeh   See *Jahi.*

Jerah
Israelite, Arab
Moon and Night; Family and Tribes
   "Moon, Bride of the Sun." Also the name of a tribe that
descended from Sham and Hagar. Alternate form: Terah.
[Sykes 1968; Tenney 1963]

Jericho Goddesses, The
Jericho
Unknown
   Neolithic female figurines that were found in an early
Mesolithic town in Israel. They are typical fertility goddessess
from that period. [Achtemeier 1985]

Kades
Canaan
Love and Sexuality; Hunting and Wild Animals; Reptiles
   She presides over sexuality and is portrayed standing
naked on the back of a lion, holding a snake in her hands. She
later became an Egyptian deity. [Lurker 1984]

Kadi
Mesopotamia; Assyria; Babylonia
Justice; Demi-animals; Reptiles
   An earth goddess and champion of justice, she witnesses
all human events, especially the taking of oaths. Often
portrayed as a snake with a human head. A form of *Ki.*
[Carlyon 1982; Leach 1992; Monaghan 1981]

Kait
Anatolia, *Hittite*
Agriculture
   A goddess of grain. See also *Kait,* Egypt. [Leach 1992;
Wedeck and Baskin 1971]

Kamrusepas
Anatolia, *Hittite*
Health and Healing; Magic
   A goddess of healing and magic, she can cure paralysis by
"loosening that which is bound." Alternate forms: Katahzippuri,
Katahzipuri. [Cotterell 1979; Durdin-Robertson 1975; Eliade
1987; Leach 1992; Stone 1979]

Ka-silim
Mesopotamia; Babylonia
Water
   A river goddess. [Hommell 1925; Leach 1992]

Katahzippuri   See *Kamrusepas.*

Katahzipuri   See *Kamrusepas.*

Kathirat, The
Mesopotamia
Education and Knowledge
   "The Wise Ones." Appearing as swallows, they provide
what is necessary for weddings and preside over births. They
celebrate these occasions with joyful song and are mentioned
in the Poem of Nikkal. Similar to the *Charites,* Greek and
Roman Empires. See also the *Kotharat.* [Durdin-Robertson
1975]

Kattahha

Anatolia, *Hittite*

Justice

"Queen." A goddess. [Wedeck and Baskin 1971]

Kaukabhta

Syria

Unknown

A goddess identified with *Astarte*. [Jobes 1962; Jones 1932]

Keb   See *Gea*.

Khi-dimme-azaga

Babylonia

Mother and Guardian

"Child of the Renowned Spirit." Mother goddess, daughter of Ea. May be identical to *Belit Seri*. [Jobes 1962]

Khusareth

Phoenicia

Order

"Harmony." [Cooper 1876]

Ki

Mesopotamia; Sumer

Earth and Nature

"Earth." Daughter of *Lahamu* and Lakhmu. Ki was originally joined together with An, the sky god, until their son Enlil, the air god, separated them. See also *Kadi*, this section, and *Nut*, Egypt. Ki was later displaced by *Nintu, Ninhursag*, and *Ninmah*. Alternate forms: Kisar, Kishar. [Carlyon 1982; Durdin-Robertson 1975; Leach 1972; Leach 1992; Lurker 1984]

Kilili   "Ishtar, the Promiscuous." See *Ishtar*.

Kimah

Near East

Stars and Planets

"The Seven Stars" or "the Pleiades." Her worship is similar to that of *Ayish*. Equivalent to the *Krittika*, Indian Subcontinent, and to the *Pleiades* and the *Vergiliae*, both Greek and Roman Empires. [Durdin-Robertson 1975]

Kindazi

Mesopotamia

Unknown

A goddess associated with the god Nin-girsu. [Jacobsen 1976; Leach 1992]

Kirisa

Elam

Unknown

"The Gilded One." [Durdin-Robertson 1975]

Kisar   See *Ki*.

Kishar   See *Ki*.

Kista

Persia

Education and Knowledge; Magic; Time; Mother and Guardian

"Religious Knowledge." A genie who presided over the eleventh day of the lunar month and was worshiped by Zarathustra and his wife. A protector of humans and provider of food and libations, she is often invoked with *Daena*. [Durdin-Robertson 1982]

Kiun   See *Chiun*.

Kôshart

Canaan

Mother and Guardian

A goddess of childbirth. Her male counterpart is Koshar. Alternate form: Kôshartu. [Albright 1968; Leach 1992]

Kôshartu   See *Kôshart*.

Kotharat, The

Canaan

Arts

"Daughters of Joyous Song" or "The Swallows." Daughters of the morning star (or the new moon). A group of divine singers and wet-nurses who appear in the Epic of Aqhat and the Poem of Nikkal. See also the *Kathirat*. [Eliade 1987]

Kozbi   See *Chasbei*.

Krumai

Afghanistan, *Kaffir*

Earth and Nature; Ceremonies

A nature deity in Kafiristan (present-day Nuristan) who watches over the snow-covered mountains. A comical dance is performed in her honor. [Leach 1992]

Kubaba

Anatolia, *Hittite*

Mother and Guardian

A goddess of Carchemish, she later became the patron of the countries conquered by the Hittites, whose people considered Carchemish to be their mother city. The Phrygians called her *Cybele* and later introduced her to the Romans. She is identified with *Hepat* and *Arinna* and associated with *Ishtar*. [Amiet 1977; Chicago 1979; Durdin-Robertson 1975; Ergener 1988; Lurker 1984]

Kubebe Kupapa   See *Hepat*.

Kubele   See *Cybele*.

Kulitta

Anatolia, *Hittite*

Unknown

One of the two attendants of *Shaushka*; the other one is *Ninatta*. [Durdin-Robertson 1975; Savill 1976]

Kun

Central Asia, *Turk*

Sun and Day

A sun goddess and consort of the moon god, Ai-ada. [Czaplicka 1969; Leach 1992]

Kupapa   See *Hepat*.

Kutbi

Mesopotamia

Unknown

A Hebrew woman who was made a goddess after delivering Bakru from death. [Teixidor 1977]

Kybele   See *Cybele*.

Labartu

Mesopotamia; Assyria

Evil; Destroyer of Life; Magic; Household Affairs; Ceremonies

A demon who hides in marshes and mountains, kidnapping children or making them sick. Boys and girls were given amulets to protect them from her. Later on, good spirits who protected households were called "Labartu." [Jobes 1962]

Lachamu   See *Lahamu.*

Lachos   See *Lahamu.*

Lady of the Abyss
Mesopotamia; Babylonia
Education and Knowledge; Creator of Life
   "Unfathomable Wisdom." Wife of the supreme god.
Alternate form: Voice of the Abyss. [Jobes 1962]

Lady of Ninab
Mesopotamia
Unknown
   A goddess and daughter of Numushda; she married the
god Martu, leader of the Martu Semites. [Durdin-Robertson
1975]

Lahamu
Mesopotamia; Babylonia
Primordial Being
   "Primeval Silt." Daughter of *Tiamat* and Apsu, mother of
Ki, she created the first matter and is invoked during
ceremonies when a building is completed. Alternate forms:
Lachamu, Lachos, Lakhamu, Lamamu. [Durdin-Robertson
1975; Jobes 1962; Monaghan 1981]

Lahar
Mesopotamia; Babylonia; Sumer
Domesticated Animals
   A goddess of domesticated animals, sister of *Ashnan.* (Also
the name of a male deity.) [Leach 1992; Monaghan 1981]

Lakhamu   See *Lahamu.*

Lalla   See *Lilith.*

Lama
Anatolia, *Hittite*
Mother and Guardian
   "Lama of the Shield." A protector of cities and animals,
she acts as an intermediary between the gods and their
worshipers. See also *Lamassu.* [Amiet 1977; Carlyon 1982;
Wedeck and Baskin 1971]

Lamamu   See *Lahamu.*

Lamashtu
Mesopotamia; Assyria
Evil
   A demon goddess who taunts the sick and infects children
with the plague. Daughter of Anu. Equivalent to *Dimme* and
Lamasthu. See also *Lamassu.* Alternate forms: Lamastu,
Lamme. [Amiet 1977; Jobes 1962; Leach 1992]

Lamassu
Mesopotamia; Sumer; Assyria
Destroyer of Life; Goodness; Ugliness; Mother and Guardian
   A goddess of the city of Susa. To the Assyrians, she was an
evil goddess who killed children; to the Semites, she was a
benevolent guardian monster. As *Lama,* she was a Sumerian
protector goddess. See also *Lamashtu.* [Amiet 1977; Guirand
1968; Savill 1976]

Lamasthu
Sumer
Hunting and Wild Animals; Demi-animals; Evil; Destroyer of
Life; Ceremonies; Reptiles
   "Daughter of Heaven." A lion-headed goddess who covets
humans and their children. She infects children with disease,
and drinks the blood and eats the flesh of adults. Lamasthu

is often portrayed carrying double-headed serpents and
suckling dogs and pigs. For protection, amulets bearing
her name were hung on all the doors of a house. See also
Lamashtu, Lamassu, Lilith, Baba Yaga, all Eastern Europe;
Lamia, Greek and Roman Empires; and *Kishimogin,* Far East.
[Durdin-Robertson 1975; Monaghan 1981]

Lamastu   See *Lamashtu.*

Lamme   See *Lamashtu.*

Lat   See *Asherah.*

Laz
Mesopotamia; Babylonia; Elam
Sun and Day
   A solar deity at Kutha or Cuthah in Babylonia who was
associated with *Esharra.* Her consort is Nergal. [Durdin-
Robertson 1975; Saggs 1962]

Leilah
Persia
Beauty; Selflessness; Love and Sexuality
   "Beauty." She represents chastity and affection. Equivalent
of *Psyche,* Greek and Roman Empires. [Jobes 1962]

Lelwani
Anatolia, *Hittite*
Heaven and Hell
   An underworld deity. Originally thought to be male who
was later considered a female deity. When threatened by
death, people would offer her surrogate images of themselves.
Also the patron deity of King Hattusilis. Alternate form:
Lelwanis. [Lurker 1984; Savill 1976]

Lelwanis   See *Lelwani.*

Levanah
Chaldea
Unknown
   A moon goddess associated with the first day of the
waning moon, she controls the tides. Equivalent to *Selene*
and *Luna,* both Greek and Roman Empires. [Durdin-
Robertson 1975; Durdin-Robertson 1982]

Leviathan
Israelite
Reptiles; Water
   A snake-shaped sea monster who appears in the Hebrew
Scriptures and the apocryphal Book of Enoch, she dwells
beneath the watery abyss and is associated with *Tiamat.*
Alternate form: Leviathanah. [Cotterell 1979; Durdin-
Robertson 1975; Monaghan 1981]

Leviathanah   See *Leviathan.*

Lilit   See *Lilith.*

Lilith
Near East; *Sumerian*
Weather; Disorder; Evil; Moon and Night; Education and
Knowledge; Justice
   Probably an early Sumerian storm demon, Lilith (Lilitu)
is mentioned in a text dating from ca. 2400 B.C.E. In Hebrew
scriptures, Isaiah called her a night monster who haunts
Edom. The Talmud describes her as a "charming woman."
In the Cabala writings she is said to have taught wisdom
to Adam. According to rabbinic legend she is Adam's first
wife, who, for some reason, flew away. To the Arabs, she is
"The Holy Lady." In feminist theology her story is expanded.

In the beginning, God formed Adam and Lilith from dust and made them equal. Adam tried to order Lilith about and she grew very tired of his attempt to control her, invoked the name of God, and flew out of the garden. God then created Eve for Adam, and for awhile she existed as his subordinate. Adam told her about the horrible demon, Lilith, who lived on the other side of the wall. One day Eve climbed the wall and happened upon Lilith. Though she was frightened, Eve did not run, but stayed and talked with her. They told each other stories and taught each other many things, and a bond of sisterhood grew between them. God and Adam were apprehensive, fearing the power of this new alliance.

See also *Lilithu* and *Mahalat.* Equivalent to *Kishijotan,* Far East, and *Hariti,* Indian Subcontinent. Alternate forms: Abyzu, Ailo, Ardat Lili, Broxa, Gelou, Gilou, Lalla, Lilit, Lilitu, Ptrotka. [Baring 1991; Cooper 1876; Durdin-Robertson 1975; Jobes 1962; Leach 1992; Monaghan 1981; Neuman 1972; Plaskow 1979; Patai 1967; Stone 1979]

Lilithu
Mesopotamia; Babylonia; Sumer
Evil; Love and Sexuality; Weather; Moon and Night
A demon who entices sleeping men; a nocturnal wind specter. She became the Hebrew *Lilith.* Alternate forms: Ardat Lili and Lilith. [Jobes 1962; Monaghan 1981]

Lilitu   See *Lilith.*

Liluri
Syria
Earth and Nature
A mountain goddess who married the weather god. [Lurker 1984]

Lilwani
Anatolia, *Hittite*
Earth and Nature; Ceremonies
An earth goddess, connected with the spring festival of *Purulli.* Solemn oaths were sworn in her temple. [Durdin-Robertson 1975; Monaghan 1981]

Lisina
Mesopotamia
Domesticated Animals
A donkey goddess, daughter of *Ninhursag.* [Jacobsen 1976; Leach 1992]

Lusin
Armenia
Moon and Night
A moon goddess. [Archaeological Institute vol. 5 1916–1932]

Ma
Anatolia
Earth and Nature; Creator of Life
"Lady of Beasts." The Romans brought her back as a goddess of agriculture and fertility. See also *Ma,* Greek and Roman Empires; and *Ma,* Africa. Ma is also the name of a Cappadocian goddess of war. Cappadocia was part of Anatolia, which is present-day Turkey. [Fairbanks 1907; Leach 1972; Leach 1992; Neumann 1972]

Maan-eno   See *Aka.*

Machalath
Hebrew
Heaven and Hell; The Four Directions
One of the *Qlippoth* and the mother of *Aggareth.* She inhabits the northeast region of the underworld. [Durdin-Robertson 1975]

Mader-akka   See *Aka.*

Maeleth   See *Mahalat.*

Mah
Persia; Sumer; Akkad, *Semite*
Earth and Nature; Creator of Life; Mother and Guardian
Earth mother and virgin queen of the gods. Sister of Enlil. She created human beings from clay and is the goddess of human and animal fertility. She was assimilated into the Roman *Bellona* and became *Mah-Bellona,* Greek and Roman Empires. The Persian Mah is a moon goddess who is the same as *Fortuna* and *Nike,* both Greek and Roman Empires. Equivalent to *Bau, Belit Ilani, Gula, Ininni,* and *Ishtar.* Alternate forms: Makh, Mami, Ninhursag, Ninmah, Ninmea, Ninsikilla, Nintur, Nunusesmea. [Ergener 1988; Jobes 1962; Leach 1992; Monaghan 1981]

Mahalat
Hebrew
Evil; Justice
A queen who commands hundreds of dancing demons. She is an enemy of *Lilith,* and they will meet in combat on the day of judgment. Alternate form: Maeleth. [Monaghan 1981]

Mahlyanag
Persia
Creator of Life
First Woman in Zoroastrianism. Equivalent to *Masyanag.* [Kramer 1961b]

Mai   See *Umai.*

Makh
Mesopotamia; Babylonia; Assyria
Creator
A goddess of fertility and procreation. At Nin-tud, her name was *Belit Ilani.* See also *Mah.* Alternate form: Belit-itani. [Jobes 1962]

Makhir
Mesopotamia; Babylonia
Intelligence and Creativity
A goddess who is invoked for favorable dreams. [Redfield 1931]

Makhut   See *Matronit.*

Malkat-shemen
Mesopotamia; Armenia
Primordial Being
"Queen of Heaven." [Eliade 1987]

Malkatu
Mesopotamia
Primordial Being
"Queen of Heaven." Associated with *Siduri* and *Ishtar.* [Durdin-Robertson 1975]

Malakuta Ashar Amaim   See *Ashtart.*

Malkuth   See *Malkuth,* Western Europe.

Mama
Israelite, Sumerian
Mother and Guardian; Immortality; Creator of Life
A Sumerian and Hebrew mother goddess who presides over childbirth. Wife of Erra and Nergal.

🔥 *After the flood, Ea ordered the death of a lesser deity so that Mama could take the dead god's blood ånd mingle it with clay to make a human being. The person she created had both divine and mortal elements: a temporal body and an immortal soul.*

See also *Gula.* Alternate forms: Am, Ama, Mami. [Jobes 1962; Leach 1992; Roberts 1972]

Mami

Mesopotamia; Babylonia; Sumer; Akkad; Assyria
Creator of Life; Mother and Guardian

A creator deity. Among her titles are "Mother Womb," "Creatrix of Destiny," and "Mistress of All the Gods." She was invoked during childbirth and was especially kind to women who were bearing a second child.

🔥 *While still above the great abyss, Mami fashioned clay images of herself. Seven of these she placed on her left, and they became women; the other seven she placed on her right, and they became men.*

Equivalent to *Nügua,* Far East; and *Ma,* Egypt. See also *Nu-Kwa,* Far East. Alternate forms: Amadubad, Amatudda, Ani, Aruru, Erua, Mah, Mama, Nagar Saga, Nindum, Ninsikilla, Sasura. [Durdin-Robertson 1975; Leach 1992; Monaghan 1981; Saggs 1962; Stone 1979]

Mamit   See *Mamitu.*

Mamitu

Mesopotamia; Chaldea; Sumer; Babylonia; Akkad; Assyria; Sumer
Fate; Mother and Guardian; Evil

"Mother of Destinies." A goddess of fate and childbirth; all must appear before her when they die. She is also a demon of irrevocable curses. She is honored at a Babylonian festival. Alternate forms: Mamit, Mammitu, Mammentun. [Carlyon 1982; Durdin-Robertson 1975; Leach 1992; Monaghan 1981]

Mammentun   See *Mamitu.*

Mammmitu   See *Mamitu.*

Manungal

Mesopotamia
Mother and Guardian

A goddess of childbirth. [Jacobsen 1970; Leach 1992]

Mara

Mesopotamia; Sumer
Water

"Great Sea." A primordial great mother personified by the sea. Equivalent to *Slacia,* Greek and Roman Empires. Alternate forms: Marah, Salacia. [Durdin-Robertson 1975]

Marah   See *Mara.*

Mashti

Mesopotamia; Elam
Unknown

A goddess who was replaced by *Ishtar.* [Durdin-Robertson 1975]

Mashyoi

Persia
Creator of Life; Family and Tribes
"First Woman."

🔥 *There once was a tree whose leaves produced ten kinds of animals, consisting of earth animals, water animals, and human animals. Mashyoi and her mate, the first man, were formed from a double leaf on this tree. For the first fifty winters, they were the prey of Druj demons. Then they had a pair of children,* whom they devoured. After that, they gave birth to seven more pairs of children, who became the progenitors of fifteen races of humans.

See also *Masyanag* and *First Woman.* [Leach 1972]

Masyanag

Persia
Creator of Life

"Mother of the World." First Woman in Persian Avestrianism. Equivalent to *Mahlyanag* in Zoroastrianism. See also *Mashyoi.* [Kramer 1961b]

Matar Kubile

Anatolia, *Phyrgia*
Earth and Nature

A mountain goddess and mother goddess. Equivalent to *Rhea,* Greek and Roman Empires. [Ker"nyi 1951; Leach 1992]

Mater Artemis

Persia
Unknown

Name for *Anāhita* in Lydia, and ancient country in Asia Minor. [Wedeck and Baskin 1971]

Mater-turrita

Anatolia
Unknown

An ancient title for *Rhea-kybele.* [Cooper 1876]

Matronethah   See *Matronethah,* Western Europe.

Matronit   See *Matronit,* Western Europe.

Meder

Ethiopia
Earth and Nature

Semitic earth mother worshiped in Ethiopia. Sometimes considered male. Alternate form: Medr. [Leach 1992]

Medr   See *Meder.*

Melita   See *Mylitta.*

Melitta   See *Mylitta.*

Meme   See *Meme,* Africa.

Meni

Phoenicia; Canaan
Fate and Luck

A goddess of fate, she can give either good or bad luck. Sometimes considered male. [Durdin-Robertson 1975; Leach 1992]

Meshiane

Persia
Creator of Life

First Woman. A name for the biblical *Eve.* [Wedeck and Baskin 1971]

Metra

Persia
Moon and Night; Creator of Life

A moon goddess and fertility deity. [Jobes 1962; Zimmerman 1964]

Metsulah

Israelite
Water; Heaven and Hell

Connected with the sea. Her region has some characteristics of the upper world and some of Sheol, the underworld, where *Leviathan* lives. Like Sheol, Metsulah swallows people. She is similar to *Tiamat*. [Durdin-Robertson 1975]

Mezulla
Anatolia, *Hittite, Hatti*
Sun and Day
   Daughter of the sun goddess, *Wurusemu*. Alternate form: Muzulla. [Durdin-Robertson 1975; Savill 1976]

Milkath
Phoenicia; Carthage
Heaven and Hell
   A chthonic deity allied with *Allat*. [Cook 1930; Leach 1992]

Minu Anni
Mesopotamia; Assyria
Fate
   A goddess of fate. [Monaghan 1981]

Molis   See *Mylitta*.

Mot
Chaldea
Mother and Guardian
   Primordial mother of the gods. [Cooper 1876]

Mother Chuber   See *Tiamat*.

Mother of Life
Persia
Unknown
   One of the *Aeons*. She created the first human beings. [Durdin-Robertson 1975]

Moymis
Mesopotamia; Babylonia
Creator of Life
   A creation goddess and daughter of *Tiamat*. [Sykes 1968]

Mu'allidtu   See *Mylitta*.

Mulishshu   See *Ninlil*.

Mulitta   See *Mylitta*.

Mulliltu   See *Ninlil*.

Mummu
Mesopotamia; Babylonia
Mother and Guardian
   "Primordial Mother." [Neumann 1972]

Muš
Persia
Evil; Moon and Night
   A demon who rules the night and causes lunar eclipses. [Gray 1930; Leach 1992]

Muzulla   See *Mezulla*.

Myletta   See *Mylitta*.

Mylitta
Phoenicia
Beauty
   A moon goddess who presides over fertility and childbirth, desire, and sacred sexuality. She has a shrine at the holy spring of Afka. She combines the forces of flowing water and heavenly fire into sexual energy. See also *Anaitis*.

Alternate forms: Afka, Aphek, Ishtar, Melita, Melitta, Molis, Myletta, Mulitta, Mu'allidtu. [Cotterell 1979; Durdin-Robertson 1975; Leach 1992; Monaghan 1981; Redfield 1931]

Myrrha
Syria; Phoenicia
Magic; Earth and Nature; Love and Sexuality; Family and Tribes; Unhappiness
   Daughter of the king of Assyria, she was changed into a myrrh tree.
   One day the Greek Goddess Aphrodite cast a spell on Myrrha that made her lust after her father, so she got him drunk and had her way with him. Afterwards, she became afraid of his anger and ran away to the gods, who changed her into a myrrh tree from which her son, Adonis, was born nine months later.
   The Adonis cult began in Babylonia and Syria, moved to Phoenicia and Cyprus, and then moved to Greece. Alternate form: Smyrna. [Bonnerjea 1927; Leach 1972; Monaghan 1981; Zimmerman 1964]

Nabarbi
Anatolia, *Hurrian*
Unknown
   A goddess. [Eliade 1987]

Nagar Saga   "Framer of the Fetus." See *Mami*.

Nahar
Mesopotamia; Ugarit
Sun and Day
   A sun goddess. [Sykes 1968]

Nahema   See *Nahema*, Western Europe.

Nahunta   See *Ishtar* and *Anāhita*.

Nammu
Mesopotamia; Sumer; Asia Minor
Primordial Being; Creator of Life
   Primeval goddess of the formless waters of creation. She created all the other deities, some of whom then created human beings. Mother of *Ki, Mami, Ninmah,* and *Ninhursag*. [Chicago 1979; Durdin-Robertson 1975; Monaghan 1981; Stone 1979]

Nana
Mesopotamia; Sumer; Babylonia; Elam
Justice
   "Queen." Mistress of the cities of Eridu, Erech, and Uruk in Sumer (southern part of Mesopotamia or Babylonia). The Elamites stole her statue from Akkad (in the northern part of Babylonia), and it was not returned until 1,635 years later. In Armenia she is called *Nanai*. See also *Nana*, Oceania, and *Nana*, Northern Europe. Alternate forms: Nina, Tashmetu. [Bonnerjea 1927; Durdin-Robertson 1975; Harding 1971; Jobes 1962; Leach 1992; Melville 1969; Monaghan 1981; Saggs 1962]

Nanai
Mesopotamia; Babylonia; Sumer; Armenia
Stars and Planets
   "Mistress of the Heavens." A stellar goddess of Ur and Uruk, in Sumer. Identified with *Nana, Nane, Anāhita* (Armenian Anāhit), and *Astghik*. She was assimilated into *Ishtar* and later surfaced as the Armenian *Nane*. [Jobes 1962]

Nanaja
Mesopotamia; Syria
Love and Sexuality; War

A goddess of love and war. Equivalent to *Tashmetu.* Her worship spread to Syria and Iran. [Lurker 1984]

Nane
Armenia
Stars and Planets; Heaven and Hell; War; Mother and Guardian

A goddess of the evening star and a mistress of heaven. She is probably the goddess *Nana,* whose worship spread over a large area. Nane became an austere, war-like goddess who fiercely protected those who worshiped her. [Eliade 1987; Jobes 1962; Jones 1932; Leach 1992]

Nanna
Mesopotamia; Babylonia; Sumer; Akkad
Moon and Night

Moon goddess. When the moon is new Nanna is called *Ashimbabbar,* and when the half moon is out her name is *Ensum.* [Jacobsen 1970; Leach 1992]

Nanshe
Mesopotamia; Babylonia; Sumer
Fishing and Water Animals; Intelligence and Creativity; Justice; Goodness

A Babylonian water goddess; daughter of Enki, sister of *Inanna* and Ningirsu; and an interpreter of dreams. Using *Nidaba's* sacred laws, she judges each person at the beginning of the new year and always shows compassion toward the poor and the weak. Great goddess of Lagash in Sumer and a goddess of fishing. Alternate forms: Nanshebargunu, Nidaba. [Amiet 1977; Durdin-Robertson 1975; Leach 1992; Monaghan 1981]

Nanshebargunu   See *Nanshe* and *Nunbarshegunu.*

Nanshebargunu-nanshe   See *Nunbarshegunu.*

Narunte
Mesopotamia; Elam
War

"Sister of the Evil-giver." A goddess of victory. Alternate form: Ninhursag. [Amiet 1977; Savill 1976]

Nasa
Persia
Evil; Insects

A demon who takes the form of a fly in order to eat dead bodies. [Monaghan 1981]

Nashak
Persia
Family and Tribes

"Grandmother" of the Arabs. Wife of Siyakmak, mother of *Fravakain.* [Jobes 1962]

Nasu
Persia
Evil; Magic; Disorder

A demon who interrupts sleep and casts spells. Equivalent to *Hexe* and *Drude,* both Northern Europe, and to *Druj,* this section. Like *Nasa,* she devours dead bodies. [Leach 1972; Leach 1992; Lurker 1984]

Nata   See *Nina.*

Nathair Parrthuis, The
Israelite
Reptiles

"The Serpent." Said to be a wily, crafty, and subtle beast, she is found in a medieval Irish and Latin version of the Book of Genesis. Alternate form: Serpent of Paradise. [Durdin-Robertson 1975]

Nazi
Mesopotamia; Sumer
Fishing and Water Animals; Intelligence and Creativity; Justice

A fish goddess who interprets dreams and champions justice. [Leach 1992; Roberts 1972]

Nephesh
Israelite
Intelligence and Creativity; Education and Knowledge

"Breath of Life." Nephesh is the seat of both physical desire and intellect. She also records facts and condenses forms. Corresponds to *Mulaprakriti,* Indian Subcontinent, and may also be associated with *Chavah.* [Durdin-Robertson 1975]

Neshamah
Near East, *Semite*
Intelligence and Creativity

"Breath." She is connected with the lighter forms of matter. She also inspires logic, intellectuality, and idealism. She corresponds to *Binah,* Western Europe. [Durdin-Robertson 1975]

Ne-zil-la
Mesopotamia; Babylonia
Wealth; Stars and Planets

"Abundance." A stellar deity. [Langdon 1931; Leach 1992]

Nhang
Armenia
Evil; Charisma; Magic

An evil spirit who may appear as either a woman or a seal. She seduces her victims and then sucks their blood. [Leach 1972]

Nicostrata
Mesopotamia; Akkad
Education and Knowledge; Fate

A goddess of writing and the alphabet. Equivalent to *Carmentis,* Greek and Roman Empires. See also *Nicostrata,* Greek and Roman Empires. [Boulding 1976; Leach 1972; Zimmerman 1964]

Nidaba
Mesopotamia; Sumer; Babylonia
Education and Knowledge; The Arts; Reptiles; Demi-animals

Sumerian goddess of writing, music, and record-keeping at Nippur, Lagash, Erech, and Umma, around 3200 B.C.E. Sister of *Inanna.* Portrayed as a serpent or a woman with a serpent's tail, she is the keeper of the sacred laws of Lagash, which *Nanshe* uses in her new year's judgments. Alternate form: Basmu Usum. [Bonnerjea 1927; Boulding 1976; Durdin-Robertson 1975; Leach 1992; Savill 1976; Stone 1979]

Nikal-mati
Anatolia
Sun and Day; Justice

A sun goddess, also a Hittite queen about 3,400 years ago. Alternate form: Nikkalmati. [Durdin-Robertson 1975; Stone 1979]

Nikkal
Canaan
Moon and Night; Earth and Nature

"Fruits of the Earth." A moon goddess who presides over fertility and fruition. Wife of Yarih, a moon god. See also *Ningal*. [Durdin-Robertson 1975; Leach 1992]

Nikkalmati   See *Nikal-mati*.

Nin Ella
Mesopotamia; Babylonia
Water
   "Great Lady of the Waters." Consort of Ea. [Jobes 1962]

Nin Si Anna   See *Ishtar* and *Ninisinna*.

Nina
Mesopotamia; Babylonia; Sumer
Demi-animals; Fishing and Water Animals
   "Queen of the Waters." A goddess of Lagash, often portrayed as a serpent- or fish-tailed woman. Also associated with the ancient town of Eridu. Alternate forms: Nana, Gestinanna, Nata. [Durdin-Robertson 1975; Leach 1992; Monaghan 1981; Stone 1979]

Nin-agid-kahadu
Mesopotamia; Babylonia
Unknown
   Local deity. [Bonnerjea 1927]

Nin-akha-guddu
Akkad; Babylonia
Unknown
   A goddess. [Cooper 1876]

Nin-akha-kuda
Mesopotamia; Babylonia
Water
   A water deity who is invoked with *Bau* and *Gula* in a magical formula to aid in healing. Associated with the god Ea and pure water. [Leach 1992; Sayce 1898]

Nin-anna
Mesopotamia; Babylonia
Heaven and Hell; Education and Knowledge
   An underworld scribe. [Leach 1992; Thompson 1903]

Ninatta
Mesopotamia, *Hittite*
Love and Sexuality; Family and Tribes
   A goddess of love and marriage. Attendant of *Shaushka*. See also *Kulitta*. [James 1960; Leach 1992]

Ninazu
Mesopotamia
Heaven and Hell; Immortality
   "Naked Death." An underworld goddess who cares for the dead like a mother. Equivalent to *Ereshkigal*. [Monaghan 1981]

Nin-dim   "The Lady of Procreation." See *Sarpanitu*.

Nindukugga
Mesopotamia; Sumer
Heaven and Hell
   An underworld goddess. [Durdin-Robertson 1975; Savill 1976]

Nindum   "Lady of Procreation." See *Mami*.

Nin-edin   "Lady of the Wasteland [the Underworld]." See *Belit Ilani*, *Belit Seri*, and *Gestinanna*.

Nin-e-i-garak
Mesopotamia; Sumer
Domesticated Animals
   A dairy goddess. Consort of Nin-exen-x-la. [Jacobsen 1970; Leach 1992]

Ninella   See *Damkina*.

Ningal
Mesopotamia; Sumer; Ugarit
Earth and Nature
   A reed goddess and probably an earth goddess, daughter of *Ningikuga* and wife of the moon god. See also *Nikkal*, which may be an alternate name for Ningal. See also *Nukarā*, Egypt. Alternate form: Ningul. [Durdin-Robertson 1975; Leach 1992; Monaghan 1981]

Nin-gelal   See *Belit*.

Ningharasag   See *Ninhursag*.

Ningikuga
Mesopotamia
Earth and Nature
   "Lady of the Pure Reeds." Vegetation goddess, mother of *Ningal*, and consort of Enki. [Jacobsen 1976; Leach 1992]

Ningirda
Mesopotamia; Sumer
Unknown
   A goddess, daughter of Enki and consort of Ninazu. [Wedeck and Baskin 1971]

Ningizzida
Mesopotamia
Heaven and Hell
   An afterworld goddess who stands at the gates to heaven. Mother of the god Tammuz. [Carlyon 1982]

Ningul   See *Ningal*.

Ninhabursildu
Mesopotamia; Babylonia
Water
   A fountain goddess. [Leach 1992]

Ninharrissi   "Lady of the Mountains." See *Ishtar*.

Ninhurra   See *Ninkurra*.

Ninhursag
Near East
Mother and Guardian
   A mother goddess and creator, consort of Enki. Her shrine at Obeid dates from circa 4000 to 3500 B.C.E. Before her marriage, she was called *Ninsikilla*; as Enki's wife, she became *Damgalnunna*; after giving birth to the gods, her name became *Nintuama Kalamma*; and as the mother of the earth and its vegetation, she is called Ninhursag.
   Ninhursag became angry when Enki ate some plants that she had invented. To punish his greed, she cursed him with death, but then, feeling remorse, she created eight different gods who healed his eight organs and brought him back to life.
   See also *Aruru*. Alternate forms: Mah, Narunte, Ningharasag, Nin-khursag, Ninnah. [Amiet 1977; Chicago 1979; Cotterell 1979; Durdin-Robertson 1975; Leach 1992; Monaghan 1981; Neumann 1972; Savill 1976; Sproul 1979]

Nini   See *Inanna*.

Ninigara
Near East
Agriculture
   A dairy goddess who married Ninhar. [Jacobsen 1970; Leach 1992]

Nin-imma
Mesopotamia
Love and Sexuality
   Goddess of female sexual organs. [Jacobsen 1976; Leach 1992]

Nininsina   See *Ninisinna.*

Ninisinna
Mesopotamia
Health and Healing
   A goddess of the city of Insin. Daughter of **Uras** and sister of **Inanna.** Patron of medicine and healing and also a war goddess. Alternate forms: Nin Si Anna, Nininsina. [Durdin-Robertson 1975; Leach 1992; Lurker 1984; Monaghan 1981; Savill 1976]

Ninkarrak
Mesopotamia; Babylonia; Assyria; Akkad
Health and Healing
   A goddess of healing and childbirth. She is invoked against slanderers and is associated with watchdogs. Identified with **Bau** and **Gula.** See also **Ninkharak.** Alternate form: Ninkarraka. [Durdin-Robertson 1975; Jobes 1962; Leach 1992]

Ninkasi
Sumer
Happiness; Agriculture; Health and Healing
   "Lady Who Fills the Mouth." A goddess of intoxicating drink. She gives pleasure and once healed Enki's sore mouth.
   Ninkasi was born in fresh water, but her liquid of choice was beer. [Durdin-Robertson 1975; Leach 1992; Monaghan 1981; Savill 1976]

Ninkharak
Mesopotamia
Health and Healing; Domesticated Animals
   "Lady of the Mountain." A goddess of healing who takes the form of a dog. Assimilated into **Ishtar.** See also **Ninkarrak.** [Monaghan 1981]

Nin-kharsak
Mesopotamia; Babylonia
Mother and Guardian; Earth and Nature
   "Mother of the Gods." A mountain goddess, consort of Bel (Mul-lil). [Leach 1992]

Nin-khursag   See *Ninhursag.*

Ninki
Mesopotamia
Unknown
   An ancient goddess similar to **Ninhursag.** Alternate form: Damkina. [Durdin-Robertson 1975; Senior 1985]

Nin-ki
Mesopotamia
Earth and Nature
   "Lady Earth." Associated with Enki. Alternate form: Damkina. [Jacobsen 1976; Leach 1992]

Ninkigal   "Lady of the Great Earth." See *Ereshkigal.*

Ninkurra
Mesopotamia; Babylonia; Sumer
Earth and Nature
   A mountain goddess who presides over plants. Daughter of **Ninsar, Ninhursag,** or **Ninmu** and the god Enki. Mother of **Uttu.** Alternate forms: Ninkurru, Ninhurra. [Durdin-Robertson 1975; Leach 1992; Monaghan 1981; Saggs 1962; Savill 1976]

Ninkurru   See *Ninkurra.*

Ninlil
Mesopotamia; Babylonia; Sumer
Weather; Earth and Nature; Heaven and Hell
   "Mistress of Winds." Ancient goddess of the earth, the air, heaven, and the underworld. Patron of the city of Nippur. Her emblems are the serpent, the heavenly mountain, the stars, and a stylized tree with interwoven branches. She was later assimilated into **Ishtar.** In Babylonia she is called **Belit** or **Belit-matate.** Daughter of **Nunbarshegunu.**
   After Ninlil had rejected the advances of Enlil, he kidnapped and raped her. The other gods were angered by this and banished him to the underworld, but Ninlil was pregnant, and, not wanting to be left alone, she followed him down to his place of exile. Ninlil and Enlil knew that she was to give birth to the moon god, and they conspired to leave the underworld. Ninlil produced three beings who became their surrogates in the underworld, and Enlil and Ninlil, who was still pregnant, were able to return to earth. After the moon god was born he rose up into the sky, where he can be seen today.
   Alternate forms: Belit, Belit-matate, Mulishshu, Mulliltu, Ninlilla, Nunbar-segunni. [Achtemeier 1985; Carlyon 1982; Cotterell 1979; Durdin-Robertson 1975; Leach 1992; Monaghan 1981; Savill 1976; Sykes 1968]

Ninlilla   See *Ninlil.*

Ninmah
Sumer
Creator of Life; Courage
   "Exalted Lady." Associated with **Ninhursag.** She took some clay from under the watery abyss and created six kinds of abnormal human beings. Said to correspond to **Aruru, Mah, Mami,** and **Nintu.**
   One day Ninmah visited her son, Ninurta, on the battlefield during an intense battle. He was so impressed by her bravery that he built a large pile of rocks and named it after her. [Durdin-Robertson 1975; Leach 1992; Monaghan 1981]

Nin-makh
Chaldea
Stars and Planets
   "The Mighty Lady." A stellar goddess. [Cooper 1876]

Ninmar
Mesopotamia; Babylonia
Mother and Guardian
   "Exalted Lady." A bird goddess worshiped in Babylon and near the Persian Gulf, as well as in the city of Buabba. [Bonnerjea 1927; Durdin-Robertson 1975; Leach 1992]

Nin-marki
Chaldea
Unknown
   A goddess whose temple at Ur was called Bitgilsa. [Cooper 1876]

Ninmea
Mesopotamia; Sumer; Akkad
Fate

A goddess of fate, another name for *Mah*. [Langdon 1931; Leach 1992]

Nin-me-sar-ra
Mesopotamia; Sumer
Primordial Being
"Lady of the Universe." Primordial goddess and consort of En-me-sar-ra. [Jacobsen 1970; Leach 1992]

Ninmu
Mesopotamia; Babylonia
Family and Tribes
A goddess who was born to *Ninhursag* and Enki after only ten days in the womb. Enki then slept with her, and she became the mother of *Ninkurra*. Alternate form: Ninsar. [Durdin-Robertson 1975; Saggs 1962]

Ninmug
Mesopotamia; Sumer
Unknown
Sister of *Inanna*. [Durdin-Robertson 1975]

Ninmuk
Mesopotamia; Akkad
Water
A goddess of the Tigris River. See also *Gatamdug*. Alternate form: Nin-muk. [Cooper 1876]

Ninmul
Chaldea
Primordial Being
A primordial goddess. [Durdin-Robertson 1975]

Ninnah   See *Ninhursag*.

Ninni
Mesopotamia; Babylonia
Creator of Life; War
An early goddess of fertility and war and a companion of *Ishtar*. She was later assimilated into *Inanna*. [Leach 1992; Sykes 1968]

Nin-nibru
Mesopotamia; Babylonia
Unknown
"Lady of Nippur." She was assimilated into the goddess *Gula*. [Saggs 1962]

Ninsaba
Mesopotamia; Babylonia; Sumer; Akkad
1) Science; Education and Knowledge; Fate; Intelligence and Creativity; 2) Agriculture
1) A goddess who brought architecture, reading and writing, and astrology to her people. She was also an oracle and an interpreter of dreams. 2) Also the name of an Akkadian corn goddess. Patron of the Sumerian city of Umma. [Amiet 1977; Durdin-Robertson 1975; Leach 1992; Monaghan 1981; Savill 1976]

Ninsar
Mesopotamia; Sumer
Earth and Nature
"Goddess Who Gives Life." Plant goddess, daughter of *Ninhursag* and Enki. Ninsar and her father, Enki, produced *Ninkurra*. Alternate forms: Ninmu, Urbadgumgum. [Durdin-Robertson 1975; Leach 1992; Monaghan 1981]

Ninshebargunu
Mesopotamia
Agriculture

A goddess of imperfect barley. Mother of *Sud*. [Jacobsen 1970; Leach 1992]

Nin-si-anna   "Lady and Eye of Heaven." See *Ishtar*.

Ninsikil   See *Ninsikilla*.

Ninsikilla
Mesopotamia; Sumer
Heaven and Hell; Immortality
"Pure Lady." She rules in heaven, or Dilmun, the Sumerian name for paradise, where there is no death. An ancient country was named after her. Also, the name of *Ninhursag* when she was still a virgin. Alternate forms: Ninsikil, Mami. [Monaghan 1981; Savill 1976]

Ninsun
Mesopotamia; Babylonia; Chaldea
Education and Knowledge; Domesticated Animals
"Great Queen." A goddess of wisdom and cows, patron of the Sumerian city of Kullab. In Babylonia she was known as "the Destructive Lady." She was the mother of Gilgamesh and the wife of Lugalbanda. Alternate form: Sirtur. [Bonnerjea 1927; Durdin-Robertson 1975; Leach 1992]

Ninsu-utud
Mesopotamia; Sumer
Health and Healing
A goddess of healing, invoked especially for toothaches. [Jobes 1962]

Ninti
Mesopotamia; Sumer
Health and Healing
"Lady of the Rib." One of the eight healing goddesses created by *Ninhursag* to heal Enki (see story under *Ninhursag*). Alternate forms: Hannahannas, Nintur. [Durdin-Robertson 1975; Monaghan 1981]

Nintu
Mesopotamia; Sumer; Chaldea, *Hittite*
Mother and Guardian
"Lady Who Gave Birth." She is also called *Belit Ilani*. Closely identified with *Ninhursag*. See also *Aruru*. [Carlyon 1982; Durdin-Robertson 1975; Leach 1992; Lurker 1984]

Nintuama Kalamma
Mesopotamia; Sumer
Mother and Guardian
"Lady Who Gives Birth." A name for *Ninhursag* when she became a mother. Alternate form: Nintu-ama-kalamma. [Dames 1979; Jobes 1962; Savill 1976]

Nintur
Mesopotamia; Babylonia
Mother and Guardian
"Lady of the Womb." A birth goddess of the city of Shirpurla. Later identified with *Ishtar*. Equivalent to *Ninhursag*. Alternate forms: Nintu, Sentu, Mah. [Leach 1992; Monaghan 1981]

Ninudzalli   See *Gula*.

Nin-ur
Mesopotamia; Babylonia
Mother and Guardian
"Lady of Ur." A mother goddess. [Jobes 1962]

Nin-zizna   "The Lady of Birth." See *Sarpanitu*.

Niritu See *Bau.*

Nirmali
Afghanistan, *Kaffir*
Mother and Guardian
   A goddess who presides over childbirth and protects
children in Kafiristan (present-day Nuristan). [Leach 1992]

Nuah
Mesopotamia; Babylonia
Moon and Night
   A moon goddess who was the universal mother. [Durdin-
Robertson 1975; Harding 1971]

Nuha See *Nukimmut.*

Nukimmut
Mesopotamia; Assyria
Mother and Guardian
   Mother of the gods Ninip and Nebo. Alternate form: Nuha.
[Cooper 1876]

Nunbar-segunni "Goddess of Agricultural Fertility."
See *Ninlil.*

Nunbarshegum See *Nunbarshegunu.*

Nunbarshegunu
Mesopotamia; Sumer, *Chaldea*
Mother and Guardian
   "Old Woman." She lived in the city of the gods before
people were created. Mother of *Ninlil* of Chaldea. Alternate
forms: Nanshebargunu, Nunbarshegum, Nanshebargunu-
nanshe. [Durdin-Robertson 1975; Savill 1976]

Nunusesmea See *Mah.*

Nutrix
Carthage
Creator of Life
   "She Who Nourishes." Supreme goddess of fertility. See
also *Tanith.* [Jobes 1962; Lurker 1984]

Nvard
Armenia
Unknown
   A goddess married to Ara, who refused to become the
lover of *Semiramis* because of his great love for Nvard.
[Jones 1932]

Odatis
Persia
Dawn and Twilight; Beauty
   "Dawn." Womanly beauty at its fullest. [Jobes 1962]

Omicle
Phoenicia
Mother and Guardian
   Mother of Potos in the creation legend of Damascus.
[Sykes 1968]

Omorca See *Tiamat.*

Onoroca See *Tiamat.*

Orore
Chaldea
Primordial Being; Demi-animals; Insects

Primordial goddess who was the original world-egg. An
insect-headed goddess who had a giant eye and was always
grossly pregnant. [Durdin-Robertson 1975; Monaghan 1981]

Oub
Near East
Immortality; Magic
   A ghost, spirit, or wizard who can communicate with the
dead. Has been known to chirp and mutter while casting
spells. (Can also be male.) [Durdin-Robertson 1975]

Pagat See *Paghat.*

Paghat
Syria; Canaan; Ugarit
Agriculture
   A goddess of wine and sister of Aqhat. The story of her
brother's death and resurrection, in which she is mentioned,
is told in the Ugaritic Ras Shamra texts. See also *Samal.*
Alternate forms: Pagat, Pughat. [Durdin-Robertson 1975;
Leach 1972; Leach 1992]

Pairikas, The
Persia
Magic; Weather; Evil; Love and Sexuality
   Evil spirits who are sorcerers and can cause droughts and
eclipses. Half-human, half-animal beings with lecherous
propensities. See also the *Pari.* [Jones 1932; Leach 1972;
Malandra 1983]

Pairimaiti
Persia
Evil; Disorder
   "Crooked-mindedness." A demon who causes religious
believers to lose their faith. [Gray 1930; Hinnells 1973; Leach
1992]

Papaya
Mesopotamia, *Hittite, Hatti*
Heaven and Hell; Fate
   Primeval underworld goddess of fate. With *Istustaya,* she
spins the thread of life. [Durdin-Robertson 1975; Kramer
1961b; Leach 1992; Stone 1979]

Paqhat
Mesopotamia; Ugarit
Fate
   A goddess and seer who foretold a seven-year drought.
[Savill 1976]

Pârendi
Persia
Wealth
   "Plenitude." One of the wives of Ahura Mazda, she
bestows material wealth. [Durdin-Robertson 1982; Leach
1992; Malandra 1983]

Pari, The
Persia
Goodness; Magic; Heaven and Hell; Fire; Immortality
   Benevolent genies who were once evil spirits identified
with the *Pairikas.* They guide human souls to paradise.
The Pari were formed out of fire and subsist on perfume.
Alternate form: The Peri.
   *The Pari are constantly at war with evil spirits who, when
   they catch Pari, put them in iron cages and then hang them
   high up in trees. Other Pari visit those who are incarcerated
and bring them delicious food to smell, and the odor provides them
food.* [Leach 1972]

Parigs, The
Persia
Magic
   Manichaean witches. [Durdin-Robertson 1975]

Pdry
Canaan
Creator of Life; Weather
   A goddess of fertility and mist. [Gray 1957; Leach 1992]

Peri, The   See the *Pari.*

Perkunas   See *Armat.*

Pessinuntica
Phyrgia
Mother and Guardian
   "Universal Mother." [Graves 1954]

Phlox   See *Phlox*, Western Europe.

Phronesia
Near East
Intelligence; Creativity; Immortality
   Gnostic creator, with *Sophia* and *Dynamis,* of principalities and angels. She is said to possess purpose, intention, thoughtfulness, good sense, and practical wisdom. [Durdin-Robertson 1975]

Pidrai
Canaan
Earth and Nature
   "The Maiden of Light." One of three nature goddesses with her sisters *Tallai* and *Arsai.* [Durdin-Robertson 1975; Leach 1992]

Pidray
Canaan
Large Size
   "The Fat One." Daughter of Baal and sister of *Arsay.* [Eliade 1987]

Pinikir
Mesopotamia; Elam
Supreme Being
   Supreme deity of the Elamite pantheon until the middle of the second millennium B.C.E., when she was replaced by the god Humban. She presided over the agricultural community and the activities of hunting, fishing, and herding. [Achtemeier 1985]

Ptrotka   "Winged Creature." See *Lilith.*

Puella   See *Zuriel.*

Pughat   See *Paghat.*

Qlippoth, The
Near East
Heaven and Hell; Directions; Intelligence and Creativity
   "The Nightmares." Four underworld spirits: *Lilith* the Elder inhabits the southeast portion of the world below, *Aggareth* the northeast, *Machalath* the northwest, and *Lilith* the Younger the southwest. Similar to *Empusae, Lamiae,* and *Mormo,* Greek and Roman Empires. [Durdin-Robertson 1975]

Qadash   See *Asherah.*

Qudshu
Canaan
Unknown
   May be similar to *Athirat.* [Eliade 1987]

Ra'alat Ashtart   See *Ashtart.*

Rabba   See *Rabbah.*

Rabbah
Israelite
Earth and Nature
   Patron of the city of Rabbah. Alternate form: Rabba. [Durdin-Robertson 1975]

Rabi'a Al-adawiya
Persia, *Islam*
Selflessness; Arts; Love and Sexuality; Education and Knowledge; Intelligence and Creativity
   A saint who is sometimes credited with founding Sufism. She lived in Basara, where she died in 801 C.E. She is buried in Jerusalem. Her poetry imparts the message that "the essence of mysticism is love." [Pike 1951]

Rachmay
Canaan
Health and Healing
   A nurse goddess. [Driver 1956; Leach 1992]

Rahmai
Anatolia
Unknown
   Daughter of *Asherah.* [Stone 1979]

Rahmaya
Syria
Unknown
   A goddess associated with *Asherah.* [Durdin-Robertson 1975]

Rasastat
Persia
Justice
   "The Right Course." She represents truth. [Gray 1930; Leach 1992]

Rata
Persia
Wealth
   "The Bountiful." See also *Rata,* Oceania. [Gray 1930; Leach 1992]

Rat-tanit   See *Tanith.*

Razishta Cista
Persia
Education and Knowledge
   "Instruction." She guides her followers along both material and spiritual paths. See also *Cista.* [Malandra 1983]

Remphan   See *Chiun.*

Reshpu
Israelite
Weather; War; Destroyer of Life; Disorder
   A Hebrew deity who was introduced into Egypt from Syria by Seti I. She is the female counterpart of the Phoenician Reseph-mikal, the god of lightning and thunder, war, and plague. [Cooper 1876; Leach 1992]

Rhea-kybele   "Mother of Towers." See *Mater-turrita*.

Ri
Mesopotamia; Babylonia; Assyria; Phoenicia
Moon and Night
   "Light." Moon goddess of Phoenicia, after whom the
Babylonian king Hammurabi named his city. [Cooper 1876;
Monaghan 1981]

Rubati
Assyria; Chaldea
Unknown
   "Lady of the Gods." [Cooper 1876]

Ruha D'qudsha
Near East
Magic; Evil; Stars and Planets
   "Holy Spirit." A Mandean demon who gave birth to the
planets and to the spirits of the zodiac who demonize time
and space. The Mandeans are a Gnostic sect that still exists in
the Near East. [Eliade 1987; Lurker 1984]

Rukho
Persia
Moon and Night; Creator of Life
   "Darkness." A Mandean goddess who creates bodies for
human beings but does not give them souls. [Drahomaniv
1961; Leach 1992]

Rusa
Syria
Mother and Guardian; Fate
   Mother goddess and goddess of fate. She is the evening
star. Alternate form: Arsa. [Jobes 1962]

Sabitu
Mesopotamia
Water; Heaven and Hell
   A seaworld and underworld goddess who guards the
"water of death." In the Epic of Gilgamesh, she is the goddess
Ishtar in disguise. [Durdin-Robertson 1975; Monaghan 1981]

Sadarnuna
Mesopotamia; Sumer
Moon and Night
   "New Moon." [Monaghan 1981]

Sadwes
Persia
Weather
   "Maiden of Light." Manichaean rain goddess who brings
violent storms with thunder and lightning, hail, and snow.
[Durdin-Robertson 1975]

Sahassaras
Anatolia, *Hittite*
Justice
   Patron of the city of Tuwanuwa. Alternate forms:
Huwassanas, Tasimis. [Durdin-Robertson 1975; Savill 1976]

Sala
Mesopotamia; Babylonia, *Kassite*
Sun and Day; Reptiles
   "Light." A sun goddess and consort of the sun gods
Tammuz, Merodach, and Rimmon. Also a Babylonian
goddess of reptiles. [Leach 1992; Monaghan 1981]

Salgusa
Hittite
Immortality

Deity who guards the bones of the dead and makes new
souls in an alembic oven (device for distillation). Equivalent
to *Baba Yaga*, Eastern Europe. [Hubbs 1988]

Saltu
Mesopotamia
Disorder
   A goddess who creates discord. She was the enemy of
Anat or *Ishtar* and the people. [Langdon 1931; Leach 1992]

Samai
Mesopotamia; Elam
Heaven and Hell
   "Heaven." There is a statue of her in Hatra, Iran.
[Durdin-Robertson 1982]

Samal
Canaan
Destroyer of Life
   A goddess of death and mother of vultures.
   *When Anath was unable to persuade Daniel's son, Aqhat,
   to give her his bow, she had him killed. Samal ate his corpse.
   Aqhat was later resurrected by either Anath or Daniel.*
   See also *Paghat.* Alternate form: Sumul. [Durdin-
Robertson 1975; Leach 1972]

Samkhat
Mesopotamia; Babylonia
Happiness
   A goddess of joy. [Redfield 1931]

Sammuramat   See *Semiramis*.

Sandalphon
Near East
Earth and Nature; Immortality
   Archangel of the earth. She presided over the elementals
who assisted in the creation of the planet. Corresponds to
Demeter, Greek and Roman Empires, and to *Isis,* Egypt.
Alternate form: Sandolphon. [Durdin-Robertson 1975]

Sandaramet   See *Spandaramet*.

Sandark   See *Spandaramet*.

Sandolphon   See *Sandalphon*.

Santaramet
Armenia
Unknown
   A goddess of the underworld, equivalent to *Spentā
Ārmaiti.* [Jones 1932]

Saoka
Persia
Wealth; Time
   A goddess of wealth and well-being who presides over the
third day of the lunar month. [Durdin-Robertson 1982; Gray
1930; Leach 1992]

Sapas
Phoenicia
Commerce and Travel
   "Torch of the Gods." A messenger for other deities.
[Carlyon 1982]

Sapientia   See *Sophia*.

Saps
Mesopotamia; Ugarit
Sun and Day
"Light of the Gods." A sun deity. [Lurker 1984]

Sarbanda
Mesopotamia; Babylonia
Hunting and Wild Animals; Ceremonies
"Queen of the Bow." Worshiped in Erech with elaborate annual ceremonies. Later merged with *Ishtar.* [Monaghan 1981]

Saris
Armenia
Unknown
Ancient goddess related to *Ishtar.* Later assimilated into *Semiramis.* [Monaghan 1981]

Sarpanit   See *Sarpanitu.*

Sarpanitu
Mesopotamia; Babylonia; Akkad; Assyria
Sun and Day; Health and Healing
"Silvery Bright One." Solar and healing goddess and consort of Marduk. She is also called *Zerpanitum* when she is the creator of seeds. As protector of the fetus she is called *Nin-dim, Nin-zizna,* or *Sasuru.* Sarpanitu assimilated the goddess *Erua* and was said to have been absorbed in turn by *Aruru.* Also an alternate name for *Zarpanitu.* Alternate forms: Sarpanit, Sarpanitum. [Bonnerjea 1927; Durdin-Robertson 1975; Jayne 1925; Jobes 1962; Leach 1992; Saggs 1962]

Sarpanitum   See *Aruru* and *Sarpanitu.*

Sartiyas
Mesopotamia, *Hittite*
Justice
"Queen of Katapa." Patron of the city of Katapa in Anatolia. [Savill 1976]

Sasura   "Protector of the Fetus." See *Mami.*

Sasuru   "Goddess of the Fetus." See *Sarpanitu.*

Sausga   See *Sauska.*

Sauska
Mesopotamia, *Hurrian*
War; Love and Sexuality; Creator of Life; Health and Healing
"She Who Is Armed." A goddess of love, fertility, healing, and war. Her reputation reached as far as Egypt. Equivalent to *Ishtar.* Alternate forms: Sawuska, Sausga. [Lehmann 1975; Lurker 1984]

Sawuska   See *Sauska.*

Schala
Mesopotamia; Babylonia; Assyria
Unknown
A goddess. [Sykes 1968]

Scorpion Woman
Mesopotamia
Heaven and Hell
She guards the gate, located in the Mountains of Mashu, that leads to the underworld. According to the Epic of Gilgamesh, Scorpion Woman was as tall as the pillars of heaven and her breasts were so large that they descended into Hades. Although her appearance terrified Gilgamesh, she let him pass through her gates. [Durdin-Robertson 1975]

Sea Goddess
Anatolia, *Hurrian*
Water
Water deity. [Savill 1976]

Seimia
Mesopotamia; Babylonia; Assyria
Fate; Mother and Guardian
"Star of Babylon." Patron of the city of Babylon. Assyrian fate goddess and mother goddess, identified with *Ashima* and *Shimti.* Alternate form: Simi. [Jobes 1962; Monaghan 1981]

Semele
Anatolia, *Phrygian*
Earth and Nature
An earth goddess identical to *Zamin.* [Jones 1932]

Semiramis
Mesopotamia; Babylonia; Assyria
Wild Birds; Creator of Life; Love and Sexuality; Unhappiness; Selfishness
A goddess queen who ruled the city of Nineveh and founded the city of Babylon. She left the earth as a dove, and was worshiped for fertility.

When Semiramis needed a lover to replace her husband, King Ninus, after he died, she chose Ara, but Ara rejected her advances because he loved his wife, Nvard. The angry Semiramis then tried to capture Ara with a large contingent of soldiers, but they killed him by mistake. Grief-stricken, Semiramis had his body taken to her palace in hopes that his life could be restored. When he did not return from the dead, she dressed another one of her lovers in Ara's clothing, and made love to him instead.

Alternate form: Sammuramat. [Chicago 1979; Durdin-Robertson 1975; Jones 1932; Leach 1972; Monaghan 1981; Woodcock 1953; Zimmerman 1964]

Sentu   See *Nintur.*

Sephira   See *Sephira,* Western Europe.

Sephiroth   See *Sephiroth,* Western Europe.

Serpent of Paradise   See the *Nathair Parrthuis.*

Seruya
Mesopotamia; Assyria
Unknown
A goddess and consort of Assur. [Cooper 1876]

Shachuth
Israelite
Heaven and Hell
She presides over the pit of Sheol, one of the divisions of the underworld. See also *Sheol.* [Durdin-Robertson 1975]

Shala
Mesopotamia; Babylonia; Sumer; Chaldea; Canaan
Goodness; Weather; Disorder
"The Compassionate Virgin." A Canaanite storm goddess often represented as carrying an ear of corn. First worshiped by the Sumerians, she was taken into the Chaldean pantheon and then into the religion of the Babylonians, where she became the consort of Adad. Alternate form: Shalash. [Durdin-Robertson 1975; Durdin-Robertson 1982; Jobes 1962; Leach 1972]

Shalash   See *Shala*.

Shalimtum
Mesopotamia; Akkad
Dawn and Twilight
   "Twilight." Consort of Shalim. [Leach 1992; Roberts 1972]

Shamash   See *Shapash*.

Shapas   See *Shapash*.

Shapash
Canaan; Palestine; Syria; Arabia; Ugarit, *Hittite*
Sun and Day
   "Torch of the Gods." An all-seeing sun goddess. When
associated with Baal, she is a fertility deity; in association
with Mot, the god of death and sterility, she burns the crops.
Equivalent to *Wurusemu*, this section; *Ama-terasu-o-mi-
gami*, Far East; *Surya*, Indian Subcontinent; and *Sonne*,
Northern Europe. Alternate forms: Shamash, Shapas.
[Durdin-Robertson 1975; Eliade 1987; Leach 1992; Monaghan
1981; Stone 1979]

Shaph
Anatolia; Ugarit
Sun and Day
   A sun goddess. [Baumgartner 1984]

Sharis   See *Ishtar*.

Sharrat Shame   "Queen of Heaven." See *Ishtar*.

Shatagat   See *Shataqat*.

Shataqat
Syria
Health and Healing
   A goddess of healing mentioned in the Ras Shamra Tablets.
   *When Shataqat was asked to cure Keret, the king of Hubur,
   of a mysterious disease, she flew over hundreds of cities and
   towns in search of the medicine that would make him well.
When she found it and had cured the king, word of her victory over
death spread throughout the kingdom.*
   Alternate form: Shatagat. [Durdin-Robertson 1975;
Monaghan 1981; Savill 1976]

Shaushga   See *Shaushka*.

Shaushka
Anatolia, *Hurrian*
Love and Sexuality; Justice; War; Hunting and Wild Animals;
Demi-animals; Mother and Guardian
   A central figure in the Hurrian pantheon who is identified
with *Ishtar*. A goddess of love, sexuality, law, and war,
Shaushka is portrayed in Anatolia seated on a lion with
wings sprouting from her shoulder blades; in one hand she
holds a golden cup and in the other a symbol representing
"good." Also called the "Mother Goddess of Nineveh." She is
attended by *Ninatta* and *Kulitta*. See also *Sauska* and
Semiramis. Alternate form: Shaushga. [Durdin-Robertson
1975; Eliade 1987; Jobes 1962; Leach 1992; Monaghan 1981;
Savill 1976]

Shedath
Anatolia, *Hittite*
Unknown
   A female counterpart of Shed. [Cooper 1876]

Shekinah
Near East; *Canaanites*
Primordial Being; Time; Supreme Being
   The tangible manifestation of God on earth, she has come
to be known as an independent deity. Mother of *Filia Vocis*,
Western Europe. Among her titles are Divine Grace, The
Music of the Spheres, Primodial Light, and The Tree of Life.
Shekinah rests on the "Mercy Seat," a chair, stool, tripod,
throne, or dolmen (momument of flat stones forming a table
or seat) that is associated with goddess worship. As the Tree
of Life she bears twelve different fruits, one for each month,
and her leaves are said to help to heal the nations. In some
traditions she is considered the personification of Israel as the
Bride. She corresponds to *Sephira*, *Matronethah*, and
Malkuth (see Western Europe), and also to *Aditi* and *Vac* (see
Indian Subcontinent). [Durdin-Robertson 1975;
Durdin-Robertson 1982; Jobes 1962; Monaghan 1981;
Neumann 1972; Patai 1967]

Sheol
Near East, *Israelite*
Heaven and Hell; Immortality
   Personification of the underworld. Sheol is also the name
for the underworld, an area beneath and within the earth
that receives the dead, the womb from which rebirth is
possible. Later Hebrew and Cabalistic cosmology describes
hell as being divided into seven regions, each having its own
degree of heat: Gehennom, The Gates of Death, The Shadow
of Death, The Pit, The Mire of Clay, Abaddon, and Sheol. Also
worshiped in Northern Europe. See also *Shachuth*.
[Durdin-Robertson 1975]

Sherua
Mesopotamia; Assyria
Creator of Life
   Creator goddess who was later assimilated into *Ishtar*.
[Monaghan 1981; Saggs 1962]

Sheve
Canaan
Destroyer of Life
   "Death." Sister of "Life" and daughter of *Allatu*. [Chicago
1979]

Shibbeta
Jewish
Evil; Health and Healing
   A demon.
   *Shibbeta causes those who do not wash their hands in the
   morning to have cramps later in the day. She especially
   affects children.* [Bonnerjea 1927; Jobes 1962]

Shid
Mesopotamia; Babylonia
Unknown
   A goddess worshiped in the ancient city of Erech. [Bonnerjea
1927]

Shiduri   See *Siduri*.

Shimti
Mesopotamia; Assyria
Fate
   A fate goddess who may be related to *Ishtar*. See also
Ashima. [Jobes 1962; Leach 1992]

Shintalimeni
Anatolia, *Hittite*
Fate; Justice

A goddess of fate who is concerned with good and evil and questions of ultimate justice. [Eliade 1987]

Shulamite
Mesopotamia; Assyria, *Israelite*
Creator of Life
Creator of heaven and earth and a personification of wisdom and fertility. The city of Shulman was named for her. In the Bible she became Shulamite, the bride of Solomon. [Jobes 1962; Monaghan 1981]

Shutu
Mesopotamia; Babylonia
Weather; Directions
"South Wind."
One day, when Adapa was out fishing, Shutu flew overhead and overturned his boat. Enraged, Adapa broke Shutu's wings, which made the wind stop blowing. After seven days, the other gods asked about the wind and discovered what he had done. Adapa repented and was forgiven, Shutu's wings healed, and the wind blew once more. [Leach 1972]

Siduri
Mesopotamia; Babylonia; Sumer; Akkad
Mother and Guardian; Agriculture; Education and Knowledge; Happiness
A goddess of wine and wisdom who encourages her followers to eat, drink, and be merry. As guardian of the "Waters of Death" in the Epic of Gilgamesh, Siduri gives Gilgamesh instructions on how to cross over them safely. She is identified with *Ishtar* (this region), and *Tenemet*, Egypt. Alternate forms: Shiduri, Siduri Sabitu. [Durdin-Robertson 1975; Jobes 1962; Leach 1992; Monaghan 1981; Savill 1976]

Siduri Sabitu   See *Siduri.*

Sige
Near East
Intelligence and Creativity; Immortality
"Silence." One of the *Aeons*. In Gnosticism, she is a form of thought and one of the angels of the square upon which Gnosis rests. [Durdin-Robertson 1975; Monaghan 1981]

Sileni
Anatolia, *Phrygian*
Water
A goddess of springs and rivers. [Dames 1979]

Silili
Mesopotamia
Domesticated Animals
"Divine Mare." A goddess mentioned in the Epic of Gilgamesh. See also *Silili*, Oceania. [Durdin-Robertson 1975; Leach 1992]

Simi   See *Seimia.*

Simorgh
Persia
Wild Birds
A bird goddess, the equivalent of *Garita,* Indian Subcontinent. [Durdin-Robertson 1976]

Sirah   See *Siris.*

Sirara
Mesopotamia; Sumer
Water
A sea goddess associated with Enki. [Kramer 1950; Leach 1992]

Sirdu   See *A.*

Siris
Mesopotamia; Babylonia; Chaldea; Sumer
Weather; Wild Birds; Ceremonies; War
"Lady of Rain and Clouds." A bird goddess who ruled the rain clouds and sent them where she wished. Once, she fiercely defended the Chaldeans by flying over their enemies and washing them away with a flood of water. Also a goddess (or god?) of banquets. Alternate form: Sirah. [Durdin-Robertson 1975; Leach 1992; Monaghan 1981]

Sirrida   See *A.*

Sirtur   See *Ninsun.*

Sister Fire
Armenia
Fire; Health and Healing
Worshiped in conjunction with Brother Spring, Sister Fire is extinguished in the bosom of her loving brother. In the same area today, a medicinal potion is made by mixing the ashes of a fired oak with water. [Jones 1932]

Smyrna   See *Myrrha.*

Sondara   See *Spandaramet.*

Sophia
Near East
Education and Knowledge; The Arts; Immortality; Primordial Being; Intelligence and Creativity
"Wisdom." The Holy Spirit, a Gnostic deity devoted to human well-being. One of the *Aeons*. Through her wisdom one learns handicrafts, the arts, and all kinds of practical skills, as well as sound judgment and political wisdom. Mother of *Sophia-achamoth, Enthumesis,* and the Elohim. She was co-creator, with *Phronesia* and *Dynamis,* of the principalities and angels. In Hellenic philosophy, she was the spirit of God. In Gnostic belief, she coexists with a God who descended to earth to assist in creation. See also the *Holy Spirit* and *Sophia Prunikos.* Equivalent to *Prajna* and *Vac* and *Vach,* both Indian Subcontinent. Alternate forms: Barbelo, Sapientia. [Durdin-Robertson 1975; Durdin-Robertson 1982; Neumann 1972]

Sophia Prunikos
Near East
Unhappiness
One of the *Aeons,* she may be the "fallen" half of *Sophia,* who was faced with distress and problems. [Carlyon 1982]

Sophia-achamoth
Near East
Primordial Being; Immortality
One of the *Aeons* and a personification of the lower Astral Light. Daughter of *Sophia* and mother of Ildabaoth and considered by some to be the mother of the God of the Hebrew Scriptures. Sophia-achamoth is responsible for spirituality within the human soul and is closely related to *Barbelo.* See also *Anael* and *Celestial Virgin.* Alternate form: Achamoth. [Carlyon 1982; Durdin-Robertson 1975]

Spandaramet
Armenia
Earth and Nature; Heaven and Hell
Earth goddess and ruler of the dead. With the advent of Christianity, her name came to mean "hell." Equivalent to *Spentā Ārmaiti.* Alternate forms: Santaramet, Sandaramet, Sandark, Sondara. [Eliade 1987; Jones 1932; Lurker 1984]

Spantaramet
Armenia
Agriculture
   Keeper of the vineyards. Translators of the Armenian
Bible used her name to render the name of Dionysus; no
mention of Spantaramet has been found anywhere else. She
is equivalent to *Spentā Ārmaiti*. [Jones 1932]

Spentā Ārmaiti
Persia
Selflessness; Earth and Nature
   "Divine Piety" or "Bountiful Devotion." A daughter of
Ahura Mazda and one of the *Amesha Spentas*, she guards the
earth and protects its vineyards. In Armenia she is known as
Santaramet. She is equivalent to *Spandaramet* and to the
Vedic goddess *Aramati*, Indian Subcontinent. See also
Armaiti. Alternate form: Asfandarmad. [Dexter 1990;
Durdin-Robertson 1982; Eliade 1987; Jones 1932; Leach 1972]

Spiritus Venereus
Near East
Immortality
   The *Holy Spirit* in its material aspect, mother of the seven
stellars in the Nazarene religion. She is similar to the Gnostic
Sophia-achamoth. [Durdin-Robertson 1982]

Subeh, The
Syria
Evil; Ugliness
   Demons who take the form of fabulous animals or ugly
women with coarse hair, large eyes, and long breasts.
[Bonnerjea 1927]

Succoth Benoth
Chaldea; Samaria
Domesticated Animals
   A goddess brought into Samaria and worshiped by the
Chaldeans. Her name is probably a Hebrew version of
Zirratbanit. She is portrayed as a hen with baby chicks.
Alternate form: Zirpanitu. [Cooper 1876; Durdin-Robertson
1975; Leach 1992; Sykes 1968]

Succubus
Jewish
Love and Sexuality; Evil; Magic
   A demon who has intercourse with men at night. If proper
prayers are said in the morning, the conception of new
demons can be prevented. *Nahema* is a Succubus. [Leach
1972; Wedeck and Baskin 1971]

Sud
Mesopotamia; Sumer
Agriculture
   A corn goddess worshiped in the cities of Shuruppak and
Eresh. Daughter of *Ninshebargunu* and consort of Enlil.
[Achtemeier 1985; Leach 1992]

Sulmanitu
Mesopotamia
Love and Sexuality; War
   A goddess of love and war. [Albright 1968; Leach 1992]

Sumul   See *Samal*.

Symbetylos   See *Ashima Baetyl*.

Taauth
Phoenicia
Unknown

"The Great Lady." Female counterpart of the god Ao.
[Cooper 1876]

Talay
Canaan
Water
   "Dew." [Eliade 1987]

Tallai
Syria; Canaan
Weather
   A goddess of dew and rain. She is a daughter of Baal and a
sister of *Arsai* and *Pidrai*. Alternate form: Talliya. [Durdin-
Robertson 1975; Leach 1992]

Talliya   See *Tallai*.

Tamtu   See *Tiamat*.

Tanais
Persia
Mother and Guardian
   Protector of slaves. [Wedeck and Baskin 1971]

Tanit   See *Tanith*.

Tanit Pene Baal
Carthage
Moon and Night; Creator of Life
   An androgynous moon and fertility goddess who created
all life by giving birth to herself. [Bell 1968; Leach 1992;
Meyerowitz 1958]

Tanith
Phoenicia
Mother and Guardian; Sky and Heavens; Ceremonies
   "Great Mother." A sky goddess of Carthage who ruled the
sun, moon, and stars. When the Romans conquered and
destroyed Carthage, they called her *Dea Caelestis*, Greek and
Roman Empires. According to one source, she had to be
propitiated by the immolation of a human child. Similar to
Malagan, Northern Europe. Alternate forms: Tanit, Thinit,
Tinnit, Rat-tanit. [Achtemeier 1985; Jayne 1925; Lurker 1984;
Monaghan 1981; Neumann 1972; Sykes 1968]

Tarkhu
Anatolia, *Hittite*
Unknown
   A goddess who may have been the predecessor of *Atargatis*.
[Monaghan 1981]

Taromati
Persia
Evil; Disorder
   "Contempt." A demon who makes people disobedient.
[Hinnells 1973; Leach 1992]

Tashmetrum
Mesopotamia
Education and Knowledge
   A goddess of writing who married Nabu, the scribe of the
gods. See also *Tashmetu*. [Carlyon 1982]

Tashmetu
Mesopotamia; Sumer; Babylonia; Assyria
Education and Knowledge
   Said to have "a wide ear," she is kind and always hears
the prayers of her followers. She had a chapel in the great
temple of Esagila, in Babylon. Wife of Nebo, the god of
teaching and writing, Tashmetu opens the ears of those

receiving instruction. See also *Tashmetrum*. Alternate forms: Nana, Tashmit, Tasmit, Urmit, Urmitu, Vanainti, Varamit. [Durdin-Robertson 1975; Jobes 1962; Leach 1992; Lurker 1984; Saggs 1962]

Tashmit   See *Tashmetu*.

Tasimis
Anatolia, *Hittite*
Weather; Disorder
   A storm goddess who was worshiped in an area north of the Taurus foothills. Alternate forms: Huwassanas, Sahassaras. [Durdin-Robertson 1975]

Tasmit   See *Tashmetu*.

Tauthe   See *Tiamat*.

Tawannannas
Anatolia
Sun and Day; Justice
   A sun goddess, also a queen of the Hatti and the high priestess of the shrine at Tahurpa. Alternate form: Twannannas. [Durdin-Robertson 1975; Stone 1979]

Tazhak
Persia
Family and Tribes
   Mother of the Arabian people, daughter of *Fravakain* and sister of *Guzhak*. [Jobes 1962]

Tebunah
Near East, *Israelite*
Intelligence and Creativity; Happiness
   Personification of understanding. Similar to *Chokmah*, Western Europe, and *Binah*, Western Europe. Mentioned in Proverbs as providing happiness to those who "getteth understanding." [Durdin-Robertson 1975]

Tehom
Mesopotamia
Mother and Guardian
   Called "Mother" in Mesopotamia and "the Deep One" by the Hebrews, she is present in the watery abyss. Equivalent to *Tiamat*. Alternate form: T'hom. [Leach 1992; Walker 1986]

Telita
Mesopotamia; Babylonia
Moon
   "Queen of the Moon." Identified with Thalath or *Tiamat*. [Durdin-Robertson 1975]

Terah   See *Jerah*.

Thalassa
Chaldea; Mesopotamia
Water
   "The Sea." Alternate name for *Tiamat*. See also *Thalassas*, Greek and Roman Empires. [Durdin-Robertson 1975; Monaghan 1981; Zimmerman 1964]

Tham   "Water." See *Tiamat*.

Thammuatz   "Wild Cow." See *Tiamat*.

Thamte   See *Tiamat*.

Tharatha   See *Atargatis*.

Thatmanitu
Phoenicia
Health and Healing
   A goddess of healing and daughter of Keret. [Albright 1968; Leach 1992]

Thavatth   See *Tiamat*.

Thepla
Armenia
Evil; Mother and Guardian
   An evil goddess of childbirth who kills infants. Equivalent to *Āl*. [Jones 1932]

Thinit   See *Tanith*.

Thisalat   See *Tiamat*.

Thisbe
Mesopotamia; Babylonia
Love and Sexuality; Unhappiness; Hunting and Wild Animals; Magic
   A goddess of love.
   When Thisbe had a secret rendezvous with her lover, Pyramus, she arrived at their meeting place to find a young lioness in his stead. The startled Thisbe dropped her cloak and the lioness began to play with it, smearing it with blood from a recent kill. Thisbe then ran away, and when Pyramus arrived and saw the bloody cloak, he thought that his beloved had been eaten by the lioness and proceeded to kill himself. When she returned and saw what had happened, Thisbe killed herself beside him; the blood of both lovers ran together and soaked into the ground by a mulberry tree, turning its berries red. [Leach 1972]

Thitmanat
Mesopotamia; Ugarit
Health and Healing
   "The Eighth One." In the Epic of Keret she helps to cure her father, King Keret, of his illness. Alternate form: Thitmanet. [Durdin-Robertson 1975; Savill 1976]

Thitmanet   See *Thitmanat*.

Thlavatth   See *Tiamat*.

Throne Goddesses, The   See the *Cow Goddesses*.

Thummim
Israelite
Unknown
   Semitic name for *Themis*, Greek and Roman Empires, and *Thmei*, Egypt. [Durdin-Robertson 1975]

Thymbris
Anatolia; Troy
Water
   A river nymph. [Leach 1992; Roscher 1965]

Tiamat
Mesopotamia; Babylonia; Chaldea; Akkad
Water; Primordial Being; Creator of Life; Reptiles; Earth and Nature; Sky and Heavens
   "Bitter Ocean." A goddess of the primordial waters, she was the first mother and, with her consort Apsu, she created the other gods.
   Before heaven and earth had been named, the little gods whom Tiamat and Apsu had created disturbed Apsu with their noisy activities, so, despite his wife's objections, he decided to kill them. But his son, Ea, drew a magic circle around himself and his siblings, and from the protection of that circle they

were able to kill their father. . . . Another time, Ea's brother, Anu, created winds that bothered Tiamat and made her give birth to a host of monstrous serpents. . . . After the gods had made Marduk their king, he killed Tiamat and cut her body in half. One half became the earth and the other half became the sky.

See also *Tihamtu.* Equivalent to *Makaris* and *Mother Earth,* both Indian Subcontinent. Alternate forms: Mother Chuber, Mumu Taimet, Omorca, Onoroca, Tamtu, Tauthe, Thalassa, Tham, Thamte, Tharavatth, Thlavatth, Thavatth, Thisalat, Thammuatz, Tiawath, Tisalat, Ummu Khubhar. [Chicago 1979; Cooper 1876; Cotterell 1979; Durdin-Robertson 1975; Jobes 1962; Leach 1992; Monaghan 1981; Neumann 1972; Stone 1979]

Tiawath See *Tiamat.*

Tif'eret See *Binah.*

Tigranuhi
Armenia
Moon and Night
"Darkness." A spirit whose demon husband, Azdahah, tried to kill her brother, Tigranes, but Tigranuhi warned her brother of Azdahah's plan, and Tigranes killed Azdahah instead. Alternate form: Tigranuki. [Jobes 1962; Jones 1932]

Tigranuki See *Tigranuhi.*

Tihamtu
Assyria
Water; Primordial Being; Reptiles
"The Sea." She emerged from the sea as a dragon with seven heads, but Bel-Merodach drove her back into the primordial darkness. See also *Tiamat.* [Cooper 1876]

Tillil
Chaldea
Unknown
A goddess equivalent to *Nephthys,* Egypt. [Durdin-Robertson 1975]

Tillili
Mesopotamia; Babylonia
Primordial Being
"Primordial Earth." Consort of Alala. [Leach 1992; Sayce 1898]

Tinnit See *Tanith.*

Tisalat See *Tiamat.*

Tiskhu "Mistress of Armies." See *Ishtar.*

Titae Aretia See *Aretia.*

Titaea Magna See *Aretia.*

Titanides, The
Phoenicia
Unknown
Seven daughters of *Astarte* and Cronus. See also *Titanides,* Greek and Roman Empires. Alternate form: Artemides. [Durdin-Robertson 1975]

Tres Mariae
Near East
Mothers and Guardians
"The Three Mothers." A female triad of goddesses that existed before the Christian era. Their names are on a tablet found at Metz: "To the Goddesses Mariae, they of the street of peace." [Durdin-Robertson 1982]

Tres Matres See *Tres Matres,* Western Europe.

Tsikhu See *Ishtar.*

Tušnamati
Persia
Intelligence and Creativity
"Meditation." Equivalent to *Armaiti.* [Gray 1930; Leach 1992]

Twannannas See *Tawannannas.*

Uda
Persia
Evil; Disorder
"Loquacity." A demon who makes people talk too much. [Gray 1930; Leach 1992]

Udai See *Vatak.*

Ukhat
Mesopotamia; Babylonia
Unknown
"Wailing Woman." A servant of Gilgamesh who helped lure Eabani into Gilgamesh's service. [Bonnerjea 1927]

Ulsiga See *Ishtar.*

Umai
Anatolia
Household Affairs; Fire
A fire deity who presides over home and hearth in Turkey. See also *Umai,* Far East and Eastern Europe. Alternate forms: Mai, Ymai. [Baumgartner 1984; Leach 1992]

Umm See *Am.*

Umm S-subyan See *Umm S-subyan,* Africa.

Ummu Khubhar See *Tiamat.*

Upanayana
Persia
Education and Knowledge
"Tradition." [Gray 1930; Leach 1992]

Uparatat
Persia
War
A victory goddess. Alternate form: Vanainti. [Carnoy 1917; Gray 1930; Jobes 1962; Leach 1992]

Uras
Mesopotamia
Earth and Nature
Ancient earth goddess, mother of *Ninisinna.* [Lurker 1984]

Urash
Mesopotamia; Sumer
War
A war goddess and consort of the god An. [Savill 1976]

Urbadgumgum See *Ninsar.*

Urmit See *Tashmetu.*

Urmitu See *Tashmetu.*

Ushharay
Near East
Insects
A scorpion goddess. Alternate form: Ishhara. [Eliade 1925]

Uthht
Canaan
Unknown
"Incense-burner." A goddess who may have originated in Mesopotamia. [Eliade 1987]

Uttu
Mesopotamia; Babylonia; Sumer
Earth and Nature; Household Affairs
A goddess of vegetation and weaving, daughter of *Ninkurra*. After consorting with Enki, she gave birth to many plants. [Durdin-Robertson 1975; Leach 1992; Monaghan 1981; Saggs 1962]

Vanainti "Conquering Superiority." See *Tashmetu* and *Uparatat*.

Varamit See *Tashmetu*.

Vatak
Persia
Evil; Love and Sexuality; Disorder
A Zoroastrian demon, half human and half monster, who makes people talk when they should be quiet and makes them commit incest. Alternate forms: Aūṭak, Udai. [Leach 1992]

Veritas See *Aletheia*.

Virgin Mary
Near East
Mother and Guardian
The Great Mother of ancient religions whom Christianity assimilated as the Virgin Mary. She is known as a birth-giving goddess, a goddess of animals, and the queen of heaven and is invoked for blessings. See also *Tres Matres*, this section; *Maryam*, Africa; *Black Virgin, Diana, Mater Dei, Proserpina,* and *Theotokos*, Greek and Roman Empires; *Avezuha, Boldogasszany, Kildisin, Luojatar, Mary-Rusalka, Mokasi, Niski-ava,* and *Sarakka*, Eastern Europe; *Ban-Chaideachaidh Moire*, Western Europe; *Isis*, Egypt; and *Bibi-Miriam*, Indian Subcontinent. [Baring and Cashford 1991; Cotterell 1979; Deen 1955; Hultkrantz 1983; Jobes 1962; Leach 1992; Pike 1951]

Vita See *Zoe*.

Voice of the Abyss See *Lady of the Abyss*.

Walanni
Anatolia
Sun and Day
Sun goddess. [Stone 1979]

Wisuriyanza
Asia Minor; Syria, *Hittite*
Magic; Ceremonies
A witch who took the place of the Hebrew *Lilith*. She demanded the sacrifice of a child in return for wealth and fertility. [Hubbs 1988]

Word, The
Near East
Primordial Being

The mother of matter. She is connected to *Filia Vocis.* She is similar to *Vac,* Indian Subcontinent; *Kwanyin,* Far East; and *Sefekh,* Egypt. [Durdin-Robertson 1975]

Wurusemu
Anatolia, *Hatti, Hittite*
Sun and Day; Family and Tribes
A sun goddess who married Taru, a weather god. She was worshiped in the city of Arinna and presided over the kingdom of the Hittites. Alternate form: Arinna. [Durdin-Robertson 1975; Leach 1992; Monaghan 1981]

Xnathaiti
Persia
Love and Sexuality
"Lust." [Gray 1930; Leach 1992]

Yaošti
Persia
Unknown
"Zeal." A wife of Ahura Mazda. [Gray 1930; Leach 1992]

Yah See *Chokmah*.

Yahveh See *Chokmah*.

Yechidah
Israelite
Heaven and Hell; Earth and Nature
"Unique." Personification of an element lighter than *Chaiah,* she is associated with the world of nature (heaven). [Durdin-Robertson 1975]

Yimak
Persia
Creator of Life
First woman. Alternate forms: Yimeh, Yimaka. [Eliade 1987; Jobes 1962]

Yimaka See *Yimak*.

Yimeh See *Yimak*.

Ymai See *Umai*.

Zaliyanu
Anatolia, *Hittite*
Earth and Nature
A mountain goddess and wife of the storm god. Mentioned in the Epic of Illuyankas. [Durdin-Robertson 1975; Kramer 1961b]

Zaltu
Mesopotamia
Unknown
A goddess associated with *Ishtar*. [Durdin-Robertson 1975]

Zam
Persia
Earth and Nature
An earth goddess identified with *Ashtart*. Alternate form: Amurdat. [Gray 1930; Grimal 1973; Leach 1992]

Zamama
Mesopotamia; Assyria
Justice
Patron goddess of the city of Kish. [Wedeck and Baskin 1971]

Zamin
Persia
Earth and Nature
   Earth goddess, equivalent to *Semele*. [Jobes 1962]

Zamyad
Persia
Earth and Nature; Time
   "The Earth." A goddess of the thirteenth day of the waning moon (the 28th day of the lunar month), she was called "the Genius of the Earth." [Durdin-Robertson 1982]

Zanaru   "Lady of the Lands." See *Ishtar*.

Zarpandit
Mesopotamia
Creator of Life; Moon and Night
   "Shining Silver" or "Seed-maker." A creator goddess worshiped at night when the moon was rising, she may be the same as *Zarpanitu*. See also *Aruru*. Alternate forms: Zerpanitu, Zerpanitum, Beltis, Beltiya, Aruru, Sarpanitu. [Monaghan 1981]

Zarpanitu
Mesopotamia; Babylonia; Chaldea
Creator of Life
   A goddess who ensures the continuation of life. Associated with *Gasmu*. May be the same as *Zarpandit*. Alternate forms: Beltia, Zerpanitum, Zirbanit, Sarpanitu. [Durdin-Robertson 1975; Jobes 1962; Leach 1992]

Zerbanit   See *Baalti*.

Zerpanitu   See *Zarpandit*.

Zerpanitum   "Lady of the Abyss." See *Sarpanitu, Zarpandit, Zarpanitu*.

Zertur
Mesopotamia; Sumer
Mother and Guardian
   "Young Maiden." The mother of Tammuz. [Wedeck and Baskin 1971]

Zhob Mother Goddess, The
Afghanistan
Unknown
   Figures of her dating from around 3000 B.C.E. have been found in the Zhob River Valley; they are goggle-eyed, hooded, and voluptuous. [Fairservis 1971]

Zib   "The Evening Star." See *Ishtar*.

Zicum
Mesopotamia; Babylonia; Assyria
Primordial Being; Creator of Life
   "Primordial Abyss." A primeval goddess worshiped at Eridu and Ur in Sumer; she gave birth to the earth, the heavens, and all the other gods. Alternate forms: Zikum, Zigara. [Harding 1971; Leach 1992; Rawlinson 1885; Sayce 1898]

Zigara   See *Zicum*.

Zigarun
Mesopotamia; Babylonia
Creator of Life
   "Mother Who Begot Heaven and Earth." [Sykes 1968]

Zikum   See *Zicum*.

Zintuhi
Anatolia, *Hatti, Hittite*
Unknown
   Granddaughter of *Wurusemu* and daughter of either *Mezulla* or *Hulla*. [Durdin-Robertson 1975; Monaghan 1981]

Zirbanit   See *Zarpanitu*.

Zirpanitu   See *Succoth Benoth*.

Zirratbanit
Mesopotamia; Babylonia; Assyria
Unknown
   Called *Succoth Benoth* in Hebrew texts, she was the wife of Marduk. After the fall of Israel, worship of her was brought to Sumeria by the Babylonians. [Cooper 1876]

Zoe
Near East
Primordial Being
   "Means of Life." One of the *Aeons*. Alternate form: Vita. [Durdin-Robertson 1975]

Zuriel
Near East
Weather; Immortality; Stars and Planets
   An angel associated with air and with the planet Venus in the constellation of Libra. Alternate form: Puella. [Durdin-Robertson 1975]

NORTH AMERICA

?Aano?ovi "Echo."   See *N̨arimamau?u.*

Aataentsic
Northeast, *Iroquois*
Creator of Life; Destroyer of Life; Immortality; Magic; Sky and Heavens

"Woman Who Fell from the Sky." Celestial deity who became First Woman. Mother of Gusts of Wind, grandmother of Iouskeha and Tawiskaron. She is also malevolent, causing fatal diseases and then taking charge of the deceased souls.

 Aataentsic's father died before she was born, but she was able to communicate with his spirit. He told her that her intended mate was Earth-holding Chief. To reach her husband-to-be, Aataentsic had to face many dangers and Earth-holding Chief's tests. When she returned to her village and gave birth to a daughter, her people threw her (or she accidentally fell) down to the blue lake below. As she was falling, her daughter Gusts of Wind returned to her mother's womb. The animals and birds of the blue lake realized that Aataentsic needed some land to rest on so she could once more give birth to Gusts of Wind and they quickly set about making land from the lake's mud.

Equivalent to *Eagentci.* See also *Awehai, Ketq Skwayne, Navajo Woman First,* and *Woman Who Fell from the Sky.* Alternate forms: Ataentsic, Ataensic, Atahensic. [Gill 1992; Leach 1972; Monaghan 1981; Redfield 1931; Savill 1978; Senior 1985]

Abalone Woman   See *Estsanatlehi.*

Ackwin
Central Woodland, *Winnebago*
Family and Tribes; Earth and Nature; Ceremonies

"Grandmother." Earth goddess who is particularly honored at medicine dances and war-bundle feasts in Wisconsin. She is also called a "babbler." [Emerson 1965; Leach 1992]

Aci'asdza   See *Ashi Esdza.*

A-ha Kachin' Mana
Southwest, *Hopi*
Ceremonies

Kachina of the *Powamu* or Bean Dance, which is performed in early February and is mostly concerned with fertility. *Kachina* broadly refers to any masked figure among the Pueblo peoples and even in other southwestern cultures. This is not its only meaning, as a kachina can also be a mediator spirit between the human and spiritual world, a masked dancer personifying a spirit being, a doll of the spirit, or a spirit of the dead. [Colton 1949; Gill 1992; Wright 1973; Wright 1977]

Ahe'a
Southwest, *Zuni*
Family and Tribes; Ceremonies

"Oh My!" Grandmother of all kachinas (see *A-ha Kachin' Mana*). Alternate forms: Jemez Old Woman, Hemokatsiki. [Bunzel 1984; Wright 1985]

Ahgishanakhou
Northwest, *Tlingit*
Earth and Nature

Chthonic goddess who protects the pillar-support of the earth. [Bancroft 1886; Leach 1992]

Ahmetolela Okya
Southwest, *Zuni*
Ceremonies; Weather

"Rainbow Dancer Girl." A kachina (see *A-ha Kachin' Mana*). Alternate form: Thlehakto Okya. [Wright 1985]

Ahöla Mana
Southwest, *Hopi*
Ceremonies; Time

"Germ God Maiden." Kachina (see *A-ha Kachin' Mana*) of the *Soyal* Ceremony, which is celebration of the Winter Solstice. She accompanies Ahola when he visits the kivas and ceremonial houses and carries a tray filled with seeds from the fields. Alternate form: Hemis Kachin' Mana. [Colton 1949; Wright 1977]

Ahsonnutli
Southwest, *Navajo*
Sky and Heavens
   "Turquoise Woman." Alternate aspect of sky goddess, *Estsanatlehi,* or she may be a separate goddess. Alternate form: Turquoise Woman. [Monaghan 1981; Sykes 1968]

Aialila'axa
Northwest, *Bella Coola*
Mother and Guardian; Moon and Night; Health and Healing
   Guardian of the moon who protects people from sickness and death. [Boas 1898; Leach 1992]

Aittsamka
Northwest, *Bella Coola*
Education and Knowledge
   "Abalone-shell Woman." Goddess at Talio. With *Atbilzaniatlliax,* she teaches the people. See also *Yolkai Estan.* [McIlwraith 1948]

Aiviliajog
Arctic, *Iglulirmiut Inuit*
Water
   Central Eskimo goddess. Equivalent to *Sedna.* [Boas 1884; Leach 1992]

Ai-Willi-Ay-O
Arctic, *Inuit*
Water
   Equivalent to *Sedna.* Ai-Willi-Ay-O is worshiped on the west coast of Hudson Bay. See also *Aywilliayoo.* [Monaghan 1990]

Akna
Arctic; Mexico, *Inuit, Lacandon*
Moon and Night
   "Moon" or "The Mother." To the Lacandon she is the wife of the sun, Qin. To the Inuit she is a goddess of childbirth. [Carlyon 1982; Leach 1992]

Akoq
Arctic, *Polar Inuit*
Sky and Heavens
   Sky goddess whose husband is the moon. Alternate form: Aqong. [Wyers 1932]

Akycha
Arctic, *Inuit*
Sun and Day; Family and Tribes; Love and Sexuality; Unhappiness
   "Sun." Sister of *Aningap.*

   Akycha was so upset that her brother, the moon, had violated her that she chased him endlessly. They are now in the sky, where the chase continues.
   See also *Greenland Sun Goddess, Siqiniq,* and *Sun Sister.* Alternate form: Seqinek. [Leach 1992; Monaghan 1981; Wyers 1932]

'Alaĥtin
California, *Chumash*
Moon and Night; Health and Healing; Luck; Time
   Moon goddess who brings good health and fortune. Providing light at night, she affects the movement of the sea,

women's menses, and the calendar. 'Alaĥtin cleanses and purifies her followers. [Leach 1992]

?Al?heleqeč
California, *Chumash*
Evil
   A Nunašiš, a demon who carries a basket of hot tar on her back. [Blackburn 1975]

Alarana
Arctic, *Point Barrow Inuit*
Earth and Nature; Hunting and Wild Animals
   Animal goddess.

   Alarana and her brother Aligunaluk were eaten by wolves. The wolves turned into humans and took the children's bones to the house of she-wolf/medicine woman, who laid Alarana's bones on the skin of a young caribou cow and her brother's on the skin of a young bull. The medicine woman sang them back to life, and they transformed themselves into caribou. [Gill 1992]

Alkuntam
Northwest, *Bella Coola*
Creator of Life; Ceremonies
   Daughter of a cannibal goddess, *Nunusomikeeqonem.* She helped create animals and people. [Leach 1992; Savill 1978]

Alo Mana
Southwest, *Hopi*
Ceremonies
   Kachina (see *A-ha Kachin' Mana*) brought from the eastern pueblos. Alternate forms: Hemis Kachin' Mana, Kocha Mana. [Colton 1949; Wright 1973; Wright 1977]

Amayicoyondi
California, *Pericu*
Mother and Guardian; Family and Tribes
   "Red Mountain." Sky goddess, mother goddess, and creator of the people. [Monaghan 1990]

Ampata Sapa
North America
Unhappiness; Love and Sexuality
   Ghost of St. Anthony's Falls.

   When Ampata Sapa's warrior husband took another wife, Ampata Sapa ran to the river. She launched a canoe into the torrent and disappeared over the falls. Sometimes on a night when the moon is bright Ampata Sapa can be seen going over the falls again. [Emerson 1965]

Ana Maria
Southwest, *Yaqui*
Commerce and Travel
   "Sea Hamut." A wise woman who determined the boundaries of the Yaqui territory with the help of a giant.

   When strange sounds were heard vibrating in the trees, Ana Maria was summoned to interpret them. She told of strange men who would come and teach them new ways.
   See also *Gefjun,* Northern Europe. [Painter 1986]

Anavigak
Arctic, *Iglulik Inuit*
Water
   At the Pond Inlet on north Baffin Island, this is a name for *Sedna.* She may also be called *Unaviga.* [Leach 1992; Nungak 1969; Wyers 1932]

Ang-chin Mana
Southwest, *Hopi*
Ceremonies; Agriculture

"White Corn Maiden." A kachina (see *A-ha Kachin' Mana*). See also *Khuntsaenyu'a'anyun*. Alternate form: Qocha Mana. [Colton 1949]

Angak'chin' Mana
Southwest, *Hopi*
Ceremonies
   "Long-haired Kachina Girl." She may also be called *Kocha Mana* and have been originally Zuni. See also *A-ha Kachin' Mana*. [Wright 1973; Wright 1977]

Angwushahai-i
Southwest, *Hopi*
Agriculture; Ceremonies; Wild Birds
   "Crow Bride." Some say this is a name for *Angwusnasomtaka* when on Third Mesa. She participates in the *Powamu* or Bean Dance fertility ceremony. [Colton 1949; Wright 1973; Wright 1977]

Angwusnasomtaka
Southwest, *Hopi*
Wild Birds; Agriculture; Ceremonies
   "Crow Mother." Appears in the *Powamu* or Bean Dance on all three mesas. Some consider her the mother of all kachinas (see *A-ha Kachin' Mana*), and she appears at the initiation of children at the kachina cult ceremony during *Powamu*. At Third Mesa she is called *Angwushahai-i*. [Wright 1973; Wright 1977]

Animal Mother
Northeast, *Iroquois, Tlingit*
Heaven and Hell; Hunting and Wild Animals
   Underworld goddess who protects animals. The Tlingit on Teslin Lake in the southeastern Yukon Territory believe she gives game animals to the people. [Burland 1975; MacNeish 1981; Tyler 1964]

Aningap   See *Tatqeq*.

Aningat   See *Tatqeq*.

'Anltani
Southwest, *Navajo*
Insects; Goodness; Creator of Life
   "Cornbeetle." Benevolent fertility deity of Arizona and New Mexico. [Leach 1992; Moon 1984]

Anog Ite
Plains, *Dakota, Oglala, Lakota*
Beauty; Ugliness; Evil; Disorder
   "Two-faced Woman." Daughter of First Woman and First Man, wife of Tate, the wind. Evil goddess who causes trouble, laziness, and bad habits in South Dakota. She teaches quilling, a form of basket-making, which is said to conflict with women's traditional roles and to lead to lesbianism.
   Anog Ite was first called Ite. When she attempted to seduce the sun, Wi, Ite was condemned by her grandfather Skan, the sky, to live with two faces, Anog Ite. One of her faces is beautiful and the other very ugly. [Gill 1992; Leach 1992]

Anoolikwotsaix
Northwest, *Bella Coola*
Ceremonies; Time; Intelligence and Creativity
   "Guardian of Secrets." She is involved in the winter ceremonial dances. [Leach 1992; McIlwraith 1948]

Anusyelaix
Northwest, *Bella Coola*
Creator of Life

Stskiitl First Woman. Her family symbol is a stake decorated with abalone shells, which she found floating in the river when she and her brother Anusyelaix were sent down to be the first people. [McIlwraith 1948]

Anya Kachin' Mana
Southwest, *Hopi*
Agriculture; Ceremonies
   "Maid Who Grinds Corn." A kachina (see *A-ha Kachin' Mana*). [Fewkes 1985]

Apache Woman
Southeast, *Apache*
Earth and Nature
   "Earth Woman." The feminine as attributed to the earth. [Opler 1941]

Apasinasee
Arctic, *Hudson Bay Inuit*
Creator of Life
   Creator goddess.
   Apasinasee had so many dog-children, she was unable to support them all. Some were sent inland, where they became giants or walrus-eating dwarfs; some disappeared aboard a sailing vessel; and a few stayed with her to become the Eskimo people. [Monaghan 1981]

Api   See *Apish*.

Apish
Plains, *Crow, Apsaroke*
Destroyer of Life
   "Corn Silk." She brings sickness. Alternate form: Api. [Curtis 1908]

Aqong   See *Akoq*.

Aquit
Mexico, *Opata*
Moon and Night
   Moon goddess. Her brother is the sun. Alternate form: Metza. [Johnson 1949; Leach 1992]

Arnaaluk Takannaaluk
Arctic, *Iglulik Inuit*
Water
   Sea goddess who presides over the sea animals. Equivalent to *Sedna*. Alternate forms: Tanakapsaluk, Takanaluk Arnaluk. [Leach 1992; Nungak 1969; Rasmussen 1929]

Arnahapshaaluk   See *Arnapkapfaluk*.

Arnapkapfaluk
Arctic, *Copper Inuit*
Water
   "Big, Bad Woman." Sea goddess at Bathurst Inlet. Equivalent to *Sedna*. Her husband is Igpiarjuk or Ikparyuak. Alternate form: Arnahapshaaluk. [Damas 1984; Leach 1992; Wyers 1932]

Arnaknagsak
Arctic, *Greenland Inuit*
Water
   "Old Mother," or "Majestic Woman" who lives at the bottom of the sea. Equivalent to *Sedna*. Alternate forms: Arnakuagsak, Arnarquagssaq, Arnarquáshaaq. [Sykes 1968; Wyers 1932]

Arnakapshaaluk   See *Arnapkapfaluk*.

Arnakuagsak See *Arnaknagsak*.

Arnaluktakanaluk See *Arnaaluk Takannaaluk*.

Arnarquagssaq See *Arnaknagsak*.

Arnarquáshaaq
West Greenland
Evil; Earth and Nature
  "Old Hag" or "The Mighty Woman." A bad woman who
has command over all sea animals. This is not a proper name
for a deity, but an epithet. See also *Sedna*. Alternate form:
Arnaknagsak. [Damas 1984; Wyers 1932]

Asdzaa Dootlijii
Southwest, *Navajo*
Unknown
  "Turquoise Woman." Sometimes a name for *Changing
Woman* and at other times a separate deity. In one story
Changing Woman (*Estsanatlehi*) creates *Turquoise Woman*
and *Whiteshell Woman* from skin that she rubs from under
her breasts. See also *Asdzaa Yoolgai* and *Estsanatlehi*.
Alternate form: Turquoise Woman. [Gill 1992]

'Asdzáá·nádle·hé See *Estsanatlehi*.

Asdzaa Yoolgai
Southwest, *Navajo*
Fishing and Water Animals
  "Whiteshell Woman." Like *Turquoise Woman,* she is
sometimes separate from *Changing Woman* (*Estsanatlehi*)
and other times an alternate name for her. As a separate
identity she is sister of *Changing Woman* and in other
instances the wife of the Sun. *Whiteshell Woman* (*Yolkai
estsanis*) also an Apache goddess. See also *Asdzaa Dootlijii*.
Alternate form: Whiteshell Woman. [Gill 1992]

Ashi esdza
Southwest, *Navajo*
Metals and Minerals
  "Salt Woman." See also *Malokatsiki, Mina Koya,* and
Ong Wuhti. Alternate form: Aci'asdza. [Turner 1974]

Asiak See *Asiaq*.

Asiaq
Arctic, *Greenland and Caribou Inuit*
Weather; Hunting and Wild Animals
  Weather goddess. She is asked to make it rain so that
hunting will be easier. To make it rain, Asiaq shakes a skin
drenched in urine above the earth. Some say she has been
wandering since the beginning of time looking for a mate.
Alternate form: Asiak. [Baumgartner 1984; Cotterell 1979;
Damas 1984; Leach 1992; Wyers 1932]

Asin
Northwest, *Alsea*
Evil; Fate; Magic
  Monster. A wood-dwelling girl who kidnaps people,
especially children. Her laughter foretells of death, and
medicine people can gain bad medicine by dreaming about
her. See also *Dzoo-noo-qua*. [Gill 1992]

Asintmah
Subarctic
Earth and Nature
  The first woman on earth, worshiped in western Canada.
  *Asintmah walked about on the beautiful earth. She
  gathered branches and wove a great earth blanket. It was
  under this blanket that Mother Earth gave birth to the*

*first living beings: mouse, rabbit, cougar, caribou, wapiti, and
moose.* [Stone 1979]

?Ašixuč
California, *Chumash*
Evil; Weather
  Demon who brings hot weather. [Blackburn 1975]

Ataensic See *Aataensic*.

Ataentsic See *Aataensic*.

Atahensic See *Aataensic*.

Atansic See *Awehai*.

Atavish
California, *Yamai, Harurai, Chatutai, Tamayowut*
Primordial Being
  "Empty." Primordial goddess who successively changed
names. She became *Yamai*, "Not in Existence," then *Harurai
Chatutai*, "Boring, Lowering," and finally *Tamayowut*,
"Earth." [Kroeber 1925; Leach 1992]

Atbilxaniatlliax
Northwest, *Bella Coola*
Fishing and Water Animals; Education and Knowledge
  "The One with Abalone on Her Hat." Goddess at the town
of Talio, and, with *Aittsamka*, a teacher of the people. See
also *Yolkai Estsan* and *Aittsamka*. [McIlwraith 1948]

Atira
Plains, *Pawnee*
Creator of Life; Stars and Planets; Life/Death Cycle
  Creator deity who is said to be the Evening Star. She is the
mother of all things, bringing forth life and into whom all life
returns. Mother of *Uti Hiata*. Atira's symbol is an ear of corn.
[Carlyon 1982; Chicago 1979; Leach 1992; Monaghan 1981]

Atitxmana
Northwest, *Bella Coola*
Unknown
  "The Clang of Copper." Sister goddess of *Kanuslaliam* at
Nusxeq. They lived in a copper house with a loon totem pole
given to them by the underwater god. [McIlwraith 1948]

Atocle See *Atoshle Suyuki*.

Atoshle See *Atoshle Suyuki*.

Atoshle Suyuki
North America, *Hopi*
Evil; Ceremonies
  Hopi kachina (see *A-ha Kachin' Mana*). An ogre who is
said to eat children. She is of Zuni origin and accompanies
Soyok Wugti. Her hair is gray with eagle down caught in it,
and she wears a white-spotted black mask, carries a stick,
and has a basket in which she puts children. See also
Awatovi Soyok Wuhti. Alternate forms: Atoshle, Suyuki,
Atocle. [Colton 1949; Fewkes 1985; Gill 1992; Tyler 1964]

Atse ataed
Southwest, *Navajo*
Unknown
  "First Girl." [Turner 1974]

Atse esdza See *Atse Esdzaa*.

Atse Esdzaa
Southwest, *Navajo*
Destroyer of Life; Magic
   The woman of the primordial pair. The pair may have been transformed by the wind from primordial ears of corn. Atse Esdzaa and Atse Hasteen raised *Changing Woman* but were not her parents.

 When Changing Woman reached maturity, Atse Esdzaa and Atse Hasteen gave her the medicine bundle of creation. They then returned to the lower world with a copy of the bundle and became the chiefs of witchcraft and death.
   See also *Estsanatlehi.* Alternate form: Atse Esdza. [Gill 1992; Jobes 1962; Monaghan 1981]

Atsentma
Subarctic, *Tahltan*
Hunting and Wild Animals
   "Meat Mother." Goddess of animals. A pregnant woman could not keep up with her migrating tribe so they left her behind. She gave birth to all the meat animals— moose, caribou, etc. Now people try not to offend her or she will keep the game animals away from them. [Bierhorst 1985; Leach 1992; Teit 1919]

Aukjuk
Arctic, *Netsilinqmiut Inuit*
Creator of Life; Justice
   "Disemboweller." Creator goddess who does not tolerate infractions of her taboos. [Leach 1992; Wyers 1932]

Avilayoq
Arctic, *Baffin Land Inuit*
Water
   Sea goddess of Cumberland Sound. Equivalent to *Sedna.* [Wyers 1932]

Aviliayuk   See *Uiniyumayuituq.*

Awatobi Soyok Wuqti   Sea *Awatovi Soyok Wuhti*

Awatovi Soyok Wuhti
Southwest, *Hopi*
Agriculture; Ceremonies
   "Ogre Woman." She dances at the *Powamu* or Bean Dance and *Soyoko,* but only on First Mesa. *Soyoko* is a ritualized event during the *Powamu* ceremony. *Powamu* is the fertility ritual in February. See also *Atoshle Suyuki.* Wuhti indicates a married woman. Alternate form: Awatobi Soyok Wuqti. [Colton 1949; Wright 1973; Wright 1977]

Awehai
Northeast, *Iroquois*
Family and Tribes; Sky and Heavens; Reptiles; Creator of Life
   Creator deity. Wife of Hanohwendjiawagi (Dehavenjawa), mother of Gaendeson.

 Awehai was originally a celestial being, but was thrown out of the skies by her husband, who thought she had been unfaithful. As she was falling she caught seeds and animals, carrying them with her. As she neared the endless water below, winged creatures slowed her descent and guided her to the back of the Great Turtle. On the turtle's back they gathered dirt and the earth was formed. Awehai scattered the seeds and let the animals run free. When the seeds sprouted and Awehai saw how beautiful the earth was, she produced children, the Iroquois.
   Alternate forms: Atansic, Awenhai. [Leach 1992; Stone 1979]

Awenhai   See *Awehai.*

Aweshi   See *Suyuki.*

Awitelin Tsita
Southwest, *Zuni*
Creator of Life; Sky and Heavens; Mother and Guardian
   "Four-fold Vessel." Earth mother who was formed by Awonawilona, a dual deity who created Awitelin Tsita and the sky by throwing pieces of his cuticle into the endless sea or from the saliva of *Shiwanokia.*

 Awitelin Tsita joined in constant intercourse with the sky until her four wombs were filled. She then gave birth to all living beings.
   Alternate form: Hatai Wuhti. [Cotterell 1979; Jobes 1962; Leach 1972; Leach 1992; Long 1963; Monaghan 1981]

Aywilliayoo
Arctic, *Iglulik Inuit*
Water
   Equivalent to *Sedna.* See also *Ai-Willi-Ay-O.* [Wyers 1932]

Badger Old Woman
Southwest, *Pueblo*
Mother and Guardian; Ceremonies; Hunting and Wild Animals
   Childbirth goddess. A badger paw is worn by or placed near the mother during delivery because a badger digs itself out quickly. Badger Woman may have opened the door of the earth and let out the kachinas (see *A-ha Kachin' Mana*). [Leach 1972; Tyler 1964]

Bah-bah-deed
Northwest, *Duwamish*
Earth and Nature
   Mountain goddess. [Clark 1953]

Bapets, The
Great Basin, *Southern Ute*
Destroyer of Life; Mother and Guardian; Evil Cannibals.
   They are ample beings with large breasts filled with poison milk. If the children they kidnap nurse from the Bapets breasts, they die instantly. A Bapet can only be killed with an obsidian-tipped arrow. [Gill 1992]

Baxbakualanuchsiwae
Northwest
Ceremonies
   Cannibal Mother. Equivalent to *Tsonoqua.* [Savill 1978]

Bear Daughter
Central Plateau, *Salish*
Earth and Nature; Evil; Hunting and Wild Animals
   Animal goddess who may be a monster. See also *Bear Woman.* [Bierhorst 1985]

Bear Maiden
North America
Hunting and Wild Animals; Magic; Mother and Guardian
   Goddess who gives food. She is also called *Bear Woman.*

 A young man hunting in the woods meets a young woman who is actually a black bear. The young man kills her enemy, the grizzly, and they live happily together until salmon-fishing time. He takes his wife to his village, but she refuses to help with the communal food activities. When the food runs out that winter, Bear Maiden reveals an underground store of dried salmon and berries, saving them from starvation. In the spring, when her husband starts to renew his acquaintance with an old sweetheart, Bear Maiden changes herself and their child back into their bear forms and disappears. Her husband searches for her, but cannot find her.
   This is a story that appears in many cultures—the disappearance of an offended supernatural wife, such as *Bear*

Woman (this region), and *Lima,* Eastern Europe, and *Allwise,* Northern Europe. [Bierhorst 1985; Leach 1972]

Bear Mother
Northwest
Justice; Ceremonies; Magic; Mother and Guardian; Hunting and Wild Animals

A woman who wandered away from her people and changed into a bear. While living in a bear den, she had bear cub children. Hunters believe if they put on bear skins the bear people will help them with their hunting.

 Bear Mother found a human boy and raised him as her own. She taught him how to differentiate between sincere and insincere prayers and returned him to his people. The boy told the people that the bears know the difference between sincere and insincere prayers and that the bears will provide food for only those who are sincere.

See also **Bear Woman** and **Rhpisunt.** [Bierhorst 1985; Burland 1975; Gill 1992; Leach 1972]

Bear Woman
Northwest, *Tlingit*
Ceremonies; Family and Tribes; Love and Sexuality; Stars and Planets; Magic; Mother and Guardian; Hunting and Wild Animals

There is a great variety of Bear Woman stories. They include adulterous relationships with bears, female bears becoming wives of humans, and women changing into bears and having bear children. The bear is a sacred animal and enters into many Native American myths, ceremonies, and beliefs among the peoples of the North Pacific Coast, California, the Plateau, Plains, Central Woodlands, and the Southwest.

 When Bear Woman commits adultery with a bear, her family kills the bear, and she changes into a bear and attacks her lover's slayers. The murderers flee through magic flight, but she follows. A bird tells her siblings Bear Woman's one vulnerable spot and they kill her. Some versions say the brother and sisters do not return home, but become the Seven Stars (Ursa Major).

See also **Bear Daughter, Bear Maiden, Bear Mother, Chilili Okya, Grizzly Bear Mother,** and **Papawa.** Alternate form: Tcikee Cac Nadleehe. [Bierhorst 1985; Burland 1975; Gill 1992; Leach 1972]

Bear Woman and the Fawns
California, *Lassik*
Justice; Hunting and Wild Animals; Family and Tribes; Destroyer of Life

Malevolent wife of Chicken Hawk.

Grizzly Bear and Deer were the wives of Chicken Hawk. Grizzly Bear killed Deer while she was pretending to delouse Deer's head. She took the head home and roasted it. Deer's children were horrified and cried. Grizzly Bear told them to go out and play. While they were playing, the hair on their mother's head warned them that they were in danger. The fawns smothered Grizzly Bear's children in a fire and took the meat home to Grizzly Bear. When they told her she had eaten her own children, Grizzly Bear chased the fawns toward the river. Old Grandfather Crane was in the river and let the fawns use his neck as a bridge to cross the water. When Grizzly Bear tried to cross, Old Grandfather Crane twisted his neck so she fell off and was carried down the river.

See also **Deer Woman.** [Gill 1992; Leach 1972]

Big Black Meteor Star
Plains, *Pawnee*
Stars and Planets; Health and Healing; Education and Knowledge

"Star of Magic." She is a teacher of medicine women and men. [Burland 1975]

Big Dog
North America
Moon and Night; Magic; Domesticated Animals

Moon goddess.

 Big Dog swallows the sun, causing an eclipse. To keep this from happening, little dogs are whipped to make them howl, which is supposed to make Big Dog desist. [Jobes 1962]

Bikeh Hozho
Southwest, *Navajo*
Happiness

"Happiness Girl." She is the personification of speech. She appears in the Navajo creation story in human-like form. Along with Sa?ah naghai, she gives life to all beings. See also **Estsanatlehi.** [Gill 1992]

Bikeh Xozo
Southwest, *Navajo*
Happiness; Sky and Heavens

"Happiness." Sky goddess. [Haile 1947; Leach 1992]

Black Butte
Northwest, *Warm Springs*
Water; Earth and Nature

Creator deity.

Black Butte and her husband were on a march through Oregon. She was carrying a bag of roots and berries on her back. One day when the sun was very heavy, Black Butte sat down to rest. Her sweat was so profuse that it formed the Metolius River and the roots and berries used the moisture to take root. These became the favorite foods of the people. [Clark 1953]

Blackfoot Earth Woman
Plains, *Blackfoot*
Earth and Nature

The first people were Earth Woman, Sun, and a dog.

Earth Woman told her husband that she would like someone else to live with them. Soon she had two sons. Sun moved far away, but he helps Earth Woman provide food for her children. [Wolf 1977]

Blackfoot First Woman
Plains, *Blackfoot*
Life/Death Cycle; Creator of Life

She was created by the Blackfoot creator god.

Blackfoot First Woman asked the creator god if she and the other people would always be alive. The creator god admitted that he had not given any consideration to the idea. Blackfoot First Woman agreed to throw a stone into the river and the decision would be made—if the stone floated, people would live forever, if it sank the people would die and stay dead. When the stone sank, the people had more sympathy for each other because they knew they would die. [Carlyon 1982; Grinnell 1892]

Blackfoot Old Woman
Plains, *Blackfoot*
Creator of Life

First Woman. She and her husband were the first inhabitants of the world. [Leach 1972]

Blue Jay
Northwest, *Snuqualmi*
Fishing and Water Animals; Wild Birds

Deity who taught the people how to make fishing nets.

Before the earth had changed, there were five women—dog salmon, tyee salmon, silver salmon, steelhead salmon, and rainbow salmon. They came from the west to Snuqualmi River Falls. Here they stole a baby, Blue Jay's grandchild. Blue Jay knew she must do something to help retrieve the child, so she flew to the end of the world and learned how to make nets for catching salmon. [Weigle 1982]

Bowutset
Southwest, *Sia Pueblo*
Creator of Life
First Mother with her sister *Utset.* [Burland 1975]

Bright-Cloud Woman
Northwest, *Tsimshian*
Fishing and Water Animals; Weather
Protector and provider of salmon. Her husband is Txamsem (Raven).

 Bright-Cloud Woman is happily married for a time and she makes her husband prosperous by providing him with lots of salmon. When he falsely accuses her of infidelity, she leaves him and takes her people, the salmon, with her. When he tries to stop her, Bright-Cloud Woman turns to smoke and vanishes. [Gill 1992]

Bright Star
Plains, *Pawnee*
Earth and Nature; Water; Stars and Planets
Mother of all things, the female principle of existence. She made the hills, valleys, trees, grass, and water. She is the mother of *Pawnee First Woman.* She is Venus, the evening star. Alternate forms: Evening Star, Pawnee. [Hultkrantz 1983; Jobes 1962; Savill 1978]

Buffalo Calf Maiden See *White Buffalo Woman.*

Buffalo-calf-road-woman
Plains, *Cheyenne*
War; Hunting and Wild Animals
Warrior goddess. [Burland 1975]

Buffalo Calf Woman See *White Buffalo Woman.*

Buffalo Girl
Plains, *Arikara*
Hunting and Wild Animals; Education and Knowledge
Animal goddess. She is a horned woman who teaches hunting. [Burland 1975]

Buffalo Old Woman
Plains, *Kiowa, Apache*
Hunting and Wild Animals
Equivalent to *White Buffalo Woman.* [Leach 1972]

Buffalo Wife
Plains
Hunting and Wild Animals; Earth and Nature
Goddess of plants and animals.

Buffalo Wife appears as a woman and marries a man. They have a child, but Buffalo Wife is not treated properly by her husband and she takes their child and returns to the buffalo herd. When her husband comes to find her, he is required to identify her and his child in order to be able to take them back. The child gives his father a signal so he can pick them out from the rest of the buffalo.
See also *Hidatsa Buffalo Woman.* [Bierhorst 1985; Leach 1972]

Cactus Grandmother
Southwest, *Tewa*
Selflessness; Ceremonies; Time; Family and Tribes
"Gives of Herself." At ceremonies during the Winter Kiva, she is passed around and around the circle until she vanishes and returns to her people. If she should be dropped during the passing, bad luck will be forthcoming. [Leach 1972]

Ca-the-ña
Southwest, *Mohave*
Love and Sexuality; Creator of Life
Goddess of love, who is called the "Mohave Venus." She promotes fertility among humans and animals. The adopted sister of Ku-yu. [Bourke 1887–1888; Jobes 1962; Leach 1992]

Chahałheeł See *Tcalyel.*

Chakwaina Asho-adta
Southwest, *Hopi*
Unknown
"Chakwaina's Grandmother." She wears an old dress and a wedding belt and appears in Pamyua at First Mesa. Similar to *He-e-e.* See also *Chakwaina Okya.* Alternate form: Chakwaina Sho-adta. [Colton 1949; Wright 1973]

Chakwaina Okya
Southwest, *Zuni*
War; Large Size; Hunting and Wild Animals
"Warrior Woman," "Giant," "Owner of All Game," "Keeper of the Game," "Warrior of the Kianakwe." Goddess of childbirth, who also increases livestock and aids in hunting. She can also exorcise evil and witchcraft. Granddaughter of *Chakwaina Asho-adta* and daughter of *Chakwina Yu-adta.* See also *Chakwena.* Alternate form: Kuyapalitsa. [Colton 1949; Leach 1992; Tyler 1964; Wright 1985]

Chakwaina Sho-adta See *Chakwaina Asho-adta.*

Chakwaina Yu-adta
Southwest, *Hopi*
Ceremonies; Hunting and Wild Animals
Kachina (see *A-ha Kachin' Mana*) who carries a rattle, bow, and arrows. Mother of *Chakwaina Okya.* Yu-adta is thought to be a Tewa name. [Colton 1949]

Chakwena
Southwest, *Laguna Pueblo*
Large Size
Giant. In an adventure the hero killed her. See also *Chakwaina Okya.* [Leach 1972]

Changing Bear Maiden See *Tcikee Cac Nadleehe.*

Changing Woman See *Estsanatlehi.*

Cherokee First Woman
Southeast, *Cherokee*
Mother and Guardian; Creator of Life
Ancestor goddess.

The animals and plants were made by an unknown spirit. The first humans were a brother and sister. First Woman was struck with a fish by her brother, after which she began to give birth to children. Every seven days she gave birth to another child and it seemed that she might overpopulate the earth. It was then decided that she should have only one child in a year and it has been that way ever since. [Mooney 1900]

Cherokee Sun Goddess
Southeast, *Cherokee*
Sun and Day
Companion of the moon god. [Leach 1992]

Cherokee Maize Mother
Southeast, *Cherokee*
Goddess who brought beans and corn to the people. See also *Corn Mother.* [Eliade 1987]

Chilili Okya
Southwest, *Zuni*
Hunting and Wild Animals
   "Bear Old Woman" or "Bear Foot Woman." The bear is a sacred animal among many Native American peoples. See also *Bear Woman.* Alternate form: Tchilili Okya. [Leach 1972; Wright 1985]

Chimon Mana
Southwest, *Hopi*
Magic; Unhappiness
   "Jimson Weed Maiden." A young, somewhat good-looking woman who preys upon males. She has the power to cause insanity. Alternate form: Maswik' Chin' Mana. [Colton 1949; Wright 1973; Wright 1977]

Chuginadak
Arctic, *Aleut Inuit*
Metals and Minerals; Earth and Nature; Fire; Disorder
   Goddess of minerals and volcanoes.

 Chuginadak was a proud woman who did not choose to marry any of the men in her village. She left her home and set out to find the man she wanted for her husband. She magically walked across the water from island to island until she finally found the man. They embraced and made love so passionately that the man died. When the man's father found that his son had died, he was very angry and sent warriors and magic spirits against Chuginadak. She was invulnerable, but she returned to the village and explained to the man's father how much she had loved his son and what had happened. Hearing this, he magically raised his son from the dead, and Chuginadak and her lover were reunited and became the leaders of the people.
   See also *Fuj,* Far East; *Aetna,* Greek and Roman Empires; *Pele,* Oceania. [Monaghan 1981]

Chuhna
California
Household Affairs
   Goddess of thread and ropes. [Weigle 1982]

Chulavete
Arizona, *Pima*
Stars and Planets
   "Morning Star." Stellar deity worshiped in Mexico and Arizona. [Alexander 1964; Leach 1992]

Chumash Moon Woman
California, *Chumash*
Moon and Night
   Moon goddess who lives in a house near that of Sun. [Blackburn 1975]

Chup
California, *Chumash*
Earth and Nature; Weather; Fire; Intelligence and Creativity; Family and Tribes
   "Mother of the Indians." Earth goddess whose aspects are wind, rain, and fire. She provides food and has the power of reason and all emotions. Her ritual name is Hutash. Alternate forms: Chupu, Shup. [Hudson 1978; Leach 1992]

Chupu   See *Chup.*

Cisiud
Northwest, *Skagit*
Household Affairs; Mother and Guardian
   "Female Siud" (guardian). Protector of the house and family members. She appears in the form of a woman with long hair that reaches the ground, covering her face and body. [Collins 1974]

Cochiti Mother
Southwest, *Cochiti Pueblo*
Heaven and Hell; Agriculture; Creator of Life
   "The Mother." Underground goddess of corn and fertility.

 When Cochiti Mother abandoned her children they sent messengers to her underground home asking for help. In return, she sent them a maize figure as a substitute mother. [Eliade 1987]

Coeur D'Alene Mother
Central Plateau, *Coeur D'Alene*
Earth and Nature
   Mother Earth. [Boas and Teit 1985]

Cold Woman
Southwest
Weather; Disorder
   Name for *Changing Woman* when she summons a storm that kills most of the gods. See also *Estsanatlehi.* [Bierhorst 1985; Moon 1984]

Copper Woman
Subarctic, *Chipewyan, Dogrib*
Metals and Minerals
   Mineral and copper goddess.

 Copper Woman was the first woman and she had sex with a dog who became a man at night. They had six puppies, three of whom remained dogs and three of whom changed into humans, becoming the ancestors of the Dogrib.
   See also *Djilaqons* and *Volcano Woman.* [Bierhorst 1985; Gill 1992; Leach 1972; MacNeish 1981]

Corn Maidens
North America, *Zuni*
Agriculture; Ceremonies; Wild Birds; Weather; Poverty
   Six Kachinas (see *A-ha Kachin' Mana*) representing yellow, blue, red, white, black, and mixed colors of corn. They arrive in the *Molawai* ceremony on the last day of the *Shalako* ceremony. (See *Sio Shalako Mana* for description of ceremony.)

 One of the Corn Maidens was offended by a bow priest. The maidens left for the ocean, taking all the corn with them. They were aided by Duck, who put them under her wings and carried them under the water. This was the beginning of seven years of famine. Newekwe Youth was sent in search of them (or, alternatively, the warrior twins went on an unsuccessful search, during which they created the Milky Way) and eventually the Corn Maidens returned.
   See also *Corn Mother* and *Corn Woman* (this region), and *Sago Woman,* Southeast Asia. [Bunzel 1984; Gill 1992; Tyler 1964; Wright 1985]

Corn Mother
Plains, *Arikara, Pawnee, Cheyenne, Mandan, Hidatsa*
Education and Knowledge; Ceremonies; Health and Healing; Agriculture
   Corn personified as woman.

In early times, the Arikara world was populated by giants. The creator god, Nesaru, was angry with the giants and destroyed them with a flood. First he turned some of the smaller people into corn and sent them and some of the animals to live underground during the flood. From the corn growing in heaven, he took an ear and turned it into Corn Mother. She went down to earth and found the people and the animals. With the help of Mouse, Mole, and Badger, a hole was dug to the surface of the earth. With Corn Mother leading them, they began their journey to the west. Before she finally left them, she taught the people many things: how to plant corn, to play games, to study the stars and planets, to honor the gods in the sky with smoke, and to make sacred medicine bundles. Mother Corn then became a cedar tree so she could stay with her people.

Corn plays a key role in the mythology and ritual of many of the corn-growing cultures and is connected with fertility and medicine. See also *Cherokee Maize Mother, Corn Maidens, Corn Woman, Creek Maize Mother, Natchez Maize Mother, Pawnee Corn Mother, Selu,* and *Tewa Corn Mother.* Alternate form: Mother Sunset Yellow. [Bierhorst 1985; Burland 1975; Curtis 1908]

Corn Soot Woman   See *Ioashkanake.*

Corn Woman
Southeast, *Abnaki, Cherokee, Huron*
Agriculture; Hunting and Wild Animals; Goodness
   Deity found in a variety of stories. Sometimes corn grows from her blood, which has been scattered on the fields after her death. She may appear as a single green stalk of corn and teach hunting secrets and the importance of generosity, or she may be one of three sisters who are responsible for corn, beans, and squash. See also *Selu, Corn Mother, Yellow Woman,* and *Corn Maidens.* See also *Uke-mochi-no-kami,* Far East, and *Hainuwule,* Oceania. [Gill 1992; Leach 1972]

Cotsipamapot
Great Basin, *Paiute, Moapa*
Creator of Life
   Creator of the whole country.
   Cotsipamapot is still living. When the people die, they go to her. The people do not know where they go when they die, but Cotsipamapot does. She also makes new people. She knows everything. She makes animals out of mud and creates all the languages. [Gill 1992; Leach 1992; Weigle 1982]

Creator Being
Northwest, *Clallams*
Water; Creator of Life
   Goddess of Puget Sound in Washington. [Tyler 1964]

Creek Maize Mother
Southeast, *Creek*
Agriculture
   Goddess who brought beans and maize to the people. See also *Corn Mother.* [Eliade 1987]

Cu-piritta-ka
Plains, *Pawnee*
Stars and Planets
   "Female White Star." Her name refers to her place in the sky, not to the belief that she is a star.
   Cu-piritta-ka sent her daughter to earth to rule over the earth lodge of the west, which contained all the animals. Wanting women to be superior to men, Cu-piritta-ka told her daughter to kill any young man who sought her attention, assuming that all other women would do the same.
   See also *Evening Star.* [Gill 1992]

Dagwanoenyent
Northeast, *Seneca*
Evil; Magic; Weather; Disorder
   Evil witch who lives in the north. Daughter of the wind, she often manifests as a whirlwind. [Gill 1992]

Dah-ko-beed
Northwest, *Duwamish*
Earth and Nature
   "Tacoma." Earth goddess of the Cascade Mountains. Alternate form: Tacoma. [Monaghan 1981]

Daughter of the Sun
Northwest, *Salish, Nisqually, Yakima*
Creator of Life
   Ancestor deity, daughter of the sun. Her husband was Yehl, the primeval bird. [Brinton 1876]

Dawn (Seneca)
Northeast, *Seneca*
Dawn and Twilight
   Light goddess. She lives at Sky Fields and turns Night Wind into Morning Star to herald her return. [de Wit 1979]

Dawn Woman
Northeast, *Algonquin, Ottawa*
Dawn and Twilight
   Daughter of the moon. Dawn Woman gives birth to the sun each day, dying in the process. [Brinton 1876; Brinton 1882]

Death-bringing-woman
Northwest, *Kwakiutl*
Destroyer of Life
   Death goddess. [Locher 1932]

Deer Mothers, The
Southwest, *Taos Pueblo*
Hunting and Wild Animals
   Goddesses of animals. See also *Deer Woman.* [Tyler 1964]

Deer Woman
Southwest, *Lassik, Zuni*
Hunting and Wild Animals; Family and Tribes
   Deity who appears in a variety of stories. She is usually a mother, sister, or wife of another animal character.
   Deer Woman married a man, but she left him because he criticized her eating habits. She departed, taking their son with her.
   See also *Bear Woman and the Fawns* and *Deer Mothers.* [Gill 1992]

Deohako
Northeast, *Seneca*
Agriculture
   Collective name for the three daughters of the Earth Mother. They are the guardians and spirits of corn, beans, and squash. See also *Onatah.* [Jobes 1962; Leach 1972]

Djabani
Southwest, *Navajo*
Directions
   Goddess of the east. Also the name of a male deity. [Leach 1992]

Dji Sisnaxitl   "Slave-owner." See *Qamaits.*

Djigonsasee
Northeast, *Huron*
Family and Tribes; Order
   Virgin mother of Degganiwada. Her son was the founder of the Six Nations. Djigonsasee participated in peace-keeping by carrying messages and treaties between the nations. [Bray 1935; Monaghan 1981]

Djilaqons
Northwest, *Haida*
Family and Tribes
   Ancestor of the Eagle clan who lives in the water. Her husband is Ka?iti, the chief of the Grizzly Bears. In stories of the peoples' migration across the Aleutian Islands, she is

portrayed as *Copper Woman, Frog Woman,* or *Volcano Woman.* See also *Dzelarhons* and *Yelu Kxinang.* [Gill 1992]

Dogrib First Woman
Subarctic, *Dogrib*
Family and Tribes; Domesticated Animals
  She gave birth to six puppies—three became the ancestors of the people, three remained dogs. [Leach 1972]

Duh-hwahk
Northwest, *Nooksakk, Lummi*
Weather
  "Clear Sky." [Clark 1953]

Dzelarhons
Northwest, *Haida*
Justice; Earth and Nature
  Ruler of the earth creatures, who punishes any humans who abuse them. Also called *Volcano Woman* and *Frog Princess.*
  Dzelarhons came out of the sea with six canoe loads of people. Since canoes could be 40 to 50 feet in length, she must have had a large group of people with her. She married the bear god. Because some fisherman insulted her, she caused a fire that destroyed a village. As a frog, she was offended by some hunters and she destroyed all the people, except one, with a volcanic eruption.
  This story is also told about *Djilaqons*—they may be the same goddess. [Bierhorst 1985; Burland 1975; Leach 1972; Monaghan 1981]

Dzoo-noo-qua
Northwest, *Kwakiutl*
Ugliness; Large Size
  Ugly giant who steals children. Sky Boy kills her and frees all the children. See also *Asin* and *Snee-nee-iq.* [Gill 1992]

Eagentci
Northeast, *Seneca*
  Seneca name for Huron *Adtaensic.* See also *Ketq Skwanya* and *Woman Who Fell from the Sky.* [Jobes 1962; Gill 1992]

Earth Altar Young Woman See *Mamzrau Mana.*

Ee-eh-ch-choo-ri-ch'ahm-nin
Southwest, *Isleta Pueblo*
Magic; Reptiles; Goodness; Agriculture
  "Yellow Corn Maidens." They were witches who turned into benevolent snakes.

Ee-loolth
Northwest, *Duwamish*
Earth and Nature
  Mountain goddess. [Clark 1953]

Eithinoha
Northeast, *Iroquois*
Earth and Nature
  "Earth Goddess." Mother of *Onatah,* the corn/wheat goddess. Similar to *Nokomis.* [Jobes 1962; Leach 1992; Savill 1978; Senior 1985]

Elihino
Southeast, *Cherokee*
Earth and Nature
  Earth Mother. Sister of *Corn Woman, Sehu Woman,* and the Sun, *Igaehinvdo.* [Durdin-Robertson 1982]

Erlaveersisoq
Arctic, *Greenland*
Water; Destroyer of Life
  "The One Who Removes Entrails." If the victim could be made to laugh, this goddess split them open and removed their entrails. See also *Irdlirvirisissong* and *Ululiarnaq.* Alternate form: Erhlaveersissoq. [Eliade 1987; Wyers 1932]

Erhlaveersissoq See *Erlaveersisoq.*

Esceheman
Plains, *Cheyenne, Arapaho*
Earth and Nature
  "Our Grandmother." Earth goddess. [Leach 1992; Powell 1969]

Esdzanata
Southwest, *Navajo*
Time
  Guardian of the calendar stone. [Turner 1974]

Estanatlehi See *Estsanatlehi.*

Estsanatlehi
Southwest, *Navajo*
Time; Magic; Life/Death Cycle; Immortality
  "Self-renewing One." Also called *Changing Woman,* Estsanatlehi can change at will from a child to a young woman to a very old woman. Daughter of *Naestan* and also said to be the sister of Changing Woman. Parent, with the Sun, of the twins Monster Slayer and Born for Water, who rid the earth of monsters. She is also called *Abalone Woman, Cold Woman, Jet Woman, Salt Woman, Turquoise Woman,* and *Whiteshell Woman* (or Yolkai Estan) which may refer to her changes of dress corresponding to the change of the seasons. She controls all fertility and sterility. The first humans are said to have been created with skin rubbed from her body. She is the essence of death and re-birth and is similar to *Niigua* and *Dao,* Far East. Also similar to *White-Painted Woman, Iatiku,* and *Moon Woman.* See also *Asdzaa Dootlijii, Bikeh Hozho Malokatsiki,* and *Ahnt Kai,* Central America and Mesoamerica. Alternate forms: Ahsonnutli, Changing Woman, Estanatlehi, Estsanatlehi, Ests'unnadlehi, Jet Woman. [Cotterell 1979; Gill 1992; Jobes 1962; Leach 1972; Leach 1992; Monaghan 1981; Moon 1984; Senior 1985; Stone 1979]

Ests'unnadlehi See *Estsanatlehi.*

Eithinoha See *Nokomis.*

Evening Star
Plains, *Skidi, Pawnee, Klamath*
Directions; Stars and Planets
  Goddess who lives in the west and holds up the sky. Companion of *Pawnee Moon Woman.*
  The creator told Evening Star to make clouds, wind, lighting, and thunder in the sky. When the storm was over there was a great ocean below. Then the earth appeared. Evening Star mated with Morning Star and their daughter became First Woman. Before they could mate, however, Morning Star had to overcome an obstacle, Evening Star's toothed vagina.
  See also *Cu-piritta-ka, Toothed Vagina, Korawini?i,* and *Poo?wavil.* [Bierhorst 1985; Carlyon 1982; Marriott 1975; Savill 1978]

Evening Star Lady
Northeast, *Winnebago*
Stars and Planets
   The fairest of all. When she rises the calendar men make a cut in their calendar sticks. She is the one to whom lovers sing happy songs and tell secrets.
 One night, Evening Star Lady ran away with Thunderbird. This made the people very sad, so the Great Spirit caught Thunderbird and returned Evening Star Lady to the sky. [de Wit 1979]

Ewauna
Northwest, *Coquille*
Creator of Life; Metals and Minerals
   Creator goddess personified by the rock formations along the Oregon coast at the mouth of the Coquille River. [Brinton 1876]

Five Sisters, The
Northeast, *Iroquois*
Agriculture
   Food goddesses. They protect the corn, squash, and pumpkins. [Burland 1975]

Foam Mother
Southwest, *Pueblos*
Water; Weather
   Water goddess. She provides rainbows, thunderbolts, and the fog that creates the clouds. [Burland 1975]

Foam Woman
Northwest, *Haida*
Family and Tribes; Water
   Creator deity. She appeared at the time of the flood and was the great-grandmother of the Raven Clan families.
 Foam Woman had twenty breasts, ten on each side. Each breast nursed one of the grandmothers of each of the future Raven Clan families. [Bierhorst 1985]

Fox Earth Goddess
Northeast, *Fox*
Hunting and Wild Animals; Earth and Nature
   The earth is a woman upon which we live. She gives us food to eat and a place to dwell. [Hultkrantz 1983]

Fox Moon Goddess
Northeast, *Sauk, Fox*
Moon and Night; Goodness; Hunting and Wild Animals
   She is beneficent and does not cause harm like the sun god. [Hultkrantz 1983]

Frog Princess   See *Dzelarhons.*

Frog Woman
California, *Luiseno*
Evil; Fishing and Water Animals; Selfishness
   Malevolent deity.
Frog Woman hated Wiyot, the guardian of earthly things, because he had more beautiful legs than hers. Frog Woman spit in the spring that he drank from and he died.
   See also *Djilaqons.* [Leach 1972]

Ga-go-sa Ho-nun-nas-tase-ta, The
Northeast, *Iroquois*
Evil
   "Mistress of the False-faces." Demons who have no bodies. [Leach 1992; Morgan 1901]

Gaende'sonk
Northeast, *Iroquois*
Weather; Sky and Heavens
   "Gusts of Wind." Daughter of *Awenhai* and Haonhwendj-iawa'qi. She created the sun and moon from her body. [Gray 1925; Leach 1992]

Gahondjidahonk
Northeast, *Seneca*
Family and Tribes; Fire; Selfishness
   "She Who Is Burned in Many Places." Gahondjidahonk belongs to a group of women who try to destroy their daughters' husbands on their wedding night. The women jump into the fire, and when the sons-in-law try to save them, they are burned to death. The women survive because they are immune to fire, and occasionally a new son-in-law is not destroyed because he knows of the trick and does not try to rescue his mother-in-law. [Gill 1992]

Gendenwitha
Northeast, *Iroquois*
Selfishness; Magic; Love and Sexuality; Stars and Planets
   "She Who Brings the Day." The Morning Star.
 Gendenwitha was beloved by the great hunter, Sosondowah. Dawn, who also loved the hunter, was jealous. She captured Gendenwitha and turned her into a star on Dawn's forehead so that she precedes dawn each day. The lovers can see each other, but can never be joined.
   See also *Morning-Star Woman.* [Burland 1975; Carlyon 1982; Guirand 1968; Leach 1992; Monaghan 1981]

Genetaska
Northeast, *Iroquois*
Order; Family and Tribes
   "Mother of Nations." Peacemaker among the Six Iroquois Nations. Alternate forms: Jigonsahseh, Yegowaneh. [Bray 1935; Monaghan 1981]

Geyaguga
Southeast, *Cherokee*
Moon and Night
   "*Nuñda* That Dwells in the Night." Sister of the sun, *Nuñda.* [Leach 1992; Maclean 1896; Spence 1925b]

Ghost-Face-Woman
Northwest, *Kwakiutl*
Heaven and Hell
   Underworld goddess. [Locher 1932]

Glisma   See *Glispa.*

Glispa
Southwest, *Navajo*
Education and Knowledge; Magic; Heaven and Hell; Ceremonies; Health and Healing
   Underworld goddess of magic. Glispa came from the lower world to teach the people ceremonies, chants, sand-painting, and the feather-prayer offerings. She gave them the gift of healing and the powers of shamans. Alternate form: Glisma. [Burland 1975]

Gnaski
Plains, *Oglala, Lakota*
Evil
   Demon. Daughter of Unk and Iya. She is frightened of medicine bags. [Leach 1992; Walker 1980]

Godasiyo
Northeast, *Seneca*
Family and Tribes; Disorder

A chief of the people when the earth was new.

 Godasiyo was the chief of the people on one side of the river. They lived peacefully with their neighbors on the other side of the river and all the people spoke the same language. Godasiyo's dog began to cause trouble so she decided to move her people upstream. They built canoes to go to their new home, building a special one for Godasiyo, a catamaran. When they reached a fork in the river, her people began to argue, and the platform Godasiyo was riding on split. Godasiyo fell into the river and became a fish. The people were upset but found they could not communicate with each other as they now spoke different languages. This is the reason there are so many languages. [Gill 1992]

Goddesses of the Eastern and Western Ocean, The
North America, *Many tribes*
Creator of Life; Water; Directions
   Creator deities.

 The Goddess of the Eastern Ocean and the Goddess of the Western Ocean met over the water on the rainbow bridge. Realizing there was nothing below but water, they concentrated together and made land appear. The Goddess of the Eastern Ocean made a little wren out of clay and together they made it come to life. They continued until they had created all the birds and animals and then they created First Woman. [Johnson 1988]

Go-gome-tha-na   See *Kokumthena.*

Gogyeng So Wuhti
Plains; Southwest, *Hopi, Kiowa*
Insects; Sun and Day; Fire
   "Spider Grandmother." The Hopi brought her with them to the Black Mesa. The Kiowa say that it was Gogyeng So Whuti who brought the sun for her people, making the world light. She saved a small piece of the sun, bringing it down to earth so her people could have fire. See also *Kokyang Wuhti* and *Spider Woman.* Alternate forms: Gogyeng sowhuti, Grandmother Spider. [Moon 1984; Stone 1979]

Grandmother
Southeast, *Creek*
Earth and Nature; Agriculture
   Earth mother. She gave the people maize. [Burland 1975]

Grandmother Datura   See *Momoy.*

Grandmother Earth
Mexico, *Kickapoo*
Earth and Nature
   Fertility goddess. She sustains herself by eating the bodies that are buried in her. She is offered tobacco at planting time so she will provide abundant crops of corn, beans, and squash. She is also a source of wisdom. [Latorre and Latorre 1976]

Grandmother Moon
Mexico, *Kickapoo*
Mother and Guardian; Moon and Night
   Moon deity who provides food.

 It is Kickapoo Grandmother Moon's face that we see in the moon. She is there stirring a kettle of food for her people, and if she stops the world will end. [Latorre and Latorre 1976]

Grandmother of Nava
Southwest, *Navajo*
Family and Tribes; Earth and Nature; Ceremonies
   Ancestor deity.

 Many years ago Grandmother of Nava brought nine races from her home in the west. They were the deer race, sand race, water race, bear race, hare race, prairie-wolf race, rattlesnake race, tobacco-plant race, and reed-grass race. Once they were placed, she transformed them into humans and their races became the special totems of their clan. [Emerson 1965]

Grandmother Spider
Southeast, *Cherokee, Tewa, Kiowa*
Creator of Life; Sun and Day; Fire; Education and Knowledge; Ceremonies; Insects
   Creator deity who brought the sun and fire to humans. She taught them how to make pottery, bows and arrows, and how to braid the bow string. She also gave instructions about sweat baths, ceremonies, and blessings. See also *Spider Woman.* Alternate form: Gogyeng So Whuti. [Bierhorst 1985]

Greenland Sun Goddess
Arctic, *Greenland Inuit*
Sun and Day
   Sun deity.

 Sun had a lover, but she did not know who he was. In the darkness, she marked her lover with some soot and she discovered he was her brother, Moon. She ran away, carrying a torch. He followed her, and now they follow each other across the sky.
   See also *Akycha, Siqiniq,* and *Sun Sister.* [Damas 1984]

Grizzly Bear Mother
Northwest, *Modoc*
Family and Tribes; Hunting and Wild Animals
   Mother goddess around Mt. Shasta area. Ancestor of all the tribes. See also *Bear Woman.* [Clark 1953]

Gyhldeptis
Northwest, *Tlingit, Haida*
Earth and Nature; Mother and Guardian
   "Hanging Hair." Forest goddess who protects people from harm. Her hair hangs from the cedar trees in the rain forest. [Burland 1975; Monaghan 1981]

Hahai-i Wuhti
Southwest, *Hopi*
Ceremonies; Demi-animals
   "Pour Water Woman," "Kachina Mother," or "Kachina Grandmother." Mother of all kachinas (see *A-ha Kachin' Mana*), along with Crow Mother. She is also the mother of the monsters, the Nataskas, and dogs. She is quite vocal, which is unusual, and is the principal actor in the Water Serpent Ceremony. She also participates in the *Niman* or Home Dance (the last dance before the kachinas depart for their home in the San Francisco Mountains). Wuhti indicates a married woman. [Colton 1949; Wright 1973; Wright 1977]

Ha-Ha-Uh

Ha-Ha-Whu Okya   See *Mukikwe Okya.*

Haialilaqs
Northwest, *Kwakiutl*
Health and Healing
   "Healing-woman and Pestilence-woman." [Locher 1932]

Haka Lasi
California
Fire; Immortality; Wild Birds
   "Loon Woman." A fire goddess.

 A young girl started a fire on earth and her family fell into it. As they burned, their hearts flew out of their bodies and Haka Lasi gathered them up, making them

into a necklace that she wore. When Haka Lasi was killed, the family was revived and lived again. [Leach 1992; Weigle 1982]

Hakulaq
Northwest, *Tsimshian, Kwakiutl*
Disorder; Destroyer of Life; Wealth; Heaven and Hell; Evil; Water
Water monster who causes storms. Also a deity of wealth and the underworld. Originally named ***Lennaxidag*** (see for story), she became the monster Hakulaq because of her child.

 Hakulaq lets her child float in the water between two islands. When travelers rescue the child, Hakulaq accuses them of kidnapping. She then causes a storm that kills the people. [Gill 1992; Locher 1932]

Han
Plains, *Lakota, Oglala Sioux*
Sun and Day; Moon and Night; Primordial Being
"Black of Darkness." Primordial goddess. The god Skan split her in two: one half became the night and the other half became the day and was given another name. [Bierhorst 1985; Leach 1992; Monaghan 1981; Walker 1980]

Hano
Northwest, *Bella Coola*
Magic; Education and Knowledge
Goddess at Qwaqmai on Schooner Pass. Hano manifested as a shaman so she could teach the people. *Sutal* and *Wilx* were her companions at the Nass River. [McIlwraith 1948]

Hano Mana
Southwest, *Hopi*
Ceremonies; Agriculture
"Tewa Girl." Fertility deity who participates in the *Pawamu* ceremony or Bean Dance. Her likeness is given to the girls at Tewa, just as *Hahai-i Wuhti* is given to the girls of Hopi. [Colton 1949; Wright 1973; Wright 1977]

Hanwi
Plains, *Oglala, Lakota Sioux*
Moon and Night; Dawn and Twilight
Sky and moon goddess. She rules the night, including dawn and twilight. Her husband is the sun, Wi.

 Hanwi was embarrassed when her husband Wi allowed Ite, who wanted to become Wi's companion, to come between them. The god Skan gave Hanwi the freedom to go her own way and made her ruler of the night. [Bierhorst 1985; Leach 1992; Monaghan 1981; Walker 1980]

Harurai Chatutai   See *Atavish.*

Has-gueme
Southeast, *Delaware*
Fate; Agriculture
Corn goddess who has the power of prophecy. [Leach 1992]

Hasinais Goddesses, The
Plains, *Hasinais*
Courage
Three deities.

 In primordial times, a woman and her two daughters confronted the devil. He ate one of the daughters, and from one drop of her blood the first male god came forth and became the ruler of the world. [Bolton 1987]

Hastseoltoi
Southwest, *Navajo*
Hunting and Wild Animals
Goddess of hunting. [Burland 1975; Leach 1992]

Hatai Wugti   See *Hatai Wuhti.*

Hatai Wuhti
Southwest, *Hopi*
Earth and Nature; Insects
Earth goddess who manifests as a large-bodied spider. Wuhti indicates a married woman. Alternate forms: Hatai Wugti, Hatai wugti, Awitelin Tsita, Spider Woman. [Burland 1975; Fewkes 1985; Monaghan 1981]

Hatcher, The
Plains, *Lakota Sioux*
Creator of Life
"First Woman."

 The Holy Mystery made his people out of clay and fired them to give them solidity and color. One day one of his figures was more pleasing to look at than the others and he called her The Hatcher. The others he called The Planters and together they were the Lakota. [LaPointe 1976]

H'ativa
Plains, *Pawnee*
Agriculture
"Mother-breathing Life." Corn goddess who is the daughter of earth mother *H'uraru*, and heaven father. [Jobes 1962]

Ha-Wha-Whoa   See *Mukikwe Okya.*

Hawichyepam Maapuch
California, *Chemehuevi*
Water; Supreme Being
"All-powerful." She manifests as a power rather than a being.

 Hawichyepam Maapuch caused the water covering the world to recede. Once the water was gone, Coyote and Puma, who had been on the top of Charleston Peak above the water, were able to descend and populate the world.
Hawichyepam Maapuch also appears in the Mohave origin tale. [Leach 1972]

Hayicanak   See *Hayicanako.*

Hayicanako
Northwest, *Tlingit*
Earth and Nature; Disorder; Ceremonies
"The Old Woman Underneath." She supports the earth either by holding it or by tending the beaver leg post that holds it. She causes earthquakes, which her people believe means she is hungry. To appease her they throw grease on the fire so it will melt and run down to her. Alternate form: Hayicanak. [Gill 1992; Leach 1972; Leach 1992; Savill 1978]

Hayoołkaał Asdzą́ą́
Southwest, *Navajo*
Dawn and Twilight; Creator of Life
Dawn Woman. Creator deity who lives in the north and is responsible for making people think. She determines which "Wind Soul" each child will have at birth. See also *Xayołká·ł 'esząˊ.* [Leach 1992; McNeley 1981]

Hé-é-e
Southwest, *Hopi*
War
"Warrior Maid." Spirit of the Oraibis Kachina (see *A-ha Kachin' Mana*), she leads the noisy, threatening kachinas in the procession to the village during the Pachavu ceremony, the dramatization of historical events.

Hé-é-e was having her hair groomed by her mother, when there was an attack on her village. Hé-é-e gathered the men and successfully fought off the enemy.
Similar to *Chakwaina Asho-adta* and *Heoto Mana.* Alternate form: He' Wuhti. [Colton 1949; Fewkes 1985; Leach 1992; Wright 1973]

He' Wuhti See *Hé-é-e.*

Heavy Woman
Plains, *Hidatsa*
Heaven and Hell
   Underworld goddess. She keeps the dead in the underworld. [Bierhorst 1985]

Hehea Mana See *Heheya Kachin' Mana.*

Heheya Kachin' Mana
Southwest, *Hopi*
Agriculture; Ceremonies
   Kachina (see *A-ha Kachin'Mana*) who appears in the *Powamu* ceremony or Bean Dance at Second Mesa. On the First Mesa, she lassos those who were delinquent in giving food gathered on the collecting trip. Alternate form: Hehea Mana. [Colton 1949; Fewkes 1985; Wright 1973]

Hekoolas
California, *Miwok*
Sun and Day; Fishing and Water Animals
   Sun goddess. Her body is covered with abalone shells.
 When Hekoolas lived in another world, our sky was dark and cold. Oye the Coyote sent some men to bring Hekoolas to our world. She did not want to come but they roped her and dragged her back so we would have sunlight.
   See also *Kanene Ski Amai Yehi.* [Monaghan 1981]

Heloha
Southeast, *Choctaw*
Weather; Wild Birds
   Goddess of thunder. A female thunderbird. [Burland 1975; Leach 1992]

Hemis Kachin' Mana
Southwest, *Hopi*
Ceremonies
   "Hemis Kachina Girl." The Hemis Kachinas (see *A-ha Kachin' Mana*) are the most common at the *Niman* ceremony (the home-going ceremony, after which the kachinas return to the San Francisco Mountains). Depending on whom she accompanies and what objects she holds in her hands, she is called by different names including *Ahöla Mana, Kachin' Mana,* and *Qoia Akachin Mana.* See also *Hona Mana* and *Hokyang Maha.* Alternate forms: Alo Mana, Hemis Mana. [Colton 1949; Wright 1973; Wright 1977]

Hemis Mana See *Hemis Kachin' Mana.*

Hemokatsiki See *Ahe'a.*

Hemushikwe Okya
Southwest, *Zuni*
Ceremonies
   Dancer and dance companion of the male, Hemushikwe. Alternate forms: Nahalic Okya, Nahalish' Okya. [Wright 1985]

Heoto Mana
Southwest, *Hopi*
War

Warrior Maiden. A kachina (see *A-ha Kachin' Mana*) who dances on all three mesas. Similar to *Hé-é-e.* [Wright 1973]

Hetethlokya
Southwest, *Zuni*
Metals and Minerals
   "Clay Woman." She gives of herself to potters. [Leach 1972]

Hidatsa Buffalo Woman
Plains, *Hidatsa*
Magic; Mother and Guardian; Hunting and Wild Animals
   Food goddess associated with the Buffalo Ceremony, *Mitĕ-kéikŭ,* to call back the herd when food is scarce.
 Traveling north with the herd, a buffalo cow injured her leg and could not continue. She stopped in a ravine where there was grass and water and she would be hidden. Very soon she delivered a bull calf and, fearing that a nearby camp might find them, she turned herself and her child into human beings. Buffalo Woman built a lodge and, because she was still lame, she sent her son to gather bark and grass that she magically turned into meat. She then sent her son to the village with pemmican and told him to make friends with the chief's daughter. The chief's wife came to visit and removed the thorn from Buffalo Woman's foot and dressed it so it would heal. Buffalo Woman asked to live in the village and to have her son marry the chief's daughter, and the chief's wife gladly consented. When food was short, Buffalo Woman turned her son back into a buffalo and sent him to find his father in the north and ask him to bring the buffalo south. His task accomplished, the son returned to the village and became a man once more. Soon the buffalo came from the north and there was food once again.
   See also *Buffalo Wife.* [Curtis 1908]

Hihankara
Plains, *Lakota Sioux*
Immortality; Stars and Planets; Justice; Wild Birds
   "Owl Maker."
 Hinhankara is an old woman who guards the Spirit Road (Milky Way), the path deceased human spirits must follow. She examines each spirit (nagi) to see if it has an identifying tattoo. If there is no mark, the spirit is pushed from the path toward earth where it lands and becomes a ghost. [Gill 1992]

Hila
Arctic, *Caribou Inuit*
Weather
   Weather deity who presides over cold weather. Sometimes seen as male. [Leach 1992; Nungak 1969; Rasmussen 1929]

Hilili Okya
Southwest, *Zuni*
Reptiles
   "Snake Dance Girl." [Wright 1985]

Hishikoyatsaspa
Southwest, *Sia Pueblo*
Earth and Nature
   Earth goddess. [Fewkes 1895c; Leach 1992]

Hoho Mana
Southwest, *Hopi*
Ceremonies
   "Zuni Kachina Girl." (See *A-ha Kachin' Mana* for definition of kachina). Imported by the Hopi from the Zuni shortly before the turn of the twentieth century. She dances with the Zuni Hemis Kachina. See also *Hemis Kachin' Mana.* [Colton 1949; Wright 1973; Wright 1977]

Hokoha Okya
Southwest, *Zuni*
Agriculture; Ceremonies

"Harvest Dance Girl." A kachina (see *A-ha Kachin' Mana*). Similar to Hopi *Yohozro Wuhti*. Alternate form: Oken'ona. [Wright 1985]

Hokyang Mana
Southwest, *Hopi*
Ceremonies; Agriculture

A kachina (see *A-ha Kachin' Mana*). She carries an ear of corn in each hand. See also *Hemis Kachin' Mana*. [Fewkes 1985; Wright 1977]

Hongak
Northeast, *Seneca*
Wild Birds

"Canadian Wild Goose." Her husband is Hagowanen, the great hunter. She is the mother of Othegwenhda, Flint.

Hongak gave Othegwenhda an amulet of flint made in the shape of a finger. The amulet has the power of Hongak, and she asks it for advice and for the ability to transform. [Gill 1992]

Hopi Shalako Mana
Southwest, *Hopi*
Unknown

"Hopi Shalako Girl." She dances with Shalako Taka, her mate. [Wright 1977]

Horo Mana
Southwest, *Hopi*
Ceremonies; Time

"Comb Hair Upwards Girl." Tewa Kachin' Mana dances during the *Powamu* or Bean Dance on First Mesa. She carries a yucca brush and musses people's hair. She appears with *Nuvak'chin' Mana,* who brings cold to the Hopi and whose winter wind messes up Horo Mana's hair. [Colton 1949; Wright 1973; Wright 1977]

Ho-Wha-Whoa   See *Mukikwe Okya.*

Hükyangkwü
Southwest, *Hopi*
Weather; War

"Wind Woman." Malevolent deity of high winds and sandstorms. Her sandstorms are helpful during war. [Leach 1992; Parsons 1939]

Hulluk Miyumko, The
California, *Miwok*
Stars and Planets; Beauty

"Morning Star and the Pleiades." Beautiful star chiefs. They were kept awake to do their job by a whistling elderberry tree. [Monaghan 1990]

H'uraru
Plains, *Pawnee*
Life/Death Cycle; Supreme Being

Mother of life and death. Her daughters are *Uti Hiata* and *H'ativa*. All-seeing and all-knowing, she creates all life and waits for humans to return to her for rebirth. [Jobes 1962; Leach 1992; Monaghan 1981]

Hürü'Ingwühti
Southwest, *Hopi*
Directions; Fishing and Water Animals; Sky and Heavens; Metals and Minerals

"Hard Beings Woman." She has a house in the east or west. According to some, this is the name of twin deities, one who lives in the east and one who lives in the west, between whom the sun travels each day. Yet others say she is the "Mother of the Universe" and to her belong the moon, the stars, and all the hard things like stones, shells, and beads. Alternate form: Huzruwauqti. [Jobes 1962; Moon 1984; Stone 1979; Tyler 1964; Wright 1977]

Ḥutash   See *Chup.*

Hutsipamamau?u
California, *Chemehuevi*
Earth and Nature; Water

"Ocean Woman." Primeval goddess who forms a triad with Wolf and Coyote.

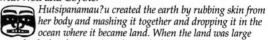 *Hutsipanamau?u created the earth by rubbing skin from her body and mashing it together and dropping it in the ocean where it became land. When the land was large enough, she lay down on it and stretched it to make it even larger. She stopped when Coyote and Wolf said it was large enough.*

Sometimes she is considered a dual deity made up of two sisters or a mother and daughter. [Leach 1992]

Huzruwauqti   See *Hürü' Ingwühti.*

Huzru Wugti
Southwest, *Tusayan*
Earth and Nature

Earth goddess. [Leach 1992]

Iatiku
Southwest, *Acoma, Laguna, Cochiti, Zia*
Creator of Life; Mother and Guardian; Ceremonies

Guardian of humans who is sometimes said to be "the breath of life."

Iatiku and her sisters were planted in the earth by Utsiti. Spider Woman gave the sisters a basket of seeds and images to assist them with creation. Iatiku also made the kachinas and the Kobictaiya (spirit beings similar to kachinas). She made the clown Koshare by rubbing her skin and placing a ball of it under a blanket.

She is prayed to at meal time. One of her sisters is *Nautsiti,* who helped Iatiku disperse the seeds and images of creation. Similar to *Estsanatlehi.* Alternate form: Iyatiku. [Burland 1975; Gill 1992]

Idliragijenget
Arctic, *Central Inuit*
Water

Sea goddess. Equivalent to *Sedna.* [Boas 1884; Leach 1992]

Iemaparu
Southwest, *Isleta Pueblo*
Agriculture

"Corn Mother." [Leach 1992; Parsons 1939]

Igaehinvdo
Southeast, *Cherokee*
Sun and Day

"Sun." Sister of the earth, *Elihino,* and corn, *Sehu Woman.* If she is given proper attention, Igaehinvdo will not burn up the earth. [Durdin-Robertson 1982]

Ignirtoq
Arctic, *Inuit*
Fire; Weather

Lightning goddess. Sister of Kadlu. See also *Ingnirtung.* [Boas 1901; Leach 1992]

Ikalu nappa
Arctic
Demi-animals; Fishing and Water Animals

Half woman and half fish. See also *Sedna.* [Gill 1992]

Ikas
Northeast, *Algonquin*
Earth and Nature
   "Mother Earth." [Jobes 1962]

Imam-shua
Arctic, *Chugach Inuit*
Fishing and Water Animals; Weather; Water
   Sea goddess. She presides over sea animals and good weather. [Leach 1992]

I-nach-tin-ak   See *Mikamatt.*

Ingnirtungl
Arctic
Weather; Fire
   Lightning goddess. See also *Ignirtoq.* [Boas 1884; Leach 1992]

Inuit Earth Mother
Arctic, *Inuit*
Creator of Life; Earth and Nature
   Creator of humans, animals, plants, and fruits in Quebec. [Damas 1984]

Ioashkanake
Southwest, *Cochiti*
Agriculture
   Corn-shuck goddess. Formerly called **Corn Soot Woman.** [Weigle 1982]

Iqalu Nappaa, The
Arctic, *Inuit*
Wealth; Demi-animals; Fishing and Water Animals; Arts
   Mermaids who give wealth to the people from the bottom of the sea and teach humans how to throat-sing. [Dumas 1984]

Iqamiaitx
Northwest, *Chinook*
Water
   Water goddess. Equivalent to *Itclixyan.* [Leach 1992; Spier 1930]

Irdlirvirisissong
Arctic, *Greenland Inuit*
Evil
   "Disemboweller." Demon clown. If you laugh when she is around, she will cut you open and give your intestines to the dogs. See also *Erlaveersisoq* and *Ululiarnaq.* [Burland 1975; Wyers 1932]

Island Woman
Great Basin
Unknown
   Goddess. [Bierhorst 1985]

Itclixyan
Northwest, *Wishram*
Hunting and Wild Animals; Water; Fishing and Water Animals
   Columbia River goddess. She guards the fishers and hunters of water animals. Equivalent to *Iqamiatx.* [Leach 1992; Spier 1930]

I'tc'ts'ity   See *Naotsete.*

Ite
Plains, *Oglala, Lakota Sioux*
Beauty; Selfishness
   Beautiful daughter of the chief of the people, *Ka.* Wife of Tate, the Wind, mother of Wani, four sons who have a combined name and who established the four cardinal directions and who control the four seasons. She was vain, and her plotting to take the place of the Moon as the Sun's companion led to her banishment and her transformation into a two-faced woman. See also *Anog Ite.* [Bierhorst 1985; Gill 1992; Walker 1980]

Itsictsiti   See *Utset.*

Ixlexwani
Northwest, *Bella Coola*
Wild Birds; Sky and Heavens; Demi-animals; Weather
   Sky goddess who came to earth in the form of a golden eagle with her sister, **Sonxwana,** and three brothers. They brought beaver as food for the people.
   When her siblings transformed to humans, Ixlexwani refused to change. She wandered about in a frenzied, semi-human form until her sister and brothers killed her. She is petrified in the valley that bears her name, and it is from here that the coldest winter winds blow. [McIlwraith 1948]

Ixuixiwi
Plains, *Ioway*
Earth and Nature
   "Our Mother, the Earth." [Leach 1992; Skinner 1920]

Iyatiku
Southwest, *Keres*
Life/Death Cycle; Mother and Guardian; Heaven and Hell; Agriculture
   "Corn Mother." She led the people out of their underground world into the sunlight. She fed them her heart, which was corn. It is said that infants come from her underground home when they are born and return to her when they die. She is the mother of **Sha'koa.** Alternate form: Iatiku. [Baumgartner 1984; Cotterell 1979; Gill 1992; Moon 1984]

Jemez Old Woman   See *Ahe'a.*

Jet Woman   See *Estsanatlehi.*

Jigonsahseh   See *Genetaska.*

Ka
Plains, *Lakota*
Creator of Life
   First Woman. Wife of Wa and mother of *Ite.* [Gill 1992]

Ka'a Mata
California, *Pomo*
Sun and Day
   Daylight deity. Her husband is Ka'a djaj, "Daylight Man." [Leach 1992; Loeb 1926]

Ka-mu-iu-dr-ma-giu-iu-e-ba
Southwest, *Havasupai*
Water
   "Mother of the Waters." She mated with rattlesnakes and had two sons, "Children of the Waters." Her sons killed the rattlesnakes, and now lead their people in Havasu Canyon. [Cushing 1882; Leach 1992]

Kachin' Mana
Southwest, *Hopi*
Ceremonies; Agriculture

"Yellow Corn Girl." A kachina (see *A-ha Kachin' Mana*). Alternate form: Hemis Kachin' Mana. [Wright 1973; Wright 1977]

Kadhutetash
Plains, *Hidatsa*
Agriculture; Immortality
"Old Woman Who Never Dies." Corn goddess. [Curtis 1908]

Kadlu
Arctic, *Central Inuit*
Weather
Thunder goddess.

 When Kadlu was a little girl, she was playing outside with her sisters. She jumped on the hollow ice and the sound became thunder. Her sister made lightning by rubbing pieces of flint together. A third sister urinated to make the rain. [Boas 1884; Monaghan 1981; Wallis 1939]

Kahaila Kachin' Mana
Southwest, *Hopi*
Reptiles
"Turtle Maiden." A kachina (see *A-ha Kachin' Mana*) who wears a Rio Grande woman's dress. [Colton 1949]

Kakash Kachina See *Quail Kachin' Mana*.

Kalxsmaknim
Northwest, *Bella Coola*
Unknown
Goddess of Stuix whose sister is *Qopimpmana*. Together their names mean "Rising Dust." Their name came from the dust their brother caused when he threw moose hides down on the floor. [McIlwraith 1948]

Kamaits
Northwest, *Bella Coola*
Directions
"Old Woman." She lives at Atsaakti, a realm in the east. [Leach 1992]

Kanaeski Anaiyehi
Southeast, *Cherokee*
Insects; Fire; Water
"Water Spider." She gave fire to the people. [Turner 1974]

Kanene Ski Amai Yehi
Southeast, *Cherokee*
Insects
"Grandmother Spider." She brought the sun to our world.

 Kanene Ski Amai Yehi made a basket and then spun a web to carry her to the other side of the world. She grabbed the sun, put it in her basket, and brought it back so we would have light.
See also *Hekoolas*. [Monaghan 1981]

Kanilkes
Northwest, *Bella Coola*
Ceremonies; Sky and Heavens
Goddess at Stuix. With O'Mielkes, she brought cone-shaped whistles to the people to use in their ceremonies.

 When Kanilkes and O'Mielkes got to earth, they were very unhappy because they wanted a house. But then night came and they thought they had a house with a beautiful roof. It was the sky covered with bright shining stars.
See also *Kimilkan*. [McIlwraith 1948]

Kannakapfaluk
Arctic, *Copper Inuit*
Water; Weather; Fishing and Water Animals
Sea goddess. She controls the animals and the weather. Equivalent to *Sedna*. [Leach 1992; Wyers 1932]

Kansa First Woman
Subarctic, *Kansa*
Creator of Life; Selfishness

 First Man was in the earth and was very lonely so the god sent him First Woman. They came to the surface and soon were very vain about their long, bushy tails. It is said that the god took away their beautiful tails and made nagging women from them. [Unrau 1971]

Kanuslaliam
Northwest, *Bella Coola*
Metals and Minerals
"Pretty Copper." She lived in the town of Nusxeq with her sister *Atitxmana*. They had a beautiful copper house. The underwater god gave them a loon totem pole. [McIlwraith 1948]

Kashatskihakatidise
Plains, *Wichita*
Agriculture; Moon and Night.
"Bright-shining-woman." Mother Corn who is also the moon. She teaches women about their monthly flow, pregnancy, calendars, and offerings. [Dorsey 1904; Leach 1992]

Kashinako
Southwest, *Sia*
Directions
"White Woman of the East." Goddess of the six directions. [Fewkes 1895c; Leach 1992]

Kato First Woman
North American, *Kato*
Creator of Life
She was made from the first man when the god took one of his legs, split it, and created her. [Thompson 1929]

Kattakju
Arctic, *Baffin Land Inuit*
Health and Healing
Healing goddess. She works with shamans to care for the sick. [Bilby 1923; Leach 1992]

Katuma
Arctic, *Iglulik Inuit*
Fishing and Water Animals; Beauty; Wild Birds; Heaven and Hell; Water
Equivalent to *Sedna*. [Wyers 1932]

Katyutayuuq
Pueblos
Evil
A bodiless monster. [Gill 1992]

Kavna
Arctic, *Nuliayuk Inuit*
Water
Sea goddess. Name for *Nuliajuk* on the coast. [Leach 1992; Nungak 1969]

Kawas
Plains, *Pawnee*
Moon and Night; Water; Wild Birds

Moon and water goddess worshiped in Nebraska. In the Hako ceremony the beneficent brown eagle personifies the female. [Fletcher 1900; Leach 1992]

Kefeliu
Southwest, *Isleta Pueblo*
Fire
Fire goddess who presides at both the hearth and kiva. [Leach 1992; Parsons 1929]

Keninqas
Northwest, *Nootka*
Wild Birds; Water
"Crow."

Keninqas owned all the fresh water and refused to share it with anyone. The chiefs summoned Raven and asked him to get the water from Keninqas. Raven, through trickery, was successful, creating a large lake and all the rivers in the world. [Gill 1992]

Keres Moon Mother
Southwest, *Keres*
Creator of Life
Creator goddess. [Gill 1992]

Keresan Sisters
Southwest, *Acoma Pueblo*
Earth and Nature
Goddesses of animals. They took the animal spirits out of Mother Goddess's basket and made them into earthly creatures. [Tyler 1964]

Ketq Skwayne
Northeast, *Huron, Salish*
Fishing and Water Animals; Creator of Life; Sky and Heavens
"Grandmother Toad." Creator and sky goddess. See also *Aataentsic, Eagentci,* and *Woman Who Fell from the Sky.* [Bierhorst 1985; Burland 1975; Leach 1992; Monaghan 1981]

Ketq Skwaye   See *Ketq Skwayne.*

Khunpinu'a'anyun
Southwest, *Tewa*
Agriculture; Directions
Goddess of red corn from the south. [Harrington 1907; Leach 1992]

Khuntasaengge'i'a'anyun
Southwest, *Tewa*
Agriculture; Directions
Corn goddess who is all colors and comes from the south. [Harrington 1907; Leach 1992]

Khuntsaenyu'a'anyun
Southwest, *Tewa*
Agriculture; Directions
Goddess of white corn from the east. See also *Ang-chin Mana.* [Harrington 1907; Leach 1992]

Khuntsanyu'a'anyun
Southwest, *Tewa*
Agriculture
Goddess of blue corn from the north. [Harrington 1907; Leach 1992]

Khuntseji'a'anyun
Southwest, *Tewa*
Agriculture
Goddess of yellow corn from the west. [Harrington 1907; Leach 1992]

Kikewei p'aide
Southwest, *Isleta Pueblo*
Moon and Night
Mother goddess of the moon. [Leach 1992; Parsons 1929]

Kimilkan
Northwest, *Bella Coola*
Ceremonies; Disorder
Goddess at the village of Atqalaxl. She brought cone-shaped whistles as gifts for the people but they quarreled so much over them that she left the earth in disgust. See also *Kanilkes.* [McIlwraith 1948]

Kivish Atakvish
California, *La Jolla*
Sky and Heavens; Earth and Nature; Mother and Guardian
Sky and earth deities.

In the beginning there were a boy and a girl and they had the same name, Kivish Atakvish. When the girl became pregnant after the boy had made her sleep, he left and became the sky. She stayed and made ready for the birth by making noises that created land. From then on the sky and the earth were separated. [Gill 1992]

Klah Klahnee
Northwest, *Yakima, Klikitat*
Earth and Nature
Goddess of the "Three Sister" mountain. [Monaghan 1981]

Köcha Kachin' Mana
Southwest, *Hopi*
Ceremonies
"White Kachina Girl." See also *Nuvak'chin' Mana.* [Wright 1977]

Kocha Mana   "White Girl." See *Alo Mana Angak'chin Mana,* and *A-ha Kachin'Mana.*

Kochinako
Southwest, *Acoma Pueblo, Sia*
Hunting and Wild Animals
"Yellow Woman." Fertility goddess and guardian of game. As a goddess of direction, she is called "Yellow Woman of the North." See also *Yellow Woman.* [Muser 1978; Tyler 1964]

Kohak Oka
Southwest, *Zuni*
Fishing and Water Animals
"White Shell Woman." Maternal grandmother or mother of the Sun Father. She lives with him in his home in the western ocean. See also *Yolkai estsan.* [Gill 1992]

Kohkang Wuhti   See *Spider Woman.*

Kok' Okya   See *Kokwele.*

Kokokshi   See *Kokwele.*

Kokomikeis
Plains, *Blackfoot*
Moon and Night
Moon goddess. Mother of Morning Star. Alternate form: Komorkis. [Cotterell 1979; Turner 1974; Sykes 1968]

Kokopell' Mana
Southwest, *Hopi*
Love and Sexuality
"Assassin Fly Girl." Fertility kachina (see *A-ha Kachin' Mana*). Erotic companion of Kokopeli.

Kokopell' Mana challenges men to race with her. After they start, she lifts her dress and quickly overtakes them. When she catches them, she throws them to the ground and simulates intercourse. [Colton 1949; Savill 1978; Wright 1973; Wright 1977]

Kokumthena
Northeast, *Shawnee*
Education and Knowledge; Creator of Life; Agriculture; Hunting and Wild Animals; Ceremonies
   "Our Grandmother." Omniscient creator deity. She is portrayed as a normal to large-sized woman with gray hair. She is said to live near or in the land of the dead. Kokumthena is present at the "Bread Dances," dances for sustenance, to make crops and game animals more plentiful. Alternate forms: Go-gome-tha-na, Paabothkwe. [Leach 1972; Leach 1992; Wright 1977]

Kokwatawu   See *Suyuki.*

Kokwelacokti   See *Kokwele.*

Kokwelashokti Oken'ona
Southwest, *Zuni*
Agriculture; Ceremonies
   "Kachina Grinding Girl." She brings corn to the women to grind and provides spiritual assistance and prayers to sustain them. See also *A-ha Kachin' Mana* for definition of kachina. Alternate form: Kokwele. [Wright 1985]

Kokwele
Southwest, *Zuni*
Ceremonies
   "Kachina Girl" or "God Girl." When she is called *Kokwelashokti Oken'ona* she is the "Corn-Grinding Kachina Girl" and when her name is *Oky'enawe* she is the "Grinding Girl." For definition of kachina see *A-ha Kachin' Mana.* Alternate forms: Kokwelacokti, Kokokshi, Okya, Kok' Okya. [Wright 1985]

Kokyan Wuhti
Southwest, *Hopi*
Goodness; Creator of Life; Insects; Earth and Nature
   "Spider Grandmother." Beneficent creator deity who is an earth mother and who created humans, plants, and animals, although some say it was Huruing Wuhti of the East and Huruing Wuhti of the West who created the plants and animals. She is equivalent to *Susistinako.* Wuhti indicates a married woman. See also *Gogyeng So Wuhti* and *Spider Woman.* [Gill 1992; Jobes 1962; Leach 1992; Stone 1979; Tyler 1964; Wright 1977]

Kolahmana
Southwest, *Zuni*
War; Ceremonies
   Warrior kachina (see *A-ha Kachin' Mana*). She killed the enemy and saved her people. [Bunzel 1984]

Komanchi Kachin' Mana
Southwest, *Hopi*
Ceremonies
   "Comanche Kachina Girl." Kachina present in a social dance setting. [Wright 1977]

Komokatsiki
Southwest, *Zuni*
Time; Mother and Guardian
   Kachina Old Woman. Mother of *Koyemshi* and *Sihwuluhtsitsa.*

 Komokatasiki lies in the middle of the lake during the winter solstice. Her mouth is open to catch sticks that the women float on the lake. When she swallows the sticks, they become babies. Infants are born to her one after another, with no discomfort. [Bunzel 1984; Wright 1985]

Komorkis   See *Kokomikeis.*

Komwidapokuwia
Southwest, *Yavapai*
Creator of Life; Health and Healing; Magic
   Creator goddess. Protector of shamans in Arizona. [Gifford 1936; Leach 1992]

Konin Kachin' Mana
Southwest, *Hopi*
Ceremonies
   "Cohonino Kachina Girl." Along with *Supai Kachin' Mana,* she represents the Havasupai, western neighbors of the Hopi. See also *A-ha Kachin' Mana* for definition of kachina. [Wright 1977]

Korawini?i
Great Basin, *Owens Valley Paiute*
Family and Tribes; Love and Sexuality; Destroyer of Life; Mother and Guardian
   Mother of all the Native American peoples.
 Korawini?i attracts many men, but when they have intercourse with her they are killed because she has teeth in her vagina. Coyote is the only man left and when he attempts to have intercourse with her he hears a tooth snap and withdraws. He transforms his penis into a hard stick. This time her teeth get caught and are pulled out. Intercourse is no longer a problem and Korawini?i has many children.
   See also *Poo?wavil, Toothed Vagina,* and *Evening Star.* [Gill 1992]

Kothlamana
Southwest, *Zuni*
War
   Warrior maiden who was the first captive of the Kianakwe spirits. Alternate forms: Kothlama, Kothlana. [Wright 1985]

Kothlana   See *Kothlamana.*

Koyemshi
Southwest, *Zuni*
Arts
   "Old Dance Woman." Daughter of *Komokatsiki.* [Wright 1985]

Ksem-wa'tsq
Northwest, *Tsimshian*
Wild Birds; Health and Healing; Magic
   "Land-otter Woman." Goddess of the shamans and the Eagle clan. [Leach 1992]

Ku Gu
Southwest, *Tewa*
Time; Ceremonies
   "Mother Kachina" (see *A-ha Kachin' Mana.*) Summer goddess of San Juan Mountains. [Laski 1958; Leach 1992]

Kumanshi Okya
Southwest, *Zuni*
Magic
   "Comanche Girl." A supernatural being. [Wright 1985]

Kunna
Arctic, *Iglulik Inuit*
Water
  Sea goddess. Equivalent to *Sedna*. [Wyers 1932]

Kurkanninako
Southwest, *Sia*
Directions
  "Red Woman of the South." Goddess of directions.
[Fewkes 1895c; Leach 1992]

Kutca mana
Southwest, *Hopi*
Ceremonies
  A kachina (see *A-ha Kachin' Mana*). [Fewkes 1985]

Kutnahin
Southeast, *Chitimacha*
Sun and Day; Weather; Education and Knowledge
  Sun goddess. She causes thunder as she travels around the
area teaching the proper way to live. Later this figure became
male. [Leach 1992; Swanton 1928]

Kuyapalitsa "Mountain Lion Girl." See *Chakwaina Okya*.

Kwa?akuyi-savepone
Southwest, *Mohave*
Education and Knowledge
  She and her brother travel around the land teaching the
people. [Gill 1992]

Kwamumu Okya
Southwest, *Zuni*
Agriculture; Ceremonies
  "Navajo Girl." She is a harvest kachina (see *A-ha Kachin'
Mana*). [Wright 1985]

Kwavonakwa
Southwest, *Hopi*
Ceremonies
  Kachina (see *A-ha Kachin' Mana* at Second Mesa. [Colton
1949]

L!äzwag·iᵋlayugwa
British Columbia, *Kwakiutl*
Wild Birds
  "Copper-maker-woman." Daughter of Q!omogwa. She
manifests as a white bird that has the odor of copper. See also
Tlaqwagi'laywga. [Boas 1935; Leach 1992]

L'etsa'aplelana
Northwest, *Bella Coola*
Ceremonies; Magic; Health and Healing
  Goddess who initiates the shamans. [Boas n.d.; Leach 1992]

La'idamlulum Ku'le
California, *Maidu*
Creator of Life; Stars and Planets
  "Morning-star Woman." First woman. [Cotterell 1979;
Long 1963]

La'pilewe Okya
Southwest, *Zuni*
Ceremonies
  "Feather String Girl," "Buffalo Dance Girl," or "Sioux Girl."
[Wright 1985]

Laliaaiauts
Northwest, *Bella Coola*
Unknown

Goddess of Satlia. Her town was made of copper and
abalone shells. Her husband was Raven. [McIlwraith 1948]

Large Woman
Plains, *Hidatsa*
Heaven and Hell; Unhappiness
  She figures in a creation story.
 *Long ago people lived under the earth by a large body of
water. There was a tree hanging down from above and a
young man had a vision that the tree should be climbed,*
which he did easily. Many people followed him until Large Woman
tried to climb the tree and broke off the root. Then no one else could
escape to the beautiful world above and the people were sad because
they were separated. [Curtis 1908]

Le-tkakawash
Northwest, *Klamath*
Wild Birds; Sky and Heavens
  Bird goddess. Mother of the moon god, Aishish. She
represents the sky at moonrise or sunrise as a red or yellow
bird. [Gatschet 1890; Leach 1992]

Leelinau
North America
Earth and Nature
  Tree deity.
 *Leelinau did not want to marry the man chosen for her. To
escape the marriage, she ran into the forest and became
the bride of Oksau, the stately pine.* [Emerson 1965]

Lennaxidaq
Northwest, *Kwakiutl*
Luck; Weather; Water
  Goddess of luck and wealth.
*Lennaxidaq traveled about with her child, bestowing
wealth and luck on anyone who saw, heard, or touched
them. When Lennaxidaq heard that her child had dug the
eyes out of a human and eaten them, she was very upset and left her
lake for the sea. In the sea she became the monster Hakulaq.*
[Locher 1932]

Liatiku See *Uretsete*.

Loha
Northwest, *Klamath*
Goodness; Beauty
  Beneficent goddess personified as a beautiful woman.
[Clark 1953]

Loo-wit
Northwest, *Multnomah, Klikitat*
Fire; Earth and Nature
  Fire goddess of Mt. St. Helens.
*The Great Spirit told her to keep her fire where the people
could get it easily. She keeps it burning as a reminder to
the people of herself and the Great Spirit.* [Clark 1953;
Monaghan 1981]

Louse Woman
Great Basin, *Chemehuevi*
Creator of Life
  Creator, with Coyote, of the first humans. [Zigmond 1980]

Luk
Northwest, *Klamath*
Hunting and Wild Animals
  "Grizzly Bear." Sometimes a male deity. [Chamberlain
1892; Gatschet 1890; Leach 1992]

Maiden Whose Clothes Rattle See *Tcikee Cac Nadleehe*.

Mahakh
Arctic, *Aleut*
Domesticated Animals
   "Bitch Mother." Parent, with Iraghdadakh, of two half-human, half-fox beings who became the parents of the humans. [Leach 1992; Monaghan 1990]

Maja
Plains, *Sioux*
Earth and Nature
   Earth mother of the Native American people from Minnesota to the Rocky Mountains. [Dorsey 1892; Leach 1992]

Maka
Plains, *Oglala Sioux, Lakota*
Earth and Nature
   "Earth." One of the Superior Gods, ancestor and protector of all that exists upon her. She shows her pleasure by giving abundant food and good medicine. If she is displeased there is scarcity and evil medicine. Maka created *Unk* to be her companion, but *Unk* is banished to deep water. Some people believe that *Wohpe* and Maka created the blunt-toothed, claw-footed animals. Alternate form: Maka-akan. [Gill 1992; Leach 1992; Walker 1980]

Maka-akan   See *Maka*.

Malaȟishishinish
California, *Chumash*
Insects; Stars and Planets; Weather
   "Scorpion Woman." Stellar goddess who can make the thunder. [Hudson 1978; Leach 1992]

Malaxšišiniš
California, *Chumash*
Evil; Insects; Demi-animals
   A Nunašiš, demon who has a scorpion tail. [Blackburn 1975]

Mallina
Arctic, *Greenland Inuit*
Sun and Day
   Sun goddess. Sister of Anningat, the moon. [Leach 1992]

Malokatsiki
Southwest, *Zuni, Cochiti, Isleta, Navajo*
Ceremonies; Magic; Metals and Minerals
   "Salt Woman, "Salt Old Woman," or "Salt Mother." Provider of salt. Salt Woman and Turquoise Man left the Zuni because their flesh was being wasted. She now lives at Salt Lake. *Salt Woman* of the Isleta Pueblo is brought in, in the form of salt, at an autumn ceremony. The ceremony consists of "cleaning her veins" and anyone present with bad thoughts may be turned into an animal. Among the Navajo, *Salt Woman* is an aspect of *Changing Woman* and she is involved with creation—she is necessary for life. See also *Ashi Esdza, Estsanatlehi, Mina Koya, Ong Wuhti,* and *Salt Woman.* [Leach 1972; Moon 1984; Tyler 1964; Wright 1985]

Mamzrau Mana
Southwest, *Hopi*
Ceremonies
   Kachina (see *A-ha Kachin' Mana*) who appears at the *Mamzrau* initiation dance. She is part of the *Mamzrau* women's society. Alternate forms: Earth Altar Young Woman, Sand Altar Woman. [Wright 1977]

Mandan Creator   See *Mandan Mother*.

Mandan Mother
Plains, *Mandan*
Creator of Life; Earth and Nature
   Mother of First Man, sometimes known as *Mandan Creator.*

   First Man decided he would be born to a Mandan woman. He transformed himself into a dead buffalo and floated down a river. A young woman saw him and pulled him ashore. After eating his kidney-fat, she became pregnant. Mandan Mother gave birth to First Man. [Curtis 1908; Farmer 1978]

Man-el
California, *Cahuilla*
Education and Knowledge; Immortality; Family and Tribes; Moon and Night
   "Moon Maiden." She shines with a bright white light. She teaches games, songs, wise living skills, and how to get through the gate to the underworld, Telmikish. She also imparts information about clan divisions. [Clebourn 1960; Leach 1992]

Masahkare
Plains, *Crow*
Moon and Night
   "Grandmother Moon." [Leach 1992; Lowie 1922]

Masakamekokiu
Northeast, *Menomini*
Earth and Nature
   "Grandmother of Everything That Breathes." Earth goddess. Mother of *Pitkamikokiu.* [Leach 1992]

Masan Wuhti
Southwest, *Hopi*
Unknown
   "Motioning Woman." Wuhti indicates she is a married woman. Similar to *Yohozro Wuhti.* [Gill 1992; Wright 1977]

Masau'u Kachin' Mana
Southwest, *Hopi*
Ceremonies; Weather
   "Death Kachina Girl." A rasping kachina who brings heavy rains when she appears. Her face is gray-brown mud. She accompanies Skeleton Kachina and participates in the *Nevenwehe* ceremony, an initiation rite. [Wright 1973; Wright 1977]

Maskikhwsu
Northeast, *Penobscot*
Fishing and Water Animals
   "Toad Woman."
   Maskikhwsu is a wood spirit who seduces men and children. Although she means no harm, her victims are put to sleep and never awaken. [Leach 1992; Speck 1935b]

Master Spirit's Daughter
Subarctic, *Tahltan*
Mother and Guardian; Magic
   She was near a spring in the forest. Raven, who had been First Man and reincarnated as a bird, made himself into a tiny leaf and floated down to her. She drank water with the leaf in it, conceived a child, and Raven was born again as a human.
   See also *Nusxemtaiana* and *Sixmana.* [Emmons 1911]

Maswik'Chin' Mana
Southwest, *Hopi*
Ceremonies

A kachina (see *A-ha Kachin' Mana*). She participates in the *Masao* ceremony by carrying sacred water in a bowl. She also participates in the *Nevenwehe* Ceremony, an initiation rite. Alternate form: Chimon Mana. [Colton 1949; Gill 1992; Wright 1973; Wright 1977]

Meghetaghna
Arctic, *Siberian Inuit*
Water
Sea goddess. Similar to *Sedna*. [Damas 1984]

Mem Loimis
California, *Wintu*
Water
"Water Woman." Primordial goddess who lives below the earth. [Bierhorst 1985; Leach 1992; Savill 1978]

Merrinako
Southwest, *Sia*
Directions
"Blue Woman of the West." Goddess of directions. [Fewkes 1895c; Leach 1992]

Mesakamigokwaha
Northeast, *Sauk, Fox*
Earth and Nature
Earth mother. [Leach 1992]

Messak Kummik Okwi   See *Mesuk Kummik Okwi.*

Me-suk-kum-me-go-kwa
North America
Hunting and Wild Animals
"Divine Mother." Goddess of the hunt. Her followers are never without meat, as she guides their arrows. [Emerson 1965]

Mesuk Kummik Okwi
Subarctic, *Cree, Algonquin, Ottawa*
Agriculture; Mother and Guardian; Ceremonies; Health and Healing
"Our Grandmother." A primal grandmother who is in charge of the earth's food. A small portion of each meal is placed on the ground in thanks to her and she is also given an offering when medicinal roots are dug up. Alternate forms: Mesukkummik O-kwi, Me-suk-kum-mik-o-kwi, Messak Kummik Okwi. [Redfield 1931; Stone 1979]

Mesukkummik O-kwi   See *Mesuk Kummik Okwi.*

Me-suk-kum-mik-o-kwi   See *Mesuk Kummik Okwi.*

Metza   See *Aquit.*

Mi-ka-k'e Hondon
Plains, *Dhegiha Osage*
Stars and Planets
"Night Star Grandmother." Goddess of the evening star. [Leach 1992]

Mi-ka-k'eu-ki-thaç'in
Plains, *Dhegiha Osage*
Stars and Planets
"Grandmother Double-star." [Leach 1992]

Micux
Southeast, *Nanchez*
Unknown
Daughter of a cannibal goddess. [Burland 1975]

Mikimatt
Northwest
Sun and Day; Creator of Life
Sun goddess who created the world. Alternate forms: I-nach-tin-ak, Nukimatt. [Ells 1886; Leach 1992; Maclean 1896]

Mina Koya
Southwest, *Pueblo*
Metals and Minerals
"Salt Woman." Goddess of the pueblos. See also *Ashi esdza, Ong Wuhti, Malokatsiki,* and *Salt Woman.* [Tyler 1964]

Minnehaha
Plains, *Blackfoot, Iroquois*
Hunting and Wild Animals; Selflessness; Magic; Family and Tribes
Young woman who saved her people from starvation.

Minnehaha went out one morning for water and looked up at the cliff where the hunters had been unable to drive the buffalo. Usually the winter supply of meat was obtained by driving the buffalo over the cliff to their deaths, but each time the men drove them toward the cliff, the buffalo turned away before they came to the edge. This morning Minnehaha saw the buffalo standing on the edge and she said aloud that she would marry one of them if they would jump off the cliff. Surprisingly the buffalo began coming over the edge, and then the shaman of the herd appeared and demanded that Minnehaha keep her promise. When the rest of the people came to the cliff, they found plenty of meat but no Minnehaha. Her footprints showed that she had left with an old buffalo.
Alternate form: Mni-haha. [Campbell 1988b; Long 1963]

Miritatsiec
Plains, *Crow*
Mother and Guardian; Health and Healing; Hunting and Wild Animals; Moon and Night
"Moon Woman." She aids the lost and deprived, teaches healing, gives medicine bundles, and directs the movement of buffalo. See also *Moon Woman.* [Gill 1992]

Mni-haha   See *Minnehaha.*

Moing'iima
Southwest, *Papago*
Agriculture
"Earth." Food goddess. Her husband is So'teknani, the Heavens. [Hatt 1951; Leach 1992; Tyler 1964]

Momoy
California, *Chumash*
Magic; Immortality; Health and Healing; Mother and Guardian; Education and Knowledge
Ancestor shaman. A wealthy old widow who ultimately plays the role of fostering grandmother or adoptive mother. She became associated with the narcotic plant *Datura meteloides*. Momoy establishes the rules of conduct and guards tradition. She has medicine that can cure the sick and revive the dead. It is said that if you drink water that she has bathed in, you will avoid death. [Bierhorst 1985; Blackburn 1975; Halifax 1981]

Mong' Wuhti
Southwest, *Hopi*
Wild Birds; Ceremonies
"Great Horned Owl Woman." A kachina (see *A-ha Kachin' Mana*). She dances in the *Powamu* ceremony or Bean Dance. Wuhti indicates a married woman. [Colton 1949; Gill 1992; Wright 1973; Wright 1977]

Mo'n-sho'n
Plains, *Osage*
Earth and Nature
"Sacred Mother Earth" of the Lower Missouri River Basin. [Leach 1992; Matthews 1982]

Moon Woman
Plains, *Pawnee*
Agriculture; Hunting and Wild Animals; Ceremonies; Moon and Night
Moon goddess. Releaser of buffalo and corn and teacher of ceremonies. See also *Estsanatlehi* and *Miritatsiec*. [Burland 1975; Gill 1992]

Morning Star Woman
California, *Maidu*
Stars and Planets; Creator of Life
First woman. She was made from the dark red earth and water by Earth-Initiate. Morning Star Woman and the first man, Ku'ksū, had black hair, very white skin, and pink eyes. See also *Gendenwitha*. [Thompson 1929]

Mother of All Eagles
Northeast
Wild Birds
Guardian of the eagles.
 Once there was a hunter who was very successful at killing deer. He would then call the eagles, telling them there was meat, but when they came he killed them and took their feathers. One day Mother of All Eagles swooped down and carried him to her eyrie. After two days, they reached an agreement—she would return him to earth if he would shoot only deer and not kill an eagle without the permission of the Spirit World. [Burland 1975]

Mother Sunset Yellow   See *Corn Mother*.

Mu Bachu Okya
Southwest, *Zuni*
Ceremonies
"Navajo Girl" or "Hopi Navajo Girl." A supernatural spirit. [Wright 1985]

Mu'satewichi Okya
Southwest, *Zuni*
Ceremonies; Insects
"Hopi Butterfly Dance Girl." A supernatural spirit. See also *Poli Kachina Mana*. [Wright 1985]

Mucaias Mana
Southwest, *Hopi*
Ceremonies
"Buffalo Maid." A kachina (see *A-ha Kachin' Mana*) who appears at the Buffalo Dance. [Colton 1949]

Mukikwe Okya
Southwest, *Zuni*
Ceremonies; Agriculture
"Hopi Harvest Dance Girl," "Hopi Girl." A supernatural spirit. Alternate forms: Ha-ha-uh, Ha-ha-whu Okya, Ho-wha-whoa, Mukiw' okya. [Bunzel 1984; Wright 1985]

Mukw'okya   See *Mukikwe Okya*.

Munainako
Southwest, *Sia*
Directions
"Dark Woman of the Nadir." Goddess of directions. [Fewkes 1895c; Leach 1992]

Mungo
North America
Agriculture
Goddess of the grain vetch. Sister of Motho. [Leach 1972]

Muyinewu mana
Southwest, *Hopi*
Metals and Minerals
Goddess of gems. [Jobes 1962]

Muyingwa Wuhti
Southwest, *Hopi*
Ceremonies; Agriculture
Kachina (see *A-ha Kachin' Mana*) of germination. Wuhti indicates a married woman. [Gill 1992; Leach 1992; Wright 1977]

Muyinwu-wugti
Southwest, *Tusayan*
Earth and Nature
Earth goddess. [Fewkes 1893; Leach 1992]

Muyiñwuh
Southwest, *Tusayan*
Ceremonies
Underworld deity associated with germs. See also *Nañoikwa* [Leach 1992]

Na'le
Southwest, *Zuni*
Ceremonies; Hunting and Wild Animals
"Deer Dance Girl." [Wright 1985]

Na?ackjeii Esdzaa
Southwest, *Navajo*
Goodness; Evil; Household Affairs; Ceremonies; Insects
"Spider Woman." She is a participant in the emergence journey. She can be beneficial and destructive. As a symbol of the textile arts, she requires woven fabrics as offerings. See also *Spider Woman*. [Gill 1992]

Naasun
Southwest, *Pueblos*
Ceremonies; Earth and Nature
"Earth Virgin." She is prominent in the Snake-Antelope ceremony celebrating fertility. [Tyler 1964]

Naëstsán
Southwest, *Navajo*
Earth and Nature; Weather
"Woman Horizontal." Earth goddess who is the source of the winds that control life and who presides over all those things that breathe. Wife of Yadilyil, "Upper Darkness," mother of *Estsanatlehi*. She is also called *Spider Woman*. See also *Nahosdzaan Esdza*. [Cotterell 1979; Dames 1979; Leach 1992]

Nahalic Okya   See *Nahalish' Okya*.

Nahalish' Okya
Southwest, *Zuni*
Agriculture; Ceremonies
"Corn Dance Girl." A kachina (see *A-ha Kachin' Mana*) who has not been seen by the people for many years. See also *Corn Maidens*. Alternate forms: Hemushikwe Okya, Nahalic Okya. [Wright 1985]

Nahkeeta
Northwest, *Nooksakk, Lummi*
Water

Goddess of Sutherland Lake in the Olympic Mountains.

 Nahkeeta was a beautiful young maiden who was killed by a wild beast. Her people were so bereaved that the Great Spirit created a lake to cover her burial place. [Clark 1953; Monaghan 1981]

Nahokhos baadi
Southwest, *Navajo*
Stars and Planets
"Who-carries-fire-in-her-basket." Stellar goddess of Cassiopeia or Ursa Minor. [Turner 1974]

Nahosdzaan Esdza
Southwest, *Navajo*
Earth and Nature; Weather; Directions
"Earth Woman." She is the controller of the winds that affect those living on earth and in the underworld.

 The creator told Nahosdzaan Esdza that her husband would be the sky. She was to face the east and he would face the west. When there was fog, Sky was visiting Earth. See also *Naëstsán.* Alternate form: Spider Woman. [Leach 1992; Turner 1974]

Nahotsoi asdzą́ą́
Southwest, *Navajo*
Dawn and Twilight; Creator of Life
"Evening Twilight Woman." Creator, with the other Holy People, of the earth, sky, sun, moon, and animals. [Leach 1992; McNeley 1981]

Nakorut
Arctic, *Copper Inuit*
Water
Sea goddess who provides water animals. [Leach 1992; Nungak 1969]

Naliayog   See *Nuliajuk.*

Nan chu Kweejo
Southwest, *Tewa*
Earth and Nature
"Clay Mother." Her gift of clay is recognized with prayers. [Naranjo-Morse 1992]

Nanaqasilakwe
Northwest, *Kwakiutl*
Education and Knowledge; Ceremonies
"Treated-like-a-chief." She teaches religious ways to the people. [Locher 1932]

Nangkwijo
Southwest, *Tewa*
Earth and Nature
"Earth." Her husband is the sky, Makowasendo. [Tyler 1964]

Nani Waiya
Southeast, *Choctaw*
Creator of Life
Creator goddess. [Bierhorst 1985]

Nañoikwia
Southwest, *Tewa*
Destroyer of Life
Goddess of germs. See also *Muyiñwuh.* [Leach 1992]

Nanoquaqsaq
Arctic, *Akuliarmiut Inuit*
Water

Sea goddess of Baffin Land. Equivalent to *Sedna.* [Leach 1992]

Naotsete
Southwest, *Cochiti Pueblo*
Mother and Guardian
Mother goddess of aliens (people other than the Native Americans). Sister of *Uretsete.* In Sia Pueblo she is called *Now'utset,* in Santa Ana Pueblo, *Nausity,* in Acoma Pueblo, *Nau'tsitic* or *Nautsiti,* and in Laguna Pueblo, *I'tc'ts'ity.* [Tyler 1964]

Nashjei Esdza   See *Spider Woman.*

Naskapi Moon Goddess
Arctic, *Montagnais, Naskapi*
Moon and Night
Moon goddess. She can be seen on the face of the moon with her brother the trickster. [MacNeish 1981]

Nastse Estsan   See *Spider Woman.*

Nataska Mana
Southwest, *Hopi*
Ceremonies; Ugliness
Monster kachina (see *A-ha Kachin' Mana*). Child of *Hahai-i Wuhti.* She begs with her brothers on East Mesa. [Fewkes 1985; Wright 1977]

Natchez Maize Mother
Southeast, *Natchez*
Agriculture
Goddess who brought beans and maize to the people. See also *Corn Mother.* [Eliade 1987]

Nausity   See *Naotsete.*

Nautsiti
Southwest, *Acoma Pueblo*
Creator of Life; Fire; Agriculture
Creator goddess. With her sister *Iatiku* she created humans, corn, fire, and tobacco. See also *Naotsete.* [Burland 1975; Leach 1992]

Nau'tsitic   See *Naotsete.*

Navajo First Woman   See *Aataentsic.*

Naxa'asdza'•n   See *Spider Woman*

Naxocoi'esza
Southwest, *Navajo*
Dawn and Twilight
Twilight deity. Mother of Calling God. [Haile 1947; Leach 1992]

Nayaanxatisei
Plains, *Arapaho*
Love and Sexuality; Insects; Weather; Disorder; Physical Prowess
"Whirlwind Woman." Her name also means "caterpillar." Caterpillars are said to cause whirlwinds. Nayaanxatisei participated in creation by spinning a piece of mud to make the earth.

 Nayaanxatisei was desired by Nihansan, a deity known for his large sexual appetites. Tired of his attentions, she challenged him to a spinning contest during which she picked him up and threw him into a stream. She departed, leaving him aware of her power. [Gill 1992]

Neegyauks

Northwest, *Tlingit*

Justice; Earth and Nature

Tlingit name for Haida *Dzelarhons*. [Burland 1975]

Nenalaatseqa

Northwest, *Kwakiutl*

Sun and Day

"Day-receptacle-woman." She hid the sun in a box. [Locher 1932]

Neoga

Northeast, *Iroquois*

Weather; Directions

"Fawn." South Wind goddess who rules the summer winds. Gentle and kind, she walks with the sun. [Turner 1974]

Nerchevik

Arctic, *Labrador Inuit*

Water

Sea goddess. See also *Sedna*. [Damas 1984]

Nerrivik

Arctic, Greenland, *Polar Inuit*

Water; Mother and Guardian

"The Food Dish" or "Place of Food." Sea goddess. Equivalent to *Sedna*. See also *Nirivik*. [Burland 1975; Jobes 1962; Wyers 1932]

Netcensta

Northwest, *Tahltan*

Earth and Nature; Disorder

Earth mother. She supports the earth, and when she shifts she causes earthquakes. [Leach 1992; Teit 1919]

Niarimamau?u

California, *Chemehuevi*

Weather

Wind Woman. She was a lustful woman. She stole Dove's son and kept him prisoner in a cave. When he escaped, she was sealed in the cave and her name became *?Aano?ovi*. [Laird 1976; Leach 1992]

Nielleltaix   See *Nuxmelnimana*.

Nipa

Northeast, *Algonquin*

Moon and Night; Life/Death Cycle

Moon goddess. She rules night, death, cold, and sleep. [Bray 1935; Jobes 1962; Leach 1992]

Nirivik

Arctic, *Tikirarmiut*

Water; Order

Sea goddess. One who can calm the sea. See also *Nerrivik*. [Leach 1992]

Nisqually Bird Goddesses

Northwest, *Nisqually*

Ceremonies; Wild Birds

Goddesses who caught a bird of many colors and gave the feathers to different birds: to the Meadowlark they gave yellow and brown; to the Robin they gave red and brown; the Wren got only brown feathers; and the little Finch got yellow and black. When they were done, all the birds had the colors that we see today. This was also the beginning of the potlatch, the first giving of gifts by the hosts to guests invited to a celebration. [Clark 1953]

Nivikkaa

Arctic, *Greenland Inuit*

Water

"Woman Thrown Backward Over the Edge." Equivalent to *Sedna*. [Wyers 1932]

Nitsabaad

Southwest, *Navajo*

Weather

"Female Rain." [Turner 1974]

Noesarnak

Arctic, *Inuit*

Earth and Nature

Earth goddess. She manifests as a spindly-legged woman dressed in deerskins. [Guirand 1968]

Nokomis

Northeast, *Algonquin, Ojibwa*

Earth and Nature; Mother and Guardian

"Grandmother." An earth goddess who feeds all living things. Also referred to as "Grandmother Moon." Alternate form: Eithinoha. [Carlyon 1982; Jobes 1962; Leach 1992; Monaghan 1981]

Nonä'osqa

Northwest, *Bella Coola*

Earth and Nature

Flower goddess. Daughter of *Snuk-panlits*. [Boas 1898; Leach 1992]

Noogumee

Northeast, *Micmac*

Fishing and Water Animals

"Whale Mother." [Monaghan 1990]

Nooliayoo

Arctic, *Iglulik Inuit*

Water

Sea goddess. Equivalent to *Sedna*. [Wyers 1932]

No'oma Cawaneyung

Northeast, *Lenape*

Health and Healing; Directions

"Grandmother at the South." Goddess of medicinal plants. [Harrington 1921; Leach 1992]

North Wind Woman

Northwest, *Tsimshian*

Weather; Directions

Cold winter wind. Her husband Nalq (mucus) travels with her when she blows hard and causes the ice. [Gill 1992]

Northeastern Swan Maidens

Northeast

Wild Birds; Magic

Bird women who marry mortals but eventually return to their swan form and fly away. See also *Swan Maidens, Northern Europe*. [Bierhorst 1985; Bonnerjea 1927]

Norwan

California, *Wintu*

Hunting and Wild Animals; Weather; Earth and Nature

"Dancing Porcupine Woman." Daughter of Earth and Sun, she is the light, warm air that dances across the surface of the earth, making the plants grow. [Leach 1992; Monaghan 1981]

No-wa-mu
Southwest, *Jemez Pueblo*
Earth and Nature
    Earth mother. [Sando 1982]

Now'utset
Southwest, *Sia*
Mother and Guardian
    Mother goddess of aliens (people other than Native
Americans). She also created the celestial bodies with her
sister **Utset**. Alternate form: Naotsete. [Jobes 1962; Leach
1992; Savill 1978; Tyler 1964]

Nuexqemalsaix
Northwest, *Bella Coola*
Mother and Guardian
    Creator goddess who cares for the unborn humans and
animals until they are born. Alternate form: Semsemeltstas
Senxalaolela. [Boas 1898; Leach 1992]

Nukimatt   See *Mikimatt*.

Nulayuuiniq
Arctic, *Eastern Hudson Bay Inuit*
Evil; Magic; Metals and Minerals; Large Size
    Malevolent deity who became a giant right after her birth.
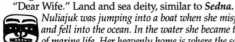 *During a time of starvation, the infant Nulayuuiniq was
found by people who had come to rescue her village. She
chased after the people, who threw sealskin scraps at her,
which the toothless Nulayuuinig swallowed whole. Eventually she
became exhausted and stopped running, whereupon she turned into
an island of solid rock.* [Gill 1992]

Nuliajajuk   See *Nuliajuk*.

Nuliajuk
Arctic, *Netsilik, Mackenzie, Baffin Land, Hudson Bay Inuit*
Fishing and Water Animals; Heaven and Hell; Justice
    "Dear Wife." Land and sea deity, similar to *Sedna*.
*Nuliajuk was jumping into a boat when she misjudged
and fell into the ocean. In the water she became the ruler
of marine life. Her heavenly home is where the souls of the
good and suicides go. When she is not there, she is in the water
guarding her animals and fish and punishing those who flaunt her
regulations.*
    Alternate forms: Aviliayuk, Kavna, Nuliayok Nuliayuk,
Nuliajajuk, Uiniyumayuituq. [Damas 1984; Hultkrantz 1983;
Leach 1992; Monaghan 1981; Muser 1978; Wyers 1932]

Nuliayok   See *Nuliajuk*.

Nuliayuk   See *Nuliajuk*.

Nuli'rahak
Arctic, *Siberian Inuit*
Water
    Sea goddess of Indian Point, Siberia. She is an old woman
who lives at the bottom of the ocean and to whom sacrifices
are offered. Alternate form: Nulirahak. [Hultkrantz 1983;
Leach 1992; Wyers 1932]

Nulixwemankta
Northwest, *Bella Coola*
Education and Knowledge
    Goddess who teaches the people at the town of Talio.
[McIlwraith 1948]

Nunam-chua
Arctic, *Chugach Inuit*
Earth and Nature

Guardian of the land animals who lives in the forests.
[Leach 1992]

Nuñda
Southeast, *Cherokee*
Sun and Day; Health and Healing; Destroyer of Life; Time
    Sun goddess who can cause headaches, fevers, and blisters.
She is also invoked to cure these maladies. She is the
"divider" of time, marking it into units. Associated with
Geyaguga. She is a favorite deity of ballplayers. Alternate
forms: Nunta, Unelanuki. [Leach 1992; Monaghan 1981;
Savill 1978]

Nunta   See *Nuñda*.

Nunuoska
Northwest, *Bella Coola*
Earth and Nature; Time
    "Mother Nature." She makes sure the flowers and trees
bloom in the spring. [McIlwraith 1948]

Nunusomikeeqonem
Northwest, *Bella Coola*
Destroyer of Life; Insects
    Cannibal goddess. Mother of *Alkuntam*. She sucks human
brains out through the ears. Later she was changed into a
mosquito. [Leach 1992; Savill 1978]

Nuptadi
Plains, *Mandan*
Ceremonies; Magic; Health and Healing
    "Young Grandmother." Cannibal goddess. After her death
her magic robe became the sacred medicine bundle. [Burland
1975]

Nuqiliaxilena
Northwest, *Bella Coola*
Creator of Life
    First Woman at Talio. [McIlwraith 1948]

Nuskitl   See *Nuxmelnimana*.

Nuskwalsikanda
Northwest, *Bella Coola*
Directions; Water
    Goddess at Snutali. She was one of the four sister
goddesses who came from the east and caused streams and
rivers to flow. [McIlwraith 1948]

Nusxemtaiana
Northwest, *Bella Coola*
Sun and Day
    Goddess at Alqalaxl. Daughter of *Skqwaluti*. She and
Raven made it possible for the people to have the sun.
 *Nusxemtaiana became the mother of Raven after he
changed himself into a ball of mud, which she
inadvertently drank with her water.*
    See also **Master Spirit's Daughter** and *Sixmana*.
[McIlwraith 1948]

Nutse'xenem
Northwest, *Bella Coola*
Sun and Day; Immortality; Ceremonies
    Solstice goddess. She appears at the solstice, and when
people see her, they faint. Their souls are taken to her house
and initiated into the mysteries of *kusiut*, the masked dancing
society. [Gill 1992; Leach 1992]

Nuvak'chin' Mana

Southwest, *Hopi*

Ceremonies; Weather

"Cold-bring Woman," "Snow Maiden." A kachina (see *A-ha Kachin' Mana*) who appears at the Snow Kachina Dance and sometimes at the *Niman* (home-going) ceremony. Her presence is a prayer for the coming of cold weather and snow to replenish the moisture in the ground. See also *Köcha Kachin' Mana*. See also *Horo Mana*. [Colton 1949; Fewkes 1985; Wright 1973; Wright 1977]

Nuxmelnimana

Northwest, *Bella Coola*

Unknown

"Stick-breaker." Goddess at Stuix. She was known for her ability to make a path through the forest. Alternate forms: Nielleltaix, Nuskitl. [McIlwraith 1948]

Nuyelelaix

Northwest, *Bella Coola*

Creator of Life

First Woman at Talio with *Snuximetlimana*. [McIlwraith 1948]

Ocean Woman

Great Basin, *Paviotso*

Water; Creator of Life

Creator goddess who came from the ocean. [Lowie 1924]

Ohoyo Osh Chishba

Southeast, *Choctaw*

Education and Knowledge; Agriculture

"Unknown Woman." Corn goddess. A wise woman who provides food.

 At first Ohoyo Osh Chishba provided food by scratching her skin. As it fell into the pot, it became cornmeal. Later she made food plants grow. [Burland 1975; Leach 1992; Monaghan 1981]

Ojibwa Daughter

Northeast, *Ojibwa*

Magic; Mother and Guardian

Mother Earth's daughter, conceived by the Winds from her body. She is worshiped in Minnesota. [Landes 1968]

Oken'ona   See *Hokoha Okya*.

Oky'enawe

Southwest, *Zuni*

Unknown

"Grinding Girl." See also *Kokwele*. [Wright 1985]

Okya   See *Kokwele*.

Old Woman Night

Plains, *Mandan, Sioux*

Moon and Night; Earth and Nature

"The Grandmother." Earth and vegetation goddess. The giver of two kettles that are the tribal fetishes, one containing the sky and the other containing the earth. [Bierhorst 1985; Curtis 1908]

Old Woman of the Sea

California, *Salinan*

Primordial Being; Water

Ancient primordial goddess. [Sproul 1979]

Old Woman of the Seasons

Central Plateau, *Kutenai*

Time

 She lived in a tipi where she kept the seasons hanging in a great moose skin bag. Winter was twelve months long, and she only let out the other seasons for a few weeks at the end of winter. Then Trickster stole the bag and let the warm spring winds escape. From then on the seasons were like they are now. [de Wit 1979]

Old Woman Who Never Dies

Plains, *Mandan*

Immortality; Earth and Nature

Earth and plant goddess. [Bierhorst 1985; Curtis 1908]

Olungwa

Arctic, *Labrador Inuit*

Fishing and Water Animals

Companion of *Sedna*. She combed Sedna's hair, and the lice became seals and her hair became seaweed. [Weigle 1982]

Omaha Earth Mother

Plains, *Omaha*

Earth and Nature

Earth goddess.

 She was covered with water until the pre-existing father caused a great rock to rise up above the water. It burst into flames and some of the water became clouds. When there was enough dry land, spirits came down from the heavens and changed into flesh and blood. [Welsch 1981]

Omamama

Subarctic, *Cree*

Creator of Life

Ancestor goddess. She was mother to Thunderbird, Frog, a Cree hero, Wolf, and Beaver. Then she gave birth to rocks and plants, making the earth look like it does now. [Monaghan 1981]

Omau-u Wuhti

Southwest, *Hopi*

Weather; Ceremonies

"Thunder Kachina." She brings rain. For definition of kachina see *A-ha Kachin' Mana*. Wuhti indicates a married woman. [Wright 1977]

Onatah

Northeast, *Seneca, Iroquois*

Agriculture

Corn or wheat goddess. Daughter of *Eithinoha* or *Nokomis*.

 Onatah went out searching for dew with which to refresh herself. An evil spirit captured and imprisoned her. When the Sun found her and took her back to the fields, she stayed there and never wandered again.

See also *Persephone*, Greek and Roman Empires, and *Deohako*. [Carlyon 1982; Guirand 1968; Jobes 1962; Leach 1972; Leach 1992; Monaghan 1981]

Onchi

Plains, *Teton Sioux*

Moon and Night

"Grandmother Moon." [Curtis 1908]

Ondoutaehte

Northeast, *Huron*

War; Small Size

"War." She is its perpetrator and appears either as an old woman or dwarf. [Gill 1992]

Onenha
Northeast, *Seneca*
Ceremonies; Agriculture; Health and Healing; Education and Knowledge
"Corn."

Onenha saved a man from death. He had always been careful to preserve corn, squash, and bean seeds, but he became ill. She came to him in a dream and told him to drink rainwater. When he recovered, she taught him a better way to care for corn and also about the Corn Harvest Ceremony. [Gill 1992]

Ong Wuhti
Southwest, *Hopi*
Goodness; Time; Metals and Minerals
"Salt Woman." Benevolent deity who provides salt and predicts the seasons. Wuhti indicates a married woman. See also *Ashi Esdza, Malokatsiki,* and *Mina Koya.* [Colton 1949; Gill 1992; Leach 1992]

Ooyarraksakju
Arctic, *Baffin Land Inuit*
Goodness; Metals and Minerals
Benevolent deity who inhabits rocks. [Leach 1992]

Ostkahakakaitshoidiaa
Plains, *Wichita*
Water; Fishing and Water Animals
Water goddess in Kansas. She heals and protects all the water animals. [Dorsey 1904; Leach 1992]

Paabothkew   See *Kokumthena.*

Pabothkwe   See *Kokumthena.*

Pachavuin Mana
Southwest, *Hopi*
Agriculture; Ceremonies
"Harvest Girl." Masked figure who brings a huge load of bean sprouts to the village during the *Pachavu* or Tribal Initiation Rites. She is not a kachina. [Colton 1949; Wright 1973; Wright 1977]

Pah
Plains, *Skidi Pawnee, Caddoan*
Moon and Night; Creator of Life
Moon goddess who lives in the west and illuminates the night. She married the sun and they created the first people. [Leach 1992; Savill 1978]

Pahpobi Kwiyo
Southwest, *Tewa*
Earth and Nature
"Fire Flower Woman." Prayers are said to her during the naming of infants and hunting. [Leach 1992; Parsons 1929]

Pahto
Northwest, *Yakima, Klickitat*
Earth and Nature
Goddess of Mt. Adams. [Monaghan 1981]

Paija
Arctic
Evil; Destroyer of Life
Evil one-legged goddess of Keewatin District, Canada. Just looking at her can cause humans to die. [Leach 1992; Mowat 1968]

Paiowa
California, *Yana*
Stars and Planets
"Evening Star." Paiute Creator Goddess, Great Basin Paiute family and tribes. She and her daughter, living in California, created the first Paiute people. [Curtin 1903; Leach 1992; Lowie 1924]

Pakhik' Mana
Southwest, *Hopi*
Ceremonies
"Water Drinking Girl." She appears at the *Mamzrau* Initiation Dance. She is often called "Butterfly Kachina Girl" and confused with *Poli Kachina Mana,* who is the real "Butterfly Girl" but not a kachina. Similar to *Shalako Mana.* [Wright 1977]

Pakimna
Arctic, *Iglulik Inuit*
Hunting and Wild Animals
"Mistress of the Caribou." [Damas 1984]

Pakitsumanga
Arctic, *Inland Inuit*
Hunting and Wild Animals; Mother and Guardian; Magic
"Mother of Caribou." Protector and guide of shamans. [Leach 1992; Rasmussen 1929]

Pakok' Okya
Southwest, *Zuni*
Ceremonies
"Navajo Kachina Girl." A supernatural spirit who dances with Pakoko. [Wright 1985]

Pakwaekasiasit
Northeast, *Penobscot*
Health and Healing
"Arrow-head Finger." Mother of medicinal plants. [Portable North American 1974]

Pana
Arctic, *Caribou, Padlermiut Inuit*
Immortality; Heaven and Hell; Weather
"Woman-up-there."

Pana lives in the sky, or heaven, where she cares for the souls of the dead. When they are reincarnated, the souls are returned to earth with the help of the moon. Pana's home is full of holes, the stars. Sometimes things are spilled in heaven and they come through the holes as rain, hail, or snow.
Alternate form: Pan•a. [Gill 1992; Leach 1972; Leach 1992]

Pan•a   See *Pana.*

Panes
California, *Acagchemen*
Wild Birds
Bird goddess. [Monaghan 1981]

Papawa
California, *Chemehuevi*
Hunting and Wild Animals
Bear goddess. See also *Bear Woman.* [Leach 1972; Leach 1992]

Pasikiapa Dese Akenona Okya
Southwest, *Zuni*
Ceremonies
"Wide Sleeves Pottery Drum Girl." Alternate form: Pasikiapa Okya. [Wright 1985]

Pasikiapa Okya   "Wide Sleeves Girl." See *Pasikiapa Dese Akenona Okya.*

Pasom Mana
Southwest, *Hopi*
Ceremonies; Earth and Nature
   "Spiderwort Maiden." Malevolent deity who can drive people insane. [Colton 1949]

Pasowee
Plains, *Kiowa*
Hunting and Wild Animals; Health and Healing; Education and Knowledge; Household Affairs
   "Buffalo Woman." She brings health and medicine and teaches the women how to build the tipis. See also *Buffalo Old Woman.* [Stone 1979]

Pawnee Corn Mother   See *Corn Mother.*

Pawnee Evening Star   See *Bright Star.*

Pawnee First Woman
Plains, *Pawnee*
Education and Knowledge; Agriculture; Household Affairs; Creator of Life
   Teacher of the people. Daughter of *Evening Star.*
   First Woman was born in heaven and came to earth on a cloud driven by a whirlwind. She knew about the earth, gardening and planting, how to make an earth lodge, and how to speak. Her mother taught her these things so she could teach the people.
   See also *Pawnee Moon Woman.* [Marriott and Rachlin 1975]

Pawnee Moon Woman
Plains, *Pawnee*
Moon and Night; Creator of Life
   She was a friend and companion to *Evening Star* when she bore *Pawnee First Woman.* Moon Woman married the sun and bore the first male. [Marriott and Rachlin 1975]

People Mother
Great Basin, *Paviotso*
Creator of Life
   Creator goddess. [Bierhorst 1985]

Peyote Woman
Plains
Ceremonies
   Ceremonial goddess of several Plains and Woodland tribes. [Leach 1972]

Pinga
Arctic, *Caribou Inuit*
Hunting and Wild Animals; Immortality; Health and Healing
   "The One Up There." Guardian of animals, ruler of the hunt, and protector of all living things who aids the medicine man. She takes the souls of the dead and then allows them to reincarnate. [Cotterell 1979; Damas 1984; Leach 1992; Savill 1978; Wyers 1932]

Piptu' Wuhti
North America, *Hopi*
Ceremonies; Disorder; Intelligence and Creativity
   Clown. She is a companion of Piptuka. They are clown dancers who appear during Plaza Dances, taunting kachinas. Their humor is ribald or obscene, often based on the reversal of norms, gluttony, or criticism of non-Hopi people. Wuhti indicates a married woman. [Colton 1949; Gill 1992; Wright 1973]

Pitkamikokiu
Northeast, *Menomini*
Weather
   "Mother of the Winds." Daughter of *Masakmekokiu.* [Leach 1992]

Plash-plash
Northwest, *Yakima, Klickitat*
Earth and Nature
   "White Spots." Goddess of Goat Rocks. One of the five mountain wives of the sun. The others are the goddesses *Wahkshum* (Simcoe Mountain), *Patho* (Mt. Adams), *Loo-wit* (Mt. St. Helens), and the goddess of Mt. Rainier. [Clark 1953; Monaghan 1981]

Po'haha
Southwest, *Tewa*
War; Ceremonies
   War kachina (see *A-ha Kachin' Mana*). [Leach 1992; Parsons 1939]

Pokinsquss
Northeast
Magic
   "Jug Woman." A witch. Alternate form: Pook-jin-skwess. [Weigle 1982]

Poli Kachina Mana
Southwest, *Hopi*
Insects; Ceremonies
   "Butterfly Girl." The masked impersonation of the kachina (see *A-ha Kachin' Mana*). She is *Poli Mana* when participating in the unmasked social dance. Because every living thing has power, insects are also important in the Hopi pantheon. Poli Kachina Mana was introduced from the pueblos of the Rio Grande. The dance is called "Tablita" because of the tablets the dancers wear on their heads. The tablets are terraced to represent clouds, and various symbols, such as the sun, are painted on them. See also *Mu'satewichi Okya.* [Colton 1949; Wright 1977]

Poli Mana   See *Poli Kachina Mana.*

Ponoya
California, *Chumash*
Stars and Planets; Unhappiness; Sun and Day
   Sun goddess. Oldest daughter of the sun, sister of *Sapigenwas.* Maker of baskets.
   Ponoya ate very little, living mostly on tobacco. She and her sister were subjected to many trials on earth and they were finally able to return to Sun's house. Their father can now watch over them as they are the two small stars that are close to the moon. [Blackburn 1975]

Pook-jin-skwess   See *Pokinsquss.*

Poo?wavi
California, *Chemehuevi*
Family and Tribes
   Creator, with Coyote, of all the Native Americans. She had a vagina with teeth and her story is the same as *Korawini?i.* See also *Evening Star* and *Toothed Vagina.* [Laird 1976; Leach 1992]

Powamu So Aum
North America
Agriculture; Ceremonies; Life/Death Cycle
   Grandmother of the Powamui Kachinas (see *A-ha Kachin' Mana*), who are associated with the Bean Dance. *Powamu* is

the bean-sprouting rite and a puberty rite. She usually appears as an old woman with a white face and scraggly hair. [Colton 1949; Leach 1972; Wright 1973; Wright 1977]

Property Woman
Northwest
Wealth
Riches come to the person who catches sight of this curly gray-haired goddess. [Bierhorst 1985]

Ptesan Winyan
Plains, *Lakota Sioux*
Hunting and Wild Animals
Equivalent to *White Buffalo Woman*. [LaPointe 1976]

Pte-ska-win   See *White Buffalo Woman*.

Pukeheh
Southwest, *Havasupai*
Creator of Life; Weather
Mother goddess. After a great flood, she was found in a hollow log. Sun fathered her son and a waterfall sired her daughter. These children became the first people. [Savill 1978]

Pukimna
Arctic, *Iglulik Inuit*
Earth and Nature
Goddess of land animals. [Monaghan 1981]

Pukjinskwes
Northeast, *Maliseet-Passamaquoddy*
Magic
Witch. She can appear as a woman or man. Pukjinskwes disliked humans so she transformed into a mosquito and became the mother of all the mosquitoes. [Gill 1992]

Pukkeenegak
Arctic, *Inuit*
Goodness; Mother and Guardian; Household Affairs
Benevolent deity who has a tattooed face. Dressed in large boots and a pretty dress, she procures food for her followers and attends births. She is also involved in the making of clothes. [Carlyon 1982; Leach 1992; Guirand 1968]

Punauaga Oloeaydili
Panama, *Cuna*
Heaven and Hell; Water
Guardian of the river that flows in the land of the dead. [Leach 1992]

Puwo-win
Northeast, *Micmac*
Magic; Goodness; Evil
Sometimes called a witch. This person, female or male, has magical powers and can be benevolent or malevolent. [Gill 1992]

Qailertetang
Arctic, *Cumberland and Baffin Land Inuit*
Time; Weather; Order
A servant of *Sedna*. Her arrival coincides with the good weather of fall. She comes to calm people's souls. [Boas 1884; Leach 1992]

Qakma
Northwest, *Bella Coola*
Creator of Life
First Woman at Nutal. See also *Siltslani*. [McIlwraith 1948]

Qamaitis
Northwest, *Bella Coola, Kwakiutl*
War; Destroyer of Life; Earth and Nature; Heaven and Hell
Chief deity who lives on the eastern end of the upper heaven. She seldom visits earth anymore, but when she does there is sickness and death.

 Qamaitis was a great warrior and at the beginning of time she came to visit earth. The mountains made the land uninhabitable, so Qamaitis changed them to make the terrain more manageable.
See also *Djisisnaxitl*. [Leach 1992; Monaghan 1981; Savill 1978; Wright 1973]

Qocha Mana   See *Ang-chin Mana*.

Qoia Akachin Mana   See *Hemis Kachin' Mana*.

Qominoqa
Northwest, *Kwakiutl*
Education and Knowledge; Mother and Guardian; Ceremonies
"Rich-woman." Cannibal goddess. She is sought for advice and warnings of danger. [Locher 1932]

Qopimpmana
Northwest, *Bella Coola*
Unknown
"Rising Dust." Goddess worshiped at Stuix with her sister *Kalxsmaknim* (see for story). [McIlwraith 1948]

Quail Kachin' Mana
Southwest, *Hopi*
Reptiles; Ceremonies
Turtle Kachina Maiden. She wears a Rio Grande woman's dress and is thought to have come from Acoma. For definition of kachina see *A-ha Kachin' Mana*. Alternate form: Kakash Kachina. [Colton 1949]

Quakuinahaba   See *Cathena*.

Queskapenek
Central Plateau, *Okanagon*
Metals and Minerals; Weather; Disorder; Creator of Life; Earth and Nature
Earth goddess who is sometimes referred to as Earth Woman.

The Great Chief made a woman into the earth. Her flesh is the soil, her hair the vegetation, her bones the rocks, and her breath the wind. She contracts when she is cold and expands when she is hot; earthquakes are her movements. We live on her and she is still alive. Humans are made from a rolled-up ball of her flesh (the soil). [Bierhorst 1976; Boas and Teit 1985; Leach 1956; Stone 1979]

Quisserrinkao
Southwest, *Sia*
Directions
"Slightly Yellow Woman of the Zenith." Goddess of directions. [Fewkes 1895c; Leach 1992]

Quootis-hooi
Northwest, *Chinook*
Creator of Life; Large Size; Wild Birds
Creator goddess. She is a giant who created people from eating thunderbird eggs. [Jobes 1962]

Rabbit Mother
Southwest, *Oraibi*
Agriculture

Fertility goddess. She is associated with squash and corn. [Tyler 1964]

Ragno
Southwest, *Pomo, Hopi*
Creator of Life
   "Old Mother Goddess." She is associated with creation. [Sykes 1968]

Rahakatittu
Plains, *Pawnee*
Ceremonies
   She represents the female principle at the *Hako* ceremony. [Jobes 1962]

Rain Goddess
Northwest, *Quinault, Chehalis, Cowlitz*
Selfishness; Weather
   Daughter of Ocean.

   Rain Goddess and her brothers, Clouds, were sent by their father to the people. The people were selfish and refused to return Rain Goddess and Clouds. The Great Spirit became angry and scooped up land, making Puget Sound and the Cascade Mountains, which then kept the moisture away from the selfish ones. [Clark 1953]

Red Dog's Wife
Arctic, *Inuit*
Domesticated Animals

An Eskimo woman married a red dog and had ten children. Five of the children were dogs that she set adrift in a boat. When they found land, the dogs became the parents of the white people. The other five children were monsters and they produced blood-drinking monsters called the Adlet by the Labrados Eskimos and Ergigdlit by the Hudson Bay Eskimos. [Cooper 1876]

Red-spider-woman
Plains, *Pawnee*
Health and Healing; Agriculture; Insects
   Old woman who lives in the center of the earth. She and her many daughters control the growth of beans and corn.

Red-spider-woman refused to allow the buffalo to spread out from their northern home. When the buffalo traveled south anyway, Red-spider-woman was killed. She sank into the ground, where the buffalo chief said she should remain, becoming the medicinal root of the squash vine.
   See also **Spider Woman.** [Gill 1992]

Red Woman
Plains, *Hidatsa, Apsaroke*
Water; Evil; Ugliness
   Ogre. A water monster who attempted to kill the hero. [Curtis 1908]

Rhpisunt
Northwest, *Haida*
Hunting and Wild Animals; Magic; Family and Tribes
   A princess. Daughter of the chief of the Wolf Clan.

Rhpisunt wandered away from her village and became the mother of bear cubs. She brought her sons back to live with her people, where they took off their bear skins and lived as humans. Many years later when their mother died, they returned to their father's people and the Wolf Clan always recognized bears as their blood relatives.
   See also **Bear Mother.** [Burland 1975; Monaghan 1981]

Rock Crystal Girl
Southwest, *Navajo*
Metals and Minerals

Deity of the east. She is worshiped at Pelado Peak. [Savill 1978]

Rukko
Plains, *Mandan*
Creator of Life
   Creator goddess. In the darkness she makes human bodies, then the male spirit adds their souls. [Monaghan 1981]

Sac First Women
Northeast, *Sac (Sauk), Ojibwa*
Creator of Life
   Two women who are the mothers of humans. [Brinton 1876]

Sakuru   See *Shakuru.*

Sakwa Mana
Southwest, *Hopi*
Agriculture; Ceremonies
   "Blue Corn Maiden." A kachina (see *A-ha Kachin' Mana*). She participates in the *Soyal* (Winter Solstice) Ceremony at First Mesa. Sakwap Mana carries a tray of ears of blue corn surrounded by spruce boughs. [Colton 1949; Wright 1973]

Sakwats Mana
North America, *Hopi*
Ceremonies
   "Runner Maiden." A kachina (see *A-ha Kachin' Mana* at Second Mesa who carries a yucca leaf whip. [Colton 1949; Wright 1977; Wright 1973]

Salt Woman   See *Malokatsiki.*

Sand Altar Woman   See *Mamzrau Mana. Tih-kuyi-wuhti,* and *Tiiwapongümsi.*

Sanihas
California, *Wintu*
Sun and Day
   Goddess of daylight. [Curtin 1903; Leach 1992]

Sanvna
Arctic, *Baffin Land Inuit*
Water
   "One-down-on-the-sea-bottom." Sea goddess. Equivalent to *Sedna.* [Wyers 1932]

Sapiqenwas
California, *Chumash*
Sun and Day
   Sun goddess. Youngest daughter of the sun, sister of *Ponoya* (see for story). [Blackburn 1975]

Sasvsuma Inua
Arctic, *Greenland Inuit*
Water
   Sea goddess. Equivalent to *Sedna.* [Wyers 1932]

Sattuma Eeva
Arctic, *Greenland Inuit*
Water
   "Spirit of the Sea Depths." Sea goddess. Equivalent to *Sedna.* [Wyers 1932]

Sedna
Arctic, *Inuit*
Fishing and Water Animals; Beauty; Wild Birds; Heaven and Hell; Water
   Sea goddess who rules over the water animals.

Sedna was a beautiful young girl who refused all suitors until Seabird came along. She went to live with him in his nest, but when her father came to visit he was horrified at the filth and took Sedna away. The bird people followed them and the sea began to rise and a storm overtook them. To calm the water, Sedna's father threw his daughter out of the kayak. She clung to the side so he chopped off her fingers, but she continued to cling to the boat. Three times he chopped at his daughter's hands until she finally let go and sank to the ocean bottom. The pieces of her hands became the sea animals. Sedna now rules Adlivin, the place where souls go after death.

Sedna is known by many different names among the Native American people. Her forms include *Ai-Willi-Ay-O, Aiviliajog, Anavigak, Arnaaluk Takannaaluk, Arnakapfaluk, Arnaknagsak, Arnarquáshaag, Avilayoq, Aywilliyoq, Idiragijenget, Ikalu nappa, Kannakapfaluk, Katuma, Kunna, Meghetaghna, Nanoquaqsaq, Nerchevik, Nerrivik, Nivikkaa, Nooliayoo, Sanvna, Sasvsuma Inua, Sattuma Eeva, Takanakapsaluk, Takanakluk arnaluk, Takanna' luk, Unaviga, Unigumisuitok,* and *Uiniyumayuituq.* [Bierhorst 1985; Burland 1975; Carlyon 1982; Cotterell 1979; Damas 1984; Eliot 1976; Leach 1992; Monaghan 1981]

Sehu Woman
Southeast, *Cherokee*
Agriculture; Ceremonies
"Corn." Sister of *Elihino* and *Igaehinudo.* The most sacred plant is celebrated in a late summer festival, Green Corn. Corn is seen as an old woman, the wife of Kanati, the hunter. Reborn each spring, she is the greatest giver of life among the plants. [Durdin-Robertson 1982]

Selu
Southeast
Agriculture; Goodness; Life/Death Cycle
Corn Mother. Her husband is Konati, Master of Game. Her heart is planted to provide food for her people. Equivalent to *Kornmutter* and *Zythiamatka,* Northern Europe.

Selu provides beans and corn for her family. One day her sons discover that she produces the corn by rubbing her stomach and the beans by rubbing her armpits. Frightened by what they think is witchcraft they decide to kill their mother. Before she dies, Selu teaches her sons how to fertilize the soil with her blood so that the maize will grow.

Similar stories about the origin of corn are told by the Creek, Natchez, Penobscot, Abnakik, Malecite, Iroquois, Huron, Ojibwa, Seneca, Shawnee, and Tuscarora peoples. See also *Corn Maidens, Corn Mother,* and *Corn Woman.* [Bierhorst 1985; Burland 1975; Gill 1992; Leach 1992; Schmidt 1951]

Semsemeltstas Senxalaolela   See *Nuexqemalsaix.*

Seqinek   See *Akycha.*

Seven Sisters
Northwest, *Nez Perce*
Stars and Planets
The Pleiades. See also the *Seven Sisters of Industry,* Far East; *Krittika,* Indian Subcontinent; and *Alcyone,* Greek and Roman Empires. [Clark 1953]

Sha'koya
Southwest, *Acoma Pueblo*
Hunting and Wild Animals
Mother of Mountain Lion Man. Daughter of *Iyatiku.* [Leach 1992]

Shakuru
Plains, *Pawnee*
Sun and Day; Creator of Life
Sun goddess. With the moon as father, she gave birth to a son. Their relatives, the Evening and Morning Stars, bore the first girl. Both children were put on the earth and became the first people. Alternate form: Sakuru. [Carlyon 1982; Jobes 1962]

Shalako Mana
Southwest, *Hopi*
Ceremonies
A kachina (see *A-ha Kachin' Mana*). She appears with a white face and square earrings. Similar to *Pakhik' Mana.* [Colton 1949; Wright 1973; Wright 1977]

Shiwanokia
North America, *Zuni*
Creator of Life; Goodness; Intelligence and Creativity
"Priest Woman." Creator of heaven and earth along with Priest Man. She made *Awitelin Tsita* from her saliva. She was concerned with hearts and minds. Alternate form *Shiwanska.* [Leach 1972; Monaghan 1981; Savill 1978; Tyler 1964]

Shiwanska   See *Shiwanokia.*

Shro-tu-na-ko
Southwest, *Keres*
Education and Knowledge
Goddess of memory. Sister of *Sussistannako.* [Leach 1992; Tyler 1964]

Shup   See *Chup.*

Sidne
Arctic, *Nugumiut Inuit*
Creator of Life
Creator goddess at Frobisher Bay, Canada. Daughter of Anguta. Sidne created all living things, while her father created the inorganic matter. [Brinton 1876; Leach 1992]

Sihwuluhtsitsa   See *Komokatsiki.*

Sila
Arctic, *Inuit*
Weather
"Ruler of the Elements." Weather deity. Described by some as a male when causing storms and female when the weather is calm and sunny. See also *Skiumyoa.* [Bierhorst 1985; Wyers 1932]

Siltslani
Northwest, *Bella Coola, Kwakiutl*
War; Destroyer of Life; Sky and Heavens
Warrior goddess. She lives in heaven beyond a bleak prairie. She rarely visits the earth because sickness and death result. She is not worshiped. See also *Qamaitis.* [McIlwraith 1948]

Simsiutaakis
Northwest, *Bella Coola*
Water
Goddess at Nusxeq who lives on the river at the North Bentinck arm where it enters Green Bay. [McIlwraith 1948]

Sinnilktok
Arctic, *Baffin Land Inuit*
Goodness; Domesticated Animals; Demi-animals; Mother and Guardian; Health and Healing

Benevolent deity who is half-woman and half-dog. She provides food and cures the ill. [Bilby 1923; Leach 1992]

Sio Mana
Southwest, *Hopi*
Ceremonies
"Zuni Kachina Maid." For definition of kachina see *A-ha Kachin' Mana.* [Fewkes 1985]

Sio Shalako Mana
Southwest, *Hopi*
Ceremonies
"Zuni Shalako Maid." Kachina (see *A-ha Kachin' Mana*) dancer who wears a maiden shawl in *Shalako* ceremony at First Mesa. The Shalako ceremony is a December ritual charaterized by tall birdlike figures called Shalakos. See also *Corn Maidens* and *Tukwinong Mana.* [Colton 1949; Wright 1973]

Siqiniq
Arctic, *Iglulik Inuit*
Sun and Day
Sun goddess.
 Siqiniq had an incestuous relationship with her brother the moon. They pursued each other with torches, but the moon's torch went out.
See also *Akycha, Greenland Sun Goddess,* and *Sun Sister.* [Damas 1984]

Sitch-tche-na-ko   See *Sussistinnako.*

Si-tcom'pa Ma-so-its
Southwest, *Kaibab*
Water
"Grandmother of the Sea." She took a sack and brought humans out of the sea and put them on the land at Kaibab Plateau, Arizona. [Leach 1992; Powell 1879]

Siwuluhtsitsa
Southwest, *Zuni*
Mother and Guardian
Mother of *Kothlamana.* [Wright 1985]

Sixmana
Northwest, *Bella Coola*
Mother and Guardian
Goddess at Snutali.
 She became the mother of Raven when he wanted to be born again as a human being. He changed himself into mud and she swallowed him with a drink of water.
See also *Master Spirit's Daughter* and *Nusxemtaiana.* [McIlwraith 1948]

Skagit Grandmother
Northwest, *Skagit*
Fishing and Water Animals; Wealth
Fish goddess.
Skagit Grandmother presided over the fishing grounds upriver from the joining of the Skagit and Cascade rivers. Fishermen who spoke to her properly were rewarded with large catches. [Collins 1974]

Skamotsxmana
Northwest, *Bella Coola*
Directions
Goddess at Snutali. She was one of the four sister goddesses who came from the east. One of her sisters caused the Bella Coola River to flow and Skamotsxmana was so upset she rocked to and fro. From this she got her Bella Coola name. See also *Tsumtlaks* and *Wiakai.* [McIlwraith 1948]

Skate Woman
California, *Yurok*
Extraterrestrial Beings
Woge goddess. Woges are the first beings who inhabited the world, but they disappeared before the first humans. [Leach 1972]

Skil-djaadai
Northwest, *Haida*
Wealth
"Property-woman." Goddess of wealth. [Locher 1932]

Sklumyoa
Arctic, *Nunivak Inuit*
Supreme Being
Supreme deity to whom prayers are addressed. Known as *Sila* in Canada. [Bierhorst 1985]

Skqwalutl
Northwest, *Bella Coola*
Unknown
Goddess at Alqualaxl. Mother of *Nusxemtaiana.* [McIlwraith 1948]

Skule
Northwest, *Klamath*
Wild Birds
"Meadowlark." Sister of Skele, wife of one of the Thunders. [Leach 1992]

Skwanat.äm.ä
Northwest, *Bella Coola*
Unhappiness
"The Mourner." Her wailing foretells of death. When she cries, mucus comes from her nose and solidifies into a crystal. Anyone who finds it will have good fortune. [Leach 1992; McIlwraith 1948]

Sky Woman
Northeast, *Seneca*
Reptiles; Creator of Life
After the world was created, Sky Woman went to the Great Earth Turtle to make the humans. See also *Awehai.* [de Wit 1979]

Snee-nee-iq
Northwest
Demi-animals; Destroyer of Life
Cannibal animal-person of ancient time who carried off children in a big basket on her back. See also *Dzoo-noo-qua, Sneneikulala.* [Gill 1992]

Sneneik
Northwest, *Bella Coola*
Destroyer of Life; Hunting and Wild Animals
Cannibal goddess. Mother of wolves.
 Sneneik steals children and robs graves. She offers food to those who visit her home, but if they partake they become paralyzed. [Jobes 1962; Monaghan 1981]

Sneneikulala
Northwest
Ceremonies
Cannibal Woman. Equivalent to *Tsonoqua.* See also *Snee-nee-iq.* [Savill 1978]

Snitsmän-a
Northwest, *Bella Coola*
Goodness; Health and Healing

Benevolent goddess. She restores people after the Stomach-cutting Dance, which involves mutilation. [Leach 1992; McIlwraith 1948]

Snowats
Northwest; Central Plateau, *Yoncalla, Kalapuya*
Hunting and Wild Animals; Creator of Life
    First Woman.

 Snowats grew from a jelly-like substance, holding a male child on a mountaintop. She traveled the world with Quartux, a wolf, and wherever they went, people appeared. [Gill 1992]

Snukpanlits
Northwest, *Bella Coola*
Time
    Goddess of Spring. Mother of *Noñ'osqa.* [Boas 1898; Leach 1992]

Snutkanals
Northwest, *Bella Coola*
Magic; Sky and Heavens; Education and Knowledge
    "Box." Goddess at Asklta.

Snutpanlits came from a supernatural box in the heavens. She was sent to earth with her two brothers to teach the people.

    See also *Sxapetl* and *Sximana.* [McIlwraith 1948]

Snutqutxals
Northwest, *Bella Coola*
Destroyer of Life
    Goddess of death. [Monaghan 1981]

Snuximetlimana
Northwest, *Bella Coola*
Creator of Life
    First Woman at Talio with *Nuyelelaix.* [McIlwraith 1948]

So Wuhti
Southwest, *Hopi*
Ceremonies
    "Grandmother." A kachina (see *A-ha Kachin' Mana*). Wuhti indicates a married woman. [Colton 1949]

Soat-saki
Plains, *Blackfoot*
Stars and Planets; Insects; Love and Sexuality
    "Feather Woman." Her lover, Morning Star, drew her to heaven with a spider's web and there she bore the star boy, Poia. [Jobes 1962]

Sohonasomtaka
Southwest, *Hopi*
War
    Warrior woman from Old Oraibi. A kachina (see *A-ha Kachin' Mana*) who appears at the Pachavu ceremony, a dramatization of historic events. [Wright 1973]

Somagalags
Northwest, *Bella Coola*
Creator of Life; Ceremonies; Education and Knowledge
    Creator goddess. First mother of the clan. She created the mountains called Kuga, Zaychissi, and Segos. Then she showed the people how to carve her totem. [Leach 1992]

Soniyawi
California, *Chemehuevi*
Stars and Planets

Star goddess. Coyote's wife who makes up the Pleiades with their son, three daughters, and a shaman. [Laird 1976; Leach 1992]

Sonxwana
Northwest, *Bella Coola*
Wild Birds; Mother and Guardian; Hunting and Wild Animals
    Eagle Goddess at Nutleax. Sister of *Ixlexwani.* They brought the beaver to the people for food. [McIlwraith 1948]

South Wind
Arctic, *Baffin Land, Iglulik Inuit*
Weather
    Weather deity. [Damas 1984]

Soyoko
Southwest, *Hopi*
Ceremonies; Destroyer of Life; Evil
    "Monster Woman." A kachina (see *A-ha Kachin' Mana*) who dresses in black and carries a blood-smeared knife. An ogre, she also carries a large basket in which she collects acceptable food. She threatens children, telling them that if they do not find game, mice, or rats for her, she will eat them instead. Alternate forms: Soyoko Mana, Soyoko Wuhti. [Colton 1949; Tyler 1964; Wright 1977]

Soyoko Mana   See *Soyoko.*

Soyoko Wuhti   See *Soyoko.*

Spider Woman
Southwest, *Hopi*
Insects; Creator of Life; Goodness; Evil
    Creator deity. Spider Woman is known among many of the Pueblo people. She has dual roles, helpful and dangerous. Her malevant aspect is called *Witch Woman.* Spider Woman traveled through the lower worlds during the emergence of humans to the earth. See also *Awitelin Tsita, Grandmother Spider, Hahai-i Wuhti, Kokyang Wuhti, Kokyangwuti, Gogyeng So Wuhti, Hatai Wuhti, Na?ackjeii Esdzaa, Naestsan, Nahosdzaan Esdza, Naste Estsan, Naxaasdza•n, Red-spider-woman, Sussistinnako, Tsitsicinako,* and *Biliku,* Indian Subcontinent. [Bierhorst 1985; Burland 1975; Cotterell 1979; Gill 1992; Monaghan 1981; Moon 1984; Stone 1979]

Spirit Woman
Arctic, *Nunivak Inuit*
Creator of Life; Hunting and Wild Animals; Magic; Unhappiness
    Creator deity.

Spirit Woman heard two brothers crying in their kayak. She came down and created earth and turned one of the brothers into a female so the earth could be populated. They lived well because there was plentiful food. One day the woman became angry because of the man's teasing and she killed him. Spirit Woman was very sad when she saw that the man was dead and the woman had fled to the sky. She turned into a wolf and her offspring became the humans that populated the earth. [Bierhorst 1976]

Sulukyi   See *Suyuki*

Sun Goddess
Northeast, *Algonquin*
Sun and Day; Destroyer of Life
    It is believed she brings death and disease to the people. [Brinton 1876]

Sun Sister

Arctic, *Inuit*

Sun and Day

There is a variety of stories about the sun as sister of the moon. They are lovers and the sister becomes angry when she finds out it is her brother. They chase each other across the sky, carrying torches. The sun's torch is much brighter than the moon's. See also *Akycha, Greenland Sun Goddess,* and *Siqiniq.* [Bierhorst 1985; Burland 1975; Stone 1979]

Sun Woman

Arctic, *Mackenzie Inuit*

Sun and Day

Sun goddess. The sun is also considered female by the Athapascas, Cherokee, Yuchi, Iroquois, Maidu, Mbocobis, and Tkupis people. [Brinton 1876; Damas 1984; Eliade 1967; Leach 1972]

Superguksoak

Arctic, *Labrador Inuit*

Earth and Nature

"Old Woman." Earth goddess who protects animals. [Damas 1984; Gill 1992; Leach 1992; Wyers 1932]

Sussistinnake   See *Sussistinnako.*

Sussistinnako

Southwest, *Keres, Sia*

Creator of Life; Family and Tribes; Fire; Weather; Mother and Guardian; Household Affairs

"Thought Woman." Primordial spider woman. Creator deity. Her daughters are *Utset,* the mother of Native Americans, and *Nowutset,* the mother of everyone else. Her sister is *Shro-tu-na-ko.* Sussistinnako produced fire, which she gave to *Tsichtinako.* She created rain, thunder, lightning, and the rainbow—and everything else. She is especially interested in weaving and childbirth. Alternate forms: Sussistinnake, Sitch-tche-na-ko. [Bierhorst 1985; Leach 1992; Moon 1984; Savill 1978; Stone 1979; Tyler 1964]

Sutal

Northwest, *Bella Coola*

Unknown

A companion of *Hano.* [McIlwraith 1948]

Su-u-ki   See *Suyuki.*

Suyuki

Southwest, *Zuni*

Evil

Cannibal Ogre Woman. Children are frightened into good behavior by stories that Suyuki puts children in her basket. Alternate forms: Su-u-ki, Sulukyi, Atoshle Suyuki, Thlamanla, Kokwatawu, Aweshi. [Bunzel 1984; Tyler 1964; Wright 1985]

Sxapetl

Northwest, *Bella Coola*

Sky and Heavens; Education and Knowledge

Goddess at Siwalos. She was sent down from the heavens with her brothers to be a teacher. See also *Sximana* and *Snutkanals.* [McIlwraith 1948]

Sximana

Northwest, *Bella Coola*

Sun and Day

"Light-bearer." Goddess at Nutsqwalt who came to earth with her brothers to be a teacher. See also *Sxapetl* and *Snutkanals.* [McIlwraith 1948]

Sye-elth

California, *Yurok*

Evil

Evil goddess who makes humans do evil things. [Leach 1992; Thompson 1916]

Ta Tha-bthin, The

Plains, *Dhegiha Osage*

Hunting and Wild Animals; Stars and Planets

"Three Deer." Star goddesses in Orion's belt worshiped in the Lower Missouri Basin. [Leach 1992]

Tacobud   See *Tacoma.*

Tacoma

Northwest, *Salish, Nisqually, Puyallup, Yakima*

Earth and Nature; Fishing and Water Animals

Earth goddess of Mt. Rainier in the Cascade Mountains. She protected the waters to permit the salmon to return. Alternate forms: Dah-ko-beed, Tacobud, Takkobad, Takobid, Tehoma. [Clark 1953; Monaghan 1981]

Tahc-I

Southeast, *Tunica*

Sun and Day; Wild Birds; Love and Sexuality

Sun goddess.

 Tahc-I lived in the dark. Kingfisher saw her and took her home. When she discovered she was in a nest and her lover would only feed her fish, she began to sing a plaintive song. As she sang, she rose into the sky, giving off a bright light. [Monaghan 1981]

Tahltan Game Mother

Subarctic, *Tahltan*

Hunting and Wild Animals

Goddess of animals. She would not release the animals to the hunters if they did not treat her with respect. Upper basin of the Stikine River in northern British Columbia. [MacNeish 1981]

Tai-mai-ya-wurt

California, *Luiseno*

Earth and Nature

Mother earth.

 Mother Earth and her brother Heaven were made by the creator. Heaven laid his hand on his sister and she trembled, giving birth to all that is terrestrial and celestial. [Gill 1987; Gill 1992]

Takanakapsaluk

Arctic, *Iglulik Inuit*

Luck; Water; Hunting and Wild Animals; Health and Healing; Justice; Heaven and Hell

Sea goddess. Equivalent to *Sedna.* She causes misfortune, but she is also sought to aid in the catching of game and for healing. The dead are said to go to her underwater home for judgment. [Jobes 1962; Leach 1992; Wyers 1932]

Takanaluk arnaluk

Unknown

"The Woman Down There." See *Arnaaluk Takannaaluk.*

Takanna' Luk   See *Sedna* and *Uiniyumayuituq.*

Takkobad   See *Tacoma.*

Takobid   See *Tacoma.*

Takursh Mana
Southwest, *Hopi*
Agriculture
    "Yellow Girl." A kachina (see *A-ha Kachin' Mana*). Corn maiden is often present with *Angak'chin Mama*. [Colton 1949; Wright 1973; Wright 1977]

Talaotumsi   See *Talatumsi*.

Talatumsi
Southwest, *Hopi*
Dawn and Twilight; Ceremonies; Mother and Guardian; Agriculture
    "Dawn Woman." Associated with the New-fire Ceremony. She acts as a mother to the novices during initiation ceremonies, the passage of children to adulthood. Talatumsi presides over childbirth and crops. [Colton 1949; Jobes 1962; Leach 1992; Tyler 1964]

Tamaayawut
California
Earth and Nature; Creator of Life
    Earth goddess. With her brother Tuukumit, she was the mother of all things. See also *Tamayowut*. [Leach 1992]

Tamambia
Great Basin, *Shoshoni*
Earth and Nature
    "Our Mother." Earth goddess. Alternate form: Tamso-Gobia. [Hultkrantz 1983; Lowie 1924]

Tamayowut
California, *Luiseno*
Creator of Life; Earth and Nature
    The Earth. Creator deity with her brother Tukomit. Mother of all things in the world, animate and inanimate. See also *Atavish* and *Tamaayawut*. Alternate form: Tomaiyowit. [Leach 1956; Leach 1992]

Tamso-Gobia   See *Tamambia*.

Tanakapsaluk   See *Sedna*.

Ta-no-wish
California, *La Jolla*
Earth and Nature; Mother and Guardian
    Mother earth.
    Ta-no-wish sat in the dark arguing with Night about who was stronger. Night made Ta-no-wish fall asleep and when she woke up she was pregnant. Everything grew within her as she sat erect and round. [Gill 1992; Muser 1978]

Tarqeq
Canada, *Iglulik*
Moon and Night; Mother and Guardian
    Moon goddess. She presides over hunting and women's fertility. Sometimes considered male. See also *Tatqeq*. [Leach 1992; Nungak 1969; Rasmussen 1931]

Tasap Kachin' Mana
Southwest, *Hopi*
Ceremonies
    "Navajo Kachina Girl." Representing the Navajo for the Hopi, she carries a rattle in the dance of the kachinas. See *A-ha Kachin' Mana* for definition of kachina. [Wright 1973; Wright 1977]

Ta-tanka-wian-ska
Plains, *Lakota Sioux*
Hunting and Wild Animals
    Equivalent to *White Buffalo Woman*. [LaPointe 1976]

Tate
Plains, *Oglala Sioux*
Weather
    "Wind." The sky god created her to keep him company. [Walker 1980]

Tatoosh
Northwest, *Okanagan*
Earth and Nature
    Island goddess at the Strait of Juan de Fuca. [Clark 1953]

Tatqeq
Arctic, *Netsilik Inuit*
Moon and Night; Mother and Guardian
    Moon goddess. She presides over women's fertility. Sometimes considered male. See also *Tarqeq*. Alternate forms: Aningat, Aningap. [Balikci 1970; Leach 1992]

Tcakwaina Mana
Southwest, *Hopi*
War
    Warrior Maiden. A kachina (see *A-ha Kachin' Mana*). She defended the pueblo when the men were away. [Fewkes 1985]

Tcakwena Okya
North America, *Zuni*
Mother and Guardian; Ceremonies
    Childbirth deity. A kachina (see *A-ha Kachin' Mana*) who gives children, presides at delivery, and blesses the infants with long life. [Bunzel 1984]

Tcalyel
Southwest, *Navajo*
Directions; Moon and Night
    "Darkness." She is associated with the east. Tcalyel is not malevolent, but she fosters foolishness and illness during the night. Alternate forms: Tcaxalxe•l, Tca•txe•l, Chahałheeł. [Leach 1992; McNeley 1981]

Tca•txe•l   See Tcalyel

Tcaxalxe•l   See Tcalyel

Tcho
Southeast, *Yuchi*
Family and Tribes; Sun and Day
    Sun goddess. Mother of Yohah, a star, and Sharpah, the moon.
    Tcho went to the east. From there she began a journey over the earth that spread sunlight everywhere. As she passed over the earth, a drop of her blood fell to the ground. From this drop of blood came the first humans—children of the sun, the Yuchis.
    Alternate forms: T-cho, Tso. [Gill 1992; Sproul 1979]

T-cho   See *Tcho*.

Tciakwenaoka
Northwest, *Zuni*
Mother and Guardian
    Goddess of fertility and childbirth. [Leach 1992]

Tcikee Cac Nadleehe
Southwest, *Navajo*
Evil
   "Changing Bear Maiden." Deity of evil. Alternate forms: Changing Bear Maiden, Maiden Whose Clothes Rattle. [Gill 1992]

Tcua-wugti
Southwest, *Moquis*
Reptiles; Heaven and Hell; Weather
   Snake goddess of underworld. She brings the rain. [Gill 1992; Leach 1992; Stephen 1888]

Tcuperekata
Plains, *Skidi Pawnee*
Stars and Planets; Creator of Life
   "Evening Star." Mother of all living things—humans, animals, birds, and plants. [Dorsey 1904b; Leach 1992]

Tehoma   See *Tacoma.*

Tepkanuset
Northeast, *Micmac*
Moon and Night; Mother and Guardian
   Moon and childbirth goddess. She protects mothers and children from the night air. [Leach 1992; Wallis 1955]

Tewa Corn Mother
Southwest, *Tewa*
Agriculture
   Corn Goddess.
   A young boy was searching for food. He heard a voice calling to him from the rafters of a house, telling him to take her and place her in a basket of corn meal. He takes the corn to all the people who have had nothing but greens to eat.
   See also *Corn Mother.* [Leach 1972]

Thlamanla   See *Suyuki.*

Thlehakto Okya   See *Ahmetolela Okya.*

Thlewekwe Okya
Southwest, *Zuni*
Ceremonies
   "Sword Swallower Girl." [Wright 1985]

Thompson Earth Mother
Northwest, *Thompson*
Earth and Nature
   She argued with her husband the sun and he changed her from a woman to the earth. Her body became features of the earth—her hair became trees and grass, her flesh became clay, her bones became rocks, and her blood became water. See also the *Thompson Goddesses.* [Long 1963]

Thompson Goddesses, The
Central Plateau, *Thompson*
Beauty; Evil; Selfishness; Goodness; Selflessness; Order; Disorder; Earth and Nature; Life/Death Cycle; Fire; Water; Education and Knowledge
   Five goddesses were created when the Old One pulled five hairs from his head. As each beautiful young woman appeared, the Old One asked her what she wished to be. The first one said she wanted to be bad and would be concerned with only her own pleasure and her descendants would fight, kill, steal, and commit adultery. The second one requested that she be good and her descendants be peaceful, wise, honest, and chaste. The third one asked to be the earth so she could give life to everything and reclaim everything in death. The fourth one wanted to be fire and to be used for the good of the people. The last one desired to be water so she could offer wisdom, cleanliness, and growth.
   See also *Thompson Earth Mother.* [Eliade 1967]

Three Kadlu Sisters, The
Arctic, *Baffin Land, Iglulik Inuit*
Weather; Fire
   Weather goddesses. They play together and bring thunder and lighting. [Damas 1984; Stone 1979]

Tih-kuyi-wuhti
North America, *Hopi*
Mother and Guardian; Hunting and Wild Animals; Unhappiness
   "Child-water Woman" and "Mother of the Game Animals." She presides over human childbirth and is the mother of antelope, deer, mountain sheep, and rabbits. She is said to have used birth blood on sand to make the rabbits. She is sometimes called *Sand Altar Woman.*
   Tih-kuyi-wuhti had a miscarriage when she was wandering with Snake Woman. This made her very sad so she wanders the earth wailing, projecting images of infants into women so they can have children.
   Wuhti indicates a married woman. [Gill 1992; Hultkrantz 1983; Jobes 1962; Leach 1972; Leach 1992; Tyler 1964]

Tikuoi Wuhti
North America, *Hopi*
Ugliness
   "The Outcast Woman." She appears at night, wearing a white wedding robe, terrifying men by appearing in their dreams. Wuhti indicates a married woman. [Colton 1949]

Tipiskawipisim
Northeast, Subarctic, *Cree, Ojibwa*
Moon and Night; Creator of Life
   "Moon." Creator of the first female after the flood. To the Cree, her brother is Sun. [Gill 1992]

Tisseyak
California, *Awant*
Disorder; Metals and Minerals
   South Dome of Yosemite Valley.
   Tisseyak and her husband came from a far-off land. When they reached the Yosemite Valley, she was very thirsty and drank all the water in Lake Awaia, causing a drought. Her husband became angry and beat Tisseyak. She, in turn, threw the basket she was carrying at him. They both turned to stone, she the South Dome and he the North Dome. The basket still lies at his feet. [Emerson 1965]

Tiwakpomatamsi   See *Tüwapongtümsi.*

Tkukwunag Kachin-mana   See *Tukwinong Mana.*

Tlakwakila
Northwest, *Bella Coola*
Ceremonies
   Goddess at Qwiyai. She came to Sea-Lion Island to sing the death songs when someone died. [McIlwraith 1948]

Tlaqwagi'layugwa
Northwest, *Kwakiutl*
Wild Birds; Metals and Minerals
   "Copper-maker-woman." She appears as a white bird, recognized because of its copper odor. She is the daughter of Qomogwa, a sea god. See also *L!äzwag·iɛlayugwa.* [Boas 1935; Leach 1992]

Tlitcaplitana
Northwest, *Bella Coola*
Sky and Heavens; Goodness; Health and Healing; Education and Knowledge; Magic
Sky goddess. Benevolent deity who heals the sick and gives secret knowledge and chants to her people. [Monaghan 1981]

Tlkelikera
California, *Yurok*
Mother and Guardian; Hunting and Wild Animals
"Mole." Goddess of childbirth. Sister of Wohpekmeu. [Kroeber 1925; Leach 1992]

Tó asdza·n
Southwest, *Navajo*
Water
Water deity. She presides over the small streams. Mother of Rain. [Leach 1992; Moon 1984]

Tomaiyowit   See *Tamayowut*.

Toodlanak
Arctic, *Baffin Land Inuit*
Goodness; Mother and Guardian; Hunting and Wild Animals
Benevolent animal mother. She provides deer for the people. [Bilby 1923; Leach 1992]

Tootega
Arctic, *Inuit*
Evil; Disorder; Magic
"Old Woman." She lives in a stone house and can walk on water. [Carlyon 1982]

Toothed Vagina
Great Basin, *Moapa*
Unknown
Goddess and daughter of *Cotsipamapot*. See also *Evening Star, Korawini?i,* and *Poo?wavil.* [Lowie 1924]

Tootooch
Northwest, *Ahts*
Wild Birds
"Thunderbird." Mother of humans, with Quawteaht as father. [Bancroft 1886; Leach 1992]

T'otowaxsemalaga
Northwest, *Kwakiutl*
Water
"Swell Woman." Sea goddess. [Boas 1935; Leach 1992]

Toxwid
Northwest, *Kwakiutl*
War; Immortality; Ceremonies; Life/Death Cycle; Earth and Nature
Warrior. She participates in *Tsetseka* ceremonies (winter ceremonial season) by begging to be killed. They "kill" her and she then dances until she is fully recovered. During current performances in the winter ceremonial season, she gives birth to a giant frog, a flock of birds, or a salmon. [Gill 1992]

Trukwinu Mana
Southwest, *Hopi*
Weather; Ceremonies
Rain kachina (see *A-ha Kachin' Mana*.) She has rain-cloud symbol on her headdress and pine boughs for hair. [Fewkes 1985]

Tsatsaquitelaku
Northwest, *Kwakiutl*
Fishing and Water Animals
Fish goddess. She protects salmon and other fish. [Locher 1932]

Tsects
Northwest
Goodness
"Grandmother White Mouse." Benevolent deity. [Burland 1975]

Tsek'any'agojo
Southwest, *Tewa*
Stars and Planets
"Evening Star." [Harrington 1907; Leach 1992]

Tsitctinako   See *Tsitsicinako*.

Tsitsicinako
Southwest, *Acoma Pueblo*
Earth and Nature; Creator of Life; Fire; Education and Knowledge
Creator deity and Earth Mother. She taught her people how to keep a fire going with the red light that fell from the sky. See also *Spider Woman*. Alternate form: Tsitctinako. [Stone 1979; Tyler 1964]

Tsi'ty'icots'a
Southwest, *Keresan*
Metals and Minerals
Salt goddess of Zuni Salt Lake. See also *Malokatsiki*. [Leach 1992; Tyler 1964]

Tsiyayoji
Southwest, *Navajo*
Wild Birds
"Meadowlark Woman." She brings the ashes necessary to make enemy scalps harmless. [Moon 1984]

Tso   See *Tcho*.

Tsonoqua
Northwest, *Kwakiutl*
Evil; Ceremonies
Cannibal Mother. Mother of wolves, she ate corpses and stolen children. See also *Sneneik*. She is called *Baxbakualanuchsiwae* and *Sneneikulala* by neighboring peoples. [Monaghan 1981; Savill 1978]

Tsore Jowa
California
Wild Birds
"Eagle." Bird goddess. [Weigle 1982]

Tsumtlaks
Northwest, *Bella Coola*
Directions; Water
Goddess at Snutali. She was one of the four sister goddesses who came from the east. One of her sisters caused the Bella Coola River to flow. Even though Tsumtlaks tried to drink the river dry, it remained a rivulet. The sisters followed the stream to the west. See also *Skamotsxmana* and *Wiakai*. [McIlwraith 1948]

Tsunukwa
Northwest, *Wakashan*
Immortality; Water; Ceremonies
She can bring the dead back to life. Her dance is slow and sleepy, leading some to say she is dim-witted.

Tsunukwa's son is killed but she cannot revive him because she doesn't have his body. A young hero recovers the body for her and she revives her son with the water of life. She thanks the hero by giving him some of the water and her mask, which he wears in her dance. [Bierhorst 1985]

Tugtut Igfianut
Arctic, *Hudson Bay, Iglulik Inuit*
Hunting and Wild Animals; Ceremonies
"Mother of Caribou." An offering of seal skin is made to her to guarantee a successful hunt. Alternate form: Tuktut Ikvait, Tukwunag Kachin-mana. [Leach 1992; Wyers 1932]

Tuktut Ikviat   See *Tugtut Igfianut.*

Tukwinong Mana
Southwest, *Hopi*
Ceremonies; Weather; Directions
"Cumulus Cloud Kachina Girl." Kachina (see *A-ha Kachin' Mana*) who dances during the *Shalako* Ceremony. The Shalako is a December ritual. See *Sio Shalako Mana.* She carries a tray of cornmeal that has been divided into four colors to represent the four directions of the clouds. Alternate form: Tukwunag Kachin-mana. [Wright 1973; Wright 1977]

Tukwunag Kachin-mana   See *Tuktut Igfianut.*

Tunica Sun Goddess
Southeast, *Tunica*
Sun and Day; Unhappiness
The disappointed bride who became the sun. [Bierhorst 1985]

Turquoise Woman
Southwest, *Navajo*
Unknown
A separate deity created by *Changing Woman* or an aspect of *Changing Woman* herself.

 Turquoise Woman and her sister Whiteshell Woman lived on the earth when the monsters came. They competed with the Corn Maidens, but lost the chance to be the wives of the Monster-slayer.

See also *Estsanatlehi* and *Asdzaa Dootlijii.* Alternate form: Ahsonnutli. [Leach 1972; Monaghan 1981; Sykes 1968]

Turtle Woman
Plains, *Arapaho*
Creator of Life
Creator goddess. In primordial times, she brought mud from the bottom of the flood to make the earth. [Marriott and Rachlin 1975]

Tuwabontsusi   See *Tüwapongtümsi.*

Tüwapongtümsi
North America, *Hopi*
Water; Ceremonies
"Earth Altar Young Woman." She represents all the moist elements in life, as well as humans, animals, and plants. Offerings are made to her at the New-fire ceremony in November. She is also called *Sand Altar Woman* and Child-water-woman (see *Tih-kuyi-wuhti*). Alternate forms: Tiwakpomatamsi, Tuwabontsusi. [Jobes 1962; Leach 1992; Tyler 1964]

Twana First Woman
Northwest, *Twana*
Creator of Life
She was made from the rib of First Man, who was made out of the ground.

 God made First Man and First Woman and told them they could eat all the fruit except a particular berry. First Woman was tempted by the King of Evil and ate some of the berries. She became the mother of Native Americans and First Man became the father of white people.

This story is similar to the Christian story of Adam and Eve and may be a combination of original myth and the biblical story. [Tyler 1964]

Two Women
Plains, *Crow, Apsaroke*
Creator of Life
First women. They were placed in the valleys with two men and told to multiply. [Curtis 1908]

Uiniyumayuituq
Arctic, *Iglulik Inuit*
Unknown
"The One Who Did Not Want a Husband." Equivalent to *Sedna.* Alternate forms: Aviliayuk, Nuliayuk, Takannaluk, Unigumsuitok, Uiniyumissuitoq. [Damas 1984]

Uiniyumissuitoq   See *Uiniyumayuituq.*

Uivarahugiyaq
Arctic, *Caribou Inuit*
Hunting and Wild Animals
"Wolf Mother." [Damas 1984]

Ukat
California, *Yauelmani*
Luck
Goddess of good luck. [Kroeber 1925; Leach 1992]

Ulala
Northwest, *Haida*
Evil; Ceremonies; Ugliness
Cannibal ogre. [Savill 1978]

Ullughmiut, The
Arctic, *Iglulik Inuit*
Heaven and Hell; Mother and Guardian
"Inhabitants of the Daytime." Women who die in childbirth become deified and live in heaven with others who died violently. [Damas 1984]

Ululiarnaq
Arctic, *Hudson Bay Inuit*
Destroyer of Life
"Disemboweller." She lives near the moon and cuts out the entrails of those she can make laugh or smile. See also *Erlaveersisoq* and *Irdlirvirisissong.* Alternate form: Ululiernang. [Leach 1992; Wyers 1932]

Ululiernang   See *Ululiarnaq.*

Unaviga   See *Anavigak.*

Unelanuki   "Apportioner of Time." See *Nuñda.*

Unhcegila, The
Plains, *Lakota Sioux*
Destroyer of Life; Reptiles
"Females of the Unktehi." Land dragons who bring death. [Leach 1992; Walker 1980]

Unigumisuitok   "The One Who Doesn't Want a Husband." See *Uiniyumayuituq.*

Unk

Plains, *Lakota, Oglala Sioux*
Fishing and Water Animals; Evil; Water
   "Contention." Goddess of the waters and ancestor of all
evil beings.

 Maka created Unk to be her companion, but Unk was
banished from the god's circle and cast into the waters.
Unk was mean and evil and created animals without
limbs. They were clothed with slime or scales and were cold; they
became the fish who live in the water.
   See also *Maka*. [Leach 1992; Walker 1980]

Uretsete

Southwest, *Cochiti*
Health and Healing; Education and Knowledge; Family and
Tribes
   Pueblo Mother Goddess. Sister of *Naotste*.

In the beginning Uretste and Naotste lived in darkness
under the earth. Sussistinnako nursed the sisters and
taught them their language. She gave them a basket
containing images of animals and seeds that were to be spread about
the world. When the roots of a tree broke through into the darkness
and allowed some light in, the sisters began their journey. They also
carried pollen and sacred corn meal and Sussistinnako taught them
prayers and the creation song and told them to thank Sun for
allowing them to come into the light. During the migration, when
there were troubles and pestilence, Uretsete taught the medicine
men so they could cure the people. Uretsete became the mother of
the Native Americans and Naotsete, the mother of the aliens (white
people).
   Among the Sia the sisters are *Utset* and *Nowutset*; the
Santa Ana have *Utctsityi* and *Nausity*; to the Acoma, the
sisters are *Liatiku* and *Nautsiti*; and the Laguna have
I'tc'ts'ity and *Nau'tsity*. See also *Uti*. [Carlyon 1982; Leach
1992; Tyler 1964]

Utctsityi

Southwest, *Santa Ana*
Family and Tribes
   "Mother of the Pueblo Indians." Her sister *Nausity* was
the mother of the aliens. See also *Uretsete*. [Tyler 1964]

Ute First Woman

Great Basin, *Ute*
Creator of Life
   Goddess.

 First Woman was created from a rib of First Man. They
were placed in a peach orchard by the creator and told not
to eat the fruit. A snake tempted First Woman to eat the
fruit and she in turn tempted First Man. When First Man realized
he had eaten the forbidden fruit, he attempted to throw it up, but it
got caught in his throat and became his "Adam's apple." First
Woman and First Man were forced to leave the orchard and earn a
living. [Lowie 1924]

Uti Hiata

Plains, *Pawnee*
Agriculture; Mother and Guardian; Education and
Knowledge
   "Mother Corn."

Father Sky sent Uti Hiata to assist with the birth of
humans from corn seeds. Thunder kidnapped her and put
her under the earth. She dug through the dirt and finally
reached the sunlight, bringing the people with her. She taught them
all they needed to know.
   See also *Uretsete* and *Mother Corn*. [Monaghan 1981]

Utlunta

Southeast, *Cherokee*
Destroyer of Life; Physical Prowess; Immortality

"Spearfinger." Cannibal.

 Utlunta liked tender, young livers to eat. To find her food,
she would disguise herself as an ordinary old woman. She
would wander about until she found someone alone.
Using the stony hard forefinger of her right hand, she would kill her
victim and eat the person's liver. She was impossible to kill with an
arrow because her skin was rock-hard. [de Wit 1979]

Utset

North America, *Sia*
Creator of Life; Stars and Planets; Insects
   First Mother with her sister, *Nowutset* or *Bowutset*.

Utset and Nowutset were children of Sussistinnako.
When the lower world was flooded, Utset led the people to
the surface of the earth through a hollow reed. She gave
Beetle a sack full of stars to carry. Beetle grew tired and sat to rest.
Curious about what was in the sack, he bit a hole so he could peek
inside. Most of the stars escaped and went to the sky, but a few
remained and Utset arranged those into the Great Bear, Orion's
belt, and the Pleiades. Utset punished Beetle by blinding him; that
is why the Sia say Beetle has no eyes.
   See also *Uretsete*. Alternate forms: Dzelarhons, Itsictsiti.
[Burland 1975; Leach 1972; Leach 1992; Monaghan 1981;
Savill 1978; Schmidt 1951; Stone 1979; Tyler 1964]

Volcano Woman

Northwest
Metals and Minerals
   Goddess of copper. See also *Djilaquons* and *Copper
Woman*. [Burland 1975]

Wah-kah-nee

Northwest, *Chinook*
Time; Wild Birds; Ceremonies
   "Drifting Maiden."

 Wah-kah-nee caused an endless winter to come to her
people by killing a bird. When she confessed to her crime,
the people set her adrift on a block of ice as an offering to
the spirits of winter. The ice crashed and summer came
immediately. Wah-kah-nee survived and returned to her people,
becoming a sacred being in her village. [Monaghan 1981]

Wahkshum

Northwest, *Yakima, Klikitat*
Earth and Nature
   Goddess of Simcoe Mountain in southwestern Washington.
[Monaghan 1981]

Wajashk

Northeast, *Algonquin, Ottawa*
Hunting and Wild Animals
   "Muskrat Woman."

 Wajashk was on a raft with the other animals, floating
about in the endless ocean that existed before the earth.
Rabbit was in charge and he sent Otter and Beaver to the
bottom of the ocean for some mud. When they were unsuccessful,
Wajashk offered to go. The other animals made fun of her, but she
returned with a speck of mud and the earth was formed. [Brinton
1882]

Wa-kon-da Hondon

Plains, *Dhegiha Osage*
Moon and Night
   Moon goddess. Grandmother of the night. [Leach 1992]

Wakwiyo

Southwest, *Tewa*
Weather; Ceremonies

"Wind Woman." In New Mexico, her exorcism can be accomplished by throwing ashes in each of the directions. [Leach 1992; Parsons 1929]

Waotunoowase

Southeast, *Delaware*
Water; Evil

Water deity. She has a woman's body and a fish's tail. She exists in every drop of water and causes drownings. [Leach 1992]

Waoyakila

Northwest, *Kwakiutl*
Water; Metals and Minerals; Magic

"Tide-woman." Sea goddess. She appears at first to be quartz, then a shadow, then a human. [Boas 1935; Leach 1992]

Wasco

Northwest, *Yakima*
Earth and Nature

Goddess of Mt. Hood. Alternate form: Wyeast. [Clark 1953; Monaghan 1981]

Whaht-kay

Northwest, *Nooksakk, Lummi*
Earth and Nature

"Fair Maiden." Spieden Island goddess. She created the land features as she traveled to reach the water. [Clark 1953]

Wheatchee

Northwest, *Nisqually*
Evil; Water

Malevolent water deity. She inhabits Lake Steilacoom near Tacoma, Washington.

 Wheatchee would sometimes lift her arm out of the water and call to people on the shore. They were so frightened that they never swam or fished in her lake. [Clark 1953]

Whistling Grandmother

Arctic, *Inuit*
Evil; Destroyer of Life

Evil goddess who causes illness and death, especially among children. [Burland 1975]

White Buffalo Calf Woman   See *White Buffalo Woman.*

White Buffalo Woman

Plains, *Lakota, Brule Sioux*
Hunting and Wild Animals; Ceremonies

Bringer of the ritual pipe and several ceremonies including the Hunkakpi, Sun Dance, and White Buffalo ceremony. She is sometimes called White Buffalo Cow Woman or White Buffalo Maiden. Equivalent to *Ptesan Winyan.*

White Buffalo Woman appeared to two young hunters as a beautiful woman. One of the men thought of having intercourse with her, and because she could read his thoughts, she encouraged him. As they embraced, they were surrounded by white smoke. The smoke cleared and all that remained of the man was his wormy skeleton. White Buffalo Woman told the second man to return to camp to tell the leaders to prepare for her arrival. She appeared in the village, presented the chief with a pipe, and instructed the people in its use. As she left, she changed into a white buffalo galloping over the hills.

Alternate forms: Buffalo Calf Woman, Ta-tanka-wian-ska, Woope. [Bierhorst 1985; Gill 1992; Leach 1972; Leach 1992; Moon 1984]

White-light Woman   See *Kochinako.*

White-painted Woman

Southwest, *Chiricahua Apache*
Mother and Guardian; Ceremonies

A girl who wanders away from her people and is impregnated by Sun. She is similar to *Changing Woman.*

 White-painted Woman and White Shell Woman were young girls together. They went away to a high mountain where they lived on fruit, staying for a long time. Sun visited and taught them how to conduct girls' puberty rites. Sun slept with White-painted Woman, while Water slept with White Shell Woman. They each bore a son, Killer of Enemies and Child of the Water, who grow up to be monster slayers. [Gill 1992; Leach 1972; Opler 1941]

White Shell Woman   See *Yolkai Estsan.*

Whobone Shelowa Okya

Southwest, *Zuni*
Ceremonies

"Santo Domingo Kokokshi Girl." [Wright 1985]

Wiakai

Northwest, *Bella Coola*
Directions; Water

Goddess at Snutali. She was one of the four sister goddesses who came from the east. Even though she did not have legs, she used her foot to make the Bella Coola River flow. See also *Skamotsxmana* and *Tsumtlaks.* [McIlwraith 1948]

Widapokwi

Southwest, *Yavapai*
Mother and Guardian; Health and Healing

She protects the people in Arizona from whirlwinds and gives them medicine songs. Grandmother of Amchitapuka.

During the emergence from the underworld into the upperworld, Widapokwi was sealed in a hollow log with some birds and provisions so she could survive the flood. The flooding occurred when the people failed to close the hole that the tree made into the underworld for their escape. When she reached the upper world, Widapokwi had a daughter whose father was Sun. She conspired to have her daughter become pregnant by Sun as well. Widapokwi's daughter had a son, Amchitapuka, who Widapokwi raised, because shortly after his birth her daughter was carried off by eagles and eaten. Amchitapuka later revenged his mother's death by changing the eagles so they could not eat humans.

In more recent times, Widapokwi has been equated with the Christian God and Amchitapuka with Jesus. [Gill 1992; Leach 1992]

Wikwanekwila

Northwest, *Bella Coola*
Justice

A chief at Nusqalst.

Wikwanekwila was captured by First Man as a gift for his potlatch. Not wanting to be a slave, Wikwanekwila promised him her name, which was a prized possession. He accepted and she escaped enslavement. [McIlwraith 1948]

Wilatsukwe Dese Akenona Okya

Southwest, *Zuni*
Ceremonies

"Apache Pottery Drum Girl." See also *Wilatsukwe Okya.* [Wright 1985]

Wilatsukwe Okya

Southwest, *Zuni*
Ceremonies

"Apache Dance Girl" or "White Mountain Apache Girl." See also *Wilatsukwe Dese Akenona Okya.* [Wright 1985]

Wild Pony

Southwest, *Jicarilla Apache*

Ceremonies; Household Affairs; Creator of Life

First Woman. Giver of the young girl's pipe ritual.

 Wild Pony and Smoke were the first humans on earth. A hatsin *[magic being] came to them and showed them where to find food and told them about the future. The* hatsin *took Wild Pony aside and showed her clay and how to make bowls and how to fire them so they would hold water. After many years the* hatsin *came to Wild Pony again, this time in a dream. It told her what she must do to teach her granddaughters how to make clay bowls. Then the* hatsin *also taught Wild Pony how to make the sacred pipe of peace and how to use the pipe.*

Since that time, eight-year-old girls have their hands rubbed with clay and are told the clay is for them to use. Then they are taught how to form the clay into pipes and how to present the pipes to their people. [Stone 1979]

Wilx

Northwest, *Bella Coola*

Unknown

Companion of **Hano.** [McIlwraith 1948]

Wind Old Woman

North America, *Hopi, Tewa*

Evil; Magic; Ceremonies

Malevolent witch-like goddess who lives at the middle of the earth. People with rheumatism give her offerings of corn meal, pollen, and a single turkey feather. [Leach 1972]

Win?namakasaama?apitsi?

California, *Chemehuevi*

Wild Birds

Bird goddess. [Laird 1976; Leach 1992]

Witch Woman

Plains, *Pawnee*

Evil; Hunting and Wild Animals; Insects; Moon and Night; Magic

Malevolent aspect of **Spider Woman.** A goddess of many disguises.

 Witch Woman had all the buffalo hidden in a cave, guarded by snakes. The people were starving and their chief asked a young man named Morning Star to help. The snakes told Morning Star that if he could conquer Witch Woman, the snakes and buffalo would be free. Morning Star successfully overpowered Witch Woman. When a spider appeared, he shot the spider to heaven on an arrow where it lives as the moon. Witch Woman then fell dead and the snakes and buffalo were released from the cave. [Gill 1992]

Wohpe

Plains, *Skidi, Lakota*

Order; Beauty; Happiness; Mother and Guardian; Time

"The Meteor." Goddess of harmony, beauty, and pleasure. Skan, the sky, created her from his own essence to be the "Mediator."

 Wohpe and Tate, the Wind, lived at the center of the world, where she cared for Yum, the rejected son of Ite. She taught Yum how to dance and play games. She also observed that the Four Winds, Tate's sons, were gone from the lodge for twelve moon cycles. When she told Skan, he established twelve moons as Wani-yetu, *a year.*

See also **Maka.** [Bierhorst 1985; Gill 1992; Leach 1992; Walker 1980]

Woman Who Fell from the Sky

Northeast, *Iroquois*

Mother and Guardian; Goodness; Evil; Creator of Life

Goddess who gave birth to twins, good and evil. She died when the evil twin burst out of her armpit. See also **Aataentsic, Eagentei, Ketq Skwayne,** and **Yatahéntshi.** [Burland 1975; Leach 1992; Savill 1978]

Woman Who Washed Her Face

Central Plateau

Water; Weather

Water goddess in Washington. She can cause floods.

A dirty woman, actually a thrush, was scolded so much that she finally washed herself. Some of the drops of water fell from her face and caused a world flood. Muskrat saved the people by diving for a piece of mud that he enlarged into the earth, where they found refuge. [Bierhorst 1985]

Woope   See *White Buffalo Woman.*

Wyeast   See *Wasco.*

Xavasumkuli

Southwest, *Yuma*

Sun and Day; Moon and Night

Goddess of daylight and darkness. [Harrington 1907; Leach 1992]

Xayołká·ł 'esẓạ·

Southwest, *Navajo*

Dawn and Twilight

"Dawn woman." Mother of Talking God. See also **Hayoołkaał Asdzą́ą́.** [Leach 1992]

Yamai   See *Atavish.*

Ya?onakka Citta

Southwest, *Zuni*

Moon and Night

"Moonlight-giving Mother." Wife of the sun. [Gill 1992]

Yaonan

Southwest, *Zuni*

Moon and Night; Creator of Life

Moon Mother. Creator deity who existed from the beginning with the sun, Awonawilona. [Leach 1992; Sayce 1898]

Yatahéntshi

Northeast, *Huron*

Heaven and Hell

"Ancient Body." Mother of humans and keeper of the dead. Equivalent to **Woman Who Fell from the Sky.** [Bierhorst 1985]

Yebaad   See *Ye'ii Baad.*

Ye'ii Baad

Southwest, *Navajo*

Ceremonies

"Female God." Alternate form: Yebaad. [Burland 1975; Monaghan 1981]

Yegowaneh   See *Jigonsahseh.*

Yellow Woman

Southwest, *Pueblo*

Ceremonies; Magic; Agriculture; Hunting and Wild Animals

Heroine of many stories. One Yellow Woman Kachina (see **A-ha Kachin' Mana**) wears a green mask, an embroidered ceremonial blanket for a dress, and a white manta on her shoulders. She may be a bride, witch, chief's daughter, bear woman, corn woman, or ogress. See also **Corn Woman** and **Kochinako.** [Gill 1992; Tyler 1964]

Yellow-going Old Woman
Southwest, *Tewa*
Stars and Planets
   Goddess of the Evening Star. [Leach 1972]

Yelukxinang
Northwest, *Haida*
Family and Tribes; Wild Birds
   Mother of the Eagle clan. Associated with *Djilaqons*. [Gill 1992]

Yo'o
Southwest, *Yaqui*
Earth and Nature
   "Elder Flower Woman." [Painter 1986]

Yohozro Wuhti
Southwest, *Hopi*
Time
   "Cold-bringing Woman." A kachina (see *A-ha Kachin' Mana*.) Similar to *Hokoha Okya, Horo Mana,* and *Masan Wuhti*. Wuhti indicates a married woman. [Colton 1949; Wright 1973; Wright 1977]

Yolkai Estsan
Southwest, *Navajo*
Agriculture; Fire; Water; Fishing and Water Animals; Moon and Night; Creator of Life
   "White Shell Woman." Moon goddess who is a primordial creator. Sister of *Estsanatlehi,* wife of Klehanoai. The abalone shell is her symbol. She created the first woman from yellow corn and the first man from white corn and gave her creations the gifts of maize and fire. White is the color of dawn and the east and she is related to the waters. See also *Atbilxaniatiliax, Aittsamka, Kohak Oka.* Alternate form: White Shell Woman. [Leach 1972; Leach 1992; Monaghan 1981; Savill 1978; Stone 1979]

Yuman Mother Earth
Southwest, *Yuman*
Creator of Life
   Mother of the creator gods.
    Mother Earth and Water had two sons. The boys separated their parents by pushing Water upward to form the sky.
   Some stories say that Mother Earth mated with Father Sky. [Bierhorst 1985]

Yung'a Mana
North America, *Hopi*
Ceremonies
   Kachina (see *A-ha Kachin' Mana*). She carries a basket containing prickly pear during the plaza dances. Alternate form: Yunya Mana. [Colton 1949; Wright 1973]

Yunya Mana   See *Yung'a Mana.*

Yu?uravatsi
California, *Chemehuevi*
Wild Birds
   Bird goddess. [Laird 1976; Leach 1992]

NORTHERN EUROPE

Aarvak
Scandinavia; North Teuton
Sun and Day
   Norse-Viking deity who is equivalent to the Roman *Aurora,* the Greek *Eos,* and the Lithuanian *Ausrine* (see Eastern Europe). [Jobes 1962]

Abundia
Scandinavia; North Teuton
Wealth
   In Medieval literature, *Fulla* was called by this name or by *Habondia.* She gives and takes back the abundance of the earth. [Jobes 1962]

Aertha   See *Hertha.*

Ahnfrau
Germany
Fate; Family and Tribes
   She warns of approaching death or disaster and is said to be a spirit/ancestor of a noble family. Nobility is a staple of Norse-Viking life, and Norse-Viking goddesses are heroic, individualistic, and part of a closely knit small group of deities with intense loyalties. [Bonnerjea 1927; Crossley-Holland 1980; Jobes 1962]

Ahrenkonigin
Austria
Agriculture
   "Queen of Corn Ears." Austrian harvest goddess. [Monaghan 1990]

Alagabiae, The
Germany
Mother and Guardian; Wealth

"Those Who Give Richly." Mother deities of the Rhineland. [Lurker 1984]

Alaisiagae, The
Germany
War
   Fierce battle-dressed warriors on horseback who are probably Teutonic goddesses. Equivalent to the *Idisi* and Norse-Viking *Valkyries.* See also *Baudihillie, Beda, Fimmilinia,* and *Friagabi.* Alternate form: Alaisiages, The. [Carlyon 1982; Guirand 1968; Savill 1977]

Alaisiages, The   See *Alaisiagae, The.*

Alfhild
Scandinavia
Physical Prowess
   Scandinavian goddess who wrestled King Alf. He had to prove himself as strong as she before she would marry him. [Monaghan 1990]

Allwise
Scandinavia; North Teuton
Demi-animals; Magic
   "All-white." A *Swan Maiden*

   Allwise, with her sisters Swanwhite and Olrun, flew from their home in Murkwood to the shores of a lake in Wolfdales. They were followed by three brothers who loved their sweet summer songs. When the brothers saw the Swan Maidens on the shore singing and weaving flax without their swan coverings, they captured the coverings and gained power over the maidens, having them for their wives. For seven years they lived happily, but in the eighth year, the swan maidens became unhappy, and in the ninth year, they regained their swan feathers and flew away forever.

Other wives liberating themselves are **Bear Woman,** North America, and **Linda,** Eastern Europe. [Leach 1972; Mackenzie 1912; Savill 1977]

Alraun
Germany; North Teuton
Luck; Magic

Priestess, goblin, or good elf. The name comes from "alraun," which is the German name for the mandrake root, used for magic. Good luck images were shaped from the roots and kept in homes. Alternate forms: Alrauna-wife; Alraune. [Jobes 1962; Leach 1972]

Alrauna-wife   See *Alraun.*

Alraune   See *Alraun.*

Amma
Scandinavia; North Teuton
Family and Tribes

"Grandmother." Mother of the Churls, a Norse-Viking race of business and trades people. A "churl" later became the ordinary free person who formed the basis of Anglo-Saxon society. [Crossley-Holland 1980; Monaghan 1981]

Angeburga
Germany
Demi-animals; Magic

Swan Maiden loved by Weiland (Voland). [Jobes 1962]

Angerbodha
Scandinavia; North Teuton
Ugliness; Destroyer of Life; Heaven and Hell; Weather

Norse monster. Daughter of *Gullveig.* She is said to be half-dead and half-alive, frequently being shown as half-black and half-white. As a ruler of the dead, she is called **Hella.** As **Hyrokkin,** she is the goddess of winter storms. [Crossley-Holland 1980; Jobes 1962; Monaghan 1981]

Angeyja
Scandinavia; North Teuton
Large Size; Water

One of the nine *Vana Mothers* or *Wave Maidens.* [Jobes 1962]

Angur-boda   See *Gullveig.*

Askefruer, The
Scandinavia; North Teuton
Earth and Nature; Health and Healing; Magic

"Ash Nymphs." They are endowed with occult powers, can cure diseases, and are portrayed as having hairy bodies, pendulant breasts, messy hair, and clothes of moss. The ash tree is particularly important in the ancient Scandinavian religion. The world tree was the ash, Yggdrasill. The first man, Ask, was transformed from an ash tree. [Bonnerjea 1927; Jobes 1962; Leach 1972]

Aslaug   See *Aslog.*

Aslog
Scandinavia; North Teuton
Weather

Spirit of the air who is the connection between deities and humans.

Daughter of *Brynhild* and Sigurd.

 Aslog was placed in the care of Baenkhild, the sister of Brynhild, and her husband, Heimer. After her father, Sigurd, was killed and her mother, Brynhild, died, Heimer

feared for Aslog's life and took her to Norway. In one version of the story, the Norwegian peasants discovered that Aslog had a treasure, so they killed Heimer and took Aslog as a slave and renamed her Krähe, "Crow." In another version, she was simply a ward of a peasant couple. In both versions, she married Ragnar Loödbrog and had either two sons, Norse kings Ingvar and Ubbe, or five sons.

Alternate forms: Aslaug, Krähe. [Jobes 1962; Leach 1972]

Asynja   See *Asynjur, The.*

Asynje   See *Asynjur, The.*

Asynjor   See *Asynjur, The.*

Asynjur, The
Scandinavia; North Teuton
Justice; Supreme Being

Companions of *Freyja* and goddesses in the Nordic pantheon. Among their number (13, 19, or 52, depending on the authority) are **Beda, Frigga, Horn, Idun(a), Nanna,** and **Sif.** They live at Asgard and form a judicial community that holds daily council with the other deities.

The Norse universe is visualized as a tricentric structure. On the top level is Asgard, realm of the Aesir, or warrior gods. Each of the deities has a separate hall within the walled citadel. Valhalla is also here. The second level is Midgard and is inhabited by humans and surrounded by an immense ocean. The world of the giants, Jotunheim, is also on this level. Their citadel is called Utgard, the outer world. The dwarfs are on this level and live in Nidavellir (Dark Home) and the dark elves live below them in Svartalfheim. Asgard and Midgard are connected by Bilfrost, a flaming rainbow bridge. On the third level is Niflheim, the world of the dead. *Asynja* or *Asnyje* is the singular of Asynjur. See also **Baduhenna.** Alternate form: Asynjor. [Jobes 1962; Leach 1972; Sykes 1968]

Atla
Scandinavia; North Teuton
Large Size; Water

One of the nine *Vana Mothers* or *Wave Maidens.* [Jobes 1962; Leach 1992]

Audhumbla
Scandinavia; North Teuton
Creator of Life; Domesticated Animals; Primordial Being

She existed before the creation of the world.

When the land of frost in the north, called Niflheim, and the land of fire in the south, called Muspelsheim, interacted in Ginnungagap, the area of emptiness between them, Audhumbla the cow and an evil giant, Ymir, were formed. Ymir fed off the four rivers of milk that flowed from Audhumbla's teats and she fed off the salty ice. As she licked the ice, the first man, who was named Buri, came forth.

Alternate forms: Audhumla, Audumbla. [Crossley-Holland 1980; Monaghan 1981]

Audhumla   See *Audhumbla.*

Audumbla   See *Audhumbla.*

Augeia
Scandinavia; North Teuton
Large Size; Water

One of the variant names of the nine *Vana Mothers* or *Wave Maidens.* [Leach 1992]

Aurboda   See *Gullveig.*

Aurgiafa   See *Eyrgjafa.*

Avfruvva   See *Havfru.*

Baduhenna
Germany; Grison; Frisian
Family and Tribes; Weather
   "The War-mad One." Ancient tribal deity of both the
Grisons in Switzerland and the Frisians on the islands off the
coast of the North Sea. Baduhenna and *Sif* live at Asgard and
participate in a judicial community that holds daily council
with the other deities. See also *Aśynjur, The.* [Jobes 1962;
Leach 1992; Wedeck 1971]

Baenkhild
Scandinavia; North Teuton
Family and Tribes
   Sister of *Brynhild.* [Jobes 1962]

Baudihillie
Germany
War
   "Ruler of Battle." A member of *The Alaisiagae* who had an
altar at Housesteads on Hadrian's Wall. The wall was erected
c. 121-127 C.E. by Roman Emperor Hadrian during the
occupation of Britain. Associated with *Friagabi.* [Bridgwater
1950; Savill 1977]

Bechtli   See *Berchta.*

Beda
Scandinavia; North Teuton
Earth and Nature
   Teutonic (ancient Germanic) deity who is one of the
Aśynjur, goddesses of the Norse-Viking pantheon and an
aspect of nature. [Davidson 1964; Sykes 1968]

Beiwe
Scandinavia; Saami
Sun and Day
   Sun goddess who brings the green color to the Arctic
spring. Mother of *Beiwe-Neida.* Associated with the fertility
of plants and animals, especially reindeer. She is invoked to
aid those who are insane. White female animals are sacrificed
to her and butter is considered her "porridge." In Norway
she is called *Paive.* [Monaghan 1990]

Beiwe-Neida
Scandinavia; Saami
Unknown
   Daughter of *Beiwe.* Each spring she travels through the
sky in an enclosure of reindeer antlers with her mother.
[Monaghan 1990]

Belsta   See *Bestla.*

Berche   See *Berchta.*

Berchta
Germany
Earth and Nature; Evil; Fate; Household Affairs; Mother and
Guardian; Ugliness
   "White Lady." The spinner of destiny who wears a mantle
of snow. She presides over plows, plants, spinners (whom she
rewards for diligence and punishes for carelessness), and the
souls of unborn children. Her German counterparts are
Holda and *Holle.* Like the Russian *Baba Yaga* of Eastern
Europe, she has been demoted to an ugly, cannibalistic ogre
who kidnaps children. In Mecklenburg she is called *Frau
Gode;* in Holland her name is *Vrou-elde;* in Bavaria it is
Berche; Berchtli in Switzerland; and in the Salzburg
Mountains, she is *Perchta* or *Perchtel.* See also *Dame Wode,*

Erda. Alternate forms: Frau Berchta, Frau Berta, Berchte,
Berkta, Bertha, Bertie, Berty, Brechta, Eisenberta, Perchata,
Percht, Precht, Vrou-Elde, White Lady, Yrou-Elde. [Bonnerjea
1927; Jobes 1962; Leach 1992; Neumann 1972]

Berchte   See *Berchta.*

Berchtli   See *Berchta.*

Berkta   See *Berchta.*

Bertha   See *Berchta.*

Bertie   See *Berchta.*

Berty   See *Berchta.*

Besla   See *Bestla.*

Bestla
Scandinavia; North Teuton
Primordial Being
   The first Norse-Viking primeval goddess personified as a
woman rather than a cow. She was seldom mentioned in the
Eddas, the compilation of Norse stories called *Tales of Great
Grandmother.* She is the daughter of Bolthorn, wife of Bor, and
mother of Odin, Vili, and Ve. Alternate forms: Bettla, Besla,
Belsta. [Cooper 1876; Crossley-Holland 1980; Sykes 1968]

Bettla   See *Bestla.*

Beyla
Scandinavia; North Teuton
Earth and Nature
   Norse-Viking earth goddess. Wife of Byggvir, a barley god.
Companion to *Freyja,* and therefore an aspect of nature. The
name "Vikings" refers collectively to ancient warriors who
lived in the areas of present-day Denmark, Norway, and
Sweden. The peak of the Viking Age was between 780 and
1070 C.E. [Crossley-Holland 1980; Jobes 1962]

Bil
Scandinavia; North Teuton
Earth and Nature
   Norse-Viking goddess who explains features of nature. She
is associated with the waning moon.
 *Bil lived on earth with her brother, Hujki. One morning
   while they were getting water for their family, Mani looked
   down from the moon and decided to kidnap them. He took
them to heaven to be his servants. They accompany Mani as he
escorts the moon across the sky. Bil and Hujki put the spots on the
moon.* [Jobes 1962; Leach 1992; Leach 1972; Wedeck 1971]

Bilwis
Germany, Southern; Austria
Evil; Magic
   Nature spirit who earlier was considered male but in the
Middle Ages became a demonic female and was considered a
witch. [Lurker 1984]

Bjort
Scandinavia; North Teuton
Sun and Day
   "Shining One." Norse-Viking personification of the
bright daylight and companion to *Freyja,* representing an
aspect of nature. Vikings were particularly noted for sun
worship—perhaps because they endured long periods of cold
and cloudy weather. [Jobes 1962]

Blid

Scandinavia; North Teuton
Earth and Nature; Happiness

"Blithe One." She is a companion to Norse-Viking *Freyja* and represents an aspect of nature. [Jobes 1962]

Borghild

Germany
Moon and Night; Weather

Personification of the evening mist or the moon. Mother of Hamund and Helgi, wife of Sigmund. A sun myth of the German *Volsung Saga*, in which Borghild kills the light of the sun, Sinfjotle, son of Sigmund. [Jobes 1962]

Brechta   See *Berchta*.

Brunhild

Scandinavia; North Teuton
Evil

See *Brynhild*. Brunhild is her name in the 13th-century German epic, *Das Nibelungenlied*. [Evans 1904; Leach 1972]

Brunhilda   See *Brunhild*.

Brunhilde   See *Brunhild*.

Brunnehilde   See *Brunhild*.

Brynhild

Scandinavia; North Teuton
War

A *Valkyrie* who appears in the *Volsung Saga*. Mother of *Aslog*.

Brynhild gives victory to a warrior not chosen by Odin. As punishment, Odin puts her into an enchanted sleep and surrounds her with fire. She is awakened by Sigurd, who wants to marry her. However, Sigurd is given a magic potion by Gundrun's mother, which makes him forget his love for Brynhild, and he marries Gundrun. Sigurd then wins Brynhild from Gunnar through trickery. Brynhild discovers the trick and provokes Gunnar to kill Sigurd, after which she commits suicide.

Alternate forms: Brunhild, Brunhilda, Brunhilde, Brunnehilde. [Jobes 1962; Mackenzie 1912; Monaghan 1981]

Buschfrauen

Europe
Earth and Nature

"Bushwomen." Guardians of the forest of central Europe who were golden-haired, baggy-skinned, and had pendant breasts and hollow backs. The peasants were protected by the Buschfrauen if they took care of the trees in the forest. See also *Buschgroþmutter* and *Bushweiber*. Alternate form: Silige Fraulein. [Monaghan 1981]

Buschgroþmutter

Europe
Earth and Nature; Health and Healing; Small Size

"Grandmother of the Bushes." Queen of the *Buschfrauen*. She was an elf with mossy feet and white hair.

With her followers, the Buschfrauen, she lives in hollow trees, guarding the forests and the people who respect her. The Buschfrauen are constantly harassed by an evil hunter and are safe only if they hide in special fallen trees. Buschgroþmutter can be encouraged to reveal the secrets of herbs and healing to those who please her. [Monaghan 1981]

Buschweiber

Germany
Earth and Nature

"Wild Maidens." German forest spirits similar to *Buschfrauen*. See also *Buschgroþmutter* [Bonnerjea 1927]

Bylgja

Scandinavia; North Teuton
Water

A *Wave-maiden*, a personification of the swell of waves. She is the daughter of Norse-Viking sea goddess, *Ran*, and Aegir. [Leach 1992]

Dag

Scandinavia; North Teuton
Sun and Day

Norse daughter of *Nat*, or Night.

Dag rides across the heavens on her horse, Skenfaxi. The horse's mane shines so brightly that it lights heaven and earth. Others say that Nat rides the horse Hrimfaxi and that her daughter, Dag, rides Skenfaxi. [Cooper 1876; Crossley-Holland 1980; Monaghan 1981]

Dame Wode

Germany
Unknown

Associated with Danish *Nerthus* or Scandinavian *Hertha*. See also *Berchta*. [Leach 1972]

Deivai

Germany
Supreme Being

Great Goddess in Preuþen (Prussia), a former state that occupied more than half of all Germany and the major part of North Germany. This territory formerly belonged to the original Baltic population until it was conquered, and largely exterminated, by the Teutonic Knights in the 13th century. [Baumgartner 1984; Bridgwater 1950]

Dis

Scandinavia; North Teuton
Family and Tribes; Fate; Ceremonies

Ancestral Norse-Viking deity of heredity who determines individual talents and defects. She is worshiped in services called *disablot* during a midwinter festival that honors ancestors with rituals, drinking, and storytelling. Also a generic term for any female deity. The ending "dis" appears in names such as *Freydis* and *Vanadis*. "Dis" is also the singular of *Disir* and a name of a male Celtic deity. [Jobes 1962; Monaghan 1981]

Disir, The

Scandinavia; North Teuton
Fate; Mother and Guardian; Immortality

"Sisters." General term for Norse-Viking deities including the *Norns*, *Valkyries*, and fate spirits who are the souls of deceased mothers. They are guardians of humans and attendants of *Urth*. Similar to Croatian *Rodjenice*, Eastern Europe. *Dis* is the singular form. Alternate form: Giptes. [Davidson 1964; Jobes 1962; Savill 1977]

Dürr-Kâring

Sweden
Household Affairs

Door spirit.

Dorr-Karing lives near the door and is afraid of light. She blows out the candles when inhabitants enter or leave the house.

Similar to the Lapp *Uks-akka*. Door spirits protect the house and its inhabitants from everything that can harm them. [Jobes 1962; Leach 1972]

Drafn
Scandinavia; North Teuton
Water
   Norse-Viking personification of the undertow. Daughter of the sea goddess *Ran* and Aegir. [Leach 1992]

Drifa
Norway
Weather
   "Loose Drifting Snow." Daughter of the snow god, Snior. [Leach 1992]

Drude
Austria; Germany
Evil; Magic
   A demon who disturbs sleep and casts spells. She has become synonymous with *Hexe*, or witch, and is similar to the Persian *Druj*, Near East, and Zoroastrian *Nasu*, Near East. *Druden* is the plural form. [Leach 1972; Lurker 1984]

Druden   See *Drude.*

Eastre
Germany
Agriculture; Ceremonies; Dawn and Twilight; Health and Healing
   "Radiant Dawn." She is celebrated during a spring festival with vigorous vegetation rites—singing, rejoicing, processionals, flowers, and ringing of bells. Pagan customs of lighting new fires at dawn for crop protection and healing still exist among peoples of Mesoamerica and Europe. Christian Easter and Jewish Passover ceremonies may have absorbed rituals of this goddess. Coloring and rolling eggs is a vestige of ancient fertility rites, as is the use of the rabbit symbol. The rabbit was an ancient escort of the Germanic and later Anglo-Saxon *Ostara.* Alternate name: *Eostre.* [Cooper 1876; Jobes 1962; Leach 1972; Redfield 1931]

Edda
Scandinavia; North Teuton
Family and Tribes
   "Great-grandmother." Ancestor of the race of Thralls (serfs). The *Eddas* are a compilation of ancient mythology called *Tales of Great Grandmother.*

   Edda, with either her husband, Ai, or the fire god, Heimdal, produced the first humans. One night, Heimdal came to Edda and Ai's cabin to visit. For three nights he slept between the couple, and nine months later Thrall was born. When he had grown, Thrall met Thir and they had many children. Their ancestors, the Thralls, became "enthralled" to be the food producers or farmers who led a very hard life. [Crossley-Holland 1980; Monaghan 1981]

Egia
Scandinavia; North Teuton
Water
   One of the nine *Vana Mothers* or *Wave Maidens.* [Leach 1992]

Eil   See *Eir.*

Einmyria
Scandinavia: North Teuton
Fire; Household Affairs
   "Ashes." Daughter of Loki, when he was god of the hearth, and *Glut*, sister of *Eisa.* [Leach 1992]

Eir
Scandinavia; North Teuton
Health and Healing; Education and Knowledge

"Care for," "Save." Sister of *Fulla*. Norse physician to the other gods and teacher of women in the art of healing. She appeared in later stories replacing Odin and Thor as physicians, using magic charms for healing. She is a companion of *Freyja* and *Frigga.* Alternate forms: Eil, Eira, Eria, Eyra. [Jobes 1962; Leach 1992]

Eira   See *Eir.*

Eisa
Scandinavia; North Teuton
Fire; Household Affairs
   "Embers." Daughter of Loki when he was god of the hearth, and *Glut.* Sister of *Einmyria.* [Leach 1992]

Eisenberta   See *Berchta.*

Eistla
Scandinavia; North Teuton
Water
   One of the nine *Vana Mothers* or *Wave Maidens.* [Jobes 1962; Leach 1992]

Elben, Die
Germany
Arts; Goodness
   Benevolent spirits who enjoy music and dancing. [Lurker 1984]

Elli
Scandinavia; North Teuton
Life/Death Cycle; Large Size; Physical Prowess; Disorder
   "Old Age."

   The dwarf, Thor, decided to travel to Utgard, the land of the giants. When he and his companions reached the hall of the giants, Loki said they must pass some tests to demonstrate their strength. One of Thor's tasks was to wrestle Elli. Thor was unable to move Elli, and she forced him to one knee. Thor was very powerful, but no one can overcome old age.
   Giants are the forces of chaos. They attempt to cause disorder through physical force, trickery, and magic. [Crossley-Holland 1980; Jobes 1962]

Embla
Scandinavia; North Teuton
Creator of Life; Earth and Nature
   "Vine." Norse first woman.

   The sons of Bor were walking on the shore of Midgard when they came across two fallen trees. One tree was ash and one was elm or elder. The sons of Bor formed the first woman and the first man from them. Some say that Embla was made from the ash, and others say she was made from the elm or elder. Odin gave her the breath of life, Vili gave her intelligence and emotions, and Ve gave her sight and hearing. Ask was also brought to life in this manner, and they lived together in Midgard. They are the ancestors to all the people of the world. [Crossley-Holland 1980; Jobes 1962; Guirand 1968; Monaghan 1981]

Eostre   See *Eastre.*

Erda
Germany
Unknown
   She was merged with *Berchta* or *Holda.* She is similar to *Hertha.* Also said to be an alternate name for *Fjorgyn.* [Leach 1972; Leach 1992; Monaghan 1981]

Eria   See *Eir.*

Eyra   See *Eir.*

Eyrgjafa
Scandinavia; North Teuton
Water
One of the nine *Vana Mothers* or *Wave Maidens*. Alternate form: Aurgiafa. [Jobes 1962; Leach 1992]

Fangge
Austria; Tyrol
Earth and Nature; Household Affairs
Tree spirit.

If her limbs are twisted or her bark is cut off, Fangge may die. If she survives, she will try to destroy her attacker. She also steals freshly baked bread, and to prevent this from happening, people bake their bread with caraway seeds, which the forest spirits dislike.

Similar to the Greek *Dryades*. The Tyroleans live in an autonomous province in west Austria, an area almost wholly alpine. See also *O-ryu*, Far East. [Monaghan 1981]

Fengi   See *Fenja*.

Fenja
Scandinavia; North Teuton
Life/Death Cycle; Physical Prowess; Water
Creation and destruction. Sometimes given as a *Wave Maiden* and one of the nine mothers of Heimdal. Daughter of *Griep*. Sister of *Menja*.

When Ivaldi and his sons revolted against the gods, Fenja and Menja stole the World-mill and turned the mill-stone called Grotte so violently that it broke and an earthquake occurred. Later, commanded by the sea king, Mysing, they ended the Golden Age by grinding an over-abundance of salt.

This is reminiscent of other patriarchal rewritings that make a beneficient goddess into a wild and evil deity. See also *Fengi*. Alternate form: Fenya. [Jobes 1962; Monaghan 1981]

Fenya   See *Fenja*.

Fimmilinia
Germany
War
One of the *Alaisiagae, The*. [Guirand 1968]

Fjorgyn
Scandinavia; North Teuton
Earth and Nature
Norse earth goddess. Also said to be the name of a husband of *Frigga*. Similar to *Hertha*. See also *Jord, Hlodyn,* and *Erda*. Alternate form: Fyorgyn. [Jobes 1962; Leach 1992; Monaghan 1981]

Folla
Scandinavia; North Teuton
Healing
Nordic deity equivalent to the Germanic *Fulla* and companion of *Frigga*. See also *Fulla*. [Leach 1992]

Fonn
Scandinavia; North Teuton
Weather
Norse-Viking personification of snow and ice who was the daughter of Snior, the god of snow and ice. [Leach 1992]

Foseta
Germany; Frisian
Creator of Life
Probably a fertility deity. She had a temple in Friesland, a group of islands along the North Sea coast belonging to the Netherlands. [Bridgwater 1950; Redfield 1931]

Frau Berchta   See *Berchta*.

Frau Berta   See *Berchta*.

Frau Fiuk
Germany
Weather
Weather deity. Alternate form: Frick. [Leach 1992]

Frau Frigg
Scandinavia; North Teuton
Arts; Earth and Nature; Disorder
With the Norse-Viking god, Odin, she is mentioned as a participant in the Giant's Dance. Same as *Frigga*. [Jobes 1962]

Frau Gode
Scandinavia; North Teuton
Hunting and Wild Animals; Luck
Norse deity associated with *Nerthus* and *Hertha*. She was worshiped in Mecklenburg. See also *Berchta*. Alternate form: Gode. [Leach 1972; Leach 1992]

Frau Holle   See *Holle*.

Frau Minne   See *Minne*.

Frau Saelde   See *Saelde*.

Frau Salida   See *Saelde*.

Frau Welt
Germany
Evil; Love and Sexuality; Small Size
Mistress of fairies. Thought to be a supernatural lover of humans. The Medieval religious hierarchy called her a devil. [Leach 1972]

Freitag
Germany
Household Affairs
German goddess of spinning. Friday is her sacred day. [Hubbs 1988]

Freya   See *Freyja*.

Freydis
Scandinavia; North Teuton
War
A Viking warrior. [Jobes 1962]

Freyia   See *Freyja*.

Freyja
Scandinavia; North Teuton
Creator of Life; Magic, Unhappiness; War; Goodness
Leader of the *Valkyries* and one of the Vanir (fertility gods). Mother of *Hnoss*. Daughter of Njord (Njorth) and sister of Frey. Sometimes confused with *Frigga* in Germany.

Freyja was rescued from Jotunheim (the land of the giants) by Svipdag. Still under the influence of spells, she was unable to show emotion. Svipdag, angered by her lack of gratitude, left her to wander. Once again Svipdag rescued Freyja, this time from the Hag, an ogre. They were married, but things did not go well. Svipdag was changed into a dragon by Odin, and Freyja searched for him, trying unsuccessfully to break the spell.

Alternate forms: Freya, Freyia, Gefn, Horn, Mardal, Moertholl, Syr, Vanadis. [Bonnerjea 1927; Jobes 1962; Leach 1972; Leach 1992; Monaghan 1981; Sykes 1968]

Fri   See *Frigga*.

Fria
Scandinavia; North Teuton
Magic
Deity who has magical charms. Also considered an
alternate name for *Frigga*. [Jobes 1962; Leach 1992]

Friagabi
Britain; Germany
Justice
"Giver of Freedom." One of the *The Alaisiagae,* who had
an altar at Housesteads on Hadrian's Wall. Hadrian's Wall
was erected c. 121-127 C.E. by Roman Emperor Hadrian
during the occupation of Britain. Associated with *Baudihillie.*
[Bridgwater 1950, Saville 1977]

Frick See *Frau Fiuk.*

Fricka See *Frigga.*

Frid
Scandinavia; North Teuton
Earth and Nature
"Fair One." Attendant of the Norse goddess *Freyja.*
Freyja's attendants represent aspects of nature. [Jobes 1962]

Frig See *Frigga.*

Frigg See *Frigga.*

Frigga
Scandinavia; North Teuton
Earth and Nature; Family and Tribes; Household Affairs;
Love and Sexuality; Mother and Guardian; Sun and Day;
Time; Weather
"Beloved," "Wife." One of the two main deities of the
Asgard, the Norse pantheon, but perhaps two aspects of the
same goddess—conjugal fertility *Frigg* and lover *Freyja.*
Frigg is old Norse; *Frig* is Anglo-Saxon; *Frija* is Old German.
One of the wives of Odin, mother of Balder, Hermod, Hoder,
and usually Tyr. Daughter of the god Fjorgyn and *Jord* or of
Odin and *Jord,* sister of Njord.

 *In her role as devoted wife, helper, and mother, she stayed
at her mansion, Fensalir, "sea-hall," spinning golden
threads (sun rays) or weaving (clouds).*
Probably an earth goddess of fertile summer. See also
Aśynjur. Alternate forms: Frau Frigg, Fri, Fria, Fricka, Frig,
Frija. [Jobes 1962; Leach 1992]

Frija See *Frigga.*

Frimla
Scandinavia; North Teuton
Earth and Nature
Nordic companion of *Frigga* and therefore an aspect of
nature. [Sykes 1968]

Frowa See *Frua.*

Frua
Scandinavia; North Teuton
Health and Healing
Deity of healing. Also considered an alternate name for
Freyja. Alternate form: Frowa. [Cooper 1876; Leach 1992]

Fulla
Scandinavia; North Teuton
Earth and Nature; Health and Healing; Wealth
"Abundance." Earth deity of the fruitful earth who was
portrayed as a young woman with her hair bound with a
gold band. Sister of *Eria.* Servant of *Frigga* who carried the

jewels and, in other versions, a sister and companion of
Freyja. In Medieval times she was called *Abundia* or
Habondia. Equivalent to Nordic *Folla.* Alternate forms:
Lin, Volla. [Cooper 1876; Jobes 1962; Monaghan 1981]

Fylgir, The
Germany
Family and Tribes; Mother and Guardian
"Following Spirit." Protective deities who are a person's
soul or guardian spirit. They may appear as an animal or
woman in dreams and give warnings or advice. They are
hereditary and pass on to another family member after death.
[Leach 1972; Lurker 1984]

Fylgia See *Fylgja.*

Fylgja
Scandinavia; North Teuton
Family and Tribes; Fate; Mother and Guardian; Immortality
Guardian spirit. Protective of families, she is considered a
forewarner of misfortune. Also said to be the Norwegian
guardian spirit who is the person's double or soul. According
to some, the plural form is *Fylgukona.* Alternate forms:
Fylgia, Hamingja. [Jobes 1962; Monaghan 1981]

Fylgukona
Norway
Family and Tribes; Fate; Mother and Guardian; Immortality
"Following-woman." Norwegian guardian spirit of an
individual or a family. Said by some to be the plural of *Fylgja.*
Alternate form: Hamingja. [Jobes 1962; Monaghan 1981]

Fyorgyn See *Fjorgyn.*

Ganglot
Scandinavia; North Teuton
Time
"Tardy." Norse servant of *Hel.* Other servants of Hel are
Delay, Slowness, Hunger, and Starvation. [Crossley-Holland
1980; Mackenzie 1912]

Garmangabi
Germany; Suevi
Goodness
Beneficent deity. The Suevi's identity as a tribe is not clear
other than that they are a southwest-central German people.
They gave their name to Swabia, the Black Forest area.
[Bridgwater 1950; Lurker 1984]

Gaude See *Gode.*

Gaue
Germany
Agriculture
Presides over harvesting of rye. Rye is an crop of early
Neolithic inhabitants. Sites dating from about 1000 B.C.E. to
500 C.E. have been found in Scandinavia containing evidence
of the cultivation of wheat, rye, oats, and barley. [Leach 1972;
Leach 1992]

Gebjon
Scandinavia; North Teuton
Earth and Nature; Health and Healing; Physical Prowess
"The Giver."
*Gebjon was an outstanding healer, which pleased the king.
As a reward, he told her she could claim as much land as she
could plow in a day and a night. Gebjon dug so deeply that
she tore away the crust of the earth, creating a lake and an island.*
See *Gefion, Gefjun.* [Chicago 1979]

Gefion

Scandinavia; North Teuton

Love and Sexuality; Mother and Guardian

Guardian of youths and virgins and those who will never wed. Attendant of *Frigga*. Her story is similar to those of *Gebjon* and *Gefjun*. Similar or equivalent to *Gefn*. [Cooper 1876; Crossley-Holland 1980]

Gefjun

Scandinavia; North Teuton

Earth and Nature; Physical Prowess; Justice

Goddess of agriculture and associated with the plough. She is also the goddess of virgins and oaths. Similar to *Freyja,* Gefjun had a beautiful necklace that was given to her by a lover.

Odin sent Gefjun in search of land. Gylfi, the king of Sweden, told Gefjun she could claim as much land as she could plow. She became the mistress of a giant and had four large sons, whom she transformed into oxen to aid her with the plowing. They dug deeply and separated Sjaeland (Zeuland) from the mainland. Then Gefjun went to live with Odin's son, Skjoldr (Scyld), in Leire when he was king of Denmark.

See also *Ann Maria,* North America. [Savill 1977]

Gefn   "The Generous One." See *Frejya.*

Geirahod

Scandinavia; North Teuton

Heaven and Hell; Sky and Heavens; War

One of the *Valkyries* who decides the victors in battle. The chosen warriors for death were brought to Asgard to share the joys of Valhalla. Victorious Valkyries were called "The Northern Lights" because "nightly the heavens flamed with their splendor." [Leach 1992; Mackenzie 1912]

Geirolul

Scandinavia; North Teuton

War

One of the *Valkyries* who decides the victors in battle. She invisibly assists those chosen so that victory will occur. [Mackenzie 1912; Sykes 1968]

Gerd   See *Gerda.*

Gerda

Scandinavia; North Teuton

Beauty; Magic; Fire; Sun and Day; Time

"The Frozen Earth." Gerda was very beautiful, the daughter of a giant and a mortal. Wife of Freyr.

Gerda lived in a house surrounded by flames and was able to shoot flames from her hands. Freyr fell in love and desired her for his wife. His servant, Skirnir, was sent to bring Gerda to him. The servant went to her and offered gifts, which she refused. He threatened to cast a spell in runes and this frightened her, so she promised to meet Freyr after nine nights had passed. After that time, she joined him in Asgard (the home of the gods).

A seasonal myth with Gerda as the stern, unyielding, but beautiful winter, conquered by the spring and the sun god, Freyr. Runes are mystery stones marked with secret writing used for divination. Alternate forms: Gerd, Gedir, Gerdr, Gerth, Gerthr. [Cooper 1876; Crossley-Holland 1980; Guirand 1968; Monaghan 1981; Pike 1957; Redfield 1931]

Gedir   See *Gerda.*

Gerdr   See *Gerda.*

Gerth   See *Gerda.*

Gerthr   See *Gerda.*

Gerutha

Scandinavia; North Teuton

Mother and Guardian

Hamlet's mother. Icelandic Hamlet was the guardian of the World-Mill, the mill that created material from which the world was formed. See also *Griep.* [Leach 1972; Mackenzie 1912]

Gialp   See *Gjalp.*

Giptes, The

Scandinavia; North Teuton

Destroyer of Life; Fate

Alternate name for Norse *Norns.* They are subjects of their sister, *Urd,* and carry out her wishes. Also known as the *Disir* or Maids of *Urd.* [Jobes 1962; Mackenzie 1912]

Gjalp

Scandinavia; North Teuton

Large Size; Physical Prowess; Water

"Howler." One of the nine *Vana Mothers* or *Wave Maidens.*

Loki (a trickster) took Thor to see Geirrod and his daughters, Gjalp and Greip. On their journey, they had to cross the river Vimur, a wide torrent of water and blood. Gjalp was standing astride the river upstream, increasing its depth with her menstrual flow, so that she might drown Thor.

Alternate form: Gialp. [Leach 1992]

Glut

Scandinavia; North Teuton

Fire; Household Affairs

"Glow." Wife of Loki, god of the hearth. Her daughters were *Einmyria* and *Eisa.* [Leach 1992]

Gna

Scandinavia; North Teuton

Immortality

Messenger of *Frigga.* Mother of *Einmyria.*

Riding on her winged horse, Hoof-Tosser, she was able to ride through both air and water into the mortal world in order to tell Frigga what the mortals were doing.

Alternate form: Gnaa. [Jobes 1962]

Gnaa   See *Gna.*

Gode   See *Frau Gode.*

Gol

Scandinavia; North Teuton

War

One of the *Valkyries.* Alternate form: Goll. [Leach 1972; Leach 1992]

Goll   See *Gol.*

Goli

Scandinavia; North Teuton

War

One of the *Valkyries.* [Sykes 1968]

Gollveig   See *Gullveig.*

Gondul

Scandinavia; North Teuton

War

One of the *Valkyries.*

Gondul's task was to search for fallen warriors who were kings and bring them to Valhalla. In the legend of Hildl, she was the instigator of an never-ending battle. [Leach 1992; Monaghan 1981]

Gonlod   See *Gunnlöd.*

Griep
Scandinavia; North Teuton
Fire; Water
   "Grasper." One of the nine *Vana Mothers* or *Wave Maidens.* She is the wife of the dwarf Ivalde, by whom she is the mother of Egil-Orvandel, Ide, and Thjasse Volund. With a second husband she had *Fenja* and *Menja.* She is also one of the fire-maids who sends off sparks from the World-Mill, the mill that created the material from which the world was formed.

 With her sister Gjalp, Griep was enlisted by their father, Geirrod, to help kill Thor. When Thor came to visit, the two sisters hid under Thor's chair. When he fell asleep, they tried to smash him against the ceiling. Thor awakened and was able to save himself.
   See also *Gerutha.* [Crossley-Holland 1980; Jobes 1962; Leach 1992]

Grid
Scandinavia; North Teuton
Large Size; Order; Physical Prowess
   Norse giant who, unlike the other giants, personifies order, not chaos. She was one of Odin's mistresses and mother of Vidar.

 On their way to see Geirrod, the king of the Goths, Thor and Loki decided to visit Grid's hall. In an effort to thwart Geirrod's desire to kill Thor, Grid offered him her own weapons to defend himself—her belt of strength, her iron gloves, and her unbreakable staff. He used her belt of strength to keep from being crushed against a magical roof tree, her iron gloves to catch a ball of iron, and her unbreakable staff to kill Geirrod's servants. [Crossley-Holland 1980]

Grimhild
Scandinavia; North Teuton
Love and Sexuality; Magic
   Sorcerer. Queen Mother of *Gudrun* and sons, Gunnar, Hogne, and Guttorm; wife of king Giuki.

 Grimhild made a magic potion that she gave to Sigurd to make him fall in love with her daughter Gudrun. In one version, they lived happily together and had a son, Sigmund. In another, after the marriage ceremony, the potion wore off and Sigurd realized that he really loved Brynhild. [Evans 1904]

Gritha
Scandinavia; North Teuton
Unknown
   One of the wives of Odin. Other wives are *Jord* and *Frigg.* [Cooper 1876; Crossley-Holland 1980]

Groa
Scandinavia; North Teuton
Demi-animals; Health and Healing; Large Size; Magic
   "To Grow or Sprout." Said to be a swan maiden, a giant, and a sorcerer. Wife of Orvandel (Aurvandil), mother of Svipdag, and sister of *Signe-Alveig.*

 During a duel with Hrungir, Thor was hit by a piece of flint that lodged in his head. He had a terrible headache and sent for Groa. She worked all night with her charms and spells and was able to loosen the fragment. Thor's headache stopped and, wanting to reward Groa, he told her that her husband was not dead and would return soon. Groa became so excited that

she could not remember the spells and was unable to finish removing the flint, so Thor angrily sent her away.
   Alternate form: Groad. [Crossley-Holland 1980; Jobes 1962]

Groad   See *Groa.*

Grydat
Scandinavia; North Teuton
Unknown
   One of the wives of Odin. [Cooper 1876]

Gudr
Scandinavia; North Teuton
War
   One of the Norse *Valkyries.* [Leach 1972; Leach 1992]

Gudrun
Scandinavia; North Teuton
Agriculture; Evil; Dawn and Twilight; Justice; Time
   In the *Volsung Saga* she is the daughter of Giuki and *Grimhild.* With her brothers, she is the personification of dark powers. Mother of *Swanhild.*

 The powers of the dark (winter) and the powers of the light (summer) are in constant battle, each victorious in the appropriate season. Gudrun is the gloaming, or harvest, who, after the death of the sun, marries the lord of autumn and then the lord of winter.
   In the *Das Nibelungenlied,* she is called *Kriemhild* and in Wagner's *Der Ring des Nibelungen* she is known as Gutrune. As the daughter of king Hettel she has a similar light and time story. In an Icelandic saga she is an independent goddess married to Thorwald, Thord, and then Bolli. [Bonnerjea 1927; Jobes 1962]

Gullveig
Scandinavia; North Teuton
Evil; Heaven and Hell; Metals; Immortality
   "Gold-might." In Iceland, she signifies a thirst for gold (or fertility). She is a goddess of evil, ruler of Iarnvid (Norse black forest on the world's edge). She is sometimes identified as *Freyja* in her underworld role. Mother of *Hella.*

 The Aesir burned Gollveig three times in the Hall of Hor and struck her with swords, but she could not be killed and lived eternally.
   See also *Volva.* Alternate forms: Angerbodha, Angur-boda, Aurboda, Gollveig, Gulveig-Hoder, Hag of Iarnvid, Heid, Orboda. [Crossley-Holland 1980; Jobes 1962; Guirand 1968; Leach 1992]

Gulweig-Hoder   See *Gullveig.*

Gunnlauth
Scandinavia; North Teuton
Unknown
   Daughter of Suttung. See also *Gunnlöd.* [Crossley-Holland 1980]

Gunnlūd
Scandinavia; North Teuton
Arts; Education and Knowledge; Fire
   Norse guardian of the mead of poetry, Odrerir, and the name of the cauldron in which the mead is brewed. Whoever drinks it will become a poet and a sage. Daughter of Suttung.

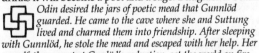 *Odin desired the jars of poetic mead that Gunnlöd guarded. He came to the cave where she and Suttung lived and charmed them into friendship. After sleeping with Gunnlöd, he stole the mead and escaped with her help. Her grandfather, upset at Gunlöd's seduction, set the world on fire.*
   See also *Gunnlauth, Gonlod.* [Crossley-Holland 1980; Jobes 1962; Guirand 1968]

Gunnr
Scandinavia; North Teuton
War
    One of the *Valkyries*. [Leach 1972; Leach 1992]

Habonde See *Habondia*.

Habondia
Germany
Wealth; Agriculture
    "Abundance." In Medieval times she was transformed
from an ancient earth goddess into a deity who was
worshiped only by witches. See also *Wanne Thekla*. Alternate
form: Habonde. [Monaghan 1981]

Hag of Iarnvid See *Gullveig*.

Hallgerda
Scandinavia; North Teuton
Beauty; Family and Tribes
    Wife of Gunnar in the *Burnt Njal*, an Icelandic Saga. She is
beautiful, selfish, and willful.

*Hallgerda quarrels with Bergthora, the wife of Gunnar's
friend, Njal. The fight between Hallgerda and Bergthora
causes a feud, which ends tragically for both families.*
*Gunnar is trapped by their enemies and begs Hallgerda for a lock of
her hair to make a new bowstring. She refuses and Gunnar is killed.*
[Jobes 1962]

Hamingja
Scandinavia; North Teuton
Luck; Mother and Guardian; Immortality
    "Caul" or "Skin." Norse guardian spirit who brings good
luck. She may appear in dreams to give counsel to her charge
and to speak for those who are dead. Alternate forms: Fylgja,
Fylgukona. [Jobes 1962; Monaghan 1981]

Hardgrep
Scandinavia; North Teuton
Magic; Mother and Guardian; Large Size
    Sorcerer. Daughter of the giant Vaganhofe. Protector of the
king of Sweden, Hadding.

*Hardgrep accompanied Hadding in all of his battles to
protect him from harm. During one battle, a great black
hand appeared and strangled her.* [Jobes 1962]

Hariasa
Germany
War
    War goddess. Alternate form: Harriasa. [Leach 1992;
Wedeck 1971]

Harimela
Germany
War
    War goddess. [Monaghan 1990]

Harimella
Germany
War
    Goddess of war. [Leach 1992]

Harriasa See *Hariasa*.

Havfru
Denmark
Demi-animals; Goodness; Evil; Water; Weather
    A mermaid. Equivalent to Finno-Ugric *Avfruvva*. She can
be helpful or harmful to humans. If fishermen see her
through sea mists, a storm is probably imminent. Havfru

returns lost drowning victims to their homes. Alternate form:
Havfrue. [Jobes 1962; Leach 1972]

Havfrue See *Havfru*.

Heartha
Scandinavia; North Teuton
Magic
    A "far-seeing witch" who has great magical powers.
Alternate form: Heitha. [Stone 1979]

Hedrun See *Heidrun*.

Heid
Scandinavia; North Teuton
Magic; Evil
    Norse sibyl or volva (prophetizing spirit), patron of evil
women. She used her evil magic and three times Odin
punished her for doing so. May be an aspect of *Freyja*. See
also *Volva*. Alternate form: Gollveig. [Jobes 1962; Monaghan
1981]

Heidrun
Scandinavia; North Teuton
Magic; Water; Weather;
    "Bright, Running Stream." The magical goat of Valhalla.
She eats from the tree that holds up the world and produces
mead (dew) for all the dead warriors who spend their time
telling the tales and songs of their battles. Personification of a
cloud. Alternate form: Hedrun. [Jobes 1962; Leach 1972;
Monaghan 1981]

Heitha See *Heartha*.

Hel
Scandinavia; North Teuton
Life/Death Cycle; War;
    Danish goddess of death. Hel is also the name of the realm
of the dead. She rides a horse, a nightmare, foretelling death.
Ganglot is her servant. See also *Hella*. Alternate form: Hela,
Hilda. [Hubbs 1988; Neumann 1972]

Hela See *Hel*.

Hella
Scandinavia; North Teuton
Destroyer of Life; Heaven and Hell; Ugliness
    "One Who Covers Up," "One Who Hides." Norse monster
who rules those who have died of old age or disease in Hel or
Nifhelheim, the realm of the dead. She is portrayed as dirty,
black, and ugly. She is the half-alive and half-dead daughter
of *Gullveig* when she is called *Angerboda,* who
was thought to be half-black and half-white. See also *Hel*.
[Crossley-Holland 1980; Monaghan 1981]

Her-fiotr See *Herfjotur*.

Herfjotur
Scandinavia; North Teuton
Charisma; Destroyer of Life
    Norse *Idisi* or *Valkyrie*. Her appearance on the battlefield
causes warriors to freeze with terror, which results in their
deaths. Alternate form: Her- fiotr. [Jobes 1962; Leach 1992]

Hertha
Scandinavia; North Teuton
Ceremonies; Domesticated Animals; Earth and Nature
    "Earth." During her ritual worship, her statue is veiled and
transported by sacred cows. The cows can only be cared for
by her priests, and her rites are celebrated in the dark.

Shrovetide processions in Christian times honor her by carrying plows, representing her fertility. In Medieval times, she was the patron of witches. Associated with **Frau Gede.** Similar to the Roman **Tellus,** Greek and Roman Empire, and Norse **Fjorgyn** or **Erda.** See also **Dame Wode.** Alternate form: Aertha. [Cooper 1876; Monaghan 1981; Redfield 1931]

Hervor
Scandinavia; North Teuton
Fire; Magic; War
Norse warrior-maiden. Daughter of Angantyr.
⌖ *Hervor rode through the fire of her father's burial mound to retrieve his sword, Tyrfing. She took the magical sword for her battles, even though her father had told her it would bring destruction.* [Jobes 1962; Monaghan 1981]

Hexe, Die
Germany
Health and Healing; Magic
Witches who can work spells to relieve illness, control nature, and nullify spells of enemies. They are usually used for positive purposes. Professional hex doctors use stock magic formulas, some very ancient. The sources now are Gypsy magic, Medieval church formulas, and ritual. See also **Drude.** [Bonnerjea 1927; Leach 1972]

Hild
Scandinavia; North Teuton
Immortality; War
Chief of the **Valkyries.** She goes each night to the battlefield to revive the dead.
⌖ *When Hild's father refused to make peace with her lover and declared war, she revived the warriors each night so they could continue the battle. In one of the battles, Dietrich struck Hild with his sword, cutting her body in two. She reunited her body before his eyes and resumed the battle. When Dietrich struck her a second time, the same thing happened, but the third time she was killed. The battle between her father and the warriors will continue until Ragnarök, the final battle between the gods and the forces of evil, which will end all creation.*
Alternate forms: Hilde, Hildr. [Crossley-Holland 1980; Leach 1992; Mackenzie 1912; Monaghan 1981]

Hilda   See **Hel.**

Hilde   See **Hild.**

Hildr   See **Hild, Hildur.**

Hildur
Scandinavia; North Teuton
War
One of the **Valkyries.** Alternate form: Hildr. [Cooper 1876; Savill 1977; Wedeck 1971]

Hiordis   See **Hjordis.**

Hiorthrimul
Scandinavia; North Teuton
War
One of the **Valkyries.** [Leach 1972; Leach 1992]

Hjordis
Scandinavia; North Teuton
Dawn and Twilight
In the *Volsung Saga,* daughter of the Eylime (Eglimi), King of the Islands. Second or third wife of Sigmund and mother of Sigurd. Probably the personification of the dawn.

⌖ *When Hjordis married Sigmund, Hundling Lygni, a former lover, was enraged and came to kill all the Volsungs. Hjordis, hearing that Sigmund was dying on the battlefield, rushed to attend his wounds. Sigmund refused her help because his death was ordained by Odin. After his death, she married Alv, the elf son of the king of Denmark, who had rescued her. Hjordis had the smith in her father-in-law's court reforge Sigmund's sword, Gram, for Sigmund's son, Sigrud.*
Alternate form: Hiordis. [Jobes 1962; Guirand 1968]

Hlif
Scandinavia; North Teuton
Earth and Nature; Mother and Guardian
"Protector." Companion to **Freyja,** representing an aspect of nature. See also **Hlin.** [Jobes 1962]

Hlin
Scandinavia; North Teuton
Mother and Guardian
"Mildness," "Warmth." Protector of those whose lives are endangered. She carries human prayers to **Frigga,** the earth goddess, and protects those whom Frigga wants protected. Perhaps an aspect of Frigga as summer. See also **Hlif.** [Cooper 1876; Monaghan 1981; Leach 1992; Jobes 1962]

Hlock
Scandinavia; North Teuton
War
One of the **Valkyries.** Alternate form: Hlokk. [Leach 1992]

Hlodyn
Scandinavia; North Teuton
Earth and Nature; Primordial Being
"Earth." Goddess of the earth before the creation of humans. Daughter of **Nat,** night, and Annar, water. One of the wives of Odin, mother of Thor. She is the personification of the "primitive, uncultivated and unpopulated earth." She is worshiped on high mountains because that is where she waits to mate with the sky. Probably similar to **Hludana.** See also **Jord.** Alternate forms: Fjorgyn, Hloldyn, Hlothyn. [Leach 1992; Lurker 1984; Monaghan 1981; Jobes 1962]

Hlokk   See **Hlock.**

Hloldyn   See **Hlodyn.**

Hlothyn   See **Hlodyn.**

Hludana
Germany
Earth and Nature; Mother and Guardian
Similar to **Hlodyn** and the model for **Frau Holle.** [Jobes 1962; Leach 1972; Leach 1992]

Hnoss
Scandinavia; North Teuton
Love and Sexuality; Metals
"Jewel." Youthful daughter of **Freyja,** the Norse goddess of sensuality. Hnoss represents infatuation. [Cooper 1876; Monaghan 1981; Jobes 1962].

Holda
Germany, *Suevi, Hessian, Thuringian*
Agriculture; Earth and Nature; Household Affairs; Mother and Guardian; Water; Weather; Ugliness
Associated with the sky, lakes, streams, maternity, and the hearth. She presides over spinning and the cultivation of flax. Holda is feared by sailors when she rides on the waves.

Holda is the leader of the "Host of the Dead," who ride through the mountains and on the air with loud screams (the wind). Wherever they pass, the fields will be especially abundant at harvest time.

In recent times she has been diminished to an ugly old woman who frightens children into good behavior. If it is raining, Holda is washing her clothes. See also *Berchta, Erda, Holla,* and *Holle.* [Bonnerjea 1927; Leach 1972; Leach 1992; Neumann 1972]

Holla
Germany
Earth and Nature; Evil; Fire; Heaven and Hell; Household Affairs; Magic

Thought to be an ancient and complex nature goddess. At first she was connected with the benevolent fire of the home hearth but was later demonized and connected to the fires of hell and considered the queen of witches and elves. See also *Holda* and *Holle.* [Stone 1979]

Holle
Germany
Evil; Mother and Guardian; Immortality; Weather

Leader of demons, the Hollen or Hulden, who can be friendly or punitive.

 Holle receives the souls of the dead and releases the newborns from the underworld. When she shakes her cushions, it snows.

She is connected with the Germanic *Hludana.* Similar to *Berchta.* See also *Holda* and *Holla.* Alternate form: Frau Holle. [Jobes 1962; Leach 1972; Lurker 1984]

Horn
Scandinavia; North Teuton
Earth and Nature

"Linen Woman." One of the names of *Freyja* and the name of one of the *Aśynjur.* [Sykes 1968]

Horsel
Germany, *Swabian*
Domesticated Animals; Moon and Night; Selflessness

Goddess associated with sacred horses. Places of horse worship are found in German towns such as Horselberg, Horselydown, and Horsenden Hill. Because she is equivalent to *Ursula,* Christians later adopted her as St. Ursula and now celebrate her feast day on October 21. See also *Ursula.* Alternate forms: Orsel, Ursel. [Jobes 1962; Leach 1992; Monaghan 1981]

Hrafn
Scandinavia; North Teuton
Water

"Despoiler." One of the *Wave Maidens.* Daughter of the sea goddess *Ran* and Aegir.

Hrede
Anglo-Saxon
Time

Anglo-Saxon spring goddess. The month of March was named for her. Alternate form: Rheda. [Monaghan 1990]

Hrist
Scandinavia; North Teuton
War

One of the *Valkyries.* [Leach 1992]

Hulda
Germany
Family and Tribes

Goddess of marriage. Mother of *Irpa.* Alternate form: Hulde. [Wedeck 1971]

Hulde   See *Hulda.*

Huldra
Scandinavia; North Teuton
Arts; Charisma; Domesticated Animals; Earth and Nature

"Hill Lady." Leader of the wood nymphs and protector of the herds that graze on the sides of mountains. She loves to dance and party, and her harp playing is hypnotic. She is attractive to humans because she is beautiful when seen straight on, but her backside can be frightening because she has a common fairy trait, a hollow back and a tail. See also *Metsänneitsyt* and *Skogsjungfru.* [Leach 1992; Monaghan 1981]

Hulle
Scandinavia; North Teuton
Domesticated Animals

Norse deity who presides over the grazing and milking of cows. [Leach 1992]

Hyldemoer
Denmark
Earth and Nature; Health and Healing

"Elder Mother" or "Elle Woman." Spirit of the elder. The elder shrub was revered as a powerful cure for illness. For example, in Bohemia its fresh juice is drunk for toothache caused by a cold. In Bavaria, if a fever patient sticks an elder twig in the ground in silence, the fever will go away. However, in some parts of Germany, an elder branch brought into the house brings ghosts. In Tyrol, an elder stick cut on St. John's Eve will detect witchcraft. [Bonnerjea 1927; Leach 1972]

Hyndla
Scandinavia; North Teuton
Fate; Family and Tribes; Large Size

"She-dog." One of the *Ivithjar,* wood giants who have the knowledge of the fates and blood lines of humans and giants. *Freyja desired "the drink of remembrance," which Hyndla controlled, so that she could determine the ancestry of her lover Ottar. Hyndla was not inclined to share this power with Freyja, so the goddess girdled Hyndla with fire (aurora of the morning) to insure her cooperation.* [Crossley-Holland 1980; Davidson 1964; Jobes 1962]

Hyrokkin
Scandinavia; North Teuton
Hunting and Wild Animals; Large Size; Weather

A giant or hag who rides a wolf with a snake bridle. As an aspect of *Angerboda,* she is a goddess of winter storms. *Hyrokkin was summoned by the gods when they were unable to launch Balder's boat, Ringhorn (Hring-horn), for his funeral pyre. She arrived on her wolf, grim-faced, and, gripping the prow of the boat, sent it racing down to the water. This made Thor angry, but the gods reminded him that she had been called for this purpose.*

Alternate form: Hyrrokin. [Crossley-Holland 1980; Jobes 1962]

Hyrrokin   See *Hyrokkin.*

Iarnsaxa   See *Jarnsaxa.*

Iarnvithjan, The
Scandinavia
Unknown

Scandinavian troll wives. [Monaghan 1990]

Idisi, The
Scandinavia; North Teuton
Fate; Mother and Guardian; Immortality; War

Spirits who include the *Norns* and the *Valkyries*. Their name is probably derived from the *Disir*, the souls of deceased mothers. *Herfjotur* is one of the Idisi.

The Idisi hover over battlefields, binding or releasing prisoners of war. Those combatants they favor find their fetters loosened; those combatants they dislike are bound tightly.

Equivalent to the *Alaisiage*. [Jobes 1962]

Idun
Scandinavia; North Teuton
Magic; Immortality; Time

She represents the earth's seasons and presides over immortality. Wife of Bragi, the god of poetry and oratory.

Idun was the keeper of the golden apples that make the gods immortal. One day Loki was snatched by a eagle and dragged across the ground for miles and miles. The eagle agreed to let Loki go if he promised to bring Idun across the Bifrost into Midgard (the world of men) in seven days. Loki convinced Idun that he had found a tree that grew golden apples just like hers, so she went with him across the Bifrost with him to see it. The eagle was waiting and swooped down and carried Idun and her apples away to Jotunheim (land of the giants). The eagle was the giant Thiazi, who wanted the gods to age while he remained young. As the gods aged and became weaker, they began to search for Idun. They discovered that she had left with Loki, so he was summoned. They told him to find Idun and return her to Asgard (the world of the gods). He asked for Freyja's falcon skin and flew to Thiazi's home, Thrymheim. He found Idun and changed her into a nut, flying with her in his claws back to Asgard. Or she may have changed into a quail and flown back to Asgard.

The nut represents autumn and the quail the spring. Idun is the personification of the seasons between September and March. See also *Asynjur*. Alternate forms: Iduna, Idunn, Ithunn, Y'dun. [Cooper 1876; Crossley-Holland 1980; Jobes 1962; Leach 1992; Stone 1979]

Iduna   See *Idun*.

Idunn   See *Idun*.

Ildico
Germany
Time; Unhappiness

Teutonic princess who is said to have killed Attila on their wedding night. The heroine of a time myth. [Bonnerjea 1927; Jobes 1962]

Imd
Scandinavia
Unknown

Scandinavian water goddess, daughter of *Ran*. See also *Imdr*. [Monaghan 1990]

Imder   See *Imdr*.

Imdr
Scandinavia; North Teuton
Fire; Water

One of the nine *Vana Mothers* or *Wave Maidens*. One of the fire maids who set off sparks of fire from the World-Mill. See also *Imd*. Alternate form: Imder. [Leach 1992; Jobes 1962; Monaghan 1990]

Ingebjorg   See *Ingeborg*.

Ingeborg
Scandinavia; North Teuton
Love and Sexuality; Sun and Day

Name of several women in solar legends. In the *Frithiof Saga*, the daughter of Norwegian King Bele, sister of Halfdan and Helge.

Ingeborg fell in love with the solar hero, Frithiof. Her brothers, however, arranged for her to marry the elderly King Ring. When her first husband died, she married Frithiof, and her brothers had to pay tribute to him. Another story says she took a mortal for a lover and blinded him so he could never love another woman.

Alternate form: Ingebjorg. [Jobes 1962; Monaghan 1981]

Ingun
Scandinavia; North Teuton
Earth and Nature

Aspect of *Freyja* as the Norse Mother Earth. Alternate form: Yngvi. [Jobes 1962]

Iord
Scandinavia; North Teuton
Earth and Nature

"The Earth." Daughter of *Nat* and her second husband, Onar. Also considered an alternate name for Germanic *Fjorgyn*. Alternate form: Jord. [Cooper 1876]

Irpa
Scandinavia; North Teuton
Weather

She can be implored to send foul weather, storms, and hail. Daughter of *Hulda* and Odin. Sister of *Thorgerdr Holgarbrudr*. [Leach 1992]

Ithunn   See *Idun*.

Ivithjar, The
Scandinavia; North Teuton
Earth and Nature; Large Size

Norse wood giants. *Hyndla* is one of the Ivithjar. [Jobes 1962]

Jarnsaxa
Scandinavia: North Teuton
Metals; Water

"Iron Cutlass." Wife of Thor and mother of Mangi. Also one of the nine *Vana Mothers* or *Wave Maidens*. Alternate form: Iarnsaxa. [Crossley-Holland 1980; Jobes 1962; Leach 1992]

Jord
Scandinavia; North Teuton
Earth and Nature; Primordial Being

"Earth." Daughter of *Nat*, one of the wives of Odin, and mother of *Frigga* and Thor. Personification of the uncultivated and unpopulated earth. See also *Fjorgyn* and *Hlodyn*. Alternate form: Iord, Jordh, Jorth. [Bonnerjea 1927; Jobes 1962; Leach 1992]

Jordegumma
Sweden
Earth and Nature; Mother and Guardian

"Old Woman of the Earth." Her name has come to mean "midwife." She is similar to *Madder-akka*. [Jobes 1962]

Jordh   See *Jord*.

Jorth   See *Jord*.

Judur
Scandinavia; North Teuton
War
   One of the *Valkyries*. [Sykes 1968]

Juks-akka
Scandinavia; Saami
Fate; Hunting and Wild Animals
   "Old Lady of the Bow." Birth goddess associated with
newborn boys. A tiny bow is placed in the porridge that is
used to honor her at the birth. This assures that the child will
be a successful hunter. She is the daughter of *Madder-akka*.
She forms a triad with her sisters *Sar-akka* and *Uks-akka*.
[Monaghan 1990]

Kajsa
Sweden
Weather
   Wind goddess. [Leach 1992]

Kara
Scandinavia; North Teuton
Charisma; Demi-animals; Physical Prowess; War
   One of the *Valkyries* and a *Swan Maiden*. Wife of the hero,
Helgi.

   *Manifested as a swan, Kara accompanied Helgi in battle.
   Flying overhead, she charmed the enemy into lethargy with
   her sweet song. During one battle, Helgi raised his sword
   and accidentally killed Kara. His life was unhappy from that day on.*
   See also *Sigrun*. [Guirand 1968; Leach 1992]

Kolga
Scandinavia; North Teuton
Water
   Personification of the untamed sea. Daughter of *Ran* and
Aegir. [Leach 1992]

Kornmutter, Die
Germany
Agriculture
   "Corn Mother." She is the spirit of the growing corn and is
incarnate in the last stalk. See also *Zytniamatka*; *Sita*, India;
Corn Mother, Iemparu, Iyatihu, the various *Maize Mothers*,
and *Selu*, North America. [Bonnerjea 1927; Leach 1972]

Krâhe
Scandinavia; North Teuton
Wild Birds
   "Crow." See *Aslog*. [Jobes 1962]

Kriemhild
Germany; North Teuton
Justice; Metals
   Mentioned in the *Das Nibelungenlied*. Sister of the king of
Burgundy, Gunther.

   *Kriemhild became the wife of Siegfried, and he gave her the
   Nibelungen gold as a wedding gift. After quarreling with
   her sister-in-law, Brynhild, Siegfried was killed and the
   gold stolen. Kriemhild mourned for three years and then married
   Etzel (Attila the Hun) to enable her to seek revenge against
   Gunther, Brynhild, and Hagen, Siegfried's murderer. This resulted
   in the deaths of everyone except Etzel.*
   See also *Gudrun*. [Bonnerjea 1927; Leach 1972]

Kunhild
Germany
Earth and Nature; Heaven and Hell; Time
   A summer maid. Similar to Greek *Persephone*.

   *Kunhild is kidnapped by Laurin, a dwarf king, and is taken
   to his underground home to be his queen. Although
   rescued by her brother, Dietlieb, and his friends, Kunhild
   returns to her wealthy husband and his magic possessions. This is a
   story of fertility, abducted by darkness, who is rescued by sun and
   spring, but who returns to darkness.* [Jobes 1962]

Kveldrida
Scandinavia; North Teuton
Magic; Moon and Night
   "Night Rider." Norse sorcerer or witch. [Jobes 1962]

Labismina
Germany
Water; Demi-animals
   Teutonic sea-serpent. May be a corruption of a French
superlative for "abyss." In folktales, she is the godmother of
Cinderella, Eastern Europe. [Jobes 1962]

Lady Wen
Wales
Water
   "White." Guardian of the wells. It is believed that wells
contain *wen*, which means "white, blessed." [Dames 1979]

Laga
Scandinavia; North Teuton
Unknown
   A wife of Odin. [Cooper 1876]

Laufey
Scandinavia; North Teuton
Earth and Nature; Large Size
   "Leafy Isle." Norse giant. As wife of the peasant Farbauti,
she was the mother of Loki, the trickster. She is so thin that
she is sometimes called *Nal*. [Jobes 1962]

Lif
Scandinavia; North Teuton
Life/Death Cycle
   A human who, with the man Lifthraser, will survive the
destruction of the world during Ragnarök (the battle of the
gods and the forces of evil) and repopulate the world.

   *Lif and Lifthraser will go to Hodmimir's forest, which is
   the only safe place from Ragnarök, and sleep until the
   world is once again covered with green vegetation. They
   will live on the dew that will fall on their lips from Yggdrasill (the
   world tree that is axis of the three levels and nine worlds of Norse
   religion.)* See also *Lifthrasir*. [Leach 1972; Senior 1985]

Lifthrasir
Scandinavia; North Teuton
Life/Death Cycle
   "Eager for Life." She will survive the final destruction by
hiding in the World Tree, Yggdrasill, and live to bring forth
new generations. See also *Lif*. [Crossley-Holland 1980]

Lilyi
Transylvania, *Gypsy*
Demi-animals; Destroyer of Life
   Daughter of Ana and wife of Melalo. The cause of catarrhal
disease, she manifests as a fish with a woman's head. [Leach
1992]

Lin
Scandinavia; North Teuton
Earth and Nature
   A companion of *Frigga*; one of her handmaidens with
Fulla and Gna. These companions are aspects of nature. Also
said to be an alternate form of *Fulla*. [Crossley-Holland 1980]

Lofe

Scandinavia; North Teuton
Family and Tribes
    She founded and presides over the ceremony of matrimony.
See *Lofn*. [Cooper 1876]

Lofn

Scandinavia; North Teuton
Earth and Nature; Love and Sexuality
    "Mild." Lofn brings together lovers who are having
difficulties by removing the obstacles to their marriage. She is
a companion of *Frigga* and one of her handmaidens. See also
Lofe, Lofua, Sjofn. Alternate form: Lofna. [Crossley-Holland
1980; Jobes 1962; Leach 1992; Monaghan 1981]

Lofna   See *Lofn*.

Lofua

Scandinavia; North Teuton
Love and Sexuality
    She reconciles lovers. See also *Lofn*. [Woodcock 1953a]

Lorelei

Germany
Charisma; Physical Prowess; Water
    Nymph of the Rhine River.
        *Perched upon a high rock on the south bank of the river at
        Hesse-Nassau, Lorelei sings and combs her hair, luring
        sailors to their deaths against the rocks.* [Bonnerjea 1927;
Leach 1972]

Madder-akka

Scandinavia; Saami
Creator of Life
    Birth goddess who lives beneath the surface of the earth.
She is associated with fertility. She has three daughters,
Juks-akka, Sar-akka, and *Uks-akka,* who live with her
and are more directly involved with the births. See also
Jordegumma. [Monaghan 1990]

Mahr   See *Mora*.

Manatar   See *Tuonetar*.

Mara   See *Mora*.

Mardal

Scandinavia; North Teuton
Earth and Nature; Sun and Day; Water
    Freyja as the golden shimmer that appears on the water at
sunset. Alternate forms: Mardoll, Moertholl. [Jobes 1962;
Monaghan 1981]

Mardoll   See *Mardal*.

Marjatta

Scandinavia; North Teuton
Mother and Guardian
    Mother of a child who supplants Vainamoinen in the
Finnish religion.
        *Marjatta hears a cranberry call out to her to be eaten.
        When she eats the berry, she conceives a child. As the time
        of delivery nears, Marjatta is sent out-of-doors and seeks
refuge in a stable.*
    This story is a combination of the Cybele-Attis and
Mary-Christ tales. [Jobes 1962]

Maruchi   See *Mora*.

Matrona

Germany, *North Teuton, Celtic*
Supreme Being; Water
    1) Scandinavian Great Mother. [Senior 1985]
    2) Celtic goddess of the river Marne. [Leach 1992; Savill
1977]

Mengi   See *Menja*.

Menglad

Scandinavia; North Teuton
Fire; Magic; Large Size
    "Necklace-glad." Similar to *Freyja* and *Frigga*. A magical
being who inhabits Jotunheim (land of the giants).
        *Svipdag was sent to win the love of Menglad. With the
        help of spells given to him by his mother Groa, he searched
        the nine worlds for her. In Jotunheim he came upon a
stronghold girdled by flame and guarded by a giant. It was here
that Menglad lived. She was reclining on the Lyfjaber, the Hill of
Healing, surrounded by her companions. When Svipdag was able to
enter the fortress, Menglad welcomed him with open arms.*
[Crossley-Holland 1980; Davidson 1964]

Menja

Scandinavia; North Teuton
Life/Death Cycle; Water; Large Size
    Giant daughter of *Griep*. Sister of *Fenja*. She creates and
destroys. She is said by some to be the personification of the
waves and one of the nine mothers of Heimdall. Giant. See
story under *Fenga*. Alternate forms: Mengi, Menya. [Jobes
1962; Monaghan 1981]

Menya   See *Menja*.

Metsânneitsyt

Finland, Western
Beauty; Earth and Nature
    "Forest Virgin." A very beautiful forest spirit who looks
like a well-dressed woman from the front but from behind
she is either a stump, a bundle of twigs, a pole, or a trough.
Sometimes she has an animal tail. She loves males and entices
them to have intercourse with her. See also *Huldra* and
Skogsjungfru. [Archaeological Institute 1916–1932; Leach
1972]

Metsola

Germany
Weather
    Mother of a frost spirit. [Savill 1977]

Mielikki

Finland
Hunting and Wild Animals; Mother and Guardian
    Deity of the forest and the hunt. She is the protector of
animals. A statue of her bears a striking resemblance to
Artemis, Greek and Roman Empire. She appears in the *Magic
Song of the Finns* and the *Kalevala*. She is said to have nurtured
a young bear, which may have a relationship to the Finnish
ritual of placing a bear skull in the forest as a sacred totem.
[Stone 1979]

Mimir

Germany; North Teuton
Primordial Being
    She is the sacred waters of destiny. [Neumann 1972]

Minne

Germany
Love and Sexuality
    Love goddess. Alternate form: Frau Minne. [Savill 1977]

Möll

Scandinavia; North Teuton
Weather
Goddess of snow and ice. Daughter of the Norse god Snior. [Leach 1992]

Mist

Scandinavia; North Teuton
War
One of the *Valkyries*. [Leach 1992]

Modgud

Scandinavia; North Teuton
Heaven and Hell; Water
Guardian of the bridge over the icy river Gjoll that leads to Hel, the realm of the newly dead. She glows with an unearthly pallor.

 When Hermod rode to Hel to look for his brother Balder, Modgud raised her arm to stop and question him. She told him that Balder had come that way and let him pass.
Alternate forms: Modgudr, Modgudhr. [Crossley-Holland 1980; Leach 1992; Monaghan 1981]

Modgudr See *Modgud*.

Modgudhr See *Modgud*.

Moertholl See *Frejya, Mardal*.

Mora

Germany
Demi-animals; Evil; Magic
Demon who torments her victims with bad dreams or strangles them and sucks their blood. She can take the form of a butterfly, a horse, or a tuft of hair. See also *Mora*, Eastern Europe. Alternate forms: Mahr, Mara, Maruchi, Smert. [Dexter 1990; Leach 1992; Monaghan 1981]

Mothir

Scandinavia; North Teuton
Family and Tribes
Ancestor of the Norse nobility, the Jarls (those who hunt, fight, and are educated). [Monaghan 1981]

Myrkrida

Scandinavia
Magic
"Dark Rider." Witch. [Monaghan 1990]

Nacht See *Nat*.

Nal See *Laufey*.

Nanna

Scandinavia; North Teuton
Earth and Nature; Family and Tribes; Love and Sexuality
Norse deity of purity, blossoms, and vegetation. Daughter of *Nef*. Wife of Balder (Baldur) and mother of Forseti.

Nanna and Balder were a devoted couple, a rare occurrence among the northern gods. When Balder was killed, Nanna died of a broken heart and was cremated with her husband on his sailing vessel, the Ringhorn. Hermod, Balder's brother, arrived in Hel (the realm of the dead) to seek the release of Balder and Nanna, but she refused to return. Instead she sent a carpet of spring flowers to Frigga and a ring to Fulla.
See also *Asynjur*. [Cooper 1876; Crossley-Holland 1980; Leach 1972]

Nat

Scandinavia; North Teuton
Happiness; Intelligence and Creativity; Metals; Moon and Night; Stars and Planets; Weather
"Night." She brings refreshment and inspiration and removes worry and care. Nat had three husbands: Naglfari, with whom she had Audr (Udr), "space or riches"; Anar (Annarr, Onar), with whom she had *Jord* (*Iord*); and Dellingr, with whom she had *Dag*.

 Each evening, Nat drives her jewel-studded chariot across the star-filled sky. It is pulled by Hrimfaxi (Frostymane), whose foam falls from his mouth to cover the earth with dew.
Alternate forms: Nott, Nacht. [Cooper 1876; Jobes 1962; Leach 1992; Monaghan 1981]

Nef

Scandinavia; North Teuton
Mother and Guardian
Mother of *Nanna*. [Sykes 1968]

Nehalennia

Scandinavia; Belgium, *Suevi, Frisian*
Mother and Guardian; Water
Protector of seafarers. She was worshiped on the Island of Walcheren in Roman times. [Davidson 1964; Leach 1992; Monaghan 1981; Redfield 1931]

Nekke

Lapland, *Saami*
Unknown
Water spirit who predicted misfortune. [Leach 1992]

Nerthus

Denmark
Earth and Nature; Order
"Mother of the Northern Earth." She is the symbol of fruitfulness and presides over peace and harmony. In Germany she is identified with *Frigga*. In Scandinavia she is associated with Njord (Niord), possibly as his sister or wife. See also *Dame Wode* and *Frau Gode*. [Cooper 1876; Crossley-Holland 1980; Davidson 1964; Monaghan 1981; Savill 1977; Stone 1979]

Nix See *Nixen, Die*.

Nixe See *Nixen, Die*.

Nixen, Die

Germany
Demi-animals; Evil; Fate; Goodness; Magic; Physical Prowess; Water
Prophetic spirits who inhabit rivers. They sing beautifully and sometimes join in dances with humans. Die Nixen are changeable beings, both in form and personality. Appearing sometimes in human form and at other times as half woman, half fish, they can be benevolent or malevolent. Frequently they kidnap humans, but will return them if given appropriate gifts. Both males and females are called "nicker" or "kelpies." To the Dutch, they are "nikker"; Old Teutonic is "nikus." Alternate forms: Nix, Nixe, Nixy. [Bonnerjea 1927; Jobes 1962; Monaghan 1981]

Nixy See *Nixen, Die*.

Norns, The

Scandinavia; North Teuton
Household Affairs; Fate; Water
The Norns—*Skuld, Urd,* and *Verdandi*—preside over the destinies of humans and gods by determining the length of

life by spinning the thread and tearing it off. They sit at the foot of Yggdrasill (the World Tree). Each day they take water from the fountain of Urd to sprinkle on the ash tree, keeping it alive. Germanic peoples consider fate a feminine power. Although the Norns gave them their fates, the Vikings could live their lives any way they chose. Not believing in an afterlife, their immortality was dependent on fame, which they sought relentlessly. See also *Disir.* Alternate form: Giptes. [Bonnerjea 1927; Crossley-Holland 1980; Durdin-Robertson 1982; Leach 1972; Leach 1992; Monaghan 1981]

Nott See *Nat.*

Oddibjord
Scandinavia; North Teuton
Fate; Luck; Wealth
   A prophet called a *Volva* or *Voluspa.*
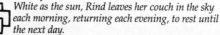   *Oddibjord travels throughout the country telling stories and fortunes. Your fortune improves as the quality and amount of food you provide her improves.*
[Monaghan 1981]

Old Woman of Germany and Scotland
Germany; Scotland
Agriculture
   Deity of the harvest who is represented by a image fashioned from stalks of grain or straw. [Eliade 1987]

Olrun
Scandinavia; North Teuton
Demi-animals
   Norse *Swan Maiden.* See also *Allwise.* [Savill 1977]

Orboda See *Gullveig.*

Orsel See *Horsel.*

Ostara See *Eastre.*

Paive See *Beiwe.*

Perchata See *Berchta.*

Percht See *Berchta.*

Perchta See *Berchta.*

Perchtel See *Berchta.*

Poshjo-akka
Scandinavia; Saami
Hunting and Wild Animals
   "She Permits Shooting." Goddess of the hunt. Skulls of the butchered animals were buried at her feet in the storage hut. If not properly buried, the animals would not reincarnate. [Monaghan 1990]

Precht See *Berchta.*

Radgrid
Scandinavia; North Teuton
War
   One of the *Valkyries.* [Leach 1992]

Radien-akka
Scandinavia; Saami
Mother and Guardian
   "Mother." One of a trinity of deities, along with a child and a father. Her likeness appears on shamans' drums. [Monaghan 1990]

Radien-kiedde
Scandinavia; Saami
Immortality
   Creator goddess who gave souls to the mother goddess *Madder-akka* to be made human. [Monaghan 1990]

Ran
Scandinavia
Water; Destroyer of Life
   Goddess of the sea. Sister/wife of Aegir, mother of the *Vana Mothers* and *Wave Maidens.* She uses a net to gather men into her realm. To drowning victims, Ran is a death goddess. [Leach 1992]

Rana Neida
Scandinavia; Saami
Time
   Goddess of spring. She turns the hills green to feed the reindeer. Sacrifices were made to her by putting blood on a spinning wheel resting against her altar. [Monaghan 1990]

Randgrid
Scandinavia; North Teuton
War
   One of the *Valkyries.* [Sykes 1968]

Reginleif
Scandinavia; North Teuton
War
   One of the *Valkyries.* [Leach 1992]

Rheda See *Hrede.*

Rhind See *Rind.*

Rind
Scandinavia; North Teuton
Earth and Nature; Large Size; Sun and Day; Weather
   A solar deity.
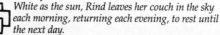   *White as the sun, Rind leaves her couch in the sky each morning, returning each evening, to rest until the next day.*
   Some authorities say that Rind is the personification of the frost-covered earth. In this form, she is a giant or a mortal and may be called *Rinde, Rinda,* or *Rhind.*
[Crossley-Holland 1980; Jobes 1962; Monaghan 1981]

Rinda See *Rind, Rindr.*

Rinde See *Rind.*

Rindr
Scandinavia; North Teuton
Earth and Nature; Justice; Time
   Personification of the surface of the earth during its dormant period. As the wife of Odin, she is the mother of Vali (Wali), who, according to this account, is the avenger of the death of Balder. Also called *Rinda.* [Cooper 1876; Leach 1992]

Risem-Edne
Norway, *Saami*
Unknown
   "Twig Mother." [Monaghan 1990]

Roggenmuhme
Germany, Scandinavia
Agriculture
   "Rye-aunt." A grain spirit who appears in human form. Rye, wheat, oats, and barley have been found dated in prehistoric times in Scandinavia, and harvested crops have

been associated with deities and have been a focus of rituals promoting fertility. [Bonnerjea 1927; Leach 1972]

Roskva
Scandinavia; North Teuton
Charisma
"The Vivacious." Daughter of Orvandel (a Norse farmer), who, with her brother Thialfi, became a servant of Thor. [Davidson 1964; Jobes 1962]

Rota
Scandinavia; North Teuton
War
One of the *Valkyries.* She is particularly associated with victory in battle. [Leach 1992]

Saelde
Germany
Mother and guardian
Goddess of protection who rewards her favorites. Alternate forms: Frau Saelde, Frau Salida, Salida. [Leach 1992]

Saga
Scandinavia; North Teuton
Arts; Education and Knowledge; Water
"All Knowing." Said by some to be an aspect of *Frigga.* Also considered a deity of the poetry, and of the narration, of history. She lives in Sokvabek, a sinking stream or waterfall. Associated with Odin, the god of poetry, battle, and death. [Crossley-Holland 1980; Jobes 1962; Leach 1992; Woodcock 1953a]

Salida   See *Saelde.*

Sangridr
Scandinavia; North Teuton
War
One of the *Valkyries.* [Leach 1992]

Sar-akka
Scandinavia; Saami
Fate; Creator of Life
Birth goddess who opens the womb for the child to be born. Daughter of *Madder-akka.* She forms a triad with her sisters *Juks-akka* and *Uks- akka.* Wood is chopped outside the birthing tent to assist her in making the opening. The mother honors Sar-akka by drinking brandy before the delivery and eating Sar-akka's porridge afterward. The porridge contains three sticks, a white one signifying good luck, a black one signifying death, and a cleft one signifying success. The sticks and how they appear in the mother's bowl indicate how Sar-akka sees the newborn's future. [Monaghan 1990]

Seidhkoma, The
Scandinavia; North Teuton
Courage; Demi-animals; Destroyer of Life; Disorder; Evil; Magic
Magicians who send human souls out of their bodies into those of animals. These fierce animals wreck havoc, destroying things, causing delusions or tempests, and depriving warriors of courage with deadly results. [Jobes 1962]

Sel
Scandinavia; North Teuton
Demi-animals; Magic; Water
She takes the form of a mermaid. It has been suggested that attacks on the feminine principal causes it to quietly

submerge, like the mermaid or the seal, occasionally surfacing through the subconscious, as on the surface of the water. Alternate form: Sil. [Dames 1979]

She-Wolf
Scandinavia; North Teuton
Earth and Nature; Hunting and Wild Animals
Norse animal. A beast who devours Volsung's sons, children of the sun.
 Signy saved the last of Volsung's sons, Sigmund, from the She-Wolf. A story of dawn, Signy, saving the sun, Sigmund, from being devoured by the earth, She-Wolf. [Jobes 1962]

Sibilja
Sweden
Demi-animals; Mother and Guardian
A deity who took the form of a cow. She was a protector of the Swedish king, Eysteinn Beli, accompanying him in battle and bellowing to frighten his enemies. [Monaghan 1981]

Sieglind
Scandinavia; North Teuton
Dawn and Twilight
According to *Der Ring des Nibelungen,* she is the wife of Sigmund and mother of Siegried. Probably a dawn deity. Alternate form: Sieglinde. [Jobes 1962]

Sieglinde   See *Sieglind.*

Sif
Scandinavia; North Teuton
Beauty; Creator of Life; Earth and Nature; Love and Sexuality;
Weather Mother of Ull, with an unknown first husband. She took Thor as her second husband and had *Thurd.* She has striking, beautiful golden hair, which is thought to represent grain or the autumn grass. On summer nights, Thor and Sif mate. His lightning strikes her fields. Besides fertility, she also is known as a deity of love and beauty. Companion of *Baduhenna.* See also *Asynjur.* [Leach 1992; Monaghan 1981]

Signe-Alveig
Scandinavia; North Teuton
Demi-animals
"Nourishing Drink." Norse *Swan Maiden.* Daughter of Sigbrygg and wife of Halfdan, a descendent of Thor. [Jobes 1962]

Signy
Scandinavia; North Teuton
Family and Tribes; Mother and Guardian
1) Wife of Loki (the trickster); mother of Nari and Vali. One of the *Asynjur.*
 Signy, trying to protect her husband, collected the venom that dripped from the poisonous snake that was suspended over Loki's head, part of his punishment by the gods for causing the death of Balder. When Signy went to empty the bowl, some poison fell on Loki's face, and his shaking caused an earthquake.
2) Also the name of a daughter of a king of Denmark, Sigar. She committed suicide after the execution of her lover. Alternate forms: Siguna, Sigyn. [Crossley-Holland 1980; Lurker 1984; Savill 1977; Sykes 1968]

Sigrdrifa
Scandinavia; North Teuton
Education and Knowledge; Health and Healing; Magic; War
"Victory Bringer." One of the *Valkyries.* Associated with healing.

Sigurdrifta angered Odin by taking a hero from battle to whom Odin had promised victory. Odin punished her by stinging her with sleep thorns, causing her to fall into a trance. Awakened for a short time by Sigurd, she taught him the wisdom of runes and sorcery.

She may be called **Brynhild** in some legends. Alternate form: Sigurdrifta. [Eliade 1987; Jobes 1962; Monaghan 1981; Savill 1977]

Sigrlinn
Scandinavia; North Teuton
War
One of the *Valkyries.* [Leach 1992]

Sigrun
Scandinavia; North Teuton
Demi-animals; War; Weather
One of the *Valkyries.* Daughter of Hogni and the lover of Helgi Hundingsbani. As a *Swan Maiden,* she may be the personification of the wind. Some say she was reborn as the Valkyrie *Kara* or *Svafa.* [Davidson 1964; Jobes 1962; Leach 1992; Savill 1977]

Siguna   See *Signy.*

Sigurdrifta   See *Sigrdrifa.*

Sigyn   See *Signy.*

Sil   See *Sel.*

Silige Fraulein
Central Europe
Earth and Nature
"Ones Who Look Like Vultures." See *Buschfrauen.* [Monaghan 1990]

Sindgund
Germany
Health and Healing; Magic
Sister of *Sunna.* She possesses magical healing charms. Alternate forms: Sinngund, Sinthgunt. [Leach 1992]

Sindur
Scandinavia; North Teuton
Water
One of the variants of the nine *Vana Mothers* or *Wave Maidens.* [Leach 1992]

Sinmora
Scandinavia; North Teuton
Fire; Large Size
Wife of Surt, the giant who guards Muspelsheim (the realm of fire), Surt guards the sword Laevateinn, the "Wounding Wand," made by Loki. [Crossley-Holland 1980]

Sinngund   See *Sindgund.*

Sinthgunt   See *Sindgund.*

Siofn
Scandinavia; North Teuton
Goodness; Love and Sexuality
Deity presiding over affection, tenderness, and sympathy. [Cooper 1876]

Sith
Scandinavia; North Teuton
Agriculture; Education and Knowledge

Norse goddess of the harvest. Second wife of Orvandel, mother of Ill.

 Sith's son, Ill, and her stepson, Svipdag, went to rescue Freyja from the giants of Jotunheim. Sith aided them in their mission by preparing the "food of wisdom" from the fat of three serpents. [Jobes 1962]

Sjofn
Scandinavia; North Teuton
Love and Sexuality
Attendant of *Frigga.* She is responsible for stirring human hearts to love. See also *Lofn.* [Crossley-Holland 1980; Leach 1992; Monaghan 1981]

Sjora
Sweden
Water; Weather
Personification of the stormy sea. Equivalent to *Ran.* Alternate form: Sjöran. [Leach 1972; Leach 1992]

Sjūran   See *Sjora.*

Skeggold
Scandinavia; North Teuton
War
One of the *Valkyries.* [Leach 1992]

Skialf
Scandinavia; North Teuton
Earth and Nature
Queen, wife of Agni. She killed her husband with her necklace. Considered by some to be a ritualistic execution carried out by Skialf as a priestess of *Freyja.* [Davidson 1964; Savill 1977]

Skogol
Scandinavia; North Teuton
War
One of the *Valkyries.* Alternate form: Skogul. [Leach 1992; Sykes 1968]

Skogsfru
Scandinavia
Charisma; Evil; Hunting and Wild Animals
A malevolent "woods-woman."

 Skogsfru lurks around the night fires of hunters, luring the unfortunate young men to follow her. [Davidson 1964; Jobes 1962]

Skogsjungfru
Sweden
Evil; Hunting and Wild Animals
Similar to Finnish *Metsänneitsyt.* [Archaeological Institute 1916–1932; Leach 1972]

Skogsnufvar, The
Scandinavia
Hunting and Wild Animals
"Wood Wives." They are responsible for the woodland animals. Hunters invoke them with coins and food before killing any game. [Monaghan 1981]

Skogul   See *Skogol.*

Skuld
Scandinavia; North Teuton
Fate; War; Water
"Shall-be." The youngest of the *Norns.* Skuld determines the length of all lives and assigns their destiny. She frequently changes the more benevolent fates given by *Urd* and *Verdandi.*

Considered a water nymph in the *Eddas,* she is also one of the *Valkyries.* [Bonnerjea 1927; Crossley-Holland 1980; Leach 1992; Monaghan 1981; Sykes 1968]

Smert See *Mora.*

Snūr
Scandinavia; North Teuton
Family and Tribes
    Norse ancestor. With her husband, Karl, son of Afi and *Amma,* Snör had ten sons and ten daughters, who were the parents of the race of peasants, Churls. [Crossley-Holland 1980]

Snorta See *Snotra.*

Snotra
Scandinavia; North Teuton
Education and Knowledge; Goodness; Health and Healing
    The wise and gentle deity of prudence and possibly cleanliness. Snotra is the most attractive of *Frigga's* handmaidens. Alternate form: Snorta. [Cooper 1876; Crossley-Holland 1980; Leach 1992; Monaghan 1981]

Sol
Germany, Scandinavia
Sun and Day
    "Mistress Sun." Daughter of Mundilfari, sister of Mani, and wife of Glaur. She is the charioteer who drives the sun across the sky. See also *Sunna.* [Cooper 1876; Leach 1992; Monaghan 1981]

Spurke
Scandinavia
Ceremonies; Time
    Deity of the month of February. Her festival is called Spurkalia. [Cooper 1876]

Sun
Scandinavia; North Teuton
Hunting and Wild Animals; Sun and Day
    A Norse girl, daughter of Mundilfari, who drives the sun on its course across the sky while a boy named Moon drives that heavenly body.

 Sun and Moon are pursued by wolves. There is a very large wolf that will one day catch them and swallow Sun, bringing about the end of the world.

    She is also called the Sun of Norse belief. [Crossley-Holland 1980; Savill 1977]

Sunna
Scandinavia; North Teuton
Health and Healing; Magic; Sun and Day
    Deity who posseses magical charms for healing. Sister of *Sindgund.* See also *Sol.* Alternate form: Sunnu. [Leach 1992; Monaghan 1981]

Sunnu See *Sunna.*

Svafa
Scandinavia; North Teuton
War
    One of the *Valkyries.* She may be an incarnation of *Sigrun.* [Savill 1977]

Svanhild See *Swanhild.*

Svava
Scandinavia; North Teuton
War
    One of the *Valkyries.* [Leach 1992]

Svipul
Scandinavia; North Teuton
War
    One of the *Valkyries.* [Leach 1992]

Swan Maidens, The
Scandinavia; Germany
Demi-animals; Magic; Time; Weather
    Air spirits who are half-supernatural and half-mortal beings and are able to interchange from woman to swan form. This usually depends upon their possession of a magic feather robe, a pair of wings, a ring, a crown, or a golden chain. They are under an enchantment that affects their relationships with humans. There is a worldwide mythological swan motif. When they remove their magic feathers (or other charms) to bathe, they become beautiful maidens. A young male steals the feather robe and claims the swan for his wife. Eventually she regains her feathers as the result of her husband breaking a taboo, and she flies away. It is suggested that this is a story of day shedding the mist and being stolen by an agricultural deity. When she flies away, summer disappears. It is also the story of divine-human marriage. See also *Allwise, Angeburga, Groa, Kara, Olrun, Signe-Alveig, Sigrun, Swanwhite, The Wunschelwybere; Zhinii,* Far East; and *Surya,* Indian Sub-continent. [Jobes 1962]

Swanhild
Scandinavia; North Teuton
Beauty; Love and Sexuality; Time; Sun and Day
    Daughter of Sigurd and *Gudrun.* The most beautiful of women.

 Swanhild is falsely accused of adultery with her stepson, Randver. Her husband, Jormunrek, has her trampled to death by horses.

    This story is interpreted as dawn, spring sunlight, or summer fertility (Swanhild) killed by winter (Jormunrek) at the instigation of storm (Sibeche). Alternate form: Svanhild. [Jobes 1962]

Swanwhite
Scandinavia; North Teuton
Weather
    A *Swan Maiden.* [Savill 1977]

Syn
Scandinavia; North Teuton
Heaven and Hell; Household Affairs; Justice
    "Denial." She is said to deny admittance to heaven of those she considers unworthy. Norse guardian of truth and justice, she presides over trials and protects against perjury. She is invoked by defendants at trials. Also a guardian of thresholds or a doorkeeper, especially at Valhalla. [Cooper 1876; Crossley-Holland 1980; Jobes 1962; Leach 1992; Monaghan 1981]

Syr
Scandinavia; North Teuton
Domesticated Animals
    The sow. A form of *Freyja.* [Monaghan 1981]

Tamfana
Germany
Agriculture
    Fertility of the harvest. [Leach 1992]

Thaukt   See *Thok*.

Thir
Scandinavia; North Teuton
Family and Tribes; Justice
   "The Drudge." Ancestor, with her husband, Thrall, to the race of thralls—the manual laborers who were never free and who lived without the protection of a patron deity. [Crossley-Holland 1980]

Thok
Scandinavia; North Teuton
Large Size; Ugliness
   A giant hag.

   When Balder (Baldur) was killed, the goddess Hel agreed to release him from her kingdom if everyone and everything in the world would weep for him. When Odin's messengers found Thok in her cave, she refused to weep, saying that she never liked Balder. Some say she was really Loki (the trickster) in disguise.
   Alternate forms: Thaukt, Thokk. [Crossley-Holland 1980; Davidson 1964; Jobes 1962; Guirand 1968; Leach 1972; Sykes 1968]

Thokk   See *Thok*.

Thora
Scandinavia; North Teuton
Dawn and Twilight; Magic; Metals; Time
   Maid of spring and possibly dawn. Daughter of Hakon or Heroth, god of fertility, and wife of Ragnar Löbrog.

   Thora raised nests of adders. She had so many that they were a threat to the public, so her husband killed them.
   Thora kept one pet snake, housing him in a box of gold. As the snake grew, so did the box, ever increasing the amount of gold.
[Jobes 1962; Leach 1972]

Thorgerd Holgabrud   See *Thorgerdr Holgarbrudr*.

Thorgerda
Scandinavia; North Teuton
Earth and Nature
   She is the "Bride of Helgi." Worshiped in Halogaland. Associated with *Freyja*. See also *Thorgerdr Holgarbrudr*. [Davidson 1964]

Thorgerdr Holgarbrudr
Scandinavia; North Teuton
Agriculture; Fates; Fishing and Water Animals; Luck; Magic; Mother and Guardian
   A deified human known for her skill in divining and sorcery. Sister of *Irpa*. As a warrior goddess, she is protector of her people.

   Thorgerdr Holgarbrudr protects her people from their enemies by sending arrows flying from each of her fingers. Each arrow kills an attacking man.
   She is also invoked for luck in fishing and farming. Her religion overlapped that of Christianity and she was denounced and called Thorgerd Holga-Troll. See also *Thorgerda*. Alternate forms: Thorgerd Holgabrud, Thorgerthr Holgarbruathr. [Davidson 1964; Monaghan 1981; Savill 1977]

Thorgerthr Holgarbruathr   See *Thorgerdr Holgarbrudr*.

Thrud
Scandinavia; North Teuton
Weather
   "Might." Daughter of *Sif* and Thor. She signifies "seed" and is considered by some to be a storm or cloud deity.

Thrudur
Scandinavia; North Teuton
War
   One of the *Valkyries*. Thrudr is a name for Odin in the *Eddas*, possibly indicating some sort of relationship between him and Thrudur. [Sykes 1968]

Tuonetar
Scandinavia; North Teuton; Finno-Ugric
Destroyer of Life; Heaven and Hell
   Deity of death. In the Norse *Kalevala*, the daughter/wife of Tuoni. See also *Tuonetar*, Eastern Europe. Alternate form: Manatar. [Jobes 1962; Leach 1972; Leach 1992; Monaghan 1981]

Uks-akka
Scandinavia; Saami
Fate
   "Old Lady of the Door." Birth goddess who welcomes the newborn into the daylight. Daughter of *Madder-akka*. She forms a triad with her sisters *Sar- akka* and *Juks-akka*. Uks-akka lives in the dark at the entrance to the tent where she blesses and protects anyone leaving and newborns arriving into the world of light. Similar to *Dörr Käring*. [Monaghan 1990]

Ulfrun
Scandinavia; North Teuton
Large Size; Water
   One of the *Wave Maidens* and *Vana Mothers* of Heimdal. She is also one of the nine giants who operate the World-Mill (the mill that created the material from which the world was formed). A personification of the waves. [Jobes 1962; Leach 1992]

Undine
Germany
Immortality; Water
   Water nymph who was created without a soul—a condition shared by all water nymphs. By marrying a mortal and having a child, Undine gained a soul and its accompanying pains and penalties. [Jobes 1962; Redfield 1931; Woodcock 1953a]

Undutar
Finland
Weather
   Personification of fog and mist who lives in the highest regions of the sky.

   Undutar has a silver sieve through which she strains the fog and mist before sending hem down to earth.
   Alternate form: Untar. [Jobes 1962; Redfield 1931]

Untar   See *Undutar*.

Urd
Scandinavia; North Teuton
Fate; Mother and Guardian
   "Past." One of the *Norns*. May have been only Urd in early belief, with *Skuld* and *Verdandi* coming later.

   It is at the Well of Urd that the three Norns gather. They care for Yggdrasill (the World Tree) so that human life and the universe can survive. The well is at the foot of Yggdrasill, which holds up the nine worlds—Asgard (the world of the Aesir) with Vanaheim (land of the Vanir) and Alfeheim (land of the Light Elves); Midgard (Middle World) with Jotunheim (land of the giants), Nidavellir (land of the dwarfs), and Svartalfheim (land of the Dark Elves); and Hel (realm of the dead) and Niflheim (world of the dead). The ninth world may be Muspelsheim (land of fire) if Hel and Niflheim are combined.

Alternate forms: Urdhr, Urdr, Urdur, Urth, Giptes. [Bonnerjea 1927; Cooper 1876; Cotterell 1979; Crossley-Holland 1980; Leach 1972; Leach 1992; Monaghan 1981; Redfield 1931]

Urdhr   See *Urd.*

Urdr   See *Urd.*

Urdur   See *Urd.*

Ursula
Scandinavia; North Teuton
Moon and Night; Selflessness
Norse moon goddess. Her attendants are 11,000 virgins (stars).

🔯 *Ursula was a fifth-century Cornish princess who was traveling to France with 11,000 virgins. Before reaching their destination they were all slain by the Huns.*
She has been adopted by the Christians as St. Ursula, and the goddess Ursula's old moon feast day became St. Ursula's Day. She is equivalent to *Horsel.* [Jobes 1962; Monaghan 1981]

Ursel   See *Ursula.*

Urth   See *Urd.*

Vala   See *Volva.*

Valkyries, The
Scandinavia; North Teuton
Beauty; Ceremonies; Fate; Heaven and Hell; War
Beautiful Norse women who choose which warriors will die in battle and then return with their bodies to Valhalla, the hall in Asgard where they await Ragnarök. Valhalla is said to have 540 doors, to accommodate 800 soldiers abreast, and to have rafters of spears and a roof of shields. The Valkyries are also said to be priests of *Freyja* and subordinates of the *Norns.* Some of their names are *Brynhild, Geirahod, Geirolul, Gol, Goli, Gondul, Gudr, Gunnr, Herfjotur, Hildur, Hiorthrimul, Hlock, Hrist, Judur, Kara, Mist, Radgrid, Randgrid, Reginleif, Rota, Sangridr, Sigrdrifa, Sigrlinn, Sigrun, Skeggold, Skogol, Skuld, Svafa, Svava, Svipul,* and *Thrudur.* The Vikings believed that the aurora borealis was the light reflected from the Valkyries' shields while they are gathering the war dead. The Valkyries reflect the fatalism that is fundamental to the Norse beliefs: the gods, not humans, decide which slain warriors are taken to Valhalla, and Ragnarök (the final battle between the gods and the forces of evil) is inescapable. See also *Disir.* Alternate form: the Alaisiagae. [Cooper 1876; Carlyon 1982; Crossley-Holland 1980; Jobes 1962; Guirand 1968; Leach 1972; Leach 1992; Monaghan 1981; Savill 1977; Sykes 1968]

Vana Mothers, The
Scandinavia; North Teuton
Creator of Life; Fire; Water
The nine daughters of *Ran* and Aegir. Also called *Wave Maidens* and fire-maids, they are personifications of waves. Together they were the mother of Heimdal. As custodians of the World-Mill, which the Norse called Grotte, they ground out the universe from Ymir's body. Resting at the bottom of the sea, the mill also grinds out fertility, seasonal changes, and universal harmony. Their names are *Angeyja, Atla, Eistla, Eyrgjafe, Gjlap, Griep, Imdr, Jarnsaxa,* and *Ulfrun,* with variants being *Augeia, Egia,* and *Sindur.* See also *Fenja.* [Jobes 1962; Leach 1992]

Vanadis   See *Freyja.*

Var
Scandinavia; North Teuton
Family and Tribes; Justice
Deity of plighted troths. She is an aspect of the all-knowing earth, who sees and knows everything. If anyone breaks an oath, she punishes them with vengence. See also *Vor.* Alternate form: Vara. [Crossley-Holland 1980; Leach 1992; Wedeck 1971]

Vara   See *Var.*

Verdandi
Scandinavia; North Teuton
Fate; Goodness; Water
One of the *Norns.* Sister of *Skuld* and *Urd.* In deciding an individual's destiny, she rules the present. She and *Urd* are considered benevolent deities and, according to the *Eddas,* are water-nymphs. Alternate form: Verthandi. [Bonnerjea 1927; Crossley-Holland 1980; Leach 1992; Monaghan 1981; Neumann 1972]

Verthandi   See *Verdandi.*

Vihansa
Germany
War
War goddess. [Leach 1992]

Vjofn
Scandinavia; North Teuton
Family and Tribes; Order
"Peacemaker." An attendant of *Frigga,* she reconciles couples who have quarreled. Alternate form: Vjofr. [Jobes 1962; Leach 1992]

Vjofr   See *Vjofn.*

Vola   See *Volva.*

Volla   See *Fulla.*

Voluspa
Scandinavia; North Teuton
Education and Knowledge; Fate; Primordial Being
Name for a seer or wise woman. There is a Norse poem titled "Völuspá" (The Sibyl's Prophecy) in the *Elder Edda.*

🔯 *Voluspa was born before the world began, so she knew the history of the world. When asked by the gods to tell the story, she recounted everything, including the end of the world and the gods at Ragnarök (the final battle between the gods and the forces of evil).*
See also *Volva.* [Crossley-Holland 1980; Monaghan 1981]

Volva
Scandinavia; North Teuton
Fate; Mother and Guardian
A Norse seer. She sings of the birth and death of deities and humans. She can be alive or dead and may be raised from her burial mound by the gods for information or to give protection to mortals. The "Völuspá" is said to be her song. See also *Gollveig, Heid, Oddibjord, Voluspa.* Alternate forms: Vala, Vola. [Crossley-Holland 1980; Jobes 1962; Monaghan 1981]

Vor
Scandinavia; North Teuton
Education and Knowledge; Family and Tribes; Justice
Omniscient deity of wisdom and knowledge. According to some, she is also the deity of marriage oaths, who punishes

those who break them. See also *Var.* [Crossley-Holland 1980; Leach 1992; Wedeck 1971]

Vrou-elde   See *Berchta.*

Wachilt
Germany
Large Size; Mother and Guardian; Water
    A giant who lives under the sea.
    ⌘ *Wachilt met King Vilcinus in the forest. She returned to the sea, where she stopped his ship and told him that she was going to have his child. Returning home with Vilcinus, she gave birth to the giant, Wade, and then disappeared. When she discovered that her grandson, Wittich, was to be killed, she came for him and took him back to the sea to protect him.* [Davidson 1964; Savill 1977]

Waldmichen
Scandinavia
Unknown
    "Wood Nymph." A form of *Freyja* in Lower Saxony. [Monaghan 1990]

Wanne Thekla
Netherlands
Unknown
    Elf Queen. May have been a form of *Habondia.* [Monaghan 1990]

Wara
Scandinavia
Family and Tribes; Justice
    She presides over social contracts. [Cooper 1876]

Wave Maidens, The
Scandinavia; North Teuton
Large Size; Water
    Nine dieties who are the personifications of waves. Daughters of *Ran.* They are said to be the joint mothers of Heimdal, a sea god. See also *Vana Mothers.* Other daughters of Ran not listed in Vana Mothers but who may also be Wave Maidens are *Bylgja, Drafn, Fenja, Hrafn, Ind,* and *Kolga.* [Leach 1992]

Weiþen Frauen, Die
Germany; Europe
Ceremonies; Fate; Magic; Mother and Guardian
    "White Women." Said to be goddess-worshiping witches or ghosts of ancient goddesses. They live in the woods, where they aid lost travelers, tell the future, and perform ritual fertility dances. [Monaghan 1981]

White Lady   See *Berchta.*

Wilden Wip, The
Germany
Health and Healing; Love and Sexuality; Magic
    Forest women. Known for their healing and magic. They enjoy sexual liaisons with human men. [Monaghan 1981]

Wode   See *Gode.*

Wunschelwybere, The
Germany
Beauty; Demi-animals; Magic; Metals; Weather
    "Shape-changers." Beautiful women who use a golden necklace to become swans. Personifications of the air or clouds, their necklace is the glow of the sunrise or sunset. Indentical to *Swan Maidens.* [Jobes 1962]

Y'dun   See *Idun.*

Yngona
Denmark
Evil
    "Anna of the Angels." Identified with the Celtic *Annis,* Western Europe. [Graves 1948]

Yngvi
Scandinavia; North Teuton
Creator of Life; Earth and Nature
    Freyja as a fertility goddess. Alternate form: Ingun. [Jobes 1962]

Yrou-elde   See *Berchta.*

Ziza
Germany
Creator of Life
    Northern deity who is the equivalent of Egyptian *Isis.* Alternate form: Zizi. [Jobes 1962; Redfield 1931]

Zizi   See *Ziza.*

Zytniamatka
Germany
Agriculture
    Prussian Corn Mother. See also *Kornmutter, Die; Sita,* India; *Corn Mother, Iemparu, Iyatihu,* the various *Maize Mothers,* and *Selu,* North America. [Monaghan 1990]

OCEANIA

Abeguwo
Melanesia: New Guinea, *Kapauka*
Weather
   Rain goddess. Her urine is the moisture. [Leach 1992; Pospisil 1958]

Abere
Melanesia
Evil
   Demon. A wild woman who attacks males. [Carlyon 1982]

Afekan
Melanesia: New Guinea, *Tifalmin*
Creator of Life; Education and Knowledge; Ceremonies
   Creator goddess. She teaches people how to live correctly. She created taro, pigs, and cultural rituals. [Leach 1992; Wheatcroft 1973]

Ahīm ū
Polynesia
Reptiles
   Lizard goddess. Also known as *Wahīmū*. [Craig 1989]

Ai Tūpua'i
Polynesia: Tahiti; Society Islands (Ta'aroa)
War; Health and Healing
   War goddess and healer. Daughter of *Tū fe'ufe'u ma i ite ra'i* and warrior god, 'Oro. [Cotterell 1979; Craig 1989; Leach 1992]

'Aiāru
Polynesia: Tahiti
Mother and Guardian; Fate
   One of the seven ancient guardians of the world. She predicts death. The others are *Fa'a'ipu, Firifiri 'Aufau,*

Nihoniho teitei, 'Ōrerorero, Tahu'a, and *Tāmaumau 'ōrero.* [Craig 1989; Henry 1928; Leach 1992]

Aka
Polynesia: Hawaii
Unknown
   Companion of *Pele.* [Craig 1989]

Aka ku a nue nue   See *Ha lo.*

Aku aku, The
Polynesia: Easter Island
Ceremonies
   Spirits who can be female or male and are often cannibalistic. About ninety Aku aku came to the island with the first settlers. They include *Kava'ara, Kava tua, Papai a taki vera,* and, the most famous, *Uka o hoheru.* [Craig 1989]

Ala muki
Polynesia: Hawaii
Water; Reptiles
   River goddess. Protector of the Waialua River. She takes the form of a dragon. [Leach 1992; Westerveldt 1963b]

'Alae a hina
Polynesia: Hawaii
Magic; Destroyer of Life; Wild Birds; War
   Sorcerer on the island of Moloka'i, who, with *Uli* and Makakūkoa'e, can cause enemies to die during wars. 'Alae a hina is also the name of the mud hen, the sacred bird of *Hina.* The mud hen is associated with sorcery, probably because of its eerie cry. [Beckwith 1940; Craig 1989; Leach 1992]

Alalahe
Polynesia
Earth and Nature; Love and Sexuality

"Fruitfulness." Goddess of vegetation and love. Alternate forms: Laka, Lake, Alalalahe. [Beckwith 1940; Craig 1989; Leach 1992]

Alalalahe See *Alalahe.*

Alinga
Australia, *Arunta*
Sun and Day
Sun goddess. Alternate form: Ochirka. [Leach 1992; Spencer and Gillen 1968]

Angarua
Polynesia: Mangaia Island
Creator of Life
Creator deity. [Sykes 1968]

Anjea
Australia
Mother and Guardian
Deity who forms infants from mud and places each in the mother's uterus. [Jobes 1962]

Anoano
Polynesia: Marquesas Islands
Unhappiness
Goddess who drives women insane. [Handy 1923; Leach 1992]

Anu mātao
Polynesia: New Zealand, *Maori*
Unknown
"Cold Space." Daughter of Rangi and *Poko ha rau te pō,* wife of Tangaroa (Kanaloa), and mother of fish deities, including Whatukura and the twins Pounamu (Te Ponaum) and Poutini. [Craig 1989; Leach 1992]

Anua
Polynesia: Tahiti
Creator of Life
Creator goddess. [Craig 1989]

'Ānuenue
Polynesia: Hawaii
Weather
Rainbow goddess. Sister of Kane and Kanaloa. [Craig 1989; Leach 1992]

Aouli
Polynesia: Tonga Islands
Sky and Heavens
Heavenly deity. Mother of *Tonga maulu'au,* grandmother of *Fakakanaoelangi.* [Craig 1989]

Apakura
Polynesia: New Zealand, *Maori*
Justice
Deity who seeks revenge for the death of her son.
 Apakura lost her loincloth (or girdle), and it was found by the sea god Rongotakawiu. He shaped a son from the cloth, and this son brought vengeance upon his mother's enemies.
The Maoris of the Chatham Islands say the death of Apakura's son, Tū, was avenged by a mountain-leaping relative, Whakatau. See also *Apekua, Apa'ula.* [Alpers 1966; Craig 1989; Eliot 1976; Leach 1972]

Apa'ula
Polynesia: Samoa
Justice

Deity who seeks revenge for the death of her son.
 Apa'ula's son, Tuiosavalalo, was murdered by Apa'ula's brothers. When she found his body, Tui's head told her she would need the help of his brother, Va'atausili, because Va'atausili could stretch to great heights. Apa'ula and Va'atausili went to Fiji and killed the murderers.
See also *Apakura, Apekua.* [Craig 1989]

Apekua
Polynesia: Marquesas Islands
Justice
Deity who seeks revenge for the death of her son.
 Apekua's son, Pota'atemau, was murdered when he went to claim his bride, the daughter of Hateamotua. Apekua enlisted the aid of her brother in avenging her son's death.
See also *Apakura, Apa'ula.* Alternate form: Pei kua. [Craig 1989]

Apu o te ra'i
Polynesia: Tahiti
Stars and Planets
Star goddess. Wife of Maunu'ura, the god of Mars, and mother of Ta'urua. [Handy 1920; Leach 1992]

'Āpua kea
Polynesia: Hawaii
Beauty; Selfishness
On the island of Oahu, 'Āpua kea and her mother were killed when 'Āpua kea compared her beauty to that of *Hi'iaka.* [Craig 1989]

Apunga
Polynesia: New Zealand, *Maori*
Earth and Nature
Goddess of small plants. Wife of Tāne. [Best 1924; Leach 1992]

Arahuta
Polynesia: New Zealand, *Maori*
Sky and Heavens
Sky deity. Daughter of lightning god Tāwhaki and *Hāpai.* [Craig 1989]

Ariki
Polynesia: New Zealand, *Maori*
Stars and Planets
Star goddess. Daughter of Puaka and *Taku rua.* [Leach 1992; White 1987]

Arimata
Polynesia: Tuamotu Islands
Fate; Unhappiness; Justice; Fishing and Water Animals
Seer.
 When her son, Niu kura, was born, Arimata told him about all of the things that he would do in the future. Arimata's sister, Huauri, was very jealous and told her son, Tahaki, the same things about his life. The jealousy between the families grew, causing Niu kura to kill Tahaki. Huauri restored her son's life and took revenge by having the ocean swallow Arimata's sons; they became porpoises. [Craig 1989]

Ārohirohi
Polynesia: New Zealand, *Maori*
Sun and Day
Sun goddess. [Craig 1989]

Arutaruta tāmaumau auahi
Polynesia: Tahiti
Fire
  Fire goddess. [Craig 1989]

Ata tangi rea
Polynesia: New Zealand, *Maori*
Earth and Nature
  Maire rau nui tree goddess. [Leach 1992; White 1987]

Atahikurangi
Polynesia: New Zealand, *Maori*
Sun and Day
  Goddess of daylight. [Craig 1989]

Atanea   See *Atanua.*

Atanua
Polynesia: Marquesas Islands
Creator of Life; Mother and Guardian; Dawn and Twilight
  "Dawn." Creator deity. Wife of *Ātea*, mother of sons and daughters, gods, birds, butterflies, and creeping things. The seas are said to be amniotic fluid that spilled when she miscarried. See also *Hakahotu*. Alternate form: Atanea. [Jobes 1962; Leach 1972; Leach 1992; Monaghan 1981]

Atarapa
Polynesia: New Zealand, *Maori*
Dawn and Twilight
  Dawn goddess. Daughter of *Atatuhi*. [Craig 1989]

Atatuhi
Polynesia: Tahiti; New Zealand, *Maori*
Sky and Heavens
  Stellar deity, the star Canopus. Mother of the moon, stars, and daylight. She is invoked for abundant harvests. Alternate form: Atutahi. [Craig 1989]

Ātea
Polynesia
Mother and Guardian
  Mother of the gods. Considered a male deity by other authors. [Wedeck and Baskin 1971]

Atea ta'o nui
Polynesia: Tahiti
Stars and Planets
  Star goddess. Mother of all the planets and stars. [Handy 1920; Leach 1992]

Atoto
Melanesia: Solomon Islands; Bougainville, *Buin*
Creator of Life; Unhappiness; Water
  Creator goddess.

 Atoto created and gave birth to her children without a husband. One day her son discovered that she cooked taro in her own urine. He was so upset that he beat her and broke all the pots that had stored her urine. It ran out and became the sea water. [Schmidt 1951]

Atua fafine
Polynesia: Tikopia
Mother and Guardian; Agriculture
  Mother of yams and guardian of women. [Firth 1967a; Leach 1992]

Atua'anua
Polynesia: Easter Island
Creator of Life
  "God-mother." Creation goddess. [Craig 1989]

Atutahi   See *Atatuhi.*

Audjal
Micronesia: Caroline Islands
Earth and Nature
  Earth goddess. [Baumgartner 1984]

Auna
Polynesia: Tahiti
Unknown
  "Solicitude." [Henry 1928; Leach 1992]

Autran
Micronesia: Ifalik
Mother and Guardian; Earth and Nature
  Mother Earth. She protects humans. She is the sister or daughter of the supreme god Aluelap. [Burrows 1947; Leach 1992]

Ava rei pua
Polynesia: Easter Island
Unknown
  Island deity. [Savill 1978]

Avin
Melanesia: New Hebrides
Sun and Day; Mother and Guardian; Commerce and Travel
  Sun goddess.

 One day, when her husband was gone, Avin mated with the moon god. The sun was so upset that he drove her from her wondrous garden. After that time, she had to work hard and live with menstrual cycles. [Guirand 1968]

Baabenga
Melanesia: Bellona Island; Rennell Island
Selfishness; Fishing and Water Animals
  Deity who appears as female or male and plays mischievous tricks. On Bellona Island, she is the daughter of Mauloko and sister of *Tehanine'angiki* and Teangaitak, and she may be associated with sharks. On Rennell Island, she is the daughter of *Tehainga'atua* and Sikingimoemore. [Craig 1989]

Babamik
Melanesia: New Guinea
Evil; Ugliness; Reptiles; Ceremonies
  An ogre who was a cannibal. After her death, she became a crocodile. [Savill 1978]

Baiangun
Australia
Mother and Guardian; Insects
  Deity who rescued her followers from a hunter, then left them, winging away in the form of a fly. [Reed 1978]

Bara
Australia: Arnhem Land
Sun and Day
  Sun goddess. Daughter of *Walo* (see *Walo* for story). [Monaghan 1981; Mounteford 1965]

Bila
Australia
Sun and Day; Ceremonies; Fire
  Cannibalistic sun deity.

 Bila provided the early light for the world by cooking her victims on a huge fire. Lizard Man was angered by her behavior and wounded her. Bila transformed herself into a ball of fire and rolled away over the horizon, leaving the land in total darkness. Lizard Man threw his boomerang, catching Bila

and making her move across the sky in a slow arc—bringing light back to the land.

Cannibalism has been practiced in all parts of the world, including Africa, India, South America, and Europe. It is practiced for various reasons: as a food source, as a religious sacrifice, as a means of gaining the strength of the person eaten, to protect the deceased's soul, to promote the cannibal to a superhuman state, and for other social or political reasons. Among some Australian coastal tribes, deceased females are eaten by their male kin and by all of the males who have had sexual intercourse with the deceased. This may be done to assuage their grief. [Leach 1972; Monaghan 1981; Roberts 1973]

Bildjiwuraroju   See *Djanggawul.*

Bima
Australia
Mother and Guardian; Unhappiness; Love and Sexuality;
Wild Birds; Magic
Early woman.

Bima had a young baby but spent much time with a lover who was not the baby's father. Each day she left her child in the shade of a tree and went into the jungle with her lover. One day she returned to find the shade had moved and her baby had died from the heat. When the father of the child found out, he decreed that all of creation must die and never come to life again. Bima was changed into a curlew. She roams the jungle, crying for her lost child and the misfortune she caused the world. [Mounteford 1965; Roberts 1973]

Bir im bir wongar
Australia
Immortality
"Spirit Dreaming." The spirit of a dead woman. [Berndt 1974]

Birra nulu
Australia
Creator of Life; Reptiles; Justice; Metals and Minerals
Creator goddess. One of the two wives of the great spirit Baiame. The other wife was *Kunan beili.*

Baiame sent his wives to gather food while he went in search of honey. He told his wives to go to the spring at Coorigil when they were finished gathering food. He said they could drink the water but should not swim in the pool, but he failed to tell them why. Birra nulu and Kunan beili were very warm when they reached the pool, and, knowing their husband would not return for a long while, they decided to go for a swim. The Kurrias, the crocodile guardians of the pool, quickly swallowed the women and carried them away. Eventually Baiame rescued them. When Baiame returned to his home in the Milky Way, he attached his wives to a crystal rock, where they would petrify and be a reminder of his time on Earth.

See also *Birrahgnooloo, Cunnembeillee.* [Reed 1973]

Birrahgnooloo
Australia, *Kamilaroi*
Water; Weather; Sky and Heavens
Water goddess. With her husband Baiame, she listens to her people's pleas for rain and sometimes sends floods. She is in the sky with her husband and his other wife, *Cunnembeillee.* Worshiped by the Kamilaroi and other tribes of South Wales. See also *Birra nulu* and *Kunanbeili.* [Leach 1972; Reed 1978]

Boaliri
Australia: Arnhem Land
Creator of Life
Creator deity. The younger of two sister goddesses in northern Australia. See also *Waimariwi.* [Senior 1985]

Bonito Maidens, The
Melanesia: Solomon Islands
Fishing and Water Animals
Fish goddesses. They are beautifully adorned with porpoise teeth, shell money, and ornaments. If properly worshiped, they bring bonito fish to the people. [Leach 1972]

Brogla
Australia
Arts; Courage; Weather
"Native Companion" and spirit of the dance.

Brogla was the best dancer in her tribe. When she danced, the people thought the Spirit of Earth had returned to them. She danced everywhere and was unafraid. The Wurrawilberoos (whirlwinds) wanted her for themselves. When they saw her dancing around her mother, who was out picking yams, the Wurrawilberoos swirled around and carried off the two women. Brogla and her mother escaped and made their way back to their camp, with the Wurrawilberoos close behind. Brogla's mother was saved, but Brogla was captured again. One day a tall, stately bird appeared in the camp in which Brogla's people lived, and when it began to dance, they knew it was Brogla. [Reed 1973]

Budyah
Australia
Destroyer of Life
Smallpox goddess. [Crooke 1894; Leach 1992]

Bulaing
Australia
Creator of Life; Heaven and Hell; Reptiles
Creation deity of the Karadjeir religion. She lives in heaven and created all things. Bulaing also refers to mythical serpents. [Lurker 1984]

Bumerali
Australia: Melville Island
Weather; Fire; Physical Prowess; Destroyer of Life
"Lightning Woman." Daughter of *Kwouk kwouk,* sister of *Tomituka.*

Bumerali travels across the skies on the thunder clouds, carrying in each hand a stone axe with which she strikes the ground, destroying things. The thunder is Bumerali speaking. When it is dry, she stays in the sky. [Leach 1992; Mounteford 1955; Mounteford 1965; Roberts 1973]

Buring une
Melanesia: Borneo; New Guinea, *Kayan*
Agriculture; Heaven and Hell; Luck
Agricultural goddess who lives underground. She determines the luck of the harvest. [Redfield 1931]

Calla filatonga
Polynesia: Tonga Islands
Weather
Wind deity. [Leach 1992; Williamson 1933]

Cassowary Mother
Melanesia: New Guinea, *Arapesh*
Hunting and Wild Animals; Life/Death Cycle; Agriculture;
Education and Knowledge
Food goddess. She teaches hunting. Her body became the vegetable food of her people. She was caught in a trap, and her bones were planted and became yams. [Schmidt 1951]

Cunnembeillee
Australia
Family and Tribes; Sky and Heavens

Ancestor of the Kamilaroi and other tribes. Wife of Baiame. She now lives in the sky with Baiame and his second wife, *Birrahgnooloo.* See also *Kunan beili, Birra nulu.* [Leach 1972]

Dama, The
Melanesia: New Guinea
Metals and Minerals; Magic
   Deities who sometimes marry human males. Their spirits are embodied in sacred stones that give power to the people. [Savill 1978]

De ai
Micronesia: Gilbert Islands
Creator of Life; Sky and Heavens
   First woman. Mother of the sun, the moon, and the sea. [Jobes 1962]

Dianggwuls   See *Djanggawul.*

Dietyi
Australia
Sun and Day
   Southeastern sun goddess. [Howitt 1904; Leach 1992]

Dilga
Australia, *Karadjeri*
Earth and Nature; Unhappiness; Mother and Guardian; Immortality; Justice
   Earth goddess worshiped in northwestern Australia.
 Dilga was very angry when two of her children, the ancestral brothers called Bagadjimbiri, were killed by Ngariman, the cat man, and his relatives. Milk came out of Dilga's breasts and flowed underground to where the murder took place. The milk drowned the murderers and revived the Bagadjimbiri. [Cotterell 1979]

Dinewan
Australia
Creator of Life; Wild Birds; Sun and Day
   Creator emu.
 Dinewan and a friend, Bralgah, had a quarrel. Bralgah threw one of Dinewan's eggs into the sky, where it became the sun. [Jobes 1962]

Dirivo
Melanesia: Torres Strait
Heaven and Hell
   Underworld goddess. [Leach 1972]

Djanggau, Djanggaus   See *Djanggawul.*

Djanggawul, The
Australia
Creator of Life; Magic; Ceremonies
   "Dreamtime Daughters of the Sun." Dreamtime refers to the mythological past. The Djanggawul are fertility deities, creators of plants, animals, sacred articles, and rituals.
 The Djanggawul sisters and their brother left the land of the immortals with sacred objects. As they traveled across the Earth, springs began to gush from the ground, trees appeared with leaves and birds, and the Djanggawul gave birth to the first humans. One day the sisters left their sacred dillybags (pouches) on the ground, and their brother and several other men stole them. The sisters soon realized that, although their emblems had been taken, the power of the emblems remained because they still had their wombs. Even the men agreed that the women should be the ritual leaders.
   See also *Junkgowa, Djunkgao.* Alternate forms: Bildjiwuraroju, Miralaidji, Dianggwuls, Djanggau, Djanggaus. [Berndt 1974; Leach 1992; Monaghan 1981; Senior 1985]

Djunkgao, The
Australia
Creator of Life
   Sister creator goddesses on the northern coast. See also *Djanggawul, Junkgowa.* [Roberts 1973]

Djugurba
Australia
Unknown
   "Mallee-hen-woman." A Dreamtime being (that is, a being from the mythological past). Alternate form: Minma Nganamara. [Savill 1978]

Dogai, The
Melanesia: Torres Strait
Selfishness; Destroyer of Life; Beauty; Magic
   Tricksters disguised as beautiful women, animals, trees, constellations, or rocks. They play tricks on people and kill children. [Leach 1972]

Dok
Australia
Stars and Planets
   Star goddess of the Southern Cross. [Reed 1978]

Dunawali
Melanesia: New Guinea
Evil; Destroyer of Life
   Evil goddess believed to be in women. She can kill males and eat their bodies. Similar to *Pinuwali, Kapiano, Walipolima.* [Savill 1978]

Dzari
Melanesia; New Guinea, *Kaean*
Earth and Nature
   Earth mother. [Leach 1992; Meiser 1963]

Eingana
Australia, *Djauan*
Creator of Life; Reptiles; Mother and Guardian; Life/Death Cycle
   Earth mother. Serpent fertility goddess who was the source of all life.
 In the beginning, Eingana gave birth by vomiting. Then she had trouble giving birth and grew large and cried. An old man heard her and speared her near the anus. First she bled, and then all of the people came out. This is how the birth process changed. When any living being is born, Eingana holds a string attached to its heel; when she lets go, death comes. [Meltzer 1981]

Ekeitehua
Melanesia: Bellona Island
Evil; Unhappiness
   Evil goddess who controls humans and causes them to go insane. Mother of *Ngeipau.* Also the name of a male deity. See also *'Iti'iti.* Alternate form: Singano. [Craig 1989]

'Elepaio
Polynesia: Hawaii
Wild Birds; Commerce and Travel; Fate
   Bird form of *Lea.*
   When canoe makers are ready to make a new canoe, they watch for a flycatcher ('Elepaio) to land on trees. If she runs up and down without stopping, the tree will be good to use. If she stops to peck, the trunk will probably be unusable from having been eaten by bugs.
   Alternate form: Lea. [Craig 1989; Leach 1992]

Emu   See *Kurikuta.*

Enda kondapala   See *Enda semangko.*

Enda semangko
Melanesia: New Guinea, *Kyaka*
War; Creator of Life; Luck
    War and fertility goddess. She is beseeched for success.
Alternate forms: Enda kondapala, Kor enda. [Leach 1992;
Savill 1978]

'Ere'ere fenua
Polynesia: Tahiti; Society Islands (Ta'aroa)
Fate; Weather; War; Disorder
    Deity whose appearance warns of storms or wars. Wife of
Tuatapuanui or Ruatupuanui. [Craig 1989; Henry 1928;
Leach 1992]

Fa'ahotu
Polynesia: Tahiti
Mother and Guardian
    Creator. Mother of Ro'o, Tahu, and many other deities. See
also *Fakahotu.* [Craig 1989]

Fa'a'ipu
Polynesia: Tahiti
Creator of Life; Mother and Guardian
    Creator goddess. She is one of the seven guardians of the
world. See *'Aiāru* for the names of the other guardians.
[Craig 1989]

Fai   See *Fai malie.*

Fai malie
Polynesia: Tonga Islands
Agriculture; Heaven and Hell
    Yam goddess.
    *Fai malie visited Pulotu, the underworld, with four
    other deities. When the forces of Pulotu were defeated,
    Fai malie swallowed the yam and secretly brought it
back to the upper world for food.*
    See also *Fehuluni, Hikuleo.* Alternate form: Fai. [Beckwith
1940; Collocott 1921; Leach 1992; Sproul 1979]

Fai tama'i
Polynesia: Samoa
Unknown
    Mother of Siamese-twin sister goddesses, *Tilafaigā* and
Taemā. [Craig 1989]

Faiga'a
Polynesia: Tonga Islands
Wild Birds
    Bird goddess. She is a heron and companion of *Jiji.*
[Collocott 1921; Leach 1992]

Faingaa
Polynesia: Tonga Islands
Love and Sexuality; Unhappiness
    Goddess.
    *Faingaa and Sisi fell in love with a Samoan who lived in
    Tonga. They loved Pasikole because of his fair hair, but
    he did not return their affection. He tried to get rid of
them by leaving them in the elements and then by entangling them
in his fishing nets. They were finally rescued by the god Tangaloa.*
[Craig 1989]

Fakahotu
Polynesia: Tonga Islands; Tuamotu Islands
Creator of Life; Ceremonies; Earth and Nature; Sky and
Heavens

"Be Fruitful." Creator deity and goddess of the feasting
mats. She controls Tonga, god of the forest and its
inhabitants. Wife of sky god Ātea in Tuamotuan legends. As
the wife of Tefatu, she gave birth to **Hina.** She is also said to
be the queen of eight heavens.
    *Fakahotu and Ātea mated; Fakahotu's masculine traits
    were transferred to Ātea, and his feminine traits were
    transferred to Fakahotu. This made them both stronger
and helped them produce mightier deities.*
    See also *Fa'ahotu, Hakahotu.* Alternate form: Papa.
[Carlyon 1982; Craig 1989; Leach 1972; Leach 1992; Long 1963]

Fanga
Polynesia: Samoa
Unknown
    Goddess. Mother of *Papa.* [Craig 1989]

Fata'a koka
Polynesia: Marquesas Islands
Magic
    Sorcerer. Grandmother of *Kua nui, Kua iti,* Taimumuhu,
Taivavena, and the eel Puhi nui a'au too. [Craig 1989]

Faumea
Polynesia: Tuamotu Islands, *Maori*
Fishing and Water Animals; Magic; Mother and Guardian
    Fertility deity and eel woman.
    *In Faumea's vagina lived eels that killed men. She
    taught the god of fish and reptiles, Tangaroa, how to
    entice the eels away. Then she and Tangaroa had two
children, Tūnuikarere and Turiafaumea. By catching the wind in
her armpit, Faumea helped Turiafaumea rescue his wife, Hina'a
rauriki, from the demon octopus.*
    Faumea is identified with the Hawaiian **Haumea.** [Craig
1989]

Faurourou
Polynesia: Tahiti
Weather
    Sky deity who rules the atmosphere and frozen clouds.
[Henry 1928; Leach 1992]

Fefafa
Polynesia: Hawaii
Earth and Nature; Life/Death Cycle
    Vegetation goddess. She cut up her daughter's body and
buried it. From the pieces grew kava and sugar cane.
[Beckwith 1940]

Fehuluni
Polynesia: Tonga Islands
Agriculture
    Yam goddess who brought yams from Samoa and planted
them to help feed her people. See also *Fai malie.* [Craig 1989]

Fenua
Polynesia: Tuamotu Islands
Earth and Nature
    Earth goddess. Also the name of a male deity. [Craig 1989]

Fire Goddess, The
Melanesia: San Cristoval
Fire; Household Affairs
    She knew how to make fire and cook food. [Leach 1972]

Firifiri 'aufau
Polynesia: Tahiti
Family and Tribes; Mother and Guardian

Genealogical deity and one of the old guardians of the world. For a list of the other guardians see *'Aiāru.* See also *Ōrerorero.* [Craig 1989]

First Woman
Melanesia: San Cristoval
Immortality; Life/Death Cycle
First Woman could change herself from an old woman to a young one whenever she wanted to.

 One day First Woman changed her skin from that of an old woman to that of a young woman. The change frightened her daughter so badly that First Woman put on her old skin again so that her daughter would recognize her. Since that time death has been in the world. [Leach 1972]

First Women
Melanesia: New Hebrides
Family and Tribes
Goddesses who emerged from the halves of a split coconut. Coconuts of various shapes and colors yielded first women with various skin color and facial characteristics. [Leach 1956]

Fue
Polynesia: Samoa
Unknown
Mother of the war god, Pava. [Craig 1989]

Fulu'ulaalematato
Polynesia: Samoa
Ceremonies; Sky and Heavens
Cannibal goddess. She inhabits the ninth heaven. [Craig 1989]

Gadjari   See *Kadjari.*

Ganabuada
Australia
Magic; Ceremonies; Education and Knowledge
Mother goddesses from Dreamtime (that is, the mythological past) who possess magical powers. During Dreamtime ritual, knowledge was given to women but denied to men. Men later took this power away from women. [Berndt 1974]

Gaueteaki
Melanesia: Bellona Island; Solomon Islands
Metals and Minerals; Creator of Life
Creation deity. A goddess worshiped in the form of a smooth, black stone. Alternate form: Gauteaki. [Bradley 1956; Craig 1989; Leach 1992]

Gauteaki   See *Gaueteaki.*

Gnowee
Australia, *Wotjabaluk*
Sun and Day; Mother and Guardian; Fire
Sun goddess.

 Gnowee lived on earth before there was any light. People carried torches wherever they went. One day Gnowee was gathering yams when her child wandered off. She set out to find him, carrying a very large torch. Gnowee never found her son, but she continues to climb in the sky each day, looking for him.

See also *Knowee.* [Monaghan 1990]

Goga
Melanesia: Ceram; Papua New Guinea, *Kiwai, Massim*
Fire; Weather; Education and Knowledge
Fire and rain goddess.

 Massim men stole the fire from her. Goga tried to douse it with rain, but some of the fire remained on the tail of a snake and was recovered by the people.

The Kiwai people believed that humans emerged as maggots from a dead wallaby. Goga taught them how to live and worship her. [Cotterell 1979; Jobes 1962; Monaghan 1981]

Goolagaya
Australia
Mother and Guardian; Disorder
Wandering spirit.

 Goolagaya liked children but had none of her own. One day she stole a baby, but she dropped it into some water, and it drowned. The people were so angry they killed Goolagaya and her white dingo. Now Goolagaya and her dingo wander the bush at twilight, stealing any wandering child. [Mounteford 1965; Roberts 1973]

Goonaroo
Australia
Wild Birds
"Whistling Duck." [Reed 1973]

Gulanundoidj   See *Mimaliwu.*

Gunabibi   See *Kunapipi.*

Gunggaranggara, The
Australia
Unknown
Goddesses of central Australia who dance diagonally across flat ground. [Berndt 1974]

Ha lo
Polynesia: Hawaii
Weather
Rainbow goddess. Alternate form: Aka ku a nue nue. [Ashdown 1971; Leach 1992]

Ha pu'u
Polynesia: Hawaii
Earth and Nature; Mother and Guardian; Metals and Minerals; Reptiles; Immortality and Magic
A dragon goddess in the Nuuanu Valley, Oahu. She and *Hau ola,* who are also forest deities, take the form of stones. Newborns are protected from evil by placing their umbilical cords under the stones. Ha pu'u is also called a goddess of necromancy. See also *Ka lei hau ola.* [Craig 1989; Leach 1992]

Haamata kee
Polynesia: Marquesas Islands
Unknown
Goddess. [Craig 1989]

Ha'apua 'inanea
Polynesia: New Zealand, *Maori*
Reptiles
Lizard woman. Companion of *Upoho,* with whom she is a servant of the goddess *Nā maka o kaha'i.* [Craig 1989]

Haere awa'awa
Polynesia: New Zealand, *Maori*
Wild Birds
Mother of the rail bird and kiwi. [Craig 1989]

Ha'i
Polynesia: Hawaii
Household Affairs; Wild Birds

Goddess of tapa makers and bird catchers. Second daughter of *Ra'i ra'i*. See also *Ha'ina kolo*. Alternate form: Ha'i wahine. [Craig 1989; Melville 1969]

Ha'i wahine

Polynesia: Hawaii
Arts; Education and Knowledge
Her symbol is a ti leaf worn around the neck. See also *Ha'ina kolo*. Alternate forms: Hina, Ha'i. [Craig 1989]

Ha'ina kolo

Polynesia: Hawaii
Unknown
Daughter of *Hina* and her husband, Kūwahailo. Ha'ina kolo is sometimes referred to in chants as *Ha'i wahine* or *Ha'i*.

 Ha'ina kolo married her nephew Keaunini (Keanini), with whom she had a son, Leimakani. They lived in a distant land, far from Waipi'o Valley, and Ha'ina kolo was not happy there. After seven years, she took Leimakani and started for Hawaii. Before reaching the island, they were shipwrecked, but they managed to swim ashore. Ha'ina kolo, distraught and confused, left Leimakani on the shore and headed to Waipi'o. Ha'ina kolo's sister, Lu'ukia, found the boy and, not knowing who he was, took him home to raise him. When he reached adulthood, she married him and they had a son, Lonokaiolohi'a. When Lu'ukia learned that Leimakani was having an affair with her younger sister, she killed Lonokaiolohi'a. At this point, Ha'ina kolo returned. Leimakani's mournful chant restored her sanity and together their prayers restored life to Lonokaiolohi'a. The family was reunited, and Leimakani and Ha'ina kolo returned to Waipi'o Valley. [Craig 1989]

Hainuwele

Melanesia: New Guinea; Ceram
Agriculture; Life/Death Cycle
Food goddess. She was killed by the men and her body planted in the earth. It produced food, particularly tubers, the people's chief food. [Leach 1992; Lurker 1984; Monaghan 1981]

Haka

Polynesia: Marquesas Islands
Creator of Life
Creator of sky and earth. [Leach 1992; Williamson 1933]

Hakahotu

Polynesia
Earth and Nature
Earth mother. One of the wives of Ātea. See also *Atanua, Fakahotu*. [Buck 1932; Leach 1992]

Hakirimaurea

Polynesia: New Zealand, *Maori*
Unknown
Ancient goddess whose husband is Tūwhakararaoa. [Craig 1989]

Hakumani

Polynesia: Niue Island of New Zealand
Household Affairs
Patron deity of tapa making. [Craig 1989; Leach 1992]

Halalamanu

Polynesia: Hawaii
Magic
Goddess of supernatural power. Daughter of *Ka onohi ula*. [Beckwith 1940]

Hale lehua   See *Moana nui ka lehua*.

Hamuri

Polynesia: Tahiti
Earth and Nature
Coconut tree goddess. [Henry 1928; Leach 1992]

Hana

Melanesia: New Guinea
Moon and Night; Love and Sexuality; Unhappiness
Moon goddess. Desiring to have sex with Hana, her brother caused her vulva to be formed. After having sex, they were so ashamed that they fled to the sky. She became the moon and he became the sun. [Savill 1978]

Hānai'ia ka malama

Polynesia: Hawaii
Goodness
Another name for *Hina*. Also a benevolent deity, wife of Hakalanileo, and mother of Kana and Nīheu. [Craig 1989]

Hanau

Polynesia: Marquesas Islands; Hawaii
Heaven and Hell
Underworld goddess. Her husband is Tonofiti. [Beckwith 1940; Leach 1992]

Hanitemau

Polynesia: Rotuma
Earth and Nature; Disorder
Deity of trees and vegetation.

 When Rotuma's first settlers came from the island of Savai'i, Samoa, they brought with them the soil that created the island of Rotuma. After they had gone back to Savai'i, Hanitemau claimed the island for herself. When the settlers returned, they quarreled with the goddess, but eventually they reached an agreement and lived peacefully. [Craig 1989]

Hanua

Polynesia: Marquesas Islands
Moon and Night
Moon goddess. [Guirand 1968]

Haoa'oa

Polynesia: Society Islands (Ta'aroa)
Unknown
"Grossness." Sister of 'Oro, god of war. [Henry 1928; Leach 1992]

Hā'oa'oa

Polynesia: Tahiti
Family and Tribes; Sky and Heavens
Heavenly deity.

 Hā'oa'oa decided to find a wife for her brother 'Oro, the war god. She descended to earth with her sister Te 'uri, and they searched many islands until they found the princess Vai rau mati on Bora-Bora. The three women then returned to heaven for the marriage. [Craig 1989]

Hāpai

Polynesia: New Zealand; Tuamotu Islands, *Maori*
Love and Sexuality; Sky and Heavens
Heavenly deity who came to earth to marry a mortal.

Hāpai fell in love with the hero Tāwhaki (sometimes considered the god of lightning) and came to earth each night to sleep with him. They had a daughter, Arahuta, whom Hāpai took back to heaven. Tāwhaki and his brother set out in search of Hāpai, and they were finally reunited in heaven.
Alternate forms: Tango tango, Tongo tongo. [Alpers 1966; Craig 1989]

Harataunga
Polynesia: New Zealand, *Maori*
Unhappiness; Evil
    Daughter of Mangamangaiatua and one of the two wives of
the Maori hero Tinirau (Kinilau) before he took *Hina* as his wife.
    *Harataunga and her sister Horotata were jealous of
    Hina and abused her so much that Hina killed them
    with her magic.* [Craig 1989]

Haria
Polynesia
Unknown
    Daughter of *Ra'i ra'i*. [Melville 1969]

Hatu atu tupun
Polynesia: Kapingamarangi
Destroyer of Life; Justice; Moon and Night
    "Darkness." She is very dangerous to males at dawn and
twilight, particularly if they are not with their wives. See also
Hetu ahin. [Emory 1965; Leach 1992]

Hatuibwari
Melanesia: San Cristoval
Mother and Guardian; Demi-animals; Reptiles
    Mother goddess. Half snake and half human, she has four
eyes and four breasts to suckle her children. [Lurker 1984]

Hau lani
Polynesia: Hawaii
Earth and Nature
    Plant goddess. Daughter of *Hina* and sister of *Haunu'u*
and Kamapua'a. [Craig 1989; Leach 1992]

Hau ola
Polynesia: Hawaii
Mother and Guardian; Earth and Nature; Reptiles; Metals
and Minerals
    Protector of newborns in the Nuuanu Valley, Oahu. She is a
dragon and forest goddess. The umbilical cord is placed
under her sacred stone. [Leach 1992; Westerveldt 1963a]

Hau wahine
Polynesia: Hawaii
Reptiles; Wealth; Fishing and Water Animals; Poverty;
Mother and Guardian; Justice; Health and Healing
    Lizard goddess who inhabits Ka'elepule and Kawainui
ponds on Oahu and provides an abundance of fish. If the
owners of the ponds oppress the poor, Hau wahine will
punish them. She also protects humans from illness. Alternate
form: Hau wahine Mo'o. [Beckwith 1940; Craig 1989; Leach
1992]

Hau wahine mo'o   See *Hau wahine*.

Hauarani
Polynesia
Magic
    Daughter of *Papa* or *Haumea*. She was born from her
mother's forehead. See also *Haunu'u, Hina ma nou rua'e,
Raumiha, Huhune, Taha'ura, Taha Taua Toto, Tu Ai Mehani*.
[Melville 1969]

Hauliparua, The
Polynesia: Samoa; Rotuma
Unknown
    Two sister goddesses.
    *The Hauliparua told Rahou to leave Samoa after his
    daughter fought with the king's daughter. Rahou took
    two baskets of sand from Samoa and created the Rotuma
Islands.* [Craig 1989]

Haumea
Polynesia: Hawaii
Mother and Guardian; Agriculture; Earth and Nature;
Disorder; Weather; Fire; Family and Tribes; Immortality
    Fertility goddess called the Mother of Hawaii. A birth deity
and goddess of edible vegetation. She also has a destructive
aspect, causing famine and sending her daughter *Pele* to
destroy everything in her path. Pele issued from Haumea's
armpit, and Haumea gave birth to many other progeny,
including the Hawaiian people. She taught women natural
childbirth. Before natural childbirth, infants were cut from
their mothers' abdomens, and their mothers died. Haumea
can rejuvenate, which she did frequently, returning to mate
with her children and grandchildren. She may form a trinity
with *Hina* and Pele. In New Zealand, she is called Haumia
tikitiki; in Tahiti, *Nona*; and in the Tuamotu Islands, she is
identified as *Faumea*. Alternate form: Ka meha i kana.
[Cotterell 1979; Craig 1989; Melville 1969; Monaghan 1981]

Haumei
Polynesia: Marquesas Islands
Ceremonies
    Cannibal goddess. [Craig 1989]

Haumia
Polynesia: New Zealand, *Maori*
Ugliness; Water; War
    Goddess of the fern root used to protect people from
witches. Ancestor of the water monster, Pai kea, and mother
of the Hawaiian war god Ke kauakahi. Also the name of a
male deity. [Craig 1989; Leach 1992]

Haunga roa
Polynesia: New Zealand, *Maori*
Unknown
    Daughter of Manaia and Kuiwai in Maori legend.
Alternate form: Haungaroa. [Alpers 1966; Craig 1989]

Haungaroa   See *Haunga roa*.

Haunu'u
Polynesia: Hawaii
Earth and Nature; Magic
    Plant goddess. Born from the forehead of her mother, *Hina*.
Sister of *Hau lani* and Kamapua'a. See also *Hauarani*.
[Beckwith 1940; Craig 1989]

Hava
Polynesia: Tuamotu Islands
Unknown
    Wife of Ataraga. [Craig 1989]

Havea lolo fonua
Polynesia: Tonga Islands
Love and Sexuality; Heaven and Hell
    Creator goddess. Daughter of Piki and *Kele*. Specifically,
the goddess of intercourse and of the underworld. [Craig
1989; Leach 1992]

Heke heki i papa
Polynesia: New Zealand, *Maori*
Unknown
    "Coming Down to Earth." Third wife of Rangi, the sky.
[Jobes 1962]

Hema
Polynesia: Hawaii; New Zealand
Creator of Life; Directions; Weather
    "South Wind." Goddess of procreation. [Best 1924; Leach
1992]

Hepeue

Polynesia: Easter Island
Metals and Minerals
Goddess of obsidian, who, with Agekai, helped to produce it. [Gray 1925; Leach 1992]

Hetu ahin

Polynesia: Kapingamarangi
Moon and Night; Dawn and Twilight
"Darkness." Very dangerous to males at twilight and dawn. See also *Hatu atu tupun*. [Emory 1965; Leach 1992]

Hi asa

Melanesia: Admiralty Islands; New Guinea
Creator of Life; Family and Tribes
Creator goddess. Wounded by a mussel shell, Hi asa took her blood and formed the first couple. They became the ancestors of all humans. [Jobes 1962]

Hiata i reia   See *Hi'iaka i reia*.

Hiata i te pori o pere   See *Hi'iaka i te pori o pere* and *Hi'iaka opio*.

Hiata kaalawamaka   See *Hi'iaka ka'a lawa maka*.

Hiata noho lani   See *Hi'iaka noho lani*.

Hiata opio   See *Hi'iaka opio*.

Hiata ta bu enaena   See *Hi'iaka tapu 'ena'ena*.

Hiata tapu enaena   See *Hi'iaka tapu 'ena'ena*.

Hiata tarei'ia   See *Hi'iaka tarei'a*.

Hiata wawahi lani   See *Hi'iaka wawahi lani*.

Hihikalani

Polynesia: Hawaii
Weather
"Female Head of the Rolling Clouds." [Beckwith 1940]

Hi'i hia

Polynesia: Marquesas Islands
War
Sister of war god Tu. [Craig 1989]

Hi'iaka

Polynesia: Hawaii
Weather
"Cloudy One." Patron of the hula. Younger sister of *Pele*. *Hi'iaka came from an egg that issued from the mouth of her mother, Haumea. Pele carried the egg in her armpit until Hi'iaka was born. For this reason, Hi'iaka was called Hi'iaka i ka poli o Pele. When Pele sent Hi'iaka to Kaua'i to escort Pele's lover, Chief Lohi'au, back to Hawaii, there were many delays. Pele had given Hi'iaka only 40 days to accomplish the task. Although Hi'iaka found Lohi'au, brought him back to life (he had died of grief for Pele), and returned him to Hawaii, she failed to do it in the allotted time. Pele took vengeance on Hi'iaka by burning Hi'iaka's friend, Hōpoe, and her forests. When Hi'iaka finally arrived, Pele surrounded her and Lohi'au with fire, killing him but not Hi'iaka. Hi'iaka restored Lohi'au to life and returned with him to Kaua'i, where they lived together, far from Pele.*
Hi'iaka's sisters are *Hi'iaka i ka'ale'i, Hi'iaka i ka 'ale moe, Hi'iaka i ka'ale po'i*, and *Hi'iaka i ka'ale'uweke*. See also *Hōpoe, Pele, Pele'ula, Uli*. Alternate form: Hi'iaka i ka poli o Pele. [Craig 1989; Leach 1992; Monaghan 1981]

Hi'iaka i ka poli o Pele   See *Hi'iaka, Hi'iaka i te pori o pere*.

Hi'iaka i ka pua'ena'ena

Polynesia: Hawaii
Unknown
One of the sisters of *Pele*. She made leis and kava, the drink of the gods, for Pele. When she is a healer and guide, she is called *Kuku 'ena i ke ahi ho'omau honua*. Alternate form: Hiata ta bu enaena. [Craig 1989]

Hi'iaka i ka'ale moe

Polynesia: Hawaii
Water
"Hi'iaka in the Low Lying Billow." Sister of *Hi'iaka*. [Craig 1989]

Hi'iaka i ka'ale po'i

Polynesia: Hawaii
Water
"Hi'iaka in the Breaking Wave." Sister of *Hi'iaka*. [Craig 1989]

Hi'iaka i ka'ale'i

Polynesia: Hawaii
Water
"Hi'iaka in the Giant Billow." Sister of *Hi'iaka*. [Craig 1989]

Hi'iaka i ka'ale'uweke

Polynesia: Hawaii
Water
"Hi'iaka in the Uncovering Billows." Sister of *Hi'iaka*. [Craig 1989]

Hi'iaka i reia

Polynesia: Hawaii
Unknown
"Garland-decked." Sister of *Pele*. Alternate form: Hiata i reia. [Leach 1992]

Hi'iaka i te pori o pere

Polynesia: Hawaii
Weather
"Cloud Kissing the Bosom of Pele." Sister of *Pele*. Alternate forms: Hiata i te pori o pere, Hi'iaka opio. [Beckwith 1940; Leach 1992]

Hi'iaka ka lei'ia   See *Hi'iaka tarei'a*.

Hi'iaka ka'a lawa maka

Polynesia: Hawaii
Weather
"Quick Glancing Eyed Cloud Holder." Sister of *Pele*. Alternate form: Hiata-kaalawamaka. [Beckwith 1940; Henry 1928; Leach 1992; Westerveldt 1963a]

Hi'iaka kapu 'ena'ena   See *Hi'iaka tapu ena'ena*.

Hi'iaka makole wawahi wa'a

Polynesia: Hawaii
Weather
"Fiery Eyed Canoe Breaker." Cloud goddess in *Pele*'s family. Alternate forms: Makole nawahi waa, Makore wawahi waa. [Beckwith 1940; Leach 1992]

Hi'iaka noho lae

Polynesia: Hawaii
Metals and Minerals

"Hi'iaka Guarding Point." She is the rock beyond the shore at Kailua, Kona. Sister of *Hi'iaka*. [Craig 1989]

Hi'iaka noho lani
Polynesia: Hawaii
Weather
"Heaven-dwelling Cloud Holder." Sister of *Pele*. Alternate form: Hiata noho lani. [Beckwith 1940; Henry 1928; Leach 1992; Westerveldt 1963a]

Hi'iaka opio
Polynesia: Hawaii
Weather
"Youthful Cloud Holder." Sister of *Pele*. Alternate forms: Hiata opio, Hi'iaka i te pori o pere. [Leach 1992]

Hi'iaka tapu'ena'ena
Polynesia: Hawaii
Weather
"Furnace-red-hot-mountain-holding-cloud." Sister of *Pele*. Alternate forms: Hiata tapu enaena, Hiata ta bu enaena, Hi'iaka kapu 'ena'ena. [Leach 1992]

Hi'iaka tarei'a
Polynesia: Hawaii
Weather
"Wreath-garlanded Cloud Holder." Sister of *Pele*. Alternate forms: Hiata tarei'ia, Hi'iaka ka lei'ia. [Beckwith 1940; Leach 1992]

Hi'iaka wawahi lani
Polynesia: Hawaii
Weather
"Heaven-rending Cloud Holder." Sister of *Pele*. Alternate form: Hiata wawahi lani. [Beckwith 1940; Leach 1992]

Hi'ilei
Polynesia: Hawaii
Unknown
Younger sister of *Hina*. Wife of Kaula wena (Red Dawn). [Beckwith 1940]

Hikuleo
Polynesia: Tonga Islands
Heaven and Hell
Goddess of Pulotu, the underworld.
 She drove out the five creatures (deities) who had come to Pulotu seeking food, but she was unable to keep them from secreting taro and yams, which they took back to the upper world.
See also *Fai malie*. [Carlyon 1982; Craig 1989; Leach 1992; Monaghan 1981]

Hina
Polynesia
Moon and Night; Household Affairs; Fishing and Water Animals; Unhappiness
Creator deity and moon goddess worshiped throughout the islands. She resides in the moon and is the patron of tapa cloth. In Tahiti she is the daughter/wife of Taaroa; in the Society Islands she is the daughter/wife of Tii, with whom she created the first humans. She is also said to be the daughter of Ātea, wife of Māui, sister of Rū or Hiro, or daughter of Ātea and *Fakahotu*.
Hina set out to find a handsome prince. She asked several sea creatures to help her, but they all failed. In anger, she beat the flounder flat and placed both of its eyes on the same side; crumpled the rock cod's head; made a lump on the turtle's back; and cracked a coconut on the whale's tail, splitting it. Later, Hina sailed to the moon in a canoe. She stepped into the moon and never returned to earth.
Equivalent to *Hine*. Alternate forms: Ha'i wahine, Ihi'ihi, Hānai'ia ka malama, Ina, Iti iti, Sina, Tapa. [Carlyon 1982; Cotterell 1979; Craig 1989; Jobes 1962; Leach 1992; Melville 1969; Monaghan 1981; Stone 1979]

Hina 'ea
Polynesia: Hawaii
Sun and Day; Health and Healing; Household Affairs
"Sunrise and Sunset." A healer and tapa maker. [Craig 1989]

Hina 'ere'ere manu'a
Polynesia: Tahiti
Arts
Goddess of tattooing. [Henry 1928; Leach 1992]

Hina hanaia'i ka malama
Polynesia: Hawaii
Moon and Night
"The Woman Who Worked in the Moon." The name of *Pele* in her human form. Identified with *Hina papa i kua*. [Beckwith 1940; Craig 1989]

Hina hele
Polynesia: Hawaii
Fishing and Water Animals
Fish goddess. See also *Hina puku 'ai, Hina puku i'a*. Alternate forms: La ea, Hina 'ulu 'ōhi'a. [Craig 1989; Leach 1992]

Hina ka'alualu moana
Polynesia: Hawaii
Water
"Hina Who Followed on the Ocean." [Beckwith 1940]

Hina kauhara
Polynesia: Easter Island
Unknown
Daughter of *Hina*. [Craig 1989]

Hina ke ahi
Polynesia: Hawaii
Fire
Fire goddess. One of the four kupua daughters of *Hina*. The other daughters are *Hina ke kai, Hina kuluua,* and *Hina mahuia*. [Beckwith 1940; Leach 1992]

Hina ke ka'ā   See *Hina'i ke kā*.

Hina ke kai
Polynesia: Hawaii
Water
Sea goddess. One of the four kupua daughters of *Hina*. [Beckwith 1940; Leach 1992]

Hina kuku kapa
Polynesia: Hawaii
Household Affairs
Goddess of tapa beaters. [Emory 1924; Leach 1992]

Hina kuluua
Polynesia: Hawaii
Weather
Rain goddess. One of the four kupua daughters of *Hina*. Alternate form: Kuliua. [Beckwith 1940; Leach 1992]

Hina lau limu kala
Polynesia: Hawaii
Water; Ceremonies; Health and Healing
Sea goddess. Patron of kahunas (priests) who specialize in sea medicines. [Beckwith 1940; Craig 1989]

Hina lei haamoa
Polynesia: Samoa
Unknown
Name for *Hina* when she is the daughter of *Lupe Pangopango*. [Craig 1989]

Hina lua'i koa
Polynesia: Hawaii
Water
Sea goddess. [Beckwith 1940; Leach 1992]

Hina ma nou rua'e
Polynesia: Hawaii
Magic
Daughter of *Papa*, born from her forehead. See also *Hauarani*. [Melville 1969]

Hina mahuia
Polynesia: Hawaii
Fire
Fire goddess of Mafuie. One of the four kupua daughters of *Hina*. [Beckwith 1940; Leach 1992]

Hina mataone
Polynesia: Marquesas Islands
Heaven and Hell
Underworld deity. [Christian 1895; Leach 1992]

Hina nui te pō   See *Hine nui te pō*.

Hina nui te'a'ara
Polynesia: Raiatea; Society Islands (Ta'aroa)
Moon and Night
Moon goddess. Alternate form: Hina tui te a'ara. [Henry 1928; Leach 1992]

Hina nui te'ara'ara
Polynesia: Tahiti
Fire; Magic
Goddess of fire walkers. See also *Hina te 'a'ara*. [Craig 1989]

Hina oio
Polynesia: Easter Island
Fishing and Water Animals
Sea goddess. Mother of water animals. Wife of Atuametua. [Craig 1989]

Hina 'ōpū hala ko'a
Polynesia: Hawaii
Fishing and Water Animals
Goddess of coral and spiny sea creatures. [Craig 1989]

Hina papa i kua
Polynesia: Tahiti
Moon and Night; Household Affairs
Moon goddess who beats tapa bark into cloth in the moonlight. Identified with *Hina hanaia'i ka malama*. [Beckwith 1940]

Hina puku 'ai
Polynesia: Hawaii
Agriculture
Goddess of vegetable food. Sister of *Hina puku i'a*. See also *Hina hele*. [Craig 1989; Leach 1992]

Hina puku i'a
Polynesia: Hawaii
Fishing and Water Animals
Goddess of fishers. Wife of Kū'ulakai, mother of 'Ai'ai, sister of *Hina puku 'ai*. See also *Hina hele*. [Craig 1989]

Hina tahu tahu
Polynesia: Tahiti
Health and Healing; Fate
Goddess of healing and divination. [Craig 1989; Leach 1992]

Hina tau miha
Polynesia: Hawaii
Magic; Love and Sexuality; Unhappiness
Goddess.

Hina tau miha found a magical, self-propelled canoe. With the canoe she found a mortal to marry, but two wild women stole him. Hina tau miha pursued him in the canoe, but when he did not return to her, she hung herself, and her spirit flew to Hawaii. [Beckwith 1940]

Hina te 'a'ara
Polynesia
Fire; Magic
Goddess of fire walkers. See also *Hina nui te'ara'ara*. [Craig 1989]

Hina te 'iva'iva
Polynesia: Tahiti
Creator of Life
Creation goddess. Wife of Rua tapua nui. [Craig 1989]

Hina tūa tua
Polynesia: Tahiti
Unknown
"Hina of the Land." [Craig 1989]

Hina tuafuaga
Polynesia: Tonga Islands
Unknown
Sent from heaven to be the first ruler with her husband, Tokilagafanua. Mother of the rain goddesses *Topukulu* and *Nafanua*. When the daughters had incestuous relationships with their father, all members of the family were changed into volcanic rocks. [Craig 1989]

Hina 'ulu 'ōhi'a
Polynesia: Hawaii
Earth and Nature
Ohia tree goddess. She supervises boat builders and protects the forest. Mother of Kā'ulu, wife of Kū ka' ōhi'a laka. Her blossoms are available only with the proper prayers. When she is the patron goddess of printing and coloring tapa, she is called *Nahinahi ana*. Alternate form: Hina hele. [Beckwith 1940; Craig 1989; Leach 1992; Westerveldt 1963a]

Hina uri
Polynesia: Hawaii; New Zealand, *Maori*
Moon and Night; Mother and Guardian
Moon and childbirth goddess. She is the moon in its dark phase. Sister of Māui. [Alpers 1966; Andersen 1928; Bray 1935; Leach 1992]

Hina'a rauriki
Polynesia: Tuamotu Islands
Unknown
   Daughter-in-law of *Faumea* (see for story). [Craig 1989]

Hina'ai ka malama
Polynesia: Hawaii
Fishing and Water Animals
   Mother goddess who gave birth to five fish goddesses: *Ka ihu koa, Ka ihu anu, Ihu koko, Ka ihu kuuna,* and *Ka ihu o pala'ai.* [Beckwith 1940]

Hina'i a'a i te marama
Polynesia: Hawaii; Tahiti
Moon and Night; Household Affairs; Earth and Nature
   "Hina-who-stepped-into-the-moon."
 Hina lived on the moon, where a large banyan tree grew—the cause of the shadows on the face of the moon. She took bark from the tree to make tapa for the other deities. One day, while climbing the tree, she broke a branch. The branch fell to earth, where it took root and became the first banyan tree. The Polynesians learned to make tapa from the bark. [Leach 1972]

Hina'i ka'uluau
Polynesia: Hawaii
Unknown
   Goddess who casts spells. [Craig 1989]

Hina'i ke ahi
Polynesia: Hawaii
Unknown
   Daughter of *Hina'ai ka malama,* wife of Akalana, mother of Māui. [Craig 1989]

Hina'i ke kā
Polynesia: Hawaii
Fishing and Water Animals
   Goddess of canoe bailers. Sister of *Hina'i ke ahi.* Similar to *Hina 'ōpū hala ko'a.* Alternate form: Hina ke ka'ā. [Craig 1989]

Hina'ōpū hala ko'a
Polynesia: Hawaii
Fishing and Water Animals
   Coral goddess. [Craig 1989]

Hina-tui te a'ara   See *Hina nui te'a'ara.*

Hine
Polynesia: New Zealand, *Maori*
Supreme Being
   Goddess of life and death who has many forms. Equivalent to *Hina.* [Savill 1978]

Hine a te po
Polynesia: New Zealand, *Maori*
Heaven and Hell
   Underworld deity. She guards the door to the netherworld. See also *Hine nui te pō.* [Andersen 1928; Leach 1992]

Hine ahiahi
Polynesia: Chatham Islands
Moon and Night
   Goddess of the evening. Daughter of the sun, Tama nui tera, and sister of *Hine ata* and *Hine aotea.* [Best 1924; Leach 1992]

Hine āhua
Polynesia: New Zealand, *Maori*
Weather; Water
   Maori goddess who appeared during the great deluge. See also *Hine apo hia.* [Craig 1989]

Hine ahuone
Polynesia: New Zealand, *Maori*
Family and Tribes; Ugliness
   "Earth-formed Maid." Ancestor of the human race. Daughter of *Papa,* mother of *Hine nui te pō.* With eyes that make the sunset red, hair like seaweed, and teeth as sharp as volcanic glass, she is a frightening deity. [Alpers 1966; Craig 1989; Eliot 1976; Monaghan 1981]

Hine ahupapa
Polynesia: New Zealand, *Maori*
Sky and Heavens
   Sky goddess and grandmother of the sun, Ra, and the moon, *Marama.* Wife of Rangi pōtiki. Mother of several sky children. [Craig 1989]

Hine aotea
Polynesia: Chatham Islands
Sun and Day
   Morning goddess. Daughter of Tama-nui-te-ra and sister of *Hine ata* and *Hine ahiahi.* [Best 1924; Leach 1992]

Hine apo hia
Polynesia: New Zealand, *Maori*
Weather; Water
   During the great deluge, she was floating on the waters. See also *Hina'āhua, Hine āhua, Hine rakatai.* Alternate form: Hine-apo-hia. [Craig 1989]

Hine ata
Polynesia: Chatham Islands
Time
   Morning goddess. Sister of *Hine aotea* and *Hine ahiahi.* [Best 1924; Leach 1992]

Hine aterepō
Polynesia: Hawaii
Unknown
   Daughter of *Hina* and the eel god, Tūnaroatetupua. [Craig 1989]

Hine i tapapauta
Polynesia: New Zealand, *Maori*
Weather; Directions; Order
   West wind deity. She makes the seas calm. Daughter of Tiu and mother of *Hine tu whenua.* [Leach 1992]

Hine i tapeka
Polynesia: New Zealand, *Maori*
Fire; Earth and Nature
   Goddess of underground fire. [Andersen 1928; Best 1924; Leach 1992]

Hine i tau ira
Polynesia
Unhappiness; Family and Tribes; Heaven and Hell
   "Dawn Maid." So angered to learn that her husband was her father, she descended to the underworld. There she became "Night," *Hine nui te pō.* See also *Hine tītama.* [Jobes 1962]

Hine i te huhi
Polynesia: New Zealand, *Maori*
Water
"Swamp Maid." [Best 1924; Leach 1992]

Hine itaitai
Polynesia: New Zealand, *Maori*
Unknown
Wife of Rakurū and mother of Tautini. [Craig 1989]

Hine kaikomako
Polynesia: New Zealand, *Maori*
Fire; Earth and Nature
"Fire Maid." Kaikomako tree (fir tree) goddess. Daughter of Tāne. [Andersen 1928; Best 1924; Leach 1992]

Hine kapua
Polynesia: New Zealand, *Maori*
Weather
"Cloud Maid." Daughter of **Hine ahuone** and Tāne. [Best 1924; Leach 1992]

Hine maki moe
Polynesia: New Zealand, *Maori*
Sky and Heavens
"Wide-spread-out Heavens." Sky deity, the mother of the sky. She is the daughter of troubled sleep. [Jobes 1962; Savill 1978]

Hine makohu
Polynesia: New Zealand, *Maori*
Weather
"Mist Maid." Daughter of Tāne. [Best 1924; Leach 1992]

Hine makura
Polynesia: New Zealand, *Maori*
Unknown
She saved the human race by consuming the waters at the time of the great flood. [Craig 1989]

Hine māru
Polynesia: New Zealand, *Maori*
Mother and Guardian
Mother of the beautiful **Hine moa.** [Craig 1989]

Hine maunga
Polynesia: New Zealand, *Maori*
Earth and Nature
Mountain deity. Wife of Tāne. [Best 1924; Leach 1992]

Hine moa
Polynesia: New Zealand, *Maori*
Beauty; Love and Sexuality
Beautiful young princess.

 Hine moa and Tūtānekai secretly fell in love. They planned to meet when Tūtānekai played his flute. The night he played to signal Hine moa to come to his island from the mainland, all the canoes were secured and she could not use them. She gathered six empty gourds, and, using them as floats, swam to Mokoia. She warmed herself in the hot springs, and then the two lovers went to the village and were married. [Craig 1989; Eliot 1976]

Hine moana
Polynesia: New Zealand, *Maori*
Water; Disorder
Sea goddess. If she becomes upset, she swamps canoes. [Best 1924; Leach 1992]

Hine nui o te kawa
Polynesia: New Zealand, *Maori*
Sky and Heavens
Heavenly goddess, wife of Paikea. After leaving heaven, she became the lover and wife of the hero Tāwhaki. [Craig 1989]

Hine nui te pō
Polynesia: Hawaii; New Zealand, *Maori*
Moon and Night; Heaven and Hell; Life/Death Cycle
"Great Hine, the Night." Guardian of the underworld. She was called **Hine i tau ira** until she went to the underworld.

Each day Hine nui te pō follows the sun as it rises in the east until it sets in the west. The god Tāne follows her, and so all living beings must also follow on her path that leads to death.

See also **Hine a te po, Hine tītamauri.** Alternate form: Hina nui te pō. [Alpers 1966; Craig 1989; Jobes 1962; Monaghan 1981]

Hine one
Polynesia: New Zealand, *Maori*
Earth and Nature
"Sand Maid." She protects Mother Earth from the ocean goddess, **Hine moana.** [Best 1924; Leach 1992]

Hine piripiri
Polynesia: New Zealand, *Maori*
Mother and Guardian
Guardian deity who rescued her husband from his violent brothers. Wife of Tāwhaki, mother of Wahieroa. [Craig 1989]

Hine popo
Polynesia: New Zealand, *Maori*
Water; Fishing and Water Animals
Water deity.

Hine popo lived on the North Island. She made friends of the tāniwhas (sea monsters) and the cod-fish god, Hapuku. On the backs of her friends, she followed her husband's canoe as he went from one island to another. [Craig 1989]

Hine pūpūmainaua
Polynesia: New Zealand, *Maori*
Unknown
Mother of Tāwhaki and Karihi. Alternate forms: Kare nuku, Pūpūmainono. [Craig 1989]

Hine rakatai
Polynesia: New Zealand, *Maori*
Weather; Water
One of the goddesses floating on the flood waters during the great deluge. See also **Hine apo hia, Kare nuku, Kare rangi.** [Craig 1989]

Hine rau wharangi   See **Hine tītamauri.**

Hine raumati
Polynesia: New Zealand, *Maori*
Agriculture; Time
"Summer Maid." Protector of food and its cultivation. Sun, her husband, lives with her only half of the year. Mother of Tānerore. See also **Hine takurua.** [Best 1924; Leach 1992]

Hine ruaki moe
Polynesia: Nairu
Heaven and Hell; Moon and Night
"Night." Underworld deity. [Craig 1989; Leach 1992]

Hine takurua

Polynesia: New Zealand, *Maori*
Fishing and Water Animals; Time
"Winter Maid." She protects the ocean fish. Her husband, the sun, lives with her only half of the year. See also *Hine raumati.* [Best 1924; Leach 1992]

Hine te aparangi

Polynesia: New Zealand, *Maori*
Unknown
Goddess. [Alpers 1966]

Hine te iwaiwa

Polynesia: New Zealand, *Maori*
Moon and Night; Mother and Guardian
"Moon." Protector of women during childbirth. Wife of the hero Tinirau. Alternate form: Hine tengarumoana. [Craig 1989; Leach 1992]

Hine te kākara

Polynesia: New Zealand, *Maori*
Commerce and Travel
Goddess who participated in the great migration of the Polynesians to New Zealand in *Arawa,* a famous canoe. Daughter of chief Kohu, wife of Ihenga. [Craig 1989]

Hine te uria

Polynesia: New Zealand, *Maori*
Fire; Weather
"Sheet Lightning." Daughter of *Hine ahuone* and Tāne. [Best 1924; Leach 1992]

Hine tengarumoana   See *Hine te iwaiwa.*

Hine tītama

Polynesia: New Zealand, *Maori*
Dawn and Twilight; Heaven and Hell; Life/Death Cycle; Family and Tribes; Unhappiness; Love and Sexuality
"Dawn Maid." Ancestor deity. Goddess who became the underworld deity, *Hine nui te pō.* Wife of Tāne nui a rangi.

 Hine tītama fled to the underworld when she discovered that she had married her own father and had borne his children. When Māui came to the underworld to seek immortality for humans, he could not escape from Hine tītama's womb, so now humans must die.
See also *Hine i tau ira.* [Alpers 1966; Craig 1989; Monaghan 1981]

Hine tītamauri

Polynesia: New Zealand, *Maori*
Earth and Nature
Vegetation deity. Daughter of Tāne and *Hine i tau ira.* See also *Hine nui te pō.* Alternate form: Hine rau wharangi. [Craig 1989; Senior 1985]

Hine tū a hōanga

Polynesia: New Zealand, *Maori*
Physical Prowess; Metals and Minerals; Commerce and Travel
"Hine-of-the-whetstone-back" or "Sandstone Maid." Goddess of the stone grinders, she sharpens knives. Daughter of Rangahua, sister of Rata.

When Rata was trying to carve a canoe, he could not get the knife to cut into the wood. Hine tū a hōanga told her brother to use her body to sharpen his knife. He did, and he was able to finish his task. [Alpers 1966; Best 1924; Craig 1989; Leach 1992]

Hine tu a kirikiri

Polynesia: New Zealand, *Maori*
Earth and Nature
"Gravel Maid." Daughter of Rangahua, a stone deity. She protects the earth from the ocean goddess *Hine moana.* [Best 1924; Leach 1992]

Hine tū a maunga

Polynesia: New Zealand, *Maori*
Earth and Nature; Mother and Guardian; Ugliness; Unhappiness
"Mountain Maid." Because she bore only rusty waters and mountain monsters, her husband, Tāne, left her. [Craig 1989; Farmer 1978; Savill 1978]

Hine tu a tai

Polynesia: New Zealand, *Maori*
Fishing and Water Animals
"Daughter of the Seacoast." Wife of Tāwhaki and mother of fish. [Leach 1992]

Hine tu whenua

Polynesia: New Zealand, *Maori*
Weather; Directions; Order
West wind goddess. She and her mother, *Hine i tapapauta,* calm the ocean. [Andersen 1928; Leach 1992; White 1987]

Hine tua tai

Polynesia: New Zealand, *Maori*
Water
Seashore goddess. [Alpers 1966]

Hine turama

Polynesia: New Zealand, *Maori*
Stars and Planets
Mother of the stars. Wife of Uru te ngangana, god of light. [Best 1924; Leach 1992]

Hine wai

Polynesia: New Zealand, *Maori*
Weather
"The Rain Maid." She is the light and misty rain. [Leach 1992]

Hine waoriki

Polynesia: New Zealand, *Maori*
Earth and Nature
"White Pine." Nature deity. [Best 1924; Leach 1992]

Hine whaitiri

Polynesia: New Zealand, *Maori*
Weather
"Thunder." Weather goddess. [Leach 1992]

Hinehaone

Polynesia: New Zealand, *Maori*
Sun and Day
"Light." Goddess of female power. [Best 1924; Henry 1928; Howells 1948]

Hintabaran

Melanesia: New Ireland
Evil
Evil goddess; sister and wife of Larunaen. [Cox 1913; Leach 1992]

Hintubuet

Melanesia: New Ireland; New Mecklenburg
Creator of Life; Moon and Night; Insects
"Our Grandmother." Creator of sky, earth, and humans. As an androgynous being, her female aspects are the moon and the butterfly. [Leach 1992; Lurker 1984]

Hit
Micronesia: Caroline Islands
Fishing and Water Animals
   Octopus goddess. [Monaghan 1981]

H'llraru
Polynesia
Earth and Nature
   Earth mother. [Savill 1978]

Hoa make i ke kula
Polynesia: Hawaii
Earth and Nature; Life/Death Cycle; Ceremonies
   Daughter of Pili and Ho'oleipalaoa.

 Hoa make i ke kula was thrown away when she was born because she looked like a taro plant. Her grandmother saved her and wrapped her in a red bark cloth. After 20 days, Hoa make i ke kula emerged from the cloth as a beautiful woman. She later had a son who was born as a wooden image. With his birth began the worship of wooden images in the Kohala district of Hawaii. [Craig 1989]

Hoi tini
Polynesia: Marquesas Islands
Earth and Nature
   Yam and ti-plant goddess. [Craig 1989; Leach 1992]

Hokiolele
Polynesia: Hawaii
Unknown
   Goddess. Sister of **Na kino wailua**.
   When Pamano is killed, the sisters Hokiolele and Na kino wailua restore him to life.
      See also **Kanaio, Keaka.** [Beckwith 1940]

Hokohoko
Polynesia: Niue Island
Unknown
   Island deity and wife of Tia. [Craig 1989]

Hoku kau opae
Polynesia: Hawaii
Stars and Planets; Fishing and Water Animals; Luck
   Goddess of the star Sirius. She determines when to catch shrimp. Alternate forms: Newe, Horo. [Emerson 1967; Leach 1992]

Honabe
Melanesia: New Guinea
Creator of Life; Fire
   Creator goddess. Her genitals created so much heat that she could cook her food with them. Mother of **Hana,** four sons, seven gods, and the first bird and possum. [Savill 1978]

Ho'o hoku i ka lani
Polynesia: Hawaii
Family and Tribes; Love and Sexuality; Unhappiness; Life/Death Cycle
   Goddess. Daughter of **Papa** and Wākea.
   Wākea slept with Ho'ohoku i ka lani, and the ali'i, the chiefly class, was born. When Papa learned of this incestuous relationship, she spit in Wākea's face and left him. This separation led to the coming of death. [Cotterell 1979; Craig 1989]

Hōpoe
Polynesia: Hawaii
Arts
   Hula deity. Friend of **Hi'iaka.**

 Hōpoe danced the first hula for Hi'iaka and Pele in the Puna district on the island of Hawaii. Hi'iaka was so pleased by the dance she planted red and white lehua trees on the island for Hōpoe.
   See also **Hi'iaka.** [Craig 1989]

Horo   See *Hoku kau opae.*

Horotata
Polynesia: New Zealand, *Maori*
Unhappiness; Evil
   Daughter of Mangamangaiatua and sister of **Harataunga** (see for story). [Craig 1989]

Hotu
Polynesia: Tahiti; New Zealand
Earth and Nature
   "Sobbing Earth." Daughter of Te-fatu and **Fa'ahotu.** Wife of Ātea and mother of many deities. [Craig 1989]

Hotukura
Polynesia: Tuamotu Islands
Unknown
   A goddess. Also a Maori chief of Hawaiki. [Craig 1989]

Hou heana
Polynesia: Marquesas Islands
Heaven and Hell; Ceremonies
   Underworld deity who teaches sacred chants. [Craig 1989]

Houmea
Polynesia: New Zealand, *Maori*
Weather; Destroyer of Life
   Drought demon. A cannibal goddess fond of food suppliers or gatherers.

 Houmea was an ogre who devoured people. She ate her own children, but her husband made her disgorge them. He then killed Houmea by throwing hot stones down her throat. [Craig 1989; Jobes 1962; Savill 1978]

Hu'a nu'u marae
Polynesia: Tahiti
Sky and Heavens
   Sky goddess and companion of Tāne. [Craig 1989]

Huahega
Polynesia: Tuamotu Islands
Unknown
   Mother of Māui. She has a dominant role in his Tuamotuan exploits. Alternate forms: Taranga, Huahenga. [Alpers 1966; Craig 1989; Monaghan 1981]

Huahenga   See *Huahega.*

Huauri   See *Arimata.*

Huhune
Polynesia
Magic
   Goddess who was born from the forehead of **Papa** or **Haumea.** See also **Hauarani.** [Melville 1969]

Huhura, The
Polynesia: Tahiti
Intelligence and Creativity
   Ingenious deities who live with Tāne. They are female and male. [Craig 1989]

Huri mai te ata
Polynesia: New Zealand, *Maori*
Earth and Nature
   Tea tree goddess. [Craig 1989; Leach 1992]

Huru te arangi
Polynesia: New Zealand, *Maori*
Weather
   Mother of snow, frost, and ice. Grandmother of the wind.
[Best 1924; Leach 1992]

Ihi
Polynesia: Tahiti; New Zealand
Education and Knowledge; Ugliness
   "Wisdom and Learning." Daughter of Ta'aroa and *Papa raharaha*. Also a monster in Lake Taupo. [Craig 1989]

Ihi awa'awa
Polynesia: Hawaii
Weather; Fire
   "Lightning." Weather deity. [Craig 1989]

Ihi lani
Polynesia: Hawaii
Weather; Fire
   "Lightning." Weather deity. [Craig 1989]

Ihiihi   See *Ihi'ihi.*

Ihi'ihi
Polynesia: New Zealand, *Maori*
Unknown
   Hina's name in New Zealand. Wife of Irawaru and mother of Pero. Alternate form: Ihiihi. [Craig 1989]

Ihu anu   See *Ka ihu anu.*

Ihu koko
Polynesia: Hawaii
Fishing and Water Animals
   Fish goddess. Her home is Waialua, where she provides the aholehole fish. Alternate form: Ka ihu koko. [Beckwith 1940]

'Ilaheva
Polynesia: Tonga Islands
Insects
   Worm goddess. Wife of Tagaloa, mother of Aho'eitu. [Cotterell 1979; Craig 1989]

Iloilokula
Melanesia: Lau Islands, *Sau*
Unknown
   Yandrana goddess who frightens men. See also *Rā marama*. [Craig 1989]

Imberombera   See *Waramurungundji.*

'Imoa
Polynesia: Samoa
Creator of Life
   First woman. [Craig 1989]

Ina   See *Hina.*

Ina maram
Micronesia: Caroline Islands; Ponape
Moon and Night
   Moon goddess. [Christian 1890; Leach 1992]

Ina'ani vai
Polynesia: Mangaia Island
Unknown
   Wife of Tangaroa and mother of Tarauri and Turi-the-Bald.
[Craig 1989]

Inacho
Micronesia: Caroline Islands; Ponape
Earth and Nature
   Forest goddess. [Christian 1890; Leach 1992]

Inemes
Micronesia: Truk Islands
Love and Sexuality
   Goddess of love and sexuality. Mother of *Ururupuin*.
Equivalent to *Venus*, Greek and Roman Empires. [Leach 1972; Leach 1992]

Ingridi
Australia
Unknown
   Dreamtime goddess. Dreamtime refers to the mythological past. [Savill 1978]

Ininguru   See *Yuguruguru, The.*

Io wahine
Polynesia: New Zealand, *Maori*
Creator of Life
   First woman. Her husband was Tikiauaha. [Craig 1989]

Ioio moa
Polynesia: Hawaii
Selflessness
   Goddess of sacred purity. [Beckwith 1940]

Iro Duget
Melanesia
Destroyer of Life
   Death goddess. [Monaghan 1981]

Iti iti
Polynesia: New Zealand, *Maori*
Unknown
   Name for sister of Rupe and possibly another name for *Hina*. [Craig 1989]

'Iti'iti
Melanesia: Bellona Island
Unknown
   Island goddess. See also *Ekeitehua*. [Craig 1989]

Jalmarida
Australia
Unknown
   Goddess. [Reed 1978]

Jari
Melanesia
Reptiles; Education and Knowledge; Fire; Agriculture; Family and Tribes
   Snake goddess. She taught the people about marriage as well as how to use fire and cultivate the earth. Trying to civilize her husband, she created his anus so that he would not smell so badly. [Savill 1978]

Jiji
Polynesia: Tonga Islands
Wild Birds
   Heron deity. [Collocott 1921; Leach 1992; Moulton 1925]

Jugumishanta
Melanesia: New Guinea, *Kamano, Usurufa, Jate, Fore*
Earth and Nature; Sky and Heavens
   Earth goddess. She made the earth from her feces and built the sky from stone. [Leach 1992; Savill 1978]

Julunggul
Australia
Weather; Reptiles; Life/Death Cycle; Water; Ceremonies; Goodness; Evil
   Rainbow snake goddess of northern territories. A fertility symbol, she can be good or evil. Sometimes seen as male or androgynous. She is embodied in freshwater and saltwater. When boys are initiated, they are told they will be swallowed by Julunggul and regurgitated, symbolizing death and rebirth. See also *Karwadi, Ngaljod, Wawilak.* Alternate forms: Yulunggul, Yurlunggur. [Berndt 1974; Leach 1992; Monaghan 1981; Poignant 1967]

Junkgowa
Australia: Arnhem Land, *Yulengor*
Family and Tribes; Agriculture; Water; Ceremonies; Education and Knowledge; Fishing and Water Animals; Weather; Fire
   Ancestor goddess. She lived during Dreamtime (the mythological past) in the spirit land called Buraklor. She has a multiple form, called the Junkgowa Sisters, who created all food and formed water holes that were the links between humans and the spirit world. The Junkgowa Sisters made the ocean, and, as they passed over it, they created all the fish and water mammals.

 The Junkgowa Sisters made a canoe to go out on the ocean they had created. When the boat went too slowly, they created the wind to speed it along. Running into a large black rock, far from land, they overturned and had to swim to shore. This was when they established spiritual rituals and symbols, implements for digging yams, and fire to warm their people. When the sisters' sons grew older, they stole their mothers' sacred totems, and the Junkgowa Sisters vanished into the sea.
   See also *Djanggawul, Djunkgao.* [Monaghan 1981]

Ka 'ahu pāhau
Polynesia: Hawaii
Fishing and Water Animals
   Shark goddess. She lives in a cave at the mouth of Pearl Harbor. Because she had human parents, she is benevolent to humans and protects them from man-eating sharks. [Beckwith 1940; Craig 1989; Emerson 1968; Leach 1992]

Ka haka ua koko
Polynesia: Hawaii
Family and Tribes
   Ancestor goddess. Mother of **Papa.** [Craig 1989]

Ka hala o māpuana
Polynesia: Hawaii
Magic; Immortality; Justice
   Sorcerer. She revives the dead and traps her enemies in the jungle. [Craig 1989]

Ka hala o puna
Polynesia: Hawaii
Weather; Magic; Immortality
   "Rainbow Maiden." On Oahu she was killed by her lover. Through magical means, her parents found her spirit and restored her to life. [Craig 1989; Leach 1992; Westerveldt 1963b]

Ka ihu anu
Polynesia: Hawaii
Fishing and Water Animals
   Fish goddess. Daughter of *Hina'ai ka malama.* Alternate form: Ihu anu. [Beckwith 1940]

Ka ihu koa
Polynesia: Hawaii
Fishing and Water Animals
   Fish goddess. She provides ulua, amber fish, and dolphins off Kaena Point. Daughter of *Hina'ai ka malama.* [Beckwith 1940]

Ka ihu koko   See *Ihu koko.*

Ka ihu kuuna
Polynesia: Hawaii
Fishing and Water Animals
   Fish goddess at Laie, where she provides the mullet. Daughter of *Hina'ai ka malama.* [Beckwith 1940]

Ka ihu o pala'ai
Polynesia: Hawaii
Fishing and Water Animals
   Fish goddess who provides mullet at Ewa. Daughter of *Hina'ai ka malama.* [Beckwith 1940]

Ka iki lani
Polynesia: Hawaii
Agriculture; Ceremonies
   Wife of Lono. Her harvest festival is called *makahiki.* [Craig 1989]

Ka 'iwa ka la meha
Polynesia: Hawaii
Wild Birds
   Bird woman of Kupua. Alternate form: Ka 'iwa ka meha. [Leach 1992; Westerveldt 1963c]

Ka 'iwa ka meha   See *Ka 'iwa ka la meha.*

Ka lama i nu'u
Polynesia: Hawaii
Reptiles; Magic
   "Lizard Grandmother." Sorcerer and ruler of the lizard population at Laie, Oahu. See also *Kalama 'ula.* Alternate form: Ka lani mai nu'u. [Craig 1989; Leach 1992]

Ka lani mai nu'u   See *Ka lama i nu'u.*

Ka lei hau ola
Polynesia: Hawaii
Immortality
   Goddess of necromancy. See also *Ha pu'u.* [Craig 1989]

Ka maunu a niho
Polynesia: Hawaii
Magic
   Sorcerer. [Craig 1989]

Ka meha i kana
Polynesia: Hawaii
Earth and Nature
   "Breadfruit Tree." A name for *Haumea* in the story of her rebirth as a woman. She turned into a breadfruit tree to save her husband. [Beckwith 1940; Leach 1992; Westerveldt 1963c]

Ka mo'o 'inanea
Polynesia: Hawaii
Reptiles; Family and Tribes; Ceremonies

Lizard goddess. She was a cannibal ancestor of the ancient Hawaiians before their migration to the islands. [Craig 1989]

Ka onohi ula
Polynesia: Hawaii
Sky and Heavens
Goddess who lives on a beautiful floating cloud, the land of Kane. She is the mother of *Halalamanu, Kuilioloa, Ioio moa,* an ordinary child, a lizard, a dog, and a caterpillar. [Beckwith 1940; Craig 1989]

Ka pū o alaka'i
Polynesia: Hawaii
Earth and Nature; Mother and Guardian
Forest goddess. She protects boatmen as they move their boats from the mountains to the sea. [Craig 1989]

Ka ua ku'āhiwa
Polynesia: Hawaii
Weather
Rain goddess from Kahiki who migrated to Hawaii. [Craig 1989; Leach 1992]

Ka wahine o ka li'ūla
Polynesia: Hawaii
Unknown
Goddess. Alternate form: Lā'ie i kawai. [Craig 1989]

Kā'ana'e like
Polynesia: Hawaii
Beauty; Family and Tribes; Love and Sexuality; Unhappiness; Justice; Fire; Weather
Beautiful goddess who lives on Uluka'a, the floating island of the gods.

Kā'ana'e like married Ke awe a'oho and they lived on Uluka'a. Her husband left her for a time to return to Hawaii. When their son, Nā ku'emake pau i keahi, grew up, he went in search of his father. He asked his father to return to Uluka'a. Ke awe a'oho fell in love with his wife's younger sister, and Kā'ana'e like caused a fiery flood to destroy Uluka'a. Only she and her son were spared. [Craig 1989]

Ka'ao melemele
Polynesia: Hawaii
Arts; Earth and Nature; Weather; Stars and Planets; Life/Death Cycle
"Maid-of-the-golden-cloud." Daughter of *Hina* and Kū. She ruled the islands with her husband/brother, Kau mā'ili'ula, and learned the hula from *Kapo.* Her dance describes the movements of nature, stars, clouds, leaves, and blossoms. [Craig 1989]

Kabo mandalat See *Kobo mandalat.*

Kadjari
Australia
Mother and Guardian
Mother goddess worshiped in northern Australia. Equivalent to *Kunapipi.* Alternate form: Gadjari. [Berndt 1974]

Kafisi
Melanesia: Trobriand Islands
Fire; Domesticated Animals; Agriculture
Goddess who cared for her brother, a snake. To reward her, the brother made fire and provided pigs and plants for her. [Carlyon 1982; Savill 1978]

Kagauraha
Melanesia: San Cristoval; Solomon Islands
Creator of Life; Reptiles; Agriculture; Health and Healing
Creator goddess in the form of a snake. She created animals and food for the people. She is not worshiped in the Solomon Islands, but the people of San Cristoval pray to her for good health and abundant crops. [Leach 1992; MacCulloch 1925]

Kahausibware
Melanesia: Solomon Islands
Life/Death Cycle; Reptiles; Mother and Guardian
Creator goddess in the form of a snake. She provided food for her people but also introduced death to the world. [Bray 1935; Cotterell 1979]

Kahoupokane
Polynesia: Hawaii
Earth and Nature; Weather
Mountain goddess. She controls the snow on Mount Hualalai. [Leach 1992; Westerveldt 1963b]

Kāhu rere moa
Polynesia: New Zealand, *Maori*
Family and Tribes
Ancestor of the Ngātipaoa tribe. Her husband is Takakōpiri. Their daughter is *Tūparahaki.* Alternate form: Te kāhu rere moa. [Craig 1989]

Kāhuitara
Polynesia: New Zealand, *Maori*
Wild Birds
Goddess of sea birds. Daughter of Kikiwai. [Craig 1989]

Kahuone
Polynesia: Marquesas Islands
Metals and Minerals
Sand goddess. Wife of Tiki. [Leach 1992; Williamson 1933]

Kai here
Polynesia: New Zealand, *Maori*
Unknown
Wife of Tūtakahinahina. [Craig 1989]

Ka'ipo
Polynesia: Hawaii
Water
"Deep Sea." Sister of *Pele.* [Ashdown 1971; Leach 1992]

Kalaia
Australia
Wild Birds; Justice; Selfishness
Emu goddess. Sister of *Kipara.*

Kalaia, the younger of the two sisters, lost social standing when Kipara had more chicks than Kalaia did. Kalaia tricked Kipara, a turkey, into killing some of her chicks by saying that she (Kalaia) had killed some of her own offspring. When Kipara found out that Kalaia had tricked her, she decided to get revenge. Kipara folded her wings tightly; she told Kalaia that she had cut them off because they were too heavy and that not having wings made her more beautiful. Kalaia cut off her wings. As a result of this rivalry, emus cannot fly, but they have more chicks than turkeys. [Berndt 1974; Mounteford 1965; Roberts 1973]

Kalama 'ula
Polynesia: Hawaii
Reptiles

Lizard grandmother who lived in a cave. Her grandson was a well-known thief, and he hid his stolen property in the cave. See also *Ka lama i nu'u*. [Craig 1989]

Kalwadi   See *Karwadi*.

Kamaunu
Polynesia: Hawaii
Magic; Wild Birds
Sorcerer. Grandmother of the hog-man Kamapua'a. She appears as a bird or flash of light. [Beckwith 1940]

Kanaio
Polynesia: Hawaii
Unknown
Goddess. Mother of Pamano. See also *Hokiolele*. [Beckwith 1940]

Kāne kua'ana
Polynesia: Hawaii
Reptiles; Fishing and Water Animals; Wealth; Ceremonies; Health and Healing
Dragon goddess of Ewa Lagoon (Pearl Harbor). Kāne kua'ana is said to have been a living person who became a *mo'o*, or lizard. If she is properly worshiped, with altars and fires, she increases the number of fish and pearl-bearing oysters in the lagoon and protects humans from illness. [Beckwith 1940; Craig 1989; Leach 1992]

Kani uhi
Polynesia: New Zealand, *Maori*
Justice
She sent the great flood to punish the wicked. [Craig 1989]

Kanikanihia
Polynesia: Hawaii
Love and Sexuality
Goddess of love. [Beckwith 1932; Leach 1992]

Ka'ōhelo
Polynesia: Hawaii
Earth and Nature
Nature goddess. Sister of *Pele*. When Ka'ōhelo died, her body became the ohelo bush, which grows on volcanic soil and produces edible red and yellow berries. [Craig 1989; Leach 1992]

Kapiano
Melanesia
Destroyer of Life
Similar to *Dunawali* of New Guinea. [Savill 1978]

Kapo
Polynesia: Hawaii
Fate; Beauty; Arts; Mother and Guardian; Destroyer of Life
"Death." A sorcerer who predicts the future. Also a beautiful goddess of the hula and goddess of childbirth and abortion. Alternate form: Kapo 'ula kīna'u. [Craig 1989; Leach 1992; Monaghan 1965]

Kapo 'ula kīna'u   See *Kapo*.

Kara ma kuna
Micronesia: Truk Islands
Water; Heaven and Hell; Immortality
Sea goddess. Protector of the underworld, Bouru. [Leach 1992; MacKenzie 1930a]

Karaia i te ata
Polynesia: Mangaia Island; Cook Islands
Heaven and Hell; Evil
Underworld demon. Daughter of *Miru*. [Sykes 1968]

Karak karak, The
Australia
Fire; Education and Knowledge; Stars and Planets
Seven goddesses of fire.

 The Karak karak held the secret of fire and would not tell how it was made. With trickery, Crow-man gathered fire from their sticks and fled. The Karak karak were very angry and left earth to become the Seven Sisters constellation, the Pleiades.
See also *Meamei*. [Roberts 1973]

Karakarook
Australia, *Kulin*
Mother and Guardian; Reptiles; Agriculture
Guardian deity. Daughter of Blunjil, the supreme being, and sister of Bimbeal, the rainbow. Karakarook has power over the sky, and she protects women working in the fields from snakes. [Leach 1992; Reed 1978]

Kare nuku
Polynesia: New Zealand, *Maori*
Weather; Water
One of the goddesses who floated upon the waters of the great flood. See also *Hine rakatai, Kare rangi*. Alternate form: Hine pūpūmainaua. [Craig 1989]

Kare rangi
Polynesia: New Zealand, *Maori*
Weather; Water
One of the goddesses who floated on the waters of the great flood. See also *Hine rakatai, Kare nuku*. Alternate form: Hine pūpūma inaua. [Craig 1989]

Karwadi
Australia, *Leagulawulmirree*
Mother and Guardian; Ceremonies; Life/Death Cycle; Immortality
"Mother of All." Worshiped in northern Australia, Karwadi figures in the rites initiating boys into adulthood. A hole in the ground or a cave is prepared in the shape of a womb. The initiates are placed in the crescent-shaped cavity and are told they will be swallowed by Karwadi and regurgitated (reborn). The boys are smeared with blood, signifying life. During the ceremony, the bull-roarer is used to emulate Karwadi's voice. Two years after this ceremony, the young men are allowed to marry. For females' puberty ritual, see *Ngaljod*. Karwadi in mortal form is called *Mujingga*.

 Karwadi took care of children, but occasionally a child in her charge would disappear—Karwadi was cannibalistic and particularly liked the flesh of infants. One day, Karwadi disappeared with a baby. The people searched for her and killed her. When they cut her open, they found all of the children she had eaten alive inside her womb, waiting to be reborn.
See also *Julunggul, Kunapipi, Wawilak*. Alternate form: Kalwadi. [Berndt 1974; Monaghan 1981]

Kau ata ata
Polynesia: New Zealand, *Maori*
Creator of Life
First Woman. Daughter of the sun god Ra and *Arohirohi*. [Craig 1989]

Kaukau
Polynesia: New Zealand, *Maori*
Fishing and Water Animals; Water

"Ocean Maid." Guardian of the realm of *Hine moana,* the sea goddess. Mother of cockles and other sea creatures. [Best 1924; Leach 1992]

Ka'ula hea
Polynesia: Hawaii
Justice; Disorder
Consort of Wākea. Also a high chief of Māui.

 Ka'ula hea was one of the many obstacles Hi'iaka encountered when she was on her voyage for Pele. [Craig 1989]

Kava tua
Polynesia: Easter Island
Magic; Ceremonies
An *Aku aku,* supernatural cannibal. (See *Kava'ara* for story.) [Craig 1989]

Kava'ara
Polynesia: Easter Island
Magic; Ceremonies
An *Aku aku,* supernatural cannibal.

Kava'ara and Kava tua captured a mortal and imprisoned him in a cave. He was saved by another Aku aku and was returned home by a girl from his village. [Craig 1989]

Kave
Micronesia: Caroline Islands
Creator of Life
Creator goddess on the Nukuoro Atoll. [Leach 1992]

Kāwelu   See *Kewelu.*

Ke aka huli lani
Polynesia: Hawaii
Creator of Life
First woman. Her husband is Kāne huli honua. See also *Lalo hāna.* [Craig 1989]

Ke ao lewa
Polynesia: Hawaii
Sky and Heavens; Wild Birds; Weather
"Moving-cloud." Sky goddess. She appears as a bird-woman to rule the birds. Ancestor of *Lepe a moa.* [Leach 1992; Wester-veldt 1963b]

Ke ao mele mele
Polynesia: Hawaii
Weather
Cloud goddess. [Leach 1992; Westerveldt 1963b]

Keaka
Polynesia: Hawaii
Unknown
Goddess. Daughter of Kai uli.

Pamano falls in love with Keaka, as does his best friend, Koolau. The two friends agree to have nothing to do with Keaka without each other's knowledge. Keaka prefers Pamano and invites him to her home. Koolau finds out and plots to kill Pamano.
See also *Hokiolele.* [Beckwith 1940]

Kearoa
Polynesia: New Zealand, *Maori*
Unknown
Goddess. She was involved in the voyage of the discovery of New Zealand. [Alpers 1966]

Kele
Polynesia: Tonga Islands
Creator of Life; Family and Tribes
Creator goddess, grandmother of the gods. With her husband, Limu, she produced the goddess *Touiafutuna.* [Craig 1989; Leach 1992]

Kena
Polynesia: Easter Island
Arts; Wild Birds
Gannet (bird) goddess. Through her sons, she taught tattooing to the people. [Leach 1992; Metraux 1940]

Keoloewa
Polynesia: Hawaii
Magic
Goddess of sorcery. [Beckwith 1940; Leach 1992]

Kepa, The
Melanesia: New Guinea
Family and Tribes
Ghosts of female ancestors. [Savill 1978]

Kewelu
Polynesia: Hawaii
Love and Sexuality; Immortality; Heaven and Hell
"White Sea Strand."

 Kewelu loved a man of the forest, but when she tried to follow him, she became entangled in vines and strangled. He went to the underworld, where he captured her spirit in a hollow coconut and restored her to life.
Alternate form: Kāwelu. [Eliot 1976; Savill 1978]

Kiha wahine
Polynesia: Hawaii
Reptiles; Demi-animals; Magic; Destroyer of Life; Fishing and Water Animals
A Māui chief who became a *mo'o* (reptile) goddess. She is human above the waist and reptile below. She can also take the form of a chicken, fish, or spider. She can cause illness. After he conquered the islands, King Kamehameha I erected a temple in her honor. Kiha wahine is said to inhabit the fish ponds on Māui and Kauai, and, if she is home when fish are caught, they will be bitter. Alternate form: Kihe wahine. [Craig 1989; Leach 1992]

Kihe wahine   See *Kiha wahine.*

Kiki pua
Polynesia: Hawaii
Magic; Reptiles; Ugliness
Witch and lizard monster on Molokai. Sister of *Pele.* Her husband was Haka' a'ano. [Craig 1989]

Kini maka
Polynesia: Hawaii
Destroyer of Life
"Many-eyed." She had the disturbing habit of eating human eyeballs. The alternate form Kini maka o kalā probably refers to the rays or eyes of the sun rather than this eye-eating goddess. Alternate forms: Kini maka o kalā, Walewale o kū. [Craig 1989]

Kini maka o kalā   See *Kini maka.*

Kipara
Australia
Wild Birds
Turkey goddess. Sister of *Kalaia* (see for story). [Berndt 1974; Mounteford 1965; Roberts 1973]

Knowee
Australia
Sun and Day
   Sun goddess. In Australia the sun is considered female and the moon as male. See also *Gnowee*. [Reed 1978]

Kobine
Micronesia: Gilbert Islands
Creator of Life; Earth and Nature; Sky and Heavens; Heaven and Hell
   Creator goddess of the sky, earth, and the first woman, *De ai*. She is also an underworld deity. Daughter of Nareau, the creation god. [Craig 1989; Jobes 1962; Leach 1992]

Kobo Mandalat
Melanesia: New Caledonia
Evil; Fishing and Water Animals; Destroyer of Life
   Demon in the form of a giant hermit crab. She causes elephantiasis. Alternate form: Kabo Mandalat. [Savill 1978]

Koevasi
Melanesia: Solomon Islands
Primordial Being; Reptiles; Creator of Life; Family and Tribes; Earth and Nature; Mother and Guardian; Education and Knowledge
   Snake mother and creator deity. With the help of her husband, Sivotohu, she established the paths of the sun and the moon. Her daughter was the ancestor of the first humans. *Koevasi sent a hornet down to the water. She told it to go under the water and make earth. When this was done, Koevasi planted two trees; then she placed wild animals there. When humans populated the land, she supplied them with the necessities of life and taught them how to speak. Her speech was difficult to understand, and each group heard it differently. That is why there are various dialects.* [Carlyon 1982; Leach 1992; Monaghan 1981; Savill 1978]

Koilasa
Melanesia: Lau Islands
Destroyer of Life
   Disease goddess. She gives rashes to those who upset her. Alternate form: Kuilasa. [Craig 1989]

Koirau na marama
Melanesia: Lau Islands
Weather; Destroyer of Life
   "Two Ladies." The winds who cause mortal death. Mothers of *Vinaka* and *Tha*. [Craig 1989]

Koke
Polynesia: New Zealand, *Maori*
Unknown
   Goddess. Her husband is Māui. See also *Rohe*. [Craig 1989]

Komeang
Melanesia: New Guinea, *Western Mejbrat*
Stars and Planets
   "Morning Star." She is associated with ceremonies involving initiation signs and markings. [Elmberg 1955; Leach 1992]

Konjini
Southwest Pacific: Rossel Island; Territory of Papua
Reptiles; Creator of Life
   Snake goddess. First she created herself; then with Mbasi, she laid an egg that hatched the first people. [Leach 1992; MacKenzie 1930a]

Kor Enda   See *Enda Semangko*.

Ku raki
Polynesia
Earth and Nature
   "White Pine Tree." [Leach 1992; White 1887–1890]

Kua iti
Polynesia: Marquesas Islands
Love and Sexuality
   Granddaughter of *Fata'a koka*. Kua iti and her sister, *Kua nui*, were seduced by their brother, Phui nui aau too, the eel. [Craig 1989]

Kua nui
Polynesia: Marquesas Islands
Love and Sexuality
   Granddaughter of *Fata'a koka*. Kua nui and her sister, *Kua iti*, were seduced by their brother, Phui nui aau too, the eel. [Craig 1989]

Kui
Polynesia: Tahiti; New Zealand, *Maori*
Weather; Ceremonies
   Blind cannibal. Probably a storm or war deity. [Jobes 1962; Savill 1978]

Kui o hina
Polynesia: Hawaii
Moon and Night
   Sky goddess. She keeps the moon stabilized as it travels through space. [Beckwith 1940]

Kuilasa   See *Koilasa*.

Kuilioloa
Polynesia: Hawaii
Fire
   Fire goddess. [Beckwith 1940]

Kuku 'ena i ke ahi ho'omau honua
Polynesia: Hawaii
Health and Healing; Commerce and Travel
   A healer who also guides lost travelers. See also *Hi'iaka i ka pua'ena'ena*. Alternate form: Hi'iaka tapu 'ena'ena. [Craig 1989]

Kūkū'ena
Polynesia: Hawaii
Commerce and Travel; Ceremonies
   Protector of travelers. Elder sister of *Pele*. She presides over the kava (drink of the gods) ceremony. [Craig 1989]

Kuliua   See *Hina kuluua*.

Kume
Polynesia: Tikopia
Heaven and Hell
   Afterlife deity. With her sister *Nau taufiti*, she cleanses the spirit of the dead. [Firth 1967b; Leach 1992]

Kumi tonga
Polynesia: Tuamotu Islands
Ceremonies
   Goddess of feasting mats. [Craig 1989]

Kumitoga
Polynesia: Vahitahi Island; Tuamotu Islands
Earth and Nature
   Vegetation deity. [Leach 1992; Stimson 1933]

Kumu tonga i te po
Polynesia: Cook Islands
Creator of Life
    Creation goddess. Daughter of **Miru**. [Sykes 1968]

Kunan beili
Australia
Creator of Life
    Creator goddess. One of the wives of the great spirit,
Baiame; the other was **Birra nulu** (see for story). See also
Birrhgnooloo, Cunnembeillee. [Reed 1973]

Kunan-beili   See *Kunan beili.*

Kunapipi
Australia, *Leagulawulmirree*
Creator of Life; Ceremonies; Weather; Reptiles
    Mother goddess worshiped in Arnhem Land in north-central
Australia. She created all living things, and she supervises
initiation and puberty rituals. She may be the rainbow snake,
Julunggul, or the rainbow snake may have preceded her and
prepared the way for her. Kunapipi is also said to be the mother
of the *Munga munga* and to be a cannibalistic deity who was
killed by Eaglehawk, a deity from Dreamtime (the mythological
past). For an explanation of cannibalism see **Bila**. See also
Kadjari, Karwadi, Moitjinka, Waramurungundji. Alternate
forms: Gunabibi, Mumuna. [Carlyon 1982; Cotterell 1979;
Leach 1992; Monaghan 1981; Savill 1978; Stone 1979]

Kunnawarra
Australia
Agriculture; Wild Birds; Love and Sexuality
    "Black Swan."

    *The creator gave Kunnawara and Kururuk a digging
    stick to use in gathering vegetables and roots. She was a
    companion and helper of men.* [Reed 1978]

Kura
Polynesia: New Zealand, *Maori*
Heaven and Hell
    Deity. Wife of Wahieroa and mother of **Rata**. Also the
name of the red wreaths worn by Maori chiefs.

    *Kura was gathering flowers with her sister when the
    earth opened and she fell into the underworld.
    Eventually Kura was rescued and returned to the upper
world.* [Alpers 1966; Craig 1989; Jobes 1962; Savill 1978]

Kura ngaituka
Polynesia: New Zealand, *Maori*
Wild Birds; Physical Prowess
    "Bird Woman." Kura ngaituka is as tall as a tree and can
cover great distances in a single stride. On her arms are
feathery wings, her fingernails are as long as spears, and she
impales birds with her lips. She lives in a cave, where she
keeps a man as a pet.
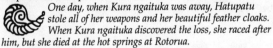
    *One day, when Kura ngaituka was away, Hatupatu
    stole all of her weapons and her beautiful feather cloaks.
    When Kura ngaituka discovered the loss, she raced after
him, but she died at the hot springs at Rotorua.*
    Alternate form: Kūrangāituka. [Alpers 1966; Craig 1989]

Kūrangāituka   See *Kura ngaituka.*

Kurikuta
Australia
Wild Birds; Weather; Fire; Disorder; Metals and Minerals
    Crow mother of the southeastern area. The eating of emu,
which is both her totem and her assistant, disturbs her.

    *When Kurikuta is upset, she descends from the sky in a
    flash of lightning and a great roll of thunder, displaying
    her quartz-crystal body.*
    See also *Emu.* [Berndt 1974]

Kurriwilban
Australia
Ceremonies; Destroyer of Life
    Cannibalistic spirit. See **Bila** for explanation of cannibalism.
Wife of Koyorowen, a cannabilistic storm deity.

    *On each shoulder Kurriwilban has an upright horn,
    which she uses to kill her victims. She kills only men;
    her husband kills women.* [Jobes 1962]

Kururuk
Australia
Agriculture; Love and Sexuality
    "Native Companion." See also **Kunnawarra.** [Reed 1978]

Kutunga
Australia
Mother and Guardian; Metals and Minerals
    Mother goddess.

    *Kutunga gave birth to children who were transformed
    into egg-shaped boulders. The boulders furnish a
    never-ending supply of spirit children called Yulanya.*
    See also *Yulanya.* [Roberts 1973]

Kwouk kwouk
Australia, *Tiwi*
Fishing and Water Animals; Weather; Disorder
    Frog deity worshiped on Melville Island. Mother of the
weather deities and **Bumarali** and **Tomituka**, as well as
Pakadringa, god of thunder.

    *Kwouk kwouk is pleased when she hears the torrential
    rain and the raging thunderstorm and sees the destructive
    lightning because she knows her children are busy.*
    Alternate form: Quork quork. [Leach 1992; Murphy 1958;
Roberts 1973]

La
Micronesia: Yap Islands
Arts
    Tattoo goddess. [Leach 1992; Muller 1917]

La ea   See *Hina hele.*

La'a hāna
Polynesia: Hawaii
Household Affairs
    Goddess of tapa makers. Her body produced the wauke
plant used to make tapa cloth. [Craig 1989]

La'ama'oma'o
Polynesia: Hawaii
Commerce and Travel
    Goddess who assisted the people's migration from Tahiti
to Hawaii. Sometimes considered a god. [Craig 1989]

La'e
Polynesia: Hawaii
Wild Birds
    Goddess of bird catchers. [Emerson 1967; Leach 1992]

Laenihi
Polynesia: Hawaii
Magic; Immortality; Demi-animals; Weather; Fishing and
Water Animals; Domesticated Animals

Sorcerer. She can restore humans to life. She takes the form of a fish or a chicken. She swims, accompanied by storms, lightning, and earthquakes. [Craig 1989]

Lahi wahine
Polynesia: Hawaii
Reptiles; Fate
Lizard goddess. She can predict the future. [Beckwith 1940; Leach 1992]

La'i la'i
Polynesia: Hawaii
Creator of Life
Primeval goddess. She cohabited with the sky god, and they produced the first humans. [Jobes 1962; Leach 1956; Monaghan 1981]

Lai'a hana
Polynesia: Hawaii
Education and Knowledge; Household Affairs
Goddess who teaches tapa makers the proper decorative patterns for dyeing. [Beckwith 1940]

Lā'ie i kawai
Polynesia: Hawaii
Weather
"Mist Maiden."

Lā'ie i kawai and her twin sister were hidden from their father, who wanted a son. She was cared for by Waka until a suitable marriage was arranged for her. Before the ceremony, Lā'ie i kawai was kidnapped by Hala aniani, who lived with her as her husband. Her patron goddesses, collectively called the Maile, then arranged for her to marry their brother, Ka ōnohi o ka lā. The couple lived on a rainbow in the land of the gods until Ka ōnohi o ka lā returned to earth and had an affair with his wife's twin. The twins' parents changed Ka ōnohi o ka lā into a wandering ghost. Lā'ie i kawai returned to earth as the goddess Ka wahine o ka li'ūla. [Craig 1989; Leach 1992]

Laka
Polynesia: Hawaii
Earth and Nature; Weather; Creator of Life; Arts; Disorder
Goddess of vegetation, guardian of the woodland, and bringer of rain. She is also the deity of fertility, reproduction, and the hula. She is alternately considered a sister, niece, or friend of *Pele*. Laka's dancers are said to represent the untamed element of human nature. Sometimes *Alalahe* is referred to as Laka. Laka is also the name of a male deity. [Beckwith 1940; Craig 1989; Jobes 1962; Leach 1972; Leach 1992; Monaghan 1981]

Lake   See *Alalahe*.

Lalo hāna
Polynesia: Hawaii
Creator of Life
First woman. A second woman also named Lalo Hāna is the mother of Laka. See also *Ke aka huli lani*. Alternate form: Lalo honua. [Craig 1989]

Lalo honua   See *Lalo hāna*.

Lani loa
Polynesia: Hawaii
Reptiles; Magic; Earth and Nature
Lizard goddess. She was killed and transformed into five small isles near a village on Oahu. [Craig 1989]

Lani wahine
Polynesia: Hawaii
Reptiles; Demi-animals; Fate
Lizard goddess who can appear as a woman and foretell disaster. She lives in Okoa Pond on Oahu. [Beckwith 1940; Craig 1989; Leach 1992]

Latmikaik
Micronesia: Pellew Islands
Water; Fishing and Water Animals; Creator of Life
Sea goddess. She was born from a wave-beaten rock. She gave birth to children and schools of fish. [Baumgartner 1984; Cotterell 1979; Leach 1992]

Lau hu iki
Polynesia: Hawaii
Education and Knowledge; Household Affairs
Goddess of tapa makers. She teaches the art of making the bark of the wauke tree into a cloth called tapa. [Beckwith 1940; Leach 1992]

Lau ka 'ie'ie
Polynesia: Hawaii
Earth and Nature
"Leaf of the Trailing Pandanus." Forest goddess and wind deity. She became the 'ie 'ie (a plant). [Craig 1989; Leach 1992]

Lau kiele 'ula
Polynesia: Hawaii
Love and Sexuality
"Sweet-scented Goddess." Sister of Makani ke oe, the love god. [Craig 1989]

Le fale i le langi
Polynesia: Samoa
Earth and Nature
Creator goddess who gave birth to several areas on the islands of Ofu and Ta'ū. These areas were named Gentle Rain, Reaching into Night, Hardly-able-to-get-down, Panting or Gasping, and Two Lands. [Craig 1989]

Le gerem
Micronesia: Yap Islands
Education and Knowledge; Time; Directions; Sky and Heavens
Goddess who taught the people about seasons and heavenly movement. [Clerk 1982; Leach 1992]

Le hev hev
Melanesia: Malekula Island in New Hebrides
Heaven and Hell; Justice; Insects; Fishing and Water Animals; Hunting and Wild Animals
"She Who Smiles So That We Draw Near and She Can Eat Us." Underworld goddess embodied as a spider, crab, rat, and female genitalia. When a departed soul approached the underworld, Le hev hev required the soul to pass certain tests before it was allowed to enter. [Monaghan 1981]

Lea
Polynesia: Hawaii
Demi-animals; Wild Birds; Commerce and Travel
Goddess of canoe makers. By appearing as a bird, and sometimes as a human, she chooses the right tree from which to make a canoe. Alternate form: 'Elepaio. [Craig 1989; Leach 1992]

Lejman
Micronesia
Insects; Creator of Life; Earth and Nature; Sky and Heavens

"Worm." Creator goddess of the Radak Group. She made the sky from the top half of a shell and the earth from the bottom half. [Leach 1972]

Lepe a moa
Polynesia: Hawaii
Family and Tribes; Wild Birds
"Bird-girl." Ancestor of **Ke ao lewa.**

 Lepe a moa was born in the form of an egg. She had the power to change from a bird to a beautiful girl. [Craig 1989; Leach 1992]

Lewa levu
Melanesia: Fiji Islands
Evil; Destroyer of Life; Justice
Evil spirit. If a person violates sacred ground, Lewa levu causes him or her to get sick. [Leach 1992; Spencer 1941]

Lewandranu
Melanesia: Lau Islands
Family and Tribes; Destroyer of Life
Goddess of the clan of Nakambuta in Nasangalau. When she is angry she can cause children to become ill. [Craig 1989]

Lewatu momo
Melanesia: Fiji Islands
Evil; Charisma; Destroyer of Life
Evil spirit who lures men to their deaths. [Leach 1992; Spencer 1941]

Lewatu ni nambua
Melanesia: Fiji Islands, *Mono-Alu*
Evil; Water; Disorder; Weather
Evil spirit. A sea goddess who can withhold the seas or cause floods. [Leach 1972; Leach 1992; Spencer 1941]

Li ara katau
Micronesia: Ponape; Caroline Islands
Earth and Nature
Forest goddess. [Christian 1890; Leach 1992]

Li arongorong pei
Micronesia: Ngatik; Ponape; Caroline Islands
Water
Sea goddess. [Christian 1890; Leach 1992]

Li au en pon tan
Micronesia: Ponape; Caroline Islands
Water
River goddess of the Paliklao. [Christian 1890; Leach 1992]

Li char
Micronesia: Ponape; Caroline Islands
Heaven and Hell
Underworld goddess. [Christian 1890; Leach 1992]

Li mot a lang
Micronesia: Ponape; Caroline Islands
Earth and Nature
Forest goddess. [Christian 1890; Leach 1992]

Lia
Australia, *Goanna*
Mother and Guardian; Water
Heavenly deity.

 Lia looked down, saw the Mother's children living in a dry desert, and decided to go to earth to help them. She married the chief of the Goanna people and began to live as they did. She quickly noticed that the men were clean but the women were dry and dusty after searching all day for roots. Each

morning the men left for the gray rocks in the distance while the women went out digging. Each night the men returned with one bag of water for their wives and daughters. Despite her husband's threats, Lia decided to search for water in the mountains while the men were gone on a journey of several days. After receiving directions from the Tukonee, or little people of a cave, Lia took all of the women into the mountains. Sinking her stick deeply into the earth, she found water. The gushing water eventually ran down the mountain, forming the Murumbidgee River. The women followed the water back to the plains. When the men returned, they were on the other side of the river, unable to cross, and so the women went away and lived in their own village. [Stone 1979]

Ligifo
Micronesia: Yap Islands
Mother and Guardian; Fate; Immortality
Guardian goddess. She knows all that happens on earth, those who live and those who die. She guides souls to Lug, the god of death. [Leach 1992; Muller 1917]

Ligoapup
Micronesia
Creator of Life
First woman. She gave birth to the first humans from her arms and her eyes. Alternate form: Ligoububfanu. [Bray 1935; Jobes 1962; Monaghan 1981]

Ligoband   See *Ligoububfanu.*

Ligobund   See *Ligoububfanu.*

Ligoububfanu
Micronesia: Truk Islands; Caroline Islands
Creator of Life; Mother and Guardian
Creator goddess. She created the first humans, then bore fruits and plants to feed them. She made the earth and its islands for their home. Alternate forms: Ligoband, Ligobund, Ligoapup. [Carlyon 1982; Leach 1956; Leach 1972; Savill 1978]

Likant e rairai   See *Likant en arum.*

Likant en arum
Micronesia: Ponape; Caroline Islands
Earth and Nature
Wood deity. Alternate form: Likant e rairai. [Leach 1992]

Likuthava
Melanesia: Lau Islands; Fiji Islands
Weather; Destroyer of Life
Goddess of Valelailai. She is invoked to prevent hurricanes but will kill if offended. [Craig 1989; Hocart 1929; Leach 1992]

Lilavatu
Melanesia: Fiji Islands
Destroyer of Life
Disease goddess who can cause death. [Savill 1978]

Lilinoe
Polynesia: Hawaii
Weather; Earth and Nature
"Mists." Goddess of snow-covered mountains, particularly Haleakala. [Craig 1989; Leach 1992]

Lilomarar   See *Liomarar.*

Limdunanij
Micronesia: Marshall Islands
Creator of Life
First woman of the Ralik Group. [Leach 1972]

Lino
Micronesia: Ratak Islands; Marshall Islands
Water; Weather
    Sea and wind goddess who is invoked for protection during high seas. Her husband is Langieli. [Knappe 1888; Leach 1992]

Liomarar
Micronesia: Yap Islands
Creator of Life
    Creator goddess. She threw sand on the water and created the island of Uithi. Mother of *Lorop*. Alternate form: Lilomarar. [Monaghan 1981; Savill 1978]

Longolongovavau
Polynesia: Tonga Islands
Heaven and Hell; Immortality; Family and Tribes
    Queen of the underworld. Daughter of *Hina* and Sinilaus.

Longolongovavau lived in the underworld until her uncle, Ofamaikiatama, found a husband, Lolomatokelau, for her in the upper world. She lived happily with her husband until the Tonga men, jealous because Lolomatokelau had such a wonderful wife, killed him. Lolomatokelau's spirit went to Pulotu (the underworld), where Ofamaikiatama found it. He returned Lolomatokelau's spirit to his body and then returned the revived man to Longolongovavau. [Craig 1989]

Lorop
Micronesia: Yap Islands
Creator of Life; Heaven and Hell; Mother and Guardian
    Creator goddess. She provided food for her children from the underworld. After she stayed in the underworld, she gave her children fish and new islands on which to live. Alternate forms: Nomoi, Mortlock. [Monaghan 1981; Savill 1978]

Lū
Polynesia: Rotuma
Stars and Planets
    Stellar goddess. Her three sons became Orion's Belt. [Craig 1989]

Lube
Polynesia: Tonga Islands
Earth and Nature
    "Dove." Goddess of the forest and woods. Alternate form: Lupe. [Collocott 1921; Leach 1992; Moulton 1925]

Lukelong
Micronesia: Caroline Islands
Creator of Life
    Creator goddess, sometimes considered a god. [Leach 1992; Savill 1978]

Lunba
Australia
Wild Birds
    "Old Kingfisher-woman." Worshiped at Ayers Rock. [Roberts 1973]

Lupe   See *Lube*.

Lupe pangopango
Polynesia: Samoa
Wild Birds
    Bird goddess who appears as a pigeon. Mother of *Hina*.
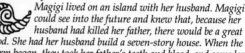
Lupe Pangopango gave Hina a dowry that was later destroyed by the god Tangaloa. After many years of separation, Hina and Tangaloa reunited, and Lupe promised to find and return Hina's dowry. [Craig 1989]

Mā 'a'a
Polynesia: Hawaii
Earth and Nature
    Wilderness goddess. She makes leis for the deities. See also *Mai 'u'u*. [Craig 1989]

Ma hui e
Polynesia: Society Islands (Ta'aroa)
Fire
    Fire goddess. [Henry 1928; Leach 1992]

Ma riko riko
Polynesia: New Zealand, *Maori*
Creator of Life
    "Glimmer," "Mirage." First woman. She was made by the sun god. [Jobes 1962]

Ma ukuuku
Polynesia: New Zealand, *Maori*
Metals and Minerals
    "White Clay." Wife of Raki. [Leach 1992; White 1987]

Madalait
Australia: Arnhem Land
Creator of Life
    Creator goddess. [Monaghan 1990]

Maeke
Polynesia: New Zealand, *Maori*
Unknown
    "Cold." She attacked the sons of *Papa*. [Best 1924; Leach 1992]

Mafuike
Polynesia
Heaven and Hell; Fire; Justice
    "Old Woman." Ruler of the underworld and goddess of fire.

    The god Māui asked Mafuike for some fire. She gave him one of her fingers, but Māui wanted more. Mafuike became angry and gave Māui all of her fingers, but this caused the earth to catch fire. Māui had to ask rain, snow, and sleet to come to keep the earth from burning up.
    See also *Mahuea*. Alternate forms: Mahuika, Makuika. [Eliot 1976; Jobes 1962; Monaghan 1981]

Mafurere
Polynesia: Tikopia
Destroyer of Life; Evil
    One of the *Pufine ma*. Goddess of sickness and evil. Twin of *Nau taufiti*. [Leach 1992]

Mafutoka   See *Nau taufiti*.

Magigi
Micronesia: Caroline Islands
Creator deity.
    Magigi lived on an island with her husband. Magigi could see into the future and knew that, because her husband had killed her father, there would be a great flood. She had her husband build a seven-story house. When the storm began, they took her father's teeth and blood, and some leaves and oil, and went into the house. After seven days of rain, the water reached the seventh story. Magigi threw her father's teeth and blood on the water. Then she put the oil in a leaf and laid it on the water. The waters stopped rising; when the storm stopped, the water receded. Because Magigi and her husband were the only people still alive, she had seven children and set them in different parts of the island to repopulate it. [Farmer 1978]

Mahora nui a rangi
Polynesia: New Zealand, *Maori*
Sky and Heavens
   Sky goddess. Alternate form: Mahora nui a tea. [Jobes 1962]

Mahora nui a tea
Polynesia: New Zealand, *Maori*
Earth and Nature; Sky and Heavens
   "Great Speeding Light." Nature goddess. Mother of the sky father, Rangi, and the four gods who prop up heaven. Alternate form: Mahora nui a rangi. [Craig 1989; Jobes 1962; Leach 1992]

Mahu fatu rau
Polynesia: Society Islands (Ta'aroa); Tahiti
War
   "Frog of Many Owners." War goddess. [Cotterell 1979; Leach 1992]

Mahuea
Polynesia: New Zealand, *Maori*
Fire
   Fire goddess. She discovered how to make fire. See also *Mafuike*. [Stone 1979]

Mahuika   See *Mafuike*.

Mai 'u'u
Polynesia: Hawaii
Earth and Nature
   Wilderness goddess who makes leis for the deities. See also *Mā 'a'a*. [Craig 1989]

Maile, The
Polynesia: Hawaii
Earth and Nature; Arts
   "Sweet-scented." Four sisters who represent four varieties of the myrtle vine, or maile. The maile vines carry the scent of the goddesses; they were used to decorate temples, and it is said their scent remains in Hawaiian temples. The goddesses are associated with the hula. Their names are *Maile ha'i wale, Maile kaluhea, Maile lauli'i, Maile pāhaka*. [Craig 1989]

Maile ha'i wale
Polynesia: Hawaii
Earth and Nature; Arts
   One of the *Maile*. [Craig 1989]

Maile kaluhea
Polynesia: Hawaii
Earth and Nature; Arts
   One of the *Maile*. [Craig 1989]

Maile lau li'i
Polynesia: Hawaii
Earth and Nature; Arts
   One of the *Maile*. [Craig 1989]

Maile pā haka
Polynesia: Hawaii
Earth and Nature; Arts
   One of the *Maile*. [Craig 1989]

Mailkun
Australia
Evil; Destroyer of Life
   Evil spirit. Wife of Koen, also an evil spirit. Mailkun kidnaps adults in a net and spears children. Alternate form: Tippakalleum. [Jobes 1962; Leach 1972; Leach 1992]

Maimoa a longona
Polynesia: Tonga Islands
Primordial Being; Creator of Life
   Primordial goddess, creator deity. Daughter of *Touiafutuna*, mother of *Valelahī*. She and her brother, Atungake, are the second set of twins in the primordial family. [Collocott 1921; Craig 1989; Leach 1992; Moulton 1925]

Mairangi
Polynesia: New Zealand, *Maori*
Reptiles
   Reptile goddess. Mother of the reptile gods (moko) and wife of Tūtewanawana. [Craig 1989]

Mairatea
Polynesia: New Zealand
Unknown
   Goddess. [Alpers 1966]

Makara, The
Australia
Wild Birds; Stars and Planets; Weather
   "Emu Women" or "Ice Maidens." Seven sisters who became the constellation Pleiades.
    As the Emu women, they had to flee a bush fire set by hunters. As they stepped over the burning plants, their legs stretched to the length they are today. They then rose to heaven as the Seven Sisters. As the Ice Maidens, the sisters' bodies are covered with icicles. When they first appear in the eastern sky, the icicles reach down to earth, covering it with frost. [Leach 1992; Mounteford 1965; Roberts 1973]

Makole nawahi waa   See *Hi'iaka makole wawahi wa'a*.

Makore wawahi waa   See *Hi'iaka makole wawahi wa'a*.

Makoro
Polynesia: New Zealand, *Maori*
Unknown
   Daughter of Kupe. Sister of *Matiu* and *Taiapua*. [Alpers 1966]

Makuika   See *Mafuike*.

Makunai
Melanesia: Bougainville; Solomon Islands
Family and Tribes
   Ancestor goddess of the Eagle people, with *Osooso*, Horomorun, and Konopia. [Leach 1992; Oliver 1967]

Mālei
Polynesia: Hawaii
Fishing and Water Animals
   Goddess of fishermen and protector of the parrot fish (uhu). [Craig 1989]

Mam
Micronesia: Yap Islands, Caroline Islands
Mother and Guardian
   Birth goddess. [Christian 1890; Leach 1992]

Mamala
Polynesia: Hawaii
Demi-animals; Reptiles
   "Kupua Goddess." A lizard, crocodile, or shark woman. [Leach 1992; Westerveldt 1963b]

Mamao
Polynesia: Samoa
Sky and Heavens

"Space." Mother of day (Ao) and night (Po). [Andersen 1928; Leach 1992]

Manana
Polynesia: Easter Island
Fishing and Water Animals
Fish goddess. Wife of the bird god, Era nuku. [Gray 1925a; Leach 1992]

Māpunai'a 'a'ala
Polynesia: Hawaii
Unknown
Daughter of *Haumea*. [Craig 1989]

Marama
Polynesia: Tahiti; Marquesas Islands; New Zealand, *Maori*
Moon and Night; Immortality
Moon goddess. Sister of Ra, the sun. Marama's body wastes away, but she restores it by bathing in the water of life. In Hawaii she is called *Uri Uri*. Alternate form: Na'vahine. [Leach 1992; Lurker 1984; Melville 1969]

Marama kai
Polynesia: Easter Island
Unknown
Goddess at Hiva. [Savill 1978]

Marei kura
Polynesia: Anaa Island; Tuamotu Islands
Agriculture; Household Affairs; Mother and Guardian
Goddess of planting, weaving, and childbirth. [Craig 1989; Leach 1992]

Mari haka
Polynesia
Unknown
Goddess. [Leach 1992; White 1987]

Mar'rallang, The
Australia
Earth and Nature
Twin earth spirits.
 Mar'rallang was the name of two sisters who were so much alike they had the same name. They met and fell in love with Wyungara, "He Who Returns to the Stars," a heavenly spirit who came to earth to aid a widow in her sorrow. Wyungara loved both sisters and married them. The marriage upset the great spirit, Nepelle, who decided to separate the wives from the husband. He started a fire, but Wyungara took his wives to the swamp. When the fire became too great, Wyungara put his wives on his spear and hurled it into the heavens. Nepelle, moved by Wyungara's devotion, let him join his wives, and the three lovers shine steadily together. [Reed 1973]

Maru a nuku
Polynesia: Anaa Island; Tuamotu Islands
Heaven and Hell
Underworld goddess. She guards the entrance of Kororupo, the underworld. [Leach 1992; Stimson 1933]

Maru a roto
Polynesia: Anaa Island; Tuamotu Islands
Heaven and Hell
Underworld goddess. She leads the dead to Kororupo, the underworld. [Leach 1992; Stimson 1933]

Matakerepo
Polynesia
Family and Tribes
"Grandmother." [Eliot 1976]

Matari'i See *Matariki*.

Matariki
Polynesia: Tahiti; Mangaia Island
Stars and Planets
Goddess who, with her six children, became the Pleiades. See also *Mayi mayi, Meamei*. Alternate form: Matari'i. [Craig 1989; Monaghan 1990]

Matiu
Polynesia
Unknown
Goddess. Daughter of Kupe and sister of *Makoro* and *Taiapua*. [Alpers 1966]

Maurea
Polynesia: New Zealand
Unknown
Goddess. [Alpers 1966]

Mayi Mayi, The
Australia
Stars and Planets
Star goddesses who form the Pleiades. See also *Matariki, Meamei*. [Monaghan 1981]

Me ha'i kana
Polynesia: Hawaii
Agriculture
Goddess of breadfruit. Alternate form: Papa. [Craig 1989]

Meamei, The
Australia
Stars and Planets; Fire; Education and Knowledge; Selfishness
"Seven Sisters." Goddesses of the Pleiades.
The Meamei were the guardians of fire. They kept the fire in their yam sticks and would not share it. Wahn the Crow devised a plan to steal the fire. Knowing the sisters liked white ants, he hid snakes in an anthill. Wahn showed the sisters where they could find the ants. When the sisters dug into the hill, the snakes attacked. As the Meamei beat at the snakes with their sticks, the ends broke off. Wahn stole the fire and kept it for himself. The Meamei went up into the sky and became the Pleiades.
See also *Karak karak, Matariki, Mayi mayi*. [Reed 1973]

Meanderi
Melanesia: New Guinea
Agriculture
Food goddess. She gave sugarcane, taro, and other food plants to her people. [Lawrence 1965; Leach 1992; Savill 1978]

Mele
Polynesia: Niue Island
Household Affairs
Goddess of weaving who is very kind to humans. [Craig 1989]

Merau
Polynesia: New Zealand, *Maori*
Unknown
"Extinction." [Andersen 1928; Leach 1992]

Mere hau
Polynesia: Tahiti
Magic
Witch. With *Nua* she abducted a young boy. She can assume the form of a duck or lizard. See also *Nua*. [Craig 1989]

Metakorab
Melanesia
Unknown
"Bogey." A spirit. [Jobes 1962; Leach 1972]

Milapukala
Australia
Wild Birds; Creator of Life; Metals and Minerals
"Cockatoo-woman."

 Milapukala lived at Cape Fourcroy on northwestern Bathurst Island. There she formed the Milapuru lagoon, with its rocky headlands and plains-like shores. She filled her creation with much food and then changed into a cleft rock on the shore of the lagoon. [Roberts 1973]

Milu
Polynesia: Hawaii
Heaven and Hell
Underworld goddess. [Beckwith 1940]

Mimaliwu
Australia
Unknown
Dreamtime goddess. Dreamtime refers to the mythological past. Alternate form: Gulanundoidj. [Savill 1978]

Mingari
Australia
Evil; Earth and Nature
"Mountain Devil-woman." She plays an important role in ritual performances in central Australia. See also *Minma mingari.* [Berndt 1974]

Minma mala
Australia
Hunting and Wild Animals
"Hare-wallaby Woman." Dreamtime goddess. Dreamtime refers to the mythological past. [Savill 1978]

Minma milbali
Australia, *Goanna*
Fate; Immortality
"White Goanna Woman."

Minma milbali, with Minma waiuda, is a spirit animator. Each child is given a spirit that has brought with it some of the life essence of Dreamtime (the mythological past). [Berndt 1974]

Minma mingari
Australia
Evil; Earth and Nature
"Mountain Devil-woman." Dreamtime goddess of the Gibson Desert. Dreamtime refers to the mythological past. See also *Mingari.* [Savill 1978]

Minma Nganamara   See *Djugurba.*

Minma waiuda
Australia
Hunting and Wild Animals
"Possum-woman." A goddess from Dreamtime (the mythological past) worshiped in central Australia. With *Minma milbali* she is a spirit animator. See also *Waiuda.* [Berndt 1974]

Minyaburu, The
Australia
Creator of Life
Creator goddesses of the northwest. [Mounteford 1965]

Miralaidji   See *Djanggawul.*

Miru
Polynesia: New Zealand; Rarotonga Island
Heaven and Hell; Immortality; Family and Tribes
Goddess of the lowest three underworlds. Her home is called Tatauotepō, the door of the night. She is also associated with kava roots. On Rarotonga she is the mother of Tau-titi and on Mangaia her children are *Karaia i teata* and *Kumu tonga i te po.*

 Tatauotepō is near the place where the spirits of the dead leap into the arms of their ancestors. Miru stands with her net to catch the departed spirits. She puts them in her ovens and eats them.

Also the name of a male deity. See also *Miru kura.* [Craig 1989; Eliot 1976; Leach 1992; Monaghan 1981; Savill 1078; Sykes 1968]

Miru kura
Polynesia: Mangaia Island
Ugliness; Heaven and Hell; Immortality; Ceremonies
Ugly old woman. The cannibal of the underworld, who devours dead souls.

 Miru kura cooks the spirits of the dead in her oven. She is assisted by Akaanga, who uses a net to catch the spirits, then feeds them worms and beetles and drugs them with kava, the drink of the gods.

See also *Miru.* [Craig 1989]

Moa kura ma nu   See *Moakura.*

Moakura
Polynesia: New Zealand, *Maori*
Mother and Guardian; Weather; Water
Goddess who saved a few humans by swallowing the floodwaters. Alternate form: Moa kura ma nu. [Craig 1989]

Moana nui ka lehua
Polynesia: Hawaii
Demi-animals; Fishing and Water Animals
Mermaid goddess. Companion of *Pele.* Alternate form: Hale lehua. [Beckwith 1940; Craig 1989; Leach 1992]

Moa'ri
Melanesia: New Guinea, *Kamano, Ururufa*
Unknown
Goddess. Counterpart of Wainako. [Berndt 1965; Leach 1992; Savill 1978]

Mo'e hau i te ra'i
Polynesia: Tahiti
Unknown
Beloved goddess. Daughter of creator god Ta'aroa and *Papa raharaha.* [Craig 1989]

Mo'e ruru'a
Polynesia: Tahiti
Creator of Life; Mother and Guardian
Creation goddess. She guards the world. [Craig 1989]

Moitjinka
Australia, *Munrinbata*
Earth and Nature
Earth mother. Similar to *Kunapipi.* [Leach 1992; Robinson 1966]

Moko
Polynesia: Easter Island
Reptiles; Arts
"Lizard Woman." She taught tattooing to the people.
[Leach 1992; Metraux 1940]

Moku hinia
Polynesia: Hawaii
Reptiles
Lizard goddess of Māui. [Beckwith 1940; Craig 1989; Leach 1992]

Mo'o, The
Polynesia
Happiness; Reptiles; Demi-animals; Fishing and Water Animals
Water nymphs or lizard deities. According to some, they are monsters. According to others, the Mo'o appear as mermaids with voluptuous bodies, and they can live on land as well as in the water. They are said to be very flirtatious, but, having no male companions, they flirt with each other. They gather flowers and vines, making garlands for themselves. When they tire of land, they swim to undersea caves to rest. They were companions of *Ra'i ra'i*. See also *Mo'o i nanea*. [Craig 1989; Melville 1969]

Mo'o i nanea
Polynesia: Hawaii
Reptiles; Family and Tribes
"Self-reliant Mo'o." Matriarch of all lizard deities, she brought her children to Oahu from the mythical land of Ke'alohilani.
 Mo'o i nanea gave guidance to 'Aukele nui a iku and helped him by eating his enemies. She also stretched her body to make a bridge that Ha'ina kolo crossed to find her husband, Kū 'ai helani.
See also *Mo'o*. [Beckwith 1940; Craig 1989; Leach 1992; Westerveldt 1963]

Mortlock
Micronesia
Creator of Life
Creator goddess similar to *Lorop*. Alternate form: Nomoi. [Monaghan 1981]

Mu mu whango   See *Mumuhanga*.

Mudungkala
Australia
Creator of Life; Earth and Nature
Creator goddess who takes the form of a blind woman.
 Mudungkala rose out of the earth, bringing three babies with her. She created the land of Tiwi. She separated Melville Island from the rest of Australia by forming a channel that filled with water. She formed the channel by circling Australia on her hands and knees. She then decreed that the island would be filled with vegetation and animals, and she left her son and two daughters to live there. [Roberts 1973; Senior 1985]

Muiu'uleapai
Polynesia: Samoa
Family and Tribes; Poverty; Agriculture; Unhappiness
Deity. Daughter of *Sināsa'umani* and Tagaloaui, granddaughter of the sun god, Tagaloa.
 Muiu'uleapai married the king of Fiji and lived on his island. Her husband's parents accused her of causing a famine that occurred shortly after she arrived. Her brother, Taeotaloga, heard of her troubles and brought breadfruit trees to Fiji. The famine ended, and Muiu'uleapa was reunited with her husband's family. [Craig 1989]

Mulu mulu
Australia, *Ungarinyin*
Magic; Destroyer of Life; Ceremonies
Witch.
 Mulu mulu lives at the bottom of wells. She catches adults and children, whom she skins and eats.
See *Bila* for an explanation of cannibalism. [Eliade 1987]

Mulukuausi, The
Melanesia: Trobriand Islands; New Guinea
Evil; Magic
Dangerous sorcerers who capture the dead and eat their organs. [Wedeck and Baskin 1971]

Mumuhanga
Polynesia: New Zealand, *Maori*
Earth and Nature
Totara tree goddess. Wife of Tāne. Alternate forms: Mu mu whango. [Best 1924; Leach 1992; White 1987]

Mumuna
Australia
Creator of Life
Ritual name of *Kunapipi*. [Monaghan 1981]

Munbakuaku
Australia, *Anula*
Wild Birds; Weather
"Dollar Bird." She makes rain. Her consort is the water-snake god, Gnurluwa, who makes rainbows. [Leach 1992; Spencer 1904]

Mundikara
Australia
Wild Birds; Unhappiness
Bird deity.
Mundikara's husband was angry with her. He vented his anger by putting her on an island and throwing rocks at her. Badly wounded, she changed into a water hen and hid in the reeds.
Aboriginal mothers tell their children this story to explain the water hen's habit of hiding in the reeds. See also *Wanatjilda*. [Roberts 1973]

Munga munga, The
Australia
Charisma
Daughters of *Kunapipi*. Kunapipi used her daughters to entice men so that she could eat them. Identified with the *Wawilak*. [Savill 1978]

Muri ranga whenua
Polynesia: New Zealand, *Maori*
Family and Tribes
Progenitor of Maori people. [Alpers 1966]

Muri whaka roto   See *Muriwhakaroto*.

Muriwhakaroto
Polynesia: New Zealand, *Maori*
Mother and Guardian; Fishing and Water Animals
Mother goddess of small fish. Alternate form: Muri whaka roto. [Alpers 1966; Craig 1989]

Murupiangkala
Australia
Sun and Day
Sun woman of Melville Island. Daughter of *Mudungkala*. [Leach 1992; Mounteford 1958]

Mutjingga   See *Karwadi*.

Nā keo lani
Polynesia: Hawaii
Health and Healing
   Goddess of healing. [Craig 1989]

Na kino wailua
Polynesia: Hawaii
Unknown
   Goddess. Sister of *Hokoiolele* (see for story). [Beckwith 1940]

Na lehua 'aka'aka
Polynesia: Hawaii
Unknown
   Goddess. [Beckwith 1940]

Na maka haha'i   See *Nā maka o kaha'i*.

Nā maka o kaha'i
Polynesia: Hawaii
Fire; Water; Earth and Nature; Justice; Magic; Immortality
   Goddess of fire, sea, and land. She rules the surface of the water. Older sister of *Pele*. Nā maka o kaha'i was born from the breasts of her mother, *Haumea*. She is associated with the romantic hero 'Au kele nui a iku. Her servants are *Ha'apua 'inanea* and *Upoho*.

   Because Nā maka o kaha'i and Pele did not get along, Pele left their home on the mythical island of Kā maka o kaha'i and went to Hawaii. Nā maka o kaha'i became the powerful chief of the Mū (first humans) and the menehune (fairies). She could fly, regenerate her body if it were cut in pieces, and turn people to ashes by raising her skirt in their direction.
   Alternate forms: Na maka haha'i, Namakaokahai. [Craig 1989; Leach 1992]

Nabudi, The
Australia: Arnhem Land
Evil; Destroyer of Life
   Malevolent goddesses of illness.

   Men who venture out alone may be shot with an invisible dart that makes them ill. It is done by a Nabudi woman. [Roberts 1973]

Nafanua
Polynesia: Samoa; Tonga Islands
War; Immortality; Heaven and Hell; Weather
   War deity and goddess of Vaiola, the rejuvenating bathing place in the afterworld that contains the water of life. Daughter of Saveasi'uleo or Leosia and *Tilafaigā* or *Taemaā*, twin sister of *Tobukulu*.

   Nafanua was born as a clot of blood, and her mother threw her away. Her father retrieved the clot and brought her to life.
   She is prayed to for success in battle and is honored with coconut fronds. In Tonga, Nafanua is a rain goddess, daughter of Tokilagafanua and *Hina tuafuaga*, mother of *Tafakula*. [Craig 1989; Leach 1992]

Nahinahi ana
Polynesia: Hawaii
Household Affairs
   Goddess of printing and coloring tapa. Alternate form: Hina 'ulu 'ōhi'a. [Craig 1989]

Namaka
Polynesia
Water
   Sea goddess. [Beckwith 1940; Monaghan 1981]

Namakaokahai   See *Na maka o kaha'i*.

Namita
Melanesia: New Guinea, *Papuan*
Creator of Life; Arts; Education and Knowledge
   Creator goddess. Fertilizing herself with her big toe, she gave birth to twins. She taught them the arts and skills necessary to survive on earth. She asked to be killed, and her blood brought forth the first humans. Alternate form: Namite. [Lurker 1984]

Namite   See *Namita*.

Narama
Australia
Evil; Weather; Reptiles; Destroyer of Life
   Malevolent rainbow serpent-woman of the Liverpool River area. She kills people who get too close to the water hole that is her home. Water holes are believed to be entrances to the world of the spirits. [Leach 1992; Mounteford 1958]

Narina
Australia
Wild Birds; Love and Sexuality; Justice; Unhappiness
   Bird deity. Wife of Yurumu, the eagle-man.

   Narina was seduced by Yurumu's friend Kilpuruna. When Yurumu found out, he planned to kill Kilpuruna. While hunting for honey, Yurumu pushed Kilpuruna out of a high tree. Kilpuruna was so flattened by the fall that he became a blanket lizard. When Narina found out her lover had been killed, she changed into a white cockatoo and flew away, calling mournfully for Kilpuruna. Yurumu also flies, searching for the lizard so he can destroy him.
   See also *Parabaruma*. [Roberts 1973]

Narpajin
Australia, *Murinbata*
Weather; Reptiles; Demi-animals; Education and Knowledge
   Rainbow snake goddess. She is half woman and half snake. She was the guardian of the ritual songs and law, but they were stolen from her. [Leach 1992; Robinson 1966]

Naruni
Australia
Wild Birds; Hunting and Wild Animals; Family and Tribes; Love and Sexuality; Justice; Unhappiness
   Mother of the platypus.

   Naruni had been promised in marriage to an elder in her tribe, but she ran away with a young lover. When she returned to the tribe, as a punishment, she was changed into a duck and banished. Living on a river with her lover, Naruni hatched two eggs. They contained strange, furry, web-footed, duck-billed creatures. Unable to return to her home, and disappointed in her offspring, Naruni died. Her children remained and increased. [Roberts 1975]

Nau fiora
Polynesia: Tikopia
Mother and Guardian
   Oven goddess. Guardian of the women who die in childbirth and who go to Rangifaerere (heaven). [Firth 1967a; Leach 1992]

Nau taufiti
Polynesia: Tikopia
Evil; Destroyer of Life
   Goddess of sickness and evil. One of the *Pufine ma*. Her twin sister is *Mafurere*. Alternate forms: Mafutoka, Rautoro. [Firth 1967a; Leach 1992]

Na'vahine
Polynesia: Hawaii
Order
   "Goddess of Serenity" or "Lady of Peace." The feminine generative force of the sun. Daughter of Teave, wife of Tāne, mother of *Rata, Tapo, Hina,* Rono, Tanaroa, and Tu. Alternate forms: Marama, Vahine te ra, Ta vahine te ra, Uri uri. [Leach 1992; Melville 1969; Wedeck and Baskin 1971]

Ndengei
Melanesia: Fiji Islands, *Na Kauvandra*
Creator of Life; Reptiles
   "Old Woman." Creator goddess in the form of a serpent. She incubated birds' eggs and hatched the first humans. [Savill 1978]

Ndimailangi
Melanesia: Lau Islands; Fiji Islands
War
   War goddess of Uruone. [Craig 1989; Leach 1992]

Ne kidong   See *Tabui kor.*

Ne te re'ere
Micronesia: Gilbert Islands
Earth and Nature
   Tree goddess. [Cotterell 1979]

Nei aro maiaki
Micronesia
Directions
   Goddess of the south. Alternate form: Nei Aro-maiaki. [Savill 1978]

Nei auti
Micronesia: Gilbert Islands
Insects; Selfishness
   She made insects to annoy the people. [Leach 1972]

Nei bairara
Micronesia
Weather
   Wind goddess. [Savill 1978]

Nei marena
Micronesia: Gilbert Islands
Unknown
   "The Woman Between." [Cotterell 1979]

Nei matamona
Micronesia
Mother and Guardian; Magic
   Tebongiroro goddess impregnated by a sunbeam. Mother of *Nei te ra'aiti.* [Savill 1978]

Nei nguiriki
Micronesia: Gilbert Islands
Creator of LIfe; Fishing and Water Animals
   "First Woman." She gave birth to fishes. [Cotterell 1979]

Nei te arei n tarawa
Micronesia
Unknown
   Island goddess. Alternate form: Nei Te-arei-n-Tarwa. [Savill 1978]

Nei te ra'aiti
Micronesia
Directions
   Goddess of the east. Daughter of *Nei matamona* of Tebongiroro. [Savill 1978]

Nei te re'ere
Micronesia: Ellice Island
Unknown
   Goddess. [Savill 1978]

Nei te tauti
Micronesia
Fishing and Water Animals
   Porcupine-fish woman. [Savill 1978]

Nevinbimba'au
Melanesia
Evil; Ugliness; Ceremonies
   Ogre who was the goddess of initiation. [Carlyon 1982; Monaghan 1981]

Newe   See *Hoku kau opae.*

Nga lalbal
Australia, *Yuin*
Unknown
   Mother of Daramulum (Thuremlin), the chief god. Mother and son lived together on earth before humans appeared. [Jobes 1962]

Ngalijod   See *Ngaljod.*

Ngaljod
Australia: Arnhem Land
Weather; Reptiles; Disorder; Destroyer of Life; Mother and Guardian; Education and Knowledge; Ceremonies
   Rainbow snake goddess. If she is disturbed, she can cause water holes to overflow, drowning people. Ngaljod created people and taught them how to find food. She is a participant in male initiation rites. (See *Karwadi* for description of rites.) She also plays a part in female puberty rites, which occur when menstruation begins. During her menstrual period, the girl goes into seclusion to keep from attracting Ngaljod's attention. At the end of this time, she is covered with red ochre, a white crescent moon is painted below her breasts to help to regulate her menstrual period, and, sometimes, a depiction of Ngaljod is painted between her breasts. See also *Julunggul.* Alternate forms: Ngalijod, Ngaloit, Numereji. [Berndt 1974; Johnson 1988; Leach 1992]

Ngaloit   See *Ngaljod.*

Ngaore
Polynesia: New Zealand, *Maori*
Earth and Nature
   "Tender One." Goddess of a rush-like grass called toetoe. Wife of Tāne. [Savill 1978]

Ngārara huarau
Polynesia: New Zealand, *Maori*
Reptiles; Demi-animals; Magic
   Part-lizard, part-human sorcerer. [Craig 1989]

Ngaumataki'one
Melanesia: Bellona Island
Family and Tribes
   Malevolent ancient goddess brought from the homeland, 'Ubea. Progenitor of two goddesses: a daughter, *Tungi'one,* and a granddaughter, *Ngaumataki'one.* All three drive people mad. [Craig 1989]

Ngeipau
Melanesia: Bellona Island
Unknown
   Goddess of Kaitu'u clan, daughter of *Ekeitehua*. [Craig 1989]

Nge'obiongo
Melanesia: Bellona Island
Household Affairs; Fire
   Goddess of ovens and protector of homes. [Craig 1989]

Nguatupu'a
Melanesia: Bellona Island
Sky and Heavens; Metals and Minerals
   Sky goddess of Tanga clan. Daughter of *Sinakibi*. She married her brother, Tepoutu'uingangi. The islanders worship them as sacred stones. [Craig 1989]

Nibora
Micronesia: Truk Islands
Directions
   "The Powerful." Goddess of the south. [Bollig 1927; Leach 1992]

Nigoubub
Micronesia: Truk Islands
Fishing and Water Animals; Creator of Life; Mother and Guardian
   Creator of the earth and humans. She is an eel that rests the earth on her breast. She is beseeched by those wanting children or help in childbirth. [Bollig 1927; Leach 1992]

Nihoniho teitei
Polynesia: Tahiti
Mother and Guardian
   Guardian of the world. See also *Tahu'a* and *Firifiri 'Aufau*. Alternate form: Nihoniho teitei. [Craig 1989]

Nihoniho tetei   See *Nihoniho teitei*.

Ningarope
Australia
Stars and Planets
   Star goddess of Encounter Bay. Mother of the star gods Pungngane and Waijungngari. [Leach 1992; Woods 1879]

Niniano
Polynesia: Marquesas Islands
Family and Tribes; Health and Healing; Fishing and Water Animals
   Ancestor of the Marquesan tribe Tui.
   Niniano gave birth to an egg that was swept away in a river. It hatched into a fishlike being, Tiu. Niniano sent her daughter, Te ipo atu, to find Tiu and to wash him with medicinal herbs. Tiu then took human form. [Craig 1989]

Niniganni
Melanesia: New Guinea, *Baga*
Creator of Life; Reptiles; Fate
   Creator goddess in the form of a python. She foretells fortune and wealth. [Johnson 1988]

Nisarere
Micronesia: Truk Islands
Household Affairs; Magic
   Goddess of weaving and sorcery. Sister of Onulap. [Bollig 1927; Leach 1992]

Nisoukepilen
Micronesia: Truk Islands
Demi-animals; Fishing and Water Animals
   Sea goddess. She is half eel and half human. [Bollig 1927; Leach 1992]

Nomoi   See *Mortlock*.

Nona
Polynesia: Tahiti; Society Islands (Ta'aroa)
Evil; Family and Tribes; Destroyer of Life; Justice; Love and Sexuality; Unhappiness
   Ogre who guards the sweet-scented oil. In Tahiti, Nona is a cannibalistic high chief in the district of Mahina.
   Nona's daughter, Hina, hid her lover in a cave, but Nona found him and ate him. Hina fled from her mother and took refuge with No'a huruhuru, who killed Nona and became Hina's husband.
   Nona is another name for *Haumea* in Tahiti. See also Roman *Nona*. [Bonnerjea 1927; Craig 1989; Jayne 1925; Redfield 1931; Savill 1978]

Nu akea
Polynesia: Hawaii
Mother and Guardian
   Goddess of nursing mothers on the island of Molokai. [Craig 1989]

Nua
Polynesia: Tuamotu Islands
Magic; Wild Birds
   Witch who could change forms. See also *Mere hau*. [Craig 1989]

Nu'a kea
Polynesia: Hawaii
Mother and Guardian
   Goddess of lactation who protects children. [Beckwith 1940; Craig 1989; Leach 1992]

Nujka'u
Polynesia: Rotuma
Destroyer of Life; Magic; Selfishness
   Sister of *Nujmaga*.
   Nujka'u and Nujmaga ate a young girl named Kau'utufia. From Kau'utufia's head grew a giant tree. Nujka'u and Nujmaga climbed the tree to the heavens because they were afraid Kau'utufia's grandmother might seek revenge. While in the heavens, the sisters played a mean trick on a pair of blind Siamese twins. Later they separated the twins and gave them their sight. [Craig 1989]

Nujmaga
Polynesia: Rotuma
Destroyer of Life; Magic; Selfishness
   Sister of *Nujka'u* (see for story). [Craig 1989]

Numereji   See *Ngaljod*.

Numma Moiyuk
Australia, *Yulengor*
Water; Mother and Guardian; Family and Tribes; Education and Knowledge
   Ocean deity.
   Numma Moiyuk appeared as a very fat woman, carrying inside of her all of the children needed to populate Australia. She gave them fresh water, food and the skill to obtain it, and tools for a spiritual life. [Monaghan 1981]

Nungeena
Australia
Mother and Guardian; Earth and Nature; Wild Birds;
Life/Death Cycle
Mother spirit who lived in a waterfall. She created the
Earth and the birds.

*At the request of Baiame, Nungeena created birds to
help control insects, which were taking over the earth
and eating all of the vegetation. Nungeena created the
lyre bird and other birds; her spirits copied Nungeena's creations
and also made water birds, night birds, swift birds, and tiny
birds—the birds that could fly fast and catch insects. The world
was saved. Baiame thought the birds were beautiful and gave them
songs to sing. Nungeena did not like the noisy voices he gave the
crow and the kookabura.* [Reed 1973; Reed 1978]

Nu'umealani
Polynesia: Hawaii
Weather
Cloud goddess. [Craig 1989]

Nu'usanga
Melanesia: Bellona Island
Unknown
Goddess. [Craig 1989]

Nuvarahu
Polynesia
Heaven and Hell
A *Turehu* (person of the underworld).

*Nuvarahu tried to leave the underworld with a sacred
garment. The guardian of the opening to the underworld
took the garment from her and allowed her to pass. As
soon as she left, he shut the door and never again granted a living
person entrance to the underworld.* [Jobes 1962]

Nyapilnu
Australia, *Yiritjashewas*
Family and Tribes; Household Affairs; Education and
Knowledge
Ancestor goddess. She discovered that tree bark could be
used to construct shelters and taught the people this craft.
[Monaghan 1981]

Ochirka   See *Alinga.*

'Ohu tū moua
Polynesia: Tahiti
Earth and Nature; Time
Earth mother. She insures the return of spring. Daughter of
Tefatu and *Fa'ahotu.* [Craig 1989]

One kea
Polynesia: Hawaii
Metals and Minerals; Time
"White Sands." In the autumn, she takes the sands to wash
them, returning them in the spring. [Ashdown 1971; Leach
1992]

One kura
Polynesia: Tuamotu Islands
Creator of Life
First woman. Wife of Tiki, the first man.

*One kura lived in the land of Havaiki te araro with her
father, Mati. One rua, Tiki's mother, came to Havaiki te
araro to find a wife for her son. She chose One kura. The
two were married. For a long time, they had no children. After
invoking the gods, One kura gave birth to Hina.*
See also *One rua.* [Craig 1989]

One rua
Polynesia: Tuamotu Islands
Unknown
Goddess in the land of Havaiki nui a, which is the original
homeland of the Polynesians. Mother of the hero Tiki. See
also *One kura.* [Craig 1989]

One u'i
Polynesia: Marquesas Islands
Earth and Nature
Earth mother. [Craig 1989]

Opae
Melanesia: New Guinea, *Kiwai*
Creator of Life
Creator goddess. Her abandoned child was cared for by a
bird who covered it with the taro plant. The taro grew and
became food for the people. [Eliade 1987]

Opopu
Polynesia: Rotuma
Unknown
Island goddess. [Craig 1989]

'Ōrerorero
Polynesia: Tahiti
Mother and Guardian
Guardian of the world. See also *Tahu'a* and *Firifiri 'aufau.*
[Craig 1989]

Oru
Polynesia: Tahiti
Creator of Life
Primordial goddess who created the earth. She and her
husband, Otaia, became the first parents. [Leach 1992;
Williamson 1933]

Osooso
Melanesia: Bougainville; Solomon Islands
Family and Tribes; Unhappiness
Goddess of suicides. Associated with *Makunai,* Horomorun,
and Konopia, they are all the ancestors of the Eagle people.
[Leach 1992; Oliver 1967]

Ouli   See *Uli.*

Pa'a o wali nu'u
Polynesia: Hawaii
Unknown
Goddess. [Craig 1989]

Paea
Polynesia: New Zealand, *Maori*
Sky and Heavens
Sky goddess. Daughter of Rangi. See also *Pāia.* [Craig
1989]

Pahula   See *Pahulu.*

Pahulu
Polynesia: Hawaii
Magic; Justice
Patron of sorcerers. She possesses *mana,* the sacred power
that embodies all the energies in the universe. She ruled
Molokai and part of Māui from her home on Lanai. Alternate
form: Pahula. [Craig 1989]

Pa'i alo
Polynesia: Hawaii
Arts
    Goddess of the hula. See also *Pa'i kua*. [Craig 1989]

Pa'i kauhale
Polynesia: Hawaii
Mother and Guardian
    Protector of villagers. [Craig 1989]

Pa'i kua
Polynesia: Hawaii
Arts
    Goddess of the hula. See also *Pa'i alo*. [Craig 1989]

Pāia
Polynesia: New Zealand, *Maori*
Mother and Guardian; Creator of Life
    Mother goddess. Daughter of Rangi, sky god, and *Papa*, earth mother. Wife of Tāne and mother of all humans. See also *Paea*. [Craig 1989]

Pakoti
Polynesia: New Zealand, *Maori*
Earth and Nature
    Mother of flax. Wife of Tāne. [Craig 1989]

Palabultjura
Australia, *Aranda*
Fishing and Water Animals; Family and Tribes
    Fish ancestor deity. [Leach 1992; Robinson 1966]

Palpinkalare
Australia
Justice
    Goddess killed by Marmoo, the "Evil One." To avenge her death, Marmoo was killed. [Reed 1973]

Pani
Polynesia: New Zealand, *Maori*
Heaven and Hell; Magic; Agriculture
    Plant deity.
    Pani was a mortal whose husband stole sweet-potato seeds from a star. When he slept with Pani, she became impregnated and gave birth to sweet potatoes. Each of her children is a different variety of sweet potato. Pani then went to the underworld, where she continues to grow sweet potatoes.
    See also *Pani tinaku*. [Carlyon 1982; Craig 1989; Monaghan 1981; Schmidt 1951]

Pani tinaku
Polynesia: Hawaii
Magic; Agriculture; Wealth
    Sweet-potato goddess. Pani tinaku steps into the waters of the Mona riki. She rubs her stomach until her baskets are full of sweet potatoes. See also *Pani*. [Beckwith 1940]

Paninduela
Australia; Tiwi
Ceremonies; Earth and Nature
    Goddess of the totemic eucalyptus tree. Wife of Tukimbini. [Leach 1992; Mounteford 1958]

Papa
Polynesia: Hawaii; New Zealand; Samoa, *Maori*
Earth and Nature; Creator of Life; Love and Sexuality; Unhappiness; Family and Tribes; Metals and Minerals; Magic
    Mother Earth.

    Papa (Mother Earth) and her husband, Rangi (Father Sky), embraced for a long time in the darkness. Between their bodies grew all living things. Finally, Mother Earth and Father Sky were forced apart. Although they are apart, they remain connected by her rising heat and his falling rain. In Hawaii, Papa is the wife of Wākea, whom she left after he committed adultery. She is often identified with Haumea as the mother of the Hawaiian people. In Samoa, Papa is a flat rock that had no vagina. Her husband carved her vagina on the stone and she became pregnant.
    See also *Papa raharaha*. Alternate forms: Papa tū a nuku, Fakahotu, Me ha'i kana, Tuanuku. [Beckwith 1940; Carlyon 1982; Cotterell 1979; Craig 1989; Eliot 1976; Leach 1992; Melville 1969; Monaghan 1981]

Papa raharaha
Polynesia: Tahiti
Mother and Guardian
    "Stratum Rock." Mother of all living things and mother of all the islands. Her husband is Tumu-nui, "Great Foundation," and her son is Te-fatu, "Lord of Hosts and of the Skies." See also *Papa*. [Craig 1989]

Papa tū a nuku   See *Papa*.

Papai a taki vera
Polynesia
Destroyer of Life; Immortality
    Death goddess, an *Aku aku*. As the soul leaves a person's body at night, she captures it, making the person ill. [Craig 1989]

Paparoa i te opunga
Polynesia: Cook Islands
Sun and Day
    "Paparoa at the Sunset." [Craig 1989]

Paparoa i tei tanga
Polynesia: Cook Islands
Creator of Life
    Creation goddess. Wife of Ātea, mother of Te Tumu. [Craig 1989]

Papatea
Polynesia: Rotuma; Samoa; Fiji Islands
Earth and Nature
    Earth goddess and primordial deity. Wife of the sky god Lagatea and mother of Tagaroa. [Craig 1989; Leach 1992]

Para whenua mea
Polynesia: New Zealand, *Maori*
Water
    Mother of waters. Daughter of *Hine tū a maunga* and Tāne. [Best 1924; Leach 1992]

Parabaruma
Australia
Wild Birds; Love and Sexuality; Unhappiness; Magic
    Bird goddess.
    Yurumu and Mudati loved Parabaruma. Yurumu devised a plan to be rid of his rival. He hid pointed sticks in a bandicoot's nest and told Mudati to jump in the nest to catch the bird. Mudati, mortally wounded, changed into a fork-tailed kite and flew away. Yumumu then proposed to Parabaruma, but, knowing of his treachery, she refused. Angry, Yurumu hit Parabaruma on the head with his club until her bleeding skin hung from her face. Parabaruma transformed herself into the masked plover, a bird who has red flaps of skin hanging from its cheeks. Its cry is like Parabaruma's screams of pain as Yurumu beat her.
    See also *Narina*. [Mounteford 1965; Roberts 1973]

Parauri

Polynesia: New Zealand, *Maori*

Wild Birds

Parson-bird goddess. Mother of birds. [Best 1924; Leach 1992]

Parawera nui

Polynesia: New Zealand, *Maori*

Weather

"Mother of the Wind Children." Her husband is Tawhiri-matea. [Best 1924; Leach 1992]

Pare

Polynesia: Hawaii; New Zealand

Fire; Earth and Nature; Disorder

Volcano goddess. Maori romantic heroine. [Monaghan 1981]

Pare arohi

Polynesia: New Zealand, *Maori*

Unknown

"Quivering Appearance of Heated Air." [Best 1924; Leach 1992]

Parekōritawa

Polynesia: New Zealand, *Maori*

Heaven and Hell; Weather

Born in the underworld to *Hine nui te pō*, she later married the sky god, Tāwhaki. Mother of Ue-nuku, the rainbow, and Whatiritiri, the thunder. [Craig 1989]

Parewhenua mea

Polynesia: New Zealand, *Maori*

Weather

Rain goddess. [Monaghan 1981]

Parihai

Polynesia: Hawaii

Family and Tribes; Magic

Daughter of **Haumea.**

With her twin brother, Paritu, Parihai sprang from the top of her mother's head to the heavens in a brilliant shaft of light. The twins did not receive physical bodies until they arrived on earth. They landed in a luxuriant garden, Hawaii. A handsome young boy and a beautiful young girl, their progeny became the Paritu dynasty. [Melville 1969; Wedeck and Baskin 1971]

Pa'u o 'pala'e

Polynesia: Hawaii

Earth and Nature

Fern goddess. [Leach 1992; Westerveldt 1963a]

Pei kua   See *Apekua.*

Pekai

Melanesia: Murray Island

Earth and Nature; Luck

Plant goddess. Worshiped for good luck in gardening. [Savill 1978]

Pele

Polynesia: Hawaii

Fire; Earth and Nature; Disorder; Ceremonies; Love and Sexuality; Beauty; Ugliness

Goddess of volcanic fire. Below the earth, Pele has light but no fire; as she leaves the earth, she erupts with much fire. Offerings are made to her when she threatens an eruption. Pele appears as a hag or a beautiful woman.

Lohi'au fell in love with Pele when she was a beautiful maiden. After only three nights, she left him, saying she would send a messenger. Pele returned to Hawaii, then sent her sister Hi'iaka to fetch Lohi'au. The story of Hi'iaka tells what happened then.

Similar to **Pere.** See also *Hi'iaka* and *Pele'ula,* this section; **Aetna,** Greek and Roman Empires; **Fuj,** Far East. [Carlyon 1982; Cotterell 1979; Eliot 1976; Leach 1992; Monaghan 1981; Stone 1979]

Pele'ula

Polynesia: Hawaii, Oahu

Fate; Love and Sexuality

Prophet on the island of Oahu.

Pele'ula was enamored of Lohi'au, the chief whom Hi'iaka was escorting to her sister Pele. Pele'ula delayed Hi'iaka by challenging her to a game of kilu, a game somewhat like spin the bottle in that it involves erotic rewards (in this case, the favors of Lohi'au). Hi'iaka won and continued her journey to Hawaii.

See also *Pele* and *Hi'iaka.* [Wedeck and Baskin 1971]

Pere

Polynesia: Tahiti; Society Islands (Ta'aroa)

Fire; Earth and Nature; Disorder

Fire goddess. Daughter of Mahu-ike. Her abode is in the bowels of the earth, where the deceased members of the royal family are her servants. Her hair is light auburn, like the fine threads of lava that erupt from her volcanoes. Similar to Hawaiian *Pele.* [Craig 1989]

Pi'i ka lalau

Polynesia: Hawaii

Reptiles; Small Size; Large Size

Lizard goddess from Kauai who can be seen as a giant, pygmy, or lizard. [Craig 1989]

Pinuwali

Melanesia

Evil; Destroyer of Life

Similar to *Dunawali* of New Guinea. [Savill 1978]

Pirili

Australia

Stars and Planets; Unhappiness

Stellar deity.

Pirili was mistreated by her lover and fled to the Milky Way for protection. The goddesses of the Milky Way placed her in the Seven Sisters constellation, the Pleiades, where she remains safely hidden. [Mounteford 1965]

Pīrīrama

Polynesia: New Zealand, *Maori*

Stars and Planets

Goddess of the Pleiades. [Craig 1989]

Pito 'ura

Polynesia: Tahiti

Earth and Nature

Goddess of first coconuts. [Craig 1989]

Po

Polynesia: Hawaii

Primordial Being; Disorder; Creator of Life; Heaven and Hell

Chaos mother. She enveloped everything in the original darkness. She was that from which creation came. Mother of *La'i la'i,* the first woman from whom all others came. Po is also the name of the underworld, the world of spirits, night, and the gods. See also *Po'ele.* [Craig 1989; Jobes 1962]

Po he'enalu mamao
Polynesia
Mother and Guardian; Creator of Life
  Mother goddess who gave birth to the first people. [Leach 1956]

Po lao uli
Polynesia
Domesticated Animals; Agriculture
  Mother of a pig child. She taught the child to cultivate taro and increase the land production. [Leach 1956]

Po ne'a 'aku
Polynesia: Hawaii
Hunting and Wild Animals
  "Night-creeping-away." Part of the sixth pair of primordial deities. Mother of Pilo'i, the rat child. [Leach 1992]

Po tangotango
Polynesia: New Zealand, *Maori*
Moon and Night
  "Gloomy Night." Daughter of *Hine nui te pō*. [Andersen 1928; Leach 1992]

Po urirui
Polynesia: New Zealand, *Maori*
Moon and Night
  "Dark Night." Daughter of *Hine nui te pō*. [Andersen 1928; Leach 1992]

Po'ele
Polynesia
Moon and Night; Earth and Nature; Fishing and Water Animals; Metals and Minerals
  "Darkness." Primordial female of the first pair of deities. Her mate was Kumulipo. Mother of coral, plants, and stone. See also *Po*. [Leach 1956; Leach 1992]

Pohaha
Polynesia: Hawaii
Dawn and Twilight; Mother and Guardian; Small Size
  "Night-just-breaking-into-dawn." Born after *Powehiewhi*. Pohaha is the mother of the tiny, frail, flitting things that are born at dawn. [Leach 1956; Leach 1992]

Poko ha rua te pō
Polynesia: New Zealand, *Maori*
Weather; Ceremonies
  Weather deity. Goddess of winds and storms, rites, and incantations. Wife of Rangi and mother of Hanui-o-rangi and *Anu mātao*. [Craig 1989; Jobes 1962; Leach 1992; Savill 1978]

Polalowehi
Polynesia: Hawaii
Wild Birds; Reptiles; Weather
  "Darkness-streaked-with-glimmering-light." She was born before *Pohaha*. Wife of Popanopano, mother of egg-laying animals and mud-dwelling creatures. [Leach 1956; Leach 1992]

Poli 'ahu
Polynesia: Hawaii
Weather; Love and Sexuality; Justice
  Snow goddess of Mauna Kea on the Big Island.
  Poli 'ahu was a rival of Pele and Hina i ka malama. Poli 'ahu fell in love with the same man that Hina loved. When Hina won the man's heart, Poli 'ahu sought revenge by separating the lovers with alternating heat and cold. [Craig 1989]

Poneiemai
Polynesia
Domesticated Animals
  "Pregnant Night." Primordial mother of the dog. [Leach 1956; Leach 1992]

Porpoise Girl
Micronesia
Demi-animals; Fishing and Water Animals; Unhappiness
  Sea goddess.
  She liked to watch humans, and she would come up onto the beach, hiding her tail. One night, a man took her tail, and she was forced to marry him and stay on land. Similar to swan-maiden tales, when she found her tail, she put it back on and returned to the sea. Her children would not eat porpoise meat for fear of harming their mother. [Carlyon 1982]

Pōti'i tā rire
Polynesia: Tahiti
Magic
  Goddess of sorcery. [Craig 1989; Leach 1992]

Pou te aniwaniwa
Polynesia: New Zealand, *Maori*
Weather
  Rainbow goddess. She represents the lower band of color. The upper, darker band is called Kahukura-pango. [Best 1924; Leach 1992]

Powehiwehi
Polynesia
Fishing and Water Animals
  "Darkness Streaked with Glimmering Light." She and Pouliuli were the second set of primordial twins. Mother of fish and ocean animals. [Leach 1992]

Pu fafine
Polynesia: Tikopia
Commerce and Travel
  "Ritual Oven." Goddess of canoe shed and sacred adz. [Firth 1967a; Leach 1992]

Pūpūmainono   See *Hine pūpūmainaua*.

Pu te hue
Polynesia: New Zealand, *Maori*
Earth and Nature
  She is either mother of the hue gourd or the gourd itself. [Leach 1992]

Pu whakahara
Polynesia: Hawaii
Earth and Nature
  Tree goddess. Associated with Tāne. [Best 1924; Leach 1992; White 1987]

Pua
Polynesia: Hawaii
Magic
  Sorcery goddess on Molokai. She can cause abdomens to swell. [Craig 1989; Leach 1992]

Pua ina noa
Polynesia: Marquesas Islands
Fishing and Water Animals
  Fish goddess. Also wife of Tāne and mother of Papa uka. [Craig 1989]

Puako mopele
Polynesia: Tonga Islands
Domesticated Animals; Demi-animals
Ruler of all the gods of Ha'apai. She has the head of a pig and the body of a woman. Alternate form: Puako-mopele. [Craig 1989]

Puanga
Polynesia: New Zealand, *Maori*
Unknown
Daughter of *Hāpai*. [Alpers 1966]

Puckowie
Australia
Family and Tribes
Grandmother spirit. [Reed 1973]

Pufine i ravenga
Polynesia: Tikopia
Fire
Fire goddess. As an oven deity, she is called *Raup enapena*. Alternate form: Ruataka. [Firth 1967b; Leach 1992]

Pufine ma, The
Polynesia: Tikopia
Destroyer of Life; Evil
Twin goddesses of sickness and evil, *Mafurere* and *Nau taufiti*. [Firth 1967b; Leach 1992]

Puhavao atua
Polynesia: Easter Island
Earth and Nature
Nature goddess. She makes sure the plants produce green leaves. Wife of Atua Metua. [Craig 1989]

Puimi
Melanesia: New Guinea
Ceremonies
Initiation goddess. Her symbol is the small, shrill bull roarer. [Leach 1972; Savill 1978]

Pulelei'ite   See *Sasa'umani*.

Puna hoa
Polynesia: Hawaii
Mother and Guardian
According to one account, the mother of *Hi'iaka*. Wife of Kai-pala-o'a. [Craig 1989]

Pūonoono
Polynesia: Tahiti
Mother and Guardian
"Persistence." Ancient goddess who guards the world. [Craig 1989]

Purlimil
Australia
Love and Sexuality; Unhappiness; Family and Tribes; Earth and Nature; Justice; Immortality; Time
Flower spirit of the dead.

 Purlimil loved a young man named Borola, but she was promised in marriage to an evil man named Tirlta.
Before her marriage to Tirlta could take place, Purlimil and Borola ran away to his people's land on the shore of a beautiful lake. After several years, Tirlta set out to avenge what he considered a great wrong. He planned to kill all of Borola's people and take Purlimil for his own, but in the confusion Purlimil was also killed. The bodies were left on the ground, and their blood covered the soil. The next year, Tirlta returned to gloat. Instead of bones, he found a carpet of scarlet flowers with black eyes, which are called Desert

Peas or Flowers of Blood. Tirlta could feel the spirits of the dead and tried to escape, but a spear from a cloud killed him. Tirlta and the spear remain as small stones on the shore of the lake, which became salty from the tears of the spirits. The spirits return each season, covering the arid plains as the Flowers of Blood. [Mounteford 1965; Roberts 1973]

Pu'uhele
Polynesia: Hawaii
Earth and Nature
Hill deity. A lesser-known sister of *Pele*.

 Pu'uhele was born prematurely and was thrown across the channel to Māui. She traveled about the island and decided to reman at Wānanalua. When she died, she became the hill Ka'uiki by the sea. [Craig 1989]

Qatgoro
Melanesia: Banks Islands
Metals and Minerals; Creator of Life
Creator goddess in the form of a large stone. When she split in two, she gave birth to the tribal hero. [Leach 1956]

Queensland First Woman
Australia
Creator of Life; Earth and Nature
The moon, which in Australia is usually considered a male deity, created First Woman.

 First Woman was made from a box tree. To make her soft and supple, the moon rubbed her with yams and mud. [Farmer 1978]

Quork quork   See *Kwouk kwouk*.

Rā marama
Melanesia: Lau Islands
Family and Tribes
Goddess of Sau clan who is feared by the males. See also *Iloilokula*. [Craig 1989]

Ra'i ra'i
Polynesia
Family and Tribes
"Spirit of Joy and Sunshine." Ra'i ra'i came from heaven to earth to be the mother of the Mu, the first humans. Her companions were the *menehune*, or tiny fairies; the *eepas*, or elves; the *Tupu'a* who lived on the ground; and the *Mo'o* who lived in the water. With the help of *Papa*, Ra'i ra'i gave birth to her first child, Mure, who was quickly followed by *Tu Rua*, *Ha'i*, *Haria*, and Hatea. [Melville 1969; Wedeck and Baskin 1971]

Rakataura
Polynesia: New Zealand, *Maori*
Weather; Arts
Air and music goddess. Daughter of Tāne and mother of *Wheke*. [Craig 1989]

Raluve
Melanesia: Loma; Nsangalau; Lau Islands
Destroyer of Life
She likes humans but gives rashes to those who anger her. [Craig 1989]

Rangahore
Polynesia: New Zealand, *Maori*
Earth and Nature; Metals and Minerals
Nature goddess who gave birth to stones. Her husband was Tāne. [Craig 1989]

Rara
Polynesia: Rotuma
Unknown
  Island goddess. [Craig 1989]

Rata
Polynesia: Hawaii
Intelligence and Creativity
  Goddess of inspiration. Daughter of Tāne and *Na'vahine*, wife of Rono and member of the third heavenly trinity.

Rata flew into the Garden of Abundance, where she inspired the children of Haumea to conquer space and to do with their lives whatever they pleased.
  See also *Rata*, Near East. [Leach 1992; Melville 1969; Wedeck and Baskin 1971]

Rau 'ata'ati
Polynesia: Tahiti
Earth and Nature
  "Prickly-leaf." Forest goddess. Daughter of *Papa raharaha* and Ta'aroa. [Henry 1928; Leach 1992]

Rau 'ata'ura
Polynesia: Tahiti
Earth and Nature
  "Leaf-of-red-stem." Forest goddess. Daughter of *Papa raharaha* and Ta'aroa. [Henry 1928; Leach 1992]

Rau kata ura
Polynesia: New Zealand, *Maori*
Arts
  Goddess of music. Mother of *Wheke*. [Craig 1989]

Rau penapena
Polynesia: Tahiti
Earth and Nature
  "Protecting Leaf." Forest goddess. As an oven goddess, she is called *Pufine i ravenga*. [Henry 1928; Leach 1992]

Rau 'ata mea
Polynesia: Tahiti
Earth and Nature
  "Leaf of Pink Stem." Forest goddess. Daughter of *Papa raharaha* and Ta'aroa. [Henry 1928; Leach 1992]

Rauei
Polynesia: Mangaia Island
Fishing and Water Animals
  Fishing goddess. [Craig 1989]

Raumiha
Polynesia
Mother and Guardian; Magic
  Daughter born from the forehead of her mother, *Haumea*. See also *Hauarani*. [Beckwith 1940; Melville 1969]

Rautoro See *Nau taufiti.*

Rea
Polynesia
Earth and Nature
  "Sheen." She was the lighter sheen of the forest greens. She protected the nature spirits below her in the forest. [Melville 1969]

Re'are'a
Polynesia: Tahiti
Happiness
  Goddess of joy. Daughter of sun god Ra and sun goddess *Tū papa*. [Craig 1989]

Rehua
Polynesia: New Zealand, *Maori*
Family and Tribes
  Ancestor goddess. [Savill 1978]

Repo
Polynesia: New Zealand, *Maori*
Mother and Guardian
  Mother of *Hina*, wife of Māui. [Craig 1989]

Rerenoa
Polynesia: New Zealand, *Maori*
Earth and Nature
  Plant goddess. Wife of Tāne. [Best 1924; Leach 1992]

Rima horo
Polynesia: Tuamotu Islands
Heaven and Hell
  Goblin who lives in the underworld, Kororupo. Mother of *Rima poto* and Rima roa. [Craig 1989]

Rima poto
Polynesia: Tuamotu Islands
Unknown
  Daughter of *Rima horo*. [Craig 1989]

Riri tuna rai
Polynesia: Easter Island
Earth and Nature
  Mother of the coconut. [Craig 1989]

Ro Lei
Melanesia
Unknown
  Island goddess. [Savill 1978]

Ro Som
Melanesia
Water; Wealth; Justice
  "Money." Sea goddess. Falling in love with the hero, she gives him wealth and good fortune. When he insults her, she leaves him penniless and returns to the sea. [Leach 1972]

Rohe
Polynesia: New Zealand, *Maori*
Heaven and Hell; Beauty
  Goddess of the underworld. Beautiful wife of Māui. Alternate form: Koke. [Craig 1989]

Rona
Polynesia: New Zealand, *Maori*
Moon and Night
  Moon goddess. [Jobes 1962; Leach 1992; Monaghan 1981]

Rua hine metua
Polynesia: New Zealand, *Maori*
Mother and Guardian; Happiness; Order
  "Old Mother." One of several ancient goddesses who guard the world. She gives joy and a sense of inner peace. See also *Ruahine nihoniho ro roa*. [Craig 1989]

Rua papa
Polynesia: Tahiti
Creator of Life; Directions
  Creator goddess who, with her husband, Ru, separated the world into the four directions. Grandmother of Māui. [Craig 1989]

Rua tamaine
Polynesia: Mangaia Island; Cook Islands
Fishing and Water Animals
    Fish goddess. [Craig 1989; Leach 1992]

Rua tupua nui
Polynesia: Tahiti
Stars and Planets
    Star goddess. Wife of Atea ta'o nui. Mother of all stars and
planets. [Handy 1920; Leach 1992]

Ruahine nihoniho ro roa
Polynesia: New Zealand, *Maori*
Mother and Guardian; War; Unhappiness
    "Old-woman-with-long-teeth." One of the many ancient
goddesses who guard the world. She brings war and pain.
See also *Rua hine metua.* [Craig 1989; Leach 1992]

Ruānge
Polynesia: Mangaia Island; Cook Islands
Creator of Life; Family and Tribes
    Creator and progenitor of the tribes. Her husband is
Akatauria. [Craig 1989; Sykes 1968]

Ruataka   See *Pufine i ravenga.*

Ruku tia
Polynesia: New Zealand, *Maori*
Unknown
    Goddess. [Savill 1978]

Ruma'u Ari'i
Polynesia: Hawaii
Earth and Nature; Mother and Guardian
    Mother goddess of four children who become coconut
trees in time of famine. Her husband is the breadfruit tree.
Alternate form: Ramau-Arii. [Beckwith 1940]

Runepai
Melanesia: New Britain, *Bola*
Agriculture; Magic
    Food goddess. She placed her body over a fire and was
changed into food for the people. The people learned to plant
and harvest food. [Schmidt 1951]

Saato   See *Sa'ato.*

Sa'ato
Polynesia: Samoa
Weather
    Rain goddess from Savai'i Island. Daughter of Foge and
Toafa. Alternate form: Saato. [Craig 1989]

Sagatea
Polynesia: Samoa
Dawn and Twilight
    "Twilight." [Craig 1989]

Sasa'umani
Polynesia: Samoa
War
    War goddess. Mother of *Pulelei'ite.* [Craig 1989]

Satene
Melanesia: New Guinea
Justice; Heaven and Hell
    "Judgment." Because humans killed *Hainuwele,* Satene
became an underworld goddess. She greeted humans after
their death. Her arms were a door through which the dead
humans attempted to pass. If they succeeded, they

reincarnated as humans; if they failed, they became animals
or spirits. [Eliot 1976]

Shaliom
Melanesia: New Britain
Wild Birds; Demi-animals; Unhappiness
    "Swan Maiden." She was forced to marry a human after he
stole her cassowary-feather apron. See also *Swan Maidens,*
Northern Europe. [Savill 1978]

Sherok
Melanesia: New Guinea, *Arapesh*
Agriculture; Education and Knowledge; Ugliness
    Yam deity.

 *Sherok survived a flood that killed all of the people and
animals of her village. After the flood, she put yams in
all of the hollow places of her body. She looked repulsive
because the yams appeared to be boils. She went to another village
and, after being accepted, she took out the yams to make soup. She
then taught the people how to grow yams.* [Schmidt 1951]

Sian pual'ekia'a   See *Sian pual'etafa.*

Sian pual'etafa
Polynesia: Rotuma
Stars and Planets
    She and her sister, *Sian pual'ekia'a,* became the Pleiades
and Orion. [Craig 1989]

Sienjarolol
Polynesia: Rotuma
Unknown
    Island goddess. [Craig 1989]

Sientafitukrou
Polynesia: Rotuma
Unknown
    Possibly an island goddess. [Craig 1989]

Sikingimoemoe
Melanesia: Bellona Island
Evil; Justice
    Punitive and cruel goddess who makes sure humans obey
her taboos and worship her. [Craig 1989]

Silili
Melanesia: New Guinea
Sky and Heavens
    "Divine Mare." A sky goddess on Normanby Island in the
Papua Gulf off New Guinea. She is an evil deity who steals
and kills people. See also *Silili,* Near East. [Durdin-Robertson
1975; Leach 1992]

Sina
Melanesia: Aniwa Island and Futuna Islands in New
Hebrides group
Moon and Night; Fishing and Water Animals; Love and
Sexuality; Justice; Life/Death Cycle
    Moon goddess. A form of *Hina.*

 *In Samoa, Sina had a pet eel. When the eel grew too
large for its pool, Sina looked for a larger pool. When she
moved him, the eel struck her and had intercourse with
her. For this he was killed. His head was buried, and it grew into the
coco palm.* [Beckwith 1940]

Sina tae o i lagi
Polynesia: Samoa
Unknown
    Goddess. [Craig 1989]

Sinafakalau
Polynesia: Tuvalu
Love and Sexuality; Unhappiness; Immortality
Daughter of *Hina* (*Sina*) and Alona, a cannibal.
 Sinafakalau's best friend was Sinafofalangi.
Sinafofalangi came down from the heavens to visit her
friend and was eaten by Alona. Sinafakalau became so
distraught that her father disgorged her friend. Three days later,
Sinafofalangi revived and flew back to her home in the heavens.
[Craig 1989]

Sinafofalangi   See *Sinafakalau.*

Sinakibi
Melanesia: Bellona Island
Justice; Creator of Life
"Blind Sina." Creator deity. Mother of *Nguatupu'a* and
Tepoutu'uingangi.
 Sinakibi prevented her children from stealing the
life-spirit from a mortal man because the man's wife had
restored Sinakibi's sight. [Craig 1989]

Sināsa'umani
Polynesia: Samoa
Sun and Day
Sun goddess. Wife of Tagaloaui and mother of six children.
Sister of *Sasa'umani.* [Craig 1989]

Sine Matanoginogi
Melanesia: Normanby Island; New Guinea
Weather
Atmosphere goddess. [Leach 1992; Roheim 1946]

Sinebomatu
Melanesia: Dobu
Heaven and Hell; Justice; Immortality
"Woman of the Northeast Wind." Chthonic deity.
Several days after someone dies, his or her spirit leaves
the body and goes to Bwebweso (the afterworld, which
is a hill of the dead on the neighboring Normanby
Island). The spirit carries a betel nut to give to the warder, who is
Sinebomatu or Kekewage. After this fee is paid, and if the spirit is
sufficiently rotted and free from the scars of disease, the spirit can
pass. If a child dies, the warders care for it until one of its parents
dies, so it will have a guardian in the afterworld. [Leach 1972]

Sinekili
Melanesia: Normanby Island; New Guinea
Agriculture
Yam goddess. Her husband is Taubewa. [Leach 1992;
Roheim 1946]

Singano   See *Ekeitehua.*

Sisi
Polynesia: Tonga Islands
Unknown
Goddess who was rescued by the god Tangaloa. (See
Faingaa for story.) [Craig 1989]

Sky Maiden
Melanesia
Demi-animals; Wild Birds; Unhappiness; Sky and Heavens
Goddess whose wings were stolen by a man. This
prevented her from returning to the sky. She cried so much
that the tears washed away the wings' hiding place. She put
them on and flew back to her home in the sky. See also *Swan*
Maidens, Northern Europe. [Bray 1935]

Star Girl
Australia, *Australoid*
Stars and Planets; Fire
Stellar deity.
 Star Girl was said to be a mortal who, when the moon
was not shining, reached into the fire and threw the hot
coals into the sky. The coals became stars that form a
trail of light to guide the people when the moon is too tired to appear.
[Stone 1979]

Sun Woman
Australia, *Arunta*
Sun and Day
Sun goddess. She returns to earth each morning with her
glowing fire. Similar to *Akewa,* South America; *Sun Sister,*
North America; *Ama terasu-o-mi- kami,* Far East; and *Allat,*
Near East. [Stone 1979]

Ta vahine te ra   See *Na'vahine.*

Tabui kor
Melanesia: New Britain
Creator of Life
Creator goddess. Mother of Tilik and Tarai. Alternate form:
Ne Kidong. [Leach 1992]

Taemā
Polynesia: Samoa
War; Arts
War goddess. She supervises tattooing.
 Taemā and Tilafaigā were Siamese twins. They would
swim to neighboring islands. One day, as they were
swimming, a floating log severed the connection that
joined their bodies. On the island of Tutuila they made war clubs
and on Fiji they learned the art of tattooing.
In eastern Samoa, it is *Titi* who is said to be the twin of
Taemā. Anything that grows double is sacred to them, and
they are offended by people sitting back to back. [Craig 1989;
Leach 1992]

Tafakula
Polynesia: Eua Island; Tonga Islands
Weather; Agriculture
Weather goddess. She is prayed to for a good growing
season. [Gifford 1929; Leach 1992]

Tagaloa fofoa
Polynesia: Niue Island
Unknown
Goddess. [Craig 1989]

Tagaloa lahi
Polynesia: Niue Island
Unknown
Goddess. [Craig 1989]

Tagaloa tati
Polynesia: Niue Island
Weather
"Near-rainbow." Wife of the god Kolua. Also mentioned as
a god. [Leach 1992; Loeb 1926]

Tagaloa ulu'ulu
Polynesia: Niue Island
Unknown
Goddess. [Craig 1989]

Tagaloamotumotu
Polynesia: Niue Island
Weather

"Spotted Rainbow." Wife of the god Kalua. Also mentioned as a god. [Leach 1992; Loeb 1926]

Tagisomenaja
Melanesia: New Guinea, *Kamano, Usurufa, Jate, Fore*
Stars and Planets
   Evening star goddess, wife of the moon, Wajubu. [Leach 1992; Savill 1978]

Taha taua toto
Polynesia
Magic; Mother and Guardian
   Born from the forehead of her mother, *Haumea*. See also *Hauarani*. [Melville 1969]

Taha'ura
Polynesia
Magic; Mother and Guardian
   Born from the forehead of her mother, *Haumea*. See also *Hauarani*. [Melville 1969]

Tahi ari'i
Polynesia: Tahiti
Stars and Planets
   Star goddess. Associated with the constellation Auriga. [Handy 1920; Leach 1992]

Tahu'a
Polynesia: Tahiti
Mother and Guardian
   "The Artificer." Ancient goddess who guards the world. The other guardians are *'Aiāru, Fa'a'ipu, Firifiri 'Aufau, Nihoniho teitei, 'Ōrerorero*, and *Tāmaumau 'ōrero*. [Craig 1989]

Tahunui
Polynesia: Vahitahi Island; Tuamotu Islands
Earth and Nature; Ceremonies
   Vegetation deity and goddess of the feasting mats. [Craig 1989; Leach 1992; Stimson 1933]

Tai tapu
Polynesia: Marquesas Islands
War
   Sister of the war god Tū. [Craig 1989]

Taiapua
Polynesia: New Zealand, *Maori*
Unknown
   Daughter of Kupe. Sister of *Matiu* and *Makoro*. [Alpers 1966]

Taio
Melanesia: New Britain, *Lukalai*
Moon and Night
   Moon goddess, wife of the sun, Haro. [Savill 1978]

Tairbu
Polynesia: Society Islands (Ta'aroa)
Weather; Disorder; Justice
   Sky goddess. With the god Veromatautoru, she controls the winds and storms, using them to punish those who forget to honor the deities. [Ellis 1853; Leach 1992]

Taisumalie
Polynesia: Samoa
War; Fishing and Water Animals; Wild Birds
   War goddess incarnated as an eel or bat. Sometimes a god. [Craig 1989]

Tākā
Polynesia: Mangaia Island
Creator of Life
   Creator goddess. Wife of Rongo and mother of *Tavake*. See also *Tavake*. [Craig 1989]

Taka rita
Polynesia: New Zealand, *Maori*
Family and Tribes; Love and Sexuality; Justice
   Adulterous wife of Chief Ue-nuku (the name of several chiefs and gods).
 When Ue-nuku discovered that his wife was committing adultery, he killed her. Her brother, Tā-wheta, took revenge by killing some of Ue-nuku's family. This led to a tribal feud. [Craig 1989]

Taku rua
Polynesia: New Zealand, *Maori*
Stars and Planets; Agriculture
   Star goddess of Sirius. She is invoked for planting and harvest. [Andersen 1928; Leach 1992; White 1987]

Tamaiti ngava ringa vari
Polynesia
Mother and Guardian
   "Soft-bodied." Mother of *Papa*. [Long 1963]

Tāmaumau 'ōrero
Polynesia: Tahiti
Education and Knowledge; Mother and Guardian
   "Tale-bearer." One of the guardians of the world. See also *'Aiāru, Fa'a'ipu, Firifiri 'Aufau, Nihoniho teitei, 'Ōreorero*, and *Tahu'a*. [Craig 1989]

Tane roroa
Polynesia: New Zealand, *Maori*
Unknown
   Daughter of *Rongorongo*. [Alpers 1966]

Tangae
Polynesia: Marquesas Islands
Unknown
   Goddess. [Craig 1989]

Tango tango
Polynesia
Creator of Life; Heaven and Hell
   Creator goddess. She retreated to heaven with her husband and grandmother, *Matakerepo*. See also *Tongo tongo*. Alternate form: Hāpai. [Beckwith 1940; Eliot 1976]

Taonoui
Polynesia: Society Islands (Ta'aroa)
Stars and Planets
   Star goddess in the creation story. [Sykes 1968]

Tapa
Polynesia
Moon and Night
   Name for *Hina* as the moon goddess. [Monaghan 1981]

Tapo
Polynesia
Unknown
   Goddess of the South Pacific. One of the third trinity. Daughter of *Na'vahine*. [Melville 1969]

Tapuitea
Polynesia: Samoa
Destroyer of Life; Evil; Stars and Planets

Cannibalistic deity. Daughter of *Sina* or Itea and Tapu.
Tapuitea married the king of Fiji and had several children. After a time, she grew horns on her head and became a cannibal demon. She ate all of her children except her son, Toivā, and returned to Samoa. Toivā followed his mother and persuaded her to flee to heaven, where she became the evening star Tapuitea or the planet Venus. [Craig 1989]

Tapuppa
Polynesia: Tahiti
Metals and Minerals
    Stone deity. Primeval goddess and mother of Totorro, Otaia, and Oru. [Leach 1992]

Taranga
Polynesia
Heaven and Hell; Agriculture; Mother and Guardian
    Underworld goddess who tends the gardens that produce food for the world. Mother of Māui. Alternate form: Huahega. [Monaghan 1981]

Tatau   See *Urutonga.*

Taua
Polynesia: Puka-puka
Mother and Guardian
    Goddess of women. She is prayed to in times of danger or trouble. [Beaglehole 1938; Leach 1992]

Tāua ki te marangai
Polynesia: New Zealand, *Maori*
Family and Tribes
    Creator goddess. She and Tāne created the first people. [Craig 1989]

Tauwhare kiokio
Polynesia: New Zealand, *Maori*
Earth and Nature
    Tree-fern goddess. [Best 1924; Leach 1992]

Tavake
Polynesia: Mangaia Island
Mother and Guardian
    Mother of Rangi, Mokoiro, and Akatauria. See also *Tākā.* [Craig 1989]

Te anoa
Polynesia: Tahiti
Earth and Nature; Fire
    "Heat of the Earth." Daughter of *Papa raharaha* and Ta'aroa. [Craig 1989]

Te anu mātao
Polynesia: New Zealand, *Maori*
Unknown
    Goddess. [Craig 1989]

Te ata tuhi
Polynesia: New Zealand, *Maori*
Dawn and Twilight
    "Early Dawn." Mother of the moon. [Leach 1992]

Te ipo atu
Polynesia: Marquesas Islands
Unknown
    Daughter of *Niniano.* [Craig 1989]

Te kāhu rere moa   See *Kāhu rere moa.*

Te ku whaka hara
Polynesia
Earth and Nature
    Totara tree goddess. [Leach 1992; White 1987]

Te kui u'uku
Polynesia
Earth and Nature
    Matai tree goddess. [Leach 1992; White 1987]

Te mehara
Polynesia: Tahiti; Society Islands (Ta'aroa)
Education and Knowledge; Water
    "Wisdom." In the district of Vaira'o, Te mehara sits by a spring called *Vai ru'ia,* or "Darkened Water." On moonlit nights she can be seen combing her long hair and conversing with women who have come to seek her favor. [Craig 1989; Leach 1992]

Te mo'o nieve
Polynesia: Marquesas Islands
Family and Tribes; Ugliness; Evil
    Ancient ancestor ogre in Taaoa Valley on Hiva Oa. [Craig 1989]

Te muri
Polynesia: Tahiti
Weather
    "Mother of Winds." [Craig 1989]

Te papa
Polynesia: Tuamotu Islands
Creator of Life
    Creator goddess. [Craig 1989]

Te ra'i tû roroa
Polynesia: Tahiti
Stars and Planets
    "Long-extended Sky." Star goddess located between the constellations of Leo and Hydra. [Handy 1920; Leach 1992]

Te vahine nui tahu ra'i
Polynesia: Raiatea
Fire; Magic; Health and Healing
    Benevolent deity of fire walkers. She dresses in ti-leaf skirts and garlands, and fire walkers use the ti plant in their ceremony. Te vahine nui tahu ra'i makes people well after a serious illness. See also *Vahine nui tahu ra'i.* [Craig 1989]

Tehahine'angiki
Melanesia: Bennell Island
Unknown
    Goddess. Sister of *Baabenga.* [Craig 1989]

Tehainga'atua
Melanesia: Rennell Island
Mother and Guardian
    Mother of *Baabenga.* Also, the name of a sky god on Bellona Island. [Craig 1989]

Tei Tituaabine
Micronesia: Gilbert Islands
Earth and Nature; Life/Death Cycle
    Tree and vegetation goddess. Portrayed as red skinned with eyes that flash like lightning. When she produced no children, she died. Out of her grave grew three trees: from her head the coconut palm, from her navel the almond, and from her feet the pandanus. [Cotterell 1979]

Tepotatango
Polynesia
Heaven and Hell
"Bottom of Hades." Wife of Rangi. [Sykes 1968]

Tere hē
Polynesia: Tahiti
Earth and Nature; Disorder; Fishing and Water Animals
Maiden who was responsible for the division of Tahiti from its original land body. Tahiti was thought to have once been part of a large piece of land that filled the space between Ra'iātea and Hu'ahine, a land called Havai'i or Hawaiki (the original land of the Polynesians).

A sacred meeting of the gods was being held at Opoa, and humans were told to stay inside. Tere hē disobeyed and went swimming. The gods were angry and drowned her. A giant eel tore the land, separating Ra'iātea and Hu'ahine, leaving an island floating free. The spirit of Tere hē, taking the form of a fish, entered the new island and swam away. As she swam, one fin formed Mount Ororhena and another broke off and formed the island of Mo'orea. As other parts of her body broke off, they formed all of the Society Islands; this is where Tere hē is today. [Craig 1989]

Tere'e fa'aari'i mai'i te Ra'i
Polynesia: Tahiti
Sky and Heavens
"Errand To Create Majesty in Heaven." Sky goddess. [Handy 1920; Leach 1992]

Tereteth
Micronesia: Yap Islands; Caroline Islands
Earth and Nature
Coconut goddess. [Christian 1890; Leach 1992]

Tesikubai
Melanesia: Bellona Island
Unknown
Goddess. Daughter of *Teu'uhi*. [Craig 1989]

Te'ura taui e pâ
Polynesia: Tahiti
Stars and Planets
Star goddess. [Handy 1920; Leach 1992]

Te'uri
Polynesia: Society Islands (Ta'aroa)
Moon and Night
"Darkness." Sister of 'Oro. [Henry 1928; Leach 1992]

Teu'uhi
Melanesia: Bellona Island
Unknown
Goddess. Sister of *Ekeitehua*, mother of *Tesikubai*. [Craig 1989]

Tha
Melanesia: Lau Islands; Fiji Islands
War; Destroyer of Life; Wild Birds; Fate; Evil
"Bad." Sister of *Vinaka*. A war goddess, daughter of the winds, who causes mortal death. Vinaka can overcome Tha's powers. Associated with birds of fate that fly in and out of houses. [Craig 1989; Leach 1992]

Tiki
Polynesia: New Zealand, *Maori*
Sun and Day
Light goddess. Wife of the twilight god, Maikoriko. [Lang 1887; Leach 1992]

Tiki kapakapa
Polynesia: New Zealand, *Maori*
Creator of Life; Mother and Guardian
First woman, mother of all humans. [Jobes 1962]

Tilafaigā
Polynesia: Samoa
War; Arts
Goddess of war and tattooing. Sister of *Taemā*, mother of *Nafanua*. [Craig 1989; Leach 1992]

Tilafainga
Polynesia: Samoa
Water; Heaven and Hell; Immortality
Water goddess in Vaiola. In the afterworld, she is the source of rebirth. [Leach 1992; Williamson 1933]

Tima te kore
Polynesia: Harvey Island
Primordial Being
Primeval goddess. Daughter of *Papa* or *Haumea*. [Jobes 1962]

Timu ateatea
Polynesia: Samoa
Unknown
Goddess. [Craig 1989]

Tippakalleum See *Mailkun*.

Titi
Polynesia: Samoa
Unknown
Siamese twin with *Taemā* in eastern Samoa. Anything that is double in shape is sacred to them; this includes such things as double yams, double bananas, and so forth. The twins do not like humans to sit back to back because they consider that a mocking behavior. [Craig 1989]

Titua'abine
Micronesia
Unknown
Goddess created by the friction of heaven and earth moving against each other. [Savill 1978]

Toa hakanorenore
Polynesia: Mangareva (Gambier Islands)
Fishing and Water Animals
Eel goddess. [Buck 1938; Leach 1992]

Toa miru
Polynesia: Mangareva (Gambier Islands)
Mother and Guardian
Childbirth goddess who guides children's souls. She lives in Pouaru, the underworld. [Craig 1989; Leach 1992]

Toafa
Polynesia: Samoa
Weather
Rain goddess. Mother of *Sa'ato*. Sometimes considered a god. [Craig 1989]

Tobukulu
Polynesia: Tonga Islands
Fishing and Water Animals; Wealth
Fish goddess. She is petitioned for a good fish harvest. Twin sister of *Nafanua*, daughter of *Hina*. [Collocott 1921; Leach 1992]

Tobunaygu
Melanesia: Trobriand Island; New Guinea
Reptiles
  Snake goddess. [Locher 1932]

Toi mata
Polynesia: Society Islands (Ta'aroa)
War
  "Axe with Eyes." War goddess to whom human sacrifices
were made. [Cotterell 1979; Leach 1992]

Tomituka
Australia; Tiwi
Weather
  "Monsoon Rain." Melville Island goddess. Daughter of
Kwouk kwouk (see for story) and sister of *Bumerali*. [Leach
1992; Mounteford 1965; Roberts 1973]

Tonga maulu'au
Polynesia: Tonga Islands
Sky and Heavens; Goodness
  Daughter of the heavenly couple *Aouli* and Aofitoki.

*Tonga maulu'au was kidnapped from heaven by a
mortal man. Her parents allowed her to stay on earth,
where she had a daughter, Fakaknaoelangi. When her
husband left her for his niece, Tonga maulu'au became angry and
started to go back to her heavenly home, but she returned when she
heard her daughter crying. She was reconciled with her husband
and stayed on earth.* [Craig 1989]

Tongo tongo
Polynesia: New Zealand, *Maori*
Creator of Life; Sky and Heavens
  Creator goddess. Mother of the moon goddess *Marama*
and sun god Ra. See also *Tango tango*. Alternate form: Hāpai.
[Craig 1989]

Tonu tai
Polynesia: Tonga Islands
Fishing and Water Animals; Water
  "Sea Turtle" or "Tortuous Water." Female of the third pair
of deities born of *Touiafutuna*. Her twin was Tonu uta,
"Tortuous Earth." Mother of *Vele si'i*. [Craig 1989; Leach
1992; Williamson 1933]

Topukulu
Polynesia: Tonga Islands
Weather; Water
  Rain goddess on 'Eua Island. [Craig 1989]

Touiafutuna
Polynesia: Tonga Islands
Metals and Minerals; Creator of Life
  "Metallic Stone." Creator deity. Daughter of Limu and
Kele. Touiafutuna appeared as a large, metallic rock that
spewed forth four sets of twins, who, in turn, were parents
of more deities. The first sets of twins were: Piki and Kele
(a child given the name of Touiafutuna's mother), Atugakai
and *Maimoa a longa*, Tonu uta and *Tonu tai*, and Lupe and
Tukuhali. [Craig 1989; Leach 1992]

Tshikaro
Polynesia
Agriculture; Love and Sexuality; Earth and Nature
  Yam goddess.

*Tshikaro was hidden under the ground. One day a man
dug a hole and unknowingly had sex with the earth.
Tshikaro became pregnant and delivered many yam
tubers.* [Eliade 1987]

Tu
Polynesia: Tahiti; Mangaia Island; Harvey Island
Unknown
  Goddess of Moorea. [Long 1963]

Tu Ai Mehani
Polynesia
Magic
  Goddess born from the forehead of her mother, *Haumea*.
See also *Hauarani*. [Melville 1969]

Tū fe'ufe'u mai i te ra'i
Polynesia: Tahiti
Metals and Minerals
  Sand goddess.

*Tū fe'ufe u mai'i te ra'i was the wife of 'Oro, a
warrior god. Mother of Ai Tūpua'i. 'Oro pushed
her out of the heavens and she landed on earth as a pile
of sand.* [Craig 1989]

Tu i te moana'urifa
Polynesia: Tahiti
Stars and Planets
  Constellation goddess of Hydra. [Handy 1920; Leach 1992]

Tū matua
Polynesia: Mangaia Island
Creator of Life
  Creator goddess. *Vari ma te takere* created her, and they
lived in Avaiki, the depths of the universe, which resembles a
coconut. [Craig 1989]

Tū metua
Polynesia: Mangaia Island
Unknown
  "Straight-speech" or "Stick-by-the-parent." She speaks no
evil. Sixth and last daughter of *Vari ma te takere*. [Craig 1989]

Tu neta   See *Tū papa*.

Tū papa
Polynesia: Cook Islands
Sun and Day
  Sun goddess. Youngest daughter of *Papa*. Mother of
Re'are'a. On Raiatea, Tū papa ("Tu-of-the-lowest-depths")
was wife of the sun god. Alternate form: Tu neta. [Craig 1989;
Sykes 1968]

Tū pari
Polynesia: New Zealand, *Maori*
Reptiles
  Mother of the lizard gods. [Craig 1989]

Tū poro mai   See *Tū poro tū*.

Tū poro tū
Polynesia: Tahiti
Ceremonies
  Proclamation deity. Daughter of *Papa raharaha* and
Ta'aroa. She makes proclamations upon the mountains for
her father and helped to create his first temple. She used his
backbone for the ridge pole, his breastbone to cap the roof,
and his thigh bone for carved ornaments. This became the
model for later temples. Alternate form: Tū poro mai. [Craig
1989]

Tū raki
Polynesia: New Zealand, *Maori*
Moon and Night
  Progenitor of the moon goddess. [Craig 1989]

Tu Rua
Polynesia
Unknown
   Daughter of *Ra'i ra'i*. [Melville 1969]

Tu wae rore
Polynesia
Earth and Nature; Water
   Tree goddess and seaweed deity. Wife of Tāne. Mother of
the kahika-tea, rimu, and tane-kaha trees. [Craig 1989; Leach
1992]

Tuanuku   See *Papa*.

Tuapu'u
Polynesia: Marquesas Islands
Evil; Fishing and Water Animals; Immortality
   Demon goddess who stores fish in an opening in her back.

*Tuapu'u's children gave her eels to eat, and she died.
She revived and chased her children, but they killed her
again.* [Craig 1989]

Tukapua
Polynesia: New Zealand, *Maori*
Weather
   Sky goddess. She takes the form of clouds. [Best 1924;
Leach 1992]

Tukuhali
Polynesia
Creator of Life; Earth and Nature
   Creator of all land and water animals on earth. Daughter
of *Touiafutuna* and twin sister of Lupe. [Craig 1989]

Tuli
Melanesia: Fiji Islands; Samoa
Wild Birds; Creator of Life; Water
   Bird deity. Tuli is a plover that carries messages for Tagaloa.
*Tuli was sent to earth to find dry land and to create
plants, animals, and humans. When Tuli was unable to
find any place without water, Tagaloa threw rocks down
to make islands so that Tuli could begin her creations.*
   Tuli is sometimes considered the same as *Hina* and is
sometimes considered a male deity. [Craig 1989; Leach 1992;
Monaghan 1981; Savill 1978]

Tulpengusu
Melanesia: Bellona Island
Reptiles
   Snake goddess. [Craig 1989]

Tumu iti
Polynesia: Tuamotu Islands (Paumotu) in Society Islands
(Ta'aroa)
Creator of Life
   Creator goddess. She and Tumu nui formed one of the
primal pairs. [Leach 1992]

Tumu te tangotango
Polynesia: Mangaia Island
Unknown
   "Echo." Goddess. [Craig 1989]

Tumuteanaoa
Polynesia: Mangaia Island
Unknown
   "Echo." The fourth goddess created by *Vari ma te takere*.
[Craig 1989; Long 1963]

Tu-neta   See *Tū papa*.

Tungi'one
Melanesia: Bellona Island
Evil; Unhappiness
   Evil goddess who drove people insane. Daughter of
Ngaumataki'one and mother of *Ngaumataki'one*. [Craig
1989]

Tūparahaki   See *Kāhu rere moa*.

Tupengusu
Melanesia: Bellona Island
Reptiles
   Snake goddess. [Craig 1989]

Tupetupe i fare one
Polynesia: Tahiti
Unknown
   Goddess who lives with Tāne. [Craig 1989]

Tupu'a, The
Polynesia
Small Size; Magic; Demi-animals; Wild Birds
   Fairies. Tiny, feminine, winged beings who live in the
branches of flowering trees. They never alight on the ground.
They were companions of *Ra'i ra'i*. [Melville 1969]

Uahea
Polynesia: Tahiti; Tuamotu Islands
Creator of Life
   Creation goddess. Daughter of *Rua papa* and Rū. Mother
of Māui. [Craig 1989]

Ubu
Melanesia: New Guinea
Fire
   Fire goddess. She produced fire in the palm of her hand
and gave the burning coals to the Australian hero. [Reed
1978]

Ufi
Polynesia: Samoa
Unknown
   Goddess. [Craig 1989]

Uhalaoa
Polynesia: Hawaii
Earth and Nature
   Goddess of the garden. [Beckwith 1940]

Ui
Polynesia: Samoa
Moon and Night; Mother and Guardian
   "Darkness."
*Ui heard that the sun was angry and was going to kill
all humans. The next morning, Ui went to the east and
straddled the sun as he began to rise. She made him
agree to go slowly so that there would be more light but not so
slowly that he would kill the people.* [Craig 1989]

Uka o hoheru
Polynesia: Easter Island
Disorder; Ceremonies
   Cannibal goddess who married a human. She left him in a
whirlwind after an argument. See also *Aku aku*. [Craig 1989]

Ukwa'anija
Melanesia: New Guinea, *Kapauka*
Evil; Earth and Nature
   Forest demon. Her husband is Tege. [Leach 1992; Pospisil
1958]

Uli
Polynesia: Hawaii
Magic; Health and Healing; Destroyer of Life
   Sorcerer. She has the power to heal and to kill. *Hi'iaka* invoked Uli to bring Lohi'au back to life. Uli's granddaughter, who is also named Uli, teaches the art of praying a person to death. Also the name of a male deity in Samoa. See also *Hi'iaka*. Alternate form: Ouli. [Beckwith 1940; Craig 1989; Leach 1992]

Uli po'ai o ka moku
Polynesia: Hawaii
Water
   Water goddess. [Beckwith 1940; Leach 1992]

Ungamilia
Australia, *Arunta*
Stars and Planets
   Evening star deity worshiped in central Australia. [Leach 1992; Spencer and Gillen 1968]

Upoho
Polynesia: Hawaii
Reptiles
   Lizard goddess. [Craig 1989]

Uri Uri
Polynesia
Unknown
   Name for *Na'Vahine* and *Marama*. [Leach 1992; Lurker 1984; Melville 1969; Wedeck and Baskin 1971]

Urunganada
Australia, *Walbiri*
Ceremonies
   One of two spirit beings associated with ritual dancing. The other is *Yabadjaudjau*. See also *Yuguruguru*. [Berndt 1974]

Ururupuin
Micronesia
Happiness; Love and Sexuality
   "Night Flirt." Loving and playful daughter of *Inemes*. [Bollig 1927; Leach 1992]

Urutahi
Polynesia: New Zealand
Wild Birds
   Bird goddess. She is the patron of the tui bird. [Craig 1989]

Urutonga
Polynesia: New Zealand, *Maori*
Water
   Sea goddess. Alternate form: Tatau. [Alpers 1966]

U'uhoa
Polynesia: Marquesas Islands
Earth and Nature
   Coconut goddess. [Handy 1923; Leach 1992]

Vahine mau i te pae fenua
Polynesia: Tahiti
Water
   Seashore goddess. She guarded the beaches. [Henry 1928; Leach 1992]

Vahine mau ni'a
Polynesia: Tahiti
Unknown

"She-who-is-responsible-for-holding-everything-together." [Craig 1989]

Vahine nautahu
Polynesia: Tuamotu Islands
Creator of Life
   "Enchantress." She molded Ātea into a recognizable form. [Craig 1989; Leach 1992]

Vahine nui tahu ra'i
Polynesia: Tahiti
Fire; Mother and Guardian; Weather
   Protector of fire walkers, who invoke her to fan them as they walk on the coals. She also controls lightning. She is a friend of *Hina*. See also *Te vahine nui tahu ra'i*. [Craig 1989; Henry 1928]

Vahine te ra   See *Na'vahine*.

Vakai a heva
Polynesia: Easter Island
Unknown
   Goddess. [Savill 1978]

Valelahī
Polynesia: Tonga Islands
Unknown
   Goddess. [Craig 1989]

Vana'ana'a
Polynesia: Tahiti
Mother and Guardian
   "Eloquence." Ancient goddess who guards the world. [Craig 1989]

Vari ma te takere
Polynesia: Mangaia Island
Mother and Guardian
   "The Beginning and Bottom." The primeval mother who tore six children from her sides. She lived in Avaiki, the bottom of the coconut shell that formed the universe. See also *Wari ma te takere*. [Craig 1989; Leach 1992; Long 1963; Savill 1978]

Vele lahi
Polynesia: Tonga Islands
Creator of Life
   Creator goddess. [Craig 1989]

Vele si'i
Polynesia: Tonga Islands
Creator of Life
   Creator goddess. [Craig 1989]

Vie kena
Polynesia: Easter Island
Unknown
   Daughter of *Vie moko*. [Craig 1989]

Vie moko
Polynesia: Easter Island
Reptiles
   Lizard goddess. Mother of *Vie kena*. [Craig 1989]

Vinaka
Melanesia: Lau Islands
War; Fate; Wild Birds; Destroyer of Life; Goodness
   "Good." A war goddess and daughter of the winds, she revives persons whom her sister, *Tha*, kills. Associated with birds of fate that fly in and out of houses. [Craig 1989]

Vinmara
Melanesia
Demi-animals; Wild Birds
  "Web Wing." Swan maiden. [Zimmerman 1964]

Vuhi atua
Polynesia: Easter Island
Unknown
  Goddess. [Craig 1989]

Waha See *Waka.*

Wahīmū See *Ahīm ū.*

Wahini hai
Polynesia
Evil; Destroyer of Life
  Demon who eats children. [Monaghan 1981]

Wai ta iki
Polynesia: Hawaii
Metals and Minerals
  One of the wives of Tama ahua.

 Wai ta iki deserted Tama ahua. He pursued her with great energy, causing changes in the topographical features of the land. He finally found her, and they returned to their cave. The other gods were angry about all the changes Tama ahua had caused, so they turned Wai ta iki and Tama ahua to stone. [Craig 1989]

Waiau
Polynesia: Hawaii
Weather
  Mauna Kea snow goddess. [Leach 1992; Westerveldt 1963c]

Waimariwi
Australia
Creator of Life
  Creator deity. The older of two sister goddesses worshiped in northern Australia. See also *Boaliri.* [Senior 1985]

Waiuda
Australia
Hunting and Wild Animals; Ceremonies; Magic
  "Possum Woman."

Waidua turned into an opossum, and, when her husband burned the tree she was in, she turned into a wooden dish. Her dish is used for drinking blood during religious ceremonies.
  See also *Minma waiuda.* [Berndt 1974]

Waka
Polynesia: Hawaii
Reptiles
  Lizard goddess, or *Mo'o.* She is venerated by female chiefs. Alternate form: Waha. [Beckwith 1940; Craig 1989]

Walewale o kū See *Kini maka.*

Wali manoanoa
Polynesia: Hawaii
Reptiles
  Lizard goddess who can make the government prosperous. Alternate form: Walinu'u. [Beckwith 1940; Craig 1989; Leach 1992]

Walinu'u See *Wali manoanoa.*

Walipolima
Melanesia
Evil
  Similar to *Dunawali* of New Guinea. [Savill 1978]

Walo
Australia
Sun and Day; Mother and Guardian
  Sun-woman. Mother of *Bara.*

 Each day, Walo and Bara traveled across the sky together from their home in the east. One day, Walo sent Bara back home because she realized that two suns traveling together were scorching the earth and the people. [Monaghan 1990; Roberts 1973]

Wanatjilda
Australia
Wild Birds; Unhappiness; Magic
  Bird deity.

 Wanatjilda's husband was very angry with her. He trapped her on an island and began throwing stones at her. To escape, Wanatjilda transformed herself into a diver duck and swam away.
  Mothers tell their children this story to explain why diver ducks can dodge stones. See also *Mundikara.* [Roberts 1973]

Wao
Polynesia: Hawaii
Water
  Water goddess. She is in the upland forests and springs. [Ashdown 1971; Leach 1992]

Waramurungundji
Australia
Creator of Life; Water
  Creator goddess who came out of the ocean. First she made the land, and then she took children, animals, and plants from her body to inhabit it. Similar to *Kunapipi.* Alternate forms: Imberombera, Waramurungundju. [Leach 1992; Monaghan 1981]

Waramurungundju See *Waramurungundji.*

Wari ma te takere
Polynesia: Cook Islands
Family and Tribes; Earth and Nature
  "The Beginning and the Bottom." From her coconut-shell body, she gave birth to the gods. See also *Vari ma te takere.* [Monaghan 1981]

Wauwalak See *Wawilak, The.*

Wawalag, The See *Wawilak, The.*

Wawalug See *Wawilak, The.*

Wawilak, The
Australia, *Murngin*
Creator of Life; Ceremonies; Education and Knowledge; Commerce and Trade; Family and Tribes; Love and Sexuality; Mother and Guardian
  Creator and fertility sister goddesses. They were responsible for civilizing the world. Their travels are the basis of the four great totemic ceremonies that are used in initiation rites.

 The sisters were forced to wander because they were said to have committed clan incest. When they happened upon the pool of Julunggul, they unknowingly let their menstrual blood get into the water, which was not allowed. Julunggul came to the surface and swallowed the sisters and their

children. A flood caused Julunggul to vomit them, but she swallowed them again and again regurgitated them. Each place this happened became a sacred spot for initiation ceremonies.

See also *Julunggul* and *Karwadi*. Alternate forms: Wawalag, Wawalug, Wauwalak. [Carlyon 1982; Leach 1972; Leach 1992; Monaghan 1981]

Wayambeh
Australia
Reptiles; Disorder; Mother and Guardian
"Tortoise Woman."

 Wayambeh married Kookaburra, a bird. This led to many arguments because Kookaburra thought eggs should be laid in nests and Wayambeh thought they should be laid in a hole in the mud. [Reed 1973]

Whaitiri
Polynesia: New Zealand, *Maori*
Heaven and Hell; Ceremonies; Weather; Magic
Cannibalistic underworld deity, goddess of thunder and lightning.

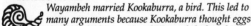 *Whaitiri's chant separated Papa and Rangi so the sky and earth could be formed and the beings that had been conceived between them could have light. Whaitiri lost her sight when her husband gave her fish to eat. He had caught the fish with a hook made of the bones of his relatives whom Whaitiri had eaten. Her sons were able to restore her vision.* [Alpers 1966; Craig 1989; Jobes 1962; Leach 1992; Savill 1978]

Wheke
Polynesia: New Zealand, *Maori*
Unknown
Goddess. [Craig 1989]

Wheṭē
Polynesia: New Zealand, *Maori*
Creator of Life
Creator goddess. She provided the parts for the first people. [Craig 1989]

Wibalu, The
Australia
Disorder; Hunting and Wild Animals; Sun and Day
Women who owned the only boomerangs in the world.

 The Wibalu were powerful because of their boomerangs. The men were jealous and devised a scheme to distract the Wibalu in order to steal the wonderful weapons. Two of the men changed into white swans and flew overhead. The women followed them, and the other men stole the boomerangs. When the Wibalu discovered the boomerangs were gone, they began to accuse one another and fight among themselves. The Wibalu were taken to the sky, and the blood from their wounds stained the clouds scarlet. When the people see a brilliant sunset, they know the Wibalu women are fighting again. [Roberts 1973]

Wirana
Australia
Wild Birds; Mother and Guardian; Metals and Minerals
Bird deity.

Wirana, an eagle-hawk, built a nest high in a tree and laid two eggs. While she was away from the nest hunting for food, a rock pigeon stole the eggs. Wirana tried to kill the thief, but an owl threw a boomerang at Wirana, killing her. Wirana transformed herself into a painting on the wall of a cave in the Kimberley Ranges and changed her eggs into boulders near its opening. [Stutley 1984]

Wulutahanga
Melanesia
Reptiles; Immortality; Weather; Water; Justice; Wealth

Snake goddess. Her father cut her into eight parts, and, after eight days of rain, her body was healed. This process was repeated until, finally, to punish the people, she covered the islands with eight waves. After the flood, only a mother and her child were left. To this pair the goddess gave wealth and food. [Monaghan 1981]

Wurdilapu
Australia, *Yiritja*
Unknown
Sister of *Nyapilnu*. [Monaghan 1980]

Wuriupranala
Australia; Tiwi
Sun and Day
Sun goddess who rises in the east with a torch made of blazing bark.

 When Wuriupranala rises in the morning, she puts powdered ochre on her body. Some falls on the clouds, coloring them red. At the top of her arc, she makes the sky very hot by lighting a fire to cook her lunch. Before she retires to the underground channel that takes her back to the east, she once again powders herself with ochre, causing the red sunset.

Alternate form: Wuriupranili. [Leach 1992; Monaghan 1981; Mounteford 1965; Roberts 1973]

Wuriupranili   See *Wuriupranala.*

Wutmara
Melanesia
Creator of Life
First woman. [Savill 1978]

Yabadjaudjau
Australia, *Walabiri*
Unknown
One of two spirit beings associated with ritual dancing in northern Australia. The other is *Urunganada.* See also *Yuguruguru.* [Berndt 1974]

Yalungur
Australia
Wild Birds; Mother and Guardian
Dreamtime Eagle-hawk. Dreamtime refers to the mythological past.

Yalungur began life as a male, but he was castrated by a god. The god then formed a baby by inserting bloodwood into Yalungur's body. This baby was the first woman. [Savill 1978]

Yam Woman
Melanesia: New Guinea
Agriculture
Food goddess. [Eliade 1987]

Yama enda
Melanesia: New Guinea
Destroyer of Life; Charisma; Earth and Nature
Disease and forest goddess who seduces and kills males. [Savill 1978]

Yeenapah
Australia
Family and Tribes; Unhappiness
Mountain devil. Wife of In-nard-dooah, a man of the Porcupine tribe.

 Yeenapah and In-nard-dooah were married and lived happily for a time, but they were very different in character. After following her husband in search of a new place to live, Yeenapah became discouraged and told

In-nard-dooah she was returning to their home. He left her in a shelter he had constructed on the dry plains and continued his journey. While he was gone, Yeenapah gave birth to five girls and five boys. When he returned, Yeenapah was gone. He followed her, but she said she no longer wanted to live with him because he had treated her badly. Even after she made a new home for herself and her children, In-nard-dooah wanted her. He sat and watched her, leaning against a spear-grass bush. He sat so long that spines grew out his back. [Reed 1973]

Yhi
Australia
Sun and Day; Life/Death Cycle; Education and Knowledge; Immortality

Sun goddess. She sent the summer and winter to make things grow and let them sleep.

 When Yhi left the earth to live in the sky, she told the people that they would die and their bodies would remain on earth but their spirits would join her in heaven. After telling them this, she rose into the sky and became a ball of light, sinking behind the western hills. [Leach 1992; Reed 1973]

Yirbaik baik
Australia
Ceremonies; Domesticated Animals; Destroyer of Life; Wild Birds; Weather

"Old Woman." A cannibalistic deity who had a large pack of dingoes. (See **Bila** for a discussion of cannibalism.)

 Yirbaik baik used her dogs to help her find and kill her victims. The people finally killed her and the dogs.

Yirbaik baik transformed herself into a small brown bird that hides in the bush and is usually seen only at night. If her call is heard during the day, Yirbaik baik is calling the rainstorms to bring water to the dry earth and its inhabitants. [Mounteford 1965]

Yirbaik-baik   See *Yirbaik baik.*

Yuguruguru, The
Australia, *Waneiga*
Unknown

Two spirit beings of northern Australia associated with ritual dancing. See also **Urunganada** and **Yabadjaudjau.** Alternate form: Ininguru. [Berndt 1974]

Yulanya
Australia
Unknown

Spirit children. See **Kutunga.** [Mounteford 1965]

Yulunggul   See *Julunggul.*

Yurlunggur   See *Julunggul.*

SOUTH AMERICA

Amara   See *Mama Pacha.*

Apolonia, Saint
Brazil, *Ita*
Health and Healing
   Goddess of healing invoked for relief of toothaches. [Leach 1992; Wagley 1964]

Asima Si
Brazil, *Mundurucu*
Water; Fishing and Water Animals
   Water and fish goddess. She inhabits the Para, the east mouth of the Amazon River. [Leach 1992; Murphy 1958]

Atoja
Peru, *Aymara*
Earth and Nature; Weather
   Mountain deity. She sends the rain. [Leach 1992; Tschopik 1951]

Axo Mama   See *Axomama.*

Axomama
Peru
Agriculture; Mother and Guardian
   "Potato Mother." She makes potatoes grow to provide food for the people. Alternate form: Axo Mama. [Leach 1992; Redfield 1951; Schmidt 1951]

Ayar
Peru
Education and Knowledge
   Collective name for four sisters and brothers who came from the heavens to earth to teach the people. The sister/wives are *Cura, Huaco, Occlo,* and *Raua* and are "Mothers." See also *Peruvian Mamas.* [Wedeck and Baskin 1971]

Beru
Brazil, *Tecuna*
Evil; Insects; Ceremonies
   Demon who appears as a butterfly at female puberty rites. [Leach 1992; Zerries 1968]

Biu Si
Brazil, *Mundurucu, Para*
Hunting and Wild Animals
   Animal mother who appears as a tapir. [Leach 1992; Murphy 1958]

Boiuna
Brazil; Amazon River
Reptiles; Magic
   Serpent goddess who has great magic. She is much feared by the people. [Senior 1985]

Caipora
Brazil
Hunting and Wild Animals
   Animal goddess. She protects them from hunters. [Senior 1985]

Calounga
Brazil
Destroyer of Life; Water
   In Maranhão, she is a death goddess. In Rio de Janeiro, she is a sea goddess. [Bastide 1978; Leach 1992]

Cavillaca
Peru, *Inca*
Metals and Minerals; Love and Sexuality; Magic; Unhappiness
   Goddess who became a rock in the sea.

✂☼ *Cavillaca was sitting beneath a tree, weaving the wool of a*
white llama, when the god Viracocha saw her. He placed
some fruit next to her, but no one knew who he was
because he was disguised as a beggar. When Cavillaca ate the fruit,
she became pregnant. When the child touched the beggar, indicating
who was his father, Cavillaca was humiliated. She threw herself and
the child into the sea, where they were changed into rocks. The
grieving Viracocha remained by the sea. [Savill 1978; Van Over
1980]

Ceiuci
Brazil
Stars and Planets; Earth and Nature
Star goddess. One of the Pleiades. She created all animal
species. [Monaghan 1981]

Chasca
Peru, *Inca*
Dawn and Twilight; Weather; Mother and Guardian
Goddess of the dawn who also appeared at twilight.
Protector of maidens. Her messengers are fleecy clouds that
drop dew. Equivalent to *Venus,* Greek and Roman Empires.
[Brinton 1882; Jobes 1962; Leach 1992; Redfield 1931]

Chokesuso
Peru
Creator of Life; Water
Fertility goddess. She protects irrigation channels.
Alternate form: Choque Suso. [Alexander 1920; Leach 1992;
Trimborn 1968]

Choque Suso   See *Chokesoso.*

Cobra Grande da Lagoa   See *Doña Rosalina.*

Cocamama
Peru
Love and Sexuality; Earth and Nature; Life/Death Cycle;
Selfishness; Health and Healing; Happiness
Mother of coca. Her plant brings health and happiness.

✂☼ *Cocamama was a woman with many lovers. A jealous*
lover cut her in half. From her body grew the coca
plant.
Alternate form: Cocomama. [Leach 1992; Monaghan 1981]

Cocha
Peru
Weather
Rain goddess. [Reville 1884]

Cocomama   See *Cocamama.*

Copacati
Peru, *Inca*
Water; Unhappiness
Lake goddess. Upset when the people worshiped other
gods, she tore down the temples around Tiahuanaco or threw
them in Lake Titicaca. [Sykes 1968]

Cori Ocllo   See *Ocllo.*

Cura
Peru, *Inca*
Sky and Heavens; Mother and Guardian
One of the *Ayar.* As one of the *Peruvian Mamas,* she is
known by several different names including *Mama Coya,*
Mama Cura, and *Mama Ipa Qora.* [Wedeck and Baskin 1971]

Doña Rosalina
Brazil, *Belem*
Reptiles
Snake goddess. Alternate form: Cobra Grande da Lagoa.
[Leach 1992; Leacock and Leacock 1972]

Dyevae
Brazil, *Tecuna*
Water
Water goddess. [Leach 1992; Zerries 1968]

First Woman
Peru, *Inca*
Family and Tribes; Immortality
Ancestor deity.

✂☼ *First man Guamansuri came down to earth and seduced a*
sister of one of the Gauchemines (darklings). Her brothers
killed Guamansuri, but First Woman was already
pregnant. She died producing two eggs, but one of the offspring
brought her back to life. [Brinton 1876]

Huaco
Peru, *Inca*
War
One of the *Ayar.* In the journey across the country of the
Peruvian Mamas, Huaco is credited with destroying all
members of an opposing tribe. See also *Peruvian Mamas.*
Alternate forms: Mama Huaco, Ipa Huaco, Topa Huaco.
[Leach 1972]

Iamanja
Brazil
Water; Ceremonies
Sea goddess. A summer solstice ritual is held in her honor.
See also *Yemanja,* Africa. [Stone 1979]

Iavure-cunha
Brazil
Earth and Nature
Forest deity in the Xingu River area. [Leach 1992; Villas
Boas and Villas Boas 1973]

Ina
Brazil
Fishing and Water Animals
Dolphin goddess who lives in the Para, the east mouth of
the Amazon River. [Leach 1992; Leacock and Leacock 1972]

Ipa Huaco   See *Huaco.*

Ituana
Brazil
Insects; Heaven and Hell; Stars and Planets; Immortality
"Mother Scorpion." She rules the afterworld from her
home on the Milky Way, and she returns the soul to newborns.
[Johnson 1988; Monaghan 1981]

Jamaina
Brazil, *Belem*
Water; Demi-animals; Fishing and Water Animals
Ocean goddess who appears as a mermaid. [Leach 1992;
Leacock and Leacock 1972]

Jandira
Brazil, *Belem*
Water
Sea goddess. [Leach 1992; Leacock and Leacock 1972]

Jarina

Brazil, *Belem*
Earth and Nature; Happiness
  Tree goddess. A joyful deity who is known to imbibe.
[Leach 1992; Leacock and Leacock 1972]

Jubbu-jang-sangne

Brazil, *Belem*
Earth and Nature; Intelligence and Creativity; Ceremonies
  Tree goddess. She is the head of the Jurema deities. Their
sacred tree, the jurema, provides a narcotic used to induce
visions. [Chowdhury 1971; Leach 1992]

Ka-ata-killa

Peru
Moon and Night; Large Size
  Moon goddess. Before the Incas arrived, the indigenous
people worshiped her on the shores of Lake Titicaca. She was
queen of the giants. Later, her followers became the Colossi of
Tiahuanak. See also *Mama Quilla*. [Sykes 1968]

Karuebak

Brazil, *Mundurucu*
Agriculture
  "Mother of Manioc." [Leach 1992; Levi-Strauss 1973]

Kilya   See *Mama Quilla*.

Llacsahuato

Peru; Huarochiri District
Health and Healing
  Goddess of healing. [Leach 1992; Trimborn 1968]

Luandinha

Brazil, *Ita*
Water; Reptiles
  Water goddess in the form of a snake who inhabits the
Amazon. [Leach 1992; Wagley 1964]

Mae D'agua

Brazil
Water
  Water goddess. [Bastide 1978]

Maisö

Brazil, *Paressi*
Metals and Minerals; Creator of Life; Family and Tribes
  "Stone Woman." First woman of the Matto Grosso area.
Mother of *Uarahiulú* and Darukavaitere and ancestor of the
Paressi people. From Maisö came all living things. [Jobes
1962; Leach 1972; Leach 1992; Sykes 1968]

Maize Mother

Peru
Agriculture; Ceremonies
  Pre-Columbian mother of maize. Effigies of her are made
from the largest ears of the harvest. Corn mothers are found
in most areas of the world. [Eliade 1987]

Mama Allpa

Peru
Earth and Nature; Agriculture; Wealth
  Earth goddess. She gives bountiful harvests. [Leach 1992;
Redfield 1931]

Mama Cocha

Peru, *Inca, Chincha*
Water; Health and Healing; Fishing and Water Animals
  "Sea Mother." Primeval deity who is the oldest known
deity in Peru. She makes her followers healthy and provides

them with fish and other food from the sea, especially
whales. Fishers, in particular, worship her. Alternate form:
Mama-Qoca. [Jobes 1962; Leach 1972; Leach 1992; Monaghan
1981]

Mama Cora

Peru
Agriculture
  Maize goddess. Equivalent to *Kore*, Greek and Roman
Empires. [Jobes 1962]

Mama Cura   See *Cura*.

Mama Huaco   See *Huaco*.

Mama Ipa Qora   "Aunt Weed." See *Cura*.

Mama Llama

Peru, *Inca*
Domesticated Animals
  Animal deity who presides over the flocks. See also *Mama
Pacha*. [Leach 1992; Markham 1969]

Mama Ocllo   See *Ocllo*.

Mama Ocllo Huaca   See *Ocllo*.

Mama Ogllo   See *Ocllo*.

Mama Pacha

Peru, *Chincha*
Earth and Nature; Agriculture; Ceremonies; Reptiles; Disorder
  Earth goddess. She is petitioned for good harvests. During
planting and harvesting, corn meal is sometimes sprinkled on
the ground as an offering to her. She is also said to be a
dragon who causes earthquakes. Llamas are sacrificed in her
honor. See also *Mama Llama*. Alternate forms: Mamapacha,
Amara, Pachamama. [Alexander 1920; Leach 1992; Markham
1969; Monaghan 1981]

Mama Qoca   See *Mama Cocha*.

Mama Quilla

Peru, *Inca*
Moon and Night; Time; Ceremonies; Family and Tribes
  "Mother Moon" or "Golden Mother." Moon goddess
associated with the calendar, feast days being established
according to the phases of the moon. Also a goddess of
marriage. *Pacsa Mama* is a name used for Mama Quilla
during one of her phases. See also *Ka-ata-killa*. Alternate
forms: Quilla, Kilya, Mama-Kilya. [Leach 1992; Lurker 1984;
Stone 1979; Sykes 1968]

Mama Rahua   See *Raua*.

Mama Raua   See *Raua*.

Mama Rawa   See *Raua*.

Mama Sara

Peru
Agriculture; Ceremonies
  "Mother Maize." She is honored at the *Aymoray* festival.
See also *Mama Zara*. Alternate form: Sara Mama. [Leach
1992; Means 1931]

Mama Zara

Peru
Agriculture

"Grain Mother." She is said to manifest in cornstalks. Images of her are made from ears of corn and dressed in women's clothes. See also *Mama Sara.* Alternate form: Zara Mama. [Monaghan 1981; Redfield 1931; Schmidt 1951]

Mama-Kilya   See *Mama Quilla.*

Mamapacha   See *Mama Pacha.*

Maret-Jikky
Brazil, *Botocudo*
Supreme Being
Supreme goddess with her husband Maretkhmakniam. [Leach 1992; Pettazzoni 1956]

Mariana
Brazil, *Belem*
Health and Healing; Mother and Guardian; Love and Sexuality; Fishing and Water Animals
Goddess of healing, children, and love. She also protects sailors. [Leach 1992; Leacock and Leacock 1972]

Mirahuato
Peru; Huarochiri District
Health and Healing
Goddess of good health. [Leach 1992; Trimborn 1968]

Munya·k Yopue
Brazil, *Botocudo*
Moon and Night
"Mother Moon." [Leach 1992; Nimuendaju 1946]

Nandecy
Brazil, *Tupinambi*
Unknown
Brazilian deity. [Guirand 1968]

Nanen
Brazil
Earth and Nature
Earth goddess. Equivalent to Yoruba *Nana* and Dahomey *Nana Buruku,* both in Africa. [Leach 1972]

Noitu
Brazil, *Camayura*
Hunting and Wild Animals; Sun and Day; Moon and Night
Jaguar goddess. Mother of the sun, Kuat, and the moon, Yai, in Matto Grosso. [Leach 1992; Oberg 1953; Weyer 1961]

Nungui
Peru, *Jivaro*
Earth and Nature; Education and Knowledge; Ceremonies; Agriculture; Metals and Minerals
Earth goddess, deity of vegetation, and giver of culture. She is said to be the soul of the manioc plant. When the manioc is planted, the women sit on the roots, and one of them holds a red-painted manioc in her lap, tenderly caressing it. Nungui is represented by a stone of an unusual shape. [Berger 1985; Leach 1992; Weigle 1982]

Ocllo
Peru, *Inca*
Household Affairs; Sky and Heavens
"Queen." One of the *Ayar.* She and her brother came to earth from the sun and the moon. She invented spinning and taught women how to spin wool.

> While searching for inhabitable land, the Peruvian Mamas found an area they desired, but people lived there. Mama Ocllo killed a man, cut him open, and removed his lungs. She carried them in her mouth into the villages. The residents fled

in terror, leaving the land for the Peruvian Mamas and their brothers.
Alternate forms: Mama Ocllo Huaca, Ogllo, Mama Ogllo, Oella, Oclo, Oullo, Ocollo, Oolle, Cori Ocllo. [Jobes 1962; Senior 1985]

Oclo   See *Ocllo.*

Ocollo   See *Ocllo.*

Oella   See *Ocllo.*

Ogllo   See *Ocllo.*

Oolle   See *Ocllo.*

Oshoun
Brazil
Water; Mother and Guardian
Water goddess. She protects youth. Wife of Oshossi. [Landes 1940; Leach 1992]

Oullo   See *Ocllo.*

Our Mother
Brazil, *Apapocuva-Guarani*
Creator of Life; Sun and Day; Moon and Night
Creator goddess. Her sons became the sun and moon. [Leach 1956]

Oya de esteira   See *Oya-Bale.*

Oya-bale
Brazil
Water
Water deity. Equivalent to African *Oya.* The Portuguese call her *Oya de esteira.* [Gleason 1987]

Pachamama   See *Mama Pacha.*

Pacsa Mama   See *Mama Quilla.*

Panda
Brazil
Water
Sea goddess. Equivalent to African *Yemanja.* [Leach 1992]

Paxsi
Peru, *Aymara*
Moon and Night; Fate; Education and Knowledge
Moon goddess. Wife of the sun, Lupi. Her advice is sought through divination. [Leach 1992; Tschopik 1951]

Perimbó
Brazil, *Surára, Pakidái*
Moon and Night; Supreme Being; Creator of Life; Goodness; Justice
Moon goddess and supreme being who created the earth and all life. She forms an inseparable union with the moon god, Poré. They are benevolent and just, but punish when it is necessary. [Leach 1992; Zerries 1968]

Peruvian Mamas
Peru
Sky and Heavens; Family and Tribes
Four mothers. They are members of the *Ayar.*

> The four women with their four brothers came to earth from the heavens. After they had lived on earth for awhile, they left their original home in caves to search for fertile

land on which to settle. They founded the city of Cuzco and became the ancestors of the Inca people.

Their names are listed variously as *Occlo, Huaco, Cura,* and *Raua,* or as *Mama Occlo, Mama Huaco, Mama Ipa Gora,* and *Mama Rawa.* They are also called *Mama Ocllo Huaca, Mama Huaco, Mama Cora,* and *Mama Rahua* or *Topa Huaco, Cori Ocllo,* and *Ipa Huaco.* [Monaghan 1981; Leach 1972; Wedeck and Baskin 1971]

Pirua
Peru
Stars and Planets
Mother of *Mama Cora.* Also the name for the planet Jupiter. [Jobes 1962]

Pomba Gira
Brazil, *Umbanda*
Evil
"The Devil." The messenger between humans and the gods. Her husband is the divine teacher. [Bastide 1978; Eliade 1987]

Princess d'Alva
Brazil, *Belem*
Dawn and Twilight
"Dawn." Daughter of Averekete. [Leach 1992; Leacock 1956]

Putcha Si
Brazil, *Mundurucu*
Earth and Nature; Justice
Animal mother. She punishes those who offend her. [Leach 1992; Murphy 1958; Zerries 1968]

Quilla   See *Mama Quilla.*

Quinoa Mother
Peru
Agriculture
Pre-Colombian goddess of grain. [Eliade 1987]

Raharariyoma
Brazil; Venezuela, *Yanomamo*
Water; Reptiles; Destroyer of Life
River goddess. Seen as a snake who can cause drowning. [Chagnon 1968; Leach 1992]

Rainha Barba
Brazil, *Belem*
Weather; Fire
Goddess of thunder and lightning. [Leach 1992; Leacock and Leacock 1972]

Rapsem Si
Brazil, *Mundurucu*
Hunting and Wild Animals
Deer mother. [Leach 1992; Murphy 1958]

Raua
Peru, *Inca*
Sky and Heavens; Mother and Guardian
One of the *Ayar.* See also *Peruvian Mamas.* Alternate forms: Mama Raua, Mama Rahua, Mama Rawa. [Leach 1972; Monaghan 1981; Wedeck and Baskin 1971]

Sara Mama   See *Mama Sara.*

Schetewuarha
Bolivia; Brazil, *Chamacoco*
Weather; Supreme Being

"Ruler of the World" and "Mother of Rain." She is all powerful and brings the rain only when she wishes. [Baumgartner 1984; Leach 1992]

Senhora Ana
Brazil, *Belem*
Health and Healing; Selflessness
Old and humble goddess. She is part of the Preto Velho gods, deities with curative powers. [Leach 1992; Leacock 1956]

Shell Woman
Brazil, *Xingu*
Family and Tribes; Fishing and Water Animals; Unhappiness; Magic
Ancestor deity.

The only man on Earth found a shell and changed it into a woman. He married her, and, when their son was born, the first man took the child and left. Shell Woman cried and cried until she turned back into a shell. [Farmer 1978]

Si
Peru, *Chimu*
Moon and Night; Ceremonies
Moon goddess. Children, animals, and birds were sacrificed to her. [Alexander 1920; Leach 1992; Loeb 1931]

Star Woman
Brazil, *Chaco, Ge, Apinaye*
Agriculture; Education and Knowledge; Stars and Planets; Family and Tribes; Magic
She taught the people how to plant maize.

A very ugly man wanted to marry a bright star. Star Woman, as a mysterious woman, came to his village and married him. Thereupon he changed into a handsome and successful man. After a long time, Star Woman returned to her home in the sky, taking her husband with her. It was too cold for him and he died. [Leach 1972; Schmidt 1951]

Tamparawa
Brazil, *Tapirape*
Moon and Night
Moon goddess. Wife of Anchopeteri. [Leach 1992; Wagley 1940]

Taru
Brazil, *Botocudo*
Water
Water deity. [Brinton 1876; Leach 1992]

Taue Si
Brazil, *Mundurucu*
Hunting and Wild Animals
Prego monkey goddess. [Leach 1992; Murphy 1958]

Temioua
Brazil, *Tupi-Guarani, Uaupes*
Creator of Life; Family and Tribes; Stars and Planets
Creation deity.

Temioua fled her family to avoid an unwanted marriage. She became the wife of a Yacami chief. Their children hatched from two eggs that she produced. The children were a girl, who became the constellation Pleiades, and a boy, who became Orion. [Sykes 1968]

Teresita, Saint   Originally the African goddess *Oya.* See *Oya,* Africa.

Topa Huaco   See *Huaco.*

Topétine

Peru; Brazil, *Tecuna*

Fire; Hunting and Wild Animals

Goddess of fire, who takes the form of a jaguar. Mother of nU'tapa. [Leach 1992; Nimuendaju 1952]

Toru-guenket

Brazil, *Tupi*

Moon and Night; Evil; Weather; Disorder

Moon goddess. She is evil, causing bad weather and other troubles. [Leach 1992; Spence 1925a]

Uarahiulú

Brazil, *Paressi*

Creator of Life; Sky and Heavens; Reptiles; Wild Birds; Magic

Creator deity. Mother of the sun, moon, and all celestial beings. Also the mother of Uazale, the first Paressi Indian.

Maisö was upset because her son, Darúkavaiteré, and Uarahiulú were creating serpents and parrots. Through magic, Maisö caused them to have a human child instead. [Leach 1972; Leach 1992]

Upore   See *Uwan.*

Urpihuachac

Peru

Fishing and Water Animals; Unhappiness; Water; Wild Birds

Sea goddess who kept all of the world's fish in a pond. Viracocha broke down the walls of the pond and emptied the fish into the sea. He was angry because Urpihuachac's daughters changed into doves to flee him. [Alexander 1920; Leach 1992; Markham 1969; Savill 1978; Van Over 1980]

Uwan

Brazil, *Tenetehara*

Evil; Water; Destroyer of Life; Fishing and Water Animals

Evil water goddess of rivers and water animals. She brings sickness. Alternate forms: Upore, Uzare. [Leach 1992; Wagley and Galvao 1948]

Uzare   See *Uwan.*

Wazeparkwa

Brazil, *Shearente*

Sun and Day

Mother of the sun. [Leach 1992; Nimuendaju 1942]

Yaca-mama

Brazil

Water; Reptiles

"Mother of the Streams." In the Issa-Japura District, she is an anaconda that obstructs the streams, keeping them from flowing. [Leach 1992; MacCulloch 1925]

Yara

Brazil

Water; Charisma

A Siren. See *Siren,* Greek and Roman Empires. [Jobes 1962]

Yemoja

Brazil

Mother and Guardian

"Mother of the Gods." In the Candomble, she is a powerful deity. [Gleason 1987]

Zara Mama   See *Mama Zara.*

SOUTHEAST ASIA

Abyang
Philippines, *Bisayan*
Sky and Heavens
    Sky deity. Sister of Suklangmalayon. [Jocano 1969; Leach 1992]

Abyang Durunuun
Philippines, *Bisayan*
Heaven and Hell; Magic
    Underworld goddess. She is in charge of the charms and works with Sumpoy and Magyan. [Jocano 1969; Leach 1992]

Ag Aganney
Philippines, *Kankanay*
Destroyer of Life
    Disease goddess. On Luzon she is a mischievous roadside spirit who can cause tumors by hitting the legs of the people passing by. [Leach 1992; Vanoverbergh 1972]

Agemem
Philippines, *Tinguian*
Sky and Heavens
    Co-creator of the earth, moon, stars and sun. Her husband and co-creator is Kadaklan. Mother of sons, Adam and Balujen. [Leach 1972]

Agusan Devi
Philippines
Supreme Being
    A Hindu goddess worshiped in the province of Agusan. See *Devi*, Indian Subcontinent. [Monaghan 1990]

Akodau
Philippines, *Nabaloi*
Heaven and Hell
    Underworld deity. [Leach 1992; Moss 1920]

Akshobhya
Indonesia
Unknown
    "Immovable" or "Imperturbable." A Dhyani-Buddha. [Eliot 1935; Getty 1962; Leach 1992; Snelgrove 1957; Waddell 1925]

Alan, The
Philippines, *Tinguian*
Earth and Nature; Demi-animals; Wild Birds
    Forest spirits. Half-human, half-bird beings with reversed toes and fingers who hang from trees. Usually they are friendly but can also be hostile. [Bray 1935; Leach 1972]

Alindodoay
Philippines, *Isneg*
Agriculture
    Rice goddess who is called on for help during harvest time. [Leach 1992; Vanoverbergh 1941]

Alunsina
Philippines, *Sulod, Bisayan*
Heaven and Hell
    Goddess of Ibabawnon (heaven) to the Sulod people and a sky goddess to the Bisayan people on Panay Island. [Jocano 1969; Leach 1992]

Amamikyu
Okinawa; Ryukyu Islands
Creator of Life
    Creation deity with her companion Shinerikyu. [Leach 1992; Lebra 1966]

Amitabha
Indonesia
Immortality

Dhyani-Buddha of "Infinite Light" or "Boundless Light" who saves souls. On the island of Bali, a goddess; in other areas a male deity. See also *Amitabha,* Far East. [Getty 1962; Hackin 1963; Leach 1992; Percheron 1953]

Ammal
Ceylon, *Tamil*
Destroyer of Life
Disease goddess who brings smallpox and skin problems. [Leach 1992]

Amoghasiddhi
Indonesia
Magic; Goodness
"Infallible Magic." In Bali, a Dhyana-Buddha of the north who represents mercy and compassion. In other areas considered a male deity. [Eliot 1935; Getty 1962; Hackin 1963; Leach 1992]

A Mong
Burma, *Karens*
Family and Tribes; Magic
Ancestor deity with her brother Lan-yien. They protected themselves with a magic drum. [Jobes 1962]

Anat
Philippines, *Isneg*
Agriculture; Goodness
Benevolent goddess who helps with the rice harvest. See also *Anat,* Near East. [Leach 1992]

Andin Bambin
Indonesia: Borneo, *Ngaju*
Creator; Immortality
Creator goddess who decided that people should die and be reborn. She decided this with Peres while her husband, Ranying Pahatara, was away. [Leach 1992; Scharer 1963]

Aninito Ad Chalom
Philippines, *Mayawyaw*
Heaven and Hell; Disorder; Earth and Nature
Chthonic goddess who causes earthquakes. [Lambrecht 1932; Leach 1992]

Aniton Tauo
Philippines, *Zambales*
Weather
Rain and wind deity. [Jocano 1969; Leach 1992]

Anitun Tabu
Philippines, *Tagalog*
Weather
Wind and rain goddess. Daughter of Dumangan and *Idianale* and sister of Dumakulem. [Jocano 1969; Leach 1992]

Annawan
Philippines, *Isneg*
Water
Sea goddess of Luzon. When typhoons come, she must be pacified in order to control the waters. [Leach 1992; Vanoverbergh 1953]

Apna
Indonesia
Earth and Nature
Mother earth, part of the primeval pair on Kisar Island. Her husband is Father Sky Apha. They are also called Uru-Wadu, "Moon-Sun." See also *Uru.* [Leach 1992]

Aponibolinayen
Philippines, *Tinguian*
Beauty; Sun and Day
Sky woman.
Aponibolinayen was carried to the heavens by a vine wrapped around her waist. She tried to enter unseen the place where the sun sleeps at night, but her beauty radiated with a bright light. The sun awakened and married her. Their children were born from her little finger.
See also *Gaygayoma.* [Bray 1935; Jobes 1962; Leach 1972; Monaghan 1981]

Arud
Malaya; Malay Peninsula, *Jakun*
Heaven and Hell
Underworld deity of the Tekai River. [Leach 1992]

Arurin
Philippines, *Isneg*
Water; Agriculture; Ceremonies
River goddess. To make sure the harvest is good, she is invited to eat with the family. [Leach 1992]

Bà Ngu'
Indonesia: Annam
Fishing and Water Animals; Ceremonies
Dolphin goddess who rescues sailors, carrying them to safety on her back. Dolphins are considered bringers of good luck, and dead ones are retrieved from the water and buried on land. After three months and ten days the bones are taken from the burial site and placed in a tomb. This guarantees the prosperity of the village. [Leach 1972]

Bà-Du'c Chu'a, The
Indonesia: Annam
Earth and Nature; Water; Weather
"Three Mothers." They represent the forests, air, and water. See also *Duc Ba* and *Duc Thanh Ba.* [Leach 1972; Leach 1992]

Baitpandi
Philippines, *Bagobo*
Household Affairs
Goddess of weavers. [Jocano 1969; Leach 1992]

Bake
Indonesia
Ugliness; Evil
Ogre. Alternate form: Inangi I Bake. [Jobes 1962]

Balintawag
Philippines, *Isneg*
Water
River goddess in Luzon. She lives in a pool near Sabangan. [Leach 1992; Vanoverbergh 1953]

Balu Adad
Indonesia: Borneo, *Milanow*
Heaven and Hell; Immortality
Underworld goddess. She brings the souls of the dead to her home. [De Crespigny 1875; Leach 1992]

Banana Maiden
Indonesia: Celebes
Earth and Nature
Vegetation goddess. Her story is similar to that of *Konohana-sakuya-hime,* Far East, and *Sita,* Indian Subcontinent. [Durdin-Robertson 1976]

Bangan
Philippines, *Ibaloy*
Love and Sexuality
Goddess of love. Daughter of Lumauwig and *Bugan,* sister of Obban. [Jocano 1969; Leach 1992]

Batara Shri
Indonesia
Creator of Life
Creator goddess. [Savill 1978]

Batoer
Indonesia: Bali
Water
Water deity who inhabits the sacred lake. Her husband is Goenoeng Agoeng, god of the highest mountain, on which the other deities live. [Belo 1949; Leach 1992]

Bawin Jata Balawang Bulau   See *Jata* and *Tambon.*

Bee Bride
Indonesia: Borneo
Insects; Creator of Life; Demi-animals
Creator bee goddess. She created humans.
Bee Bride took human form and her husband promised to keep her original form secret. When he broke his promise, he turned into a bee man. [Eliot 1976]

Benih Lela Punggang Tengian Dara Bintang Tiga Datai Ka Jelan
Indonesia: Borneo, *Dyak*
Household Affairs
Goddess of weaving in Sarawak who makes her followers experts. Daughter of Pulang Gana, god of earth, soil, and rice farming, and *Srintun Tanah Tumboh Yak Srindak Tanggi Buloh.* [Leach 1992]

Bhulli Buri   See *Mainao,* Indian Subcontinent.

Bia-ka-pusud-an-langit
Philippines, *Bagobo*
Heaven and Hell
"Lady of the Navel of Heaven" who inhabits the sixth heaven. [Benedict 1916; Leach 1992]

Bia-t'oden
Philippines, *Bagobo*
Heaven and Hell
Goddess of the fifth heaven. Her husband is Salamiawan, god of the second heaven. [Benedict 1916; Leach 1992]

Biku Indu Antu
Indonesia: Borneo, *Iban Dyak*
Agriculture; Wealth
Rice goddess who is invoked for abundant harvests in Sarawak. Sister of Batara. [Leach 1992; Nyuak 1906]

Biliku   Malaysian goddess. See *Biliku,* Indian Subcontinent.

Bintang
Indonesia: Borneo, *Dyak*
Love and Sexuality; Magic
Love goddess worshiped in Sarawak. She gives power to love potions and charms. [Leach 1992]

Bisan
Malaya; Malay Peninsula
Insects; Earth and Nature
Spirit of camphor who manifests as a cicada. She is propitiated with food. [Leach 1972; Leach 1992]

Boru Deak Parudjar
Malaya; Malay Peninsula; Bali; Java; Sumatra
Creator of Life
Deity who was the mother of the first humans. Daughter of Batāra Guru.
Boru Deak Parudjar leaped from the upperworld into the limitless sea. Her father Batāra Guru sent a handful of earth down and when it landed on the water it grew larger. It grew so large that it made dark the undersea home of Naga Padoha, a serpent. He became angry and started pushing the earth about. Her father then sent down more earth and a hero to capture the serpent. The serpent wiggled about, creating the mountains and valleys, and his movements still cause earthquakes. [Leach 1972]

Bounmagyi
Burma, *Yeigyi*
Agriculture
Agricultural deity. She is called on during harvest on the threshing floor or the granary. [Leach 1992; Spiro 1967]

Bugan
Philippines, *Ifugao, Igorot*
Mother and Guardian; Creator of Life; Insects
Goddess of obstetrics. With her brother/husband Wigan, she begat the first humans after the great flood. She is associated with Balitok, a god of obstetrics. Prayers for women are addressed to her. The Igorot sometimes call her the goddess of locusts. See also *Bugan inWigan.* [Bray 1935; Evans 1904; Jobes 1962; Leach 1992; Monaghan 1981]

Bugan inBulul
Philippines, *Ifugao*
Agriculture
Goddess of agriculture. Her husband is Bulul, god of the granary. [Barton 1946; Leach 1992]

Bugan inIntongnin
Philippines, *Ifugao*
Creator of Life
Fertility goddess. She encourages reproduction. Her husband is Intongnin, god of reproduction. [Barton 1946; Leach 1992]

Bugan inKinulhudan
Philippines, *Ifugao*
Household Affairs
Weaving goddess. Her husband is Kinulhudan, god of weaving and dysentery. [Barton 1946; Leach 1992]

Bugan inMagnad
Philippines, *Ifugao*
Destroyer of Life
Disease goddess. She causes the liver to malfunction. Her husband is Mágnad. [Barton 1946; Leach 1992]

Bugan inManahaut
Philippines, *Ifugao*
War
War goddess. Her husband is Manahaut. [Barton 1946; Leach 1992]

Bugan inMonkulabe
Philippines, *Ifugao*
Household Affairs
Weaving goddess. [Barton 1946; Leach 1992]

Bugan inNgilin
Philippines, *Ifugao*
Life/Death Cycle
    Fertility goddess. She is benevolent but if she wishes, she can cause sickness. Her husband is Ngilin, god of reproduction. [Barton 1946; Leach 1992]

Bugan inPati
Philippines, *Ifugao*
Destroyer of Life; Ceremonies
    Disease goddess. She must be offered sacrifices to avert illness. [Leach 1992]

Bugan inPunholdaiyan
Philippines, *Ifugao*
Household Affairs
    Primal ancestor of the weaving deities. Her husband is Punholdaiyan. [Barton 1946; Leach 1992]

Bugan inUldi
Philippines, *Ifugao*
Household Affairs
    Weaving goddess. Her husband is Uldi. [Barton 1946; Leach 1992]

Bugan inWigan
Philippines, *Ifugao*
Creator of Life
    Fertility goddess. Her brother/husband is Wigan. See also *Bugan.* [Barton 1946; Leach 1992]

Bugan Nak Amtalao
Philippines
Magic; Fate
    Goddess of magic and good omens. [Barton 1946; Leach 1992]

Bugan Nak Hinumbian
Philippines, *Ifugao*
Magic; Fate
    Goddess of magic and omens. [Barton 1946; Leach 1992]

Bulan
Philippines, *Bagobo*
Moon and Night; Mother and Guardian
    Moon goddess who guards the earth with her husband the sun. [Jocano 1969; Leach 1992]

Chalonarang
Indonesia; Bali
Magic; Destroyer of Life
    Sorcerer and companion of *Durga,* Indian Subcontinent. *Durga* encouraged her to spread plague among the people. Alternate form: Rangda. [Savill 1978]

Chang-hko
Burma, *Kachins*
Creator of Life
    "Primeval Mother."
    Chang-hko was saved in a boat during the great flood. She became the mother of all humans. [Leach 1972; Leach 1992]

Chemioi
Malay Peninsula, *Kenta*
Sky and Heavens
    Heavenly deity worshiped in Kedah. Her husband is Begjag, a sky god who rules the winds. [Leach 1992; Schebesta 1927]

Chinoi Sagar
Malaya; Malay Peninsula
Immortality
    She cares for the souls of the dead near Belet, the underworld. [Leach 1992]

Chitsa Numjan
Burma, *Kachins*
Hunting and Wild Animals
    Deer mother. Her parents are Ningthoi wa and *Ningsin majan.* [Gilhodes 1908; Leach 1992]

Con Tinh
Indonesia: Annam
Evil; Immortality
    Malevolent spirits who inhabit old trees. They are young women who have died prematurely and they attack passersby, robbing them of their souls. Alternate form: Con-tinh. [Jobes 1962; Leach 1972]

Cunda
Indonesia: Java
Education and Knowledge
    Buddhist Bodhisatva. See also *Cunda,* Indian Subcontinent. [Durdin-Robertson 1992; Getty 1962; Jobes 1962]

Dagau
Philippines, *Manobo*
Agriculture; Disorder; Earth and Nature; Reptiles
    Rice goddess. She can bring abundance or famine. Also a goddess who lives at the foundation of the earth with her pet python whose writhing can cause earthquakes. [Leach 1992; Raats 1969]

Dagdagamiyan
Philippines, *Isneg*
Destroyer of Life; Agriculture
    Disease goddess. She looks particularly for children who are present during the harvest. [Leach 1992; Vanoverbergh 1941]

Dao
Indonesia
Creator of Life
    Primordial mother of Batu Island. With her husband, the wind, she bore the first pairs of deities and humans. See also *Dao,* Far East. [Leach 1992]

Dara Ensing Tamaga
Indonesia: Borneo, *Undup Dyaks*
Fate; Wild Birds
    Fate deity. She is a bird who can bring good omens. [Leach 1992]

Dara Rambai Geruda
Indonesia: Borneo, *Iban Dyak*
Water; Destroyer of Life; Goodness
    Water goddess worshiped in Sarawak who can be benevolent. When malevolent, she causes drownings. Equivalent to *Muni Mental Batu* and *Minti Dara Bunsu.* [Leach 1992]

Darago
Philippines
Fire; Earth and Nature; War; Disorder; Luck; Ceremonies
    Volcano deity who controls the fortunes of warriors and demands sacrifices. Also name of male god. [Jobes 1962; Leach 1992; Monaghan 1981]

Daterata

Burma

Goodness; Mother and Guardian; Insects

Benevolent goddess of Mt. Meru. She protects from the evil gnats. [Leach 1992; Spiro 1967]

Dewi Amisani

Indonesia

Unknown

Goddess who is a co-wife with *Dewi Hasin* and *Dewi Paya.* [Savill 1978]

Dewi Cri

Indonesia: Java; Bali

Agriculture

Rice deity. She is worshiped in the form of rice.

Dewi Cri disappeared from sight and on that spot cultivated rice and coco palms grew.

See also *Dewi Sri* and *Saning Sari.* [Leach 1992; Schmidt 1951]

Dewi Danu

Indonesia: Bali

Water; Ceremonies

Water goddess. She inhabits the crater lake on Mt. Balu. Ducks, pigs, coins, and coconuts are offered to her by farmers as thanks for the water they use. [Leach 1992]

Dewi Gangga

Indonesia: Bali

Water

Water goddess who inhabits rivers and lakes. Her husband is Siwa. [Covarrubias 1937; Leach 1992]

Dewi Hasin   See *Dewi Amisani.*

Dewi Melanting

Indonesia: Bali

Creator; Heaven and Hell

Fertility goddess and chthonic deity. She lives part of the year under the earth and promotes the growth of seeds. Benefactor of gardens and markets. Daughter of Wisnu and *Dewi Sri.* Equivalent to *Persephone,* Greek and Roman Empires. [Leach 1992]

Dewi Paya   See *Dewi Amisani.*

Dewi Pertimah

Indonesia: Java

Mother and Guardian; Ceremonies

Childbirth goddess to whom offerings are made before the birth. [Geertz 1960; Leach 1992]

Dewi Ratih

Indonesia: Bali

Moon and Night

Moon goddess who is sought for protection at weddings. Her husband is Semara. [Covarrubias 1937; Hooykaas 1964; Leach 1992]

Dewi Seri   See *Dewi Sri.*

Dewi Sri

Indonesia: Bali; Celebes

Agriculture; Wealth; Beauty

Rice goddess. She promotes abundance and beauty. See also *Dewi Cri, Sri.* Alternate form: Dewi Seri. [Friederich 1959; Hooykaas 1964; Leach 1992]

Dinawagan

Philippines, *Apayao*

Health and Healing

Goddess of health and healing. Her husband is Hatan. [Leach 1992; Wilson 1947]

Dinonganan

Philippines, *Ifugao*

Goodness; Fate

Benevolent goddess who brings omens. [Barton 1946; Leach 1992]

Djalai

Malaya; Malay Peninsula, *Kenta*

Sky and Heavens

Sky deity. [Leach 1992; Pettazzoni 1956]

Djata

Indonesia: Borneo, *Ngadju-Dyak*

Heaven and Hell; Reptiles

Underworld goddess who rules the crocodiles. She is a water snake and frequently appears to people in this form. Originally her name was *Tambon.* Alternate form: Putir. [Lurker 1984]

Doh Tenangan

Indonesia: Borneo, *Kayans*

Mother and Guardian

Goddess worshiped by women. Her husband is Laki Tenangan. [Leach 1992; Monaghan 1981]

Dua Nggae

Indonesia: Flores Island

Supreme Being; Education and Knowledge; Earth and Nature; Sky and Heavens; Moon and Night

Supreme being. A dual omniscient being who is the earth goddess, *Nggae,* and sky god, Dua. Sometimes the names are reversed. See also *Nggae.* Alternate form: Vula Ledza. [Leach 1992; Pettazzoni 1956]

Duan Luteh

Indonesia: Kei Archipelago

Moon and Night

Moon goddess. Her husband is the sun god, Duadlerwuan. [Frazer 1926; Leach 1992]

Duc Ba

Indonesia: Annam

Earth and Nature; Ceremonies; Time

Spirits of feminine trees. They are worshiped on the first and fifteenth of each month, mostly by women. See also *Duc Thanh Ba* and *Bà Du'c Chu'a.* [Leach 1972; Leach 1992]

Duc Thanh Ba

Indonesia: Annam

Earth and Nature

"Spirit of the Forests." See also *Duc Ba* and *Bà Du'c Chu'a.* [Leach 1972]

E U

Burma

Creator of Life

First woman. [Jobes 1962]

Empung Luminuut

Indonesia: Celebes Island, *Minahasa*

Creator of Life; Magic

Creator deity.

Empung Luminuut came out of the earth, possibly as the sweat of a stone. The west wind impregnated her and she gave birth to the sun. The sun and Empung Luminuut were married and from them came all the gods and humans. [Lurker 1984]

Entelanying

Indonesia: Borneo, *Iban Dyak*

Goodness; Mother and Guardian; Household Affairs

Benevolent goddess of Sarawak who empowers males against their enemies and empowers women to weave creatively. See also **Muni Mental Batu.** Equivalent to *Gitir, Indai Abang, Mendona, Puyu,* and *Singgar.* [Leach 1992]

Female Spectres, The

Malaya; Malay Peninsula

Beauty; Ceremonies; Wealth; Education and Knowledge

Goddesses who appear as two beautiful women during ceremonies for the novice. They reveal the secrets and treasures of the earth. [Durdin-Robertson 1976]

Fire Woman

Indonesia: Borneo, *Sea Dyak*

Fire; Mother and Guardian; Magic; Family and Tribes; Education and Knowledge; Reptiles

Goddess of fire.

Fire Woman and a group of women and children were in the jungle close to a river when they found a snake and killed it to feed themselves. As soon as they began to eat, a torrential rain started and the river rose. Fire Woman ran toward higher ground with her infant and they survived. When night came and the winds blew, Fire Woman rubbed her body against a tree, and much to her surprise, a fire started. As time went by, she became more adept at making fire, and when her son grew up, the water had receded and they were able to return to the land where they had once lived. Fire Woman took her son for her husband and they became the parents of the Dyak people. She taught them how to make fire and warned them about killing sacred snakes, for she now knew that was what had caused the flood. [Stone 1979]

First Woman

Indonesia: Borneo, *Kyan*

Creator of Life

First Woman of the Kyan people descended from a tree.

One day a spade handle fell out of the sky to earth. It took root and grew into a tree. Then a vine stretched down from the moon and wrapped itself around the tree. A girl and boy were born and they became the parents of the first people. [Farmer 1978]

Funan

Indonesia: Timor Island

Moon and Night

Moon goddess. Her consort is the sun. [Frazer 1926; Leach 1992]

Gaiyun

Philippines, *Ifugao*

Creator of Life; Mother and Guardian; Destroyer of Life; War

Fertility goddess. She is protective but can also cause sickness and death. Also a war goddess. Her husband is Pinyuhon, god of reproduction. [Barton 1946; Leach 1992]

Gayak, The

Malaya; Malay Peninsula, *Bera*

Heaven and Hell

Rulers of the underworld, a goddess and god. [Evans 1923; Leach 1992]

Gaygayoma

Philippines, *Tinguian*

Stars and Planets; Magic; Mother and Guardian; Family and Tribes; Selfishness

Star goddess. Daughter of Bagbagak, Big Star, and Sinag, the Moon. Mother of Takyayen.

Gaygayoma came down from the heavens in her star-dress seeking sugar cane that grew in Aponitolau's garden. Wanting Aponitolau for herself, she told him that her companion stars would eat him if he refused to go with her. Later she let him visit his earthly wife, Aponibolinayen, and allowed her son, Takyayen (born from his mother's last two fingers), to visit with Aponibolinayen's son, Kanga (born from his mother's little finger).

See also *Aponibolinayen.* [Bray 1935]

Gendui Lanyut

Malaya; Malay Peninsula, *Sakai*

Heaven and Hell; Immortality

Underworld goddess. In hell, she washes the souls. [Leach 1992; Skeat 1906]

Gimokodan

Philippines, *Bogobo*

Large Size; Immortality

Giant underworld deity.

The Gimokodan Woman lives beside the dark river that surrounds the nether world. Her body is covered with nipples and she breast feeds the spirits of deceased infants before they enter her world. [Cotterell 1979]

Girinatha

Indonesia: Bali

Agriculture

Young rice plant. Associated with *Sri* when she is the goddess of rice. [Leach 1992; Levi 1933]

Giriputri

Indonesia: Bali

Earth and Nature

Mountain goddess, a name for *Sri.* [Danileou 1964; Leach 1992; Redfield 1931; Stutley 1984]

Gitir

Indonesia: Borneo, *Iban Dyaks*

Goodness; Household Affairs; Mother and Guardian

Benevolent deity of Sarawak who empowers women to weave creatively and men to overcome their enemy's weapons. Equivalent to *Entelanying, Indai Abang, Puyu,* and *Singgar.* [Leach 1992]

Hainuwele

Indonesia: Ceram

Agriculture; Wealth; Ceremonies; Life/Death Cycle

"Coco-palm Branch." She brought wealth to the people.

Hainuwele grew from a coconut that Ameta found and planted. There had been no coco-palms before this. Hainuwele grew very quickly and participated in the Maro festival, where she gave gifts to the dancers. The people grew jealous of her wealth and decided to kill her. On the ninth night of the Maro festival they threw her into a hole they had dug in the center of the dance ground. When her father discovered her body he cut it into pieces and buried them in the dancing ground. They grew into wonderful plants that became the principal food for the people.

See also *Satine.* [Long 1963; Neumann 1972; Schmidt 1951]

Hanan

Philippines, *Tagalog*

Sun and Day

"Morning." Daughter of Bathala and a mortal, sister of *Mayari* and *Tala.* [Jocano 1969; Leach 1992]

Hnit Ma Daw See *Shwe Myet Hna*.

Hnitma Dawgyi
Indochina (Vietnam)
Creator of Life
   Creator goddess. [Jobes 1962]

Hpi Bi Yaw
Burma, *Karens*
Agriculture
   Agriculture goddess. She promotes the fertility of the crops and rice paddy. [Leach 1992]

Hukloban
Philippines, *Tagalog*
Evil; Health and Healing
   Evil goddess who can also heal those she hurts. [Jocano 1969; Leach 1992]

Humitau
Philippines, *Tinguian*
Water
   Sea goddess, guardian of Tau-mariu, lord of the sea. When she was abducted, a great flood ensued. [Leach 1992]

Ibabasag
Philippines, *Bukidnon*
Mother and Guardian
   Deity of pregnant women who invoke her during childbirth. [Cole 1956; Jocano 1969; Leach 1992]

Ibu
Philippines, *Manobo*
Heaven and Hell; Immortality
   Underworld goddess. She cares for the dead. [Jocano 1969; Leach 1992; Raats 1969]

Ibu Pertiwi
Indonesia: Bali
Earth and Nature
   "Mother Earth." Name for *Sri*. [Covarrubias 1937; Grader 1960; Leach 1992]

Idianale
Philippines, *Tagalog*
Goodness; Commerce and Travel
   Goddess of hard work and good deeds. Her husband is Dumangan, and her children are Dumakulem and Anitun Tabu. [Jocano 1969; Leach 1992]

Ikapati
Philippines, *Tagalog*
Agriculture; Domesticated Animals
   "Giver of Food." Fertility goddess who promotes abundance of the crops, fields, and herds. [Leach 1992]

Imbulu Man
Indonesia: Sumatra, *Battak*
Wild Birds; Mother and Guardian
   Bird goddess. Mother of humans. [Leach 1992; MacKenzie 1930a]

Ina
Indonesia: Ambon Island; Moluccas
Earth and Nature
   Mother earth. Alternate form: Upu Ume. [Leach 1992]

Ina Onian
Indonesia: Sumatra
Goodness; Water
   "Mother of Water." Benevolent river deity. [Savill 1978]

Inada Dao
Indonesia: South Nias
Creator of Life
   Creator goddess. Mother of Lowalani and Latura Dano. [Leach 1992; Suzuki 1959]

Ina Da Samadulo Hose
Indonesia, *Nias*
Creator of Life; Metals and Minerals
   "Mother of the Gods." Also mother of all humans.
   Ina Da Samadulo Hose came from a splitting stone. She had two sets of mixed twins and from these came all the races of the world. [Leach 1972; Savill 1978]

Ina Da Samihara Luwo
Indonesia
Primordial Being
   Primeval goddess.
   Ina Da Samihara Luwo was born from the parting of the formless chaos. She created the world. When one of the stones in her world split, Ina Da Samadulo Hose, mother of humans, was born. [Savill 1978]

Inaka See *Upu Ume*.

Inan Oinan
Indonesia, *Pageh*
Water
   "Mother of the Waters" on Mentawei Island. [Leach 1992; Savill 1978]

Inangi I Bake See *Bake*.

Inawen
Philippines, *Tinguian*
Water; Ceremonies
   Sea goddess. Her help can be sought by offerings of chicken blood and rice. [Cole 1922; Leach 1992]

Inchin Temaga
Indonesia: Borneo, *Sea Dyaks*
Sky and Heavens
   Heavenly deity. Daughter of Singalang Buron on Sarawak. [Leach 1992]

Indai Abang
Indonesia: Borneo; Sarawak, *Iban Dyak*
Goodness; Household Affairs; Mother and Guardian
   Benevolent goddess of Sarawak. She protects men from the weapons of their enemies and aids women in weaving. Equivalent to *Entelanying, Gitir, Puyu,* and *Singgar*. [Leach 1992]

Indara
Indonesia: Celebes Island, *Torajas*
Supreme Being; Earth and Nature; Creator of Life
   "Maiden." Supreme goddess and earth goddess who created people but not plants and animals, although, as *Ndara*, she is said to be a fertility goddess and rice deity. [Leach 1992; Monaghan 1981]

Indo I Laoe
Indonesia: Celebes Island
Heaven and Hell; Agriculture

Underworld goddess associated with rice. Sister of *Indo I Losi.* [Downs 1920; Leach 1992]

Indo I Losi

Indonesia: Celebes Island
Agriculture
Goddess of rice. Sister of *Indo I Laoe.* [Downs 1920; Leach 1992]

Indo I Tuladidi

Indonesia: Celebes Island
Creator of Life; Agriculture
Fertility goddess. She has hair of rice. Her husband is Pue Mpalaburu, the supreme being. [Downs 1920; Leach 1992]

Indo nTegolili

Indonesia: Celebes Island
Moon and Night; Mother and Guardian
Moon goddess. She watches over people and reports their activities to Pue Mpalaburu. [Downs 1920; Leach 1992; Pettazzoni 1956]

Indoea Padi

Indonesia: Sumatra, *Minangkabau*
Agriculture
Rice mother. She is represented by special plants. [Eliade 1987]

Indudun inPundaikuhan

Philippines, *Ifugao*
Creator of Life; Agriculture; Insects
"Grasshoppered." Fertility goddess of the fields at Kalinugan. Her husband is Pundaikuhan, god of a vine that is a charm against locusts. [Leach 1992]

Ineno Pae

Malaya; Malay Peninsula; Celebes, *Tomori*
Agriculture; Ceremonies
"Mother of Rice." At the beginning of the harvest selected stalks of rice are tied together in a sheaf and are called Ineno Pae. Offerings are made to her, and when all the rice is harvested, Ineno Pae is cut and placed on the rice-barn floor and the rest of the harvest is piled on top of her. [Durdin-Robertson 1976]

Ini Andan

Indonesia: Borneo, *Dyaks*
Sky and Heavens; Luck; Agriculture; Ceremonies; Wealth
Heavenly deity worshiped in Sarawak. She brings good luck to farmers and blesses them with abundance and skill. She is associated with the "Feast of the Whetstones," which is celebrated before land is cleared for farming. See also *Ini Manang.* [Leach 1992]

Ini Manang

Indonesia: Borneo; Sarawak (colony of Borneo), *Dyak*
Health and Healing; Sky and Heavens; Ceremonies
"Medicine Woman." Sarawak celestial sister of Singalang Burong who is invoked during the "Feast of the Whetstones." See also *Ini Andan.* Alternate form: Manang Jaban. [Leach 1992]

Inoltagon

Philippines, *Ifugao*
Weather
Wind goddess. Her husband is Nunanud. [Barton 1946; Leach 1992]

Intombangol

Philippines, *Bukidnon*
Reptiles
Two serpents, one female and one male, upon whom the earth rests. [Leach 1992]

Ipamahandi

Philippines, *Bukidnon*
Luck
"Goddess of Accident." [Jocano 1969; Leach 1992]

Ja Najek

Indonesia, *Kerau*
Moon and Night; Education and Knowledge
Moon goddess. She knows everything and cannot be fooled by people. [Leach 1992; Pettazzoni 1956]

Jalang

Malaya; Malay Peninsula, *Semang*
Supreme Being; Mother and Guardian
Supreme goddess. She is one of the three grandmothers who live underground and protect the stone which supports the sky. Daughter of Yak Lepeh. [Leach 1972]

Jara Meng

Indonesia, *Semang*
Moon and Night; Immortality; Life/Death Cycle
Moon goddess of Lenggong in North Perak who rejuvenates and grows younger after a period of growing older. [Leach 1992]

Jata

Indonesia: Borneo, *Dyaks*
Earth and Nature; Reptiles; Supreme Being; Heaven and Hell
Earth deity who lived in the primeval waters as a snake. She created the world with the sun Mahatala (Mahatara) and together they form a dual supreme being. She represents the underworld, he the upperworld, and they are the duality of all things. Alternate forms: Bawin Jata Balawang Bulau, Tambon. [Leach 1992]

Jingjan Numjan

Burma, *Katchins*
Insects
Ant Mother. Daughter of Ningthoi wa and *Ningsin majan.* [Leach 1992]

Ju Puteur

Malaya; Malay Peninsula, *Ple*
Heaven and Hell; Magic
Underworld sorcerer. [Leach 1992]

Kabagiyawan

Philippines, *Isneg*
Weather; Disorder
Atmosphere goddess. She causes typhoons whenever she is naked. [Leach 1992; Vanoverbergh 1953]

Kadeyuna

Philippines, *Bagobo*
Sky and Heavens
Goddess of the seventh heaven. Sister of *Tiun.* Her husband is Malaki Lunsud, god of the eighth heaven. [Leach 1992]

Kakiadan

Philippines, *Manobo*
Agriculture
Rice goddess. [Jocano 1969; Leach 1992]

Kalcheng
Malaya; Malay Peninsula, *Menik Kaien, Kintak Bong*
Earth and Nature; Order
   Earth goddess. She is sought to alleviate thunderstorms caused by Tapern, the weather god. [Evans 1937; Leach 1992]

Kameian
Indonesia: Sumatra
Evil; Water
   "Father's Sister." An evil river goddess. [Savill 1978]

Kant Jan
Burma, *Katchins*
Metals and Minerals
   Mother goddess of valuable stones. Daughter of *Phungkam Janun.* [Gilhodes 1908; Leach 1992]

Kapaä
Indonesia: Java, *Ongtong*
Water
   Sea goddess. Her husband is Peave and her children are Keloguei and Keheari. [Chadwick 1930; Leach 1992]

Karokung
Philippines, *Bogobo*
Water; Destroyer of Life
   River goddess who can cause fever and chills. [Benedict 1916; Leach 1992]

Katsin Numka Majan
Burma, *Katchins*
Health and Healing
   "Mother of Vital Organs." She protects the heart, liver, lungs, etc. Daughter of *Phungkam Janun.* [Gilhodes 1908; Leach 1992]

Kayamanan
Philippines
Wealth
   Goddess who brings wealth. [Leach 1992]

Keheari
Indonesia: Java, *Ongtong*
Water
   Sea goddess. Daughter of Peave and *Kapaä* and sister of Keloguei. [Chadwick 1930; Leach 1992]

Khmoc Pray, The
Cambodia
Mother and Guardian; Destroyer of Life; Immortality
   Malevolent spirits of women who died in childbirth. They inhabit trees and torment passersby, sometimes killing them with rocks. An even more fearful ghost is the woman accompanied by the ghost of her fetus. She died during her pregnancy. [Leach 1972]

Kibayen
Philippines, *Tinguian*
Evil; Destroyer of Life
   Evil goddess. She comes to healing ceremonies to try to steal the sick person's life. [Cole 1922; Leach 1992]

Klang
Malaya; Malay Peninsula
Creator of Life; Wild Birds
   First woman.
   Klang lived in a house. One day a young child was misbehaving outside and when Klang looked out she became dizzy and fell. Falling through space, she changed into a hawk. [Eliot 1976]

Kok Lir
Indonesia: Borneo, *Iban Dyak*
Mother and Guardian
   Goddess worshiped in Sarawak who harms men but not women. [Leach 1992]

Kolkolibag, The
Philippines, *Ifugao*
Mother and Guardian
   "Spirits of Birth." Childbirth goddesses who can cause difficult labors unless they are appeased properly. [Jocano 1969; Leach 1992]

Kumang
Indonesia: Borneo, *Iban, Sea Dyak*
Fate; War; Wealth; Heaven and Hell
   Mother goddess worshiped in Sarawak who is also a goddess of prophecy. Her husband is Kling, a rice god. She gives aid in war and makes her followers prosperous.
   Kumang was in charge of paradise where the first Iban lived. She was easily recognizable because her back was white—bleached by the sun. [Cotterell 1979; Leach 1992]

Kundui
Malaya; Malay Peninsula, *Mantra*
Moon and Night
   Moon goddess. Her husband was the evil god, Moyang Bertang. [Leach 1992; Skeat 1906]

Lai-oid
Malaya; Malay Peninsula, *Bateg*
Earth and Nature; Justice; Disorder; Water
   Earth goddess. She causes flooding to destroy homes of people who have offended her. Her husband is Jawait. [Evans 1937; Leach 1992]

Langaan
Philippines
Weather
   Atmosphere deity. She brings rain and wind. Mother of Aponitolau. [Jocano 1969; Leach 1992]

Langhui   See *Langsuir.*

Langsuir, The
Malaya; Malay Peninsula
Destroyer of Life; Evil; Ceremonies; Mother and Guardian
   Death demons. Women who die in childbirth become Langsuir. They dress in green robes and have long nails and very long, jet-black hair. The hair hides the hole in the back of the neck where they suck children's blood. When a woman dies in childbirth, glass beads are put in her mouth, needles in the palms of her hands, and eggs are placed in each armpit to prevent her from becoming a Langsuir. Alternate forms: Langhui, Langsuyar. [Bonnerjea 1927; Leach 1972]

Langsuyar   See *Langsuir.*

Larai Majan
Burma, *Katchins*
Domesticated Animals
   Bird goddess. She protects domestic birds. Daughter of *Phungkam Janun.* [Gilhodes 1908; Leach 1992]

Latu Hila la Balaa
Indonesia: Watubela Island
Earth and Nature
   Mother earth. [Frazer 1926; Leach 1992]

Lepeh
Malaya; Malay Peninsula, *Negritos*
Heaven and Hell; Water; Disorder
"Grandmother." Underworld goddess who can bring underground water up to the surface, causing floods. See also *Yak Lepeh.* [Evans 1937; Leach 1992]

Lingan
Philippines, *Mayawyaw, Ifugao*
Moon and Night
Moon goddess. [Barton 1946; Leach 1992]

Lingkambene
Indonesia: Celebes Island
Sky and Heavens; Ceremonies
Creator goddess.
Lingkambene angered her parents and went to heaven where she was sacrificed by roasting. When she died, the sun came from her forehead and the moon from the back of her head, her eyes and internal organs became the constellations, while her flesh formed all of the stars. [Eliot 1976]

Lise
Indonesia: Celebes Island
Agriculture
Rice goddess. [Adriani and Kruyt 1950; Downs 1920; Leach 1992]

Loupgarous, The
Indonesia
Magic; Destroyer of Life; Insects
Sorcerer. Fate determines if a woman is to become a Loupgarou. If so, she flies through the air at night, landing on the thatch houses. She then takes a mosquito form and wriggles into the house where she sucks the blood and the life from a child. See also *Penanggalan.* [Savill 1978]

Lulong
Indonesia: Borneo, Sarawak (colony of Borneo), *Dyak*
Mother and Guardian; Household Affairs; Love and Sexuality; Magic
Goddess of women. She teaches them to weave and make tribal patterns on cloth. Also a goddess of love associated with charms and potions. [Leach 1992]

Lumaknak inLukbuban
Philippines, *Ifugao*
Agriculture
Goddess of agriculture at Binuyuk. Her husband is Lukbuban, an agricultural deity. [Leach 1992]

Lumimuut
Indonesia
Earth and Nature; Creator of Life
Earth goddess who was born from the sweat of a rock.
A crane told Lumimuut where to find some soil which she used to cover a stone, forming the earth. Then she planted seeds that grew into trees and plants. When she climbed to the top of a mountain she had made, the west wind came and impregnated her. She became the mother of the gods and the ancestor of humans. [Bray 1935; Jobes 1962; Leach 1992; Monaghan 1981; Savill 1978]

Luyong Baybay
Philippines, *Sulod*
Moon and Night; Heaven and Hell
Moon goddess who controls the tides. Also an underworld deity. Her husband is Paigrab, ruler of the afterworld. [Jocano 1969; Leach 1992]

Luyong Kabig
Philippines, *Sulod*
Heaven and Hell; Reptiles
Underworld deity who cares for the stream of snakes at its entrance. [Jocano 1969; Leach 1992]

Machin Tungku
Burma, *Katchins*
Water
"Mother of Water." Daughter of *Phungkam Janun.* [Gilhodes 1908; Leach 1992]

Madun Pungren Majan
Burma, *Katchins*
Arts
"Mother of Flutes." Daughter of *Phungkam Janun.* [Gilhodes 1908; Leach 1992]

Mae Phosop
Thailand (Siam)
Agriculture
Rice deity. Alternate form: Posop. [Hanks 1963; Leach 1992]

Mae Phra Phloeng
Thailand (Siam)
Fire; Mother and Guardian
"Fire." She is called on during pregnancy. [Leach 1992]

Magapid
Philippines, *Ifugao*
Fate
Fate goddess associated with omens. [Barton 1946; Leach 1992]

Magtatangal
Philippines, *Tagalog*
Destroyer of Life; Ugliness
Death deity who frightens people to death. Sister of Silangan. [Jocano 1969; Leach 1992]

Maize Mother
Indonesia: Celebes Island
Agriculture
Food goddess. [Schmidt 1951]

Makarom Mawakhu
Keisar Island
Primordial Being
Primordial goddess. Her male counterpart was Makarom Manouwe. [Eliade 1958; Leach 1992]

Makawalang
Indonesia: Celebes, *Minahassa*
Heaven and Hell
Afterworld goddess who is its guardian. [Kruijt 1925; Leach 1992; MacKenzie 1930a]

Manamoan
Philippines, *Mandaya*
Earth and Nature; Mother and Guardian
Earth goddess who protects women in childbirth. [Leach 1992; Raats 1969]

Manang Jaban
Indonesia: Borneo, *Iban Dyak*
Sky and Heavens; Luck; Health and Healing; Agriculture
Heavenly goddess worshiped in Sarawak who brings good luck and health. She is also invoked by farmers before they clear the land. Alternate form: Ini Manang. [Leach 1992]

Mande Rubiah

Indonesia: Sumatra

Health and Healing

"Good Spirit." A djinn who is sought in a trance for healing. [Savill 1978]

Mangagaway

Philippines, *Tagalog*

Destroyer of Life

Disease goddess who can bring death. [Jocano 1969; Leach 1992]

Manik Galih

Indonesia: Bali

Agriculture

She protects the crops against harm. [Leach 1992]

Manoid

Indonesia, *Djahai, Jehai, Kenta*

Earth and Nature; Creator of Life; Immortality; Ceremonies

Earth goddess. Her husband is Karei, god of lightning and the supreme being who created everything except the earth and humans. Humans can assuage their sins by pouring blood on the ground for her and by throwing it skyward for him. To the Kenta people she is the creator of the first humans. [Evans 1937; Leach 1992; Pettazzoni 1956; Roheim 1972]

Manolge inBahiwag

Philippines, *Ifugao*

Heaven and Hell

Underworld goddess. Her husband is Bahiwag, god of the underworld. [Leach 1992]

Manuk Manuk

Indonesia: Sumatra

Domesticated Animals

"Blue Chicken." Deity who produced the three eggs from which the sons of the supreme being, Mula djadi na bolon, were born. [Savill 1978]

Mapatal Bugan inAmalgo

Philippines, *Mayawyaw*

Sun and Day

Sun goddess on Luzon. Her husband is Mapatal, a sun god. [Lambrecht 1932; Leach 1992]

Maran Junti Majan

Burma, *Katchins*

Metals and Minerals

"Mother of Salt." Daughter of *Phungkam Janun*. [Gilhodes 1908; Leach 1992]

Mayari

Philippines, *Tagalog*

Moon and Night

Moon goddess. Daughter of Bathala and a mortal father, beautiful sister of *Hanan* and *Tala*. [Jocano 1969; Leach 1992]

Mebuyan

Philippines; Burma, *Bagobo, Kachins*

Destroyer of Life; Heaven and Hell; Life/Death Cycle

Goddess of death and Gimokudan (the underworld). For the Bagobo, Mebuyan affects the life and death rhythms by shaking the tree of life. The Kachins believe that a slender bamboo, which is easily shaken, forms a bridge over the boiling cauldrons of death. [Leach 1972; Leach 1992]

Mekala

Thailand (Siam)

Fire; Weather

Goddess of lightning. [Jobes 1962]

Mele

Indonesia: Bali

Household Affairs

Goddess of weaving. [Leach 1992]

Mendong

Indonesia: Borneo, *Iban Dyak*

Goodness; Household Affairs; Mother and Guardian

Benevolent goddess worshiped in Sarawak who aids women with weaving and makes men invulnerable to their enemies. Equivalent to *Entelanying*. [Leach 1992]

Minti Dara Bunsu

Indonesia: Borneo, *Iban Dyak*

Water; Mother and Guardian; Destroyer of Life

Water goddess worshiped in Sarawak who aids divers. She is sometimes malevolent, causing drownings. See also *Muni Mental Batu* and *Dara Rambai Geruda*. [Leach 1992]

Mona   See *Tuglibong*.

Moon Mother

Indonesia: Celebes Island

Moon and Night; Earth and Nature

"Moon." The goddess who gave birth to the earth and who will bring forth other worlds. [Durdin-Robertson 1976]

Muk Jauk

Cambodia

Earth and Nature

"Black Lady." Earth deity. [Monaghan 1981]

Mulua Satene

Indonesia: Ceram, *Welame*

Heaven and Hell; Life/Death Cycle

Afterworld deity who sends children to earth so they can die and return to populate her abode. [Leach 1992; Raats 1969]

Muni Mental Batu

Indonesia: Borneo, *Iban Dyak*

Water; Mother and Guardian; Destroyer of Life

Water goddess worshiped in Sarawak who aids divers but sometimes causes drowning. See also *Dara Rambai Geruda, Entelanying,* and *Minti Dara Bunsu*. [Leach 1992]

Munsumundok

Indonesia: Borneo, *Dusun*

Creator of Life; Sky and Heavens; Life/Death Cycle

Creator deity worshiped in Sarawak, with her husband Kinharingan, a creator god.

Mumsumundok and Kinharingan came out of a rock in the middle of the sea and walked across the water until they came to the house of Bisagit, the god of smallpox. Bisagit gave them earth and after it was placed, Kinharingan made the Dusuns (Dusans) and Munsumundok made the sky. Together they created the sun, moon, and constellations. Because there was no food, they killed one of their children, cut her into small pieces, and planted her in the earth. From the pieces grew all the plants and animals.

See also *Nunsumnundok*. [Leach 1972; Leach 1992]

Na Ina

Philippines, *Ifugao*

Creator of Life; War

Fertility goddess at Kapungahan who is also a war deity. [Barton 1946; Leach 1992]

Nama Djang Ad Chalom
Philippines, *Ifugao*
Heaven and Hell; Creator of Life
   Underworld goddesses who creates fetuses. [Leach 1992]

Nana Buruku   See *Nana Buruku*, Africa.

Nang Pyek Kha Yeh Khi
Burma
Mother and Guardian; Demi-animals; Hunting and Wild Animals
   Mother goddess who has the ears and legs of a tiger. Daughter of Ta-Hsek-Khi and *Yahsek Khi.* Her husband was Khun Hsang L'rong.
   Nang Pyek Kha Yeh Khi was given the earth and water. When her parents died from eating one of the gourds of life and death, she became the guardian of the gourds. When Khun Hsang L'rong cut the gourds open, animals and people came out of them.
   See also *Wang Pyekkha Yek Khi.* [Jobes 1962]

Nang Tholani
Laos
Earth and Nature
   Earth goddess. [Deydier 1952; Leach 1992]

Nat   See *Nat*, Northern Europe.

Ndara
Indonesia: Celebes Island
Earth and Nature; Disorder; Heaven and Hell
   Chthonic earth goddess. Her husband is Toara-lino, an earth deity who is invoked for children. She supports the earth on her head and when she moves there are earthquakes. [Downs 1920; Leach 1992; Wales 1957]

Ndo I Ronda Eo
Indonesia: Celebes Island, *To Plande, To Onda'e*
Creator of Life; Directions
   Fertility goddess of the east for the To Plande. A name for *Siladi* to the To Onda'e people. [Downs 1920; Leach 1992]

Nenak Kebajan
Indonesia, *Mantra Jukudn*
Moon and Night; Education and Knowledge
   Moon goddess who knows all that is happening. [Leach 1992; Pettazzoni 1956]

Nggae
Indonesia: Flores Island
Creator of Life
   Supreme being. A dual omniscient being who is the earth goddess, Nggae, and sky god, Dua. Sometimes the names are reversed. See also *Dua Nggae.* Alternate form: Vula Ledz. [Leach 1992; Pettazzoni 1956]

Nimli Numjan
Burma, *Katchins*
Wild Birds
   Bird Mother. Daughter of Ningthoi wa and *Ningsin majan.* [Gilhodes 1908; Leach 1992]

Ningpang Majan
Burma, *Katchins*
Creator of Life
   Primordial mother of all the deities. [Leach 1992]

Ningsin Majan
Burma, *Katchins*
Moon and Night; Wild Birds; Creator of Life
   Goddess of night who belongs to the second generation of deities. With her brother/husband Ningthoi Wa, the god of light, she became the mother of the third generation of gods. At her death, she was transformed into a bird and called **U Kaukon.** [Gilhodes 1908; Leach 1992]

Ningthet Majan
Burma, *Katchins*
Justice
   "Heat." She takes part in the judgment of the accused with her husband Ninglum lawa. They take the part of the plaintiff during the testing of the accused, whose hand is plunged into boiling water. See also *Ningtsi Majan* and *Tara Majan.* [Gilhodes 1908; Leach 1992]

Ningtsi Majan
Burma, *Katchins*
Justice
   "Cold." She and her husband, Ningshung lawa, protect the accused when his hand is plunged into boiling water. See also *Ningthet Majan* and *Tara Majan.* [Gilhodes 1908; Leach 1992]

Nini Anteh
Indonesia
Moon and Night
   "Little Girl in the Moon." Equivalent to *Bil,* Northern Europe. [Jobes 1962]

Niwa
Burma, *Tangsas, Khemsing*
Creator of Life
   Creator goddess. She and her husband, Dombe, created all things. [Leach 1992]

Njai
Indonesia: Java
Water
   Sea goddess who rules the other sea spirits. She lives in a beautiful palace at the bottom of the ocean and is given great reverence. See also *Njai Lora Kidoul.* Alternate form: Ratu Loro Kidul. [Leach 1992; Redfield 1931]

Njai Lora Kidoul
Indonesia: Java
Water; Justice; Fate
   Goddess of the Indian Ocean. She rules the deities from her palace on the rocky coast of south Java. At the grotto of Karang, people come to consult her oracle. See also *Njai.* [Savill 1978]

Nunsumnundok
Indonesia: Borneo
Creator of Life; Metals and Minerals
   First woman. She emerged from a living rock. The rock was in the sea and it opened its mouth to allow the first woman and man to merge. See also *Munsumundok.* [Eliot 1976]

Obban
Philippines, *Bontok, Kankanay*
Creator of Life
   Fertility goddess. Daughter of *Bugan* and Lumauwig. [Jocano 1969; Leach 1992]

Oltagon
Philippines, *Ifugao*
Agriculture

Goddess of agriculture at Namtogan. [Barton 1946; Leach 1992]

Omonga
Indonesia: Celebes Island, *Timori*
Agriculture; Moon and Night
Rice goddess who lives in the moon. [Redfield 1931]

Oshun   See *Oshun*, Africa.

Paja Yan   See *Pajau Yan*.

Pajau Tan   See *Pajau Yan*.

Pajau Yan
Vietnam, *Chams*
Goodness; Health and Healing; Luck; Ceremonies; Time; Immortality; Moon and Night
Benevolent goddess of health, healing, and good fortune. Offerings are made to her on the first day of the waning moon.
Pajau Yan lived on earth, but she was sent to the moon to live because she was healing and raising all the dead. On the moon Pajau Yan honors the sun by a lunar eclipse and provides flowers for the dead to ease their transition from life to death.
Alternate forms: Paja Yan, Pajau Tan, Pajan Yan. [Leach 1972; Leach 1992; Monaghan 1981; Redfield 1931]

Pajan Yan   See *Pajau Yan*.

Pandan Rumari
Indonesia: Sumatra, *Battak*
Agriculture
Fertility goddess pertaining to agriculture. Sister of Batāra Guru. [Leach 1992; MacKenzie 1930a]

Panglang
Philippines, *Bukidnon*
Mother and Guardian
Childbirth goddess. She and her servant Mangoñoyamo protect pregnant woman, unborn children, and midwives. [Leach 1992]

Pantan Ini Andan
Indonesia: Borneo, *Iban Dyak*
Agriculture; Wealth
Agriculture goddess invoked in Sarawak for a good rice harvest. [Leach 1992; Nyuak 1906]

Pantang Mayang
Indonesia: Borneo, *Dyak*
Goodness; Love and Sexuality; Magic
Benevolent goddess of love in Sarawak who is associated with charms and potions. [Leach 1992]

Penaban Sari
Indonesia: Bali
Heaven and Hell; Creator of Life
Pair of chthonic deities of fertility, one female and one male. [Grader 1969; Leach 1992]

Penanggalan
Malaya; Malay Peninsula
Destroyer of Life
Vampire who attacks newborns. She is believed to take human form and can be caught and killed. A bunch of thistle is used to catch her. See also *Loupgarous, The.* [Bonnerjea 1927]

Pheebee Yau
Burma, *Karens*
Agriculture
Agricultural fertility deity who protects corn and rice fields. [Leach 1992; McMahon 1876]

Phra Naret
Siam (Thailand)
Unknown
Equivalent of *Lakshmi*, Indian Subcontinent. [Jobes 1962]

Phraw Majan
Burma, *Katchins*
Beauty
"Mother of Beauty." Daughter of *Phungkam Janun*. [Gilhodes 1908; Leach 1992]

Phungkam Janun
Burma
Earth and Nature
Earth goddess. Mother of *Phraw Majan* and *Katsin Numka Majan*. When she died, she became known as *Shadip*. [Gilhodes 1908; Leach 1992]

Phy Wam Numjan
Burma, *Katchins*
Hunting and Wild Animals
"Mother of the Porcupine." Daughter of *Ningsin majan* and Ningthoi wa. [Gilhodes 1908; Leach 1992]

Po Bya Tikuh
Cambodia
Evil
"Mouse Queen." Malevolent deity, daughter of *Po Ino Nogar*. [Monaghan 1981]

Po Ino Nogar
Cambodia; Vietnam; Annam, *Chams*
Creator of Life; Agriculture
"Great One." World fertility goddess who brought rice to the people and protects the fields and harvests. She was born from the sea foam or clouds and has 97 husbands and 38 daughters. Two of her daughters are *Po Bya Tikuh* and *Po Yan Dari*. Alternate forms: Po Yan Ino Nogar Taha, Po Nagar. [Leach 1992; Monaghan 1981]

Po Nagar   See *Po Ino Nogar*.

Po Sah Ino
Cambodia; Indonesia; Annam, *Chams*
Commerce and Travel
Goddess of merchants. Mother of Po Klon Garai. [Cabaton 1925; Leach 1992]

Po Yan Dari
Cambodia
Destroyer of Life; Health and Healing
Goddess of disease. Daughter of *Po Ino Nogar*, sister of *Po Bya Tikuh*. She lives in caves and grottoes where her worshipers come seeking cures for sickness. [Leach 1992; Monaghan 1981]

Po Yan Ino Nogar Taha   See *Po Ino Nogar*.

Poee Ura
Indonesia: Celebes Island
Weather; Agriculture
Rain and agriculture deity. Alternate form: Pue ura. [Downs 1920; Leach 1992; Wales 1957]

Posop   See *Mae Phosop*.

Prah Thorni
Cambodia
Earth and Nature
   Earth goddess. [Leach 1992; Marchall 1963]

Prithivi
Indonesia: Bali
Earth and Nature; Domesticated Animals
   "Broad One." Earth goddess seen as a cosmic cow. See also
Prithivi, Indian Subcontinent. [Leach 1992; Monaghan 1981;
Stutley 1984]

Pudau
Malaya; Malay Peninsula, *Lanoh*
Mother and Guardian; Household Affairs
   Goddess who protects the eastern horizon where the sun
rises. [Evans 1937; Leach 1992]

Pue Ura   See *Poee Ura*.

Pungtang Majan
Burma, *Katchins*
Agriculture
   Deity who is the mother of rice and cotton. Daughter of
Phungkam Janun. [Gilhodes 1908; Leach 1992]

Putir
Indonesia: Borneo, *Ngaju*
Creator of Life
   "Life Producer." Creator goddess. Her brother/husband is
Mahatala, who is the supreme deity with *Jata*. Alternate
forms: Djata, Putir Selong Tamanang. [Leach 1992; Lurker
1984]

Putir Selong Tamanang   See *Putir*.

Puyu
Indonesia: Borneo, *Iban Dyak*
Goodness; Household Affairs; Mother and Guardian
   Benevolent goddess of Sarawak who empowers women to
weave creatively and men to overcome their enemy's
weapons. Equivalent to *Entelanying, Gitir, Indai Abang,* and
Singgar. [Leach 1992]

Rabia
Indonesia: Ceram
Moon and Night; Earth and Nature; Family and Tribes;
Ceremonies; Immortality
   Moon goddess who is also associated with the earth. Some
consider her identical to *Hainuwele* and *Mulua Satene*. Wife
of Tuwale, a sky deity.
   *Originally Rabia lived on earth with her parents. She was
   promised in marriage to Tuwale, but when the marriage did
   not happen, he caused Rabia to sink below the earth. Rabia's
mother had a pig slaughtered and instituted the death feast. After
three days Rabia rose into the sky as the moon.*
   Alternate form: Rabie. [Leach 1992; Monaghan 1981]

Rabie   See *Rabia*.

Rajah Jewata
Indonesia: Borneo, *Sea Dyak*
Fishing and Water Animals
   Fish goddess worshiped in Sarawak. [Leach 1992]

Rangda
Indonesia: Bali
Heaven and Hell; Creator of Life; Love and Sexuality; Magic

Chthonic deity who is a goddess of fertility, sexuality and
lust, and the temple of the dead. She is associated with magic
potions and charms. Rangda is a manifestation of *Durga*,
Indian Subcontinent. See also *Rangda*, Indian Subcontinent.
Alternate form: Chalonarang. [Leach 1992; Savill 1978]

Ratih
Indonesia: Bali
Moon and Night; Mother and Guardian; Family and Tribes
   Moon goddess who is sought for protection at weddings.
Her husband is Semara. [Covarrubias 1937; Hooykaas 1964;
Leach 1992]

Ratu Loro Kidul
Java
Water
   Sea goddess. See *Njai*. [Leach 1992]

Rice Mother
Indonesia, *Toraja*
Agriculture; Magic
   Rice plant deity of Sulawesi. See also *Sago Woman*. [Eliade
1987]

Rock Maiden
Indonesia: Celebes Island
Metals and Minerals
   A goddess who is personified as a rock.
[Durdin-Robertson 1976]

Roembanggea
Indonesia: Celebes Island, *Toraja*
Agriculture
   Rice goddess. [Adriani and Kruyt 1950; Leach 1992]

Sagar
Malaya; Malay Peninsula, *Grik*
Heaven and Hell
   Underworld goddess. She guards the bridge of Belelt.
[Evans 1937; Leach 1992]

Sago Woman
Indonesia: Celebes Island
Agriculture; Magic; Life/Death Cycle
   Agriculture goddess.
   *Everyone in Sago Woman's house enjoyed her delicious dish
   made from sago palm, but they could not understand where it
   came from, as she never left the house. Spying on her one day,
   they discovered that she merely had to rub her hands above the
cooking pot and sago would fall into the pot. (In other variations of
the story, she scrapes her vagina or dirt from her body to produce
the sago.) Thinking she must be a witch to make sago appear so
magically, they decided to kill her. Before her death, Sago Woman
told the people to come to her grave a week later. They did so, and
found a sago palm growing.*
   See also *Rice Mother* and *Corn Woman*, North America.
[Schmidt 1951]

Salampandai
Indonesia: Borneo, *Sea Dyaks*
Creator of Life
   Creator goddess of Sarawak. She makes people out of clay.
Each child chooses its own gender by choosing the tools it
wants to use. Alternate form: Selampandai. [Gomes 1911;
MacKenzie 1930b; Roth 1968]

Sampny Nang
Burma, *Katchins*
Life/Death Cycle

Goddess of life. Daughter of *Ningpang Majan*. [Gilhodes 1908; Leach 1992]

Sanghyang Ibu Pertiwi
Philippines, *Manobo*
Heaven and Hell
Underworld goddess. She cares for the dead. [Jocano 1969; Leach 1992; Ratts 1969]

Sangiang Serri   See *Sangiyan Sari*.

Sangiyan Sari
Indonesia: Celebes Island, *Buginese*
Agriculture; Justice
Rice goddess.
Sangiyan Sari decided to leave earth forever because the people were so careless and wasteful of her rice. She was persuaded to return from heaven to earth by a benevolent deity who wanted to prevent a famine.
Alternate form: Sangiang Serri. [Eliade 1987; Leach 1992; Schmidt 1951]

Saning Sari
Indonesia: Java; Sumatra, *Minang-kabauers*
Agriculture
Mother of rice who influences its growth. In Java she is the guardian of rice. See also *Dewi Cri*. [Durdin-Robertson 1976; Leach 1992]

Saptapetala
Indonesia: Bali
Earth and Nature
Earth goddess. [Belo 1949; Leach 1992]

Saputan
Indonesia: Celebes Island; North Minahassa
Fire; Earth and Nature; Disorder
Volcano goddess. [Leach 1992]

Sarengge
Indonesia: Celebes Island
Creator of Life; Weather
Fertility goddess who is sought to bring rain. Her husband is Sareo. [Leach 1992]

Satene   See *Satine*.

Satine
Indonesia: Ceram
Justice; Heaven and Hell; Earth and Nature; Magic
Goddess who emerged from an unripe banana and ruled those who had emerged from the ripe bananas. She became the queen of the underworld after the death of *Hainuwele*.
Satine was so angry when the people killed Hainuwele that she built a great ninefold spiral gate on the spot where Hainuwele was killed. She stood inside the gate and told the people that they must come through the gate. Those who failed to get through were turned into pigs, deer, birds, fish, and the many spirits who now inhabit the earth. Those who got through had to jump over either five or nine bamboo sticks and became the Fivers or Niners. They had to stay on earth. When they died they would get to see Satine again but only after a difficult journey. Satine lives on the mountain of the dead, and whoever dies must first cross eight other mountains to reach her.
See also *Hainuwele*. Alternate form: Satene. [Long 1963; Monaghan 1981]

Sautu Majan
Burma, *Kachins*
Unknown

"Mother of Fat and Grease." Daughter of *Phungkam Janun*. [Gilhodes 1908; Leach 1992]

Saw Meya   See *Shwe Myet Hna*.

Saweigh
Philippines, *Bilaan*
Heaven and Hell; Creator of Life
Chthonic deity who is a creator goddess. She lives with her husband, Melu, in the earth. [Leach 1992; Ratts 1969]

Sedaw Thakmina
Burma, *Yeigyi*
Water
Water goddess. She protects the irrigation waters around Sedaw. [Leach 1992; Spiro 1967]

Selampandai   See *Salampandai*.

Seri
Malaya; Malay Peninsula, *Kelantan*
Creator of Life
Fertility goddess. See also *Sri*. [Hill 1951; Leach 1992]

Setesuyara
Indonesia: Bali
Heaven and Hell
Underworld goddess. [Covarrubias 1937; Leach 1992]

Shadip
Burma, *Katchins*
Earth and Nature; Weather
Earth goddess who makes the rainbow after Woi Shun sends the rain. When *Phungkam Janun* died, she became Shadip. [Gilhodes 1908; Leach 1992]

Shangkam Majan
Burma, *Katchins*
Insects
"Mother of the Bees." Daughter of Kringkrong Wa and Ynong Majan. [Gilhodes 1908; Leach 1992]

Shawa Unti Majan
Burma, *Katchins*
Earth and Nature
Mother of thatch. [Gilhodes 1908; Leach 1992]

Shindwe Hla   See *Shwe Myet Hna*.

Shwe Myet Hna
Indonesia
Earth and Nature; Creator of Life
"Golden-faced One." Fertility goddess who personifies the scorched earth. Alternate forms: Hnit Ma Daw, Saw Meya, Shindwe Hla, Taunggyi Shin, Thon Pan Hla. [Jobes 1962]

Shwe Na Be
Indonesia
Earth and Nature
Nature deity. [Jobes 1962]

Si Dayang
Indonesia: Sumatra, *Karo Battas*
Earth and Nature; Agriculture
"The Maker of Man" or "The All-life." Nature mother and rice goddess. [Keane 1925a; Leach 1992]

Siberu Dayang Mata Ni Ari
Indonesia: Sumatra
Creator of Life; Agriculture

"Light-of-the-sky." Fertility and rice goddess. Her husband is Ketengahen. [Leach 1992]

Sidapa
Philippines, *Bisaya*
Destroyer of Life
   Death goddess. She and Makaptan rule over all the earthly deities of Kamariitan. [Kroeber 1918; Leach 1992]

Sigrutan
Philippines, *Isneg*
Evil; Destroyer of Life
   Evil goddess who strangles people. [Leach 1992; Vanoverbergh 1953]

Sik Sawp
Burma
Sky and Heavens
   She represents heaven while Hkrip Hkrawkp represents earth. Mother of Chanun and Woi-shun who were the creators of all things in heaven and earth. [Jobes 1962]

Siladi
Indonesia: Sumatra, *Karo Battas, To Onda'e*
Agriculture
   Rice goddess. Alternate form: Ndo I Ronda Eo. [Downs 1920; Leach 1992]

Silat
Indonesia
Magic; Weather; Fire; Evil; Earth and Nature
   Forest deity. Pre-Islamic djinn of lightning. Also the name of a demon who is the ancestor of the Amr B Yarbu. [Sykes 1968]

Silewe Nazarata
Indonesia: Nias Island
Creator of Life; Education and Knowledge; Intelligence and Creativity; Evil; Moon and Night
   Creator deity who gave wisdom and understanding when she made the world and humans. She also causes fear because she is sometimes malevolent. She dwells in the loftiest sphere of heaven, the moon. [Leach 1992; Lurker 1984]

Simei
Malaya; Malay Peninsula, *Semong; Senoi*
Mother and Guardian
   Childbirth deity who protects women and babies. Her brother/husband is Ple, creator of the earth and humans. [Leach 1992; Schebesta 1952–1957; Skeat 1906]

Singan
Philippines, *Nabaloi*
Agriculture
   Rice goddess. [Kroeber 1918; Leach 1992]

Singgar
Indonesia: Borneo; Sarawak (colony of Borneo), *Iban Dyak*
Goodness; Household Affairs; Mother and Guardian
   Benevolent deity who empowers women to weave creatively and men to overcome their enemy's weapons. See also *Entelanying, Gitir, Indai Abang,* and *Puyu.* [Leach 1992]

Si Rapan
Philippines, *Isneg*
Order; Family and Tribes
   Goddess of marriage, affecting its harmony. See also *Sisina.* [Leach 1992; Vanoverbergh 1938]

Sisina
Philippines, *Isneg*
Family and Tribes; Order
   Goddess of marriage. Offerings to Sisina protect the married couple and ensure marital harmony. See also *Si Rapan.* [Leach 1992; Vanoverbergh 1938]

Sitapi
Indonesia: Sumatra, *Battak*
Creator of Life; Sky and Heavens; Earth and Nature
   Heavenly deity. Daughter of Batāra Guru.
   When swallows were sent to earth to be the first living things there, the earth was barren. Sitapi lowered seven hen's eggs and a magic ring to earth and from these grew vegetation and animals and anything else that was needed. [Leach 1992; MacKenzie 1930a]

Siti Permani
Indonesia: Borneo, *Sea Dyaks*
Agriculture; Life/Death Cycle
   Food goddess worshiped in Sarawak. Her body became pumpkins and other food plants. [Leach 1992]

Sri
Malaya; Malay Peninsula; Indonesia: Bali
Agriculture; Creator of Life; Wealth; Luck
   Goddess of rice and good fortune. She presides over fertility and prosperity. Wife of Visnu. See also *Dewi Sri,* this section, and *Sri,* Indian Subcontinent. Alternate forms: Giriputri, Ibu Pertiwi, Seri. [Leach 1992; Skeat 1925]

Srintun Tanah Tumboh Yak Srindak Tanggi Buloh
Indonesia: Borneo, *Dyaks*
Household Affairs
   Goddess of weaving worshiped in Sarawak. Mother of *Benih Lela Punggang Tengian Dara Bintang Tiga Datai Ka Jelan.* Her husband is Pulang Gana. [Leach 1992]

Suklang-malayon
Philippines, *Bisayan*
Sky and Heavens; Household Affairs; Happiness
   Sky goddess who protects households, bringing them happiness. [Jocano 1969; Leach 1992]

Suvarnamacha
Siam (Thailand)
Demi-animals; Fishing and Water Animals
   "Queen of the Sea" who appears as a mermaid. [Jobes 1962]

Ta La
Burma, *Karen*
Earth and Nature
   Mountain goddess of Thaw Thai. [Leach 1992]

Tabindain Thakinma
Burma, *Yeigyi*
Agriculture; Mother and Guardian; Reptiles
   Agriculture goddess. She is asked to keep snakes away during the transplanting season in the paddy fields. [Leach 1992; Spiro 1967]

Tagabayan
Philippines, *Monobo*
Evil; Love and Sexuality
   Evil goddess who encourages incest and adultery in Mindanao. [Jocano 1969; Leach 1992]

Tagamaling
Philippines, *Monobo*
Agriculture
Agriculture goddess of all crops but rice. [Jocano 1969; Leach 1992]

Takel
Malaya; Malay Peninsula, *Semang, Menri, Negritos*
Agriculture; Heaven and Hell; Earth and Nature
Agriculture goddess who presides over the tuber harvest. Among the Menri she is an earth goddess and her husband is Karei, the supreme being who created everything except the earth and humans. Some people consider her a chthonic deity who is a guardian of the pillar that supports heaven. [Leach 1992; Schebesta 1927]

Tala
Philippines, *Tagalog*
Stars and Planets
Star goddess. Daughter of Bathala and a mortal father. Sister of **Mayari** and **Hanan**. [Leach 1992]

Tambon
Indonesia: Borneo, *Ngaju*
Water
Water goddess. See also **Djata, Jata.** Alternate form: Bawin Jata Balawang Bulau. [Leach 1992; Lurker 1984]

Tana Ekan
Indonesia: East Flores; Solar Island
Supreme Being; Earth and Nature
"The Earth." Supreme goddess and partner of Lera Wulan. [Leach 1992; Pettazzoni 1956]

Tangkam Majan
Burma, *Katchins*
Mother and Guardian; Domesticated Animals; Agriculture
Mother goddess who provided domestic animals and vegetables. [Leach 1992]

Taphagan
Philippines, *Manobo*
Agriculture
Harvest deity who guards the harvested rice. [Leach 1992]

Tara Majan
Burma, *Katchins*
Justice
"Justice." The innocent are protected by her when they must submit to the boiling water test. See also **Ningtsi Majan** and **Ningthet Majan.** [Leach 1992]

Tarai
Malaya; Malay Peninsula, *Semang*
Weather; Disorder
Storm goddess. Wife or daughter of the god Biliku. Tarai can also be a male deity. [Leach 1992]

Taunggyi Shin See *Shwe Myet Hna.*

Teu Kweh
Burma, *Karen*
Directions; Weather
Eastern rainbow goddess. Her husband is Hkü Te, an underworld god who appears in the western rainbow. [Leach 1992]

Teze
Indonesia: Flores Island, *Riung*
Creator of Life; Magic; Mother and Guardian; Life/Death Cycle
Creator deity.
Teze lived alone for a long time. One day, as she slept beneath a flowering tree, a flower fell on her and she became pregnant. She had a son who later became her husband. One of their children was killed and when its blood, skin, and bones were put in a field, food plants grew from them. [Schmidt 1951]

Thabet, The
Burma
Immortality; Mother and Guardian; Large Size; Ugliness
Ghosts of women who died in childbirth. They are much feared by men. They have huge bodies and long, slimy tongues. [Jobes 1962; Leach 1972]

Thevadas, The
Cambodia
Unknown
Goddesses at Angkor. Equivalent to **Devatas,** Indian Subcontinent. [Durdin-Robertson 1976]

Thon Pan Hla See *Shwe Myet Hna.*

Thusandi
Burma, *Palaung*
Reptiles; Family and Tribes
Ancestor deity who appears as a serpent. [Leach 1992; Scott 1964]

Tinguian "Dawn." See *Aponibolinayen.*

Tiguianes
Philippines, *Gianges*
Creator of Life
Creator goddess in Cotabato who created the world. [Jocano 1969; Leach 1992]

Tisna Wati
Indonesia: Java, Bali
Agriculture; Life/Death Cycle; Love and Sexuality
Agricultural deity. Goddess of the dry mountain rice and the coco palm.
Tisna Wati was born from a pot. Her father, Batāra Guru, was desirous of his daughter, and when she finally surrendered to him, she died. From her body sprung food plants, the mountain rice and the coco palm. [Leach 1992; Schmidt 1951]

Tiun
Philippines, *Bagobo*
Sky and Heavens
Goddess of the fourth heaven. Sister of **Kadeyuna.** [Leach 1992]

Todlibon
Philippines, *Bagobo*
Family and Tribes
Goddess of marriage. Her husband is Todlay. [Leach 1992]

Toiron Numjan
Burma, *Katchins*
Insects
Mother of the crickets. Daughter of **Ningsin majan** and Ningthoi Wa. [Leach 1992]

Tolus Ka Talegit
Philippines, *Bagobo*
Household Affairs
Goddess of women's weaving. [Leach 1992]

Trung Nhi
Indonesia
Weather; Mother and Guardian
Rain goddess and protective deity. Sister of *Trung Trac*.
[Jobes 1962; Monaghan 1981]

Trung Trac
Indonesia
Weather; War; Justice
Rain goddess. Sister of *Trung Nhi*.
Trung Trac and her sister were originally warrior women who led a successful revolt against a tyrannical Chinese governor. Later, the Chinese returned and conquered the people. When Trung Trac and Trung Nhi died, they were deified. [Jobes 1962; Monaghan 1981]

Tuglibong
Philippines, *Bagobo*
Creator of Life; Agriculture
Primeval goddess and creator deity with Tuglay.
When Tuglibong and Tuglay were first on earth, the sky was very low. Tuglibong made Tuglay move the sky higher so it would not interfere with the rice pounding. [Leach 1992; Raats 1969]

U Kaukon See *Ningsin Majan*.

Uban Sanane
Indonesia: Buru Island; Moluccas
Earth and Nature
"Grandmother Earth." Partner of Uban Langi, a sky god.
[Leach 1992; Pettazzoni 1956]

Ungap
Indonesia: Borneo, *Punans*
Heaven and Hell
Guardian of the afterworld. She can be bribed to let people into heaven. [Leach 1992; Moss 1925]

Upu Tapene
Indonesia
Justice; Earth and Nature
Earth goddess who is invoked when taking oaths. Associated with Upu Langi, a sky god connected with the sun. [Leach 1992]

Upu Ume
Indonesia
Earth and Nature; Justice
"Mother Earth." She is invoked when taking oaths. Associate of Upu Lanito, sky god associated with the elements. Alternate forms: Ina, Inaka. [Leach 1992]

Upunusa
Indonesia: Leti Islands; Moa Island; Lakor Island
Earth and Nature; Creator of Life
"Grandmother Earth." Female principle and partner of Dudilaa, the sun god and male principle. [Leach 1992]

Uru See *Apna*.

Usi Afu
Indonesia
Earth and Nature; Creator of Life

"Lady Earth." Her husband is Usi-Neno, "Lord Sun." Creation was a result of their union and their continued relationship imparts fertility and growth to all living things. [Leach 1992; Redfield 1931]

Vula Ledz "Moon-Sun." See *Dua Nggae, Nggae*.

Wang Pyekkha Yek-khi
Indonesia, *Wa*
Creator of Life; Demi-animals; Hunting and Wild Animals
First woman. Daughter of *Yatai*. She has tiger ears and legs. See also *Nang Pyek Kha Peh Khi*. [Farmer 1978]

Warunsasadun
Indonesia: Borneo, *Dusun*
Creator of Life; Sky and Heavens; Life/Death Cycle
Creator goddess who lives in the sky. Consort of Kinorohingan, creator god. She killed her child and buried it to make the soil fertile. [Leach 1992; Raats 1969]

Wetar
Indonesia: Amboina Island
Creator of Life
First woman. She emerged from a tree that was fertilized by a bird. [Savill 1978]

Winia
Indonesia: Ceram Island; Gorrmon
Creator of Life; Beauty
First woman. She is known for her great beauty. [Savill 1978]

Ya Monoij
Malaya; Malay Peninsula, *Semang*
Heaven and Hell; Justice
Ruler of the underworld. [Leach 1992; Schebesta 1952–1957]

Ya Tangoi
Malaya; Malay Peninsula, *Semang*
Earth and Nature
"Rambu-tan Tree." Her husband is Ta Piago. [Leach 1992; Schebesta 1952–1957]

Yahsang Kahsi "Grandmother All-powerful." See *Yahsek Khi*.

Yahsek Khi
Indonesia, *Shan, Wa*
Creator of Life; Life/Death Cycle
First being. A tadpole-shaped being. She and Tahsek-khi, were the first beings. They ate the gourd of death and died. Their daughter *Nang Pyek Kha Yek Khi* became the guardian of the gourds of life and death. Yahsek-Khi was renamed *Yahsang Kahsi* by the creator, Hkun Hsang Long. Alternate form: Yatai. [Jobes 1962]

Yak
Malaya; Malay Peninsula, *Semang*
Earth and Nature
Earth mother worshiped in Kedah. Mother of Ta Ponn. [Leach 1992; Monaghan 1981]

Yak Chin
Malaya; Malay Peninsula, *Lanoh*
Heaven and Hell
Goddess of Paradise. [Leach 1992]

Yak Lepeh

Malaya; Malay Peninsula, *Semang, Kintak Bong, Menik Kaien*

Heaven and Hell; Water; Earth and Nature

Underworld goddess. One of the grandmothers who can bring water to the surface of the earth. She is also the guardian of the roots of the stone that holds up the heavens. See also *Lepeh*. [Leach 1972; Leach 1992]

Yak Tanggoi

Malaya; Malay Peninsula, *Negritos*

Family and Tribes; Sky and Heavens

Ancestor deity who became a sky goddess. Her husband is Tak Piagok. [Leach 1992]

Yara Meng

Malaya; Malay Peninsula, *Lanoh*

Sky and Heavens; Immortality; Ceremonies

Sky goddess who is very old and white. She is an intermediary, accepting the sacrifices of blood that are thrown skyward to the gods during thunderstorms.

Yara Meng is rejuvenated by her grandson Jamoi when she gets too old. He sprinkles her with the sap of wild ginger leaves. [Leach 1992]

Yatai   See *Yahsek Khi*.

Yu Kantang

Burma, *Katchins*

Hunting and Wild Animals

Mother of squirrels. Daughter of *Ningsin Majan* and Ningthoi wa. [Leach 1992]

Yuang Sori

Indonesia, *Bahnar*

Sky and Heavens; Agriculture

Sky goddess who protects the harvest. Her partner is Bok Glaih, the god of lightning. [Leach 1992]

WESTERN EUROPE

Abnoba
France
Earth and Nature; Mother and Guardian
  Goddess of childbirth who is the deification of the Black
Forest. Identified with the Roman *Diana*. [Baumgartner 1984;
Jayne 1925; Leach 1992]

Abunciada See *Habonde*.

Abundia See *Habonde*.

Achall
Ireland, *Celtic*
Earth and Nature; Unhappiness.
  Irish deity who died when she learned her brother was
dead. The Hill of Achall near Tara is named for her. See also
Habonde. [Monaghan 1990]

Achtan
Ireland, *Celtic*
Hunting and Wild Animals
  Legendary daughter of an evil Irish druid smith.
  ✚✚ *When the king of Ireland was about to leave for his*
  ━ *final battle, he slept with Achtan. From this liaison*
  ✚✚ *she conceived a son, whom she named after his father,*
*Cormac mac Art. After being inadvertently separated from his
mother and suckled by a wolf, mother and son were reunited.
Cormac ultimately became king of Ireland, taking his father's place.*
[Monaghan 1981]

Adsullata
Unknown
Water
  River goddess. [Sykes 1968]

Aebh See *Aobh*.

Aeife See *Aoife*.

Aeracura
Germany
Earth and Nature
  Earth goddess of the Rhine Valley. [Jobes 1962; Monaghan
1990]

Aerfon
France, *Celtic*
Water; Fate
  Goddess of the river Dee. Alternate form: Dyfridwy.
[Johnson 1988]

Aeron
Wales, *Celtic*
War
  Welsh goddess of war. [Monaghan 1990]

Aeval
Ireland, *Celtic*
Love and Sexuality; Magic; Small Size
  Fairy queen of Munster.
  ✚✚ *Aeval held a "midnight court" when the men of her*
  ━ *district were accused of not satisfying their mates' sexual*
  ✚✚ *desires. After hearing both the men's and the women's*
*presentation, Aeval declared that the men must learn to be more
open and creative in their sexual relations.* [Monaghan 1981]

Agnes See *Annis*.

Agness See *Annis*.

Agrona
Wales, *Celtic*
Destroyer of Life

499

Goddess of slaughter who was worshiped in Wales.
[Leach 1992]

Ahes   See *Dahut.*

Aibell, *Celtic*
Ireland, *Celtic*
Beauty; Arts; Magic; Destroyer of Life; Mother and Guardian;
Education and Knowledge; Small Size
   "Beautiful." Guardian spirit who inhabits the Craig Laity,
the gray rock, two miles north of Killaloe, Ireland. Music
from her magic harp brings death to those who hear it. Before
being made into a fairy, she had been a ruler of a *sídhe* in
north Munster. Some say fairies, particularly green ones, love
playing and teaching the music of pipes and especially
reward human pipers. Alternate form: Aoibhell. [Ellis 1987;
Leach 1972]

Aibheaog
Ireland, *Celtic*
Fire
   Irish fire goddess in County Donegal. [Monaghan 1981]

Aide
Ireland, *Celtic*
Magic; Water
   Wife of the Irish god, Enna.
   ✚✚ *Aide and her family were drowned by the magic*
   ✚✚ *of Enna's other wife, Dubh.* [Ellis 1987; Jobes
   ✚✚ 1962]

Aideen   See *Aidín.*

Aidín
Ireland, *Celtic*
Love and Sexuality
   A foreigner who married Oscar, a warrior of the Fianna
and son of the goddess *Sadb.* Aidín died of grief when her
husband was killed in battle and she was buried on Ben Edar
(Howth) by her father-in-law, Oisín. An Ogham (the earliest
form of Irish writing) stone was erected at the spot in her
memory. Alternate form: Aideen. [Ellis 1987]

Aife   See *Aoife.*

Aige
Ireland, *Celtic*
Demi-animals; Water; Unhappiness
   When Aige was maliciously changed into a fawn, she
wandered until she was either slain by warriors of the Celtic
king or drowned by throwing herself into water. Today there
is a bay named for her in Ireland. [Ellis 1987; Monaghan 1981]

Ailbe
Ireland, *Celtic*
Creativity and Intelligence
   Daughter of Cormac mac Art, who became the lover of
Fionn Mac Cumhail. She won his attention by answering his
riddles. [Ellis 1987]

Ailinn
Ireland, *Celtic*
Love and Sexuality; Magic; Unhappiness
   Princess of Leinster.
   ✚✚ *Ailinn and Baile, a prince of northern Ireland, fell in love*
   ✚✚ *and agreed to meet secretly. A rogue discovered their secret*
   ✚✚ *and got to the meeting place before Ailinn and told Baile*
   that Ailinn was dead. Baile immediately died from grief, whereupon
   the rogue met Ailinn and told her that Baile was dead, and she too
died from grief. They were buried in adjoining graves, and from
their memorial markers grew intertwining trees.
   Alternate form: Aillinn. [Bray 1935; Ellis 1987; Jobes 1962;
Monaghan 1981]

Áille
Ireland, *Celtic*
Justice
   When her husband, Meargach of Green Spears, was killed
in battle, she sought revenge. When her attempt was unsuccess-
ful, Áille committed suicide. [Ellis 1987]

Aillinn   See *Ailinn.*

Aima
Spain, *Celtic*
Mother and Guardian; Sky and Heavens
   "Great Mother." She appears in the the *Johannie Revelation*
in heaven, clothed with the sun and the moon under her feet,
wearing a crown of twelve stars. A Cabala deity who was
also worshiped in the Near East, her symbol is the Hebrew
letter *He* or *Heh.* Equivalent to *Maut,* Egypt. See also *Aima,*
Near East. Alternate forms: Aima Elohim, Aimah. [Durdin-
Robertson 1975; Jobes 1962]

Aima Elohim   See *Aima.*

Aimah   See *Aima.*

Aimend
Ireland, *Celtic*
Sun and Day
   Sun goddess. Daughter of the king of Corco Loigde. [Ellis
1987]

Ain
Ireland, *Celtic*
Justice
   One of two sisters said to be responsible for the high status
of women in ancient Ireland. Women's rights were established
in the "Brehon Laws," which spelled out women's property
rights and freedom. The Norman occupation put an end to
these laws. [Monaghan 1990]

Áine
Ireland, *Celtic*
Love and Sexuality; Agriculture; Earth and Nature; Creator of
Life; Luck; Magic; Mother and Guardian; Ceremonies; Small
Size
   "Bright." Sun goddess of love and fertility, associated with
the moon, who is said to have planted a whole hill with peas
in one night. Áine is worshiped on Midsummer Eve, when
torches of hay and straw are waved over crops and cattle. She
brings luck and increase to fields and pastures while
guarding humans against illness and infertility. She inhabits
Cnoc Áine in County Kerry, where sacred rites are celebrated.
   ✚✚ *One St. John's Night a group of girls lingered on the*
   ✚✚ *hill watching the torches and participating in the games.*
   ✚✚ *Suddenly, Áine appeared among them, thanking them for*
honoring her. She told them to look through a ring, and when they
did, they saw an apparently empty hill crowded with people.
   She survived into 14th-century legend as the fairy Aine
with a mortal lover and into modern times as the queen of
the fairies in south Munster. Possibly the twin sister of *Grian.*
[Durdin-Robertson 1982; Ellis 1987; Graves 1948; Jobes 1962;
Leach 1972; Leach 1992]

Airmed
Ireland, *Celtic*
Health and Healing; Immortality

Irish goddess of medicine. Daughter of Dian Cécht, god of medicine and sister of Miach. She helps her father guard the secret Well of Healing.

✛|✛ *When Dian Cécht discovered that his son, Miach, was*
✛|✛ *a better physician then he was, he killed his son. His daughter, Airmid, gathered the herbs that grew on Miach's grave and used them to cure illnesses of the nervous system. Once, when Airmid had the herbs laid out on her cloak, Dian Cécht overturned the cloak so the herbs were mixed up, preventing any humans from learning the secret of immortality that was possible with their use.*

Alternate form: Airmid. [Ellis 1987; Monaghan 1981]

Airmid   See *Airmed.*

Akerbeltz
Spain, *Basque*
Health and Healing; Earth and Nature
   Basque goddess of healing. She cares for animals and represents the goddess *Mari.* [Eliade 1987]

Albina
Britain, *Celtic*
Moon and Night; Creator of Life
   "White Goddess" of fertility. She is represented by the white moon and the white chalk seen in British fields. Also a fairy who appears at dawn and is associated with *Aurora,* Greek and Roman Empires. [Dames 1979; Durdin-Robertson 1982; Graves 1948]

Albuferetan Mother Goddess
Spain, *Celtic*
Mother and Guardian
   Iberian goddess at Albufereta. [Eliade 1987]

Alicantean Mother Goddess
Spain, *Celtic*
Mother and Guardian
   Iberian goddess found at Alicante. [Eliade 1987]

Almha
Ireland, *Celtic*
Unknown
   One of the deities of the Tuatha Dé Danaan. See also *Danu.* Alternate form: Almu. [Monaghan 1990]

Almu   See *Almha.*

Ama   See *Ëire.*

Amagandar, The
Unknown
Mother and Guardian
   Protective spirits. Alternate form: Orokannar. [Baumgartner 1984]

Amboto Lady
Spain, *Basque*
Wild Birds
   Vulture goddess. [Eliade 1987]

Ameipicer
Spain, *Basque*
Water
   Basque goddess of a fountain or spring in Spain. [Leach 1992]

Amilamia
Spain, *Basque*
Goodness

"Golden Yellow Lady." Basque benevolent deity in Spain. [Eliade 1987]

Amona
Spain
Unknown
   One of the *Sephiroth.* Similar to *Binah,* she is also worshiped in the Near East. [Durdin-Robertson 1975]

Ana   See *Anu.*

Anan   See *Ëire.*

Andarta
Gaul
War; Hunting and Wild Animals
   "Strong Bear." A victory goddess worshiped in Gaul. [Jobes 1962; Johnson 1988; Leach 1992]

Andate   See *Andrasta.*

Andrasta
Britain, *Iceni*
War
   "Invincible One." Goddess of victory who was worshiped by the famous Queen Boudicca of the Iceni tribe. Alternate forms: Andate, Andraste. [Leach 1992; Wedeck and Baskin 1971]

Andraste   See *Andrasta.*

Anith   See *Ëire.*

Anna Livia Plurabelle
Ireland, *Celtic*
Creator of Life; Water
   Great mother. Personification of the female principle in nature. In Dublin, she is the personification of the Liffey River in Ireland. [Jobes 1962]

Anna Perenna   See *Anu.*

Annan   See *Anu.*

Annis
British Isles, *Celtic*
Wild Birds; Destroyer of Life; Ugliness
   "Blue Hag." She assumes the form of an owl and is said to suck the blood from children. Similar to *Blodeuwedd.* Originally thought to be *Inanna,* Near East creator goddess, as *Inanna* gradually evolved into a horned moon goddess and finally into the Brythonic Annis, the bloodsucker of children. Identified with Danish *Yngona,* Northern Europe. See also *Anu.* Alternate forms: Agnes, Agness. [Carlyon 1982; Graves 1948; Jobes 1962]

Anu
Ireland, *Celtic*
Creator of Life; Earth and Nature; Wealth; Mother and Guardian; Sky and Heaven
   Irish mother goddess of the earth and moon. She provides prosperity and plenty and is the mother of all the heroes or deities. It is assumed that she is the same deity as *Dana* or *Danu* and Ireland itself. The mountains, The Paps of Anu in County Kerry, are named for her. Identical to *Black Annis,* she also parallels the goddess *Anna Perenna,* Greek and Roman Empires. See also *Búanann* and *Ëire,* and *Ana,* Indian Subcontinent. Alternate names: *Ana, Annan, Annis, Black Annis, Iath n'Anann.* [Ellis 1987; Jobes 1962; Senior 1985]

Aobh
Ireland, *Celtic*
Weather; Magic; Evil; Demi-animals; Mother and Guardian
Goddess of the mist. Daughter of Ailill of Aran, sister of *Aoife* and *Arbha,* and wife of the ocean god Lir (Llyr).

✛✛ *Aobh had four children by Lir. When Aobh died in childbirth with her second set of twins, Lir married her sister Aoife. Because Aoife was jealous of Aobh's children, she cast a spell on them, turning them into swans who must fly from lake to lake forever. Aobh returned to her children as the mist, but Aoife dissolved Aobh with her warm rays, separating Aobh from her children again.*

Alternate form: Aebh. [Ellis 1987; Jobes 1962]

Aoibhell   See *Aibell.*

Aoife
Scotland, *Celtic*
Evil; Demi-animals; Magic; Education and Knowledge
There are several women with this name in Celtic religion. One Aoife is a warrior princess of the Land of Shadows, daughter of Árd-Greimne and sister of *Scáthach.* Another Aoife is a daughter of Ailill of Aran and sister of *Aobh.* She married Lir (Llyr), the ocean god, after her sister died. This Aoife was changed into a demon of the air for her treatment of her stepchildren. A third Aoife was a lover of Ilbrec. She was changed into a crane. Killed in that form, her skin was used to make the Treasure Bag of Fianna (the king's guards). This Aoife may have been the consort of the sea god Mananan. When she stole the secret alphabet of the gods to give to humans, she was punished by being changed into a crane. See also *Arbha.* Alternate forms: Aeife, Aife. [Ellis 1987; Jobes 1962; Monaghan 1981]

Aonach   See *Ëire.*

Arbha
British Isles, *Celtic*
Family and Tribes
Youngest daughter of Celtic Ailill of Aran. Sister of *Aoife* and *Aobh.* [Ellis 1987]

Arco   See *Artio.*

Arduinna
Gaul, *Celtic*
Earth and Nature; Mother and Guardian; Hunting and Wild Animals
Justice goddess of childbirth and of the Ardennes Forest of Gaul. She demands a "fine" for animals killed on her land. Similar to the Roman *Diana.* Alternate form: Ardwinna. [Jayne 1925; Leach 1992; Monaghan 1981; Redfield 1931; Wedeck and Baskin 1971]

Ardwinna   See *Arduinna.*

Arenmetia
Britain, *Celtic*
Health and Healing
Goddess of healing waters. [Leach 1992]

Argante
Britain, *Celtic*
Health and Healing
Queen of Avalon who is known for her healing powers. [Monaghan 1981]

Arianhod   See *Arianrhod.*

Arianrhod
Wales, *Celtic*
Mother and Guardian; Moon and Night; Love and Sexuality; Fate; Creator of Life; Magic; Justice
"Silver Wheel." She is called a goddess of childbirth, the moon, fertility, and fate. In the "Mabinogion," she insisted she was a virgin. Math tested her and proved her a liar; furthermore, the birth of twin sons, Llew Llaw Gyffes and Dylan, rather disproved her claim. There is a reef off the Carnavon coast of Britain still called Caer Arianrhod, which some believe is the remains of her island castle. Arianrhod may have played the dual role of virgin plus fertility goddess. In goddess belief, the word "virgin" means "not belonging to a man" and has nothing to do with sexual behavior. She was later relegated to the status of a sorcerer. Alternate forms: Arianhod, Margawse, Morgause. [Chicago 1979; Jobes 1962; Leach 1972; Monaghan 1981; Senior 1985]

Arnamentia
Britain, *Celtic*
Water
British goddess of springs. [Monaghan 1990]

Artio
Britain; Switzerland, *Celtic*
Hunting and Wild Animals
Goddess of wildlife who is associated with the Bear Clan. She is worshiped in Celtic Gaul, Britain, and Switzerland. Similar to Greek *Artemis.* In Spain she is called *Arco.* Alternate forms: Dea Artio. [Leach 1992; Monaghan 1981; Wedeck and Baskin 1971]

Asiah
Spain
Earth and Nature
A Cabalistic deity, a realm of nature which has a dense materiality. It is the lowest of the worlds of emanations and is said to correspond to the earth. Asiah is associated with *Malkuth* and is worshiped in the Near East. She is frequently not personified. See also *Briah.* [Durdin-Robertson 1975]

Assa
Ireland, *Celtic*
Goodness
"Gentle One." She later became *Nessa,* "the Ungentle One." [Monaghan 1981]

Astiya, The
Spain, *Basque*
Magic
Basque witches of Spain. Since the introduction of Christianity, stories have been told of humans who can interrupt the witches' Sabbat celebration and overhear some information that allows breaking the witches' or the devil's spell on their victims. [Leach 1972]

Ataecina
Iberia, *Celtic*
Heaven and Hell
Goddess of the underworld and the city of Turobriga, Iberia. [Leach 1992; Lurker 1984]

Aufaniae, The
Rhineland; Spain
Family and Tribes
Mother deities. [Lurker 1984]

Auge
Spain
Fire; Creator of Life
  Spanish goddess of heat and fertility. [Leach 1992]

Aughty   See *Echtghe.*

Avantia
Gaul, *Celtic*
Health and Healing; Water
  Goddess of water associated with Grannos, the healing
god of thermal springs. Alternate form: Aventia. [Leach 1992]

Aventia   See *Avantia.*

Axona
Gaul, *Celtic*
Water
  Goddess of the Aisne River in Gaul. [Leach 1992]

Badb
Ireland, *Celtic*
War; Wild Birds; Fate; Magic; Water
  Irish war goddess who presides over battles. She appears
after dark as a tiny woman with red webbed feet to wash the
bloody battlefield clothing. Her name signifies a crow, the
symbol of war goddesses. She is part of a triune with *Macha*
and *Mórrígán.* She is sometimes called *Badb Catha.* A second
Badb was a handmaiden to *Niamh,* the wife of Conall of the
Victories. See also *Badba, Ban Nighechain, Bodua, Nigheag
Na H-ath.* [Ellis 1987; Jobes 1962; Redfield 1931]

Badb Catha   See *Badb.*

Badba
Ireland, *Celtic*
War
  War goddess who frequents battlefields. She is linked with
the war goddess *Badb.* [Ellis 1987]

Badh
Ireland, *Celtic*
Small Size; Magic
  A *Bean Sídhe,* or *Banshee,* in Munster, Ireland. [Ellis 1987]

Bainleannan
Ireland, *Celtic*
Unknown
  Celtic spirit. [Ellis 1987]

Balma
Unknown
Unknown
  Goddess in creation stories involving a flood myth. [Sykes
1968]

Ban Naomha
Ireland, *Celtic*
Fishing and Water Animals; Education and Knowledge;
Demi-animals
  Irish fish goddess who manifests herself as a trout. She
inhabits an ancient well in Kil-na-Greina in County Cork,
where she will answer questions if the proper ritual is
performed. Alternate form: Banna Naomha. [Monaghan
1981]

Ban Nighechain
Scotland, *Celtic*
Water

"Little Washerwoman." She washes the bloody clothes
after battle. See *Badb, Caoineag, Nigheag Na H-ath.* Also
called *Washer of the Ford.* [Leach 1972]

Banba
Ireland
Family and Tribes; Destroyer of Life
  "Land Unplowed for a Year." With *Fótla* and *Ëire,* she
forms a triad representing the spirit of Ireland. All three
names are synonyms for Ireland, but the country takes its
modern name from *Ëire.* Banba tried unsuccessfully to keep
the invading Milesians out of Ireland. Banba is also
considered by some to be a death goddess. Alternate form:
Bandha. See also Cathubodia. [Ellis 1987; Jobes 1962]

Ban-chuideachaidh Moire
Ireland
Mother and Guardian; Selflessness
  "Aid Woman." Title of Irish *Bridget* as a saint. Refers to her
acting as a midwife to the *Virgin Mary,* Near East.
[Monaghan 1990]

Band Goddesses, The
Iberia, *Celtic*
Family and Tribes
  Twenty-four Iberian goddesses, all of whose names begin
with "Band," were worshiped on the land between the
Guadiana and Mino rivers. Associated with *Tyche,* Greek and
Roman Empires. [Eliade 1987]

Bandha   See *Banba.*

Banna
Ireland, *Celtic*
Water; Creativity; Immortality
  Goddess of the River Bann. [Monaghan 1981]

Banna Naomha   See *Ban Naomha.*

Banschi
Ireland, *Celtic*
Small Size
  "White Lady." Irish queen of the elves. See also *Banshees,
The.* [Jobes 1962]

Banshees, The
Ireland, *Celtic*
Small Size; Magic
  "Fairies." Companions of mortals, to whom the Banshees
become greatly attached.
  ✠✠ *A Banshee would visit Fingin Mac Luchta, king of South
✠✠ Munster in the second century, during the festival of
    Samhain (Samain). The Banshee would take the king to
visit the shees (storage areas), to see all the treasures they contained.*
  See also *Badh, Caoineag* and *Banschi.* Alternate forms:
Banshie, Bansith. [Durdin-Robertson 1982]

Banshie   See *Banshees, The.*

Bansith   See *Banshees, The.*

Basa-Andre
Spain, *Basque*
Earth and Nature
  Wood and mountain spirit. She sits at the entrance to her
cave, combing her luxuriant hair, enticing men to their ruin.
[Leach 1972]

Be Bind   See *Bebhionn.*

Bē Find

Ireland, *Celtic*

Fate; Small Size

Sister of the goddess *Boann,* and mother of the Irish hero, Fraoch. According to some, she is one of three fairies who are present at every birth, predicting the future and bestowing good and evil gifts. Alternate form: Bebind. See also *Boann.* [Ellis 1987; Jobes 1962; Leach 1972]

Beag

Ireland, *Celtic*

Magic; Water; Education and Knowledge

Owner of a magic well. Anyone who drinks the water in Beag's well will become wise. Beag was one of the Dé Danaan, people of the goddess *Danu.*

✠✠ *Fionn Mac Cumhail came to Beag's well to get a drink.*
✠✠ *Beag's three daughters tried to keep him from drinking by throwing water on him. Some of the water got in his mouth and Fionn became wise.* [Ellis 1987]

Bean Nighe, The

Ireland; Scotland, *Celtic*

Household Affairs; Destroyer of Life

A form of the *Bean Sídhe.* They are Irish and Highland Scottish women who died in childbirth with their laundry undone and who, as punishment, must remain on earth as ghosts. [Monaghan 1981]

Bean Sôdhe

Ireland, *Celtic*

Fate; Destroyer of Life; Small Size; Family and Tribes

"Woman of the Hills" or "Woman of the Fairies." When the Irish deities were driven underground by other emerging religions, these goddesses became fairies. Their mound- like homes are called *sídhes.* They are identified with particular families, and their eerie wails warn of an approaching death. Their more popular English name is *Banshee.* See also *Bean Nighe, Caoineag.* [Ellis 1987; Jobes 1962]

Bebhionn

Ireland, *Celtic*

Large Size; Dawn and Twilight; Beauty; Justice

A beautiful giant from the Land of the Maidens, Ireland.

✠✠ *Pledged to wed the giant Aedh against her will, Bebhionn*
✠✠ *fled. Although she sought the help of Fionn Mac Cumhail and the Fianna (the king's guards), Aedh was able to follow and kill her. She was buried on the Ridge of the Dead Woman. Bebhionn is described as the dawn, Aedh as a storm wind, and Fionn, whose help she sought, as the sun.*

Alternate form: Be Bind. [Ellis 1987; Jobes 1962]

Bebind See *Bé Find.*

Bebo

Ireland, *Celtic*

Small Size

Fairy queen. [Ellis 1987]

Bec Fola

Ireland, *Celtic*

Magic

A wife of Diarmuid, a king.

✠✠ *Early one morning Bec Fola left her sleeping husband and*
✠✠ *went to visit the Otherworld. After being gone a day and a night, she returned to find Diarmuid just awakening and that it was still the morning of her departure.*

Bēcuma

Ireland, *Celtic*

Heaven and Hell; Magic; Dawn and Twilight; Moon and Night; Weather

Celtic deity who lived in the Land of Promise, Ireland. She was later banished to the human world.

✠✠ *She lives on the Hill of Tara, where kings desiring*
✠✠ *sovereignty would sleep with her. The Tuatha Dé Danaan (see Danu) ostracized her, but they were banished, and the kings remained.*

According to some, she is the goddess of the magic boat, or a dawn or moon goddess associated with dew. [Ellis 1987; Jobes 1962; Monaghan 1981]

Belisama

Gaul, *Celtic*

Sky and Heavens; Water

Queen of Heaven. A river goddess of the Mersey or Ribble River, Gaul. Identified with the Roman *Minerva.* Also known as *Coventina.* [Leach 1992; Lurker 1984; Wedeck 1971; Woodcock 1953a]

Belisma

Gaul, *Celtic*

Fire

Thought to be a goddess of Beltaine fires. See also *Medb.* [Durdin-Robertson 1982]

Benvarry

Isle of Man, *Celtic*

Demi-animals; Fishing and Water Animals

Mermaid of the Manx-speaking peoples. [Monaghan 1990]

Benzozia

Spain, *Basque*

Family and Tribes

Basque mother goddess of the provinces of Alava, Guipuzcoa, and Vizcaya of northern Spain.

✠✠ *An account of the creation of the world says, "In the*
✠✠ *beginning a great fire-serpent lived under the world. Restless in its sleep, it threw up the Pyrenees mountains as it turned its heavy coils. From its seven gaping jaws flowed forth fire which destroyed all the world, purifying everything; then out of the fire the Basques were born."* [Leach 1972; Sykes 1968]

Bera

Spain, *Celtic*

Unknown

Goddess of Spain who was absorbed by the Celts. Similar to *Scota.* See also *Cailleach Beara.* Alternate form: Hag of Beara. [Graves 1948]

Berecynthia

Gaul, *Celtic*

Creator of Life

Fertility goddess and earth mother of Gaul. Another name for the Phrygian *Cybele.* [Leach 1992; Wedeck and Baskin 1971]

Bibi

Europe, *Gypsy*

Destroyer of Life; Health and Healing

"Cholera Itself." She causes disease, but can also be invoked to prevent it. [Leach 1992]

Biddy Mannion

Ireland, *Celtic*

Health and Healing

Midwife of Inishshark.

✚|✚ *Biddy was a great healer as well as a midwife. One day*
✚|✚ *the king and queen of the fairies spirited her away to help*
✚|✚ *their ill child. Biddy made the child well and returned*
home, where she found that a double had been left in her place so
her family would not know she was gone. [Monaghan 1981]

Bidhgoe
Ireland, *Celtic*
Love and Sexuality
"Female of Illusion." She resembles the *Biducht*, Near East.
Alternate form: Eo-Anu. [Jobes 1962]

Bina See *Binah*.

Binah
Spain
Goodness; Mother and Guardian
"Understanding." One of the *Sephiroth* who was also wor-
shiped in the Near East. As a supreme mother she is sometimes
called Elohim and Jehova Elohim and is represented by the
color black. One of four divine elements that form the deity.
The others are *Chokhma, Tiphereth,* and *Malkuth*. See also
Matronit. Alternate form: Bina. [Durdin-Robertson 1975;
Jobes 1962; Monagahan 1981; Patai 1967]

Birog
Ireland, *Celtic*
Fomorii Arts; Mother and Guardian
A druid associated with the Fomorii (see *Danu*). She was
involved in the conception of and, later, saving the life of the
god of arts and crafts, Lugh Lámhfada. [Ellis 1987]

Black Annis
Gaul
Evil; Goodness; Demi-animals
As a conquered deity, *Anu* or *Cat Ana* evolved into a
horrible monster who sometimes appears as a deformed
black cat that devours children and lives in the Dane Hills of
Leicester. Her more temperate aspect is *Gentle Annie*.
Alternate forms: Cat Ana, Cat Anna. [Durdin-Robertson
1982; Monaghan 1981]

Blai See *Sadb*.

Blanaid
Ireland, *Celtic*
Magic
Deity with the power of enchantment. No one can enter
her fortress because she keeps it revolving continuously,
perhaps suggesting the wind-swept skies. [Jobes 1962]

Blanid See *Blathnát*.

Blathine See *Blathnát*.

Blathnát
Ireland, *Celtic*
Time
Princess and daughter of a king of Inis Fer Falga.
✚|✚ *She was carried off by Cú Roí to be his wife, but she*
✚|✚ *betrayed him to Cúchulainn. She was killed by Cú Roí's*
✚|✚ *bard. Considered by some to be a time myth. Blathnát is*
the daughter of darkness, who betrays the storm demon Cú Roí to
the sun hero, Cúchulainn.
Similar to *Blodeuwedd*. Alternate form: Blanid, Blathine.
[Ellis 1987; Jobes 1962]

Blodenwedd See *Blodeuwedd*.

Blodeuedd See *Blodeuwedd*.

Blodeuwedd
Wales, *Celtic*
Love and Sexuality; Demi-animals; Earth and Nature
"Flower Maiden." Earth goddess, wife of the Welsh sun
god, Lleu (Lugh). In midsummer, the festival of Lughnasadh
celebrated the marriage of Blodeuwedd and Lleu (Lugh).
It was the custom to make a great bonfire on a high hilltop
and to heat a wagon-wheel that was then rolled down the
hill. Those watching below would foretell the season's
happenings by the course the wheel took. The fiery wheel
symbolized the descent of the sun from its midsummer
height. Blodeuwedd is similar to *Blathnát* and *Deianeira,*
and to *Delilah* and *Ishtar,* Near East. Blodeuwedd later was
considered to be treacherous and was changed into an owl
called *Twyll Huan*. In this form, she was said to be similar to
Annis; Athena, Greek and Roman Empires; and *Lilith,* Near
East. Alternate forms: Blodenwedd, Blodeuedd, Blodewedd,
Deianeira. [Durdin-Robertson 1982; Jobes 1962; Leach 1992;
Senior 1985]

Blodewedd See *Blodeuwedd*.

Bo Find
Ireland, *Celtic*
Domesticated Animals; Magic
"A Magical White Cow." She came from the western sea to
Ireland and gave birth to cattle for the people. She then
disappeared. [Monaghan 1981]

Board See *Boann*.

Boann
Ireland, *Boii*
Water; Domesticated Animals; Family and Tribes
"She of the White Cattle." Water goddess of the river
Boyne. Wife of Nechtan, sister of Bé Find. Ancestor of the
Celtic Boii tribe. She lived in the city of the Boyne, the great
city of the Dagda of the Tuatha Dé Danann (see *Danu*), the
round underground fort (sídhe) on the river Boyne near
Stackallen Bridge in Leinster, Ireland. Alternate form: Boinn.
See also Bé Find, Breg. Alternate forms: Board, Boinn. [Ellis
1987; Jobes 1963; Leach 1972; Stone 1979]

Bobd
Ireland, *Celtic*
War; Demi-animals
Irish goddess of battle who manifested as a bird.
[Davidson 1964]

Bodua
Gaul, *Celtic*
War
War goddess of Gaul. Equivalent to Irish *Badb*. [Leach
1992]

Bói See *Cailleach Beara*.

Boinn See *Boann*.

Bonnes Dames, The
Brittany
Small Size; Magic
Fairies still believed in along the eastern coast of Brittany
who are reminiscent of the ancient Celtic cult of *Matres* or
Welsh *Y Mamau*. Alternate form: Nos Bonnes Mères les Fées.
[Leach 1972]

Bormana
Gaul, *Celtic*
Health and Healing; Water

Goddess of healing. Associated with the hot springs at Bouche-du-Rhone in Gaul and the god of hot springs, Bormanus. [Leach 1992]

Borvonia
Gaul, *Celtic*
Health and Healing; Water
Goddess of a healing fountain in Gaul. [Leach 1992]

Braciaca
Gaul, *Celtic*
Agriculture
Gaelic goddess of ale. [Jobes 1962]

Brangwaine
Wales; Ireland
Love and Sexuality
Welsh goddess of love. A later form of *Branwen.* [Jobes 1962]

Branwen
Wales; Ireland
Love and Sexuality; Moon and Night; Selflessness
"White-breasted" or "White Cow." Moon and love goddess. Daughter of the sea god, Lir (Llyr). Similar to *Aphrodite,* Greek and Roman Empires. As *Brynwyn* or *Dwynwen,* she was called the patron saint of lovers. Alternate forms: Bronwen, Brangwaine, Dwynwen. [Jobes 1962]

Breg
Ireland, *Celtic*
Evil
"Lie, Guile, Disgrace." Wife of Dagda. She appears to form a triune goddess with her other names, *Meng* and *Meabal.* Frequently confused with *Boann.* [Ellis 1987; Jobes 1962]

Brenach　See *Bronach.*

Bri
Ireland
Small Size; Magic
Irish queen of the fairies. [Monaghan 1990]

Briah
Spain
Primordial Being; Earth and Nature
"The Throne." Her world is called the Briatic. She is associated with *Neshamah.* [Durdin-Robertson 1975]

Briant
Unknown
Water
River goddess of the river Briant. [Monaghan 1981]

Bricia　See *Brixia.*

Bride　See *Brigid.*

Bridget, Saint　See *Brigid.*

Bridgit　See *Brigid.*

Brig　See *Brigid.*

Brigantia
Ireland, *Brigantes*
Fire; Immortality; Family and Tribes
Powerful tutelary goddess who was the strength of the new moon, the spring of the year, and the flowing sea. In early times, the people carried her statue in a chariot and

then floated it in the sea or on a lake to celebrate her festival. To others, she was a goddess of fire born at sunrise and whose breath could revive the dead.

✛✛ *An effigy of a bride was made out of corn straw on the Eve of Brigantia, February 2. It was said to come alive with the spirit of Brigantia during the night and in its travel around the countryside. Offerings of food and drink were left for the bride as she journeyed about the land on her eve.*

This festival has become the modern Fire-Festival of Imbolc. She is equivalent to the Irish *Brigid* or *Brighid.* (Durdin-Robertson 1982; Ellis 1987; Leach 1992; Sykes 1968)

Brigentis　See *Brigid.*

Brighid　See *Brigid.*

Brigid
Ireland, *Celtic*
Health and Healing; Creator of Life; Arts; Household Affairs; Ceremonies; Fire; Selflessness; Mother and Guardian
"High One." Celtic triune goddess. She presides as goddess of healing, of fertility and poetry, and of smiths. She is portrayed as standing next to a cow, holding either a tree branch, corn, or a pan of milk. Men are excluded from her worship and her priesthood is entirely female. Her festival is one of the four great feasts in Celtic religion and is held on February 1. She is also considered a goddess of fire and the hearth, similar to the Roman *Vesta.* The Christian St. Brigid, known in Ireland as "Mary of the Gaels" or *Muime Chriosda,* has many ceremonies and traditions associated with her predecessor, including her feast day of February 1.

✛✛ *The goddess Brigit was associated with the ritual fires of purification, whereas the Christian saint was believed to tend the holy fire along with nineteen nuns. (She may have been a priestess of the goddess.) After her death, the nuns kept the fire at the shrine of St. Brigit alight.*

See also *Ban-Chuideachaidh Moire.* Alternate forms: Bride, Bridgit, Brig, Brighid; Brigantia, Brigentis, Brighid, Brigidu, Briginda, Brigindo, Brigit. [Cotterell 1989; Ellis 1987; Harding 1971; Jayne 1925; Jobes 1962; Preston 1982; Stone 1979]

Brigidu　See *Brigid.*

Briginda　See *Brigid.*

Brigindo
Gaul, *Celtic*
Household Affairs
Goddess of fire and the hearth in Gaul. Same as Irish *Brigid* or British *Brigantia.* [Ellis 1987; Jayne 1925; Leach 1992]

Brigit　See *Brigid.*

Britannia
Britain
Family and Tribes
Goddess who is the personification of the British Empire. [Jobes 1962]

Brixia
Gaul
Water
Water goddess who is associated with Luxovius, god of the thermal springs at Luxeuil, Haute-Saone in Gaul. Alternate form: Bricia. [Leach 1992]

Bronach
Ireland, *Celtic*
Ugliness

A form of *Cailleach Beara.* She is called *Brenach* in the West of Ireland, especially in the area of the Cliffs of Mohor, and is considered a hag. See also *Mal.* Alternate form: Caileach Cinn Boirne. [Monaghan 1990]

Bronwen   See *Branwen.*

Brynwyn   See *Branwen.*

Buan
Ireland, *Celtic*
Magic
When her husband's head was brought home to her, Buan had such psychic powers that she could communicate with him. The Cult of the Severed Head was predominant in Celtic belief. The head was thought to be the true being of a person and to be imbued with supernatural powers that allowed it to remain alive after the body's death. Evidence of this head cult appeared at Roquepertuse and Entremont, where human skulls were dramatically and starkly exhibited in stone niches. [Ellis 1987; Monaghan 1981; Norton-Taylor 1974]

Bj anann
Wales, *Celtic*
Creator of Life; Mother and Guardian; War
"The Lasting One." She is a Welsh goddess of fertility, a mother goddess, and a warrior goddess who is the "Mother of Heroes." See also *Anu.* [Ellis 1987; Leach 1992]

Buan-ann
Ireland, *Celtic*
Mother and Guardian; Wealth
"Good Mother." Goddess of plenty who gradually evolved into *Ana* or *Danu,* meaning "Plenty." [Jobes 1962]

Bubona   "Goddess of Herdsmen." See *Epona.*

Buô   "Yellow." See *Cailleach Beara.*

Cáer
Ireland, *Celtic*
Demi-animal
Swan maiden.
✚|✚ *Aonghus (Aengus), the god of love, dreamed about a*
✚|✚ *beautiful maiden and fell helplessly in love with her. When*
✚|✚ *he found her, he discovered that she lived as a swan on the Lake of the Dragon's Mouth. Cáer agreed to live with him on his sídhe in human form for part of the year if Aonghus would live with her as a swan the rest of the year.*
Alternate form: Cáer Ibormeith. [Ellis 1987; Jobes 1962]

Cáer Ibormeith   See *Cáer.*

Caileach Cinn Boirne   "The Hag of Black Head." See *Bronach.*

Cailleach   See *Cailleach Beara.*

Cailleach Beara
Ireland, *Celtic*
Earth and Nature; Agriculture; Family and Tribes; Education and Knowledge; Charisma
"Old Woman." A hag (wise old woman), she was the divine ancestor of Scotland. Originally she formed a triad with her sisters, *Cailleach Bolus* and *Cailleach Corca Duibhne.* She inhabits the Beara peninsula on the Cork-Kerry border on the north side of Bantry Bay, Scotland. She is said to have "let loose the rivers, shaped the hills, and waved her hammer over the growing grass." She has power over the three months of winter. In Scotland she is called *Cailleach*

Bheur and is also known as *Carline* or *Mag- Moullach.* In northern Ireland she is called *Cally Berry.* See also *Bronach.* Alternate forms: Cailleach; Caillech Bherri, Cailliach, Cailliaeċ, Digde, Dige, Dirra, Dirri, Duineach, Hag of Beara, Mala Liath, Nicnevin. [Durdin-Robertson 1982; Ellis 1987; Monaghan 1981; Jobes 1962; Leach 1972; Leach 1992; Stone 1979]

Cailleach Bheur
Scotland, *Celtic*
Sky
"Hag of Winter." Sky goddess. A wise old woman who created stone monuments. See also *Cailleach Beara.* [Monaghan 1981; Stone 1979]

Cailleach Bolus
Ireland, *Celtic*
Unknown
Sister of *Cailleach Beara* and *Cailleach Corca Duibhne.* The three sisters form a triad. [Ellis 1987]

Cailleach Corca Duibhne
Ireland, *Celtic*
Unknown
Sister of *Cailleach Beara* and *Cailleach Bolus.* The three sisters form a triad. [Ellis 1987]

Cailleach Mor
Scotland, *Celtic*
Weather; Mother and Guardian
"Big Old Wife." Scottish mother goddess who sends the south-westerly gales. May be the same as *Cailleach Beara.* [Jobes 1962]

Caillech Bherri   See *Cailleach Beara.*

Cailliach   See *Cailleach Beara.*

Cailliaeê   See *Cailleach Beara.*

Caireen
Ireland, *Celtic*
Mother and Guardian
Irish mother goddess. [Monaghan 1990]

Cally Berry   See *Cailleach Beara.*

Cameira
Celtic
Family and Tribes
Celtic goddess who was the sister of *Linda* and *Ialysa.* See also *Cameira,* Greek and Roman Empires. [Bell 1991; Graves 1948]

Campestres, The
Celtic
Agriculture
Latin name for Celtic goddesses of the fields. [Monaghan 1990]

Cannered Noz
Unknown
Immortality; Destroyer of Life
"Washerwomen of the Night." Ghostly figures who are heard about midnight on the banks of pools or streams, beating their shrouds to get them clean. This is their form of penance. [Leach 1972]

Canola
Ireland, *Celtic*
Arts; Creativity
   Ancient diety who constructed the first harp out of a whale skeleton. [Monaghan 1981]

Caoineag
Britain, *Celtic*
Fate; Destroyer of Life; Family and Tribes; Weather
   "Wailing Woman." Priestess of the dead. Popular name for *Bean Sídhe*, one of the *Banshees*. Caoineag was usually associated with the primitive earth goddess of the district in which she was found. She is heard in the hilly areas and by bodies of water, and her wailing is thought to announce the death of someone in the royal family. This association as a family spirit and wind spirit occurred later in her history. See also *Badb*, *Ban Nighechain,* and *Nigheag Na H-ath.* [Ellis 1987; Jobes 1962; Leach 1972]

Carlin
Scotland, *Celtic*
Ceremonies; Immortality; Time; Mother and Guardian
   "Old Woman." Spirit of Hallowmas Eve. During the festival of *Samain,* a representation of Carlin is made from the last stalk of harvested corn and is displayed in each farm household for protection from evil spirits. *Samain* is a very ancient festival held around November 1 in Ireland and Gaelic Scotland. Many rituals of this Hallowmas festival survive to this time, such as extinguishing fires in the homes and then rekindling them from the flame of the *Samain* bonfire. [Leach 1972; Monaghan 1981]

Carline   See *Cailleach Beara.*

Carmán
Ireland, *Celtic*
Magic; War; Ceremonies
   Celtic goddess who came from Athens to Ireland. She used sorcery to win battles. Her sons, described as ferocious, are Calma (Valiant), Dubh (Black), and Olc (Evil); sometimes they are named Dian, Dub, and Douthur. A Festival of Carmán was celebrated in Leinster on August 1, *Lugnasad. Lugnasad* is a seasonal celebration that exhibits the magical powers of the female as opposed to the physical force of the male. This festival continued through the years as the conquering peoples retained the local deities. It may be the basis for the current Wexford Festival. [Durdin-Robertson 1982; Ellis 1987; Leach 1992]

Carpunda
Gaul, *Celtic*
Water
   Goddess of a well in Gaul. [Leach 1992]

Carpundia   See *Carpunda.*

Carravogue
Ireland, *Celtic*
Reptiles; Magic
   Possibly the name for *Cailleach Beara* in eastern Ireland.

✛✛ *A woman ate berries on her way to church and was turned*
✛✛ *into a huge snake. St. Patrick sprinkled her with holy*
✛✛ *water and she slithered into a lake.*

   The snake is an ancient symbol of the goddess tradition, and this may have been a way for Christianity to try to rid the island of an earlier religion. Alternate forms: Garbhog, Gheareagain. [Monaghan 1990]

Cartimandua
Britain, *Brigantes*
War
   Descendant of the goddess *Brigantia* who, with her tribe, fought the Romans. [Monaghan 1981; Savill 1977]

Cat Ana   See *Black Annis.*

Cat Anna   See *Black Annis.*

Cathubodia
Britain, *Celtic*
Earth and Nature
   Continental goddess. Similar to the earth goddess *Banba.* [Monaghan 1981]

Cathubodua
Gaul, *Celtic*
War; Wild Birds
   Goddess of war worshiped at Haute-Savoie, Gaul. Also a name for the crow or raven of battle, the symbol of war goddesses. [Ellis 1987; Leach 1992]

Ceacht
Ireland, *Celtic*
Health and Healing
   Goddess of medicine. [Jobes 1962]

Ceasar   See *Cesair.*

Ceasara   See *Cesair.*

Ceasg
Scotland, *Celtic*
Demi-animals; Water
   Half-woman, half-salmon mermaid who was the mother of sea captains after liaisons with mortal men. [Monaghan 1981]

Ceibhfhionn
Ireland, *Celtic*
Intelligence and Creativity; Education and Knowledge; Water
   Irish goddess of inspiration who tended the Well of Knowledge and often prevented mortals from securing the water. [Monaghan 1981]

Ceithlenn   See *Cethlenn.*

Celiborca
Spain, *Celtic*
Water
   Deity associated with thermal pools. [Leach 1992; Martinez 1962]

Ceridwen   See *Cerridwen.*

Cerridwen
British Isles, *Celtic*
Education and Knowledge; Arts; Agriculture; Intelligence; Creativity; Destroyer of Life; Magic
   Brythonic goddess of wisdom, poetry, and grain. Giving and taking away verdure (the green of growing things) led to her being called the "White Lady of Inspiration and Death." As the enemy of Gwion, she ritually kills him, their battle mimicking the changing seasons. She lives in the "Elysium" at the bottom of Lake Tegid. A ritual involving Cerridwen includes a cauldron, filled with water and decorated with flowers, that is placed before an altar. The High Priestess then casts the Circle, and, standing in front of the cauldron, raises her wand, saying: "Dance ye about the Cauldron of Cerridwen, the Goddess, and be ye blessed with the touch of

this consecrated water." Then Cerridwen is celebrated with cakes, wine, dances, and games. She is considered an insular Brythonic goddess, meaning that she is of the Celtic region of Wales and Cornwall, or a Continental Brythonic (or Brittany) goddess. The third region, to which she does not belong, is Goidelic, which includes Ireland, the Isle of Man, and the western highlands and islands of Scotland. Alternate forms: Ceridwen, Keridwen. [Jobes 1962; Leach 1972; Leach 1992; Pike 1951; Stone 1979]

Cesair
Ireland, *Celtic*
Family and Tribes; Weather
Mother of the Irish people, sometimes called their "Magna Mater."

✚✚ *Anticipating a flood, she built an ark and landed in*
✚✚ *Ireland. Or she was Noah's granddaughter, who was*
✚✚ *refused a place on the ark and was forced to build her own.*
She and her 50 female companions repopulated the earth.

This may have been ancient legend changed to incorporate the new traditions of the colonizing Christians. Associated with *Inde*, Indian Subcontinent. Alternate forms: Ceasar, Ceasara, Cesar, Cesara, Cesarea, Cessair, Kesara. [Durdin-Robertson 1982; Ellis 1987; Jobes 1962]

Cesar   See *Cesair*.

Cesara   See *Cesair*.

Cesarea   See *Cesair*.

Cessair   See *Cesair*.

Cethlenn
Ireland, *Fomorii*
Family and Tribes; Fate
"Crooked Tooth." Goddess of death, wife of Balor of the Evil Eye, the god of death. She was the queen of the Fomorii (see *Danu*) who prophesied that they would be overcome by the Tuatha Dé Danann. Alternate forms: Ceithlenn, Cethlion, Cethlionn, Kethlenda. [Ellis 1987]

Cethlion   See *Cethlenn*.

Cethlionn   See *Cethlenn*.

Cetnenn
Ireland
War
Irish warrior goddess. [Monaghan 1990]

Chlaus Haistic
Ireland
Magic
Irish witch. [Monaghan 1990]

Chochmah   See *Chokmah*.

Chokmah
Spain
Education and Knowledge; Science; Order; Primordial Being
"Wisdom." The supreme mother who manifests in many forms, including administrative and technical skills, and religious and ethical knowledge. Known for giving divine spirit to her Cabalistic followers, she was worshiped in Spain and the Near East. She corresponds to *Binah* and to *Tebunah*, Near East. In Gnostic and other traditions, she is similar to *Sophia*, Near East. Equivalent to *Prajna*, *Vac*, and *Vach*, Indian Subcontinent. See also *Chokmoth*. Alternate forms: Chochmah, Hokmah. [Durdin-Robertson 1975; Durdin-Robertson 1982; Jobes 1962]

Chokmoth
Spain
Unknown
Plural for *Chokmah*. [Durdin-Robertson 1975]

Chwinbian   See *Viviane*.

Cigfa
Wales, *Celtic*
Unknown
Celtic deity; wife of Prydavi, the son of *Rhiannon*. [Savill 1977]

Clidna   See *Cliodhna*.

Cliodhna
Ireland, *Celtic*
Magic; Small Size; Heaven and Hell; Water; Beauty; Charisma
Goddess of beauty who lives in the Land of Promise, Ireland. She was later demoted to a fairy.

✚✚ *Cliodhna fell in love with a mortal named Ciabhan of the*
✚✚ *Curling Locks. They left the Land of Promise and landed*
✚✚ *in Glandore, County Cork. Ciabhan went off to hunt and*
Cliodhna remained on the shore. A great wave came and swept her
back to the Land of Promise. The "Wave of Cliodhna" is one of
"The Three Great Waves of Ireland."

Cliodhna brought the magic of "blarney," or the gift of a cajoling tongue, to the Celts.

✚✚ *The owner of Blarney Castle in County Cork, Ireland, was*
✚✚ *worried about confronting people who were suing him.*
✚✚ *Cliodhna revealed herself and said, "Kiss the stone you*
come face to face with in the morning, and the words will pour out
of you." He did and won his case. Today the Blarney Stone can be
kissed if one climbs up to the castle parapet and is lowered head
down over the edge to reach it.

Alternate forms: Clidna, Cliodna. [Ellis 1987; Leach 1972; Monaghan 1981]

Cliodna   See *Cliodhna*.

Clota
Scotland, *Celtic*
Water
Goddess of the Clyde River. [Leach 1992; MacCulloch 1911]

Clothra
Ireland, *Celtic*
Creator of Life
Goddess of fertility. By her three brothers, she became the mother of Lugaid Riab nDerg of the Red Stripes. His body was divided by two red stripes and the three sections alternately resembled one of the brothers, indicating that all three were his father. Alternate form: Clothru. [Ellis 1987; Jobes 1962]

Clothru   See *Clothra*.

Clud
British Isles, *Celtic*
Water
Possibly a Brythonic goddess of the river Clyde. Mother of Gwawl, god of light. [Jobes 1962]

Clutoida
Gaul; Scotland, *Celtic*
Water

A spring nymph at Nièvre in Gaul. Also said to be a goddess of the river Clyde in Scotland. Alternate forms: Dirri, Dirra. [Leach 1972; Leach 1992; Monaghan 1981]

Coinchend
Ireland, *Celtic*
War
 Warrior woman who was the wife of Morgan, king of the Land of Wonder. [Ellis 1987]

Conan of Cuala
Ireland, *Celtic*
Family and Tribes
 Queen of Leinster. Daughter of **Medb** of Leinster. Nine successive kings of Ireland were her husband; kings gained sovereignty by "marrying" a goddess. [Ellis 1987]

Conchenn
Ireland, *Celtic*
Love and Sexuality
 Deity who was loved by a mortal. [Jobes 1962]

Corchen
Ireland, *Celtic*
Reptile
 Irish snake goddess. [Monaghan 1990]

Cordeilla   See *Cordelia*.

Cordelia
Britain, *Celtic*
Earth and Nature; Ceremonies; Water; Time
 Brythonic goddess of spring or the summer flowers who was originally a sea goddess. Daughter of Lir (Llyr), the sea god. Similar to Greek **Persephone**.
 ✚✚ *On May 1, when Cordelia appears, Gwythr, the god*
 ✚✚ *of air, and Gwyn, god of the underworld, engage in a*
 ✚✚ *battle over her.*
 The celebration is called *Beltane* or *Bealtaine*, for an ancient pastoral festival held when the herds were turned out into the fields for the summer. The fertility rituals attracted witches and fairies, and celebrants had to be careful not to sleep outside on that night. This festival is still celebrated in the Scottish Highlands, Wales, Brittany, and the Isle of Man. Alternate forms: Cordeilla, Cordelie, Cordula, Creiddylad, Creudylad. [Jobes 1962; Leach 1972; Leach 1992; Monaghan 1981]

Cordelie   See *Cordelia*.

Cordula   See *Cordelia*.

Cornaby   See *Kernababy*.

Cornbaby   See *Kernababy*.

Corra
Scotland, *Celtic*
Fate; Magic; Demi-animals; Small Size; Evil
 Goddess of prophecy who is said to take the form of a "crane-woman." [Monaghan 1981]

Corrigan, The
Britain, *Celtic*
Fate; Magic; Demi-animals; Small Size; Evil
 Ancient druids in Brittany who later became fairy beings. It is said they intensely dislike Christian priests, so they kidnap children and leave changelings in their places. A changeling is a deformed, ugly, imbecilic child believed to be

the offspring of fairies, gnomes, or dwarfs. [Jobes 1962; Leach 1972]

Cosunea
Spain
War
 War goddess of the city of Eiriz. [Leach 1992]

Coventina
Britain; Spain, *Celtic*
Water; Fate; Ceremonies; Creation of Life
 "Goddess of the Water-shed." Water goddess who is chthonic and prophetic. She is found in Spain and in the Carrawburgh River in England. Similar to **Boann** of the Boyne River, **Belisama** of the Mersey, and **Sinann** of the Shannon. On the Spanish Island of Majorca, dancers perform the "baile de la xisterna" or "dance of the well" and celebrate ancient fertility rites that worship water, wells, and rain. Some of the steps of the dance form a zigzag path typical of fertility dances around the world. See also **Sulis**. [Leach 1972; Leach 1992; Monaghan 1981]

Creiddylad   See *Cordelia*.

Crēide Fôrálaind
Ireland, *Celtic*
Heaven and Hell; Magic
 Goddess who possessed a magic mantle, which she used to try to persuade Art, son of Conn, to stay in the Otherworld with her. [Ellis 1987]

Creirwy
Ireland, *Celtic*
Life/Death Cycle; Beauty
 Spirit of growth. Daughter of **Cerridwen**, Creirwy is called the most beautiul girl in the world. [Jobes 1962]

Creudylad   See *Cordelia*.

Crobh Dearg
Ireland, *Celtic*
Unknown
 "Red Claw." Goddess who may be a sister of **Latiaran**. Possibly a form of **Badb**. [Monaghan 1990]

Cuimne
Ireland, *Celtic*
Ugliness; Magic; Beauty
 Spectral "Hag." She assisted Mongán in rescuing his wife.
 ✚✚ *Mongán changed Cuimne into a beautiful princess so that*
 ✚✚ *Brandubh would exchange Mongán's wife, Dubh Lacha,*
 ✚✚ *for Cuimne. Once the exchange was completed, Cuimne*
 changed back into a hag (a wise old woman). [Ellis 1987]

Cyhiraeth
Wales, *Celtic*
Fate; Weather; Destroyer of Life
 Spectral demon who is an aspect of the wind or a storm. Her screech fortells impending death. [Jobes 1962]

Cymidei Cymeinfol
Britain, *Celtic*
Creator of Life; War
 Goddess of fertility known for her "war-like vigor." [Leach 1992]

Daath
Spain
Magic

One of the *Sephiroth,* the mirror containing all the *Sephiroth.* She is said to be "hidden" or "concealed" but also assertive. Her function seems to be making a variety of forms for different kinds of beings. Among her followers are angels and other beings of the denser lower realms. She is also worshiped in the Near East. Associated with *Malkuth* and identified with *Sothis,* Egypt. [Durdin-Robertson 1975]

Dahut
Britain, *Celtic*
Love and Sexuality; Evil
Continental Brythonic goddess of Brittany.

✠✠ *She was a beautiful and spoiled daughter of the king. To further her own ends, she caused the downfall of the kingdom by favoring her lover over her father. The lover opened the city floodgates and let in the waters of the sea. A great flood ensued, and Dahut and her father tried to escape the torrent on horseback. Finally, when the king saw that they were being overcome, he threw his she-devil daughter into the waves and he escaped. Dahut still haunts the seas in the form of a lovely siren, luring fishermen to their death.*
Alternate form: Ahes. [Leach 1972; Monaghan 1981]

Dame Habondia   See *Habonde.*

Dames Vertes
Gaul
Charisma; Evil
Forest spirits who lure travelers to their death. Similar to *Parooa,* Indian Subcontinent. [Monaghan 1981]

Damona
Gaul, *Celtic*
Domesticated Animals; Water; Health and Healing
Cow goddess of Gaul. Also connected with oxen and sheep. She may be a healing divinity, as she is associated with Borvo, god of the hot springs. [Jayne 1925; Jobes 1962; Leach 1992]

Dana   See *Danu.*

Danann   See *Danu.*

Danu
Ireland, *Celtic*
Mother and Guardian; Education and Knowledge; Sun and Day; Family and Tribes; Water
"Mother of the Gods." Equivalent to *Anu.* Ancestor of the Tuatha Dé Danaan. Dé Danaans were the fourth of the prehistoric colonies (overcoming the Fomorii, the powers of darkness) that arrived in Ireland many centuries before the Christian era. They were forces of knowledge and light, magicians, and highly skilled in science and metal working. After inhabiting Ireland for about 200 years, they were conquered by the people of the fifth and last colony—the Milesians (Gaels). After the defeat of the Dé Danaans, several chiefs and followers took up residence in hills—the *sídhe* (underground forts) or elf-mounds—all over the country, where they live free from observation or molestation. See also *Almha, Bécuma, Birog, Boann, Buan-ann.* Alternate forms: Dana, Danann, Danube, Don, Donann, Donau, Dunav. [Bonnerjea 1927; Dames 1979; Durdin-Robertson 1982; Ellis 1987; Jobes 1962; Senior 1985; Stone 1979]

Danube   See *Danu.*

Dawen
Ireland, *Celtic*
Domesticated Animals; Dawn and Twilight; Weather

Sacred cow related to dawn. Dawn goddesses are often the guardians of herds of heaven (clouds) that provide earth with nourishing dew. [Jobes 1962]

Dea Arduenna
Gaul, *Celtic*
Hunting and Wild Animals
Mother of forests and hunting in the Ardenne, Gaul. [Ergener 1988]

Dea Artia
France, *Celtic*
Hunting and Wild Animals
Bear goddess. See also *Dea Artio.* [Johnson 1988]

Dea Artio
Switzerland, *Celtic*
Hunting and Wild Animals
"Bear." A statue with this name was unearthed near Bern, Switzerland. See also *Artio, Dea Artia.* [Johnson 1988; Monaghan 1981]

Dea Domnann
Ireland, *Formor*
Heaven and Hell; Creator of Life
Chthonic goddess. She may also be a fertility goddess. [Leach 1992]

Dea Domnu   See *Dea Domnann.*

Dea Nutrix
France, *Celtic*
Mother and Guardian
"Nurturing Mother." Roman name for Celtic goddess. [Monaghan 1990]

Dechtirē
Ireland, *Celtic*
Demi-animals; Mother and Guardian; Heaven and Hell; Magic
Moon goddess. Daughter of the sun god, Lugh. Mother of the Irish hero Cúchulainn, a sun god. Wife of Sualtaim.

✠✠ *At her wedding feast, Dechtiré swallowed a fly that had flown into her cup and she fell into a deep sleep. She and her 50 handmaidens were changed into birds and flew away with Lugh, the sun god, to the underworld. Here the fly developed into a baby, Sdétanta, who, when grown, became Cúchulainn, the infant sun god. Dechtiré then returned to her husband, Sualtaim, the earth god, who raised the child as his own.*
Alternate forms: Dectera, Dectere, Deichtine. [Ellis 1987; Jobes 1962; Monaghan 1981]

Dectera   See *Dechtiré.*

Dectere   See *Dechtiré.*

Dee
Scotland, *Celtic*
War; Water; Fate
War goddess. Identified with the river Dee, which was said to be oracular with prophecies that are based on the river's flow. [Jobes 1962]

Deianeira   See *Blodeuwedd.*

Deichtine   See *Dechtiré.*

Deirdre
Ireland, *Celtic*
Beauty; Fate; Love and Sexuality

"Deirdre of Sorrows."

✛✛ *At her birth, the Celtic druid Cathbad foretold her future. Deirdre would be a beautiful woman, but would bring death and ruin upon Ireland. Some wanted her put to death, but King Conchobhar saved her and said he would wed her to prevent the prophecy. When she was old enough to wed, Conchobhar was very old, and Deirdre fell in love with Naoise, a handsome young warrior. They fled with his brothers to Alba. Conchobhar, feigning forgiveness, invited them back to Ulster so he could kill Naoise and his brothers. Deirdre killed herself (either by throwing herself in her lover's grave or by throwing herself from a chariot). From Naoise's and Deirdre's graves grew two pine trees, which were so intertwined that nothing could separate them.*

Alternate form: Derdriu. [Ellis 1987; Jobes 1962; Savill 1977; Senior 1985]

Derbforgaille   See *Derbhorgill.*

Derbhorgill
Scandinavia, *Celtic*
Love and Sexuality; Demi-animals; Magic
   Daughter of a king of Lochlann (country of the Norsemen).

✛✛ *Derbhorgill had been left on the beach as a payment to the Fomorii (see Danu). Cúchulainn rescued her and killed the Fomorii. She fell in love with him, and turning herself and her handmaiden into swans, followed Cúchulainn back to Ireland. He unknowingly shot her with his slingshot. He sucked out the stone and healed her, but because that united them by blood, they could not marry.*

Alternate forms: Derbforgaille, Devorgilla. [Ellis 1987; Jobes 1962; Monaghan 1981]

Derdriu   See *Deirdre.*

Dervonnae, The
Europe, *Celtic*
Life/Death Cycle; Earth and Nature
   "Oak Spirits." Triune mother goddesses of birth, growth, and death. [Jobes 1962]

Deva
Britain, *Celtic*
Water
   Goddess of the river Dee. [Leach 1992]

Devona
Ireland, *Celtic*
Water
   Goddess of the river Devon. [Monaghan 1981]

Devorgilla   See *Derbhorgill.*

Dia Griene
Scotland, *Celtic*
Sun and Day
   "Sun's Tear." Scottish daughter of the sun. [Monaghan 1990]

Dichtire
Ireland, *Celtic*
Unknown
   Celtic deity. [Davis 1971]

Digde   See *Cailleach Beara.*

Dige   See *Cailleach Beara.*

Dil
Ireland, *Celtic*
Domesticated Animals
   Irish cattle goddess. [Monaghan 1990]

Dirona   See *Sirona.*

Dirra   See *Cailleach Beara, Clutoida.*

Dirri   See *Cailleach Beara, Clutoida.*

Divona
Gaul, *Celtic*
Water
   River goddess worshiped at Cahors and Bordeaux, Gaul. [Leach 1992]

Dobhinia
Ireland, *Celtic*
Family and Tribes
   Ancestor of the people of Corco Duibhne in Kerry. [Ellis 1987]

Domnu
Ireland, *Fomorii*
Family and Tribes; Water
   Mother goddess of the Fomorii (see *Danu*). Her name refers to an abyss or deep sea. There are many tales and sagas of the struggles between the Children of Domnu, darkness and evil, and the Children of Dana, light and goodness. [Ellis 1987; Jobes 1962]

Don
Welsh, *Celtic*
Stars and Planets; Creator of Life
   Brythonic sky goddess associated with the constellation Cassiopea and ancestor of the gods. Sister of Math; wife of Beli; mother of Arianrod, Gwidyon, and Nudd. Her name was later masculinized. May be equivalent to *Danu.* [Bonnerjea 1927; Jobes 1962; Leach 1992; Stone 1979]

Donann   See *Danu.*

Donau   See *Danu.*

Doon Buidhe
Celtic
Arts
   Goddess of minstrels. [Jobes 1962]

Dornoll
Ireland, *Celtic*
Weather; Ugliness; Physical Prowess
   "Bigfist." Storm or wind diety. The ugly daughter of Domhnall (Domnal). Her feet, shins, and knees are reversed in her body, which is said to give her strength and swiftness. She fell in love with Cúchulainn, but he rejected her. See also *Levarcham.* Alternate form: Dornolla. [Ellis 1987; Jobes 1962]

Dornolla   See *Dornoll.*

Druantia
Britain, *Celtic*
Earth and Nature
   "Fir Tree." [Monaghan 1990]

Dub
Ireland, *Celtic*
Magic; Water
   "Black." A druid who is the wife of Enna, High King.

✠✠ *When Dubh discovered that Enna had another wife, she used her magic and drowned Aide. Enna then killed Dubh* ✠✠ *and she fell into a pool. The pool was called Dubh's pool, Dubhlinn, and that's how Ireland's capital got its name.*
Alternate form: Dubh. [Ellis 1987; Jobes 1962]

Dubh   See *Dub.*

Dubh Lacha
Ireland, *Celtic*
Fate; Moon and Night; Water
   Moon goddess. Also a sea goddess. [Jobes 1962; Monaghan 1990]

Dubhlaing
Celtic
Fate; Magic; Love and Sexuality
   Prophet, lover of Aoibhell.
✠✠ *Dubhlaing prophesied that Aoibhell would die in battle unless he wore a "cloak of invisibility" that she gave him.* ✠✠ [Ellis 1987]

Duillae, The
Spain
Earth and Nature
   Nature goddesses. They appear in pairs and protect vegetation. Similar to the **Matres, The.** [Leach 1992; Lurker 1984]

Duineach   "Strong" or "Having a Large Following." See *Cailleach Beara.*

Dunav   See *Danu.*

Dwynwen   See *Branwen.*

Dyfridwy   "Water of the Divinity." See *Aerfon.*

Eadna   See *Ëire.*

Eadon
Ireland, *Celtic*
Arts
   Irish goddess of poetry. [Monaghan 1990]

Ebhlenn   See *Ebhlinne.*

Ebhlinne
Ireland, *Celtic*
Earth and Nature; Ceremonies
   Irish mountain goddess of Tipperary. Honored at midsummer celebrations. Alternate form: Ebhlenn. [Monaghan 1990]

Echaid
Ireland, *Celtic*
Unknown
   Irish goddess. [Savill 1977]

Echtghe
Ireland, *Celtic*
Earth and Nature
   Mountain goddess, a form of **Ana,** known as the Mother of the gods. Daughter of Nuada Silver-Arm, supreme leader of the gods. Alternate form: Aughty. [Ellis 1987; Monaghan 1990]

Edain   See *Ëtain, Ëtain Echraidhe.*

Edain Echraidhe   See *Ëtain Echraidhe.*

Edar   See *Ëtain Echraidhe.*

Eguski
Gaul; Spain
Sun and Day
   "The Sun." Eguski is the daylight or sunlight. Alternate forms: Euzki, Iguzki, Iuzki. [Leach 1992]

Eigin
Britain, *Celtic*
Creator of Life; Selflessness
   Fertility goddess. Daughter of a god of the underworld. She evolved into a saint in Britain. [Jobes 1962]

Eile   See *Ele.*

Ëire, *Celtic*
Ireland
Family and Tribes; Earth and Nature; Moon and Night; Ceremonies
   "Night and Obscurity." Dé Danaan goddess for whom Ireland is named. Daughter of *Ëirinn* and Delbáeth.
✠✠ *When the Milesians landed in Ireland, she greeted them with her sisters Banba and Fótla. All three wished to have* ✠✠ *their island named for them. The sons of Mil promised each goddess in turn that the land should bear her name if she favored them. Ëire became the principal name and the others were used in poetic reference to Ireland.*
   See also **Anu, Ith.** Alternate forms: Ama, Anan, Anith, Aonach, Anu, Eadna, Ëirean, Eirin, Eoghana, Eriu, Iath, Momo, Mumham, Nannan, Nanu, Nau, Ops, Sibhol, Tlachgo, Tlacht. [Ellis 1987; Jobes 1962; Leach 1972; Savill 1977]

Ëirean   See *Ëire.*

Eirin   See *Ëire.*

Ëirinn
Ireland, *Celtic*
Mother and Guardian
   Mother of *Ëire, Banba,* and *Fótla.* Also given as a name for *Ëire.* [Ellis 1987]

Eithne   See *Ethné.*

Eithniu   See *Ethné.*

Ekhi
Spain, *Basque*
Sun and Day; Goodness
   "Sun." Goddess who is the personification of the sun. Her rays dissipate evil. [Eliade 1987; Lurker 1984]

Elamite
Unknown
Water; Demi-animals
   Fish-tailed goddess. [Dames 1979]

Ele
Ireland, *Celtic*
Unknown
   Sister of *Maeve.* Alternate form: Eile. [Monaghan 1990]

Emer
Ireland, *Celtic*
Sun and Day; Beauty; Household Affairs; Education and Knowledge; Physical Prowess
   Irish goddess of dawn who is the wife of the sun god, Cúchulainn. She possessed the recognized female traits of

the time: beauty, chastity, sweet speech, the ability to do needlework, the gift of voice, and the gift of wisdom. [Ellis 1987; Jobes 1962]

Eo-Anu
Ireland, *Celtic*
Heaven and Hell
Irish goddess of darkness and the underworld. Similar to *Persephone,* Greek and Roman Empires, and *Biducht,* Near East. Alternate forms: Bidhgoe, Ith. [Jobes 1962]

Eodain   See *Leanan Sidhe.*

Eoghana   See *Ëire.*

Epona
Britain; France, *Celtic*
Domesticated Animals; Water
British horse goddess, the child of a mortal and a mare. She may have originally been a spring or river goddess. She is also said to protect asses, mules, cows, and oxen. Replicas of her are placed in buildings occupied by the animals. She is the only Celtic goddess adopted by the Romans. Also associated with birds and widely worshiped in Britain and Gaul. Alternate form: Bubona. [Jobes 1962; Leach 1992; Senior 1985; Zimmerman 1964]

Erditse
Spain, *Basque*
Mother and Guardian
Basque goddess of maternity. [Leach 1972; Leach 1992]

Eri
Ireland, *Celtic*
Mother and Guardian
Irish daughter of a goddess of the Tuatha Dé Danaan (see *Danu*). Wife of Cethor and lover of the Fomorii king, Elatha, by whom she had Bres, the god of agriculture. [Ellis 1987; Jobes 1962]

Eriu   See *Ëire.*

Erni
Ireland, *Celtic*
Wealth
Keeper of the treasures of *Medb.* [Ellis 1987]

Essylt   See *Isolt.*

Estiu
Ireland, *Celtic*
War; Wild Birds
Irish warrior and bird goddess. [Monaghan 1990]

Ëtain
Ireland, *Celtic*
Health and Healing; Magic; Demi-animals
Sun goddess and horse deity. Also Irish goddess of medicine. Daughter of Dian Cécht and wife of Ogma, god of eloquence and literature. Also the name of the daughter of Olc Acha the Smith. See also *Ëtain Echraidhe.* Alternate forms: Edain, Etan. [Ellis 1987]

Ëtain Echraidhe
Ireland, *Celtic*
Moon and Night; Magic; Demi-animals; Weather
"Shining One." Moon goddess. Wife of Midir, god of the underworld.

✛✛ *Ëtain Echraidhe became Midir's second wife. Fuanmach,*
✛✛ *his first wife, was very jealous and had Ëtain Echraidhe*
✛✛ *turned into a fly. Even in her new form, Midir continued*
to communicate with her. Then Fuanmach created a wind to carry Ëtain Echraidhe away. For years she was blown about the world, until one day she landed in a cup of liquid and was swallowed. Ëtain Echraidhe was reborn and became the wife of Eochaid, a god of fertility. Midir, still desiring his former wife, challenged Eochaid to a game of chess to win her back. Now Ëtain Echraidhe lives with Midir part of the year and Eochaid the rest of the year.

This is a seasonal myth similar to that of the Greek *Persephone.* See also *Ëtain.* Alternate forms: Edain, Edain Echraidhe, Edar. [Bray 1935; Ellis 1987; Jobes 1962]

Ëtain Óig
Ireland, *Celtic*
Unknown
Daughter of *Ëtain Echraidhe.* Mother of *Mess Buachalla.* [Ellis 1987]

Etan   See *Ëtain.*

Ethlenn   See *Ethlinn.*

Ethlinn
Ireland, *Fomorii*
Fate; Mother and Guardian
Fomorii (see *Danu*) goddess. Daughter of Balor of the Evil Eye.

✛✛ *Ethlinn was imprisoned in a tower by her father because of*
✛✛ *a prophecy that he would be slain by his grandson. Cian,*
✛✛ *disguised as a woman, gained entry to the tower and*
impregnated Ethlinn. She conceived triplets, one of whom escaped the death his grandfather ordered. He was fostered by the sea god Manannán Mac Lir and became the god of arts and crafts, Lugh.

Alternate forms: Ethlenn, Ethné, Ethnea, Ethniu. [Ellis 1987; Monaghan 1981]

Ethnē
Ireland, *Celtic*
Selflessness

✛✛ *After being raped, she became a pure spirit and existed*
✛✛ *without nourishment until she found she could drink the*
✛✛ *milk of two enchanted cows.*

Ethné was also the name of several other women in Celtic religion and may be a name for *Ethlinn.* Alternate forms: Eithne, Eithniu. [Ellis 1987; Jobes 1962]

Ethnea   See *Ethlinn.*

Ethniu   See *Ethlinn.*

Euzki   See *Eguski.*

Fachea
Ireland, *Celtic*
Arts
Irish goddess of poetry. [Monaghan 1990]

Fairies, The
Brittany
Magic; Small Size
Early goddesses who were demoted to fairies in later times. Along the coast of Brittany they are called *Bonnes Dames* or *Nos Bonnes Mères les Fées.* Similar to the Iberian *Matres* and the Welsh *Y Mamau.* [Ellis 1987; Leach 1972]

Falerina
Italy
Magic

Italian sorcerer who made a magic sword that cuts through enchanted materials. [Jobes 1962]

Fand
Ireland, *Celtic*
Health and Healing; Happiness; Beauty; Demi-animals; Charisma
"Pearl of Beauty." Irish goddess of healing and pleasure. Wife of the sea god, Manannán.

✛|✛ *Fand would often leave her kingdom of the*
✛|✛ *Land-over-Wave and, taking the form of a seabird, fly to*
✛|✛ *earth looking for human lovers to snare.* [Ellis 1987; Jobes 1962; Leach 1992; Monaghan 1981]

Fangge
Austria
Earth and Nature
Tree spirit who was the wife of the Tyrol of Austria. Similar to a Greek *Dryad*. [Monaghan 1981]

Fata Morgana   See *Morgan Le Fay*.

Fays, The
Europe
Ceremonies; Family and Tribes
Spirits of pre-Celtic matrilineal races. Associated with the priesthood or druids. [Sykes 1968]

Fea
Ireland, *Celtic*
War; Unhappiness
"The Hateful." War goddess and wife of Nuada. [Ellis 1987; Jobes 1962; Leach 1992]

Fedelm
Ireland, *Celtic*
Fate
Prophet and daughter of Conchobhar. Also the name of a *sídhe* dweller who loved Cúchulainn. [Ellis 1987; Jobes 1962]

Fedelma
Ireland
Fate
Prophet. Woman of the *sídhe* Cruachan, Hell's Gateway. (A *sídhe* is an underground fort or an elf-mound.) She prophesied to *Medb* that the invasion of Ulster to obtain the Brown Bull would not be successful. She is described as having long blond hair. See also *Feithline*. [Ellis 1987]

Feithline
Ireland, *Celtic*
Fate; Heaven and Hell
Prophet. She lives in the *sídhe* of Cruachan, Hell's Gateway. She prophesied the death of *Maeve*. She is said to have "seven burnt-gold braids hanging down to her shoulders." See also *Fedelma*. [Monaghan 1981]

Fflur
Unknown
Small Size
Daughter of a dwarf. [Sykes 1968]

Fideal
Scotland
Water; Evil; Charisma
Scottish water demon. Like some other demons, Fideal would lure mortal lovers to their deaths by appearing as a beautiful maiden. The men would follow her into the water and drown. [Monaghan 1981]

Filia Vocis
Spain
Education and Knowledge; Ceremonies; Justice
"Daughter of a Voice." In the Cabala literature she is the daughter of *Shekinah*, Near East. She may speak out loud or in someone's mind, giving guidance. Her voice emanates from the "Mercy Seat" where her mother sits. She inspired the Hebrew prophets and chief priests, pronouncing traditions and laws. She was also worshiped in the Near East. [Durdin-Robertson 1975]

Finbar   See *Findbhair*.

Finchoem   See *Findchaem*.

Findabar   See *Findbhair*.

Findbar   See *Findbhair*.

Findbhair
Ireland, *Celtic*
Moon and Night
"Fair Eyebrows." Daughter of *Medb* and Ailill who aided Fraoch in killing a water demon. She is probably a personification of an aspect of the moon. Alternate forms: Finbar, Findabar, Findbar. [Ellis 1987; Jobes 1962; Leach 1972; Monaghan 1981]

Findchaem
Ireland, *Celtic*
Mother and Guardian
Deity who was the daughter of the druid Cathbad and sister of *Dechtiré*. Said to have become the mother of Conall Caernach by swallowing a worm. She was the foster mother of Cúchulainn. Alternate name: *Finchoem*. [Ellis 1987; Monaghan 1981]

Finncaev
Ireland
Small Size; Love and Sexuality; Magic
"Fair Love." Irish Queen of Fairies. [Monaghan 1990]

Finoguala   See *Fionnuala*.

Fiongalla   See *Fionnuala*.

Fionnuala
Ireland, *Celtic*
Weather; Dawn and Twilight; Demi-animals
Irish goddess of the mist or dawn. Daughter of Lir (Llyr), the ocean god. She was transformed into a swan by her stepmother, *Aoife*. Alternate forms: Finoguala, Fiongalla. [Ellis 1987; Jobes 1962; Monaghan 1981]

Firamodor
Britain, *Anglo-Saxon*
Earth and Nature
British earth goddess. Equivalent to Greek *Demeter*. [Cooper 1876]

Fland
Ireland, *Celtic*
Water; Charisma; Evil
"Lake Maiden." Daughter of *Flidais*. She lives beneath the waters and lures humans to their death. [Monaghan 1981]

Flidais
Ireland, *Celtic*
Hunting and Wild Animals; Domesticated Animals

Irish goddess of wild animals who protects herds of deer. She is said to have a cow that can provide milk in one night for 300 people. Alternate form: Flidhais. [Jobes 1962; Leach 1992]

Flidhais   See *Flidais.*

Fódhla   See *Fótla.*

Fodla   See *Fótla.*

Fótla
Ireland, *Celtic*
Earth and Nature; Family and Tribes
Sister of *Ëire* and *Banba.* Her name is a poetic synonym for Ireland. In Ireland a province is named for her, Áth-Fhótla (New Ireland). Alternate forms: Fodla, Fódhla. [Ellis 1987; Jobes 1962; Leach 1972; Monaghan 1981]

Frovida
Spain
Water
River goddess. An altar honoring her was found in Braga. [Leach 1992; Martinez 1962]

Fuamhnach   See *Fuamnach.*

Fuamnach
Ireland, *Celtic*
Magic; Unhappiness
Sorcerer who was the first wife of Midir.

✚✚ *Jealous of Midir's second wife, Ëtain Echraidhe, Fuamnach turned her into a pool of water, a worm, and finally a fly that she blew about the world for years.*
✚✚
Alternate form: Fuamhnach. [Ellis 1987; Jobes 1962; Savill 1977]

Fuwch Frech
Wales
Health and Healing; Education and Knowledge; Happiness; Domesticated Animals; Mother and Guardian
"Brindled Cow." She fills the pails of those in need with milk.

✚✚ *Once a wicked hag milked her dry and she fled the country. Another story says that when an avaricious farmer wanted to kill the magical cow for meat, his arm was paralyzed by a fairy, who took the cow and her offspring and disappeared into a lake.*
See also *Fuwch Gyfeilioru.* [Leach 1972]

Fuwch Gyfeilioru
Wales
Health and Healing; Education and Knowledge; Happiness; Domesticated Animals; Mother and Guardian
Welsh deity in the form of an elfin cow. Her endless supply of milk can heal, and it provides wisdom and happiness. Similar to Scandinavian *Audhumbla,* Irish *Glasgavlen,* and Egyptian *Shilluk.* See also *Fuwch Frech.* [Stutley 1984]

Garbh Ogh
Ireland, *Celtic*
Large Size; Ceremonies
"Queen Bee." An ageless giant. Her priests practice self-castration. [Jobes 1962]

Garbhog   See *Carravogue.*

Geburah
Spain
Unknown

"Severity." One of the *Sephiroth.* She is coupled with *Gedulah.* [Durdin-Robertson 1975]

Gedulah
Spain
Unknown
"Greatness" or "Majesty." One of the *Sephiroth.* Coupled with *Geburah.* [Durdin-Robertson 1975]

Geniti Glinne, The
Ireland, *Celtic*
Evil; War; Disorder
Irish air demons. They aided the men of Ulster in battle by confusing *Medb's* army. [Jobes 1962]

Gentle Annie
British
Weather
British goddess of weather. The temperate aspect of *Black Annis.* [Monaghan 1981]

Gevurah
Spain
Supreme Being
"Severity." One of the *Sephiroth,* she is coupled with *Gedullah.* [Durdin-Robertson 1975]

Gheareagain   See *Carravogue.*

Gillagriene
Ireland, *Celtic*
Sun and Day
Irish sun goddess. [Monaghan 1990]

Giolla Grēine
Ireland, *Celtic*
Unhappiness
Daughter of a mortal father and a sunbeam.

✚✚ *Giolla Gréine was very disturbed when she learned the manner of her birth. Jumping into Loch Gréine, the lake of the sun, she floated to Daire Gréine, the oak grove of the sun. Her death occurred at Tuam Gréine, the tomb of the suns.* [Ellis 1987]

Glaisrig
Isle of Man, *Celtic*
Demi-animals
Demon who was half-human, half-beast, known to the speakers of Manx. [Bonnerjea 1927]

Glaistig
Scotland
Household Affairs; Domesticated Animals
Scottish guardian of houses and cattle. She is "a thin grey little woman, with yellow hair reaching to her heels, dressed in green." [Bonnerjea 1927]

Glas
Ireland
Magic; Domesticated Animals
"Blue One." Irish milch-cow that had magical powers. [Monaghan 1990]

Glas Gaibleann
Ireland, *Celtic*
Creator of Life; Agriculture
"Gray White-loined Cow." Fertility goddess. She gives an unending supply of milk. When fields in Ireland are exceptionally fertile, it is said that "The Gray Cow slept there." [Leach 1972]

Glasgavlen
Ireland
Magic; Demi-animals; Domesticated Animals
    Irish cow goddess who grants wishes. [Stutley 1984]

Goiko   See *Ilazki.*

Gorddu
British Isles, *Celtic*
Heaven and Hell; Magic
    Brythonic sorcerer who is associated with hell. [Jobes 1962]

Grania   See *Grainne.*

Grainne
Ireland, *Celtic*
Sun and Day; Love and Sexuality
    Irish daughter of King Cormac mac Art.

✠✠ *She did not want to marry the sun-hero, an old man*
✠✠ *named Finn, so at the betrothal feast, she eloped with*
✠✠ *Diarmaid, the moon-hero. He refused to don her mantle of*
invisibility and was killed.

    A light myth of the sun overcoming the moon. Grainne
personifies the gloaming. Alternate form: Grania. [Jobes
1962; Monaghan 1981; Senior 1985]

Grian
Ireland, *Celtic*
Sun and Day
    "Sun." Irish goddess of the sun. Queen of the *sídhe*
(underground fort or elf-mound) Cnoc Gréine at Pallas Green
in County Limerick. Possibly the twin sister of *Áine.* Also
said to be a name for *Macha.* [Ellis 1987; Leach 1992]

Griselicae Nymphae, The
Gaul
Health and Healing; Water
    Healing nymphs who inhabit the thermal springs of
Basses-Alpes in Provence, bordering on Italy. [Jayne 1925]

Guanhumara   See *Gwenhwyfar.*

Guener   See *Gwen.*

Guenever   See *Gwenhwyfar.*

Guenhuvara   See *Gwenhwyfar.*

Guinevere   See *Gwenhwyfar.*

Gvenn Teir Bronn
Wales, *Celtic*
Mother and Guardian
    Welsh goddess of motherhood who had three breasts,
which allowed her to nurse her triplet sons all at the same
time. [Carlyon 1982]

Gvenour   *Gwenhwyfar.*

Gwen
Ireland, *Celtic*
Happiness
    Irish goddess of smiles. Similar to Greek *Venus.* Alternate
form: Guener. [Jobes 1962]

Gwenhwyfar
Wales
Creator of Life; Mother and Guardian
    Goddess of childbirth and fertility. She appears in Arthurian
legend as three wives of Arthur: one the daughter of the god
of death, one the daughter of the god of light, and the third
a daughter of a deity of unknown attributes. As a triune
goddess, she is connected with birth, growth, and death.

✠✠ *Gwenhwyfar told the knights of the Round Table that on*
✠✠ *the following day (May Day, when fairies have special*
✠✠ *power), they were to accompany her "a-maying." The*
knights were warned to be well-horsed and dressed in green, the
color that nearly all the fairy-folk of Britain and Ireland wear. Green
is said to symbolize eternal youth and re-birth, nature's springtime
characteristics.

    Alternate forms: Guanhumara, Guenever, Guenhuvara,
Guinevere, Gvenour, Gwenhwyvar. [Jobes 1962; Leach 1972;
Leach 1992; Monaghan 1981; Senior 1985]

Gwenhwyvar   See *Gwenhwyfar.*

Gwrach y Rhibyn
Ireland, *Celtic*
Fate; Evil; Beauty; Ugliness; Magic; Water
    "Washer of the Ford." Death goddess.

✠✠ *She appears as a beautiful maiden or an ugly hag, washing*
✠✠ *bloody garments in a stream. When observed, she*
✠✠ *announces whose garments she is washing, foretelling of*
their death.

    Welsh female in black with the wings of bat. An aspect of
Morgan Le Fay. Alternate form: Mórrígán. [Leach 1972]

Gwragedd Annwn, The
Wales
Water
    Welsh spirits of lakes and streams. In later times,
Christians said they were descendants of villagers who
reviled St. Patrick and were punished by being drowned.
[Jobes 1962]

Gwyar
Wales
Dawn and Twilight
    "Gore." Personification of the red dawn or gloaming.
Welsh wife of the sky god, Lludd, and sister of Arthur, by
whom she was the mother of Gwalchmei. [Jobes 1962;
Monaghan 1981]

Gwyllion, The
Wales
Earth and Nature; Evil; Magic; Metals
    Welsh mountain spirits who are fierce and cruel. As
protection against their magic it is necessary to carry
something made of iron. [Jobes 1962; Monaghan 1981]

Habetrot
Britain
Health and Healing; Household Affairs
    British goddess of spinning and healing. [Monaghan 1981]

Habonde
British Isles, *Celtic*
Agriculture; Magic; Ceremonies
    "Abundance." A goddess of Germanic or Celtic origin. She
is the goddess of witches. Beltane is a special holiday to Celtic
witches, the Celtic May Day, whose rites are said to point to a
very early female fertility cult. Still celebrated today in
Ireland, the Scottish Highlands, Wales, Brittany, and the Isle
of Man, it is intended to increase fertility of the herds, fields,
and home. The main event is the building of the Beltane
bonfire. People dance sunwise around it and cattle are driven
through it. Sometimes two fires are built and people creep
between them to ensure good health and luck. In Denmark,
Habonde distributes gifts. Also a name for the Norse goddess
of the earth's harvests, *Fulla,* Northern Europe. See also

Habonde, Northern Europe. Alternate forms: Abunciada, Abundia, Dame Habondia, Habondia. [Jobes 1962; Leach 1972; Monaghan 1981]

Habondia   See *Habonde.*

Hag
Scotland
Magic; Ugliness; Evil; Destroyer of Life
Scottish spirit of darkness and storms; a sorcerer. An evil, ugly, old woman who is the enemy of life, who became known as a witch. Associated with the devil and death. [Jobes 1962]

Hag of Beara   See *Cailleach Beara, Bera.*

Helliougmounis
Gaul
Sun and Day
An Aquitainian sun goddess in Gaul. Aquitaine was a kingdom in southwest France at the time of Julius Caesar. [Bridgwater 1950; Leach 1992]

Henwen
Britain
Creator of Life; Domesticated Animals; Insects; Agriculture
British sow goddess who appeared early in the creation period. Henwen wandered about the land giving birth in various places to wheat, barley, a bee, a kitten, an eagle, and a wolf. [Monaghan 1981]

Hod
Spain
Unknown
"Splendor." The Cabala call her Elohim Tzabaoth, one of the *Sephiroth.* [Jobes 1962]

Hokmah   See *Chokmah.*

Ialysa
Celtic
Family and Tribes
Goddess who was the sister of *Cameira* and *Linda.* [Graves 1949]

Iath   See *Ëire.*

Iath n'Anann   See *Anu.*

Icauna
Gaul
Water
Goddess of the river Yonne in Gaul. [Leach 1992]

Idetargi   See *Ilazki.*

Ignis Fatuus
Ireland
Weather; Disorder
Irish mist or light goddess. She creates a mirage in the marsh, causing people to lose their way. [Jobes 1962]

Iguzki   See *Eguski.*

Ilazki
Spain; France, *Basque*
Moon and Night; Family and Tribes
"Moon," "Grandmother." Daughter of the earth and sister of the sun. Alternate forms: Goiko, Idetargi, Illargi, Illargui, Iratagi, Iretagi, Iretargui. [Leach 1992; Lurker 1984]

Illargi   See *Ilazki.*

Illargui
Spain, *Basque*
Moon and Night
"Light of the Dead." The light (possibly of the moon) that shines for the souls of the dead. Alternate form: Illargi. See also *Ilazki.* [Leach 1992; Lurker 1984]

Inghean Bhuidhe
Ireland, *Celtic*
Selflessness; Agriculture; Ceremonies; Time; Creator of Life; Life/Death Cycle
"Yellow-haired Girl." Sister of *Latiaran* and *Lasair.* She rules the beginning of summer as a fertility goddess. She is honored at her festival on May 6. Later sainted by the Christian church along with her sisters. [Monaghan 1990]

Iratagi   See *Ilazki.*

Iretagi   See *Ilazki.*

Iretargui   See *Ilazki.*

Irnan
Ireland, *Celtic*
Magic
Sorcerer of the Dé Danaan. Daughter of Conaran. Irnan and her two sisters spun a magic web to capture the Fianna (the king's guards). [Ellis 1987]

Isolde   See *Isolt.*

Isolt
Ireland, *Celtic*
Love and Sexuality
Irish lover of Tristan.
✝✝ *Their love life was fraught with problems and Tristan eventually crossed the sea to France, where he met and married Isolt of the White Hands. There was a dramatic confrontation between Isolt the wife and Isolt the lover.*
Reduplication of character was common in mythology and folklore. Alternate forms: Essylt, Isolde, Yseut. [Leach 1972]

Isolt of the White Hands
France, *Celtic*
Love and Sexuality
Wife of Tristan. See also *Isolt.* [Leach 1972]

Ith
Ireland, *Celtic*
Earth and Nature
"Hunger for Fertility." Name of *Ëire* and *Eo-Anu.* Also the name of an Irish god. [Jobes 1962]

Iuzki   See *Eguski.*

Ivilia
Spain
Water
Spanish goddess of healing springs. [Leach 1992a]

Iweridd
Ireland, *Celtic*
Earth and Nature; Family and Tribes
"Ireland." Brythonic earth goddess. Mother of *Branwen.* [Jobes 1962]

Keridwen   See *Cerridwen.*

Kernababy
England; Scotland, *Celtic*
Earth and Nature; Agriculture; Ceremonies
An image of an earth goddess fashioned from the last gleanings of the cornfield. Probably used in fertility rites in England and Scotland and related to *Persephone*, Greek and Roman Empires. Alternate forms: Cornaby, Cornbaby, Kernbaby, Kirnababy. [Jobes 1962]

Kernbaby   See *Kernababy*.

Kesara   See *Cesair*.

Kethlenda   See *Cethlenn*.

Kicva
British Isles
Agriculture
Brythonic fertility goddess who was thought to change with the seasons. Wife of Pryderi, with whom she lived in the enchanted land of Dyfed. Alternate form: Kieva. [Jobes 1962; Sykes 1968]

Kieva   See *Kicva*.

Kirnababy   See *Kernababy*.

Korrigan
Gaul, *Celtic*
Water
Goddess of underground springs in Gaul. [Monaghan 1981]

Lady of Baza
Spain, *Turdetan*
Earth and Nature; Family and Tribes
Turdetan goddess of Granada, Spain. The Turdetan people were contemporaries of the Iberians and lived in the southern part of the Iberian Peninsula from the late 6th century B.C.E. to the arrival of the Romans at the end of the 3rd century B.C.E. [Eliade 1987]

Lady of the Lake
Wales
Water
Name for Welsh *Nimue*. See also *Vivian*. [Monaghan 1981]

Laha
Unknown
Health and Healing
Possibly a goddess of health. [Jayne 1925]

Lahe
Spain, *Basque*
Health and Healing
Basque goddess invoked to prevent or cure illness. [Eliade 1987; Leach 1992]

Lamia
Spain, *Basque*
Water; Goodness
Benevolent Basque water sprite. [Leach 1972]

Lamin
Spain, *Basque*
Demi-animals; Domesticated Animals
Basque spirit who has chicken feet. She inhabits caves, wells, and old castles. She disappears when there are oxen present. [Eliade 1987]

Laminaks
Spain, *Basque*
Demi-animals; Domesticated Animals
Basque spirit of the western Pyrenees. She sometimes manifests as a mermaid and other times as half-bird, half-woman. [Eliade 1987]

Lasair
Ireland
Time; Selflessness; Creator of Life
"Flame." Irish fertility goddess of spring. Sister of *Latiaran* and *Inghean Bhuidhe*. The three goddesses were sainted by the Christian church. [Monaghan 1990]

Latiaran
Ireland
Agriculture; Selflessness
Irish harvest goddess. Sister of *Lasair* and *Inghean Bhuidhe*. Later, all three became Christian saints. *Crobh Dearg* is sometimes also listed as Latiaran's sister. [Monaghan 1990]

Latis
Britain
Water
Water goddess found in British pools or bogs. [Leach 1992]

Lavercam   See *Lebharcham*.

Leanan Sidhe
Ireland, *Celtic*
Intelligence and Creativity; Arts; Magic; Love and Sexuality; Unhappiness
"Fairy Sweetheart" who inspires singers. Irish sister and opposite of *Bean Sídhe*. Because of her unearthly beauty, her mate would be distraught when she was not with him and would die from depression, which led to the belief that she was destructive. Alternate form: Lhianna-shee. [Ellis 1987; Monaghan 1981]

Lebharcham
Ireland, *Celtic*
Health and Healing; Arts
Nurse of Deirdre. Also a poet.
✠ ✠ *Lebharcham tried to protect Deirdre by lying to Conchobhar. She told him that Deirdre's beauty had faded while she lived in Alba with Naoise. She knew Conchobhar still thought about vengeance against Naoise for eloping with his bride-to-be.*
Alternate forms: Lavercam, Lebhorcham. [Ellis 1987; Monaghan 1981; Savill 1977]

Lebhorcham   See *Lebharcham*.

Levarcham
Ireland, *Celtic*
Weather; Fate; Physical Prowess
Irish prophet and wind spirit. Her feet, shins, and knees are reversed, making her strong and swift. See also *Dornoll*. [Jobes 1962]

Lhianna-shee   See *Leanan Sidhe*.

LôBan
Ireland, *Celtic*
Beauty; Water; Demi-animals
"Beauty of Women." Sister of *Fand*. Also the name of a mermaid that lives in Lough Neagh. Alternate form: Liban. [Ellis 1987; Monaghan 1981]

Liban   See *Lí Ban*.

Lilith   See *Lilith*, Near East.

Linda
Celtic
Family and Tribes
Goddess along with her sisters *Cameira* and *Ialysa*. See also *Linda*, Eastern Europe. [Graves 1948]

Litavis
Gaul
War
War goddess in Gaul. Associated with Mars Cicollius (Celtic name for the Roman Mars). [Leach 1992]

Little Van Lake Lady   See *Modron*.

Logia
Ireland, *Celtic*
Water
Irish goddess of the Lagan River. [Monaghan 1990]

Long Meg
Britain
Destroyer of Life; Large Size
British demon of disease and plague. She is a giant who can throw large boulders. Sometimes called *Mons Meg,* it is from this name that large guns get their name. Alternate form: Meg. [Jobes 1962]

Lot
Ireland
War; Physical Prowess
Fomori (the powers of darkness) war goddess. She has bloated lips in her breast, has four eyes in her back, and is extremely strong. [Ellis 1987]

Luaths Lurgann
Ireland, *Celtic*
Physical Prowess; Earth and Nature
"Speedy Foot." The fastest of all the runners and aunt of Finn.

When Finn was born, Luaths Lurgann spirited him away to protect him from those who would harm him. After many years, Luaths Lurgann had grown old and was unable to run very fast. While being pursued by an enemy, Finn picked up his aunt so he could carry her to safety. Instead, Finn ran so fast that Luaths Lurgann was torn apart. Her nephew planted her thighbones in the earth and they formed Loch Lurgann. [Monaghan 1981]

Lur
Spain, *Basque*
Creator of Life; Supreme Being
"Earth." She is the Basque mother of the sun and the moon. Lur contains the wealth of the earth. Alternate form: Lurbira. [Leach 1992; Lurker 1984]

Lurbira   See *Lur*.

Lurgorr
Spain, *Basque*
Earth and Nature
"Red Earth." Basque/Pyrennean goddess worshiped in Roman times. [Lurker 1984]

Lusitanian Goddess
Iberia, *Lusitanian*
Family and Tribes
Iberian peninsular tribal goddess related to *Artemis*, Greek and Roman Empires. [Eliade 1987]

Mab   See *Medb*.

Macha
Ireland, *Celtic*
War; Family and Tribes; Health and Healing
Triune goddess with *Badb* and *Neman*. As goddess of war, she personifies battle and slaughter. Heads cut off in battle are called "Macha's acorn crop."

As wife of Crunniuc Mac Agnomain of Ulster, Macha was forced to race against the king's horses even though she was pregnant. At the end of the race she gave birth to twins, and the place was named Emain Macha. Before she died, she cursed the men of Ulster, saying they would suffer the pangs of childbirth for five days and four nights during times of Ulster's greatest difficulties and for nine times nine generations.
Macha of the Red Tresses is said to have been the seventy-sixth monarch of Ireland who built the Emain Macha and established the first hospital in Ireland 400 years before the first hospital in Rome. Alternate form: Grian. [Ellis 1987; Leach 1972; Monaghan 1981; Stone 1979]

Maeve   See *Medb*.

Ma Gog   See *Magog*.

Maga
Ireland, *Celtic*
Mother and Guardian
Goddess and daughter of the love god, Aonghus Óg. Her husband is Ross the Red. [Ellis 1987]

Mag-Moullach   See *Cailleach Beara*.

Magog
Britain
Earth and Nature; Mother and Guardian
"Mother God." British mountain goddess. Alternate form: Ma Gog. [Monaghan 1990]

Maid Marian
Britain
Time
Goddess of spring, the British Queen of the May. Equivalent to *Myrrha*, Near East. [Leach 1972]

Mal
Ireland, *Celtic*
Unknown
Irish goddess of Hag's Head on the Cliffs of Moher. See also *Bronach*. [Monaghan 1990]

Mala Liath
Scotland
Sky and Heavens
"Gray Mare" or "Gray Eyebrows." Sky goddess who is said to have been the caretaker of pigs. May be an alternate name for *Cailleach Beara*. [Monaghan 1990; Stone 1979]

Malagan Mother Goddess
Iberia
Mother and Guardian
An Iberian goddess similar to Phoenician *Tanit* who appeared in the Valley of Abdalajis (Malaga) and in the sanctuary of Castellar de Santisteban (Jaen). [Eliade 1987]

Malkuth
Spain
Family and Tribes; Earth and Nature
"Queen." Personification of Israel. She is personified as the throne of justice, one of the *Sephiroth*. The Cabala writings

say she is connected with the earth, both on its surface and within it, the densest manifestation of matter. Associated with *Matronethah* and said to correspond to *Shekinah*, Near East. Malkuth is also worshiped in the Near East. [Durdin-Robertson 1975; Jobes 1962]

Margawse   See *Morgause.*

Mari
Spain, *Basque*
Water; Justice; Demi-animals
    Basque goddess who presides over rains and drought, and punishes those guilty of lies, stealing, and pride. Sometimes she lives in caves, assuming the physical characteristics of different animals, such as cloven hooves or claws. She sometimes appears as a wealthy woman. She rides through the air in a horse-drawn chariot and lives in a richly appointed palace, which she replaces every seven years. She can also appear as a burning tree, a white cloud, or a rainbow. She is pleased by offerings of sheep. See also *Mari,* Indian Subcontinent. [Eliade 1987]

Mari Morgan, The
British Isles, *Celtic*
Weather; Justice; Demi-animals
    To the continental Brythonic Celts, these are sirens of the western seaboard and islands. Alternate forms: Morgan, Morganes. [Leach 1972]

Matres, The
Iberia
Mother and Guardian
    "Mother." Goddesses of the central part of the Iberian Peninsula with such names as Matres Aufaniae in Seville and Matres Brigaecae, Matres Galaicae, and Matres Monitucinae in Burgos. Also known as *Matronae.* See also *Bonnes Dames Duillae, Fairies;* and *Matris,* Indian Subcontinent. [Eliade 1987]

Matronae   See *Matres, The.*

Matronethah
Spain
Mother and Guardian
    "The Mother," "The Way." Her husband is Metatron. She is mentioned in the *Zohar,* the "Book of Brightness," the universal code of the Cabala. She is associated with *Malkuth* and said to correspond to *Shekinah,* Near East. Alternate form: Matronitha. [Durdin-Robertson 1975; Monaghan 1981; Patai 1967]

Matronit
Spain
Love and Sexuality; Mother and Guardian; Evil; Selflessness
    The Daughter of the Cabalistic tetrad, which consisted of Father, Mother, Son, and Daughter. She is the link between The Divine and humans. In the *Zohar,* she takes Jacob, and then Moses, as her husband. Her four traits are said to be chastity, promiscuity, motherliness, and bloodthirstiness. Alternate forms: Matronita, Makhut. [Monaghan 1981; Patai 1967]

Matronita   See *Matronit.*

Matronitha   See *Matronetha.*

Meabal   See *Breg.*

Meadhbh   See *Medb.*

Meave   See *Medb.*

Medb
Ireland, *Celtic*
War; Love and Sexuality; Supreme Being; Magic; Small Size
    Irish goddess of sovereignty. A king must be ritually married to her to legitimize his reign. Considered a triune goddess, presiding over war, sovereignty, and sexuality and intoxication. She became the goddess of Beltaine in whose honor the May Queen is crowned and the ceremonial dance around the Maypole is held. She has been demoted to a fairy queen, *Mab.* See also *Belisma, Conan of Cuala.* Alternate forms: Maeve, Meadhbh, Meave, Medhbh, Medhbha. [Durdin-Robertson 1982; Ellis 1987; Jobes 1962; Leach 1992; Monaghan 1981; Savill 1977; Senior 1985; Stone 1979]

Medhbh   See *Medb.*

Medhbha   See *Medb.*

Meg   See *Long Meg.*

Melusina   See *Melusine.*

Melusine
Gaul
Demi-animals; Justice
    Daughter of the water goddess *Pressina.*

✝✝   *Each Sunday Melusine turns into a serpent,*
✝✝   *punishment given her by her mother for attacking*
✝✝   *her father.*

    In France, one of the most famous fairies, who is still honored by bakers for the May Fair in the neighborhood of Lusignan near Poitiers. They make gingerbread cakes (*melusines*) bearing her impression and a serpent's tail. Alternate form: Melusina. [Durdin-Robertson 1982; Monaghan 1981]

Meng   See *Breg.*

Mermaids, The
Ireland; Europe
Demi-animals; Water
    Sea deities who are half-human, half-fish. They can be benevolent or malevolent. Similar to the *Sirens,* Greek and Roman Empires. [Ellis 1987; Jobes 1962]

Merrow
Ireland
Demi-animals; Water
    An Irish *Mermaid.* [Bonnerjea 1927]

Mess Buachalla
Ireland, *Celtic*
Charisma; Mother and Guardian
    "The Cowherd's Foster Child."

✝✝   *Mess Buachalla was the daughter of Ëtain Óig and*
✝✝   *Cormac. Cormac wanted a son, so he ordered his daughter*
✝✝   *killed. She captivated the hearts of her killers and they left*
her in the barn of the cowherd of the High King Eterscél. She married Eterscél, but on her wedding eve, she was visited by Nemglan, the bird god, and Conaire was born of this union. Eterscél raised Conaire as his son.
    Others say she was a child of incest. [Ellis 1987; Jobes 1962]

Minerva Medica
France
Health and Healing
    Goddess of healing absorbed by the Romans. [Monaghan 1990]

Miranda
Britain
Dawn and Twilight; Time
   Possibly a dawn or spring maiden from an old English myth. [Jobes 1962]

Modron
British Isles, *Celtic*
Water; Health and Healing
   Brythonic water goddess. Wife of the underworld god, Urien, and mother of the sun god, Mabon. She presides over medicinal herbs. Alternate form: Little Van Lake Lady. [Jobes 1962; Leach 1972]

Mogfind   See *Mongfhinn.*

Momo   See *Ëire.*

Momu
Scotland, *Celtic*
Waters; Earth and Nature
   Goddess of wells and hills. [Monaghan 1990]

Moncha
Ireland, *Celtic*
Ceremonies
   Irish druidic priestess. [Monaghan 1990]

Moneiba
Canary Islands
Weather; Mother and Guardian
   Goddess and protector of Hierro Island. She is worshiped by women and invoked for rain. [Leach 1992; Lurker 1984]

Mongfhinn
Ireland, *Celtic*
Magic; Evil; Ceremonies
   Malevolent goddess of sorcery.
   ✠✠ *She accidentally consumed poison that she had intended for her stepson. She died on Samain Eve, which came to be known as the Festival of Mongfhinn. On this night she searches the countryside, trying to find children's souls.*
   Also said to be a snow goddess. Alternate form: Mogfind. [Durdin-Robertson 1982; Ellis 1987; Jobes 1962]

Mons Meg   See *Long Meg.*

Mór   See *Mughain.*

Mor Muman
Ireland, *Celtic*
Sun and Day
   Sun goddess. [Ellis 1987]

Morey Ba
Canary Islands
Unknown
   Goddess of women. [Basset 1925; Leach 1992]

Morgain La Fee   See *Morgan Le Fay.*

Morgaine La Faye   See *Morgan Le Fay.*

Morgan   See *Mari Morgan, The.*

Morgan Le Fay
Britain; Wales
Water; Magic; Small Size
   Sea goddess who evolved into an English and Welsh enchantress. A fairy queen who evolved from the earlier goddess, *Mórrígán.* She is known in France as *Morgain La Fee*; in Denmark, she is called *Morgana*; and in Italy *Fata Morgana.* She is called the queen of Avalon on the Isle of Women. Sometimes spelled *Morgaine La Faye.* See also *Morgana.* Alternate form: Fata Morgana. [Bonnerjea 1927; Monaghan 1981; Stone 1979]

Morgana   See *Morgan Le Fay.*

Morganes   See *Mari Morgan, The.*

Morgause
Ireland, *Celtic*
Moon and Night
   Moon goddess who was a later form of *Arianhod.* Alternate form: Margawse. See also Arianrhod. [Jobes 1962]

Morgay
Britain
Agriculture
   North British harvest goddess. [Monaghan 1990]

Moriath
Ireland, *Celtic*
Water; Magic; Arts; Health and Healing
   "Sea-land." She crafts magical music that puts people to sleep and restores speech to those who have lost it. See also *Muiriath.* Alternate form: Moriath Morce. [Ellis 1987; Monaghan 1981]

Moriath Morce   See *Moriath.*

Mórrîgán
Ireland, *Celtic*
War; Magic; Demi-animals; Mother and Guardian
   "Great Queen." Irish goddess of the Tuatha Dé Danaan (see *Danu*). She is a triune goddess of war who does not fight, but uses magic to assist her warriors. The triune is said to be formed with *Badb* and *Macha*; or *Macha, Badb,* and *Anu*; or *Macha, Badb,* and *Nemain.* The latter two groupings are called The Mórrígán, whose three attributes are variously given as the three phases of the moon; the Three Mothers; or maiden, matron, and crone.
   ✠✠ *It was Mórrígán who provided fog and rain clouds so the Tuatha Dé Danaan could land undetected on the coast of Ireland. She aided them in their battle against the earlier inhabitants of Ireland, the Formorii and Fir Bolgs. She became the enemy of Cúchulainn when he refused her love and she left him in the form of a raven, predicting his short and grim life.*
   See also *Morgan Le Fay.* Alternate form: Gwrach y Rhibyn. [Ellis 1987; Leach 1992; Monaghan 1981; Stone 1979]

Moruach   See *Moruadh.*

Moruadh
Ireland, *Celtic*
Demi-animals; Water
   Irish sea maiden. She drinks brandy, and her appearance is like that of a merman (a male sea-dweller), half-human and half-fish, with green hair, a red nose, and pig's eyes. Alternate form: Moruach. [Ellis 1987; Monaghan 1981]

Mugain   See *Mughain.*

Mughain
Ireland
Family and Tribes
   A queen of Munster, Ireland. Also the name of several other deities. Alternate forms: Mór, Mugain. [Ellis 1987; Leach 1972; Savill 1977]

Muime Chriosda   See *Brigid*.

Muirdris
Ireland, *Celtic*
Evil; Ugliness; Water
   "Having Teats." Water monster. She was killed by Fergus
Mac Léide. Alternate form: Sineach. [Ellis 1987]

Muireartach
Ireland, *Celtic*
Water; Weather
   "Eastern Sea." Irish sea goddess. [Monaghan 1981]

Muirenn
Ireland, *Celtic*
Health and Healing
   Nurse of the Celtic hero Cael, a warrior of the Fianna (the
king's guards). [Ellis 1987]

Muiriath
Ireland, *Celtic*
Water
   "Sea-land." See Irish *Moriath*. [Monaghan 1981]

Mumham   See *Ëire*.

Munanna
Ireland
Demi-animals; Justice
   Irish spirit who appears crane-like, circling the cliffs of
Inishkea.
✛✛ *Munanna tired of her husband and formed an alliance*
   ✛✛ *with a Scandinavian pirate. They killed her husband and*
   ✛✛ *escaped to Norway. The pirate tired of Munanna and*
*drowned her. She changed into a crane and flies about screaming
"revenge, revenge."* [Monaghan 1981]

Murigen
Ireland, *Celtic*
Water
   Irish lake goddess. Possibly the same as *Morgan*. [Sykes
1968]

Murna of the White Neck
Ireland, *Celtic*
Mother and Guardian
   "The Fair One." Mother of Fionn Mac Cumhail, the
greatest leader of the Fianna (the king's guards). [Ellis 1987]

Naas
Ireland, *Celtic*
Family and Tribes
   Irish wife of the god Lugh. Naas in County Kildare is
named for her. [Ellis 1987]

Nabia
Iberia
Family and Tribes; Ceremonies
   Iberian goddess of various tribes, worshiped from Tagus to
the Cantabrico. Lambs were sacrificed to her. [Eliade 1987]

Nahema
Spain
Evil
   "Mother of Spirits and Demons." One of the Inverse
Sephiroth, a *Succubus*. She is the opposite of *Malkuth*.
[Durdin-Robertson 1975]

Náir
Ireland, *Celtic*
Selflessness; Earth and Nature; Heaven and Hell; Weather
   Goddess of modesty. Also said to be an Irish earth goddess.
Any king who slept with Náir died. Some scholars suggest
that the legend records a time of "ritual kingship" when the
king "married" the earth goddess and then was sacrificed,
assuring her fertility.
✛✛ *She took King Crebhán to the Otherworld (lands of the*
   ✛✛ *gods and where one is reborn after death) where he found*
   ✛✛ *wonderful treasures.*
   Alternate form: Nar. [Ellis 1987; Monaghan 1981]

Nannan   See *Ëire*.

Nantosvelta
Britain; Gaul
Household Affairs; War; Water
   British water goddess, goddess of domesticity, and of war.
In her various roles she is associated with the sun god, with a
dovecote, and with the raven in Britain and Gaul. Alternate
forms: Nantotsuelta, Natosuelta. [Leach 1992; Redfield 1931]

Nantotsuelta   See *Nantosvelta*.

Nanu   See *Ëire*.

Nar   See *Náir*.

Nath
Ireland, *Celtic*
Education and Knowledge
   Irish goddess of wisdom. [Jobes 1962]

Natosuelta   See *Nantosvelta*.

Nau   See *Ëire*.

Navia
Spain, *Gallacian*
Water
   Gallacian water goddess. [Leach 1992]

Navia Arconunieca
Spain
Water
   Spanish water goddess. [Leach 1992]

Nechtan Scëne
Ireland, *Celtic*
Mother and Guardian; Magic
   Mother of three supernatural sons—Foill, Fannell, and
Tuache—who were killed by Cúchulainn. [Ellis 1987]

Neeve of the Golden Hair   See *Niamh*.

Nemain
Ireland, *Celtic*
War; Unhappiness
   "Venomous," "Frenzy." One of five Irish war goddesses
who provoke warriors to madness in battle. The others
are *Fea, Badb, Macha,* and the *Mórrígán*. Nemain is also
considered one of the triune of the *Mórrígán*. Associated with
the British *Nemotoma*. Alternate forms: Neman, Nemon,
Nenhain. [Ellis 1987; Leach 1972; Leach 1992; Monaghan
1981]

Neman   See *Nemain*.

Nemetona
Britain; Germany
War
   British war goddess and "goddess of the sacred grove." Similar to *Nemain*. Associated with Mars, she is also worshiped in the Rhine country. See also *Sulis*. [Leach 1992; Monaghan 1981]

Nemon   See *Nemain*.

Nenhain   See *Nemain*.

Nessa
Ireland, *Celtic*
Mother and Guardian
   Irish princess and mother of Conchobhar.
✠✠ *Conchobhar is said by some to have been a miraculous birth; others say the druid Cathbad is his father. It may have been Cathbad who changed Assa, "the gentle one," to Nessa, "the ungentle one."* [Ellis 1987; Monaghan 1981]

Niamh
Ireland, *Celtic*
Health and Healing; Love and Sexuality; Heaven and Hell
   Among the Irish goddesses with this name are: a daughter of Celtchair; a wife of Conall, who nursed Cúchulainn; and Niamh "Of the en Hair," who took her lover, Oisín, to Tír Tairnigiri, the Land of Promise. Alternate form: Neeve of the Golden Hair. See also Badb. [Ellis 1987; Jobes 1962; Monaghan 1981]

Nicnevin
Scotland, *Celtic*
Agriculture
   "Bone Mother." Scottish name for *Cailleach Beara*. See also *Juno*, Greek and Roman Empires. [Durdin-Robertson 1982; Monaghan 1990]

Nigheag Na H-ath
Scotland, *Celtic*
Fate
   "Little Washer of the Ford." A small Scottish woman with red webbed feet who foretells death by washing clothes at night after a battle. See also *Badb, Ban Nighechain, Caoineag*. [Leach 1972]

Nimue
Wales
Supreme Being; Water
   Welsh goddess of sovereignty. She invested Arthur as king and carried him to Avalon when he died. Welsh name for *Lady of the Lake*. See also *Rhiannon, Viviane*. [Monaghan 1981]

Niskai
Europe
Mother and Guardian; Life/Death Cycle
   Triune mother goddess of southern and western Europe. Goddess of birth, growth, and death. See also *Niskai*. [Bonnerjea 1927; Delaney 1980; Jobes 1962]

Niskai, The
Europe
Water
   Water spirits. See also *Niskai*. [Bonnerjea 1927; Delaney 1980; Jobes 1962]

Nos Bonnes Mëres les Fëes   See *Bonnes Dames, The*.

Oanuava
Gaul
Earth and Nature
   Earth goddess in Gaul. [Monaghan 1990]

Odras
Ireland, *Celtic*
Water
   When she made demands of *Mórrígán*, the Irish queen of death, she was turned into a pool of water. [Ellis 1987; Monaghan 1981]

Ollototae
Britain
Mother and Guardian
   "Pertaining to All People." Refers to the mother goddesses on an inscription in Binchester, Britain. [Jayne 1925]

Olwen
Wales
Sun and Day
   "Leaving White Foot-prints" or "Golden Wheel." Welsh sun goddess. Daughter of *Goleuddydd* and the giant, Ysbaddeden.
✠✠ *Chulhwch, a cousin of King Arthur, asked for Arthur's help in meeting and marrying Olwen. Ysbaddaden, Olwen's father, attempted to prevent the marriage by imposing innumerable impossible conditions. Chulhwch completed all the tasks with Arthur's help, and killed Ysbaddaden. Olwen became Chulhwch's only wife.* [Monaghan 1981; Savill 1977; Senior 1985]

Onagh   See *Oonagh*.

Onaugh
Ireland, *Celtic*
Small Size; Magic
   Irish fairy queen. See *Oonagh*. [Monaghan 1981]

Ondine
Gaul
Water
   Water-spirit. [Bonnerjea 1927]

Onuava
Gaul
Earth and Nature
   Earth goddess worshiped at Gironde. [Leach 1992]

Oona   See *Oonagh*.

Oonagh
Ireland, *Celtic*
Small Size; Magic
   Ancient Irish goddess of the Dé Danaan. Wife of Fionnbharr. In later times she was relegated to "queen of all the fairies in Ireland." Alternate forms: Onagh, Onaugh, Oona. [Ellis 1987; Monaghan 1981]

Ops   See *Ëire*.

Orokannar   See *Amagandar*.

Ortz   See *Urtz*.

oShion
Europe, *Gypsy, Kalderdash*
Time; Luck
   Goddess of time and good fortune among the Kalderdash. Sometimes a male god. [Leach 1992]

Ost   See *Urtz.*

Penardun
Wales, *Celtic*
Sky and Heavens
    Brythonic sky goddess. Wife of the Welsh sea god, Lir (Llyr), and mother of Manawyaddan. [Jobes 1962; Leach 1992]

Phlox
Spain
Fire
    "Most Vigorous Flame." In some Cabalistic traditions, she is the quintessence of the elements. [Durdin-Robertson 1975]

Plur na mBan
Ireland, *Celtic*
Earth and Nature
    "The Flower of Women." Daughter of *Niamh.* [Ellis 1987]

Pressina
Gaul
Water; Mother and Guardian; Unhappiness; Magic; Justice; Demi-animals
    Water spirit.
✛✛   *Pressina married a mortal king. When he forgot his promise not to see her during childbirth and came into the room during the delivery of triplets—Melusine, Melior, and Palatina— Pressina was angry and left him. When she grew up, Melusine decided to punish her father, and with the help of her sisters she covered him, his palace, and his servants with magic, burying them in a mountain. Pressina then punished Melusine by putting a curse on her, which changed her into a serpent each Sunday.* [Durdin-Robertson 1982; Monaghan 1981]

Primum Mobile
Europe
Creator of Life; Primordial Being
    "First Beginning." Neolithic mother goddess and the "Original Mother." [Dames 1979]

Proximae, The
Europe
Mother and Guardian; Life/Death Cycle
    "Kinswomen." Mother goddesses of southern and western Europe. Triune mother goddesses of birth, growth, and death. [Jobes 1962]

Quadriviae
Europe
Mother and Guardian; Travel; Life/Death Cycle
    "Goddess of the Cross-roads." She is a triune goddess of birth, growth, and death who is self-creating and self-sustaining. [Jobes 1962]

Ratis
Britain
War
    British goddess of the fortress. [Monaghan 1990]

Re
Ireland; Scandinavia, *Celtic*
Moon and Night
    "Light." Irish goddess of the moon who may be of Phoenician origin. Golden crescents found in the bogs of Ireland are thought to have been carried by Druids (men or women who preside at Celtic religious functions) and to be associated with moon worship. Alternate form: Ri. [Durdin-Robertson 1975; Ellis 1987; Monaghan 1981]

Regina   See *Rhiannon, Rigantona.*

Rhiannon
Wales, *Celtic*
Domesticated Animals; Charisma
    Welsh moon goddess who may have evolved from *Rigantona.* Wife of Pwyll and mother of Pryderi. In later times she was called an enchantress and may have evolved into *Nimue* or *Viviane* It is said that she rides on a beautiful white mare and that the birds fly about her, welcoming the seasons.
✛✛   *Rhiannon was the wife of Pwyll, the king of Dyfed. After four years of marriage, a son was born to them on the first of May. That night, while Rhiannon and her attendants slept, the baby disappeared. When they awoke and found the baby gone, the women caring for Rhiannon were frightened. Thinking they would be blamed, they killed a puppy and smeared Rhiannon with blood to make it appear that she had killed her son. As punishment the Druid told Rhiannon that she must meet anyone coming to the palace, tell them of her terrible deed, and ask to carry them into the hall on her back. This she did for several years. One day a farmer who lived in the kingdom appeared at the palace bearing her son. He explained how, several years earlier, on May 1st, a foal on his farm had been stolen by a demon. While pursuing the demon, he found a child the demon had dropped. Since he and his wife had no children, they kept the boy and called him Guri. When they finally heard the story about Rhiannon, they realized the child must be her lost son and they quickly brought him to the palace. When Rhiannon saw her son, she cried out that her grief had ended. The Druid (man or woman who presides at Celtic religious functions) said his name should henceforth be Pryderi, Welsh for "anxiety."*
    Alternate forms: Regina, Riannon. [Jobes 1962; Leach 1992; Monaghan 1981; Stone 1979]

Ri   See *Re.*

Riannon   See *Rhiannon.*

Rigantona
Britain, *Celtic*
Creator of Life; Supreme Being
    "Great Queen." Brythonic mother goddess of fertility. She was later known as *Rhiannon.* Alternate form: Regina. [Jobes 1962; Leach 1972; Stone 1979]

Rosmerta
Gaul
Wealth
    Goddess of material wealth in Gaul. [Savill 1977]

Saar   See *Sadb.*

Saba   See *Sadb.*

Sabia   See *Sadb.*

Sabra
Unknown
Courage; Selflessness
    Mythical daughter of an Egyptian king, she was rescued from a dragon by St. George, who married her. She became an example of the perfect citizen with saintly virtues. This story possibly reflects Christianity "rescuing" the lady from polytheism or paganism. [Jobes 1962]

Sabrina
Britain
Water
    Goddess of the Severn River in Britain. [Jobes 1962; Leach 1992]

Sadb
Ireland, *Celtic*
Moon and Night; Creator of Life; Demi-animals; Mother and
Guardian; Hunting and Wild Animals
   Moon goddess. She presides over fertility.
   ✝✝ *Sadb was turned into a fawn by the Dark Druid. Escaping
   ✝✝ the spell for awhile, she became the mistress of Fionn, but
   ✝✝ the Dark Druid found her and changed her back into a
fawn. She had a son, whom she raised until Fionn, realizing it was
his son, took over his care.*
   Alternate forms: Blai, Saar, Saba, Sabia, Sadhbh. [Ellis
1987; Jobes 1962; Monaghan 1981]

Sadhbh   See *Sadb*.

Saman   See *Samhain*.

Samhain
Ireland; Phoenicia, *Celtic*
Ceremonies; Agriculture; Heaven and Hell; Time
   Cabirian (Greek) deity worshiped in ancient Ireland and
Phoenicia. The festival of Samhain occurs at harvest time and
marks one of the four divisions of the Irish year. It is also the
time when the otherworld becomes visible to humans. This
celebration has been absorbed by Christianity as St. Martin's
Mass (Martinmas). It is also called All Saints' Day or
All-Hallows. Samhain is also the name of a male deity. See
also *Tlachtga*. Alternate forms: Saman, Samhuin, Sanhin.
[Durdin-Robertson 1975; Ellis 1987]

Samhuin   See *Samhain*.

Sanhin   See *Samhain*.

Scáthach
Scotland, *Celtic*
War; Fate; Mother and Guardian; Physical Prowess;
Education and Knowledge; Magic
   "Shadow." Scottish warrior goddess, mother goddess, and
prophet. Warriors would travel long distances to study with
her, learning magical battle skills. One of her students was
Cúchulainn. She is also called Scáthach Buanand (victory)
and Scáthach nUanaind. [Ellis 1987; Leach 1992]

Scota
Scotland; Gaul; Egypt
Family and Tribes
   Possibly the name of two goddesses: One is the ancestor of
the Scots and the Gaels, who was an Egyptian princess who
became a Gaelic queen. Her name is found in Egypt, Thracia,
Spain, Ireland, and Scotland. There is also a daughter of the
Egyptian Pharaoh Nectanebus, who married Milesius. She
was killed when fighting with the Milesians against the Dé
Danaan and is buried in Scotia's Glen. See also *Bera*.
[Durdin-Robertson 1975; Ellis 1987]

Seang
Scythia
Unknown
   Wife of Milesius. She was the daughter of a Scythian king.
When she died, Milesius went to Egypt and married *Scota*.
[Ellis 1987]

Segeta
Gaul
Health and Healing; Water
   Goddess of the healing springs at Aquae Segetae near
Loire in Gaul. [Jayne 1925; Leach 1992]

Segomanna
Gaul
Water
   Possibly a goddess of springs in Gaul. [Leach 1992]

Sel   See *Sul*.

Sephira
Spain
Intelligence and Creativity
   "Divine Intelligence." Primodial mother of the *Sephiroth* in
Cabalistic tradition. She forms a triad with *Binah* and
Chokmah. She is described "as an active potency spreading
in every direction." She is worshiped in the Near East where
she is indentified with *Shekinah* and *Sophia*. [Durdin-
Robertson 1975; Durdin-Robertson 1982]

Sephiroth
Spain
Supreme Being
   The ten attributes or emanations of the divine listed in
Cabalistic writings who are also worshiped in the Near East.
They include *Amona, Binah, Chokma, Daath, Geburah,
Gedulah, Hod, Sephira,* and *Tiphereth*. See also *Matronit*.
There are also Inverse Sephiroth, one of whom is *Nahema*.
[Durdin-Robertson 1975; Durdin-Robertson 1982]

Sequana
Gaul, *Sequani*
Water; Health and Healing; Family and Tribes
   Goddess of the River Seine, which has a shrine at its
headwaters where she practices healing. Ancestor of the
Sequani tribe. [Jayne 1925; Leach 1992; Stone 1979]

Serreta de Alcoy Mother Goddess
Iberia
Family and Tribes; Ceremonies
   Goddess of the Iberians at Serreta de Alcoy, Spain. The
worship of this goddess included music and religious dances
as evidenced by the artifacts found at this location. [Eliade
1987]

Setlocenia
Britain
Health and Healing
   British goddess of long life. [Leach 1992]

Sgeimh Solais
Ireland, *Celtic*
Beauty; War
   "Light of Beauty." Her marriage started a war that resulted
in the destruction of the Fianna (the king's guards). [Ellis
1987]

Sheela-na-gig   See *Sheila-na-gig*.

Sheelanagyg   See *Sheila-na-gig*.

Sheila-na-gig
Ireland, *Celtic*
Creator of Life
   Irish fertility goddess. "Gyg" is the name in Norse for a
female Jotun or Giantess, that is, an image of the female.
"Sheela" was the patron of women. She is depicted in petro-
glyphs holding her vagina open with both hands. Carvings of
her are also found on Christian churches. Alternate forms:
Sheela-na-gig, Sheelanagyg, Shela-no-gig. [Dames 1979;
Durdin-Robertson 1982; Jobes 1962; Monaghan 1981]

Shela-no-gig   See *Sheila-na-gig*.

Sheol   See *Sheol*, Near East.

Sibhol   See *Ëire*.

Silkie
Scotland
Household Affairs; Order; Disorder
   Scottish goddess of the home.
   ✝✝ *Wearing silk clothes, she went into homes to check on
   the housekeeping of the women. If it was too neat, she
   ✝✝ created disorder; if too dirty, she cleaned the house.*
[Monaghan 1981]

Silly Wychtis, The
Scotland; Wales
Small Size; Magic
   Scottish and Welsh fairies. [Dames 1979]

Sin
Ireland
Small Size; Magic
   Irish fairy. She creates wine and pigs from leaves. She uses
them to feed the many soldiers whom she also created with
magic spells. Her powers indicate that she had probably been
a goddess. [Monaghan 1981]

Sinann
Ireland, *Celtic*
Water; Education and Knowledge
   Irish goddess of the Shannon River.
   ✝✝ *Like Boann, Sinann tried to get information from the
   "Well of Knowledge." The water rose up and, flooding
   ✝✝ westward, drowned her, forming the river Shannon.*
   Alternate forms: Sinend, Sinnan, Sionan. [Ellis 1987; Leach
1992; Savill 1977]

Sineach   See *Muirdris*.

Sinend   See *Sinann*.

Sinnan   See *Sinann*.

Sionan   See *Sinann*.

Sirona
Gaul
Stars and Planets; Water
   "Star." Associated with Grannus. Also the name of a
deified fountain in Bironde, Gaul. Alternate form: Dirona.
[Leach 1992; Savill 1977; Sykes 1968]

Smirgat
Ireland, *Celtic*
Fate
   Prophet and wife of Fionn. Smirgat prophesied that Fionn
would die if he drank from a horn. From then on, he drank
only from a goblet or bowl. [Ellis 1987]

Souconna
Gaul, *Celtic*
Water
   Goddess of the river Saône in Gaul. [Leach 1992; Savill
1977]

Sovranty
Ireland
Supreme Being; Ugliness; Beauty
   Irish goddess who bestows kingship. She first appears as
an ugly crone but then turns into a lovely maiden, frequently

after being kissed by a male. Possibly a patriarchal rewriting
of the times when goddesses chose their mates. [Ellis 1987]

Stratteli
Switzerland, *Celtic*
Evil; Earth and Nature; Agriculture; Ceremonies; Time
   "Witch" and "Nightmare." Wood spirits at Brunnen on
Lake Lucerne, these evil spirits are expelled between
Christmas and Epiphany. If too little noise is made on Twelfth
Night, and the evil spirits are not driven away, the fruit crop
will not be good. This is an overlapping of earlier religious
beliefs with Christian holidays that continues to present
times. Alternate form: Strudeli. [Johnson 1988]

Strudeli   See *Stratteli*.

Sul
Britain
Health and Healing
   Goddess of health at Aquae Salis, Bath, England. Identified
with **Minerva**, Greek and Roman Empires, and perhaps the
Suleviae of Gaul. She is also the equivalent of **Bridgid**,
Eastern Europe. Sul's name is derived from the Celtic words
for eye and seeing. She is possibly related to the Goddess of
Silbury Hill, for whom there is a procession at Candlemass to
the sacred spring at Suilohead. Alternate forms: Sel, Sulla,
Sulis, Sullis. [Dames 1979; Jayne 1925; Leach 1992; Monaghan
1981]

Suleviae, The
Gaul
Mother and Guardian; Goodness
   Beneficent and protecting mothers or matrons of the Gauls.
May be a triad which includes *Sul* and *Brigid*. The name is
found at healing shrines associated with water in England
and France. [Jayne 1925; Monaghan 1981]

Sulis   See *Sul*.

Sulla   See *Sul*.

Sullis   See *Sul*.

Tabiti
Unknown
Supreme Being
   Great goddess who possibly evolved from *Tibirra*, a more
ancient goddess. [Davis 1971]

Taillate   See *Tailtu*.

Taillte   See *Tailtu*.

Tailtu
Ireland, *Celtic*
Earth and Nature; Ceremonies
   Irish earth goddess. Daughter of Firbolg, king of the Great
Plain. Tailtu made the plain by clearing the forest of Breg.
Teltown (Tailltin or Teltin), between Navan and Kells, is
named for her. Her foster son Lugh decreed an agrarian feast
in her honor, *Lughnasadh*. Celebrated beginning August 1, it is
said to have originally lasted fifteen days. Christianity now
celebrates this feast as Lamas, the feast of first fruits.
Alternate forms: Taillate, Taillte, Tailtiu, Tallte. [Ellis 1987;
Monaghan 1981]

Tailtiu   See *Tailtu*.

Tallte   See *Tailtu*.

Tamesis
Britain; France
Water
   British goddess of the river Thames and the Tamise (Scheldt) in France. [Sykes 1968]

Taranis
Gaul
Destroyer of Life; Ceremonies
   Possibly a death goddess of Gaul. She requires human sacrifices. [Jobes 1962]

Taranus   See *Taranis.*

Tea
Ireland, *Celtic*
Family and Tribes
   Irish goddess of the Dé Danaan. Wife of the first Milesian king, Eremon. The ancient capital of Ireland, Tara (Tea-mhair), was named for her. With her sister, *Tephi,* she founded Tara, the ancient religious and political center of Ireland. Parts of Tara have been dated to 2000 B.C.E. [Durdin-Robertson 1982; Ellis 1987]

Tephi
Ireland, *Celtic*
Family and Tribes
   Sister of *Tea,* with whom she founded Tara, an ancient Irish religious and cultural center. They were patrons of the Assemblies of Tara. [Durdin-Robertson 1982]

Tertiana
Britain
Destroyer of Life
   British goddess of illness. She is responsible for "the three day recurrent fever." [Leach 1992]

Tibirra   See *Tabiti.*

Tif'eret   See *Tiphereth.*

Tiphereth
Spain
Sun and Day; Stars and Planets
   "Magnificence." One of the *Sephiroth,* the ten attributes of God in Cabalistic tradition. She is associated with the sun and the planets Venus and Mars. [Durdin-Robertson 1975]

Tlachgo   See *Ëire.*

Tlacht   See *Ëire.*

Tlachtga
Ireland, *Celtic*
Magic; Ceremonies
   Goddess of magic. Daughter of the druid Mug Ruith. The Hill of Tlachta (now the Hill of Ward) is named for her. The hill is associated with the Samhain festival. See also *Samhain.* [Ellis 1987]

Tres Matres
Spain
Weather; Water; Fire
   "The Three Mothers." In the Cabalistic *Book for Formation,* they represent air, water, fire. According to some scholars, a feminine trinity preceded a masculine trinity. The Three Mothers may be an archetype of the "Tres Maries," the *Virgin Mary, Mary Magdalene,* and *Mary Cleopas.* There continues to be a group of goddess worshipers today at Arles in Provence. Their triad is called "The Three Maries of Provence" or "The

Three Maries of the Sea," and they celebrate with a festival May 24th to 28th. [Durdin-Robertson 1975; Durdin-Robertson 1982]

Triduana
Scotland, *Celtic*
Water; Selflessness
   Scottish name for *Bridgit* in the Edinburgh area. She had a sacred well beneath an oak tree. [Monaghan 1990]

Triple Goddess
Europe, *Celtic*
Life/Death Cycle; Time
   The Celts have a number of triune goddesses. They represent several kinds of triads of creator, protector, and destroyer: as earth mother she is birth, growth, and death or spring, summer, and winter; as goddess of the moon she is the lady of the earth (waxing), the sky (full), and the underworld (waning). There is also a triad of the aspects of womanhood: maiden, mother, and crone. See also *Badb, Banba, Breg, Brigid, Cailleach Beara, Dervonnae, The, Gwenhwyfar, Macha, Medb, Mórrígán, Nemain, Niskai, Proximae, The, Quadriviae, Suliviae, The.* [Jobes 1962]

Tryanon
Unknown
Magic; Small Size
   Fairy princess. [Jobes 1962]

Tuag
Ireland, *Celtic*
Dawn and Twilight
   Irish dawn goddess. [Jobes 1962]

Tuireann
Ireland, *Celtic*
Demi-animals; Hunting and Wild Animals
   Irish wolf-hound goddess. She was turned into a wolf-hound by *Uctdealbh.* Alternate form: Tureann. [Ellis 1987; Monaghan 1981]

Tureann   See *Tuireann.*

Twyll Huan   See *Blodeuwedd.*

Uairebhuidhe
Ireland, *Celtic*
Wild Birds
   Irish bird goddess. [Monaghan 1990]

Uathach
Ireland, *Celtic*
Dawn and Twilight
   "Spectre." Daughter of *Scáthach.* She became Cúchulainn's lover when he came to be trained as a warrior by her mother. [Ellis 1987; Jobes 1962]

Uchtcelbh
Ireland, *Celtic*
Earth and Nature; Beauty
   "Shapely Bosom." Irish earth goddess. [Jobes 1962]

Uchtdealbh
Ireland, *Celtic*
Evil; Magic; Small Size; Demi-animals; Hunting and Wild Animals
   Malevolent fairy. She turned *Tuireann* into a wolf-hound. [Monaghan 1981]

Ura
Gaul
Water
   Well or spring goddess in Gaul. [Leach 1992]

Urganda
Unknown
Goodness; Magic; Small Size
   Benevolent fairy. [Bonnerjea 1927]

Urisks, The
Unknown
Magic; Small Size
   Supernatural women. Said to be the children of liaisons between fairies and humans. Solitary by nature, they live in lonely and mountainous areas. [Bonnerjea 1927]

Urnia
Gaul
Water
   Water goddess at Ourne in Gaul. [Leach 1992]

Urtz
France; Spain, *Basque*
Water; Sky and Heavens
   Sky goddess of the Basques in France and Spain. Benevolent and malevolent, she brings the light rains or destructive storms. Alternate forms: Ortz, Ost. [Leach 1992]

Valencian Mother Goddess
Spain
Mother and Guardian
   Iberian goddess at Valencia. [Eliade 1987]

Veleda
Germany, *Celtic*
War; Fate; Family and Tribes
   Warrior queen of the continental Celts. Said by some to have been a deified human. She is the leader of the Bructeri tribe and has oracular powers. She lives in a tower on the Lipee River. [Frazer 1959; Monaghan 1981]

Venus of Quinipily
France
Unknown
   Beseeched to ease the pains of childbirth. [Leach 1972]

Verbeia
Celtic
Water
   Goddess of the river Wharfe. [Monaghan 1981]

Vercana
Gaul
Water
   Water goddess with a spring named for her in Gaul. [Leach 1992]

Visuna
Germany
Water; Health and Healing
   Goddess of healing who inhabits the springs at Baden Baden in the Black Forest. [Leach 1992]

Viviane
Wales
Magic

An earlier goddess who evolved into a Welsh sorcerer who cast a spell on Merlin. Also called *Lady of the Lake*. Alternate forms: Chwinbian, Nimue, Vivien, Vivienne. [Jobes 1962; Leach 1972; Monaghan 1981]

Vivien   See *Viviane*.

Vivienne   See *Viviane*.

Washer of the Ford   See *Badb*.

Weird Sisters
Britain
Fate
   Name for the three *Fates*. See also *Wyrdes, The*. [Leach 1992]

Wylgeforte, Saint
Portugal, *Christian*
Selflessness; Love and Sexuality; Family and Tribes; Heaven and Hell
   Daughter of the queen of Portugal.
   ✠✠ *Wylgeforte wanted to remain a virgin, so she prayed for a beard. When a beard grew, men were no longer interested in her. The prince of Sicily was angered by her ploy and had her crucified.*
   She provides horses to take evil husbands to the devil. Sometimes called Saint Uncumber, she encumbers women of bad husbands. [Jobes 1962]

Wyrdes, The
Scotland
Fate
   Name for Scottish goddesses of fate. See also *Weird Sisters*. [Leach 1972]

Wyvach
Wales
Water; Life/Death Cycle; Evil
   Woman in a pre-Christian legend who, with her husband, built the Welsh Ark to escape a deluge sent by the monster, Addanc. [Savill 1977]

Y Mamau
Wales
Mother and Guardian; Life/Death Cycle; Magic; Small Size
   "The Mothers." Triune goddesses of birth, growth, and death. They are considered self-creating and self-sustaining. Also the name given to fairies in Wales. See also *Bonnes Dames, The, Matres, The*. [Jobes 1962]

Ygerna
British Isles
Mother and Guardian; Magic; Love and Sexuality
   Queen and mother of Arthur.
   ✠✠ *Ygerna was a beautiful queen who was desired by King Uther Pendragon. He asked Merlin to make him look like the queen's husband so he could sleep with her. When her real husband was killed in battle, Uther married Ygerna.* [Savill 1977]

Yseut   See *Isolt*.

Zaden
Iberia
Fishing and Water Animals
   Iberian goddess of fishers. [Leach 1992]

BIBLIOGRAPHY

Achtemeier, Paul J., ed. 1985. *Harper's Bible Dictionary*. San Francisco: Harper & Row.

Adriani, N. and Albert C. Kruyt. 1950. *Bare'e-Speaking Toradja of Central Celebes (The East Toradja)*, 2d ed., vol. 1. Amsterdam: Noord-Hollandsche Uitgeners Maatschappij.

Alagoa, Ebiegberi Joe. 1964. "Idu: A Creator Festival at Okpoma (Brass) in the Niger Delta." *Africa* 34 (January): 1–8.

Albright, William Foxwell. 1968. *Yahweh and the Gods of Canaan*. Garden City, New York: Doubleday.

Alexander, Hartley Burr. 1916. *North America*. Vol 10, *Mythology of All Races*. Boston: Marshall Jones.

Alpers, Antony. 1966. *Maori Myths and Tribal Legends*. Boston and Cambridge: Riverside Press/Houghton Mifflin.

Ames, Delano. 1965. *Egyptian Mythology*. London: Hamlyn.

Amiet, Pierre. 1977. *Art of the Ancient Near East*. New York: Harry N. Abrams.

Anankian, Mardiros H. 1925. "Armenian." In *Armenian-African*. Vol. 7, *Mythology of All Races*. Boston: Marshall Jones.

Andersen, Johannes C. 1928. *Myths and Legends of the Polynesians*. London: George G. Harrap.

Anderson, R. B. 1891. *Norse Mythology*. Chicago: S. C. Griggs.

Anthes, Rudolf. 1961. "Mythology of Ancient Egypt." In *Mythologies of the Ancient World*, ed. Samuel Noah Kramer. Chicago: Quadrangle Books.

Anwyl, Edward. 1906. *Celtic Religion*. London: Archibald Constable.

Anzaludúa, Gloria. 1989. "Entering into the Serpent." In *Weaving the Visions*, ed. Carol P. Christ and Judith Plaskow. San Francisco: Harper & Row.

Archaeological Institute of America. 1916–1932. *Mythology of All Races*. 13 vols. Boston: Marshall Jones.

Ashdown, Inez. 1971. *The Broad Highway of Maui*. Wailuku, HI: Ace Printing.

Avery, Catherine B., ed. 1962. *New Century Classical Handbook*. New York: Appleton-Century-Crofts.

Balikci, Asen. 1970. *The Netsilik Eskimo*. Garden City, NY: Natural History Press.

Bancroft, Hubert Howe. 1886. *The Works of Hubert Howe Bancroft*. 38 vols. San Francisco: The History Company.

Baring, Anne and Jules Cashford. 1991. *Myth of the Goddess: Evolution of an Image*. London: Viking Arkana.

Barns, Thomas. 1925. "Trees and Plants." In *Encyclopaedia of Religion and Ethics*, ed. James Hastings, vol. 12. New York: Scribner's.

Barthell, Edward E. 1971. *Gods and Goddesses of Ancient Greece*. Coral Gables, FL: University of Miami Press.

Barton, Roy Franklin. 1946. "The Religion of the Ifugaos." In *Memoirs of the American Anthropological Association* 65.

Basak, Radhagovinda. 1953. "The Hindu Concept of the Natural World." In *The Religion of the Hindus*, ed. Kenneth Morgan. New York: Ronald Press.

Basset, Rene. 1925. "The Berbers and North Africa." In *Encyclopaedia of Religion and Ethics*, ed. James Hastings, vol. 2. New York: Scribner's.

Bastide, Roger. 1978. *The African Religions of Brazil: Toward a Sociology of the Interpenetration of Civilizations*. Baltimore: Johns Hopkins University Press.

Batchelor, John. 1894. "Items of Ainu Folklore." *Journal of American Folklore* 7: 15–44.

———. 1925. "Ainus." In *Encyclopaedia of Religion and Ethics*, ed. James Hastings, vol. 1. New York: Scribner's.

———. ca. 1927. *Ainu Life and Lore: Echoes of a Departing Race*. Tokyo: Japan Advertiser Press.

Baumgartner, Anne S. 1984. *Ye Gods!* Secaucus, NJ: Lyle Stuart.

Beaglehole, Ernest and Pearl Beaglehole. 1938. *Ethnology of Pukapuka*. Bernice P. Bishop Museum Bulletin, no. 150. Honolulu, HI: Bishop Museum Press.

Becher, Hans. "The Sura and the Pakidai, Two Yanomamo Tribes in Northwest Brazil." In *Mitteilungen* 16: 1–133.

Beckwith, Martha Warren. 1932. *Kepelino's Traditions of Hawaii.* Bernice P. Bishop Museum Bulletin, no. 95. Honolulu, HI: Bishop Museum Press.

———. 1940. *Hawaiian Mythology.* Honolulu, HI: University of Hawaii Press.

Begg, Ean. 1985. *The Cult of the Black Virgin.* New York: Penguin.

Beier, Ulli, ed. 1966. *The Origin of Life and Death: African Creation Myths.* London: Heinemann.

Bel, Alfred. 1968. *La religion musulmani en berberie.* Paris: Librairie Orientaliste, Paul Guethner.

Bell, Robert E. 1991. *Women of Classical Mythology: A Biographical Dictionary.* Santa Barbara, CA: ABC-CLIO.

Bell, Charles. 1931. *The Religion of Tibet.* Oxford, England: Clarendon Press.

Belo, Jane. 1949. *Bali: Temple Festival.* Locust Valley, NY: J. J. Augustin.

Benedict, Laura Watson. 1916. *A Study of Bagobo Ceremonial, Magic, and Myth.* New York: New York Academy of Sciences.

Bennett, Wendell C. and Robert M. Zingg. 1935. *The Tarahumara: An Indian Tribe of Northern Mexico.* Chicago: University of Chicago Press.

Berger, Pamela. 1985. *The Goddess Obscured: Transformation of the Grain Protectress from Goddess to Saint.* Boston: Beacon.

Berndt, Ronald M. 1965. "The Kamano, Usurufa, Jate and Fore of the Eastern Highlands." In *Gods, Ghosts, and Men in Melanesia,* ed. Peter Lawrence and M. J. Meggett. Melbourne, Australia: Oxford University Press.

———. 1974. *Australian Aboriginal Religion.* Leiden, the Netherlands: E. J. Brill.

Best, Elsdon. 1924a. *The Maori.* Wellington, New Zealand: Harry H. Tombs.

———. 1924b. *Maori Religion and Mythology.* New York: AMS Press.

Bhattacharji, Sukumari. 1970. *The Indian Theogony.* Cambridge: Cambridge University Press.

Bierhorst, John. 1976. *The Red Swan: Myths and Tales of the American Indians.* New York: Farrar, Straus & Giroux.

———. 1985. *Mythology of North America.* New York: William Morrow.

———. 1988. *Mythology of South America.* New York: William Morrow.

Bilby, Julian W. 1923. *Among Unknown Eskimos.* London: Seeley Service.

Biswas, P. D. 1956. *Santals of the Santal Parganas.* New Delhi: Bharatiya Adimjati Sevak Sangh.

Blackburn, Thomas C., ed. 1975. *December's Child: A Book of Chumash Oral Narratives.* Los Angeles: University of California Press.

Boas, Franz. 1888. "The Central Eskimo." *Annual Report of the Bureau of American Ethnology* 6: 399–669.

———. 1898. "Mythology of the Bella Coola Indians." *Memoirs of the American Museum of Natural History* 2: 25–127.

———. 1901. *The Eskimo of Baffin Land and Hudson Bay.* American Museum of Natural History, bulletin 15. New York: American Museum of Natural History.

———. 1935. *Kwakiutl Culture as Reflected in Mythology,* vol. 12. New York: G. E. Stechert.

Boas, Franz and James Teit. 1985. *Coeur D'Alene, Flathead and Okanogan Indians.* Fairfield, WA: Ye Galleon Press.

Bogoras, Waldemar. 1904. "The Chukchee." In *Memoirs of the American Museum of Natural History* 11(1–3).

Bolen, Jean Shinoda. 1984. *Goddesses in Everywoman: A New Psychology of Women.* New York: Harper & Row.

Bollig, Laurentius. 1927. *The Inhabitants of the Truk Islands: Religion, Life and a Short Grammar of a Micronesian People.* Munster, Germany: Aschendorffsche Verlagsbuchhandlung.

Bonnerjea, Biren. 1927. *A Dictionary of Superstitions and Mythology.* London: Folk Press.

Bosi, Roberto. 1960. *The Lapps.* London: Thames and Hudson.

Boulding, Elise. 1976. *The Underside of History: A View of Women through Time.* Boulder, CO: Westview.

Bourke, John G. 1887–1888. "The Medicine-Men of the Apache." *Annual Report of the Bureau of American Ethnology* 9: 451–603.

———. 1889. "Cosmogony and Theogony of the Mojave Indians." *Journal of American Folklore* 2: 169–189.

Boyd, Maurice. 1969. *Tarascan Myths and Legends.* Fort Worth: Texas Christian University Press.

Bradley, Diana. 1956. "Notes and Observations from Rennell and Bellona Islands, British Solomon Islands." *Polynesian Society Journal* 65: 332–341.

Branston, Brian. 1955. *Gods of the North.* London: Thames and Hudson.

Bratton, Fred Gladstone. 1970. *Myths and Legends of the Ancient Near East.* New York: Thomas Y. Crowell.

Bray, Frank Chapin. 1935. *The World of Myths: Dictionary of Mythology.* New York: Thomas Y. Crowell.

Bridgwater, William, ed. 1950. *Columbia Encyclopedia in One Volume,* 2d ed. Morningside Heights, NY: Columbia University Press.

Briggs, George Weston. 1920. *The Chamars.* London: Oxford University Press.

———. 1953. *The Doms and Their Near Relations.* Mysore, India: Wesley Press and Publishing House.

Brinton, Daniel G. 1876. *Myths of the New World: A Treatise on the Symbolism and Mythology.* New York: Greenwood.

———. 1882. *American Hero-Myths: A Study in the Native Religions of the Western Continent.* Philadelphia: H. C. Watts.

Browning, Iain. 1973. *Petra.* Park Ridge, NJ: Noyes Press.

Brundage, Burr Cartwright. 1979. *The Fifth Sun: Aztec Gods, Aztec World.* Austin: University of Texas Press.

Buck, Peter H. 1932. *Ethnology of Manihiki and Kakahanga.* Bernice P. Bishop Museum Bulletin, no. 99. Honolulu, HI: Bishop Museum Press.

———. 1938. *Ethnology of Magareva.* Bernice P. Bishop Museum Bulletin, no. 157. Honolulu, HI: Bishop Museum Press.

Buckley, Jorunn Jacobsen. 1986. *Female Fault and Fulfilment in Gnosticism.* Chapel Hill: University of North Carolina Press.

Budge, E. A. Wallis. 1969. *Gods of the Egyptians or Studies in Egyptian Mythology.* 2 vols. New York: Dover.

———. 1989. *From Fetish to God in Ancient Egypt.* Salem, NH: Ayer Company.

Bulfinch, Thomas. 1898. *The Age of Fable.* Philadelphia: David McKay.

Bunzel, Ruth L. 1984. *Zuni Katcinas: An Analytical Study.* Glorieta, NM: Rio Grande Press.

Burkert, Walter. 1985. *Greek Religion.* Cambridge, MA: Harvard University Press.

Burland, Cottie. 1975. *North American Indian Mythology.* New York: Hamlyn.

Burrows, Edwin G. 1949. "The People of Ifalik: A Little-Disturbed Atoll Culture." Unpublished manuscript. Coordinated Investigation of Micronesian Anthropology, Pacific Science Board, National Research Council. Washington, DC.

Cabaton, Antoine. 1925. "Annam (Popular Religion)." In *Encyclopaedia of Religion and Ethics,* ed. James Hastings, vol. 3. New York: Scribner's.

Campbell, Joseph. 1949. *The Hero with a Thousand Faces.* Bollingen Series, no. 17. Princeton, NJ: University Press.

———. 1974. *Mythic Image.* Princeton, NJ: Princeton University Press.

———. 1988a. "The Way of the Animal Powers." *Historical Atlas of the World Mythology*, vol. 1. New York: Harper & Row.

———. 1988b. *The Power of Myth*. New York: Doubleday.

Campbell, W. "Formosa." 1925. In *Encyclopaedia of Religion and Ethics*, ed. James Hastings, vol. 6. New York: Scribner's.

Carlyon, Richard. 1982. *A Guide to the Gods*. New York: Quill.

Carnoy, Albert J. 1917. "Iranian." In *Indian Iranian*. Vol. 6, *Mythology of All Races*. Boston: Marshall Jones.

Carrasco, David. 1990. *Religions of Mesoamerica: Cosmovision and Ceremonial Centers*. San Francisco: Harper & Row.

Casson, Lionel. 1965. *Ancient Egypt*. New York: Time.

Cavendish, Richard. 1980. *Mythology: An Illustrated Encyclopedia*. New York: Rizzoli.

Ceram, C. W. 1956. *Secret of the Hittites: Discovery of an Ancient Empire*. New York: Knopf.

Chadwick, John. 1976. *The Mycenaean World*. Cambridge: Cambridge University Press.

Chadwick, Nora K. 1930. "Notes on Polynesian Mythology." *Journal of the Royal Anthropological Institute of Great Britain and Ireland* 66: 75–112.

Chagnon, Napoleon A. 1968. *Yanomamo*. New York: Holt, Rinehart & Winston.

Chamberlain, Alexander F. 1982. "Review of *The Klamath Indians of Southwestern Oregon*." *Journal of American Folklore* 5: 252–255.

———. 1990. "Biographical Notes." *Journal of American Folklore* 13: 304–306.

Chamberlain, Basil Hall. 1887. *The Language, Mythology, and Geographical Nomenclature of Japan Viewed in the Light of Aino Studies*. Tokyo: Imperial University.

Chang, K. C. 1976. *Early Chinese Civilization: Anthropological Perspectives*. Cambridge, MA: Harvard University Press.

———. 1983. *Art, Myth, and Ritual: The Path to Political Authority in Ancient China*. Cambridge, MA: Harvard University Press.

Chavannes, Édouard. 1910. *Le t'ai chan: Essai de monographie d'un culte chinois*. Paris: E. Leroux.

Chicago, Judy. 1979. *The Dinner Party: A Symbol of Our Heritage*. Garden City, NY: Anchor/Doubleday.

Chowdhury, J. N. 1971. *A Comparative Study of Adi Religion*. Shillong, India: North-East Frontier Agency.

Christ, Carol P. and Judith Plaskow. 1979. *Womanspirit Rising: A Feminist Reader in Religion*. New York: Harper & Row.

Christian, F. W. 1895. "Notes on the Marquesans." *Polynesian Society Journal* 4: 187–202.

Clark, Charles Allen. 1932. *Religions of Old Korea*. New York: Fleming H. Revell.

Clark, Ella E. 1953. *Indian Legends of the Pacific Northwest*. Berkeley, CA: University of California Press.

Clebert, Jean-Paul. 1967. *The Gypsies*. Baltimore: Penguin.

Clebourn, James. 1960. *The Cahuilla Indians*. Los Angeles: Western Lore Press.

Clendinnen, Inga. 1991. *The Aztecs: An Interpretation*. Cambridge: Cambridge University Press.

Clerk, Christian. 1982. "Polynesia and Micronesia." In *Legends of the World*, ed. Richard Cavendish. New York: Schocken.

Cline, Howard. 1944. "Lore and Deities of the Lacandon Indians, Chiapas, Mexico." *Journal of American Folklore* 57: 107–115.

Coe, Michael. 1987. *The Mayan*. London: Thames and Hudson.

Cole, Fay-Cooper. 1922. *The Tinguian*. Anthropological Series, vol. 14, no. 2. Chicago: Field Museum of Natural History.

———. 1945. *Peoples of Malaysia*. New York: Van Nostrand.

Coleman, Charles. 1832. *Mythology of the Hindus*. London: Parbury, Allen.

Collins, June McCormick. 1974. *Valley of the Spirits: The Upper Skagit Indians of Western Washington*. Seattle and London: University of Washington Press.

Collocott, E. E. V. 1921. "Notes on Tongan Religion." *Polynesian Society Journal* 30: 152–163, 227–240.

Colton, Harold S. 1949. *Hopi Kachina Dolls*. Albuquerque, NM: University of New Mexico Press.

Cook, Stanley A. 1930. *The Religion of Ancient Palestine in the Light of Archaeology*. London: Oxford University Press.

Cooke, G. A. 1925. "Nabataeans." In *Encyclopaedia of Religion and Ethics*, ed. James Hastings, vol. 9. New York: Scribner's.

Coolidge, Dane and Mary Roberts Coolidge. 1939. *The Last of the Seris*. New York: Dutton.

Cooper, W. R. 1876. *An Archaic Dictionary: Biographical, Historical and Mythological, from the Egyptian, Assyrian, and Etruscan Monuments and Papyri*. London: Samuel Bagster and Sons.

Cotterell, Arthur. 1979. *Dictionary of World Mythology*. New York: Peridee/Putnam.

———. 1989. *Macmillan Illustrated Encyclopedia of Myths and Legends*. New York: Macmillan.

Courlander, Harold. 1973. *Tales of Yoruba Gods and Heroes*. New York: Crown.

———. 1975. *A Treasury of African Folklore: The Oral Literature, Traditions, Myths, Legends, Epics, Tales, Recollections, Wisdom, Sayings, and Humor of Africa*. New York: Crown.

Covarrubias, Miguel. 1937. *Island of Bali*. New York: Knopf.

Cox, George W. 1970. *The Mythology of the Aryan Nations*. 2 vols. London: Longmans.

Cox, W. H. 1913. "New Ireland (New Mecklenburg) Myths." In *Man* 13: 195–199.

Craig, Robert D. 1989. *Dictionary of Polynesian Mythology*. New York: Greenwood.

Crim, Keith, ed. 1981. *Abingdon Dictionary of Living Religions*. Nashville, TN: Parthenon Press.

Crooke, W. 1894. *An Introduction to the Popular Religion and Folklore of Northern India*. Allahabad, India: Government Press of the Northwestern Provinces and Oudh Province.

Crossley-Holland, Kevin. 1980. *The Norse Myths*. New York: Pantheon.

Curtin, Jeremiah. 1903. *Creation Myths of Primitive America*. Boston: Little, Brown.

———. 1909. *A Journey in Southern Siberia*. Boston: Little, Brown.

Curtis, Edward S. 1970 *North American Indian*. Landmarks in Anthropology Series. 12 vols. New York: Johnson Reprint Corp.

Cushing, Frank Hamilton. 1882. "The Nation of the Willows." *Atlantic Monthly* 50: 263–374, 541–559.

Czaplicka, M. A. 1969. *Aboriginal Siberia: A Study in Anthropology*. Oxford: Clarendon Press.

Damas, David, ed. 1984. *Handbook of North American Indians*. Vol. 5: *Arctic*. Washington, DC: Smithsonian Institution.

Dames, Michael. 1979. *Silbury Treasure: The Great Goddess Rediscovered*. London: Thames and Hudson.

Danielou, Alain. 1964. *Hindu Polytheism*. New York: Bollingen Foundation. Distributed by Pantheon Books.

Davidson, H. R. Ellis. 1964. *Gods and Myths of the Viking Age*. New York: Bell.

Davis, Elizabeth Gould. 1971. *The First Sex*. New York: G. P. Putnam's Sons.

Day, Clarence Burton. 1940. *Chinese Peasant Cults, Being a Study of Chinese Paper Gods*. Shanghai: Kelly and Walsh.

de Barandiaran, Jose Miguel. 1972. *Obras completas, diccionario illustrado de mitologia vasca y algunas de sus fuentes*. Vol. 1, *La Gran Enciclopedia Vasca*. Bilbao, Spain: Graficas Ellacuria.

De Crespigny, Lieut. 1875. "On the Milanows of Borneo." *Journal of the Royal Anthropological Institute of Great Britain and Ireland* 5: 34–37.

De Groot, J. J. M. 1925. "Confucian Religion." In *Encyclopaedia of Religion and Ethics*, ed. James Hastings, vol. 4. New York: Scribner's.

de Kay, Charles. 1898. *Bird Gods*. New York: A. S. Barnes.

de Nebesky-Wojkowitz, Rene. 1952. "Ancient Funeral Ceremonies of the Lepchas." *Eastern Anthropologist* 5(1): 27–40.

de Wit, Dorothy, ed. 1979. *Talking Stone*. New York: Greenwillow.

Deen, Edith. 1955. *All of the Women of the Bible*. New York: Harper & Brothers.

Deive, Carlos Esteban. 1988. *Vodun and Magic in Santo Domingo*. Santo Domingo, Dominican Republic: Fundacion Cultural Dominicana.

Del Re, Arundel. ca. 1951. *Creation Myths of the Formosan Natives*. Tokyo: Hokuseido Press.

Delaney, John J. 1980. *Dictionary of Saints*. New York: Doubleday.

Der Nersessian, Serarpie. 1969. *The Armeneans*. London: Thames and Hudson.

Dexter, Miriam Robbins. 1990. *Whence the Goddesses: A Source Book*. New York: Pergamon.

Deydier, Henri. 1952. *Introduction to the Knowledge of Laos*. Saigon: Imprimerie Francaise d'Outre-Mer.

Diamond, Norma. 1969. *K'un Shen, a Taiwan Village*. New York: Holt, Rinehart & Winston.

Dioszegl, V. 1968. *Popular Beliefs and Folklore Tradition in Siberia*. Bloomington, IN: Indiana University Press.

Dorsey, F. Owen. 1892. "Nanibozhu in Siouan Mythology." *Journal of American Folklore* 5: 293–304.

Dorsey, George A. 1904a. *The Mythology of the Witchita*. Washington, DC: Carnegie Institute of Washington.

———. 1904b. *Traditions of the Skidi Pawnee*. Boston: Houghton Mifflin.

———. 1904c. "Witchita Tales III." *Journal of American Folklore* 17: 153–160.

Downs, Richard Erskine. 1920. *The Religion of the Bare'e-Speaking Toradja of Central Celebes*. 'S-Gravenhage, the Netherlands: Excelsior.

Drahomaniv, M. P. 1961. *Notes on the Slavic Religio-Ethical Legends: The Dualistic Creation of the World*. Bloomington, IN: Indiana University Press.

Driver, G. R. 1956. *Canaanite Myths and Legends*. Edinburgh, Scotland: T. and T. Clark.

Dubose, Hampdon C. 1886. *The Dragon: Image and Demon*. London: Partridge.

Duran, Fray Diego. 1971. *Book of the Gods and Rites and the Ancient Calendar*. Trans. Fernando Horcasitas and Doris Heyden. Norman: University of Oklahoma Press.

Durdin-Robertson, Lawrence. 1975. *The Goddesses of Chaldaea, Syria and Egypt*. Carlow, Ireland: Cesara.

———, Lawrence. 1976. *The Goddesses of India, Tibet, China and Japan*. Carlow, Ireland: The Nationalist.

———, Lawrence. 1982. *Juno Covella: Perpetual Calendar of the Fellowship of Isis*. Clonegal Castle, Enniscorthy, Ireland: Cesara.

———, Lawrence. 1990. *The Year of the Goddess: A Perpetual Calendar of Festivals*. Wellingborough, Northamptonshire, England: Aquarian Press.

Eells, Myron. 1886. *The Twana, Chemakum, and Klallam Indians of Washington Territory*. Smithsonian Institution Annual Report. Washington, DC: Smithsonian Institution.

Eliade, Mircea. 1958. *Patterns in Comparative Religion*. Trans. Rosemary Sheed. New York: Meridan.

———. 1964. *Shamanism*. Bollingen Series, no. 76. Princeton, NJ: Princeton University Press.

———. 1967. *Gods, Goddesses, and Myths of Creation: A Thematic Source Book of the History of Religions*. Part I, Primitives to Zen. New York: Harper & Row.

———. 1987. *Encyclopedia of Religion*. New York: Macmillan.

Eliot, Alexander. 1976. *Myths*. New York: McGraw-Hill.

Eliot, Charles. 1932. *Japanese Buddhism*. London: Routledge & Kegan Paul.

Eliseev, Serge. 1932. "The Mythology of Japan." In *Asiatic Mythology, a Detailed Description and Explanation of the Mythologies of All the Great Nations of Asia*, by J. Hackin et al. Trans. F. M. Atkinson. London: G. G. Harrap.

Ellis, Peter Berresford. 1987. *A Dictionary of Irish Mythology*. Santa Barbara, CA: ABC-CLIO.

Ellis, William. 1853. *Polynesian Researches*, vol. 1. London: Henry G. Bohn.

Ells, Myron. 1886. *The Twana, Chemakum, and Klallam Indians of Washington Territory*. Smithsonian Institution Annual Report. Washington, DC: Smithsonian Institution.

Elmberg, John-Erik. 1955. "Field Notes on the Mejbrat People, Western New Guinea." *Ethnos* 20, 1:3–102.

Elwin, Verrier. 1939. *The Baiga*. London: John Murray.

———. 1942. *The Agaria*. London: Oxford University Press.

———. 1949. *Myths of Middle India*. Madras, India: Geoffrey Cumberlege, Oxford University Press.

———. 1954. *Tribal Myths of Orissa*. Oxford: Oxford University Press.

Emerson, Ellen Russell. 1965. *Indian Myths or Legends, Traditions and Symbols of the Aborigines of America Compared with Those of Other Countries, Including Hindostan, Egypt, Persia, Assyria, and China*. Minneapolis, MN: Ross & Haines.

Emerson, J. S. 1967. "The Lesser Hawaiian Gods." *The (San Francisco) Revue* 1 (December): 37–60.

———. 1968. "The Lesser Hawaiian Gods." In *The Kahunas*, ed. Sibley S. Morrill. San Francisco: Sibley S. Morrill, 1968.

Emmons, G. T. 1911. *The Tahltan Indians*. Philadelphia: University of Pennsylvania, University Museum.

Emory, Kenneth P. 1924. *The Island of Lanai*. Bernice P. Bishop Museum Bulletin, no. 135. Honolulu, HI: Bishop Museum Press.

———. 1965. *Kapingamarangi: Social and Religious Life of a Polynesian Atoll*. Bernice P. Bishop Museum Bulletin, no. 228. Honolulu, HI: Bishop Museum Press.

Ergener, Resit. 1988. *Anatolia: Land of Mother Goddess*. Ankara, Turkey: Hitit Publications.

Er-Wei, J. Tu. 1959. "A Contribution to the Mythology of the Tsou, Formosa." *Anthropos* 54, 3–4: 536–541.

Evans, Bergen. 1904. *Dictionary of Mythology, Mainly Classical*. Lincoln, NE: Centennial Press.

Evans, Ivor H. N. 1923. *Studies in Religion, Folklore, and Custom in British North Borneo and the Malay Peninsula*. Cambridge: Cambridge University Press.

———. 1937. *The Negritos of Malaya*. Cambridge: Cambridge University Press.

Evans-Wentz, W. Y. 1960. *Tibetan Book of the Dead: Or, the After-Death Experiences on the Bardo Plane, According to Lama Kazi Dawa-Samdup's English Rendering*. Oxford: Oxford University Press.

Fairbanks, Arthur. 1907. *The Mythology of Greece and Rome*. New York: D. Appleton.

Fairservis, Walter A., Jr. 1971. *The Roots of Ancient India: The Archaeology of Early Indian Civilization*. New York: Macmillan.

Farmer, Penelope. 1978. *Beginnings: Creation Myths of the World*. West Hanover, MA: Halliday Lithograph.

Ferguson, John. 1970. *The Religions of the Roman Empire*. Ithaca, NY: Cornell University Press.

Ferguson, John C. 1937. "Chinese." In *Chinese-Japanese*. Vol. 8, *Mythology of All Races*. Boston: Marshall Jones.

Ferm, Vergilius, ed. 1950. *Ancient Religions*. New York: Philosophical Library.

Fernandez, Adela. 1985. *Diccionario ritual de voces nahuas: Definiciones de palabras que expresan el pensamiento mitico y religioso de los nahuas prehispanicos*. Mexico City, Mexico: Panorama Editorial.

Fewkes, Jesse Walter. 1895a. "Oraibi Flute Altar." *Journal of American Folklore* 8: 265–284.

————. 1895b "Hopi Shrines near the East Mesa, Arizona." *American Anthropologist New Series* 8: 346–875.

————. 1895c. "A Comparison of Sia and Tusayan Snake Ceremonies." *American Anthropologist* 8, 2: 118–141.

————. 1897. "Tusayan Katcinas." *Annual Report of the Bureau of American Ethnology* 15.

————. 1985. *Hopi Katchinas.* New York: Dover.

Firth, Raymond William. 1967a. *Tikopia Ritual and Belief.* Boston: Beacon.

————. 1967b. *The Work of the Gods in Tikopia.* New York: Humanities Press.

Fletcher, Alice C. 1900–1901. "The Hako: A Pawnee Ceremony." *Annual Report of the Bureau of American Ethnology* 22(2): 5–372.

Franck, Adolphe. 1967. *The Kabbalah: The Religious Philosophy of the Hebrews.* Secaucus, NJ: Citadel.

Francke, A. H. 1923. *Tibetan Wedding Songs.* Hagen und Darmstadt: Folkwang Verlag.

Frazer, James George. 1926. *The Worship of Nature.* New York: Macmillan.

————. 1951. *The Golden Bough.* New York: Macmillan.

————. 1959. *The New Golden Bough.* New York: New American Library.

————. 1961. *Adonis, Attis, Osiris.* New Hyde Park, NY: University Books.

Friederich, R. 1959. *The Civilization and Culture of Bali.* Calcutta: Susil Gupta.

Gadon, Elinor W. 1989. *The Once and Future Goddess: A Sweeping Visual Chronicle of the Sacred Female and Her Reemergence in the Cult Mythology of Our Time.* San Francisco: Harper & Row.

Gardiner, Alan H. 1925. "Personification (Egyptian)." In *Encyclopaedia of Religion and Ethics,* ed. James Hastings, vol. 9. New York: Scribner's.

Gardner, E. A. 1925. "Personification (Greek)." In *Encyclopaedia of Religion and Ethics,* ed. James Hastings, vol. 9. New York: Scribner's.

Gatschet, Albert S. 1890. *The Klamath Indians of Southwestern Oregon.* Washington, DC: Department of the Interior.

Geertz, Clifford. 1960. *The Religion of Java.* Glencoe, IL: Free Press.

Getty, Alice. 1962. *The Gods of Northern Buddhism: Their History, Iconography and Progressive Evolution through the Northern Buddhist Countries.* Rutland, VT: Charles E. Tuttle.

Ghurye, G. S. 1962. *Gods and Men.* Bombay, India: Popular Book Depot.

Gifford, Edwin Winslow. 1929. *Tongan Society.* Bernice P. Bishop Museum Bulletin, no. 61. Berkeley, CA: University of California Press.

————. 1936. "Northeastern and Western Yavapai." *University of California Publications in American Archaeology and Ethnology* 34.

Gilhodes, P. Ch. 1908. "Mythologie et religion des katchins (birmanie)." *Anthropos* 3(2): 672–699.

Gill, Sam D. 1987. *Mother Earth: An American Story.* Chicago: University of Chicago Press.

Gill, Sam D. and Irene F. Sullivan. 1992. *Dictionary of Native American Mythology.* Santa Barbara, CA: ABC-CLIO.

Gillon, Werner. 1984. *A Short History of African Art.* New York: Facts on File.

Gimbutas, Marija. 1963. *The Balts.* New York: Praeger.

————. 1971. *The Slavs.* New York: Praeger.

————. 1989. *Language of the Goddess.* San Francisco: Harper & Row.

Gleason, Judith. 1987. *Oya: In Praise of the Goddess.* Boston: Shambhala.

Goldziher, Ignac. 1877. *Mythology among the Hebrews.* Trans. Russell Martineau. London: Longman, Green.

Gomes, Edwin H. 1911. *Seventeen Years among the Sea Dyaks of Borneo.* London: Seeley.

Gonzalez-Wippler, Migene. 1985. *Tales of the Orishas.* New York: Original Publications.

————. 1989. *Santeria: African Magic in Latin America.* New York: Harmony.

Gorer, Geoffrey. 1911. *Himalayan Village.* London: Michael Joseph.

Grader, C. J. 1961. "The State Temples of Mengwi." *Selected Studies in Indonesian Archaeology* 5: 155–186. The Hague, the Netherlands: B. M. Nijhoff.

————. 1969. "Pura Meduwe Karang at Kubutambahan." *Selected Studies in Indonesian Archeology* 8: 131–174. The Hague, the Netherlands: B. M. Nijhoff.

Graham, David Crockett. 1928. *Religion in Szechuan Province, China.* Smithsonian Institution Miscellaneous Collections 80(4). Washington, DC: Smithsonian Institution.

————. 1937. "Ceremonies and Customs of the Chu'an Miao." *Journal of the West China Border Research Society* 9.

————. 1958. *The Customs and Religion of the Ch'iang.* Smithsonian Institution Miscellaneous Collections 135(1). Washington, DC: Smithsonian Institution.

————. 1961. *Folk Religion in Southwest China.* Smithsonian Institution Miscellaneous Collections, 142(2). Washington, DC: Smithsonian Institution.

Graves, Robert. 1948. *The White Goddess.* New York: Farrar, Straus & Giroux.

Gray, Florence L. 1925. "Easter Island." In *Encyclopaedia of Religion and Ethics,* vol. 5, ed. James Hastings. New York: Scribner's.

Gray, John. 1957. *The Legacy of Canaan.* Leiden, the Netherlands: E. J. Brill.

Gray, Louis H. 1925. "Iroquois." In *Encyclopaedia of Religion and Ethics,* ed. James Hastings, vol. 7. New York: Scribner's.

————. 1930. *The Foundations of the Iranian Religions.* Bombay: D. B. Taraporevala Sons.

Grimm, Jacob. 1880–1888. *Teutonic Mythology.* 4 vols. London: B. W. Swan Sonnenschein & Allen.

Grimal, Pierre, ed. 1973. *Larousse World Mythology.* London: Hamlyn.

Grinnell, George B. 1892. *Blackfoot Lodge Tales: The Story of a Prairie People.* New York: Charles Scribner & Sons.

Guerber, H. A. 1895. *Myths of Northern Lands.* New York: American Book.

Guirand, Felix, ed. 1968. *New Larousse Encyclopedia of Mythology.* New York: Putnam.

Gurdon, Philip Richard Thornhaugh. 1907. *The Khasis.* London: D. Nutt.

————. 1914. *The Khasis.* 2d ed. London: Macmillan.

————. 1925. "Ahoms." In *Encyclopaedia of Religion and Ethics,* ed. James Hastings, vol. 1. New York: Scribner's.

Gurney, O. R. 1952. *The Hittites.* Baltimore: Penguin.

Hackin, J., et al. 1932. *Asiatic Mythology, a Detailed Description and Explanation of the Mythologies of All the Great Nations of Asia.* Trans. F. M. Atkinson. London: G. G. Harrap.

Haile, Berard. 1947. *Head and Face Masks in Navaho Ceremonialism.* St. Michaels, AZ: St. Michaels Press.

Halifax, Joan. 1981. *Shaman, the Wounded Healer.* London: Thames and Hudson.

Hamilton, Edith. 1940. *Mythology: Timeless Tales of Gods and Heroes.* Boston: Little, Brown.

Hammond, Norman. 1990. *Ancient Maya Civilization.* New Brunswick, NJ: Rutgers University Press.

Handy, E. S. Craighill. 1923. *The Native Culture in the Marquesas.* Bernice P. Bishop Museum Bulletin, no. 9. Honolulu, HI: Bishop Museum Press.

Hanks, Jane Richardson. 1963. *Maternity and Its Rituals in Bang Chan.* Ithaca, NY: Cornell University, Department of Asian Studies.

Harding, M. Esther. 1971. *Woman's Mysteries, Ancient and Modern.* New York: Harper & Row.

Harrington, John Peabody. 1907. "The Ethnography of the Tewa Indians." *Annual Report of the Bureau of American Ethnology* 19: 29–636.

Harrington, M. R. 1921. *Religions and Ceremonies of the Lenape.* Contributions, Museum of the American Indian, Heye Foundation, 19. New York: Museum of the American Indian, Heye Foundation.

Hartland, E. Sidney. 1925. "Death and the Disposal of the Dead (Introductory)." In *Encyclopaedia of Religion and Ethics,* ed. James Hastings, vol. 4. New York: Scribner's.

Hastings, James, ed. 1925. *Encyclopaedia of Religion and Ethics.* New York: Scribner's.

Hatt, Gudmund. 1951. "The Corn Mother in America and Indonesia." *Anthropos* 46: 853–914.

Haydon, Eustace. 1941. *Bibliography of the Gods.* New York: Macmillan.

Henry, Jules. 1941. *Jungle People: A Kaingang Tribe of the Highlands of Brazil.* Richmond, VA: William Byrd Press.

Henry, Teuira. 1920. "Tahitian Astronomy." *Polynesian Society Journal* 29.

———. 1928. *Ancient Tahiti.* Bernice P. Bishop Museum Bulletin, no. 48.

Herbert, Jean. 1967. *Shinto: At the Fountain-head of Japan.* London: George Allen and Unwin.

Herm, Gerhard. 1975. *The Phoenicians: The Purple Empire of the Ancient World.* New York: William Morrow.

Herskovits, Melville J. 1937. *Life in a Haitian Valley.* New York: Knopf.

Hesiod. 1981. *Theogony,* Trans. Norman O. Brown. Indianapolis: Bobbs-Merrill.

Hill, A. H. 1951. "Kelantan Padi Planting." *Journal of the Royal Anthropological Institute of Great Britain* (Malaysian Branch) 24: 56–76.

Hinnells, John R. 1973. *Persian Mythology.* New York: Hamlyn.

Hocart, A. M. 1929. *Lau Islands, Fiji.* Bernice P. Bishop Museum Bulletin, no. 62. Honolulu, HI: Bishop Museum Press.

Hoffman, Helmut. 1956. *The Religions of Tibet.* London: George Allen and Unwin.

Holmberg, Uno. 1925. "Lapps." In *Encyclopaedia of Religion and Ethics,* ed. James Hastings, vol. 7. New York: Scribner's.

Holmes, D. C. 1902. "Notes on the Religious Ideas of the Elema Tribe of the Papuan Gulf." *Journal of the Royal Anthropological Institute of Great Britain and Ireland* 32: 426–431.

Holtom, D. C. 1931. "Some Notes on Japanese Tree Worship." *Transactions of the Asiatic Society of Japan* 2d ser., 8: 1–19.

———. 1965. *The National Faith of Japan: A Study in Modern Shinto.* New York: Paragon Book Reprint Corp.

Hommell, Fr. 1925. "Calendar (Babylonian)." In *Encyclopaedia of Religion and Ethics,* ed. James Hastings, vol. 3. New York: Scribner's.

Hooykaas, C. 1964. *Agama tirtha.* Amsterdam: N. V. Noord-Hollandsche Uitgevers Maatschappij.

Hori, Ichiro. 1959. "Japanese Folk-Beliefs." *American Anthropologist* 61: 405–424.

———. 1968. *Folk Religion in Japan: Continuity and Change.* Chicago: University of Chicago Press.

Horowitz, Michael M. 1963. "The Worship of South Indian Deities in Martinique." *Ethnology* 2: 349–345.

Howell, F. Clark. 1968. *Early Man.* New York: Time-Life Books.

Howells, William. 1948. *The Heathens: Primitive Man and His Religions.* Garden City, NY: Doubleday.

Howitt, A. W. 1904. *The Native Tribes of Southeast Australia.* London: Macmillan.

Huart, Clement. "The Mythology of Persia." In *Asiatic Mythology, a Detailed Description and Explanation of the Mythologies of All the Great Nations of Asia,* by J. Hackin et al. Trans. F. M. Atkinson. London: G. G. Harrap.

Hubbs, Joanna. 1988. *Mother Russia: The Feminine Myth in Russian Culture.* Bloomington, IN: Indiana University Press.

Hudson, D. Travis and Ernest Underhay. 1978. *Crystals in the Sky: An Intellectual Odyssey Involving Chumash Astronomy, Cosmology and Rock Art.* Santa Barbara, CA: Ballena Press and Santa Barbara History Museum.

Hultkrantz, Ake. 1983. *The Book of the Goddesses.* New York: Crossroad.

Hutton, J. H. 1921. *The Angami Nagas.* London: Macmillan.

———. 1968. *The Sema Nagas.* London: Oxford University Press.

Ibn-al-kalbi, Hisham. 1952. *The Books of Idols, Being a Translation from the Arabic of the Kitab Al-assnam.* Princeton, NJ: Princeton University Press.

Ions, Veronica. 1967. *Indian Mythology.* London: Hamlyn.

———. 1982. *Egyptian Mythology.* New York: Peter Bedrick Books.

Jacobsen, Thorkild. 1970. *Toward the Image of Tammuz.* Cambridge, MA: Harvard University Press.

———. 1976. *The Treasures of Darkness.* New Haven, CT: Yale University Press.

James, E. O. 1958. *Myth and Ritual in the Ancient Near East, An Archaeological and Documentary Study.* New York: Praeger.

———. 1959. *The Cult of the Mother Goddess.* New York: Barnes & Noble.

———. 1960. *The Ancient Gods.* London: Weidenfeld and Nicolson.

Janashia, N. S. 1937. "The Religious Beliefs of the Abkhasians." *Georgica* 4–5: 117–153.

Jayne, Walter Addison. 1925. *The Healing Gods of Ancient Civilizations.* New Hyde Park, NY: University Books.

———. 1962. *The Healing Gods of Ancient Civilizations.* New York: University Books.

Jobes, Gertrude. 1962. *Dictionary of Mythology, Folklore and Symbols.* New York: Scarecrow.

Jocano, F. Landa. 1969. *Outline of Philippine Mythology.* Manilla, Phillippines: Centro Escolar University Research and Development Center.

Jochelson, Waldemar. 1908. "The Koryak." *Memoirs of the American Museum of Natural History* 10(1).

Johnson, Buffie. 1988. *Lady of the Beasts: Ancient Images of the Goddess and Her Sacred Animals.* San Francisco: Harper & Row.

Johnson, Jean B. 1949. *The Opata: An Inland Tribe of Sonora.* University of New Mexico Publications in Anthropology 6. Albuquerque, NM: University of New Mexico Press.

Jordan, David K. 1972. *Gods, Ghosts, and Ancestors.* Berkeley and Los Angeles: University of California Press.

Karsten, Rafael. 1926. *The Civilization of the South American Indians.* New York: Knopf.

———. 1955. *The Religion of the Samek.* Leiden, The Netherlands: E. J. Brill.

Kato, Genchi. 1971. *Study of Shinto: The Religion of the Japanese Nation.* New York: Barnes & Noble.

Keane, A. H. 1925a. "Asia." In *Encyclopaedia of Religion and Ethics,* ed. James Hastings, vol. 2. New York: Scribner's.

———. 1925b. "Australasia." In *Encyclopaedia of Religion and Ethics,* ed. James Hastings, vol. 2. New York: Scribner's.

Keeler, Clyde E. 1960. *Secrets of the Cuna Earth-Mother.* New York: Exposition Press.

Keith, A. Berriedale. 1917. "Indian." In *Indian-Iranian.* Vol. 6, *Mythology of All Races.* Boston: Marshall Jones.

Kelley, David Humiston. 1976. *Deciphering the Maya Script.* Austin: University of Texas Press.

Kerenyi, K. 1951. *The Gods of the Greeks.* London: Thames and Hudson.

Klementz, Demetrius. 1925. "Buriats." In *Encylaopedia of Religion and Ethics,* ed. James Hastings, vol. 3. New York: Scribner's.

Knappe, C. 1888. "Religious View of the Marshall Islanders." *Mitteilungen von Forschungsreisenden und Gelehrten aus den deutschen Schutzgebeiten* 1: 63–81.

Kramer, Samuel Noah. 1950. "Sumerian Religion." In *Ancient Religions*, ed. Vergilius Ferm. New York: Philosophical Library.

———. 1961a. "Mythology of Sumer and Akkad." In *Mythologies of the Ancient World*, ed. Samuel Noah Kramer. Chicago: Quadrangle Books.

——— 1961b. *Mythologies of the Ancient World.* Chicago: Quadrangle Books.

Krickeberg, Walter. "Mesoamerica." In *Pre-Columbian American Religions*, ed. E. O. James. New York: Holt, Rinehart & Winston.

Kroeber, A. L. 1905. "Wishosk Myths." *Journal of American Folklore* 18: 85–107.

———. 1918. *History of Philippine Civilization as Reflected in Religious Nomenclature.* Anthropological Papers of the American Museum of Natural History 19(2). New York: American Museum of Natural History.

———. 1925. "Handbook of the Indians of California." *Annual Report of the Bureau of American Ethnology* 78.

Krohn, Kaarle. 1925. "Finns (Ancient)." In *Encyclopaedia of Religion and Ethics*, ed. James Hastings, vol. 6. New York: Scribner's.

Kruijt, Alb. C. 1925. "Indonesians." In *Encyclopaedia of Religion and Ethics*, ed. James Hastings, vol. 7. New York: Scribner's.

Laird, Carobeth. 1976. *The Chemehuevis.* Banning, CA: Malki Museum Press.

Lambrecht, Francis. 1932. "The Mayawyaw Ritual." In *Publications of the Catholic Anthropological Conference.* Washington, DC: Catholic Anthropological Conference.

Lamy, Lucie. 1981. *Egyptian Mysteries.* New York: Crossroad.

Landes, Ruth. 1940. "Fetish Worship in Brazil." *Journal of American Folklore* 53: 261–270.

———. 1968. *Ojibwa Religion and the Midewiwin.* Madison: University of Wisconsin Press.

Langdon, Stephen Herbert. 1931. *Semitic.* Vol. 5, *Mythology of All Races.* Boston: Marshall Jones.

LaPointe, James. 1976. *Legends of the Lakota.* San Francisco: Indian Historian Press.

Larson, Gerald J., ed. 1974. *Myth in Indo-European Antiquity.* Berkeley and Los Angeles: University of California Press.

Laski, Vera. 1958. "Seeking Life." *Memoirs of the American Folklore Society* 10.

Latorre, Felipe A. and Dolores L. Latorre. 1976. *The Mexican Kickapoo Indians.* Austin: University of Texas Press.

Lawrence, Peter and M. J. Meggett, eds. 1965. *Gods, Ghosts and Men in Melanesia.* Melbourne: Oxford University Press.

Leach, Maria. 1956. *The Beginning: Creation Myths around the World.* New York: Funk & Wagnalls.

Leach, Maria, ed. 1949–1950. *Funk and Wagnalls Standard Dictionary of Folklore, Mythology, and Legend,* 2 vols. New York: Funk and Wagnalls.

Leach, Marjorie. 1992. *Guide to the Gods.* Santa Barbara, CA: ABC-CLIO.

Leacock, Seth. 1956. *The Beginning.* New York: Funk & Wagnalls.

Leacock, Seth and Ruth Leacock. 1972. *Spirits of the Deep: An Afro-Brazilian Cult.* Garden City, NY: Doubleday Natural History Press.

Lebra, William P. 1966. *Okinawan Religion: Belief, Ritual, and Social Structure.* Honolulu: University of Hawaii Press.

Leeming, David Adams. 1981. *Mythology: The Voyage of the Hero.* New York: Harper & Row.

Lehmann, Johannes. 1975. *The Hittites: People of a Thousand Gods.* New York: Viking.

Leroi-Gourhan, Andre. 1967. *Treasures of Prehistoric Art.* New York: Harry N. Abrams.

Lessa, William A. 1961. *Tales from the Ulithi Atoll: A Comparative Study in Oceanic Folklore.* Folklore Studies, vol. 13. Berkeley and Los Angeles: University of California Press.

Levi, Sylvain. 1933. *Sanskrit Texts from Bali.* Baroda, India: Oriental Institute.

Levi-Strauss, Claude. 1973. *From Honey to Ashes.* New York: Harper & Row.

———. 1975. *The Raw and Cooked.* New York: Harper & Row.

Levin, M. G. and L. P. Potapov, eds. 1964. *Peoples of Siberia.* Chicago: University of Chicago Press.

Lewis, Ethel Clark. 1956. *Portraits of Bible Women.* New York: Vintage.

Li Anche. 1948. "Bon: The Magico-Religious Belief of the Tibetan- Speaking Peoples." *Southwestern Journal of Anthropology* 4: 31–42.

Linossier, Raymonde. 1963. "The Mythology of Buddhism in India." In *Asiatic Mythology, a Detailed Description and Explanation of the Mythologies of all the Great Nations of Asia,* ed. J. Hackin et al. Trans. F. M. Atkinson. London: G. G. Harrap.

Littleton, C. Scott. 1965. *Georges Dumezil and the New Comparative Indo-European Mythology.* Los Angeles: University of California Press.

Littmann, E. 1925. "Abyssinia." In *Encyclopaedia of Religion and Ethics*, ed. James Hastings, vol. 1. New York: Scribner's.

Locher, G. W. 1932. *The Serpent in Kwakiutl Religion: A Study in Primitive Culture.* Leyden, The Netherlands: E. J. Brill.

Lockyer, Herbert. 1967. *The Women of the Bible.* Grand Rapids, MI: Zondervan.

Loeb, Edwin M. 1926. "History and Traditions of Niue." *Bernice P. Bishop Museum Bulletin* 32.

———. 1931. "The Religious Organization of North Central California and Tierra del Fuego." *American Anthropologist* 33: 517–556.

Long, Charles H. 1963. *Alpha: The Myths of Creation.* New York: George Braziller.

Lothrop, Samuel Kirkland. 1926. *Pottery of Costa Rica and Nicaragua.* Contributions, Museum of the American Indian, Heye Foundation, vol. 8, no 1. New York: Museum of the American Indian, Heye Foundation.

Lovén, Sven. 1935. *Origins of the Tainan Culture, West Indies.* Goteborg, Sweden: Elanders Bokfrycheri Akfiebolag.

Lowie, Robert H. 1922. *Religion of the Crow.* Anthropological Papers of the American Museum of Natural History, vol. 25, no. 2. New York: American Museum of Natural History.

Lumholtz, Carl. 1902. *Unknown Mexico: A Record of Five Years' Exploration among the Tribes of the Western Sierra Madre; in the Tierra Caliente of Tepic and Jalisco; and among the Tarascos of Michoacan.* New York: Scribner's.

Lurker, Manfred. 1984. *Gods and Goddesses, Devils and Demons.* New York: Routledge & Kegan Paul.

Mac Cana, Proinseas. 1970. *Celtic Mythology.* London: Hamlyn.

MacCulloch, John Arnott. 1925. "Cross-Roads." In *Encyclopeedia of Religion and Ethics*, ed. James Hastings, vol. 4. New York: Scribner's.

———. 1930. *Eddic.* Vol. 2, *Mythology of All Races.* Boston: Marshall Jones.

Macdonell, A. A. 1897. *Vedic Mythology.* Strassburg, France: Karl J. Trubner.

Machal, Jan. 1918. *Slavic.* Vol. 3, *Mythology of All Races*, ed. Louis Herbert Gray. Boston: Marshall Jones.

McIlwraith, T. F. 1948. *The Bella Coola Indians.* Toronto: University of Toronto Press.

Mackenzie, Donald A. 1912. *Teutonic Myth and Legend.* London: Gresham.

———. 1913. *Egyptian Myth and Legend.* London: Greshman.

———. 1930a. *Myths and Traditions of the South Sea Islands.* London: Gresham.

————. 1930b. *Myths from Melanesia and Indonesia*. London: Gresham.

MacLagen, P. J. 1925. "Heroes and Hero-Gods." In *Encyclopaedia of Religion and Ethics*, ed. James Hastings, vol. 6. New York: Scribner's.

Maclean, John. 1896. *Canadian Savage Folk: The Native Tribes of Canada*. Toronto: William Briggs.

McMahon, A. R. 1876. *The Karens of the Golden Chersonnese*. London: Harrison.

MacNeish, June Helm, ed. 1981. *Handbook of North American Indians. Vol. 6: Subarctic*. Washington, DC: Smithsonian Institution.

McNeley, James Kale. 1981. *Holy Wind in Navajo Philosophy*. Tucson, AZ: University of Arizona Press.

Majumdar, Dhirenda Nath. 1950. *The Affairs of a Tribe*. Lucknow, India: Lucknow University, Department of Anthropology.

Malandra, William W. 1983. *An Introduction to Ancient Iranian Religion*. Minneapolis: University of Minnesota Press.

Mansikka, V. J. 1925. "Demons and Spirits (Slavic)." In *Encyclopaedia of Religion and Ethics*, ed. James Hastings, vol. 4. New York: Scribner's.

Marchall, Charles-Henri. 1963. "The Mythology of Indo-China and Java in Asiatic Mythology," ed. J. Hackin et al. New York: Thomas Crowell.

Marriott, Alice and Carol K. Rachlin. 1975. *Plains Indian Mythology*. New York: Thomas Y. Crowell.

Markham, Clements R. 1969. *The Incas of Peru*. Lima, Peru: Librerias A. B. C.

Marsh, Gordon H. 1967. "Eskimo-Aleut Religion." In *North American Indians: A Sourcebook*, ed. Roger C. Owen. New York: Macmillan.

Marshall, Harry Ignatius. "The Karen People of Burma: Contributions in History and Political Science." Ohio State University Bulletin, vol. 26, no. 13.

Martin, E. Osborn. 1914. *The Gods of India*. New York: Dutton.

Martinez, Jose M. B. 1962. *Religiones primitivas de hispania*. Rome, Italy: Consejo Superior de Investigaciones Cientificas.

Matthews, John Joseph. 1982. *The Osages, Children of the Middle Waters*. Norman: University of Oklahoma Press.

Matthews, Washington. 1889. "Nogoilpi, the Gambler: A Navajo Myth." *Journal of American Folklore* 2: 89–94.

Matthiae, Paolo. 1981. *Ebla: An Empire Rediscovered*. New York: Doubleday.

Mbiti, John S. 1970. *Concepts of God in Africa*. New York: Praeger.

Means, Philip Ainsworth. 1931. *Ancient Civilizations of the Andes*. New York: Scribner's.

Meiser, Leo. 1963. "Raran, the High Spirit of the Kaean." *Anthropos* 58: 905–906.

Mellaart, James. 1970. *Excavations at Hacilar*. Edinburgh, Scotland: Edinburgh University Press.

Meltzer, David. 1981. *Birth: An Anthology of Ancient Texts, Songs, Prayers, and Stories*. San Francisco: North Point.

Melville, Leinani. 1969. *Children of the Rainbow*. Wheaton, IL: Theosophical Publishing House.

Mercer, S. A. B. 1925a. "War, War-Gods (Semitic)." In *Encyclopaedia of Religion and Ethics*, ed. James Hastings, vol. 12. New York: Scribner's.

————. 1925b. "Water, Water-Gods (Babylonia, Egypt)." In *Encyclopaedia of Religion and Ethics*, ed. James Hastings, vol. 12. New York: Scribner's.

Merriam, C. Hart. 1910. *The Dawn of the World: Myths and Weird Tales Told by the Mewan Indians of California*. Cleveland, OH: Arthur Cleark.

Metraux, Alfred. 1940. *Ethnology of Easter Island*. Bernice P. Bishop Museum Bulletin, no. 160.

Meyerowitz, Eva L. R. 1958. *The Akan of Ghana*. London: Faber and Faber.

Michael, Henry N. 1963. *Studies in Siberian Shamanism*. Toronto: University of Toronto Press.

Mills, J. P. 1937. *The Rengma Nagas*. London: Macmillan.

Moes, Robert. 1983. *Auspicious Spirits: Korean Folk Paintings and Related Objects*. Washington, DC: The Foundation.

Mole, William. 1966. *Gods, Men and Wine*. London: Wine and Food Society.

Monaghan, Patricia. 1981. *Book of Goddesses and Heroines*. New York: Dutton.

————. 1990. *Book of Goddesses and Heroines*, rev. ed. St. Paul, MN: Lewellyn, 1990.

Moon, Sheila. 1984. *Changing Woman and Her Sisters: Feminine Aspects of Selves and Deities*. San Francisco: Guild for Psychological Studies Publication House.

Mooney, James. 1900. *Myths of the Cherokee*. New York: Johnson Reprint Company.

Morgan, Lewis H. 1901. *League of the Ho-de-no-sau-nee or Iroquois*. New York: Dodd, Mead.

Moscati, Sabatino. 1960. *Ancient Semitic Civilizations*. New York: Capricorn.

————. 1962. *The Face of the Ancient Orient*. Garden City, NY: Anchor Books.

Moss, C. R. 1920. "Nabaloi Law and Ritual." *University of California Publications in American Archaeology and Ethnology* 15.

Moss, Rosalind. 1925. *The Life after Death in Oceania*. Oxford: Oxford University Press.

Moulton, J. Egan. 1925. "Tongans." In *Encyclopaedia of Religion and Ethics*, ed. James Hastings, vol. 12. New York: Scribner's.

Mountford, Charles P. 1955. "The Lightning Man in Australian Mythology." *Man* 55: 129–130.

————. 1958. *The Tiwi: Their Art, Myth, and Ceremony*. London: Phoenix House.

————. 1965. *Dreamtime: The Australian Aboriginal Myths*. Adelaide, Australia: Rigby.

Mowat, Farley. 1968. *People of the Deer*. New York: Pyramid Books.

Mudiraj, G. N. R. 1970. "Folk Deities of Telangana." *Folklore* (Calcutta) 11(2): 47–50.

Mukherjea, Charulal. 1962. *The Santals*. Calcutta: A. Mukherjee.

Müller, Wilhelm. 1917–1918. "Yap, von Dr. Wilhelm Müller (Wismar)." In *Ergebnisse der Südsee-expedition, 1908–1910*, vol. 2(1–2). Hamburg: Friederichsen.

Munro, Neil Gordon. 1963. *Ainu Creed and Cult*. New York: Columbia University Press.

Murphy, Robert F. 1958. "Mundurucu Religion." *University of California Publications in American Archaeology and Ethnology* 49.

Murray, Alexander S. 1882. *Manual of Mythology: Greek and Roman, Norse, and Old German, Hindoo and Egyptian Mythology*. New York: Scribner's.

Muser, Curt. 1978. *Facts and Artifacts of Ancient Middle America: A Glossary of Terms and Words Used in the Archaeology and Art History of Pre-Columbian Mexico and Central America*. New York: Dutton.

Myerhoff, Barbara. 1974. *Peyote Hunt: The Sacred Journey of the Huichol Indians*. Ithaca, NY: Cornell University Press.

Naik, T. B. 1956. *The Bhils: A Study*. New Delhi: Bharatiya Adimjati Sevak Sangh.

Naranjo-Morse, Nora. 1992. *Mud Woman: Poems from the Clay*. Tucson: University of Arizona Press.

Nash, June C. 1970. *The Change of Officials in Tzo'ontahal, Chiapas, Mexico: An Analysis of Behavior as a Key to Structure and Process*. New Orleans: Tulane University, Middle American Research.

————. 1978. "The Aztecs and the Ideology of Male Dominance." *Signs* 4(2).

Negev, Avraham. 1986. *Nabataean Archaeology Today*. New York: New York University Press.

Neumann, Erich. 1972. *The Great Mother: An Analysis of the Archetype*. Princeton, NJ: Princeton University Press.

Nicholson, Henry B. 1971. "Religion in Pre-Hispanic Central Mexico." In *Handbook of Middle American Indians* Vol. 2: 395–446. Austin: University of Texas Press.

Nimuendaju, Curt. 1942. *The Serente*. Trans. Robert Lowie. Los Angeles: Southwest Museum.

———. 1946. "Social Organiztion and Beliefs of the Botocudo of Eastern Brazil." *Southwestern Journal of Anthropology* 2(1): 93–115.

———. 1952. "The Tukuna," trans. William D. Hohenthal. *University of California Publications in American Archaeology and Ethnology* 45.

Norbeck, Edward. 1954. *Takashima: A Japanese Fishing Community*. Salt Lake City: University of Utah Press.

Nordenskiold, Erland. 1930. *Picture-Writing and Other Documents: Parts 1–2*. Goteborg, Sweden: Goteborg Museum.

———. 1938. *An Historical and Ethnological Survey of the Cuna Indians*. Goteborg, Sweden: Goteborg Museum.

Norton-Taylor, Duncan. 1974. *The Celts*. New York: Time-Life Books.

Nungak, Zebedee and Eugene Arima. 1969. *Eskimo Stories from Povungnituk, Quebec*. National Museum of Canada Anthropological Series, Bulletin 235, no. 90. Ottawa: National Museum of Canada.

Nunnally-Cox, Janice. 1981. *Foremothers: Women of the Bible*. New York: Seabury Press.

Nyuak, Leo. 1906. "Religious Rites and Customs of the Iban or Dyaks of Sarawak," trans. Edmund Dunn. *Anthropos* 1: 11–24, 165–184, 403–425.

Oberg, Kalervo. 1953. *Indian Tribes of the Northern Mato Grosso, Brazil*. Smithsonian Institution, Institute of Social Anthropology, Publication 15. Washington, DC: Smithsonian Institution.

Oldenberg, H. 1969. *Ancient India*. Chicago: Open Court.

Oliver, Douglas L. 1967. *A Solomon Island Society*. Boston: Beacon.

Olson, Carl, ed. 1983. *The Book of the Goddess Past and Present: An Introduction to Her Religion*. New York: Crossroad.

Ono, Yasuhiro, et al., eds. 1985. *Nihonshukyojiten (Encyclopedia of Japanese Religion)*. Tokyo: Kobundo.

Opler, Morris Edward. 1941. *An Apache Life-way: The Economic, Social and Religious Institutions of the Chiricahua Indians*. Chicago: University of Chicago Press.

O'Rahilly, Thomas F. 1946. *Early Irish History and Mythology*. Dublin: Dublin Institute for Advanced Studies.

Ortiz, Alfonso, ed. 1979. *Handbook of North American Indians. Vol. 9: Southwest*. Washington, DC: Smithsonian Institution.

———. 1983. *Handbook of North American Indians. Vol. 10: Southwest*. Washington, DC: Smithsonian Institution.

Paasonen, H. "Mordvins." 1925. In *Encyclopaedia of Religion and Ethics*, ed. James Hastings, vol. 8. New York: Scribner's.

Painter, Muriel Thayer. 1986. *With Good Heart: Yaqui Beliefs and Ceremonies in Pascua Village*. Tucson: University of Arizona Press.

Pal, Pratapaditya. 1981. *Hindu Religion and Iconology*. Los Angeles: Vichitra Press.

Pal, Pratapaditya and Dipak Chandra Phattacharyya. 1969. *The Astral Divinities of Nepal*. Varanasi, India: Prithivi Prakashan.

Parrinder, Geoffrey. 1967. *African Mythology*. London: Hamlyn.

Parsons, Elsie Clews. 1916. "The Zuni Molawia." *Journal of American Folklore* 29: 392–399.

———. 1929. "The Social Organization of the Tewa of New Mexico." *Memoirs of the American Anthropological Association* 36.

———. 1932. "Isleta, New Mexico." *Annual Report of the Bureau of American Ethnology* 47: 193–466.

———. 1939. *Pueblo Indian Religion*. Vol. 1. Chicago: University of Chicago Press.

Pasztory, Esther. 1983. *Aztec Art*. New York: Harry N. Abrams.

Patai, Raphael. 1967. *The Hebrew Goddess*. New York: Ktav Publishing.

Pelton, Robert W. 1972. *Complete Book of Voodoo*. New York: G. P. Putnam's Sons.

Percheron, Maurice. 1953. *Dieux et demons, lamas et sourciers de mongolie*. Paris: de Noel.

Peredo, Miguel Guzman. 1974. "Exploring the Sacred Well." *Américas* 26(8): 17–23.

Perera, Victor and Robert D. Bruce. 1982. *The Last Lords of Palenque: The Lacandon Mayas of the Mexican Rain Forest*. Berkeley and Los Angeles: University of California Press.

Pettazzoni, Raffaele. 1956. *The All-Knowing God: Researches into Early Religion and Culture*. London: Methuen.

Philippi, Donald L. 1982. *Songs of Gods, Songs of Humans*. San Francisco: North Point.

———. 1968. *Kojiki*. Tokyo: University of Tokyo Press.

Phillips, John A. 1984. *Eve: The History of an Idea*. San Francisco: Harper & Row.

Plaskow, Judith. 1979. "The Coming of Lilith: Toward a Feminist Theology." In *Womanspirit Rising: A Feminist Reader in Religion*, eds. Carol P. Christ and Judith Plaskow. San Francisco: Harper & Row.

Poignant, Roslyn. 1967. *Oceanic Mythology*. London: Hamlyn.

Pospisil, Leopold. 1958. *Kapauku Papuans and Their Law*. Yale University Publications in Anthropology 54. New Haven, CT: Yale University Press.

Powell, J. W. 1879–1880. "Sketch of the Mythology of the North American Indians." In *Annual Report of the Bureau of American Ethnology* 1.

Powell, Peter J. 1969. *Sweet Medicine*. Norman: University of Oklahoma Press.

Preston, James J., ed. 1982. *Mother Worship: Themes and Variations*. Chapel Hill: University of North Carolina Press.

Prokof'yeva, E. D. 1964. "The Nentsy." In *Peoples of Siberia*, eds. M. G. Levin and L. P. Potapov. Chicago: University of Chicago Press.

Puhvel, Jaan, ed. 1974. *Myth in Indo-European Antiquity*. Berkeley and Los Angeles: University of California Press.

Puini, C. and F. V. Dickens. 1880. "The Seven Gods of Happiness." *Transactions of the Asiatic Society of Japan* 8–9.

Punekar, Vijaya B. 1959. *The Son Kolis of Bombay*. Bombay: Popular Book Depot.

Putnam, John J. 1971. "The Ganges, River of Faith." *National Geographic* 140 (October): 445–482.

Queval, Jean. 1968. *Lexique des dieux*. Paris: Delpire.

Raats, Pieter Jan. 1969. *A Structural Study of Bagobo Myths and Rites*. Cebu City, Philippines: University of San Carlos.

Radcliffe-Brown, A. R. 1967. *The Andaman Islanders*. New York: Free Press.

Radice, Betty, ed. 1975. *Hindu Myths: A Sourcebook Translated from the Sanskrit*. New York: Penguin.

Rasmussen, Knud. 1929. *Intellectual Culture of the Iglulik Eskimos*. Report of the Fifth Thule Expedition, 1921–1924, vol. 7, no. 1. Copenhagen: Gyldendal.

———. 1930. *Observations on the Intellectual Culture of the Caribou Eskimos*. Report of the Fifth Thule Expedition, 1921–1924, vol. 7, no. 2. Copenhagen: Gyldendal.

———. 1931. *The Netsilik Eskimos: Social Life and Spiritual Culture*. Report of the Fifth Thule Expedition, 1921–1924, vol. 8, no. 1–2. Copenhagen: Gyldendal.

Rawlinson, George. 1885. *The Religions of the Ancient World*. New York: John B. Alden.

Redfield, Bessie G., ed. 1931. *Gods: A Dictionary of the Deities of All Lands, Including Supernatural Beings, Mythical Heroes and Kings, Sacred Books of Principal Religions.* New York: G. P. Putnam's Sons.

Reed, A. W. 1973. *Myths and Legends of Australia.* New York: Taplinger.

————. 1978. *Aboriginal Myths: Tales of the Dreamtime.* Sydney, Australia: A. H. & A. W. Reed.

Renel, Ch. 1906. *Les religions de la gauls avant le christianisme.* Paris: Ernest Leroux.

Reville, Albert D. D. 1884. *The Native Religions of Mexico and Peru.* New York: Scribner's.

Revon, M. "Nature." 1925. In *Encyclopaedia of Religion and Ethics,* ed. James Hastings, vol. 9. New York: Scribner's.

Ribbach, Samuel Heinrich. 1940. *Drogpa Namgyal: The Life of a Tibetan.* München-Planegg, Germany: Otto Wilhelm Barth Verlag.

Rigaud, Milo. 1969. *Secrets of Voodoo.* San Francisco: City Lights Books.

Rivers, W. H. R. "Todas." 1925. In *Encyclopaedia of Religion and Ethics,* ed. James Hastings, vol. 12. New York: Scribner's.

Roberts, Ainslie and Charles P. Mountford. 1973. *The Dreamtime Book: Australian Aboriginal Myths.* Englewood Cliffs, NJ: Prentice-Hall.

Roberts, Ainslie and Melva Jean Roberts. 1975. *Dreamtime Heritage: Australian Aboriginal Myths.* Adelaide, Australia: Rigby.

Roberts, J. J. M. 1972. *The Earliest Semitic Pantheon.* Baltimore: Johns Hopkins University Press.

Robertson, George Scott. 1925. "Kafiristan." In *Encyclopaedia of Religion and Ethics,* ed. James Hastings, vol. 7. New York: Scribner's.

Robertson, John M. 1911. *Pagan Christs.* London: Watts.

Robinson, Roland. 1966. *Aboriginal Myths and Legends.* Melbourne: Sun Books.

Rock, Joseph F. 1936. "The Origin of the Tso-la Books, or Books of Divination of the Na-khi or Mo-so Tribe." *Journal of the West China Border Research Society* 8.

————. 1947. *Ancient Na-khi Kingdom of Southwest China.* Cambridge: Harvard University Press.

————. 1959. "Contributions of the Shamanism of the Tibetan-Chinese Borderland." *Anthropos* 54: 796–818.

Roheim, Geza. 1946. "Yaboaine, a War God of Normanby Island." *Oceania* 16(4): 319–336.

————. 1954. *Hungarian and Vogul Mythology.* Locust Valley, NY: J. J. Augustin.

————. 1972. *The Panic of the Gods.* New York: Harper & Row.

Roscher, W. H. 1965. *Ausfuhrliches lexikon der greichischen und romischen mythologie.* Hildesheim, Germany: Georg Olms Verlagsbuchhandlung.

Ross, Anne. 1967. *Pagan Celtic Britain.* New York: Columbia University Press.

Roth, Henry Ling. 1968. *The Natives of Sarawak and British North Borneo.* Singapore: University of Malaya Press.

Roy, Sarat Chandra. 1928. *Oraon Religion and Customs.* Shambazar, Calcutta: Industry Press.

Rudolph, Kurt. 1983. *Gnosis.* San Francisco: Harper & Row.

Ruhela, Satya Pal. 1971. "Lohars: Bullock-Cart Blacksmiths of India's Rajasthan State." In *Nomads of the World.* Washington, DC: National Geographic Society.

Russell, R. V. 1916. *The Tribes and Castes of the Central Provinces of India.* 4 vols. London: Macmillan.

————. 1925. "Central Provinces (India)." In *Encyclopaedia of Religion and Ethics,* ed. James Hastings, vol. 3. New York: Scribner's.

Saggs, H. W. F. 1962. *The Greatness That Was Babylon.* New York: Hawthorn Books.

Sahagun, Fray Bernardino de. 1950–1982. *General History of the Things of New Spain: Florentine Codex.* Trans. Charles E. Dibble and Arthur J. O. Anderson. 13 vols. Monographs of the School of American Research 14. Santa Fe, NM: School of American Research.

Sakamoto, Toro, Saburo Ienaga, Mitsusoda Ienaga, and Susumn Ono, eds. 1967. *Nihonshoki.* Tokyo: Iwanami-Shoten.

Samuel, Alan E. 1966. *The Mycenaeans in History.* Englewood Cliffs, NJ: Prentice-Hall.

Sando, Joe S. 1982. *Nee Hemish—A History of the Jemez Pueblo.* Albuquerque: University of New Mexico Press.

Savill, Sheila. 1977. *Pears Encyclopaedia of Myths and Legends: Northern Europe, Southern and Central Africa.* London: Pelham.

————. 1978. *Pears Encyclopaedia of Myths and Legends: Oceania and Australia, The Americas.* London: Pelham.

Sayce, A. H. 1898. *Lectures on the Origin and Growth of Religion as Illustrated by the Religion of the Ancient Babylonians.* Hibbert Lectures. Oxford: Williams and Norgate.

Schafer, Edward. 1973. *The Divine Woman.* Berkeley and Los Angeles: University of California Press.

Scharer, Hans. 1963. *Ngaju Religion.* Trans. Rodney Needham. The Hague: Martinus Nijhoff.

Schebesta, Paul. 1927. *Among The Forest Dwarfs of Malaya.* London: Hutchinson.

————. 1952–1957. *Die Negrito Asiens.* Vienna- Modling: St.-Gabriel Verlag.

Schele, Linda and Mary Ellen Miller. 1986. *The Blood of Kings: Dynasty and Ritual in Maya Art.* Fort Worth, TX: Kimbell Art Museum.

Schmidt, P. W. 1951. "The Corn Mother in America and in Indonesia." *Anthropos* 46.

Schoeps, Hans-Joachim. 1961. *The Religions of Mankind.* Garden City, NY: Doubleday.

Schrader, O. 1925. "Aryan Religion." In *Encyclopaedia of Religion and Ethics,* ed. James Hastings, vol. 2. New York: Scribner's.

Schram, Louis M. J. 1957. "The Mongurs of the Kansu-Tibetan Border." *Transactions of the American Philosophical Society* 47(2).

Schulze, F. V. P. 1912. *The Religion of the Kuvi-Konds, Their Customs and Folklore.* Madras, India: Gravaes, Cookson.

Scott, James George. 1964. *Indo-Chinese.* Vol. 12, *Mythology of All Races.* New York: Cooper Square.

Seler, Edward. 1925. "Huichols." In *Encyclopaedia of Religion and Ethics,* ed. James Hastings, vol. 6. New York: Scribner's.

Seligmann, Kurt. 1948. *Magic, Supernaturalism, and Religion.* New York: Grosset and Dunlap.

Senior, Michael. 1985. *Illustrated Who's Who in Mythology.* New York: Macmillan.

Shternberg, Lev Iakoblevich. 1933. *The Gilyak, Orochi, Goldi, Negidal, Ainu: Articles and Materials.* Khabarovsk, USSR: Dal'giz.

Sierksma, F. 1960. *The Gods as We Shape Them.* London: Routledge and Kegan Paul.

————. 1966. *Tibet's Terrifying Deities.* The Hague: Mouton.

Siiger, Halfdan. 1967. "The Lepchas: Culture and Religion of a Himalayan People." *National Museum of Denmark* 11(1–2).

Siméon, Rémi. 1988. *Diccionario de la lengua nahuatl o mexicana.* Trans. Josefina Oliva de Coll. Mexico City: Siglo Veintiuno Editores.

Sjoestedt, Marie-Louise. 1982. *Gods and Heroes of the Celts.* Berkeley, CA: Turtle Island Foundation.

Skeat, Walter Wm. 1906. *Pagan Races of the Malay Peninsula.* London: Macmillan.

————. 1925. "Malay Peninsula." In *Encyclopaedia of Religion and Ethics,* ed. James Hastings, vol. 8. New York: Scribner's.

Skinner, Alanson. 1920. *The Medicine Ceremony of the Menomini, Iowa, and Wahpeton Dakota, with Notes on the Ceremony among Theponca, Bungi, Ojibwa, and Potawatomi.* Museum of the American Indian, Heye Foundation, *Indian Notes and Monographs* 4.

Snellgrove, David L. 1957. *Buddhist Himalaya.* Oxford: Bruno Cassirer.

Speck, Frank G. 1935a. "Penobscot Tales and Religious Beliefs." *Journal of American Folklore* 48: 1–107.

———. 1935b *Naskapi*. Norman: University of Oklahoma Press.

Spence, Lewis. 1925a. "Brazil." In *Encyclopaedia of Religion and Ethics*, ed. James Hastings, vol. 2. New York: Scribner's.

———. 1925b. "Cherokees." In *Encyclopaedia of Religion and Ethics*, ed. James Hastings, vol. 3. New York: Scribner's.

———. 1925c. "Chinooks." In *Encyclopaedia of Religion and Ethics*, ed. James Hastings, vol. 3. New York: Scribner's.

———. 1925d. "Choctaws." In *Encyclopaedia of Religion and Ethics*, ed. James Hastings, vol. 3. New York: Scribner's.

Spencer, Baldwin. 1904. *Northern Tribes of Central Australia*. London: Macmillan.

Spencer, Baldwin and F. J. Gillen. 1968. *The Native Tribes of Central Australia*. New York: Dover.

Spencer, Dorothy M. 1941. *Disease, Society and Religion in Fiji Islands*. Locust Valley, NY: J. J. Augustin.

Spier, Leslie and Edward Sapir. 1930. "Wishram Ethnography." *University of Washington Publications in Anthropology* 3(3): 151–300.

Spiro, Melford. 1967. *Burmese Supernaturalism*. Englewood Cliffs, NJ: Prentice-Hall.

Spretnak, Charlene, ed. 1982. *Politics of Women's Spirituality*. Garden City, NY: Anchor.

Sproul, Barbara C. 1979. *Primal Myths: Creating the World*. San Francisco: Harper & Row.

Stegmiller, P. F. 1921. "The Religious Life of the Khasi." *Anthropos* 16: 407–441.

Stephen, Alexander M. 1888. "Legend of the Snake Order of the Moqui, as Told by Outsiders." *Journal of American Folklore* 1: 109–114.

Stimson, J. Frank. 1933. *Tuamotan Religion*. Bernice P. Bishop Museum Bulletin, no. 103.

Stone, Merlin. 1979. *Ancient Mirrors of Womanhood*. Boston: Beacon.

Stout, David B. 1947 *San Blas Cuna Acculturation: An Introduction*. New York: Viking Fund.

Street, C. 1804. Whittingham Dean. *A Dictionary of Polite Literature or, Fabulous History of the Heathen Gods and Illustrious Heroes*. London: Scatcherd and Letterman.

Stutley, Margaret and James Stutley. 1984. *Harper's Dictionary of Hinduism: Its Mythology, Folklore, Philosophy, Literature, and History*. New York: Harper & Row.

Suzuki, Peter. 1959. *The Religious System and Culture of Nias, Indonesia*. The Hague: Excelsior.

Swanton, John R. 1904–1905. "Social Conditions, Beliefs, Linguistic Relationships of the Tlingit Indians." *Annual Report of the Bureau of American Ethnology* 26: 391–486.

———. 1928. "Sun Worship in the Southeast." *American Anthropologist* 30(2): 206–213.

Sykes, Egerton, ed. 1968.*Everyman's Dictionary of Non-classical Mythology*. New York: Dutton.

Szabo, A. 1925. "Hungarians." In *Encyclopaedia of Religion and Ethics*, ed. James Hastings, vol. 6. New York: Scribner's.

Tedlock, Dennis. 1985. *Popol Vuh: The Definitive Edition of the Mayan Book of the Dawn of Life and the Glories of Gods and Kings*. New York: Simon and Schuster.

Teish, Luisah. 1985. *Jambalaya: The Natural Woman's Book*. San Francisco: Harper & Row.

Teit, James A. 1919. "Tahltan Tales." *Journal of American Folklore* 32: 198–259.

Teixidor, Javier. 1977. *The Pagan God: Popu Religion in the Greco-Roman Near East*. Princeton, NJ: Princeton University Press.

Tenney, Merrill C., ed. 1963. *Zondervan Pictorial Bible Dictionary*. Grand Rapids, MI: Zondervan.

Thaliath, Joseph. 1956. "Notes on Some Pulaya Customs and Beliefs." *Anthropos* 52(5–6): 1029–1054.

Thompson, J. Eric S. 1930. *Ethnology of the Mayas of Southern and Central British Honduras*. Field Museum of Natural History Anthropological Series. Chicago: Field Museum of Natural History.

———. 1970. *Maya History and Religion*. Norman: University of Oklahoma Press.

Thompson, Lucy. 1916. *To the American Indian*. Eureka, CA: Cummins Print Shop.

Thompson, R. Campbell. 1903. *The Devils and Evil Spirits of Babylonia*, vol. 1. London: Luzac.

Thompson, Stith. 1929. *Tales of the North American Indians*. Bloomington: Indiana University Press.

Thramer, E. 1925. "Health and Gods of Healing." In *Encyclopaedia of Religion and Ethics*, ed. James Hastings, vol. 6. New York: Scribner's.

Thurston, Edgar. 1909. *Castes and Tribes of Southern India*. 7 vols. Madras, India: Government Press.

Tod, James. 1920. *Annals and Antiquities of Rajastan*. Oxford: Oxford University Press.

Tozzer, Alfred M. 1937. "Landa's Relacion de las Cosas de Yucatan." *Peabody Museum of Archaeology and Ethnology Memoirs* 18.

Trigg, Elwood B. 1973. *Gypsy Demons and Divinities*. Secaucus, NJ: Citadel.

Trimborn, Hermann. 1968. "South Central America and the Andean Civilizations." In *Pre-Columbian American Religions*, ed. Walter Krickeberg. New York: Holt, Rinehard and Winston.

Tschopik, Harry, Jr. 1951. "The Aymara of Chucuito, Peru." *Anthropological Papers of the American Museum of Natural History* 44(2).

Tucci, Giuseppe. 1980. *The Religions of Tibet*. Trans. Geoffrey Samuel. Berkeley and Los Angeles: University of California Press.

Turner, Frederick W., III. 1974. *The Portable North American Indian Reader*. New York: Viking.

Turner, George. 1884. *Samoa, a Hundred Years Ago and Long Before: Together with Notes on the Cults and Customs of Twenty- three Other Islands in the Pacific*. London: Macmillan.

Tyler, Hamilton A. 1964. *Pueblo Gods and Myths*. Norman: University of Oklahoma Press.

Unrau, William E. 1971. *The Kansa Indians: A History of the Wind People, 1673–1873*. Norman: University of Oklahoma Press.

Van Over, Raymond, ed. 1980. *Sun Songs: Creation Myths from around the World*. New York: Meridian, New American Library.

Vanoverbergh, Morice. 1938. "The Isneg Life Cycle II: Marriage, Death, and Burial." *Publications of the Catholic Anthropological Conference* 3(3): 187–280.

———. 1941. "The Isneg Farmer." *Publications of the Catholic Anthropological Conference* 3(4): 281–386.

———. 1953. "Religion and Magic among the Isneg." *Anthropos* 48(1–2): 71–104.

———. 1972. "Kankanay Religion (Northern Luzon, Philippines)." *Anthropos* 67(1–2): 72–128.

Villa Rojas, Alfonso. 1968. "The Tzeltal." In *Handbook of Middle American Indians*, ed. R. Wauchope. Austin: University of Texas Press.

Villas Boas, Orlando and Claudio Villas Boas. 1973. *Xingu: The Indians, Their Myths*. New York: Farrar, Straus & Giroux.

Von Furer-Haimendorf, Christoph. 1964. *The Sherpas of Nepal*. Berkeley and Los Angeles: University of California Press.

Waddell, L. Austine. 1925. "Demons and Spirits (Tibetan)." In *Encyclopaedia of Religion and Ethics*, ed. James Hastings, vol. 4. New York: Scribner's.

Wagley, Charles. 1940. "World View of the Tapirape Indians." *Journal of American Folklore* 53: 252–260.

———. 1964. *Amazon Town*. New York: Knopf.

Wagley, Charles and Eduardo Galvão. 1948. "The Tenetehara." In *Handbook of South American Indians*, ed. Julian H. Steward, vol. 3. Washington, DC: Government Printing Office.

Wagner, W. 1882. *Asgard and the Gods*. London: W. Swan Sonnenschein.

Wales, H. G. Quaritch. 1957. *Prehistory and Religion in Southeast Asia*. London: Bernard Quaritch.

Walker, Barbara G. 1983. *The Woman's Encyclopedia of Myths and Secrets*. San Francisco: Harper & Row.

———. 1986. *The I Ching of the Goddess*. San Francisco: Harper & Row.

———. 1988. *The Woman's Dictionary of Symbols and Sacred Objects*. San Francisco: Harper & Row.

Walker, James R. 1980. *Lakota Belief and Ritual*. Lincoln: University of Nebraska Press.

Wallis, Wilson D. 1939. *Religion in Primitive Society*. New York: F. S. Crofts.

Wallis, Wilson D. and Ruth Sawtell Wallis. 1955. *The Micmac Indians of Eastern Canada*. Minneapolis: University of Minnesota Press.

Wedeck, H. E. and Wade Baskin. 1971. *Dictionary of Pagan Religions*. New York: Philosophical Library.

Weigle, Marta. 1982. *Spiders and Spinsters: Women and Mythology*. Albuquerque: University of New Mexico Press.

Welsch, Roger L. 1981. *Omaha Tribal Myths and Trickster Tales*. Chicago: Sage Books, 1981.

Welsford, Enid. 1925a. "Nature (Lettish, Lithuanian, Old Prussian, Slavic)." In *Encyclopaedia of Religion and Ethics*, ed. James Hastings, vol. 9. New York: Scribner's.

———. 1925b. "Sun, Moon, and Stars (Teutonic and Balto-Slavic)." In *Encyclopaedia of Religion and Ethics*, ed. James Hastings, vol. 12. New York: Scribner's.

Werner, Alice. 1964. "African." In *Armenian-African*. Vol. 7, *Mythology of All Races*. New York: Cooper Square.

Werner, E. T. C. 1961. *A Dictionary of Chinese Mythology*. New York: Julian Press.

Westerveldt, W. D. 1912. "Lepe-a-moa." *Thrum, Hawaiian Annual*, 38: 105–117.

———. 1915. *Legends of Gods and Ghosts (Hawaiian Mythology)*. London: Constable.

———. 1963a. *Hawaiian Legends of Ghosts and Ghost- Gods*. Rutland, VT: Charles E. Tuttle.

———. 1963b. *Hawaiian Legends of Old Honolulu*. Rutland, VT: Charles E. Tuttle.

———. 1963c. *Hawaiian Legends of Volcanoes*. Rutland, VT: Charles E. Tuttle.

Weyer, Edward, Jr. 1961. *Primitive Peoples Today*. Garden City, NY: Doubleday.

Wheatcroft, Wilson. 1973. "Tifalmin." In *Primitive Worlds: People Lost in Time*. Washington, DC: National Geographic Society.

White, John. 1887–1890. *The Ancient History of the Maori, His Mythology and Traditions*, vols. 1, 3. Wellington, New Zealand: G. Didsbury, Government Printer.

Whitecotton, Joseph W. 1977. *The Zapotecs: Princes, Priests, and Peasants*. Norman: University of Oklahoma Press.

Wiesinger, R. 1967. "The Women's Part in the Religious Life of the Bhil." *Anthropos* 62(3–4): 497–508.

Williams, C. A. S. 1976. *Outlines of Chinese Symbolism and Art Motives*, 3d rev. ed. New York: Dover.

Williamson, Robert W. 1933. *Religious and Cosmic Beliefs in Central Polynesia*. 2 vols. Cambridge: Cambridge University Press.

Wilson, Laurence Lee. 1947. *Apayo Life and Legends*. Baguio, P.I.: Human Relations Area Files OA5, OA1. New Haven, CT: HRAF Press.

Wolf, Adolf Hungry. 1977. *The Blood People: A Division of the Blackfoot Confederacy. An Illustrated Interpretation of the Old Ways*. New York: Harper & Row.

Woodcock, Percival George. 1953. *Dictionary of Mythology*. New York: Philosophical Library.

Woods, J. D. 1879. *Native Tribes of South Australia*. Adelaide, Australia: E. S. Wigg and Son.

Wright, Barton. 1973. *Kachinas: A Hopi Artist's Documentary*. Flagstaff, AZ: Northland.

———. 1977. *Hopi Kachinas: The Complete Guide to Collecting Kachina Dolls*. Flagstaff, AZ: Northland.

———. 1985. *Kachinas of the Zuni*. Flagstaff, AZ: Northland.

Wu Che-lin, Ch'en Kuo-chun, et al. 1942. *Studies of Miao-i Societies in Kweichow*. Human Relations Area Files AE5. Kweiyang, China: Wen-t'ung Book Company.

Wyers, Edward Moffat, Jr. 1932. *The Eskimos: Their Environment and Folkways*. New Haven, CT: Yale University Press.

Yasumaro, Inoue Shunji. 1965. *Kojiki*. Tokyo: Kojiki Preparatory Association.

Yasumaro, Yaichiro Isobe. 1928. *The Story of Ancient Japan*. Tokyo: San Kaku Sha.

Zimmer, Heinrich. 1955. *Art of Indian Asia, Its Mythology and Transformations*. Bollingen Series, no. 39. New York: Pantheon.

Zimmerman, J. E. 1964. *Dictionary of Classical Mythology*. New York: Bantam/Harper & Row.

INDEX OF GODDESSES BY NAME

A – Near East
A Hsiang. *See* A Xiang – Far East
A Mong – Southeast Asia
A Nyit A Jom – Indian Subcontinent
A Xiang – Far East
Aahmes-nefertari – Egypt
Aakhabit. *See* Gate-keeping
　Goddesses – Egypt
?Aano?ovi. *See* Niarimamau?u – North
　America
Aarvak – Northern Europe
Aa-sheft – Egypt
Aasith – Egypt
Aat-aatet – Egypt
Aataentsic – North America
Aat-khu – Egypt
Aba Khatun – Far East
Ababa – Africa
Aba-khatun – Eastern Europe
Abalone Woman. *See* Estsanatlehi –
　North America
Abarbarea – Greek and Roman Empires
Abe – Africa
Abe – Central America and
　Mesoamerica
Abeguwo – Oceania
Abena Budu – Africa
Abenawa – Africa
Abeona – Greek and Roman Empires
Abere – Oceania
Aberewa – Africa
Aberewa Awukuwa – Africa
Abet-neteru-s – Egypt
Abhraganga. *See* Ganga – Indian
　Subcontinent
Abhramu – Indian Subcontinent

Abnoba – Western Europe
Abowie – Africa
Abrayanti – Indian Subcontinent
aBru-gu-ma – The Himalaya
Absusu. *See* Ishtar – Near East
Abtagigi. *See* Ishtar – Near East
Abuk – Africa
Abu-mehsu – Africa
Abunciada. *See* Habonde – Western
　Europe
Abundantia – Greek and Roman
　Empires
Abundia – Northern Europe
Abundia. *See* Habonde – Western
　Europe
Abundita. *See* Abundantia – Greek and
　Roman Empires
Abyang – Southeast Asia
Abyang Durunuun – Southeast Asia
Abyss Lady – Near East
Abyzu – Near East
Acacalis – Greek and Roman Empires
Acacallis. *See* Acacalis – Greek and
　Roman Empires
Acalanthis – Greek and Roman Empires
Acalle. *See* Acacalis – Greek and Roman
　Empires
Acantha – Greek and Roman Empires
Acasta. *See* Acaste – Greek and Roman
　Empires
Acaste – Greek and Roman Empires
Acaviser – Greek and Roman Empires
Acca – Greek and Roman Empires
Acca Larentia – Greek and Roman
　Empires

Acca Laurentia. *See* Acca Larentia –
　Greek and Roman Empires
Acco – Greek and Roman Empires
Acek – Africa
Achaea – Greek and Roman Empires
Achaia. *See* Achaea – Greek and Roman
　Empires
Achaiva. *See* Demeter – Greek and
　Roman Empires
Achall – Western Europe
Achamoth. *See* Sophia-achamoth –
　Near East
Acheloides, The – Greek and Roman
　Empires
Achelois – Greek and Roman Empires
Acheri, The – Indian Subcontinent
Achiroe – Greek and Roman Empires
Achlys – Greek and Roman Empires
Acholoe – Greek and Roman Empires
Achtan – Western Europe
Achvistr. *See* Acaviser – Greek and
　Roman Empires
Aci'asdza. *See* Ashi Esdza – North
　America
Acidalia – Greek and Roman Empires
Acidusa – Greek and Roman Empires
Ackwin – North America
Acleme. *See* Alcmena – Greek and
　Roman Empires
Acme – Greek and Roman Empires
Acmenes, The – Greek and Roman
　Empires
Acna – Central America and
　Mesoamerica
Acraea – Greek and Roman Empires

Acrea. *See* Acraea – Greek and Roman Empires

Acria. *See* Acraea – Greek and Roman Empires

Actaea – Greek and Roman Empires

Acuecueyotlcihuatl – Central America and Mesoamerica

Ada – Near East

Adamah – Near East

Adamanteia. *See* Adamanthea – Greek and Roman Empires

Adamanthea – Greek and Roman Empires

Adamina – Near East

Adamisil Wedo – Central America and Mesoamerica

Adamu – Near East

Adanari – Indian Subcontinent

Adb-isi – Near East

Adda-nari. *See* Adanari – Indian Subcontinent

Adda. *See* Ida – Indian Subcontinent

Addephagia. *See* Adephagia – Greek and Roman Empires

Addittee. *See* Aditi – Indian Subcontinent

Adeona – Greek and Roman Empires

Adephagia – Greek and Roman Empires

Aderenosa – Near East

Adhararani – Indian Subcontinent

Adhidevatas, The – Indian Subcontinent

Adicia – Greek and Roman Empires

Adimata. *See* Manasa – Indian Subcontinent

Adiona. *See* Adeona – Greek and Roman Empires

Adishakti. *See* Shakti – Indian Subcontinent

Adit. *See* Aditi – Indian Subcontinent

Aditi – Indian Subcontinent

Aditya, The – Indian Subcontinent

Adkaya. *See* Prithivi – Indian Subcontinent

Admeta – Greek and Roman Empires

Admete – Greek and Roman Empires

Adnigkishar – Near East

Adra Nedefa – Near East

Adraste – Greek and Roman Empires

Adrastea – Greek and Roman Empires

Adrasteia. *See* Adrastea – Greek and Roman Empires

Adrija. *See* Parvati – Indian Subcontinent

Adrika – Indian Subcontinent

Adryades, The. *See* The Dryades – Greek and Roman Empires

Adsullata – Western Europe

Aea – Greek and Roman Empires

Aeaea – Greek and Roman Empires

Aeaga. *See* Aega – Greek and Roman Empires

Aeantis – Greek and Roman Empires

Aebh. *See* Aobh – Western Europe

Aedos – Greek and Roman Empires

Aeetias – Greek and Roman Empires

Aeetine. *See* Aeetias – Greek and Roman Empires

Aeetis. *See* Aeetias – Greek and Roman Empires

Aega – Greek and Roman Empires

Aegea. *See* Aega – Greek and Roman Empires

Aegeria – Greek and Roman Empires

Aegia. *See* Aega – Greek and Roman Empires

Aegiale – Greek and Roman Empires

Aegialeia. *See* Aegiale – Greek and Roman Empires

Aegilae. *See* Aigle – Greek and Roman Empires

Aegina – Greek and Roman Empires

Aeginaea – Greek and Roman Empires

Aegle. *See* Aigle – Greek and Roman Empires

Aegophaga – Greek and Roman Empires

Aegophagos – Greek and Roman Empires

Aeife. *See* Aoife – Western Europe

Aello – Greek and Roman Empires

Aellopos – Greek and Roman Empires

Aeolis. *See* Alcyone – Greek and Roman Empires

Aeons, The – Near East

Aer – Greek and Roman Empires

Aeracura – Western Europe

Aerfon – Western Europe

Aero. *See* Merope – Greek and Roman Empires

Aeron – Western Europe

Aertha. *See* Hertha – Northern Europe

Aesa – Greek and Roman Empires

Aestas – Greek and Roman Empires

Aesyle – Greek and Roman Empires

Aetae, The. *See* The Litae – Greek and Roman Empires

Aeterna. *See* Vesta – Greek and Roman Empires

Aether – Greek and Roman Empires

Aetheria – Greek and Roman Empires

Aethra – Greek and Roman Empires

Aethre. *See* Aether – Greek and Roman Empires

Aethyia – Greek and Roman Empires

Aetna – Greek and Roman Empires

Aetole – Greek and Roman Empires

Aeval – Western Europe

Afekan – Oceania

Afiong Edem – Africa

Afka – Near East

Afrékété – Africa

Ag Aganney – Southeast Asia

Agada – Africa

Agaman Nibo – Central America and Mesoamerica

Agamede – Greek and Roman Empires

Aganippe – Greek and Roman Empires

Aganippides, The – Greek and Roman Empires

Agasaya – Near East

Agathe Tyche – Greek and Roman Empires

Agave – Greek and Roman Empires

Agdistis – Greek and Roman Empires

Agdos – Greek and Roman Empires

Ageleia – Greek and Roman Empires

Ageleis. *See* Ageleia – Greek and Roman Empires

Agemem – Southeast Asia

Aggareth. *See* the Qlippoth – Near East

Aginvati – Indian Subcontinent

Aglaia – Greek and Roman Empires

Aglaope – Greek and Roman Empires

Aglaopheme – Greek and Roman Empires

Agnayi – Indian Subcontinent

Agnes. *See* Annis – Western Europe

Agness. *See* Annis – Western Europe

Agni. *See* Varsus – Indian Subcontinent

Agno – Greek and Roman Empires

Agoraea – Greek and Roman Empires

Agoraia. *See* Agoraea – Greek and Roman Empires

Agraea. *See* Agrotera – Greek and Roman Empires

Agrat Bat Mahalat – Near East

Agraulids, The. *See* The Augralids – Greek and Roman Empires

Agraulos – Greek and Roman Empires

Agriculture Goddess, The – Far East

Agrona – Western Europe

Agrotera – Greek and Roman Empires

Agrotora. *See* Agrotera – Greek and Roman Empires

Agusan Devi – Southeast Asia

Agusaya – Near East

Agwani – Indian Subcontinent

Agwe – Central America and Mesoamerica

Agweta – Central America and Mesoamerica

Ah Uaynih – Central America and Mesoamerica

Ah Wink-ir Masa – Central America and Mesoamerica

A-ha Kachin' Mana – North America

Aha Njoku – Africa

Ahabit – Egypt

Ahalya – Indian Subcontinent

Ahana – Indian Subcontinent

Aharišvang – Near East

Ahat – Egypt

Ahe'a – North America

Ahīm ū – Oceania

Ahemait – Egypt

Ahera. *See* Asherah – Near East

Ahes. *See* Dahut – Western Europe

Ahgishanakhou – North America

Ahi – Egypt

Ahmes-nefertari. *See* Aahmes-nefertari – Egypt

Ahmetolela Okya – North America

Ahnfrau – Northern Europe

Ahnt Ahs Pok' – Central America and Mesoamerica

Ahnt Kai' – Central America and Mesoamerica

Ahöla Mana – North America

Ahrenkonigin – Northern Europe

Ahsonnutli – North America

Ahti – Egypt

Ahuic – Central America and Mesoamerica

Ahurani – Near East

Ai Tūpua'i – Oceania

Ai. *See* A – Near East

Äi. *See* Ajatar – Eastern Europe

Aialila'axa – North America

'Aiāru – Oceania

Aibell – Western Europe

Aibheaog – Western Europe
Aida Wedo – Central America and Mesoamerica
Aide – Western Europe
Aideen. *See* Aidí n – Western Europe
Aidí n – Western Europe
Aidos – Greek and Roman Empires
Aie Lacha – Indian Subcontinent
Aife. *See* Aoife – Western Europe
Aige – Western Europe
Aigina. *See* Aegina – Greek and Roman Empires
Aigle – Greek and Roman Empires
Äijo – Eastern Europe
Ailbe – Western Europe
Ailinn – Western Europe
Áille – Western Europe
Aillinn. *See* Ailinn – Western Europe
Ailo. *See* Lilith – Near East
Aima – Western Europe
Aima Elohim. *See* Aima – Western Europe
Aimah. *See* Aima – Western Europe
Aimend – Western Europe
Ain – Western Europe
Aindri. *See* Saci – Indian Subcontinent
Áine – Western Europe
Aingini. *See* Ganesani – Indian Subcontinent
Aino – Eastern Europe
Airmed – Western Europe
Airmid. *See* Airmed – Western Europe
Aisera. *See* Asera – Near East
'Aisha Qandisha – Africa
Aisyt. *See* Ayisit – Eastern Europe
Aitan – Indian Subcontinent
Aither. *See* Aether – Greek and Roman Empires
Aithuia – Greek and Roman Empires
Aittsamka – North America
Aiviliajog – North America
Ai-Willi-Ay-O – North America
Aiyjsyt – Eastern Europe
Aiyulaniza. *See* Niseginyu – Indian Subcontinent
Aizu – Africa
Aja – Africa
Aja – Near East
Ajatar – Eastern Europe
Äjätär. *See* Ajatar – Eastern Europe
Ajattara. *See* Ajatar – Eastern Europe
Aje – Africa
Ajy-khoton. *See* Ajysit – Eastern Europe
Ajysit – Eastern Europe
Ajysit-ijaksit-khotan. *See* Ajysit – Eastern Europe
Ajysit-ijäksit. *See* Ajysit – Eastern Europe
Ajysit-khotun. *See* Ajysit – Eastern Europe
Ajysyt. *See* Ajysit – Eastern Europe
Ajysyt-ijäksit-khotun – Eastern Europe
Aka – Near East
Aka – Oceania
Aka ku a nue nue. *See* Ha lo – Oceania
Akarkhentkats – Egypt
Akaru-hime – Far East
Akasa – Indian Subcontinent
Akasaganga. *See* Ganga – Indian Subcontinent

Akasagarabha – Indian Subcontinent
âkâsha-dahatû-ishvarî – The Himalaya
Akaste. *See* Acaste – Greek and Roman Empires
Akazu – Africa
Akerbeltz – Western Europe
Akert-khentet-auset-s – Egypt
Akeso – Greek and Roman Empires
Akhet – Egypt
Akhuvitr – Greek and Roman Empires
Akhvizer. *See* Akhuvitr – Greek and Roman Empires
Aki-bime-no-kami – Far East
Akka. *See* Aka – Near East
Akkan, The – Eastern Europe
Akko. *See* Rauni – Eastern Europe
Akkruva – Eastern Europe
Akna – North America
Akodau – Southeast Asia
Akoq – North America
Akpitoko – Africa
Akraia – Greek and Roman Empires
Aksara – Indian Subcontinent
Aksaya. *See* Prithivi – Indian Subcontinent
Akshobhya – Southeast Asia
Aku aku, The – Oceania
Akusaa – Egypt
Akuti – Indian Subcontinent
Akycha – North America
Āl – Near East
Al Shua – Indian Subcontinent
Ala – Africa
Ala muki – Oceania
'Alae a hina – Oceania
Alagabiae, The – Northern Europe
Alaghom Naum – Central America and Mesoamerica
Alaisiagae, The – Northern Europe
Alaisiages, The. *See* Alaisiagae, The – Northern Europe
Alajeru – Africa
Alakhani – Indian Subcontinent
Alakshmi – Indian Subcontinent
Alala – Greek and Roman Empires
Alalahe – Oceania
Alalalahe. *See* Alalahe – Oceania
Alalcomene – Greek and Roman Empires
Alalcomenia. *See* Alalkomenia – Greek and Roman Empires
Alalkomenia – Greek and Roman Empires
Alambusha – Indian Subcontinent
Alan, The – Southeast Asia
'Alaĥtin – North America
Alarana – North America
Alasho-Funfun – Africa
Alat. *See* Asherah – Near East
Alath – Near East
Albasta – Eastern Europe
Albina – Western Europe
Albina – Greek and Roman Empires
Albuferetan Mother Goddess – Western Europe
Albuna – Greek and Roman Empires
Albunea. *See* Albuna – Greek and Roman Empires
Alceste. *See* Alcestis – Greek and Roman Empires

Alcestis – Greek and Roman Empires
Alcimache – Greek and Roman Empires
Alcippe – Greek and Roman Empires
Alcis – Greek and Roman Empires
Alcmena – Greek and Roman Empires
Alcyone – Greek and Roman Empires
Ale. *See* Ala – Africa
Alea – Greek and Roman Empires
Alecto – Greek and Roman Empires
Alectrona – Greek and Roman Empires
Alencica – Eastern Europe
Aletheia – Near East
Aletheia. *See* Alethia – Greek and Roman Empires
Alethia – Greek and Roman Empires
Aletis. *See* Erigone – Greek and Roman Empires
Alexida – Greek and Roman Empires
Alexirrhoe – Greek and Roman Empires
Alfhild – Northern Europe
Algea – Greek and Roman Empires
Algia. *See* Algea – Greek and Roman Empires
?Al?heleqeč – North America
Alicantean Mother Goddess – Western Europe
Alimede – Greek and Roman Empires
Alindodoay – Southeast Asia
Alinga – Oceania
Alitia. *See* Aletheia – Near East
Alkmene. *See* Alcmena – Greek and Roman Empires
Alkonost – Eastern Europe
Alkuntam – North America
Allat – Near East
Allatu – Near East
All-bringing-forth – Africa
Allekto. *See* Alecto – Greek and Roman Empires
Allwise – Northern Europe
Alma – Greek and Roman Empires
Alma Mammosa. *See* Ceres – Greek and Roman Empires
Almha – Western Europe
Almoshi – Eastern Europe
Almu. *See* Almha – Western Europe
Alo – Africa
Alo Mana – North America
âloka. *See* sNang-gsal-ma – The Himalaya
âloke. *See* sNang-gsal-ma – The Himalaya
Alopurbi – Indian Subcontinent
Alpan – Greek and Roman Empires
Alpanu – Greek and Roman Empires
Alphaea – Greek and Roman Empires
Alpheias – Greek and Roman Empires
Alphito – Greek and Roman Empires
Alpnu. *See* Alpanu – Greek and Roman Empires
Alraun – Northern Europe
Alrauna-wife. *See* Alraun – Northern Europe
Alraune. *See* Alraun – Northern Europe
Alseides, The – Greek and Roman Empires
Altan-telgey – The Himalaya
Altan-telgey. *See* Teleglen-edzen – Eastern Europe

Altan-telgey. *See* Teleglen-edzen – Far
East
Altria – Greek and Roman Empires
Alukah. *See* Allatu – Near East
Alunsina – Southeast Asia
Alvasta. *See* Ovda – Eastern Europe
Alwantin – Indian Subcontinent
Am – Near East
Ama – Africa
Ama – Eastern Europe
Ama. *See* Äre – Western Europe
Ama Usum Gal Ana. *See* Inanna – Near
East
Amadubad. *See* Mami – Near East
Amagandar, The – Eastern Europe
Amagandar, The – Western Europe
Amakiri – Africa
Amalthea – Greek and Roman Empires
Amaltheia. *See* Amalthea – Greek and
Roman Empires
Amamikyu – Southeast Asia
Amanjah. *See* Emanja – Central
America and Mesoamerica
Amanoro – Near East
Ama-no-sagu-me – Far East
Amara. *See* Mama Pacha – South
America
Amari De – Indian Subcontinent
Ama-terasu-ō-mi-kami – Far East
Ama-terasu-oho-hiru-me-no-mikoto.
See Ama-terasu-ō-mi-kami – Far East
Amathaon. *See* Amathaounta – Greek
and Roman Empires
Amathaounta – Greek and Roman
Empires
Amatheia – Greek and Roman Empires
Amathuntia. *See* Amathusia – Greek
and Roman Empires
Amathusia – Greek and Roman Empires
Amat-isi – Near East
Ama-tsu-otome, The – Far East
Amatudda. *See* Mami – Near East
Amauneit – Africa
Amaunet – Egypt
Amavasya – Indian Subcontinent
Amayicoyondi – North America
Amba – Indian Subcontinent
Amba Bai – Indian Subcontinent
Ambabachi. *See* Bhudevi – Indian
Subcontinent
Amber. *See* Amba – Indian Subcontinent
Amberella – Eastern Europe
Ambika – Indian Subcontinent
Ambologera – Greek and Roman
Empires
Amboto Lady – Western Europe
Ambrosia – Greek and Roman Empires
Ambulia – Greek and Roman Empires
Ame-chikaru-mizu-hime – Far East
Ameipicer – Western Europe
Amelenwa – Africa
Amelia – Central America and
Mesoamerica
Amemait. *See* Ammit – Egypt
Amemet – Egypt
Amenet – Egypt
Amenit. *See* Ament – Egypt
Ame-no-sade-yori-hime – Far East
Ame-no-tanabata-hime-no-mikoto –
Far East

Ame-no-toko – Far East
Ame-no-toko-tachi-no-kami – Far East
Ame-no-tsudoe-chine-no-kami – Far
East
Ame-no-uzume – Far East
Ame-no-uzume-no-mikoto. *See*
Ame-no-uzume – Far East
Ament – Near East
Ament – Egypt
Amentet. *See* Ament – Egypt
Amenti – Egypt
Amentit. *See* Ament – Egypt
Ament-semu-set – Egypt
Ameretāt – Near East
Amerodat. *See* Ameretāt – Near East
Amesha Spentas, The – Near East
Ami Goddess, The – Far East
Amica – Greek and Roman Empires
Amida. *See* Amitabha – Far East
Amilamia – Western Europe
Amins. *See* Lusin – Eastern Europe
Amirini – Africa
Amit – Egypt
Amitabha – Far East
Amitabha – Southeast Asia
Ami-tanne-mat – Far East
Amma – Northern Europe
Amma – Indian Subcontinent
Amma Attar. *See* Asherat – Near East
Ammal – Southeast Asia
Ammal. *See* Parvati – Indian
Subcontinent
Ammarik – Eastern Europe
Ammas. *See* Amma – Indian
Subcontinent
Ammavaru – Indian Subcontinent
Am-met. *See* Ammit – Egypt
Ammit – Egypt
Ammut. *See* Ammit – Egypt
Amn – Egypt
Amnisiades, The – Greek and Roman
Empires
Amoghasiddhi – Southeast Asia
Amona – Western Europe
Amonit. *See* Amaunet – Egypt
Ampata Sapa – North America
Amphictyonis – Greek and Roman
Empires
Amphilogea – Greek and Roman
Empires
Amphinome – Greek and Roman
Empires
Amphiro – Greek and Roman Empires
Amphissa. *See* Metope – Greek and
Roman Empires
Amphithoe – Greek and Roman
Empires
Amphitrite – Greek and Roman
Empires
Ampithoe. *See* Amphithoe – Greek and
Roman Empires
Amponyinamoa – Africa
Amra – Eastern Europe
Amrit – Indian Subcontinent
Amritika. *See* Amrita – Indian
Subcontinent
Amunet – Egypt
Amunta – Egypt
Amurdat. *See* Zam – Near East
Amymone – Greek and Roman Empires

Ana – Near East
Ana – Indian Subcontinent
Ana Maria – North America
Ana. *See* Anu – Western Europe
Anadyomene – Greek and Roman
Empires
Anaea. *See* Anaitis – Greek and Roman
Empires
Anael – Near East
Anagke. *See* Ananke – Greek and
Roman Empires
Anagtia – Greek and Roman Empires
Anagtia Diiva. *See* Anagtia – Greek and
Roman Empires
Anahid – Near East
Anāhit. *See* Anāhita – Near East
Anāhita – Near East
Anaitis – Near East
Anaitis – Greek and Roman Empires
Anakhai, The – Eastern Europe
Anakulam-Bhagavathi – Indian
Subcontinent
Anala – Indian Subcontinent
An-alai-chotoun – Eastern Europe
An-alai-khotun. *See* An-alai-chotoun –
Eastern Europe
Änäm Jajuci – Eastern Europe
Anan. *See* Ana – Near East
Anan. *See* Äre – Western Europe
Anana-gunda – Eastern Europe
Ananke – Greek and Roman Empires
Anapel – Eastern Europe
Anapurna. *See* Annapurna – Indian
Subcontinent
Anasuya – Indian Subcontinent
Anat – Near East
Anat – Southeast Asia
Anat-bethel – Near East
Anat-yaw. *See* Anat-bethel – Near East
Anata. *See* Anat – Near East
Anath – Near East
Anatha Baetyl – Egypt
Anatha. *See* Anath – Near East
Anatha. *See* Anatha Baetyl. – Egypt
Anatis – Egypt
Anatole – Greek and Roman Empires
Anatu – Near East
Anavigak – North America
Anaxarete – Greek and Roman Empires
Anaxibia – Greek and Roman Empires
Anaxiroe – Greek and Roman Empires
Anaxo – Greek and Roman Empires
Anaxšti – Near East
Anceta – Greek and Roman Empires
Anchiale – Greek and Roman Empires
Anchinoe. *See* Achiroe – Greek and
Roman Empires
Anchiroe – Greek and Roman Empires
An-darkhan-khotun. *See*
An-alai-chotoun – Eastern Europe
Andarta – Western Europe
Andate. *See* Andrasta – Western Europe
Andin Bambin – Southeast Asia
Andrasta – Western Europe
Andraste. *See* Andrasta – Western
Europe
Andriamahilala – Africa
Androctasia – Greek and Roman
Empires

Androktiasi, The – Greek and Roman Empires
Andromeda – Greek and Roman Empires
Ane – Africa
Aneitis. See Anaitis – Greek and Roman Empires
Anemotis – Greek and Roman Empires
Anenit, The – Egypt
Anesidora – Greek and Roman Empires
Ang-chin Mana – North America
Angak'chin' Mana – North America
Angana – Indian Subcontinent
Angarmati Bhawani – Indian Subcontinent
Angarua – Oceania
Angeburga – Northern Europe
Angelos – Greek and Roman Empires
Angerbodha – Northern Europe
Angerona – Greek and Roman Empires
Angeronia. See Angerona – Greek and Roman Empires
Angeyja – Northern Europe
Anghairya – Near East
Angina – Greek and Roman Empires
Angitia – Greek and Roman Empires
Anguitia. See Angitia – Greek and Roman Empires
Angur-boda. See Gullveig – Northern Europe
Angwushahai-i – North America
Angwusnasomtaka – North America
Ani – Africa
Ani. See Mami – Near East
Anieros – Greek and Roman Empires
Anigriades, The. See Anigrides – Greek and Roman Empires
Anigrides, The – Greek and Roman Empires
Anila – Indian Subcontinent
Anima Mundi – Greek and Roman Empires
Animal Mother – North America
Aningap. See Tatqeq – North America
Aningat. See Tatqeq – North America
Aninito Ad Chalom – Southeast Asia
Anippe – Greek and Roman Empires
Anit – Near East
Anit – Egypt
Anith. See Ếre – Western Europe
Aniton Tauo – Southeast Asia
Anitun Tabu – Southeast Asia
Anjana. See Angana – Indian Subcontinent
Anjea – Oceania
Ank. See Anuket – Egypt
Anka – Egypt
Ankamma – Indian Subcontinent
Ankhet – Egypt
Ankhtith – Egypt
Ankushâ. See Chags-kyu-ma – The Himalaya
'Anltani – North America
Anlu-lebie-landet Numakiedeil Emei – Eastern Europe
Anna Kuari – Indian Subcontinent
Anna Kurari. See Anna Kuari – Indian Subcontinent
Anna Livia Plurabelle – Western Europe
Anna-nin. See Anat – Near East

Anna Perenna – Greek and Roman Empires
Anna Perenna. See Anu – Western Europe
Annal. See Parvati – Indian Subcontinent
Annallja Tu Bari – Africa
Annan. See Anu – Western Europe
Annapatni – Indian Subcontinent
Annapurna – Indian Subcontinent
Annawan – Southeast Asia
Anne, Saint – Central America and Mesoamerica
Annis – Western Europe
Anoano – Oceania
Anog Ite – North America
Anoi Diggan Juje – Indian Subcontinent
Anoolikwotsai – North America
Anouke. See Anuket – Egypt
Anoukis. See Anuket – Egypt
Anpet – Egypt
Anqa-naut – Eastern Europe
Ānqet. See Anuket, Isis – Egypt
Anqt. See Anuket – Egypt
Anquet. See Anuket – Egypt
Anrita – Indian Subcontinent
Anrn – Egypt
Anta – Egypt
Anta. See Anāhita, Anthat, Anaitis – Near East
Antaea – Greek and Roman Empires
Antaeus – Near East
Antai – Indian Subcontinent
Antariksha – Indian Subcontinent
Antarta – Egypt
Āntat – Egypt
Anteia – Greek and Roman Empires
Antevorta – Greek and Roman Empires
Anthat – Near East
Anthat. See Anta – Egypt
Anthea. See Antheia – Greek and Roman Empires
Anthedon – Greek and Roman Empires
Antheia – Greek and Roman Empires
Anthracia – Greek and Roman Empires
Anthrathi – Egypt
Ānthretju – Near East
Ānthretju – Egypt
Anthyt – Near East
Anticleia – Greek and Roman Empires
Antigone – Greek and Roman Empires
Antinoe – Greek and Roman Empires
Antioche – Greek and Roman Empires
Antiope – Greek and Roman Empires
Antu. See Anat – Near East
Antum. See Anat – Near East
Anu – Western Europe
Anu mātao – Oceania
Anu. See Ana – Indian Subcontinent
Anu. See Ana – Near East
Anua – Oceania
Anucis. See Anka – Greek and Roman Empires
'Ānuenue – Oceania
Anuke – Egypt
Anuket – Egypt
Anukit. See Anuket – Egypt
Anumati – Indian Subcontinent
Anuna – Near East
Anunit – Near East

An-unsser – Egypt
Anuqet. See Anuket – Egypt
Anush – Near East
Anushakti – Indian Subcontinent
Anushayini – Indian Subcontinent
Anusyelai – North America
Anya Kachin' Mana – North America
Anyigba – Africa
An.zu – Near East
Aobh – Western Europe
Aoede – Greek and Roman Empires
Aoibhell. See Aibell – Western Europe
Aoife – Western Europe
Aonach. See Ếre – Western Europe
Aonides, The – Greek and Roman Empires
Ao-numa-nu-oshi-hime – Far East
Aouli – Oceania
Ap, The – Indian Subcontinent
Apa. See Ap – Indian Subcontinent
Apa'ula – Oceania
Apache Woman – North America
Apah. See Ap – Indian Subcontinent
Apakura – Oceania
Apala – Indian Subcontinent
Apanchomene – Greek and Roman Empires
Aparajita – Indian Subcontinent
Aparna – Indian Subcontinent
Apas. See Ap – Indian Subcontinent
Apasinasee – North America
Apaturia – Greek and Roman Empires
Ape-huchi – Far East
Apekua – Oceania
Apemeru-ko-yan-mat Unameru-ko-yan-mat – Far East
Apet – Egypt
Aphacitis. See Aphrodite – Greek and Roman Empires
Aphaea – Greek and Roman Empires
Aphaia. See Aphaea – Greek and Roman Empires
Aphek. See Mylitta – Near East
Aphrodite – Greek and Roman Empires
A-phyi-gung-rgyal – The Himalaya
Api – Eastern Europe
Api. See Apet, Taueret, Ta-urt – Egypt
Api. See Apish – North America
Apia – Near East
Apish – North America
Apito. See Atabei – Central America and Mesoamerica
Apitus – Egypt
Apna – Southeast Asia
Apnapurna – Indian Subcontinent
Apo, The – Near East
Apoconallotl. See Apozanolotl – Central America and Mesoamerica
Apollonis – Greek and Roman Empires
Apolonia, Saint – South America
Aponibolinayen – Southeast Asia
Apostrophia – Greek and Roman Empires
Apotrophia. See Apostrophia – Greek and Roman Empires
Apozanolotl – Central America and Mesoamerica
Appiades, The – Greek and Roman Empires
Appias – Greek and Roman Empires

Aprija – Africa
Apsarases, The – Indian Subcontinent
Apseudes – Greek and Roman Empires
Apt – Egypt
Ap-taui. *See* Uadjet, Uatchet – Egypt
Apteros – Greek and Roman Empires
Apt-hent – Egypt
Apt-renpit – Egypt
Apu – Indian Subcontinent
Apu o te ra'i – Oceania
'Āpua kea – Oceania
Apunga – Oceania
Apvā – Indian Subcontinent
Aqong. *See* Akoq – North America
Aquaba – Africa
Aquit – North America
Ara. *See* Arai – Greek and Roman
    Empires
Aracynthias. *See* Aphrodite – Greek
    and Roman Empires
Arae. *See* Arai – Greek and Roman
    Empires
Arahuta – Oceania
Arai – Greek and Roman Empires
Aramati – Indian Subcontinent
Arani – Indian Subcontinent
Arantides, The. *See* Erinyes – Greek and
    Roman Empires
Aranya – Indian Subcontinent
Aranyani – Indian Subcontinent
Arapap – Eastern Europe
Ararat – Near East
Ara-seshap – Egypt
Araua – Africa
Arava – Africa
Arayi, The – Indian Subcontinent
Arbha – Western Europe
Arcadian – Greek and Roman Empires
Arce – Greek and Roman Empires
Arche – Greek and Roman Empires
Archiroe. *See* Achiroe – Greek and
    Roman Empires
Arco. *See* Artio – Western Europe
Ardalides, The – Greek and Roman
    Empires
Ardaliotides. *See* The Ardalides – Greek
    and Roman Empires
Ardat Lili. *See* Lilith and Lilithu, Near
    East
Ardhanari – Indian Subcontinent
Ardokhsho – Near East
Arduinna – Western Europe
Arduisur – Near East
Ardvī Surā Anāhita. *See* Anāhita – Near
    East
Ardvi Anahita. *See* Anāhita – Near East
Ardvi Vaxsha – Near East
Ardwinna. *See* Arduinna – Western
    Europe
Area. *See* Areia – Greek and Roman
    Empires
Aredvi Sura Anahita. *See* Anāhita –
    Near East
Areia – Greek and Roman Empires
Arenmetia – Western Europe
Areta. *See* Arete – Greek and Roman
    Empires
Arete – Greek and Roman Empires
Arethusa – Greek and Roman Empires
Aretia – Near East

Aretz – Near East
Argante – Western Europe
Arge – Greek and Roman Empires
Argeia – Greek and Roman Empires
Argennis. *See* Aphrodite – Greek and
    Roman Empires
Argimpasa – Greek and Roman
    Empires
Argiope – Greek and Roman Empires
Argyra – Greek and Roman Empires
Aria. *See* Furies – Greek and Roman
    Empires
Ariadne – Greek and Roman Empires
Arianhod. *See* Arianrhod – Western
    Europe
Arianrhod – Western Europe
Aricina – Greek and Roman Empires
Aridela. *See* Ariadne – Greek and
    Roman Empires
Ariel – Near East
Ariki – Oceania
Arimata – Oceania
Ariniddu. *See* Arinna – Near East
Arinitti. *See* Arinna – Near East
Arinna – Near East
Ariste – Greek and Roman Empires
Aristobule – Greek and Roman Empires
Arisya – Near East
Aritatheth – Egypt
Armaita. *See* Armaiti – Near East
Armaiti – Near East
Armat – Near East
Armata – Greek and Roman Empires
Arnaaluk Takannaaluk – North
    America
Arnahapshaaluk. *See* Arnapkapfaluk –
    North America
Arnakapshaaluk. *See* Arnapkapfaluk –
    North America
Arnaknagsak – North America
Arnakuagsak. *See* Arnaknagsak –
    North America
Arnaluktakanaluk. *See* Arnaaluk
    Takannaaluk – North America
Arnamentia – Western Europe
Arnapkapfaluk – North America
Arnarquagssaq. *See* Arnaknagsak –
    North America
Arnarquáshaaq – North America
Arne – Greek and Roman Empires
Ārohirohi – Oceania
Arrhippe – Greek and Roman Empires
Arsa. *See* Rusa – Near East
Arsai – Near East
Arsay – Near East
Arsinoe – Egypt
Arsinoe – Greek and Roman Empires
Arsiya – Near East
Arstât – Near East
Aršti. *See* Arstât – Near East
Arsy. *See* Arsai – Near East
Artemides. *See* the Titanides – Near East
Artemidos, Saint – Near East
Artemis – Greek and Roman Empires
Artemis Ephesus – Near East
Artimpasa – Greek and Roman Empires
Artio – Western Europe
Arubani – Near East
Arud – Southeast Asia
Aruna – Indian Subcontinent

Arundhati – Indian Subcontinent
Arurin – Southeast Asia
Aruru – Near East
Aruru-ishtar. *See* Ishtar – Near East
Arusyak – Near East
Arutaruta tāmaumau auahi – Oceania
Arwut – Indian Subcontinent
Arya. *See* Sarasvati – Indian
    Subcontinent
Aryajangulitara. *See* Sitatara – Indian
    Subcontinent
As. *See* Isis – Egypt
Asa Poorna – Indian Subcontinent
Asaase Aberewa – Africa
Asaase Afua. *See* Asase Afua – Africa
Asaase Yaa. *See* Asase Yaa – Africa
Asakhira. *See* Ishara – Near East
Asa-ma. *See* Konohana-sakuya-hime –
    Far East
Asapishachikis, The – Indian
    Subcontinent
Asapura – Indian Subcontinent
Asapurna – Indian Subcontinent
Asase Afua – Africa
Asase Efua. *See* Asase Yaa – Africa
Asase Yaa – Africa
As-ava – Eastern Europe
Asdoulos – Near East
Asdzaa Dootlijii – North America
Asdzaa Yoolgai – North America
'Asdzaá•nádle•hé. *See* Estsanatlehi –
    North America
Asenath. *See* As-neit, Egypt – Near East
Asera – Near East
Aserat. *See* Asera – Near East
Aset. *See* Isis – Egypt
Asfandarmad. *See* Spentā Ārmaiti –
    Near East
Ashdar – Near East
Asherah – Near East
Asherat. *See* Asherah – Near East
Asherath. *See* Asherah – Near East
Asheratian. *See* Asherah – Near East
Asherat-of-the-sea. *See* Asherah – Near
    East
Ashertu. *See* Asherah – Near East
Ashi – Near East
Ashi – Indian Subcontinent
Ashi esdza – North America
Ashi Vanguhi. *See* Ashish Vanuhi –
    Near East
Ashi Yast. *See* Ashish Vanuhi – Near
    East
Ashiakle – Africa
Ashima – Near East
Ashima Baetyl – Near East
Ashima Baetyl – Egypt
Ashima. *See* Amathaounta – Greek and
    Roman Empires
Ashimbabbar – Near East
Ashi-nadaka-no-kami – Far East
Ashi-oxsho – Near East
Ashirat – Near East
Ashirtu. *See* Ashirat – Near East
Ashis – Indian Subcontinent
Ashish Vanuhi – Near East
Ashishang. *See* Ashish Vanuhi – Near
    East
Ashke-tanne-mat – Far East
Ashmunikal – Near East

Ashnan – Near East
Ashtar-kemosh – Near East
Ashtarchemosh – Near East
Ashtaroth, The – Near East
Ashtaroth. *See* Ashtoreth – Egypt
Ashtart – Near East
Ashtarthet. *See* Ashtoreth – Egypt
Ashtartu – Near East
Ashtharoth, The. *See* Ashtoreth and The
    Ashtaroth – Near East
Ashtoreth – Near East
Ashtoreth – Egypt
Ashuritu. *See* Belit – Near East
Ashva – Indian Subcontinent
Asi – Near East
Aši – Near East
Asia – Africa
Asia – Greek and Roman Empires
Asiah – Western Europe
Asiak. *See* Asiaq – North America
Asiaq – North America
Asikni. *See* Virini – Indian Subcontinent
Asima Si – South America
Asin – North America
Asine – Greek and Roman Empires
Asintmah – North America
Asirat. *See* Asherah – Near East
Asirtu. *See* Asherah – Near East
Āsit – Egypt
Asiti. *See* Asi – Near East
?Ašixuč – North America
Askefruer, The – Northern Europe
Aslaug. *See* Aslog – Northern Europe
Aslik – Near East
Aslog – Northern Europe
Asmodaeus. *See* Asmodeus – Near East
Asmodeus – Near East
Asmun Nikal – Near East
Asnan – Near East
As-neit – Egypt
Aso – Egypt
Aso. *See* Niseginyu – Indian
    Subcontinent
Asokakanta – Indian Subcontinent
Asopo – Greek and Roman Empires
Aspelenie – Eastern Europe
Asra – Indian Subcontinent
Asrapas. *See* Dakinis – Indian
    Subcontinent
Asrath. *See* Asherah – Near East
Asratu. *See* Asherah – Near East
Asri – Indian Subcontinent
Asrušti – Near East
Assa – Western Europe
Assam Mother Earth – Indian
    Subcontinent
Assaros – Greek and Roman Empires
Asseneth – Greek and Roman Empires
Assesia – Greek and Roman Empires
Assuras. *See* The Asuris – Indian
    Subcontinent
Ast – Egypt
Astabhuja Kurukulla. *See* Kurukulla –
    Indian Subcontinent
Astar. *See* Ishtar – Near East
Astart. *See* Astarte – Near East
Astarte – Near East
Asteria – Greek and Roman Empires
Asterodeia – Greek and Roman Empires

Asterodia. *See* Asterodeia – Greek and
    Roman Empires
Asterope – Greek and Roman Empires
Asteropeia – Greek and Roman Empires
Astert. *See* Astarte – Near East
Astghik – Near East
Astiya, The – Western Europe
Astraea – Greek and Roman Empires
Astrateia – Greek and Roman Empires
Astratu. *See* Asherah – Near East
Astrea. *See* Astraea – Greek and Roman
    Empires
Astrik – Eastern Europe
Astronoe – Near East
Astyageia – Greek and Roman Empires
Asu Mainao – Indian Subcontinent
Asuniti – Indian Subcontinent
Asura. *See* The Asuris – Indian
    Subcontinent
Asuri. *See* The Asuris – Indian
    Subcontinent
Asuris, The – Indian Subcontinent
Asvini – Indian Subcontinent
Asynja. *See* Aś ynjur, The – Northern
    Europe
Asynje. *See* Aś ynjur, The – Northern
    Europe
Asynjor. *See* Aś ynjur, The – Northern
    Europe
Aś ynjur, The – Northern Europe
Ata – Far East
Ata tangi rea – Oceania
Atabei – Central America and
    Mesoamerica
Atae. *See* Ate – Greek and Roman
    Empires
Ataecina – Western Europe
Ataensic. *See* Aataensic – North
    America
Ataentsic. *See* Aataensic – North
    America
Atahensic. *See* Aataensic – North
    America
Atahikurangi – Oceania
Atai – Africa
Atalanta – Greek and Roman Empires
Atalante. *See* Atalanta – Greek and
    Roman Empires
Atanea. *See* Atanua – Oceania
Atansic. *See* Awehai – North America
Atanua – Oceania
Atar. *See* Atargatis – Near East
Atarapa – Oceania
Atarate. *See* Atargatis – Near East
Atargata. *See* Atargatis – Near East
Atargatis – Near East
Atatuhi – Oceania
Atavish – North America
Atbilxaniatllia – North America
Ate – Near East
Ate – Greek and Roman Empires
Atea ta'o nui – Oceania
Ātea – Oceania
At-em. *See* Atem – Egypt
Atem – Egypt
Atergatis. *See* Atargatis – Near East
Atet – Egypt
Atete – Africa
Athana Lindia – Greek and Roman
    Empires

Atharate. *See* Atargatis – Near East
Atheh. *See* Ate – Near East
Athena – Greek and Roman Empires
Athena of Ilium. *See* Anāhita – Greek
    and Roman Empires
Athenaia. *See* Athena – Greek and
    Roman Empires
Athene Boarmia – Greek and Roman
    Empires
Athene. *See* Athena – Greek and Roman
    Empires
Atherat. *See* Asherah – Near East
Athi. *See* Atargatis – Near East
Athirat – Near East
Athor. *See* Hathor – Egypt
Athra. *See* Aethra – Greek and Roman
    Empires
Athtarath. *See* Astarte – Near East
Athtor – Egypt
Athyr. *See* Hathor – Egypt
Ati-canda – Indian Subcontinent
Aticpac Calqui Cihuatl – Central
    America and Mesoamerica
Atida – Africa
Atira – North America
Atitxmana – North America
Atla – Northern Europe
Atlacamani – Central America and
    Mesoamerica
Atlacoya – Central America and
    Mesoamerica
Atlantia – Greek and Roman Empires
Atlantides, The – Greek and Roman
    Empires
Atlantis. *See* Maia – Greek and Roman
    Empires
Atlatona – Central America and
    Mesoamerica
Atlatonin – Central America and
    Mesoamerica
Ato – Africa
Atocle. *See* Atoshle Suyuki – North
    America
Atoja – South America
Ator. *See* Hathor – Egypt
Atoshle Suyuki – North America
Atoshle. *See* Atoshle Suyuki – North
    America
Atoto – Oceania
Atropos – Greek and Roman Empires
Atse ataed – North America
Atse esdza. *See* Atse Esdzaa – North
    America
Atse Esdzaa – North America
Atsentma – North America
Attabeira. *See* Atabei – Central America
    and Mesoamerica
Atthis – Greek and Roman Empires
Atua fafine – Oceania
Atua'anua – Oceania
Atugan – The Himalaya
Atum – Near East
Atutahi. *See* Atatuhi – Oceania
Au Sept. *See* Auset – Egypt
Au Set. *See* Auset, Isis – Egypt
Audhumbla – Northern Europe
Audhumla. *See* Audhumbla – Northern
    Europe
Audjal – Oceania

Audumbla. *See* Audhumbla – Northern
    Europe
Aufaniae, The – Western Europe
Auge – Western Europe
Auge – Greek and Roman Empires
Augeia – Northern Europe
Aughty. *See* Echtghe – Western Europe
Augralids, The – Greek and Roman
    Empires
Aukert – Egypt
Aukjuk – North America
Auksagandhi – Indian Subcontinent
Aulis – Greek and Roman Empires
Auloniades, The – Greek and Roman
    Empires
Auna – Oceania
Aunt Piety – Far East
Aura – Greek and Roman Empires
Aurae. *See* Aura – Greek and Roman
    Empires
Aurboda. *See* Gullveig – Northern
    Europe
Aurgiafa. *See* Eyrgjafa – Northern
    Europe
Aurita – Greek and Roman Empires
Aurora – Greek and Roman Empires
Auroras, The – Eastern Europe
Ausca – Eastern Europe
Auseklis – Eastern Europe
Ausera. *See* Ausra, Ausrine – Eastern
    Europe
Auset – Egypt
Aushrine. *See* Ausrine – Eastern Europe
Ausinari – Indian Subcontinent
Ausra – Eastern Europe
Ausrine – Eastern Europe
Austheia – Eastern Europe
Austrine. *See* Ausrine – Eastern Europe
Aũtak. *See* Vatak – Near East
Auteb. *See* Autyeb – Egypt
Automatia – Greek and Roman Empires
Autonoe – Greek and Roman Empires
Autran – Oceania
Aut-yeb. *See* Autyeb – Egypt
Autyeb – Egypt
Auxesia – Greek and Roman Empires
Auxo – Greek and Roman Empires
Ava – Eastern Europe
Ava rei pua – Oceania
Avalokita – Far East
Avantia – Western Europe
Avantimatrikas. *See* The Avantimatris –
    Indian Subcontinent
Avantimatris, The – Indian
    Subcontinent
Avany – Indian Subcontinent
Avaris – Egypt
Avas, The – Eastern Europe
Aventia. *See* Avantia – Western Europe
Aventina – Greek and Roman Empires
Avernales – Greek and Roman Empires
Averruncus – Greek and Roman
    Empires
Aversa – Greek and Roman Empires
Avezuha – Eastern Europe
Avfruvva – Eastern Europe
Avfruvva. *See* Havfru – Northern
    Europe
Avilayoq – North America

Aviliayuk. *See* Uiniyumayuituq – North
    America
Avin – Oceania
Avlekete – Africa
Awa – Eastern Europe
Awa-nami-no-kami – Far East
Awatobi Soyok Wuqti – North America
Awatovi Soyok Wuhti – North America
Awehai – North America
Awejsirdenee – Indian Subcontinent
Awenhai. *See* Awehai – North America
Aweshi. *See* Suyuki – North America
Awitelin Tsita – North America
Axieros – Greek and Roman Empires
Axiocersa. *See* Axiokersa – Greek and
    Roman Empires
Axioche – Greek and Roman Empires
Axiokersa – Greek and Roman Empires
Axiopoenos – Greek and Roman
    Empires
Axo Mama. *See* Axomama – South
    America
Axomama – South America
Axona – Western Europe
Axšti – Near East
Aya – Africa
Aya – Near East
Ayaba – Africa
Aya-eke – Africa
Aya-kashiko-ne-no-kami – Far East
Ayar – South America
Ayauhteotl – Central America and
    Mesoamerica
Aye. *See* Aya – Africa
Ayeba – Africa
Ayepi – Indian Subcontinent
Ayida Oueddo. *See* Aida Wedo –
    Central America and Mesoamerica
Ayida. *See* Aida Wedo – Central
    America and Mesoamerica
Ayish – Near East
Ayisit – Eastern Europe
Ayizan – Central America and
    Mesoamerica
Ayizan Velequete. *See* Ayizan – Central
    America and Mesoamerica
Ayopechcatl – Central America and
    Mesoamerica
Ayopechtli. *See* Ayopechcatl – Central
    America and Mesoamerica
Aywilliayoo – North America
Ayyysyt. *See* Ayisit – Eastern Europe
Az – Near East
Azele Yaba – Africa
Azelekel. *See* Cherlak – Eastern Europe
Azer-ava – Eastern Europe
Azesia – Greek and Roman Empires
A-zi-mu-a – Near East
Aziri – Africa
Azuiti – Near East
Ba – Far East
Bà Ngu' – Southeast Asia
Baäbai – Far East
Baabenga – Oceania
Ba'alat. *See* Beltis – Near East
Ba'alat Ashtart – Near East
Baalath – Near East
Ba'alath Gebal – Near East
Ba'alatu Darkati. *See* Anat – Near East
Ba'alatu Mulki. *See* Anat – Near East

Ba'alatu Samen Ramen. *See* Anat –
    Near East
Baalith – Near East
Baalti – Near East
Baaltis. *See* Beltis – Near East
Baau. *See* Bau – Near East
Baba – Near East
Baba Yaga – Eastern Europe
Babaia – Near East
Baba-Jaga. *See* Baba Yaga – Eastern
    Europe
Babamik – Oceania
Babayanmi. *See* Bayanni – Africa
Bab'e Kasha – Eastern Europe
Babelah – Near East
Babia. *See* Babaia – Near East
Babu. *See* Bau – Near East
Bacchae, The. *See* The Maenades –
    Greek and Roman Empires
Bacchantes, The. *See* The Maenades –
    Greek and Roman Empires
Bacche – Greek and Roman Empires
Badb – Western Europe
Badb Catha. *See* Badb – Western Europe
Badba – Western Europe
Badger Old Woman – North America
Badh – Western Europe
Badi Mata – Indian Subcontinent
Bà-Du'c Chu'a, The – Southeast Asia
Baduhenna – Northern Europe
Baei've. *See* Beive-neida – Eastern
    Europe
Baenkhild – Northern Europe
Baev. *See* Bau – Near East
Bagala – Indian Subcontinent
Bagbarti – Near East
Bagmashtu – Near East
Bagmasti – Near East
Bagula – Indian Subcontinent
Bagvarti – Near East
Bah-bah-deed – North America
Bahet – Egypt
Bahu – Near East
Bahu – Indian Subcontinent
Bahucharaji – Indian Subcontinent
Bai Haldahin – Indian Subcontinent
Bai Mundan – Far East
Baiangun – Oceania
Baihi – Indian Subcontinent
Baiji – Far East
Bainleannan – Western Europe
Baitpandi – Southeast Asia
Bakchetis. *See* Begoe – Greek and
    Roman Empires
Bake – Southeast Asia
Bala – Indian Subcontinent
Balambika – Indian Subcontinent
Balini – Indian Subcontinent
Balintawag – Southeast Asia
Balma – Western Europe
Balneorum – Greek and Roman Empires
Balthi – Near East
Balu Adad – Southeast Asia
Baluchistan Goddesses – Indian
    Subcontinent
Bamya – Near East
Ban – Near East
Ban Naomha – Western Europe
Ban Nighechain – Western Europe
Banana Maiden – Southeast Asia

Banasamkari. *See* Banasankari – Indian Subcontinent
Banasankari – Indian Subcontinent
Ban-ava – Eastern Europe
Banba – Western Europe
Ban-chuideachaidh Moire – Western Europe
Band Goddesses, The – Western Europe
Bandha. *See* Banba – Western Europe
Bangan – Southeast Asia
Banit – Near East
Banjari – Indian Subcontinent
Banka Mundi – Indian Subcontinent
Banna – Western Europe
Banna Naomha. *See* Ban Naomha – Western Europe
Bansapti – Indian Subcontinent
Banschi – Western Europe
Banshees, The – Western Europe
Banshie. *See* Banshees, The – Western Europe
Bansith. *See* Banshees, The – Western Europe
Banzhen – Far East
Baowa. *See* Nüwa – Far East
Bapets, The – North America
Bara – Oceania
Barbata – Greek and Roman Empires
Barbelo – Near East
Barbmo-akka – Eastern Europe
Bardaichila – Indian Subcontinent
Bardo Goddesses – The Himalaya
Barhishmati – Indian Subcontinent
Bar-juchne – Near East
Baruth. *See* Beruth – Near East
Basa-Andre – Western Europe
Basanti – Indian Subcontinent
Basany – Indian Subcontinent
Baski Mata – Indian Subcontinent
Basmu Usum. *See* Nidaba – Near East
Bassarae, The – Greek and Roman Empires
Bassarides, The. *See* The Bassarae – Greek and Roman Empires
Bast – Egypt
Bastet. *See* Bast – Egypt
Bastis. *See* Bast – Egypt
Basuli – Indian Subcontinent
Basumati – Indian Subcontinent
Basundhara. *See* Bhudevi – Indian Subcontinent
Bat – Egypt
Batara Shri – Southeast Asia
Bateia – Greek and Roman Empires
Bathkol – Near East
Batoer – Southeast Asia
Bau – Near East
Baubo – Near East
Baudihillie – Northern Europe
Bauri Bai – Indian Subcontinent
Bawin Jata Balawang Bulau. *See* Jata and Tambon – Southeast Asia
Bawu. *See* Baba – Near East
Baxbakualanuchsiwae – North America
Bayanni – Africa
bDud-mo-gshin-rej-mgo-dgu-ma – The Himalaya
bDud-mo-gshin-rje-lag-brgya-ma – The Himalaya

bDud-mo-gsod-mo-gsod-byed-ma – The Himalaya
bDud-mo-phung-khrol-ma – The Himalaya
bDud-mo-rno-myur – The Himalaya
bDug-spös-ma – The Himalaya
Be Bind. *See* Bebhionn – Western Europe
Bé Find – Western Europe
Beag – Western Europe
Bean Nighe, The – Western Europe
Bean Sí dhe – Western Europe
Bear Daughter – North America
Bear Maiden – North America
Bear Mother – North America
Bear Woman – North America
Bear Woman – Far East
Bear Woman and the Fawns – North America
Bebhionn – Western Europe
Bebind. *See* Bé Find – Western Europe
Bebo – Western Europe
Bec Fola – Western Europe
Bechtli. *See* Berchta – Northern Europe
Bécuma – Western Europe
Beda – Northern Europe
Bee Bride – Southeast Asia
Befana – Greek and Roman Empires
Begoe – Greek and Roman Empires
Behbet – Egypt
Beive-neida – Eastern Europe
Beiwe – Eastern Europe
Beiwe – Northern Europe
Beiwe-Neida – Northern Europe
Beiwe-neida. *See* Beive-neida – Eastern Europe
Bela Pinnu – Indian Subcontinent
Belatsunat – Near East
Bele Alua – Africa
Belet. *See* Baalath – Near East
Beletekallim – Near East
Beletersetim. *See* Belit Seri – Near East
Beletseri. *See* Belit Seri – Near East
Beli Sheri. *See* Belit Seri – Near East
Belili – Near East
Belisama – Western Europe
Belisheri. *See* Belit Seri – Near East
Belisma – Western Europe
Belit – Near East
Belit Ilani – Near East
Belit Ile. *See* Balthi and Belit Ilani – Near East
Belit Seri – Near East
Belit-itani. *See* Makh – Near East
Belit-matate. *See* Ninlil – Near East
Bellona – Greek and Roman Empires
Belsta. *See* Bestla – Northern Europe
Belti. *See* Baalti, Beltis – Near East
Beltia. *See* Beltis and Zarpanitu – Near East
Beltis – Near East
Beltiya. *See* Zarpandit – Near East
Beltu. *See* Beltis and Belit – Near East
Bendis – Greek and Roman Empires
Benih Lela Punggang Tengian Dara Bintang Tiga Datai Ka Jelan – Southeast Asia
Bentakumari – Indian Subcontinent
Benten – Far East
Benvarry – Western Europe

Benzaiten. *See* Benten – Far East
Benzai-tennyo. *See* Benten – Far East
Benzozia – Western Europe
Bera – Western Europe
Bera Pennu. *See* Tari Pennu – Indian Subcontinent
Berche. *See* Berchta – Northern Europe
Berchta – Northern Europe
Berchte. *See* Berchta – Northern Europe
Berchtli. *See* Berchta – Northern Europe
Berecynthia – Western Europe
Berecynthia – Greek and Roman Empires
Berecynthia. *See* Cybele – Near East
Beregina – Eastern Europe
Bereginy, The – Eastern Europe
Bereguini. *See* Bereginy – Eastern Europe
Berenice – Egypt
Berenice Euergetes. *See* Berenice – Egypt
Berenike. *See* Berenice – Egypt
Berenise. *See* Berenice – Egypt
Bergoia. *See* Begoe – Greek and Roman Empires
Berit. *See* Beruth – Near East
Berith. *See* Beruth – Near East
Berkta. *See* Berchta – Northern Europe
Bernice. *See* Berenice – Egypt
Beroe – Greek and Roman Empires
Beroth. *See* Beruth – Near East
Bertha. *See* Berchta – Northern Europe
Bertie. *See* Berchta – Northern Europe
Berty. *See* Berchta – Northern Europe
Beru – South America
Beruth – Near East
Beset – Egypt
Besla. *See* Bestla – Northern Europe
Bestla – Northern Europe
Bettada Chicama – Indian Subcontinent
Bettla. *See* Bestla – Northern Europe
Beyla – Northern Europe
Bhadrā – Indian Subcontinent
Bhadrakali – Indian Subcontinent
Bhagadevi – Indian Subcontinent
Bhagavathi – Indian Subcontinent
Bhagavati – Indian Subcontinent
Bhageseri – Indian Subcontinent
Bhagirathamma – Indian Subcontinent
Bhagirathi – Indian Subcontinent
Bhagvati. *See* Mindhal – Indian Subcontinent
Bhairava, The – Indian Subcontinent
Bhairavi – Indian Subcontinent
Bhandarin – Indian Subcontinent
Bharadi – Indian Subcontinent
Bharati – Indian Subcontinent
Bhasa. *See* Bhasi – Indian Subcontinent
Bhasi – Indian Subcontinent
Bhattarika. *See* Durga – Indian Subcontinent
Bhaumi. *See* Sita – Indian Subcontinent
Bhavani – The Himalaya
Bhavani(s) – Indian Subcontinent
Bhawani. *See* Bhavani – Indian Subcontinent
Bherunda. *See* Kali and Yakshi – Indian Subcontinent
Bhgavati – Indian Subcontinent
Bhgavatiamman – Indian Subcontinent
Bhima – Indian Subcontinent

Bhisana – Indian Subcontinent
Bhogavati – Indian Subcontinent
Bhowani. *See* Bhavani – Indian
    Subcontinent
Bhrkuti – Indian Subcontinent
Bhudevi – Indian Subcontinent
Bhukhi Mata – Indian Subcontinent
Bhulli Buri. *See* Mainao – Indian
    Subcontinent
Bhumi – Indian Subcontinent
Bhumidevi. *See* Bhumi – Indian
    Subcontinent
Bhumiya Rani – Indian Subcontinent
Bhumme Nari – Indian Subcontinent
Bhutamatri – Indian Subcontinent
Bhuti. *See* Lakshmi – Indian
    Subcontinent
Bhuvanesvari – Indian Subcontinent
Bhuyian – Indian Subcontinent
Bia – Greek and Roman Empires
Bia-ka-pusud-an-langit – Southeast Asia
Bia-t'oden – Southeast Asia
Bibi – Western Europe
Bibi Miriam – Indian Subcontinent
Biblis. *See* Byblis – Greek and Roman
    Empires
Biddy Mannion – Western Europe
Bidhgoe – Western Europe
Biducht – Near East
Big Black Meteor Star – North America
Big Dog – North America
Bigoe. *See* Begoe – Greek and Roman
    Empires
Bigone. *See* Begoe – Greek and Roman
    Empires
Bija-garaba. *See* Sarasvati – Indian
    Subcontinent
Bijaldeo Kanya – Indian Subcontinent
Bijloki – Indian Subcontinent
Bikeh Hozho – North America
Bikeh Xozo – North America
Biku Indu Antu – Southeast Asia
Bil – Northern Europe
Bila – Oceania
Bildjiwuraroju. *See* Djanggawul –
    Oceania
Bilig-un cinadu-kijaghar-a kuruksen –
    Far East
Biliku – Indian Subcontinent
Bilit – Near East
Bilit Taauth. *See* Bilit – Near East
Bilwis – Northern Europe
Bima – Oceania
Bina. *See* Binah – Western Europe
Binah – Western Europe
Bintang – Southeast Asia
Bir im bir wongar – Oceania
Bird and Eye Goddess – Eastern Europe
Birog – Western Europe
Birra nulu – Oceania
Birrahgnooloo – Oceania
Bisal Mariamna – Indian Subcontinent
Bisam Thakurani – Indian Subcontinent
Bisan – Southeast Asia
Bisari – Indian Subcontinent
Bitabok – Africa
Bithia – Eastern Europe
Bithiah – Near East
Biu Si – South America

Bixia Yuangun. *See* Bixia Yuanjin – Far
    East
Bixia Yuanjin – Far East
Bixia Yuanjun. *See* Bixia Yuanjin – Far
    East
Bixiao – Far East
Bjort – Northern Europe
bKur-dman-rgyalmo – The Himalaya
Black Annis – Western Europe
Black Butte – North America
Black Crow-headed One – The
    Himalaya
Black Cuckoo-headed Mystic
    Goddess – The Himalaya
Black Petali – The Himalaya
Black Sow-headed Sow Goddess – The
    Himalaya
Black Virgin – Greek and Roman
    Empires
Black Vixen-headed One – The
    Himalaya
Blackfoot Earth Woman – North
    America
Blackfoot First Woman – North America
Blackfoot Old Woman – North America
Blai. *See* Sadb – Western Europe
Blanaid – Western Europe
Blanid. *See* Blathnát – Western Europe
Blathine. *See* Blathnát – Western Europe
Blathnát – Western Europe
Blid – Northern Europe
Blodenwedd. *See* Blodeuwedd –
    Western Europe
Blodeuedd. *See* Blodeuwedd – Western
    Europe
Blodeuwedd – Western Europe
Blodewedd. *See* Blodeuwedd – Western
    Europe
Blue Jay – North America
Blue Lotus – Far East
Blue Monkey-headed Goddess of
    Inquisitiveness – The Himalaya
Blue Serpent-headed Water Goddess –
    The Himalaya
Blue Wolf-headed Wind Goddess – The
    Himalaya
Bo Find – Western Europe
Boaliri – Oceania
Búanann – Western Europe
Boand. *See* Boann – Western Europe
Boann – Western Europe
Boarmia – Greek and Roman Empires
Bobd – Western Europe
Bodua – Western Europe
Boeotia – Greek and Roman Empires
Boginki. *See* The Bereginy – Eastern
    Europe
Bogoda. *See* Dziewanna – Eastern
    Europe
Bói. *See* Cailleach Beara – Western
    Europe
Boinn. *See* Boann – Western Europe
Boiuna – South America
Bolbe – Greek and Roman Empires
Boldogasszony – Eastern Europe
Bomong. *See* Bong – Indian
    Subcontinent
Bomu Rambi – Africa
Bona – Greek and Roman Empires
Bona Dea – Greek and Roman Empires

Bona Oma – Greek and Roman Empires
Bong – Indian Subcontinent
Bonga – Indian Subcontinent
Bonito Maidens, The – Oceania
Bonnes Dames, The – Western Europe
Bonto – Eastern Europe
Boodh. *See* Buddhi – Indian
    Subcontinent
Boorbi Pennu – Indian Subcontinent
Borghild – Northern Europe
Bormana – Western Europe
Bormonia – Greek and Roman Empires
Boru Deak Parudjar – Southeast Asia
Borvonia – Western Europe
Borysthenis – Greek and Roman
    Empires
Bosumabla – Africa
Boulaia – Greek and Roman Empires
Bounmagyi – Southeast Asia
Bouto. *See* Buto – Egypt
Bowutset – North America
Bozaloshtsh – Eastern Europe
Braciaca – Western Europe
Brahmani – Indian Subcontinent
Brahmi. *See* Sarasvati and Savitri –
    Indian Subcontinent
Brangwaine – Western Europe
Branwen – Western Europe
Brauronia – Greek and Roman Empires
brDa'i 'phrad – The Himalaya
Brechta. *See* Berchta – Northern Europe
Breg – Western Europe
Breksta – Eastern Europe
Brenach. *See* Bronach – Western Europe
Bri – Western Europe
Briah – Near East
Briah – Western Europe
Briant – Western Europe
Bribsun – The Himalaya
Bricia. *See* Brixia – Western Europe
Bride of the Barley – Africa
Bride. *See* Brigid – Western Europe
Bridget, Saint. *See* Brigid – Western
    Europe
Bridgit. *See* Brigid – Western Europe
Brieẑu-māte – Eastern Europe
Brig. *See* Brigid – Western Europe
Brigantia – Western Europe
Brigentis. *See* Brigid – Western Europe
Brigette – Central America and
    Mesoamerica
Brighid. *See* Brigid – Western Europe
Bright Star – North America
Bright-Cloud Woman – North America
Brigid – Western Europe
Brigidu. *See* Brigid – Western Europe
Briginda. *See* Brigid – Western Europe
Brigindo – Western Europe
Brigit. *See* Brigid – Western Europe
Brimo – Greek and Roman Empires
Brisa – Greek and Roman Empires
Brisaya – Indian Subcontinent
Briseis – Greek and Roman Empires
Britannia – Western Europe
Britomartis – Greek and Roman
    Empires
Brixia – Western Europe
Brizo – Greek and Roman Empires
'Brog-bza'-lha-icam-ma – The Himalaya
Brogla – Oceania

Brome – Greek and Roman Empires
Bronach – Western Europe
Bronwen. *See* Branwen – Western Europe
Broxa – Near East
brTan-ma – The Himalaya
brTar-byed-ma. *See* sKyabs-mdun – The Himalaya
'Brug-gi-sgra-sgrog-ma – The Himalaya
Brunhild – Northern Europe
Brunhilda. *See* Brunhild – Northern Europe
Brunhilde. *See* Brunhild – Northern Europe
Brunnehilde. *See* Brunhild – Northern Europe
Brynhild – Northern Europe
Brynwyn. *See* Branwen – Western Europe
bStan-ma. *See* Tan-ma – The Himalaya
bTsan-ldan-blo-sgron-ma – The Himalaya
Buan – Western Europe
Buan-ann – Western Europe
Bubastis. *See* Bast, Sekhet, Uat – Egypt
Bubastos – Greek and Roman Empires
Bubona – Greek and Roman Empires
Bubona. *See* Epona – Western Europe
Bubrostis – Near East
Buddha Dahinis. *See* Buddha Dakinis – Indian Subcontinent
Buddha Dakinis – The Himalaya
Buddha Krotishaurima – The Himalaya
Buddhadakini – Indian Subcontinent
Buddhi – Indian Subcontinent
Buddhi Nagin – Indian Subcontinent
Budeia – Greek and Roman Empires
Budhi Pallien – Indian Subcontinent
Budung-yihe-ibe – Eastern Europe
Budyah – Oceania
Buffalo Calf Maiden. *See* White Buffalo Woman – North America
Buffalo Calf Woman. *See* White Buffalo Woman – North America
Buffalo Girl – North America
Buffalo Old Woman – North America
Buffalo Wife – North America
Buffalo-calf-road-woman – North America
Bugan – Southeast Asia
Bugan inBulul – Southeast Asia
Bugan inIntongnin – Southeast Asia
Bugan inKinulhudan – Southeast Asia
Bugan inMagnad – Southeast Asia
Bugan inManahaut – Southeast Asia
Bugan inMonkulabe – Southeast Asia
Bugan inNgilin – Southeast Asia
Bugan inPati – Southeast Asia
Bugan inPunholdaiyan – Southeast Asia
Bugan inUldi – Southeast Asia
Bugan inWigan – Southeast Asia
Bugan Nak Amtalao – Southeast Asia
Bugan Nak Hinumbian – Southeast Asia
Bugarik – Indian Subcontinent
Buí . *See* Cailleach Beara – Western Europe
Buk – Africa
Bukura-e Dheut – Eastern Europe
Bulaing – Oceania

Bulan – Southeast Asia
Bulia – Greek and Roman Empires
Bumerali – Oceania
Bunzi – Africa
Burhi Mata – Indian Subcontinent
Burhi Thakurani – Indian Subcontinent
Buring une – Oceania
Bursung – Indian Subcontinent
Buruku – Africa
Buschfrauen – Northern Europe
Buschgroßmutter – Northern Europe
Buschweiber – Northern Europe
Bushongo Earth Mother – Africa
Bushyasta – Near East
Buto – Egypt
Bwalya Chabala – Africa
Byblis – Greek and Roman Empires
Bylgja – Northern Europe
Byzyge – Greek and Roman Empires
C – Near East
Cabeiri. *See* Cabeiriae – Greek and Roman Empires
Cabeiria – Greek and Roman Empires
Cabeiriae – Greek and Roman Empires
Cabeiro – Greek and Roman Empires
Cabira – Near East
Caca – Greek and Roman Empires
Cacce-jienne – Eastern Europe
Cacia. *See* Caca – Greek and Roman Empires
Cactus Grandmother – North America
Caecilia. *See* Tanaquil – Greek and Roman Empires
Caelestis – Near East
Caelestis. *See* Dea Caelestis – Greek and Roman Empires
Caeneus. *See* Caenis – Greek and Roman Empires
Caenis – Greek and Roman Empires
Cáer – Western Europe
Cáer Ibormeith. *See* Cáer – Western Europe
Caha Paluna – Central America and Mesoamerica
Caha-Paluma. *See* Caha Paluna – Central America and Mesoamerica
Caileach Cinn Boirne. *See* Bronach – Western Europe
Cailleach. *See* Cailleach Beara – Western Europe
Cailleach Beara – Western Europe
Cailleach Bheur – Western Europe
Cailleach Bolus – Western Europe
Cailleach Corca Duibhne – Western Europe
Cailleach Mor – Western Europe
Caillech Bherri. *See* Cailleach Beara – Western Europe
Cailliach. *See* Cailleach Beara – Western Europe
Cailliaeč. *See* Cailleach Beara – Western Europe
Caipora – South America
Caireen – Western Europe
Cajiah. *See* Chaiah – Near East
Caksusi – Indian Subcontinent
Calaene – Greek and Roman Empires
Calaeno. *See* Celaeno – Greek and Roman Empires
Cale – Greek and Roman Empires

Caliadne – Greek and Roman Empires
Caligo – Greek and Roman Empires
Calla filatonga – Oceania
Callianassa – Greek and Roman Empires
Callianeira – Greek and Roman Empires
Calligeneia – Greek and Roman Empires
Calliope – Greek and Roman Empires
Callipygos – Greek and Roman Empires
Callirhoe. *See* Callirrhoe – Greek and Roman Empires
Callirrhoe – Greek and Roman Empires
Calliste – Greek and Roman Empires
Callisto – Greek and Roman Empires
Cally Berry. *See* Cailleach Beara – Western Europe
Calounga – South America
Calva – Greek and Roman Empires
Calybe – Greek and Roman Empires
Calypso – Greek and Roman Empires
Camdhen. *See* Kamadhenu – Indian Subcontinent
Cameira – Western Europe
Camenae, The – Greek and Roman Empires
Camise – Greek and Roman Empires
Campe – Greek and Roman Empires
Campestres, The – Western Europe
Camunda – Indian Subcontinent
Camundi. *See* Camunda and Candi – Indian Subcontinent
Can Nü – Far East
Cana Aulola – Indian Subcontinent
Cana Palak – Indian Subcontinent
Cancala. *See* Lakshmi and Lola – Indian Subcontinent
Canda – Indian Subcontinent
Candanayika – Indian Subcontinent
Candasya Naptyas, The – Indian Subcontinent
Candavati – Indian Subcontinent
Candelaria – Central America and Mesoamerica
Candelifera – Greek and Roman Empires
Candi – Indian Subcontinent
Candika. *See* Candi – Indian Subcontinent
Candit – Africa
Candogra – Indian Subcontinent
Canente – Greek and Roman Empires
Canidia – Greek and Roman Empires
Cannered Noz – Western Europe
Canola – Western Europe
Caoineag – Western Europe
Capheira – Greek and Roman Empires
Capita. *See* Capta – Greek and Roman Empires
Capta – Greek and Roman Empires
Caraki – Indian Subcontinent
Cardea – Greek and Roman Empires
Caridad – Central America and Mesoamerica
Carlin – Western Europe
Carline. *See* Cailleach Beara – Western Europe
Carmán – Western Europe
Carme – Greek and Roman Empires

Carmenta. *See* Carmentis – Greek and Roman Empires

Carmentis – Greek and Roman Empires

Carna – Greek and Roman Empires

Carpo – Greek and Roman Empires

Carpophori – Greek and Roman Empires

Carpunda – Western Europe

Carpundia. *See* Carpunda – Western Europe

Carravogue – Western Europe

Cartimandua – Western Europe

Carvi. *See* Bhadrā – Indian Subcontinent

Caryatid. *See* Caryatis – Greek and Roman Empires

Caryatis – Greek and Roman Empires

Caryotis. *See* Caryatis – Greek and Roman Empires

Casmenae, The. *See* The Camenae – Greek and Roman Empires

Cassiopeia – Greek and Roman Empires

Cassotis – Greek and Roman Empires

Cassowary Mother – Oceania

Castalia – Greek and Roman Empires

Castalides, The – Greek and Roman Empires

Castitas – Greek and Roman Empires

Cat Ana. *See* Black Annis – Western Europe

Cat Anna. *See* Black Annis – Western Europe

Cataclothes, The – Greek and Roman Empires

Çatal Hüyük Goddesses, The – Near East

Ca-the-ña – North America

Catherine, Saint – Central America and Mesoamerica

Cathubodia – Western Europe

Cathubodua – Western Europe

Cavillaca – South America

Ceacht – Western Europe

Ceasar. *See* Cesair – Western Europe

Ceasara. *See* Cesair – Western Europe

Ceasg – Western Europe

Cedreatis. *See* Artemis – Greek and Roman Empires

Ceibhfhionn – Western Europe

Ceithlenn. *See* Cethlenn – Western Europe

Ceiuci – South America

Celaeno – Greek and Roman Empires

Celedones, The – Greek and Roman Empires

Celeno. *See* Celaeno – Greek and Roman Empires

Celestial Sow, The – Egypt

Celestial Virgin – Near East

Celestial Waterer, The – Egypt

Celiborca – Western Europe

Centeotl – Central America and Mesoamerica

Centeotlcihuatl. *See* Centeotl – Central America and Mesoamerica

Cephisso – Greek and Roman Empires

Cer – Greek and Roman Empires

Cerceïs – Greek and Roman Empires

Cercyra – Greek and Roman Empires

Cerdo. *See* Alphito, Peitho, and Teledice – Greek and Roman Empires

Ceres – Greek and Roman Empires

Ceres Africana – Africa

Ceres Punica. *See* Ceres Africana – Africa

Ceridwen. *See* Cerridwen – Western Europe

Cerridwen – Western Europe

Cesair – Western Europe

Cesar. *See* Cesair – Western Europe

Cesara. *See* Cesair – Western Europe

Cesarea. *See* Cesair – Western Europe

Cessair. *See* Cesair – Western Europe

Cethlenn – Western Europe

Cethlion. *See* Cethlenn – Western Europe

Cethlionn. *See* Cethlenn – Western Europe

Cetnenn – Western Europe

Ceto – Greek and Roman Empires

Chaabou – Near East

Chaabu. *See* Chaabou – Near East

Chade – Africa

Cha-dog-ma – The Himalaya

Chags-kyu-ma – The Himalaya

Chahałheeł. *See* Tcalyel – North America

Chaiah – Near East

Chak-yu-ma. *See* Chags-kyu-ma – The Himalaya

Chakrisvari – Indian Subcontinent

Chakwaina Asho-adta – North America

Chakwaina Okya – North America

Chakwaina Sho-adta. *See* Chakwaina Asho-adta – North America

Chakwaina Yu-adta – North America

Chakwena – North America

Chala – Indian Subcontinent

Chalchihitlicue. *See* Chalchiuhtlicue – Central America and Mesoamerica

Chalchiuhcihuatl – Central America and Mesoamerica

Chalchiuhcueye. *See* Chalchiuhtlicue – Central America and Mesoamerica

Chalchiuhtlicue – Central America and Mesoamerica

Chalchiutlicue. *See* Chalchiuhtlicue – Central America and Mesoamerica

Chalcioecos – Greek and Roman Empires

Chalcioecus. *See* Chalcioecos – Greek and Roman Empires

Chalinitis – Greek and Roman Empires

Challalamma – Indian Subcontinent

Chalmecacihuatl – Central America and Mesoamerica

Chalmecacihutl. *See* Chalmecacihuatl – Central America and Mesoamerica

Chalonarang – Southeast Asia

Chamariya – Indian Subcontinent

Chamconda Mata – Indian Subcontinent

Chamunda. *See* Durga – Indian Subcontinent

Chamundi – Indian Subcontinent

Chamyne – Greek and Roman Empires

Chandi – Indian Subcontinent

Chandi Mata – Indian Subcontinent

Chandika. *See* Devi – Indian Subcontinent

Chandra – Indian Subcontinent

Chandragupta – Indian Subcontinent

Chang-bu – Far East

Chang E – Far East

Chang-hko – Southeast Asia

Chang Hsi. *See* Zhang Xi – Far East

Chang Ngo. *See* Chang E – Far East

Chang O. *See* Chang E – Far East

Chang Xi – Far East

Chang Yong – Far East

Ch'ang Yung. *See* Chang Yong – Far East

Changing Bear Maiden. *See* Tcikee Cac Nadleehe – North America

Changing Woman. *See* Estsanatlehi – North America

Chantico – Central America and Mesoamerica

Chao San Niang. *See* Zhao Sanniang – Far East

Chaos – Near East

Chaos – Greek and Roman Empires

Chapala – Indian Subcontinent

Charani Devi – Indian Subcontinent

Chariboea – Greek and Roman Empires

Chariclo – Greek and Roman Empires

Charis – Greek and Roman Empires

Charites, The – Greek and Roman Empires

Charity. *See* the Aeons – Near East

Charlotte, Mademoiselle – Central America and Mesoamerica

Charme. *See* Carme – Greek and Roman Empires

Charmel. *See* Carme – Greek and Roman Empires

Charybdis – Greek and Roman Empires

Chasbei – Near East

Chasca – South America

Chaurashi Devi – Indian Subcontinent

Chausath Joginis. *See* Chausathi Yoginis – Indian Subcontinent

Chausathi – Indian Subcontinent

Chausathi Yoginis, The – Indian Subcontinent

Chauturopayini – Indian Subcontinent

Chavah – Near East

Chavva. *See* Chavah – Near East

Chaya – Indian Subcontinent

Chebel Yax. *See* Ix Chebel Ya – Central America and Mesoamerica

Chedi Furen – Far East

Chekechani – Africa

Chelone – Greek and Roman Empires

Chemioi – Southeast Asia

Chemnis. *See* Khoemnis – Egypt

Chemnu. *See* Khoemnis – Egypt

Chen – Far East

Chên, Queen. *See* Mi Fei – Far East

Chen Furen. *See* Bixia Yuanjin – Far East

Chen-te P'u-sa. *See* Zhende Pusa – Far East

Chensit – Egypt

Chera – Greek and Roman Empires

Cherlak – Eastern Europe

Cherokee First Woman – North America

Cherokee Maize Mother – North America

Cherokee Sun Goddess – North America

Cherubim, The – Near East

Ch'e-Ti Fu-jen. *See* Chedi Furen – Far East

Chhatmata – Indian Subcontinent

Chhaya – Indian Subcontinent

Chhotimai – Indian Subcontinent

Chi – Africa

Ch'i Ku-tzu. *See* The Qi Guzi – Far East

Chia Shih. *See* Jia Shi – Far East

Chiang, The Empress – Far East

Chibilias – Central America and Mesoamerica

Chich Cohel – Central America and Mesoamerica

Chi-chi-gyal-mo – The Himalaya

Chíchipáchu – Central America and Mesoamerica

Chicomecoatl – Central America and Mesoamerica

Chieh. *See* Jie – Far East

Chigrinad – Indian Subcontinent

Chih Nu. *See* Zhinü – Far East

Chih-nii. *See* Zhinnü – Far East

Ch'i-hsien-niangniang. *See* Qixian Niangniang – Far East

Chikisani-kamui – Far East

Chikisanti. *See* Chikisani-kamui – Far East

Chilili Okya – North America

Chilkin Piri – Indian Subcontinent

Chimaera – Greek and Roman Empires

Chimaira. *See* Chimaera – Greek and Roman Empires

Chimalma – Central America and Mesoamerica

Chimalman. *See* Chimalma – Central America and Mesoamerica

Chimalmat – Central America and Mesoamerica

Chimera. *See* Chimaera – Greek and Roman Empires

Chimon Mana – North America

Chin Ku. *See* Jin Gu – Far East

Chin Mu. *See* Jin Mu – Far East

Chin Nü. *See* Zhinü – Far East

Chineke. *See* Chi – Africa

Chingan Mata – Indian Subcontinent

Chin-hua Niang-niang. *See* Jinhua Niangniang – Far East

Chinnamasta – Indian Subcontinent

Chinnamastaka. *See* Chinnamasta – Indian Subcontinent

Chinnintamma – Indian Subcontinent

Chinoi Sagar – Southeast Asia

Chione – Greek and Roman Empires

Chi-shiki-no-ō-kami. *See* Izanami-no-kami – Far East

Chit – Indian Subcontinent

Chitarhai Devi – Indian Subcontinent

Chiti. *See* Chit – Indian Subcontinent

Chitkuar Devi – Indian Subcontinent

Chitone – Greek and Roman Empires

Chitsa Numjan – Southeast Asia

Chitti – Indian Subcontinent

Chiu T'ien Hou Mu. *See* Jiutian Houmu – Far East

Chiu T'ien Hsuan-nu. *See* Jiutinan Xuannu – Far East

Chiun – Near East

Chiun. *See* Ken – Egypt

Chiu-rang-guru, The – Far East

Ch'iung Hsiao. *See* Qiongxiao – Far East

Chi-wara. *See* Tji-wara – Africa

Chiwash-kor-kamui – Far East

Chiwashekot-mat – Far East

Chlaus Haistic – Western Europe

Chlidanope – Greek and Roman Empires

Chloe – Greek and Roman Empires

Chloris – Greek and Roman Empires

Chochmah. *See* Chokmah – Western Europe

Chokesuso – South America

Chokmah – Western Europe

Chokmoth – Western Europe

Chola Pacho – Indian Subcontinent

Choorail – Indian Subcontinent

Choque Suso. *See* Chokesoso – South America

Choro – Greek and Roman Empires

Chowa – Indian Subcontinent

Christalline – Central America and Mesoamerica

Chryse – Greek and Roman Empires

Chryseis – Greek and Roman Empires

Chrysopeleia – Greek and Roman Empires

Chthonia – Greek and Roman Empires

Chthoniae, The – Greek and Roman Empires

Chuan Hou – Far East

Ch'uang Mu. *See* Chuang Mu – Far East

Chuang Mu – Far East

Chuginadak – North America

Chuh Kamuy – Far East

Chuhna – North America

Chu'i lha mo – The Himalaya

Chu'i lha mo Mamaki – The Himalaya

Chui-shen Niangniang. *See* Juishen Niangniang – Far East

Chulavete – Central America and Mesoamerica

Chulavete – North America

Chu-lcam-rgyal-mo – The Himalaya

Chulmetic – Central America and Mesoamerica

Chuma – Eastern Europe

Chumash Moon Woman – North America

Chun T'i. *See* Jun Ti – Far East

Chunda – Indian Subcontinent

Chup – North America

Chu'phrul can – The Himalaya

Chupu. *See* Chup – North America

Chupunika – Indian Subcontinent

Churalin – Indian Subcontinent

Churel – Indian Subcontinent

Churelin Mata – Indian Subcontinent

Chu-shêng Niangniang. *See* Bixia Yuanjin – Far East

Chwinbian. *See* Viviane – Western Europe

Cidaria – Greek and Roman Empires

Cigfa – Western Europe

Cigoro – Africa

Cihuacoatl – Central America and Mesoamerica

Cihuapipiltin, The – Central America and Mesoamerica

Cihuateotl – Central America and Mesoamerica

Cihuateteo, The – Central America and Mesoamerica

Cihuatzin – Central America and Mesoamerica

Cilich Colel – Central America and Mesoamerica

Cilla – Greek and Roman Empires

Cinderella – Eastern Europe

Cinei-new – Eastern Europe

Cinxia – Greek and Roman Empires

Cipactónal – Central America and Mesoamerica

Cipattoval. *See* Cipactónal – Central America and Mesoamerica

Circe – Greek and Roman Empires

Cirrha – Greek and Roman Empires

Cisiud – North America

Cisseis – Greek and Roman Empires

Cista – Near East

Citherides, The – Greek and Roman Empires

Citlalcueyetl. *See* Citlalicue – Central America and Mesoamerica

Citlalicue – Central America and Mesoamerica

Citlalinicue. *See* Citlalicue – Central America and Mesoamerica

Ciuateteo. *See* Cihuateteo – Central America and Mesoamerica

Claire, Saint – Central America and Mesoamerica

Clairmé, Mademoiselle – Central America and Mesoamerica

Clairmeziné – Central America and Mesoamerica

Clear-light Mother – The Himalaya

Cleeia. *See* Cleia – Greek and Roman Empires

Cleia – Greek and Roman Empires

Cleidouchos. *See* Athena – Greek and Roman Empires

Cleio. *See* Clio – Greek and Roman Empires

Cleis – Greek and Roman Empires

Cleochareia – Greek and Roman Empires

Cleone – Greek and Roman Empires

Cleta – Greek and Roman Empires

Clidna. *See* Cliodhna – Western Europe

Clio – Greek and Roman Empires

Cliodhna – Western Europe

Cliodna. *See* Cliodhna – Western Europe

Cloacina – Greek and Roman Empires

Clonia – Greek and Roman Empires

Clota – Western Europe

Clother – Egypt

Clotho – Greek and Roman Empires

Clothra – Western Europe

Clothru. *See* Clothra – Western Europe

Cluacina – Greek and Roman Empires

Clud – Western Europe

Clutoida – Western Europe

Clymene – Greek and Roman Empires

Clytia – Greek and Roman Empires
Clytie. *See* Clytia – Greek and Roman
　　Empires
Cnagia – Greek and Roman Empires
Cnidia – Greek and Roman Empires
Cnossia – Greek and Roman Empires
Coatlalopeuh. *See* Virgin of
　　Guadalupe – Central America and
　　Mesoamerica
Coatlaxopeuh. *See* Virgin of
　　Guadalupe – Central America and
　　Mesoamerica
Coatlicue – Central America and
　　Mesoamerica
Coatrischie – Central America and
　　Mesoamerica
Cobra Grande da Lagoa. *See* Doña
　　Rosalina – South America
Cocamama – South America
Coccymo – Greek and Roman Empires
Cocha – South America
Cochana. *See* Pitao Huichaana – Central
　　America and Mesoamerica
Cochiti Mother – North America
Cocomama. *See* Cocamama – South
　　America
Cocythiae, The – Greek and Roman
　　Empires
Coeur D'Alene Mother – North America
Coinchend – Western Europe
Coinquenda – Greek and Roman
　　Empires
Colaenis – Greek and Roman Empires
Cold Woman – North America
Colel Cab – Central America and
　　Mesoamerica
Colias – Greek and Roman Empires
Collatina – Greek and Roman Empires
Colleda – Eastern Europe
Colocasia – Greek and Roman Empires
Comitia – Greek and Roman Empires
Comizahual – Central America and
　　Mesoamerica
Con Tinh – Southeast Asia
Conan of Cuala – Western Europe
Conchenn – Western Europe
Conciliatri – Greek and Roman Empires
Concordia – Greek and Roman Empires
Condyleates – Greek and Roman
　　Empires
Conservatrix. *See* Fortuna – Greek and
　　Roman Empires
Copacati – South America
Copia – Greek and Roman Empires
Copper Woman – North America
Cora. *See* Core – Greek and Roman
　　Empires
Corchen – Western Europe
Corcyra. *See* Cercyra – Greek and
　　Roman Empires
Cordaca – Greek and Roman Empires
Cordeilla. *See* Cordelia – Western
　　Europe
Cordelia – Western Europe
Cordelie. *See* Cordelia – Western Europe
Cordula. *See* Cordelia – Western Europe
Core – Greek and Roman Empires
Cori Ocllo. *See* Ocllo – South America
Corinna. *See* Core – Greek and Roman
　　Empires

Corinne. *See* Core – Greek and Roman
　　Empires
Corn Maidens – North America
Corn Mother – North America
Corn Mother – Eastern Europe
Corn Soot Woman. *See* Ioashkanake –
　　North America
Corn Woman – North America
Cornaby. *See* Kernababy – Western
　　Europe
Cornbaby. *See* Kernababy – Western
　　Europe
Corner Goddess – Far East
Coronides, The – Greek and Roman
　　Empires
Coronis – Greek and Roman Empires
Corpse Goddesses – Far East
Corra – Western Europe
Corrigan, The – Western Europe
Corycia – Greek and Roman Empires
Coryciae, The – Greek and Roman
　　Empires
Coryphaea – Greek and Roman Empires
Coryphasia – Greek and Roman
　　Empires
Corythallia – Greek and Roman
　　Empires
Cosbi. *See* Chasbei – Near East
Cosmic Waters, The – Indian
　　Subcontinent
Cosunea – Western Europe
Coti – Africa
Cotsipamapot – North America
Cotton Mother – Indian Subcontinent
Cotys – Near East
Cotys – Greek and Roman Empires
Cotytto. *See* Cotys – Greek and Roman
　　Empires
Cotytto. *See* Cotys – Near East
Coventina – Western Europe
Cow Goddesses, The – Near East
Coyolxauhqui – Central America and
　　Mesoamerica
Cranto – Greek and Roman Empires
Crataeis – Greek and Roman Empires
Creator Being – North America
Creek Maize Mother – North America
Creiddylad. *See* Cordelia – Western
　　Europe
Créide Fí ráland – Western Europe
Creirwy – Western Europe
Creneis – Greek and Roman Empires
Creta. *See* Crete – Greek and Roman
　　Empires
Cretan Snake Goddess – Greek and
　　Roman Empires
Crete – Greek and Roman Empires
Creudylad. *See* Cordelia – Western
　　Europe
Creusa – Greek and Roman Empires
Crinaiae, The – Greek and Roman
　　Empires
Crobh Dearg – Western Europe
Crocodile Woman – Africa
Cteis – Greek and Roman Empires
Ctesylla – Greek and Roman Empires
Cuba – Greek and Roman Empires
Cudel – Indian Subcontinent
Cueravaperi – Central America and
　　Mesoamerica

Cuerohperi. *See* Cueravaperi – Central
　　America and Mesoamerica
Cui Sheng – Far East
Cuimne – Western Europe
Cuisheng Sheng Mu – Far East
Culsa – Greek and Roman Empires
Culsu. *See* Culsa – Greek and Roman
　　Empires
Cunda – Far East
Cunda – Indian Subcontinent
Cunda – Southeast Asia
Cunina – Greek and Roman Empires
Cunnembeillee – Oceania
Cunti. *See* Cunda – Indian Subcontinent
Cu-piritta-ka – North America
Cupra – Greek and Roman Empires
Cura – South America
Curche – Eastern Europe
Curiatia – Greek and Roman Empires
Curissia – Greek and Roman Empires
Curitis – Greek and Roman Empires
Curotrophos – Greek and Roman
　　Empires
Cutzi – Central America and
　　Mesoamerica
Cuvto-ava – Eastern Europe
Cyane – Greek and Roman Empires
Cybele – Near East
Cybele – Greek and Roman Empires
Cycladic Goddesses, The – Greek and
　　Roman Empires
Cydippe – Greek and Roman Empires
Cydonia – Greek and Roman Empires
Cyhiraeth – Western Europe
Cylla. *See* Cilla – Greek and Roman
　　Empires
Cyllene – Greek and Roman Empires
Cymatolege – Greek and Roman
　　Empires
Cymidei Cymeinfol – Western Europe
Cymo – Greek and Roman Empires
Cymodoce – Greek and Roman Empires
Cymothoe – Greek and Roman Empires
Cynosura – Greek and Roman Empires
Cynthia – Greek and Roman Empires
Cypete. *See* Ocypete – Greek and
　　Roman Empires
Cypria – Greek and Roman Empires
Cypridos – Greek and Roman Empires
Cyprigeneia. *See* Cypria – Greek and
　　Roman Empires
Cypris. *See* Cypria – Greek and Roman
　　Empires
Cyprogenes. *See* Cypria – Greek and
　　Roman Empires
Cyrene – Greek and Roman Empires
Cythera – Greek and Roman Empires
Cytherea. *See* Cythera – Greek and
　　Roman Empires
Cythereia. *See* Cythera – Greek and
　　Roman Empires
Cytherias. *See* Cythera – Greek and
　　Roman Empires
Da – Greek and Roman Empires
Da Ma Niangniang. *See* Deo Ma
　　Niangniang – Far East
Da'an Nü – Far East
Daath – Western Europe
Dabaiaba. *See* Dabaiba – Central
　　America and Mesoamerica

Dabaiba – Central America and
    Mesoamerica
Dabiancai Tiannü – Far East
Dactyli. See Dactyls – Greek and Roman
    Empires
Dactyls, The – Greek and Roman
    Empires
Dada – Africa
Dadju – Indian Subcontinent
Dadmish – Near East
Daeira – Greek and Roman Empires
Daena – Near East
Dag – Northern Europe
Dagau – Southeast Asia
Dagdagamiyan – Southeast Asia
Daginis, The. See The Dakinis – Indian
    Subcontinent
Dagon – Near East
Dagwanoenyent – North America
Dah-ko-beed – North America
Dahomean Moon Woman – Africa
Dahut – Western Europe
Daiboth, The Female – Far East
Daini – Indian Subcontinent
Dainichi-nyorai – Far East
Daintary – Indian Subcontinent
Dais – Greek and Roman Empires
Daityas, The – Indian Subcontinent
Daiviprakriti – Indian Subcontinent
Daiyou Taiping Xiang Yuxian
    Niangniang. See Yu Nü – Far East
Daji – Far East
Dakini – Indian Subcontinent
Dakini Guru – The Himalaya
Dakini Queen. See Khadoma Queen –
    The Himalaya
Dakinis, The – Indian Subcontinent
Dakshina – Indian Subcontinent
Daksinakalika. See Durga – Indian
    Subcontinent
Dama, The – Oceania
Damake. See Damkina – Near East
Damasippus – Greek and Roman
    Empires
Damatres, The – Greek and Roman
    Empires
Damayanti – Indian Subcontinent
Damballah – Central America and
    Mesoamerica
Dame Habondia. See Habonde –
    Western Europe
Dame Wode – Northern Europe
Dames Vertes – Western Europe
Damgalnunna – Near East
Damia – Greek and Roman Empires
Dam-ki. See Damkina – Near East
Damkina – Near East
Damoia. See Damia – Greek and Roman
    Empires
Damona – Western Europe
Da-mu-gal. See Gula – Near East
Dam-tshig-mkha'-'gro-ma – The
    Himalaya
Damwamwit – Africa
Dan – Africa
Dana. See Danu – Western Europe
Danai Furen – Far East
Danais. See Axioche – Greek and
    Roman Empires
Danann. See Danu – Western Europe

Danavis, The – Indian Subcontinent
Dangira – Africa
Dantesvari. See Mata – Indian
    Subcontinent
Danu – Western Europe
Danu – Greek and Roman Empires
Danu – Indian Subcontinent
Danube. See Danu – Western Europe
Danuna. See Danu – Greek and Roman
    Empires
Danus, The – Indian Subcontinent
Dao – Far East
Dao – Southeast Asia
Dao Mu. See Dou Mou – Far East
Daphnaea – Greek and Roman Empires
Daphne – Greek and Roman Empires
Dara Eke – Far East
Dara Ensing Tamaga – Southeast Asia
Dara Rambai Geruda – Southeast Asia
Darago – Southeast Asia
Dariya – Africa
Dark Maid, The – Far East
Dark-blue Owl-headed One – The
    Himalaya
Dark-blue Smasha – The Himalaya
Dark-blue Wolf-headed One – The
    Himalaya
Dark-brown Lion-headed One – The
    Himalaya
Dark-brown Yak-headed Rakshasa
    Goddess – The Himalaya
Dark-green Fox-headed Baton
    Goddess – The Himalaya
Dark-green Ghasmari – The Himalaya
Darmit – Indian Subcontinent
Darzamat. See Dārzu-māte – Eastern
    Europe
Dārzu-māte – Eastern Europe
Dasabhuja. See Durga – Indian
    Subcontinent
Dasara – Indian Subcontinent
Da-shi-zhi. See Dashizhi – Far East
Dashizhi – Far East
Dasse – Africa
Data – Africa
Daterata – Southeast Asia
Daughter of the Sky. See Nambi – Africa
Daughter of the Sun – North America
Daukina. See Damkina – Near East
Daulis – Greek and Roman Empires
Dauthe. See Damkina – Near East
Davata – Indian Subcontinent
Davcina – Near East
Davke. See Davcina – Near East
Davkina. See Damkina – Near East
Dawen – Western Europe
Dawi – Near East
Dawkina. See Damkina – Near East
Dawn (Seneca) – North America
Dawn Woman – North America
Daxian Furen – Far East
Daya – Indian Subcontinent
Dayan – Indian Subcontinent
Dazimus – Near East
dBang-bsdud-ma – The Himalaya
dBang-sdud-kyi-mkha'-'gro-ma – The
    Himalaya
dByangs-can-ma – The Himalaya
dByans-can-ma. See dByangs-can-ma –
    The Himalaya

dByar-gyi-rgyal-mo – The Himalaya
Ddrvaspa – Near East
De ai – Oceania
De Develski. See Amari De – Indian
    Subcontinent
Dea Arduenna – Western Europe
Dea Artia – Western Europe
Dea Artio – Western Europe
Dea Caelestis – Greek and Roman
    Empires
Dea Dia – Greek and Roman Empires
Dea Domnann – Western Europe
Dea Domnu. See Dea Domnann –
    Western Europe
Dea Febris. See Febris – Greek and
    Roman Empires
Dea Marica – Greek and Roman
    Empires
Dea Matuta. See Mater Matuta – Greek
    and Roman Empires
Dea Nutri – Western Europe
Dea Quartana. See Febris – Greek and
    Roman Empires
Dea Syria – Greek and Roman Empires
Dea Tertiana. See Febris – Greek and
    Roman Empires
Deae Matres, The – Greek and Roman
    Empires
Death-bringing-woman – North
    America
Death Goddess – Africa
Debee. See Devi – Indian Subcontinent
Debena – Eastern Europe
Dechtiré – Western Europe
Decima. See Decuma – Greek and
    Roman Empires
Dectera. See Dechtiré – Western Europe
Dectere. See Dechtiré – Western Europe
Decuma – Greek and Roman Empires
Dee – Western Europe
Deer Mothers, The – North America
Deer Woman – North America
Deianeira – Greek and Roman Empires
Deianeira. See Blodeuwedd – Western
    Europe
Deichtine. See Dechtiré – Western
    Europe
Deima – Greek and Roman Empires
Deino – Greek and Roman Empires
Deiois. See Deione – Greek and Roman
    Empires
Deione – Greek and Roman Empires
Deiope. See Chione – Greek and Roman
    Empires
Deiopea – Greek and Roman Empires
Deipara – Greek and Roman Empires
Deiphobe – Greek and Roman Empires
Deirdre – Western Europe
Deities of the Third Earthly
    Generation – Far East
Deivai – Northern Europe
Dejanira. See Deianeira – Greek and
    Roman Empires
Dekla – Eastern Europe
Dekle. See The Divje Devojke – Eastern
    Europe
Delia – Greek and Roman Empires
Deliades, The – Greek and Roman
    Empires
Delight – Greek and Roman Empires

Delight Goddess, The – Indian
  Subcontinent
Delka. *See* Dekla – Eastern Europe
Delphinia – Greek and Roman Empires
Demeter – Greek and Roman Empires
Demo. *See* Demeter – Greek and Roman
  Empires
Demon Protector of the Grand Lama –
  The Himalaya
Dendritus – Greek and Roman Empires
Deo – Near East
Deo – Greek and Roman Empires
Deo Ma Niangniang – Far East
Deohako – North America
Deoine. *See* Deione – Greek and Roman
  Empires
Derbforgaille. *See* Derbhorgill –
  Western Europe
Derbhorgill – Western Europe
Dercetis. *See* Derketo – Near East
Derceto. *See* Derketo – Near East
Derdriu. *See* Deirdre – Western Europe
Derfintos – Eastern Europe
Derketo – Near East
Dero – Greek and Roman Empires
Derrhiatis. *See* Artemis – Greek and
  Roman Empires
Dervonnae, The – Western Europe
Desahai Devi – Indian Subcontinent
Deshtri – Indian Subcontinent
Desini. *See* Durga – Indian Subcontinent
Despoena – Greek and Roman Empires
Despoina. *See* Despoena – Greek and
  Roman Empires
Deung Abok – Africa
Deva – Western Europe
Deva Kanyakas. *See also* Devis. –
  Indian Subcontinent
Deva Kanyas. *See* Deva Kanyakas –
  Indian Subcontinent
Devabhuti. *See* Ganga – Indian
  Subcontinent
Devaki – Indian Subcontinent
Devala – Indian Subcontinent
Devana – Eastern Europe
Devananda – Indian Subcontinent
Devanganas, The. *See* Devis – Indian
  Subcontinent
Devasena – Indian Subcontinent
Devasuni. *See* Sarama – Indian
  Subcontinent
Devatas, The – Indian Subcontinent
Devayani – Indian Subcontinent
Devayoshas, The. *See* Devis – Indian
  Subcontinent
Devee. *See* Devi – Indian Subcontinent
Deverra – Greek and Roman Empires
Devi – Indian Subcontinent
Devikas, The. *See* Devis – Indian
  Subcontinent
Devis, The – Indian Subcontinent
Devona – Western Europe
Devorgilla. *See* Derbhorgill – Western
  Europe
Dewaite Szwenta – Eastern Europe
Dewel – Indian Subcontinent
Dewi Amisani – Southeast Asia
Dewi Cri – Southeast Asia
Dewi Danu – Southeast Asia
Dewi Gangga – Southeast Asia

Dewi Hasin. *See* Dewi Amisani –
  Southeast Asia
Dewi Melanting – Southeast Asia
Dewi Paya. *See* Dewi Amisani –
  Southeast Asia
Dewi Pertimah – Southeast Asia
Dewi Ratih – Southeast Asia
Dewi Seri. *See* Dewi Sri – Southeast Asia
Dewi Sri – Southeast Asia
Dewy – Near East
Dexamene – Greek and Roman Empires
Deywuckee. *See* Devaki – Indian
  Subcontinent
dGra-lha-ma-lha-bu-rdzi – The
  Himalaya
dGra-lha-thab-lha-g•yu-mo – The
  Himalaya
Dhahu Dhukan – Indian Subcontinent
Dhanada – Indian Subcontinent
Dhanesvari. *See* Sarasvati – Indian
  Subcontinent
Dhara – Indian Subcontinent
Dharani – Indian Subcontinent
Dharni Deota – Indian Subcontinent
Dharni Pinnu – Indian Subcontinent
Dharti Mai. *See* Dharti Mata and
  Bhudevi – Indian Subcontinent
Dharti Mata – Indian Subcontinent
Dharti. *See* Dharti Mata – Indian
  Subcontinent
Dhavata – Eastern Europe
Dhisana – Indian Subcontinent
Dhriti – Indian Subcontinent
Dhrtarastri – Indian Subcontinent
Dhrti. *See* Dhriti – Indian Subcontinent
Dhruva – Indian Subcontinent
Dhumavati – Indian Subcontinent
Dhumorna – Indian Subcontinent
Dhupa – Indian Subcontinent
Dhupema. *See* bDug-spös-ma – The
  Himalaya
Dhupema. *See* Dhupa – Indian
  Subcontinent
Di Mu – Far East
Di Ya – Far East
Dia – Greek and Roman Empires
Dia Griene – Western Europe
Diablesse, The – Central America and
  Mesoamerica
Diana – Greek and Roman Empires
Diana of Ephesians – Greek and Roman
  Empires
Dianggwuls. *See* Djanggawul – Oceania
Dianoia – Near East
Diarrhoea – Indian Subcontinent
Dice – Greek and Roman Empires
Dichtire – Western Europe
Dicte – Greek and Roman Empires
Dictynna – Greek and Roman Empires
Didilia – Eastern Europe
Dido – Near East
Dido Anna. *See* Dido – Near East
Didon. *See* Dido – Near East
Didone. *See* Dido – Near East
Didun – The Himalaya
Dierra – Africa
Dietyi – Oceania
Digde. *See* Cailleach Beara – Western
  Europe
Digdevatas – Indian Subcontinent

Dige. *See* Cailleach Beara – Western
  Europe
Diiwica – Eastern Europe
Dik-kanya – Indian Subcontinent
Dikaiosyne – Egypt
Dike. *See* Dice – Greek and Roman
  Empires
Dikkumari, The – Indian Subcontinent
Diktynna. *See* Dictynna – Greek and
  Roman Empires
Dil – Western Europe
Dilbah – Near East
Dilbali. *See* Ishtar – Near East
Dilga – Oceania
Dilli Polasi – Indian Subcontinent
Dimme – Near East
Dimtabba – Near East
Dinawagan – Southeast Asia
Dindymene – Greek and Roman
  Empires
Dinewan – Oceania
Dingirmah. *See* Hannahannas – Near
  East
Dinka First Woman – Africa
Dinonganan – Southeast Asia
Dinsangma – The Himalaya
Dionaea – Greek and Roman Empires
Dione – Near East
Dione – Greek and Roman Empires
Dionea. *See* Dionaea – Greek and
  Roman Empires
Dios – Greek and Roman Empires
Dioxippe – Greek and Roman Empires
Dirae, The – Greek and Roman Empires
Dirce – Greek and Roman Empires
Dirivo – Oceania
Dirona. *See* Sirona – Western Europe
Dirra. *See* Cailleach Beara, Clutoida –
  Western Europe
Dirri. *See* Cailleach Beara, Clutoida –
  Western Europe
Dis – Northern Europe
Disciplina – Greek and Roman Empires
Discord. *See* Discordia – Greek and
  Roman Empires
Discordia – Greek and Roman
  Empires
Dishai Devi – Indian Subcontinent
Disir, The – Northern Europe
Dispirir Mata – Indian Subcontinent
Diti – Indian Subcontinent
Diuturna. *See* Juturna – Greek and
  Roman Empires
Dive Zeny – Eastern Europe
Diviana – Greek and Roman Empires
Divine Queen – Africa
Divi-te Zeni, The – Eastern Europe
Divi-te Zheny, The. *See* Divi-te Zeni –
  Eastern Europe
Divja Davojke, The – Eastern Europe
Divje Devojke, The – Eastern Europe
Divo Duhita – Indian Subcontinent
Divona – Western Europe
Divoženky, The – Eastern Europe
Diwali – Indian Subcontinent
Diwja. *See* Diwya – Greek and Roman
  Empires
Diwya – Greek and Roman Empires
Dizane – Near East
Djabani – North America

Djaga Woman – Africa
Djalai – Southeast Asia
Djanggau, Djanggaus. See
   Djanggawul – Oceania
Djanggawul, The – Oceania
Djata – Southeast Asia
Djet – Egypt
Dji Sisnaxitl. See Qamaits – North
   America
Djigonsasee – North America
Djilaqons – North America
Djugurba – Oceania
Djunkgao, The – Oceania
dKar-mo – Far East
dMag-zor-ma – The Himalaya
Dobaya. See Dobayba – Central
   America and Mesoamerica
Dobayba – Central America and
   Mesoamerica
Dobhinia – Western Europe
Doda – Eastern Europe
Dodah – Near East
Dodola. See Doda – Eastern Europe
Dodone – Greek and Roman Empires
Dodonides, The – Greek and Roman
   Empires
Dogai, The – Oceania
Dogon Earth Mother – Africa
Dogon Sun Goddess – Africa
Dogrib First Woman – North America
Doh Tenangan – Southeast Asia
Doini – Indian Subcontinent
Dok – Oceania
Dol Jyang. See Bribsun – The Himalaya
Dolja. See Dolya – Eastern Europe
Doljang – Indian Subcontinent
Dolma – The Himalaya
Dolma. See Tara – Indian Subcontinent
Dolya – Eastern Europe
Dom-gdon-can – The Himalaya
Domiduca – Greek and Roman Empires
Domnu – Western Europe
Don – Western Europe
Donann. See Danu – Western Europe
Donau. See Danu – Western Europe
Dong Mu – Far East
Dongar Dai – Indian Subcontinent
Donyi – Indian Subcontinent
Doon Buidhe – Western Europe
Doorga. See Parvati and Durga – Indian
   Subcontinent
Dorides, The – Greek and Roman
   Empires
Dorina – Africa
Doris – Greek and Roman Empires
Dorje Naljorma – The Himalaya
Dorje Phagmo – The Himalaya
Dorje-pa-mo – The Himalaya
Dornoll – Western Europe
Dornolla. See Dornoll – Western Europe
Dörr-käring – Northern Europe
Dosangma – The Himalaya
Doto – Greek and Roman Empires
Dou Mou – Far East
Dou Mu. See Dou Mou – Far East
Doña Rosalina – South America
Douizhen. See Doushen Niangniang –
   Far East
Doushen Niangniang – Far East

Dove Goddess – Greek and Roman
   Empires
dPal-gyi-pho-nya-las-mkhan-mo – The
   Himalaya
dPal-ldan Lha-mo – The Himalaya
dPyid-kyi-rgyal-mo. See
   Chi-chi-gyal-mo – The Himalaya
Drafn – Northern Europe
Dragon Mother, The – Far East
Drag-ppo'i-klog-khyung-ma – The
   Himalaya
Draupadi – Indian Subcontinent
Dri-chab-ma. See Dri-chha-ma – The
   Himalaya
Dri-chha-ma – The Himalaya
Drifa – Northern Europe
Dril-bu-ma. See Til-bu-ma – The
   Himalaya
Dröl-ma – The Himalaya
Drimo – Greek and Roman Empires
Druantia – Western Europe
Drude – Eastern Europe
Drude – Northern Europe
Druden. See Drude – Northern Europe
Druh – Indian Subcontinent
Druj – Near East
Druxsans, The – Near East
Drvaspa – Near East
Dryades, The – Greek and Roman
   Empires
Dryads, The. See The Dryades – Greek
   and Roman Empires
Drymo. See Drimo – Greek and Roman
   Empires
Dryope – Greek and Roman Empires
Dsovinar – Near East
Dsovinar – Eastern Europe
Dua Nggae – Southeast Asia
Duan Luteh – Southeast Asia
Dub – Western Europe
Dubh. See Dub – Western Europe
Dubh Lacha – Western Europe
Dubhlaing – Western Europe
Duc Ba – Southeast Asia
Duc Thanh Ba – Southeast Asia
Dudu Hepa – Near East
Dugbo – Africa
Dughda – Near East
Dughdhova. See Dughda – Near East
Dugnai – Eastern Europe
Dug-po-ma. See bDug-spös-ma – The
   Himalaya
Duh-hwahk – North America
Duhkharni Mai – Indian Subcontinent
Duillae, The – Western Europe
Duineach. See Cailleach Beara –
   Western Europe
Dula – Indian Subcontinent
Dumuziabzu – Near East
Dunav. See Danu – Western Europe
Dunawali – Oceania
Dundubhi. See Manthara – Indian
   Subcontinent
Dunna Musun – Eastern Europe
Durga – Indian Subcontinent
Durga Mata – Indian Subcontinent
Durgamma – Indian Subcontinent
Durgapunja. See Kali – Indian
   Subcontinent

Durja. See Parvati and Durga – Indian
   Subcontinent
Dur-khrod-kyi-bdag-mo-khros-ma-
   nag-mo – The Himalaya
Dur-khrod-lha-mo – The Himalaya
Durpatta Mata – Indian Subcontinent
Duttur – Near East
Dvang-phyng-ma. See
   Wang-Chugmas – The Himalaya
Dwynwen. See Branwen – Western
   Europe
Dyaush-pitir – Indian Subcontinent
Dyava-matar. See Prithivi – Indian
   Subcontinent
Dyava-Prthivi – Indian Subcontinent
Dyevae – South America
Dyfridwy. See Aerfon – Western Europe
Dynamene – Greek and Roman Empires
Dynamis – Near East
Dysis – Greek and Roman Empires
Dysnomia – Greek and Roman Empires
Dyu – Indian Subcontinent
Dzari – Oceania
Dzelarhons – North America
Dzewana. See Dziewona – Eastern
   Europe
Dzidzielia – Eastern Europe
Dzievona. See Dziewona – Eastern
   Europe
Dziewanna – Eastern Europe
Dziewona – Eastern Europe
Dziparu-māte – Eastern Europe
Dziva – Africa
Dziwica. See Diiwica – Eastern Europe
Dziwożony – Eastern Europe
Dziwuje Zony. See The Divje Dvojke –
   Eastern Europe
Dzoo-noo-qua – North America
Dzurawu – Indian Subcontinent
Dzydzilelya – Eastern Europe
E Ú – Southeast Asia
Eadna. See Ħre – Western Europe
Eadon – Western Europe
Eagentci – North America
Earth Altar Young Woman. See
   Mamzrau Mana – North America
Earth Cow, The – Far East
Earth Goddess – The Himalaya
Earth Goddess – Indian Subcontinent
Earth Goddess. See Tartary and Cathay
   Earth Goddess – Far East
Earth Mother of Hrusso – Indian
   Subcontinent
Earth Woman of Dogon. See Dogon
   Earth Mother – Africa
Eastern Mother – Far East
Eastre – Northern Europe
Ebhlenn. See Ebhlinne – Western
   Europe
Ebhlinne – Western Europe
Ecclesia – Near East
Echaid – Western Europe
Echenais – Greek and Roman Empires
Echidna – Greek and Roman Empires
Echo – Greek and Roman Empires
Echtghe – Western Europe
Edain Echraidhe. See Ħain Echraidhe –
   Western Europe
Edain. See Ħain, Ħain Echraidhe –
   Western Europe

Edar. *See* Ḥain Echraidhe – Western Europe

Edda – Northern Europe

Edem – Near East

Eden – Near East

Edinkira – Africa

Edji – Far East

Edji – Eastern Europe

Edjo. *See* Buto – Egypt

Edulica – Greek and Roman Empires

Edusa – Greek and Roman Empires

Ee-eh-ch-choo-ri-ch'ahm-nin – North America

Ee-loolth – North America

Egattala – Indian Subcontinent

Egeria. *See* Aegeria – Greek and Roman Empires

Egia – Northern Europe

Egitummal – Near East

Egle – Eastern Europe

Egungun-oya – Africa

Eguski – Western Europe

Ehe – Egypt

Ehe Tazar – Eastern Europe

Eidothea – Greek and Roman Empires

Eidyia. *See* Idyia – Greek and Roman Empires

Eigin – Western Europe

Eil. *See* Eir – Northern Europe

Eile. *See* Ele – Western Europe

Eileithyea. *See* Eileithyia – Greek and Roman Empires

Eileithyia – Greek and Roman Empires

Eilethyia. *See* Eileithyia – Greek and Roman Empires

Eimaramene – Near East

Eingana – Oceania

Einmyria – Northern Europe

Eione – Greek and Roman Empires

Eir – Northern Europe

Eira. *See* Eir – Northern Europe

Ḥire, Celtic – Western Europe

Ḥrean. *See* Ḥire – Western Europe

Eirene – Greek and Roman Empires

Eirin. *See* Ḥire – Western Europe

Ḥrinn – Western Europe

Eisa – Northern Europe

Eisenberta. *See* Berchta – Northern Europe

Eistla – Northern Europe

Eithinoha – North America

Eithinoha. *See* Nokomis – North America

Eithne. *See* Ethné – Western Europe

Eithniu. *See* Ethné – Western Europe

Eka Abassi – Africa

Ekadzati – The Himalaya

Ekajata – Indian Subcontinent

Ekajati. *See* Ekajata – Indian Subcontinent

Ekanamsa. *See* Durga – Indian Subcontinent

Ekaparna – Indian Subcontinent

Ekapatala – Indian Subcontinent

Ekash-Taka – Indian Subcontinent

Ekastaka – Indian Subcontinent

Ekeitehua – Oceania

Ekhi – Western Europe

Ekineba – Africa

Ekki. *See* Aka – Near East

Ekumoke – Africa

Elais – Greek and Roman Empires

Elamadichi – Indian Subcontinent

Elamite – Western Europe

Elasii, The – Greek and Roman Empires

Elat. *See* Asherah – Near East

Elate – Greek and Roman Empires

Elath. *See* Asherah – Near East

Elben, Die – Northern Europe

Ele – Western Europe

Electra – Greek and Roman Empires

Electryone – Greek and Roman Empires

Eleionomae – Greek and Roman Empires

Eleithyia. *See* Eileithyia – Greek and Roman Empires

Elektra. *See* Electra – Greek and Roman Empires

Eleos – Greek and Roman Empires

'Elepaio – Oceania

Eleusina – Greek and Roman Empires

Eleusina. *See* Eleusinia – Greek and Roman Empires

Eleuthera – Greek and Roman Empires

Eleutho. *See* Eileithyia – Greek and Roman Empires

Elihino – North America

Elionia – Greek and Roman Empires

Elisabeth, Saint – Central America and Mesoamerica

Elissa – Near East

Ella. *See* Cinderella – Eastern Europe

Ellamma – Indian Subcontinent

Elli – Northern Europe

Elpis – Greek and Roman Empires

Emanja – Central America and Mesoamerica

Emanjah. *See* Emanja – Central America and Mesoamerica

Embla – Northern Europe

Embroidery Goddess – Far East

Emenet. *See* Ahat – Egypt

Emer – Western Europe

Emmer – Near East

Empanada – Greek and Roman Empires

Empung Luminuut – Southeast Asia

Empusa – Greek and Roman Empires

Empusae – Greek and Roman Empires

Empusae. *See* Ghuls – Indian Subcontinent

Emu. *See* Kurikuta – Oceania

Enakhsys – Eastern Europe

Enarete – Greek and Roman Empires

Enda kondapala. *See* Enda semangko – Oceania

Enda semangko – Oceania

Endeis – Greek and Roman Empires

Enekpe – Africa

Enenet-hemset. *See* Kerhet – Egypt

Enhydria – Greek and Roman Empires

Enkrateia – Greek and Roman Empires

Ennit. *See* Kerhet – Egypt

Ennoe. *See* Ennoia – Near East

Ennoia – Near East

Enodia – Greek and Roman Empires

Ensum. *See* Nanna – Near East

Entelanying – Southeast Asia

Enthumesis – Near East

Enthymese. *See* Enthumesis – Near East

Enyo – Greek and Roman Empires

Eo-Anu – Western Europe

Eodain. *See* Leanan Sidhe – Western Europe

Eoghana. *See* Ḥire – Western Europe

Eos – Greek and Roman Empires

Eostre. *See* Eastre – Northern Europe

Epaine – Greek and Roman Empires

Epeione. *See* Epione – Greek and Roman Empires

Êpet – Egypt

Ephesia – Greek and Roman Empires

Epimelides. *See* Meliades – Greek and Roman Empires

Epinoia – Near East

Epione – Greek and Roman Empires

Epipole – Greek and Roman Empires

Epipyrgidia – Greek and Roman Empires

Epistrophia – Greek and Roman Empires

Epitragia. *See* Aphrodite – Greek and Roman Empires

Epitymbia – Greek and Roman Empires

Epitymbria. *See* Epitymbia – Greek and Roman Empires

Epona – Western Europe

Epona – Greek and Roman Empires

Equestris – Greek and Roman Empires

Erato – Greek and Roman Empires

Erce – Eastern Europe

Erda – Northern Europe

Erditse – Western Europe

'Ere'ere fenua – Oceania

Eres Ki Gala. *See* Ereshkigal – Near East

Ereshkigal – Near East

Eretz. *See* Aretz – Near East

Ergane – Greek and Roman Empires

Ergatis – Greek and Roman Empires

Erhlaveersissoq. *See* Erlaveersisoq – North America

Eri – Western Europe

Eria. *See* Eir – Northern Europe

Eriboea – Greek and Roman Empires

Erigone – Greek and Roman Empires

Erinnys, The. *See* Erinyes – Greek and Roman Empires

Erinyes, The – Greek and Roman Empires

Erinys – Greek and Roman Empires

Eripha – Greek and Roman Empires

Eriphyle – Greek and Roman Empires

Eris – Greek and Roman Empires

Eriskegal. *See* Ereshkigal – Near East

Eriu. *See* Ḥire – Western Europe

Erkir. *See* Armat – Near East

Erlaveersisoq – North America

Ermutu – Egypt

Erni – Western Europe

Ernutet – Egypt

Ernutit. *See* Ernutet – Egypt

Erpuit Goddesses, The – Egypt

Ersa – Greek and Roman Empires

Erse. *See* Ersa – Greek and Roman Empires

Erua – Near East

Erycina – Greek and Roman Empires

Erythea – Greek and Roman Empires

Erytheia. *See* Erythea – Greek and Roman Empires

Erytheis. *See* Erythea – Greek and Roman Empires
Erzilie of Damballa. *See* Erzulie – Central America and Mesoamerica
Erzilie Topicanare. *See* Erzulie – Central America and Mesoamerica
Erzilie Zandor. *See* Erzulie Mapiangueh – Central America and Mesoamerica
Erzulie – Central America and Mesoamerica
Erzulie Mapiangueh – Central America and Mesoamerica
Erzulie Toho. *See* Erzulie Mapiangueh – Central America and Mesoamerica
Erzulie Vestry. *See* Erzulie Mapiangueh – Central America and Mesoamerica
Erzulie-Freda-Dahomey. *See* Erzulie – Central America and Mesoamerica
Esceheman – North America
Esdzanata – North America
Ese. *See* Isis – Egypt
Esenchebis – Greek and Roman Empires
Esesar – Africa
Eset. *See* Isis – Egypt
Esharra – Near East
Eshtar – Near East
Esi. *See* Isis – Egypt
Essylt. *See* Isolt – Western Europe
Estanatlehi. *See* Estsanatlehi – North America
Estiu – Western Europe
Ests'unnadlehi. *See* Estsanatlehi – North America
Estsanatlehi – North America
Ḧain – Western Europe
Ḧain Echraidhe – Western Europe
Ḧain Óig – Western Europe
Etan. *See* Ḧain – Western Europe
Eterna – Far East
Eternal Mother – Indian Subcontinent
Ethausva – Greek and Roman Empires
Ether – Eastern Europe
Ether. *See* Aether – Greek and Roman Empires
Ethlenn. *See* Ethlinn – Western Europe
Ethlinn – Western Europe
Ethné – Western Europe
Ethnea. *See* Ethlinn – Western Europe
Ethniu. *See* Ethlinn – Western Europe
Etna – Greek and Roman Empires
Etogon – Far East
Etugen – Far East
Etugen – Eastern Europe
Euadne – Greek and Roman Empires
Euagora. *See* Evagora – Greek and Roman Empires
Euarne. *See* Evarne – Greek and Roman Empires
Euboea – Greek and Roman Empires
Eucharis – Greek and Roman Empires
Eucleia – Greek and Roman Empires
Eucrante – Greek and Roman Empires
Eudaimonia – Greek and Roman Empires
Eudane. *See* Evadne – Greek and Roman Empires
Eudia – Greek and Roman Empires
Eudora – Greek and Roman Empires

Eugora – Greek and Roman Empires
Eukrante. *See* Eucrante – Greek and Roman Empires
Eukrate. *See* Eucrante – Greek and Roman Empires
Eulimene – Greek and Roman Empires
Eumenides, The. *See* The Erinyes – Greek and Roman Empires
Eumolpe – Greek and Roman Empires
Euneike. *See* Eunike – Greek and Roman Empires
Eunice. *See* Eunike – Greek and Roman Empires
Eunike – Greek and Roman Empires
Eunoe – Greek and Roman Empires
Eunomia – Greek and Roman Empires
Eunoste – Greek and Roman Empires
Eunostos – Greek and Roman Empires
Euonyme – Greek and Roman Empires
Eupheme – Greek and Roman Empires
Euphrosyne – Greek and Roman Empires
Euploia – Greek and Roman Empires
Eupompe – Greek and Roman Empires
Euporia – Greek and Roman Empires
Europa – Greek and Roman Empires
Euryale – Greek and Roman Empires
Eurybia – Greek and Roman Empires
Eurydice – Greek and Roman Empires
Eurynome – Greek and Roman Empires
Euryphaessa – Greek and Roman Empires
Euryphassa. *See* Euryphaessa – Greek and Roman Empires
Eurysternos – Greek and Roman Empires
Euryte – Greek and Roman Empires
Eus-os. *See* Saosis – Egypt
Euterpe – Greek and Roman Empires
Eutychia – Greek and Roman Empires
Euzki. *See* Eguski – Western Europe
Evadne – Greek and Roman Empires
Evagora – Greek and Roman Empires
Evan – Greek and Roman Empires
Evarne – Greek and Roman Empires
Eve – Near East
Evening Star – North America
Evening Star Lady – North America
Eveningstar of Wakaranga – Africa
Ewauna – North America
Ewe Goddesses, The. *See* The Cow Goddesses – Near East
Ewuraba – Africa
Eyra. *See* Eir – Northern Europe
Eyrgjafa – Northern Europe
Ey-vet'ne Kimtaran. *See* Tarn – Eastern Europe
Ezili – Africa
Ezili Freda Dahomey. *See* Ezili – Africa
Ezili Freda Dahomey. *See* Erzulie – Central America and Mesoamerica
Ezili. *See* Erzulie – Central America and Mesoamerica
Ezilie-Freda-Dahomey. *See* Erzulie – Central America and Mesoamerica
Ezinu – Near East
Ezo Goddess – Far East
Ezum Mezum – Africa
Fa. *See* Gbadu and Minona – Africa
Fa'a'ipu – Oceania

Fa'ahotu – Oceania
Fachea – Western Europe
Fadza-mama – Eastern Europe
Fai. *See* Fai malie – Oceania
Fai malie – Oceania
Fai tama'i – Oceania
Faiga'a – Oceania
Faingaa – Oceania
Fairies, The – Western Europe
Fakahotu – Oceania
Falerina – Western Europe
Fama – Greek and Roman Empires
Fand – Western Europe
Fanga – Oceania
Fangge – Northern Europe
Fangge – Western Europe
Faraony. *See* The Navki – Eastern Europe
Fata – Greek and Roman Empires
Fata Alcina – Greek and Roman Empires
Fata Morgana – Greek and Roman Empires
Fata Morgana. *See* Morgan Le Fay – Western Europe
Fata'a koka – Oceania
Fates, The. *See* Parcae – Greek and Roman Empires
Fatit, The – Eastern Europe
Fatua. *See* Bona Dea, Fauna – Greek and Roman Empires
Fatuella. *See* Fauna – Greek and Roman Empires
Fatum – Greek and Roman Empires
Faula. *See* Fauna – Greek and Roman Empires
Faumea – Oceania
Fauna – Greek and Roman Empires
Faurourou – Oceania
Fays, The – Western Europe
Fea – Western Europe
Febris – Greek and Roman Empires
Februa – Greek and Roman Empires
Februlis – Greek and Roman Empires
Fecunditas – Greek and Roman Empires
Fecundity Lady – Far East
Fedelm – Western Europe
Fedelma – Western Europe
Fefafa – Oceania
Fehuluni – Oceania
Fei, Lady – Far East
Feithline – Western Europe
Felicitas – Greek and Roman Empires
Female Spectres, The – Southeast Asia
Feminine Powers, The – Near East
Feng Po – Far East
Feng Popo. *See* Feng Po – Far East
Fengi. *See* Fenja – Northern Europe
Fenja – Northern Europe
Fenua – Oceania
Fenya. *See* Fenja – Northern Europe
Feraŝti – Near East
Ferentina – Greek and Roman Empires
Feronia – Greek and Roman Empires
Fevroniia – Eastern Europe
Fflur – Western Europe
Fideal – Western Europe
Fides – Greek and Roman Empires
Fifth Hour Goddess – Egypt
Filia Vocis – Western Europe

Filia Vocis. *See* Filia Vocis, Western Europe – Near East
Fimmilinia – Northern Europe
Finbar. *See* Findbhair – Western Europe
Finchoem. *See* Findchaem – Western Europe
Findabar. *See* Findbhair – Western Europe
Findbar. *See* Findbhair – Western Europe
Findbhair – Western Europe
Findchaem – Western Europe
Finncaev – Western Europe
Finoguala. *See* Fionnuala – Western Europe
Fiongalla. *See* Fionnuala – Western Europe
Fionnuala – Western Europe
Firamodor – Western Europe
Fire Goddess, The – Oceania
Fire Mother – Eastern Europe
Fire Woman – Southeast Asia
Firebird, The – Eastern Europe
Firifiri 'aufau – Oceania
First Mothers – Central America and Mesoamerica
First Woman – South America
First Woman – Eastern Europe
First Woman – Oceania
First Woman – Southeast Asia
First Woman, The – Near East
First Women – Oceania
Five Sisters, The – North America
Fjorgyn – Northern Europe
Fland – Western Europe
Flidais – Western Europe
Flidhais. *See* Flidais – Western Europe
Flora – Greek and Roman Empires
Flower Goddesses – Far East
Fluona. *See* Fluonia – Greek and Roman Empires
Fluonia – Greek and Roman Empires
Fluvinoa. *See* Fluonia – Greek and Roman Empires
Foam Mother – North America
Foam Woman – North America
Fódhla. *See* Fótla – Western Europe
Fodla. *See* Fótla – Western Europe
Fohsu – Africa
Folla – Northern Europe
Fonn – Northern Europe
Fons – Greek and Roman Empires
Forna – Greek and Roman Empires
Fors – Greek and Roman Empires
Fortuna – Greek and Roman Empires
Foseta – Northern Europe
Fótla – Western Europe
Four Uaipu Cow Goddesses – Egypt
Fox Earth Goddess – North America
Fox Moon Goddess – North America
Frasasti – Near East
Frau Berchta. *See* Berchta – Northern Europe
Frau Berta. *See* Berchta – Northern Europe
Frau Fiuk – Northern Europe
Frau Frigg – Northern Europe
Frau Gode – Northern Europe
Frau Holle. *See* Holle – Northern Europe

Frau Minne. *See* Minne – Northern Europe
Frau Saelde. *See* Saelde – Northern Europe
Frau Salida. *See* Saelde – Northern Europe
Frau Welt – Northern Europe
Fraud – Greek and Roman Empires
Fraus. *See* Fraud – Greek and Roman Empires
Fravakain – Near East
Fravashis, The – Near East
Freitag – Northern Europe
Freya. *See* Freyja – Northern Europe
Freydis – Northern Europe
Freyia. *See* Freyja – Northern Europe
Freyja – Northern Europe
Fri. *See* Frigga – Northern Europe
Fria – Northern Europe
Friagabi – Northern Europe
Frick. *See* Frau Fiuk – Northern Europe
Fricka. *See* Frigga – Northern Europe
Frid – Northern Europe
Frig. *See* Frigga – Northern Europe
Frigg. *See* Frigga – Northern Europe
Frigga – Northern Europe
Friis Avfruvva. *See* Akkruva – Eastern Europe
Frija. *See* Frigga – Northern Europe
Frimla – Northern Europe
Frog Princess. *See* Dzelarhons – North America
Frog Woman – North America
Frost Goddess – Far East
Frovida – Western Europe
Frowa. *See* Frua – Northern Europe
Frua – Northern Europe
Fšeratu – Near East
Fuamhnach. *See* Fuamnach – Western Europe
Fuamnach – Western Europe
Fuchi. *See* Fuji – Far East
Fue – Oceania
Fuji – Far East
Fulgora – Greek and Roman Empires
Fulla – Northern Europe
Fulu'ulaalematato – Oceania
Funadama-sama – Far East
Funan – Southeast Asia
Fupao – Far East
Furiae. *See* The Furies – Greek and Roman Empires
Furies, The – Greek and Roman Empires
Furina – Greek and Roman Empires
Furrina. *See* Furina – Greek and Roman Empires
Fute-mimi-no-kami – Far East
Fuwch Frech – Western Europe
Fuwch Gyfeilioru – Western Europe
Fuzhou Princess – Far East
Fylgia. *See* Fylgja – Northern Europe
Fylgir, The – Northern Europe
Fylgja – Northern Europe
Fylgukona – Northern Europe
Fyorgyn. *See* Fjorgyn – Northern Europe
Gabeta. *See* Gabija – Eastern Europe
Gabieta. *See* Gabija – Eastern Europe
Gabija – Eastern Europe
Gabjauja – Eastern Europe

Gadjari. *See* Kadjari – Oceania
Gaea – Greek and Roman Empires
Gaeeochos – Greek and Roman Empires
Gaende'sonk – North America
Ga-go-sa Ho-nun-nas-tase-ta, The – North America
Gahondjidahonk – North America
Gaia. *See* Gaea – Greek and Roman Empires
Gaiyun – Southeast Asia
Gajalakshmi. *See* Lakshmi – Indian Subcontinent
Galadevi – Indian Subcontinent
Galatea – Greek and Roman Empires
Galateia. *See* Galatea – Greek and Roman Empires
Galaxaura – Greek and Roman Empires
Galaxaure. *See* Galaxaura – Greek and Roman Empires
Galene – Greek and Roman Empires
Gallathaea. *See* Galateia – Greek and Roman Empires
Gamelia – Greek and Roman Empires
Gan Gaur – Indian Subcontinent
Ganabuada – Oceania
Ganapatihrdaya – Indian Subcontinent
Ganda First Woman – Africa
Gandha. *See* Dri-chha-ma, The Himalaya – Indian Subcontinent
Gandhari – Indian Subcontinent
Gandharvadatta – Indian Subcontinent
Gandharvi – Indian Subcontinent
Gandharvis – Indian Subcontinent
Gandhema. *See* Dri-chha-ma – The Himalaya
Gandini – Indian Subcontinent
Ganesani – Indian Subcontinent
Ganga – Indian Subcontinent
Ganga Devi – Indian Subcontinent
Gangaji – Indian Subcontinent
Gangamma – Indian Subcontinent
Gangammal – Indian Subcontinent
Gangkar Shame – The Himalaya
Ganglot – Northern Europe
Gangs-dkar-sha-med – The Himalaya
Ganis – Eastern Europe
Ganna – Africa
Ganymeda. *See* Hebe – Greek and Roman Empires
Ganymede. *See* Hebe. Alternate form: Ganymeda – Greek and Roman Empires
Ganzir. *See* Ereshkigal – Near East
Gao Lanying – Far East
Gaomei. *See* Nüwa – Far East
Gaon Mataa. *See* Ujali – Indian Subcontinent
Gara Satamai – Indian Subcontinent
Garbh Ogh – Western Europe
Garbhog. *See* Carravogue – Western Europe
Garita – Indian Subcontinent
Gar-ma – The Himalaya
Garmangabi – Northern Europe
Gasain Era – Indian Subcontinent
Gashan-ki. *See* Damkina – Near East
Gasmu – Near East
Gatamdug – Near East
Gate-keeping Goddesses – Egypt
Ga-tum-dug – Near East

Gau – Indian Subcontinent
Gaude. See Gode – Northern Europe
Gaue – Northern Europe
Gaueteaki – Oceania
Gauri – Indian Subcontinent
Gauri Sankara – Indian Subcontinent
Gauris. See Gauri – Indian Subcontinent
Gautami. See Durga, Kripi, and
   Rakshasi – Indian Subcontinent
Gauteaki. See Gaueteaki – Oceania
Gavariamma – Indian Subcontinent
Gayak, The – Southeast Asia
Gayatri – Indian Subcontinent
Gaygayoma – Southeast Asia
Gbadu – Africa
Gbenebeka – Africa
Gcagcile – Africa
Ge. See Gaea – Greek and Roman
   Empires
Ge. See Ghe – Near East
Ge Gu – Far East
Gea – Near East
Gebjon – Northern Europe
Geburah – Western Europe
Gedir. See Gerda – Northern Europe
Gedulah – Western Europe
Gefion – Northern Europe
Gefjun – Northern Europe
Gefn. See Frejya – Northern Europe
Geirahod – Northern Europe
Geirolul – Northern Europe
Gello – Greek and Roman Empires
Gelou. See Lilith – Near East
Gemeter. See Demeter – Greek and
   Roman Empires
Gendenwitha – North America
Gendui Lanyut – Southeast Asia
Genea – Near East
Genetaska – North America
Genetri – Greek and Roman Empires
Genetyllides, The – Greek and Roman
   Empires
Genetyllis – Greek and Roman Empires
Genita Mana – Greek and Roman
   Empires
Geniti Glinne, The – Western Europe
Gennaides. See The Genetyllides –
   Greek and Roman Empires
Gentle Annie – Western Europe
Gephen – Near East
Gerd. See Gerda – Northern Europe
Gerda – Northern Europe
Gerdr. See Gerda – Northern Europe
Gerth. See Gerda – Northern Europe
Gerthr. See Gerda – Northern Europe
Gerutha – Northern Europe
Geshtin – Near East
Geshtinanna. See Geshtin and
   Gestinanna – Near East
Gestinanna – Near East
Geush Urvan – Near East
Gevurah – Western Europe
Geyaguga – North America
Ghar Jenti – Indian Subcontinent
Ghasmari. See Dark-Green Ghasmari –
   The Himalaya
Ghatchindan – Indian Subcontinent
Ghe – Near East
Gheareagain. See Carravogue –
   Western Europe

Ghihadevatas. See Devatas – Indian
   Subcontinent
Ghirdhima. See gLu-ma Ghirdhima –
   The Himalaya
Ghoshinis. See Ghosinis – Indian
   Subcontinent
Ghosinis – Indian Subcontinent
Ghost-Face-Woman – North America
Ghritachi. See Ghrtaci – Indian
   Subcontinent
Ghrtaci – Indian Subcontinent
Ghuls – Indian Subcontinent
Gialp. See Gjalp – Northern Europe
Giane – Greek and Roman Empires
Gidne. See Ganis – Eastern Europe
Gigantia – Greek and Roman Empires
Gillagriene – Western Europe
Gilou. See Lilith – Near East
Giltine – Eastern Europe
Gimokodan – Southeast Asia
Ginoo moong – Indian Subcontinent
Giolla Gréine – Western Europe
Giptes, The – Northern Europe
Girija. See Parvati – Indian Subcontinent
Girinatha – Southeast Asia
Giriputri – Southeast Asia
Girl Twin of Mithuna – Indian
   Subcontinent
Gita. See gLu-ma Ghirdhima – The
   Himalaya
Gitir – Southeast Asia
Gjalp – Northern Europe
Glaisrig – Western Europe
Glaistig – Western Europe
Glas – Western Europe
Glas Gaibleann – Western Europe
Glasgavlen – Western Europe
Glauce – Greek and Roman Empires
Glaucia – Greek and Roman Empires
Glauconome – Greek and Roman
   Empires
Glaucopis – Greek and Roman Empires
Glauke – Greek and Roman Empires
Glaukonome – Greek and Roman
   Empires
Glaukopis – Greek and Roman Empires
Glisma. See Glispa – North America
Glispa – North America
Glog-bdag-mo – The Himalaya
gLu-ma Ghirdhima – The Himalaya
Glut – Northern Europe
Gna – Northern Europe
Gnaa. See Gna – Northern Europe
gNam-Iha-byang-sman-mthing-gi-go-zu
   -can – The Himalaya
gNam-Iha dkar-mo – The Himalaya
gNam-lcags-thog-'bebs-ma – The
   Himalaya
gNam-phyi-gung-rgyal. See
   A-phyi-gung-rgyal – The Himalaya
Gnas, The – Indian Subcontinent
Gnaski – North America
Gnowee – Oceania
Godasiyo – North America
Godavari – Indian Subcontinent
Goddess-greatly-beloved-with-red-hair –
   Egypt
Goddess-joined-unto-life-with-flowing-h
   air – Egypt
Goddess of Papremis – Egypt

Goddess "I" – Central America and
   Mesoamerica
Goddess "O" – Central America and
   Mesoamerica
Goddesses of the Eastern and Western
   Ocean, The – North America
Gode. See Frau Gode – Northern Europe
Goga – Oceania
Gogome. See Yomo-tsu-shiko-me – Far
   East
Go-gome-tha-na. See Kokumthena –
   North America
Gogyeng So Wuhti – North America
Goiko. See Ilazki – Western Europe
Gokarmo – The Himalaya
Gol – Northern Europe
Goli – Northern Europe
Goll. See Gol – Northern Europe
Gollveig. See Gullveig – Northern
   Europe
Gomaj – Indian Subcontinent
Gondul – Northern Europe
Gonlod. See Gunnlöd – Northern
   Europe
Gonti – Indian Subcontinent
Gontiyalamma. See Gonti – Indian
   Subcontinent
Good Sight Lady – Far East
Goolagaya – Oceania
Goonaroo – Oceania
Goose Goddess – Egypt
Gopis, The – Indian Subcontinent
Gopya – Indian Subcontinent
Gorddu – Western Europe
Gorgons, The – Greek and Roman
   Empires
Gorgopa – Greek and Roman Empires
Gorska Makva – Eastern Europe
Gosae-era – Indian Subcontinent
Gos-dhar-mo. See Gokarmo – The
   Himalaya
Gös-dkar-mo. See Gokarmo – The
   Himalaya
Gos-ster-ma-dkar-mo – The Himalaya
Gouri. See Gauri and Isani – Indian
   Subcontinent
Graces, The. See The Charites – Greek
   and Roman Empires
Graeae, The – Greek and Roman
   Empires
Grahamatrka – The Himalaya
Grahis, The – Indian Subcontinent
Graiai. See The Graeae – Greek and
   Roman Empires
Grainne – Western Europe
Gramadevatas, The – Indian
   Subcontinent
Grande Brigette. See Brigette – Central
   America and Mesoamerica
Grande Ezili – Central America and
   Mesoamerica
Grandmother – North America
Grandmother Datura. See Momoy –
   North America
Grandmother Earth – North America
Grandmother Moon – North America
Grandmother of Nava – North America
Grandmother Spider – North America
Grania. See Grainne – Western Europe

Gratiae, The – Greek and Roman Empires

Greedy Woman – Africa

Green Deer-headed Wealth-guardian Goddess – The Himalaya

Green Dolma. *See* Bribsun – The Himalaya

Green Tara. *See* Bribsun and Khadiravani Tara – The Himalaya

Greenish-black Elephant-headed Big-nosed Goddess – The Himalaya

Greenish-black Leopard-headed Great Goddess – The Himalaya

Greenish-black Serpent-headed Mystic Goddess – The Himalaya

Greenish-black Vulture-headed Eater Goddess – The Himalaya

Greenland Sun Goddess – North America

Grhadevi – Indian Subcontinent

Grhalaksmi – Indian Subcontinent

Grian – Western Europe

Grid – Northern Europe

Griep – Northern Europe

Grihadeva – Indian Subcontinent

Grilya Burhin – Indian Subcontinent

Grimhild – Northern Europe

Griselicae Nymphae, The – Western Europe

Grismadevi – Indian Subcontinent

Gritha – Northern Europe

Grizzly Bear Mother – North America

Groa – Northern Europe

Groad. *See* Groa – Northern Europe

Grogopa. *See* Gorgopa – Greek and Roman Empires

Grydat – Northern Europe

gshin-rje-mo – The Himalaya

gSum-brag-ma – The Himalaya

Guabance – Central America and Mesoamerica

Guabonito – Central America and Mesoamerica

Guacarapita. *See* Atabei – Central America and Mesoamerica

Gu-lang. *See* Pashupatî – The Himalaya

Guamaonocon – Central America and Mesoamerica

Guanhumara. *See* Gwenhwyfar – Western Europe

Guanyin – Far East

Guatauva – Central America and Mesoamerica

Gubarra – Near East

Gudiri-mumi – Eastern Europe

Gudr – Northern Europe

Gudrun – Northern Europe

Gudyri-mumy. *See* Gudiri-mumi – Eastern Europe

Guédé l'Oraille – Central America and Mesoamerica

Guede Masaka – Central America and Mesoamerica

Guener. *See* Gwen – Western Europe

Guenever. *See* Gwenhwyfar – Western Europe

Guenhuvara. *See* Gwenhwyfar – Western Europe

Guggulu – Indian Subcontinent

Guiling Shenamu – Far East

Guimazoa. *See* Atabei – Central America and Mesoamerica

Guinevere. *See* Gwenhwyfar – Western Europe

Gula – Near East

Gula Bau. *See* Gula – Near East

Gulanundoidj. *See* Mimaliwu – Oceania

Gullveig – Northern Europe

Gulsalia Mata – Indian Subcontinent

Gulses, The – Near East

Gulweig-Hoder. *See* Gullveig – Northern Europe

Gum Lin – Far East

Gumshea – Near East

Gunabibi. *See* Kunapipi – Oceania

Gundhary. *See* Gandhari – Indian Subcontinent

Gung. *See* Ganga – Indian Subcontinent

Gunga. *See* Ganga – Indian Subcontinent

Gunggaranggara, The – Oceania

Gungu – Indian Subcontinent

Gunnlauth – Northern Europe

Gunnlöd – Northern Europe

Gunnr – Northern Europe

Guodeng – Far East

Gur. *See* Bau – Near East

Guzhak – Near East

Gvenn Teir Bronn – Western Europe

Gvenour – Western Europe

Gwen – Western Europe

Gwenhwyfar – Western Europe

Gwenhwyvar. *See* Gwenhwyfar – Western Europe

Gwrach y Rhibyn – Western Europe

Gwragedd Annwn, The – Western Europe

Gwyar – Western Europe

Gwyllion, The – Western Europe

Gyangya'di – Africa

Gyhldeptis – North America

'Gying-dkar-ma – The Himalaya

Gymnasia – Greek and Roman Empires

Ha lo – Oceania

Ha pu'u – Oceania

Haamata kee – Oceania

Ha'apua 'inanea – Oceania

Habetrot – Western Europe

Habonde – Western Europe

Habonde. *See* Habondia – Northern Europe

Habondia – Northern Europe

Habondia. *See* Habonde – Western Europe

Hachi-kazuki-hime – Far East

Hacilar Goddess – Near East

Hada Bai – Indian Subcontinent

Hadakai – Indian Subcontinent

Hadphoran Marhi – Indian Subcontinent

Haere awa'awa – Oceania

Haero. *See* Merope – Greek and Roman Empires

Hag – Western Europe

Hag of Beara. *See* Cailleach Beara, Bera – Western Europe

Hag of Iarnvid. *See* Gullveig – Northern Europe

Hagar – Egypt

Hagno – Greek and Roman Empires

Hahai-i Wuhti – North America

Ha-Ha-Uh – North America

Ha-Ha-Whu Okya. *See* Mukikwe Okya – North America

Ha'i – Oceania

Ha'i wahine – Oceania

Haialilaqs – North America

Haimavati. *See* Devi – Indian Subcontinent

Ha'ina kolo – Oceania

Haine – Africa

Hainuwele – Oceania

Hainuwele – Southeast Asia

Hak – Egypt

Haka – Oceania

Haka Lasi – North America

Hakahotu – Oceania

Hakini – Indian Subcontinent

Hakirimaurea – Oceania

Hakulaq – North America

Hakumani – Oceania

Hala – Near East

Halalamanu – Oceania

Halcyon. *See* Alcyone – Greek and Roman Empires

Halcyone. *See* Alcyone – Greek and Roman Empires

Hale lehua. *See* Moana nui ka lehua – Oceania

Halia – Greek and Roman Empires

Haliae, The – Greek and Roman Empires

Halimede – Greek and Roman Empires

Hallgerda – Northern Europe

Halmssuitta – Near East

Halsodyne – Greek and Roman Empires

Haltia – Eastern Europe

Hamadryades, The – Greek and Roman Empires

Hamadryads. *See* Hamadryades – Greek and Roman Empires

Hamadryas – Greek and Roman Empires

Hamaelides, The – Greek and Roman Empires

Hambarus, The – Near East

Hamingja – Northern Europe

Hamsadhirudha. *See* Sarasvati – Indian Subcontinent

Hamsika – Indian Subcontinent

Hamuri – Oceania

Hamuxa. *See* Tatei Hamuxa – Central America and Mesoamerica

Ham-vareti – Near East

Han – North America

Hana – Oceania

Hānai'ia ka malama – Oceania

Hanan – Southeast Asia

Hanata – Near East

Hanau – Oceania

Hana-yama-hime. *See* Hani-yasu-bime-no-kami – Far East

Hanitemau – Oceania

Hani-yasu-bime-no-kami – Far East

Haniyasu-hime. *See* Hani-yasu-bime-no-kami – Far East

Hannahannas – Near East

Hano – North America

Hano Mana – North America

Hanua – Oceania

Hanwasuit – Near East
Hanwi – North America
Haoa'oa – Oceania
Hā'oa'oa – Oceania
Hap Cow, The – Egypt
Hāpai – Oceania
Hapantili – Near East
Hap-tcheserts – Egypt
Harahvaiti – Indian Subcontinent
Haramara. See Tatei Haramara –
    Central America and Mesoamerica
Harappan Goddesses – Indian
    Subcontinent
Harataunga – Oceania
Harbadevi – Indian Subcontinent
Hardahin. See Bai Haldahin – Indian
    Subcontinent
Hardgrep – Northern Europe
Hari – Indian Subcontinent
Haria – Oceania
Hariasa – Northern Europe
Harimela – Northern Europe
Harimella – Northern Europe
Harini – Indian Subcontinent
Haritei-mo. See Helidi – Far East
Hariti – Indian Subcontinent
Harits, The – Indian Subcontinent
Hariyali – Indian Subcontinent
Hariyari Mata – Indian Subcontinent
Harmonia – Greek and Roman Empires
Harpies, The – Greek and Roman
    Empires
Harrakoi Dikko – Africa
Harriasa. See Hariasa – Northern
    Europe
Harsiddh Mata – Indian Subcontinent
Harurai Chatutai. See Atavish – North
    America
Has-gueme – North America
Hash-inau-uk-kamui – Far East
Hashat – Near East
Hashepsowe. See Hatshepsut – Egypt
Hashinau-kor-kamui – Far East
Hashinau-uk-kamui. See
    Hash-inau-uk-kamui – Far East
Hasinais Goddesses, The – North
    America
Hast – Egypt
Hastakamala. See Lakshmi – Indian
    Subcontinent
Hastimukha. See Jyestha – Indian
    Subcontinent
Hastseoltoi – North America
Hatai Wugti. See Hatai Wuhti – North
    America
Hatai Wuhti – North America
Hatasu. See Hatshepsut – Egypt
Hatcher, The – North America
Hatepinu – Near East
Hathay – Indian Subcontinent
Hathor – Egypt
Hathors, The – Egypt
H'ativa – North America
Hat-mehi – Egypt
Hat-mehit. See Hatmehit – Egypt
Hatmehit – Egypt
Hatschihime. See Hachi-kazuki-hime –
    Far East
Hatshepsut – Egypt
Hatshopsiti. See Hatshepsut – Egypt

Hatti Throne Goddess – Near East
Hatu atu tupun – Oceania
Hatuibwari – Oceania
Hau lani – Oceania
Hau ola – Oceania
Hau wahine – Oceania
Hau wahine mo'o. See Hau wahine –
    Oceania
Hauarani – Oceania
Hauhet – Egypt
Hauket. See Hauhet – Egypt
Hauliparua, The – Oceania
Haumea – Oceania
Haumei – Oceania
Haumia – Oceania
Haunga roa – Oceania
Haungaroa. See Haunga roa – Oceania
Haunu'u – Oceania
Haurvatāt – Near East
Hautse Kupúri. See Tāté Hautse
    Kupúri – Central America and
    Mesoamerica
Hava – Oceania
Havaafru. See Avfruvva – Eastern
    Europe
Havea lolo fonua – Oceania
Havfru – Northern Europe
Havfrue. See Havfru – Northern Europe
Havirbhu – Indian Subcontinent
Ha-Wha-Whoa. See Mukikwe Okya –
    North America
Hawichyepam Maapuch – North
    America
Haya-aki-tsu-hime-no-kami – Far East
Hayicanak. See Hayicanako – North
    America
Hayicanako – North America
Hayoołkaał Asdzą́ą́ – North America
He Ku – Far East
He Xiangu – Far East
He. See Xi Wang mu – Far East
He' Wuhti. See Hé-é-e – North America
Hea – Near East
Heartha – Northern Europe
Heavy Woman – North America
Heba. See Hebat – Near East
Hebat – Near East
Hebatu. See Hebat – Near East
Hebe – Greek and Roman Empires
Heb-i – Egypt
Hecaerge – Greek and Roman Empires
Hecate – Near East
Hecate – Greek and Roman Empires
Hedetet – Egypt
Hedrun. See Heidrun – Northern
    Europe
Hé-é-e – North America
Hegemone – Greek and Roman Empires
Hegetoria – Greek and Roman Empires
Heh – Egypt
Hehea Mana. See Heheya Kachin'
    Mana – North America
Hehet – Egypt
Heheya Kachin' Mana – North America
Hehut. See Hauhet – Egypt
Heid – Northern Europe
Heidrun – Northern Europe
Heimarmene – Greek and Roman
    Empires

Heimarmene. See Eimaramene – Near
    East
Heitha. See Heartha – Northern Europe
Heka. See Hak – Egypt
Heke heki i papa – Oceania
Hekenth – Egypt
Heket – Egypt
Hekoolas – North America
Hekt. See Heqet – Egypt
Hel – Northern Europe
Hela. See Hel – Northern Europe
Helen – Greek and Roman Empires
Helena – Greek and Roman Empires
He-li Di. See Hariti – Indian
    Subcontinent
Helia – Greek and Roman Empires
Heliadae, The – Greek and Roman
    Empires
Helice – Greek and Roman Empires
Heliconides, The – Greek and Roman
    Empires
Helidi – Far East
Helike – Greek and Roman Empires
Hella – Northern Europe
Helle – Greek and Roman Empires
Helliougmounis – Western Europe
Hellotia – Greek and Roman Empires
Helmund – Near East
Heloha – North America
Hema – Oceania
Hemambika – Indian Subcontinent
Hemantadevi – Indian Subcontinent
Hemaprabha – Indian Subcontinent
Hemera – Greek and Roman Empires
Hemeresia – Greek and Roman Empires
Hemis Kachin' Mana – North America
Hemis Mana. See Hemis Kachin'
    Mana – North America
Hemithea – Greek and Roman Empires
Hemokatsiki. See Ahe'a – North
    America
Hemsut, The – Egypt
Hemuset. See The Hemsut – Egypt
Hemushikwe Okya – North America
Henemet-em-anh-annuit – Egypt
Heng E. See Chang E – Far East
Heng O. See Chang E – Far East
Henioche – Greek and Roman Empires
Hentet-arqiu – Egypt
Henti – Near East
Hent-nut-s – Egypt
Henwen – Western Europe
Heos. See Aurora, Eos – Greek and
    Roman Empires
Heoto Mana – North America
Hepat – Near East
Hepatu. See Hebat – Near East
Hepeue – Oceania
Hepit. See Hebat and Hepat – Near East
Heptapora – Greek and Roman Empires
Heptet – Egypt
Heqet – Egypt
Heqt. See Heqet – Egypt
Heqtit. See Heqet – Egypt
Hequet. See Heqet – Egypt
Hequit. See Heqet – Egypt
Hera – Greek and Roman Empires
Hercyna – Greek and Roman Empires
Her-fiotr. See Herfjotur – Northern
    Europe

Herfjotur – Northern Europe
Herit – Egypt
Herkyna. *See* Hercyna – Greek and
  Roman Empires
Hermiona. *See* Harmonia – Greek and
  Roman Empires
Hermione – Greek and Roman Empires
Herse – Greek and Roman Empires
Her-sha-s – Egypt
Her-tep-aha-her-neb-s – Egypt
Her-tept – Egypt
Hert-erman – Egypt
Hertha – Northern Europe
Hert-ketit-s – Egypt
Heru-pa-kaut – Egypt
Heru-sekha – Egypt
Hervor – Northern Europe
Hesa – Egypt
Hesamut. *See* Reret – Egypt
Hesat. *See* Hesa – Egypt
Hesi. *See* Isis – Egypt
Hespera – Greek and Roman Empires
Hesperia. *See* Asterope, Hespera –
  Greek and Roman Empires
Hesperides, The – Greek and Roman
  Empires
Hesperie. *See* Hespera – Greek and
  Roman Empires
Hesperis – Greek and Roman Empires
Hestia – Greek and Roman Empires
Hetemitet – Egypt
Hetep-sekhus – Egypt
Hetepet. *See* Hetpet – Egypt
Hetethlokya – North America
Hether. *See* Hathor – Egypt
Het-hert – Egypt
Het-kau-nebt-er-tcher – Egypt
Hetpet – Egypt
Hettsui-no-kami – Far East
Hetu ahin – Oceania
Heurippe – Greek and Roman Empires
Hexe, Die – Northern Europe
Hi asa – Oceania
Hiata i reia. *See* Hi'iaka i reia – Oceania
Hiata i te pori o pere. *See* Hi'iaka i te
  pori o pere and Hi'iaka opio –
  Oceania
Hiata kaalawamaka. *See* Hi'iaka ka'a
  lawa maka – Oceania
Hiata noho lani. *See* Hi'iaka noho lani –
  Oceania
Hiata opio. *See* Hi'iaka opio – Oceania
Hiata ta bu enaena. *See* Hi'iaka tapu
  'ena'ena – Oceania
Hiata tapu enaena. *See* Hi'iaka tapu
  'ena'ena – Oceania
Hiata tarei'ia. *See* Hi'iaka tarei'a –
  Oceania
Hiata wawahi lani. *See* Hi'iaka wawahi
  lani – Oceania
Hidaba – Near East
Hidatsa Buffalo Woman – North
  America
Hidimba – Indian Subcontinent
Hidimva. *See* Hidimba – Indian
  Subcontinent
Hihankara – North America
Hi-haya-bi-no-kami. *See*
  Hi-no-haya-hi-no-mikoto – Far East
Hihikalani – Oceania

Hi'i hia – Oceania
Hi'iaka – Oceania
Hi'iaka i ka poli o Pele. *See* Hi'iaka,
  Hi'iaka i te pori o pere – Oceania
Hi'iaka i ka pua'ena'ena – Oceania
Hi'iaka i ka'ale moe – Oceania
Hi'iaka i ka'ale po'i – Oceania
Hi'iaka i ka'ale'i – Oceania
Hi'iaka i ka'ale'uweke – Oceania
Hi'iaka i reia – Oceania
Hi'iaka i te pori o pere – Oceania
Hi'iaka ka lei'ia. *See* Hi'iaka tarei'a –
  Oceania
Hi'iaka ka'a lawa maka – Oceania
Hi'iaka kapu 'ena'ena. *See* Hi'iaka tapu
  ena'ena – Oceania
Hi'iaka makole wawahi wa'a – Oceania
Hi'iaka noho lae – Oceania
Hi'iaka noho lani – Oceania
Hi'iaka opio – Oceania
Hi'iaka tapu'ena'ena – Oceania
Hi'iaka tarei'a – Oceania
Hi'iaka wawahi lani – Oceania
Hi'ilei – Oceania
Hi-kawa-hime – Far East
Hikuleo – Oceania
Hila – North America
Hilaeira – Greek and Roman Empires
Hilaira. *See* Hilaeira – Greek and
  Roman Empires
Hilara. *See* Hilaeira – Greek and Roman
  Empires
Hild – Northern Europe
Hilda. *See* Hel – Northern Europe
Hilde. *See* Hild – Northern Europe
Hildr. *See* Hild, Hildur – Northern
  Europe
Hildur – Northern Europe
Hilili Okya – North America
Hima – Indian Subcontinent
Himalia – Greek and Roman Empires
Himalis – Greek and Roman Empires
Himbuto. *See* Uadjet – Egypt
Hime-jima – Far East
Himera. *See* Hemera – Greek and
  Roman Empires
Himeropa – Greek and Roman Empires
Hime-shima. *See* Hime-jima – Far East
Hime-tatara-isuke-yori-hime. *See*
  Hoto-tatara-isusuki-hime-no-mikoto –
  Far East
Hime-tatara-isuzu-himen-no-mikoto.
  See
  Hoto-tatara-isusuki-hime-no-mikoto –
  Far East
Himsa – Indian Subcontinent
Hina – Oceania
Hina 'ea – Oceania
Hina 'ere'ere manu'a – Oceania
Hina hanaia'i ka malama – Oceania
Hina hele – Oceania
Hina ka'alualu moana – Oceania
Hina kauhara – Oceania
Hina ke ahi – Oceania
Hina ke ka'ā. *See* Hina'i ke kā – Oceania
Hina ke kai – Oceania
Hina kuku kapa – Oceania
Hina kuluua – Oceania
Hina lau limu kala – Oceania
Hina lei haamoa – Oceania

Hina lua'i koa – Oceania
Hina ma nou rua'e – Oceania
Hina mahuia – Oceania
Hina mataone – Oceania
Hina nui te pō. *See* Hine nui te pō –
  Oceania
Hina nui te'a'ara – Oceania
Hina nui te'ara'ara – Oceania
Hina oio – Oceania
Hina 'ōpū hala ko'a – Oceania
Hina papa i kua – Oceania
Hina puku 'ai – Oceania
Hina puku i'a – Oceania
Hina tahu tahu – Oceania
Hina tau miha – Oceania
Hina te 'a'ara – Oceania
Hina te 'iva'iva – Oceania
Hina tūa tua – Oceania
Hina tuafuaga – Oceania
Hina 'ulu 'ōhi'a – Oceania
Hina uri – Oceania
Hina'a rauriki – Oceania
Hina'ai ka malama – Oceania
Hi-naga-hime – Far East
Hina'i a'a i te marama – Oceania
Hina'i ka'uluau – Oceania
Hina'i ke ahi – Oceania
Hina'i ke kā – Oceania
Hina'ōpū hala ko'a – Oceania
Hi-narashi-bime – Far East
Hina-teri-nukata-bichi-o-ikochini-no-
  kami – Far East
Hina-tui te a'ara. *See* Hina nui te'a'ara –
  Oceania
Hindi. *See* Durga – Indian Subcontinent
Hindira. *See* Durga – Indian
  Subcontinent
Hine – Oceania
Hine a te po – Oceania
Hine ahiahi – Oceania
Hine āhua – Oceania
Hine ahuone – Oceania
Hine ahupapa – Oceania
Hine aotea – Oceania
Hine apo hia – Oceania
Hine ata – Oceania
Hine aterepō – Oceania
Hine i tapapauta – Oceania
Hine i tapeka – Oceania
Hine i tau ira – Oceania
Hine i te huhi – Oceania
Hine itaitai – Oceania
Hine kaikomako – Oceania
Hine kapua – Oceania
Hine maki moe – Oceania
Hine makohu – Oceania
Hine makura – Oceania
Hine māru – Oceania
Hine maunga – Oceania
Hine moa – Oceania
Hine moana – Oceania
Hine nui o te kawa – Oceania
Hine nui te pō – Oceania
Hine one – Oceania
Hine piripiri – Oceania
Hine popo – Oceania
Hine pūpūmainaua – Oceania
Hine rakatai – Oceania
Hine rau wharangi. *See* Hine
  tītamauri – Oceania

Hine raumati – Oceania
Hine ruaki moe – Oceania
Hine takurua – Oceania
Hine te aparangi – Oceania
Hine te iwaiwa – Oceania
Hine te kākara – Oceania
Hine te uria – Oceania
Hine tengarumoana. See Hine te iwaiwa – Oceania
Hine tītama – Oceania
Hine tītamauri – Oceania
Hine tū a hōanga – Oceania
Hine tū a maunga – Oceania
Hine tu a kirikiri – Oceania
Hine tu a tai – Oceania
Hine tu whenua – Oceania
Hine tua tai – Oceania
Hine turama – Oceania
Hine wai – Oceania
Hine waoriki – Oceania
Hine whaitiri – Oceania
Hinehaone – Oceania
Hinglajin – Indian Subcontinent
Hi-no-haya-hi-no-mikoto – Far East
Hinomahe-no-kami – Far East
Hintabaran – Oceania
Hintubuet – Oceania
Hiordis. See Hjordis – Northern Europe
Hiorthrimul – Northern Europe
Hippe – Greek and Roman Empires
Hippeia. See Hippe – Greek and Roman Empires
Hippia – Greek and Roman Empires
Hippias. See Hippia – Greek and Roman Empires
Hippo – Greek and Roman Empires
Hippocrenides, The – Greek and Roman Empires
Hippodameia – Greek and Roman Empires
Hippolaitis – Greek and Roman Empires
Hippona – Greek and Roman Empires
Hipponoe – Greek and Roman Empires
Hippothoe – Greek and Roman Empires
Hiqit. See Heqet – Egypt
Hiquit. See Heqet – Egypt
Hir Nineveh – Near East
Hira. See Lakshmi – Indian Subcontinent
Hiranyavaksas. See Vasudhara – Indian Subcontinent
Hirose-no-kawaai-no-kami. See Waka-uka-no-me-no-mikoto – Far East
Hisa-me, The – Far East
Hishikoyatsaspa – North America
Hit – Oceania
Hiyoi Kwan-non – Far East
Hjordis – Northern Europe
Hlamos, The – The Himalaya
Hlif – Northern Europe
Hlin – Northern Europe
H'llraru – Oceania
Hlock – Northern Europe
Hlodyn – Northern Europe
Hlokk. See Hlock – Northern Europe
Hloldyn. See Hlodyn – Northern Europe
Hlothyn. See Hlodyn – Northern Europe
Hludana – Northern Europe

Hnit Ma Daw. See Shwe Myet Hna – Southeast Asia
Hnitma Dawgyi – Southeast Asia
Hnoss – Northern Europe
Ho Hsien-ku. See He Xiangu – Far East
Ho Ku – Far East
Ho Sian Gu. See He Xiangu – Far East
Hoa make i ke kula – Oceania
Hoatziqui – Central America and Mesoamerica
Hod – Western Europe
Hod-zer-can-ma – The Himalaya
Hoh – Egypt
Hoho Mana – North America
Hoi tini – Oceania
Hokiolele – Oceania
Hokmah. See Chokmah – Western Europe
Hokoha Okya – North America
Hokohoko – Oceania
Hoku kau opae – Oceania
Hokyang Mana – North America
Holda – Northern Europe
Holdja. See Haltia – Eastern Europe
Holi – Indian Subcontinent
Holika – Indian Subcontinent
Holla – Northern Europe
Holle – Northern Europe
Holy Ghost, The. See the Holy Spirit – Near East
Holy Spirit, The – Near East
Honabe – Oceania
Hongak – North America
Hongatar – Eastern Europe
Hongluan Xingjun – Far East
Honoured High Mistress – Eastern Europe
Ho'o hoku i ka lani – Oceania
Hopi Shalako Mana – North America
Hōpoe – Oceania
Hora – Greek and Roman Empires
Horae, The – Greek and Roman Empires
Horai. See The Horae – Greek and Roman Empires
Horchia. See Aretia – Near East
Hore – Near East
Horit – Egypt
Horkeu-kamui – Far East
Horme – Greek and Roman Empires
Horn – Northern Europe
Horo Mana – North America
Horo. See Hoku kau opae – Oceania
Horokariyep – Far East
Horotata – Oceania
Horsel – Northern Europe
Horsel. See Ursula – Eastern Europe
Horta – Greek and Roman Empires
Hosia – Greek and Roman Empires
Hostilina – Greek and Roman Empires
Hotogov Mailgan – Eastern Europe
Hoto-tatara-isusuki-hime-no-mikoto – Far East
Hotra – Indian Subcontinent
Hottentot Mother Goddess – Africa
Hotu – Oceania
Hotukura – Oceania
Hou heana – Oceania
Hou T'u Kuo Huang. See Houtu Guohuang – Far East

Hou Tu Nainai – Far East
Hou Tu. See Hou Tu Nainai and Hu Tu – Far East
Houmea – Oceania
Houri, The – Near East
Houtu Guohuang – Far East
Hov-ava – Eastern Europe
How Kung. See Hoy Kong – Far East
Howanmata – Indian Subcontinent
Ho-Wha-Whoa. See Mukikwe Okya – North America
Hoy Kong – Far East
Hphreng-ba-ma – The Himalaya
Hpi Bi Yaw – Southeast Asia
Hrafn – Northern Europe
Hrede – Northern Europe
Hri – Indian Subcontinent
Hrist – Northern Europe
Hsi Ho. See Xi Hou – Far East
Hsi Shih. See Xi Shi – Far East
Hsi Wang Mu. See Xi Wangmu – Far East
Hsiang, Lady. See Xiang, Lady – Far East
Hsieh Jên Hsing Chün. See Xieren Xingjun – Far East
Hsieh, Lady. See Xie, Lady – Far East
Hsi-ling Shih. See Xiling Shi – Far East
Hsiu-chi. See Xiu Zhi – Far East
Hsü T'ien-chu. See Xu Tianju – Far East
Hsueh Hu Niang Niang. See Xuehu Niangniang – Far East
Hsuk'ung Tsang. See Xu Kongcang – Far East
Htamenmas – The Himalaya
Hu Tu – Far East
Hua Hsien. See Hua Xian – Far East
Hu'a nu'u marae – Oceania
Hua Xian – Far East
Huaco – South America
Huahega – Oceania
Huahenga. See Huahega – Oceania
Huang – Far East
Huang Daopo – Far East
Huang Tao-p'o. See Huang Daopo – Far East
Huauri. See Arimata – Oceania
Hubar. See Hubur – Near East
Hubur – Near East
Huchi-fuchi – Far East
Huchu Xing. See Yuefu Taiyin – Far East
Huechaana – Central America and Mesoamerica
Hueytonantzin. See Tonantzin – Central America and Mesoamerica
Huh. See Heh – Egypt
Huhune – Oceania
Huhura, The – Oceania
Huiçana. See Pitao Huichaana. – Central America and Mesoamerica
Huichanatao – Central America and Mesoamerica
Huixtocihuatl – Central America and Mesoamerica
Hukloban – Southeast Asia
Hükyangkwü – North America
Hulda – Northern Europe
Hulde. See Hulda – Northern Europe
Huldra – Northern Europe
Huliamma – Indian Subcontinent

Huligama – Indian Subcontinent
Huligavva – Indian Subcontinent
Hulka Devi – Indian Subcontinent
Hulki Mai – Indian Subcontinent
Hulla – Near East
Hulle – Northern Europe
Hulluk Miyumko, The – North America
Humitau – Southeast Asia
Hunahpu-Vuch – Central America and
    Mesoamerica
Hundi. *See* Bursung – Indian
    Subcontinent
Hung Luan Hsing Chün. *See* Hongluan
    Xingjun – Far East
Huntheth – Egypt
Huntu Katt! Katten – Africa
Hunwarmata – Indian Subcontinent
Huoling Shengmu – Far East
H'uraru – North America
Huri mai te ata – Oceania
Huriya – Near East
Hur-ki – Near East
Hurriya. *See* Huriya – Near East
Huru te arangi – Oceania
Hürü'Ingwühti – North America
Husbishag – Near East
Hushan Dashi. *See* Zhende Pusa – Far
    East
Hu-shan Ta-shih. *See* Zhende Pusa –
    Far East
Hushbishag. *See* Husbishag – Near East
Hushiti – Near East
Ḥutash. *See* Chup – North America
Hutena. *See* the Gulses – Near East
Hutsipamamau?u – North America
Huwassanas – Near East
Huyairya – Near East
Huzi. *See* Fuji – Far East
Huzru Wugti – North America
Huzruwauqti. *See* Hürü' Ingwühti –
    North America
Hyades, The – Greek and Roman
    Empires
Hyale – Greek and Roman Empires
Hybla – Greek and Roman Empires
Hydra – Greek and Roman Empires
Hydria – Greek and Roman Empires
Hygea. *See* Hygeia – Greek and Roman
    Empires
Hygeia – Greek and Roman Empires
Hygieia. *See* Hygeia – Greek and
    Roman Empires
Hyldemoer – Northern Europe
Hymnia – Greek and Roman Empires
Hyndla – Northern Europe
Hypate – Greek and Roman Empires
Hypercheiria – Greek and Roman
    Empires
Hypereia – Greek and Roman Empires
Hypermestra. *See* Mestra – Greek and
    Roman Empires
Hyrania – Indian Subcontinent
Hyra – Africa
Hyrmine. *See* Hermione – Greek and
    Roman Empires
Hyrokkin – Northern Europe
Hyrrokin. *See* Hyrokkin – Northern
    Europe
Iaera – Greek and Roman Empires
Iahu – Near East

Iahu Anat – Near East
Iaira. *See* Iaera – Greek and Roman
    Empires
Ialysa – Western Europe
Iamanja – South America
Iambe – Greek and Roman Empires
Ianassa – Greek and Roman Empires
Ianeira – Greek and Roman Empires
Ianira. *See* Ianeira – Greek and Roman
    Empires
Ianthe – Greek and Roman Empires
Iarila – Eastern Europe
Iarnsaxa. *See* Jarnsaxa – Northern
    Europe
Iarnvithjan, The – Northern Europe
Iasis – Greek and Roman Empires
Iaso – Greek and Roman Empires
Iasonia – Greek and Roman Empires
Iath. *See* Ïre – Western Europe
Iath n'Anann. *See* Anu – Western
    Europe
Iatiku – North America
Iavure-cunha – South America
Ibabasag – Southeast Asia
Ibu – Southeast Asia
Ibu Pertiwi – Southeast Asia
Icauna – Western Europe
Ichar-tsirew – Africa
Ichchhashakti – Indian Subcontinent
Ichiki-shima-hime-no-mikoto – Far East
Ichnaea. *See* Themis – Greek and
    Roman Empires
Ichpuchtli – Central America and
    Mesoamerica
Id – Near East
Ida – Greek and Roman Empires
Ida – Indian Subcontinent
Idaea – Greek and Roman Empires
Idalia – Greek and Roman Empires
Idavida – Indian Subcontinent
Ideal Nature – Indian Subcontinent
Idem-huva – Eastern Europe
Idem-kuva. *See* Idem-huva – Eastern
    Europe
Idetargi. *See* Ilazki – Western Europe
Idianale – Southeast Asia
Idisi, The – Northern Europe
Idliragijenget – North America
Idothea. *See* Eidothea – Greek and
    Roman Empires
Idumo Pantheon Deities. *See* Izumo
    Pantheon Deities – Far East
Idun – Northern Europe
Iduna. *See* Idun – Northern Europe
Idunn. *See* Idun – Northern Europe
Idunome-no-kami. *See*
    Izu-no-me-no-kami – Far East
Idya. *See* Idyia – Greek and Roman
    Empires
Idyia – Greek and Roman Empires
Idzu-no-me-no-kami. *See*
    Izu-no-mo-no-kami – Far East
Iella. *See* Atabei – Central America and
    Mesoamerica
Iemaparu – North America
Igaehinvdo – North America
Igbarun – Africa
Igirit. *See* Agrat Bat Mahalat – Near East
Ignea. *See* Vesta – Greek and Roman
    Empires

Ignirtoq – North America
Ignis Fatuus – Western Europe
Igoni – Africa
Igrath Bath Mahalath – Near East
Iguanuptigili – Central America and
    Mesoamerica
Iguzki. *See* Eguski – Western Europe
Iha-naga-hime. *See* Iwa-naga-hime. –
    Far East
Ihatsutsu-nome. *See*
    Iwa-tsutsu-no-me-no-mikoto – Far
    East
Ihi – Oceania
Ihi awa'awa – Oceania
Ihi lani – Oceania
Ihi'ihi – Oceania
Ihiihi. *See* Ihi'ihi – Oceania
Ihu anu. *See* Ka ihu anu – Oceania
Ihu koko – Oceania
Ii – Africa
Ijäksit-khotun. *See* Ajysit – Eastern
    Europe
Ije – Africa
Ikalu nappa – North America
Ikapati – Southeast Asia
Ikas – North America
Ikosatana. *See* Inkosazana – Africa
Iku Oteganaka. *See* Tāté Ikū
    Otegañaka – Central America and
    Mesoamerica
Ikuguhi. *See* Iku-gui-no-kami – Far East
Iku-gui-no-kami – Far East
Iku-kuhi-no-mikotu. *See*
    Iku-gui-no-kami – Far East
Iku-tama-saki-tama-hime-no-kami –
    Far East
Iku-tama-yori-bime – Far East
Ila – Indian Subcontinent
Ilaeira. *See* Hilaeira – Greek and Roman
    Empires
'Ilaheva – Oceania
Ilamatecihuatl. *See* Ilamatecuhtli –
    Central America and Mesoamerica
Ilamatecuhtli – Central America and
    Mesoamerica
Ilancueitl – Central America and
    Mesoamerica
Ilat. *See* Athirat – Near East
Ilavija. *See* Idavida – Indian
    Subcontinent
Ilavila. *See* Idavida – Indian
    Subcontinent
Ilazki – Western Europe
Ildico – Northern Europe
Ilena – Eastern Europe
Ile-neut. *See* Ilena – Eastern Europe
i-lha-mo – Indian Subcontinent
Ilia – Greek and Roman Empires
Ilissiades, The – Greek and Roman
    Empires
Ilithyia. *See* Eileithyia – Greek and
    Roman Empires
Illargi. *See* Ilazki – Western Europe
Illargui – Western Europe
Illibem Berti – Eastern Europe
Ilma – Eastern Europe
Ilmatar. *See* Ilmater – Eastern Europe
Ilmater – Eastern Europe
Iloilokula – Oceania
Ilura – Indian Subcontinent

Ilythyia-Leucothea – Greek and Roman
Empires
Imam-shua – North America
Imberombera. *See* Waramurungundji –
Oceania
Imbrasia – Greek and Roman Empires
Imbulu Man – Southeast Asia
Imd – Northern Europe
Imder. *See* Imdr – Northern Europe
Imdr – Northern Europe
Imo – Africa
'Imoa – Oceania
In – Far East
Ina – South America
Ina – Southeast Asia
Ina. *See* Hina – Oceania
Ina Da Samadulo Hose – Southeast Asia
Ina Da Samihara Luwo – Southeast Asia
Ina maram – Oceania
Ina Onian – Southeast Asia
Ina'ani vai – Oceania
Inacho – Oceania
I-nach-tin-ak. *See* Mikamatt – North
America
Inada Dao – Southeast Asia
Inada-hime – Far East
Inagami-hime. *See* Kushi-nada-hime –
Far East
Inaka. *See* Upu Ume – Southeast Asia
Inan Oinan – Southeast Asia
Inangi I Bake. *See* Bake – Southeast Asia
Inanna – Near East
Inanupdikile – Central America and
Mesoamerica
Inaras – Near East
Inari – Far East
Inari-m'yojim. *See* Inari – Far East
Inawen – Southeast Asia
Inchin Temaga – Southeast Asia
Indai Abang – Southeast Asia
Indara – Southeast Asia
Inde – Indian Subcontinent
Indira. *See* Lakshmi – Indian
Subcontinent
Indo I Laoe – Southeast Asia
Indo I Losi – Southeast Asia
Indo I Tuladidi – Southeast Asia
Indo nTegolili – Southeast Asia
Indoea Padi – Southeast Asia
Indrani – Indian Subcontinent
Indudun inPundaikuhan – Southeast
Asia
Inemes – Oceania
Ineno Pae – Southeast Asia
Ine-shki-ava. *See* Nishke-ava – Eastern
Europe
Inferna – Greek and Roman Empires
Ingebjorg. *See* Ingeborg – Northern
Europe
Ingeborg – Northern Europe
Inghean Bhuidhe – Western Europe
Ingnirtungl – North America
Ingridi – Oceania
Ingun – Northern Europe
Ini Andan – Southeast Asia
Ini Manang – Southeast Asia
Ini-herit – Egypt
Inin – Near East
Ininguru. *See* Yuguruguru, The –
Oceania

Ininni – Near East
Inkosazana – Africa
Inkosazana-ye-zulu. *See* Inkosazana –
Africa
Inkosikasi – Africa
'Inna – Africa
Innin. *See* Inanna and Innini – Near East
Ino – Greek and Roman Empires
Ino-hime – Far East
Inoltagon – Southeast Asia
Inoshishi – Far East
Intercidona – Greek and Roman
Empires
Interduca – Greek and Roman Empires
Intombangol – Southeast Asia
Inuit Earth Mother – North America
Invidia – Greek and Roman Empires
Iny – Greek and Roman Empires
Io wahine – Oceania
Ioashkanake – North America
Iodama – Greek and Roman Empires
Ioio moa – Oceania
Iole – Greek and Roman Empires
Ione – Greek and Roman Empires
Ioniades, The. *See* The Ionides – Greek
and Roman Empires
Ionides, The – Greek and Roman
Empires
Iope. *See* Cassiopeia – Greek and
Roman Empires
Iophossa. *See* Chalciope – Greek and
Roman Empires
Iord – Northern Europe
Ioulo, The – Greek and Roman Empires
Iou-s-aas – Egypt
Ipa Huaco. *See* Huaco – South America
Ipamahandi – Southeast Asia
Ipet – Egypt
Iphianassa – Greek and Roman Empires
Iphiboe. *See* Hermione – Greek and
Roman Empires
Iphigeneia – Greek and Roman Empires
Iphimedeia – Greek and Roman
Empires
Iphthime – Greek and Roman Empires
Ipi. *See* Ipet – Egypt
Iqalu Nappaa, The – North America
Iqamiait – North America
Ira – Indian Subcontinent
Iratagi. *See* Ilazki – Western Europe
Iravati – Indian Subcontinent
Irdlirvirisissong – North America
Irene. *See* Eirene – Greek and Roman
Empires
Iresu-huchi – Far East
Iretagi. *See* Ilazki – Western Europe
Iretargui. *See* Ilazki – Western Europe
Iris – Greek and Roman Empires
Irkalla – Near East
Irlek-khan – Eastern Europe
Irnan – Western Europe
Irnina – Near East
Irnini – Near East
Iro Duget – Oceania
Irpa – Northern Europe
Irsirra – Near East
Iš – Near East
Isa – Far East
Isa – Eastern Europe
Isamba – Africa

Isana. *See* Durga – Indian Subcontinent
Isani – Indian Subcontinent
Isdustaya. *See* Istustaya – Near East
Ises – Africa
Ishara – Near East
Ishhara. *See* Ushharay – Near East
Ishi-kori-dome-no-mikoto – Far East
Ish-khanna – Near East
Ishkhara – Near East
Ishtar – Near East
Isi – Indian Subcontinent
Isia – Greek and Roman Empires
Isidore, Saint – Central America and
Mesoamerica
Isidoulos – Near East
Isis – Egypt
Island Paradise Lady – Near East
Island Woman – North America
Isolde. *See* Isolt – Western Europe
Isolt – Western Europe
Isolt of the White Hands – Western
Europe
Isong – Africa
Issoria – Greek and Roman Empires
Istara. *See* Ishtar – Near East
Istehar – Near East
Isthar – Near East
Istsel – Central America and
Mesoamerica
Istustaya – Near East
Isuke-yori-hime. *See*
Hoto-tatara-isusuki-hime-no-mikoto –
Far East
It Mu – Indian Subcontinent
Itaba Tahuana – Central America and
Mesoamerica
Itchita – Eastern Europe
Itclixyan – North America
I'tc'ts'ity. *See* Naotsete – North America
Ite – North America
Ith – Western Europe
Ithome – Greek and Roman Empires
Ithunn. *See* Idun – Northern Europe
Iti iti – Oceania
Itiba Tahuvava. *See* Itaba Tahuana –
Central America and Mesoamerica
'Iti'iti – Oceania
Itiki-sima-pime-no-mikoto. *See*
Ichiki-shima-hime-no-mikoto – Far
East
Itoki – Central America and
Mesoamerica
Itonia – Greek and Roman Empires
Itonias. *See* Itonia – Greek and Roman
Empires
Itonis. *See* Itonia – Greek and Roman
Empires
Itsictsiti. *See* Utset – North America
Ituana – South America
Itzcueye – Central America and
Mesoamerica
Itzpapalotl – Central America and
Mesoamerica
Itzpapalotlcihuatl. *See* Itzpapalotl –
Central America and Mesoamerica
Itzpapalotzin. *See* Itzpapalotl – Central
America and Mesoamerica
Iuno. *See* Juno – Greek and Roman
Empires
Iusaaset – Egypt

Iusas. *See* Iusaset, Juesaes, Saosis – Egypt
Iusaset – Egypt
Iusasit. *See* Saosis – Egypt
Iustitia. *See* Justitia – Greek and Roman Empires
Iuturna. *See* Juturna – Greek and Roman Empires
Iuventas. *See* Juventas – Greek and Roman Empires
Iuzki. *See* Eguski – Western Europe
Ivilia – Western Europe
Ivithjar, The – Northern Europe
Iwa-naga-hime – Far East
Iwasubime-no-kami. *See* Iwa-su-hime-no-kami – Far East
Iwa-su-hime-no-kami – Far East
Iwatsutsu-nome. *See* Iwa-tsutsu-no-me-no-mikoto – Far East
Iwa-tsutsu-no-me-no-mikoto – Far East
Iweridd – Western Europe
Ix Ahau – Central America and Mesoamerica
Ix Bolon Yol Nicté – Central America and Mesoamerica
Ix Ch'up – Central America and Mesoamerica
Ix Chancab – Central America and Mesoamerica
Ix Chebel Ya – Central America and Mesoamerica
Ix Chel – Central America and Mesoamerica
Ix Chuah – Central America and Mesoamerica
Ix Dziban Yol Nicté – Central America and Mesoamerica
Ix Dzoy – Central America and Mesoamerica
Ix Hun Tah Dz'ib. *See* Ix Chebel Ya – Central America and Mesoamerica
Ix Hun Tah Nok – Central America and Mesoamerica
Ix Hun Zipit Caan. *See* Ix Chel – Central America and Mesoamerica
Ix Kan Citam Thul – Central America and Mesoamerica
Ix Kan Itzam Thul – Central America and Mesoamerica
Ix Kanyultá – Central America and Mesoamerica
Ix Ku – Central America and Mesoamerica
Ix Pucyolá – Central America and Mesoamerica
Ix Saclactun – Central America and Mesoamerica
Ix Tab – Central America and Mesoamerica
Ix Tan Yol – Central America and Mesoamerica
Ix Tan Yol Ha – Central America and Mesoamerica
Ix Tol Och – Central America and Mesoamerica
Ix Tub Tan – Central America and Mesoamerica
Ix U Sihnal – Central America and Mesoamerica

Ix Ual Cuy – Central America and Mesoamerica
Ix Ual Icim – Central America and Mesoamerica
Ix Zacal Nok. *See* Ix Hun Tah Nok – Central America and Mesoamerica
Ixchel. *See* Ix Chel – Central America and Mesoamerica
Ixcuina – Central America and Mesoamerica
Ixcuiname, The – Central America and Mesoamerica
Ixhunieta. *See* Ix Chebel Ya – Central America and Mesoamerica
Ixlexwani – North America
Ixma Chucbeni – Central America and Mesoamerica
Ixquic. *See* Xquic – Central America and Mesoamerica
Ixtab – Central America and Mesoamerica
Ixuixiwi – North America
Ixzaluoh. *See* Ix Chebel Ya – Central America and Mesoamerica
Iyalode. *See* Oshun – Central America and Mesoamerica
Iya-maase – Africa
Iyanla – Africa
Iyatiku – North America
Iyerugame. *See* Yerugami – Central America and Mesoamerica
Iza – Near East
Izanami-no-kami – Far East
Izanami-no-mikoto. *See* Izanami-no-kami – Far East
Iztaccenteol – Central America and Mesoamerica
Iztaccihuatl – Central America and Mesoamerica
Iztat Ix. *See* Alaghom Naum – Central America and Mesoamerica
Izumo Pantheon Deities – Far East
Izu-no-me-no-kami – Far East
Izushi-otome-no-kami – Far East
Izushio-tome. *See* Izushi-otome-no-kami – Far East
Ja Najek – Southeast Asia
Jabme-akka – Eastern Europe
Jabmeks – Eastern Europe
Jaga-baba. *See* Jezinky – Eastern Europe
Jagad-dhatri. *See* Parvati, Sarasvati, and Durga – Indian Subcontinent
Jagadgauri – Indian Subcontinent
Jagad-yoni – Indian Subcontinent
Jaganmatr. *See* Durga and Lakshmi – Indian Subcontinent
Jaher Era – Indian Subcontinent
Jahi – Near East
Jahira Buru – Indian Subcontinent
Jaja – Eastern Europe
Jakhamata. *See* Jakhmata – Indian Subcontinent
Jakhmata – Indian Subcontinent
Jaki. *See* Jahi – Near East
Jaladhija. *See* Lakshmi – Indian Subcontinent
Jalang – Southeast Asia
Jalia – Indian Subcontinent
Jalkamni – Indian Subcontinent
Jalmarida – Oceania

Jalpa Mai – Indian Subcontinent
Jamadagni – Indian Subcontinent
Jamai Sashthi. *See* Aranya – Indian Subcontinent
Jamaina – South America
Jamants – Indian Subcontinent
Jameakka. *See* Jabmeks – Eastern Europe
Jami – Indian Subcontinent
Jami-ajmo-ollmaj. *See* Jabmeks – Eastern Europe
Jana – Greek and Roman Empires
Jandira – South America
Ja-neb'a – Eastern Europe
Janguli – Indian Subcontinent
Japanese Mother Goddess – Far East
Jappi Mata – Indian Subcontinent
Jar Goddesses, The. *See* Cow Goddesses – Near East
Jara – Indian Subcontinent
Jara Meng – Southeast Asia
Jari – Oceania
Jarina – South America
Jarnsaxa – Northern Europe
Jassuju – Indian Subcontinent
Jata – Southeast Asia
Jatavedasi – Indian Subcontinent
Jatila – Indian Subcontinent
Jauthe – Near East
Jaya – Indian Subcontinent
Jayani. *See* Jayanti – Indian Subcontinent
Jayanti – Indian Subcontinent
Jayini – Indian Subcontinent
Jedza – Eastern Europe
Jeh. *See* Jahi – Near East
Jejamo-karpo – The Himalaya
Jemez Old Woman. *See* Ahe'a – North America
Jen, Queen. *See* Mi Fei – Far East
Jende Pusa. *See* Zhende Pusa – Far East
Jendzi-baba. *See* Jezinky – Eastern Europe
Jendzyna. *See* Jezinky – Eastern Europe
Jerah – Near East
Jericho Goddesses, The – Near East
Jesodha. *See* Yashoda – Indian Subcontinent
Jet Woman. *See* Estsanatlehi – North America
Jewel Goddesses – The Himalaya
Jezanna – Africa
Jezenky. *See* Jezinky – Eastern Europe
Jezibaba – Eastern Europe
Jezinky, The – Eastern Europe
Jhulan Devi – Indian Subcontinent
Jia Shi – Far East
Jian Lao – Far East
Jiang Yuan – Far East
Jibbi-Jang-Sangne – Indian Subcontinent
Jie – Far East
Jigonsahseh. *See* Genetaska – North America
'Jig-rten-mkha'-'gro-ma – The Himalaya
'Jigs-pa'i-zer-mo-mig-gcig – The Himalaya
Jiji – Oceania
Jin Gu – Far East
Jin Mu – Far East
Jin Nü. *See* Zhinü – Far East

Jingjan Numjan – Southeast Asia
Jinhua Niangniang – Far East
Jiutian Houmu – Far East
Jiutinan Xuannu – Far East
Jnanashakti – Indian Subcontinent
Joda-māte – Eastern Europe
Jogan Mata. *See* Holi – Indian
   Subcontinent
Jokwa – Far East
Joli-taren – Eastern Europe
Joli-torem. *See* Joli-Taren – Eastern
   Europe
Jo-mo-lha-ri – The Himalaya
Jonaji Belachina – Central America and
   Mesoamerica
Jord – Northern Europe
Jordegumma – Northern Europe
Jordh. *See* Jord – Northern Europe
Jorth. *See* Jord – Northern Europe
Joukahainen – Eastern Europe
Ju Puteur – Southeast Asia
Jubbu-jang-sangne – South America
Judur – Northern Europe
Judy, The. *See* Vila – Eastern Europe
Juesaes – Egypt
Juga – Greek and Roman Empires
Jugalis. *See* Juga – Greek and Roman
   Empires
Jugumishanta – Oceania
Juishen Niangniang – Far East
Juks-akka – Northern Europe
Juksakka – Eastern Europe
Julunggul – Oceania
Jumala. *See* Slatababa – Eastern Europe
Jumna Ji – Indian Subcontinent
Jumna. *See* Yami – Indian Subcontinent
Jumon-ava – Eastern Europe
Jun-tei Kwan-non – Far East
Jun Ti – Far East
Jūni-sama – Far East
Junit – Egypt
Junkgowa – Oceania
Juno – Greek and Roman Empires
Juno Coelestis – Africa
Juras Māte – Eastern Europe
Jurasmat. *See* Juras Māte – Eastern
   Europe
Jurate – Eastern Europe
Jurt-ava – Eastern Europe
Jurt-azerava – Eastern Europe
Jusas. *See* Juesaes – Egypt
Justitia – Greek and Roman Empires
Juturna – Greek and Roman Empires
Juventas – Greek and Roman Empires
Juventus. *See* Juventas – Greek and
   Roman Empires
Jyaya. *See* Jyestha. – Indian
   Subcontinent
Jyestha – Indian Subcontinent
Jyestha Alakshmi – Indian Subcontinent
Jyotsna – Indian Subcontinent
Ka – North America
Ka 'ahu pāhau – Oceania
Ka Blai Synshar – Indian Subcontinent
Ka Blei Sam Um – Indian Subcontinent
Ka Di – Indian Subcontinent
Ka Ding – Indian Subcontinent
Ka Duba – Indian Subcontinent
Ka haka ua koko – Oceania
Ka hala o māpuana – Oceania

Ka hala o puna – Oceania
Ka ihu anu – Oceania
Ka ihu koa – Oceania
Ka ihu koko. *See* Ihu koko – Oceania
Ka ihu kuuna – Oceania
Ka ihu o pala'ai – Oceania
Ka iki lani – Oceania
Ka 'iwa ka la meha – Oceania
Ka 'iwa ka meha. *See* Ka 'iwa ka la
   meha – Oceania
Ka Khlam – Indian Subcontinent
Ka Ksaw Ka Jirngam – Indian
   Subcontinent
Ka lama i nu'u – Oceania
Ka lani mai nu'u. *See* Ka lama i nu'u –
   Oceania
Ka 'Lei Aitan – Indian Subcontinent
Ka lei hau ola – Oceania
Ka 'Lei Iing – Indian Subcontinent
Ka 'Lei Synshar – Indian Subcontinent
Ka maunu a niho – Oceania
Ka meha i kana – Oceania
Ka mo'o 'inanea – Oceania
Ka Niangriang – Indian Subcontinent
Ka onohi ula – Oceania
Ka pū o alaka'i – Oceania
Ka Ram-ew – Indian Subcontinent
Ka Rasong – Indian Subcontinent
Ka Rih – Indian Subcontinent
Ka Ron – Indian Subcontinent
Ka Shwar – Indian Subcontinent
Ka Singi – Indian Subcontinent
Ka Smer – Indian Subcontinent
Ka Sngi – Indian Subcontinent
Ka Syrtieh – Indian Subcontinent
Ka Taben – Indian Subcontinent
Ka Taro. *See* Ka Taroh – Indian
   Subcontinent
Ka Taroh – Indian Subcontinent
Ka ua ku'āhiwa – Oceania
Ka Um – Indian Subcontinent
Ka wahine o ka li'ūla – Oceania
Ka'a Mata – Indian Subcontinent
Kā'ana'e like – Oceania
Ka'ao melemele – Oceania
Ka-ata-killa – South America
Kabagiyawan – Southeast Asia
Kabeiroi, The. *See* Cabeiriae – Greek
   and Roman Empires
Kabo mandalat. *See* Kobo mandalat –
   Oceania
Kabyle First Woman – Africa
Kachin' Mana – North America
Kades – Near East
Kadesh. *See* Qetesh – Egypt
Kadeyuna – Southeast Asia
Kadhutetash – North America
Kadi – Near East
Kadjari – Oceania
Kadlu – North America
Kadomas. *See* Khahdoma – The
   Himalaya
Kadru – Indian Subcontinent
Kafisi – Oceania
Kagauraha – Oceania
Kagayo-hime – Far East
Kaguya-hime-no-mikoto – Far East
Kahaila Kachin' Mana – North America
Ka-harus-apu-saru-ma-hakar-uma. *See*
   Bast – Egypt

Kahasumma – Indian Subcontinent
Kahausibware – Oceania
Kahi – Egypt
Kahoupokane – Oceania
Kāhu rere moa – Oceania
Kāhuitara – Oceania
Kahuone – Oceania
Kai here – Oceania
Kaiala – Africa
Kaika – Indian Subcontinent
Kaikara – Africa
Kaikeyi – Indian Subcontinent
Kairadeshahi – Indian Subcontinent
Kait – Near East
Kait – Egypt
Ka'ipo – Oceania
Kaiwan – Africa
Kajsa – Northern Europe
Kakash Kachina. *See* Quail Kachin'
   Mana – North America
Kaki – Indian Subcontinent
Kakia – Greek and Roman Empires
Kakiadan – Southeast Asia
Kakini – Indian Subcontinent
Kakit. *See* Kauket – Egypt
Kakubh – Indian Subcontinent
Kala Pidari. *See* Pidari – Indian
   Subcontinent
Kaladi. *See* Jyestha – Indian
   Subcontinent
Kalaia – Oceania
Kalaka – Indian Subcontinent
Kalama 'ula – Oceania
Kalamahichandi – Indian Subcontinent
Kalapiat – Far East
Kalaratri – Indian Subcontinent
Kalcheng – Southeast Asia
Kaldas-ava – Eastern Europe
Kaldyni-mumas – Eastern Europe
Kali – Indian Subcontinent
Kaliamma – Indian Subcontinent
Kalika – Indian Subcontinent
Kalilika. *See* Kalika – Indian
   Subcontinent
Kalimata – Indian Subcontinent
Kalimulore – Africa
Kaliyani – Indian Subcontinent
Kallianassa – Greek and Roman
   Empires
Kallianeira – Greek and Roman Empires
Kalliphaeira – Greek and Roman
   Empires
Kallirhoe. *See* Callirrhoe – Greek and
   Roman Empires
Kalliste. *See* Callisto – Greek and
   Roman Empires
Kallisto. *See* Callisto – Greek and
   Roman Empires
Kalma – Eastern Europe
Kaltas-anki – Eastern Europe
Kaltes – Eastern Europe
Kalumaiamman – Indian Subcontinent
Kaluvaliamma – Indian Subcontinent
Kalwadi. *See* Karwadi – Oceania
Kalxsmaknim – North America
Kalypso. *See* Calypso – Greek and
   Roman Empires
Kamadhenu – Indian Subcontinent
Kamaits – North America
Kamakhya – Indian Subcontinent

Kamaksi – Indian Subcontinent
Kamala – Indian Subcontinent
Kamashi – Indian Subcontinent
Kamasshi. *See* Parvati – Indian Subcontinent
Kamaugarunga – Africa
Kamaunu – Oceania
Kamdhen. *See* Kamadhenu – Indian Subcontinent
Kameian – Southeast Asia
Kamennaia Baba, The – Eastern Europe
Kamennye Baby, The. *See* The Kamennaia Baba – Eastern Europe
Kamesvari – Indian Subcontinent
Kami. *See* Rati – Indian Subcontinent
Kami-ata-ka-shi-tsu-hime. *See* Konohana-sakuya-hime – Far East
Kami-mima-subi. *See* Kami-musubi-no-kami – Far East
Kami-musubi-no-kami – Far East
Kaminari – Far East
Kami-naru. *See* Naru-kami – Far East
Kamrusepas – Near East
Kamthi Mata – Indian Subcontinent
Kamu-ata-kashi-tsu-hime. *See* Konohana-sakuya-hime – Far East
Kamu-ata-tsu-hime. *See* Konohana-sakuya-hime – Far East
Kamu-hata-hime – Far East
Kamui-fuchi – Far East
Kamui-fuji. *See* Kamui-fuchi – Far East
Kamui-huchi – Far East
Kamui-matne-po – Far East
Kamui-menoko – Far East
Ka-mu-iu-dr-ma-giu-iu-e-ba – North America
Kamu-mimusubi. *See* Kami-musubi-no-kami – Far East
Kamu-ō-ichi-hime – Far East
Kamu-ya-tate-hime-no-mikoto – Far East
Kamuy-fuchi. *See* Kamui fuchi – Far East
Kanaeski Anaiyehi – North America
Kanaio – Oceania
Kanaka Durgamma – Indian Subcontinent
Kana-yama-bime-no-kami – Far East
Kana-yama-hiko – Far East
Kanayama-hime. *See* Kana-yama-bime-no-kami – Far East
Kando-ye-shes-chogyel – The Himalaya
Kandralekel. *See* Cherlak – Eastern Europe
Kāne kua'ana – Oceania
Kanene Ski Amai Yehi – North America
Kangra Goddess, The – Indian Subcontinent
Kani uhi – Oceania
Kani. *See* Ganis – Eastern Europe
Kanikanihia – Oceania
Kanilkes – North America
Kankali – Indian Subcontinent
Kankar Mata – Indian Subcontinent
Kannae. *See* Kanyā – Indian Subcontinent
Kannagi – Indian Subcontinent
Kannakapfaluk – North America
Kanni Amma – Indian Subcontinent
Kanni, The – Indian Subcontinent

Kanniha Paramesvare – Indian Subcontinent
Kannimar, The – Indian Subcontinent
Kanro-o. *See* Amitabha – Far East
Kansa First Woman – North America
Kant Jan – Southeast Asia
Kanti – Indian Subcontinent
Kanuslaliam – North America
Kanyā – Indian Subcontinent
Kanyā Kumārī – Indian Subcontinent
Kanyabara. *See* Kanyā – Indian Subcontinent
Kanym – Eastern Europe
Kao Lan-ying. *See* Gao Lanying – Far East
Kao Mei. *See* Nüwa – Far East
Ka'ōhelo – Oceania
Kapaä – Southeast Asia
Kapalini – Indian Subcontinent
Kapenopfu – Indian Subcontinent
Kapiano – Oceania
Kapila-patni. *See* Jyestha – Indian Subcontinent
Kapisha – Indian Subcontinent
Kapni Piri – Indian Subcontinent
Kapo 'ula kīna'u. *See* Kapo – Oceania
Kapo – Oceania
Kapu Māte – Eastern Europe
Kara – Northern Europe
Kara ma kuna – Oceania
Karaia i te ata – Oceania
Karaikkal Asmmaiyar – Indian Subcontinent
Karak karak, The – Oceania
Karakarook – Oceania
Karala. *See* Parvati – Indian Subcontinent
Karali – Indian Subcontinent
Karama – Africa
Kararat – Far East
Kardas-ś Arko – Eastern Europe
Kare nuku – Oceania
Kare rangi – Oceania
Karicag – Indian Subcontinent
Karili. *See* Karali – Indian Subcontinent
Karisini. *See* Lakshmi – Indian Subcontinent
Karitei-mo. *See* Hariti – Indian Subcontinent
Karitei-mo. *See* Kichi-jō-ten – Far East
Karma Dakinis – The Himalaya
Karma Kro-ti-shvr-ri-ma. *See* Karma-krotishaurima – The Himalaya
Karmadakini – Indian Subcontinent
Karma-krotishaurima – The Himalaya
Karokung – Southeast Asia
Karous – Central America and Mesoamerica
Karpophoros – Greek and Roman Empires
Karta – Eastern Europe
Kartek. *See* Thoeris – Egypt
Karttiki – Indian Subcontinent
Karuebak – South America
Karu-no-ō-iratsume – Far East
Karwadi – Oceania
Kasenko – Far East
Kashatskihakatidise – North America
Kashinako – North America

Ka-silim – Near East
Kastha – Indian Subcontinent
Katahzippuri. *See* Kamrusepas – Near East
Katahzipuri. *See* Kamrusepas – Near East
Kataputanas, The – Indian Subcontinent
Katarwiri – Africa
Kateri – Indian Subcontinent
Katesch – Egypt
Kathirat, The – Near East
Kathshchar-ekva – Eastern Europe
Kati Ankamma – Indian Subcontinent
Kato First Woman – North America
Katsin Numka Majan – Southeast Asia
Kattahha – Near East
Kattakju – North America
Katukilal – Indian Subcontinent
Katuma – North America
Katyutayuuq – North America
Kau ata ata – Oceania
Kaukabhta – Near East
Kaukasis – Greek and Roman Empires
Kaukau – Oceania
Kauket – Egypt
Ka'ula hea – Oceania
Kaulesi – Indian Subcontinent
Kaumari – Indian Subcontinent
Kaumudi. *See* Jyotsna – Indian Subcontinent
Kauni. *See* Kanya – Indian Subcontinent
Kausalya – Indian Subcontinent
Kausiki – Indian Subcontinent
Kava tua – Oceania
Kava'ara – Oceania
Kave – Oceania
Kaveri – Indian Subcontinent
Kavna – North America
Kawalkamata – Indian Subcontinent
Kawas – North America
Kāwelu. *See* Kewelu – Oceania
Kaxiwari. *See* Tatei Kaxiwari – Central America and Mesoamerica
Kayamanan – Southeast Asia
Kayanohime – Far East
Kaya-no-hime-no-kami – Far East
Ke aka huli lani – Oceania
Ke ao lewa – Oceania
Ke ao mele mele – Oceania
Keaka – Oceania
Kearoa – Oceania
Keb. *See* Gea – Near East
Kebechet – Egypt
Kebehut – Egypt
Keca Aba – Eastern Europe
Kedesh. *See* Qetesh – Egypt
Kefa – Egypt
Kefeliu – North America
Keheari – Southeast Asia
Kek-t – Egypt
Kekit. *See* Kauket – Egypt
Kekiut. *See* Kauket – Egypt
Kekuit – Egypt
Kelaino – Greek and Roman Empires
Kele – Oceania
Kele-yin ükin tegri – Far East
Kelikila. *See* Rati – Indian Subcontinent
Kelu Devaru – Indian Subcontinent
Ken – Egypt
Kena – Oceania

Kenat – Egypt
Kenemet – Egypt
Kenet – Egypt
Keng San Gu – Far East
Keng San Guniang – Far East
K'eng San Hu-niang. See Keng San Guniang – Far East
K'eng San-ku. See Keng San Gu – Far East
Keninqas – North America
Kenken-ur. See Ser-t – Egypt
Kenmut – Egypt
Kenru-katkimat – Far East
Kent – Egypt
Keoloewa – Oceania
Kep. See Kefa – Egypt
Kepa, The – Oceania
Kepha. See Kefa – Egypt
Ker. See Cer – Greek and Roman Empires
Keraunia – Greek and Roman Empires
Keren Sotskon Pas. See Kud-ava – Eastern Europe
Kerep-nove – Far East
Keres Moon Mother – North America
Keres, The – Greek and Roman Empires
Keresan Sisters – North America
Kerhet – Egypt
Keridwen – Western Europe
Kerimas – The Himalaya
Kerkeis. See Cerceïs – Greek and Roman Empires
Kernababy – Western Europe
Kernbaby. See Kernababy – Western Europe
Kerres – Greek and Roman Empires
Kerub of Air – Egypt
Kesara. See Cesair – Western Europe
Keshini – Indian Subcontinent
Kesora – Indian Subcontinent
Kesou Niangniang – Far East
Ketche Avalon. See Keca Aba – Eastern Europe
Kethlenda. See Cethlenn – Western Europe
Ketq Skwaye. See Ketq Skwayne – North America
Ketq Skwayne – North America
Ketse-awa – Eastern Europe
Kewelu – Oceania
Keyûrî. See Kerimas – The Himalaya
Keyum – Indian Subcontinent
Keyuri – Indian Subcontinent
Khadhomas. See Khahdoma – The Himalaya
Khadiravani Tara – The Himalaya
Khadoma Queen – The Himalaya
Khados. See Khahdoma – The Himalaya
Khaft – Egypt
Khahdoma – The Himalaya
Khahdomas. See Dakinis – Indian Subcontinent
Khala Kumari – Indian Subcontinent
Kha-la-me-'bar-ma – The Himalaya
Khandros. See Khahdoma – The Himalaya
Khania Shkwakwa – Eastern Europe
Kha-ra-ta-nek-ha – Egypt
Khasias Celestial Woman – Indian Subcontinent

Khaya. See Chaya and Chhaya – Indian Subcontinent
Khebent – Egypt
Kheftes-hau-hesqet-neha-her – Egypt
Khekaris, The – Indian Subcontinent
Khemit – Egypt
Khenememtit – Egypt
Khent – Egypt
Kheperu – Egypt
Khera – Egypt
Khermai. See Bhagavati – Indian Subcontinent
Khermata – Indian Subcontinent
Khesef-khemt – Egypt
Khi-dimme-azaga – Near East
Khir Bhawani – Indian Subcontinent
Khmoc Pray, The – Southeast Asia
Khnemet-urt – Egypt
Khoemnis – Egypt
Khoemnu. See Khoemnis – Egypt
Khôn-ma – The Himalaya
Khosadam – Eastern Europe
Khosedabam. See Khosadam – Eastern Europe
Khosodam – Eastern Europe
Khotun – Eastern Europe
Khrag-gi-ser-'bebs-ma – The Himalaya
Khulungma – Indian Subcontinent
Khunpinu'a'anyun – North America
Khuntasaengge'i'a'anyun – North America
Khuntsaenyu'a'anyun – North America
Khuntsanyu'a'anyun – North America
Khuntseji'a'anyun – North America
Khusareth – Near East
Khut – Egypt
Khwora!ma – Africa
Ki – Near East
Kiang Yuan. See Jiang Yuan – Far East
Kibayen – Southeast Asia
Kichi-jō-ten – Far East
Kicva – Western Europe
Kidaria – Greek and Roman Empires
Kieva. See Kicva – Western Europe
Kiha wahine – Oceania
Kihe wahine. See Kiha wahine – Oceania
Kikewei p'aide – North America
Kiki pua – Oceania
Kikimora – Eastern Europe
Kildisin – Eastern Europe
Kildisin-mumy. See Kildisin – Eastern Europe
Kilili. See Ishtar – Near East
Kilya. See Mama Quilla – South America
Kimah – Near East
Kimilkan – North America
Kimnaris, The – Indian Subcontinent
Kindazi – Near East
Kine Nane – Indian Subcontinent
Kine. See Ganis – Eastern Europe
Kini maka – Oceania
Kini maka o kalā. See Kini maka – Oceania
Kinkin – Indian Subcontinent
Kinkini-dharî. See Til-bu-ma – The Himalaya

Kinnaris. See Kimnaris – Indian Subcontinent
Kipara – Oceania
Kipu-tytto – Eastern Europe
Kirati. See Durga and Ganga – Indian Subcontinent
Kirisa – Near East
Kirke. See Circe – Greek and Roman Empires
Kirnababy. See Kernababy – Western Europe
Kirteka, The. See Krittikas – Indian Subcontinent
Kirti – Indian Subcontinent
Kiru – The Himalaya
Kisagai-hime – Far East
Kisar. See Ki – Near East
Kisboldogasszony. See Boldogasszony – Eastern Europe
Kishar. See Ki – Near East
Kishijo-ten. See Kichi-jō-ten – Far East
Kishijoten – Far East
Kishimojin. See Helidi, Lamasthu, Near East – Far East
Kisshō-ten. See Kichi-jō-ten – Far East
Kissiang – Far East
Kista – Near East
Kitchen Range Goddess – Far East
Kitro Bai – Indian Subcontinent
Kiun. See Chiun – Near East
Kiun. See Ken – Egypt
Kivish Atakvish – North America
Kivutar – Eastern Europe
Kiyo-hime – Far East
Klah Klahnee – North America
Klang – Southeast Asia
Kleio. See Clio – Greek and Roman Empires
Klothes – Greek and Roman Empires
Klotho. See Clotho – Greek and Roman Empires
Klu-mo-dung-skyong-ma – The Himalaya
Klymene. See Clymene – Greek and Roman Empires
Klytia. See Clytia – Greek and Roman Empires
Knowee – Oceania
Ko – Africa
Ko Ku. See Ge Gu – Far East
Kobine – Oceania
Kobo Mandalat – Oceania
Köcha Kachin' Mana – North America
Kocha Mana. See Alo Mana Angak'chin Mana, and A-ha Kachin'Mana – North America
Kochinako – North America
Kodamata – Indian Subcontinent
Koevasi – Oceania
Kohak Oka – North America
Kohkang Wuhti. See Spider Woman – North America
Koilasa – Oceania
Koirau na marama – Oceania
Kok Lir – Southeast Asia
Kokamukha. See Durga – Indian Subcontinent
Koke – Oceania

Koki – Africa
Kokkalamma – Indian Subcontinent
Koko Mwezi. *See* Mweji – Africa
Kokobi – Africa
Kokokshi. *See* Kokwele – North
    America
Kok' Okya. *See* Kokwele – North
    America
Kokomikeis – North America
Kokopell' Mana – North America
Kokumthena – North America
Kokuzo – Far East
Kokwatawu. *See* Suyuki – North
    America
Kokwelacokti. *See* Kokwele – North
    America
Kokwelashokti Oken'ona – North
    America
Kokwele – North America
Kokyan Wuhti – North America
Kol First Woman – Indian Subcontinent
Kolahmana – North America
Kolapuriamma – Indian Subcontinent
Kolga – Northern Europe
Koliada – Eastern Europe
Kolias – Greek and Roman Empires
Kolin Sutti Bhavani – Indian
    Subcontinent
Koljada. *See* Koliada – Eastern Europe
Kolkolibag, The – Southeast Asia
Komanchi Kachin' Mana – North
    America
Komeang – Oceania
Komodia – Greek and Roman Empires
Komokatsiki – North America
Komorkis. *See* Kokomikeis – North
    America
Komwidapokuwia – North America
Kongde – Far East
Kongtsun Demo – The Himalaya
Konin Kachin' Mana – North America
Konjini – Oceania
Kono – Africa
Kono First Woman – Africa
Konohana-chiru-hime – Far East
Konohana-no-sakuya-bime. *See*
    Konohana-sakuya-hime – Far East
Konohana-sakuya-hime – Far East
Konshana-sakuya-hime. *See*
    Konohana-sakuya-hime – Far East
Koo-mah'mm hahs-ay' Tahm – Central
    America and Mesoamerica
Kooshelya. *See* Kausalya – Indian
    Subcontinent
Kor Enda. *See* Enda Semangko –
    Oceania
Korawini?i – North America
Kore – Greek and Roman Empires
Kore-Arethusa – Greek and Roman
    Empires
Kornmutter, Die – Northern Europe
Koros – Greek and Roman Empires
Korraval – Indian Subcontinent
Korrawi – Indian Subcontinent
Korrigan – Western Europe
Koš La-kuva – Eastern Europe
Kôshart – Near East
Kôshartu. *See* Kôshart – Near East
Kostroma – Eastern Europe
Kostrubonko – Eastern Europe

Kotari. *See* Kottavei – Indian
    Subcontinent
Kotavi. *See* Kottavei – Indian
    Subcontinent
Kotharat, The – Near East
Kothlamana – North America
Kothlana. *See* Kothlamana – North
    America
Koti-sri. *See* Jun-tei Kwan-non – Far East
Kotma Ma – Indian Subcontinent
Kottavei – Indian Subcontinent
Kottutto. *See* Cotys – Greek and Roman
    Empires
Kotus. *See* Cotys – Greek and Roman
    Empires
Kotyto. *See* Cotys – Greek and Roman
    Empires
Kourotrophos – Greek and Roman
    Empires
Kov-ava – Eastern Europe
Koyasu Kwan-non – Far East
Koyemshi – North America
Kozbi. *See* Chasbei – Near East
Krachi Woman – Africa
Krähe – Northern Europe
Kranto – Greek and Roman Empires
Krasnyi – Eastern Europe
Kratesis – Greek and Roman Empires
Kraunca – Indian Subcontinent
Kriemhild – Northern Europe
Kriksy – Eastern Europe
Krimba – Eastern Europe
Kripi – Indian Subcontinent
Krisna. *See* Draupadi – Indian
    Subcontinent
Krittika, The – Indian Subcontinent
Kritya – Indian Subcontinent
Krityakas, The – Indian Subcontinent
Kriya – Indian Subcontinent
Kriyashakti – Indian Subcontinent
Krodha – Indian Subcontinent
Krodhesvari – The Himalaya
Krumai – Near East
Ksama – Indian Subcontinent
Ksem-wa'tsq – North America
Ksetrasya Patni – Indian Subcontinent
Kshama – Indian Subcontinent
Kshanti – Indian Subcontinent
Kshiti-apsarases, The – Indian
    Subcontinent
Ksirabdhitanaya. *See* Lakshmi – Indian
    Subcontinent
Ksudha. *See* Mahakali and
    Mahalakshmki – Indian
    Subcontinent
Kteis. *See* Cteis – Greek and Roman
    Empires
Ku Gu – North America
Ku raki – Oceania
Kua iti – Oceania
Kua nui – Oceania
Kuan Yin. *See* Guanyin – Far East
Kuanja – Africa
Kuapla. *See* Kupalo – Eastern Europe
Kubaba – Near East
Kubai-khotun – Eastern Europe
Kubaiko – Eastern Europe
Kubay-khotun-la. *See* Nalban-Aiy –
    Eastern Europe
Kubebe Kupapa. *See* Hepat – Near East

Kubele. *See* Cybele – Near East
Kubjika – Indian Subcontinent
Kucedre. *See* Kulshedra – Eastern
    Europe
Kud-ava – Eastern Europe
Kud-azerava. *See* Kud-ava – Eastern
    Europe
Kudo-jurtava. *See* Kud-ava – Eastern
    Europe
Ku-doku-niyo – Far East
Kuei-ling Sheng-mu. *See* Guiling
    Shenamu – Far East
Kuga – Eastern Europe
Kugu Shotshen-ava – Eastern Europe
Kuguri-gami – Far East
Kuhu – Indian Subcontinent
Kui – Oceania
Kui o hina – Oceania
Kuilasa. *See* Koilasa – Oceania
Kuilioloa – Oceania
Kujaku-myō-ō – Far East
Kujaku-myō-ō. *See* Mahamayuri –
    Indian Subcontinent
Kujum-Chantu – Indian Subcontinent
Kukar Mari – Indian Subcontinent
Kuku 'ena i ke ahi ho'omau honua –
    Oceania
Kukudhi. *See* Kukuth – Eastern Europe
Kūkū'ena – Oceania
Kukuri-hime-no-kami – Far East
Kukuru 'Uimari. *See* Tatei Kukuru
    'Uimari – Central America and
    Mesoamerica
Kukuth – Eastern Europe
Kul – Eastern Europe
Kul Devi – Indian Subcontinent
Kul Gosain – Indian Subcontinent
Kulagollamma – Indian Subcontinent
Kulanthalamman – Indian Subcontinent
Kule – The Himalaya
Kuleswari – Indian Subcontinent
Kulitta – Near East
Kuliua. *See* Hina kuluua – Oceania
Kulmu. *See* Kulsu – Greek and Roman
    Empires
Kulshedra – Eastern Europe
Kulsu – Greek and Roman Empires
Kumang – Southeast Asia
Kumanshi Okya – North America
Kumari – Indian Subcontinent
Kumbhamata – Indian Subcontinent
Kumbhi. *See* Jyestha – Indian
    Subcontinent
Kumbhinasa – Indian Subcontinent
Kume – Oceania
Kumi tonga – Oceania
Kumitoga – Oceania
Kumu tonga i te po – Oceania
Kun – Far East
Kun – Near East
Kun – Indian Subcontinent
Kunan beili – Oceania
Kunan-beili. *See* Kunan beili – Oceania
Kunapipi – Oceania
Kun-bzang-ma – The Himalaya
Kunda. *See* Cunda – Indian
    Subcontinent
Kundalini – Indian Subcontinent
Kundalini Shakti – Indian Subcontinent
Kundui – Southeast Asia

Kung-te. *See* Kongde – Far East
Kunhild – Northern Europe
Kuni-no-kuhiza-mochi-no-kami – Far East
Kuni-no-kura-do-no-kami – Far East
Kuni-no-mi-hashira – Far East
Kuni-no-mi-kumari-no-kami – Far East
Kuni-no-sa-giri-no-kami – Far East
Kuni-no-sa-zuchi-no-kami – Far East
Kunna – North America
Kunnawarra – Oceania
Kunnyan. *See* Kanya – Indian Subcontinent
Kun-syo-ming-wang – Far East
Kunti – Indian Subcontinent
Kuntu-bzang-mo – The Himalaya
Kuo-teng. *See* Guodeng – Far East
Kupal'nitsa – Eastern Europe
Kupalo – Eastern Europe
Kupapa. *See* Hepat – Near East
Kupli – Indian Subcontinent
Kura – Oceania
Kura ngaituka – Oceania
Kura-mitsu-ha-no-kami – Far East
Kūrangāituka. *See* Kura ngaituka – Oceania
Kurikuta – Oceania
Kurkanninako – North America
Kurmar Devis, The – Indian Subcontinent
Kurriwilban – Oceania
Kurukule. *See* Kurukulla – Indian Subcontinent
Kurukulla – Indian Subcontinent
Kurukulle – The Himalaya
Kurumbai – Indian Subcontinent
Kururuk – Oceania
Kushi-nada-hime – Far East
Kusumamodini – Indian Subcontinent
Kutamangari – Indian Subcontinent
Kutbi – Near East
Kutca mana – North America
Kutnahin – North America
Kuttuto. *See* Cotys – Greek and Roman Empires
Kutug:a – Eastern Europe
Kutumbini – Indian Subcontinent
Kutunga – Oceania
Kuutar – Eastern Europe
Kuyapalitsa. *See* Chakwaina Okya – North America
Kuzo-no-ha – Far East
Kveldrida – Northern Europe
Kwa?akuyi-savepone – North America
Kwamumu Okya – North America
Kwannon – Far East
Kwannung. *See* Kwannon – Far East
Kwanseieun – Far East
Kwanyin. *See* Guanyin – Far East
Kwavonakwa – North America
Kwee-kee'kai es-scop'-oh – Central America and Mesoamerica
Kwelopunyai – Central America and Mesoamerica
Kwouk kwouk – Oceania
Kwuyuniza. *See* Niseginyu – Indian Subcontinent
Kyanwa – Africa
Kybäi-khotun – Eastern Europe
Kybele. *See* Cybele – Near East

Kyewimoka. *See* Tāté Kyewimóka – Central America and Mesoamerica
Kymathea – Greek and Roman Empires
Kymatolege – Greek and Roman Empires
Kymo. *See* Cymo – Greek and Roman Empires
Kymodoce. *See* Cymodoce – Greek and Roman Empires
Kymothoe. *See* Cymothoe – Greek and Roman Empires
Kyohime. *See* Kiyo-hime – Far East
Kypris – Greek and Roman Empires
L!äzwag•ilayugwa – North America
L'etsa'aplelana – North America
La – Oceania
La ea. *See* Hina hele – Oceania
La Strega – Greek and Roman Empires
La Vecchia – Greek and Roman Empires
La'a hāna – Oceania
La'ama'oma'o – Oceania
Labartu – Near East
Labismina – Northern Europe
Lachamu. *See* Lahamu – Near East
Lachesis – Greek and Roman Empires
Lachos. *See* Lahamu – Near East
Lacinia – Greek and Roman Empires
Lactura – Greek and Roman Empires
Lada – Eastern Europe
Lada-dida. *See* Lada – Eastern Europe
Lady of Amenta – Egypt
Lady of Baza – Western Europe
Lady of Life. *See* Isis – Egypt
Lady of Ninab – Near East
Lady of Punt. *See* Hathor – Egypt
Lady of the Abyss – Near East
Lady of the Lake – Western Europe
Lady Wen – Northern Europe
La'e – Oceania
Laenihi – Oceania
Laga – Northern Europe
Laha – Western Europe
Lahamu – Near East
Lahar – Near East
Lahe – Western Europe
Lahi wahine – Oceania
La-hkima Oqla – Africa
La'i la'i – Oceania
Lai'a hana – Oceania
La'idamlulum Ku'le – North America
Lā'ie i kawai – Oceania
Laima – Eastern Europe
Laima-dalia. *See* Laima – Eastern Europe
Laimas-māte – Eastern Europe
Laime. *See* Laima – Eastern Europe
Lai-oid – Southeast Asia
Lairmena – Indian Subcontinent
Lajja – Indian Subcontinent
Laka – Oceania
Lake. *See* Alalahe – Oceania
Lakhamu. *See* Lahamu – Near East
Lakini – Indian Subcontinent
Lakshmi – Indian Subcontinent
Lakshmi mahisasuramardini. *See* Durga – Indian Subcontinent
Laksmana – Indian Subcontinent
Lala. *See* Losna – Greek and Roman Empires
Lalal – Greek and Roman Empires

Lalbai Phulbai – Indian Subcontinent
Laliaaiauts – North America
Lalita – Indian Subcontinent
Lalita Tripurasundari – Indian Subcontinent
Lalitalochana – Indian Subcontinent
Lalla Ta Bullat – Africa
Lalla. *See* Lilith – Near East
Lalo hāna – Oceania
Lalo honua. *See* Lalo hāna – Oceania
Laloue-diji – Central America and Mesoamerica
Lama – Near East
Lamamu. *See* Lahamu – Near East
Lamaria – Eastern Europe
Lamashtu – Near East
Lamassu – Near East
Lamasthu – Near East
Lamastu. *See* Lamashtu – Near East
Lambodari – Indian Subcontinent
Lamia – Western Europe
Lamia – Greek and Roman Empires
Lamiae, The – Greek and Roman Empires
Lamin – Western Europe
Laminaks – Western Europe
Lamkariya – Indian Subcontinent
Lamme. *See* Lamashtu – Near East
Lampado – Greek and Roman Empires
Lampatho – Greek and Roman Empires
Lampethusa – Greek and Roman Empires
Lampetia – Greek and Roman Empires
Lan Caihe – Far East
Lan Ts ai-ho. *See* Lan Caihe – Far East
Langaan – Southeast Asia
Langhui. *See* Langsuir – Southeast Asia
Langsuir, The – Southeast Asia
Langsuyar. *See* Langsuir – Southeast Asia
Lani loa – Oceania
Lani wahine – Oceania
Lankini – Indian Subcontinent
Laodice – Greek and Roman Empires
Laomedeia – Greek and Roman Empires
Laonome – Greek and Roman Empires
Laosoos – Greek and Roman Empires
Laphria – Greek and Roman Empires
La'pilewe Okya – North America
Lara – Greek and Roman Empires
Larai Majan – Southeast Asia
Larentia. *See* Acca Larentia and Lara – Greek and Roman Empires
Lares, The – Greek and Roman Empires
Large Woman – North America
Larissaea – Greek and Roman Empires
Larunda – Greek and Roman Empires
Larymna – Greek and Roman Empires
Lasa – Greek and Roman Empires
Lasa-Rakuneta – Greek and Roman Empires
Lasair – Western Europe
Lasas, The – Greek and Roman Empires
Lasema. *See* Sgeg-mo-ma – The Himalaya
Las-kyi-mkha'-'gro-ma – The Himalaya
Las-kyi-mkhah-hgro – The Himalaya
Lâsyâ. *See* Sgeg-mo-ma – The Himalaya
Lat. *See* Asherah – Near East

Lata – Indian Subcontinent
Latiaran – Western Europe
Latis – Western Europe
Latmikaik – Oceania
Lato. *See* Leto – Greek and Roman
  Empires
Latona – Greek and Roman Empires
Latu Hila la Balaa – Southeast Asia
Lau hu iki – Oceania
Lau ka 'ie'ie – Oceania
Lau kiele 'ula – Oceania
Laufey – Northern Europe
Laugo-edne – Eastern Europe
Lauka-māte – Eastern Europe
Laukosargas – Eastern Europe
Laukumāte – Eastern Europe
Lauma – Eastern Europe
Laumé – Eastern Europe
Laurentia. *See* Acca Larentia – Greek
  and Roman Empires
Lavangi – Indian Subcontinent
Lavercam. *See* Lebharcham – Western
  Europe
Laverna – Greek and Roman Empires
Lavinia – Greek and Roman Empires
Laxmi. *See* Lakshmi – Indian
  Subcontinent
Laz – Near East
Lazdu-māte – Eastern Europe
Le fale i le langi – Oceania
Le gerem – Oceania
Le hev hev – Oceania
Lea – Oceania
Leagore – Greek and Roman Empires
Leanan Sidhe – Western Europe
Lebharcham – Western Europe
Lebhorcham. *See* Lebharcham –
  Western Europe
Leda – Greek and Roman Empires
Ledaea. *See* Hermione – Greek and
  Roman Empires
Leelinau – North America
Leiagora – Greek and Roman Empires
Leiagore. *See* Leiagora – Greek and
  Roman Empires
Leilah – Near East
Leirioessa. *See* Leiriope – Greek and
  Roman Empires
Leiriope – Greek and Roman Empires
Lei-tsu. *See* Lei-zi – Far East
Lei-zi – Far East
Lejman – Oceania
Lelaino – Greek and Roman Empires
Lelwani – Near East
Lelwanis. *See* Lelwani – Near East
Lengdin – Far East
Lenju – Indian Subcontinent
Lennaxidaq – North America
Lepe a moa – Oceania
Lepeh – Southeast Asia
Leprea – Greek and Roman Empires
Lernaea – Greek and Roman Empires
Lesini. *See* Durga – Indian Subcontinent
Lesni Zenka, The – Eastern Europe
Letham – Greek and Roman Empires
Lethe – Greek and Roman Empires
Le-tkakawash – North America
Leto – Greek and Roman Empires
Letogeneia – Greek and Roman Empires
Leuce – Greek and Roman Empires

Leucippe – Greek and Roman Empires
Leucophryne – Greek and Roman
  Empires
Leucosia – Greek and Roman Empires
Leucothea – Greek and Roman Empires
Leucothoe – Greek and Roman Empires
Levana – Greek and Roman Empires
Levanah – Near East
Levarcham – Western Europe
Leviathan – Near East
Leviathanah. *See* Leviathan – Near East
Lewa levu – Oceania
Lewandranu – Oceania
Lewatu momo – Oceania
Lewatu ni nambua – Oceania
Leza. *See* Lisa – Africa
Lghags-sgrog-ma. *See* Cha-dog-ma –
  The Himalaya
Lha-ma-yin – The Himalaya
Lha-mo – The Himalaya
Lha-mo-gos-dkar-ma – The Himalaya
Lha-mo-kar-po. *See* Lha-mo – The
  Himalaya
Lhianna-shee. *See* Leanan Sidhe –
  Western Europe
Li – Far East
Li ara katau – Oceania
Li arongorong pei – Oceania
Li au en pon tan – Oceania
Lí Ban – Western Europe
Li char – Oceania
Li mot a lang – Oceania
Lia – Oceania
Liatiku. *See* Uretsete – North America
Liban. *See* Lí Ban – Western Europe
Libentina – Greek and Roman Empires
Libera – Greek and Roman Empires
Liberalitas – Greek and Roman Empires
Libertas – Greek and Roman Empires
Libethrides, The. *See* The Muses –
  Greek and Roman Empires
Libitina – Greek and Roman Empires
Libya – Greek and Roman Empires
Liderc, The – Eastern Europe
Liella. *See* Atabei – Central America
  and Mesoamerica
Lif – Northern Europe
Lifthrasir – Northern Europe
Ligankdikei. *See* Lignaco De – Greek
  and Roman Empires
Ligea. *See* Ligeia – Greek and Roman
  Empires
Ligeia – Greek and Roman Empires
Ligifo – Oceania
Lignaco De – Greek and Roman
  Empires
Ligoapup – Oceania
Ligoband. *See* Ligoububfanu – Oceania
Ligobund. *See* Ligoububfanu – Oceania
Ligoububfanu – Oceania
Likant e rairai. *See* Likant en arum –
  Oceania
Likant en arum – Oceania
Likho – Eastern Europe
Likuthava – Oceania
Lilaea – Greek and Roman Empires
Lilaia. *See* Lilaea – Greek and Roman
  Empires
Lilavatu – Oceania
Lilinoe – Oceania

Lilit. *See* Lilith – Near East
Lilith – Near East
Lilithu – Near East
Lilitu. *See* Lilith – Near East
Lilomarar. *See* Liomarar – Oceania
Liluri – Near East
Lilwani – Near East
Lilyi – Northern Europe
Limdunanij – Oceania
Limenia – Greek and Roman Empires
Limnades, The – Greek and Roman
  Empires
Limnaea – Greek and Roman Empires
Limnate – Indian Subcontinent
Limnatides, The – Greek and Roman
  Empires
Limnatis – Greek and Roman Empires
Limniace. *See* Limnate – Indian
  Subcontinent
Limnoreia – Greek and Roman Empires
Limoniades, The – Greek and Roman
  Empires
Lin – Northern Europe
Lina – Greek and Roman Empires
Lincui Hu – Far East
Lin-cui-hu-zin. *See* Lincui Hu – Far East
Linda – Eastern Europe
Linda – Western Europe
LIndian Subcontinent – Greek and
  Roman Empires
Lingan – Southeast Asia
Lingkambene – Southeast Asia
Lino – Oceania
Linos – Greek and Roman Empires
Linu-māte – Eastern Europe
Liomarar – Oceania
Lips – Greek and Roman Empires
Liriope. *See* Leiriope – Greek and
  Roman Empires
Lisa – Africa
Lise – Southeast Asia
Lisina – Near East
Lissa – Africa
Litae, The – Greek and Roman Empires
Litai, The. *See* The Litae – Greek and
  Roman Empires
Litavis – Western Europe
Little Van Lake Lady. *See* Modron –
  Western Europe
Liu Tsu. *See* Liu Zu – Far East
Liu Zu – Far East
Living Goddess – The Himalaya
Ljubi – Eastern Europe
Llacsahuato – South America
Llorona, La – Central America and
  Mesoamerica
Lo Shen – Far East
Loa – Africa
Loa – Central America and
  Mesoamerica
Lobsangma – The Himalaya
Locana – The Himalaya
Locheia – Greek and Roman Empires
Lochia. *See* Locheia – Greek and Roman
  Empires
Locid-epie – Eastern Europe
Loddiš-edne – Eastern Europe
Lofe – Northern Europe
Lofn – Northern Europe
Lofna. *See* Lofn – Northern Europe

Lofua – Northern Europe
Logia – Western Europe
Loha – North America
Lohasur – Indian Subcontinent
Loka-mata. See Lakshmi – Indian Subcontinent
Lola – Indian Subcontinent
Lolita. See Lalita – Indian Subcontinent
Long Meg – Western Europe
Longatis – Greek and Roman Empires
Longji Kongju – Far East
Long-life Sisters – The Himalaya
Longolongovavau – Oceania
Longzhi Kongju. See Longji Kongju – Far East
Longzhi Kongju. See Longji Kongju – Far East
Loo-wit – North America
Lopamudra – Indian Subcontinent
Lopemat – Eastern Europe
Lorelei – Northern Europe
Lorop – Oceania
Losna – Greek and Roman Empires
Lot – Western Europe
Lotis – Greek and Roman Empires
Louhi – Eastern Europe
Loupgarous, The – Southeast Asia
Louse Woman – North America
Loviatar – Eastern Europe
Loxo – Greek and Roman Empires
Loy Yi Lung. See Yi Long – Far East
Lu – The Himalaya
Lū – Oceania
Lua – Greek and Roman Empires
Lua Mater. See Lua – Greek and Roman Empires
Lua Saturni. See Lua – Greek and Roman Empires
Luakamat. See Lauka-māte – Eastern Europe
Luamerava – Africa
Luandinha – South America
Luaths Lurgann – Western Europe
Lube – Oceania
Lubentia. See Libentina – Greek and Roman Empires
Lubentina. See Libentina – Greek and Roman Empires
Lucania – Greek and Roman Empires
Luceria – Greek and Roman Empires
Lucetia. See Luceria – Greek and Roman Empires
Lucifera – Greek and Roman Empires
Lucina – Greek and Roman Empires
Lucna – Greek and Roman Empires
Luk – North America
Lukelong – Oceania
Lulong – Southeast Asia
Lu-ma. See gLu-ma Ghirdhima – The Himalaya
Lumaknak inLukbuban – Southeast Asia
Lumimuut – Southeast Asia
Luna – Greek and Roman Empires
Lunba – Oceania
Lung-chi Kung-chu. See Longji Kongju – Far East
Luojatar – Eastern Europe
Luonnotar – Eastern Europe

Luot-chozjik. See Luot-hozjik – Eastern Europe
Luot-hozjik – Eastern Europe
Lupa – Greek and Roman Empires
Lupe pangopango – Oceania
Lupe. See Lube – Oceania
Luperca. See Lupa – Greek and Roman Empires
Lur – Western Europe
Lurbira. See Lur – Western Europe
Lurgorr – Western Europe
Lusin – Near East
Lusin – Eastern Europe
Lusitanian Goddess – Western Europe
Lust Goddess – Indian Subcontinent
Lutchmeen. See Lakshmi – Indian Subcontinent
Luyong Baybay – Southeast Asia
Luyong Kabig – Southeast Asia
Lybica – Greek and Roman Empires
Lyce – Greek and Roman Empires
Lyceia – Greek and Roman Empires
Lycippe – Greek and Roman Empires
Lyco – Greek and Roman Empires
Lycoatis – Greek and Roman Empires
Lycorias – Greek and Roman Empires
Lygodesma – Greek and Roman Empires
Lykorias – Greek and Roman Empires
Lymniades, The. See The Limnades – Greek and Roman Empires
Lympha – Greek and Roman Empires
Lymphae. See Lympha – Greek and Roman Empires
Lymyzn-mam – Eastern Europe
Lysianassa – Greek and Roman Empires
Lysidice – Greek and Roman Empires
Lysimache – Greek and Roman Empires
Lysizona – Greek and Roman Empires
Lyssa – Greek and Roman Empires
Ma – Africa
Ma – Near East
Ma – Egypt
Ma – Greek and Roman Empires
Ma Dharti – Indian Subcontinent
Ma Gog. See Magog – Western Europe
Ma Gu – Far East
Ma hui e – Oceania
Ma Ku. See Ma Gu – Far East
Ma Ming Shêng Mu. See Maming Shengmu – Far East
Ma Niangniang. See Deo Ma Niangniang – Far East
Ma Nu – Indian Subcontinent
Ma Paudi – Indian Subcontinent
Ma riko riko – Oceania
Ma Shi – Far East
Ma Shih. See Ma Shi – Far East
Ma Tsu P'o. See Ma Zupo – Far East
Ma Tsu. See Ma Zu – Far East
Ma ukuuku – Oceania
Ma Zu – Far East
Ma Zupo – Far East
Mā 'a'a – Oceania
Maa-ema. See Ma-emma – Eastern Europe
Maa-emae. See Maan-emo – Eastern Europe
Maan-emo – Eastern Europe

Maan-emoinen. See Maan-emo – Eastern Europe
Maan-eno – Eastern Europe
Maan-eno. See Aka – Near East
Maât – Egypt
Maati. See Maât – Egypt
Maau. See Atet – Egypt
Mab. See Medb – Western Europe
Mabisalira – Africa
Macha – Western Europe
Ma-cha Shên. See Mazha Shen – Far East
Machalath – Near East
Machandri – Indian Subcontinent
Machanitis – Greek and Roman Empires
Machi-pal Lha-mo – The Himalaya
Machin Tungku – Southeast Asia
Mac-ig-dpal. See Machi-pal Lha-mo – The Himalaya
Ma-cig-dpal-lho-mo. See Lha-mo – The Himalaya
Macouas First Woman – Africa
Macris – Greek and Roman Empires
Madalait – Oceania
Maddar-aka. See Maddarakka – Eastern Europe
Maddarakka – Eastern Europe
Madder-akka – Northern Europe
Madder-akku – Eastern Europe
Madeleine – Central America and Mesoamerica
Mader-akka. See Aka – Near East
Madhava – Indian Subcontinent
Madhavi Devi – Indian Subcontinent
Madhukasa – Indian Subcontinent
Madhusri – Indian Subcontinent
Madira – Indian Subcontinent
Madri – Indian Subcontinent
Madu-Ammal – Indian Subcontinent
Madun Pungren Majan – Southeast Asia
Mae D'agua – South America
Mae Phosop – Southeast Asia
Mae Phra Phloeng – Southeast Asia
Maeke – Oceania
Maeleth. See Mahalat – Near East
Ma-emma – Eastern Europe
Maenades, The – Greek and Roman Empires
Maenads, The. See Maenades – Greek and Roman Empires
Maeonides, The – Greek and Roman Empires
Maera – Greek and Roman Empires
Maerope. See Merope – Greek and Roman Empires
Ma'et – Egypt
Maet. See Maât – Egypt
Maîtresse Philomêne. See Phillomena, Saint – Central America and Mesoamerica
Maeve. See Medb – Western Europe
Mafdet – Egypt
Mafiet – Egypt
Maftet. See Mafdet – Egypt
Mafuike – Oceania
Mafurere – Oceania
Mafutoka. See Nau taufiti – Oceania
Mag-Moullach. See Cailleach Beara – Western Europe
Maga – Western Europe
Magapid – Southeast Asia

Magarsia – Greek and Roman Empires
Ma-gcig-dpal-lha-mo – The Himalaya
Maghayanti – Indian Subcontinent
Magigi – Oceania
Magna Dea. *See* Ceres – Greek and
  Roman Empires
Magna Mater – Greek and Roman
  Empires
Magog – Western Europe
Magtatangal – Southeast Asia
Mah – Near East
Mahadevi – Indian Subcontinent
Mahagramadevata – Indian
  Subcontinent
Mahakali – Indian Subcontinent
Mahakh – North America
Mahalakshmi – Indian Subcontinent
Mahalat – Near East
Mahalaya – Indian Subcontinent
Mahamai – Indian Subcontinent
Mahamantranusarini – Indian
  Subcontinent
Mahamari. *See* Mahakali,
  Mahalakshmi, and Mahamaya –
  Indian Subcontinent
Mahamaya – Indian Subcontinent
Mahamayuri – Indian Subcontinent
Mahanidra. *See* Uma – Indian
  Subcontinent
Mahapratisara – Indian Subcontinent
Mahari – Indian Subcontinent
Mahasahasrapramardani – Indian
  Subcontinent
Mahasarasvati – Indian Subcontinent
Mahasitaviti – Indian Subcontinent
Mahasveta – Indian Subcontinent
Mahavani. *See* Sarasvati – Indian
  Subcontinent
Mahavidya – Indian Subcontinent
Mahavidya. *See* Grahamatrka – The
  Himalaya
Mahavidyas, The – Indian Subcontinent
Mahavyahriti, The – Indian
  Subcontinent
Mah-Bellona – Greek and Roman
  Empires
Mahendri – Indian Subcontinent
Mahesvari – Indian Subcontinent
Mahi – Indian Subcontinent
Mahisasuramardini – Indian
  Subcontinent
Mahlaima. *See* Hphreng-ba-ma – The
  Himalaya
Mahlyanag – Near East
Mahm-m – Central America and
  Mesoamerica
Mahora nui a rangi – Oceania
Mahora nui a tea – Oceania
Mahr. *See* Mora – Northern Europe
Mahte – Eastern Europe
Mahu – Africa
Mahu fatu rau – Oceania
Mahuea – Oceania
Mahuika. *See* Mafuike – Oceania
Mai Dharitri – Indian Subcontinent
Mai 'u'u – Oceania
Mai. *See* Umai – Near East
Maia – Greek and Roman Empires
Maia. *See* Maya – Indian Subcontinent
Maid Marian – Western Europe

Maiden Whose Clothes Rattle. *See*
  Tcikee Cac Nadleehe – North
  America
Mai-hesa – Egypt
Maile ha'i wale – Oceania
Maile kaluhea – Oceania
Maile lau li'i – Oceania
Maile pā haka – Oceania
Maile, The – Oceania
Mailkun – Oceania
Maimoa a longona – Oceania
Maimungma – Indian Subcontinent
Mainao – Indian Subcontinent
Maing Jini – Far East
Maira – Greek and Roman Empires
Mairangi – Oceania
Mairatea – Oceania
Maisamma – Indian Subcontinent
Maisö – South America
Mait. *See* Maât – Egypt
Maitresse Amelia. *See* Amelia – Central
  America and Mesoamerica
Maitresse Erzulie Freda. *See* Erzulie –
  Central America and Mesoamerica
Maitresse Erzulie. *See* Erzulie – Central
  America and Mesoamerica
Maitresse Karous. *See* Karous – Central
  America and Mesoamerica
Maitresse Madeleine. *See* Madeleine –
  Central America and Mesoamerica
Maitreyi. *See* Ahalya – Indian
  Subcontinent
Maitri – Indian Subcontinent
Maiya Andhiyari – Indian Subcontinent
Maize Mother – South America
Maize Mother – Southeast Asia
Maja – North America
Majesta. *See* Maia – Greek and Roman
  Empires
Majky, The. *See* Navki – Eastern Europe
Maka – North America
Maka-akan. *See* Maka – North America
Makara – Indian Subcontinent
Makara, The – Oceania
Makaravaktra – Indian Subcontinent
Makaris, The – Indian Subcontinent
Makarom Mawakhu – Southeast Asia
Makasa – Africa
Makawalang – Southeast Asia
Makh – Near East
Makhir – Near East
Makhut. *See* Matronit – Near East
Mak-nebt-s – Egypt
Makole nawahi waa. *See* Hi'iaka
  makole wawahi wa'a – Oceania
Makore wawahi waa. *See* Hi'iaka
  makole wawahi wa'a – Oceania
Makoro – Oceania
Makosh – Eastern Europe
Makuika. *See* Mafuike – Oceania
Makunai – Oceania
Mal – Western Europe
Mâlâ. *See* Hphreng-ba-ma – The
  Himalaya
Mala Liath – Western Europe
Malagan Mother Goddess – Western
  Europe
Malaňishishinish – North America
Malakuta Ashar Amaim. *See* Ashtart –
  Near East

Malaviskh – Greek and Roman Empires
Malaxšišiniš – North America
Mālei – Oceania
Maliades. *See* Meliades – Greek and
  Roman Empires
Malin Budhi – Indian Subcontinent
Malini – Indian Subcontinent
Malkat-shemen – Near East
Malkatu – Near East
Malkuth – Western Europe
Mallana Devi – Indian Subcontinent
Mallina – North America
Mallinatha – Indian Subcontinent
Malokatsiki – North America
Malophorus – Greek and Roman
  Empires
Mam – Oceania
Mama – Near East
Mama Allpa – South America
Mama Cocha – South America
Mama Cora – South America
Mama Cura. *See* Cura – South America
Mama Huaco. *See* Huaco – South
  America
Mama Ipa Qora. *See* Cura – South
  America
Mama-Kilya. *See* Mama Quilla – South
  America
Mama Llama – South America
Mama Nono – Central America and
  Mesoamerica
Mama Ocllo Huaca. *See* Ocllo – South
  America
Mama Ocllo. *See* Ocllo – South America
Mama Ogllo. *See* Ocllo – South America
Mama Pacha – South America
Mama Qoca. *See* Mama Cocha – South
  America
Mama Quilla – South America
Mama Rahua. *See* Raua – South
  America
Mama Raua. *See* Raua – South America
Mama Rawa. *See* Raua – South America
Mama Sara – South America
Mama Zara – South America
Mama. *See* Ma – Egypt
Mâmakî – The Himalaya
Mamala – Oceania
Mamaldi – Far East
Mamaldi – Eastern Europe
Maman Brigitte. *See* Brigette – Central
  America and Mesoamerica
Maman Simbi – Central America and
  Mesoamerica
Mamao – Oceania
Mamapacha. *See* Mama Pacha – South
  America
Mamata – Indian Subcontinent
Mami – Near East
Mamili – Indian Subcontinent
Maming Shengmu – Far East
Mamit. *See* Mamitu – Near East
Mamitu – Near East
Mammentun. *See* Mamitu – Near East
Mammitu. *See* Mamitu – Near East
Ma-mo – The Himalaya
Mamona. *See* Atabei – Central America
  and Mesoamerica
Mamony – Eastern Europe
Ma-mo-sgam-pa-ma – The Himalaya

Mampadurei – Eastern Europe
Mamzrau Mana – North America
Mana – Greek and Roman Empires
Mana Geneta. *See* Mana – Greek and Roman Empires
Manamoan – Southeast Asia
Manana – Oceania
Manang Jaban – Southeast Asia
Manasa – Indian Subcontinent
Manasi – Indian Subcontinent
Manatar. *See* Tuonetar – Northern Europe
Mandakini. *See* Ganga – Indian Subcontinent
Mandan Creator. *See* Mandan Mother – North America
Mandan Mother – North America
Mandaradevi – Indian Subcontinent
Mandaramala – Indian Subcontinent
Mandarava – Indian Subcontinent
Mande Rubiah – Southeast Asia
Ma-ndəə – Africa
Mandodari – Indian Subcontinent
Mandwa Rani – Indian Subcontinent
Mane Hennu Devaru. *See* Kelu Devaru – Indian Subcontinent
Mane Manchamma. *See* Mane Manchi – Indian Subcontinent
Mane Manchi – Indian Subcontinent
Manefertrā – Egypt
Man-el – North America
Mang Ching'i. *See* Maing Jini – Far East
Mangadevatas – Indian Subcontinent
Mangagaway – Southeast Asia
Mangalamai – Indian Subcontinent
Mangu-srî. *See* Manjusris – The Himalaya
Mania – Greek and Roman Empires
Maniae. *See* The Erinyes – Greek and Roman Empires
Manideakdili – Central America and Mesoamerica
Manik Galih – Southeast Asia
Maninupdikili – Central America and Mesoamerica
Manjusris – The Himalaya
Mannu – Eastern Europe
Manoid – Southeast Asia
Manolge inBahiwag – Southeast Asia
Manota – Indian Subcontinent
Manthara – Indian Subcontinent
Manto – Greek and Roman Empires
Mantradevatas – Indian Subcontinent
Mantrikashakti – Indian Subcontinent
Manuk Manuk – Southeast Asia
Manungal – Near East
Manusha-Rakshasis, The – Indian Subcontinent
Manzan Gormo – Far East
Manzan Görmö – Eastern Europe
Mao Tzu Shên Chüu. *See* Maozi Shenju – Far East
Maozi Shenju – Far East
Mapatal Bugan inAmalgo – Southeast Asia
Māpunai'a 'a'ala – Oceania
Mara – Near East
Marà – Eastern Europe
Mara. *See* Mora – Northern Europe
Marah. *See* Mara – Near East

Marahi Devi. *See* Marai Mata – Indian Subcontinent
Marai Mata – Indian Subcontinent
Maraki – Indian Subcontinent
Marama – Oceania
Marama kai – Oceania
Maramma – Indian Subcontinent
Maran Junti Majan – Southeast Asia
Maras, The – Eastern Europe
Mardal – Northern Europe
Mardeq Avalon – Eastern Europe
Mardez-awa – Eastern Europe
Mardoll. *See* Mardal – Northern Europe
Marei kura – Oceania
Marena – Eastern Europe
Maret-Jikky – South America
Margavati – Indian Subcontinent
Margawse. *See* Morgause – Western Europe
Marhai Devi. *See* Marai Mata – Indian Subcontinent
Marhai Mata – Indian Subcontinent
Mari – Western Europe
Mari – Indian Subcontinent
Mari Bhavani – Indian Subcontinent
Mari haka – Oceania
Mari Mai – Indian Subcontinent
Mari Mata – Indian Subcontinent
Mari Morgan, The – Western Europe
Mariai. *See* Mariamma and Mari – Indian Subcontinent
Mariama. *See* Mariamma – Indian Subcontinent
Mariamma – Indian Subcontinent
Mariamman – Indian Subcontinent
Mariana – South America
Mariatha. *See* Mahari – Indian Subcontinent
Marica – Greek and Roman Empires
Marichi – Indian Subcontinent
Marici – Indian Subcontinent
Maridama – Indian Subcontinent
Maridiamma. *See* Maridama – Indian Subcontinent
Marōdo – Far East
Marie Madeleine, Saint – Central America and Mesoamerica
Marie-aimée – Central America and Mesoamerica
Marimba – Africa
Marinette – Central America and Mesoamerica
Marinette Bois Cheche. *See* Marinette – Central America and Mesoamerica
Marinette Bwa Cheche. *See* Marinette – Central America and Mesoamerica
Marisha – Indian Subcontinent
Marishi. *See* Marichi – Indian Subcontinent
Marishi-ten – Far East
Maritchi – Indian Subcontinent
Mariyammai – Indian Subcontinent
Mariyamman – Indian Subcontinent
Mariyayi – Indian Subcontinent
Marjatta – Eastern Europe
Marjatta – Northern Europe
Marpessa – Greek and Roman Empires
Mar'rallang, The – Oceania
Marsha. *See* Marisha – Indian Subcontinent

Maru a nuku – Oceania
Maru a roto – Oceania
Maru Devi – Indian Subcontinent
Maruchi – Eastern Europe
Maruchi. *See* Mora – Northern Europe
Marulupolamma – Indian Subcontinent
Maruttaruni – Indian Subcontinent
Maruwa. *See* Marwe – Africa
Marwe – Africa
Mary, Star of the Sea – Central America and Mesoamerica
Maryam – Africa
Maryatale – Indian Subcontinent
Mary-rusalka – Eastern Europe
Marzana – Eastern Europe
Marzyana – Eastern Europe
Masahkare – North America
Masai Moon Goddess – Africa
Masakamekokiu – North America
Masan – Indian Subcontinent
Masan Wuhti – North America
Masani – Indian Subcontinent
Masanyatha – Indian Subcontinent
Masau'u Kachin' Mana – North America
Masaya – Central America and Mesoamerica
Mashongavudzi – Africa
Mashti – Near East
Mashyoi – Near East
Maskhonit. *See* Meskhent – Egypt
Maskikhwsu – North America
Maslenitsa – Eastern Europe
Massassi – Africa
Master Spirit's Daughter – North America
Mastor-ava – Eastern Europe
Maswasi – Indian Subcontinent
Maswik'Chin' Mana – North America
Masyanag – Near East
Mat' Syra Zemlya. *See* Mati-syra-zemlya – Eastern Europe
Mata – Indian Subcontinent
Mata Devi. *See* Mata – Indian Subcontinent
Mata Januvi – Indian Subcontinent
Matabai – Indian Subcontinent
Matakerepo – Oceania
Matamgi. *See* Matangi Shakti – Indian Subcontinent
Matangi – Indian Subcontinent
Matangi Shakti – Indian Subcontinent
Matar Kubile – Near East
Mataras, The – Indian Subcontinent
Matari'i. *See* Matariki – Oceania
Matariki – Oceania
Māte – Eastern Europe
Mater Artemis – Near East
Mater Larum. *See* Lara – Greek and Roman Empires
Mater Magna. *See* Magna Mater – Greek and Roman Empires
Mater Matuta – Greek and Roman Empires
Mater-turrita – Near East
Mater Turrita – Greek and Roman Empires
Matergabia – Eastern Europe
Matergabiae. *See* Matergabia – Eastern Europe

Mathyalamma. *See* Mutyalamma – Indian Subcontinent

Matinieri, The. *See* The Tatei Matinieri – Central America and Mesoamerica

Mati-syra-zemlya – Eastern Europe

Matiu – Oceania

Matlalcueye – Central America and Mesoamerica

Matnau – Far East

Matou Niang – Far East

Matres Britanne – Greek and Roman Empires

Matres, The – Western Europe

Matres. *See* Matres Britanne – Greek and Roman Empires

Matrikas, The. *See* Matris – Indian Subcontinent

Matrikas. *See* Hlamos – The Himalaya

Matrioshka – Eastern Europe

Matri-Padma – Indian Subcontinent

Matris – Indian Subcontinent

Matrix of the Universe – Indian Subcontinent

Matrona – Northern Europe

Matrona – Greek and Roman Empires

Matronae. *See* Matres, The – Western Europe

Matronethah – Western Europe

Matronit – Western Europe

Matronita. *See* Matronit – Western Europe

Matronitha. *See* Matronetha – Western Europe

Matsu. *See* Mazu – Far East

Matu – Africa

Matuta. *See* Mater Matuta – Greek and Roman Empires

Mauit. *See* Mut – Egypt

Maura Mata – Indian Subcontinent

Maurea – Oceania

Maut. *See* Mut – Egypt

Mauthia – Eastern Europe

Mavje, The. *See* Navki – Eastern Europe

Mavky, The. *See* Navki – Eastern Europe

Mawa – Africa

Mawshai – Indian Subcontinent

Mawu – Africa

Mawu Sodza – Africa

Mawu-Lisa – Africa

Maya – Indian Subcontinent

Maya Mayuri. *See* Mahamayuri – Indian Subcontinent

Mayadevi. *See* Maya and Mahamaya – Indian Subcontinent

Mayahuel – Central America and Mesoamerica

Mayarani – Indian Subcontinent

Mayari – Southeast Asia

Mayavati. *See* Rati and Maya – Indian Subcontinent

Mayavva – Indian Subcontinent

Mayet. *See* Maât – Egypt

Mayi Mayi, The – Oceania

Mayramu – Africa

Mazha Shen – Far East

Mazu – Far East

Mbaba Mwana Waresa – Africa

Mbache – Africa

Mbale – Africa

Mbongwe – Africa

Mboze – Africa

Mbuya. *See* Dziva – Africa

Me ha'i kana – Oceania

Meabal. *See* Breg – Western Europe

Meadhbh. *See* Medb – Western Europe

Meamei, The – Oceania

Mean – Greek and Roman Empires

Meana. *See* Mena – Indian Subcontinent

Meanderi – Oceania

Meave. *See* Medb – Western Europe

Mebeli – Africa

Mebuyan – Southeast Asia

Mechanitis – Greek and Roman Empires

Medb – Western Europe

Medea – Greek and Roman Empires

Medeine – Eastern Europe

Meder – Near East

Medha – Indian Subcontinent

Medhbh. *See* Medb – Western Europe

Medhbha. *See* Medb – Western Europe

Medini – Indian Subcontinent

Meditrina – Greek and Roman Empires

Medr. *See* Meder – Near East

Medusa – Greek and Roman Empires

Mefitis. *See* Mephitis – Greek and Roman Empires

Meg. *See* Long Meg – Western Europe

Megaera – Greek and Roman Empires

Megaira – Greek and Roman Empires

Megale – Greek and Roman Empires

Megatra. *See* Megaira – Greek and Roman Empires

Meghetaghna – North America

Megisto – Greek and Roman Empires

Meh Urit. *See* Hathor – Egypt

Mehen – Egypt

Mehenit – Egypt

Mehet – Egypt

Mehet-uret. *See* Hathor, Isis, Mehet – Egypt

Mehi – Egypt

Mehit – Egypt

Mehiti – Egypt

Meh-khebitet-seh-neter – Egypt

Mehueret – Egypt

Mehuerit. *See* Mehueret – Egypt

Meh-urt. *See* Ahat, Mehueret – Egypt

Mehurt. *See* Mehueret – Egypt

Meiboia – Greek and Roman Empires

Me'-ilha-mo Gos-dkar-mo – The Himalaya

Meilichia – Greek and Roman Empires

Meilinoe. *See* Melinoe – Greek and Roman Empires

Mejdejn – Eastern Europe

Mekala – Southeast Asia

Melaenis – Greek and Roman Empires

Melanaegis, The – Greek and Roman Empires

Melande-awa – Eastern Europe

Melanippe – Greek and Roman Empires

Mele – Oceania

Mele – Southeast Asia

Meleagrian – Greek and Roman Empires

Melete – Greek and Roman Empires

Melia – Greek and Roman Empires

Meliades – Greek and Roman Empires

Meliae, The – Greek and Roman Empires

Meliboea – Greek and Roman Empires

Melides. *See* Meliades – Greek and Roman Empires

Melinaea – Greek and Roman Empires

Melinoe – Greek and Roman Empires

Melissa – Greek and Roman Empires

Melissae, The – Greek and Roman Empires

Melita. *See* Mylitta – Near East

Melite – Greek and Roman Empires

Melitodes – Greek and Roman Empires

Melitta. *See* Mylitta – Near East

Mella – Africa

Mellona – Greek and Roman Empires

Mellonia. *See* Mellona – Greek and Roman Empires

Melobosis – Greek and Roman Empires

Melobote. *See* Melobosis – Greek and Roman Empires

Melpomene – Greek and Roman Empires

Melusina. *See* Melusine – Western Europe

Melusine – Western Europe

Mem Loimis – North America

Meme – Africa

Meme. *See* Meme, Africa – Near East

Memphis – Greek and Roman Empires

Mena – Indian Subcontinent

Menaka. *See* Mena – Indian Subcontinent

Menanippe. *See* Melanippe – Greek and Roman Empires

Menat – Egypt

Mendeis – Greek and Roman Empires

Mendis. *See* Bendis – Greek and Roman Empires

Mendong – Southeast Asia

Mene – Greek and Roman Empires

Meneruva – Greek and Roman Empires

Menerva. *See* Meneruva – Greek and Roman Empires

Menestho – Greek and Roman Empires

Meng. *See* Breg – Western Europe

Meng Chiang Nü. *See* Meng Jiangnü – Far East

Meng Jiangnü – Far East

Meng Po Niangniang – Far East

Mengi. *See* Menja – Northern Europe

Mengk, The – Eastern Europe

Menglad – Northern Europe

Menhenet – Egypt

Menhet – Egypt

Menhit – Egypt

Meni – Near East

Menippe – Greek and Roman Empires

Menja – Northern Europe

Menkheret – Egypt

Menluzipu – Far East

Menqet – Egypt

Menrfa – Greek and Roman Empires

Menrva. *See* Menrfa – Greek and Roman Empires

Mens – Greek and Roman Empires

Menstro. *See* Antiope – Greek and Roman Empires

Mentha. *See* Menthe – Greek and Roman Empires

Menthe – Greek and Roman Empires
Menya. *See* Menja – Northern Europe
Mephitis – Greek and Roman Empires
Merau – Oceania
Mera-māte – Eastern Europe
Mere hau – Oceania
Mere-ama – Eastern Europe
Mereneiu. *See* Näkineiu – Eastern
   Europe
Merenneito. *See* Näkki – Eastern Europe
Meresger. *See* Merseger – Egypt
Meret – Egypt
Meri – Egypt
Meri-en-sekar. *See* Rannu – Egypt
Merit – Egypt
Mermaids, The – Western Europe
Merna. *See* Mena – Indian Subcontinent
Meroe – Greek and Roman Empires
Merope – Greek and Roman Empires
Merrinako – North America
Merrow – Western Europe
Merseger – Egypt
Mersekhnet. *See* Atet – Egypt
Mert – Egypt
Merte. *See* Mert – Egypt
Merti, The – Egypt
Mertseger. *See* Merseger – Egypt
Mesabai – Indian Subcontinent
Mesakamigokwaha – North America
Mesako. *See* Mesabai – Indian
   Subcontinent
Meschamaat – Eastern Europe
Mese – Greek and Roman Empires
Mesembria – Greek and Roman
   Empires
Mesenet – Egypt
Meshiane – Near East
Meshkent – Egypt
Meshkenet. *See* Meskhent – Egypt
Meskhenit. *See* Meskhent – Egypt
Meskhent – Egypt
Meskhoni. *See* Meshkent – Egypt
Mesma – Greek and Roman Empires
Mess Buachalla – Western Europe
Messak Kummik Okwi. *See* Mesuk
   Kummik Okwi – North America
Messeis – Greek and Roman Empires
Messene – Greek and Roman Empires
Messia – Greek and Roman Empires
Mesta – Egypt
Mestra – Greek and Roman Empires
Mesuk Kummik Okwi – North America
Me-suk-kum-me-go-kwa – North
   America
Metakorab – Oceania
Meža-māte – Eastern Europe
Meter – Greek and Roman Empires
Meteres – Greek and Roman Empires
Methe – Greek and Roman Empires
Methyer – Egypt
Me?tik Čič?u – Central America and
   Mesoamerica
Metioche – Greek and Roman Empires
Metis – Greek and Roman Empires
Me-tog-ma – The Himalaya
Metope – Greek and Roman Empires
Metra – Near East
Metsänneitsyt – Eastern Europe
Metsänneitsyt – Northern Europe
Metsarhatija – Eastern Europe

Metsola – Northern Europe
Metsola Mother – Eastern Europe
Metsulah – Near East
Metza. *See* Aquit – North America
Mezulla – Near East
Mgigalekha – Indian Subcontinent
Mhatzuu. *See* Mazu – Far East
Mhaya – Africa
Mht wr.t – Egypt
Mi-bou-do – Far East
Mi Fei – Far East
Mi-ka-k'e Hondon – North America
Mi-ka-k'eu-ki-thaç'in – North America
Miao Qing – Far East
Miao Shan – Far East
Miao Yin – Far East
Miao Yin Fomu – Far East
Miao Yu. *See* Miao Qing – Far East
Mictanteot – Central America and
   Mesoamerica
Mictecacihuatl – Central America and
   Mesoamerica
Mictlancihuatl – Central America and
   Mesoamerica
Micu – North America
Mida – Greek and Roman Empires
Mideatis – Greek and Roman Empires
Mideia – Greek and Roman Empires
Midwives, Goddess of – Far East
Midzuha-no-me-no-kami. *See*
   Mitsu-ha-no-me-no-kami – Far East
Mielikki – Eastern Europe
Mielikki – Northern Europe
Mielus. *See* Mielikki – Eastern Europe
Mier-iema. *See* Mere-ama – Eastern
   Europe
Mieulutar. *See* Mielikki – Eastern
   Europe
Mifuto-hime – Far East
Migonitis – Greek and Roman Empires
Mihi-uirit. *See* Mehueret – Egypt
Mihit – Egypt
Mihotsu-hime – Far East
Miketsu-kami – Far East
Mikimatt – North America
Miko – Far East
Mikura-tana-no-kami – Far East
Milapukala – Oceania
Militaris – Greek and Roman Empires
Milkath – Near East
Milt. *See* Mert – Egypt
Milu – Oceania
Milun – Far East
Mimaliwu – Oceania
Mimallones, The – Greek and Roman
   Empires
Mimi Biliku. *See* Biliku – Indian
   Subcontinent
Mimir – Northern Europe
Min Jok – Africa
Mina – Indian Subcontinent
Mina Koya – North America
Minachiamman – Indian Subcontinent
Minaksi – Indian Subcontinent
Minceskro – Eastern Europe
Mindhai Devi. *See* Mindal – Indian
   Subcontinent
Mindhal – Indian Subcontinent
Minerva – Greek and Roman Empires
Minerva Medica – Western Europe

Ming, Lady – Far East
Mingari – Oceania
Minma mala – Oceania
Minma milbali – Oceania
Minma mingari – Oceania
Minma Nganamara. *See* Djugurba –
   Oceania
Minma waiuda – Oceania
Minne – Northern Europe
Minnehaha – North America
Minona – Africa
Mintha. *See* Menthe – Greek and
   Roman Empires
Minthe. *See* Mentha – Greek and
   Roman Empires
Minti Dara Bunsu – Southeast Asia
Mintuchi-kamui – Far East
Minu Anni – Near East
Minyaburu, The – Oceania
Mï öll – Northern Europe
Mirahuato – South America
Miralaidji. *See* Djanggawul – Oceania
Miranda – Western Europe
Miren, The. *See* The Fatit – Eastern
   Europe
Mirgi Devi – Indian Subcontinent
Miritatsiec – North America
Miru – Oceania
Miru kura – Oceania
Mirume – Far East
Mirzapore Forest Goddess – Indian
   Subcontinent
Mis-khum – Eastern Europe
Misa – Greek and Roman Empires
Miseke – Africa
Miseria – Greek and Roman Empires
Mishima-no-mizo-kui-hime – Far East
Misrakesi – Indian Subcontinent
Mist – Northern Europe
Mistress Ezili. *See* Erzulie – Central
   America and Mesoamerica
Mitsu-ha-no-me-no-kami – Far East
Mixoparthenos, The – Greek and
   Roman Empires
Miyazu-hime – Far East
Miysis – Greek and Roman Empires
Mizohuhi hime. *See* Mizo-kuhi-hime –
   Far East
Mizo-kuhi-hime – Far East
Mizuha-no-me. *See*
   Mitsu-ha-no-me-no-kami – Far East
Mizunoe. *See* Oto – Far East
Mizu-tsu-hime – Far East
Mkhah-hgro-ma. *See* Khahdoma – The
   Himalaya
Mlakukh – Greek and Roman Empires
Mnasa – Greek and Roman Empires
Mneiae, The – Greek and Roman
   Empires
Mneme – Greek and Roman Empires
Mnemonides, The – Greek and Roman
   Empires
Mnemosyne – Greek and Roman
   Empires
Mngilamma – Indian Subcontinent
Mni-haha. *See* Minnehaha – North
   America
Mo. *See* Nok – Far East
Mo Bo – Far East
Mo Ye – Far East

Mo Yeh. *See* Mo Ye – Far East
Moa kura ma nu. *See* Moakura – Oceania
Moakura – Oceania
Moana nui ka lehua – Oceania
Moa'ri – Oceania
Mobokomu – Africa
Mocihuaquetzque – Central America and Mesoamerica
Modgud – Northern Europe
Modgudhr. *See* Modgud – Northern Europe
Modgudr. *See* Modgud – Northern Europe
Modron – Western Europe
Mo'e hau i te ra'i – Oceania
Mo'e ruru'a – Oceania
Moera, The. *See* The Moirae – Greek and Roman Empires
Moerae, The. *See* The Moirae – Greek and Roman Empires
Moertholl. *See* Frejya, Mardal – Northern Europe
Mogfind. *See* Mongfhinn – Western Europe
Mohani – Indian Subcontinent
Mohenjo-Daro Goddesses – Indian Subcontinent
Mohini – Indian Subcontinent
Moing'iima – North America
Moirae, The – Greek and Roman Empires
Moirai, The. *See* The Moirae – Greek and Roman Empires
Moire-mat – Far East
Moitjinka – Oceania
Moko – Oceania
Mokos. *See* Mokosi – Eastern Europe
Mokosh – Eastern Europe
Mokosi – Eastern Europe
Moksha – Eastern Europe
Moku hinia – Oceania
Mokum – The Himalaya
Mokusa. *See* Mokuskha – Eastern Europe
Mokusha. *See* Mokuskha – Eastern Europe
Mokuskha – Eastern Europe
Molae, The – Greek and Roman Empires
Mo-lha-mo – The Himalaya
Molis. *See* Mylitta – Near East
Molpadia – Greek and Roman Empires
Molpe – Greek and Roman Empires
Mombu – Central America and Mesoamerica
Momo. *See* Ïre – Western Europe
Momoy – North America
Momu – Western Europe
Mona. *See* Tuglibong – Southeast Asia
Moncha – Western Europe
Moneiba – Western Europe
Moneta – Greek and Roman Empires
Mong' Wuhti – North America
Mongfhinn – Western Europe
Monkey Goddess of Hampi – Indian Subcontinent
Mons Meg. *See* Long Meg – Western Europe
Mo'n-sho'n – North America

Mo'o, The – Oceania
Mo'o i nanea – Oceania
Moombi – Africa
Moon Mother – Southeast Asia
Moon Woman – North America
Mooth. *See* Mut – Egypt
Moothevi – Indian Subcontinent
Mór. *See* Mughain – Western Europe
Mor Muman – Western Europe
Mora – Eastern Europe
Mora – Northern Europe
Morae, The. *See* The Moirae – Greek and Roman Empires
Morana – Eastern Europe
Mor-ava – Eastern Europe
Moravaya Panna – Eastern Europe
Morey Ba – Western Europe
Morgain La Fee. *See* Morgan Le Fay – Western Europe
Morgaine La Faye. *See* Morgan Le Fay – Western Europe
Morgan Le Fay – Western Europe
Morgan. *See* Mari Morgan, The – Western Europe
Morgana. *See* Morgan Le Fay – Western Europe
Morganes. *See* Mari Morgan, The – Western Europe
Morgause – Western Europe
Morgay – Western Europe
Moriath – Western Europe
Moriath Morce. *See* Moriath – Western Europe
Morimi – Africa
Mormo – Greek and Roman Empires
Morning Star Woman – North America
Morningstar of Wakaranga – Africa
Morongo – Africa
Morpho – Greek and Roman Empires
Mórrí gán – Western Europe
Mors – Greek and Roman Empires
Morta – Greek and Roman Empires
Mortlock – Oceania
Moruach. *See* Moruadh – Western Europe
Moruadh – Western Europe
Moshir-huchi – Far East
Mot – Near East
Mother Chuber. *See* Tiamat – Near East
Mother Earth – Indian Subcontinent
Mother Fish – Indian Subcontinent
Mother Friday. *See* Paraskeva – Eastern Europe
Mother Globes – Indian Subcontinent
Mother Khahdoma – The Himalaya
Mother of All Eagles – North America
Mother of Food – Africa
Mother of Life – Near East
Mother of Mannu. *See* Mannu – Eastern Europe
Mother of Metsola – Eastern Europe
Mother of Ten Thousand Things – Far East
Mother Space – Indian Subcontinent
Mother Sunset Yellow. *See* Corn Mother – North America
Mother Water – Indian Subcontinent
Mothir – Northern Europe
Motho – Indian Subcontinent
Moti Mata – Indian Subcontinent

Mt. Unebi Goddess – Far East
Mousso Koroni Koundye – Africa
Mout. *See* Mut – Egypt
Mou-t'u. *See* Moutu – Far East
Moutu. *See* Hou Tu Nainai. Alternate form: Mou-t'u – Far East
Moye. *See* Mo Ye – Far East
Moymis – Near East
Mrtyu – Indian Subcontinent
mThing-gi-zhal-bzang-ma – The Himalaya
mTsho-sman-g•yu-thang-cho-longs-ma – The Himalaya
mTsho-sman-gzi-ldan-ral-gcig-ma – The Himalaya
mTsho-sman-klu-yi-rgyal-mo – The Himalaya
mTsho-sman-mthing-gi-lha-mo – The Himalaya
mTsho-sman-nyi-ma'i-byan-goig-ma – The Himalaya
mTsho-sman-rgyal-mo-mkhro'i-gtso – The Himalaya
mTsho-sman-ru-phyug-rgyal-mo – The Himalaya
Mu – Central America and Mesoamerica
Mu. *See* Nok – Far East
Mu Alesop – Central America and Mesoamerica
Mu Aligisai. *See* Mu Alesop – Central America and Mesoamerica
Mu Bachu Okya – North America
Mu Je. *See* Mu Re – Far East
Mu mu whango. *See* Mumuhanga – Oceania
Mu Olokukurtlisop – Central America and Mesoamerica
Mu Olokundil – Central America and Mesoamerica
Mu Olotagisop – Central America and Mesoamerica
Mu Olotakiki – Central America and Mesoamerica
Mu Re – Far East
Mu Sobia – Central America and Mesoamerica
Mu'allidtu. *See* Mylitta – Near East
Mucaias Mana – North America
Mudevi – Indian Subcontinent
Mudungkala – Oceania
Mugadi. *See* Jyestha – Indian Subcontinent
Mugain. *See* Mughain – Western Europe
Mughain – Western Europe
Muhongo – Africa
Muhurta – Indian Subcontinent
Muime Chriosda. *See* Brigid – Western Europe
Muirdris – Western Europe
Muireartach – Western Europe
Muirenn – Western Europe
Muiriath – Western Europe
Muit. *See* Mut – Egypt
Muiu'uleapai – Oceania
Mujaji – Africa
Muk Jauk – Southeast Asia
Mukasa – Africa
Mukhambika – Indian Subcontinent
Mukikwe Okya – North America

Muksort – Eastern Europe
Mukta Devi – Indian Subcontinent
Muktakesi – Indian Subcontinent
Mukw'okya. *See* Mukikwe Okya –
    North America
Mukylcin – Eastern Europe
Mulaprakriti – Indian Subcontinent
Muliebris – Greek and Roman Empires
Mulishshu. *See* Ninlil – Near East
Mulitta. *See* Mylitta – Near East
Mulliltu. *See* Ninlil – Near East
Mulu mulu – Oceania
Mulua Satene – Southeast Asia
Mulukuausi, The – Oceania
Mumham. *See* Ëre – Western Europe
Mummu – Near East
Mumuhanga – Oceania
Mumuna – Oceania
Munainako – North America
Munakata Goddesses – Far East
Munanna – Western Europe
Munbakuaku – Oceania
Mundikara – Oceania
Munga munga, The – Oceania
Mungo – North America
Mungo – Indian Subcontinent
Muni Mental Batu – Southeast Asia
Mun-lu-dzi-pu. *See* Menluzipu – Far
    East
Munsumundok – Southeast Asia
Munthkh. *See* Munthukh – Greek and
    Roman Empires
Munthukh – Greek and Roman Empires
Munya – Eastern Europe
Munya•k Yopue – South America
Munychia – Greek and Roman Empires
Murala – Indian Subcontinent
Murava – Eastern Europe
Murcia – Greek and Roman Empires
Muri ranga whenua – Oceania
Muri whaka roto. *See* Muriwhakaroto –
    Oceania
Murigen – Western Europe
Muriwhakaroto – Oceania
Murna of the White Neck – Western
    Europe
Murtea. *See* Murcia – Greek and Roman
    Empires
Murtia. *See* Murcia – Greek and Roman
    Empires
Murupiangkala – Oceania
Muryoju. *See* Amitabha – Far East
Muryoka. *See* Amitabha – Far East
Musae, The. *See* The Muses – Greek and
    Roman Empires
Mu'satewichi Okya – North America
Muses, The – Greek and Roman
    Empires
Musike – Greek and Roman Empires
Musso Koroni – Africa
Mut – Egypt
Muta – Greek and Roman Empires
Muth. *See* Mut – Egypt
Mutjingga. *See* Karwadi – Oceania
Mut-neb-set – Egypt
Mut-ubastet. *See* Ubastet – Egypt
Mutyalamma – Indian Subcontinent
Muyinewu mana – North America
Muyingwa Wuhti – North America
Muyiñwuh – North America

Muyinwu-wugti – North America
Muyt – Egypt
Muzamuza – Indian Subcontinent
Muzem-mumi. *See* Muzem-mumy –
    Eastern Europe
Muzem-mumy – Eastern Europe
Muzjem-mumi. *See* Muzem-mumy –
    Eastern Europe
Muzulla. *See* Mezulla – Near East
Muš – Near East
Mwarega. *See* Namboa – Africa
Mweji – Africa
Mwezi. *See* Mweji – Africa
Mycalessia – Greek and Roman Empires
Mycalessides, The – Greek and Roman
    Empires
Myesyats – Eastern Europe
Myletta. *See* Mylitta – Near East
Mylitta – Near East
Myrkrida – Northern Europe
Myrrha – Near East
Myrtis of Anthedon – Greek and
    Roman Empires
Myrtoessa – Greek and Roman Empires
Mysia – Greek and Roman Empires
Mysterious Female – Far East
Mystis – Greek and Roman Empires
Nã Afiye – Africa
Nã Bake – Africa
Na Dede Oyeadu – Africa
Na Ina – Southeast Asia
Na kino wailua – Oceania
Na lehua 'aka'aka – Oceania
Na maka haha'i. *See* Nã maka o
    kaha'i – Oceania
Na Rip Nom – Indian Subcontinent
Na Yo – Africa
Na Zong Nyo. *See* It Mu – Indian
    Subcontinent
Nã keo lani – Oceania
Nã maka o kaha'i – Oceania
Na?ackjeii Esdzaa – North America
Naaliwámi. *See* Tãté Naaliwámi –
    Central America and Mesoamerica
Naas – Western Europe
Naasun – North America
Nabarbi – Near East
Nabia – Western Europe
Nabudi, The – Oceania
Nabuzana – Africa
Nacht. *See* Nat – Northern Europe
Nadi – Indian Subcontinent
Nae. *See* Naete – Africa
Naedona. *See* Naete – Africa
Naenia – Greek and Roman Empires
Naëstsán – North America
Naete – Africa
Nafanua – Oceania
Nagadya – Africa
Nagar Saga. *See* Mami – Near East
Nagawonyi – Africa
Nage-bonga – Indian Subcontinent
Nage-Era – Indian Subcontinent
Naginis, The. *See* the Nagis – Indian
    Subcontinent
Nagis, The – Indian Subcontinent
Nagnis. *See* Nagis – Indian Subcontinent
Nagodya – Africa
Nagyboldogasszony. *See*
    Boldogasszony – Eastern Europe

Nahab – Egypt
Nahalic Okya. *See* Nahalish' Okya –
    North America
Nahalish' Okya – North America
Naham-ua – Egypt
Nahar – Near East
Nahema – Western Europe
Nahinahi ana – Oceania
Nahkeeta – North America
Nahmauit – Egypt
Nahokhos baadi – North America
Nahosdzaan Esdza – North America
Nahotsoi asdzáá – North America
Nahunta. *See* Ishtar and Anāhita – Near
    East
Nai Mu – Far East
Naiades, The – Greek and Roman
    Empires
Naiads. *See* The Naiades – Greek and
    Roman Empires
Naikin Bai – Indian Subcontinent
Naimetzabok – Central America and
    Mesoamerica
Naina Devi – Indian Subcontinent
Nai-orun-kamui – Far East
Náir – Western Europe
Nais. *See* Menthe – Greek and Roman
    Empires
Naivedya. *See* Zhal-zas-ma – The
    Himalaya
Najade – Eastern Europe
Nakawe. *See* Takótsi Nakawé – Central
    America and Mesoamerica
Nakime – Far East
Näkineitsi. *See* Näkineiu – Eastern
    Europe
Näkineiu – Eastern Europe
Näkinneito – Eastern Europe
Näkinpiika. *See* Näkki – Eastern Europe
Naki-saha-me-no-kami. *See*
    Naki-sawa-me-no-kami – Far East
Naki-saha-no-me-no-mikoto. *See*
    Naki-sawa-me-no-kami – Far East
Naki-sawame-no-mikoto. *See*
    Naki-sawa-me-no-kami – Far East
Nakith – Egypt
Nakiwulo – Africa
Näkki – Eastern Europe
Nakorut – North America
Nakshatras, The – Indian Subcontinent
Naktamcharis, The – Indian
    Subcontinent
Nakti Devi – Indian Subcontinent
Nal. *See* Laufey – Northern Europe
Naladi – Indian Subcontinent
Nalban-aiy – Eastern Europe
Na'le – North America
Naliayog. *See* Nuliajuk – North America
Nalongo – Africa
Nalwanga – Africa
Nalygyr-aissyt-khotun – Eastern Europe
Nama Djang Ad Chalom – Southeast
    Asia
Namagiri – Indian Subcontinent
Namaka – Oceania
Namakaokahai. *See* Na maka o kaha'i –
    Oceania
Namamdamma – Indian Subcontinent
Nambi – Africa

Namboa – Africa
Namita – Oceania
Namite. *See* Namita – Oceania
Nam-kha-ing-kya-wang-chug-ma –
　The Himalaya
Nam-mk'ahi-snin-po – The Himalaya
Nam-mkha'g•yu-mdog-snang-srid-
　mdzod – The Himalaya
Nam-mkh-ah-dvyings-kyi-dvang-phyug
　-ma. *See* Nam-kha-ing-kya-wang-
　chug-ma – The Himalaya
Nam-mkha'i-lha-mo-gsal-byed-ma –
　The Himalaya
Nam-mkha'i-lha-mo-Kun-tu-bzang-mo –
　The Himalaya
Nam-mkha'i-lha-mo-snyoms-byed-ma –
　The Himalaya
Nam-mkha'i-lha-mo-sprin-tshogs-ma –
　The Himalaya
Nam-mkha'i-lha-mo-tsha-gsang-snyoms
　– The Himalaya
Nam-mkha'i-lha-mo-tshod-'dzin-ma –
　The Himalaya
Nammu – Near East
Nan – Eastern Europe
Nan chu Kweejo – North America
Nan Tummat. *See* Olokukurtilisop –
　Central America and Mesoamerica
Nana – Near East
Nana. *See* Nana Buruku – Africa
Nana. *See* Nana Buruku – Central
　America and Mesoamerica
Nana Buluku – Africa
Nana Buruku – Africa
Nana Buruku – Central America and
　Mesoamerica
Nana Enna – Africa
Nana Jakpa – Africa
Nana Olokegepiai – Central America
　and Mesoamerica
Nana Olomaguyriai – Central America
　and Mesoamerica
Nana-buluku. *See* Nana Buluku – Africa
Nanaburucu. *See* Nana Buruku – Africa
Nanaburucu. *See* Nana Buruku –
　Central America and Mesoamerica
Nanaea. *See* Anaitis – Greek and
　Roman Empires
Nanai – Near East
Nanaja – Near East
Nanaki. *See* Nakime – Far East
Na-naki-me. *See* Nakime – Far East
Nanan. *See* Nana Buruku – Africa
Nanan. *See* Nana Buruku – Central
　America and Mesoamerica
Nanaolonupippisopi – Central America
　and Mesoamerica
Nanaqasilakwe – North America
Nanda Devi – Indian Subcontinent
Nandecy – South America
Nandi – Indian Subcontinent
Nandini – Indian Subcontinent
Nane – Near East
Nanen – South America
Nang Pyek Kha Yeh Khi – Southeast
　Asia
Nang Tholani – Southeast Asia
Nanga Baigin – Indian Subcontinent
Nangkwijo – North America

Nang-sal-ma. *See* sNang-gsal-ma – The
　Himalaya
Nani Waiya – North America
Nanna – Near East
Nanna – Northern Europe
Nannan. *See* Ëre – Western Europe
Nañoikwia – North America
Nanoquaqsaq – North America
Nanshe – Near East
Nanshebargunu-nanshe. *See*
　Nunbarshegunu – Near East
Nanshebargunu. *See* Nanshe and
　Nunbarshegunu – Near East
Nantosvelta – Western Europe
Nantotsuelta. *See* Nantosvelta –
　Western Europe
Nanu. *See* Ëre – Western Europe
Naotsete – North America
Napaea, The – Greek and Roman
　Empires
Napaeae, The. *See* The Napaea – Greek
　and Roman Empires
Naprit – Egypt
Napuri-kor-kamui-kor-matnepo – Far
　East
Nar. *See* Náir – Western Europe
Narama – Oceania
Narasimhi – Indian Subcontinent
Narayani Mai – Indian Subcontinent
Nar-azerava – Eastern Europe
Narcaea – Greek and Roman Empires
Narechnitsa – Eastern Europe
Nari – Indian Subcontinent
Narina – Oceania
Narmada – Indian Subcontinent
Naro-kha-choma – The Himalaya
Naro-mk-a-spyod-ma. *See*
　Naro-kha-choma – The Himalaya
Narpajin – Oceania
Narucnici, The – Eastern Europe
Naru-kami – Far East
Naruni – Oceania
Narunte – Near East
Nasa – Near East
Nascio – Greek and Roman Empires
Nashak – Near East
Nashjei Esdza. *See* Spider Woman –
　North America
Nasilele – Africa
Naskapi Moon Goddess – North
　America
Nastasija – Eastern Europe
Nastse Estsan. *See* Spider Woman –
　North America
Nasu – Near East
Nat – Northern Europe
Nata. *See* Nina – Near East
Natalis – Greek and Roman Empires
Nataska Mana – North America
Natchez Maize Mother – North America
Nath – Western Europe
Nathair Parrthuis, The – Near East
Nathum – Greek and Roman Empires
Natosuelta. *See* Nantosvelta – Western
　Europe
Natsu-no-me-no-kami. *See*
　Natsu-taka-tsu-hi-no-kami – Far East
Natsu-taka-tsu-hi-no-kami – Far East
Nau – Egypt
Nau fiora – Oceania

Nau taufiti – Oceania
Nau. *See* Ëre – Western Europe
Nau'tsitic. *See* Naotsete – North
　America
Naunet – Egypt
Nausithoe – Greek and Roman Empires
Nausity. *See* Naotsete – North America
Nautsiti – North America
Navadurgas, The – Indian Subcontinent
Na'vahine – Oceania
Navajo First Woman. *See* Aataentsic –
　North America
Navapatrikas, The. *See* Navadurgas –
　Indian Subcontinent
Nãves-mãte – Eastern Europe
Navi, The. *See* The Navki – Eastern
　Europe
Navia – Western Europe
Navia Arconunieca – Western Europe
Navirilis – Greek and Roman Empires
Navki, The – Eastern Europe
Navky. *See* The Navki – Eastern Europe
Nawandyo – Africa
Naxa'asdza'•n. *See* Spider Woman –
　North America
Naxocoi'esza – North America
Nayaanxatisei – North America
Nay-Ekva – Eastern Europe
Nayikas, The – Indian Subcontinent
Nazi – Near East
Nazit – Egypt
Ndako Gboya – Africa
Nda-la-a-ssaw-mi – Far East
Ndara – Southeast Asia
Ndengei – Oceania
Ndimailangi – Oceania
Ndo I Ronda Eo – Southeast Asia
Ndoi – Africa
Ndwanga – Africa
Ne kidong. *See* Tabui kor – Oceania
Ne te re'ere – Oceania
Neaera – Greek and Roman Empires
Neb-ankhet – Egypt
Neb-anu – Egypt
Nebele – Africa
Nebetu. *See* Nebtuu – Egypt
Nebhat. *See* Nephthys – Egypt
Nebheb-ka. *See* Nehebka – Egypt
Nebhet Hotep – Egypt
Nebhet-hotep. *See* Nebhet Hotep –
　Egypt
Neb-oo – Egypt
Neb-senti – Egypt
Nebt – Egypt
Nebt-er-tcher – Egypt
Nebthet. *See* Nephthys – Egypt
Nebt-hot. *See* Nephthys – Egypt
Nebthotpit. *See* Nebhet Hotep – Egypt
Neb-ti. *See* The Nebti – Egypt
Nebti, The – Egypt
Nebt-mat – Egypt
Nebt-nehi – Egypt
Nebt-setau – Egypt
Nebt-shat – Egypt
Nebt-shefshefet – Egypt
Nebt-thehent – Egypt
Nebt-unnut – Egypt
Nebtusha – Egypt
Nebtuu – Egypt
Necessitas – Greek and Roman Empires

Nechbet. *See* Nekhebet – Egypt
Nechmetawaj – Egypt
Nechtan Scéne – Western Europe
Neda – Greek and Roman Empires
Nedolya – Eastern Europe
Nedusia – Greek and Roman Empires
Neegyauks – North America
Neeve of the Golden Hair. *See* Niamh –
   Western Europe
Nef – Northern Europe
Nefertem – Egypt
Neg. *See* Neith – Egypt
Nehalennia – Northern Europe
Nehebka – Egypt
Nehebkath. *See* Nehebka – Egypt
Nehemāuit – Egypt
Nehemcou – Egypt
Nehimeou – Egypt
Nehmet-awai. *See* Nechmetawaj – Egypt
Nei aro maiaki – Oceania
Nei auti – Oceania
Nei bairara – Oceania
Nei marena – Oceania
Nei matamona – Oceania
Nei nguiriki – Oceania
Nei te arei n tarawa – Oceania
Nei te ra'aiti – Oceania
Nei te re'ere – Oceania
Nei te tauti – Oceania
Neilo – Greek and Roman Empires
Neis – Greek and Roman Empires
Neit. *See* Neith – Egypt
Neiterogob – Africa
Neith – Egypt
Neither. *See* Neith – Egypt
Nejky, The. *See* The Navki – Eastern
   Europe
Nejma – Africa
Nekhabit. *See* Nekhebet – Egypt
Nekhbet. *See* Nekhebet – Egypt
Nekhebet – Egypt
Nekhebit. *See* Nekhebet – Egypt
Nekhen – Egypt
Nekiu – Egypt
Nekke – Northern Europe
Nelaima – Eastern Europe
Nemain – Western Europe
Neman. *See* Nemain – Western Europe
Nemanous. *See* Nahmauit – Egypt
Nemea – Greek and Roman Empires
Nemertes – Greek and Roman Empires
Nemesis – Greek and Roman Empires
Nemetona – Western Europe
Nemodilky, The – Eastern Europe
Nemon. *See* Nemain – Western Europe
Nemorensis – Greek and Roman
   Empires
Nen – Egypt
Nena – Central America and
   Mesoamerica
Nenak Kebajan – Southeast Asia
Nenalaatseqa – North America
Nenhain. *See* Nemain – Western Europe
Nenia. *See* Naenia – Greek and Roman
   Empires
Neoga – North America
Neomeris – Greek and Roman Empires
Nephele – Greek and Roman Empires
Nephesh – Near East
Nephthys – Egypt

Nephys. *See* Nephthys – Egypt
Nepit – Egypt
Neprit – Egypt
Nepte. *See* Nephthys – Egypt
Nepthys. *See* Nephthys – Egypt
Neptunine – Greek and Roman Empires
Nerchevik – North America
Nereides, The – Greek and Roman
   Empires
Nereis – Greek and Roman Empires
Nerine – Greek and Roman Empires
Nerio – Greek and Roman Empires
Nerrivik – North America
Nerthus – Northern Europe
Nesaea – Greek and Roman Empires
Nesaia. *See* Nesaea – Greek and Roman
   Empires
Nesbet – Egypt
Neserit – Egypt
Nesert. *See* Neserit – Egypt
Neshamah – Near East
Neshtu – Egypt
Nesi-khonsu – Egypt
Neske-pas – Eastern Europe
Neš keper-ava – Eastern Europe
Neso – Greek and Roman Empires
Nesreča – Eastern Europe
Nessa – Western Europe
Net. *See* Ahat, Mehenit, Nut – Egypt
Netcensta – North America
Nete – Greek and Roman Empires
Netert-en-khentet-ra – Egypt
Netet – Egypt
Netheth – Egypt
Netpe – Egypt
Netsika. *See* The Tatei Netsika – Central
   America and Mesoamerica
Nevinbimba'au – Oceania
Newe. *See* Hoku kau opae – Oceania
Ne-zil-la – Near East
Nga lalbal – Oceania
Ngalijod. *See* Ngaljod – Oceania
Ngaljod – Oceania
Ngaloit. *See* Ngaljod – Oceania
Ngame – Africa
Ngaore – Oceania
Ngārara huarau – Oceania
Ngaumataki'one – Oceania
Ngeipau – Oceania
Nge'obiongo – Oceania
Nggae – Southeast Asia
Nguatupu'a – Oceania
Nguntre – The Himalaya
Nhang – Near East
Niachero – Africa
Niamh – Western Europe
Niang-niang Sung-tzu. *See* Niangniang
   Songzi – Far East
Niangniang – Far East
Niangniang Songzi – Far East
Niaɍimamau?u – North America
Nibora – Oceania
Nibu-tsu-hime – Far East
Nice – Greek and Roman Empires
Nicephorus – Greek and Roman
   Empires
Nichta. *See* Nikta – Greek and Roman
   Empires
Nicnevin – Western Europe
Nicostrata – Near East

Nicostrata – Greek and Roman Empires
Nicostrate. *See* Nicostrata – Greek and
   Roman Empires
Nicothoe – Greek and Roman Empires
Nidaba – Near East
Nidhema. *See* Zhal-zas-ma – The
   Himalaya
Nidra – Indian Subcontinent
Nielleltaix. *See* Nuxmelnimana – North
   America
Nigheag Na H-ath – Western Europe
Nigoubub – Oceania
Nihoniho teitei – Oceania
Nihoniho tetei. *See* Nihoniho teitei –
   Oceania
Nikaiva – Africa
Nikal-mati – Near East
Nike – Greek and Roman Empires
Nikkal – Near East
Nikkalmati. *See* Nikal-mati – Near East
Nikta – Greek and Roman Empires
Nikumbhila – Indian Subcontinent
Nimba – Africa
Nimli Numjan – Southeast Asia
Nimm – Africa
Nimue – Western Europe
Nin Ella – Near East
Nin Si Anna. *See* Ishtar and Ninisinna –
   Near East
Nina – Near East
Nin-agid-kahadu – Near East
Nin-akha-guddu – Near East
Nin-akha-kuda – Near East
Nin-anna – Near East
Ninatta – Near East
Ninavanhu-ma – Africa
Ninazu – Near East
Ninda Kando (Chando) – Indian
   Subcontinent
Nin-dim. *See* Sarpanitu – Near East
Nindukugga – Near East
Nindum. *See* Mami – Near East
Nin-edin. *See* Belit Ilani, Belit Seri, and
   Gestinanna – Near East
Nin-e-i-garak – Near East
Ninella. *See* Damkina – Near East
Ning-Bonga – Indian Subcontinent
Ningal – Near East
Ningarope – Oceania
Nin-gelal. *See* Belit – Near East
Ningharasag. *See* Ninhursag – Near
   East
Ningikuga – Near East
Ningirda – Near East
Ningizzida – Near East
Ningpang Majan – Southeast Asia
Ningsin Majan – Southeast Asia
Ningthet Majan – Southeast Asia
Ningtsi Majan – Southeast Asia
Ningul. *See* Ningal – Near East
Ni-ngurre – The Himalaya
Ningyo, The – Far East
Ninhabursildu – Near East
Ninharrissi. *See* Ishtar – Near East
Ninhurra. *See* Ninkurra – Near East
Ninhursag – Near East
Nini Anteh – Southeast Asia
Nini. *See* Inanna – Near East
Niniano – Oceania
Niniganni – Oceania

Ninigara – Near East
Nin-imma – Near East
Nininsina. See Ninisinna – Near East
Ninisinna – Near East
Ninit – Egypt
Ninkarrak – Near East
Ninkasi – Near East
Nin-kharsak – Near East
Ninkharak – Near East
Nin-khursag. See Ninhursag – Near East
Nin-ki – Near East
Ninki – Near East
Ninkigal. See Ereshkigal – Near East
Ninkurra – Near East
Ninkurru. See Ninkurra – Near East
Ninlil – Near East
Ninlilla. See Ninlil – Near East
Ninmah – Near East
Nin-makh – Near East
Ninmar – Near East
Nin-marki – Near East
Ninmea – Near East
Nin-me-sar-ra – Near East
Ninmu – Near East
Ninmug – Near East
Ninmuk – Near East
Ninmul – Near East
Ninnah. See Ninhursag – Near East
Ninni – Near East
Nin-nibru – Near East
Ninsaba – Near East
Ninsar – Near East
Ninshebargunu – Near East
Nin-si-anna. See Ishtar – Near East
Ninsikil. See Ninsikilla – Near East
Ninsikilla – Near East
Ninsu-utud – Near East
Ninsun – Near East
Ninti – Near East
Nintu – Near East
Nintuama Kalamma – Near East
Nintur – Near East
Ninudzalli. See Gula – Near East
Nin-ur – Near East
Nin-zizna. See Sarpanitu – Near East
Nipa – North America
Nirantali – Indian Subcontinent
Niritu. See Bau – Near East
Nirivik – North America
Nirmali – Near East
Nirriti – Indian Subcontinent
Nirrti. See Nirriti – Indian Subcontinent
Nisacharis, The – Indian Subcontinent
Nisarere – Oceania
Niseginyu – Indian Subcontinent
Nish-kan-ru-mat – Far East
Nishem. See Seben – Egypt
Nishke-ava – Eastern Europe
Nishtigri – Indian Subcontinent
Niskai – Western Europe
Niskai, The – Western Europe
Niski-ava – Eastern Europe
Nisoukepilen – Oceania
Nisqually Bird Goddesses – North
    America
Nissa – Greek and Roman Empires
Nit – Egypt
Nitatui – Indian Subcontinent
Nitat-unarabe – Far East
Niti – Indian Subcontinent

Nitsabaad – North America
Nitya – Indian Subcontinent
Niu She – Far East
Niu. See Nok – Far East
Nivikkaa – North America
Niwa – Southeast Asia
Niwetukame. See Tatei Niwetukame –
    Central America and Mesoamerica
Nix. See Nixen, Die – Northern Europe
Nixe. See Nixen, Die – Northern Europe
Nixen, Die – Northern Europe
Nixi Dii, The. See The Nixi – Greek and
    Roman Empires
Nixi, The – Greek and Roman Empires
Nixy. See Nixen, Die – Northern Europe
Niyati – Indian Subcontinent
Njai – Southeast Asia
Njai Lora Kidoul – Southeast Asia
Nkike – Africa
Nochiu-e-rant-mat – Far East
Nocnitsa – Eastern Europe
Noctiluca – Greek and Roman Empires
Noesarnak – North America
Nohuicana. See Pitao Huichaana –
    Central America and Mesoamerica
Nohuichana – Central America and
    Mesoamerica
Noitu – South America
Nok – Far East
Nokomis – North America
Nomia – Greek and Roman Empires
Nomkubulwana – Africa
Nomkubulwane – Africa
Nommo – Africa
Nomoi. See Mortlock – Oceania
Nona – Greek and Roman Empires
Nona – Oceania
Nona Chamari – Indian Subcontinent
Nonã'osqa – North America
Noogumee – North America
Nooliayoo – North America
No'oma Cawaneyung – North America
Noot. See Nut – Egypt
Norns, The – Northern Europe
Norov-ava – Eastern Europe
Norov-pas. See Norov-ava – Eastern
    Europe
Nor-rgyun-ma – The Himalaya
Nor-ster-ma-sngon-mo – The Himalaya
North Wind Woman – North America
Northeastern Swan Maidens – North
    America
Nortia – Greek and Roman Empires
Norwan – North America
Nos Bonnes Mères les Fées. See Bonnes
    Dames, The – Western Europe
Nostu Nopantu – Indian Subcontinent
Nott. See Nat – Northern Europe
Noub – Egypt
Novjaci, The. See The Navki – Eastern
    Europe
No-wa-mu – North America
Now'utset – North America
No – Greek and Roman Empires
No-zuchi-no-kami. See
    Kaya-no-hime-no-kami – Far East
Nrtya – Indian Subcontinent
Nsomeka. See Songi – Africa
Ntoa – Africa
Nts'ai Hwa – Far East

Nü – Far East
Nu akea – Oceania
Nü Chün. See He Ku – Far East
Nu Hsi. See Nüwa – Far East
Nü Kua. See Nügua – Far East
Nu Kwa. See Nügua – Far East
Nü She – Far East
Nua – Oceania
Nu'a kea – Oceania
Nuah – Near East
Nubait – Egypt
Nubit. See Mut – Egypt
Nubt. See Noub – Egypt
Nu-chiao. See Nüjiao – Far East
Nuexqemalsai – North America
Nügua – Far East
Nuha. See Nukimmut – Near East
Nuit. See Nut – Egypt
Nüjiao – Far East
Nujka'u – Oceania
Nujmaga – Oceania
Nukalamma – Indian Subcontinent
Nukarā – Egypt
Nukimatt. See Mikimatt – North
    America
Nukimmut – Near East
Nukulamma – Indian Subcontinent
Nulayuuiniq – North America
Nuliajajuk. See Nuliajuk – North
    America
Nuliajuk – North America
Nuliayok. See Nuliajuk – North America
Nuliayuk. See Nuliajuk – North
    America
Nuli'rahak – North America
Nulixwemankta – North America
Nümei. See Nügua – Far East
Nümei. See Nüwa – Far East
Numereji. See Ngaljod – Oceania
Numeria – Greek and Roman Empires
Numina, The – Greek and Roman
    Empires
Numma Moiyuk – Oceania
Nummo – Africa
Numod-emei – Eastern Europe
Nunakawa-hime – Far East
Nunam-chua – North America
Nunbar-segunni. See Ninlil – Near East
Nunbarshegum. See Nunbarshegunu –
    Near East
Nunbarshegunu – Near East
Nuñda – North America
Nundina – Greek and Roman Empires
Nunet – Egypt
Nungeena – Oceania
Nungui – South America
Nunit. See Nunet – Egypt
Nunsumnundok – Southeast Asia
Nunta. See Nuñda – North America
Nunuoska – North America
Nunurao – Far East
Nunusesmea. See Mah – Near East
Nunusomikeeqonem – North America
Nunut – Egypt
Nupka-ush-ma – Far East
Nupki-ot-mat – Far East
Nuptadi – North America
Nuqiliaxilena – North America
Nursia. See Nortia – Greek and Roman
    Empires

Nurtia. *See* Nortia – Greek and Roman
Empires
Nusa-kor-huchi – Far East
Nuset-i-malit, The – Eastern Europe
Nushim – Egypt
Nuskitl. *See* Nuxmelnimana – North
America
Nuskwalsikanda – North America
Nustoo – Indian Subcontinent
Nusxemtaiana – North America
Nut – Egypt
Nutri – Near East
Nutri – Greek and Roman Empires
Nutse'xenem – North America
Nu'umealani – Oceania
Nu'usanga – Oceania
Nuvak'chin' Mana – North America
Nuvarahu – Oceania
Nuwa. *See* Nügua – Far East
Nüwa – Far East
Nüxi. *See* Nüwa – Far East
Nuxmelnimana – North America
Nuyelelai – North America
Nvard – Near East
Nyabahasa – Africa
Nyabibuya – Africa
Nyabingi. *See* Nyabibuya – Africa
Nyadeang – Africa
Nyakala – Africa
Nyakarembe – Africa
Nyale – Africa
Nyaliep – Africa
Nyame – Africa
Nyamwezi First Woman – Africa
Nyante – Africa
Nyapilnu – Oceania
Nycheia – Greek and Roman Empires
Nye-pha'i-btsun-mo – The Himalaya
Nyinawhira – Africa
Nyingwan Mebege – Africa
Nymphae Infernae Paludis – Greek and
Roman Empires
Nymphae, The. *See* The Nymphs –
Greek and Roman Empires
Nymphaea – Greek and Roman
Empires
Nymphes – Greek and Roman Empires
Nympheuomene – Greek and Roman
Empires
Nymphs, The – Greek and Roman
Empires
Nyohwe Ananu – Africa
Nysa – Greek and Roman Empires
Nyseides, The – Greek and Roman
Empires
Ny – Greek and Roman Empires
Nzambi – Africa
Nzambi-si. *See* Nzambi – Africa
Nzima Mother – Africa
Oanuava – Western Europe
Oba – Africa
Oba – Central America and
Mesoamerica
Obaneñe. *See* Bayanni – Africa
Obasi Nsi – Africa
Obassi Nsi. *See* Obasi Nsi – Africa
Obatala – Central America and
Mesoamerica
Obban – Southeast Asia
O-be-hime-no-kami – Far East

Obosom – Africa
Obsequens – Greek and Roman Empires
Obyda – Eastern Europe
Ocean Woman – North America
Oceanides, The – Greek and Roman
Empires
Oceanids, The. *See* The Oceanides –
Greek and Roman Empires
Ochirka. *See* Alinga – Oceania
Ochu – Central America and
Mesoamerica
Ochumare – Central America and
Mesoamerica
Ochun. *See* Oshun – Central America
and Mesoamerica
Ocllo – South America
Oclo. *See* Ocllo – South America
Ocollo. *See* Ocllo – South America
Oculata Lucifera – Greek and Roman
Empires
Ocypete – Greek and Roman Empires
Ocypode. *See* Ocypete – Greek and
Roman Empires
Ocyrhoë. *See* Ocyrrhoë – Greek and
Roman Empires
Ocyrrhoë – Greek and Roman Empires
Ocythoe. *See* Ocypete – Greek and
Roman Empires
Odame – Africa
Odatis – Near East
Oddibjord – Northern Europe
Oddudua – Central America and
Mesoamerica
Odras – Western Europe
Odu – Africa
Odudua – Africa
Oduduwa. *See* Odudua – Africa
Oduwa. *See* Odudua – Africa
Odyne – Greek and Roman Empires
Od-zer-'c'an-ma. *See* Hod-zer-can-ma –
The Himalaya
Oella. *See* Ocllo – South America
Oeno – Greek and Roman Empires
Oenoatis – Greek and Roman Empires
Oenoe – Greek and Roman Empires
Oenoie – Greek and Roman Empires
Oenotropae, The – Greek and Roman
Empires
Oeroe – Greek and Roman Empires
Ogboinba – Africa
O-getsu-hime. *See*
Uke-mochi-no-kami – Far East
O-ge-tsu-hime-no-kami – Far East
'Og-gis-bdag – The Himalaya
Ogllo. *See* Ocllo – South America
Ogress of Lust – The Himalaya
Ogtarghui-in jiruken – Far East
Ogu-māte – Eastern Europe
Ō-hiru-me-no muchi. *See*
Ama-terasu-ō-mi-kami – Far East
Ō-hiru-no muchi. *See*
Ama-terasu-ō-mi-kami – Far East
Oho-to-no-be-no-kami. *See*
Ō-to-no-be-no-mikoto – Far East
Ohoyatsu-hime. *See* Ō-yatsu hime – Far
East
Ohoyo Osh Chishba – North America
'Ohu tū moua – Oceania
Ohyn – Eastern Europe
Oia. *See* Oya – Africa

Ō-ichi-hime – Far East
Oichi-hime. *See* Ō-ichi-hime – Far East
Oimi-no-kami. *See*
Waka-uka-no-me-no-mikoto – Far
East
Oizys – Greek and Roman Empires
Ojibwa Daughter – North America
Ojid-emei – Eastern Europe
Okame – Far East
Okeaninai, The. *See* The Oceanides –
Greek and Roman Empires
Oken'ona. *See* Hokoha Okya – North
America
Oki-tsu-hime – Far East
Oki-tsu-shima-hime-no-mikoto. *See*
Takiri-bime-no-mikoto – Far East
Okikurmi kot tureshi – Far East
Okitsu-hime-no-mikoto. *See*
Oki-tsu-hima – Far East
Okya. *See* Kokwele – North America
Oky'enawe – North America
Okypete. *See* Ocypete – Greek and
Roman Empires
Okyrhoe. *See* Ocyrrhoë – Greek and
Roman Empires
Okyrrhoë. *See* Ocyrrhoë – Greek and
Roman Empires
Ola Bibi – Indian Subcontinent
Ola Chandi. *See* Ola Bibi – Indian
Subcontinent
Olabibib. *See* Ola Bibi – Indian
Subcontinent
Ol-apa – Africa
Old Woman Night – North America
Old Woman of Germany and
Scotland – Northern Europe
Old Woman of the Sea – North America
Old Woman of the Seasons – North
America
Old Woman Who Never Dies – North
America
Olla – Central America and
Mesoamerica
Ollototae – Western Europe
Olodeakdili – Central America and
Mesoamerica
Olokanigidilisop – Central America
and Mesoamerica
Olokikadiryae – Central America and
Mesoamerica
Olokukurtilisop – Central America and
Mesoamerica
Olokum – Africa
Olokum – Central America and
Mesoamerica
Olomakriai – Central America and
Mesoamerica
Olonupdikili. *See* Olonuptigile –
Central America and Mesoamerica
Olonuptigile – Central America and
Mesoamerica
Olosa – Africa
Olosa – Central America and
Mesoamerica
Oloueaidili – Central America and
Mesoamerica
Olouiknidilisop – Central America and
Mesoamerica
Olrun – Northern Europe
Oltagon – Southeast Asia

Olungwa – North America
Olwen – Western Europe
Olympiades, The – Greek and Roman Empires
Omaha Earth Mother – North America
Omamama – North America
Omanjah. See Amanjah – Central America and Mesoamerica
Omau-u Wuhti – North America
Omecihuatl – Central America and Mesoamerica
Omeciuatl. See Omecihuatl – Central America and Mesoamerica
Omeyacigoat – Central America and Mesoamerica
Omeyatecigoat. See Omeyacigoat – Central America and Mesoamerica
Omicle – Near East
Omiya-hime – Far East
Omonga – Southeast Asia
Omorca. See Tiamat – Near East
Onagh. See Oonagh – Western Europe
Onatah – North America
Onaugh – Western Europe
Onca – Greek and Roman Empires
Oncaea – Greek and Roman Empires
Onchi – North America
Ondine – Western Europe
Ondoutaehte – North America
One kea – Oceania
One kura – Oceania
One rua – Oceania
One u'i – Oceania
Onenha – North America
Ong Wuhti – North America
Onga. See Onca – Greek and Roman Empires
Onile – Africa
Onmun-emei – Eastern Europe
Onne-chip-kamui – Far East
Ō-no-de-hime – Far East
Onoroca. See Tiamat – Near East
Onuava – Western Europe
Onuris. See Ini-herit – Egypt
Oolle. See Ocllo – South America
Oona. See Oonagh – Western Europe
Oonagh – Western Europe
Ooyarraksakju – North America
Opae – Oceania
Opet. See Apet, Taueret, Ta-urt – Egypt
Ophthalmitis – Greek and Roman Empires
Opifera. See Ops and Diana – Greek and Roman Empires
Opigena – Greek and Roman Empires
Opis – Greek and Roman Empires
Opopu – Oceania
Opora – Greek and Roman Empires
Ops – Greek and Roman Empires
Ops. See Ēire – Western Europe
Optiletis – Greek and Roman Empires
Ora – Eastern Europe
Orans – Eastern Europe
Oraon Earth Goddess – Indian Subcontinent
Orboda. See Gullveig – Northern Europe
Orbona – Greek and Roman Empires
Ore, The – Eastern Europe

Oreadai, The. See The Oreades – Greek and Roman Empires
Oreades, The – Greek and Roman Empires
Orehu – Africa
Orehu – Central America and Mesoamerica
Oreilochia – Greek and Roman Empires
Oreithyia – Greek and Roman Empires
'Orerorero – Oceania
Ori-hime. See Shokujo – Far East
Orisha Oko. See Wife of Orisha Oko – Africa
Orisnici, The. See The Narucnici – Eastern Europe
Orithyia. See Oreithyia – Greek and Roman Empires
Orodemniades, The. See The Oreades – Greek and Roman Empires
Orokannar, The. See The Amagandar – Eastern Europe
Orokannar. See Amagandar – Western Europe
Orore – Near East
Orseis – Greek and Roman Empires
Orsel. See Horsel – Northern Europe
Orsel. See Ursula – Eastern Europe
Orthia – Greek and Roman Empires
Orthosia – Greek and Roman Empires
Ortygia – Greek and Roman Empires
Ortz. See Urtz – Western Europe
Oru – Oceania
Orusandiamma – Indian Subcontinent
O-ryu – Far East
Os Keca Aba. See Keca Aba – Eastern Europe
Osaka – Africa
oShion – Western Europe
Oshoun – South America
Oshu – Africa
Oshun – Africa
Oshun – Central America and Mesoamerica
Oshun Ana. See Oshun – Africa
Oshun Telargo. See Oshun – Africa
Oshun Yeye Moro. See Oshun – Africa
Oshupa. See Oshu – Africa
Osooso – Oceania
Ossa – Greek and Roman Empires
Ossilago. See Ossipaga – Greek and Roman Empires
Ossipaga – Greek and Roman Empires
Ossipagina. See Ossipaga – Greek and Roman Empires
Ossipago. See Ossipaga – Greek and Roman Empires
Ossipanga. See Ossipaga – Greek and Roman Empires
Ost. See Urtz – Western Europe
Ostara. See Eastre – Northern Europe
Ostkahakakaitshoidiaa – North America
Osu. See Oshu – Africa
Osun. See Oshun – Central America and Mesoamerica
Ot – Far East
Ot – Eastern Europe
Ot-änä – Eastern Europe
Otafuku. See Ame-no-uzume – Far East
Oto – Far East

Oto-hime. See Karu-no-ō-iratsume and So-tohoshi-no-iratsume – Far East
Oto-matoiko. See Ō-to-matohi-me-no-kami – Far East
Ō-to-ma-hime-no-mikoto. See Ō-to-no-be-no-kami – Far East
Otomatoime. See Ō-to-matohi-me-no-kami – Far East
Ō-to-mato-hime-no-kami. See Ō-to-no-be-no-kami – Far East
Oto-tachibana-hime-no-mikoto – Far East
Ō-tsuchi-no-kami – Far East
Ot's'uved-azerava. See Otsuved-azer-ava – Eastern Europe
Otsuved-azer-ava – Eastern Europe
Otygen – Far East
Otygen – Eastern Europe
Ouati. See Sekhet – Egypt
Oub – Near East
Ouli. See Uli – Oceania
Oullo. See Ocllo – South America
Our Lady of Candelaria. See Candelarra – Central America and Mesoamerica
Our Lady of Hope – Central America and Mesoamerica
Our Lady of La Caridad of Cobre – Central America and Mesoamerica
Our Lady of Mercy – Central America and Mesoamerica
Our Lady of Regla – Central America and Mesoamerica
Our Mother – South America
Ourania. See Urania – Greek and Roman Empires
Ovda – Eastern Europe
Ovia – Africa
Oxomoco – Central America and Mesoamerica
Oxomogo. See Oxomoco – Central America and Mesoamerica
Oxomuco. See Oxomoco – Central America and Mesoamerica
Oxum. See Oshun – Central America and Mesoamerica
Oxun – Africa
Oxun – Central America and Mesoamerica
Oxun Doco. See Oxun – Africa
Oxun Doco. See Oxun – Central America and Mesoamerica
Oxun Panda. See Oxun – Africa
Oxun Panda. See Oxun – Central America and Mesoamerica
Oxyderces. See Oxydercis – Greek and Roman Empires
Oxydercis – Greek and Roman Empires
Oya – Africa
Oya – Central America and Mesoamerica
Oya de esteira. See Oya-Bale – South America
Oya-ajere – Africa
Oya-bale – South America
Oyame. See Nyame – Africa
Ō-ya-tsu-hime-no-mikoto – Far East
Oynyena Maria – Eastern Europe
Pa. See Ba – Far East

Pa Janjali. *See* Pae Devi – Indian Subcontinent
Pa'a o wali nu'u – Oceania
Pa'u o 'pala'e – Oceania
Paabothkew. *See* Kokumthena – North America
Pabothkwe. *See* Kokumthena – North America
Pachamama. *See* Mama Pacha – South America
Pachavuin Mana – North America
Pacht. *See* Bast – Egypt
Pacsa Mama. *See* Mama Quilla – South America
Padma. *See* Lakshmi, Manasa, Matris, and Sri – Indian Subcontinent
Padma Dakinis – The Himalaya
Padma Krotishaurima – The Himalaya
Padma Kro-ti-shvr-ri-ma. *See* Padma Krotishaurima – The Himalaya
Padma mkha' 'gro ma – The Himalaya
Padmadakini – Indian Subcontinent
Padmavati – Indian Subcontinent
Paduri. *See* Illibem Berti – Eastern Europe
Pae Devi – Indian Subcontinent
Paea – Oceania
Paedotrophus – Greek and Roman Empires
Paeonia – Greek and Roman Empires
Pagat. *See* Paghat – Near East
Paghat – Near East
Pags-ma-gdugs-dkar – The Himalaya
Pah – North America
Paharon – Indian Subcontinent
Pahpobi Kwiyo – North America
Pahto – North America
Pahula. *See* Pahulu – Oceania
Pahulu – Oceania
Pa'i alo – Oceania
Pai Chi. *See* Baiji – Far East
Pa'i kauhale – Oceania
Pa'i kua – Oceania
Pai Mu-tan. *See* Bai Mundan – Far East
Pāia – Oceania
Paija – North America
Paiowa – North America
Pairikas, The – Near East
Pairimaiti – Near East
Pais – Greek and Roman Empires
Paivatar – Eastern Europe
Paive. *See* Beiwe – Eastern Europe
Paive. *See* Beiwe – Northern Europe
Paja Yan. *See* Pajau Yan – Southeast Asia
Pajan Yaṅ. *See* Pajau Yan – Southeast Asia
Pajau Tan. *See* Pajau Yan – Southeast Asia
Pajau Yan – Southeast Asia
Pakhet. *See* Pakhit – Egypt
Pakhik' Mana – North America
Pak-hit. *See* Pakhit – Egypt
Pakhit – Egypt
Pakht. *See* Bast – Egypt
Pakimna – North America
Pakitsumanga – North America
Pakok' Okya – North America
Pakoti – Oceania
Paks-av – Eastern Europe

Pakwaekasiasit – North America
Palabultjura – Oceania
Palato – Greek and Roman Empires
Pales – Greek and Roman Empires
Pallas – Greek and Roman Empires
Pallenis – Greek and Roman Empires
Pallor – Greek and Roman Empires
Palpinkalare – Oceania
Pamphile – Greek and Roman Empires
P'an Chin-lien. *See* Pan Jinlian – Far East
Pan Dong Cyu – Indian Subcontinent
Pan Jinlian – Far East
P'an Kin-lien. *See* Pan Jinlian – Far East
Pan Niang – Far East
Pan•a. *See* Pana – North America
Pana – North America
Panacea – Greek and Roman Empires
Panaceia. *See* Panacea – Greek and Roman Empires
Panachaea – Greek and Roman Empires
Panakeia. *See* Panacea – Greek and Roman Empires
Panatis – Greek and Roman Empires
Pancaraksa, The – Indian Subcontinent
Pan-chen. *See* Banzhen – Far East
Panda – Africa
Panda – South America
Pandan Rumari – Southeast Asia
Pandara – Indian Subcontinent
Pandeia – Greek and Roman Empires
Pandemos – Greek and Roman Empires
Pandia – Greek and Roman Empires
Pandora – Greek and Roman Empires
Pandrosos – Greek and Roman Empires
Pândurâ – The Himalaya
Panes – North America
Pang Che – Far East
P'ang Chiao. *See* Pang Jiao – Far East
P'ang Chu. *See* Pang Zhu – Far East
Pang Jiao – Far East
Pang Zhu – Far East
Panglang – Southeast Asia
Pani – Oceania
Pani tinaku – Oceania
Paniharin – Indian Subcontinent
Panike – Eastern Europe
Paninduela – Oceania
Panope – Greek and Roman Empires
Panopea. *See* Panope – Greek and Roman Empires
Panopeia. *See* Panope – Greek and Roman Empires
Pansahi Mata – Indian Subcontinent
Pantan Ini Andan – Southeast Asia
Pantang Mayang – Southeast Asia
Panteleia – Greek and Roman Empires
Panthoibi – Indian Subcontinent
Papa – Oceania
Papa raharaha – Oceania
Papa tū a nuku. *See* Papa – Oceania
Papai a taki vera – Oceania
Paparoa i te opunga – Oceania
Paparoa i tei tanga – Oceania
Papatea – Oceania
Papawa – North America
Papaya – Near East
Paphia – Greek and Roman Empires
Paqhat – Near East
Para whenua mea – Oceania
Parabaruma – Oceania

Paraca. *See* Parca – Greek and Roman Empires
Parashakti, The – Indian Subcontinent
Paraskeva – Eastern Europe
Paraskeva Griaznaia – Eastern Europe
Paraskeva Piatnitsa. *See* Paraskeva – Eastern Europe
Parasu-pani. *See* Bhavani – Indian Subcontinent
Parauri – Oceania
Para-vac – Indian Subcontinent
Parawera nui – Oceania
Parbutta – Indian Subcontinent
Parca – Greek and Roman Empires
Parcae, The – Greek and Roman Empires
Pare – Oceania
Pare arohi – Oceania
Paregoros – Greek and Roman Empires
Pareia – Greek and Roman Empires
Parekōritawa – Oceania
Parendi – Indian Subcontinent
Pârendi – Near East
Parewhenua mea – Oceania
Pari, The – Near East
Parigs, The – Near East
Parihai – Oceania
Parnasavari – Indian Subcontinent
Parnassa. *See* Metope – Greek and Roman Empires
Parnassides, The – Greek and Roman Empires
Par-neferu-en-neb-set – Egypt
Parooa – Indian Subcontinent
Parrapotamma – Indian Subcontinent
Partenope. *See* Parthenope – Greek and Roman Empires
Parthenia – Greek and Roman Empires
Parthenope – Greek and Roman Empires
Parthenos – Greek and Roman Empires
Partula – Greek and Roman Empires
Parvati – Indian Subcontinent
Pâshadharî. *See* Zhag-pa-ma – The Himalaya
Pasht – Egypt
Pashupatî – The Himalaya
Pasikiapa Dese Akenona Okya – North America
Pasikiapa Okya. *See* Pasikiapa Dese Akenona Okya – North America
Pasiphae – Greek and Roman Empires
Pasithea – Greek and Roman Empires
Pasithoe – Greek and Roman Empires
Pasom Mana – North America
Pasowee – North America
Pasupati – Indian Subcontinent
Patelina. *See* Patella – Greek and Roman Empires
Patella – Greek and Roman Empires
Pathya – Indian Subcontinent
Pathya Svasti – Indian Subcontinent
Pathyarevati – Indian Subcontinent
Patrinia – Far East
Paulomi. *See* Indrani – Indian Subcontinent
Pauri Pat – Indian Subcontinent
Paurnamasi – Indian Subcontinent
Pavanarekha – Indian Subcontinent
Pavor – Greek and Roman Empires

Pawnee Corn Mother. *See* Corn Mother – North America
Pawnee Evening Star. *See* Bright Star – North America
Pawnee First Woman – North America
Pawnee Moon Woman – North America
Pa – Greek and Roman Empires
Pax Augusta. *See* Pa – Greek and Roman Empires
Paxsi – South America
Pdry – Near East
Pe – Africa
Pecunia – Greek and Roman Empires
Pedile – Greek and Roman Empires
Pegaeae, The – Greek and Roman Empires
Pegaia, The. *See* The Pegaeae – Greek and Roman Empires
Pegasides, The – Greek and Roman Empires
Pei kua. *See* Apekua – Oceania
Peirene – Greek and Roman Empires
Peisdice – Greek and Roman Empires
Peisinoe – Greek and Roman Empires
P'ei-t'ai Niang-niang. *See* Peitai Niangniang – Far East
Peitai Niangniang – Far East
Peitho – Greek and Roman Empires
P'ei-yang. *See* Peiyang – Far East
Peiyang – Far East
Pekai – Oceania
Pekhet. *See* Pakhit – Egypt
Pekheth. *See* Pakhit – Egypt
Pelagia – Greek and Roman Empires
Pelasga – Greek and Roman Empires
Pelasgian Goddess. *See* Pelasga – Greek and Roman Empires
Pelasgis. *See* Pelasga – Greek and Roman Empires
Pelden Lhamo – The Himalaya
Pele – Oceania
Pele'ula – Oceania
Peliades, The – Greek and Roman Empires
Pelonia – Greek and Roman Empires
Pelopeia – Greek and Roman Empires
Pemphredo – Greek and Roman Empires
Penaban Sari – Southeast Asia
Penanggalan – Southeast Asia
Penardun – Western Europe
Peng Po. *See* Meng Po Niangniang – Far East
Penia – Greek and Roman Empires
Penteteris – Greek and Roman Empires
People Mother – North America
Pephredo. *See* Pemphredo – Greek and Roman Empires
Pe-poso-koshimpuk – Far East
Pepromene – Greek and Roman Empires
P'er Ndzi Ssaw Ma – Far East
Per Uadjit – Egypt
Perasia – Far East
Perchata. *See* Berchta – Northern Europe
Percht. *See* Berchta – Northern Europe
Perchta. *See* Berchta – Northern Europe
Perchtel. *See* Berchta – Northern Europe
Percunatele – Eastern Europe
Pere – Oceania

Pereplut – Eastern Europe
Peri, The. *See* the Pari – Near East
Periboea. *See* Curissa – Greek and Roman Empires
Perimbó – South America
Perit – Egypt
Perit, The – Eastern Europe
Perke – Eastern Europe
Perkunas. *See* Armat – Near East
Perkune Tete – Eastern Europe
P'erna-azor-ava – Eastern Europe
Pero – Greek and Roman Empires
Perse – Greek and Roman Empires
Persea. *See* Perse – Greek and Roman Empires
Perseides, The. *See* Perse – Greek and Roman Empires
Perseis – Greek and Roman Empires
Persephatta. *See* Persephone – Greek and Roman Empires
Persephone – Greek and Roman Empires
Persephoneia. *See* Persephone – Greek and Roman Empires
Persian Artemis – Greek and Roman Empires
Perso – Greek and Roman Empires
Persphassa. *See* Persephone – Greek and Roman Empires
Pertunda – Greek and Roman Empires
Peruvian Mamas – South America
Pessinuntia – Greek and Roman Empires
Pessinuntica – Near East
Petali. *See* Black Petali – The Himalaya
Pet-etok-mat – Far East
Petni – Indian Subcontinent
Petorush-mat. *See* Pet-ru-ush-mat – Far East
Petraea – Greek and Roman Empires
Petraia. *See* Petraea – Greek and Roman Empires
Pet-ru-ush-mat – Far East
Peyote Woman – North America
Phace – Greek and Roman Empires
Phaea – Greek and Roman Empires
Phaedra – Greek and Roman Empires
Phaenna – Greek and Roman Empires
Phaeno – Greek and Roman Empires
Phaeo – Greek and Roman Empires
Phaethonides, The – Greek and Roman Empires
Phaethontiades, The. *See* The Phaethonides – Greek and Roman Empires
Phaethontides, The. *See* The Phaethonides – Greek and Roman Empires
Phaethusa – Greek and Roman Empires
Pharka Undharan Mata – Indian Subcontinent
Pharmaceia – Greek and Roman Empires
Pharmacides, The – Greek and Roman Empires
Pharmen-ma. *See* Htamenmas – The Himalaya
Pharygaea – Greek and Roman Empires
Phatusa – Greek and Roman Empires
Pheebee Yau – Southeast Asia

Phe-ma-du-kar. *See* Pags-ma-gdugs-dkar – The Himalaya
Pheme – Greek and Roman Empires
Phemonoe – Greek and Roman Empires
Pheraea – Greek and Roman Empires
Pheraia. *See* Pheraea – Greek and Roman Empires
Pherousa. *See* Pherusa – Greek and Roman Empires
Pherusa – Greek and Roman Empires
Phigalia – Greek and Roman Empires
Philia – Greek and Roman Empires
Philomena, Saint – Central America and Mesoamerica
Philotes – Greek and Roman Empires
Philyra – Greek and Roman Empires
Phlo – Western Europe
Phobos – Greek and Roman Empires
Phoebe – Greek and Roman Empires
Phoki Mata – Indian Subcontinent
Phonos – Greek and Roman Empires
Phorcides, The – Greek and Roman Empires
Phorcis – Indian Subcontinent
Phorcydes, The. *See* Phorcides – Greek and Roman Empires
Phorcynides, The. *See* The Phorcides – Greek and Roman Empires
Phosphoros – Greek and Roman Empires
Pho-zem-na-po. *See* Jejamo-karpo – The Himalaya
Phra Naret – Southeast Asia
Phratria – Greek and Roman Empires
Phraw Majan – Southeast Asia
Phreng-ta-ma. *See* Hphreng-ba-ma – The Himalaya
'Phrog-'chang-ma – The Himalaya
Phronesia – Near East
Phrygia – Greek and Roman Empires
Phulmata – Indian Subcontinent
Phulmati – Indian Subcontinent
Phungkam Janun – Southeast Asia
'Phur-'debs-ma – The Himalaya
Phut – Egypt
Phy Wam Numjan – Southeast Asia
Phyllodoce – Greek and Roman Empires
Phyllodoke. *See* Phyllodoce – Greek and Roman Empires
Physis – Greek and Roman Empires
Phytalus – Greek and Roman Empires
Phytia – Greek and Roman Empires
Phyto – Greek and Roman Empires
Phyugs-bdag-btsun-mo – The Himalaya
Pi hia yuan kiun. *See* Bixia Yuanjin – Far East
Picchanto – Central America and Mesoamerica
Pidari – Indian Subcontinent
Pidrai – Near East
Pidray – Near East
Piegulas māte – Eastern Europe
Pieria – Greek and Roman Empires
Pietas – Greek and Roman Empires
Pi'i ka lalau – Oceania
Pi-hia-yü-kün. *See* Bixia Yuanjin – Far East

Pi-hsia Yuan-chin. *See* Bixia Yuanjin – Far East
Pi-hsia Yuan-chun. *See* Bixia Yunajin – Far East
Pi-hsiao. *See* Bixiao – Far East
Pilnitis. *See* Piluitus – Eastern Europe
Piluitus – Eastern Europe
Pilumnus – Greek and Roman Empires
Piluuytis. *See* Piluitus – Eastern Europe
Pilwittus. *See* Piluitus – Eastern Europe
Pimpleia. *See* Pipleia – Greek and Roman Empires
Pimpleides, The – Greek and Roman Empires
Pinga – North America
Pingala – Indian Subcontinent
Pingeela. *See* Pingala – Indian Subcontinent
Pingela. *See* Pingala – Indian Subcontinent
Pinikir – Near East
Pinuwali – Oceania
Pipleia – Greek and Roman Empires
Piptu' Wuhti – North America
Pirene. *See* Pyrene – Greek and Roman Empires
Pīrīrama – Oceania
Pirili – Oceania
Pirts-māte – Eastern Europe
Pirua – South America
Pisaca. *See* Pishacha – Indian Subcontinent
Pisacas. *See* Pishacha and Pisachis – Indian Subcontinent
Pisachis, The – Indian Subcontinent
Pishacha – Indian Subcontinent
Pishachakis. *See* Pisachis – Indian Subcontinent
Pishachis. *See* Pisachis – Indian Subcontinent
Pistis – Greek and Roman Empires
Pitali. *See* Pidari – Indian Subcontinent
Pitanatis – Greek and Roman Empires
Pitane – Greek and Roman Empires
Pitao Huichaana – Central America and Mesoamerica
Piteri – Indian Subcontinent
Pitho. *See* Peitho – Greek and Roman Empires
Pithys. *See* Pitys – Greek and Roman Empires
Pitkamikokiu – North America
Pito 'ura – Oceania
Pitys – Greek and Roman Empires
Placida – Greek and Roman Empires
Plaksy. *See* Kriksy, Nocnitsa – Eastern Europe
Plash-plash – North America
Pleiades, The – Greek and Roman Empires
Pleias. *See* Maia – Greek and Roman Empires
Pleione – Greek and Roman Empires
Plexaura. *See* Plexaure – Greek and Roman Empires
Plexaure – Greek and Roman Empires
Ploto – Greek and Roman Empires
Plouto – Greek and Roman Empires
Plur na mBan – Western Europe
Pluto – Greek and Roman Empires

Po – Oceania
Po Bya Tikuh – Southeast Asia
Po he'enalu mamao – Oceania
Po Ino Nogar – Southeast Asia
Po lao uli – Oceania
Po Nagar. *See* Po Ino Nogar – Southeast Asia
Po ne'a 'aku – Oceania
Po Sah Ino – Southeast Asia
Po tangotango – Oceania
Po urirui – Oceania
Po Yan Dari – Southeast Asia
Po Yan Ino Nogar Taha. *See* Po Ino Nogar – Southeast Asia
Pochamma – Indian Subcontinent
Podamata – Indian Subcontinent
Podarge – Greek and Roman Empires
Poee Ūra – Southeast Asia
Po'ele – Oceania
Poena – Greek and Roman Empires
Poenae, The. *See* The Furies – Greek and Roman Empires
Poene – Greek and Roman Empires
Poetry Goddess – Far East
Pogoda – Eastern Europe
Po'haha – North America
Pohaha – Oceania
Pohjan-akka – Eastern Europe
Poi-soya-un-mat – Far East
Pokinsquss – North America
Poko ha rua te pō – Oceania
Polalowehi – Oceania
Polamde – Indian Subcontinent
Poldunica – Eastern Europe
Polednica. *See* Poldunica – Eastern Europe
Polednice, The – Eastern Europe
Polengabia – Eastern Europe
Poleramma – Indian Subcontinent
Polevik. *See* Polevoi – Eastern Europe
Polevoi – Eastern Europe
Poli Kachina Mana – North America
Poli Mana. *See* Poli Kachina Mana – North America
Poli 'ahu – Oceania
Polias – Greek and Roman Empires
Poliatas – Greek and Roman Empires
Polimastos. *See* Polymastus – Greek and Roman Empires
Poliuchos – Greek and Roman Empires
Pollamma – Indian Subcontinent
Pölöznitsa – Eastern Europe
Poludnitsa. *See* Poldunica – Eastern Europe
Poludnitsy, The – Eastern Europe
Poludnitza. *See* Poldunica – Eastern Europe
Polyboulos – Greek and Roman Empires
Polydora – Greek and Roman Empires
Polyhymnia. *See* Polymnia – Greek and Roman Empires
Polyhymno – Greek and Roman Empires
Polymastus – Greek and Roman Empires
Polymatheia – Greek and Roman Empires
Polymnia – Greek and Roman Empires
Polynoe – Greek and Roman Empires

Polynome – Greek and Roman Empires
Polyxo – Greek and Roman Empires
Pomba Gira – South America
Pomona – Greek and Roman Empires
Poneiemai – Oceania
Ponniyayi – Indian Subcontinent
Ponoya – North America
Pontia – Greek and Roman Empires
Pontomedusa – Greek and Roman Empires
Pontopereia – Greek and Roman Empires
Ponyke – Eastern Europe
Pook-jin-skwess. *See* Pokinsquss – North America
Poo?wavi – North America
Populonia – Greek and Roman Empires
Poramai – Indian Subcontinent
Porpoise Girl – Oceania
Porrima – Greek and Roman Empires
Pört-kuva – Eastern Europe
Poru Mai. *See* Poramai – Indian Subcontinent
Pos Bai – Indian Subcontinent
Poshjo-akka – Eastern Europe
Poshjo-akka – Northern Europe
Posidaeia – Greek and Roman Empires
Posop. *See* Mae Phosop – Southeast Asia
Possjo-akka – Eastern Europe
Postvorta – Greek and Roman Empires
Potameides, The – Greek and Roman Empires
Potamia – Greek and Roman Empires
Pōti'i tā rire – Oceania
Potina – Greek and Roman Empires
Potnia – Greek and Roman Empires
Potnia Theron – Greek and Roman Empires
Pots-hozjik – Eastern Europe
Pou te aniwaniwa – Oceania
Powamu So Aum – North America
Powehiwehi – Oceania
Poza-mama – Eastern Europe
Prabha – Indian Subcontinent
Prabhasa – Indian Subcontinent
Prabhata. *See* Prabha – Indian Subcontinent
Pracanda – Indian Subcontinent
Pracriti – Indian Subcontinent
Praenestina – Greek and Roman Empires
Pragna. *See* Prajna – Indian Subcontinent
Prah Thorni – Southeast Asia
Prajna – Indian Subcontinent
Prajnaparamita – The Himalaya
Prajnaparamita – Indian Subcontinent
Prajnapti – Indian Subcontinent
Prakriti – Indian Subcontinent
Prakrti. *See* Prakriti – Indian Subcontinent
Pramandani – Indian Subcontinent
Pramlocha – Indian Subcontinent
Pratyusha – Indian Subcontinent
Praxidicae, The – Greek and Roman Empires
Praxidice – Greek and Roman Empires
Praxidikae, The. *See* The Praxidicae – Greek and Roman Empires

Praxidike. *See* Praxidice – Greek and Roman Empires
Praxithea – Greek and Roman Empires
Precht. *See* Berchta – Northern Europe
Pregnant Woman – Africa
Prema – Greek and Roman Empires
Prende – Eastern Europe
Prenne. *See* Prende – Eastern Europe
Pressina – Western Europe
Pretasana. *See* Camunda – Indian Subcontinent
Prez-poludnica. *See* Poldunica – Eastern Europe
Primigenia – Greek and Roman Empires
Primum Mobile – Western Europe
Princess d'Alva – South America
Prisca – Greek and Roman Empires
Prishni – Indian Subcontinent
Pritha. *See* Kunti and Prithivi – Indian Subcontinent
Prithivi – Indian Subcontinent
Prithivi – Southeast Asia
Priti – Indian Subcontinent
Privata – Greek and Roman Empires
Priyadarsana – Indian Subcontinent
Priyakarini – Indian Subcontinent
Prodromia – Greek and Roman Empires
Proet – Egypt
Promachorma – Greek and Roman Empires
Promachus – Greek and Roman Empires
Pronaea – Greek and Roman Empires
Pronoë – Greek and Roman Empires
Pronoea. *See* Pronaea – Greek and Roman Empires
Pronoia – Greek and Roman Empires
Pronubia – Greek and Roman Empires
Property Woman – North America
Prorsa – Greek and Roman Empires
Proserpina – Greek and Roman Empires
Proserpine. *See* Proserpina – Greek and Roman Empires
Prosymna – Greek and Roman Empires
Protageneia. *See* Protogenia – Greek and Roman Empires
Protho – Greek and Roman Empires
Protis – Greek and Roman Empires
Proto – Greek and Roman Empires
Protogenia – Greek and Roman Empires
Protomedea. *See* Protomedeia – Greek and Roman Empires
Protomedeia – Greek and Roman Empires
Proversa – Greek and Roman Empires
Providentia – Greek and Roman Empires
Proximae, The – Western Europe
Prsni. *See* Prishni – Indian Subcontinent
Prymno – Greek and Roman Empires
Psamathe – Greek and Roman Empires
Psezpolnica – Eastern Europe
Psyche – Greek and Roman Empires
Ptesan Winyan – North America
Pte-ska-win. *See* White Buffalo Woman – North America
Ptitsy-siriny – Eastern Europe
Ptrotka. *See* Lilith – Near East
Pu fafine – Oceania
Pu te hue – Oceania

Pu whakahara – Oceania
Pua – Oceania
Pua ina noa – Oceania
Puako mopele – Oceania
Puanga – Oceania
Publica – Greek and Roman Empires
Puckowie – Oceania
Pudau – Southeast Asia
Pudicitia – Greek and Roman Empires
Pue Ura. *See* Poee Ura – Southeast Asia
Puella. *See* Zuriel – Near East
Pufine i ravenga – Oceania
Pufine ma, The – Oceania
Puges – Eastern Europe
Pughat. *See* Paghat – Near East
Pugna – Greek and Roman Empires
Pu'gud-emei – Eastern Europe
Puhavao atua – Oceania
Puikani – Africa
Puimi – Oceania
Puirsho – Eastern Europe
Pukeheh – North America
Pukimna – North America
Pukjinskwes – North America
Pukkase – The Himalaya
Pukkeenegak – North America
Pulelei'ite. *See* Sasa'umani – Oceania
Puloma – Indian Subcontinent
Puluga. *See* Biliku – Indian Subcontinent
Puna hoa – Oceania
Punauaga Oloeaydili – Central America and Mesoamerica
Punauaga Oloeaydili – North America
Punauaga Oloesgidili – Central America and Mesoamerica
Punauaga Oloibiyalisop – Central America and Mesoamerica
Punauaga Olokurgililiae – Central America and Mesoamerica
Punauaga Oloniskidilisop – Central America and Mesoamerica
Punauaga Olopunalisop – Central America and Mesoamerica
Punauaga Olouagaidili – Central America and Mesoamerica
Punauaga Uisogdili – Central America and Mesoamerica
Punauagauisogdilli. *See* Punauaga Uisogdili – Central America and Mesoamerica
Pungtang Majan – Southeast Asia
Pūonoono – Oceania
Pūpūmainono. *See* Hine pūpūmainaua – Oceania
Puramdhi – Indian Subcontinent
Purandhi – Indian Subcontinent
Puranjani – Indian Subcontinent
Purikh – Greek and Roman Empires
Purlimil – Oceania
Pururavas – Indian Subcontinent
Purvachitti – Indian Subcontinent
Purvadevatas – Indian Subcontinent
Pushpâ. *See* Me-tog-ma – The Himalaya
Pushpema – Me-tog-ma – The Himalaya
Pushti – Indian Subcontinent
Puspa – Indian Subcontinent
Puta – Greek and Roman Empires
Puta Santa, La. *See* Oshun – Central America and Mesoamerica

Putana – Indian Subcontinent
Putcha Si – South America
Putir – Southeast Asia
Putir Selong Tamanang. *See* Putir – Southeast Asia
Pu'uhele – Oceania
Puwo-win – North America
Puyu – Southeast Asia
Pyatnitsa Prascovia – Eastern Europe
Pylaitis – Greek and Roman Empires
Pylotis – Greek and Roman Empires
Pyrene – Greek and Roman Empires
Pyronia – Greek and Roman Empires
Pyrrha – Greek and Roman Empires
Qadash. *See* Asherah – Near East
Qadash. *See* Qetesh – Egypt
Qadesh. *See* Qetesh – Egypt
Qailertetang – North America
Qakma – North America
Qamaitis – North America
Qandisa – Africa
Qatgoro – Oceania
Qebhsnuf – Egypt
Qedeshet. *See* Qetesh – Egypt
Qetesh – Egypt
Qetshu. *See* Qetesh – Egypt
Qi Guzi, The – Far East
Qiongxiao – Far East
Qixian Niangniang – Far East
Qlippoth, The – Near East
Qocha Mana. *See* Ang-chin Mana – North America
Qodshu. *See* Qetesh – Egypt
Qoia Akachin Mana. *See* Hemis Kachin' Mana – North America
Qominoqa – North America
Qopimpmana – North America
Quabso – Africa
Quadriviae – Western Europe
Quail Kachin' Mana – North America
Quakuinahaba. *See* Cathena – North America
Quan Hou – Far East
Quati. *See* Isis – Egypt
Qudshu – Near East
Quedesh. *See* Qetesh – Egypt
Queen of the Grain – Eastern Europe
Queensland First Woman – Oceania
Queskapenek – North America
Quetzalmalin – Central America and Mesoamerica
Quetzaltetlatl – Central America and Mesoamerica
Quiamucame – Central America and Mesoamerica
Quies – Greek and Roman Empires
Quilaztli – Central America and Mesoamerica
Quilla. *See* Mama Quilla – South America
Quinoa Mother – South America
Quiritis – Greek and Roman Empires
Quisserrinkao – North America
Quootis-hooi – North America
Quork quork. *See* Kwouk kwouk – Oceania
Ra – Africa
Rā marama – Oceania
Ra'alat Ashtart. *See* Ashtart – Near East
Rabba. *See* Rabbah – Near East

Rabbah – Near East
Rabbit Mother – North America
Rab-brtan-ma – The Himalaya
Rabi'a Al-adawiya – Near East
Rabia – Southeast Asia
Rabie. *See* Rabia – Southeast Asia
Rachmay – Near East
Radegasta – Eastern Europe
Radgrid – Northern Europe
Radha – Indian Subcontinent
Radien-akka – Eastern Europe
Radien-akka – Northern Europe
Radien-kiedde – Eastern Europe
Radien-kiedde – Northern Europe
Rafu-sen – Far East
Rafusne. *See* Rafu-sen – Far East
Ragalata. *See* Rati – Indian Subcontinent
Ragana – Eastern Europe
Ragno – North America
Rahabasin Mata – Indian Subcontinent
Rahakatittu – North America
Raharariyoma – South America
Rahmai – Near East
Rahmaya – Near East
Rain Goddess – North America
Rainha Barba – South America
Ra'i ra'i – Oceania
Rait – Egypt
Rajah Jewata – Southeast Asia
Rajamma – Indian Subcontinent
Rajarajeshvari – Indian Subcontinent
Rajyadidevatas, The – Indian
  Subcontinent
Rajyasri – Indian Subcontinent
Raka – Indian Subcontinent
Rakataura – Oceania
Rakembaranu – Africa
Rakini – Indian Subcontinent
Raksasis. *See* Rakshasis – Indian
  Subcontinent
Rakshasis, The – Indian Subcontinent
Rakshodhidevatas, The – Indian
  Subcontinent
Raksin Mata – Indian Subcontinent
Raktadantika – Indian Subcontinent
Raktadhara – Indian Subcontinent
Raktipurbi – Indian Subcontinent
Ral-gcig-ma – The Himalaya
Raluve – Oceania
Rama – Indian Subcontinent
Ramaladevi – Indian Subcontinent
Rambha – Indian Subcontinent
Ramchandi – Indian Subcontinent
Ramuit. *See* Renenet – Egypt
Ran – Northern Europe
Rana Nedia – Eastern Europe
Rana Neida – Northern Europe
Ranaghanti – Indian Subcontinent
Rana-neidda. *See* Rana Nedia – Eastern
  Europe
Randa – Africa
Randeng – Far East
Randgrid – Northern Europe
Ranen. *See* Renenet – Egypt
Rangahore – Oceania
Rangda – Indian Subcontinent
Rangda – Southeast Asia
Raninit. *See* Renenet – Egypt
Ranno. *See* Renen, Renenet – Egypt
Rannu – Egypt

Rannut. *See* Renenet, Renenutet – Egypt
Ranpu – Egypt
Ranu Bai – Indian Subcontinent
Ranuit. *See* Renenet – Egypt
Rapawiyema. *See* Tãté Rapawiyama –
  Central America and Mesoamerica
Rapsem Si – South America
Rara – Oceania
Rasastat – Near East
Rat – Egypt
Rat Devi. *See* Maiya Andhiyari – Indian
  Subcontinent
Rat Mai. *See* Maiya Andhiyari – Indian
  Subcontinent
Rata – Near East
Rata – Oceania
Ratainicza – Eastern Europe
Ratainitsa. *See* Ratainicza – Eastern
  Europe
Rati – Indian Subcontinent
Ratih – Southeast Asia
Ratis – Western Europe
Ratna Dakinis – The Himalaya
Ratna Krotishaurima – The Himalaya
Ratna Kro-ti-shavr-ri-ma. *See* Ratna
  Krotishaurima – The Himalaya
Ratnadakini – Indian Subcontinent
Ratnamangari – Indian Subcontinent
Ra-to. *See* Ritho – Egypt
RatriIndian Subcontinent – Indian
  Subcontinent
Ratta – Egypt
Rat-tanit. *See* Tanith – Egypt
Rat-taoui. *See* Rat-taui – Egypt
Rat-taui – Egypt
Ratu Loro Kidul – Southeast Asia
Rau 'ata mea – Oceania
Rau 'ata'ati – Oceania
Rau 'ata'ura – Oceania
Rau kata ura – Oceania
Rau penapena – Oceania
Raua – South America
Raudna – Eastern Europe
Raudri. *See* Ambika and Matris –
  Indian Subcontinent
Rauei – Oceania
Raumiha – Oceania
Rauni – Eastern Europe
Rautoro. *See* Nau taufiti – Oceania
Rav-ava – Eastern Europe
Ravdna – Eastern Europe
Raz-ajk – Eastern Europe
Razishta Cista – Near East
Rddhi – Indian Subcontinent
rDerje-mkhah-hgro. *See* Vajradakini,
  Indian Subcontinentn
  Subcontinent – The Himalaya
rDo-rje-dpal-gyi yum – The Himalaya
rDo-rje-drag-mo-rgyal – The Himalaya
rDo-rje-mkha'-'gro-ma – The Himalaya
rDo-rje-ne-ne-gnam-sman-sgron – The
  Himalaya
rDo-rje-rnal-hbyor-ma – The Himalaya
Re – Western Europe
Rea – Oceania
Re'are'a – Oceania
Red Crow-headed Thunderbolt
  Goddess – The Himalaya
Red Dog's Wife – North America

Red Hoopoe-headed Desire Goddess –
  The Himalaya
Red Horse-headed Delight Goddess –
  The Himalaya
Red Ibex-headed Woman Goddess –
  The Himalaya
Red Lion-headed Mystic Goddess –
  The Himalaya
Red Makara-headed Peaceful
  Goddess – The Himalaya
Red Pramoha – The Himalaya
Red Pukhase – The Himalaya
Red Scorpion-headed Amrita
  Goddess – The Himalaya
Red Snow-bear-headed Virgin
  Goddess – The Himalaya
Red-spider-woman – North America
Red Tara. *See* Kurukulle – The
  Himalaya
Red Tiger-headed One – The Himalaya
Red Woman – North America
Reddish-yellow Serpent-headed
  Brahma Goddess – The Himalaya
Redu – Greek and Roman Empires
Regina – Greek and Roman Empires
Regina. *See* Rhiannon, Rigantona –
  Western Europe
Rehua – Oceania
Remati – The Himalaya
Rembha – Indian Subcontinent
Remphan. *See* Chiun – Near East
Remute. *See* Renenutet – Egypt
Renen – Egypt
Renenet – Egypt
Renenit. *See* Renenet – Egypt
Renenti – Egypt
Renen-utet. *See* Renenet, Renenutet –
  Egypt
Renenutet – Egypt
Rennute. *See* Renenet – Egypt
Rennutet – Egypt
Renpa – Egypt
Renpet – Egypt
Renph. *See* Renpet – Egypt
Renpit. *See* Renpet – Egypt
Renuka – Indian Subcontinent
Renuntet. *See* Renenet – Egypt
Renute. *See* Renenet – Egypt
Renutet. *See* Rennutet – Egypt
Repa – Egypt
Repo – Oceania
Rerenoa – Oceania
Reret – Egypt
Rerit. *See* Taueret – Egypt
Rert. *See* Apet, Taueret, Ta-urt – Egypt
Rertu. *See* Apet, Taueret, Ta-urt – Egypt
Reschep – Egypt
Reshpu – Near East
Reva – Indian Subcontinent
Revali – Indian Subcontinent
Revati – Indian Subcontinent
Rhamnusia – Greek and Roman
  Empires
Rharias – Greek and Roman Empires
Rhea – Greek and Roman Empires
Rhea Silvia – Greek and Roman
  Empires
Rhea Sylvia. *See* Rhea Silvia – Greek
  and Roman Empires

Rhea-kybele. *See* Mater-turrita – Near East
Rheda. *See* Hrede – Northern Europe
Rhene – Greek and Roman Empires
Rhiannon – Western Europe
Rhind. *See* Rind – Northern Europe
Rhode – Greek and Roman Empires
Rhodea. *See* Rhodeia – Greek and Roman Empires
Rhodeia – Greek and Roman Empires
Rhodia – Greek and Roman Empires
Rhododactylos – Greek and Roman Empires
Rhodope – Greek and Roman Empires
Rhodos – Greek and Roman Empires
Rhoeo – Greek and Roman Empires
Rhpisunt – North America
Ri – Near East
Ri. *See* Re – Western Europe
Riannon. *See* Rhiannon – Western Europe
Ri-bu-mo – The Himalaya
Ricana – Africa
Rice Mother – Southeast Asia
Riddhi. *See* Rddhi – Indian Subcontinent
Rigantona – Western Europe
Rigiu Boba – Eastern Europe
Rigs-bu-mo. *See* Ri-bu-mo – The Himalaya
Rima horo – Oceania
Rima poto – Oceania
Rin-chen-mkha'-'gro-ma – The Himalaya
Rin-chen-mkhah-ngro – The Himalaya
Rind – Northern Europe
Rinda. *See* Rind, Rindr – Northern Europe
Rinde. *See* Rind – Northern Europe
Rindr – Northern Europe
Riri tuna rai – Oceania
Ririt. *See* Taueret – Egypt
Risem-edne – Eastern Europe
Risem-Edne – Northern Europe
Ritha. *See* Prithivi – Indian Subcontinent
Ritho – Egypt
Rksavaktradakini – Indian Subcontinent
Rlung-gi-lha-mo-dam-tshig-sgrol-ma – The Himalaya
rMa-bya-c'en-mo – The Himalaya
Ro Lei – Oceania
Ro Som – Oceania
Robigo – Greek and Roman Empires
Rochanî – The Himalaya
Rock Crystal Girl – North America
Rock Maiden – Southeast Asia
Rodasi – Indian Subcontinent
Rohina. *See* Rohini – Indian Subcontinent
Rohini – Indian Subcontinent
Rojenice, The. *See* The Rodjenice – Eastern Europe
Ro-kha-ma – The Himalaya
Rokime – Indian Subcontinent

Roma – Greek and Roman Empires
Rona – Oceania
Rong gi Jo-mo-kha-rag. *See* rDo-rje-dpal-gyi yum – The Himalaya
Ronkini – Indian Subcontinent
Ronpet – Egypt
Röönikkä. *See* Rauni – Eastern Europe
Roskva – Northern Europe
Rosmerta – Western Europe
Rosna – Central America and Mesoamerica
Rota – Northern Europe
Ro-tara-ni-bi – Far East
Rõugutaja – Eastern Europe
Rozanice – Eastern Europe
Rozdenici – Eastern Europe
Rozenitsa. *See* Rozhenitsa – Eastern Europe
Rozhanitsy, The – Eastern Europe
Rozhdenitsa. *See* Rozhenitsa – Eastern Europe
Rozhenitsa – Eastern Europe
Rtuharika – Indian Subcontinent
Rua hine metua – Oceania
Rua papa – Oceania
Rua tamaine – Oceania
Rua tupua nui – Oceania
Ruahine nihoniho ro roa – Oceania
Ruānge – Oceania
Ruataka. *See* Pufine i ravenga – Oceania
Rubati – Near East
Ru-be-sei – Far East
Rudrani – Indian Subcontinent
Ruha D'qudsha – Near East
Rukho – Near East
Rukko – North America
Rukmini – Indian Subcontinent
Ruku tia – Oceania
Ruma'u Ari'i – Oceania
Rumia Dea – Greek and Roman Empires
Rumina – Greek and Roman Empires
Rumor – Greek and Roman Empires
Runcina – Greek and Roman Empires
Runeeka. *See* Renuka – Indian Subcontinent
Runepai – Oceania
Rusa – Near East
Rusalka, The – Eastern Europe
Rusalki, The. *See* Rusalka – Eastern Europe
Rusalki-siriny, The – Eastern Europe
Rusalky, The. *See* Rusalka – Eastern Europe
Rusina – Greek and Roman Empires
Russian Mother Earth – Eastern Europe
Rutbe – Central America and Mesoamerica
Sa – Egypt
Saar. *See* Sadb – Western Europe
Sa'ato – Oceania
Saato. *See* Sa'ato – Oceania
Saba. *See* Sadb – Western Europe
Sabaga – Eastern Europe
Sabbath – Africa
Sabia. *See* Sadb – Western Europe
Sabitu – Near East
Sabra – Western Europe
Sabrina – Western Europe

Sabulana – Africa
Sac First Women – North America
Sachmet – Egypt
Saci – Indian Subcontinent
Sacontala. *See* Sakuntala – Indian Subcontinent
Sacra. *See* Vesta – Greek and Roman Empires
Sacti. *See* Shakti – Indian Subcontinent
Sadanvas, The – Indian Subcontinent
Sadarnuna – Near East
Sadb – Western Europe
Sadbhavasri – Indian Subcontinent
Sadhbh. *See* Sadb – Western Europe
Sadsta-akka – Eastern Europe
Sadwes – Near East
Saelde – Northern Europe
Safekh-aabut – Egypt
Safekh-abui. *See* Seshat – Egypt
Safkhitabui. *See* Seshat – Egypt
Sag – Egypt
Saga – Northern Europe
Sagar – Southeast Asia
Sagaris – Greek and Roman Empires
Sagaritis – Greek and Roman Empires
Sagatea – Oceania
Sago Woman – Southeast Asia
Sah – Egypt
Sahaganya – Indian Subcontinent
Sahassaras – Near East
Sahk Kays' Es Yo Sees' Kak Aht – Central America and Mesoamerica
Saho-yama-hime – Far East
Sa'i-lha-mo Sangs-rgyas-spyan-ma – The Himalaya
Saint Paraskeva. *See* Paraskeva – Eastern Europe
Saint Prende. *See* Prende – Eastern Europe
Saint Thecla. *See* Dekla, Karta – Eastern Europe
Sais – Greek and Roman Empires
Saitis – Greek and Roman Empires
Saiva-neida, The – Eastern Europe
Saivo-neita – Eastern Europe
Sakambhari – Indian Subcontinent
Sakhala – Eastern Europe
Sakhala-khatun. *See* Sakhala – Eastern Europe
Sakhmet. *See* Sekhmet – Egypt
Sakhmis – Egypt
Saki – Indian Subcontinent
Sakis. *See* Krittika – Indian Subcontinent
Saki-tama-hime – Far East
Sakunadevatas – Indian Subcontinent
Sakunadhisthatri – Indian Subcontinent
Sakuni – Indian Subcontinent
Sakuntala – Indian Subcontinent
Sakuru. *See* Shakuru – North America
Sakuya-bime. *See* Konohana-no-sakuya-bime – Far East
Sakwa Mana – North America
Sakwats Mana – North America
Sala – Near East
Salacia – Greek and Roman Empires
Salampandai – Southeast Asia
Salatia. *See* Salacia – Greek and Roman Empires
Salgusa – Near East

Sali Minao – Indian Subcontinent
Salida. *See* Saelde – Northern Europe
Salmacis – Greek and Roman Empires
Salmaone – Greek and Roman Empires
Salpin – Greek and Roman Empires
Salt Woman. *See* Malokatsiki – North America
Saltu – Near East
Salus – Greek and Roman Empires
Salus Hygeia. *See* Salus – Greek and Roman Empires
Salus Publica. *See* Salus – Greek and Roman Empires
Salutaris – Greek and Roman Empires
Sama Bolowa – Africa
Samai – Near East
Samaiya – Indian Subcontinent
Samal – Near East
Samalamma – Indian Subcontinent
Saman. *See* Samhain – Western Europe
Samanta-Bhadra. *See* Kuntu-bzang-mo – The Himalaya
Sambata – Africa
Sambatu. *See* Sambata – Africa
Sambhu – Indian Subcontinent
Sambhuti. *See* Sambhu – Indian Subcontinent
Samdhya. *See* Sandhya – Indian Subcontinent
Samgna – Indian Subcontinent
Samhain – Western Europe
Samhuin. *See* Samhain – Western Europe
Samjna. *See* Samgna – Indian Subcontinent
Samjuna – Indian Subcontinent
Samkhat – Near East
Sammuramat. *See* Semiramis – Near East
Samnati – Indian Subcontinent
Samovila. *See* The Vila – Eastern Europe
Samovily. *See* The Vila – Eastern Europe
Sampny Nang – Southeast Asia
Samriddhi – Indian Subcontinent
Samundra – Indian Subcontinent
San Fu Jên. *See* The San Furen – Far East
San Furen, The – Far East
San Gufuren – Far East
San Ku. *See* San Gu – Far East
San Ku Fu Jen. *See* San Gufuren – Far East
Sandalphon – Near East
Sandaramet. *See* Spandaramet – Near East
Sandark. *See* Spandaramet – Near East
Sandhya – Indian Subcontinent
Sandi – Indian Subcontinent
Sandili – Indian Subcontinent
Sandolphon. *See* Sandalphon – Near East
Sanghyang Ibu Pertiwi – Southeast Asia
Sangia-mama – Eastern Europe
Sangiang Serri. *See* Sangiyan Sari – Southeast Asia
Sangiyan Sari – Southeast Asia
Sangridr – Northern Europe
Sangs-rgyas-mkha'-'gro-ma – The Himalaya
Sangs-rgyas-spyan-ma – The Himalaya
Sangvo Nimu – Indian Subcontinent

Sangyay Chanma. *See* Sangs-rgyas-spyan-ma – The Himalaya
Sangye-khado – The Himalaya
Sanhin. *See* Samhain – Western Europe
Sanihas – North America
Saning Sari – Southeast Asia
Sanjna. *See* Samgna – Indian Subcontinent
Sankata – Indian Subcontinent
Sankchinni – Indian Subcontinent
Sankini – Indian Subcontinent
Sannati. *See* Samnati – Indian Subcontinent
Sansari Mai – Indian Subcontinent
Sans-rgyas-mkhah-hgro. *See* Sangye-khado – The Himalaya
Santa – Indian Subcontinent
Santaramet – Near East
Santaramet – Eastern Europe
Sanumati – Indian Subcontinent
Sanvna – North America
Sao – Greek and Roman Empires
Sao Ch'ing Niang. *See* Saoqing Niang – Far East
Saoka – Near East
Saoqing Niang – Far East
Saosis – Egypt
Sao-ts'ing Niang. *See* Saoqing Niang – Far East
Sapas – Near East
Sapientia – Greek and Roman Empires
Sapientia. *See* Sophia – Near East
Sapientia-Sophia. *See* Sapientia – Greek and Roman Empires
Sapiqenwas – North America
Saps – Near East
Sapt – Egypt
Sapta-koti-buddha-matri-cunti-devi – Indian Subcontinent
Sapta-koti-buddha-matri-cunti-devi. *See* Jun-tei Kwan-non – Far East
Saptamatrakas – Indian Subcontinent
Saptapetala – Southeast Asia
Saputan – Southeast Asia
Sara Mama. *See* Mama Sara – South America
Sara. *See* Amari De – Indian Subcontinent
Sara. *See* Isis – Egypt
Sarada. *See* Sarasvati – Indian Subcontinent
Saraddevi – Indian Subcontinent
Saradvadhu – Indian Subcontinent
Sara-kali. *See* Amari De – Indian Subcontinent
Sar-akka – Northern Europe
Sarakka – Eastern Europe
Sarak-kamui – Far East
Sarama – Indian Subcontinent
Saranjus – Indian Subcontinent
Saranya. *See* Sumjuna – Indian Subcontinent
Saranyu – Indian Subcontinent
Sarassouadi – Indian Subcontinent
Sarasvati – Indian Subcontinent
Saraswati. *See* Sarasvati – Indian Subcontinent
Sarawniya – Africa
Sarbanda – Near East

Sarduli – Indian Subcontinent
Sarengge – Southeast Asia
Sa-rgyal-dong-gi-dbal-mo – The Himalaya
Saris – Near East
Sarmishtha. *See* Sarmistha – Indian Subcontinent
Sarmistha – Indian Subcontinent
Sarna Burhia – Indian Subcontinent
Saronia – Greek and Roman Empires
Saronis. *See* Saronia – Greek and Roman Empires
Sarpanit. *See* Sarpanitu – Near East
Sarpanitu – Near East
Sarpanitum. *See* Aruru and Sarpanitu – Near East
Sarparajni – Indian Subcontinent
Sarpedonia – Greek and Roman Empires
Sarpis, The – Indian Subcontinent
Sarset – Egypt
Sartiyas – Near East
Sarvabuddhadakini – Indian Subcontinent
Sarvakamadugha – Indian Subcontinent
Sarvari – Indian Subcontinent
Sarvasavaaranaam-bhagavati. *See* Parnasavari – Indian Subcontinent
Sarvayoni – Indian Subcontinent
Sarveshvari – Indian Subcontinent
Sasana-devi – Indian Subcontinent
Sasa'umani – Oceania
Sasilekha – Indian Subcontinent
Sasthi – Indian Subcontinent
Sasti – Indian Subcontinent
Sasura. *See* Mami – Near East
Sasuru. *See* Sarpanitu – Near East
Sasvsuma Inua – North America
Sat Matra – Indian Subcontinent
Satarupa – Indian Subcontinent
Satel – Egypt
Satene – Oceania
Satene. *See* Satine – Southeast Asia
Satet – Egypt
Sati – Egypt
Sati – Indian Subcontinent
Sati-abut – Egypt
Sati-arut – Egypt
Satine – Southeast Asia
Satis – Egypt
Satit. *See* Satet – Egypt
Sattuma Eeva – North America
Satvai – Indian Subcontinent
Satyabhama – Indian Subcontinent
Satyavati – Indian Subcontinent
Saudamani – Indian Subcontinent
Saule – Eastern Europe
Saules Meitas – Eastern Europe
Saules-māte – Eastern Europe
Sausga. *See* Sauska – Near East
Sauska – Near East
Sautu Majan – Southeast Asia
Savadamma – Indian Subcontinent
Savala. *See* Kamadhenu – Indian Subcontinent
Savari – Indian Subcontinent
Savarna – Indian Subcontinent
Savior – Greek and Roman Empires
Savitri – Indian Subcontinent

Saw Meya. *See* Shwe Myet Hna –
   Southeast Asia
Saweigh – Southeast Asia
Sawuska. *See* Sauska – Near East
Sa-yi-lha-mo-bstan-ma – The Himalaya
Say-say ai-khai ai'pay. *See* Mahm-m –
   Central America and Mesoamerica
Sayo-hime – Far East
Sayori-bime-no-mikoto. *See*
   Ichiki-shima-hime-no-mikoto – Far
   East
Scabies – Greek and Roman Empires
Scáthach – Western Europe
Schala – Near East
Schastie – Eastern Europe
Schent – Egypt
Schetewuarha – South America
Schilalyi – Eastern Europe
Sciras – Greek and Roman Empires
Scorpion Woman – Near East
Scota – Western Europe
Scotia – Greek and Roman Empires
Scylla – Greek and Roman Empires
Sea Goddess – Near East
Seang – Western Europe
Seb-tet – Egypt
Seba – Egypt
Seben – Egypt
Sebit – Egypt
Secia – Greek and Roman Empires
Second Earthly Generation Deities – Far
   East
Sedaw Thakmina – Southeast Asia
Sedhu – Indian Subcontinent
Sedi – Indian Subcontinent
Sedi-Irkong-Bomong – Indian
   Subcontinent
Sedi-Irkong-Bong – Indian Subcontinent
Sedna – North America
Seewa – Eastern Europe
Sefchet. *See* Seshat – Egypt
Sefek-aabui. *See* Seshat – Egypt
Sefekh. *See* Seshat – Egypt
Sefekh-seshat. *See* Seshat – Egypt
Sefk-het-abut. *See* Seshat – Egypt
Sefkh-tābui. *See* Seshat – Egypt
Sefkhabu – Egypt
Segeta – Western Europe
Segetia – Greek and Roman Empires
Segomanna – Western Europe
Seher-tut – Egypt
Sehmet. *See* Sekhmet – Egypt
Sehu Woman – North America
Seia – Greek and Roman Empires
Seidhkoma, The – Northern Europe
Seimia – Near East
Sei-o-bo – Far East
Seirenes. *See* Sirens – Greek and Roman
   Empires
Seitho. *See* Pitho – Greek and Roman
   Empires
Seja – Greek and Roman Empires
Sekhemet-ren-s-em-abet-s – Egypt
Sekhet – Egypt
Sekhet-aanru – Egypt
Sekhet-aaru. *See* Sekhet-aanru – Egypt
Sekhet-bast-ra – Egypt
Sekhet-hetepet – Egypt
Sekhet-metu – Egypt
Sekhment. *See* Sekhet – Egypt

Sekhmet – Egypt
Sekmet. *See* Sekhmet – Egypt
Sekseket – Egypt
Sel – Northern Europe
Sel. *See* Sul – Western Europe
Sela – Africa
Selampandai. *See* Salampandai –
   Southeast Asia
Selci-syt-emysyt – Eastern Europe
Selena. *See* Selene – Greek and Roman
   Empires
Selene – Greek and Roman Empires
Selk – Egypt
Selket – Egypt
Selkhet. *See* Selket – Egypt
Selkit. *See* Selket – Egypt
Selqet. *See* Selket – Egypt
Selquet. *See* Selket – Egypt
Selu – North America
Semargla – Eastern Europe
Semele – Near East
Semele – Greek and Roman Empires
Semik – Eastern Europe
Semiramis – Near East
Semmesmaat – Eastern Europe
Semnai Theai, The – Greek and Roman
   Empires
Semsemeltstas Senxalaolela. *See*
   Nuexqemalsai – North America
Semt – Egypt
Sena – Indian Subcontinent
Senamuki – Indian Subcontinent
Senb-kheperu – Egypt
Seneb – Egypt
Senecta – Greek and Roman Empires
Senectus. *See* Senecta – Greek and
   Roman Empires
Seng-ge Dolma – The Himalaya
Seng-ge Ga-mu – Far East
Seng-ge Karmo – Far East
Seng-ge'i-gdong-can – The Himalaya
Senga-dong-ma – The Himalaya
Sengdroma – The Himalaya
Sengen-sama – Far East
Sengi-mama – Eastern Europe
Senhora Ana – South America
Senjo, The. *See* The Senyo – Far East
Sentait – Egypt
Sentu. *See* Nintur – Near East
Sānu-māte – Eastern Europe
Senyo, The – Far East
Se-o-nyo – Far East
Seoritsu-hime – Far East
Sepeo. *See* Speio – Greek and Roman
   Empires
Sephira – Western Europe
Sephiroth – Western Europe
Sept. *See* Sothis – Egypt
Septet. *See* Sothis – Egypt
Seqinek. *See* Akycha – North America
Sequana – Western Europe
Seret – Egypt
Seri – Southeast Asia
Serket. *See* Selket – Egypt
Serkhit. *See* Selket – Egypt
Serpent of Paradise. *See* the Nathair
   Parrthuis – Near East
Serq. *See* Selket – Egypt
Serqet – Egypt
Serque-edne – Eastern Europe

Serreta de Alcoy Mother Goddess –
   Western Europe
Ser-t – Egypt
Seruya – Near East
Sesat. *See* Seshat – Egypt
Sesenet-khu – Egypt
Seshait-safkhitabui. *See* Seshat – Egypt
Sesha't. *See* Seshat – Egypt
Seshat – Egypt
Seshatu. *See* Seshat – Egypt
Sesheta. *See* Seshat – Egypt
Seshetat – Egypt
Seshetet – Egypt
Ses-rab-kyi-pha-rol-ta-phyin-pa. *See*
   Prajnaparamita – The Himalaya
Seta – Africa
Setesuyara – Southeast Asia
Setlocenia – Western Europe
Sevasti-devi – Indian Subcontinent
Seven Females, The – Indian
   Subcontinent
Seven Kine-deities – Egypt
Seven Sisters – North America
Seven Sisters of Industry – Far East
Seventeen Generations Deities – Far
   East
Seya-tatara-hime – Far East
Sgeg-mo-ma – The Himalaya
Sgeimh Solais – Western Europe
sGrol-dkar-po. *See* Sitatara, Indian
   Subcontinentn Subcontinent – The
   Himalaya
sGrol-ma. *See* sGrol-mas – The
   Himalaya
sGrol-mas – The Himalaya
Shabari. *See* Jatila – Indian Subcontinent
Shachuth – Near East
Shadip – Southeast Asia
Shait – Egypt
Shaivi. *See* Manasa – Indian
   Subcontinent
Shakini – Indian Subcontinent
Shakinis, The – Indian Subcontinent
Sha'koya – North America
Shakti – The Himalaya
Shakti – Indian Subcontinent
Shaktis, The – Indian Subcontinent
Shaktiyasas – Indian Subcontinent
Shakuntala. *See* Sakuntala – Indian
   Subcontinent
Shakuru – North America
Shala – Near East
Shalako Mana – North America
Shalash. *See* Shala – Near East
Shalimtum – Near East
Shaliom – Oceania
Shal-za-ma. *See* Zhal-zas-ma – The
   Himalaya
Shamash. *See* Shapash – Near East
Shamidevi – Indian Subcontinent
Shandian Pozi – Far East
Shan-tien P'o-tzu. *See* Shandian Pozi –
   Far East
Shangkam Majan – Southeast Asia
Shanti – Indian Subcontinent
Shapas. *See* Shapash – Near East
Shapash – Near East
Shaph – Near East
Sharis. *See* Ishtar – Near East
Sharrat Shame. *See* Ishtar – Near East

Shashaya – Africa
Shashthi. See Shasti – Indian Subcontinent
Shasthi – Indian Subcontinent
Shasti – Indian Subcontinent
Shastradevatas – Indian Subcontinent
Shatagat. See Shataqat – Near East
Shataqat – Near East
Shatarupa. See Vac – Indian Subcontinent
Shaterany – Indian Subcontinent
Shatshektshe, The. See The Shotshen – Eastern Europe
Shaushga. See Shaushka – Near East
Shaushka – Near East
Shavasi – Indian Subcontinent
Shawa Unti Majan – Southeast Asia
She Mu – Far East
She Sang Neu. See Shesang Nü – Far East
Shedath – Near East
Shedi. See Sedi – Indian Subcontinent
Sheela-na-gig. See Sheila-na-gig – Western Europe
Sheelanagyg. See Sheila-na-gig – Western Europe
Sheila-na-gig – Western Europe
Shekinah – Near East
Shela-no-gig. See Sheila-na-gig – Western Europe
Shell Woman – South America
Shemat-khu – Egypt
Shen Deity – Far East
Shen Mu. See Bixia Yuanjin – Far East
Shenat-pet-utheset-neter – Egypt
Shêng Mu. See Shengmu – Far East
Sheng-ku. See Shenggu – Far East
Shenggu – Far East
Shengmu – Far East
Shenty – Egypt
Sheol – Near East
Sheol. See Sheol, Near East – Western Europe
Shepe – Far East
She-p'er. See Shepe – Far East
Sheput – Egypt
Sherok – Oceania
Sherua – Near East
Shesang Nü – Far East
Shesat-makey-neb-s – Egypt
Shesemtet – Egypt
Sheshat – Egypt
Shes-kentet – Egypt
Sheta – Egypt
Sheve – Near East
She-Wolf – Northern Europe
Shi – Far East
Shibbeta – Near East
Shid – Near East
Shidkin-kede – Indian Subcontinent
Shiduri. See Siduri – Near East
Shih Hu Shih. See Shihu Shi – Far East
Shih-chi Niang-niang. See Shiji Niangniang – Far East
Shihu Shi – Far East
Shiji Niangniang – Far East
Shiko-me. See Yomo-tsu-shiko-me – Far East
Shilluk – Egypt
Shimti – Near East

Shinatsuhime – Far East
Shindwe Hla. See Shwe Myet Hna – Southeast Asia
Shing Moo. See Xing Mu – Far East
Shing-rum – Indian Subcontinent
Shintalimeni – Near East
Shi-nun-manuri – Far East
Shi-nish-e-ran-mat – Far East
Shio-mi-ma – Far East
Shir-kor-kamui – Far East
Shitala. See Sitala – Indian Subcontinent
Shitateru-hime-no-mikoto. See Takahime-no-mikoto – Far East
Shitla. See Sitala – Indian Subcontinent
Shiu-mu Niang-niang. See Xiumu Niangniang – Far East
Shiwanokia – North America
Shiwanska. See Shiwanokia – North America
Shokujo – Far East
Shotshen, The – Eastern Europe
Shozu-ga-no-baba – Far East
Shraddha – Indian Subcontinent
Shri – Indian Subcontinent
Shri-devi. See Lha-mo – The Himalaya
Shro-tu-na-ko – North America
Shrutavati – Indian Subcontinent
Shtrige – Eastern Europe
Shuci – Indian Subcontinent
Shuhiji-no-kami. See Su-hiji-ni-no-kami – Far East
Shui-i Shih. See Shuiyi Shi – Far East
Shui-mu Niang-niang. See Shuimu Niangniang – Far East
Shuimu Niangniang – Far East
Shuiyi Shi – Far East
Shuki – Indian Subcontinent
Shu-koyan-mat – Far East
Shulamite – Near East
Shun I Fu-jen. See Shunyi Furen – Far East
Shundimumi – Eastern Europe
Shunyi Furen – Far East
Shup. See Chup – North America
Shurpanakha – Indian Subcontinent
Shushtee – Indian Subcontinent
Shuska-Revati – Indian Subcontinent
Shutu – Near East
Shwe Myet Hna – Southeast Asia
Shwe Na Be – Southeast Asia
Shyavi – Indian Subcontinent
Shyeni – Indian Subcontinent
Si – South America
Si – Eastern Europe
Si Adaman. See Adamisil Wedo – Central America and Mesoamerica
Si Dayang – Southeast Asia
Si Ling She. See Siling Shen – Far East
Si Rapan – Southeast Asia
Si Wang Mu. See Xi Wangmu – Far East
Sia Jatta Bari – Africa
Sian pual'ekia'a. See Sian pual'etafa – Oceania
Sian pual'etafa – Oceania
Si-Bavas. See Si. – Eastern Europe
Siberu Dayang Mata Ni Ari – Southeast Asia
Sibhol. See Ëre – Western Europe
Sibilja – Northern Europe
Sichi – Indian Subcontinent

Sidapa – Southeast Asia
Siddha-Yoginis, The – Indian Subcontinent
Siddhanganas – Indian Subcontinent
Siddhikari – Indian Subcontinent
Siddhis – Indian Subcontinent
Sidne – North America
Siduri – Near East
Siduri Sabitu. See Siduri – Near East
Sieglind – Northern Europe
Sieglinde. See Sieglind – Northern Europe
Siella. See Atabei – Central America and Mesoamerica
Sienjarolol – Oceania
Sientafitukrou – Oceania
Sien-tsan. See Xiancan – Far East
Sieou Wen-yin. See Xiu Wenyin – Far East
Sierra Leone Goddess – Africa
Sif – Northern Europe
Sige – Near East
Signe-Alveig – Northern Europe
Signy – Northern Europe
Sigrdrifa – Northern Europe
Sigrlinn – Northern Europe
Sigrun – Northern Europe
Sigrutan – Southeast Asia
Siguna. See Signy – Northern Europe
Sigurdrifta. See Sigrdrifa – Northern Europe
Sigyn. See Signy – Northern Europe
Sihwuluhtsitsa. See Komokatsiki – North America
Sik Sawp – Southeast Asia
Sikingimoemoe – Oceania
Sil. See Sel – Northern Europe
Sila – North America
Sila – Indian Subcontinent
Siladi – Southeast Asia
Silat – Southeast Asia
Sileni – Near East
Silewe Nazarata – Southeast Asia
Silige Fraulein – Northern Europe
Silili – Near East
Silili – Oceania
Siling Shen – Far East
Silkie – Western Europe
Silla – Africa
Silla Mountain Goddess – Far East
Silly Wychtis, The – Western Europe
Siltslani – North America
Silvia. See Rhea Silvia – Greek and Roman Empires
Simaethis – Greek and Roman Empires
Simei – Southeast Asia
Simhavahini. See Durga – Indian Subcontinent
Simhavaktra – Indian Subcontinent
Simhika – Indian Subcontinent
Simi. See Seimia – Near East
Simorgh – Near East
Simsiutaakis – North America
Sin – Western Europe
Sina – Oceania
Sina tae o i lagi – Oceania
Sinafakalau – Oceania
Sinafofalangi. See Sinafakalau – Oceania
Sinakibi – Oceania
Sinann – Western Europe

Sināsa'umani – Oceania
Sinavali – Indian Subcontinent
Sindgund – Northern Europe
Sindhu – Indian Subcontinent
Sindur – Northern Europe
Sine Matanoginogi – Oceania
Sineach. *See* Muirdris – Western Europe
Sinebomatu – Oceania
Sinekili – Oceania
Sinend. *See* Sinann – Western Europe
Singan – Southeast Asia
Singano. *See* Ekeitehua – Oceania
Singarmati Devi – Indian Subcontinent
Singgar – Southeast Asia
Singhbahani – Indian Subcontinent
Singhbahini – Indian Subcontinent
Singhinî – The Himalaya
Siniboi – Indian Subcontinent
Sinivali – Indian Subcontinent
Sinmora – Northern Europe
Sinnan. *See* Sinann – Western Europe
Sinngund. *See* Sindgund – Northern
     Europe
Sinnilktok – North America
Sinoe – Greek and Roman Empires
Sinthgunt. *See* Sindgund – Northern
     Europe
Sio Mana – North America
Sio Shalako Mana – North America
Siofn – Northern Europe
Sionan. *See* Sinann – Western Europe
Sipe Gyalmo – The Himalaya
Sipna – Greek and Roman Empires
Siqiniq – North America
Sirah. *See* Siris – Near East
Sirara – Near East
Sirdu. *See* A – Near East
Sirêne, La – Central America and
     Mesoamerica
Sirens, The – Greek and Roman Empires
Siriny, The – Eastern Europe
Siris – Near East
Sirona – Western Europe
Sirrida. *See* A – Near East
Sirsootee – Indian Subcontinent
Sirtur. *See* Ninsun – Near East
Sisi – Oceania
Sisina – Southeast Asia
Sister Fire – Near East
Sita – Indian Subcontinent
Sitala – Indian Subcontinent
Sitala Devi. *See* Sitala – Indian
     Subcontinent
Sitala Mata. *See* Sitala – Indian
     Subcontinent
Sitalamma – Indian Subcontinent
Sitapi – Southeast Asia
Sitatapatra Aparajita – Indian
     Subcontinent
Sitatara – Indian Subcontinent
Sitch-tche-na-ko. *See* Sussistinnako –
     North America
Si-tcom'pa Ma-so-its – North America
Sith – Northern Europe
Siti Permani – Southeast Asia
Sitking-Kedding – Indian Subcontinent
Sitla. *See* Sitala – Indian Subcontinent
Sitlamata – Indian Subcontinent
Sito – Greek and Roman Empires
Siva – Eastern Europe

Siva – Indian Subcontinent
Siwuluhtsitsa – North America
Sixmana – North America
Sixty-four Yoginis, The. *See* Chausathi
     Yoginis – Indian Subcontinent
Sjantaik – Eastern Europe
Sjofn – Northern Europe
Sjojungfru – Eastern Europe
Sjora – Northern Europe
Sjöran. *See* Sjora – Northern Europe
Skagit Grandmother – North America
Skamotsxmana – North America
Skandamata. *See* Sasthi – Indian
     Subcontinent
Skate Woman – North America
Skeggold – Northern Europe
Skialf – Northern Europe
Skil-djaadai – North America
Sklumyoa – North America
Skogol – Northern Europe
Skogsfru – Northern Europe
Skogsjungfru – Northern Europe
Skogsnufvar, The – Northern Europe
Skogul. *See* Skogol – Northern Europe
Skqwalutl – North America
Skuld – Northern Europe
Skule – North America
Skwanat.äm.ä – North America
Sky Maiden – Oceania
Sky Woman – North America
Sky Woman of Nuer – Africa
sKyabs-mdun – The Himalaya
Skyes-bu-ber – The Himalaya
Slatababa – Eastern Europe
Sleparis – Greek and Roman Empires
Smamet – Egypt
Smasha – The Himalaya
Smashali. *See* Smasha – The Himalaya
Smert – Eastern Europe
Smert. *See* Mora – Northern Europe
Smilšu-māte – Eastern Europe
Smirgat – Western Europe
Smriti – Indian Subcontinent
Smrtnice – Eastern Europe
Smyrna – Greek and Roman Empires
Smyrna. *See* Myrrha – Near East
sNa tshogs nkha' 'gro ma – The
     Himalaya
Snake Goddess of Knossos – Greek and
     Roman Empires
sNang-gsal-ma – The Himalaya
Snee-nee-iq – North America
Sneneik – North America
Sneneikulala – North America
Snitsmän-a – North America
Snör – Northern Europe
Snorta. *See* Snotra – Northern Europe
Snotra – Northern Europe
Snowats – North America
Snukpanlits – North America
Snutkanals – North America
Snutqutxals – North America
Snuximetlimana – North America
So – Africa
So Wang-mo – Far East
So Wuhti – North America
Soat-saki – North America
Sobha – The Himalaya
Sobkit – Egypt
Sochet – Egypt

Sochit. *See* Sochet – Egypt
Sodasi – Indian Subcontinent
Sodza – Africa
Sofh – Egypt
Sogbo – Africa
Sohonasomtaka – North America
Sojenice, The – Eastern Europe
Sokarahita – Indian Subcontinent
Sokhet – Egypt
Sokhit. *See* Sekhmet – Egypt
Sol – Northern Europe
Solbon – Eastern Europe
Solntse – Eastern Europe
Soma Cow. *See* Mahi – Indian
     Subcontinent
Soma. *See* Vasus – Indian Subcontinent
Somagalags – North America
Somber Maiden – Far East
Somlai – Indian Subcontinent
Sondara. *See* Spandaramet – Near East
Song Tseu Niang Naing. *See* Songzi
     Niangniang – Far East
Song Tsi Kuan Yin. *See* Songzi
     Guanyin – Far East
Songi – Africa
Song-tsen-gam-po. *See* Dolma – The
     Himalaya
Songzi – Far East
Songzi Guanyin – Far East
Songzi Niangniang – Far East
Soniyawi – North America
Sonnolipenu – Indian Subcontinent
Sonxwana – North America
Sookhmurna. *See* Sushumna – Indian
     Subcontinent
Soora. *See* Sura – Indian Subcontinent
Soorenjnaree. *See* Pingala – Indian
     Subcontinent
Sopd. *See* Sothis – Egypt
Sopdet. *See* Sothis – Egypt
Sopdit. *See* Sothis – Egypt
Sophia – Near East
Sophia Prunikos – Near East
Sophia-achamoth – Near East
Sophrosyne – Greek and Roman
     Empires
Sor-ava – Eastern Europe
Soris. *See* !Urisis – Africa
Sororia – Greek and Roman Empires
Sospita – Greek and Roman Empires
Soteira – Greek and Roman Empires
Sothis – Egypt
Sotohori-irat-sume. *See*
     So-tohoshi-no-iratsume – Far East
So-tohoshi-no-iratsume – Far East
Souban – Egypt
Souconna – Western Europe
South Wind – North America
Sovranty – Western Europe
Soyoko – North America
Soyoko Mana. *See* Soyoko – North
     America
Soyoko Wuhti. *See* Soyoko – North
     America
Spandaramet – Near East
Spantaramet – Near East
Sparta – Greek and Roman Empires
Speio – Greek and Roman Empires
Spentā Ārmaiti – Near East

Speo. *See* Speio – Greek and Roman Empires
Spermo – Greek and Roman Empires
Spes – Greek and Roman Empires
Sphinx, The – Egypt
Sphragitides, The – Greek and Roman Empires
Spider Woman – North America
Spirit Woman – North America
Spiritus Venereus – Near East
Sponde – Greek and Roman Empires
Spurke – Northern Europe
Sreča – Eastern Europe
Sree. *See* Lakshmi – Indian Subcontinent
Sri – Indian Subcontinent
Sri – Southeast Asia
Sri Lakshmi. *See* Lakshmi – Indian Subcontinent
Sridevi – The Himalaya
Srid-pa'i-sman. *See* A-phyi-gung-rgyal – The Himalaya
Srimati – The Himalaya
Sringatpadini – Indian Subcontinent
Sring-mo-no-chung-gzi-byin-ma – The Himalaya
Srinmo – The Himalaya
Srintun Tanah Tumboh Yak Srindak Tanggi Buloh – Southeast Asia
Srog-bdag-mo – The Himalaya
Sruta-Kriti – Indian Subcontinent
Sse – Far East
Star Girl – Oceania
Star Woman – South America
Stata Mater – Greek and Roman Empires
Statua Mater. *See* Stata Mater – Greek and Roman Empires
Stella Maris. *See* Isis – Egypt
Sterope – Greek and Roman Empires
Sthalidevatas – Indian Subcontinent
Sthenele – Greek and Roman Empires
Sthenias – Greek and Roman Empires
Sthenno. *See* Stheno – Greek and Roman Empires
Stheno – Greek and Roman Empires
Sthenoboea. *See* Antea – Greek and Roman Empires
Stilbe – Greek and Roman Empires
Stilbo – Greek and Roman Empires
Stimula – Greek and Roman Empires
Sti-per-sei – Far East
Stiria – Greek and Roman Empires
Stiritis. *See* Stiria – Greek and Roman Empires
Ston-gyi-rgyal-mo – The Himalaya
Stonychia – Greek and Roman Empires
Stratteli – Western Europe
Strenia – Greek and Roman Empires
Strenua – Greek and Roman Empires
Strudeli. *See* Stratteli – Western Europe
Strymo – Greek and Roman Empires
Stymphalia – Greek and Roman Empires
Sty – Greek and Roman Empires
Suada – Greek and Roman Empires
Suadela. *See* Suada – Greek and Roman Empires
Suaha – Indian Subcontinent
Subbu Khai Thung – Indian Subcontinent

Subeh, The – Near East
Subhadra – Indian Subcontinent
Subhangi. *See* Rati – Indian Subcontinent
Substance Mother – Indian Subcontinent
Succoth Benoth – Near East
Succubus – Near East
Sud – Near East
Sudakshina – Indian Subcontinent
Sudbina – Eastern Europe
Sudesna. *See* Tara – Indian Subcontinent
Sudice, The – Eastern Europe
Sudička – Eastern Europe
Sudicky, The – Eastern Europe
Sudjaje, The – Eastern Europe
Sudjenice, The – Eastern Europe
Sudzenici, The – Eastern Europe
Sugrivi – Indian Subcontinent
Su-hiji-ni-no-kami – Far East
Suimado. *See* Atabei – Central America and Mesoamerica
Sukanthi – Indian Subcontinent
Sukanya – Indian Subcontinent
Sukarapreyasi – Indian Subcontinent
Sukhajamma – Indian Subcontinent
Suki – Indian Subcontinent
Sukias, The – Central America and Mesoamerica
Sukkamielli – Eastern Europe
Suklang-malayon – Southeast Asia
Š ukš endal – Eastern Europe
Sukuyan – Central America and Mesoamerica
Sul – Western Europe
Suleviae, The – Western Europe
Sulis. *See* Sul – Western Europe
Sulla. *See* Sul – Western Europe
Sullis. *See* Sul – Western Europe
Sulmanitu – Near East
Sulochana – Indian Subcontinent
Sulukyi. *See* Suyuki – North America
Sumati – Indian Subcontinent
Sumaya – Indian Subcontinent
Sumitra – Indian Subcontinent
Sumu Mung – Indian Subcontinent
Sumul. *See* Samal – Near East
Sun – Northern Europe
Sun and Moon, Goddess of the – Far East
Sun Goddess – North America
Sun Goddess – Far East
Sun Goddess, Formosan – Far East
Sun Sister – North America
Sun Virgin – Eastern Europe
Sun Woman – North America
Sun Woman – Oceania
Sundari – Indian Subcontinent
Sundi-mumi. *See* Sundy-mumy – Eastern Europe
Sundy-mumy – Eastern Europe
Sung Tzi Liang Liang. *See* Songzi Niangniang – Far East
Sung Tzü. *See* Songzi – Far East
Sung Tzü Kuan-yin. *See* Songzi Guanyin – Far East
Sung-tsi Niang-niang. *See* Songzi Niangniang – Far East
Sung-tzu Niang Niang. *See* Songzi Niangniang – Far East

Sunkalamma – Indian Subcontinent
Sunna – Northern Europe
Sunnu. *See* Sunna – Northern Europe
Sunrta – Indian Subcontinent
Sun-tzu Niang Niang. *See* Songzi Niangniang – Far East
Suonetar – Eastern Europe
Suoyatar – Eastern Europe
Superguksoak – North America
Sura – Indian Subcontinent
Surabhi. *See* Kamadhenu – Indian Subcontinent
Surabhidatta – Indian Subcontinent
Suradevi. *See* Sura – Indian Subcontinent
Š urali – Eastern Europe
Surapamsula – Indian Subcontinent
Surasa – Indian Subcontinent
Suraswati. *See* Bharadi – Indian Subcontinent
Suratamangari – Indian Subcontinent
Suris, The – Indian Subcontinent
Sur-mumy – Eastern Europe
Surupa – Indian Subcontinent
Surya – Indian Subcontinent
Surya-Bai. *See* Surya – Indian Subcontinent
Suryasya Duhita – Indian Subcontinent
Susana – Indian Subcontinent
Suseri-bime-no-mikoto – Far East
Suserihime – Far East
Sushakti – Indian Subcontinent
Sushumna – Indian Subcontinent
Susime – Indian Subcontinent
Sussistinnake. *See* Sussistinnako – North America
Sussistinnako – North America
Susumna. *See* Sushumna – Indian Subcontinent
Sutal – North America
Sutrooka – Indian Subcontinent
Suttibhavani – Indian Subcontinent
Sutudri – Indian Subcontinent
Su-u-ki. *See* Suyuki – North America
Suvan – Egypt
Suvarnamacha – Southeast Asia
Suyuki – North America
Svadha – Indian Subcontinent
Svafa – Northern Europe
Svaha – Indian Subcontinent
Svahariti – Indian Subcontinent
Svanhild. *See* Swanhild – Northern Europe
Svarnarekha – Indian Subcontinent
Svava – Northern Europe
Svayamvaraprabha – Indian Subcontinent
Svipul – Northern Europe
Swadha – Indian Subcontinent
Swaha. *See* Svaha and Suaha – Indian Subcontinent
Swan Maidens, The – Northern Europe
Swanhild – Northern Europe
Swanwhite – Northern Europe
Sweigs-dunka – Eastern Europe
Sxapetl – North America
Sximana – North America
Syama – Indian Subcontinent
Syamatara. *See* Tara – Indian Subcontinent

Sycamore Tree Goddess – Egypt
Sye-elth – North America
Syllis – Greek and Roman Empires
Symbetylos. *See* Ashima Baetyl – Near East
Syn – Northern Europe
Synallaxis, The. *See* The Ionides – Greek and Roman Empires
Synnytar. *See* Luonnotar – Eastern Europe
Syr – Northern Europe
Syrin – Greek and Roman Empires
Syt-kul-amine – Eastern Europe
Syzygia – Greek and Roman Empires
Szelanya – Eastern Europe
Szepasszonyok, The – Eastern Europe
Ta Hsien Fu Jên. *See* Daxian Furen – Far East
Ta La – Southeast Asia
Ta Tha-bthin, The – North America
Ta vahine te ra. *See* Na'vahine – Oceania
Taauth – Near East
Tab'a. *See* Umm S-subyan – Africa
Tabaminarro – Central America and Mesoamerica
Tabhi-yiri – Africa
Tabindain Thakinma – Southeast Asia
Tabiti – Eastern Europe
Tabiti – Western Europe
Tabliope – Greek and Roman Empires
Tabui kor – Oceania
Tachi. *See* Daji – Far East
Tachibana. *See* Oto-tachibana-hime-no-mikoto – Far East
Tacita – Greek and Roman Empires
Tacobud. *See* Tacoma – North America
Tacoma – North America
Tadaka – Indian Subcontinent
Tadatagei – Indian Subcontinent
Ta-dehnet. *See* Merseger – Egypt
Taemā – Oceania
Tafakula – Oceania
Tafne – Egypt
Tafner – Egypt
Tafnu. *See* Tafne – Egypt
Tafnuit – Egypt
Tagabayan – Southeast Asia
Tagaloa fofoa – Oceania
Tagaloa lahi – Oceania
Tagaloa tati – Oceania
Tagaloa ulu'ulu – Oceania
Tagaloamotumotu – Oceania
Tagamaling – Southeast Asia
Tagisomenaja – Oceania
Tagi-tsu-hime. *See* Takitsu-hime-no-mikoto – Far East
Tagorihime. *See* Takiri-bime-no-mikoto – Far East
Taha taua toto – Oceania
Taha'ura – Oceania
Tahc-I – North America
Tahi ari'i – Oceania
Tahltan Game Mother – North America
Tahu'a – Oceania
Tahunui – Oceania
T'ai Chün Hsien Niang. *See* Taijun Xianniang – Far East
Tai Shan Niangniang. *See* Bixia Yuanjin – Far East

Tai tapu – Oceania
Tai Yuan – Far East
Taiapua – Oceania
Taijun Xianniang – Far East
Taillate. *See* Tailtu – Western Europe
Taillte. *See* Tailtu – Western Europe
Tailtiu. *See* Tailtu – Western Europe
Tailtu – Western Europe
Tai-mai-ya-wurt – North America
Taio – Oceania
Tairbu – Oceania
Taisumalie – Oceania
Tait – Egypt
Taiyin – Far East
Tai-yo T'ai-p'ing-hsiang Yu-hsien Niangniang. *See* Yu Nü – Far East
Taiyuan – Far East
Tākā – Oceania
Taka rita – Oceania
Tāké Vêlika Uimáli – Central America and Mesoamerica
Takahime-no-mikoto – Far East
Takanakapsaluk – North America
Takanaluk arnaluk – North America
Takanna' Luk. *See* Sedna and Uiniyumayuituq – North America
Takel – Southeast Asia
Takiri-bime-no-mikoto – Far East
Takitsu-hime-no-mikoto – Far East
Takitu-pime-no-mikoto. *See* Takitsu-hime-no-mikoto – Far East
Takkobad. *See* Tacoma – North America
Takobid. *See* Tacoma – North America
Takótsi Nakawé – Central America and Mesoamerica
Taku rua – Oceania
Takurani. *See* Ganga Devi – Indian Subcontinent
Takursh Mana – North America
Tala – Southeast Asia
Talaira. *See* Hilaeira – Greek and Roman Empires
Talaotumsi. *See* Talatumsi – North America
Talatumsi – North America
Talay – Near East
Tallai – Near East
Talliya. *See* Tallai – Near East
Tallte. *See* Tailtu – Western Europe
Táltos – Eastern Europe
Tama-yori-bime-no-mikoto – Far East
Tamaayawut – North America
Tamaiti ngava ringa vari – Oceania
Talyeu Nimu – Indian Subcontinent
Tamambia – North America
Tamamo-no-maye – Far East
Tamara – Africa
Tāmaumau 'ōrero – Oceania
Tamayorihime. *See* Tama-yori-bime-no-mikoto – Far East
Tamayowut – North America
Tambon – Southeast Asia
Tamesis – Western Europe
Tamfana – Northern Europe
Tamfana – Greek and Roman Empires
Tamil Mountain Fairies, The – Indian Subcontinent
Tamparawa – South America
Tamra – Indian Subcontinent

Tamso-Gobia. *See* Tamambia – North America
Tamtu. *See* Tiamat – Near East
Tamun. *See* Amunta – Egypt
Tamuno – Africa
Tana Ekan – Southeast Asia
Tanabata hime. *See* Shokujo – Far East
Tanabata tsume. *See* Shokujo – Far East
Tanais – Near East
Tanais. *See* Anaitis – Greek and Roman Empires
Tanakapsaluk. *See* Sedna – North America
Tanaquil – Greek and Roman Empires
Tane roroa – Oceania
Tanenet. *See* Taninit – Egypt
Tanenit – Egypt
T'ang. *See* Tang – Far East
Tang – Far East
Tangae – Oceania
Tangkam Majan – Southeast Asia
Tango tango – Oceania
Taninit – Egypt
Tanit – Greek and Roman Empires
Tanit Pele Baal. *See* Tanit – Greek and Roman Empires
Tanith. *See* Tanit – Greek and Roman Empires
Tanith – Near East
Tan-ma – The Himalaya
Tanmatra – Indian Subcontinent
Tanmatras. *See* Seven Females – Indian Subcontinent
Tano – Africa
Ta-no-wish – North America
Tanum – Indian Subcontinent
Tao. *See* Dao – Far East
Tao Mu. *See* Dao Mu – Far East
Taonoui – Oceania
Taourt – Egypt
Tapa – Oceania
Tapati – Indian Subcontinent
Taphagan – Southeast Asia
Ta-pien-ts'ai-t'ien-nü. *See* Dabiancai Tiannü – Far East
Tapo – Oceania
Tapuitea – Oceania
Tapuppa – Oceania
Tara – The Himalaya
Tara – Indian Subcontinent
Tara Bai – Indian Subcontinent
Tara Bosatsu. *See* Ro-tara-ni-bi – Far East
Tara Majan – Southeast Asia
Tarai – Indian Subcontinent
Tarai – Southeast Asia
Taraka – Indian Subcontinent
Taranga – Oceania
Taranis – Western Europe
Taranus. *See* Taranis – Western Europe
Ta-repy – Egypt
Tari Pennu – Indian Subcontinent
Tarkhu – Near East
Tarn – Eastern Europe
Taromati – Near East
Tarqeq – North America
Tartary and Cathay Earth Goddess – Eastern Europe
Tartary and Cathay Earth Goddess – Far East

Taru – South America
Tasap Kachin' Mana – North America
Tashitsheringma – The Himalaya
Tashmetrum – Near East
Tashmetu – Near East
Tashmit. *See* Tashmetu – Near East
Tasimis – Near East
Tasmit. *See* Tashmetu – Near East
Ta-tanka-wian-ska – North America
Tatau. *See* Urutonga – Oceania
Tate – North America
Tātē Haútse Kupúri – Central America
    and Mesoamerica
Tātē Ikū Otegañaka – Central America
    and Mesoamerica
Tātē Kyewimóka – Central America
    and Mesoamerica
Tātē Naaliwámi – Central America and
    Mesoamerica
Tātē Rapawiyama – Central America
    and Mesoamerica
Tātē Tulirkita – Central America and
    Mesoamerica
Tatei Hamuxa – Central America and
    Mesoamerica
Tatei Haramara – Central America and
    Mesoamerica
Tatei Kaxiwari – Central America and
    Mesoamerica
Tatei Kukuru 'Uimari – Central
    America and Mesoamerica
Tatei Matinieri, The – Central America
    and Mesoamerica
Tatei Netsika, The – Central America
    and Mesoamerica
Tatei Niwetukame – Central America
    and Mesoamerica
Tatei Utuanaka – Central America and
    Mesoamerica
Tatei Werika – Central America and
    Mesoamerica
Tatei Werika'Uimari. *See* Tatei Werika –
    Central America and Mesoamerica
Tatei Xapawiyelkame – Central
    America and Mesoamerica
Tatei Xuturi Iwiekame – Central
    America and Mesoamerica
Tatei Yurienaka – Central America and
    Mesoamerica
Tateima, The – Central America and
    Mesoamerica
Tathagata mahavai-rokana. *See*
    Dainichi-nyorai – Far East
Tatoosh – North America
Tatqeq – North America
Tatsu-ta-hime – Far East
Tatsuta-hime. *See* Tatsu-ta-hime – Far
    East
Taua – Oceania
Tāua ki te marangai – Oceania
Taue Si – South America
Taueret – Egypt
Taunggyi Shin. *See* Shwe Myet Hna –
    Southeast Asia
Taur – Egypt
Ta-ur. *See* Taur – Egypt
Tauret. *See* Taur – Egypt
Taurian Artemis. *See* Tauropolis and
    Trivia – Greek and Roman Empires

Taurione. *See* Tauropolis – Greek and
    Roman Empires
Taurit. *See* Taueret – Egypt
Tauro – Greek and Roman Empires
Tauropolis – Greek and Roman Empires
Tauropolos. *See* Tauropolis – Greek and
    Roman Empires
Tauropos. *See* Tauropolis – Greek and
    Roman Empires
Ta-urt – Egypt
Tauthe. *See* Tiamat – Near East
Tauvai. *See* Jyestha – Indian
    Subcontinent
Tauwhare kiokio – Oceania
Tava-ajk – Eastern Europe
Tavake – Oceania
Tavisi. *See* Jayanti – Indian Subcontinent
Tawannannas – Near East
Taxankpada Agodales – Far East
Taygete – Greek and Roman Empires
Tayt – Egypt
Taytet. *See* Tayt – Egypt
Tazhak – Near East
Tcakwaina Mana – North America
Tcakwena Okya – North America
Tcalyel – North America
Tcaridyi – Eastern Europe
Tca•txe•l. *See* Tcalyel – North America
Tcaxalxe•l. *See* Tcalyel – North America
Tcheser-shetat – Egypt
Tchesert – Egypt
T-cho. *See* Tcho – North America
Tcho – North America
Tciakwenaoka – North America
Tcikee Cac Nadleehe – North America
Tcua-wugti – North America
Tcuperekata – North America
Te anoa – Oceania
Te anu mātao – Oceania
Te ata tuhi – Oceania
Te ipo atu – Oceania
Te kāhu rere moa. *See* Kāhu rere moa –
    Oceania
Te ku whaka hara – Oceania
Te kui u'uku – Oceania
Te mehara – Oceania
Te mo'o nieve – Oceania
Te muri – Oceania
Te papa – Oceania
Te ra'i tû roroa – Oceania
Te vahine nui tahu ra'i – Oceania
Tea – Western Europe
Tebunah – Near East
Techne – Greek and Roman Empires
Teeree – Indian Subcontinent
Tefenet. *See* Tefnut – Egypt
Tefent – Egypt
Tefnoot. *See* Tefnut – Egypt
Tefnuit. *See* Tefnut – Egypt
Tefnut – Egypt
Tega – Africa
Tehahine'angiki – Oceania
Tehainga'atua – Oceania
Tehenut. *See* Neith – Egypt
Tehom – Near East
Tehoma. *See* Tacoma – North America
Tei Tituaabine – Oceania
Teikirzi – Indian Subcontinent
Teisiphone. *See* Tisiphone – Greek and
    Roman Empires

Tekaharesapusaremkakaremet – Egypt
Tekarpada – Far East
Tekh-heb. *See* Tekhi – Egypt
Tekhi – Egypt
Telchinia – Greek and Roman Empires
Telecleia – Greek and Roman Empires
Teledice – Greek and Roman Empires
Teleglen-edzen – Far East
Teleglen-edzen – Eastern Europe
Teleglen-Edzen. *See* Altan-telgey – The
    Himalaya
Teleia – Greek and Roman Empires
Telephassa – Greek and Roman
    Empires
Teles – Greek and Roman Empires
Telesto – Greek and Roman Empires
Telete – Greek and Roman Empires
Teleze-awa – Eastern Europe
Telita – Near East
Tellus – Greek and Roman Empires
Tellus Mater. *See* Tellus – Greek and
    Roman Empires
Telphusa – Greek and Roman Empires
Telphusia – Greek and Roman Empires
Temazcalteci – Central America and
    Mesoamerica
Temioua – South America
Tempestates – Greek and Roman
    Empires
Temtith – Egypt
Temu – Egypt
Te-na-zuchi-no-kami – Far East
Ten'gono – Africa
Tenemet – Egypt
Tenemit. *See* Tenemet – Egypt
Tenenit. *See* Tenemet – Egypt
Tenga – Africa
Tenga – Eastern Europe
Tenith – Egypt
Tennin, The – Far East
Tensho. *See* Ama-terasu-ō-mi-kami –
    Far East
Ten-sho-dai-jin. *See*
    Ama-terasu-ō-mi-kami – Far East
Tent-baiu – Egypt
Tentenit-uhert-khakabu – Egypt
Tenth Aunt – Far East
Tentyris – Egypt
Tenye Te'en – Africa
Tephi – Western Europe
Tepkanuset – North America
Tepotatango – Oceania
Terah. *See* Jerah – Near East
Tere hē – Oceania
Tere'e fa'aari'i mai'i te Ra'i – Oceania
Teresa, Santa – Central America and
    Mesoamerica
Teresita, Saint. *See* Oya, Africa – South
    America
Tereteth – Oceania
Tergemina – Greek and Roman Empires
Terpsichore – Greek and Roman
    Empires
Terra. *See* Tellus – Greek and Roman
    Empires
Terra Mater. *See* Tellus – Greek and
    Roman Empires
Tertiana – Western Europe
Tesana – Greek and Roman Empires
Tesert – Egypt

Tesert-ant – Egypt
Tesikubai – Oceania
Teteoinnan – Central America and
  Mesoamerica
Teteoninnan. See Teteoinnan – Central
  America and Mesoamerica
Tetevinan – Central America and
  Mesoamerica
Tētewan – Central America and
  Mesoamerica
Tethys – Greek and Roman Empires
Teu Kweh – Southeast Asia
Te'ura taui e pâ – Oceania
Te'uri – Oceania
Teu'uhi – Oceania
Tewa Corn Mother – North America
Teze – Southeast Asia
Tha – Oceania
Thab-lha-g•ui-mo – The Himalaya
Thab-lha-g•yu-mo – The Himalaya
Thabet, The – Southeast Asia
Thadha Pennu – Indian Subcontinent
Thakurani Bakorani – Indian
  Subcontinent
Thakurani Mai – Indian Subcontinent
Thakurani Mata. See Thakurani
  Bakorani and Burhi Mata – Indian
  Subcontinent
Thalaeia. See Thaleia – Greek and
  Roman Empires
Thalana – Greek and Roman Empires
Thalassa – Near East
Thalassa – Greek and Roman Empires
Thalassa Erythra. See Thalassa – Greek
  and Roman Empires
Thaleia – Greek and Roman Empires
Thalia. See Thaleia – Greek and Roman
  Empires
Thallo – Greek and Roman Empires
Thalna – Greek and Roman Empires
Tham. See Tiamat – Near East
Thammuatz. See Tiamat – Near East
Thamte. See Tiamat – Near East
Thamuatz – Africa
Thana – Greek and Roman Empires
Thanr – Greek and Roman Empires
Tharatha. See Atargatis – Near East
Thatmanitu – Near East
Thaukt. See Thok – Northern Europe
Thavatth. See Tiamat – Near East
Thceser-shetat – Egypt
Thea. See Theia – Greek and Roman
  Empires
Thebe – Greek and Roman Empires
Thebean Goddess – Egypt
Thei. See Theia – Greek and Roman
  Empires
Theia – Greek and Roman Empires
Theisoa – Greek and Roman Empires
Thelchtereia – Greek and Roman
  Empires
Thelpusa. See Telphusa – Greek and
  Roman Empires
Thelxiepeia – Greek and Roman
  Empires
Thelxinoe – Greek and Roman Empires
Thelxinoea – Greek and Roman Empires
Themath – Egypt
Themis – Greek and Roman Empires
Themisto – Greek and Roman Empires

Thenenet – Egypt
Theotokos – Greek and Roman Empires
Thepla – Near East
Theresa, Saint. See Teresa, Santa –
  Central America and Mesoamerica
Theria – Greek and Roman Empires
Therma – Greek and Roman Empires
Thermaia – Greek and Roman Empires
Thermia – Greek and Roman Empires
Thermuthis – Greek and Roman
  Empires
Thermuthis. See Renenet – Egypt
Thesan – Greek and Roman Empires
Thesmia. See Thesmophoros – Greek
  and Roman Empires
Thesmophoros – Greek and Roman
  Empires
Thesmorphonius – Greek and Roman
  Empires
Thespeia – Greek and Roman Empires
Thetis – Greek and Roman Empires
Thevadas, The – Southeast Asia
Thinggishalsangma – The Himalaya
Thinit. See Tanith – Near East
Thir – Northern Europe
Third Lady – Far East
Thirst Goddess – Indian Subcontinent
Thisalat. See Tiamat – Near East
Thisbe – Near East
Thisbe – Greek and Roman Empires
Thitmanat – Near East
Thitmanet. See Thitmanat – Near East
Thlamanla. See Suyuki – North America
Thlavatth. See Tiamat – Near East
Thlehakto Okya. See Ahmetolela
  Okya – North America
Thlewekwe Okya – North America
Thmei – Egypt
Tho-ag. See Tho-og – The Himalaya
Thoantea. See Tauropolis – Greek and
  Roman Empires
Thoë – Greek and Roman Empires
Thoeris – Egypt
Thog-ag. See Tho-og – The Himalaya
Thog-gi-bu-yug – The Himalaya
Thok – Northern Europe
Thokk. See Thok – Northern Europe
Thompson Earth Mother – North
  America
Thompson Goddesses, The – North
  America
Thon Pan Hla. See Shwe Myet Hna –
  Southeast Asia
Tho-og – The Himalaya
Thora – Northern Europe
Thorgerd Holgabrud. See Thorgerdr
  Holgarbrudr – Northern Europe
Thorgerda – Northern Europe
Thorgerdr Holgarbrudr – Northern
  Europe
Thorgerthr Holgarbruathr. See
  Thorgerdr Holgarbrudr – Northern
  Europe
Thoueris – Egypt
Three Kadlu Sisters, The – North
  America
Thriae – Greek and Roman Empires
Thriai. See Thriae – Greek and Roman
  Empires

Throne Goddesses, The. See the Cow
  Goddesses – Near East
Thrud – Northern Europe
Thrudur – Northern Europe
Thummim – Near East
Thurgai. See Minachiamman – Indian
  Subcontinent
Thusandi – Southeast Asia
Thya – Greek and Roman Empires
Thyades. See The Thyiades – Greek and
  Roman Empires
Thyene – Greek and Roman Empires
Thyia – Greek and Roman Empires
Thyiades, The – Greek and Roman
  Empires
Thymbris – Near East
Thyone. See Semele – Greek and Roman
  Empires
Ti Mu. See Di Mu – Far East
Tia Shan Niang-niang. See Bixia
  Yuanjin – Far East
Tiamat – Near East
Tian Fei – Far East
Tian Hou – Far East
Tian Hou niangniang. See Tian Hou –
  Far East
Tian Mu. See Dou Mou – Far East
Tian Mu Niangniang – Far East
Tian Nü, The – Far East
Tiangong Dimu – Far East
Tianxian Songzi. See Bixia Yuanjin – Far
  East
Tiawath. See Tiamat – Near East
Tibetan Sarasvati – The Himalaya
Tibirra. See Tabiti – Western Europe
Tiburtis – Greek and Roman Empires
'Ti Kita – Central America and
  Mesoamerica
Tie – Egypt
T'ien Fei. See Tian Fei – Far East
Tien Hou. See Tian Hou – Far East
T'ien Hou. See Jun Ti and Tian Hou –
  Far East
T'ien Kung Ti Mu. See Tiangong
  Dimu – Far East
T'ien Mu. See Dou Mou – Far East
Tien Mu Niang Niang. See Tian Mu
  Niangniang – Far East
Tien Nu. See The Tian Nü – Far East
T'ien-hsien Sung-tzu. See Bixia
  Yuanjin – Far East
Tif'eret. See Binah – Near East
Tif'eret. See Tiphereth – Western Europe
Tigranuhi – Near East
Tigranuki. See Tigranuhi – Near East
Tiguianes – Southeast Asia
Tihamtu – Near East
Tih-kuyi-wuhti – North America
Tiki – Oceania
Tiki kapakapa – Oceania
Tikuoi Wuhti – North America
Tilafaigā – Oceania
Tilafainga – Oceania
Tilan Xian. See Bixia Yuanjin – Far East
Til-bu-ma – The Himalaya
Tillil – Near East
Tillili – Near East
Tilottama – Indian Subcontinent
Tima te kore – Oceania
Timandra – Greek and Roman Empires

Timu ateatea – Oceania
Tingoi, The – Africa
Tinguian. *See* Aponibolinayen – Southeast Asia
Tinnit. *See* Tanit – Greek and Roman Empires
Tinnit. *See* Tanith – Near East
Tintai – Africa
Tinten. *See* Tintai – Africa
Tipanu – Greek and Roman Empires
Tiphanati – Greek and Roman Empires
Tiphereth – Western Europe
Tipiskawipisim – North America
Tipoplo – Greek and Roman Empires
Tippakalleum. *See* Mailkun – Oceania
Tisalat. *See* Tiamat – Near East
Tisiphone – Greek and Roman Empires
Tiskhu. *See* Ishtar – Near East
Tisna Wati – Southeast Asia
Tisseyak – North America
Titae Aretia. *See* Aretia – Near East
Titaea – Greek and Roman Empires
Titaea Magna. *See* Aretia – Near East
Titaia. *See* Titaea – Greek and Roman Empires
Titan Rhea. *See* Rhea – Greek and Roman Empires
Titan Theia. *See* Theia – Greek and Roman Empires
Titania – Greek and Roman Empires
Titanides, The – Near East
Titanides, The – Greek and Roman Empires
Titanids, The. *See* The Titanides – Greek and Roman Empires
Titanis – Greek and Roman Empires
Tithorea – Greek and Roman Empires
Titi – Oceania
Tito. *See* Eos – Greek and Roman Empires
Titua'abine – Oceania
Tiun – Southeast Asia
Tiv – Egypt
Tiwakpomatamsi. *See* Tüwapongtümsi – North America
Tji-wara – Africa
Tkukwunag Kachin-mana. *See* Tukwinong Mana – North America
Tlachgo. *See* Ére – Western Europe
Tlacht. *See* Ére – Western Europe
Tlachtga – Western Europe
Tlacolteutl – Central America and Mesoamerica
Tlakwakila – North America
Tlaltecuhtli – Central America and Mesoamerica
Tlaqwagi'layugwa – North America
Tlatlauhquicenteotl. *See* Centeotl – Central America and Mesoamerica
Tlazolteotl – Central America and Mesoamerica
Tlitcaplitana – North America
Tlkelikera – North America
Tmei – Egypt
Tñe-ceivune – Eastern Europe
Tó asdza•n – North America
Toa hakanorenore – Oceania
Toa miru – Oceania
Toafa – Oceania
Tobukulu – Oceania

Tobunaygu – Oceania
Toci – Central America and Mesoamerica
Todlibon – Southeast Asia
Toeris. *See* Taueret – Egypt
Togo Musun – Eastern Europe
Tohar-tsiereur – Africa
Toho-tsu-machi-ne-no-kami – Far East
Toi mata – Oceania
Toikunrari-mat – Far East
Toi-kura-puni-mat – Far East
Toiron Numjan – Southeast Asia
Tokpodun – Africa
Tola. *See* Tula – Indian Subcontinent
Tol-ava – Eastern Europe
T'o-lo – Far East
Tolus Ka Talegit – Southeast Asia
Toma – The Himalaya
Tomaiyowit. *See* Tamayowut – North America
Tomam – Eastern Europe
Tomituka – Oceania
Tonacacíhuatl – Central America and Mesoamerica
Tonagma – The Himalaya
Tonalcacihuatl – Central America and Mesoamerica
Tonan. *See* Tonantzin – Central America and Mesoamerica
Tonantsi. *See* Tonantzin – Central America and Mesoamerica
Tonantzin. *See also* Virgin of Guadalupe – Central America and Mesoamerica
Tonga maulu'au – Oceania
Tongo tongo – Oceania
Tonu tai – Oceania
Toodlanak – North America
Tootega – North America
Toothed Vagina – North America
Tootooch – North America
Topa Huaco. *See* Huaco – South America
Topétine – South America
Topogh – Africa
Topukulu – Oceania
Tori-mimi-no-kami – Far East
Torom Anki – Eastern Europe
Torone – Greek and Roman Empires
Tortoise Goddess – Far East
Toru-guenket – South America
Toses – Egypt
Totala – Indian Subcontinent
Totole – Africa
T'otowaxsemalaga – North America
Totsu-machine-no-kami. *See* Toho-tsu-machi-ne-no-kami – Far East
Tou Mou. *See* Dou Mou and Jun Ti – Far East
Touiafutuna – Oceania
Tou-shen Niang-niang. *See* Doushen Niangniang – Far East
Toxwid – North America
Toyonkenime-no-kami. *See* Uke-mochi-no-kami – Far East
Toyotama. *See* Toyo-tama-bime-no-mikoto – Far East
Toyo-tama-bime-no-mikoto – Far East

Toyo-uke-bime-no-kami – Far East
Toyouke-Daijin – Far East
Toyoukehime-no-Kami – Far East
Toyu-uke-no-kami. *See* Toyo-uke-bime-no-kami – Far East
Tragasia – Greek and Roman Empires
Travel Goddess – Far East
Tres Mariae – Near East
Tres Matres – Western Europe
Triclaria – Greek and Roman Empires
Triduana – Western Europe
Trigana – Indian Subcontinent
Trigata – Indian Subcontinent
Trijata – Indian Subcontinent
Triple Goddess – Western Europe
Triple Pussa – Far East
Tripura. *See* Gauri and Parvati – Indian Subcontinent
Tripura Bhairavi – Indian Subcontinent
Tripurasundari – Indian Subcontinent
Trisala – Indian Subcontinent
Trito. *See* Tritogeneia – Greek and Roman Empires
Tritogeneia – Greek and Roman Empires
Tritogenis. *See* Tritogeneia – Greek and Roman Empires
Tritone – Greek and Roman Empires
Tritonia – Greek and Roman Empires
Tritonis. *See* Tritogeneia – Greek and Roman Empires
Tritopatores – Greek and Roman Empires
Tritopatreis. *See* Tritopatores – Greek and Roman Empires
Trivia – Greek and Roman Empires
Trsa. *See* Trsna – Indian Subcontinent
Trsna – Indian Subcontinent
Trukwinu Mana – North America
Trung Nhi – Southeast Asia
Trung Trac – Southeast Asia
Tryanon – Western Europe
Ts'an Nü. *See* Da'an Nü and Can Nü – Far East
Tsandhali – The Himalaya
Tsatsaquitelaku – North America
Tsects – North America
Tsek'any'agojo – North America
Tse-ring Chhe-nga – The Himalaya
Tse-Sun. *See* Zesun – Far East
Tsetse – Africa
Tsetse Bumba. *See* Tsetse – Africa
Tseu Souen Nai Nai. *See* Songzi Niangniang and Zesun Nainai – Far East
Tseurima – The Himalaya
Tseurima – Indian Subcontinent
Tsha-ba'i-brtan-ma-chen-mo – The Himalaya
Tshadze-ienne – Eastern Europe
Tshatse-neida – Eastern Europe
Tshikaro – Oceania
Tsho-gyalma – The Himalaya
Tshuma – Eastern Europe
Tsi – Eastern Europe
Ts'i Kuan Niang – Far East
Ts'i Ma Niang Tsai – Far East
Tsikhu. *See* Ishtar – Near East
Tsilah Wedo – Central America and Mesoamerica

Tsi-pas. *See* Tsi. – Eastern Europe
Tsitctinako. *See* Tsitsicinako – North America
Tsitsicinako – North America
Tsi'ty'icots'a – North America
Tsiyayoji – North America
Tso. *See* Tcho – North America
Tsonoqua – North America
Tsont-nofre. *See* Isis – Egypt
Tsore Jowa – North America
Tsua Sen Niang Niang – Far East
Ts'uai-shen Niang Niang – Far East
Tsubura-hime – Far East
Tsuchi-no-mi-oya-no-kami. *See* O-tsuchi-no-kami – Far East
Ts'ui sheng Niang-niang. *See* Ts'uai-shen-niang-niang – Far East
Ts'ui Shêng Shêng-mu. *See* Cuisheng Sheng Mu – Far East
Tsukisakaki hime – Far East
Tsuma-tsu-hime-no-mikoto – Far East
Tsumtlaks – North America
Tsun Kyanske – Indian Subcontinent
Tsunukwa – North America
Tsura-nami-no-kami – Far East
Tu – Oceania
Tu Ai Mehani – Oceania
Tū fe'ufe'u mai i te ra'i – Oceania
Tu i te moana'urifa – Oceania
Tū matua – Oceania
Tū metua – Oceania
Tu neta. *See* Tū papa – Oceania
Tū papa – Oceania
Tū pari – Oceania
Tū poro mai. *See* Tū poro tū – Oceania
Tū poro tū – Oceania
Tū raki – Oceania
Tu Rua – Oceania
T'u Ti Fu Jên. *See* Tudi Furen – Far East
T'u Ti Nai-nai. *See* Tudi Nainai – Far East
Tu wae rore – Oceania
Tuag – Western Europe
Tuanuku. *See* Papa – Oceania
Tuapu'u – Oceania
Tuatt-makel-neb-s – Egypt
Tuchulcha – Greek and Roman Empires
Tudi Furen – Far East
Tudi Nainai – Far East
Tueret. *See* Êpet, Taueret – Egypt
Tueris. *See* Taueret – Egypt
Tuglibong – Southeast Asia
Tugtut Igfianut – North America
Tui – Far East
Tuima – Indian Subcontinent
Tuireann – Western Europe
Tukapua – Oceania
Tuktut Ikviat. *See* Tugtut Igfianut – North America
Tukuhali – Oceania
Tukwinong Mana – North America
Tukwunag Kachin-mana. *See* Tuktut Igfianut – North America
Tula – Indian Subcontinent
Tul-awa – Eastern Europe
Tuli – Oceania
Tulirkita. *See* Tāté Tulirkita – Central America and Mesoamerica
Tulpengusu – Oceania
Tulsi – Indian Subcontinent

Tumu iti – Oceania
Tumu te tangotango – Oceania
Tumuteanaoa – Oceania
Tunder Ilona. *See* Tundr Ilona – Eastern Europe
Tundr Ilona – Eastern Europe
Tung Mu. *See* Dong Mu – Far East
Tungi'one – Oceania
Tunica Sun Goddess – North America
Tuonetar – Eastern Europe
Tuonetar – Northern Europe
Tūparahaki. *See* Kāhu rere moa – Oceania
Tupengusu – Oceania
Tupetupe i fare one – Oceania
Tupu'a, The – Oceania
Turan – Greek and Roman Empires
Tureann. *See* Tuireann – Western Europe
Tūrem Mother – Eastern Europe
Turesh – Far East
Turesh machi – Far East
Turkic Earth Mother – Eastern Europe
Turquoise Woman – North America
Tursa – Greek and Roman Empires
Turtle Woman – North America
Tushan, Lady – Far East
Tushti – Indian Subcontinent
Tušnamati – Near East
Tutela. *See* Vesta – Greek and Roman Empires
Tutelina. *See* Tutilina – Greek and Roman Empires
Tutilina – Greek and Roman Empires
Tutulina. *See* Tutilina – Greek and Roman Empires
Tuulikki – Eastern Europe
Tuurman – Eastern Europe
Tuwabontsusi. *See* Tüwapongtümsi – North America
Tüwapongtümsi – North America
Tvastri. *See* Samgna – Indian Subcontinent
Twana First Woman – North America
Twannannas. *See* Tawannannas – Near East
Twelve Goddesses of Life and Strength – Egypt
Two Women – North America
Twumpuduro. *See* Tano – Africa
Twyll Huan. *See* Blodeuwedd – Western Europe
Tyche – Greek and Roman Empires
Typho – Egypt
Tzapotla Tenan – Central America and Mesoamerica
Tzaputaltena. *See* Tzapotla Tenan – Central America and Mesoamerica
Tzinteotl. *See* Centeotl – Central America and Mesoamerica
Tzitzimime, The – Central America and Mesoamerica
Tzitzimitl – Central America and Mesoamerica
Tzŭ Kou. *See* Zi Gou – Far East
Tzu Sun Niang Niang. *See* Zisun Niangniang – Far East
Tzu-ku Shën. *See* Zigu Shen and Keng San Gu – Far East

Tzultacaj, The – Central America and Mesoamerica
U – Central America and Mesoamerica
U Colel Caan – Central America and Mesoamerica
U Kaukon. *See* Ningsin Majan – Southeast Asia
Ua – Egypt
Ua Zit. *See* Uazit – Egypt
Uadgit. *See* Uadjet – Egypt
Uadjet – Egypt
Uadjit. *See* Uadjet – Egypt
Uahea – Oceania
Uairebhuidhe – Western Europe
Uajyt. *See* Buto – Egypt
Uarahiulú – South America
Uat – Egypt
Uatchet – Egypt
Uatchit. *See* Uatchet – Egypt
Uatch-ura – Egypt
Uathach – Western Europe
Uati – Egypt
Uatit. *See* Bast – Egypt
Uazet. *See* Buto – Egypt
Uazit – Egypt
Uba-gami – Far East
Uban Sanane – Southeast Asia
Ubast. *See* Bast – Egypt
Ubastet – Egypt
Ubu – Oceania
Uchtcelbh – Western Europe
Uchtdealbh – Western Europe
Uda – Near East
Udai. *See* Vatak – Near East
Udelnicy, The. *See* The Narucnici – Eastern Europe
Udens-māte – Eastern Europe
Udjat. *See* Buto, Uadjet – Egypt
Udzume. *See* Ame-no-uzume – Far East
Uêret. *See* Êpet – Egypt
Uert-hekeu. *See* Saosis – Egypt
Uertheku – Egypt
Ufi – Oceania
Ugadama – Far East
Ugly Females of Yomi – Far East
Ugracanda – Indian Subcontinent
Ugratara – Indian Subcontinent
Ugsakka. *See* Uksakka – Eastern Europe
Ugtsho Yamasil – The Himalaya
Uguns-māte – Eastern Europe
Uhalaoa – Oceania
Ui – Oceania
Ui Tango – The Himalaya
Uiniyumayuituq – North America
Uiniyumissuitoq. *See* Uiniyumayuituq – North America
Uivarahugiyaq – North America
Uixtocihuatl. *See* Huixtocihuatl – Central America and Mesoamerica
Ujali – Indian Subcontinent
Ujali Mata – Indian Subcontinent
Uka o hoheru – Oceania
Uka-no-kami. *See* Inari – Far East
Uka-no-mitama-no-kami. *See* Ugadama – Far East
Uka-no-mitama. *See* O-ge-tsu-hime-no-kami – Far East
Ukat – North America
Uke-mochi-no-kami – Far East
Uke-no-kami. *See* Inari – Far East

Ukepenopfu – Indian Subcontinent
Ukhat – Near East
Uks-akka – Northern Europe
Uksakka – Eastern Europe
Ukwa'anija – Oceania
Ulala – North America
Uldda – Eastern Europe
Ulfrun – Northern Europe
Ulgen Ekhe – Eastern Europe
Uli – Oceania
Uli po'ai o ka moku – Oceania
Ullughmiut, The – North America
Ulsiga. See Ishtar – Near East
Ululiarnaq – North America
Ululiernang. See Ululiarnaq – North
    America
Ulupi – Indian Subcontinent
Um – Far East
Uma – Indian Subcontinent
Uma Kanya. See Kanyā – Indian
    Subcontinent
Umai – Far East
Umai – Near East
Umai – Eastern Europe
Umariya Mata – Indian Subcontinent
Uminai-gami – Far East
Umm. See Am – Near East
Umm s-Subyan – Egypt
Umm S-subyan – Africa
Ummu Khubhar. See Tiamat – Near East
Umugai-hime. See Umugi-hime – Far
    East
Umugi-hime – Far East
Unaviga. See Anavigak – North
    America
Unchi-ahchi – Far East
Unchi-ahchi – Eastern Europe
Undine – Northern Europe
Undutar – Northern Europe
Unelanuki. See Nuñda – North America
Unen-em-hetep – Egypt
Ungamilia – Oceania
Ungap – Southeast Asia
Unhcegila, The – North America
Uni – Greek and Roman Empires
Unigumisuitok. See Uiniyumayuituq –
    North America
Unk – North America
Unkulunkulu – Africa
Unnit – Egypt
Unnut – Egypt
Unt. See Isis – Egypt
Untar. See Undutar – Northern Europe
Untombinde – Africa
Unun-emei – Eastern Europe
Unut. See Unnit – Egypt
Unxia – Greek and Roman Empires
Upanayana – Near East
Uparatat – Near East
Upis – Greek and Roman Empires
Upoho – Oceania
Upore. See Uwan – South America
Upu Tapene – Southeast Asia
Upu Ume – Southeast Asia
Upunusa – Southeast Asia
Ura – Western Europe
Uradamma – Indian Subcontinent
Urania – Greek and Roman Empires
Urara-e-ran-mat – Far East
Uras – Near East

Urash – Near East
Uravari – Indian Subcontinent
Urbadgumgum. See Ninsar – Near East
Urd – Northern Europe
Urdhr. See Urd – Northern Europe
Urdr. See Urd – Northern Europe
Urdur. See Urd – Northern Europe
Uresici, The. See The Narucnici –
    Eastern Europe
Uretsete – North America
Urganda – Western Europe
Uri Uri – Oceania
Urinanka. See Tatei Utuanaka – Central
    America and Mesoamerica
!Urisis – Africa
Urisks, The – Western Europe
Urisnici, The. See The Narucnici –
    Eastern Europe
Urja. See Urjani – Indian Subcontinent
Urjani – Indian Subcontinent
Urme, The – Eastern Europe
Ur-mertu-s-teshert-sheni – Egypt
Urmila – Indian Subcontinent
Urmit. See Tashmetu – Near East
Urmitu. See Tashmetu – Near East
Urmya – Indian Subcontinent
Urnia – Western Europe
Urpihuachac – South America
Ursel. See Ursula – Eastern Europe
Ursel. See Ursula – Northern Europe
Ursitory, The. See The Urme – Eastern
    Europe
Ursula – Northern Europe
Ursule – Central America and
    Mesoamerica
Urth. See Urd – Northern Europe
Urt-hekau – Egypt
Urt-hikeu – Egypt
Urt-sekhemu – Egypt
Urtz – Western Europe
Uru. See Apna – Southeast Asia
Uruasi. See Urvasi – Indian
    Subcontinent
Uruki. See Urvasi – Indian Subcontinent
Urunganada – Oceania
Ururupuin – Oceania
Urutahi – Oceania
Urutonga – Oceania
Urvashi. See Urvasi – Indian
    Subcontinent
Urvasi – Indian Subcontinent
Usas – Indian Subcontinent
Usert – Egypt
Ushas. See Usas – Indian Subcontinent
Ushharay – Near East
Ushmet-hatu-kheftiu-rā – Egypt
Ushnishavijaya – The Himalaya
Ushnishavijaya – Indian Subcontinent
Ushodevatas – Indian Subcontinent
Usi Afu – Southeast Asia
Usiququmadevu – Africa
Usit – Egypt
Usnisavijaya – Indian Subcontinent
Ut – Eastern Europe
Utctsityi – North America
Ute First Woman – North America
Uthht – Near East
Uti – Africa
Uti Hiata – North America
Utlunta – North America

Uto – Egypt
Utset – North America
Uttararani – Indian Subcontinent
Uttu – Near East
Utuanaka. See Tatei Utuanaka – Central
    America and Mesoamerica
U'uhoa – Oceania
Uwan – South America
'Uwardaw – Africa
Uzare. See Uwan – South America
Uzoit. See Buto, Uadjet, Uazit – Egypt
Uzume. See Ame-no-uzume – Far East
Vac – Indian Subcontinent
Vach. See Vac – Indian Subcontinent
Vacha. See Vac – Indian Subcontinent
Vacuna – Greek and Roman Empires
Vadaba – Indian Subcontinent
Vadava. See Vadaba – Indian
    Subcontinent
Vadra-Kali – Indian Subcontinent
Vagisvara. See Sarasvati – Indian
    Subcontinent
Vagitanus – Greek and Roman Empires
Vagneg-imi – Eastern Europe
Vahine mau i te pae fenua – Oceania
Vahine mau ni'a – Oceania
Vahine nautahu – Oceania
Vahine nui tahu ra'i – Oceania
Vahine te ra. See Na'vahine – Oceania
Vaidarbhiganani – Indian Subcontinent
Vais. See Vasa – Eastern Europe
Vaisnavi – Indian Subcontinent
Vajar Mata – Indian Subcontinent
Vajra Dakinis – The Himalaya
Vajra Krotishaurima – The Himalaya
Vajradakini – Indian Subcontinent
Vajra-Shringkhala. See Cha-dog-ma –
    The Himalaya
Vajra-Vārāhī – The Himalaya
Vajravarahi – Indian Subcontinent
Vajravaraki – The Himalaya
Vajrayâna Devatas – The Himalaya
Vajrayogini – Indian Subcontinent
Vajrayogini. See Dorje Naljorma and
    rDo-rje-rnal-hbyor-ma – The
    Himalaya
Vakai a heva – Oceania
Vakarine – Eastern Europe
Vakš-oza – Eastern Europe
Va-kul – Eastern Europe
Vala. See Volva – Northern Europe
Valelahī – Oceania
Valencian Mother Goddess – Western
    Europe
Valetudo – Greek and Roman Empires
Valkyries, The – Northern Europe
Valli – Indian Subcontinent
Vama – Indian Subcontinent
Vammatar – Eastern Europe
Vana – Indian Subcontinent
Vana Mothers, The – Northern Europe
Vana'ana'a – Oceania
Vanadevatas – Indian Subcontinent
Vanadis. See Freyja – Northern Europe
Vanainti. See Tashmetu and Uparatat –
    Near East
Vanaspati Mai – Indian Subcontinent
Vandya – Indian Subcontinent
Vanth – Greek and Roman Empires

Vanths, The – Greek and Roman Empires
Var – Northern Europe
Vara. *See* Var – Northern Europe
Varahi – Indian Subcontinent
Varamit. *See* Tashmetu – Near East
Vari ma te takere – Oceania
Varma-ava – Eastern Europe
Varshayanti – Indian Subcontinent
Varu-dasa-rabbi – Indian Subcontinent
Varunani – Indian Subcontinent
Varuni. *See* Varunani – Indian Subcontinent
Varutri(s) – Indian Subcontinent
Vasa – Eastern Europe
Vasanta – Indian Subcontinent
Vasantadevi. *See* Vasanta – Indian Subcontinent
Vasillissa – Eastern Europe
Vasistha – Indian Subcontinent
Vassanti. *See* Vasanta – Indian Subcontinent
Vasudhara – Indian Subcontinent
Vasudhara. *See* Vasudhara, Indian Subcontinentn Subcontinent – The Himalaya
Vasus, The – Indian Subcontinent
Vatak – Near East
Vatiaz – Far East
Vatsasur – Indian Subcontinent
Vayu. *See* Vasus – Indian Subcontinent
Vechernyaya Zvezda – Eastern Europe
Vedagarbha. *See* Mahalakshmi and Mahasarasvati – Indian Subcontinent
Ved-ava – Eastern Europe
Ved-azer-ava. *See* Ved-ava – Eastern Europe
Ved-azerava. *See* Ved-ava – Eastern Europe
Veden emä – Eastern Europe
Vedenemäntä – Eastern Europe
Vedenneito – Eastern Europe
Ved'ma – Eastern Europe
Ved-mastor-ava – Eastern Europe
Veela. *See* The Vila – Eastern Europe
Veele. *See* The Vila – Eastern Europe
Veeneiu – Eastern Europe
Vegavati – Indian Subcontinent
Vegoia. *See* Begoe – Greek and Roman Empires
Vĕja-mãte – Eastern Europe
Vel'-ava – Eastern Europe
Vele lahi – Oceania
Vele si'i – Oceania
Veleda – Western Europe
Vellamo – Eastern Europe
Velu-mãte – Eastern Europe
Venilia – Greek and Roman Empires
Venus – Greek and Roman Empires
Venus of Quinipily – Western Europe
Vîras – The Himalaya
Verbeia – Western Europe
Vercana – Western Europe
Verdandi – Northern Europe
Verdatchamma – Indian Subcontinent
Vergiliae, The – Greek and Roman Empires
Veritas – Greek and Roman Empires
Veritas. *See* Aletheia – Near East

Verthandi. *See* Verdandi – Northern Europe
Verticordia – Greek and Roman Empires
Veshianka – Eastern Europe
Veshtitze. *See* Vyestitsa – Eastern Europe
Vesna – Eastern Europe
Vesta – Greek and Roman Empires
Vestice, The – Eastern Europe
Vesuna Erinia – Greek and Roman Empires
Vetca-neut – Eastern Europe
Vete-ema. *See* Mere-ama – Eastern Europe
Veyyi Kannula Ammavaru – Indian Subcontinent
Viaratri. *See* Chinnamasta – Indian Subcontinent
Vibudhastris, The – Indian Subcontinent
Victoria – Greek and Roman Empires
Victri – Greek and Roman Empires
Vidhava. *See* Dhumavati and Mahavidyas – Indian Subcontinent
Vidya. *See* Chinnamasta – Indian Subcontinent
Vidyadevis, The – Indian Subcontinent
Vidyadharis, The – Indian Subcontinent
Vidyavadhus, The – Indian Subcontinent
Vidyujjvalakarali – Indian Subcontinent
Vie kena – Oceania
Vie moko – Oceania
Vielona – Eastern Europe
Vierge Caridad, La – Central America and Mesoamerica
Vigayavati – Indian Subcontinent
Vighaparsada. *See* Jyestha – Indian Subcontinent
Vihansa – Northern Europe
Vijagarbha. *See* Sarasvati – Indian Subcontinent
Vijaya. *See* Durga and Vijayasri – Indian Subcontinent
Vijaya Sakti – Indian Subcontinent
Vijayasri – Indian Subcontinent
Vikesi – Indian Subcontinent
Vila, The – Eastern Europe
Vile. *See* Vila – Eastern Europe
Viljaneitsi, The – Eastern Europe
Vimala – Indian Subcontinent
Vinaka – Oceania
Vinasa – The Himalaya
Vinata – Indian Subcontinent
Vinayika. *See* Ganesani – Indian Subcontinent
Vindhya – Indian Subcontinent
Vindhyacalavasini. *See* Vindhyavasini – Indian Subcontinent
Vindhyavasini – Indian Subcontinent
Vindhyesvari. *See* Vindhya – Indian Subcontinent
Vinmara – Oceania
Vipas – Indian Subcontinent
Viraj – Indian Subcontinent
Viranakka – Eastern Europe
Virani. *See* Virini – Indian Subcontinent
Vir-ava – Eastern Europe
Vir-azerava. *See* Vir-ava – Eastern Europe

Virgin Jasper – Far East
Virgin Mary – Near East
Virgin of Guadalupe – Central America and Mesoamerica
Virginalis – Greek and Roman Empires
Virginensis – Greek and Roman Empires
Virginia – Greek and Roman Empires
Virgo – Greek and Roman Empires
Virilis – Greek and Roman Empires
Virini – Indian Subcontinent
Viriplaca – Greek and Roman Empires
Virtus – Greek and Roman Empires
Virudha – Indian Subcontinent
Visadhari. *See* Manasa – Indian Subcontinent
Visahari. *See* Manasa – Indian Subcontinent
Visanti. *See* Vasanta – Indian Subcontinent
Vishnupadi – Indian Subcontinent
Vishpala – Indian Subcontinent
Visuna – Western Europe
Visvadakini – Indian Subcontinent
Vita. *See* Zoe – Near East
Vit'š a-kuva – Eastern Europe
Viviane – Western Europe
Vivien. *See* Viviane – Western Europe
Vivienne. *See* Viviane – Western Europe
Viz-anya – Eastern Europe
Vizi-leany – Eastern Europe
Vjofn – Northern Europe
Vjofr. *See* Vjofn – Northern Europe
Vodianiani. *See* The Navki – Eastern Europe
Vodni Panny, The – Eastern Europe
Vodyanoi, The – Eastern Europe
Vodyanoy. *See* The Vodyanoi – Eastern Europe
Voice of the Abyss. *See* Lady of the Abyss – Near East
Vola. *See* Volva – Northern Europe
Volcano Woman – North America
Voleta – Greek and Roman Empires
Volla. *See* Fulla – Northern Europe
Voltumna – Greek and Roman Empires
Volumna – Greek and Roman Empires
Volupia. *See* Angerona – Greek and Roman Empires
Volupta – Greek and Roman Empires
Voluptas – Greek and Roman Empires
Voluspa – Northern Europe
Volva – Northern Europe
Vor – Northern Europe
Vrikdevatsas, The – Indian Subcontinent
Vrishakapayi – Indian Subcontinent
Vrou-elde. *See* Berchta – Northern Europe
Vu-ava – Eastern Europe
Vuhi atua – Oceania
Vula Ledz. *See* Dua Nggae, Nggae – Southeast Asia
Vumdhati – Indian Subcontinent
Vüt-kuva – Eastern Europe
Vyaghravaktradakini – Indian Subcontinent
Vyaghrini – The Himalaya
Vyestitsa – Eastern Europe
Wachilt – Northern Europe

Wadjet. *See* Uadjet – Egypt
Waelcyrge. *See* The Furies – Greek and Roman Empires
Wagadu – Africa
Waghai Devi – Indian Subcontinent
Waha. *See* Waka – Oceania
Wahīmū. *See* Ahīm ū – Oceania
Wahini hai – Oceania
Wah-kah-nee – North America
Wahkshum – North America
Wai ta iki – Oceania
Waiau – Oceania
Waimariwi – Oceania
Waiuda – Oceania
Wajashk – North America
Waka – Oceania
Wakahirume. *See* Wakahirume-no-mikoto – Far East
Wakahirume-no-mikoto – Far East
Wakarine. *See* Vakarine – Eastern Europe
Waka-sana-me-no-kami – Far East
Waka-uka-hime waka-uke-nome – Far East
Waka-uka-no-me-no-mikoto – Far East
Wakka-ush-kamui. *See* Pet-ru-ush-mat – Far East
Wa-kon-da Hondon – North America
Wakwiyo – North America
Walanni – Near East
Waldmichen – Northern Europe
Walewale o kū. *See* Kini maka – Oceania
Wali manoanoa – Oceania
Walinu'u. *See* Wali manoanoa – Oceania
Walipolima – Oceania
Walo – Oceania
Walrus Mother – Eastern Europe
Wanatjilda – Oceania
Wang. *See* Xi Wangmu – Far East
Wang Pyekkha Yek-khi – Southeast Asia
Wang-Chugmas – The Himalaya
Wangmu Niangniang – Far East
Wanne Thekla – Northern Europe
Wao – Oceania
Waotunoowase – North America
Waoyakila – North America
Wara – Northern Europe
Waramurungundji – Oceania
Waramurungundju. *See* Waramurungundji – Oceania
Wari ma te takere – Oceania
Warunsasadun – Southeast Asia
Wasco – North America
Washer of the Ford. *See* Badb – Western Europe
Watamaraka – Africa
Watch Merti – Egypt
Wauwalak. *See* Wawilak, The – Oceania
Wave Maidens, The – Northern Europe
Wawalag, The. *See* Wawilak, The – Oceania
Wawalug. *See* Wawilak, The – Oceania
Wawilak, The – Oceania
Wayambeh – Oceania
Wazeparkwa – South America
Wazit. *See* Uadjet – Egypt
Weird Sisters – Western Europe
Weiwobo. *See* Xi Wangmu. – Far East
Weiƀen Frauen, Die – Northern Europe

Wejamaat. *See* Vêja-māte – Eastern Europe
Wellamo. *See* Vellamo – Eastern Europe
Wen Cheng – Far East
Wen Ch'iao. *See* Wen Qiao – Far East
Wen Qiao – Far East
Wenchen – Far East
Werethekau – Egypt
Werika. *See* Tatei Werika – Central America and Mesoamerica
Werika 'Uimari. *See* Tatei Werika 'Uimari – Central America and Mesoamerica
Wesna – Eastern Europe
Western Mother – Far East
Wetar – Southeast Asia
Whaht-kay – North America
Whaitiri – Oceania
Wheatchee – North America
Wheke – Oceania
Whetē – Oceania
Whistling Grandmother – North America
White Bear-headed Indra Goddess – The Himalaya
White Buffalo Calf Woman. *See* White Buffalo Woman – North America
White Buffalo Woman – North America
White Eagle-headed Mighty Goddess – The Himalaya
White Kerima – The Himalaya
White Kite-headed Moon Goddess – The Himalaya
White Lady. *See* Berchta – Northern Europe
White Shell Woman. *See* Yolkai Estsan – North America
White Wave – Far East
White Woman – Central America and Mesoamerica
White-light Woman. *See* Kochinako – North America
White-painted Woman – North America
Whobone Shelowa Okya – North America
Whose-name-is-mighty-in-her-works – Egypt
Wiakai – North America
Wibalu, The – Oceania
Widapokwi – North America
Wife of Orisha Oko – Africa
Wikwanekwila – North America
Wilatsukwe Dese Akenona Okya – North America
Wilatsukwe Okya – North America
Wild Pony – North America
Wilden Wip, The – Northern Europe
Willi – Eastern Europe
Wil – North America
Winagu-gami. *See* Uminai-gami – Far East
Wind Old Woman – North America
Winia – Southeast Asia
Win?namakasaama?apitsi? – North America
Wiosna – Eastern Europe
Wirana – Oceania
Wisuriyanza – Near East
Witch Woman – North America
Wode. *See* Gode – Northern Europe

Wohpe – North America
Woman in a Ship – Indian Subcontinent
Woman Who Fell from the Sky – North America
Woman Who Washed Her Face – North America
Woman with Cord – Indian Subcontinent
Woman-light of the Shadows, The – Egypt
Woo Neu. *See* Nok – Far East
Woope. *See* White Buffalo Woman – North America
Word, The – Near East
Wosyet – Egypt
Woyengi – Africa
Wulutahanga – Oceania
Wunschelwybere, The – Northern Europe
Wurdilapu – Oceania
Wuriupranala – Oceania
Wuriupranili. *See* Wuriupranala – Oceania
Wurusemu – Near East
Wüt-awa – Eastern Europe
Wüt-ian uder – Eastern Europe
Wutmara – Oceania
Wyeast. *See* Wasco – North America
Wylgeforte, Saint – Western Europe
Wyrdes, The – Western Europe
Wyvach – Western Europe
Xantho – Greek and Roman Empires
Xapawiyekame. *See* Tatei Xapawiyelkame – Central America and Mesoamerica
Xapawiyelkame. *See* Tatei Xapawiyelkame – Central America and Mesoamerica
Xaratanga – Central America and Mesoamerica
Xatel-ekwa – Eastern Europe
Xavasumkuli – North America
Xayołká•l 'eszą• – North America
Xbaquiyalo – Central America and Mesoamerica
Xcanil – Central America and Mesoamerica
Xcanul – Central America and Mesoamerica
Xenia – Greek and Roman Empires
Xhau. *See* Ix Ahau – Central America and Mesoamerica
Xi Hou – Far East
Xi Shi – Far East
Xi Wangmu – Far East
Xiancan – Far East
Xiang, Lady – Far East
Xie, Lady – Far East
Xieren Xingjun – Far East
Xiling Shi – Far East
Xilonen – Central America and Mesoamerica
Xing Mu – Far East
Xitzam – Central America and Mesoamerica
Xiu Wenyin – Far East
Xiu Zhi – Far East
Xiumu Niangniang – Far East
Xixiquipilihui – Central America and Mesoamerica

Xkan Le O – Central America and
  Mesoamerica
Xkitza – Central America and
  Mesoamerica
Xmucane – Central America and
  Mesoamerica
Xnathaiti – Near East
Xochiquetzal – Central America and
  Mesoamerica
Xochiquetzalli. See Xochiquetzal –
  Central America and Mesoamerica
Xoli-katess – Eastern Europe
Xonaxi Gualapag. See Xonaxi
  Quecuya – Central America and
  Mesoamerica
Xonaxi Peochina Coyo. See Jonaji
  Belachina – Central America and
  Mesoamerica
Xonaxi Quecuya – Central America and
  Mesoamerica
Xonaxihuilia. See Xonaxi Quecuya –
  Central America and Mesoamerica
Xotsadam – Eastern Europe
Xpuch – Central America and
  Mesoamerica
Xquic – Central America and
  Mesoamerica
Xquiq. See Xquic – Central America and
  Mesoamerica
Xtabai. See The Xtabay – Central
  America and Mesoamerica
Xtabay, The – Central America and
  Mesoamerica
Xtah – Central America and
  Mesoamerica
Xtoh – Central America and
  Mesoamerica
Xu Kongcang – Far East
Xu Tianju – Far East
Xuehu Niangniang – Far East
Xuturi Iwiekame. See Tatei Xuturi
  Iwiekame – Central America and
  Mesoamerica
Y Mamau – Western Europe
Ya Hsek Khi – Far East
Ya Monoij – Southeast Asia
Ya Tangoi – Southeast Asia
Yabadjaudjau – Oceania
Yabme-akka – Eastern Europe
Yaca-mama – South America
Yachimata-hime – Far East
Ya-gami-hime – Far East
Yagas, The – Indian Subcontinent
Yaga-vasilisa. See Baba Yaga – Eastern
  Europe
Yagawa-e-hime. See
  Ashi-nadaka-no-kami – Far East
Yah. See Chokmah – Near East
Ya'hal-na'ut – Eastern Europe
Yahsang Kahsi. See Yahsek Khi –
  Southeast Asia
Yahsek Khi – Southeast Asia
Yahveh. See Chokmah – Near East
Yak – Southeast Asia
Yak Chin – Southeast Asia
Yak Lepeh – Southeast Asia
Yak Tanggoi – Southeast Asia
Yakami – Far East
Yakshi, The – Indian Subcontinent

Yakshini. See the Yakshi – Indian
  Subcontinent
Yalode – Africa
Yal-un eke – Far East
Yalungur – Oceania
Yam Woman – Oceania
Yama enda – Oceania
Yama-hime – Far East
Yamai. See Atavish – North America
Yama-no-Shinbo – Far East
Yama-omba – Far East
Yamato-hime – Far East
Yamato-hime-no-mikoto – Far East
Yama-uba. See Yama-omba – Far East
Yambe-akka. See Yabme-akka – Eastern
  Europe
Yametsu-hime – Far East
Yami – The Himalaya
Yami – Indian Subcontinent
Yamni-huchi – Far East
Yamuna. See Yami – Indian
  Subcontinent
Ya-nebya – Eastern Europe
Yang. See Xi Wangmu – Far East
Yang Chen – Far East
Yang Shih – Far East
Yang T'ai Chün. See Yang Taijun – Far
  East
Yang Taijun – Far East
Yanguang Nainai. See Yanjing
  Niangniang – Far East
Yanguang Pusa – Far East
Yanjing Niangniang – Far East
Yanta – Indian Subcontinent
Yao Chi. See Yao Ji – Far East
Yao Ji – Far East
Yaocihuatl – Central America and
  Mesoamerica
Ya?onakka Citta – North America
Yaonan – North America
Yaoshkep-kamui – Far East
Yaošti – Near East
Yaparamma – Indian Subcontinent
Yara – South America
Yara Meng – Southeast Asia
Yasak-no-iri-bime-no-mikoto – Far East
Yasasvati – Indian Subcontinent
Yashoda – Indian Subcontinent
Yashodhara – Indian Subcontinent
Yasodha. See Yashoda – Indian
  Subcontinent
Yatahéntshi – North America
Yatai. See Ya Hsek Khi – Far East
Yatai. See Yahsek Khi – Southeast Asia
Yatudhanis, The – Indian Subcontinent
Yaumau-hadaku – Eastern Europe
Yaumau-haddaku. See
  Yaumau-hadaku – Eastern Europe
Yauni – Indian Subcontinent
Yaye-zakura – Far East
Y'dun. See Idun – Northern Europe
Yebaad. See Ye'ii Baad – North America
Yechidah – Near East
Yechu – Indian Subcontinent
Yeenapah – Oceania
Yegiled-emei – Eastern Europe
Yegowaneh. See Jigonsahseh – North
  America
Ye'ii Baad – North America

Yellow Bat-headed Delight Goddess –
  The Himalaya
Yellow Dog-headed Rakshasi – The
  Himalaya
Yellow Goat-headed Mystic Goddess –
  The Himalaya
Yellow Tseurima – The Himalaya
Yellow Woman – North America
Yellow-going Old Woman – North
  America
Yellowish Bird-headed One – The
  Himalaya
Yellowish-black Tiger-headed
  Rakshasi – The Himalaya
Yellowish-white Tsandhali – The
  Himalaya
Yelukxinang – North America
Yemaja. See Yemanja – Central America
  and Mesoamerica
Yemanja – Central America and
  Mesoamerica
Yemanja. See Yemonja – Africa
Yemaya – Central America and
  Mesoamerica
Yemoja – South America
Yemojá – Africa
Yemonja – Africa
Yemonja. See Yemanja – Central
  America and Mesoamerica
Yen Tsing Niang Niang. See Yanjing
  Niangniang – Far East
Yen-kuang P'u-sa. See Yanguang Pusa –
  Far East
Yept – Egypt
Yept Hemet. See Yept – Egypt
Yerenamma – Indian Subcontinent
Yerra Gadipati Ganga – Indian
  Subcontinent
Yerugami – Central America and
  Mesoamerica
Yeshe-khahdoma – The Himalaya
Ye-she-tsho-gyal – The Himalaya
Ye-shes-mkha'-'gro-ma – The Himalaya
Yeye Kari. See Oshun – Central
  America and Mesoamerica
Ygerna – Western Europe
Yhi – Oceania
Yi Long – Far East
Yid-'prog-ma – The Himalaya
Yimak – Near East
Yimaka. See Yimak – Near East
Yimeh. See Yimak – Near East
Yimeng Niangniang – Far East
Yin – Far East
Yine'a-ne'ut – Eastern Europe
Ying Hsi-niang. See Yingxi Niang – Far
  East
Yingxi Niang – Far East
Yin-meng Niang-niang. See Yimeng
  Niangniang – Far East
Yirbaik baik – Oceania
Yirbaik-baik. See Yirbaik baik – Oceania
Y-lyunda Kotta – Eastern Europe
Ymai. See Umai – Near East
Ymoja – Africa
Ynakhsyt – Eastern Europe
Yngona – Northern Europe
Yngvi – Northern Europe
Yoganidra – Indian Subcontinent
Yogini – The Himalaya

Yoginis, The – Indian Subcontinent
Yohozro Wuhti – North America
Yohualticitl – Central America and
    Mesoamerica
Yolkai Estsan – North America
Yomo-tsu-hisame. *See*
    Yomo-tsu-shiko-me – Far East
Yomo-tsu-ō-kami. *See*
    Izanami-no-kami – Far East
Yomo-tsu-shiko-me – Far East
Yoni – Indian Subcontinent
Yo'o – North America
Yorozu-hatatoya-akitsushi-hime-no-
    mikoto – Far East
Yrou-elde. *See* Berchta – Northern
    Europe
Yseut. *See* Isolt – Western Europe
Ysodha. *See* Yashoda – Indian
    Subcontinent
Yu, Lady – Far East
Yu Kantang – Southeast Asia
Yu Mu Sei – Far East
Yu Neu. *See* Yu Nü – Far East
Yu Nü – Far East
Yu Nü Daxian. *See* Yu Nü and Tai Shan
    Niangniang – Far East
Yu-nu Ta-hsien. *See* Yu Nü Daxian –
    Far East
Yuan, Lady – Far East
Yuang Sori – Southeast Asia
Yuede Xingjun. *See* Yuefu Taiyin – Far
    East
Yuefu Taiyin – Far East
Yueh Fu T'ai Yin. *See* Yuefu Taiyin –
    Far East
Yuguruguru, The – Oceania
Yukanye – Africa
Yuki-onne – Far East
Yulanya – Oceania
Yulunggul. *See* Julunggul – Oceania
Yum – The Himalaya
Yum-chen-mo – The Himalaya
Yuman Mother Earth – North America
Yun Hsiao. *See* Yunxiao – Far East
Yun Hwa Fu-jen. *See* Yunhua Furen –
    Far East
Yung'a Mana – North America
Yunhua Furen – Far East
Yunxiao – Far East
Yunya Mana. *See* Yung'a Mana – North
    America

Yurienaka. *See* Tatei Yurienaka –
    Central America and Mesoamerica
Yurlunggur. *See* Julunggul – Oceania
Yu?uravatsi – North America
Zaden – Western Europe
Zaliyanu – Near East
Zallus – Eastern Europe
Zaltu – Near East
Zam – Near East
Zamama – Near East
Zamin – Near East
Zamyad – Near East
Zana – Greek and Roman Empires
Zanaru. *See* Ishtar – Near East
Zapotlantenan – Central America and
    Mesoamerica
Zara Mama. *See* Mama Zara – South
    America
Zarpandit – Near East
Zarpanitu – Near East
Zarya – Eastern Europe
Zarya Utrennyaya. *See* Zorya
    Utrennyaya – Eastern Europe
Zarya Vechernyaya. *See* Zorya
    Veckernyaya – Eastern Europe
Zas-ster-ma-dmar-mo – The Himalaya
Zat-badar – Africa
Zeme – Eastern Europe
Zemes-māte. *See* Zeme – Eastern Europe
Zemyna – Eastern Europe
Zemynele. *See* Zemyna – Eastern
    Europe
Zendere. *See* Dziva – Africa
Zenenet – Egypt
Zephyritis – Greek and Roman Empires
Zerbanit. *See* Baalti – Near East
Zerpanitu. *See* Zarpandit – Near East
Zerpanitum. *See* Sarpanitu, Zarpandit,
    Zarpanitu – Near East
Zertur – Near East
Zerynthis – Greek and Roman Empires
Zesun – Far East
Zesun Nainai. *See* Songzi Niangniang –
    Far East
Zeuxippe – Greek and Roman Empires
Zeuxo – Greek and Roman Empires
Zhag-pa-ma – The Himalaya
Zhags-pa-ma. *See* Zhag-pa-ma – The
    Himalaya
Zhal-zas-ma – The Himalaya
Zhang Xi – Far East
Zhao Sanniang – Far East

Zhende Pusa – Far East
Zhinnü. *See* Zhinü – Far East
Zhinü – Far East
Zhiva – Eastern Europe
Zhob Mother Goddess, The – Near East
Zhuseng Niang-niang. *See* Bixia
    Yuanjin – Far East
Zi Gou – Far East
Zib. *See* Ishtar – Near East
Zicum – Near East
Ziedkele – Eastern Europe
Ziedu-māte – Eastern Europe
Zigara. *See* Zicum – Near East
Zigarun – Near East
Zigu Shen – Far East
Zikum. *See* Zicum – Near East
Zimarzla – Eastern Europe
Zintuhi – Near East
Zipaltonal – Central America and
    Mesoamerica
Zirbanit. *See* Zarpanitu – Near East
Zirna – Greek and Roman Empires
Zirpanitu. *See* Succoth Benoth – Near
    East
Zirratbanit – Near East
Zisong Nai Nai. *See* Songzi
    Niangniang – Far East
Zisun Niangniang – Far East
Zitna-atka – Eastern Europe
Ziva – Eastern Europe
Ziza – Northern Europe
Zizi. *See* Ziza – Northern Europe
Zizilia – Eastern Europe
Zleja – Eastern Europe
Zlotababa – Eastern Europe
Zodiacal Virgins, The – Egypt
Zoe – Near East
Zorya, The – Eastern Europe
Zorya Utrennyaya – Eastern Europe
Zorya Vechernyaya – Eastern Europe
Zosteria – Greek and Roman Empires
Zumiang Nui – Indian Subcontinent
Zuriel – Near East
Zveyda Dennitsa. *See* Zvezda
    Dennitsa – Eastern Europe
Zvezda Dennitsa – Eastern Europe
Zvoruna – Eastern Europe
Zygia – Greek and Roman Empires
Zylvie. *See* Dziewanna – Eastern Europe
Zytniamatka – Northern Europe
Zywie – Eastern Europe

INDEX OF GODDESSES BY ATTRIBUTE

Agriculture

Africa
Abuk, Acek, Aha Njoku, Ala, Ani, Anyigba, Aprija, Ayaba, Aya-eke, Bride of the Barley, Bunzi, Ceres Africana, Chade, Dinka First Woman, Dogon Sun Goddess, Dziva, Fohsu, Greedy Woman, Ii, Inkosazana, 'Inna, Kaikara, Macouas First Woman, Mawu Sodza, Minona, Morimi, Morningstar of Wakaranga, Mother of Food, Mukasa, Na Dede Oyeadu, Na Yo, Nambi, Nyakarembe, Nzima Mother, Puikani, Tji-wara, Wife of Orisha Oko, Yalode

Central America and Mesoamerica
Centeotl, Chalchiuhcihuatl, Chalchiuhtlicue, Chicomecoatl, Cueravaperi, Iztaccenteol, Loa, Nena, Tāté Ikū Otegañaka, Tāté Rapawiyama, Tatei Netsika, Tatei Utuanaka, Tatei Yurienaka, Tonantzin, Tzultacaj, Xaratanga, Xcanil, Xilonen

Eastern Europe
Azer-ava, Bab'e Kasha, Corn Mother, Curche, Divja Davojke, Dziewanna, Erce, Gabjauja, Idem-huva, Jaja, Kildisin, Lauka-māte, Laukosargas, Maan-emo, Makosh, Marzyana, Maslenitsa, Mastor-ava, Mati-syra-zemlya, Mukylcin, Norov-ava, Paks-av, Pereplut, Piluitus, Pogoda, Poldunica, Polevoi, Pölöznitsa, Poludnitsy, Pszepolnica, Pyatnitsa Prascovia, Queen of the Grain, Rigiu Boba, Seewa,

Sor-ava, Sreča, Vakš-oza, Vila, Viljaneitsi, Zitna-atka

Egypt
Ernutet, Naprit, Nehebka, Nepit, Neprit, Renen, Renenet, Renenti, Renenutet, Rennutet, Sekhet-hetepet, Shenty, Ubastet

Far East
Agriculture Goddess, Aki-bime-no-kami, Baäbai, Di Mu, Earth Cow, Etugen, Izumo Pantheon Deities, Jiang Yuan, Kushi-nada-hime, Ma Gu, Mazha Shen, Meng Jiangnü, Mikura-tana-no-kami, Natsu-taka-tsu-hi-no-kami, Nügua, Ru-be-sei, Shi, Tatsu-ta-hime, Tenth Aunt, Toyoukehime-no-Kami, Tudi Furen, Ugadama, Uke-mochi-no-kami, Waka-sana-me-no-kami, Waka-uka-no-me-no-mikoto, Yachimata-hime, Yu, Yuefu Taiyin

Greek and Roman Empires
Agraulos, Alphito, Athana Lindia, Auxesia, Azesia, Boarmia, Budeia, Carpophori, Ceres, Dais, Damia, Dea Dia, Demeter, Eunostos, Fornax, Hegemone, Herse, Himalia, Himalis, Hostilina, Karpophoros, Lactura, Libera, Meliades, Mellona, Messia, Numina, Ops, Pandrosos, Patella, Pomona, Proserpina, Robigo, Runcina, Rusina, Salus, Secia, Segetia, Seia, Seja, Sito, Spermo, Tamfana, Tutilina

Indian Subcontinent
A Nyit A Jom, Ambika, Anala, Anna Kuari, Annapatni, Annapurna, Asu Mainao, Basumati, Bhandarin, Bhumiya Rani, Bhutamatri, Boorbi Pennu, Challalamma, Chamconda Mata, Chitkuar Devi, Cotton Mother, Dharti Mata, Hariyari Mata, Hinglajin, Ida, Ira, Isani, Karttiki, Kul Gosain, Kulagollamma, Ma Dharti, Machandri, Madira, Maimungma, Mainao, Maisamma, Mamili, Mari Mai, Motho, Mungo, Nakti Devi, Navadurgas, Niseginyu, Raka, Rangda, Rokime, Sakambhari, Sali Minao, Sangvo Nimu, Sarna Burhia, Sita, Sonnolipenu, Talyeu Nimu, Tari Pennu, Thadha Pennu, Varunani

Near East
Armaiti, Ashnan, Asnan, Deo, Dizane, Egitummal, Emmer, Ezinu, Kait, Ninigara, Ninkasi, Ninsaba, Ninshebargunu, Paghat, Siduri, Spantaramet, Sud

North America
Ang-chin Mana, Angwushahai-i, Angwusnasomtaka, Anya Kachin' Mana, Awatovi Soyok Wuhti, Cochiti Mother, Corn Maidens, Corn Mother, Corn Woman, Creek Maize Mother, Deohako, Ee-eh-ch-choo-ri-ch'ahm-nin, Five Sisters, Grandmother, Hano Mana, Has-gueme, H'ativa, Heheya Kachin' Mana, Hokoha Okya, Hokyang Mana, Iemaparu, Ioashkanake, Iyatiku,

Kachin' Mana, Kadhutetash, Kashatskihakatidise, Khunpinu'a'anyun, Khuntasaengge'i'a'anyun, Khuntsaenyu'a'anyun, Khuntsanyu'a'anyun, Khuntseji'a'anyun, Kokumthena, Kokwelashokti Oken'ona, Kwamumu Okya, Mesuk Kummik Okwi, Moing'iima, Moon Woman, Mukikwe Okya, Mungo, Muyingwa Wuhti, Nahalish' Okya, Natchez Maize Mother, Nautsiti, Ohoyo Osh Chishba, Onatah, Onenha, Pachavuin Mana, Pawnee First Woman, Powamu So Aum, Rabbit Mother, Red-spider-woman, Sakwa Mana, Sehu Woman, Selu, Takursh Mana, Talatumsi, Tewa Corn Mother, Uti Hiata, Yellow Woman, Yolkai Estsan

Northern Europe
Ahrenkonigin, Eastre, Gaue, Gudrun, Habondia, Holda, Kornmutter, Old Woman of Germany and Scotland, Roggenmuhme, Sith, Tamfana, Thorgerdr Holgarbrudr, Zytniamatka

Oceania
Atua fafine, Buring une, Cassowary Mother, Fai malie, Fehuluni, Hainuwele, Haumea, Hina puku 'ai, Hine raumati, Jari, Junkgowa, Ka iki lani, Kafisi, Kagauraha, Karakarook, Kunnawarra, Kururuk, Marei kura, Me ha'i kana, Meanderi, Muiu'uleapai, Pani, Pani tinaku, Po lao uli, Runepai, Sherok, Sinekili, Tafakula, Taku rua, Taranga, Tshikaro, Yam Woman

South America
Axomama, Karuebak, Maize Mother, Mama Allpa, Mama Cora, Mama Pacha, Mama Sara, Mama Zara, Nungui, Quinoa Mother, Star Woman

Southeast Asia
Alindodoay, Anat, Arurin, Biku Indu Antu, Bounmagyi, Bugan inBulul, Dagau, Dagdagamiyan, Dewi Cri, Dewi Sri, Girinatha, Hainuwele, Hpi Bi Yaw, Ikapati, Indo I Laoe, Indo I Losi, Indo I Tuladidi, Indoea Padi, Indudun inPundaikuhan, Ineno Pae, Ini Andan, Kakiadan, Lise, Lumaknak inLukbuban, Mae Phosop, Maize Mother, Manang Jaban, Manik Galih, Oltagon, Omonga, Pandan Rumari, Pantan Ini Andan, Pheebee Yau, Po Ino Nogar, Poee Ura, Pungtang Majan, Rice Mother, Roembanggea, Sago Woman, Sangiyan Sari, Saning Sari, Si Dayang, Siberu Dayang Mata Ni Ari, Siladi, Singan, Siti Permani, Sri, Tabindain Thakinma, Tagamaling, Takel, Tangkam Majan, Taphagan, Tisna Wati, Tuglibong, Yuang Sori

Western Europe
Áine, Braciaca, Cailleach Beara, Campestres, Cerridwen, Glas Gaibleann, Habonde, Henwen, Inghean

Bhuidhe, Kernababy, Kicva, Latiaran, Morgay, Nicnevin, Samhain, Stratteli

Arts

Africa
Akpitoko, Ekineba, Marimba

Central America and Mesoamerica
Ahnt Kai'

Eastern Europe
Saule

Egypt
Bast, Seshat

Far East
Benten, Dabiancai Tiannü, Jinhua Niangniang, Karu-no-ō-iratsume, Lan Caihe, Miao Yin Fomu, Naru-kami, Poetry Goddess, Tennin

Greek and Roman Empires
Achelois, Aoede, Aonides, Apollonis, Arche, Ardalides, Asopo, Athena, Borysthenis, Calliope, Celedones, Cephisso, Dactyls, Erato, Euterpe, Heptapora, Hippocrenides, Hypate, Iambe, Ilissiades, Komodia, Maeonides, Melete, Melpomene, Mese, Mneiae, Mneme, Mnemonides, Muses, Myrtis of Anthedon, Neilo, Nete, Parnassides, Pegasides, Phemonoe, Pimpleides, Polymatheia, Polymnia, Rhodia, Syrinx, Techne, Terpsichore, Thaleia, Thelxinoe, Tipoplo, Tritone, Urania

The Himalaya
dByangs-can-ma, gLu-ma Ghirdhima

Indian Subcontinent
Biliku, Charani Devi, Devala, Gandharvis, Gosae-era, Jaher Era, Karaikkal Asmmaiyar, Mantrikashakti, Sarasvati, Satarupa, Vidyadevis, Vidyavadhus

Near East
Kotharat, Rabi'a Al-adawiya

North America
Iqalu Nappaa, Koyemshi

Northern Europe
Elben, Frau Frigg, Gunnlöd, Huldra, Saga

Oceania
Brogla, Ha'i wahine, Hina 'ere'ere manu'a, Hōpoe, Ka'ao melemele, Kapo, Kena, La, Laka, Maile, Maile ha'i wale, Maile kaluhea, Maile lau li'i, Maile pā haka, Moko, Namita, Pa'i alo, Pa'i kua, Rakataura, Rau kata ura, Taemā, Tilafaigā

Southeast Asia
Madun Pungren Majan

Western Europe
Aibell, Birog, Brigid, Canola, Cerridwen, Doon Buidhe, Eadon,

Fachea, Leanan Sidhe, Lebharcham, Moriath

Beauty

Africa
Ezili

Central America and Mesoamerica
Erzulie, Ichpuchtli, Koo-mah'mm hahs-ay' Tahm, Oshun, Tsilah Wedo, Xochiquetzal

Eastern Europe
Bukura-e Dheut, Krasnyi, Laima, Metsänneitsyt, Näkineiu, Näkinneito, Näkki, Nemodilky, Prende, Vasa, Vu-ava

Egypt
Hatshepsut

Far East
Bai Mundan, Hachi-kazuki-hime, Hoto-tatara-isusuki-hime-no-mikoto, Kaguya-hime-no-mikoto, Karu-no-ō-iratsume, Kichi-jō-ten, Pan Jinlian, So-tohoshi-no-iratsume, Wangmu Niangniang

Greek and Roman Empires
Actaea, Aello, Agave, Aglaope, Aglaopheme, Aigle, Alimede, Amphinome, Amphithoe, Amphitrite, Andromeda, Aphrodite, Apseudes, Arethusa, Asia, Auxo, Beroe, Cale, Callianassa, Callianeira, Callipygos, Cassiopeia, Charis, Charites, Choro, Clymene, Cranto, Cydippe, Cymatolege, Deiopea, Dero, Dexamene, Dione, Dorides, Doris, Doto, Drimo, Eudia, Eudora, Eugora, Eumolpe, Eurydice, Evagora, Evarne, Glauce, Glauconome, Glauke, Glaukonome, Gratiae, Halsodyne, Helen, Helice, Hipponoe, Hippothoe, Ianassa, Ianeira, Ione, Iphianassa, Iphthime, Kallianassa, Kallianeira, Kranto, Kymatolege, Laomedeia, Leiagora, Leucosia, Leucothoe, Ligeia, Lilaea, Limnoreia, Lycorias, Lykorias, Lysianassa, Maera, Maira, Melite, Menippe, Molpe, Nausithoe, Neomeris, Nereides, Nereis, Nesaea, Neso, Oreithyia, Panope, Parthenope, Pasithea, Peitho, Pherusa, Phyllodoce, Plexaure, Ploto, Polynoe, Polynome, Pontomedusa, Pronoë, Protho, Proto, Protogenia, Scylla, Sirens, Speio, Thaleia, Thalna, Thelxiepeia, Thoë, Venus, Xantho, Zana

The Himalaya
Hlamos, Khadoma Queen, Rochanî, Sgeg-mo-ma

Indian Subcontinent
Ahalya, Churel, Gavariamma, Hidimba, Jara, Kumbhinasa, Lakshmi, Minachiamman, Mohini, Nirriti, Pisachis, Priyadarsana, Rakshasis, Ramaladevi, Rambha, Sruta-Kriti, Sulochana, Sundari, Tapati, Tilottama,

Trigata, Trijata, Tripurasundari,
Urmila, Urvasi, Vandya

Near East
Leilah, Mylitta, Odatis

North America
Anog Ite, Hulluk Miyumko, Ite,
Katuma, Loha, Sedna, Thompson
Goddesses, Wohpe

Northern Europe
Gerda, Hallgerda, Metsänneitsyt, Sif,
Swanhild, Valkyries, Wunschelwybere

Oceania
'Āpua kea, Dogai, Hine moa, Kā'ana'e
like, Kapo, Pele, Rohe

Southeast Asia
Aponibolinayen, Dewi Sri, Female
Spectres, Phraw Majan, Winia

Western Europe
Aibell, Bebhionn, Cliodhna, Creirwy,
Cuimne, Deirdre, Emer, Fand, Gwrach
y Rhibyn, Lí Ban, Sgeimh Solais,
Sovranty, Uchtcelbh

Birds

Africa
Kono

Central America and Mesoamerica
Goddess "O", Itzpapalotl, Ix Chel,
Marinette, Quilaztli, Tāké Vêlika
Uimáli, Tatei Kukuru 'Uimari, Tatei
Werika, White Woman

Eastern Europe
Alkonost, Barbmo-akka, Bereginy,
Firebird, Gabija, Laima, Linda,
Loddiš-edne, Luonnotar, Mary-rusalka,
Ptitsy-siriny, Tomam, Tshuma, Tundr
Ilona, Vasillissa, Vēja-māte, Vyestitsa,
Zhiva

Egypt
Kerub of Air, Nekhebet, Nephthys

Far East
Kararat, Kujaku-myō-ō,
Kun-syo-ming-wang, Nakime,
Takahime-no-mikoto, Tennin, Wangmu
Niangniang, Xie, Zhinü

Greek and Roman Empires
Acholoe, Aglaope, Aglaopheme,
Aithuia, Alcyone, Celaeno, Erato,
Harpies, Inyx, Kelaino, Lelaino,
Leucosia, Ligeia, Molpe, Nicothoe,
Parthenope, Podarge, Rumor, Sirens,
Thelxiepeia

The Himalaya
Black Crow-headed One, Black
Cuckoo-headed Mystic Goddess,
Dark-blue Owl-headed One,
Greenish-black Vulture-headed Eater
Goddess, Htamenmas, Red
Crow-headed Thunderbolt Goddess,
Red Hoopoe-headed Desire Goddess,
rMa-bya-c'en-mo, White Eagle-headed

Mighty Goddess, Yellowish
Bird-headed One

Indian Subcontinent
Bhasi, Biliku, Dhrtarastri, Garita,
Gayatri, Kaki, Kraunca, Mahamayuri,
Nirriti, Shuci, Shuki, Shyeni, Surya,
Tamra, Tanum, Thadha Pennu,
Vidyadharis, Vinata

Near East
Ate, Bar-juchne, Broxa, Cherubim,
Semiramis, Simorgh, Siris

North America
Angwushahai-i, Angwusnasomtaka,
Blue Jay, Corn Maidens, Haka Lasi,
Heloha, Hihankara, Hongak,
Ixlexwani, Katuma, Kawas, Keninqas,
Ksem-wa'tsq, L!äzwag•ilayugwa,
Le-tkakawash, Mong' Wuhti, Mother of
All Eagles, Nisqually Bird Goddesses,
Northeastern Swan Maidens, Panes,
Quootis-hooi, Sedna, Skule, Sonxwana,
Tahc-I, Tlaqwagi'layugwa, Tootooch,
Tsiyayoji, Tsore Jowa, Wah-kah-nee,
Win?namakasaama?apitsi?,
Yelukxinang, Yu?uravatsi

Northern Europe
Krähe

Oceania
'Alae a hina, Bima, Dinewan, 'Elepaio,
Faiga'a, Goonaroo, Haere awa'awa,
Ha'i, Jiji, Ka 'iwa ka la meha,
Kāhuitara, Kalaia, Kamaunu, Ke ao
lewa, Kena, Kipara, Kunnawarra, Kura
ngaituka, Kurikuta, La'e, Lea, Lepe a
moa, Lunba, Lupe pangopango,
Makara, Milapukala, Munbakuaku,
Mundikara, Narina, Naruni, Nua,
Nungeena, Parabaruma, Parauri,
Polalowehi, Shaliom, Sky Maiden,
Taisumalie, Tha, Tuli, Tupu'a, Urutahi,
Vinaka, Vinmara, Wanatjilda, Wirana,
Yalungur, Yirbaik baik

South America
Uarahiulú, Urpihuachac

Southeast Asia
Alan, Dara Ensing Tamaga, Imbulu
Man, Klang, Nimli Numjan, Ningsin
Majan

Western Europe
Amboto Lady, Annis, Badb,
Cathubodua, Estiu, Uairebhuidhe

Ceremonies

Africa
Ala, Aprija, Asaase Aberewa, Asase
Afua, Asase Yaa, Bayanni, Bride of the
Barley, Bwalya Chabala, Damwamwit,
Ekineba, Harrakoi Dikko, Imo,
Iya-maase, Iyanla, Kaikara, Katarwiri,
Kono, Lisa, Mawu Sodza, Mbaba
Mwana Waresa, Minona, Morimi,
Mother of Food, Mujaji, Nã Bake,
Nagodya, Nasilele, Ndako Gboya,

Nikaiva, Nimm, Nomkubulwane,
Nyakala, Nzima Mother, Randa,
Ricana, 'Uwardaw, Yalode

Central America and Mesoamerica
Agaman Nibo, Ahnt Kai', Aida
Wedo, Centeotl, Chalmecacihuatl,
Cueravaperi, Guabonito, Huixtocihuatl,
Itzpapalotl, Jonaji Belachina, Loa,
Marinette, Masaya, Mayahuel, Mu
Olokukurtlisop, Sukuyan, Toci,
Tonantzin, Virgin of Guadalupe, Xcanil

Eastern Europe
Ajysit, Bab'e Kasha, Bereginy,
Cacce-jienne, Cherlak, Colleda, Corn
Mother, Divje Devojke, Dziewanna,
Erce, Gabija, Ilmater, Jabme-akka,
Kildisin, Koliada, Kulshedra,
Kupal'nitsa, Kupalo, Lada, Ljubi,
Marzana, Maslenitsa, Matergabia,
Mati-syra-zemlya, Mielikki, Mokosh,
Moksha, Mokuskha, Nocnitsa, Ot,
P'erna-azor-ava, Pirts-māte, Pogoda,
Pört-kuva, Prende, Pyatnitsa Prascovia,
Queen of the Grain, Rauni, Ravdna,
Rigiu Boba, Rodjenice, Rozanice,
Rusalka, Seewa, Semik, Slatababa,
Smert, Sundy-mumy, Tartary and
Cathay Earth Goddess, Tol-ava,
Vakš-oza, Vila, Vit'ša-kuva, Vüt-kuva,
Yabme-akka, Yaumau-hadaku,
Ynakhsyt, Zhiva, Zlotababa

Egypt
Hap Cow, Hathors, Isis, Seshat, Shenty,
Thoeris, Tie, Uadjet

Far East
Ame-no-uzume, Apemeru-ko-yan-mat
Unameru-ko-yan-mat, Benten,
Chiwash-kor-kamui, Chuh Kamuy,
Corpse Goddesses, Di Mu, Earth Cow,
Ge Gu, Hachi-kazuki-hime, Hettsui-
no-kami, Hi-kawa-hime, Jiutinan
Xuannu, Kamui-fuchi, Kararat,
Konohana-sakuya-hime, Ma Gu,
Midwives, Miko, Pang Che, Pang Jiao,
Pang Zhu, Perasia, Pet-ru-ush-mat,
Saoqing Niang, She Mu, Shokujo,
Takahime-no-mikoto, Tartary and
Cathay Earth Goddess, Western
Mother, Yamato-hime, Yamato-
hime-no-mikoto, Zisun Niangniang

Greek and Roman Empires
Acca Larentia, Admeta, Alcmena,
Amphictyonis, Angerona, Anna
Perenna, Befana, Calligeneia,
Concordia, Cordaca, Cotys, Cybele,
Despoena, Eudaimonia, Flora, Fornax,
Hebe, Hecate, Hellotia, Hosia, Juturna,
Lares, Libera, Libitina, Lupa, Mater
Matuta, Meditrina, Melissae, Naenia,
Nortia, Nundina, Ops, Pandemos, Pax,
Phytia, Saronia, Tauropolis, Telesto,
Tellus, Thesmophoros, Vesta

The Himalaya
Khahdoma, Kiru, Living Goddess,
Ma-gcig-dpal-lha-mo,
Nam-mkha'i-lha-mo-Kun-tu-bzang-mo,

Ogress of Lust, Ro-kha-ma, Sangye-khado, Sa-yi-lha-mo-bstan-ma, Sengdroma, Skyes-bu-ber, Tonagma, Vajra Dakinis, Vîras

Indian Subcontinent
Aksara, Amavasya, Amba, Anna Kuari, Arani, Asapurna, Asuniti, Bahucharaji, Bardaichila, Barhishmati, Bhagavathi, Bharati, Bhavani(s), Bhutamatri, Bisal Mariamna, Buddhadakini, Burhi Mata, Chigrinad, Chinnamasta, Chitkuar Devi, Damayanti, Dharti Mata, Dhumorna, Diwali, Draupadi, Ellamma, Ganapatihrdaya, Gandini, Ganga Devi, Gangaji, Gara Satamai, Gauri, Gayatri, Gopis, Gramadevatas, Hariyari Mata, Havirbhu, Hemambika, Holika, Hotra, Huligavva, Ida, Isani, Jamants, Ka Blei Sam Um, Ka 'Lei Synshar, Kali, Kalika, Kamakhya, Kamaksi, Kanni, Kaveri, Kelu Devaru, Khala Kumari, Kumari, Kumbhamata, Kupli, Lakshmi, Ma Dharti, Mahi, Makara, Mallana Devi, Mamili, Manasa, Mariamma, Matabai, Minaksi, Namamdamma, Narmada, Nikumbhila, Oraon Earth Goddess, Parvati, Prajnaparamita, Raka, Rangda, Ronkini, Rudrani, Sadanvas, Sandili, Sarasvati, Sarna Burhia, Sasana-devi, Sati, Sedhu, Sinivali, Sita, Sitala, Subhadra, Sura, Susime, Svaha, Svahariti, Swadha, Tari Pennu, Teikirzi, Thakurani Bakorani, Totala, Ugracanda, Ujali Mata, Urvasi, Vajravarahi, Vindhyavasini

Near East
Ahurani, Apo, Atargatis, Ba'alat Ashtart, Bau, Beltis, Cotys, Dizane, Krumai, Labartu, Lamasthu, Lilwani, Sarbanda, Siris, Tanith, Wisuriyanza

North America
Ackwin, A-ha Kachin' Mana, Ahe'a, Ahmetolela Okya, Ahöla Mana, Alkuntam, Alo Mana, Ang-chin Mana, Angak'chin' Mana, Angwushahai-i, Angwusnasomtaka, Anoolikwotsaix, Anya Kachin' Mana, Atoshle Suyuki, Awatovi Soyok Wuhti, Badger Old Woman, Baxbakualanuchsiwae, Bear Mother, Bear Woman, Cactus Grandmother, Chakwaina Yu-adta, Corn Maidens, Corn Mother, Glispa, Grandmother of Nava, Grandmother Spider, Hahai-i Wuhti, Hano Mana, Hayicanako, Heheya Kachin' Mana, Hemis Kachin' Mana, Hemushikwe Okya, Hoho Mana, Hokoha Okya, Hokyang Mana, Horo Mana, Iatiku, Kachin' Mana, Kanilkes, Kimilkan, Köcha Kachin' Mana, Kokumthena, Kokwelashokti Oken'ona, Kokwele, Kolahmana, Komanchi Kachin' Mana, Konin Kachin' Mana, Ku Gu, Kutca mana, Kwamumu Okya, Kwavonakwa, L'etsa'aplelana, La'pilewe Okya, Malokatsiki, Mamzrau Mana, Masau'u Kachin' Mana, Maswik'Chin' Mana,

Mesuk Kummik Okwi, Mong' Wuhti, Moon Woman, Mu Bachu Okya, Mu'satewichi Okya, Mucaias Mana, Mukikwe Okya, Muyingwa Wuhti, Muyiñwuh, Na'le, Na?ackjeii Esdzaa, Naasun, Nahalish' Okya, Nanaqasilakwe, Nataska Mana, Nisqually Bird Goddesses, Nuptadi, Nutse'xenem, Nuvak'chin' Mana, Omau-u Wuhti, Onenha, Pachavuin Mana, Pakhik' Mana, Pakok' Okya, Pasikiapa Dese Akenona Okya, Pasom Mana, Peyote Woman, Piptu' Wuhti, Po'haha, Poli Kachina Mana, Powamu So Aum, Qominoqa, Quail Kachin' Mana, Rahakatittu, Sakwa Mana, Sakwats Mana, Sehu Woman, Shalako Mana, Sio Mana, Sio Shalako Mana, Sneneikulala, So Wuhti, Somagalags, Soyoko, Talatumsi, Tasap Kachin' Mana, Tcakwena Okya, Thlewekwe Okya, Tlakwakila, Toxwid, Trukwinu Mana, Tsonoqua, Tsunukwa, Tugtut Igfianut, Tukwinong Mana, Tüwapongtümsi, Ulala, Wah-kah-nee, Wakwiyo, White Buffalo Woman, White-painted Woman, Whobone Shelowa Okya, Wilatsukwe Dese Akenona Okya, Wilatsukwe Okya, Wild Pony, Wind Old Woman, Ye'ii Baad, Yellow Woman, Yung'a Mana

Northern Europe
Dis, Eastre, Hertha, Spurke, Valkyries, Weiþen Frauen

Oceania
Afekan, Aku aku, Babamik, Bila, Djanggawul, Fakahotu, Fulu'ulaalematato, Ganabuada, Haumei, Hina lau limu kala, Hoa make i ke kula, Hou heana, Julunggul, Junkgowa, Ka iki lani, Ka mo'o 'inanea, Kāne kua'ana, Karwadi, Kava tua, Kava'ara, Kui, Kūkū'ena, Kumi tonga, Kunapipi, Kurriwilban, Miru kura, Mulu mulu, Nevinbimba'au, Ngaljod, Paninduela, Pele, Poko ha rua te pō, Puimi, Tahunui, Tū poro tū, Uka o hoheru, Urunganada, Waiuda, Wawilak, Whaitiri, Yirbaik baik

South America
Beru, Iamanja, Jubbu-jang-sangne, Maize Mother, Mama Pacha, Mama Quilla, Mama Sara, Nungui, Si

Southeast Asia
Arurin, Bà Ngu', Bugan inPati, Darago, Dewi Danu, Dewi Pertimah, Duc Ba, Female Spectres, Hainuwele, Inawen, Ineno Pae, Ini Andan, Ini Manang, Langsuir, Lingkambene, Manoid, Pajau Yan, Rabia, Yara Meng

Western Europe
Áine, Brigid, Carlin, Carmán, Cordelia, Coventina, Ebhlinne, Ëire, Fays, Filia Vocis, Garbh Ogh, Habonde, Inghean Bhuidhe, Kernababy, Moncha, Mongfhinn, Nabia, Samhain, Serreta de

Alcoy Mother Goddess, Stratteli, Tailtu, Taranis, Tlachtga

Charisma

Africa
Qandisa

Central America and Mesoamerica
Ayauhteotl

Eastern Europe
Cacce-jienne, Mis-khum, Nemodilky, Saiva-neida, Šurali, Vasa

Far East
Bai Mundan

Greek and Roman Empires
Aglaia, Aglaope, Aglaopheme, Aigle, Auxo, Cale, Calypso, Charis, Charites, Gratiae, Himeropa, Laosoos, Leagore, Leucosia, Ligeia, Molpe, Paregoros, Parthenope, Pasithea, Peisinoe, Peitho, Pheme, Sirens, Suada, Thaleia, Thelchtereia, Thelxiepeia

Indian Subcontinent
Bharati, Delight Goddess, Gandharvadatta, Gandharvi, Gavariamma, Hidimba, Jara, Kirti, Kuhu, Kumbhinasa, Minaksi, Nirriti, Parooa, Pisachis, Rakshasis, Rama, Ramaladevi, Saki, Trigata, Trijata, Vajravarahi, Yashodhara

Near East
Frasasti, Nhang

Northern Europe
Herfjotur, Huldra, Kara, Lorelei, Roskva, Skogsfru

Oceania
Lewatu momo, Munga munga, Yama enda

South America
Yara

Western Europe
Cailleach Beara, Cliodhna, Dames Vertes, Fand, Fideal, Fland, Mess Buachalla, Rhiannon

Commerce and Travel

Central America and Mesoamerica
Ayizan

Eastern Europe
Vakš-oza

Far East
Dou Mou, Hani-yasu-bime-no-kami, Inari, Ishi-kori-dome-no-mikoto, Mo Ye, Onne-chip-kamui, Poi-soya-un-mat, Se-o-nyo, Shozu-ga-no-baba, Tian Fei, Tian Hou, Ugadama, Xi Shi, Yachimata-hime, Zhao Sanniang, Zi Gou

Greek and Roman Empires
Abeona, Empusae, Enodia, Ergane, Eulimene, Euploia, Eupompe, Fama, Juno, Limnades, Mater Matuta, Pylaitis, Trivia

The Himalaya
Sring-mo-no-chung-gzi-byin-ma

Indian Subcontinent
Bettada Chicama, Jamants, Ka Rasong, Kaliamma, Kaluvaliamma, Kanniha Paramesvare, Kulanthalamman, Kurumbai, Lohasur, Mangalamai, Margavati, Mari Mai, Masan, Matris, Mawshai, Narayani Mai, Nona Chamari, Parooa, Pathya, Pauri Pat, Poleramma, Samaiya, Sansari Mai, Shamidevi, Singhbahani, Yaparamma

Near East
Sapas

North America
Ana Maria

Oceania
Avin, 'Elepaio, Hine te kākara, Hine tū a hōanga, Kuku 'ena i ke ahi ho'omau honua, Kūkū'ena, La'ama'oma'o, Lea, Pu fafine, Wawilak

Southeast Asia
Idianale, Po Sah Ino

Western Europe
Quadriviae

Courage

Africa
Mella, Ogboinba

Eastern Europe
Alencica, Kubaiko

Egypt
Gate-keeping Goddesses, Sekhmet

Far East
Konohana-sakuya-hime, Oto-tachibana-hime-no-mikoto, Yakami

Greek and Roman Empires
Alcestis, Deima, Iphimedeia, Menippe, Pallor, Pavor, Phobos, Virtus, Zana

The Himalaya
Vîras

Indian Subcontinent
Apvā, Banka Mundi, Draupadi, Kali, Rahabasin Mata, Raka

Near East
Ninmah

North America
Hasinais Goddesses

Northern Europe
Seidhkoma

Oceania
Brogla

Western Europe
Sabra

Creator of Life

Africa
Acek, Alasho-Funfun, Andriamahilala, Asase Afua, Atai, Atete, Ayeba, Bride of the Barley, Buruku, Ceres Africana, Chi, Coti, Dogon Earth Mother, Dziva, Eka Abassi, Ekumoke, Eveningstar of Wakaranga, Ezum Mezum, Isong, Kabyle First Woman, Kamaugarunga, Ma, Macouas First Woman, Mashongavudzi, Mawu, Mawu-Lisa, Mbale, Mbongwe, Meme, Minona, Moombi, Morningstar of Wakaranga, Mousso Koroni Koundye, Nalwanga, Nasilele, Ndwanga, Nebele, Ninavanhu-ma, Nummo, Nyabahasa, Nyabibuya, Nyakala, Nyale, Nyamwezi First Woman, Nyingwan Mebege, Nyohwe Ananu, Nzambi, Odudua, Panda, Pe, Quabso, Sela, Songi, Tamuno, Unkulunkulu, Woyengi

Central America and Mesoamerica
Caha Paluna, Cipactónal, Comizahual, First Mothers, Huechaana, Ix Hun Tah Nok, Mu Alesop, Mu Olokukurtlisop, Mu Olokundil, Mu Olotagisop, Mu Olotakiki, Mu Sobia, Nana Olokegepiai, Nana Olomaguyriai, Nohuichana, Oxomoco, Pitao Huichaana, Xkan Le Ox, Xmucane, Xquic, Zipaltonal

Eastern Europe
Akkan, Amra, Ava, Didilia, Dzidzielia, Edji, First Woman, Hotogov Mailgan, Iarila, Ilmater, Joli-taren, Kostrubonko, Lazdu-māte, Linu-māte, Luonnotar, Mahte, Mamaldi, Nalban-aiy, Nan, Paraskeva, Puirsho, Radien-kiedde, Rusalka, Shotshen, Tundr Ilona, Ved-ava

Egypt
Amenti, Anka, Auset, Goose Goddess, Heket, Hemsut, Heqet, Maât, Merit, Mut, Muyt, Nekhebet, Ser-t, Taueret

Far East
Ame-no-toko-tachi-no-kami, Aya-kashiko-ne-no-kami, Edji, Hu Tu, In, Izanami-no-kami, Jūni-sama, Kami-musubi-no-kami, Mother of Ten Thousand Things, Mysterious Female, Nügua, Nunurao, Ō-ichi-hime, Peitai Niangniang, Ro-tara-ni-bi, Sse, Tiangong Dimu, Uminai-gami, Xi Wangmu, Ya Hsek Khi, Yin

Greek and Roman Empires
Agraulos, Anaitis, Ariadne, Cotys, Gaea, Populonia

The Himalaya
Bhavani, Nguntre, Ni-ngurre, Shakti, Ui Tango, Yum

Indian Subcontinent
Aditi, Anoi Diggan Juje, Anushakti, Ap, Arundhati, Asa Poorna, Bhagavati, Bhavani(s), Biliku, Bisal Mariamna, Brahmani, Bursung, Camunda, Chauturopayini, Dakshina, Dayan, Devi, Dyava-Prthivi, Earth Goddess, Earth Mother of Hrusso, Ganapatihrdaya, Ganesani, Ganga, Gauri, Gnas, Gopis, Gramadevatas, Hinglajin, Huligama, Ichchhashakti, Ideal Nature, Indrani, Ira, It Mu, Jagad-yoni, Jassuju, Jatavedasi, Kahasumma, Kali, Kamaksi, Kangra Goddess, Kapenopfu, Kaumari, Keyum, Kine Nane, Kotma Ma, Kumbhamata, Lakini, Lakshmi, Lalita Tripurasundari, Mahadevi, Mahalakshmi, Mahendri, Mahesvari, Malin Budhi, Manasa, Matri-Padma, Matrix of the Universe, Maya, Mohenjo-Daro Goddesses, Mother Fish, Mother Water, Mukta Devi, Nari, Nidra, Nirantali, Nostu Nopantu, Nustoo, Oraon Earth Goddess, Parvati, Piteri, Prajna, Puramdhi, Rangda, Ranu Bai, Rati, Saptamatrakas, Sarasvati, Sarvayoni, Shaktis, Sichi, Sinavali, Sitala, Sodasi, Sutrooka, Teeree, Totala, Tripura Bhairavi, Uma, Vaisnavi, Varahi, Varunani, Yami, Yashodhara, Zumiang Nui

Near East
Aeons, Am, Anāhita, Anath, Ararat, Aretia, Armaiti, Artemis Ephesus, Arubani, Aruru, Ashi, Ashtar-kemosh, Ashtart, Ashtoreth, Astarte, Atargatis, Bagmasti, Ban, Barbelo, Bau, Cybele, Dumuziabzu, Feminine Powers, First Woman, Fravashis, Genea, Hacilar Goddess, Holy Spirit, Inanna, Ishtar, Lady of the Abyss, Ma, Mah, Mahlyanag, Makh, Mama, Mami, Mashyoi, Masyanag, Meshiane, Metra, Moymis, Nammu, Ninmah, Ninni, Nutrix, Pdry, Rukho, Sauska, Semiramis, Sherua, Shulamite, Tanit Pene Baal, Tiamat, Yimak, Zarpandit, Zarpanitu, Zicum, Zigarun

North America
Aataentsic, Alkuntam, 'Anltani, Anusyelaix, Apasinasee, Atira, Aukjuk, Awehai, Awitelin Tsita, Blackfoot First Woman, Blackfoot Old Woman, Bowutset, Ca-the-ña, Cherokee First Woman, Cochiti Mother, Cotsipamapot, Creator Being, Daughter of the Sun, Ewauna, Goddesses of the Eastern and Western Ocean, Grandmother Spider, Hatcher, Hayoołkaał Asdzáá, Iatiku, Inuit Earth Mother, Ka, Kansa First Woman, Kato First Woman, Keres Moon Mother, Ketq Skwayne, Kokumthena, Kokyan Wuhti, Komwidapokuwia, La'idamlulum Ku'le, Louse Woman, Mandan Mother, Mikimatt, Morning Star Woman, Nahotsoi asdzáá, Nani

Waiya, Nautsiti, Nuqiliaxilena, Nuyelelaix, Ocean Woman, Omamama, Pah, Pawnee First Woman, Pawnee Moon Woman, People Mother, Pukeheh, Qakma, Queskapenek, Quootis-hooi, Ragno, Rukko, Sac First Women, Shakuru, Shiwanokia, Sidne, Sky Woman, Snowats, Snuximetlimana, Somagalags, Spider Woman, Spirit Woman, Sussistinnako, Tamaayawut, Tamayowut, Tcuperekata, Tipiskawipisim, Tsitsicinako, Turtle Woman, Twana First Woman, Two Women, Ute First Woman, Utset, Wild Pony, Woman Who Fell from the Sky, Yaonan, Yolkai Estsan, Yuman Mother Earth

Northern Europe
Audhumbla, Embla, Foseta, Freyja, Madder-akka, Sar-akka, Sif, Vana Mothers, Yngvi, Ziza

Oceania
Afekan, Angarua, Anua, Atanua, Atoto, Atua'anua, Birra nulu, Boaliri, Bulaing, De ai, Dinewan, Djanggawul, Djunkgao, Eingana, Enda semangko, Fa'a'ipu, Fakahotu, Gaueteaki, Haka, Hema, Hi asa, Hina te 'iva'iva, Hintubuet, Honabe, 'Imoa, Io wahine, Kagauraha, Kau ata ata, Kave, Ke aka huli lani, Kele, Kobine, Koevasi, Konjini, Kumu tonga i te po, Kunan beili, Kunapipi, La'i la'i, Laka, Lalo hāna, Latmikaik, Lejman, Ligoapup, Ligoububfanu, Limdunanij, Liomarar, Lorop, Lukelong, Ma riko riko, Madalait, Magigi, Maimoa a longona, Milapukala, Minyaburu, Mo'e ruru'a, Mortlock, Mudungkala, Mumuna, Namita, Ndengei, Nei nguiriki, Nigoubub, Niniganni, One kura, Opae, Oru, Pāia, Papa, Paparoa i tei tanga, Po, Po he'enalu mamao, Qatgoro, Queensland First Woman, Rua papa, Ruānge, Sinakibi, Tabui kor, Tākā, Tango tango, Te papa, Tiki kapakapa, Tongo tongo, Touiafutuna, Tū matua, Tukuhali, Tuli, Tumu iti, Uahea, Vahine nautahu, Vele lahi, Vele si'i, Waimariwi, Waramurungundji, Wawilak, Whetē, Wutmara

South America
Chokesuso, Maisö, Our Mother, Perimbó, Temioua, Uarahiulú

Southeast Asia
Amamikyu, Andin Bambin, Batara Shri, Bee Bride, Boru Deak Parudjar, Bugan, Bugan inIntongnin, Bugan inWigan, Chang-hko, Dao, Dewi Melanting, E U, Empung Luminuut, First Woman, Gaiyun, Hnitma Dawgyi, Inada Dao, Ina Da Samadulo Hose, Indara, Indo I Tuladidi, Indudun inPundaikuhan, Klang, Lumimuut, Manoid, Munsumundok, Na Ina, Nama Djang Ad Chalom, Ndo I Ronda Eo, Nggae, Ningpang Majan, Ningsin

Majan, Niwa, Nunsumnundok, Obban, Penaban Sari, Po Ino Nogar, Putir, Rangda, Salampandai, Sarengge, Saweigh, Seri, Shwe Myet Hna, Siberu Dayang Mata Ni Ari, Silewe Nazarata, Sitapi, Sri, Teze, Tiguianes, Tuglibong, Upunusa, Usi Afu, Wang Pyekkha Yek-khi, Warunsasadun, Wetar, Winia, Yahsek Khi

Western Europe
Áine, Albina, Anna Livia Plurabelle, Anu, Arianrhod, Auge, Berecynthia, Brigid, Búanann, Clothra, Coventina, Cymidei Cymeinfol, Dea Domnann, Don, Eigin, Glas Gaibleann, Gwenhwyfar, Henwen, Inghean Bhuidhe, Lasair, Lur, Primum Mobile, Rigantona, Sadb, Sheila-na-gig

Dawn and Twilight

Central America and Mesoamerica
Hunahpu-Vuch, Tabaminarro

Eastern Europe
Ammarik, Ausca, Auseklis, Ausra, Ausrine, Laumé, Tñe-ceivune, Xoli-katess, Zorya, Zorya Vechernyaya

Egypt
Kekuit

Far East
Bixia Yuanjin, Jun Ti, Tian Hou, Wakahirume-no-mikoto

Greek and Roman Empires
Albina, Anteia, Anticleia, Antigone, Antiope, Atthis, Aurora, Eos, Euryphaessa, Iole, Mater Matuta, Phosphoros, Tesana

The Himalaya
Hod-zer-can-ma

Indian Subcontinent
Ahana, Ashva, Harits, Jyotsna, Marichi, Marici, Prabha, Rukmini, Sandhya, Sarama, Sati, Urvasi, Usas, Ushodevatas

Near East
Aja, Aya, Bamya, Dido, Odatis, Shalimtum

North America
Dawn (Seneca), Dawn Woman, Hanwi, Hayoołkaał Asdzą́ą́, Nahotsoi asdzą́ą́, Naxcoi'esza, Talatumsi, Xayołká·ł 'eszą·

Northern Europe
Eastre, Gudrun, Hjordis, Sieglind, Thora

Oceania
Atanua, Atarapa, Hetu ahin, Hine tītama, Pohaha, Sagatea, Te ata tuhi

South America
Chasca, Princess d'Alva

Western Europe
Bebhionn, Bécuma, Dawen, Fionnuala, Gwyar, Miranda, Tuag, Uathach

Demi-Animals

Africa
'Aisha Qandisha, All-bringing-forth, Asaase Aberewa, Bunzi, Crocodile Woman, Kalimulore, Ndwanga, Nimm, Nummo, Olokum, Oxun, Yukanye

Central America and Mesoamerica
Chíchipáchu, Itzpapalotl, Ix Kan Citam Thul, Ix Kan Itzam Thul, Ix Tol Och, Ix Ual Cuy, Ix Ual Icim, Olokum, Oxun, Quilaztli

Eastern Europe
Ajatar, Akkruva, Alkonost, Avfruvva, Bereginy, Gorska Makva, Laima, Liderc, Luot-hozjik, Siriny

Egypt
Ahemait, Ahti, Amaunet, Ammit, Ankhtith, Ashtoreth, Bast, Êpet, Hak, Hauhet, Hekenth, Heket, Heptet, Heqet, Her-tept, Hert-ketit-s, Hoh, Kerub of Air, Mehi, Mehueret, Menhet, Merseger, Mihit, Mut, Nahab, Nazit, Neith, Nekhebet, Nepit, Neshtu, Nut, Pakhit, Sag, Sekhet, Sekhmet, Selket, Sesenet-khu, Shesemtet, Souban, Sphinx, Taourt, Taueret, Ta-urt, Tefnut, Tesert, Tie, Uadjet, Ubastet

Far East
Hi-naga-hime, Matou Niang, Ningyo, Nügua, Nüwa, Tamamo-no-maye, Tennin, Xi Wangmu

Greek and Roman Empires
Acholoe, Aello, Aglaope, Aglaopheme, Aphaea, Celaeno, Chimaera, Echidna, Empusa, Fraud, Harpies, Hippo, Kelaino, Lasa-Rakuneta, Lelaino, Leucosia, Ligeia, Lupa, Maera, Magna Mater, Molpe, Nicothoe, Parthenope, Podarge, Rumor, Sirens, Thelxiepeia, Tuchulcha, Vanth

The Himalaya
Black Cuckoo-headed Mystic Goddess, Black Sow-headed Sow Goddess, Blue Monkey-headed Goddess of Inquisitiveness, Blue Serpent-headed Water Goddess, Blue Wolf-headed Wind Goddess, Cha-dog-ma, Chags-kyu-ma, Dark-brown Yak-headed Rakshasa Goddess, Dark-green Fox-headed Baton Goddess, Dom-gdon-can, Dorje Phagmo, Green Deer-headed Wealth-guardian Goddess, Greenish-black Elephant-headed Big-nosed Goddess, Greenish-black Leopard-headed Great Goddess, Greenish-black Serpent-headed Mystic Goddess, Greenish-black Vulture-headed Eater Goddess, Htamenmas, Lu, Red Crow-headed Thunderbolt Goddess, Red Hoopoe-headed Desire Goddess, Red Horse-headed Delight Goddess, Red Ibex-headed Woman Goddess, Red Lion-headed Mystic Goddess, Red Makara-headed Peaceful Goddess, Red Scorpion-headed Amrita Goddess, Red

Snow-bear-headed Virgin Goddess, Reddish-yellow Serpent-headed Brahma Goddess, Senga-dong-ma, Sengdroma, Seng-ge'i-gdong-can, Til-bu-ma, White Bear-headed Indra Goddess, White Eagle-headed Mighty Goddess, White Kite-headed Moon Goddess, Yellow Bat-headed Delight Goddess, Yellow Dog-headed Rakshasi, Yellow Goat-headed Mystic Goddess, Yellowish-black Tiger-headed Rakshasi, Zhag-pa-ma

Indian Subcontinent
Bagala, Ganapatihrdaya, Gandharvis, Ganga, Grismadevi, Kimnaris, Nagis, Narasimhi, Rksavaktradakini, Sarpis, Sringatpadini, Surya, Vidyadharis

Near East
Atargatis, Cherubim, Dagon, Deo, Derketo, Eden, Kadi, Lamasthu, Nidaba, Nina, Orore, Shaushka

North America
Hahai-i Wuhti, Ikalu nappa, Iqalu Nappaa, Ixlewani, Malaxšišinɨš, Sinnilktok, Snee-nee-iq

Northern Europe
Allwise, Angeburga, Groa, Havfru, Kara, Labismina, Lilyi, Mora, Nixen, Olrun, Seidhkoma, Sel, Sibilja, Signe-Alveig, Sigrun, Swan Maidens, Wunschelwybere

Oceania
Hatuibwari, Kiha wahine, Laenihi, Lani wahine, Lea, Mamala, Moana nui ka lehua, Mo'o, Narpajin, Ngārara huarau, Nisoukepilen, Porpoise Girl, Puako mopele, Shaliom, Sky Maiden, Tupu'a, Vinmara

South America
Jamaina

Southeast Asia
Alan, Bee Bride, Nang Pyek Kha Yeh Khi, Suvarnamacha, Wang Pyekkha Yek-khi

Western Europe
Aige, Aobh, Aoife, Ban Naomha, Benvarry, Black Annis, Blodeuwedd, Bobd, Cáer, Ceasg, Corra, Corrigan, Dechtiré, Derbhorgill, Elamite, Étain, Ëtain Echraidhe, Fand, Fionnuala, Glaisrig, Glasgavlen, Lamin, Laminaks, Lí Ban, Mari, Mari Morgan, Melusine, Mermaids, Merrow, Mórrígán, Moruadh, Munanna, Pressina, Sadb, Tuireann, Uchtdealbh

Destroyer of Life

Africa
Abena Budu, Atai, Cigoro, Dangira, Dariya, Death Goddess, Dinka First Woman, Djaga Woman, Ganda First Woman, Gyangya'di, Karama, Loa, Makasa, Mayramu, Nalongo,

Nomkubulwane, Osaka, Pregnant Woman, Ricana, Sarawniya, Tabhi-yiri, Umm S-subyan, Yalode

Central America and Mesoamerica
Agaman Nibo, Chíchipáchu, Cihuateteo, Guédé l'Oraille, Ix Tab, Llorona, Marie-aimée, Mictecacihuatl, Tzitzimime, Xonaxi Quecuya

Eastern Europe
Ajatar, Anlu-lebie-landet Numakiedeil Emei, Baba Yaga, Bozaloshtsh, Cacce-jienne, Chuma, Giltine, Jabme-akka, Kalma, Kapu Māte, Khania Shkwakwa, Khosadam, Khosodam, Kipu-tytto, Kukuth, Kulshedra, Louhi, Loviatar, Marzana, Mera-mäte, Meschamaat, Minceskro, Morana, Moravaya Panna, Nāves-mäte, Navki, Ovda, Schilalyi, Smert, Šukšendal, Tarn, Tcaridyi, Tshuma, Vammatar, Vyestitsa, Yabme-akka, Zitna-atka

Egypt
Ahemait, Ammit, Fifth Hour Goddess, Gate-keeping Goddesses, Hathor, Sekhet, Umm s-Subyan

Far East
Banzhen, Doushen Niangniang, Napuri-kor-kamui-kor-matnepo, Nü She, She Mu, Xi Wangmu, Yama-omba

Greek and Roman Empires
Aello, Aglaope, Aglaopheme, Arai, Brimo, Cer, Ceres, Charybdis, Gorgopa, Leucosia, Libitina, Ligeia, Limnades, Lua, Meleagrian, Molpe, Mors, Morta, Parthenope, Scylla, Sirens, Thelxiepeia, Tuchulcha, Vanth, Vanths

The Himalaya
Chu'phrul can, dBang-bsdud-ma, Dur-khrod-kyi-bdag-mo-khros-ma-nag-mo, Dur-khrod-lha-mo, gshin-rje-mo, gSum-brag-ma, 'Jigs-pa'i-zer-mo-mig-gcig, Kerimas, Kha-la-me-'bar-ma, Lha-mo, Ma-mo, Ma-mo-sgam-pa-ma, Srinmo, Srog-bdag-mo

Indian Subcontinent
Acheri, Agwani, Alwantin, Angarmati Bhawani, Ankamma, Arayi, Badi Mata, Bai Haldahin, Baihi, Basanti, Bauri Bai, Bettada Chicama, Bhadrakali, Bhageseri, Bhgavati, Bhgavatiamman, Bhumiya Rani, Bisari, Bugarik, Burhi Mata, Chamariya, Chhotimai, Chilkin Piri, Chingan Mata, Chinnamasta, Churalin, Churelin Mata, Dakinis, Dayan, Dhahu Dhukan, Dhumavati, Diarrhoea, Dispirir Mata, Duhkharni Mai, Durga Mata, Durpatta Mata, Galadevi, Gandhari, Gangammal, Gavariamma, Ghatchindan, Ginoo moong, Grahis, Gulsalia Mata, Hadphoran Marhi, Hidimba, Hulka Devi, Hulki Mai, Jalia, Jalpa Mai, Jappi Mata, Jara, Jyestha, Jyestha Alakshmi, Ka Duba, Ka Khlam, Ka Niangriang,

Ka Rih, Ka Shwar, Ka Smer, Ka Taroh, Kairadeshahi, Kalamahichandi, Kaluvaliamma, Kamthi Mata, Kankar Mata, Kanti, Kapni Piri, Kateri, Kati Ankamma, Keyuri, Kokkalamma, Kuleswari, Kumbhinasa, Lamkariya, Mahakali, Mahamai, Mahari, Mangalamai, Manthara, Marai Mata, Maraki, Maramma, Marhai Mata, Mari, Mari Bhavani, Mari Mai, Mari Mata, Mariamma, Mariamman, Maridama, Mariyammai, Mariyayi, Masan, Masani, Mata, Matangi Shakti, Matris, Maura Mata, Mirgi Devi, Moti Mata, Mrtyu, Mutyalamma, Nage-bonga, Nage-Era, Naikin Bai, Namamdamma, Narayani Mai, Nirriti, Nukalamma, Nukulamma, Ola Bibi, Paharon, Pansahi Mata, Pharka Undharan Mata, Phoki Mata, Phulmata, Phulmati, Pisachis, Pochamma, Polamde, Poleramma, Pollamma, Putana, Rahabasin Mata, Rakshasis, Raksin Mata, Rtuharika, Rudrani, Sakuni, Sankata, Sansari Mai, Satarupa, Satvai, Shakti, Sitala, Sukhajamma, Sunkalamma, Sushakti, Tari Pennu, Thakurani Bakorani, Trigata, Trijata, Tripura Bhairavi, Tseurima, Tsun Kyanske, Ugratara, Ujali, Ujali Mata, Umariya Mata, Vinata

Near East
Anath, Dimme, Ereshkigal, Gula, Inanna, Jahi, Labartu, Lamassu, Lamasthu, Reshpu, Samal, Sheve

North America
Aataentsic, Apish, Atse Esdzaa, Bapets, Bear Woman and the Fawns, Death-bringing-woman, Erlaveersisoq, Hakulaq, Korawini?i, Nañoikwia, Nuñda, Nunusomikeeqonem, Paija, Qamaitis, Siltslani, Snee-nee-iq, Sneneik, Snutqutxals, Soyoko, Sun Goddess, Ululiarnaq, Unhcegila, Utlunta, Whistling Grandmother

Northern Europe
Angerbodha, Giptes, Hella, Herfjotur, Lilyi, Ran, Seidhkoma, Tuonetar

Oceania
'Alae a hina, Budyah, Bumerali, Dogai, Dunawali, Hatu atu tupun, Houmea, Iro Duget, Kapiano, Kapo, Kiha wahine, Kini maka, Kobo Mandalat, Koilasa, Koirau na marama, Kurriwilban, Lewa levu, Lewandranu, Lewatu momo, Likuthava, Lilavatu, Mafurere, Mailkun, Mulu mulu, Nabudi, Narama, Nau taufiti, Ngaljod, Nona, Nujka'u, Nujmaga, Papai a taki vera, Pinuwali, Pufine ma, Raluve, Tapuitea, Tha, Uli, Vinaka, Wahini hai, Yama enda, Yirbaik baik

South America
Calounga, Raharariyoma, Uwan

Southeast Asia
Ag Aganney, Ammal, Bugan inMagnad, Bugan inPati, Chalonarang, Dagdagamiyan, Dara Rambai Geruda, Gaiyun, Karokung, Khmoc Pray, Kibayen, Langsuir, Loupgarous, Magtatangal, Mangagaway, Mebuyan, Minti Dara Bunsu, Muni Mental Batu, Penanggalan, Po Yan Dari, Sidapa, Sigrutan

Western Europe
Agrona, Aibell, Annis, Banba, Bean Nighe, Bean Sídhe, Bibi, Cannered Noz, Caoineag, Cerridwen, Cyhiraeth, Hag, Long Meg, Taranis, Tertiana

Directions

Africa
Agada, Dierra, Ganna, Silla, Wagadu

Central America and Mesoamerica
Mictlancihuatl, Tāté Haútse Kupúri, Tāté Kyewimóka, Tāté Naaliwámi, Tāté Rapawiyama

Eastern Europe
Bozaloshtsh, Haltia, Khosodam, Tomam, Tshadze-ienne, Tshatse-neida

Egypt
Ament, Herit, Kenat, Mehet, Mehit, Netheth, Uatch-ura

Far East
In, Isa, Matnau, Milun, Nügua, Sei-o-bo, Shuiyi Shi, Taxankpada Agodales, Tekarpada, Xi Wangmu

Greek and Roman Empires
Aello, Lips, Palato, Salmaone

The Himalaya
Black Cuckoo-headed Mystic Goddess, Black Petali, Black Sow-headed Sow Goddess, Blue Monkey-headed Goddess of Inquisitiveness, Blue Serpent-headed Water Goddess, Blue Wolf-headed Wind Goddess, Cha-dog-ma, Chags-kyu-ma, Dark-blue Smasha, Dark-brown Yak-headed Rakshasa Goddess, Dark-green Fox-headed Baton Goddess, Dark-green Ghasmari, Green Deer-headed Wealth-guardian Goddess, Greenish-black Elephant-headed Big-nosed Goddess, Greenish-black Leopard-headed Great Goddess, Greenish-black Serpent-headed Mystic Goddess, Greenish-black Vulture-headed Eater Goddess, Karma Dakinis, Karma-krotishaurima, Kule, Kurukulle, Mâmakî, Nam-mkha'i-lha-mo-snyoms-byed-ma, Nam-mkha'i-lha-mo-sprin-tshogs-ma, Nam-mkha'i-lha-mo-tsha-gsang-snyoms, Nam-mkha'i-lha-mo-tshod-'dzin-ma, Ogress of Lust, Padma Dakinis, Padma Krotishaurima, 'Phrog-'chang-ma, 'Phur-'debs-ma, Pukkase, Ratna Krotishaurima, Red Crow-headed Thunderbolt Goddess, Red Hoopoe-headed Desire Goddess, Red Horse-headed Delight Goddess, Red Ibex-headed Woman Goddess, Red Lion-headed Mystic Goddess, Red Makara-headed Peaceful Goddess, Red Pramoha, Red Pukhase, Red Scorpion-headed Amrita Goddess, Red Snow-bear-headed Virgin Goddess, Reddish-yellow Serpent-headed Brahma Goddess, Sangs-rgyas-spyan-ma, Smasha, sNang-gsal-ma, Til-bu-ma, Tsandhali, Tseurima, Vajra Krotishaurima, White Bear-headed Indra Goddess, White Eagle-headed Mighty Goddess, White Kerima, White Kite-headed Moon Goddess, Yellow Bat-headed Delight Goddess, Yellow Dog-headed Rakshasi, Yellow Goat-headed Mystic Goddess, Yellow Tseurima, Yellowish-black Tiger-headed Rakshasi, Yellowish-white Tsandhali, Zhal-zas-ma

Indian Subcontinent
Biliku, Desahai Devi, Dikkumari, Hamsika, Namamdamma, Pathya, Sarvakamadugha, Subhadra, Surupa, Vijaya Sakti

Near East
Arduisur, Qlippoth, Shutu

North America
Djabani, Evening Star, Goddesses of the Eastern and Western Ocean, Hürü'Ingwühti, Kamaits, Kashinako, Khunpinu'a'anyun, Khuntasaengge'i'a'anyun, Khuntsaenyu'a'anyun, Kurkanninako, Merrinako, Munainako, Nahosdzaan Esdza, Neoga, No'oma Cawaneyung, North Wind Woman, Nuskwalsikanda, Quisserrinkao, Skamotsxmana, Tcalyel, Tsumtlaks, Tukwinong Mana, Wiakai

Oceania
Hema, Hine i tapapauta, Hine tu whenua, Le gerem, Nei aro maiaki, Nei te ra'aiti, Nibora, Rua papa

Southeast Asia
Ndo I Ronda Eo, Teu Kweh

Disorder

Africa
Atai, Bushongo Earth Mother, Damwamwit, Gcagcile, Lissa, Masai Moon Goddess, Mobokomu, Mousso Koroni Koundye, Musso Koroni

Central America and Mesoamerica
Coatrischie, Erzulie, Guabancex, Guédé l'Oraille, Guede Masaka, Iguanuptigili, Itaba Tahuana, Ix Chel, Ixtab, Maninupdikili, Masaya, Mombu, Olonuptigile, Punauaga Olopunalisop, Xcanul

Eastern Europe
Dive Zeny, Divje Devojke, Divoženky, Dziwożony, Mamony, Pszepolnica, Saule, Sukkamielli, Šukšendal, Suoyatar, Šurali, Vakš-oza, Vestice, Zallus

Egypt
Rait

Far East
Chiu-rang-guru, Chiwash-kor-kamui, Fuji, Horokariyep, Kalapiat, Matnau, Shenggu, Takitsu-hime-no-mikoto

Greek and Roman Empires
Acidalia, Adephagia, Ate, Discordia, Dysnomia, Erinys, Eris, Hipponoe, Melinoe, Methe, Mimallones, Pugna, Rumor

The Himalaya
gNam-lha-byang-sman-mthing-gi-go-zu-can, Nam-mkha'g•yu-mdog-snang-srid-mdzod

Indian Subcontinent
Bardaichila, Ghosinis, Parooa, Taraka, Vegavati

Near East
Anat, Anaxšti, Asrušti, Dsovinar, Ennoia, Huwassanas, Lilith, Nasu, Pairimaiti, Reshpu, Saltu, Shala, Taromati, Tasimis, Uda, Vatak

North America
Anog Ite, Chuginadak, Cold Woman, Dagwanoenyent, Godasiyo, Hakulaq, Hayicanako, Kimilkan, Nayaanxatisei, Netcensta, Piptu' Wuhti, Queskapenek, Thompson Goddesses, Tisseyak, Tootega

Northern Europe
Elli, Frau Frigg, Seidhkoma

Oceania
'Ere'ere fenua, Goolagaya, Hanitemau, Haumea, Hine moana, Ka'ula hea, Kurikuta, Kwouk kwouk, Laka, Lewatu ni nambua, Ngaljod, Pare, Pele, Pere, Po, Tairbu, Tere hē, Uka o hoheru, Wayambeh, Wibalu

South America
Mama Pacha, Toru-guenket

Southeast Asia
Aninito Ad Chalom, Dagau, Darago, Kabagiyawan, Lai-oid, Lepeh, Ndara, Saputan, Tarai

Western Europe
Geniti Glinne, Ignis Fatuus, Silkie

Domesticated Animals

Africa
Deung Abok, Morongo

Central America and Mesoamerica
Chíchipáchu, Tāté Haútse Kupúri, Tāté Naaliwámi, Tatei Xuturi Iwiekame

Eastern Europe
Almoshi, Enakhsys, Gorska Makva, Haltia, Illibem Berti, Kaldas-ava, Kaltes, Kamennaia Baba, Kikimora, Koš

La-kuva, Lopemat, Marà, Mokosi, Näkki, Ratainicza, Sreča, Tartary and Cathay Earth Goddess, Vit'ša-kuva, Ynakhsyt

Egypt
Ahat, Akarkhentkats, An-unsser, Ashtoreth, Celestial Sow, Ehe, Four Uaipu Cow Goddesses, Hap Cow, Hathor, Heb-i, Heru-sekha, Hesa, Mafdet, Mehueret, Neith, Sentait, Shenty, Shilluk, Smamet, Tchesert

Far East
Baiji, Earth Cow, Matou Niang, Tartary and Cathay Earth Goddess, Uke-mochi-no-kami

Greek and Roman Empires
Aega, Aeginaea, Aegophaga, Aegophagos, Albina, Alcippe, Athene Boarmia, Bubona, Chalinitis, Damasippus, Epona, Equestris, Heurippe, Hippia, Hippodameia, Hippona, Lampetia, Malophorus, Meliades, Nomia, Pales, Phaea

The Himalaya
Black Sow-headed Sow Goddess, Dorje Phagmo, Nye-pha'i-btsun-mo, Phyugs-bdag-btsun-mo, Red Horse-headed Delight Goddess, Sengdroma, Vajravaraki, Yellow Dog-headed Rakshasi, Yellow Goat-headed Mystic Goddess, Zhag-pa-ma

Indian Subcontinent
Ashva, Asokakanta, Asvini, Bettada Chicama, Bhadrā, Dakshina, Dishai Devi, Gandharvadatta, Gandharvi, Gandini, Ganga Devi, Gauri, Gopis, Hadakai, Harits, Ida, Ila, It Mu, Kalumaiamman, Kamadhenu, Kanaka Durgamma, Kastha, Kukar Mari, Kurmar Devis, Madu-Ammal, Mahi, Mallana Devi, Marici, Naikin Bai, Naina Devi, Nandini, Parrapotamma, Phoki Mata, Phorcis, Prabha, Prishni, Prithivi, Rohini, Samgna, Sarama, Saranyu, Sarvakamadugha, Sasthi, Shasti, Sinivali, Sitala, Sugrivi, Suki, Thakurani Bakorani, Totala, Vac, Vadaba, Vasudhara, Vatsasur, Yerra Gadipati Ganga

Near East
Ashtoreth, Cow Goddesses, Daena, Ddrvaspa, Deo, Duttur, Geush Urvan, Lahar, Lisina, Nin-e-i-garak, Ninkharak, Ninsun, Silili, Succoth Benoth

North America
Big Dog, Dogrib First Woman, Mahakh, Red Dog's Wife, Sinnilktok

Northern Europe
Audhumbla, Hertha, Horsel, Huldra, Hulle, Syr

Oceania
Kafisi, Laenihi, Po lao uli, Poneiemai, Puako mopele, Yirbaik baik

South America
Mama Llama

Southeast Asia
Ikapati, Larai Majan, Manuk Manuk, Prithivi, Tangkam Majan

Western Europe
Bo Find, Boann, Damona, Dawen, Dil, Epona, Flidais, Fuwch Frech, Fuwch Gyfeilioru, Glaistig, Glas, Glasgavlen, Henwen, Lamin, Laminaks, Rhiannon

Earth and Nature

Africa
Aberewa, Aja, Aje, Ala, Alo, Ama, Amakiri, Amponyinamoa, Ane, Ani, Aprija, Asase Yaa, Asia, Atete, Azele Yaba, Bele Alua, Bushongo Earth Mother, Chi, Divine Queen, Dogon Earth Mother, Dugbo, Edinkira, Esesar, Huntu Katt! Katten, Ii, Ije, Isong, Kaiwan, Krachi Woman, Ma, Ma-ndəə, Maryam, Mbache, Morningstar of Wakaranga, Nana Buruku, Ndoi, Neiterogob, Nimba, Nkike, Nommo, Ntoa, Nyame, Nyohwe Ananu, Nzambi, Obasi Nsi, Odudua, Oshun, Tega, Tenga, Ten'gono, Tingoi, Tintai, 'Uwardaw

Central America and Mesoamerica
Ah Wink-ir Masa, Atabei, Chalchiuhcihuatl, Chulmetic, Cihuacoatl, Coatlicue, Colel Cab, Cueravaperi, Guamaonocon, Ichpuchtli, Ilamatecuhtli, Itzcueye, Itzpapalotl, Iztaccihuatl, Mama Nono, Marinette, Masaya, Mayahuel, Mu Olokukurtlisop, Nana Buruku, Nanaolonupippisopi, Olokukurtilisop, Olomakriai, Omecihuatl, Punauaga Olopunalisop, Quetzalmalin, Rosna, Takótsi Nakawé, Tāté Haútse Kupúri, Tāté Kyewimóka, Tatei Utuanaka, Tatei Yurienaka, Teteoinnan, Tlaltecuhtli, Toci, Tonantzin, Tsilah Wedo, Xaratanga, Xcanul, Xilonen, Xochiquetzal, Zapotlantenan

Eastern Europe
Äijo, Albasta, An-alai-chotoun, Api, Bereginy, Cuvto-ava, Dārzu-māte, Debena, Diiwica, Dive Zeny, Divi-te Zeni, Divja Davojke, Divje Devojke, Divoženky, Dunna Musun, Dziewona, Dziwožony, Ehe Tazar, Erce, Etugen, Fevroniia, Ganis, Gudiri-mumi, Honoured High Mistress, Itchita, Ja-neb'a, Joli-taren, Kaltes, Kamennaia Baba, Kathshchar-ekva, Kildisin, Koš La-kuva, Kupal'nitsa, Lauma, Lesni Zenka, Louhi, Luonnotar, Maan-emo, Maan-eno, Maddarakka, Ma-emma, Mamony, Mampadurei, Mannu, Marena, Mary-rusalka, Marzana,

Mastor-ava, Mati-syra-zemlya, Medeine, Mejdejn, Melande-awa, Mengk, Meschamaat, Metsänneitsyt, Metsarhatija, Metsola Mother, Meža-māte, Mielikki, Mis-khum, Mokosh, Mother of Metsola, Muzem-mumy, Nar-azerava, Nuset-i-malit, Obyda, Ogu-māte, Otygen, Ovda, Perit, Rana Nedia, Raudna, Rauni, Raz-ajk, Risem-edne, Rusalki-siriny, Russian Mother Earth, Sangia-mama, Sengi-mama, Sēnu-māte, Sjantaik, Šurali, Tava-ajk, Teleglen-edzen, Tenga, Turkic Earth Mother, Tuulikki, Uldda, Ulgen Ekhe, Vēja-māte, Vila, Vir-ava, Willi, Yabme-akka, Ya-nebya, Zeme, Zemyna, Ziedu-māte

Egypt
Aasith, Anatha Baetyl, Anatis, Bast, Hagar, Her-sha-s, Isis, Mehueret, Nebtuu, Repa, Saosis, Satis, Sokhet, Usert

Far East
Ama-no-sagu-me, Chikisani-kamui, Dao, Di Mu, Di Ya, dKar-mo, Etogon, Etugen, Ezo Goddess, Flower Goddesses, Fuji, Hani-yasu-bime-no-kami, Hime-jima, Hou Tu Nainai, Houtu Guohuang, Hua Xian, Huang Daopo, Izanami-no-kami, Jian Lao, Jin Mu, Kaya-no-hime-no-kami, Kayanohime, Konohana-chiru-hime, Konohana-sakuya-hime, Kun, Kuni-no-mi-hashira, Lan Caihe, Lengdin, Mamaldi, Mi-bou-do, Milun, Mt. Unebi Goddess, Naru-kami, Niangniang, Ō-no-de-hime, O-ryu, Ō-to-matohi-me-no-kami, Ō-to-no-be-no-kami, Ō-tsuchi-no-kami, Otygen, Ō-ya-tsu-hime-no-mikoto, Qi Guzi, Rafu-sen, Ru-be-sei, San Gufuren, Second Earthly Generation Deities, Seng-ge Ga-mu, Seng-ge Karmo, Sengen-sama, Shen Deity, Shir-kor-kamui, Shuiyi Shi, Su-hiji-ni-no-kami, Teleglen-edzen, Toi-kura-puni-mat, Tsukisakaki hime, Tsuma-tsu-hime-no-mikoto, Tudi Furen, Tudi Nainai, Ya Hsek Khi, Yama-hime, Yametsu-hime, Yaye-zakura, Yunhua Furen

Greek and Roman Empires
Acacalis, Acantha, Acca Larentia, Achaea, Acmenes, Admete, Adrastea, Aegiale, Aganippe, Agdos, Agno, Aigle, Akraia, Alalkomenia, Alcimache, Alexirrhoe, Alseides, Amymone, Anchiale, Anthedon, Antheia, Anthracia, Antiope, Arcadian, Arethusa, Arge, Argiope, Artemis, Asterodeia, Atlantia, Atlantides, Auloniades, Aura, Axieros, Axiokersa, Axioche, Bassarae, Bendis, Brisa, Brome, Cabeiriae, Carme, Caryatis, Castitas, Chamyne, Chelone, Chloe, Chloris, Chryse, Chrysopeleia, Chthonia, Chthoniae, Cirrha, Cisseis,

Citherides, Clonia, Clytia, Cnossia, Cocythiae, Coinquenda, Collatina, Coronis, Corycia, Coryciae, Coryphaea, Coryphasia, Cteis, Cyane, Cyllene, Cynosura, Da, Daphnaea, Daulis, Dea Marica, Deiopea, Deliades, Dendritus, Diana, Dicte, Dodonides, Dryades, Dryope, Echo, Endeis, Ephesia, Erato, Eripha, Erycina, Erythea, Eucharis, Eunoste, Eurydice, Euryte, Fauna, Feronia, Flora, Furina, Gaeeochos, Giane, Glauce, Hagno, Hamadryades, Hamaelides, Hegetoria, Helike, Hemera, Hespera, Hesperides, Hestia, Hippe, Hora, Horta, Hyale, Hybla, Iaera, Ida, Idaea, Inyx, Iodama, Ithome, Kalliphaeira, Karpophoros, Kolias, Laodice, Laonome, Lavinia, Leucippe, Leucophryne, Ligeia, Lignaco Dex, Limoniades, Linos, Lotis, Lyce, Maenades, Maia, Malophorus, Manto, Matres Britanne, Melanippe, Melia, Meliades, Meliae, Melissae, Mendeis, Menthe, Mideia, Mycalessides, Napaea, Neaera, Nissa, Nomia, Nycheia, Nymphes, Nymphs, Nysa, Nyseides, Ocyrrhoë, Oenoe, Oncaea, Oreades, Orseis, Ortygia, Ossa, Pandora, Pareia, Parthenia, Phigalia, Philia, Phoebe, Physis, Pieria, Pipleia, Pitys, Polyhymno, Polymastus, Potnia, Potnia Theron, Prosymna, Puta, Pyrrha, Rhea, Rhene, Rhodope, Rhodos, Rusina, Sagaris, Sagaritis, Salmacis, Semnai Theai, Sinoe, Speio, Sphragitides, Syllis, Syrinx, Teledice, Tellus, Thallo, Thebe, Theisoa, Thespeia, Thisbe, Thriae, Titaea, Tithorea, Tyche, Xenia, Zephyritis

The Himalaya
aBru-gu-ma, Altan-telgey, Atugan, bDud-mo-rno-myur, brTan-ma, Gangkar Shame, Jo-mo-lha-ri, Khadiravani Tara, Kongtsun Demo, Kun-bzang-ma, Me-tog-ma, Mokum, mThing-gi-zhal-bzang-ma, 'Og-gis-bdag, Pashupatī, Rab-brtan-ma, rDo-rje-dpal-gyi yum, rDo-rje-drag-mo-rgyal, Sa'i-lha-mo Sangs-rgyas-spyan-ma, Sa-rgyal-dong-gi-dbal-mo, sKyabs-mdun, Tse-ring Chhe-nga, Tsha-ba'i-brtan-ma-chen-mo, Ugtsho Yamasil

Indian Subcontinent
Adanari, Alakhani, Amari De, Apala, Aramati, Arani, Aranyani, Ardhanari, Asapurna, Assam Mother Earth, Auksagandhi, Banasankari, Bansapti, Baski Mata, Basuli, Bela Pinnu, Bhadrakali, Bhogavati, Bhumi, Bhumiya Rani, Bhumme Nari, Bhuyian, Bonga, Buddhi, Buddhi Pallien, Chakrisvari, Chola Pacho, Devatas, Dharani, Dharni Pinnu, Digdevatas, Diti, Dongar Dai, Durga, Dyava-Prthivi, Earth Mother of Hrusso, Gandharvis, Ganga, Gasain Era, Gau, Gauri Sankara, Gopya, Grilya Burhin,

Guggulu, Ida, Ila, i-lha-mo, Ira, Jahira Buru, Jibbi-Jang-Sangne, Ka Ram-ew, Kalika, Kaliyani, Kamala, Karicag, Katukilal, Khermata, Kine Nane, Ksama, Ksetrasya Patni, Kshiti-apsarases, Kujum-Chantu, Kusumamodini, Kutamangari, Lakshmi, Lata, Lavangi, Ma Dharti, Machandri, Madhavi Devi, Mahasitaviti, Mahasveta, Mahendri, Mahi, Mai Dharitri, Manasa, Mandaramala, Mandwa Rani, Mantradevatas, Matris, Medini, Mirzapore Forest Goddess, Mngilamma, Mother Earth, Motho, Mungo, Murala, Muzamuza, Naladi, Nanda Devi, Nanga Baigin, Nishtigri, Pan Dong Cyu, Parvati, Petni, Poramai, Pracriti, Prakriti, Pramandani, Prishni, Prithivi, Raktadantika, Ramchandi, Ratnamangari, Ronkini, Saci, Sandhya, Sansari Mai, Sanumati, Sarna Burhia, Sarparajni, Sarpis, Saudamani, Sedi, Seven Females, Shamidevi, Shasti, Shidkin-kede, Shushtee, Sita, Sitking-Kedding, Siva, Sokarahita, Sri, Sringatpadini, Subbu Khai Thung, Sukarapreyasi, Sulochana, Sundari, Tadaka, Talyeu Nimu, Tamil Mountain Fairies, Tari Pennu, Thakurani Mai, Tripura Bhairavi, Tulsi, Uma, Uravari, Valli, Vana, Vanadevatas, Vanaspati Mai, Vandya, Varu-dasa-rabbi, Vasudhara, Vikesi, Vindhya, Virudha, Vrikdevatsas, Yakshi

Near East
Adamah, Adamina, Aja, Ameretāt, Amesha Spentas, Anatu, An.zu, Apia, Aretia, Aretz, Arisya, Armaiti, Armat, Arsai, Arsiya, Aruru, Asherah, Baalath, Ba'alath Gebal, Baubo, Briah, Chaabou, Cotys, Cybele, Davcina, Dumuziabzu, Eden, Epinoia, Fravashis, Ga-tum-dug, Gea, Gephen, Geshtin, Geush Urvan, Ghe, Gubarra, Gumshea, Hea, Houri, Inanna, Ininni, Irnini, Ki, Krumai, Liluri, Lilwani, Ma, Mah, Matar Kubile, Meder, Myrrha, Nikkal, Ningal, Ningikuga, Nin-kharsak, Nin-ki, Ninkurra, Ninlil, Ninsar, Pidrai, Rabbah, Sandalphon, Semele, Spandaramet, Spentā Ārmaiti, Tiamat, Uras, Uttu, Yechidah, Zaliyanu, Zam, Zamin, Zamyad

North America
Ackwin, Ahgishanakhou, Alarana, Apache Woman, Arnarquáshaaq, Asintmah, Bah-bah-deed, Bear Daughter, Black Butte, Blackfoot Earth Woman, Bright Star, Buffalo Wife, Chuginadak, Chup, Coeur D'Alene Mother, Dah-ko-beed, Dzelarhons, Ee-loolth, Eithinoha, Elihino, Escheman, Fox Earth Goddess, Grandmother, Grandmother Earth, Grandmother of Nava, Gyhldeptis, Hatai Wuhti, Hayicanako, Hishikoyatsaspa, Hutsipamamau?u,

Huzru Wugti, Ikas, Inuit Earth Mother, Ixuixiwi, Keresan Sisters, Kivish Atakvish, Klah Klahnee, Kokyan Wuhti, Leelinau, Loo-wit, Maja, Maka, Mandan Mother, Masakamekokiu, Mesakamigokwaha, Mo'n-sho'n, Muyinwu-wugti, Naasun, Naëstsán, Nahosdzaan Esdza, Nan chu Kweejo, Nangkwijo, Neegyauks, Netcensta, Noesarnak, Nokomis, Nonā'osqa, Norwan, No-wa-mu, Nunam-chua, Nunuoska, Old Woman Night, Old Woman Who Never Dies, Omaha Earth Mother, Pahpobi Kwiyo, Pahto, Pasom Mana, Plash-plash, Pukimna, Qamaitis, Queskapenek, Superguksoak, Tacoma, Tai-mai-ya-wurt, Tamaayawut, Tamambia, Tamayowut, Ta-no-wish, Tatoosh, Thompson Earth Mother, Thompson Goddesses, Toxwid, Tsitsicinako, Wahkshum, Wasco, Whaht-kay, Yo'o

Northern Europe
Askefruer, Beda, Berchta, Beyla, Bil, Blid, Buschfrauen, Buschgroḇmutter, Buschweiber, Embla, Fangge, Fjorgyn, Frau Frigg, Frid, Frigga, Frimla, Fulla, Gebjon, Gefjun, Hertha, Hlif, Hlodyn, Hludana, Holda, Holla, Horn, Huldra, Hyldemoer, Ingun, Iord, Ivithjar, Jord, Jordegumma, Kunhild, Laufey, Lin, Lofn, Mardal, Metsänneitsyt, Nanna, Nerthus, Rind, Rindr, She-Wolf, Sif, Silige Fraulein, Skialf, Thorgerda, Yngvi

Oceania
Alalahe, Apunga, Ata tangi rea, Audjal, Autran, Dilga, Dzari, Fakahotu, Fefafa, Fenua, Ha pu'u, Hakahotu, Hamuri, Hanitemau, Hau lani, Hau ola, Haumea, Haunu'u, Hina 'ulu 'ōhi'a, Hina'i a'a i te marama, Hine i tapeka, Hine kaikomako, Hine maunga, Hine one, Hine tītamauri, Hine tu a kirikiri, Hine tū a maunga, Hine waoriki, H'llraru, Hoa make i ke kula, Hoi tini, Hotu, Huri mai te ata, Inacho, Jugumishanta, Ka meha i kana, Ka pū o alaka'i, Ka'ao melemele, Kahoupokane, Ka'ōhelo, Kobine, Koevasi, Ku raki, Kumitoga, Laka, Lani loa, Lau ka 'ie'ie, Le fale i le langi, Lejman, Li ara katau, Li mot a lang, Likant en arum, Lilinoe, Lube, Mā 'a'a, Mahora nui a tea, Mai 'u'u, Maile, Maile ha'i wale, Maile kaluhea, Maile lau li'i, Maile pā haka, Mar'rallang, Mingari, Minma mingari, Moitjinka, Mudungkala, Mumuhanga, Nā maka o kaha'i, Ne te re'ere, Ngaore, Nungeena, 'Ohu tū moua, One u'i, Pakoti, Paninduela, Papa, Papatea, Pare, Pa'u o 'pala'e, Pekai, Pele, Pere, Pito 'ura, Po'ele, Pu te hue, Pu whakahara, Puhavao atua, Purlimil, Pu'uhele, Queensland First Woman, Rangahore, Rau 'ata'ati, Rau 'ata'ura, Rau penapena, Rau 'ata mea, Rea, Rerenoa, Riri tuna rai, Ruma'u Ari'i, Tahunui, Tauwhare kiokio, Te anoa, Te

ku whaka hara, Te kui u'uku, Tei
Tituaabine, Tere hē, Tereteth, Tshikaro,
Tu wae rore, Tukuhali, Uhalaoa,
Ukwa'anija, U'uhoa, Wari ma te takere,
Yama enda

South America
Atoja, Ceiuci, Cocamama,
Iavure-cunha, Jarina,
Jubbu-jang-sangne, Mama Allpa,
Mama Pacha, Nanen, Nungui, Putcha Si

Southeast Asia
Alan, Aninito Ad Chalom, Apna,
Bà-Du'c Chu'a, Banana Maiden, Bisan,
Dagau, Darago, Dua Nggae, Duc Ba,
Duc Thanh Ba, Giriputri, Ibu Pertiwi,
Ina, Indara, Jata, Kalcheng, Lai-oid,
Latu Hila la Balaa, Lumimuut,
Manamoan, Manoid, Moon Mother,
Muk Jauk, Nang Tholani, Ndara,
Phungkam Janun, Prah Thorni,
Prithivi, Rabia, Saptapetala, Saputan,
Satine, Shadip, Shawa Unti Majan,
Shwe Myet Hna, Shwe Na Be, Si
Dayang, Silat, Sitapi, Ta La, Takel, Tana
Ekan, Uban Sanane, Upu Tapene, Upu
Ume, Upunusa, Usi Afu, Ya Tangoi,
Yak, Yak Lepeh

Western Europe
Abnoba, Achall, Aeracura, Áine,
Akerbeltz, Anu, Arduinna, Asiah,
Basa-Andre, Blodeuwedd, Briah,
Cailleach Beara, Cathubodia, Cordelia,
Dervonnae, Druantia, Duillae,
Ebhlinne, Echtghe, Éire, Fangge,
Firamodor, Fótla, Gwyllion, Ith,
Iweridd, Kernababy, Lady of Baza,
Luaths Lurgann, Lurgorr, Magog,
Malkuth, Momu, Náir, Oanuava,
Onuava, Plur na mBan, Stratteli, Tailtu,
Uchtcelbh

Education and Knowledge

Africa
Aja, Ekineba, Inkosazana, Minona

Central America and Mesoamerica
Ahnt Kai', Alaghom Naum,
Comizahual, Grande Ezili, Ix Chebel
Yax, Kwee-kee'kai es-scop'-oh

Eastern Europe
Vila

Egypt
Safekh-aabut, Selk, Seshat, Sofh, Tie

Far East
Ama-terasu-ō-mi-kami, Amitabha,
Aunt Piety, Bilig-un cinadu-kijaghar-a
kuruksen, Chiwash-kor-kamui,
Dashizhi, Dou Mou, Dragon Mother,
Guanyin, Kele-yin ükin tegri, Mirume,
Niu She, Nügua, P'er Ndzi Ssaw Ma,
Pet-ru-ush-mat, Randeng, Turesh
machi, Xiancan, Xiling Shi, Yang Chen,
Zesun

Greek and Roman Empires
Aristobule, Budeia, Carmentis, Circe,
Clio, Daeira, Halimede, Hecate, Mystis,
Polyboulos

The Himalaya
Buddha Dakinis, Dakini Guru, Dorje
Naljorma, Dri-chha-ma, Ekadzati,
Hphreng-ba-ma,
Kando-ye-shes-chogyel, Khadiravani
Tara, Khahdoma, Khadoma Queen,
Manjusris, Prajnaparamita,
rDo-rje-rnal-hbyor-ma, Sangye-khado,
Skyes-bu-ber, Tibetan Sarasvati,
Tsho-gyalma, Vajrayâna Devatas,
Vinasa, Yeshe-khahdoma,
Ye-she-tsho-gyal, Yum-chen-mo,
Zhal-zas-ma

Indian Subcontinent
Anasuya, Ashi, Bharadi, Deshtri,
Devaki, Jatila, Kali, Mahavidya,
Mahavidyas, Mantrikashakti, Medha,
Niti, Prajna, Prajnaparamita,
Priyakarini, Rajarajeshvari, Samjuna,
Sarasvati, Siddha-Yoginis, Siddhis,
Sitatara, Smriti, Vac, Vibudhastris,
Vidyadevis, Vidyadharis

Near East
Abyss Lady, Artemis Ephesus, Aši,
Ecclesia, Ennoia, Ferašti, Gasmu, Hea,
Hidaba, Kathirat, Kista, Lady of the
Abyss, Lilith, Nephesh, Nicostrata,
Nidaba, Nin-anna, Ninsaba, Ninsun,
Rabi'a Al-adawiya, Razishta Cista,
Siduri, Sophia, Tashmetrum, Tashmetu,
Upanayana

North America
Aittsamka, Atbilxaniatlliax, Big Black
Meteor Star, Buffalo Girl, Corn Mother,
Glispa, Grandmother Spider, Hano,
Kokumthena, Kutnahin, Kwa?akuyi-
savepone, Man-el, Momoy,
Nanaqasilakwe, Nulixwemankta,
Ohoyo Osh Chishba, Onenha, Pasowee,
Pawnee First Woman, Qominoqa,
Shro-tu-na-ko, Snutkanals, Somagalags,
Sxapetl, Thompson Goddesses,
Tlitcaplitana, Tsitsicinako, Uretsete,
Uti Hiata

Northern Europe
Eir, Gunnlöd, Saga, Sigrdrifa, Sith,
Snotra, Voluspa, Vor

Oceania
Afekan, Cassowary Mother,
Ganabuada, Goga, Ha'i wahine, Ihi,
Jari, Junkgowa, Karak karak, Koevasi,
Lai'a hana, Lau hu iki, Le gerem,
Meamei, Namita, Narpajin, Ngaljod,
Numma Moiyuk, Nyapilnu, Sherok,
Tāmaumau 'ōrero, Te mehara,
Wawilak, Yhi

South America
Ayar, Nungui, Paxsi, Star Woman

Southeast Asia
Cunda, Dua Nggae, Female Spectres,
Fire Woman, Ja Najek, Nenak Kebajan,
Silewe Nazarata

Western Europe
Aibell, Aoife, Ban Naomha, Beag,
Cailleach Beara, Ceibhfhionn,
Cerridwen, Chokmah, Danu, Emer,
Filia Vocis, Fuwch Frech, Fuwch
Gyfeilioru, Nath, Scáthach, Sinann

Evil

Africa
Greedy Woman, Katarwiri, La-hkima
Oqla, Minona, Qandisa, Tabhi-yiri,
Usiququmadevu, Watamaraka

Central America and Mesoamerica
Christalline, Cihuapipiltin, Diablesse,
Guede Masaka, Iguanuptigili,
Maninupdikili, Olonuptigile, Sukuyan,
Tzitzimime, Tzitzimitl

Eastern Europe
Äijo, Ajatar, Albasta, Anakhai, Arapap,
Avezuha, Baba Yaga, Bithia, Bonto,
Bozaloshtsh, Bukura-e Dheut, Dolya,
Gabjauja, Irlek-khan, Jaja, Jedza,
Jezibaba, Jezinky, Joda-māte,
Khosadam, Khosodam, Kostroma,
Kriksy, Kulshedra, Lauma, Laumé,
Liderc, Likho, Ljubi, Loviatar, Maras,
Mengk, Navki, Nedolya, Nesreča,
Nocnitsa, Ovda, Poldunica, Polednice,
Schilalyi, Šukšendal, Suoyatar,
Szepasszonyok, Tcaridyi, Uldda,
Va-kul, Ved'ma, Vestice, Vodyanoi,
Vyestitsa

Egypt
Ahti, Sag, Sekhet, Serqet, Taourt

Far East
Daxian Furen, Helidi, Kiyo-hime,
Napuri-kor-kamui-kor-matnepo,
Nitat-unarabe, Nupki-ot-mat,
Sarak-kamui, She Mu, Toikunrari-mat,
Ugly Females of Yomi, Yama-omba

Greek and Roman Empires
Acco, Achelois, Aonides, Apaturia,
Apollonis, Arche, Ardalides, Asopo,
Borysthenis, Caca, Cephisso, Empusa,
Empusae, Erato, Eriphyle, Euryale,
Fata, Fata Alcina, Fata Morgana, Fraud,
Gello, Gorgons, Heptapora,
Hippocrenides, Hypate, Ilissiades,
Kakia, Lamia, Lamiae, Laverna,
Maeonides, Melete, Mneiae, Mneme,
Mnemonides, Mormo, Muses, Myrtis of
Anthedon, Neilo, Pandora, Parnassides,
Pegasides, Phaea, Phorcides,
Pimpleides, Polymatheia, Polymnia,
Pyrene, Rhodia, Scylla, Thaleia,
Thelxinoe, Tipoplo, Tritone, Tursa,
Urania

The Himalaya
brDa'i 'phrad, Chu'phrul can,
dBang-bsdud-ma, gSum-brag-ma,

'Gying-dkar-ma, 'Jigs-pa'i-zer-mo-mig-gcig, Khahdoma, Khôn-ma, Lha-ma-yin, Ma-mo, rDo-rje-dpal-gyi yum, Ri-bu-mo, Singhinî, Srinmo, Srog-bdag-mo, Tan-ma, Tonagma, Vyaghrini, Yid-'prog-ma, Yogini

Indian Subcontinent

Arayi, Asapishachikis, Asuris, Bagala, Bhairava, Bhairavi, Bhgavatiamman, Bhima, Bhisana, Bhumiya Rani, Bonga, Bursung, Canda, Caraki, Chakrisvari, Chausathi Yoginis, Churalin, Churel, Cudel, Dakini, Dakinis, Danavis, Danus, Dayan, Devi, Dewel, Durga, Gara Satamai, Gavariamma, Ghosinis, Ghuls, Grahis, Hariti, Hidimba, Himsa, Jalia, Jara, Ka Niangriang, Ka Rih, Ka Ron, Ka Taroh, Karali, Kataputanas, Kati Ankamma, Kinkin, Kottavei, Krodha, Kumbhinasa, Mahasahasrapramardani, Makaris, Manthara, Manusha-Rakshasis, Maridama, Minachiamman, Mohani, Moothevi, Muzamuza, Nagis, Naktamcharis, Nirriti, Nisacharis, Nukulamma, Petni, Pisachis, Pishacha, Pramlocha, Puloma, Putana, Rakshasis, Rakshodhidevatas, Rtuharika, Rudrani, Sadanvas, Sandhya, Sankchinni, Sansari Mai, Saudamani, Shakini, Shakinis, Sringatpadini, Sulochana, Sumu Mung, Tadaka, Taraka, Tari Pennu, Trigata, Trijata, Vandya, Vatsasur, Vinata, Yakshi, Yatudhanis, Yoginis

Near East

Abyzu, Agrat Bat Mahalat, Anaxšti, Ariel, Asmodeus, Asrušti, Az, Broxa, Bushyasta, Celestial Virgin, Dawi, Druǰ, Druxsans, Dughda, Edem, Gula, Hubur, Jahi, Labartu, Lamashtu, Lamasthu, Lilith, Lilithu, Mahalat, Mamitu, Mu•, Nasa, Nasu, Nhang, Pairikas, Pairimaiti, Ruha D'qudsha, Shibbeta, Subeh, Succubus, Taromati, Thepla, Uda, Vatak

North America

?Al?heleqeč, Anog Ite, Arnarquáshaaq, Asin, ?Ašixuč, Atoshle Suyuki, Bapets, Bear Daughter, Dagwanoenyent, Frog Woman, Ga-go-sa Ho-nun-nas-tase-ta, Gnaski, Hakulaq, Irdlirvirisissong, Katyutayuuq, Malaxšišiniš, Na?ackjeii Esdzaa, Nulayuuiniq, Paija, Puwo-win, Red Woman, Soyoko, Spider Woman, Suyuki, Sye-elth, Tcikee Cac Nadleehe, Thompson Goddesses, Tootega, Tsonoqua, Ulala, Unk, Waotunoowase, Wheatchee, Whistling Grandmother, Wind Old Woman, Witch Woman, Woman Who Fell from the Sky

Northern Europe

Berchta, Bilwis, Brunhild, Drude, Frau Welt, Gudrun, Gullveig, Havfru, Heid, Holla, Holle, Mora, Nixen, Seidhkoma, Skogsfru, Skogsjungfru, Yngona

Oceania

Abere, Babamik, Dunawali, Ekeitehua, Harataunga, Hintabaran, Horotata, Julunggul, Karaia i te ata, Kobo Mandalat, Lewa levu, Lewatu momo, Lewatu ni nambua, Mafurere, Mailkun, Mingari, Minma mingari, Mulukuausi, Nabudi, Narama, Nau taufiti, Nevinbimba'au, Nona, Pinuwali, Pufine ma, Sikingimoemoe, Tapuitea, Te mo'o nieve, Tha, Tuapu'u, Tungi'one, Ukwa'anija, Wahini hai, Walipolima

South America

Beru, Pomba Gira, Toru-guenket, Uwan

Southeast Asia

Bake, Con Tinh, Hukloban, Kameian, Kibayen, Langsuir, Po Bya Tikuh, Sigrutan, Silat, Silewe Nazarata, Tagabayan

Western Europe

Aobh, Aoife, Black Annis, Breg, Corra, Corrigan, Dahut, Dames Vertes, Fideal, Fland, Geniti Glinne, Gwrach y Rhibyn, Gwyllion, Hag, Matronit, Mongfhinn, Muirdris, Nahema, Stratteli, Uchtdealbh, Wyvach

Family and Tribes

Africa

Ababa, Abuk, Amauneit, Ani, Aquaba, Bwalya Chabala, Deung Abok, Enekpe, Iyanla, Kono, Kono First Woman, Moombi, Mother of Food, Muhongo, Mweji, Nana Buluku, Niachero, Nummo, Nzima Mother, Odu, Rakembaranu, Unkulunkulu, Uti

Central America and Mesoamerica

Aida Wedo, Claire, Itaba Tahuana, Koo-mah'mm hahs-ay' Tahm, Rutbe, Xmucane

Eastern Europe

Bab'e Kasha, Boldogasszony, Colleda, Dzidzielia, Egle, First Woman, Jumon-ava, Kaldyni-mumas, Kybäi-khotun, Lada, Ot, Togo Musun, Vel'-ava

Egypt

Auset, Hatshepsut, Kahi, Khoemnis, Neith, Selket, Tentyris

Far East

Ama-terasu-ō-mi-kami, Ame-no-uzume, Apemeru-ko-yan-mat Unameru-ko-yan-mat, Bear Woman, Chikisani-kamui, Di Mu, Dou Mou, Eterna, Fuzhou Princess, He Ku, Hongluan Xingjun, Iku-tama-yori-bime, Kamui-fuchi, Meng Jiangnü, Miao Shan, Miyazu-hime, Mu Re, Nü, Nügua, Nunakawa-hime, Nüwa, Ot, Seya-tatara-hime, Ts'i Kuan Niang, Tushan, Xie, Ya-gami-hime, Yu, Yuan, Zhinü

Greek and Roman Empires

Alcmena, Amathaounta, Andromeda, Antinoe, Argimpasa, Assaros, Chthoniae, Cinxia, Cloacina, Conciliatrix, Creusa, Domiduca, Eleuthera, Enarete, Erinyes, Europa, Gaea, Gamelia, Hera, Hestia, Interduca, Juga, Juno, Lares, Larunda, Megaera, Mixoparthenos, Moneta, Orseis, Phratria, Roma, Syzygia, Telphusia, Unxia, Venus, Viriplaca, Zygia

The Himalaya

Mo-lha-mo

Indian Subcontinent

Arani, Arundhati, Avantimatris, Bhagavathi, Bhumiya Rani, Chandi Mata, Chaya, Diti, Gauri, Ghrtaci, Hathay, Inde, Kaikeyi, Kamadhenu, Kannagi, Kanni, Kannimar, Keshini, Kol First Woman, Mariyamman, Na Rip Nom, Rukmini, Sahaganya, Sakuntala, Sarmistha, Satarupa, Sedi, Sena, Sutrooka, Svadha, Tapati, Totala, Ukepenopfu, Virini

Near East

Adnigkishar, Ariel, Beruth, Cybele, Dynamis, Ecclesia, Fravakain, Gephen, Guzhak, Jerah, Mashyoi, Myrrha, Nashak, Ninatta, Ninmu, Tazhak, Wurusemu

North America

Ackwin, Ahe'a, Akycha, Amayicoyondi, Awehai, Bear Woman, Bear Woman and the Fawns, Cactus Grandmother, Chup, Deer Woman, Djigonsasee, Djilaqons, Dogrib First Woman, Foam Woman, Gahondjidahonk, Genetaska, Godasiyo, Grandmother of Nava, Grizzly Bear Mother, Korawini?i, Man-el, Minnehaha, Poo?wavi, Rhpisunt, Sussistinnako, Tcho, Uretsete, Utctsityi, Yelukxinang

Northern Europe

Ahnfrau, Amma, Baduhenna, Baenkhild, Dis, Edda, Frigga, Fylgir, Fylgja, Fylgukona, Hallgerda, Hulda, Hyndla, Lofe, Mothir, Nanna, Signy, Snör, Thir, Var, Vjofn, Vor, Wara

Oceania

Cunnembeillee, Firifiri 'aufau, First Women, Hā'oa'oa, Haumea, Hi asa, Hine ahuone, Hine i tau ira, Hine tītama, Ho'o hoku i ka lani, Jari, Junkgowa, Ka haka ua koko, Ka mo'o 'inanea, Kā'ana'e like, Kāhu rere moa, Kele, Kepa, Koevasi, Lepe a moa, Lewandranu, Longolongovavau, Makunai, Matakerepo, Miru, Mo'o i nanea, Muiu'uleapai, Muri ranga whenua, Naruni, Ngaumataki'one, Niniano, Nona, Numma Moiyuk, Nyapilnu, Osooso, Palabulṭjura, Papa, Parihai, Puckowie, Purlimil, Rā marama, Ra'i ra'i, Rehua, Ruānge, Taka rita, Tāua ki te marangai, Te mo'o nieve, Wari ma te takere, Wawilak, Yeenapah

South America
First Woman, Maisö, Mama Quilla, Peruvian Mamas, Shell Woman, Star Woman, Temioua

Southeast Asia
A Mong, Fire Woman, Gaygayoma, Rabia, Ratih, Si Rapan, Sisina, Thusandi, Todlibon, Yak Tanggoi

Western Europe
Arbha, Aufaniae, Banba, Band Goddesses, Bean Sídhe, Benzozia, Boann, Brigantia, Britannia, Cailleach Beara, Cameira, Caoineag, Cesair, Cethlenn, Conan of Cuala, Danu, Dobhinia, Domnu, Ëire, Fays, Fótla, Ialysa, Ilazki, Iweridd, Lady of Baza, Linda, Lusitanian Goddess, Macha, Malkuth, Mughain, Naas, Nabia, Scota, Sequana, Serreta de Alcoy Mother Goddess, Tea, Tephi, Veleda, Wylgeforte

Fate

Africa
Atida, Egungun-oya, Gbadu, Minona, Nana Jakpa, Nomkubulwana, Odu, Ogboinba, Tamuno

Central America and Mesoamerica
Aida Wedo, Chantico, Masaya, Oxomoco, Xmucane

Eastern Europe
Ajysit, Ayisit, Bozaloshtsh, Caccejienne, Chuma, Dekla, Dolya, Fatit, Kaltas-anki, Karta, Kikimora, Kuga, Kybäi-khotun, Laima, Laumé, Mora, Narechnitsa, Narucnici, Nelaima, Nesreča, Ore, Pört-kuva, Puges, Rodjenice, Rozanice, Rozdenici, Rozhanitsy, Smrtnice, Sojenice, Sreča, Sudbina, Sudice, Sudička, Sudicky, Sudjaje, Sudjenice, Urme, Vagneg-imi, Viz-anya, Vizi-leany

Egypt
Meshkent, Meskhent, Shait

Far East
Ame-no-sade-yori-hime, Corner Goddess, Dou Mou, Maozi Shenju, Mifuto-hime, Omiya-hime, Shi-nun-manuri, Ts'i Kuan Niang

Greek and Roman Empires
Acaviser, Achaea, Actaea, Adrastea, Aegeria, Aesa, Agave, Aglaope, Aglaopheme, Albuna, Alimede, Amphinome, Amphithoe, Amphitrite, Ananke, Anna Perenna, Antevorta, Antinoe, Aphrodite, Apseudes, Arethusa, Asia, Atropos, Avernales, Bateia, Beroe, Brizo, Cale, Caliadne, Callianassa, Callianeira, Carmentis, Cassotis, Cataclothes, Cer, Ceres, Chlidanope, Choro, Cleochareia,

Clotho, Clymene, Cranto, Cydippe, Cymatolege, Decuma, Deiopea, Deiphobe, Dero, Dexamene, Dione, Dorides, Doris, Doto, Drimo, Echenais, Eleionomae, Eudia, Eudora, Eugora, Eumolpe, Eurydice, Evagora, Evan, Evarne, Fatum, Glauce, Glauconome, Glauke, Glaukonome, Halsodyne, Harmonia, Heimarmene, Helice, Hera, Hipponoe, Hippothoe, Ianassa, Ianeira, Ione, Iphianassa, Iphthime, Kallianassa, Kallianeira, Kranto, Kymatolege, Lachesis, Laomedeia, Lasa, Lasas, Leiagora, Leucosia, Leucothoe, Ligeia, Lilaea, Limnatides, Limnoreia, Lybica, Lyco, Lycorias, Lykorias, Lysianassa, Maera, Maira, Manto, Mean, Melite, Menippe, Moirae, Molpe, Moneta, Naiades, Nausithoe, Necessitas, Neomeris, Nereides, Nereis, Nesaea, Neso, Nete, Nymphae Infernae Paludis, Ocyrrhoë, Oenoie, Oreithyia, Panope, Parcae, Parthenope, Pasithea, Pepromene, Pherusa, Phyllodoce, Plexaure, Ploto, Polynoe, Polynome, Polyxo, Pontomedusa, Porrima, Pronoë, Prorsa, Protho, Proto, Protogenia, Proversa, Sirens, Speio, Thaleia, Thelxiepeia, Thoë, Thriae, Tiburtis, Timandra, Xantho

The Himalaya
'Brog-bza'-lha-icam-ma, bTsan-Idan-blo-sgron-ma, dMag-zor-ma, Kurukulle, Lha-mo-gos-dkar-ma, mThing-gi-zhal-bzang-ma, Nor-rgyun-ma, Pelden Lhamo, Ral-gcig-ma, Srimati

Indian Subcontinent
Hidimba, Kolapuriamma, Lairmena, Mahakali, Mata, Niyati, Purvachitti, Putana, Trisala

Near East
Ashi-oxsho, Bathkol, Eimaramene, Gatamdug, Gulses, Husbishag, Irsirra, Istustaya, Mamitu, Meni, Minu Anni, Nicostrata, Ninmea, Ninsaba, Papaya, Paqhat, Rusa, Seimia, Shimti, Shintalimeni

North America
Asin, Has-gueme

Northern Europe
Ahnfrau, Berchta, Dis, Disir, Fylgja, Fylgukona, Giptes, Hyndla, Idisi, Juks-akka, Nixen, Norns, Oddibjord, Sar-akka, Skuld, Thorgerdr Holgarbrudr, Uks-akka, Urd, Valkyries, Verdandi, Voluspa, Volva, Weißen Frauen

Oceania
'Aiāru, Arimata, 'Elepaio, 'Ere'ere fenua, Hina tahu tahu, Kapo, Lahi wahine, Lani wahine, Ligifo, Minma milbali, Niniganni, Pele'ula, Tha, Vinaka

South America
Paxsi

Southeast Asia
Bugan Nak Amtalao, Bugan Nak Hinumbian, Dara Ensing Tamaga, Dinonganan, Kumang, Magapid, Njai Lora Kidoul

Western Europe
Aerfon, Arianrhod, Badb, Bé Find, Bean Sídhe, Caoineag, Cethlenn, Corra, Corrigan, Coventina, Cyhiraeth, Dee, Deirdre, Dubh Lacha, Dubhlaing, Ethlinn, Fedelm, Fedelma, Feithline, Gwrach y Rhibyn, Levarcham, Nigheag Na H-ath, Scáthach, Smirgat, Veleda, Weird Sisters, Wyrdes

Fire

Africa
Ewuraba, Mousso Koroni Koundye, Randa, Tsetse

Central America and Mesoamerica
Anne, Candelaria, Chantico, Dabaiba, Grande Ezili, Masaya, Takótsi Nakawé, Tāté Naaliwámi, Xcanul

Eastern Europe
Aspelenie, Colleda, Dhavata, Fadza-mama, Firebird, Gabija, Kupal'nitsa, Kupalo, Kutug:a, Lamaria, Liderc, Locid-epie, Munya, Nay-Ekva, Ot, Ot-änä, Oynyena Maria, Panike, Perkune Tete, Polengabia, Ponyke, Poza-mama, Sabaga, Sakhala, Tabiti, Tarn, Togo Musun, Tol-ava, Tul-awa, Tuurman, Uguns-māte, Umai, Unchi-ahchi, Ut, Vir-ava, Yegiled-emei

Egypt
Amit, Gate-keeping Goddesses, Khoemnis, Neserit, Sekhmet, Uatchet

Far East
Apemeru-ko-yan-mat Unameru-ko-yan-mat, Fuji, Hettsui-no-kami, Hi-no-haya-hi-no-mikoto, Huchi-fuchi, Iresu-huchi, Iwa-tsutsu-no-me-no-mikoto, Jie, Kalapiat, Kamui-fuchi, Konohana-sakuya-hime, Li, Ot, Perasia, Shandian Pozi, Tian Mu Niangniang, Unchi-ahchi, Xiu Wenyin, Yal-un eke

Greek and Roman Empires
Aetna, Caca, Camenae, Hestia, Phosphoros, Pyronia, Vesta, Vesuna Erinia

The Himalaya
dGra-lha-thab-lha-g•yu-mo, dPal-gyi-pho-nya-las-mkhan-mo, Glog-bdag-mo, gLu-ma Ghirdhima, Me'-ilha-mo Gos-dkar-ma, sNang-gsal-ma, Thab-lha-g•ui-mo, Thab-lha-g•yu-mo

Indian Subcontinent
Adhararani, Agnayi, Agwani, Angarmati Bhawani, Arani, Assam Mother Earth, Ausinari, Biliku, Davata,

Dhisana, Dhumavati, Durga, Holika, Ka Ding, Pandara, Parashakti, Rangda, Saudamani, Shamidevi, Urvasi, Uttararani, Vana, Vidyujjvalakarali

Near East
Āl, Pari, Sister Fire, Umai

North America
Chuginadak, Chup, Gahondjidahonk, Gogyeng So Wuhti, Grandmother Spider, Haka Lasi, Ignirtoq, Ingnirtungl, Kanaeski Anaiyehi, Kefeliu, Loo-wit, Nautsiti, Sussistinnako, Thompson Goddesses, Three Kadlu Sisters, Tsitsicinako, Yolkai Estsan

Northern Europe
Einmyria, Eisa, Gerda, Glut, Griep, Gunnlöd, Hervor, Holla, Imdr, Menglad, Sinmora, Vana Mothers

Oceania
Arutaruta tāmaumau auahi, Bila, Bumerali, Fire Goddess, Gnowee, Goga, Haumea, Hina ke ahi, Hina mahuia, Hina nui te'ara'ara, Hina te 'a'ara, Hine i tapeka, Hine kaikomako, Hine te uria, Honabe, Ihi awa'awa, Ihi lani, Jari, Junkgowa, Kā'ana'e like, Kafisi, Karak karak, Kuilioloa, Kurikuta, Ma hui e, Mafuike, Mahuea, Meamei, Nā maka o kaha'i, Nge'obiongo, Pare, Pele, Pere, Pufine i ravenga, Star Girl, Te anoa, Te vahine nui tahu ra'i, Ubu, Vahine nui tahu ra'i

South America
Rainha Barba, Topétine

Southeast Asia
Darago, Fire Woman, Mae Phra Phloeng, Mekala, Saputan, Silat

Western Europe
Aibheaog, Auge, Belisma, Brigantia, Brigid, Phlox, Tres Matres

Fishing and Water Animals

Africa
Abenawa, Afrékété, Dada, Mukasa, Olosa

Central America and Mesoamerica
Centeotl, Chalchiuhtlicue, Huechaana, Kwelopunyai, Nohuichana, Olokum, Olosa, Tlaltecuhtli

Eastern Europe
Akkruva, Avfruvva, Bereginy, Cherlak, Cinei-new, Kul, Mere-ama, Mokosh, Näkki, Ragana, Siriny, Veden emä, Vüt-kuva, Yaumau-hadaku

Egypt
Hatmehit, Heket, Heru-pa-kaut, Mehiti, Naham-ua, Nehemcou

Far East
Ami-tanne-mat, Chiwashekot-mat, Funadama-sama, He Ku, Ichiki-shima-hime-no-mikoto,

Kisagai-hime, Kwannon, Ma Zu, Ma Zupo, Ningyo, Pet-ru-ush-mat, Takiri-bime-no-mikoto, Takitsu-hime-no-mikoto, Tian Hou, Turesh, Umugi-hime

Greek and Roman Empires
Amphitrite, Britomartis, Brizo, Chelone, Dictynna, Doto

Indian Subcontinent
Adrika, Alambusha, Angana, Anoi Diggan Juje, Apsarases, Auksagandhi, Bhagirathamma, Bhairava, Caksusi, Cana Aulola, Cana Palak, Chaurashi Devi, Gara Satamai, Ghrtaci, Gramadevatas, Guggulu, Harbadevi, Harini, Ira, Jamadagni, Jassuju, Ka Blei Sam Um, Keshini, Khala Kumari, Kshiti-apsarases, Lavangi, Madhava, Mahadevi, Mahagramadevata, Makaris, Malini, Manasi, Marisha, Mena, Mina, Misrakesi, Mother Fish, Naladi, Orusandiamma, Pae Devi, Pramandani, Pramlocha, Pururavas, Purvachitti, Rajamma, Rambha, Rati, Sahaganya, Samalamma, Sanumati, Sasilekha, Saudamani, Sukanthi, Surabhidatta, Surapamsula, Tilottama, Uravari, Urvasi, Vadaba, Vasistha, Veyyi Kannula Ammavaru, Yerenamma

Near East
Atargatis, Dagon, Derketo, Ishara, Nanshe, Nazi, Nina

North America
Asdzaa Yoolgai, Atbilxaniatlliax, Blue Jay, Bright-Cloud Woman, Frog Woman, Hekoolas, Hürü'Ingwühti, Ikalu nappa, Imam-shua, Iqalu Nappaa, Itclixyan, Kannakapfaluk, Katuma, Ketq Skwayne, Kohak Oka, Maskikhwsu, Noogumee, Nuliajuk, Olungwa, Ostkahakakaitshoidiaa, Sedna, Skagit Grandmother, Tacoma, Tsatsaquitelaku, Unk, Yolkai Estsan

Northern Europe
Thorgerdr Holgarbrudr

Oceania
Arimata, Baabenga, Bonito Maidens, Faumea, Hau wahine, Hina, Hina hele, Hina oio, Hina 'ōpū hala ko'a, Hina puku i'a, Hina'ai ka malama, Hina'i ke kā, Hina'ōpū hala ko'a, Hine popo, Hine takurua, Hine tu a tai, Hit, Hoku kau opae, Ihu koko, Junkgowa, Ka 'ahu pāhau, Ka ihu anu, Ka ihu koa, Ka ihu kuuna, Ka ihu o pala'ai, Kāne kua'ana, Kaukau, Kiha wahine, Kobo Mandalat, Kwouk kwouk, Laenihi, Latmikaik, Le hev hev, Mālei, Manana, Moana nui ka lehua, Mo'o, Muriwhakaroto, Nei nguiriki, Nei te tauti, Nigoubub, Niniano, Nisoukepilen, Palabultjura, Po'ele, Porpoise Girl, Powehiwehi, Pua ina noa, Rauei, Rua tamaine, Sina, Taisumalie, Tere hē, Toa hakanorenore, Tobukulu, Tonu tai, Tuapu'u

South America
Asima Si, Ina, Jamaina, Mama Cocha, Mariana, Shell Woman, Urpihuachac, Uwan

Southeast Asia
Bà Ngu', Rajah Jewata, Suvarnamacha

Western Europe
Ban Naomha, Benvarry, Zaden

Goodness

Africa
Dziva, Mawu, Mella, Minona, Obasi Nsi, Sabulana, Tingoi

Central America and Mesoamerica
Coyolxauhqui, Grande Ezili, Ix Chel, Loa

Eastern Europe
Budung-yihe-ibe, Bukura-e Dheut, Cinderella, Dolya, Ja-neb'a, Kostroma, Lauma, Lesni Zenka, Madder-akku, Nalban-aiy, Nalygyr-aissyt-khotun, Ore, Ot, Vir-ava, Ya-nebya

Egypt
Merseger, Nahmauit, Reret, Thoeris, Tmei

Far East
Dainichi-nyorai, Dara Eke, Guanyin, Hashinau-kor-kamui, Kongde, Ku-doku-niyo, Kwannon, Kwanseieun, Ma Gu, Okame, Ot, Patrinia, Ro-tara-ni-bi, T'o-lo, Ts'i Ma Niang Tsai, Turesh, Umai, Wenchen, White Wave, Xiang, Zhao Sanniang

Greek and Roman Empires
Anesidora, Athena, Befana, Chloris, Cupra, Eleos, Empanada, Eudora, Eulimene, Euploia, Eupompe, Fides, Hecate, Keres, Litae, Macris, Melitodes, Melobosis, Paregoros, Pistis, Salus

The Himalaya
Chags-kyu-ma, Dolma, Dröl-ma, Khadiravani Tara, Ratna Dakinis, Yid-'prog-ma

Indian Subcontinent
Aditya, Adrika, Alakhani, Alambusha, Anala, Angana, Anila, Annapurna, Antariksha, Apsarases, Apu, Auksagandhi, Bhairava, Bibi Miriam, Biliku, Bursung, Caksusi, Camunda, Chakrisvari, Chandra, Daya, Devi, Dhara, Dhruva, Dyu, Ghrtaci, Guggulu, Harini, Hariti, Ira, Jahira Buru, Jamadagni, Kamaksi, Kapenopfu, Keshini, Kripi, Kshama, Kshanti, Kshiti-apsarases, Lavangi, Madhava, Mahamantranusarini, Mahamayuri, Mahapratisara, Mahasahasrapramardani, Mahasitaviti, Maitri, Malini, Manasi, Marisha, Mena, Misrakesi, Mrtyu, Nage-bonga, Nakshatras, Naladi, Narmada, Pancaraksa, Prabhasa, Pramandani, Pramlocha, Pratyusha, Prithivi,

Pururavas, Purvachitti, Rambha, Rati, Sahaganya, Sandhya, Sandi, Sanumati, Sasilekha, Saudamani, Savitri, Sila, Sita, Sri, Sringatpadini, Sruta-Kriti, Sukanthi, Sulochana, Sumitra, Surabhidatta, Surapamsula, Tilottama, Trigana, Trisala, Uravari, Urvasi, Ushnishavijaya, Vadaba, Vandya, Vasistha, Vasus, Yakshi, Yechu

Near East
Asherah, Bau, Celestial Virgin, Dughda, Enthumesis, Ereshkigal, Lamassu, Nanshe, Pari, Shala

North America
'Anltani, Corn Woman, Ee-eh-ch-choo-ri-ch'ahm-nin, Fox Moon Goddess, Kokyan Wuhti, Loha, Na?ackjeii Esdzaa, Ong Wuhti, Ooyarraksakju, Pukkeenegak, Puwo-win, Selu, Shiwanokia, Sinnilktok, Snitsmän-a, Spider Woman, Thompson Goddesses, Tlitcaplitana, Toodlanak, Tsects, Woman Who Fell from the Sky

Northern Europe
Elben, Freyja, Garmangabi, Havfru, Nixen, Siofn, Snotra, Verdandi

Oceania
Hānai'ia ka malama, Julunggul, Tonga maulu'au, Vinaka

South America
Perimbó

Southeast Asia
Amoghasiddhi, Anat, Dara Rambai Geruda, Daterata, Dinonganan, Entelanying, Gitir, Idianale, Ina Onian, Indai Abang, Mendong, Pajau Yan, Pantang Mayang, Puyu, Singgar

Western Europe
Amilamia, Assa, Binah, Black Annis, Ekhi, Lamia, Suleviae, Urganda

Happiness

Africa
Mawu

Central America and Mesoamerica
Ochumare, Xilonen, Xochiquetzal

Eastern Europe
Lada

Egypt
Autyeb, Bast, Hathor, Hetpet

Far East
Ame-no-uzume, Benten, Tui, Yingxi Niang

Greek and Roman Empires
Anna Perenna, Celedones, Elpis, Euphrosyne, Eutychia, Felicitas, Iambe, Komodia, Koros, Spes

The Himalaya
Dorje Naljorma, Red Horse-headed Delight Goddess, Tsho-gyalma, Yellow Bat-headed Delight Goddess

Indian Subcontinent
Asa Poorna, Asapurna, Ashis, Chunda, Devananda, Diwali, Ekajata, Ganga, Grhalaksmi, Hari, Holi, Ka Blai Synshar, Lalita, Nandi, Priti, Rembha, Sitatara

Near East
Ninkasi, Samkhat, Siduri, Tebunah

North America
Bikeh Hozho, Bikeh Xozo, Wohpe

Northern Europe
Blid, Nat

Oceania
Mo'o, Re'are'a, Rua hine metua, Ururupuin

South America
Cocamama, Jarina

Southeast Asia
Suklang-malayon

Western Europe
Fand, Fuwch Frech, Fuwch Gyfeilioru, Gwen

Health and Healing

Africa
Abowie, Aja, Amponyinamoa, Anyigba, Masai Moon Goddess, Mella, Meme, Nawandyo, Nejma, Ogboinba, Oshun, Quabso, 'Uwardaw

Central America and Mesoamerica
Ah Uaynih, Ahnt Kai', Erzulie, Guabonito, Ix Chel, Ix U Sihnal, Ixtab, Loa, Marie-aimée, Orehu, Oshun, Temazcalteci, Teteoinnan, Tlazolteotl, Toci, Tzapotla Tenan

Eastern Europe
Almoshi, Haltia, Maddarakka, Mamaldi, Mastor-ava, Mati-syra-zemlya, Nastasija, Numod-emei, Perit, Piluitus, Pört-kuva, Suonetar, Vila, Yegiled-emei, Zarya, Ziva, Zywie

Egypt
Bast, Isis, Mut, Thoeris, Ubastet

Far East
Ame-no-sade-yori-hime, Baiji, Bixia Yuanjin, Cuisheng Sheng Mu, Deo Ma Niangniang, Dou Mou, Eastern Mother, Ge Gu, Good Sight Lady, Guanyin, Huchi-fuchi, Izu-no-me-no-kami, Kesou Niangniang, Lincui Hu, Ma Gu, Mintuchi-kamui, Nts'ai Hwa, Pan Niang, P'er Ndzi Ssaw Ma, Qi Guzi, Songzi Niangniang, Tama-yori-bime-no-mikoto, Ts'uai-shen Niang Niang, Uba-gami,

Western Mother, Yanguang Pusa, Yanjing Niangniang

Greek and Roman Empires
Agamede, Agrotera, Aigle, Akeso, Alexida, Anagtia, Anceta, Angina, Angitia, Anigrides, Anna Perenna, Aurita, Bateia, Bona Dea, Bormonia, Calaene, Caliadne, Carmentis, Carna, Caryatis, Chlidanope, Cleochareia, Curitis, Echenais, Elasii, Eleionomae, Epione, Febris, Februa, Februlis, Harmonia, Helena, Hygeia, Iasis, Iaso, Iodama, Ionides, Lethe, Leto, Lilaea, Limnatides, Lympha, Maera, Meditrina, Melite, Mephitis, Munthukh, Naiades, Nortia, Oculata Lucifera, Oenoie, Ophthalmitis, Orbona, Ossipaga, Paeonia, Panacea, Pegaeae, Persephone, Pharmacides, Polyxo, Pronoë, Salus, Scabies, Strenia, Thermaia, Thermia, Volumna

The Himalaya
Lha-ma-yin, sGrol-mas, Tan-ma, Vinasa, Yid-'prog-ma

Indian Subcontinent
Aditya, Anala, Anila, Antai, Antariksha, Ap, Apala, Apu, Apvā, Aranya, Aranyani, Asapura, Ashi, Asuris, Bahucharaji, Bhadrakali, Bhagadevi, Bhagirathamma, Bhagirathi, Bisam Thakurani, Chandra, Chigrinad, Chowa, Dhara, Dharni Pinnu, Dhruva, Dyu, Ekastaka, Elamadichi, Ellamma, Ganga, Ganga Devi, Gangamma, Gavariamma, Grhalaksmi, Hadakai, Hakini, Hariti, Howanmata, Huligavva, Hunwarmata, Janguli, Kakini, Kali, Kalumaiamman, Kanaka Durgamma, Kawalkamata, Kodamata, Lakini, Lakshmi, Lalbai Phulbai, Mahakali, Mallana Devi, Manasa, Mayavva, Mena, Moothevi, Mother Globes, Mutyalamma, Nakshatras, Narmada, Nidra, Nona Chamari, Nukalamma, Nukulamma, Pan Dong Cyu, Parnasavari, Parrapotamma, Podamata, Ponniyayi, Prabha, Prabhasa, Pratyusha, Prithivi, Rajamma, RatriIndia, Revali, Rohini, Samaiya, Samalamma, Sasthi, Sat Matra, Sitala, Sitlamata, Sura, Sushumna, Susime, Thakurani Bakorani, Vasus

Near East
Ahurani, Ashi, Aši, Baba, Bau, Dazimus, Drvaspa, Geush Urvan, Gula, Hala, Haurvatāt, Ishtar, Kamrusepas, Ninisinna, Ninkarrak, Ninkasi, Ninkharak, Ninsu-utud, Ninti, Rachmay, Sarpanitu, Sauska, Shataqat, Shibbeta, Sister Fire, Thatmanitu, Thitmanat

North America
Aialila'axa, 'Alaĥtin, Big Black Meteor Star, Corn Mother, Glispa, Haialilaqs, Kattakju, Komwidapokuwia, Ksem-wa'tsq, L'etsa'aplelana, Mesuk

Kummik Okwi, Miritatsiec, Momoy, No'oma Cawaneyung, Nuñda, Nuptadi, Onenha, Pakwaekasiasit, Pasowee, Pinga, Red-spider-woman, Sinnilktok, Snitsmän-a, Takanakapsaluk, Tlitcaplitana, Uretsete, Widapokwi

Northern Europe
Askefruer, Buschgroþmutter, Eastre, Eir, Folla, Frua, Fulla, Gebjon, Groa, Hexe, Hyldemoer, Sigrdrifa, Sindgund, Snotra, Sunna, Wilden Wip

Oceania
Ai Tūpua'i, Hau wahine, Hina 'ea, Hina lau limu kala, Hina tahu tahu, Kagauraha, Kāne kua'ana, Kuku 'ena i ke ahi ho'omau honua, Nā keo lani, Niniano, Te vahine nui tahu ra'i, Uli

South America
Apolonia, Cocamama, Llacsahuato, Mama Cocha, Mariana, Mirahuato, Senhora Ana

Southeast Asia
Dinawagan, Hukloban, Ini Manang, Katsin Numka Majan, Manang Jaban, Mande Rubiah, Pajau Yan, Po Yan Dari

Western Europe
Airmed, Akerbeltz, Arenmetia, Argante, Avantia, Bibi, Biddy Mannion, Bormana, Borvonia, Brigid, Ceacht, Damona, Ëtain, Fand, Fuwch Frech, Fuwch Gyfeilioru, Griselicae Nymphae, Habetrot, Laha, Lahe, Lebharcham, Macha, Minerva Medica, Modron, Moriath, Muirenn, Niamh, Segeta, Sequana, Setlocenia, Sul, Visuna

Heaven and Hell

Africa
Ama, Ani, Asaase Aberewa, Asase Afua, Asase Yaa, Marwe, Nyale, Sama Bolowa

Central America and Mesoamerica
Chalmecacihuatl, Cihuateteo, Citlalicue, Ixtab, Manideakdili, Mictanteot, Mictecacihuatl, Mictlancihuatl, Mu Alesop, Mu Olokundil, Mu Olotagisop, Mu Olotakiki, Mu Sobia, Nana Olokegepiai, Nana Olomaguyriai, Olodeakdili, Olokanigidilisop, Olokikadiryae, Olokukurtilisop, Olonuptigile, Oloueaidili, Olouiknidilisop, Punauaga Oloeaydili, Punauaga Oloesgidili, Punauaga Oloibiyalisop, Punauaga Olokurgililiae, Punauaga Oloniskidilisop, Punauaga Olouagaidili, Punauaga Uisogdili, Tëtewan, Xonaxi Quecuya, Xquic

Eastern Europe
Ajysit, Alencica, Alkonost, Ama, Bukura-e Dheut, Jabme-akka, Jabmeks, Kipu-tytto, Pohjan-akka, Puges,

Santaramet, Tuonetar, Vammatar, Velu-māte

Egypt
Ahemait, Akert-khentet-auset-s, Amaunet, Amemet, Amenet, Ament, Amenti, Amit, Ammit, Amn, Anenit, Apet, Aukert, Clother, Erpuit Goddesses, Gate-keeping Goddesses, Goddess-greatly-beloved-with-red-hair, Goddess-joined-unto-life-with-flowing-hair, Hak, Hast, Hathor, Henemet-em-anh-annuit, Hentet-arqiu, Her-tept, Hert-ketit-s, Hetep-sekhus, Het-kau-nebt-er-tcher, Kebechet, Khebent, Khemit, Khenememtit, Khera, Khoemnis, Lady of Amenta, Ma, Maât, Manefertrā, Mehen, Mehenit, Meh-khebitet-seh-neter, Mehueret, Menkheret, Menqet, Merseger, Mert, Merti, Meshkent, Meskhent, Nebt, Nebt-er-tcher, Nebt-unnut, Nehebka, Neith, Nephthys, Nesi-khonsu, Qebhsnuf, Renenet, Rennutet, Repa, Sa, Sah, Satet, Seba, Sefkhabu, Sekhemet-ren-s-em-abet-s, Sekhet, Sekhet-bast-ra, Sekhet-hetepet, Sekhmet, Sekseket, Selket, Sentait, Sesenet-khu, Seshat, Seshetet, Seven Kine-deities, Shenat-pet-utheset-neter, Sheta, Sothis, Sycamore Tree Goddess, Tait, Taninit, Taourt, Taueret, Tayt, Tchesert, Tefnut, Tenemet, Tesert, Thenenet, Thoeris, Tmei, Ua, Uadjet, Uatchet, Unen-em-hetep, Ur-mertu-s-teshert-sheni, Whose-name-is-mighty-in-her-works

Far East
Ame-no-toko, Blue Lotus, Can Nü, Corpse Goddesses, Eterna, Hisa-me, Izanami-no-kami, Jiutinan Xuannu, Ma Gu, Mazu, Meng Po Niangniang, Miao Shan, Ming, Oto, Pang Che, Pang Jiao, Pang Zhu, Shandian Pozi, Suseri-bime-no-mikoto, Tai Yuan, Xuehu Niangniang, Yomo-tsu-shiko-me

Greek and Roman Empires
Acholoe, Avernales, Campe, Celaeno, Cretan Snake Goddess, Culsa, Erinyes, Harpies, Inferna, Kelaino, Kulsu, Lara, Lelaino, Lethe, Lyssa, Mania, Megaera, Meilichia, Melinoe, Menthe, Mixoparthenos, Nicothoe, Nymphae Infernae Paludis, Nyx, Persephone, Podarge, Proserpina, Prosymna, Snake Goddess of Knossos, Styx, Telphusia, Tuchulcha

The Himalaya
Bardo Goddesses, bDug-spös-ma, Black Crow-headed One, Black Cuckoo-headed Mystic Goddess, Black Petali, Black Sow-headed Sow Goddess, Black Vixen-headed One, Blue Monkey-headed Goddess of Inquisitiveness, Blue Serpent-headed Water Goddess, Blue Wolf-headed Wind Goddess, Buddha Krotishaurima, Cha-dog-ma, Chags-kyu-ma,

Clear-light Mother, Dark-blue Owl-headed One, Dark-blue Smasha, Dark-blue Wolf-headed One, Dark-brown Lion-headed One, Dark-brown Yak-headed Rakshasa Goddess, Dark-green Fox-headed Baton Goddess, Dark-green Ghasmari, gLu-ma Ghirdhima, Gokarmo, Green Deer-headed Wealth-guardian Goddess, Greenish-black Elephant-headed Big-nosed Goddess, Greenish-black Leopard-headed Great Goddess, Greenish-black Serpent-headed Mystic Goddess, Greenish-black Vulture-headed Eater Goddess, Hphreng-ba-ma, Htamenmas, Karma Dakinis, Karma-krotishaurima, Khahdoma, Kuntu-bzang-mo, Lha-ma-yin, Mâmakî, Manjusris, Me-tog-ma, Nam-kha-ing-kya-wang-chug-ma, Padma Dakinis, Padma Krotishaurima, Pândurâ, Pukkase, Ratna Krotishaurima, Red Crow-headed Thunderbolt Goddess, Red Hoopoe-headed Desire Goddess, Red Horse-headed Delight Goddess, Red Ibex-headed Woman Goddess, Red Lion-headed Mystic Goddess, Red Makara-headed Peaceful Goddess, Red Pramoha, Red Pukhase, Red Scorpion-headed Amrita Goddess, Red Snow-bear-headed Virgin Goddess, Red Tiger-headed One, Reddish-yellow Serpent-headed Brahma Goddess, Sangs-rgyas-spyan-ma, Sangye-khado, sGrol-mas, Smasha, sNang-gsal-ma, Til-bu-ma, Tsandhali, Tseurima, Vajra Krotishaurima, Wang-Chugmas, White Bear-headed Indra Goddess, White Eagle-headed Mighty Goddess, White Kerima, White Kite-headed Moon Goddess, Yellow Bat-headed Delight Goddess, Yellow Dog-headed Rakshasi, Yellow Goat-headed Mystic Goddess, Yellow Tseurima, Yellowish Bird-headed One, Yellowish-black Tiger-headed Rakshasi, Yellowish-white Tsandhali, Zhag-pa-ma

Indian Subcontinent
Asuris, Devayani, Ganga, Kine Nane, Lakshmi, Manasa, Nagis, Nirriti, Prajnaparamita, Sarparajni, Sarpis, Sasana-devi, Satyabhama, Siddhanganas, Sodasi, Tripura Bhairavi, Tsun Kyanske, Ulupi, Vinata, Yanta

Near East
Allat, Allatu, Ana, Aretz, Arsai, Arsay, Astarte, Atum, A-zi-mu-a, Baalith, Belili, Belit Seri, Daena, Ereshkigal, Eve, Fravashis, Gestinanna, Houri, Husbishag, Inanna, Irkalla, Ishtar, Istehar, Istustaya, Lelwani, Machalath, Metsulah, Milkath, Nane, Nin-anna, Ninazu, Nindukugga, Ningizzida, Ninlil, Ninsikilla, Papaya, Pari, Qlippoth, Sabitu, Samai, Scorpion

Woman, Shachuth, Sheol, Spandaramet, Yechidah

North America
Animal Mother, Cochiti Mother, Ghost-Face-Woman, Glispa, Hakulaq, Heavy Woman, Iyatiku, Katuma, Large Woman, Nuliajuk, Pana, Punauaga Oloeaydili, Qamaitis, Sedna, Takanakapsaluk, Tcua-wugti, Ullughmiut, Yatahéntshi

Northern Europe
Angerbodha, Geirahod, Gullveig, Hella, Holla, Kunhild, Modgud, Syn, Tuonetar, Valkyries

Oceania
Bulaing, Buring une, Dirivo, Fai malie, Hanau, Havea lolo fonua, Hikuleo, Hina mataone, Hine a te po, Hine i tau ira, Hine nui te pō, Hine ruaki moe, Hine tītama, Hou heana, Kara ma kuna, Karaia i te ata, Kewelu, Kobine, Kume, Kura, Le hev hev, Li char, Longolongovavau, Lorop, Mafuike, Maru a nuku, Maru a roto, Milu, Miru, Miru kura, Nafanua, Nuvarahu, Pani, Parekōritawa, Po, Rima horo, Rohe, Satene, Sinebomatu, Tango tango, Taranga, Tepotatango, Tilafainga, Whaitiri

South America
Ituana

Southeast Asia
Abyang Durunuun, Akodau, Alunsina, Aninito Ad Chalom, Arud, Balu Adad, Bia-ka-pusud-an-langit, Bia-t'oden, Dewi Melanting, Djata, Gayak, Gendui Lanyut, Ibu, Indo I Laoe, Jata, Ju Puteur, Kumang, Lepeh, Luyong Baybay, Luyong Kabig, Makawalang, Manolge inBahiwag, Mebuyan, Mulua Satene, Nama Djang Ad Chalom, Ndara, Penaban Sari, Rangda, Sagar, Sanghyang Ibu Pertiwi, Satine, Saweigh, Setesuyara, Takel, Ungap, Ya Monoij, Yak Chin, Yak Lepeh

Western Europe
Ataecina, Bécuma, Cliodhna, Créide Fírálaind, Dea Domnann, Dechtiré, Eo-Anu, Feithline, Gorddu, Náir, Niamh, Samhain, Wylgeforte

Household Affairs

Africa
Ayaba

Central America and Mesoamerica
Anne, Chantico, Goddess "O", Grande Ezili, Ichpuchtli, Ix Chebel Yax, Ix Chel, Ix Hun Tah Nok, Ixtab, Nohuichana, Teresa, Tlazolteotl, Xochiquetzal

Eastern Europe
Aspelenie, Dugnai, Gabija, Haltia, Jurt-ava, Jurt-azerava, Kardas-ś Arko, Kikimora, Krimba, Kud-ava, Kuutar,

Lamaria, Laugo-edne, Lauma, Laumé, Lymyzn-mam, Marà, Maruchi, Matergabia, Mokosh, Mokuskha, Nishke-ava, Niski-ava, Numod-emei, Ot-änä, Paivatar, Polengabia, Pört-kuva, Possjo-akka, Rana Nedia, Sarakka, Saule, Šukšendal, Tartary and Cathay Earth Goddess, Tuurman, Uksakka, Unchi-ahchi, Ut

Egypt
Mafdet, Neith

Far East
Apemeru-ko-yan-mat Unameru-ko-yan-mat, Bixiao, Chuang Mu, Embroidery Goddess, Fuji, Guodeng, Hani-yasu-bime-no-kami, Hettsui-no-kami, Huchi-fuchi, Izumo Pantheon Deities, Jie, Kamu-hata-hime, Kamui-fuchi, Keng San Gu, Keng San Guniang, Kenru-katkimat, Kitchen Range Goddess, Lei-zi, Liu Zu, Maozi Shenju, Moire-mat, Oki-tsu-hime, Qiongxiao, Qixian Niangniang, Shi, Shu-koyan-mat, Tartary and Cathay Earth Goddess, Turesh machi, Unchi-ahchi, Wakahirume-no-mikoto, Xiancan, Xu Tianju, Yunxiao, Zhinü, Zigu Shen

Greek and Roman Empires
Athena, Cardea, Dactyls, Deverra, Ergatis, Giane, Hestia, Intercidona, Klothes, Lina, Minerva, Molae, Numina, Panatis, Pandrosos, Pilumnus, Tanaquil, Vesta, Vesuna Erinia

The Himalaya
dGra-lha-thab-lha-g•yu-mo, Mo-lha-mo, Thab-lha-g•ui-mo, Thab-lha-g•yu-mo

Indian Subcontinent
Ankamma, Annapurna, Ayepi, Bagula, Bala, Bettada Chicama, Candasya Naptyas, Chigrinad, Chinnintamma, Devatas, Digdevatas, Dilli Polasi, Ghar Jenti, Grhadevi, Grhalaksmi, Grihadeva, Jakhmata, Jara, Ka Ksaw Ka Jirngam, Ka 'Lei Iing, Ka Rasong, Ka Taben, Kelu Devaru, Khulungma, Kitro Bai, Kubjika, Kul Devi, Kumbhamata, Kumbhinasa, Lohasur, Ma Dharti, Mainao, Mantradevatas, Paniharin, Pos Bai, Sadanvas, Savadamma, Sevasti-devi, Siniboi

Near East
Hambarus, Hushiti, Labartu, Umai, Uttu

North America
Chuhna, Cisiud, Na?ackjeii Esdzaa, Pasowee, Pawnee First Woman, Pukkeenegak, Sussistinnako, Wild Pony

Northern Europe
Berchta, Dörr-Käring, Einmyria, Eisa, Fangge, Freitag, Frigga, Glut, Holda, Holla, Norns, Syn

Oceania
Fire Goddess, Ha'i, Hakumani, Hina, Hina 'ea, Hina kuku kapa, Hina papa i kua, Hina'i a'a i te marama, La'a hāna, Lai'a hana, Lau hu iki, Marei kura, Mele, Nahinahi ana, Nge'obiongo, Nisarere, Nyapilnu

South America
Ocllo

Southeast Asia
Baitpandi, Benih Lela Punggang Tengian Dara Bintang Tiga Datai Ka Jelan, Bugan inKinulhudan, Bugan inMonkulabe, Bugan inPunholdaiyan, Bugan inUldi, Entelanying, Gitir, Indai Abang, Lulong, Mele, Mendong, Pudau, Puyu, Singgar, Srintun Tanah Tumboh Yak Srindak Tanggi Buloh, Suklang-malayon, Tolus Ka Talegit

Western Europe
Bean Nighe, Brigid, Brigindo, Emer, Glaistig, Habetrot, Nantosvelta, Silkie

Hunting and Wild Animals

Africa
Anyigba, Atida, Coti, Dorina, Eveningstar of Wakaranga, Huntu Katt! Katten, Ises, Kuanja, Kyanwa, Morongo, Thamuatz

Central America and Mesoamerica
Ah Wink-ir Masa, Comizahual, Hunahpu-Vuch, Nohuichana, Quilaztli, Xmucane

Eastern Europe
Bereginy, Bird and Eye Goddess, Briežu-māte, Debena, Devana, Diiwica, Dziewona, Ganis, Illibem Berti, Louhi, Luot-hozjik, Mary-rusalka, Mielikki, Poshjo-akka, Pots-hozjik, Rana Nedia, Sarakka, Schilalyi, Tuulikki, Viranakka, Vir-ava, Zvoruna

Egypt
Anatha Baetyl, Apet, Êpet, Hentet-arqiu, Ipet, Kenemet, Mafdet, Mehit, Menat, Menhit, Mihit, Neith, Nit, Renenet, Reret, Satet, Sekhet, Sekhmet, Ser-t, Sheput, Taueret, Thoeris, Ubastet, Unnit, Urt-hekau

Far East
Feng Po, Hashinau-kor-kamui, Hash-inau-uk-kamui, Horkeu-kamui, Inari, Inoshishi, Kamui-menoko, Kerep-nove, Kuzo-no-ha, Napuri-kor-kamui-kor-matnepo, Pet-ru-ush-mat, Poi-soya-un-mat, Tamamo-no-maye, Toikunrari-mat, Xi Wangmu

Greek and Roman Empires
Acalanthis, Acca Larentia, Aea, Agrotera, Amnisiades, Arcadian, Arge, Arrhippe, Artemis, Atalanta, Brauronia, Callisto, Chitone, Circe, Curotrophos, Diana, Lyceia, Pheraea, Psamathe

The Himalaya

Black Vixen-headed One, Blue
Wolf-headed Wind Goddess,
Cha-dog-ma, Chags-kyu-ma, Dark-blue
Wolf-headed One, Dark-brown
Lion-headed One, Dark-brown
Yak-headed Rakshasa Goddess,
Dark-green Fox-headed Baton
Goddess, Dom-gdon-can,
Greenish-black Elephant-headed
Big-nosed Goddess, Greenish-black
Leopard-headed Great Goddess,
Htamenmas, Lobsangma, Red
Ibex-headed Woman Goddess, Red
Lion-headed Mystic Goddess, Red
Snow-bear-headed Virgin Goddess,
Red Tiger-headed One,
Senga-dong-ma, Sengdroma,
Seng-ge'i-gdong-can, Tan-ma,
Vajra-Vārāhī, White Bear-headed Indra
Goddess, Yellowish-black Tiger-headed
Rakshasi

Indian Subcontinent

Abhramu, Adanari, Alopurbi,
Ammavaru, Anakulam-Bhagavathi,
Angana, Banka Mundi, Buddhi Pallien,
Chandi, Dadju, Dzurawu, Hari,
Hariyali, Huliamma, Iravati, Ka Ksaw
Ka Jirngam, Kapenopfu, Kolin Sutti
Bhavani, Mahasitaviti, Maswasi,
Matangi, Nirriti, Raktipurbi, Sarduli,
Shing-rum, Simhika, Singhbahini,
Sukarapreyasi, Suttibhavani, Tanum,
Varahi, Waghai Devi

Near East

Anath, Ate, Cybele, Hebat, Kades,
Lamasthu, Sarbanda, Shaushka, Thisbe

North America

Alarana, Animal Mother, Asiaq,
Atsentma, Badger Old Woman, Bear
Daughter, Bear Maiden, Bear Mother,
Bear Woman, Bear Woman and the
Fawns, Buffalo-calf-road-woman,
Buffalo Girl, Buffalo Old Woman,
Buffalo Wife, Chakwaina Okya,
Chakwaina Yu-adta, Chilili Okya, Corn
Woman, Deer Mothers, Deer Woman,
Fox Earth Goddess, Fox Moon
Goddess, Grizzly Bear Mother,
Hastseoltoi, Hidatsa Buffalo Woman,
Itclixyan, Kochinako, Kokumthena,
Luk, Me-suk-kum-me-go-kwa,
Minnehaha, Miritatsiec, Moon Woman,
Na'le, Norwan, Pakimna,
Pakitsumanga, Papawa, Pasowee,
Pinga, Ptesan Winyan, Rhpisunt,
Sha'koya, Sneneik, Snowats, Sonxwana,
Spirit Woman, Ta Tha-bthin, Tahltan
Game Mother, Takanakapsaluk,
Ta-tanka-wian-ska, Tih-kuyi-wuhti,
Tlkelikera, Toodlanak, Tugtut Igfianut,
Uivarahugiyaq, Wajashk, White Buffalo
Woman, Witch Woman, Yellow Woman

Northern Europe

Frau Gode, Hyrokkin, Juks-akka,
Mielikki, Poshjo-akka, She-Wolf,

Skogsfru, Skogsjungfru, Skogsnufvar,
Sun

Oceania

Cassowary Mother, Le hev hev, Minma
mala, Minma waiuda, Naruni, Po ne'a
'aku, Waiuda, Wibalu

South America

Biu Si, Caipora, Noitu, Rapsem Si, Taue
Si, Topétine

Southeast Asia

Chitsa Numjan, Nang Pyek Kha Yeh
Khi, Phy Wam Numjan, Wang Pyekkha
Yek-khi, Yu Kantang

Western Europe

Achtan, Andarta, Arduinna, Artio, Dea
Arduenna, Dea Artia, Dea Artio,
Flidais, Sadb, Tuireann, Uchtdealbh

Immortality

Africa

Djaga Woman, Ntoa, Obosom, Tamuno

Central America and Mesoamerica

Brigette, Cihuapipiltin, Hoatziqui, Itoki,
Mictanteot, Mocihuaquetzque, Tatei
Niwetukame, Tlaltecuhtli, Tlazolteotl

Eastern Europe

Änäm Jajuci, Anapel, Ayisit,
Kaltas-anki, Maddarakka, Navki,
Puges, Rusalka, Semik, Semmesmaat,
Serque-edne, Suonetar, Togo Musun,
Türem Mother, Vielona, Vila,
Vodyanoi, Zhiva

Egypt

Akert-khentet-auset-s, Ament, Amit,
Hak, Hap Cow, Hathors,
Henemet-em-anh-annuit, Heptet,
Heqet, Her-tept, Hesa, Isis, Kebechet,
Khenememtit, Khnemet-urt, Lady of
Amenta, Maât, Mehenit,
Meh-khebitet-seh-neter, Menqet, Mut,
Nephthys, Nut, Qebhsnuf, Renpet, Sa,
Satet, Selket, Sentait, Seshat, Seven
Kine-deities, Shenat-pet-utheset-neter,
Shenty, Tait, Taueret, Tayt, Tenemet,
Unen-em-hetep

Far East

Blue Lotus, Chang E, Chang Yong,
Corpse Goddesses, He Ku, He Xiangu,
Jin Mu, Kaguya-hime-no-mikoto,
Kisagai-hime, Ma Gu, Meng Po
Niangniang, Miao Shan,
Napuri-kor-kamui-kor-matnepo,
Ningyo, Seoritsu-hime, Shenggu,
Shozu-ga-no-baba, So Wang-mo,
Tennin, Umugi-hime, Xi Wangmu,
Yamni-huchi

Greek and Roman Empires

Alcestis, Alcmena, Ambologera,
Ambulia, Anima Mundi, Calypso, Eos,
Hydra, Lara, Lethe, Mana, Mania,
Mormo, Paeonia, Peliades, Pelopeia,
Psyche, Snake Goddess of Knossos,
Tellus

The Himalaya

Bardo Goddesses, Gokarmo, Seng-ge
Dolma

Indian Subcontinent

Acheri, Adrika, Alambusha, Alwantin,
Amrit, Angana, Ap, Apsarases,
Assam Mother Earth, Asuniti,
Auksagandhi, Bettada Chicama,
Bhairava, Bhutamatri, Bonga, Caksusi,
Choorail, Churalin, Churel, Devayani,
Devis, Ghrtaci, Guggulu, Harini,
Indrani, Ira, Jamadagni, Jara, Keshini,
Kshiti-apsarases, Lavangi, Madhava,
Malini, Manasi, Marisha, Mena,
Misrakesi, Mother Globes, Naladi,
Nandini, Pidari, Pisachis, Pramandani,
Pramlocha, Pururavas, Purvachitti,
Rambha, Rati, Sahaganya, Sanumati,
Sarama, Sarvakamadugha, Sasilekha,
Saudamani, Savitri, Shamidevi,
Sitatara, Sukanthi, Sukanya,
Surabhidatta, Surapamsula, Tara,
Teikirzi, Tilottama, Uma, Uravari,
Urvasi, Usas, Vadaba, Vasistha

Near East

Ameretāt, Amesha Spentas, Anael,
Artemis Ephesus, Cherubim, Daena,
Drvaspa, Dynamis, Fravashis, Mama,
Ninazu, Ninsikila, Oub, Pari,
Phronesia, Salgusa, Sandalphon, Sheol,
Sige, Sophia, Sophia-achamoth, Spiritus
Venereus, Zuriel

North America

Aataentsic, Estsanatlehi, Haka Lasi,
Hihankara, Kadhutetash, Man-el,
Momoy, Nutse'xenem, Old Woman
Who Never Dies, Pana, Pinga, Toxwid,
Tsunukwa, Utlunta

Northern Europe

Disir, Fylgja, Fylgukona, Gna, Gullveig,
Hamingja, Hild, Holle, Idisi, Idun,
Radien-kiedde, Undine

Oceania

Bir im bir wongar, Dilga, First Woman,
Ha pu'u, Haumea, Ka hala o māpuana,
Ka hala o puna, Ka lei hau ola, Kara ma
kuna, Karwadi, Kewelu, Laenihi,
Ligifo, Longolongovavau, Marama,
Minma milbali, Miru, Miru kura, Nā
maka o kaha'i, Nafanua, Papai a taki
vera, Purlimil, Sinafakalau,
Sinebomatu, Tilafainga, Tuapu'u,
Wulutahanga, Yhi

South America

First Woman, Ituana

Southeast Asia

Amitabha, Andin Bambin, Balu Adad,
Chinoi Sagar, Con Tinh, Gendui
Lanyut, Gimokodan, Ibu, Jara Meng,
Khmoc Pray, Manoid, Pajau Yan,
Rabia, Thabet, Yara Meng

Western Europe

Airmed, Banna, Brigantia, Cannered
Noz, Carlin

Insects

Africa
Eveningstar of Wakaranga, Khwora!ma, Ko, Koki

Central America and Mesoamerica
Itoki, Ix Chancab, Mu Olokukurtlisop, Punauaga Olokurgililiae

Eastern Europe
Anana-gunda, Austheia, Curche, Fatit, Khosodam, Neske-pas, Neškeper-ava, Orans, P'erna-azor-ava, Tcaridyi, Vyestitsa

Egypt
Hedetet, Selket, Serqet

Far East
Ashke-tanne-mat, Can Nü, Da'an Nü, Lei-zi, Maming Shengmu, Matou Niang, Mazha Shen, Moire-mat, San Gufuren, Siling Shen, White Wave, Xiancan, Xiling Shi, Yaoshkep-kamui

Greek and Roman Empires
Meiboia

The Himalaya
Red Scorpion-headed Amrita Goddess

Indian Subcontinent
Biliku, Mahasitaviti, Nostu Nopantu, Singarmati Devi, Singhbahini, Subbu Khai Thung

Near East
Hannahannas, Ishara, Ish-khanna, Nasa, Orore, Ushharay

North America
'Anltani, Gogyeng So Wuhti, Grandmother Spider, Hatai Wuhti, Kanaeski Anaiyehi, Kanene Ski Amai Yehi, Kokyan Wuhti, Malaŧshishinish, Malaxšišiniš, Mu'satewichi Okya, Na?ackjeii Esdzaa, Nayaanxatisei, Nunusomikeeqonem, Poli Kachina Mana, Red-spider-woman, Soat-saki, Spider Woman, Utset, Witch Woman

Oceania
Baiangun, Hintubuet, 'Ilaheva, Le hev hev, Lejman, Nei auti

South America
Beru, Ituana

Southeast Asia
Bee Bride, Bisan, Bugan, Daterata, Indudun inPundaikuhan, Jingjan Numjan, Loupgarous, Shangkam Majan, Toiron Numjan

Western Europe
Henwen

Intelligence and Creativity

Africa
Ogboinba

Central America and Mesoamerica
Alaghom Naum

Eastern Europe
Isa, Maras, Zitna-atka

Egypt
Sphinx, Tie

Far East
Ama-no-sagu-me, Xing Mu

Greek and Roman Empires
Achelois, Aganippe, Aonides, Apollonis, Arche, Ardalides, Asopo, Autonoe, Avernales, Bateia, Boarmia, Borysthenis, Brizo, Caliadne, Caryatis, Cephisso, Chlidanope, Cleochareia, Echenais, Eleionomae, Erato, Harmonia, Heptapora, Hippocrenides, Hypate, Ilissiades, Isia, Lilaea, Limnatides, Machanitis, Maeonides, Melete, Melite, Minerva, Misa, Mneiae, Mneme, Mnemonides, Mnemosyne, Muses, Myrtis of Anthedon, Naiades, Neilo, Nete, Nymphae Infernae Paludis, Oenoie, Oxydercis, Pandora, Parnassides, Pegasides, Pimpleides, Polymatheia, Polymnia, Polynoe, Polyxo, Pronoë, Rhodia, Suada, Thaleia, Thelxinoe, Tipoplo, Tritone, Urania, Voleta

The Himalaya
Bardo Goddesses, Black Cuckoo-headed Mystic Goddess, Blue Monkey-headed Goddess of Inquisitiveness, Buddha Dakinis, Clear-light Mother, Ekadzati, Greenish-black Serpent-headed Mystic Goddess, Red Lion-headed Mystic Goddess, Toma, Ushnishavijaya, Vajra Dakinis, Yellow Goat-headed Mystic Goddess

Indian Subcontinent
Akuti, Anumati, Bettada Chicama, Buddhi, Chit, Durga, Ichchhashakti, Jnanashakti, Kriyashakti, Lairmena, Mahamaya, Manasa, Manasi, Matangi, Maya, Medha, Mother Globes, Namagiri, Parvati, Prajna, Puranjani, Samgna, Shraddha, Somlai, Uma, Ushnishavijaya, Vac

Near East
Am, Chaiah, Dianoia, Epinoia, Gestinanna, Inaras, Istehar, Makhir, Nanshe, Nazi, Nephesh, Neshamah, Ninsaba, Phronesia, Qlippoth, Rabi'a Al-adawiya, Sige, Sophia, Tebunah, Tušnamati

North America
Anoolikwotsaix, Chup, Piptu' Wuhti, Shiwanokia

Northern Europe
Nat

Oceania
Huhura, Rata

South America
Jubbu-jang-sangne

Southeast Asia
Silewe Nazarata

Western Europe
Ailbe, Banna, Canola, Ceibhfhionn, Cerridwen, Leanan Sidhe, Sephira

Justice

Africa
Ala, Amelenwa, Ani, Atai, Azele Yaba, Dziva, Imo, 'Inna, Nakiwulo, Nyamwezi First Woman, Nzambi, Osaka, Tenga, Untombinde

Central America and Mesoamerica
Diablesse, Erzulie Mapiangueh, Hoatziqui, Ixtab, Loa

Eastern Europe
Aino, Alkonost, Azer-ava, Mati-syra-zemlya, Perit, Pölöznitsa, Pyatnitsa Prascovia, Si, Tenga, Tsi, Vila

Egypt
Aahmes-nefertari, Ahemait, Ammit, Amn, Apet, Aso, Buto, Hathor, Hatshepsut, Hert-ketit-s, Ini-herit, Lady of Amenta, Ma, Maât, Ma'et, Merseger, Meshkent, Meskhent, Nechmetawaj, Nehebka, Nekhen, Nephthys, Sekhet, Sekhmet, Taueret, Tefnut, Thmei, Thoeris, Tmei, Uadjet, Uatchet

Far East
Chang Yong, Corpse Goddesses, Daji, Dou Mou, Doushen Niangniang, Jokwa, Kiyo-hime, Kongde, Meng Po Niangniang, Mirume, Mo Ye, Pan Jinlian, Pang Che, Pang Jiao, Pang Zhu, Shandian Pozi, Siling Shen, Tang, Travel Goddess, Turesh, Xiling Shi

Greek and Roman Empires
Acholoe, Adicia, Agoraea, Alalcomene, Alcippe, Alecto, Alethia, Amphictyonis, Anaxarete, Arai, Arete, Astraea, Ate, Axiopoenos, Begoe, Boulaia, Bulia, Celaeno, Cer, Ceres, Chelone, Curiatia, Cyrene, Demeter, Dice, Disciplina, Epipole, Erigone, Erinyes, Eugora, Eunomia, Feronia, Furies, Harpies, Hegemone, Juno, Justitia, Kelaino, Kratesis, Laomedeia, Leagore, Lelaino, Libertas, Litae, Lucania, Lysianassa, Megaera, Mida, Mixoparthenos, Nemertes, Nemesis, Nicothoe, Nomia, Peitho, Peliades, Pelopeia, Pietas, Podarge, Poena, Populonia, Praxidice, Praxidicae, Pronoë, Protomedeia, Rhodope, Styx, Tellus, Telphusia, Thelxinoea, Themis, Themisto, Thesmophoros, Tisiphone, Veritas, Virginia, Voltumna, Xenia

The Himalaya
Buddha Dakinis, Buddha Krotishaurima, dPal-ldan Lha-mo, Mother Khahdoma, mTsho-sman-rgyal-mo-mkhro'i-gtso, mTsho-sman-ru-phyug-rgyal-mo, Ral-gcig-ma, Sipe Gyalmo, Sridevi

Indian Subcontinent
Adanari, Ahalya, Amba, Anasuya,
Ashi, Ausinari, Bhadrā, Chit,
Damayanti, Darmit, Durga,
Gandhari, Ila, Ka Blai Synshar,
Ka Sngi, Kannagi, Kausalya, Keshini,
Madri, Mahamaya, Mandodari,
Masanyatha, Minachiamman, Nirriti,
Niti, Padmavati, Pavanarekha,
Rajarajeshvari, Rajyadidevatas,
Rajyasri, Rakshodhidevatas, Satyavati,
Shuska-Revati, Sudakshina, Sumitra,
Teikirzi, Yanta

Near East
Aharišvang, Aletheia, Allatu,
Ardokhsho, Aretz, Arstât, Artemis
Ephesus, Asherah, Ashi, Ashima,
Ashish Vanuhi, Ashmunikal, Astarte,
Balthi, Belatsunat, Belit Seri, Daena,
Damgalnunna, Gestinanna, Hepat,
Houri, Ishtar, Iza, Kadi, Kattahha,
Lilith, Mahalat, Nana, Nanshe, Nazi,
Nikal-mati, Rasastat, Sahassaras,
Sartiyas, Shaushka, Shintalimeni,
Tawannannas, Zamama

North America
Aukjuk, Bear Mother, Bear Woman and
the Fawns, Dzelarhons, Hihankara,
Neegyauks, Nuliajuk, Takanakapsaluk,
Wikwanekwila

Northern Europe
Aśynjur, Friagabi, Gefjun, Gudrun,
Kriemhild, Rindr, Syn, Thir, Var, Vor,
Wara

Oceania
Apakura, Apa'ula, Apekua, Arimata,
Birra nulu, Dilga, Hatu atu tupun,
Hau wahine, Ka hala o māpuana,
Kā'ana'e like, Kalaia, Kani uhi,
Ka'ula hea, Le hev hev, Lewa levu,
Mafuike, Nā maka o kaha'i, Narina,
Naruni, Nona, Pahulu, Palpinkalare,
Poli 'ahu, Purlimil, Ro Som, Satene,
Sikingimoemoe, Sina, Sinakibi,
Sinebomatu, Tairbu, Taka rita,
Wulutahanga

South America
Perimbó, Putcha Si

Southeast Asia
Lai-oid, Ningthet Majan, Ningtsi
Majan, Njai Lora Kidoul, Sangiyan Sari,
Satine, Tara Majan, Trung Trac, Upu
Tapene, Upu Ume, Ya Monoij

Western Europe
Áille, Ain, Arianrhod, Bebhionn, Filia
Vocis, Mari, Mari Morgan, Melusine,
Munanna, Pressina

Large Size

Far East
Daiboth

Greek and Roman Empires
Elate

Indian Subcontinent
Daintary, Daityas, Danavis,
Gavariamma, Hidimba, Jara,
Kumbhinasa, Nirriti, Pisachis,
Rakshasis, Shurpanakha, Trigata, Trijata

Near East
Azuiti, Pidray

North America
Chakwaina Okya, Chakwena,
Dzoo-noo-qua, Nulayuuiniq,
Quootis-hooi

Northern Europe
Angeyja, Atla, Augeia, Elli, Gjalp, Grid,
Groa, Hardgrep, Hyndla, Hyrokkin,
Ivithjar, Laufey, Menglad, Menja, Rind,
Sinmora, Thok, Ulfrun, Wachilt, Wave
Maidens

Oceania
Pi'i ka lalau

South America
Ka-ata-killa

Southeast Asia
Gimokodan, Thabet

Western Europe
Bebhionn, Garbh Ogh, Long Meg

Life/Death Cycle

Africa
Asaase Aberewa, Asase Yaa, Djaga
Woman, Isamba, Nasilele, Nyame,
Nyamwezi First Woman, Obasi Nsi,
Odame, Onile, Quabso, Sierra Leone
Goddess, Sky Woman of Nuer

Central America and Mesoamerica
Coatlicue, Tlaltecuhtli, Tonacacíhuatl

Eastern Europe
Baba Yaga, Dunna Musun, Kostroma,
Rusalka, Russian Mother Earth,
Vagneg-imi, Yabme-akka, Ziva

Egypt
Kebehut, Renpet

Far East
Ame-no-uzume, Helidi, Inari,
Iwa-naga-hime, Omiya-hime, Oto,
Yuki-onne

Greek and Roman Empires
Chloe, Cupra, Demeter, Eos, Genita
Mana, Hebe, Juventas, Moirae,
Persephone, Pyrrha, Senecta, Teleia,
Tergemina, Theria, Venus

The Himalaya
Srinmo, Yid-'prog-ma

Indian Subcontinent
Anumati, Assam Mother Earth, Baski
Mata, Bhairavi, Devi, Durga, Gan
Gaur, Grhalaksmi, Grilya Burhin,
Hariti, Jyestha Alakshmi,
Kalamahichandi, Kalaratri, Kali,
Kumari, Mahamantranusarini,
Mahamayuri, Mahapratisara,

Mahasahasrapramardani, Mahasitaviti,
Pancaraksa, Panthoibi, Prakriti,
Prithivi, Rangda, Sadbhavasri,
Sarparajni, Usas, Yoganidra

Near East
An.zu

North America
Atira, Blackfoot First Woman,
Estsanatlehi, H'uraru, Iyatiku, Nipa,
Powamu So Aum, Selu, Thompson
Goddesses, Toxwid

Northern Europe
Elli, Fenja, Hel, Lif, Lifthrasir, Menja

Oceania
Cassowary Mother, Eingana, Fefafa,
First Woman, Hainuwele, Hine nui te
pō, Hine tītama, Hoa make i ke kula,
Ho'o hoku i ka lani, Julunggul, Ka'ao
melemele, Kahausibware, Karwadi,
Nungeena, Sina, Tei Tituaabine, Yhi

South America
Cocamama

Southeast Asia
Bugan inNgilin, Hainuwele, Jara Meng,
Mebuyan, Mulua Satene,
Munsumundok, Sago Woman, Sampny
Nang, Siti Permani, Teze, Tisna Wati,
Warunsasadun, Yahsek Khi

Western Europe
Creirwy, Dervonnae, Inghean Bhuidhe,
Niskai, Proximae, Quadriviae, Triple
Goddess, Wyvach, Y Mamau

Love and Sexuality

Africa
'Aisha Qandisha, Annallja Tu Bari,
Dogon Earth Mother, Ezili, Hottentot
Mother Goddess, Juno Coelestis,
Luamerava, Mhaya, Morongo, Nambi,
Oba, Odudua, Oshun, Tenye Te'en,
Yemonja

Central America and Mesoamerica
Diablesse, Erzulie, Ichpuchtli, Ix Chel,
Ixcuina, Ixcuiname, Oba, Olokum,
Oshun, Tlazolteotl, Tsilah Wedo,
Ursule, Xochiquetzal, Xpuch, Xtabay,
Xtah

Eastern Europe
Auseklis, Dzydzilelya, Ganis, Lada,
Lesni Zenka, Liderc, Meschamaat,
Prende, Saiva-neida, Sukkamielli,
Šukšendal, Vasa, Zizilia

Egypt
Anatha Baetyl, Isis, Ken, Qetesh,
Zodiacal Virgins

Far East
Akaru-hime, Bai Mundan, Iku-tama-
yori-bime, Inada-hime, Inari, Izushi
-otome-no-kami, Jiutinan Xuannu,
Ō-ichi-hime, Pan Jinlian, Suseri-bime-
no-mikoto

Greek and Roman Empires

Albina, Alcippe, Alcyone, Anaxarete, Antigone, Aphrodite, Argimpasa, Ariadne, Asteria, Byblis, Caenis, Callisto, Canente, Chimaera, Cloacina, Echenais, Echidna, Eos, Eurydice, Galatea, Leda, Libentina, Machanitis, Maia, Marpessa, Medea, Medusa, Mlakukh, Nomia, Peisinoe, Pertunda, Philia, Philotes, Prema, Pyrene, Salmacis, Selene, Semele, Turan, Venus, Verticordia, Virginensis, Virilis, Voluptas

The Himalaya

Cha-dog-ma, Dolma, Hlamos, Kurukulle, Me-tog-ma, Ogress of Lust, Padma Dakinis, Zhag-pa-ma

Indian Subcontinent

Ahalya, Amrit, Anasuya, Arani, Aruna, Arundhati, Ati-canda, Balini, Bonga, Camunda, Canda, Candanayika, Candavati, Candi, Candogra, Damayanti, Durga, Ghrtaci, Gnas, Hemambika, Hidimba, Indrani, Jayini, Ka Sngi, Kamakhya, Kamashi, Kamesvari, Kaulesi, Khasias Celestial Woman, Kurukulla, Lalita, Lopamudra, Lust Goddess, Madhava, Madhavi Devi, Maitri, Mamata, Medini, Mena, Minaksi, Murala, Nayikas, Parvati, Pracanda, Pramlocha, Radha, Rati, Renuka, Reva, Rohini, Samgna, Saranyu, Sarveshvari, Shakti, Suaha, Sumu Mung, Suratamangari, Sushakti, Thirst Goddess, Trigana, Trsna, Ugracanda, Urvasi, Vikesi, Vimala

Near East

Anāhita, Anat, Anat-bethel, Arusyak, Ashtar-kemosh, Ashtart, Aslik, Asmodeus, Astarte, Baalith, Babelah, Belili, Beltis, Biducht, Cotys, First Woman, Ishara, Ishtar, Istehar, Jahi, Kades, Leilah, Lilithu, Myrrha, Nanaja, Ninatta, Nin-imma, Pairikas, Rabi'a Al-adawiya, Sauska, Semiramis, Shaushka, Succubus, Sulmanitu, Thisbe, Vatak, Xnathaiti

North America

Akycha, Ampata Sapa, Bear Woman, Ca-the-ña, Gendenwitha, Kokopell' Mana, Korawini?i, Nayaanxatisei, Soat-saki, Tahc-I

Northern Europe

Frau Welt, Frigga, Gefion, Grimhild, Hnoss, Ingeborg, Lofn, Lofua, Minne, Nanna, Sif, Siofn, Sjofn, Swanhild, Wilden Wip

Oceania

Alalahe, Bima, Faingaa, Hana, Hāpai, Havea lolo fonua, Hina tau miha, Hine moa, Hine tītama, Ho'o hoku i ka lani, Inemes, Kā'ana'e like, Kanikanihia, Kewelu, Kua iti, Kua nui, Kunnawarra, Kururuk, Lau kiele 'ula, Narina, Naruni, Nona, Papa, Parabaruma, Pele, Pele'ula, Poli 'ahu, Purlimil, Sina,

Sinafakalau, Taka rita, Tshikaro, Ururupuin, Wawilak

South America

Cavillaca, Cocamama, Mariana

Southeast Asia

Bangan, Bintang, Lulong, Pantang Mayang, Rangda, Tagabayan, Tisna Wati

Western Europe

Aeval, Aidín, Ailinn, Áine, Arianrhod, Bidhgoe, Blodeuwedd, Brangwaine, Branwen, Conchenn, Dahut, Deirdre, Derbhorgill, Dubhlaing, Finncaev, Grainne, Isolt, Isolt of the White Hands, Leanan Sidhe, Matronit, Medb, Niamh, Wylgeforte, Ygerna

Luck

Africa

Anyigba

Central America and Mesoamerica

Erzulie, Jonaji Belachina, Loa, Mahm-m, Tsilah Wedo

Eastern Europe

Cinderella, Haltia, Khosadam, Laima, Laimas-māte, Mati-syra-zemlya, Mis-khum, Nedolya, Nesreča, Pereplut, Pört-kuva, Schastie, Viz-anya, Vizi-leany

Far East

Benten, Bixia Yuanjin, Ichiki-shima-hime-no-mikoto, Iku-tama-saki-tama-hime-no-kami, Iku-tama-yori-bime, Kaguya-hime-no-mikoto, Kichi-jō-ten, Okame, Saki-tama-hime, Yama-no-Shinbo

Greek and Roman Empires

Agathe Tyche, Automatia, Ceto, Eucrante, Eunike, Fortuna, Navirilis, Nortia, Polydora, Primigenia, Proto, Protogenia, Redux, Tabliope, Tyche, Upis, Virgo

Indian Subcontinent

Alakshmi, Anna Kuari, Anumati, Ap, Asri, Bhadrā, Chala, Chapala, Chigrinad, Ekajata, Ellamma, Ghar Jenti, Hada Bai, Ka Ksaw Ka Jirngam, Kali, Kamadhenu, Kankali, Lakshmi, Lola, Nukulamma, Pathya Svasti, Pauri Pat, Radha, Rajamma, Sakunadevatas, Sakunadhisthatri, Tari Pennu, Uradamma

Near East

Meni

North America

'Alaĥtin, Lennaxidaq, Takanakapsaluk, Ukat

Northern Europe

Alraun, Frau Gode, Hamingja, Oddibjord, Thorgerdr Holgarbrudr

Oceania

Buring une, Enda semangko, Hoku kau opae, Pekai

Southeast Asia

Darago, Ini Andan, Ipamahandi, Manang Jaban, Pajau Yan, Sri

Western Europe

Áine, oShion

Magic

Africa

Abuk, 'Aisha Qandisha, Bitabok, Divine Queen, Hottentot Mother Goddess, Mabisalira, Minona, Nakiwulo, Ndako Gboya, Nyale, Ogboinba, Orehu, Qandisa

Central America and Mesoamerica

Agwe, Amelia, Clairmé, Coatlicue, Comizahual, Elisabeth, Erzulie, Grande Ezili, Guédé l'Oraille, Isidore, Ix Chel, Ix Kan Itzam Thul, Karous, Laloue-diji, Madeleine, Maman Simbi, Marie Madeleine, Marinette, Mombu, Philomena, Quilaztli, Sirêne, Sukias, 'Ti Kita, Tlazolteotl, Tsilah Wedo, Ursule, Vierge Caridad, White Woman

Eastern Europe

Anapel, Bithia, Bukura-e Dheut, Cinderella, Drude, Egle, Juksakka, Kubaiko, Kupalo, Laima, Lauma, Laumé, Liderc, Louhi, Maddarakka, Mamaldi, Marjatta, Murava, Näkki, Ohyn, Ragana, Sadsta-akka, Shtrige, Suonetar, Szepasszonyok, Táltos, Uksakka, Ved'ma, Vestice, Vila, Vodyanoi, Vyestitsa

Egypt

Khoemnis, Merseger, Mut, Nebti, Neserit, Sekhmet, Thoeris, Tie, Urt-hekau, Urt-hikeu

Far East

Akaru-hime, Ame-no-sade-yori-hime, Ami Goddess, Ami-tanne-mat, Ashke-tanne-mat, Aunt Piety, Baiji, Can Nü, Dragon Mother, Eastern Mother, Eterna, Fupao, He Ku, Iwa-tsutsu-no-me-no-mikoto, Jin Gu, Jiutinan Xuannu, Kana-yama-bime-no-kami, Kiyo-hime, Kura-mitsu-ha-no-kami, Ma Gu, Meng Jiangnü, Menluzipu, Miao Shan, Mitsu-ha-no-me-no-kami, Mo Ye, Naki-sawa-me-no-kami, Nüjiao, Omiya-hime, Oto, Perasia, Se-o-nyo, Senyo, Shenggu, Shengmu, Suseri-bime-no-mikoto, Tai Yuan, Taiyuan, Tamamo-no-maye, Tama-yori-bime-no-mikoto, Third Lady, Tortoise Goddess, Tushan, Virgin Jasper, Western Mother, White Wave, Xie, Xiu Zhi, Yamato-hime, Yu, Yuan

Greek and Roman Empires

Aea, Aeaea, Aegiale, Aetheria, Agraulos, Aigle, Alcyone, Amalthea, Amphinome, Anaxarete, Andromeda, Angitia, Apostrophia, Asteria, Asterope, Asteropeia, Atlantides, Befana, Caenis, Callisto, Canidia, Celaeno, Celedones, Chelone, Circe, Coccymo, Dactyls, Dioxippe, Elais, Electra, Electryone, Erato, Euadne, Fata, Fata Alcina, Fata Morgana, Flora, Fluonia, Galatea, Gello, Hecate, Heliadae, Hippothoe, Inyx, Lamiae, Lampatho, Leda, Lotis, Mania, Medea, Meditrina, Medusa, Meliae, Meroe, Merope, Mestra, Nortia, Oeno, Oenotropae, Pamphile, Parthenia, Peisdice, Pelonia, Perse, Perseis, Phaethonides, Phaethusa, Pharmaceia, Pharmacides, Phatusa, Phytia, Pitys, Pleiades, Protis, Psamathe, Pyrene, Pyrrha, Rhodope, Scylla, Spermo, Sterope, Stonychia, Syrinx, Taygete

The Himalaya

Buddha Dakinis, Dakini Guru, Demon Protector of the Grand Lama, Dom-gdon-can, Dorje Phagmo, Khahdoma, Khadoma Queen, Kongtsun Demo, Las-kyi-mkhah-hgro, Naro-kha-choma, Rin-chen-mkhah-ngro, rMa-bya-c'en-mo, Sangye-khado, Sa-yi-lha-mo-bstan-ma, Seng-ge'i-gdong-can, Skyes-bu-ber, Vajravaraki, Vinasa, Yogini

Indian Subcontinent

Abhramu, Adanari, Adrika, Aginvati, Alambusha, Amrit, Angana, Anumati, Apala, Apsarases, Auksagandhi, Avany, Bhairava, Buddhadakini, Caksusi, Daini, Dakinis, Dayan, Delight Goddess, Gandhari, Gayatri, Ghrtaci, Grhadevi, Guggulu, Harini, Hemaprabha, Hidimba, Ila, Ira, Jamadagni, Jara, Kanni, Karmadakini, Keshini, Khekaris, Kritya, Krityakas, Kshiti-apsarases, Kurukulla, Kutamangari, Lalitalochana, Lavangi, Lopamudra, Madhava, Mahamantranusarini, Mahamayuri, Mahapratisara, Mahasahasrapramardani, Mahasitaviti, Makaravaktra, Malini, Mallinatha, Manasi, Mandaradevi, Mandarava, Marisha, Matangi, Matris, Maya, Mena, Mgigalekha, Misrakesi, Mohini, Naladi, Nikumbhila, Nitya, Padmadakini, Pancaraksa, Prajnapti, Pramandani, Pramlocha, Pururavas, Purvachitti, Rambha, Rangda, Rati, Ratnadakini, Ratnamangari, Rksavaktradakini, Sahaganya, Samgna, Sandhya, Sanumati, Saranyu, Sarvabuddhadakini, Sarvakamadugha, Sasilekha, Saudamani, Shaktiyasas, Siddhanganas, Siddha-Yoginis, Siddhikari, Siddhis, Simhavaktra, Sringatpadini, Suaha, Sukanthi, Sukanya, Surabhidatta, Surapamsula,

Suratamangari, Svarnarekha, Tara Bai, Thirst Goddess, Tilottama, Trisala, Uravari, Urvasi, Vac, Vadaba, Vajradakini, Vajravarahi, Varutri(s), Vasistha, Vidyadharis, Visvadakini, Vyaghravaktradakini, Yagas, Yashodhara, Yoginis

Near East

Abyzu, Druxsans, Ennoia, Hir Nineveh, Istehar, Kamrusepas, Kista, Labartu, Myrrha, Nasu, Nhang, Oub, Pairikas, Pari, Parigs, Ruha D'qudsha, Succubus, Thisbe, Wisuriyanza

North America

Aataentsic, Asin, Atse Esdzaa, Bear Maiden, Bear Mother, Bear Woman, Big Dog, Chimon Mana, Dagwanoenyent, Ee-eh-ch-choo-ri-ch'ahm-nin, Estsanatlehi, Gendenwitha, Glispa, Hano, Hidatsa Buffalo Woman, Komwidapokuwia, Ksem-wa'tsq, Kumanshi Okya, L'etsa'aplelana, Malokatsiki, Master Spirit's Daughter, Minnehaha, Momoy, Northeastern Swan Maidens, Nulayuuiniq, Nuptadi, Ojibwa Daughter, Pakitsumanga, Pokinsquss, Pukjinskwes, Puwo-win, Rhpisunt, Snutkanals, Spirit Woman, Tlitcaplitana, Tootega, Waoyakila, Wind Old Woman, Witch Woman, Yellow Woman

Northern Europe

Allwise, Alraun, Angeburga, Askefruer, Bilwis, Drude, Freyja, Fria, Gerda, Grimhild, Groa, Hardgrep, Heartha, Heid, Heidrun, Hervor, Hexe, Holla, Idun, Kveldrida, Menglad, Mora, Myrkrida, Nixen, Seidhkoma, Sel, Sigrdrifa, Sindgund, Sunna, Swan Maidens, Thora, Thorgerdr Holgarbrudr, Weiþen Frauen, Wilden Wip, Wunschelwybere

Oceania

'Alae a hina, Bima, Dama, Djanggawul, Dogai, Fata'a koka, Faumea, Ganabuada, Ha pu'u, Halalamanu, Hauarani, Haunu'u, Hina ma nou rua'e, Hina nui te'ara'ara, Hina tau miha, Hina te 'a'ara, Huhune, Ka hala o māpuana, Ka hala o puna, Ka lama i nu'u, Ka maunu a niho, Kamaunu, Kava tua, Kava'ara, Keoloewa, Kiha wahine, Kiki pua, Laenihi, Lani loa, Mere hau, Mulu mulu, Mulukuausi, Nā maka o kaha'i, Nei matamona, Ngārara huarau, Nisarere, Nua, Nujka'u, Nujmaga, Pahulu, Pani, Pani tinaku, Papa, Parabaruma, Parihai, Pōti'i tā rire, Pua, Raumiha, Runepai, Taha taua toto, Taha'ura, Te vahine nui tahu ra'i, Tu Ai Mehani, Tupu'a, Uli, Waiuda, Wanatjilda, Whaitiri

South America

Boiuna, Cavillaca, Shell Woman, Star Woman, Uarahiulú

Southeast Asia

Abyang Durunuun, Amoghasiddhi, A Mong, Bintang, Bugan Nak Amtalao, Bugan Nak Hinumbian, Chalonarang, Empung Luminuut, Fire Woman, Gaygayoma, Ju Puteur, Loupgarous, Lulong, Pantang Mayang, Rangda, Rice Mother, Sago Woman, Satine, Silat, Teze

Western Europe

Aeval, Aibell, Aide, Ailinn, Áine, Aobh, Aoife, Arianrhod, Astiya, Badb, Badh, Banshees, Beag, Bec Fola, Bécuma, Blanaid, Bo Find, Bonnes Dames, Bri, Buan, Carmán, Carravogue, Cerridwen, Chlaus Haistic, Cliodhna, Corra, Corrigan, Créide Fírálaind, Cuimne, Daath, Dechtiré, Derbhorgill, Dub, Dubhlaing, Ëtain, Ëtain Echraidhe, Fairies, Falerina, Finncaev, Fuamnach, Glas, Glasgavlen, Gorddu, Gwrach y Rhibyn, Gwyllion, Habonde, Hag, Irnan, Leanan Sidhe, Medb, Mongfhinn, Morgan Le Fay, Moriath, Mórrígán, Nechtan Scéne, Onaugh, Oonagh, Pressina, Scáthach, Silly Wychtis, Sin, Tlachtga, Tryanon, Uchtdealbh, Urganda, Urisks, Viviane, Y Mamau, Ygerna

Metals and Minerals

Central America and Mesoamerica

Chantico, Huixtocihuatl, Ix Saclactun, Ix Tub Tan, Sukuyan, Xtabay

Eastern Europe

Kardas-ś Arko, Mokosh, Smilśu-māte

Egypt

Nebhet Hotep, Noub

Far East

Akaru-hime, Hachi-kazuki-hime, Iwa-su-hime-no-kami, Kana-yama-bime-no-kami, Kana-yama-hiko, Mo Ye, Nüjiao, Sayo-hime, Tushan

The Himalaya

Khadoma Queen, Lobsangma

Indian Subcontinent

Danavis, Lalbai Phulbai, Lohasur, Mindhal, Moti Mata, Ranaghanti, Sat Matra, Teeree, Tilottama, Tripura Bhairavi

Near East

Ba'alat Ashtart

North America

Ashi esdza, Chuginadak, Copper Woman, Ewauna, Hetethlokya, Hürü'Ingwühti, Kanuslaliam, Malokatsiki, Mina Koya, Muyinewu mana, Nulayuuiniq, Ong Wuhti, Ooyarraksakju, Queskapenek, Rock Crystal Girl, Tisseyak, Tlaqwagi'layugwa, Tsi'ty'icots'a, Volcano Woman, Waoyakila

Northern Europe
Gullveig, Hnoss, Jarnsaxa, Kriemhild, Nat, Thora, Wunschelwybere

Oceania
Birra nulu, Dama, Gaueteaki, Ha pu'u, Hau ola, Hepeue, Hi'iaka noho lae, Hine tū a hōanga, Kahuone, Kurikuta, Kutunga, Ma ukuuku, Milapukala, Nguatupu'a, One kea, Papa, Po'ele, Qatgoro, Rangahore, Tapuppa, Touiafutuna, Tū fe'ufe'u mai i te ra'i, Wai ta iki, Wirana

South America
Cavillaca, Maisö, Nungui

Southeast Asia
Ina Da Samadulo Hose, Kant Jan, Maran Junti Majan, Nunsumnundok, Rock Maiden

Western Europe
Gwyllion

Moon and Night

Africa
Araua, Arava, Bomu Rambi, Buruku, Chekechani, Dahomean Moon Woman, Haine, Isamba, Jezanna, Lisa, Mahu, Masai Moon Goddess, Mawa, Mawu, Mweji, Namboa, Nasilele, Nyadeang, Nyame, Nyingwan Mebege, Obosom, Ol-apa, Oshu, Pe, Quabso, So, Tano

Central America and Mesoamerica
Acna, Citlalicue, Coyolxauhqui, Cutzi, Erzulie, Ilamatecuhtli, Itzcueye, Ix Ahau, Ix Chebel Yax, Ix Chel, Ix Ch'up, Ix U Sihnal, Ixcuina, Ixcuiname, Ixtab, Mayahuel, Me?tik Čič?u, Mictecacihuatl, Ochu, Oxomoco, Tetevinan, Tētewan, U, White Woman, Xaratanga, Xquic, Yemaya, Yerugami, Yohualticitl

Eastern Europe
Breksta, Hov-ava, Kov-ava, Kuutar, Lusin, Myesyats, Piegulas māte, Poludnitsy, Teleze-awa, Vyestitsa

Egypt
Anatis, Ashtoreth, Athtor, Bast, Buto, Celestial Sow, Hagar, Isis, Kauket, Kek-t, Kerhet, Nephthys, Qetesh, Woman-light of the Shadows

Far East
Chang E, Chang Xi, Chiang, Chuh Kamuy, Kaguya-hime-no-mikoto, Rafu-sen, Somber Maiden, Sun and Moon, Taiyin, Yuefu Taiyin, Zhang Xi

Greek and Roman Empires
Achlys, Anna Perenna, Antevorta, Aphaea, Artemis, Asterodeia, Atropos, Bendis, Briseis, Britomartis, Brizo, Caligo, Canidia, Cassiopeia, Diana, Electryone, Furina, Hecate, Helena, Hilaeira, Jana, Lalal, Losna, Lucifera, Lucna, Luna, Melaenis, Mene, Munychia, Nikta, Noctiluca, Nox, Nyx,

Pamphile, Pandia, Pasiphae, Phoebe, Prosymna, Selene, Tanit, Zirna

The Himalaya
Sobha, White Kite-headed Moon Goddess

Indian Subcontinent
Anumati, Assam Mother Earth, Brisaya, Candi, Chandi Mata, Dhisana, Gomaj, Gungu, Ilura, Jyotsna, Ka Sngi, Khasias Celestial Woman, Kuhu, Maiya Andhiyari, Mata, Matangi, Mgigalekha, Nakshatras, Naktamcharis, Ninda Kando (Chando), Ning-Bonga, Nisacharis, Paurnamasi, Pisachis, Raka, Ramaladevi, RatriIndia, Sankchinni, Sasilekha, Shyavi, Sinavali, Sinivali, Sushumna, Susime, Urmya

Near East
A, Anāhita, Ashima, Ashimbabbar, Astarte, Baalith, Belili, C, Caelestis, Derketo, Ereshkigal, Hapantili, Hur-ki, Jerah, Lilith, Lilithu, Lusin, Metra, Mu•, Nanna, Nikkal, Nuah, Ri, Rukho, Sadarnuna, Tanit Pene Baal, Telita, Tigranuhi, Zarpandit

North America
Aialila'axa, Akna, 'Alaĥtin, Aquit, Big Dog, Chumash Moon Woman, Fox Moon Goddess, Geyaguga, Grandmother Moon, Han, Hanwi, Kashatskihakatidise, Kawas, Kikewei p'aide, Kokomikeis, Man-el, Masahkare, Miritatsiec, Moon Woman, Naskapi Moon Goddess, Nipa, Old Woman Night, Onchi, Pah, Pawnee Moon Woman, Tarqeq, Tatqeq, Tcalyel, Tepkanuset, Tipiskawipisim, Wa-kon-da Hondon, Witch Woman, Xavasumkuli, Ya?onakka Citta, Yaonan, Yolkai Estsan

Northern Europe
Borghild, Horsel, Kveldrida, Nat, Ursula

Oceania
Hana, Hanua, Hatu atu tupun, Hetu ahin, Hina, Hina hanaia'i ka malama, Hina nui te'a'ara, Hina papa i kua, Hina uri, Hina'i a'a i te marama, Hine ahiahi, Hine nui te pō, Hine ruaki moe, Hine te iwaiwa, Hintubuet, Ina maram, Kui o hina, Marama, Po tangotango, Po urirui, Po'ele, Rona, Sina, Taio, Tapa, Te'uri, Tū raki, Ui

South America
Ka-ata-killa, Mama Quilla, Munya•k Yopue, Noitu, Our Mother, Paxsi, Perimbó, Si, Tamparawa, Toru-guenket

Southeast Asia
Bulan, Dewi Ratih, Dua Nggae, Duan Luteh, Funan, Indo nTegolili, Ja Najek, Jara Meng, Kundui, Lingan, Luyong Baybay, Mayari, Moon Mother, Nenak Kebajan, Ningsin Majan, Nini Anteh, Omonga, Pajau Yan, Rabia, Ratih, Silewe Nazarata

Western Europe
Albina, Arianrhod, Bécuma, Branwen, Dubh Lacha, Ëire, Ëtain Echraidhe, Findbhair, Ilazki, Illargui, Morgause, Re, Sadb

Mother and Guardian

Africa
Abuk, Ala, Amauneit, Amirini, Anyigba, Aprija, Crocodile Woman, Dahomean Moon Woman, Enekpe, Gbenebeka, Ichar-tsirew, Imo, Lalla Ta Bullat, Masai Moon Goddess, Mawu, Mboze, Minona, Morongo, Mukasa, Nã Afiye, Nã Bake, Na Yo, Nabuzana, Nalongo, Nalwanga, Nana Enna, Ndwanga, Ngame, Nimba, Ninavanhu-ma, Nyabahasa, Nyabibuya, Nyakala, Nyame, Nyinawhira, Nzambi, Ogboinba, Oshun, Oya, Thamuatz, Tohar-tsiereur, Woyengi, Yemonja, Ymoja, Yukanye

Central America and Mesoamerica
Acna, Acuecueyotlcihuatl, Ahnt Kai', Atlatonin, Ayopechcatl, Chalchiuhtlicue, Cihuacoatl, Cihuateotl, Cihuateteo, Cihuatzin, Citlalicue, Coatlicue, Dobayba, Emanja, Goddess "O", Huechaana, Huichanatao, Istsel, Itoki, Itzpapalotl, Ix Chebel Yax, Ix Chel, Ix U Sihnal, Ixtab, Iztaccihuatl, Jonaji Belachina, Kwelopunyai, Llorona, Loa, Mahm-m, Mama Nono, Mayahuel, Mocihuaquetzque, Mu, Mu Olokukurtlisop, Nohuichana, Oddudua, Omecihuatl, Picchanto, Pitao Huichaana, Quilaztli, Rutbe, Sahk Kays' Es Yo Sees' Kak Aht, Sirêne, Tāke Vêlika Uimáli, Takótsi Nakawé, Tāté Tulirkita, Tatei Niwetukame, Tatei Xuturi Iwiekame, Teteoinnan, Tetevinan, Tlazolteotl, Toci, Tonantzin, Virgin of Guadalupe, White Woman, Xaratanga, Xbaquiyalo, Xmucane, Xochiquetzal, Xquic, Yemaya, Yerugami, Yohualticitl, Zapotlantenan

Eastern Europe
Aiyjsyt, Ajysit, Ajysyt-ijäksit-khotun, Amagandar, Änäm Jajuci, Anapel, Avas, Awa, Ayisit, Boldogasszony, Dekla, Dolya, Dunna Musun, Fatit, Fire Mother, Gabija, Hongatar, Honoured High Mistress, Juksakka, Jumon-ava, Kaldyni-mumas, Kaltas-anki, Kaltes, Karta, Khotun, Kildisin, Koš La-kuva, Kubai-khotun, Kugu Shotshen-ava, Kupal'nitsa, Kupalo, Kybäi-khotun, Lamaria, Laumé, Maan-emo, Maan-eno, Maddarakka, Madder-akku, Manzan Görmö, Marjatta, Māte, Mati-syra-zemlya, Matrioshka, Metsola Mother, Meža-māte, Mokosi, Moksha, Nalygyr-aissyt-khotun, Narechnitsa, Narucnici, Nishke-ava, Niski-ava, Nocnitsa, Ojid-emei, Ora, Ore, Ot-änä, Perke, Piegulas māte, Pirts-māte,

Pört-kuva, Pu'gud-emei, Puges, Radien-akka, Rodjenice, Rodnaia Matushka, Rõugutaja, Rozhanitsy, Rozhenitsa, Rusalki-siriny, Sadsta-akka, Sarakka, Saule, Serque-edne, Sjantaik, Sudbina, Sudice, Sudička, Syt-kul-amine, Tol-ava, Torom Anki, Uksakka, Umai, Urme, Vagneg-imi, Ya-nebya, Zorya

Egypt
Aahmes-nefertari, Akarkhentkats, Amenet, Anuket, Apet, Atet, Bast, Bat, Beset, Buto, Celestial Waterer, Êpet, Ermutu, Hathor, Hathors, Heket, Hemsut, Heqet, Heru-pa-kaut, Ipet, Isis, Kenemet, Mesenet, Meshkent, Meskhent, Mut, Naunet, Nefertem, Neith, Nekhebet, Netet, Nut, Ratta, Renenet, Renenutet, Ritho, Seneb, Sycamore Tree Goddess, Taourt, Taueret, Ta-urt, Temu, Thebean Goddess, Thoeris, Thoueris, Typho, Uadjet, Uati, Uazit, Ubastet, Unnit, Uto, Wosyet

Far East
Akaru-hime, Ama-terasu-ō-mi-kami, Ame-no-uzume, Ami-tanne-mat, Ashke-tanne-mat, Benten, Bixia Yuanjin, Chen, Chiwash-kor-kamui, Chang-bu, Chuang Mu, Cui Sheng, Cuisheng Sheng Mu, Dong Mu, Dou Mou, Dragon Mother, Fupao, Ge Gu, Good Sight Lady, Guanyin, Gum Lin, Hash-inau-uk-kamui, He Xiangu, Helidi, Huchi-fuchi, Inoshishi, Japanese Mother Goddess, Juishen Niangniang, Kamui-fuchi, Kishijoten, Koyasu Kwan-non, Kuguri-gami, Kujaku-myō-ō, Kun-syo-ming-wang, Lincui Hu, Ma Zu, Ma Zupo, Maing Jini, Manzan Gormo, Menluzipu, Midwives, Miketsu-kami, Ming, Miyazu-hime, Mo Bo, Mo Ye, Nai Mu, Niangniang, Niangniang Songzi, Nügua, Nüjiao, Omiya-hime, Ō-to-no-be-no-kami, Peitai Niangniang, Peiyang, Qi Guzi, San Furen, Shepe, Shi-nun-manuri, Silla Mountain Goddess, Songzi, Songzi Guanyin, Songzi Niangniang, Sti-per-sei, Suseri-bime-no-mikoto, Tai Yuan, Taijun Xianniang, Taiyuan, Tama-yori-bime-no-mikoto, Tatsu-ta-hime, Te-na-zuchi-no-kami, Tenth Aunt, Tian Fei, Tian Hou, Toikunrari-mat, Toyo-tama-bime-no-mikoto, Toyo-uke-bime-no-kami, Toyouke-Daijin, Ts'i Ma Niang Tsai, Tsua Sen Niang Niang, Ts'uai-shen Niang Niang, Tushan, Uke-mochi-no-kami, Umai, Virgin Jasper, Waka-uka-hime waka-uke-nome, Xi Hou, Xie, Xieren Xingjun, Xiu Zhi, Yang Taijun, Yaoshkep-kamui, Yi Long, Yimeng Niangniang, Yu Mu Sei, Yu, Yuan, Zesun, Zhende Pusa

Greek and Roman Empires
Abeona, Acca Larentia, Acraea, Adamanthea, Adeona, Adrastea,

Aegeria, Agno, Agrotera, Aigle, Angerona, Antevorta, Aphrodite, Arethusa, Ariadne, Arsinoe, Artemis, Assaros, Atlantides, Augralids, Averruncus, Brisa, Brizo, Brome, Calligeneia, Candelifera, Capheira, Cardea, Carmentis, Cisseis, Cleta, Colias, Comitia, Cuba, Cunina, Curitis, Curotrophos, Cybele, Cynosura, Damia, Danu, Deae Matres, Demeter, Deverra, Diana, Dodonides, Edulica, Edusa, Eidothea, Eileithyia, Elionia, Empanada, Enyo, Erato, Eripha, Erythea, Ethausva, Euboea, Eupheme, Februa, Februlis, Fecunditas, Ferentina, Genetyllides, Genetyllis, Genita Mana, Hagno, Hera, Hespera, Hesperides, Hestia, Hippe, Hypercheiria, Ida, Intercidona, Ithome, Juno, Kerres, Kourotrophos, Leda, Leto, Levana, Libya, Locheia, Luceria, Lucina, Lupa, Lysizona, Macris, Magna Mater, Mana, Mater Matuta, Matrona, Meliae, Melissa, Mens, Meter, Meteres, Molpadia, Muliebris, Mystis, Nascio, Neda, Nemorensis, Nephele, Nixi, Nona, Numeria, Numina, Nundina, Nutrix, Nysa, Nyseides, Oenoe, Opigena, Ops, Orbona, Ossipaga, Paedotrophus, Parca, Partula, Pelonia, Persephone, Perso, Philia, Philyra, Phosphoros, Phytia, Pilumnus, Polyhymno, Postvorta, Potina, Prema, Prorsa, Prosymna, Quiritis, Rhea, Rumia Dea, Rumina, Salmaone, Sao, Sospita, Soteira, Strenia, Thanr, Theisoa, Theotokos, Uni, Upis, Vagitanus, Vesta, Volumna

The Himalaya
bDud-mo-gshin-rej-mgo-dgu-ma, bDud-mo-gshin-rje-lag-brgya-ma, bDud-mo-gsod-mo-gsod-byed-ma, bDud-mo-phung-khrol-ma, Bribsun, Demon Protector of the Grand Lama, dGra-lha-ma-lha-bu-rdzi, Dorje Naljorma, Dorje-pa-mo, Gar-ma, Gokarmo, Green Deer-headed Wealth-guardian Goddess, Karma Dakinis, Kiru, Kuntu-bzang-mo, Ma-gcig-dpal-lha-mo, Mo-lha-mo, Mother Khahdoma, Padma Krotishaurima, Pags-ma-gdugs-dkar, Pelden Lhamo, Prajnaparamita, Ratna Krotishaurima, rDo-rje-drag-mo-rgyal, Remati, rMa-bya-c'en-mo, Sa-yi-lha-mo-bstan-ma, Sengdroma, sGrol-mas, Vajravaraki, Vinasa, Yid-'prog-ma, Yogini

Indian Subcontinent
Abrayanti, Acheri, Adhidevatas, Aditya, Adrika, Akasa, Alwantin, Amari De, Amavasya, Amba, Amba Bai, Ambika, Amma, Ammavaru, Ana, Anakulam-Bhagavathi, Anala, Anila, Antariksha, Anumati, Apu, Aramati, Aranya, Aranyani, Asa Poorna, Asapura, Avany, Bahu, Banjari, Bharati, Bhudevi, Bibi Miriam,

Brahmani, Bursung, Camunda, Candi, Chamundi, Chandra, Chandragupta, Choorail, Chupunika, Churalin, Churel, Cudel, Dakinis, Dakshina, Devaki, Devi, Dhara, Dharni Pinnu, Dharti Mata, Dhisana, Dhruva, Dhupa, Dula, Durgamma, Dyu, Egattala, Ekash-Taka, Ekastaka, Elamadichi, Gandhari, Gasain Era, Gramadevatas, Grhalaksmi, Gungu, Harappan Goddesses, Hariti, Hemambika, Huligavva, Idavida, Indrani, Jagadgauri, Jami, Jhulan Devi, Ka Di, Ka Rasong, Kairadeshahi, Kali, Kalika, Kamadhenu, Kapisha, Kateri, Kaumari, Kottavei, Krittika, Ksetrasya Patni, Kunti, Lankini, Maghayanti, Mahamantranusarini, Mahamayuri, Mahapratisara, Mahasahasrapramardani, Mahasitaviti, Mahendri, Mahesvari, Maisamma, Mamata, Mandwa Rani, Mangadevatas, Margavati, Mariamma, Mata, Mata Januvi, Matabai, Mataras, Matris, Mena, Monkey Goddess of Hampi, Mother Earth, Mother Globes, Mukhambika, Nakshatras, Nikumbhila, Nitatui, Nrtya, Padmavati, Pancaraksa, Paniharin, Parnasavari, Pasupati, Phorcis, Pidari, Ponniyayi, Prabhasa, Pratyusha, Prithivi, Puspa, Putana, Radha, Rajamma, Rajyadidevatas, Raka, Ranaghanti, Ranu Bai, Rati, RatriIndia, Samaiya, Sambhu, Sandi, Sapta-koti-buddha-matri-cunti-devi, Saptamatrakas, Sarama, Sarvayoni, Sasthi, Sasti, Sati, Savitri, Sedi, Sevasti-devi, Shasthi, Shasti, Shavasi, Sichi, Sinavali, Sinivali, Sitala, Sitatapatra Aparajita, Sitlamata, Subbu Khai Thung, Subhadra, Substance Mother, Sumati, Susana, Tara, Trisala, Urmya, Vac, Vaisnavi, Vajar Mata, Vama, Varahi, Varshayanti, Varutri(s), Vasus, Yasasvati, Yashoda, Yerenamma, Yoginis, Yoni

Near East
Ada, Adamu, Aka, Am, Anāhita, Anghairya, Anthat, Artemis Ephesus, Asera, Ashdar, Asherah, Ashima Baetyl, Astarte, Astronoe, Ate, Athirat, Baalti, Babaia, Bau, Beletekallim, Belit, Belit Ilani, Beltis, Bilit, Cabira, Caelestis, Çatal Hüyük Goddesses, Celestial Virgin, Chaabou, Chaos, Chavah, Cybele, Daena, Damkina, Derketo, Dughda, Dumuziabzu, Eden, Eshtar, Eve, Gula, Ham-vareti, Hannahannas, Huriya, Hushiti, Ininni, Ishkhara, Ishtar, Jauthe, Khi-dimme-azaga, Kista, Kôshart, Kubaba, Lama, Lamassu, Mah, Mama, Mami, Mamitu, Manungal, Mot, Mummu, Nane, Ninhursag, Nin-kharsak, Ninmar, Nintu, Nintuama Kalamma, Nintur, Nin-ur, Nirmali, Nukimmut, Nunbarshegunu, Omicle, Pessinuntica, Rusa, Seimia, Shaushka, Siduri, Tanais,

Tanith, Tehom, Thepla, Tres Mariae, Virgin Mary, Zertur

North America
Aialila'axa, Amayicoyondi, Awitelin Tsita, Badger Old Woman, Bapets, Bear Maiden, Bear Mother, Bear Woman, Cherokee First Woman, Cisiud, Grandmother Moon, Gyhldeptis, Hidatsa Buffalo Woman, Iatiku, Iyatiku, Kivish Atakvish, Komokatsiki, Korawini?i, Master Spirit's Daughter, Mesuk Kummik Okwi, Miritatsiec, Momoy, Naotsete, Nerrivik, Nokomis, Now'utset, Nuexqemalsaix, Ojibwa Daughter, Pakitsumanga, Pukkeenegak, Qominoqa, Sinnilktok, Siwuluhtsitsa, Sixmana, Sonxwana, Sussistinnako, Talatumsi, Ta-no-wish, Tarqeq, Tatqeq, Tcakwena Okya, Tciakwenaoka, Tepkanuset, Tih-kuyi-wuhti, Tlkelikera, Toodlanak, Ullughmiut, Uti Hiata, White-painted Woman, Widapokwi, Wohpe, Woman Who Fell from the Sky

Northern Europe
Alagabiae, Berchta, Disir, Frigga, Fylgir, Fylgja, Fylgukona, Gefion, Gerutha, Hamingja, Hardgrep, Hlif, Hlin, Hludana, Holda, Holle, Idisi, Jordegumma, Marjatta, Mielikki, Nef, Nehalennia, Radien-akka, Saelde, Sibilja, Signy, Thorgerdr Holgarbrudr, Urd, Volva, Wachilt, Weiþen Frauen

Oceania
'Aiāru, Anjea, Atanua, Ātea, Atua fafine, Autran, Avin, Baiangun, Bima, Dilga, Eingana, Fa'ahotu, Fa'a'ipu, Faumea, Firifiri 'aufau, Gnowee, Goolagaya, Ha pu'u, Hatuibwari, Hau ola, Hau wahine, Haumea, Hina uri, Hine māru, Hine piripiri, Hine te iwaiwa, Hine tū a maunga, Ka pū o alaka'i, Kadjari, Kahausibware, Kapo, Karakarook, Karwadi, Koevasi, Kutunga, Lia, Ligifo, Ligoububfanu, Lorop, Mam, Marei kura, Moakura, Mo'e ruru'a, Muriwhakaroto, Nau fiora, Nei matamona, Ngaljod, Nigoubub, Nihoniho teitei, Nu akea, Nu'a kea, Numma Moiyuk, Nungeena, 'Orerorero, Pa'i kauhale, Pāia, Papa raharaha, Po he'enalu mamao, Pohaha, Puna hoa, Pūonoono, Raumiha, Repo, Rua hine metua, Ruahine nihoniho ro roa, Ruma'u Ari'i, Taha taua toto, Taha'ura, Tahu'a, Tamaiti ngava ringa vari, Tāmaumau 'ōrero, Taranga, Taua, Tavake, Tehainga'atua, Tiki kapakapa, Toa miru, Ui, Vahine nui tahu ra'i, Vana'ana'a, Vari ma te takere, Walo, Wawilak, Wayambeh, Wirana, Yalungur

South America
Axomama, Chasca, Cura, Mariana, Oshoun, Raua, Yemoja

Southeast Asia
Bugan, Bulan, Daterata, Dewi Pertimah, Doh Tenangan, Entelanying, Fire Woman, Gaiyun, Gaygayoma, Gitir, Ibabasag, Imbulu Man, Indai Abang, Indo nTegolili, Jalang, Khmoc Pray, Kok Lir, Kolkolibag, Langsuir, Lulong, Mae Phra Phloeng, Manamoan, Mendong, Minti Dara Bunsu, Muni Mental Batu, Nang Pyek Kha Yeh Khi, Panglang, Pudau, Puyu, Ratih, Simei, Singgar, Tabindain Thakinma, Tangkam Majan, Teze, Thabet, Trung Nhi

Western Europe
Abnoba, Aibell, Aima, Áine, Albuferetan Mother Goddess, Alicantean Mother Goddess, Amagandar, Anu, Aobh, Arduinna, Arianrhod, Ban-chuideachaidh Moire, Binah, Birog, Brigid, Búanann, Buan-ann, Cailleach Mor, Caireen, Carlin, Danu, Dea Nutrix, Dechtiré, Éirinn, Erditse, Eri, Ethlinn, Findchaem, Fuwch Frech, Fuwch Gyfeilioru, Gvenn Teir Bronn, Gwenhwyfar, Maga, Magog, Malagan Mother Goddess, Matres, Matronethah, Matronit, Mess Buachalla, Moneiba, Mórrígán, Murna of the White Neck, Nechtan Scéne, Nessa, Niskai, Ollototae, Pressina, Proximae, Quadriviae, Sadb, Scáthach, Suleviae, Valencian Mother Goddess, Y Mamau, Ygerna

Order

Africa
Dan, Gbadu, Ichar-tsirew, Oya

Central America and Mesoamerica
Tsilah Wedo

Eastern Europe
Derfintos, Poldunica, Pyatnitsa Prascovia

Egypt
Hatshepsut, Ini-herit, Maât, Merseger, Tefnut

Far East
Awa-nami-no-kami, Chuang Mu, Feng Po, Jokwa, Kukuri-hime-no-kami, Meng Jiangnü, Nügua, Nüwa, Oto-tachibana-hime-no-mikoto, Tsura-nami-no-kami, Zhinü

Greek and Roman Empires
Acme, Anatole, Angerona, Argimpasa, Athena, Auge, Auxo, Conciliatrix, Concordia, Cymodoce, Cypridos, Damasippus, Dice, Eirene, Eunomia, Euporia, Galaxaura, Gymnasia, Horae, Kymatolege, Menestho, Metis, Musike, Muta, Nymphes, Nyx, Orthosia, Pax, Pheraea, Pherusa, Sophrosyne, Sponde, Tacita, Telete, Themis, Themisto, Titanis, Venus

The Himalaya
Chags-kyu-ma, Gar-ma, gLu-ma Ghirdhima, Locana, Red Makara-headed Peaceful Goddess

Indian Subcontinent
Aditya, Anala, Anila, Antariksha, Apu, Chandra, Danu, Dhara, Dhriti, Dhruva, Dyu, Ma Paudi, Matangi, Nakshatras, Prabhasa, Pratyusha, Prithivi, Sambhu, Samgna, Santa, Sarassouadi, Shamidevi, Shanti, Sodasi, Tushti, Vasus

Near East
Axšti, Khusareth

North America
Djigonsasee, Genetaska, Nirivik, Qailertetang, Thompson Goddesses, Wohpe

Northern Europe
Grid, Nerthus, Vjofn

Oceania
Hine i tapapauta, Hine tu whenua, Na'vahine, Rua hine metua

Southeast Asia
Kalcheng, Si Rapan, Sisina

Western Europe
Chokmah, Silkie

Physical Prowess

Africa
Wagadu

Central America and Mesoamerica
First Mothers

Eastern Europe
Cacce-jienne

Egypt
Gate-keeping Goddesses, Nut, Sekhmet, Wosyet

Far East
Guanyin, Kasenko, Suseri-bime-no-mikoto, Vatiaz

Greek and Roman Empires
Aello, Aellopos, Alcis, Bia, Echo, Hecaerge, Hippothoe, Horme, Optiletis, Oxydercis, Rumor, Sthenias, Stheno, Strenua, Thoë

Indian Subcontinent
Bugarik, Parooa, Pushti, Saci, Saki, Sarvakamadugha, Seven Females, Sitatapatra Aparajita, Subhadra, Sukanthi, Surupa, Tadatagei, Tara, Tara Bai, Urjani

Near East
Aretz, Cista

North America
Nayaanxatisei, Utlunta

Northern Europe
Alfhild, Elli, Fenja, Gebjon, Gefjun, Gjalp, Grid, Kara, Lorelei, Nixen

Oceania
Bumerali, Hine tū a hōanga, Kura
ngaituka

Western Europe
Dornoll, Emer, Levarcham, Lot, Luaths
Lurgann, Scáthach

Poverty

Africa
Aberewa, Dziva

Eastern Europe
Curche

Far East
Moshir-huchi, Shunyi Furen

Greek and Roman Empires
Miseria, Penia

Indian Subcontinent
Aie Lacha, Alakshmi, Bhukhi Mata,
Nirriti

North America
Corn Maidens

Oceania
Hau wahine, Muiu'uleapai

Primordial Being

Africa
Eka Abassi, Mebeli, Mousso Koroni
Koundye, Nana Buluku, Nyante

Egypt
Amaunet, Amunet, Goose Goddess,
Hauhet, Heh, Hehet, Heqet, Kait, Maât,
Mehueret, Methyer, Mht wr.t, Nen,
Nunet, Rait

Far East
Avalokita, Chang E, Chang Yong,
Kokuzo, Shen Deity

Greek and Roman Empires
Achlys, Chaos, Gaea

The Himalaya
Nam-mk'ahi-snin-po, Shakti, Tho-og

Indian Subcontinent
Aditi, Akasagarabha, Ammavaru,
Anushakti, Asa Poorna, Bisal
Mariamna, Daiviprakriti, Devi, Eternal
Mother, Ganapatihrdaya, Ganesani,
Ichchhashakti, Ideal Nature, Kali,
Kamaksi, Kundalini, Kundalini Shakti,
Lakini, Lalita Tripurasundari, Ma Nu,
Mahadevi, Mahalakshmi, Mahalaya,
Mahendri, Matri-Padma, Mulaprakriti,
Para-vac, Parvati, Prajna,
Purvadevatas, Saci, Sarparajni, Shakti,
Shaktis, Sitala, Substance Mother,
Sushakti, Tripura Bhairavi, Uma, Viraj,
Yashodhara

Near East
An.zu, Arubani, Baalath, Ba'alath
Gebal, Bagmashtu, Briah, Chaiah,
Fšeratu, Holy Spirit, Hubur, Lahamu,

Malkat-shemen, Malkatu, Nammu,
Nin-me-sar-ra, Ninmul, Orore,
Shekinah, Sophia, Sophia-achamoth,
Tiamat, Tihamtu, Tillili, Word, Zicum,
Zoe

North America
Atavish, Han, Old Woman of the Sea

Northern Europe
Audhumbla, Bestla, Hlodyn, Jord,
Mimir, Voluspa

Oceania
Koevasi, Maimoa a longona, Po, Tima
te kore

Southeast Asia
Ina Da Samihara Luwo, Makarom
Mawakhu

Western Europe
Briah, Chokmah, Primum Mobile

Reptiles

Africa
Dan, Eveningstar of Wakaranga,
Mother of Food, Nikaiva

Central America and Mesoamerica
Aida Wedo, Ayizan, Ayopechcatl,
Cihuacoatl, Coatlicue, Erzulie, Ix Tub
Tan, Mu Olokukurtlisop, Olosa, Takótsi
Nakawé, Tāté Haútse Kupúri, Tāté
Kyewimóka, Tāté Naaliwámi, Tāté
Rapawiyama, Tatei Hamuxa, Tatei
Kaxiwari, Tatei Xapawiyelkame, Xitzam

Eastern Europe
Aspelenie, Egle, Kamennaia Baba,
Marà, Rusalka, Selci-syt-emysyt,
Suoyatar

Egypt
Ankhtith, Buto, Chensit, Ernutet, Heh,
Kebechet, Khut, Mehen, Mehenit,
Menhenet, Merti, Nehebka, Renenutet,
Rennutet, Selk, Thoeris, Uatchet, Uazit,
Uertheku

Far East
Ami Goddess, Benten, Chang E,
Guiling Shenamu, Hi-naga-hime,
Inoshishi, Kiyo-hime,
Kushi-nada-hime, Nügua,
Nusa-kor-huchi, Nüwa, Shandian Pozi,
She Mu, Shihu Shi,
Toyo-tama-bime-no-mikoto

Greek and Roman Empires
Paeonia, Pyrene

The Himalaya
Blue Serpent-headed Water Goddess,
Greenish-black Serpent-headed Mystic
Goddess, Lu, Reddish-yellow
Serpent-headed Brahma Goddess,
Til-bu-ma

Indian Subcontinent
Bhogavati, Bhumiya Rani, Buddhi
Nagin, Durgamma, Gara Satamai,
Janguli, Ka Di, Kadru, Mahamayuri,

Manasa, Mane Manchi, Narmada,
Nona Chamari, Pidari, Sarparajni,
Sarpis, Singhbahini, Surasa, Ulupi,
Vigayavati

Near East
Āl, Anush, Ba'alat Ashtart, Eden,
Inaras, Ininni, Kades, Kadi, Lamasthu,
Leviathan, Nathair Parrthuis, Nidaba,
Sala, Tiamat, Tihamtu

North America
Awehai, Ee-eh-ch-choo-ri-ch'ahm-nin,
Hilili Okya, Kahaila Kachin' Mana,
Quail Kachin' Mana, Sky Woman,
Tcua-wugti, Unhcegila

Oceania
Ahīm ū, Ala muki, Babamik, Birra
nulu, Bulaing, Eingana, Ha pu'u,
Ha'apua 'inanea, Hatuibwari, Hau ola,
Hau wahine, Jari, Julunggul, Ka lama i
nu'u, Ka mo'o 'inanea, Kagauraha,
Kahausibware, Kalama 'ula, Kāne
kua'ana, Karakarook, Kiha wahine,
Kiki pua, Koevasi, Konjini, Kunapipi,
Lahi wahine, Lani loa, Lani wahine,
Mairangi, Mamala, Moko, Moku hinia,
Mo'o, Mo'o i nanea, Narama, Narpajin,
Ndengei, Ngaljod, Ngārara huarau,
Niniganni, Pi'i ka lalau, Polalowehi,
Tobunaygu, Tū pari, Tulpengusu,
Tupengusu, Upoho, Vie moko, Waka,
Wali manoanoa, Wayambeh,
Wulutahanga

South America
Boiuna, Doña Rosalina, Luandinha,
Mama Pacha, Raharariyoma,
Uarahiulú, Yaca-mama

Southeast Asia
Dagau, Djata, Fire Woman,
Intombangol, Jata, Luyong Kabig,
Tabindain Thakinma, Thusandi

Western Europe
Carravogue

Sciences

Greek and Roman Empires
Achelois, Aonides, Apollonis, Arche,
Ardalides, Borysthenis, Cephisso,
Erato, Hippocrenides, Hypate,
Ilissiades, Maeonides, Melete, Mneiae,
Mneme, Mnemonides, Muses, Myrtis of
Anthedon, Neilo, Nete, Parnassides,
Pegasides, Pimpleides, Polymatheia,
Polymnia, Rhodia, Thaleia, Thelxinoe,
Tipoplo, Tritone, Urania

Indian Subcontinent
Dhisana, Sarassouadi

Selfishness

Central America and Mesoamerica
Ayauhteotl, Erzulie

Eastern Europe
Šurali

Greek and Roman Empires
Calaene, Maera, Ossa, Rumor, Selene

Indian Subcontinent
Alakhani, Lopamudra

Near East
Az, Semiramis

North America
Frog Woman, Gahondjidahonk, Gendenwitha, Ite, Kansa First Woman, Rain Goddess, Thompson Goddesses

Oceania
'Āpua kea, Baabenga, Dogai, Kalaia, Meamei, Nei auti, Nujka'u, Nujmaga

South America
Cocamama

Southeast Asia
Gaygayoma

Selflessness

Africa
Nana Buruku, Oya

Central America and Mesoamerica
Anne, Apozanolotl, Candelaria, Catherine, Claire, Grande Ezili, Huixtocihuatl, Isidore, Ixtab, Marie Madeleine, Nana Buruku, Oba, Oddudua, Our Lady of Hope, Our Lady of La Caridad of Cobre, Our Lady of Mercy, Our Lady of Regla, Philomena, Teresa, Virgin of Guadalupe, Xpuch

Eastern Europe
Dekla, Karta, Kildisin, Luojatar, Mokosh, Mokosi, Nishke-ava, Niski-ava, Paraskeva, Prende

Egypt
Qetesh, Sati, Thmei

Far East
Miao Shan, Tai Yuan, Yakami, Yu Nü

Greek and Roman Empires
Aedos, Alcestis, Apostrophia, Astraea, Befana, Black Virgin, Enkrateia, Fides, Leprea, Muliebris, Pandora, Protogenia, Rhea Silvia, Telete, Virgo

Indian Subcontinent
Aparna, Aramati, Diti, Jatila, Kannagi, Karaikkal Asmmaiyar, Kausalya, Ksama, Kujum-Chantu, Lajja, Renuka, Shrutavati, Uma, Usnisavijaya

Near East
Anāhita, Artemidos, Leilah, Rabi'a Al-adawiya, Spentā Ārmaiti

North America
Cactus Grandmother, Minnehaha, Thompson Goddesses

Northern Europe
Horsel, Ursula

Oceania
Ioio moa

South America
Senhora Ana

Western Europe
Ban-chuideachaidh Moire, Branwen, Brigid, Eigin, Ethné, Inghean Bhuidhe, Lasair, Latiaran, Matronit, Náir, Sabra, Triduana, Wylgeforte

Sky and Heavens

Africa
Aizu, Akazu, Andriamahilala, Gbenebeka, Inkosazana, Inkosikasi, Mobokomu, Morongo, Nambi, Nomkubulwana, Nomkubulwane, Tokpodun

Central America and Mesoamerica
Obatala, Omecihuatl, Our Lady of Mercy, U Colel Caan

Eastern Europe
Auroras, Azer-ava, Ban-ava, Hotogov Mailgan, Ilmater, Kanym, Luonnotar, Mokosh, Nalban-aiy, Nalygyr-aissyt-khotun, Rana Nedia, Serque-edne

Egypt
Abet-neteru-s, Anatha Baetyl, Anta, Aritatheth, Buto, Djet, Hathor, Horit, Huntheth, Mehueret, Neith, Netpe, Nut, Shesemtet, Sothis, Tefnut, Themath

Far East
Ama-tsu-otome, Ame-chikaru-mizu-hime, Ame-no-tsudoe-chine-no-kami, Fupao, He Xiangu, Kisagai-hime, Mu Re, Nts'ai Hwa, Nügua, Nüwa, Shi-nun-manuri, Shio-mi-ma, Ts'i Ma Niang Tsai, Zhinü

Greek and Roman Empires
Aer, Aether, Aphrodite, Diwya, Eudora, Meiboia, Merope, Olympiades, Regina

The Himalaya
âkâsha-dahatû-ishvarî, A-phyi-gung-rgyal, bKur-dman-rgyalmo, 'Brug-gi-sgra-sgrog-ma, Didun, gNam-Iha dkar-mo, gNam-Iha-byang-sman-mthing-gi-go-zu-can, Khahdoma, Klu-mo-dung-skyong-ma, Nam-mkha'i-lha-mo-gsal-byed-ma, Nam-mkha'i-lha-mo-Kun-tu-bzang-mo, Nam-mkha'i-lha-mo-snyoms-byed-ma, Nam-mkha'i-lha-mo-sprin-tshogs-ma, Nam-mkha'i-lha-mo-tsha-gsang-snyoms, Nam-mkha'i-lha-mo-tshod-'dzin-ma, Ogress of Lust, rDo-rje-ne-ne-gnam-sman-sgron, Sangye-khado, Thog-gi-bu-yug

Indian Subcontinent
Aditi, Adrika, Alambusha, Angana, Antariksha, Apsarases, Auksagandhi, Bhairava, Bong, Caksusi, Devis, Dik-kanya, Dyava-Prthivi, Dyu, Earth Mother of Hrusso, Gandharvis, Ganga, Gayatri, Ghrtaci, Guggulu, Hamsika, Harini, Hima, Ira, Jamadagni, Kakubh,

Keshini, Kimnaris, Kujum-Chantu, Madhava, Malini, Manasi, Marisha, Mena, Misrakesi, Mother Space, Naladi, Pathya, Pramandani, Pramlocha, Pururavas, Purvachitti, Raktadhara, Rambha, Rati, Sahaganya, Sakuntala, Sanumati, Saranjus, Sarparajni, Sarpis, Sarvakamadugha, Sasilekha, Saudamani, Simhika, Subhadra, Sukanthi, Surabhidatta, Surapamsula, Surupa, Tapati, Tilottama, Tripura Bhairavi, Uravari, Urvasi, Vadaba, Vasistha, Vibudhastris

Near East
Anatu, Ashtart, Asi, Damkina, Tanith, Tiamat

North America
Aataentsic, Ahsonnutli, Akoq, Awehai, Awitelin Tsita, Bikeh Xozo, Gaende'sonk, Hürü'Ingwühti, Ixlexwani, Kanilkes, Ketq Skwayne, Kivish Atakvish, Le-tkakawash, Siltslani, Snutkanals, Sxapetl, Tlitcaplitana

Northern Europe
Geirahod

Oceania
Aouli, Arahuta, Atatuhi, Birrahgnooloo, Cunnembeillee, De ai, Fakahotu, Fulu'ulaalematato, Hā'oa'oa, Hāpai, Hine ahupapa, Hine maki moe, Hine nui o te kawa, Hu'a nu'u marae, Jugumishanta, Ka onohi ula, Ke ao Iewa, Kobine, Le gerem, Lejman, Mahora nui a rangi, Mahora nui a tea, Mamao, Nguatupu'a, Paea, Silili, Sky Maiden, Tere'e fa'aari'i mai'i te Ra'i, Tonga maulu'au, Tongo tongo

South America
Cura, Ocllo, Peruvian Mamas, Raua, Uarahiulú

Southeast Asia
Abyang, Agemem, Chemioi, Djalai, Dua Nggae, Inchin Temaga, Ini Andan, Ini Manang, Kadeyuna, Lingkambene, Manang Jaban, Munsumundok, Sik Sawp, Sitapi, Suklang-malayon, Tiun, Warunsasadun, Yak Tanggoi, Yara Meng, Yuang Sori

Western Europe
Aima, Anu, Belisama, Mala Liath, Penardun, Urtz

Small Size

Africa
Aya

Central America and Mesoamerica
Ahnt Ahs Pok'

Eastern Europe
Maruchi

Far East

Kaguya-hime-no-mikoto, Maing Jini, Senyo, So Wang-mo, White Wave

Indian Subcontinent

Aginvati, Hemaprabha, Khekaris, Kutamangari, Lalitalochana, Mandaradevi, Maruttaruni, Mgigalekha, Ratnamangari, Shaktiyasas, Suratamangari, Svarnarekha

Near East

Aslik

North America

Ondoutaehte

Northern Europe

Buschgroḅmutter, Frau Welt

Oceania

Pi'i ka lalau, Pohaha, Tupu'a

Western Europe

Aeval, Aibell, Aine, Badh, Banschi, Banshees, Bé Find, Bean Sídhe, Bebo, Bonnes Dames, Bri, Cliodhna, Corra, Corrigan, Fairies, Fflur, Finncaev, Medb, Morgan Le Fay, Onaugh, Oonagh, Silly Wychtis, Sin, Tryanon, Uchtdealbh, Urganda, Urisks, Y Mamau

Stars and Planets

Africa

Asase Afua, Massassi, Morongo, Ntoa, Seta, Shashaya, Topogh

Central America and Mesoamerica

Chimalmat, Chulavete, Citlalicue, Itoki, Mu Olokukurtlisop, Olomakriai, Tabaminarro, Tāké Vēlika Uimáli, Tzitzimime, Xbaquiyalo

Eastern Europe

Astrik, Khotun, Kubai-khotun, Perkune Tete, Solbon, Sweigs-dunka, Vakarine, Vechernyaya Zvezda, Vetca-neut, Zvezda Dennitsa

Egypt

Auset, Berenice, Isis, Kefa, Kenmut, Reret, Seret, Serqet, Ta-repy, Taueret, Thoeris, Zodiacal Virgins

Far East

Ame-no-tanabata-hime-no-mikoto, Can Nü, Chedi Furen, Dou Mou, Gao Lanying, Hongluan Xingjun, Hoy Kong, Huang, Huoling Shengmu, Jia Shi, Longji Kongju, Ma Shi, Manzan Gormo, Nish-kan-ru-mat, Niu She, Nochiu-e-rant-mat, Nok, Saoqing Niang, Seven Sisters of Industry, Shesang Nü, Shiji Niangniang, Shokujo, Tian Nü, Xieren Xingjun, Xiu Zhi, Yang Shih, Yu Nü, Zhinü

Greek and Roman Empires

Adraste, Aesyle, Amalthea, Ambrosia, Amphinome, Andromeda, Asteria, Asterope, Asteropeia, Astraea, Atlantides, Bacche, Callisto, Celaeno,

Cisseis, Cleia, Cleis, Coccymo, Coronis, Cynosura, Dione, Dodonides, Eidothea, Electra, Eos, Erato, Erigone, Eripha, Euadne, Eudora, Helice, Hippothoe, Hyades, Lampatho, Maia, Medusa, Merope, Nysa, Nyseides, Parthenia, Pedile, Peisdice, Phaeo, Phyto, Pleiades, Polyxo, Protis, Selene, Sterope, Stonychia, Taygete, Thyene, Urania, Vergiliae

The Himalaya

Grahamatrka

Indian Subcontinent

Abrayanti, Al Shua, Amba, Arundhati, Bahu, Chupunika, Dhisana, Dula, Girl Twin of Mithuna, Isi, Kanyā, Krittika, Maghayanti, Mahavidya, Mahi, Medini, Nitatui, Rohini, Sarama, Savari, Tara, Tara Bai, Tula, Urjani, Varshayanti, Vishnupadi, Vumdhati, Woman in a Ship, Woman with Cord

Near East

Aderenosa, Adra Nedefa, Anael, Anat-bethel, Anunit, Ashirat, Aslik, Astghik, Ayish, Ba'alat Ashtart, Celestial Virgin, Chiun, Cista, Eshtar, Istehar, Isthar, Kimah, Nanai, Nane, Ne-zil-la, Nin-makh, Ruha D'qudsha, Zuriel

North America

Atira, Bear Woman, Big Black Meteor Star, Bright Star, Chulavete, Cu-piritta-ka, Evening Star, Evening Star Lady, Gendenwitha, Hihankara, Hulluk Miyumko, La'idamlulum Ku'le, Malaḧshishinish, Mi-ka-k'e Hondon, Mi-ka-k'eu-ki-thaç'in, Morning Star Woman, Nahokhos baadi, Paiowa, Ponoya, Seven Sisters, Soat-saki, Soniyawi, Ta Tha-bthin, Tcuperekata, Tsek'any'agojo, Utset, Yellow-going Old Woman

Northern Europe

Nat

Oceania

Apu o te ra'i, Ariki, Atea ta'o nui, Dok, Hine turama, Hoku kau opae, Ka'ao melemele, Karak karak, Komeang, Lū, Makara, Matariki, Mayi Mayi, Meamei, Ningarope, Pirili, Pīrīrama, Rua tupua nui, Sian pual'etafa, Star Girl, Tagisomenaja, Tahi ari'i, Taku rua, Taonoui, Tapuitea, Te ra'i tû roroa, Te'ura taui e pâ, Tu i te moana'urifa, Ungamilia

South America

Ceiuci, Ituana, Pirua, Star Woman, Temioua

Southeast Asia

Gaygayoma, Tala

Western Europe

Don, Sirona, Tiphereth

Sun and Day

Africa

Lissa, Loa, Nummo, !Urisis, Zat-badar

Central America and Mesoamerica

Cihuateteo, Citlalicue, Olomakriai, Tatei Kukuru 'Uimari, Tlacolteutl, Tlaltecuhtli, Tzitzimime, Xmucane

Eastern Europe

Amra, Beive-neida, Beiwe, Firebird, Iarila, Keca Aba, Ketse-awa, Koliada, Krasnyi, Perkune Tete, Poldunica, Polednice, Pszepolnica, Pu'gud-emei, Rodnaia Matushka, Saule, Saules-māte, Saules Meitas, Shundimumi, Si, Solntse, Sun Virgin, Sundy-mumy, Tsi, Xatel-ekwa, Yine'a-ne'ut, Zleja, Zorya Utrennyaya

Egypt

Ahi, Akusaa, Amunta, Ara-seshap, Atet, Bast, Gate-keeping Goddesses, Hathor, Iusaaset, Kenat, Kerhet, Khut, Mht wr.t, Rat, Rat-taui, Satet

Far East

Ama-terasu-ō-mi-kami, Chuh Kamuy, Dainichi-nyorai, Hi-kawa-hime, Marishi-ten, Somber Maiden, Sun and Moon, Sun Goddess, Sun Goddess, Xi Hou

Greek and Roman Empires

Aega, Albina, Cupra, Dysis, Helia, Hemera, Phaenna, Telephassa, Theia

The Himalaya

Indian Subcontinent

Angarmati Bhawani, Anushayini, Assam Mother Earth, Bisal Mariamna, Chhatmata, Chhaya, Cosmic Waters, Dhisana, Doini, Donyi, Dyaush-pitir, Jamadagni, Ka Singi, Ka Sngi, Maya, Panthoibi, Parashakti, Pingala, Sedi-Irkong-Bomong, Sedi-Irkong-Bong, Suki, Surya, Tari Pennu, Ugracanda, Vijaya Sakti, Yatudhanis

Near East

Anit, Arinna, Ashirat, Asmun Nikal, Bar-juchne, Dudu Hepa, Hebat, Henti, Kun, Laz, Mezulla, Nahar, Nikal-mati, Sala, Saps, Sarpanitu, Shapash, Shaph, Tawannannas, Walanni, Wurusemu

North America

Akycha, Cherokee Sun Goddess, Gogyeng So Wuhti, Grandmother Spider, Greenland Sun Goddess, Han, Hekoolas, Igaehinvdo, Ka'a Mata, Kutnahin, Mallina, Mikimatt, Nenalaatseqa, Nuñda, Nusxemtaiana, Nutse'xenem, Ponoya, Sanihas, Sapiqenwas, Shakuru, Siqiniq, Sun Goddess, Sun Sister, Sun Woman, Sximana, Tahc-I, Tcho, Tunica Sun Goddess, Xavasumkuli

Northern Europe
Aarvak, Beiwe, Bjort, Dag, Frigga, Gerda, Ingeborg, Mardal, Rind, Sol, Sun, Sunna, Swanhild

Oceania
Alinga, Ārohirohi, Atahikurangi, Avin, Bara, Bila, Dietyi, Dinewan, Gnowee, Hina 'ea, Hine aotea, Hinehaone, Knowee, Murupiangkala, Paparoa i te opunga, Sināsa'umani, Sun Woman, Tiki, Tū papa, Walo, Wibalu, Wuriupranala, Yhi

South America
Noitu, Our Mother, Wazeparkwa

Southeast Asia
Aponibolinayen, Hanan, Mapatal Bugan inAmalgo

Western Europe
Aimend, Danu, Dia Griene, Eguski, Ekhi, Emer, Gillagriene, Grainne, Grian, Helliougmounis, Mor Muman, Olwen, Tiphereth

Supreme Being

Africa
Ayeba, Buruku, Inkosikasi, Mawu, Mebeli, Nyakala, Nzambi, Tamara

Central America and Mesoamerica
Omeyacigoat

Eastern Europe
Tabiti, Xotsadam, Y-lyunda Kotta

Far East
Ama-terasu-ō-mi-kami

Greek and Roman Empires
Gaea, Hera, Panteleia, Phoebe, Titanides

Indian Subcontinent
Aditi, Bhagavati, Bhuvanesvari, Devi, Ekajata, Kapenopfu, Mahadevi, Mahalakshmi, Mahasarasvati, Mahesvari, Nitya

Near East
Abyss Lady, Halmssuitta, Hanwasuit, Hatti Throne Goddess, Pinikir, Shekinah

North America
Hawichyepam Maapuch, H'uraru, Sklumyoa

Northern Europe
Aśynjur, Deivai, Matrona

Oceania
Hine

South America
Maret-Jikky, Perimbó, Schetewuarha

Southeast Asia
Agusan Devi, Dua Nggae, Indara, Jalang, Jata, Tana Ekan

Western Europe
Gevurah, Lur, Medb, Nimue, Rigantona, Sephiroth, Sovranty, Tabiti

Time

Central America and Mesoamerica
Chalchiuhcihuatl, Chalchiuhtlicue, Mictecacihuatl, Oxomoco, Tlacolteutl, Tlazolteotl, Tonantzin, Xmucane

Eastern Europe
Colleda, Dziewanna, Erce, Koliada, Kupalo, Lada, Marena, Marzana, Morana, Myesyats, Paraskeva, Perit, Poldunica, Polednice, Prende, Pszpolnica, Pyatnitsa Prascovia, Rana Nedia, Veshianka, Vesna, Wesna, Wiosna, Wüt-ian uder, Zitna-atka

Egypt
Aa-sheft, Aat-aatet, Aat-khu, Ahabit, Akhet, Ament-semu-set, Ankhtith, Anpet, Apt, Apt-hent, Apt-renpit, Ast, Atem, Fifth Hour Goddess, Hap-tcheserts, Hekenth, Hent-nut-s, Her-tep-aha-her-neb-s, Hert-erman, Hert-ketit-s, Hetemitet, Het-hert, Isis, Kefa, Khefet-hau-hesqet-neha-her, Khemit, Khent, Kheperu, Khesef-khemt, Mak-nebt-s, Manefertrā, Mehi, Menhit, Mert, Merti, Mut-neb-set, Nakith, Nau, Neb-ankhet, Neb-senti, Nebt-mat, Nebt-setau, Nebt-shat, Nebt-shefshefet, Nebt-thehent, Nebtusha, Nekiu, Nesbet, Netert-en -khentet-ra, Netheth, Nunut, Par-neferu-en-neb-set, Perit, Proet, Rennutet, Renpa, Renpet, Ronpet, Sarset, Sati-abut, Sati-arut, Sebit, Seher-tut, Sekhet, Sekhet-metu, Semt, Senb-kheperu, Sesenet-khu, Seshetat, Shemat-khu, Shesat-makey-neb-s, Sothis, Tcheser-shetat, Tefnut, Tekhi, Temtith, Tenith, Tent-baiu, Tentenit-uhert-khakabu, Tesert-ant, Thceser-shetat, Tuatt-makel-neb-s, Twelve Goddesses of Life and Strength, Uadjet, Uatchet, Unnut, Urt-sekhemu, Ushmet-hatu-kheftiu-rā, Yept

Far East
Aki-bime-no-kami, Flower Goddesses, Frost Goddess, Haya-aki-tsu-hime-no-kami, Izushi-otome-no-kami, Jūni-sama, Li, Marōdo, Patrinia, Saho-yama-hime, She Mu, Tatsu-ta-hime, Yuefu Taiyin, Zhinü

Greek and Roman Empires
Acme, Aestas, Anatole, Angerona, Auge, Auxo, Carpo, Cypridos, Demeter, Euporia, Flora, Gymnasia, Horae, Luna, Mene, Mesembria, Musike, Nymphes, Opora, Orthosia, Penteteris, Pherusa, Sponde, Telete, Thallo, Thalna, Titanis

The Himalaya
bDug-spös-ma, Buddha Krotishaurima, Cha-dog-ma, Chags-kyu-ma, Chi-chi-gyal-mo, Dark-green Ghasmari, dByar-gyi-rgyal-mo, gLu-ma Ghirdhima, Gokarmo, Hphreng-ba-ma, Karma Dakinis, Karma-krotishaurima, Kuntu-bzang-mo, Lha-mo, Me-tog-ma,

Padma Krotishaurima, Pukkase, Ratna Krotishaurima, Red Pramoha, Red Pukhase, Sangs-rgyas-spyan-ma, sGrol-mas, Smasha, sNang-gsal-ma, Ston-gyi-rgyal-mo, Tsandhali, Tseurima, Vajra Krotishaurima, Wang-Chugmas, White Kerima, Yellow Tseurima, Yellowish-white Tsandhali, Zhag-pa-ma, Zhal-zas-ma

Indian Subcontinent
Ekastaka, Grismadevi, Hariyali, Hemantadevi, Jamadagni, Kalaratri, Kali, Kalika, Madhusri, Mata, Muhurta, Pan Dong Cyu, Parvati, Saraddevi, Saradvadhu, Satarupa, Sati, Tilottama, Vasanta

Near East
Daena, Huyairya, Kista, Saoka, Shekinah, Zamyad

North America
Ahöla Mana, 'Alaĥtin, Anoolikwotsaix, Cactus Grandmother, Esdzanata, Estsanatlehi, Horo Mana, Komokatsiki, Ku Gu, Nuñda, Nunuoska, Old Woman of the Seasons, Ong Wuhti, Qailertetang, Snukpanlits, Wah-kah-nee, Wohpe, Yohozro Wuhti

Northern Europe
Frigga, Ganglot, Gerda, Gudrun, Hrede, Idun, Ildico, Kunhild, Rana Neida, Rindr, Spurke, Swan Maidens, Swanhild, Thora

Oceania
Hine ata, Hine raumati, Hine takurua, Le gerem, 'Ohu tū moua, One kea, Purlimil

South America
Mama Quilla

Southeast Asia
Duc Ba, Pajau Yan

Western Europe
Blathnát, Carlin, Cordelia, Inghean Bhuidhe, Lasair, Maid Marian, Miranda, oShion, Samhain, Stratteli, Triple Goddess

Ugliness

Africa
Nummo, Usiququmadevu

Central America and Mesoamerica
Coatlicue, Erzulie Mapiangueh, Tlaltecuhtli

Eastern Europe
Bozaloshtsh, Gorska Makva, Kalma, Kipu-tytto, Kriksy, Kulshedra, Loviatar, Metsänneitsyt, Navki, Nedolya, Shtrige, Vammatar

Egypt
Thoeris

Far East
Ame-no-uzume, Hisa-me,
Izanami-no-kami, Okame, Turesh, Ugly
Females of Yomi, Yomo-tsu-shiko-me

Greek and Roman Empires
Acholoe, Adicia, Alecto, Celaeno,
Chariboea, Chimaera, Curissia,
Echidna, Empusa, Empusae, Enyo,
Erinyes, Euryale, Gorgons, Graeae,
Harpies, Kelaino, Lamia, Lamiae,
Lelaino, Medusa, Megaera,
Mixoparthenos, Nicothoe, Perso, Phaea,
Phorcides, Podarge, Scylla, Telphusia,
Tuchulcha

The Himalaya
dPal-ldan Lha-mo,
Gangs-dkar-sha-med,
'Jigs-pa'i-zer-mo-mig-gcig

Indian Subcontinent
Arayi, Camunda, Dhumavati, Ghuls,
Kutumbini, Makaris, Marichi,
Naktamcharis, Nisacharis, Rangda,
Vidyujjvalakarali

Near East
An.zu, Lamassu, Subeh

North America
Anog Ite, Dzoo-noo-qua, Nataska
Mana, Red Woman, Tikuoi Wuhti, Ulala

Northern Europe
Angerbodha, Berchta, Hella, Holda,
Thok

Oceania
Babamik, Haumia, Hine ahuone, Hine
tū a maunga, Ihi, Kiki pua, Miru kura,
Nevinbimba'au, Pele, Sherok, Te mo'o
nieve

Southeast Asia
Bake, Magtatangal, Thabet

Western Europe
Annis, Bronach, Cuimne, Dornoll,
Gwrach y Rhibyn, Hag, Muirdris,
Sovranty

Unhappiness

Africa
Dariya, Mhaya, Qandisa, Sia Jatta Bari,
Yemonja

Central America and Mesoamerica
Oba

Eastern Europe
Aino, Dekla, Egle, First Woman,
Kivutar, Loviatar, Shtrige, Vammatar

Far East
Akaru-hime, Ama-terasu-ō-mi-kami,
Baiji, Iwa-naga-hime, Konohana-
sakuya-hime, Nakime, Naki-sawa-
me-no-kami, Takahime-no-mikoto

Greek and Roman Empires
Achlys, Aegiale, Aetheria, Agraulos,
Aidos, Aigle, Alcyone, Algea,
Anaxarete, Andromeda, Angerona,
Antigone, Arsinoe, Byblis, Calaene,
Canente, Castalia, Demeter, Dioxippe,
Elate, Electryone, Eos, Erato, Erigone,
Eurydice, Heliadae, Invidia, Lamia,
Maera, Megaira, Melpomene, Merope,
Miseria, Naenia, Nemesis, Odyne,
Oizys, Pallas, Peirene, Phaethonides,
Phaethusa, Phatusa, Pitys

The Himalaya
brDa'i 'phrad,
'Jigs-pa'i-zer-mo-mig-gcig, Kerimas,
Krodhesvari, Pukkase, Smasha, Toma,
Tonagma, Tsandhali, Tseurima

Indian Subcontinent
Assam Mother Earth, Baihi, Bauri Bai,
Bhrkuti, Candi, Dakinis, Ginoo moong,
Hathay, Hri, Ka Syrtieh, Khasias
Celestial Woman, Krodha, Kurukulla,
Lajja, Mamata, Mandodari, Mrtyu,
Murala, Muzamuza, Nirriti, Pidari,
Pramlocha, Rohini, Rudrani, Samgna,
Sedi

Near East
Inanna, Myrrha, Semiramis, Sophia
Prunikos, Thisbe

North America
Akycha, Ampata Sapa, Chimon Mana,
Large Woman, Ponoya, Skwanat.äm.ä,
Spirit Woman, Tih-kuyi-wuhti, Tunica
Sun Goddess

Northern Europe
Freyja, Ildico

Oceania
Anoano, Arimata, Atoto, Bima, Dilga,
Ekeitehua, Faingaa, Hana, Harataunga,
Hina, Hina tau miha, Hine i tau ira,
Hine tītama, Hine tū a maunga, Ho'o
hoku i ka lani, Horotata, Kā'ana'e like,
Muiu'uleapai, Mundikara, Narina,
Naruni, Nona, Osooso, Papa,
Parabaruma, Pirili, Porpoise Girl,
Purlimil, Ruahine nihoniho ro roa,
Shaliom, Sinafakalau, Sky Maiden,
Tungi'one, Wanatjilda, Yeenapah

South America
Cavillaca, Copacati, Shell Woman,
Urpihuachac

Western Europe
Achall, Aige, Ailinn, Fea, Fuamnach,
Giolla Gréine, Leanan Sidhe, Nemain,
Pressina

Unknown

Africa
Abe, Afiong Edem, Alajeru, Ato, Dasse,
Hyrax, Kaiala, Matu, Miseke, Sabbath,
Sambata, Yemojá

Central America and Mesoamerica
Charlotte, Chich Cohel, Cilich Colel,
Guatauva, Ilancueitl, Ix Bolon Yol
Nicté, Ix Chuah, Ix Dziban Yol Nicté, Ix
Dzoy, Ix Kanyultá, Ixma Chucbeni,
Quetzaltetlatl, Tonalcacihuatl, Xkitza

Eastern Europe
Beregina, Dziparu-māte, Joukahainen,
Mauthia, Siva

Egypt
Anit, Ankhet, Anrn, Antarta, Anthrathi,
Apitus, Arsinoe, Ashima Baetyl,
As-neit, Avaris, Behbet, Dikaiosyne,
Goddess of Papremis, Hat-mehi,
Iou-s-aas, Iusaset, Juesaes, Junit,
Katesch, Kenet, Kent, Khaft,
Kha-ra-ta-nek-ha, Mai-hesa, Mesta,
Neb-anu, Neb-oo, Nebt-nehi,
Nehemāuit, Nehimeou, Ninit, Nubait,
Nukarā, Nushim, Pasht, Phut, Rannu,
Reschep, Sakhmis, Sapt, Seben, Seb-tet,
Sheshat, Shes-kentet, Sobkit, Suvan,
Tafne, Tafner, Tafnuit, Tanenit, Taur,
Tefent, Tekaharesapusaremkakaremet,
Tiv, Toses, Usit, Watch Merti,
Werethekau, Zenenet

Far East
Ashi-nadaka-no-kami, Deities of the
Third Earthly Generation, Fecundity
Lady, Fei, Fute-mimi-no-kami,
Hi-narashi-bime, Hina-teri-nukata-
bichi-o-ikochini-no-kami, Hinomahe-
no-kami, Hiyoi Kwan-non, Iku-gui-
no-kami, Ino-hime, Jiutian Houmu,
Jun-tei Kwan-non, Kagayo-hime, Kamu-
ō-ichi-hime, Kamu-ya-tate-hime-no-
mikoto, Kuni-no-kura-do-no-kami,
Kuni-no-sa-zuchi-no-kami, Miao Qing,
Miao Yin, Mihotsu-hime, Munakata
Goddesses, Nibu-tsu-hime, Nupka-ush-
ma, Ogtarghui-in jiruken, Okikurmi
kot tureshi, Ō-to-mato-hime-no-kami,
Seventeen Generations Deities,
Suserihime, Toho-tsu-machi-ne-no-
kami, Tori-mimi-no-kami, Triple Pussa,
Um, Wen Cheng, Wen Qiao, Xu
Kongcang, Yasak-no-iri-bime-no-
mikoto, Yorozu-hatatoya-akitsushi-
hime-no-mikoto

Greek and Roman Empires
Acca, Achiroe, Acidusa, Aeantis,
Aeetias, Aegina, Aetole, Agdistis,
Ageleia, Aigle, Akhuvitr, Alea,
Alectrona, Alma, Alpan, Alpanu,
Alphaea, Altria, Amatheia, Amathusia,
Amica, Amphilogea, Anaxibia,
Anaxiroe, Anaxo, Androctasia,
Androktiasi, Angelos, Anieros, Antaea,
Antioche, Apanchomene, Apteros,
Arce, Argeia, Aricina, Ariste, Armata,
Arne, Artimpasa, Asia, Asine, Assesia,
Astyageia, Aventina, Aversa,
Balneorum, Barbata, Berecynthia,
Beroe, Boeotia, Bona, Bona Oma,
Bubastos, Byzyge, Cabeiria, Calliste,
Capta, Cercyra, Chalcioecos, Chera,
Chione, Chloris, Chryse, Cidaria, Cilla,
Cluacina, Cnagia, Cnidia, Colaenis,
Colocasia, Condyleates, Core,
Coronides, Coronis, Corythallia,
Crataeis, Creneis, Crete, Ctesylla,

Cupra, Cycladic Goddesses, Cydonia, Cynthia, Damatres, Daphne, Dea Caelestis, Dea Syria, Deianeira, Deione, Deipara, Delia, Delight, Delphinia, Deo, Dia, Diana of Ephesians, Dindymene, Dionaea, Dione, Dios, Dirae, Diviana, Dove Goddess, Electryone, Eleusina, Epaine, Epipyrgidia, Epistrophia, Epitymbia, Eriboea, Esenchebis, Euadne, Euboea, Eunoe, Eunomia, Euonyme, Europa, Eurynome, Eurysternos, Evadne, Fors, Genetrix, Gigantia, Glaucopis, Glaukopis, Halsodyne, Hamadryas, Harmonia, Helen, Heliconides, Hemithea, Henioche, Hercyna, Hermione, Hesperis, Hippe, Hippolaitis, Hymnia, Iasonia, Idaea, Idalia, Ilia, Ilythyia-Leucothea, Ioulo, Iphigeneia, Iphthime, Issoria, Itonia, Kaukasis, Keraunia, Kidaria, Kore, Kore-Arethusa, Kourotrophos, Kymathea, Kypris, La Strega, La Vecchia, Lacinia, Lampado, Lampethusa, Laphria, Larissaea, Larymna, Latona, Leiriope, Lernaea, Letham, Letogeneia, Leucophryne, Liberalitas, Limnatis, Lindia, Longatis, Loxo, Lycippe, Lycoatis, Lygodesma, Lysidice, Lysimache, Ma, Magarsia, Malaviskh, Mater Turrita, Megale, Megisto, Melanaegis, Meliboea, Melinaea, Melissa, Meneruva, Menrfa, Messene, Metioche, Mideatis, Migonitis, Militaris, Miysis, Mnasa, Morpho, Murcia, Mycalessia, Mysia, Narcaea, Natalis, Nathum, Nedusia, Neis, Nemea, Neptunine, Nerine, Nicostrata, Nymphaea, Nympheuomene, Obsequens, Oenoatis, Onca, Opis, Oreilochia, Orthia, Orthosia, Pais, Pallenis, Panachaea, Pandeia, Paphia, Parthenia, Parthenope, Parthenos, Pasiphae, Patella, Peisdice, Pelagia, Pelasga, Pero, Perseis, Persian Artemis, Pessinuntia, Phace, Phaedra, Pharygaea, Phonos, Phrygia, Phytalus, Pitanatis, Pitane, Placida, Poena, Poene, Polias, Poliatas, Poliuchos, Posidaeia, Praenestina, Prisca, Privata, Pronaea, Pronoia, Providentia, Psamathe, Publica, Pudicitia, Purikh, Pylotis, Pyrene, Quies, Quiritis, Rhamnusia, Rharias, Rhode, Rhododactylos, Sais, Saitis, Salpinx, Salutaris, Sapientia, Sarpedonia, Savior, Sciras, Sipna, Sleparis, Smyrna, Sororia, Sparta, Stata Mater, Sterope, Sthenele, Stilbe, Stimula, Stiria, Stymphalia, Tauro, Telchinia, Telecleia, Teles, Thalana, Thana, Thebe, Thermuthis, Thesan, Thesmorphonius, Thya, Thyia, Thyiades, Tipanu, Tiphanati, Tisiphone, Titania, Tragasia, Triclaria, Tritogeneia, Tritonia, Upis, Valetudo, Virginalis, Volupta, Zephyritis, Zerynthis

The Himalaya
Dinsangma, Dosangma, Earth Goddess, Jejamo-karpo, Jewel Goddesses, Long-life Sisters, Machi-pal Lha-mo, Tara, Tashitsheringma, Thinggishalsangma

Indian Subcontinent
Anrita, Aparajita, Arwut, Awejsirdenee, Balambika, Baluchistan Goddesses, Basany, Chausathi, Chitti, Cunda, Devasena, Dharni Deota, Divo Duhita, Doljang, Ekaparna, Ekapatala, Hyrania, Jayanti, Kalaka, Kanyā Kumārī, Kapalini, Kesora, Kriya, Laksmana, Lambodari, Mahavyahriti, Manota, Maritchi, Maru Devi, Maryatale, Mudevi, Rakini, Samnati, Sankini, Savarna, Shri, Sthalidevatas, Sumaya, Suris, Suryasya Duhita, Svayamvaraprabha, Syama, Tanmatra, Vadra-Kali, Vaidarbhiganani, Vajrayogini, Vrishakapayi

Near East
Adb-isi, Alath, Amat-isi, Ament, Asdoulos, Ashtartu, Bagbarti, Bagvarti, Bahu, Banit, Bithiah, Bubrostis, Chasbei, Dilbah, Dimtabba, Dione, Dodah, Elissa, Hashat, Hatepinu, Hecate, Hulla, Iahu, Iahu Anat, Igrath Bath Mahalath, Iš, Isidoulos, Island Paradise Lady, Jericho Goddesses, Kaukabhta, Kindazi, Kirisa, Kulitta, Kutbi, Lady of Ninab, Levanah, Mashti, Mater Artemis, Mater-turrita, Mother of Life, Nabarbi, Nin-agid-kahadu, Nin-akha-guddu, Ningirda, Ninki, Nin-marki, Ninmug, Nin-nibru, Nvard, Qudshu, Rahmai, Rahmaya, Rubati, Santaramet, Saris, Schala, Seruya, Shedath, Shid, Taauth, Tarkhu, Thummim, Tillil, Titanides, Ukhat, Uthht, Yaošti, Zaltu, Zhob Mother Goddess, Zintuhi, Zirratbanit

North America
Asdzaa Dootlijii, Atitxmana, Atse ataed, Chakwaina Asho-adta, Hopi Shalako Mana, Island Woman, Kalxsmaknim, Laliaaiauts, Masan Wuhti, Micux, Nuxmelnimana, Oky'enawe, Qopimpmana, Skate Woman, Skqwalutl, Sutal, Takanaluk arnaluk, Toothed Vagina, Turquoise Woman, Uiniyumayuituq, Wilx

Northern Europe
Beiwe-Neida, Dame Wode, Erda, Gritha, Grydat, Gunnlauth, Iarnvithjan, Imd, Laga, Nekke, Risem-Edne, Waldmichen, Wanne Thekla

Oceania
Aka, Anu mātao, Auna, Ava rei pua, Djugurba, Fai tama'i, Fanga, Fue, Gunggaranggara, Haamata kee, Ha'ina kolo, Hakirimaurea, Haoa'oa, Haria, Hauliparua, Haunga roa, Hava, Heke heki i papa, Hi'iaka i ka pua'ena'ena, Hi'iaka i reia, Hi'ilei, Hina kauhara, Hina lei haamoa, Hina tūa tua, Hina

tuafuaga, Hina'a rauriki, Hina'i ka'uluau, Hina'i ke ahi, Hine aterepō, Hine itaitai, Hine makura, Hine pūpūmainaua, Hine te aparangi, Hokiolele, Hokohoko, Hotukura, Huahega, Ihi'ihi, Iloilokula, Ina'ani vai, Ingridi, Iti iti, 'Iti'iti, Jalmarida, Ka wahine o ka li'ūla, Kai here, Kanaio, Keaka, Kearoa, Koke, Maeke, Mairatea, Makoro, Māpunai'a 'a'ala, Marama kai, Mari haka, Matiu, Maurea, Merau, Metakorab, Mimaliwu, Moa'ri, Mo'e hau i te ra'i, Na kino wailua, Na lehua 'aka'aka, Nei marena, Nei te arei n tarawa, Nei te re'ere, Nga lalbal, Ngeipau, Nu'usanga, One rua, Opopu, Pa'a o wali nu'u, Pare arohi, Puanga, Rara, Rima poto, Ro Lei, Ruku tia, Sienjarolol, Sientafitukrou, Sina tae o i lagi, Sisi, Tagaloa fofoa, Tagaloa lahi, Tagaloa ulu'ulu, Taiapua, Tane roroa, Tangae, Tapo, Te anu mātao, Te ipo atu, Tehahine'angiki, Tesikubai, Teu'uhi, Timu ateatea, Titi, Titua'abine, Tu, Tū metua, Tu Rua, Tumu te tangotango, Tumuteanaoa, Tupetupe i fare one, Ufi, Uri Uri, Vahine mau ni'a, Vakai a heva, Valelahī, Vie kena, Vuhi atua, Wheke, Wurdilapu, Yabadjaudjau, Yuguruguru, Yulanya

South America
Nandecy

Southeast Asia
Akshobhya, Dewi Amisani, Phra Naret, Sautu Majan, Thevadas

Western Europe
Adsullata, Almha, Amagandar, Amona, Bainleannan, Balma, Bera, Briant, Cailleach Bolus, Cailleach Corca Duibhne, Cannered Noz, Chokmoth, Cigfa, Crobh Dearg, Dichtire, Echaid, Elamite, Ele, Ētain Óig, Fflur, Geburah, Gedulah, Hod, Laha, Mal, Morey Ba, Sabra, Seang, Tabiti, Tryanon, Urganda, Urisks, Venus of Quinipily

War

Africa
Anyigba, Atida, Enekpe

Central America and Mesoamerica
Chantico, Chimalma, Coyolxauhqui, Itzpapalotl, Quilaztli, Yaocihuatl

Eastern Europe
Radegasta, Rozhanitsy, Tarn

Egypt
Aasith, Anatha Baetyl, Anta, Āntat, Ānthretju, Anuke, Ashtoreth, Āsit, Bast, Berenice, Mafiet, Menhit, Neith, Ranpu, Sachmet, Sekhmet

Far East
Ata, Ba, Chedi Furen, Dou Mou, Frost Goddess, Huoling Shengmu, Jokwa, Jun Ti, Marishi-ten, Mi Fei, Mifuto-hime

Greek and Roman Empires

Alala, Alcimache, Aphrodite, Areia, Artemis, Astrateia, Athena, Bellona, Caenis, Discordia, Enyo, Epipole, Eris, Eucleia, Helen, Kratesis, Lua, Mah-Bellona, Minerva, Nerio, Nice, Nicephorus, Nike, Prodromia, Promachus, Vacuna, Victoria, Victrix, Zosteria

Indian Subcontinent

Apvā, Bhadrakali, Chandi, Devi, Durga, Jaya, Kali, Korraval, Korrawi, Kottavei, Mahisasuramardini, Muktakesi, Parbutta, Ranaghanti, Rukmini, Sena, Senamuki, Shastradevatas, Shaterany, Tadatagei, Vijayasri, Vishpala

Near East

Agasaya, Agusaya, Aja, Anahid, Anāhita, Anaitis, Anat, Anat-bethel, Anath, Antaeus, Anthat, Ānthretju, Anthyt, Anuna, Anunit, Ariel, Ashtarchemosh, Ashtar-kemosh, Ashtaroth, Ashtart, Cybele, Dadmish, Ham-vareti, Hanata, Hore, Inin, Ininni, Irnina, Ishtar, Nanaja, Nane, Narunte, Ninni, Reshpu, Sauska, Shaushka, Siris, Sulmanitu, Uparatat, Urash

North America

Buffalo-calf-road-woman, Chakwaina Okya, Hé-é-e, Heoto Mana, Hūkyangkwū, Kolahmana, Kothlamana, Ondoutaehte, Po'haha, Qamaitis, Siltslani, Sohonasomtaka, Tcakwaina Mana, Toxwid

Northern Europe

Alaisiagae, Baudihillie, Brynhild, Fimmilinia, Freydis, Freyja, Geirahod, Geirolul, Gol, Goli, Gondul, Gudr, Gunnr, Hariasa, Harimela, Harimella, Hel, Hervor, Hild, Hildur, Hiorthrimul, Hlock, Hrist, Idisi, Judur, Kara, Mist, Radgrid, Randgrid, Reginleif, Rota, Sangridr, Sigrdrifa, Sigrlinn, Sigrun, Skeggold, Skogol, Skuld, Svafa, Svava, Svipul, Thrudur, Valkyries, Vihansa

Oceania

Ai Tūpua'i, 'Alae a hina, Enda semangko, 'Ere'ere fenua, Haumia, Hi'i hia, Mahu fatu rau, Nafanua, Ndimailangi, Ruahine nihoniho ro roa, Sasa'umani, Taemā, Tai tapu, Taisumalie, Tha, Tilafaigā, Toi mata, Vinaka

South America

Huaco

Southeast Asia

Bugan inManahaut, Darago, Gaiyun, Kumang, Na Ina, Trung Trac

Western Europe

Aeron, Andarta, Andrasta, Badb, Badba, Bobd, Bodua, Búanann, Carmán, Cartimandua, Cathuboduia, Cetnenn, Coinchend, Cosunea, Cymidei Cymeinfol, Dee, Estiu, Fea,

Geniti Glinne, Litavis, Lot, Macha, Medb, Mórrígán, Nantosvelta, Nemain, Nemetona, Ratis, Scáthach, Sgeimh Solais, Veleda

Water

Africa

Abena Budu, Abenawa, Aberewa Awukuwa, Abuk, Abu-mehsu, Afrékété, All-bringing-forth, Amelenwa, Asase Yaa, Ashiakle, Atete, Avlekete, Aziri, Bosumabla, Buk, Candit, Dada, Data, Ewuraba, Ezili, Harrakoi Dikko, Ichar-tsirew, Igbarun, Igoni, Imo, Katarwiri, Kokobi, La-hkima Oqla, Mukasa, Naete, Nagodya, Nana Buruku, Nimm, Nommo, Nummo, Nyaliep, Oba, Olokum, Orehu, Oshun, Ovia, Oya, Qandisa, Rakembaranu, Tabhi-yiri, Tingoi, Tokpodun, Totole, Yemojá, Yemonja, Ymoja

Central America and Mesoamerica

Abe, Acuecueyotlcihuatl, Adamisil Wedo, Agweta, Ahuic, Aida Wedo, Anne, Apozanolotl, Atlacamani, Atlacoya, Atlatona, Ayauhteotl, Ayopechcatl, Caridad, Chalchiuhtlicue, Christalline, Clairmé, Clairmeziné, Coatrischie, Dabaiba, Damballah, Dobayba, Elisabeth, Emanja, Erzulie, Goddess "I", Grande Ezili, Guabancex, Guabonito, Huixtocihuatl, Iguanuptigili, Inanupdikile, Ix Chel, Ix Kan Itzam Thul, Ix Ku, Ix Pucyolá, Ix Tan Yol, Ix Tan Yol Ha, Ix U Sihnal, Ixtab, Maman Simbi, Manideakdili, Mary, Matlalcueye, Nana Buruku, Oba, Olodeakdili, Olokikadiryae, Olokum, Olonuptigile, Orehu, Oshun, Oya, Punauaga Oloeaydili, Punauaga Oloesgidili, Punauaga Oloniskidilisop, Punauaga Olouagaidili, Punauaga Uisogdili, Quiamucame, Sirêne, Tāté Haútse Kupúri, Tatei Hamuxa, Tatei Haramara, Tatei Kaxiwari, Tatei Matinieri, Tatei Xapawiyelkame, Tatei Xuturi Iwiekame, Tateima, Tzultacaj, Vierge Caridad, Xaratanga, Xixiquipilihui, Xkan Le Ox, Xtoh, Yemanja

Eastern Europe

Aba-khatun, Amberella, Anqa-naut, As-ava, Bereginy, Cacce-jienne, Cherlak, Cinei-new, Egle, Ilmater, Juras Māte, Jurate, Kul, Kupal'nitsa, Luonnotar, Makosh, Mokosh, Mor-ava, Najade, Näkineiu, Näkinneito, Näkki, Nemodilky, Ojid-emei, Onmun-emei, Otsuved-azer-ava, Rav-ava, Rusalka, Saiva-neida, Sjojungfru, Sur-mumy, Tshadze-ienne, Tshatse-neida, Udens-māte, Unchi-ahchi, Unun-emei, Va-kul, Vasa, Ved-ava, Vellamo, Viz-anya, Vizi-leany, Vodni Panny, Vodyanoi, Vu-ava, Vüt-kuva, Walrus Mother, Wüt-awa, Wüt-ian uder, Zarya

Egypt

Akhet, Anuket, Celestial Waterer, Hast, Heqet, Kebechet, Mehen, Meret, Meri, Methyer, Naunet, Neith, Nen, Nephthys, Nunet, Proet, Satel, Satet, Sphinx, Uat

Far East

Aba Khatun, Ao-numa-nu-oshi-hime, Awa-nami-no-kami, Benten, Chiu-rang-guru, Chiwashekot-mat, Chiwash-kor-kamui, Chuan Hou, Haya-aki-tsu-hime-no-kami, He Ku, Hi-kawa-hime, Ho Ku, Horokariyep, Kamui-matne-po, Kissiang, Kuguri-gami, Kuni-no-kuhiza-mochi-no-kami, Kuni-no-mi-kumari-no-kami, Kwannon, Lo Shen, Mazu, Mintuchi-kamui, Mishima-no-mizo-kui-hime, Mitsu-ha-no-me-no-kami, Mizo-kuhi-hime, Mizu-tsu-hime, Moshir-huchi, Nai-orun-kamui, Nitat-unarabe, Nügua, Nupki-ot-mat, Oto, Pet-etok-mat, Quan Hou, Sarak-kamui, Seoritsu-hime, Shenggu, Shuimu Niangniang, Takitsu-hime-no-mikoto, Tama-yori-bime-no-mikoto, Toyo-tama-bime-no-mikoto, Tsubura-hime, Tsura-nami-no-kami, Tui, Turesh, Xiumu Niangniang, Yao Ji

Greek and Roman Empires

Abarbarea, Acantha, Acaste, Acheloides, Acraea, Actaea, Aethra, Aethyia, Aganippe, Aganippides, Agave, Alcyone, Alimede, Alpheias, Amalthea, Amathaounta, Amnisiades, Amphinome, Amphiro, Amphithoe, Amphitrite, Anadyomene, Anchiroe, Andromeda, Anigrides, Anippe, Aphaea, Appiades, Appias, Apseudes, Arethusa, Argeia, Argiope, Argyra, Asia, Asterope, Atalanta, Avernales, Bateia, Begoe, Beroe, Bolbe, Byblis, Cabeiro, Cale, Caliadne, Callianassa, Callianeira, Callirrhoe, Calybe, Calypso, Camenae, Camise, Canente, Cassotis, Castalia, Castalides, Cerceïs, Ceto, Chariboea, Chariclo, Charybdis, Chlidanope, Choro, Chryseis, Cleochareia, Cleone, Clymene, Clytia, Cranto, Creusa, Crinaiae, Curissia, Cyane, Cydippe, Cymatolege, Cymo, Cymodoce, Cymothoe, Cypria, Cythera, Daphne, Dea Marica, Deino, Deiopea, Dero, Dexamene, Diana, Dione, Dirce, Dodone, Dorides, Doris, Doto, Drimo, Echenais, Eidothea, Eione, Electra, Eleionomae, Enhydria, Enyo, Etna, Euadne, Eucrante, Eudia, Eudora, Eugora, Eumolpe, Eunike, Europa, Eurybia, Eurydice, Eurynome, Evagora, Evarne, Ferentina, Fons, Galaxaura, Galene, Glauce, Glaucia, Glauconome, Glauke, Glaukonome, Graeae, Halia, Haliae, Halimede, Halsodyne, Harmonia, Helice, Helle, Hemeresia, Hercyna, Hippo, Hipponoe, Hippothoe, Hydra, Hypereia, Ianassa,

Ianeira, Ianthe, Iasis, Idyia, Imbrasia, Ino, Ione, Ionides, Iphianassa, Iphthime, Juturna, Kallianassa, Kallianeira, Kranto, Kymatolege, Laomedeia, Leiagora, Leuce, Leucippe, Leucothea, Leucothoe, Libya, Ligeia, Lilaea, Limenia, Limnades, Limnaea, Limnatides, Limnoreia, Lycorias, Lykorias, Lysianassa, Maera, Maira, Marica, Mater Matuta, Melia, Meliboea, Melite, Melobosis, Memphis, Menippe, Merope, Mesma, Messeis, Metis, Metope, Myrtoessa, Naiades, Nausithoe, Neaera, Neda, Neis, Neomeris, Nereides, Nereis, Nesaea, Neso, Nymphae Infernae Paludis, Nymphs, Oceanides, Ocyrrhoë, Oeroe, Oreithyia, Panope, Pasiphae, Pasithea, Pasithoe, Pegaeae, Pegasides, Peirene, Peitho, Pemphredo, Perse, Perseis, Perso, Petraea, Phaeno, Pharmaceia, Pherusa, Phorcides, Phyllodoce, Pleione, Plexaure, Ploto, Plouto, Pluto, Polynoe, Polynome, Polyxo, Pontia, Pontomedusa, Pontopereia, Potameides, Potamia, Praxithea, Promachorma, Pronoë, Protho, Proto, Protogenia, Proversa, Prymno, Rhodeia, Rhodope, Rhoeo, Salacia, Sao, Scotia, Scylla, Simaethis, Speio, Stilbe, Stilbo, Strymo, Styx, Telphusa, Tethys, Thalassa, Thaleia, Therma, Thermia, Thetis, Thoë, Tiburtis, Timandra, Torone, Tyche, Urania, Venilia, Xantho, Zeuxippe, Zeuxo

The Himalaya
bDud-mo-gshin-rej-mgo-dgu-ma, bDud-mo-gshin-rje-lag-brgya-ma, bDud-mo-gsod-mo-gsod-byed-ma, bDud-mo-phung-khrol-ma, brDa'i 'phrad, Chu-lcam-rgyal-mo, Chu'i lha mo, Chu'i lha mo Mamaki, Chu'phrul can, dBang-bsdud-ma, 'Gying-dkar-ma, Khrag-gi-ser-'bebs-ma, Lu, mTsho-sman-g•yu-thang-cho-longs-ma, mTsho-sman-gzi-ldan-ral-gcig-ma, mTsho-sman-klu-yi-rgyal-mo, mTsho-sman-mthing-gi-lha-mo, mTsho-sman-nyi-ma'i-byan-goig-ma, mTsho-sman-rgyal-mo-mkhro'i-gtso, mTsho-sman-ru-phyug-rgyal-mo, Yami

Indian Subcontinent
Adrika, Aitan, Alambusha, Amrit, Angana, Ap, Apsarases, Asra, Assam Mother Earth, Auksagandhi, Bentakumari, Bhagirathi, Bhairava, Bugarik, Burhi Thakurani, Caksusi, Daityas, Danavis, Dasara, Gandharvadatta, Gandharvi, Ganga, Gangaji, Gauri, Ghrtaci, Godavari, Guggulu, Harahvaiti, Harini, Harsiddh Mata, Ira, Jalkamni, Jamadagni, Jumna Ji, Ka Blei Sam Um, Ka 'Lei Aitan, Ka Um, Kanni Amma, Kausiki, Kaveri, Keshini, Khir Bhawani, Kshiti-apsarases, Kupli, Lavangi, Lenju, Limnate, Madhava, Mahendri, Malini,

Manasi, Marisha, Marulupolamma, Matri-Padma, Matris, Maya, Mayarani, Mena, Mesabai, Misrakesi, Mother Earth, Mother Water, Nadi, Nage-bonga, Naladi, Narmada, Orusandiamma, Pae Devi, Pramandani, Pramlocha, Pururavas, Purvachitti, Rambha, Ranu Bai, Rati, Reva, Sahaganya, Samundra, Sanumati, Sarasvati, Sarvari, Sasilekha, Saudamani, Sindhu, Sirsootee, Sitalamma, Sukanthi, Surabhidatta, Surapamsula, Surasa, Sutudri, Tapati, Tilottama, Totala, Tuima, Uravari, Urvasi, Vadaba, Vasistha, Verdatchamma, Vipas, Viraj, Yami, Yauni

Near East
A, Afka, Ahurani, Amanoro, Amesha Spentas, Anāhita, An.zu, Apo, Arduisur, Ardvi Vaxsha, Asera, Astarte, Athirat, Belili, Dsovinar, Dumuziabzu, Erua, Gasmu, Gatamdug, Gestinanna, Haurvatāt, Helmund, Id, Ininni, Ka-silim, Leviathan, Mara, Metsulah, Nin Ella, Nin-akha-kuda, Ninhabursildu, Ninmuk, Sabitu, Sea Goddess, Sileni, Sirara, Talay, Thalassa, Thymbris, Tiamat, Tihamtu

North America
Aiviliajog, Ai-Willi-Ay-O, Anavigak, Arnaaluk Takannaaluk, Arnapkapfaluk, Arnaknagsak, Avilayoq, Aywilliayoo, Black Butte, Bright Star, Creator Being, Erlaveersisoq, Foam Mother, Foam Woman, Goddesses of the Eastern and Western Ocean, Hakulaq, Hawichyepam Maapuch, Hutsipamamau?u, Idliragijenget, Imam-shua, Iqamiaitx, Itclixyan, Ka-mu-iu-dr-ma-giu-iu-e-ba, Kanaeski Anaiyehi, Kannakapfaluk, Katuma, Kavna, Kawas, Keninqas, Kunna, Lennaxidaq, Meghetaghna, Mem Loimis, Nahkeeta, Nakorut, Nanoquaqsaq, Nerchevik, Nerrivik, Nirivik, Nivikkaa, Nooliayoo, Nuli'rahak, Nuskwalsikanda, Ocean Woman, Old Woman of the Sea, Ostkahakakaitshoidiaa, Punauaga Oloeaydili, Red Woman, Sanvna, Sasvsuma Inua, Sattuma Eeva, Sedna, Simsiutaakis, Si-tcom'pa Ma-so-its, Takanakapsaluk, Thompson Goddesses, Tó asdza•n, T'otowaxsemalaga, Tsumtlaks, Tsunukwa, Tüwapongtümsi, Unk, Waotunoowase, Waoyakila, Wheatchee, Wiakai, Woman Who Washed Her Face, Yolkai Estsan

Northern Europe
Angeyja, Atla, Augeia, Bylgja, Drafn, Egia, Eistla, Eyrgjafa, Fenja, Gjalp, Griep, Havfru, Heidrun, Holda, Hrafn, Imdr, Jarnsaxa, Kolga, Labismina, Lady Wen, Lorelei, Mardal, Matrona, Menja, Modgud, Nehalennia, Nixen, Norns,

Ran, Saga, Sel, Sindur, Sjora, Skuld, Ulfrun, Undine, Vana Mothers, Verdandi, Wachilt, Wave Maidens

Oceania
Ala muki, Atoto, Birrahgnooloo, Haumia, Hi'iaka i ka'ale moe, Hi'iaka i ka'ale po'i, Hi'iaka i ka'ale'i, Hi'iaka i ka'ale'uweke, Hina ka'alualu moana, Hina ke kai, Hina lau limu kala, Hina lua'i koa, Hine āhua, Hine apo hia, Hine i te huhi, Hine moana, Hine popo, Hine rakatai, Hine tua tai, Julunggul, Junkgowa, Ka'ipo, Kara ma kuna, Kare nuku, Kare rangi, Kaukau, Latmikaik, Lewatu ni nambua, Li arongorong pei, Li au en pon tan, Lia, Lino, Moakura, Nā maka o kaha'i, Namaka, Numma Moiyuk, Para whenua mea, Ro Som, Te mehara, Tilafainga, Tonu tai, Topukulu, Tu wae rore, Tuli, Uli po'ai o ka moku, Urutonga, Vahine mau i te pae fenua, Wao, Waramurungundji, Wulutahanga

South America
Asima Si, Calounga, Chokesuso, Copacati, Dyevae, Iamanja, Jamaina, Jandira, Luandinha, Mae D'agua, Mama Cocha, Oshoun, Oya-bale, Panda, Raharariyoma, Taru, Urpihuachac, Uwan, Yaca-mama, Yara

Southeast Asia
Annawan, Arurin, Bà-Du'c Chu'a, Balintawag, Batoer, Dara Rambai Geruda, Dewi Danu, Dewi Gangga, Humitau, Ina Onian, Inan Oinan, Inawen, Kameian, Kapaä, Karokung, Keheari, Lai-oid, Lepeh, Machin Tungku, Minti Dara Bunsu, Muni Mental Batu, Njai, Njai Lora Kidoul, Ratu Loro Kidul, Sedaw Thakmina, Tambon, Yak Lepeh

Western Europe
Adsullata, Aerfon, Aide, Aige, Ameipicer, Anna Livia Plurabelle, Arnamentia, Avantia, Axona, Badb, Ban Nighechain, Banna, Beag, Belisama, Boann, Bormana, Borvonia, Briant, Brixia, Carpunda, Ceasg, Ceibhfhionn, Celiborca, Cliodhna, Clota, Clud, Clutoida, Cordelia, Coventina, Damona, Danu, Dee, Deva, Devona, Divona, Domnu, Dub, Dubh Lacha, Elamite, Epona, Fideal, Fland, Frovida, Griselicae Nymphae, Gwrach y Rhibyn, Gwragedd Annwn, Icauna, Ivilia, Korrigan, Lady of the Lake, Lamia, Latis, Lí Ban, Logia, Mari, Mermaids, Merrow, Modron, Momu, Morgan Le Fay, Moriath, Moruadh, Muirdris, Muireartach, Muiriath, Murigen, Nantosvelta, Navia, Navia Arconunieca, Nimue, Niskai, Odras, Ondine, Pressina, Sabrina, Segeta, Segomanna, Sequana, Sinann, Sirona, Souconna, Tamesis, Tres Matres, Triduana, Ura, Urnia, Urtz, Verbeia, Vercana, Visuna, Wyvach

Wealth

Africa
Abowie, Aizu, Akazu, Dan, Dziva, Imo, Kaiwan, Marwe, Nyingwan Mebege, Oshun, Songi

Central America and Mesoamerica
Chalchiuhcihuatl, Oshun

Eastern Europe
Gabjauja, Jaja, Khotun, Kubai-khotun, Laimas-māte, Poludnitsy, Pört-kuva, Schastie, Slatababa, Vila, Yaumau-hadaku

Egypt
Bahet, Hatshepsut, Mert

Far East
Bai Mundan, Benten, Etugen, Ichiki-shima-hime-no-mikoto, Inari, Yama-no-Shinbo

Greek and Roman Empires
Abundantia, Anna Perenna, Copia, Doto, Hecate, Moneta, Pecunia, Plouto, Salus

The Himalaya
Gos-ster-ma-dkar-mo, Green Deer-headed Wealth-guardian Goddess, Kurukulle, Nor-ster-ma-sngon-mo, Ratna Krotishaurima, Yid-'prog-ma, Zas-ster-ma-dmar-mo

Indian Subcontinent
Aditya, Alambusha, Anala, Angana, Anila, Annapurna, Antariksha, Anumati, Apnapurna, Apu, Ashi, Ayepi, Chandra, Chitarhai Devi, Dhara, Dharani, Dhisana, Dhruva, Dyu, Ganga, Gauri, Grhalaksmi, Hada Bai, Hariti, Ida, Idavida, Isani, Ka Blai Synshar, Ka Taroh, Kine Nane, Kuhu, Kun, Kurukulla, Lakshmi, Madhukasa, Mahi, Matangi, Naina Devi, Nakshatras, Nandini, Parendi, Pathya, Pathyarevati, Pathya Svasti, Prabhasa, Pratyusha, Prithivi, Purandhi, Raka, Rddhi, Revati, Rodasi, Sakambhari, Samriddhi, Sarasvati, Sasthi, Sevasti-devi, Siddhis, Sri, Sunrta, Susime, Totala, Trigana, Usas, Vasudhara, Vasus, Yechu

Near East
Aharišvang, Ahurani, Ashi, Ashish Vanuhi, Aši, Chiun, Esharra, Ne-zil-la, Pârendi, Rata, Saoka

North America
Hakulaq, Iqalu Nappaa, Property Woman, Skagit Grandmother, Skil-djaadai

Northern Europe
Abundia, Alagabiae, Fulla, Habondia, Oddibjord

Oceania
Hau wahine, Kāne kua'ana, Pani tinaku, Ro Som, Tobukulu, Wulutahanga

South America
Mama Allpa

Southeast Asia
Biku Indu Antu, Dewi Sri, Female Spectres, Hainuwele, Ini Andan, Kayamanan, Kumang, Pantan Ini Andan, Sri

Western Europe
Anu, Buan-ann, Erni, Rosmerta

Weather

Africa
All-bringing-forth, Atida, Bunzi, Dan, Inkosazana, Mbaba Mwana Waresa, Min Jok, Morningstar of Wakaranga, Mousso Koroni Koundye, Mujaji, Mukasa, Nagadya, Nagawonyi, Oya, Quabso, Ra, Sodza, Sogbo, Tsetse

Central America and Mesoamerica
Atlacoya, Ayauhteotl, Candelaria, Chibilias, Chicomecoatl, Coatrischie, Cueravaperi, Dabaiba, Guabancex, Guédé l'Oraille, Huixtocihuatl, Inanupdikile, Itaba Tahuana, Ix Ku, Ix Tub Tan, Ixtab, Loa, Maninupdikili, Matlalcueye, Mombu, Naimetzabok, Ochumare, Olonuptigile, Oya, Takótsi Nakawé, Tāté Haútse Kupúri, Tāté Kyewimóka, Tāté Naaliwámi, Tāté Rapawiyama, Tatei Yurienaka, Xixiquipilihui, Xkan Le Ox, Xtoh

Eastern Europe
Azer-ava, Bereginy, Budung-yihe-ibe, Dewaite Szwenta, Divje Devojke, Doda, Dsovinar, Dziewanna, Ether, Gudiri-mumi, Ilena, Ilma, Kulshedra, Ljubi, Louhi, Maan-emo, Mardeq Avalon, Mardez-awa, Mokosh, Munya, Percunatele, Perkune Tete, Pogoda, Polednice, Rauni, Ravdna, Rusalka, Semargla, Solbon, Szelanya, Tarn, Varma-ava, Vēja-māte, Vir-ava, Ya'hal-na'ut, Zimarzla

Egypt
Nebt, Nephthys, Sachmet, Sag, Satel, Sekhet-aanru, Sekhet-hetepet, Tefnut

Far East
A Xiang, Ba, Dark Maid, Etugen, Feng Po, Frost Goddess, Kalapiat, Kaminari, Kujaku-myō-ō, Kuni-no-sa-giri-no-kami, Lei-zi, Ma Zupo, Matnau, Naru-kami, Nda-la-a-ssaw-mi, Niangniang, Nügua, Qi Guzi, Ru-be-sei, Saoqing Niang, Shandian Pozi, Shenggu, Shi-nish-e-ran-mat, Shinatsuhime, Shuimu Niangniang, Shunyi Furen, Takiri-bime-no-mikoto, Tatsu-ta-hime, Taxankpada Agodales, Tian Mu Niangniang, Urara-e-ran-mat, Waka-uka-no-me-no-mikoto, Xiu

Wenyin, Xiumu Niangniang, Yao Ji, Yuki-onne

Greek and Roman Empires
Acholoe, Adraste, Aello, Aesyle, Agraulos, Amphitrite, Anemotis, Aura, Bacche, Begoe, Celaeno, Chione, Cleia, Cleis, Coronis, Dais, Dione, Dodonides, Eidothea, Eos, Erato, Ersa, Eudora, Fulgora, Harpies, Hera, Herse, Hyades, Iris, Kelaino, Lelaino, Lips, Nephele, Nicothoe, Nysa, Ocypete, Palato, Pedile, Phaeo, Phaethusa, Phyto, Pitys, Podarge, Polyxo, Pyrrha, Tempestates, Thyene, Tritopatores, Venilia

The Himalaya
bDud-mo-gshin-rej-mgo-dgu-ma, bDud-mo-gshin-rje-lag-brgya-ma, bDud-mo-gsod-mo-gsod-byed-ma, bDud-mo-phung-khrol-ma, Blue Wolf-headed Wind Goddess, 'Brug-gi-sgra-sgrog-ma, Dam-tshig-mkha'-'gro-ma, dBang-sdud-kyi-mkha'-'gro-ma, dPal-gyi-pho-nya-las-mkhan-mo, Drag-ppo'i-klog-khyung-ma, Glog-bdag-mo, gNam-lha-byang-sman-mthing-gi-go-zu-can, gNam-lcags-thog-'bebs-ma, 'Jig-rten-mkha'-'gro-ma, 'Jigs-pa'i-zer-mo-mig-gcig, Khrag-gi-ser-'bebs-ma, Las-kyi-mkha'-'gro-ma, Nam-mkha'g•yu-mdog-snang-srid-mdzod, Naro-kha-choma, Padma mkha' 'gro ma, rDo-rje-mkha'-'gro-ma, rDo-rje-rnal-hbyor-ma, Rin-chen-mkha'-'gro-ma, Rin-chen-mkhah-ngro, Rlung-gi-lha-mo-dam-tshig-sgrol-ma, Sangs-rgyas-mkha'-'gro-ma, sNa tshogs nkha' 'gro ma, Ye-shes-mkha'-'gro-ma

Indian Subcontinent
Abhramu, Aditya, Adrika, Anala, Anila, Antariksha, Apsarases, Apu, Auksagandhi, Bardaichila, Bhairava, Bhasi, Bijaldeo Kanya, Bijloki, Biliku, Buddhadakini, Buddhi Nagin, Caksusi, Chakrisvari, Chandra, Chola Pacho, Cosmic Waters, Dhanada, Dhara, Dhruva, Dhumavati, Druh, Dyu, Gauri, Ghrtaci, Gonti, Guggulu, Harini, Hima, Ira, Jamadagni, Keshini, Kshiti-apsarases, Lavangi, Lola, Madhava, Madhukasa, Mahasahasrapramardani, Malini, Manasi, Mari, Mariamman, Marisha, Maruttaruni, Mena, Misrakesi, Nakshatras, Naladi, Padmadakini, Pan Dong Cyu, Parooa, Prabhasa, Pramandani, Pramlocha, Pratyusha, Prishni, Prithivi, Pururavas, Purvachitti, Rambha, Rati, Ratnadakini, Rksavaktradakini, Rodasi, Sahaganya, Sanumati, Saranjus, Saranyu, Sarparajni, Sarpis, Sarvabuddhadakini, Sasilekha, Saudamani, Savari, Simhavaktra, Sringatpadini, Sukanthi, Sulochana, Surabhidatta, Surapamsula, Tarai, Tilottama, Totala, Uravari, Urvasi, Vadaba, Vajradakini, Vandya, Varshayanti, Vasistha, Vasus,

Vidyujjvalakarali, Visvadakini,
Vyaghravaktradakini, Yakshi

Near East
Dewy, Ham-vareti, Huwassanas, Lilith,
Lilithu, Ninlil, Pairikas, Pdry, Reshpu,
Sadwes, Shala, Shutu, Siris, Tallai,
Tasimis, Zuriel

North America
Ahmetolela Okya, Asiaq, ?Ašixuč,
Bright-Cloud Woman, Chup, Cold
Woman, Corn Maidens,
Dagwanoenyent, Duh-hwahk, Foam
Mother, Gaende'sonk, Heloha, Hila,
Hükyangkwü, Ignirtoq, Imam-shua,
Ingnirtungl, Ixlexwani, Kadlu,
Kannakapfaluk, Kutnahin, Lennaxidaq,
Malaȟshishinish, Masau'u Kachin'
Mana, Naëstsán, Nahosdzaan Esdza,
Nayaanxatisei, Neoga, Nɫarɨmamau?u,
Nitsabaad, North Wind Woman,
Norwan, Nuvak'chin' Mana, Omau-u
Wuhti, Pana, Pitkamikokiu, Pukeheh,
Qailertetang, Queskapenek, Rain
Goddess, Sila, South Wind,
Sussistinnako, Tate, Tcua-wugti, Three
Kadlu Sisters, Trukwinu Mana,
Tukwinong Mana, Wakwiyo, Woman
Who Washed Her Face

Northern Europe
Angerbodha, Aslog, Baduhenna,
Borghild, Drifa, Fonn, Frau Fiuk,
Frigga, Havfru, Heidrun, Holda, Holle,
Hyrokkin, Irpa, Kajsa, Metsola, Mïöll,
Nat, Rind, Sigrun, Sjora, Swan
Maidens, Swanwhite, Thrud, Undutar,
Wunschelwybere

Oceania
Abeguwo, 'Ānuenue, Birrahgnooloo,
Brogla, Bumerali, Calla filatonga,
'Ere'ere fenua, Faurourou, Goga, Ha lo,
Haumea, Hema, Hihikalani, Hi'iaka,
Hi'iaka i te pori o pere, Hi'iaka ka'a
lawa maka, Hi'iaka makole wawahi
wa'a, Hi'iaka noho lani, Hi'iaka opio,
Hi'iaka tapu'ena'ena, Hi'iaka tarei'a,
Hi'iaka wawahi lani, Hina kuluua,
Hine āhua, Hine apo hia, Hine i
tapapauta, Hine kapua, Hine makohu,
Hine rakatai, Hine te uria, Hine tu
whenua, Hine wai, Hine whaitiri,
Houmea, Huru te arangi, Ihi awa'awa,
Ihi lani, Julunggul, Junkgowa, Ka hala
o puna, Ka ua ku'āhiwa, Kā'ana'e like,
Ka'ao melemele, Kahoupokane, Kare
nuku, Kare rangi, Ke ao lewa, Ke ao
mele mele, Koirau na marama, Kui,
Kunapipi, Kurikuta, Kwouk kwouk,
Laenihi, Lā'ie i kawai, Laka, Lewatu ni
nambua, Likuthava, Lilinoe, Lino,
Makara, Moakura, Munbakuaku,
Nafanua, Narama, Narpajin, Nei
bairara, Ngaljod, Nu'umealani,
Parawera nui, Parekōritawa,
Parewhenua mea, Poko ha rua te pō,
Polalowehi, Poli 'ahu, Pou te
aniwaniwa, Rakataura, Sa'ato, Sine
Matanoginogi, Tafakula, Tagaloa tati,
Tagaloamotumotu, Tairbu, Te muri,
Toafa, Tomituka, Topukulu, Tukapua,
Vahine nui tahu ra'i, Waiau, Whaitiri,
Wulutahanga, Yirbaik baik

South America
Atoja, Chasca, Cocha, Rainha Barba,
Schetewuarha, Toru-guenket

Southeast Asia
Aniton Tauo, Anitun Tabu, Bà-Du'c
Chu'a, Inoltagon, Kabagiyawan,
Langaan, Mekala, Poee Ura, Sarengge,
Shadip, Silat, Tarai, Teu Kweh, Trung
Nhi, Trung Trac

Western Europe
Aobh, Bécuma, Cailleach Mor,
Caoineag, Cesair, Cyhiraeth, Dawen,
Dornoll, Étain Echraidhe, Fionnuala,
Gentle Annie, Ignis Fatuus, Levarcham,
Mari Morgan, Moneiba, Muireartach,
Náir, Tres Matres